LITERATURE AND
the writing process

LITERATURE AND
the writing process
CANADIAN EDITION

ELIZABETH McMAHAN
Illinois State University

SUSAN X DAY
Iowa State University

ROBERT FUNK
Eastern Illinois University

MARLET ANN ASHLEY
Kwantlen University College

Toronto

> *This book is dedicated to Pieter and to my sons:*
> *Joel, Michael, Philip, and never forgetting our Peter.*
>
> Marlet Ann Ashley

National Library of Canada Cataloguing in Publication

  Literature and the writing process / Elizabeth McMahan ... [et al.]. — Canadian ed.

Includes index.
ISBN 0-13-120309-6

  1. College readers. 2. English language—Rhetoric—Problems, exercises, etc.
3. Report writing—Problems, exercises, etc.
4. Literature—Collections. I. McMahan, Elizabeth

PE1417.L57 2005   808'.0427   C2004-901501-X

Copyright © 2005 Pearson Education Canada, a division of Pearson Canada Inc., Toronto, Ontario.

Original edition published by Pearson Education, Inc., Upper Saddle River, NJ 07458.
Copyright © 2002. This edition is authorized for sale only in Canada.

Pearson Prentice Hall. All rights reserved. This publication is protected by copyright and permission should be obtained from the publisher prior to any prohibited reproduction, storage in a retrieval system, or transmission in any form or by any means, electronic, mechanical, photocopying, recording, or likewise. For information regarding permission, write to the Permissions Department.

ISBN 0-13-120309-6

Vice President, Editorial Director: Michael J. Young
Executive Acquisitions Editor: Jessica Mosher
Signing Representative: Carmen Batsford
Marketing Manager: Toivo Pajo
Senior Developmental Editor: Lise Dupont
Production Editor: Söğüt Y. Güleç
Copy Editor: Karen Alliston
Proofreader: Barbara Czarnecki
Production Manager: Wendy Moran
Page Layout: Carolyn E. Sebestyen
Permissions Research: Jane McWhinney
Art Director: Mary Opper
Cover and Interior Design: Lisa Lapointe
Cover Image: Susan Dobson, courtesy of Tatar Gallery, Toronto

  3 4 5   09 08 07 06

Printed and bound in Canada.

Brief Contents

Preface xxi

PART I Composing: An Overview 1

    CHAPTER 1 The Prewriting Process 2
    CHAPTER 2 The Writing Process 19
    CHAPTER 3 The Rewriting Process 37

PART II Writing about Short Fiction 61

    CHAPTER 4 How Do I Read Short Fiction? 62
    CHAPTER 5 Writing about Structure 68
    CHAPTER 6 Writing about Imagery and Symbolism 89
    CHAPTER 7 Writing about Point of View 119
    CHAPTER 8 Writing about Setting and Atmosphere 129
    CHAPTER 9 Writing about Theme 147

    Anthology of Short Fiction 163

PART III Writing about Poetry 347

    CHAPTER 10 How Do I Read Poetry? 348
    CHAPTER 11 Writing about Persona and Tone 352
    CHAPTER 12 Writing about Poetic Language 370
    CHAPTER 13 Writing about Poetic Form 388

    Anthology of Poetry 405

PART IV Writing about Drama 475

    CHAPTER 14 How Do I Read a Play? 476
    CHAPTER 15 Writing about Dramatic Structure 481
    CHAPTER 16 Writing about Character 533
    CHAPTER 17 Drama for Writing: The Research Paper 578

    Anthology of Drama 669

Appendix 819

The Pearson Education Canada **COMPANION WEBSITE**

A Great Way to Learn and Instruct Online

The Pearson Education Canada Companion Website is easy to navigate and is organized to correspond to the chapters in this textbook. Whether you are a student in the classroom or a distance learner you will discover helpful resources for in-depth study and research that empower you in your quest for greater knowledge and maximize your potential for success in the course.

[www.pearsoned.ca/mcmahan]

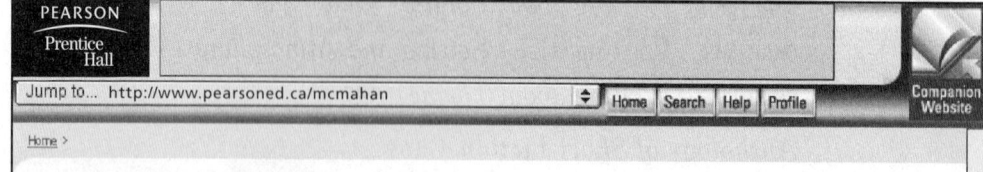

Home >

Companion Website

Literature and the Writing Process, Canadian Edition, by Elizabeth McMahan, Susan X Day, Robert Funk, and Marlet Ann Ashley

Student Resources

The modules in this section provide students with tools for learning course material. These modules include:
- Online Study Guide
- Web Destinations for some authors discussed in the text
- Interactive Timeline

In the quiz modules students can send answers to the grader and receive instant feedback on their progress through the Results Reporter. Coaching comments and references to the textbook may be available to ensure that students take advantage of all available resources to enhance their learning experience.

Contents

Contents by Genre xxii
Thematic Contents xxvi
Preface xxxi

PART I Composing: An Overview 1

CHAPTER 1 The Prewriting Process 2
Reading for Writing 2
    Joy Kogawa, "Obasan" 3
Who Are My Readers? 9
    Analyze the Audience 9
    Prewriting Exercise 9
Why Am I Writing? 10
    Reasons for Writing 10
    Prewriting Exercise 10
What Ideas Should I Use? 11
    Thinking Critically 11
    Self-Questioning 11
    Directed Freewriting 13
    Problem Solving 13
    FIGURE 1–1 Directed Freewriting 14
    Clustering 15
What Point Should I Make? 15
    FIGURE 1–2 Clustering 16
    Relate a Part to the Whole 16
How Do I Find the Theme? 17
    Stating the Thesis 17

CHAPTER 2 The Writing Process 19
How Should I Organize My Ideas? 19
The Basic Approach: Devising a Plan 19
Ordering the Ideas 21
How Do I Argue an Interpretation? 21
Developing with Details 22
    CHART 2–1 Checklist for Arguing an Interpretation 22
    Questions for Consideration 23
Maintaining a Critical Focus 23

Distinguishing Critical Comments from Plot Details 23
How Should I Begin? 24
 Postpone If Nothing Comes 24
 Write an Appealing Opening 25
 State the Thesis 25
How Should I End? 26
 Relate the Discussion to Theme 26
 Postpone or Write Ahead 26
 Write an Emphatic Final Sentence 26
Composing the First Draft 27
 Pausing to Rescan 27
 Quoting from Your Sources 27
Sample Student Paper: First Draft 28
Suggestions for Writing 35
Ideas for Writing 36
 Ideas for Responsive Writing 36
 Ideas for Critical Writing 36

CHAPTER 3 *The Rewriting Process* 37
What Is Revision? 37
Getting Feedback: Peer Review 38
 Revising in Peer Groups 38
 CHART 3-1 Peer Evaluation Checklist for Revision 39
What Should I Add or Take Out? 40
 Outlining after the First Draft 40
 Making the Outline 40
 Checking the Outline 40
 Sample After-Writing Outline 41
 Examining the Sample Outline 42
 Outlining Exercise 42
What Should I Rearrange? 43
Does It Flow? 44
What Is Editing? 45
Which Sentences Should I Combine? 45
 CHART 3-2 Transitional Terms for All Occasions 45
 CHART 3-3 Revising Checklist 46
 Combining for Conciseness 46
 Sentence Combining Exercise 47
Rearranging for Emphasis and Variety 47
 Varying the Pattern 47
 Exercise on Style 48
Which Words Should I Change? 49
 Check Your Verbs 49
 Exercise on Word Choice 49

CONTENTS   ix

          Use Active Voice Most of the Time   50
          Use Passive Voice If Appropriate   50
          Exercise on Passive Voice   50
          Feel the Words   51
          Attend to Tone   51
          Use Standard English   52
     What Is Proofreading?   52
          Try Reading It Backward   52
          Look for Your Typical Errors   53
          Read the Paper Aloud   53
          Find a Friend to Help   53
          CHART 3-4   Proofreading Checklist   54
     Sample Student Paper: Final Draft   54

PART II   *Writing about Short Fiction*   61

CHAPTER 4   *How Do I Read Short Fiction?*   62

     Notice the Structure   62
          Subplots   63
     Consider Point of View and Setting   63
     Study the Characters   64
          Foils   65
     Look for Specialized Literary Techniques   65
     Examine the Title   66
     Continue Questioning to Discover Theme   66
          CHART 4-1   Critical Questions for Reading the Short Story   67

CHAPTER 5   *Writing about Structure*   68

     What Is Structure?   68
     How Do I Discover Structure?   68
     Looking at Structure   69
          Timothy Findley, "Stones"   70
     Prewriting   83
          Finding Patterns   83
     Writing   83
          Grouping Details   83
          Relating Details to Theme   84
     Ideas for Writing   84
          Ideas for Responsive Writing   84
          Ideas for Critical Writing   84
     Rewriting   85
          Integrating Quotations Gracefully   85
          Exercise on Integrating Quotations   85
     A Critical Interpretation   86
          Lorraine M. York, "Epilogue: *Stones*"   87

CONTENTS

CHAPTER 6 *Writing about Imagery and Symbolism* 89
   What Are Images? 89
   What Are Symbols? 90
      Archetypal Symbols 90
      Phallic and Yonic Symbols 90
   How Will I Recognize Symbols? 91
      Reference Works on Symbols 91
   Looking at Images and Symbols 91
      Margaret Laurence, "To Set Our House in Order" 92
   Prewriting 102
      Interpreting Symbols 102
   Writing 102
      Producing a Workable Thesis 103
      Exercise on Thesis Statements 103
   Ideas for Writing 103
      Ideas for Responsive Writing 103
      Ideas for Critical Writing 104
   Rewriting 104
      Sharpening the Introduction 104
   Sample Student Paper 105

CHAPTER 7 *Writing about Point of View* 119
   What Is Point of View? 119
      Describing Point of View 120
      Shifting and Unreliable Narrators 120
   Looking at Point of View 121
      Eugene McNamara, "Falling in Place" 122
   Prewriting 126
      Identifying Point of View 126
   Writing 126
      Relating Point of View to Theme 126
   Ideas for Writing 127
      Ideas for Responsive Writing 127
      Ideas for Critical Writing 127
   Rewriting 127
      Sharpening the Conclusion 128

CHAPTER 8 *Writing about Setting and Atmosphere* 129
   What Are Setting and Atmosphere? 129
   Looking at Setting and Atmosphere 129
      Alistair MacLeod, "The Boat" 130
   Prewriting 142
      Prewriting Exercise 142

Writing   142
   Discovering an Organization   143
Ideas for Writing   143
   Ideas for Responsive Writing   143
   Ideas for Critical Writing   143
Rewriting: Organization and Style   144
   Checking Your Organization   144
   Improving the Style: Balanced Sentences   144
   Sentence Modelling Exercise   145

CHAPTER 9 *Writing about Theme*   147

What Is Theme?   147
Looking at Theme   148
   Alice Munro, "Boys and Girls"   149
Prewriting   158
   Figuring Out the Theme   158
   Stating the Theme   158
Writing   158
   Choosing Supporting Details   159
Ideas for Writing   159
   Ideas for Responsive Writing   159
   Ideas for Critical Writing   160
Rewriting   160
   Achieving Coherence   160
   Checking for Coherence   160
Editing: Improving Connections   161
   Repeat Words and Synonyms   161
   Try Parallel Structure   161

Anthology of Short Fiction   163

Nathaniel Hawthorne (1804–1864)
   Young Goodman Brown   163
Kate Chopin (1851–1904)
   The Story of an Hour   172
Willa Cather (1873–1947)
   Paul's Case   174
James Joyce (1882–1941)
   Araby   187
   Eveline   191
Ethel Wilson (1888–1980)
   The Window   194
Katherine Anne Porter (1890–1980)
   The Jilting of Granny Weatherall   203
Ernest Hemingway (1899–1961)
   Hills like White Elephants   210
John Steinbeck (1902–1968)
   The Chrysanthemums   214

Richard Wright (1908–1960)
    The Man Who Was Almost a Man 221
Sinclair Ross (1908–1996)
    The Lamp at Noon 230
Sheila Watson (1909–1998)
    Antigone 237
Eudora Welty (1909–2001)
    A Worn Path 243
Hisaye Yamamoto (b. 1921)
    Seventeen Syllables 249
Flannery O'Connor (1925–1964)
    A Good Man Is Hard to Find 258
Margaret Laurence (1926–1987)
    To Set Our House in Order *(in Chapter 6)*
Chinua Achebe (b. 1930)
    Dead Men's Path 269
Timothy Findley (1930–2002)
    Stones *(in Chapter 5)*
Eugene McNamara (b. 1930)
    Falling in Place *(in Chapter 7)*
Alice Munro (b. 1931)
    Boys and Girls *(in Chapter 9)*
Rudy Wiebe (b. 1934)
    Where Is the Voice Coming From? 272
Joy Kogawa (b. 1935)
    Obasan *(in Chapter 1)*
Alistair MacLeod (b. 1936)
    The Boat *(in Chapter 8)*
Joyce Carol Oates (b. 1938)
    Where Are You Going, Where Have You Been? 278
Bharati Mukherjee (b. 1940)
    The Management of Grief 289
Sandra Birdsell (b. 1942)
    The Wednesday Circle 300
Thomas King (b. 1943)
    Borders 307
David Adams Richards (b. 1950)
    A Rural Place 315
Louise Erdrich (b. 1954)
    The Red Convertible 330
Russell Smith (b. 1963)
    Serotonin 337

PART III *Writing about Poetry* 347

CHAPTER 10 *How Do I Read Poetry?* 348

Get the Literal Meaning First: Paraphrase 348
Make Associations for Meaning 349
    CHART 10-1 Critical Questions for Reading Poetry 350

CHAPTER 11 *Writing about Persona and Tone* 352

Who Is Speaking? 352

What Is Tone?   352
    Recognizing Verbal Irony   353
    Describing Tone   353
Looking at Persona and Tone   353
    Theodore Roethke, "My Papa's Waltz"   354
    Thomas Hardy, "The Ruined Maid"   354
    Pauline Johnson, "A Cry from an Indian Wife"   355
    Edmund Waller, "Go, Lovely Rose"   356
    Dorothy Parker, "One Perfect Rose"   357
Prewriting   357
    Asking Questions about the Speaker in
      "My Papa's Waltz"   357
    Devising a Thesis   358
    Describing the Tone in "The Ruined Maid"   359
    Discovering a Thesis   359
    Describing the Tone in "A Cry from an Indian Wife"   360
    Discovering a Thesis   360
    Discovering the Tone in "Go, Lovely Rose"   361
    Discovering the Tone in "One Perfect Rose"   361
Writing   361
    Explicating and Analyzing   362
Ideas for Writing   362
    Ideas for Responsive Writing   362
    Ideas for Critical Writing   363
Editing   363
    Quoting Poetry in Essays   363
Sample Student Paper   365
    Analyzing the Student Essay   369

CHAPTER 12 *Writing about Poetic Language*   370

What Do the Words Suggest?   370
    Connotation and Denotation   370
    Figures of Speech   370
    Metaphor and Simile   371
    Personification   372
    Imagery   372
    Symbol   372
    Paradox   372
    Oxymoron   373
    Other Figures of Speech   373
Looking at Poetic Language   373
    Walt Whitman, "A Noiseless Patient Spider"   373
    William Shakespeare, "Shall I Compare Thee to a
      Summer's Day?"   374

xiv   CONTENTS

        Archibald Lampman, "Voices of Earth"   374
        Dorothy Livesay, "Bartok and the Geranium"   375
        Lorna Crozier, "Poem about Nothing"   376
        Donald Hall, "My Son My Executioner"   378
Prewriting   378
        Examining Poetic Language   378
Writing   379
        Comparing and Contrasting   379
Ideas for Writing   379
        Ideas for Responsive Writing   379
        Ideas for Critical Writing   380
Rewriting: Style   380
        Choosing Vivid, Descriptive Terms   380
        Finding Lively Words   380
        Exercise on Diction   381
Sample Comparison Paper   381

CHAPTER 13 *Writing about Poetic Form*   388

What Are the Forms of Poetry?   388
        Rhythm and Rhyme   388
        CHART 13–1   Rhythm and Meter in Poetry   389
        Alliteration, Assonance, and Consonance   390
        Exercise on Poetic Form   390
        Stanzas: Closed and Open Forms   390
        Poetic Syntax   391
Looking at the Forms of Poetry   392
        Gwendolyn Brooks, "We Real Cool"   392
        bp Nichol, "landscape: 1"   392
        E. E. Cummings, "anyone lived in a pretty how town"   393
        Phyllis Webb, "Treblinka Gas Chamber"   394
        William Wordsworth, "Nuns Fret Not"   394
Prewriting   395
        Experimenting with Poetic Forms   395
Writing   397
        Relating Form to Meaning   398
Ideas for Writing   398
        Ideas for Expressive Writing   398
        Ideas for Critical Writing   400
Rewriting: Style   400
        Finding the Exact Word   401
Sample Published Essay on Poetic Form   402
        David Huddle, "The 'Banked Fire' of Robert Hayden's 'Those Winter Sundays'"   403

Anthology of Poetry 405

William Shakespeare (1564–1616)
Let Me Not to the Marriage of True Minds 405
My Mistress' Eyes Are Nothing Like the Sun 405
Shall I Compare Thee to a Summer's Day? (*in Chapter 12*)

John Donne (1572–1631)
The Flea 406
Death, Be Not Proud 406

Ben Jonson (1572–1637)
On My First Son 407

Edmund Waller (1606–1687)
Go, Lovely Rose (*in Chapter 11*)

Richard Lovelace (1618–1657)
To Lucasta, on Going to the Wars 407

Andrew Marvell (1621–1678)
To His Coy Mistress 407

William Blake (1757–1827)
The Lamb 409
The Tyger 409
The Sick Rose 410

William Wordsworth (1770–1850)
Nuns Fret Not (*in Chapter 13*)
The World Is Too Much with Us 410

George Gordon, Lord Byron (1788–1824)
She Walks in Beauty 411

Percy Bysshe Shelley (1792–1822)
Ozymandias 411

John Keats (1795–1821)
Ode on a Grecian Urn 411

Susanna Moodie (1803–1885)
XI. Brian, the Still-Hunter 413

Alfred, Lord Tennyson (1809–1892)
The Eagle 413

Robert Browning (1812–1889)
My Last Duchess 413

Walt Whitman (1819–1892)
A Noiseless Patient Spider (*in Chapter 12*)

Matthew Arnold (1822–1888)
Dover Beach 415

Emily Dickinson (1830–1886)
Safe in Their Alabaster Chambers 416
Because I Could Not Stop for Death 416

Thomas Hardy (1840–1928)
The Ruined Maid (*in Chapter 11*)

Gerard Manley Hopkins (1844–1889)
Pied Beauty 417
Spring and Fall 417

A. E. Housman (1859–1936)
    To an Athlete Dying Young   418
Sir Charles G. D. Roberts (1860–1943)
    The Flight of the Geese   419
Pauline Johnson (1861–1913)
    The Song My Paddle Sings   419
    A Cry from an Indian Wife (*in Chapter 11*)
Archibald Lampman (1861–1899)
    Voices of Earth (*in Chapter 12*)
    Winter Evening   420
William Butler Yeats (1865–1939)
    The Second Coming   421
    Sailing to Byzantium   421
Stephen Crane (1871–1900)
    War Is Kind   422
Paul Laurence Dunbar (1872–1906)
    We Wear the Mask   423
Robert Frost (1874–1963)
    Design   423
Carl Sandburg (1878–1967)
    Fog   424
    Grass   424
Wallace Stevens (1879–1955)
    The Emperor of Ice-Cream   425
E. J. Pratt (1882–1964)
    From Stone to Steel   425
Marjorie Pickthall (1883–1922)
    The Bird in the Room   426
William Carlos Williams (1883–1963)
    The Red Wheelbarrow   426
Ezra Pound (1885–1972)
    In a Station of the Metro   427
T. S. Eliot (1888–1965)
    The Love Song of J. Alfred Prufrock   427
Edna St. Vincent Millay (1892–1950)
    First Fig   430
Dorothy Parker (1893–1967)
    One Perfect Rose (*in Chapter 11*)
Wilfred Owen (1893–1918)
    Dulce et Decorum Est   431
E. E. Cummings (1894–1962)
    anyone lived in a pretty how town (*in Chapter 13*)
F. R. Scott (1899–1985)
    Laurentian Shield   431
Langston Hughes (1902–1967)
    Harlem (A Dream Deferred)   432
A. J. M. Smith (1902–1980)
    The Wisdom of Old Jelly Roll   433
Stevie Smith (1902–1971)
    Not Waving but Drowning   433

Earle Birney (1904–1995)
   Anglosaxon Street   433
Pablo Neruda (1904–1973)
   The United Fruit Co.   435
W. H. Auden (1907–1973)
   Musée des Beaux Arts   436
Theodore Roethke (1908–1963)
   My Papa's Waltz (*in Chapter 11*)
Dorothy Livesay (1909–1996)
   Bartok and the Geranium (*in Chapter 12*)
Irving Layton (b. 1912)
   The Bull Calf   437
Robert Hayden (1913–1980)
   Those Winter Sundays   437
Randall Jarrell (1914–1965)
   The Death of the Ball Turret Gunner   438
Dylan Thomas (1914–1953)
   Do Not Go Gentle into That Good Night   438
P. K. Page (b. 1916)
   Stories of Snow   439
Gwendolyn Brooks (1917–2000)
   We Real Cool (*in Chapter 13*)
Miriam Waddington (1917–2004)
   Ten Years and More   440
Margaret Avison (b. 1918)
   The Swimmer's Moment   441
Al Purdy (1918–2000)
   The Dead Poet   441
Lawrence Ferlinghetti (b. 1919)
   Constantly Risking Absurdity   442
Howard Nemerov (1920–1991)
   The Goose Fish   443
Philip Larkin (1922–1985)
   Home Is So Sad   444
Denise Levertov (1923–1997)
   O Taste and See   445
Lisel Mueller (b. 1924)
   Things   445
Allen Ginsberg (1926–1997)
   A Supermarket in California   446
James Reaney (b. 1926)
   The School Globe   447
Phyllis Webb (b. 1927)
   Sitting   448
   Treblinka Gas Chamber (*in Chapter 13*)
Donald Hall (b. 1928)
   My Son My Executioner (*in Chapter 12*)
Adrienne Rich (b. 1929)
   Aunt Jennifer's Tigers   448

Sylvia Plath (1932–1963)
   Daddy 448
Alden Nowlan (1933–1983)
   I, Icarus 451
   The Middle-Aged Man in the Supermarket 451
Leonard Cohen (b. 1934)
   A Kite Is a Victim 452
Joy Kogawa (b. 1935)
   Where There's a Wall 453
Michele Lalonde (b. 1937)
   Speak White 453
Margaret Atwood (b. 1939)
   Death of a Young Son by Drowning 456
   Dream 2: Brian the Still-Hunter 457
Seamus Heaney (b. 1939)
   Digging 457
Patrick Lane (b. 1939)
   The Bird 458
John Lennon (1940–1980) and Paul McCartney (b. 1942)
   Eleanor Rigby 459
Gwendolyn MacEwen (1941–1987)
   Icarus 460
Daphne Marlatt (b. 1942)
   retrieving madrone 462
Don McKay (b. 1942)
   Glenn Gould, Humming 462
   Icarus 463
Michael Ondaatje (b. 1943)
   The Cinnamon Peeler 464
bp Nichol (1944–1988)
   Blues 465
   landscape: 1 (*in Chapter 13*)
Bronwen Wallace (1945–1989)
   The Woman in This Poem 465
Patrick Friesen (b. 1946)
   pa poem 4: naked and nailed 467
Lorna Crozier (b. 1948)
   Poem about Nothing (*in Chapter 12*)
Jim Wong-Chu (b. 1949)
   old chinese cemetery kamloops 468
Anne Carson (b. 1950)
   God's Work 469
Dionne Brand (b. 1953)
   Land to Light On 469
Louise Erdrich (b. 1954)
   Indian Boarding School: The Runaways 472
Jan Zwicky (b. 1955)
   Musicians 472
Anne Michaels (b. 1958)
   There Is No City That Does Not Dream 473

George Elliott Clarke (b. 1960)
   Blank Sonnet   473
Billie Livingston (b. 1965)
   Paperweight   474

PART IV   *Writing about Drama*   475

CHAPTER 14 *How Do I Read a Play?*   476
  Listen to the Lines   476
  Visualize the Scene   477
  Envision the Action   478
  Drama on Film   479
      CHART 14–1   Critical Questions for Reading Plays   480

CHAPTER 15 *Writing about Dramatic Structure*   481
  What Is Dramatic Structure?   481
  Looking at Dramatic Structure   482
    Sophocles, *Antigone*   484
  Prewriting   521
    Analyzing Dramatic Structure   521
  Writing   521
    Discovering a Workable Argumentative Thesis   522
    Quoting from a Play   523
  Ideas for Writing   523
    Ideas for Responsive Writing   523
    Ideas for Critical Writing   523
  Rewriting   524
    Avoiding Unclear Language   524
  Sample Student Paper   525
    Questions for Discussion   532

CHAPTER 16 *Writing about Character*   533
  What Is the Modern Hero?   533
    The Classical Tragic Hero   533
    The Modern Tragic Hero   534
  Looking at the Modern Hero   534
    Michael Healey, *The Drawer Boy*   535
  Prewriting   574
    Analyzing the Characters   574
  Writing   574
    Choosing a Structure   575
  Ideas for Writing   575
    Ideas for Responsive Writing   575

xx   CONTENTS

        Ideas for Critical Writing   575
    Rewriting   576
        Developing Paragraphs Specifically   576
        Exercise on Providing Quotations   577
    Questions for Discussion   577

CHAPTER 17   *Drama for Writing: The Research Paper*   578
    What Is Cultural Analysis?   578
    Looking at Cultural Issues   579
        David Henry Hwang, *M. Butterfly*   580
    Using Library Sources in Your Writing   631
        A Student Researcher's Process   631
    Prewriting   632
        Finding a Thesis   632
        Locating Sources   632
        FIGURE 17–1   Reading Notes   633
        The Online Catalogue   634
        Indexes and Databases   634
        Using the Internet   634
        Reference Works in Print   635
        Taking Notes   635
    Writing   635
        CHART 17–1   Guides to Criticism of Poetry,
                            Drama, and Fiction   636
        Developing a Plan   637
        Writing before Researching   637
        Avoiding Plagiarism   638
        Introducing Quotations   639
    Ideas for Researched Writing   640
        About Short Stories   640
        About Poetry   641
        About Drama   641
    Rewriting   642
        Citing Sources   642
        Including Informational Notes   642
    Editing   642
    Sample Documented Papers by Students   642
        Paper on Drama   642
        CHART 17–2   Checklist for Accurate Documentation   643
        Paper on a Short Story   654
    Explanation of the MLA Documentation Style   661
        Sample Entries for a Works Cited List   663
        Citing Works in Electronic Form   667
        Citing Sources from the Internet   667

Anthology of Drama 669

Sophocles (ca. 496–ca. 405 BCE)
  Antigone (*in Chapter 15*)
William Shakespeare (1564–1616)
  Othello 669
Anton Chekhov (1860–1904)
  The Proposal 760
Daniel David Moses (b. 1952)
  Almighty Voice and His Wife 771
Joan MacLeod (b. 1954)
  The Shape of a Girl 803
David Henry Hwang (b. 1957)
  M. Butterfly (*in Chapter 17*)
Michael Healey (b. 1963)
  The Drawer Boy (*in Chapter 16*)

APPENDIX: ## Critical Approaches for Interpreting Literature 819

Formalism 819
Historical Approaches 820
  Biographical 820
  Cultural 820
  Marxist 821
Psychological Approaches 821
Mythological and Archetypal Approaches 822
Gender Focus 822
Reader Response 823
Deconstruction 823
Where Do You Stand? 824

Glossary of Literary and Rhetorical Terms 825
Biographical Notes 834
Credits 853
Index of Authors, Titles, and First Lines of Poems 859
Subject Index 863

Contents by Genre

Short Fiction

Chinua Achebe, *Dead Men's Path*   269
Sandra Birdsell, *The Wednesday Circle*   300
Willa Cather, *Paul's Case*   174
Kate Chopin, *The Story of an Hour*   172
Louise Erdrich, *The Red Convertible*   330
Timothy Findley, *Stones*   70
Nathaniel Hawthorne, *Young Goodman Brown*   163
Ernest Hemingway, *Hills like White Elephants*   210
James Joyce, *Araby*   187
James Joyce, *Eveline*   191
Thomas King, *Borders*   307
Joy Kogawa, *Obasan*   3
Margaret Laurence, *To Set Our House in Order*   92
Alistair MacLeod, *The Boat*   130
Eugene McNamara, *Falling in Place*   122
Bharati Mukherjee, *The Management of Grief*   289
Alice Munro, *Boys and Girls*   149
Joyce Carol Oates, *Where Are You Going, Where Have You Been?*   278
Flannery O'Connor, *A Good Man Is Hard to Find*   258
Katherine Anne Porter, *The Jilting of Granny Weatherall*   203
David Adams Richards, *A Rural Place*   315
Sinclair Ross, *The Lamp at Noon*   230
Russell Smith, *Serotonin*   337
John Steinbeck, *The Chrysanthemums*   214
Sheila Watson, *Antigone*   237
Eudora Welty, *A Worn Path*   243
Rudy Wiebe, *Where Is the Voice Coming From?*   272
Ethel Wilson, *The Window*   194
Richard Wright, *The Man Who Was Almost a Man*   221
Hisaye Yamamoto, *Seventeen Syllables*   249

Poetry

Matthew Arnold, *Dover Beach*   415
Margaret Atwood, *Death of a Young Son by Drowning*   456
Margaret Atwood, *Dream 2: Brian the Still-Hunter*   457
W. H. Auden, *Musée des Beaux Arts*   436
Margaret Avison, *The Swimmer's Moment*   441
Earle Birney, *Anglosaxon Street*   433
William Blake, *The Lamb*   409
William Blake, *The Sick Rose*   410
William Blake, *The Tyger*   409
Dionne Brand, *Land to Light On*   469
Gwendolyn Brooks, *We Real Cool*   392

Robert Browning, *My Last Duchess*   413
George Gordon, Lord Byron, *She Walks in Beauty*   411
Anne Carson, *God's Work*   472
George Elliott Clarke, *Blank Sonnet*   473
Leonard Cohen, *A Kite Is a Victim*   452
Stephen Crane, *War Is Kind*   422
Lorna Crozier, *Poem about Nothing*   376
E. E. Cummings, *anyone lived in a pretty how town*   393
Emily Dickinson, *Because I Could Not Stop for Death*   416
Emily Dickinson, *Safe in Their Alabaster Chambers*   416
John Donne, *Death, Be Not Proud*   406
John Donne, *The Flea*   406
Paul Laurence Dunbar, *We Wear the Mask*   423
T. S. Eliot, *The Love Song of J. Alfred Prufrock*   427
Louise Erdrich, *Indian Boarding School: The Runaways*   471
Lawrence Ferlinghetti, *Constantly Risking Absurdity*   442
Patrick Friesen, *pa poem 4: naked and nailed*   467
Robert Frost, *Design*   423
Allen Ginsberg, *A Supermarket in California*   446
Donald Hall, *My Son My Executioner*   378
Thomas Hardy, *The Ruined Maid*   354
Robert Hayden, *Those Winter Sundays*   437
Seamus Heaney, *Digging*   457
Gerard Manley Hopkins, *Pied Beauty*   417
Gerard Manley Hopkins, *Spring and Fall*   417
A. E. Housman, *To an Athlete Dying Young*   418
Langston Hughes, *Harlem (A Dream Deferred)*   432
Randall Jarrell, *The Death of the Ball Turret Gunner*   438
Pauline Johnson, *A Cry from an Indian Wife*   355
Pauline Johnson, *The Song My Paddle Sings*   419
Ben Jonson, *On My First Son*   407
John Keats, *Ode on a Grecian Urn*   411
Joy Kogawa, *Where There's a Wall*   453
Michele Lalonde, *Speak White*   453
Archibald Lampman, *Voices of Earth*   374
Archibald Lampman, *Winter Evening*   420
Patrick Lane, *The Bird*   458
Philip Larkin, *Home Is So Sad*   444
Irving Layton, *The Bull Calf*   437
John Lennon and Paul McCartney, *Eleanor Rigby*   459
Denise Levertov, *O Taste and See*   445
Dorothy Livesay, *Bartok and the Geranium*   375
Billie Livingston, *Paperweight*   474
Richard Lovelace, *To Lucasta, on Going to the Wars*   407
Gwendolyn MacEwen, *Icarus*   460
Daphne Marlatt, *retrieving madrone*   462
Andrew Marvell, *To His Coy Mistress*   407
Don McKay, *Glenn Gould, Humming*   462
Don McKay, *Icarus*   463

Anne Michaels, *There Is No City That Does Not Dream* 473
Edna St. Vincent Millay, *First Fig* 430
Susanna Moodie, *XI. Brian, the Still-Hunter* 413
Lisel Mueller, *Things* 445
Howard Nemerov, *The Goose Fish* 443
Pablo Neruda, *The United Fruit Co.* 435
bp Nichol, *Blues* 465
bp Nichol, *landscape: 1* 392
Alden Nowlan, *The Middle-Aged Man in the Supermarket* 451
Alden Nowlan, *I, Icarus* 451
Michael Ondaatje, The Cinnamon Peeler 464
Wilfred Owen, *Dulce et Decorum Est* 431
P. K. Page, *Stories of Snow* 439
Dorothy Parker, *One Perfect Rose* 357
Marjorie Pickthall, *The Bird in the Room* 426
Sylvia Plath, *Daddy* 448
Ezra Pound, *In a Station of the Metro* 427
E. J. Pratt, *From Stone to Steel* 425
Al Purdy, *The Dead Poet* 441
James Reaney, *The School Globe* 447
Adrienne Rich, *Aunt Jennifer's Tigers* 448
Sir Charles G. D. Roberts, *The Flight of the Geese* 419
Theodore Roethke, *My Papa's Waltz* 354
Carl Sandburg, *Fog* 424
Carl Sandburg, *Grass* 424
F. R. Scott, *Laurentian Shield* 431
William Shakespeare, *Let Me Not to the Marriage of True Minds* 405
William Shakespeare, *My Mistress' Eyes Are Nothing Like the Sun* 405
William Shakespeare, *Shall I Compare Thee to a Summer's Day?* 374
Percy Bysshe Shelley, *Ozymandias* 411
A. J. M. Smith, *The Wisdom of Old Jelly Roll* 433
Stevie Smith, *Not Waving but Drowning* 433
Wallace Stevens, *The Emperor of Ice-Cream* 425
Alfred, Lord Tennyson, *The Eagle* 413
Dylan Thomas, *Do Not Go Gentle into That Good Night* 438
Miriam Waddington, *Ten Years and More* 440
Bronwen Wallace, *The Woman in This Poem* 465
Edmund Waller, *Go, Lovely Rose* 356
Phyllis Webb, *Sitting* 448
Phyllis Webb, *Treblinka Gas Chamber* 394
Walt Whitman, *A Noiseless Patient Spider* 373
William Carlos Williams, *The Red Wheelbarrow* 426
Jim Wong-Chu, *old chinese cemetery kamloops* 468
William Wordsworth, *Nuns Fret Not* 394
William Wordsworth, *The World Is Too Much with Us* 410
William Butler Yeats, *Sailing to Byzantium* 421
William Butler Yeats, *The Second Coming* 421
Jan Zwicky, *Musicians* 472

Drama

Anton Chekhov, *The Proposal*   760
Michael Healey, *The Drawer Boy*   535
David Henry Hwang, *M. Butterfly*   580
Joan MacLeod, *The Shape of a Girl*   803
Daniel David Moses, *Almighty Voice and His Wife*   771
William Shakespeare, *Othello, the Moor of Venice*   669
Sophocles, *Antigone*   484

Thematic Contents

Rebellion and Conformity
Short Stories
Paul's Case
Eveline
The Window
The Man Who Was Almost a Man
The Lamp at Noon
Antigone
To Set Our House in Order
Boys and Girls
Obasan
The Boat
Borders

Poems
We Wear the Mask
anyone lived in a pretty how town
Harlem (A Dream Deferred)
Not Waving but Drowning
Anglosaxon Street
We Real Cool
The Swimmer's Moment
Daddy
Where There's a Wall
Speak White
Eleanor Rigby
Icarus (McKay)
The Woman in This Poem
pa poem 4: naked and nailed

Drama
Antigone
Almighty Voice and His Wife
The Shape of a Girl

Illusion and Reality
Short Stories
Young Goodman Brown
Araby
The Jilting of Granny Weatherall
A Good Man Is Hard to Find
Where Is the Voice Coming From?
Where Are You Going, Where Have You Been?
A Rural Place
Serotonin

Poems
Ozymandias
Ode on a Grecian Urn
My Last Duchess
The Ruined Maid
War Is Kind
Design
Grass
Dulce et Decorum Est
Constantly Risking Absurdity
Eleanor Rigby
Poem about Nothing

Drama
Almighty Voice and His Wife
M. Butterfly
The Drawer Boy

Love and Loss
Short Stories
Araby
Hills like White Elephants
The Lamp at Noon
Seventeen Syllables
Stones
Falling in Place
Boys and Girls
The Boat
The Management of Grief
A Rural Place
The Red Convertible
Serotonin

Poems
Let Me Not to the Marriage of True Minds

THEMATIC CONTENTS xxvii

My Mistress' Eyes Are Nothing
  Like the Sun
On My First Son
Go, Lovely Rose
To His Coy Mistress
She Walks in Beauty
Dover Beach
Winter Evening
The Love Song of J. Alfred
  Prufrock
One Perfect Rose
Aunt Jennifer's Tigers
Blues
The Woman in This Poem
Blank Sonnet
Paperweight

Drama

Othello
The Proposal
M. Butterfly
The Drawer Boy

Nature and Technology
Short Stories

Hills like White Elephants
The Lamp at Noon
Dead Men's Path
Falling in Place
The Red Convertible

Poems

Shall I Compare Thee to a
  Summer's Day?
The Flea
The Lamb
The Tyger
The Sick Rose
The World Is Too Much with Us
She Walks in Beauty
XI. Brian, the Still-Hunter
The Eagle
A Noiseless Patient Spider
Pied Beauty
The Flight of the Geese
The Song My Paddle Sings
Voices of Earth
Winter Evening

Design
Fog
Grass
From Stone to Steel
The Bird in the Room
The Red Wheelbarrow
In a Station of the Metro
Laurentian Shield
The United Fruit Co.
Bartok and the Geranium
The Bull Calf
The Death of the Ball Turret
  Gunner
Stories of Snow
The Swimmer's Moment
The Goose Fish
O Taste and See
Things
Sitting
A Kite Is a Victim
Where There's a Wall
Death of a Young Son by
  Drowning
Dream 2: Brian the Still-Hunter
The Bird
Glenn Gould, Humming
The Cinnamon Peeler
landscape: 1
God's Work
There Is No City That Does Not
  Dream

Drama

Almighty Voice and His Wife
The Drawer Boy

Male and Female
Short Stories

The Story of an Hour
Eveline
Hills like White Elephants
The Chrysanthemums
The Lamp at Noon
Antigone
Seventeen Syllables
Boys and Girls
The Boat
Where Are You Going, Where
  Have You Been?

The Wednesday Circle
A Rural Place
Serotonin

Poems

My Mistress' Eyes Are Nothing
  Like the Sun
The Flea
Go, Lovely Rose
To His Coy Mistress
She Walks in Beauty
My Last Duchess
The Ruined Maid
One Perfect Rose
Ten Years and More
Aunt Jennifer's Tigers
A Middle-Aged Man in the
  Supermarket
retrieving madrone
The Cinnamon Peeler
The Woman in This Poem
Blank Sonnet
Paperweight

Drama

Antigone
Othello
The Proposal
Almighty Voice and His Wife
M. Butterfly

Youth and Maturity
Short Stories

Young Goodman Brown
Paul's Case
Araby
Eveline
The Jilting of Granny Weatherall
The Man Who Was Almost a
  Man
A Worn Path
Antigone
To Set Our House in Order
Stones
Boys and Girls
The Boat
Where Are You Going, Where
  Have You Been?
The Wednesday Circle

A Rural Place
The Red Convertible
Serotonin

Poems

Shall I Compare Thee to a
  Summer's Day?
The Lamb
Spring and Fall
To an Athlete Dying Young
Sailing to Byzantium
My Papa's Waltz
The Bull Calf
Those Winter Sundays
Ten Years and More
Home Is So Sad
The School Globe
My Son My Executioner
I, Icarus
The Middle-Aged Man in the
  Supermarket
Death of a Young Son by
  Drowning
Eleanor Rigby
Icarus (MacEwen)
Icarus (McKay)
pa poem 4: naked and nailed
old chinese cemetery kamloops

Drama

The Shape of a Girl
The Drawer Boy

Death and Rebirth
Short Stories

The Jilting of Granny Weatherall
The Lamp at Noon
A Worn Path
A Good Man Is Hard to Find
Stones
Falling in Place
The Boat
The Management of Grief
The Red Convertible

Poems

Death, Be Not Proud
On My First Son
Ozymandias

XI. Brian, the Still-Hunter
Safe in Their Alabaster
  Chambers
Because I Could Not Stop for
  Death
Spring and Fall
To an Athlete Dying Young
The Flight of the Geese
Winter Evening
The Second Coming
Design
The Emperor of Ice-Cream
The Bird in the Room
First Fig
Dulce et Decorum Est
Not Waving but Drowning
Musée des Beaux Arts
The Bull Calf
The Death of the Ball Turret
  Gunner
Do Not Go Gentle into That
  Good Night
Stories of Snow
Ten Years and More
The Swimmer's Moment
The Dead Poet
Treblinka Gas Chamber
Death of a Young Son by
  Drowning
Dream 2: Brian the
  Still-Hunter
Glenn Gould, Humming
old chinese cemetery
  kamloops

Drama

Antigone
The Shape of a Girl

Prejudice and Acceptance
Short Stories

Paul's Case
The Man Who Was Almost a
  Man
Dead Men's Path
Stones
Obasan
The Boat
Borders

A Rural Place
The Red Convertible

Poems

A Cry from an Indian Wife
We Wear the Mask
Harlem (A Dream Deferred)
Anglosaxon Street
The United Fruit Co.
Stories of Snow
We Real Cool
Treblinka Gas Chamber
Where There's a Wall
Poem about Nothing
old chinese cemetery kamloops
Land to Light On
Indian Boarding School: The
  Runaways

Drama

Othello
Almighty Voice and His Wife
The Shape of a Girl
M. Butterfly

War and Violence
Short Stories

Stones
Falling in Place
Where Is the Voice Coming
  From?
The Red Convertible

Poems

To Lucasta, on Going to the Wars
A Cry from an Indian Wife
War Is Kind
Grass
Dulce et Decorum Est
The Death of the Ball Turret
  Gunner
Treblinka Gas Chamber

Drama

Othello
Almighty Voice and His Wife
The Shape of a Girl
The Drawer Boy

Power and Powerlessness
Short Stories

Eveline
The Man Who Was Almost a Man
The Lamp at Noon
Antigone
Seventeen Syllables
To Set Our House in Order
Stones
Where Is the Voice Coming From?
Obasan
The Wednesday Circle
A Rural Place

Poems

Death, Be Not Proud
Ozymandias
XI. Brian, the Still-Hunter
The United Fruit Co.
The Bull Calf
Treblinka Gas Chamber
Daddy
A Kite Is a Victim
Dream 2: Brian the Still-Hunter
pa poem 4: naked and nailed

old chinese cemetery kamloops
Indian Boarding School: The Runaways

Drama

Antigone
The Shape of a Girl
The Drawer Boy

On Poetry, Music, and Poets
Poems

Shall I Compare Thee to a Summer's Day?
Nuns Fret Not
The Wisdom of Old Jelly Roll
The Dead Poet
A Supermarket in California
A Kite Is a Victim
Digging
The Bird
Icarus (MacEwen)
retrieving madrone
Glenn Gould, Humming
Musicians
Blank Sonnet

Preface

This text grew out of our long-standing interest in the possibilities of integrating the study of literature with the practice of composition. Many of our students have learned to write perceptively and well using literature as their subject matter. Great literature is always thought-provoking, always new. Why not utilize it in the pursuit of critical thinking and improved writing? Toward that end, we have combined an introduction to literature with instruction in writing.

Literature and the Writing Process, Canadian Edition, presents literary selections as materials for students to read and write about, not as models for them to emulate. The text is designed to guide students through the allied processes of analytical reading and critical writing. To provide a wide range of options for writing, we have included responsive writing topics as well as critical writing topics in each chapter.

The writing instruction, concurrent with the literary study, follows the widely accepted order of beginning with larger questions of content and organization and proceeding to the particular matters, such as word choice, sentence structure, and manuscript form. On the difficult matters of devising a sound thesis and discovering theme in a literary work, we provide detailed guidance. In order to furnish a clear understanding of writing as process, we produce as illustrations throughout Part I the complete protocol that one of our students followed in preparing an essay; we include samples of her prewriting, drafting, postwriting outlining, revising, editing, and final draft. In Chapter 17 on researched writing, we have included a summary of the steps another student followed in preparing his research paper on a contemporary play. His reading notes show how he arrived at a thesis for his documented paper, which also appears. Three additional student essays are included: one illustrates the incorporation of library resources in analyzing a short story; one offers an unusual response to a group of poems; and a third demonstrates the revising process by showing the annotated first draft followed by the finished version.

This Canadian edition of *Literature and the Writing Process* provided us with a wonderful opportunity to expand the diversity of the literary selections by presenting both new and familiar Canadian works. We heard the insistent demand for more of our own short stories, poems, and plays that draw from and reflect the geography, history, and culture of Canada. Now, along with a selection of the best literature of other nations, is a selection of some of the best of our own. Chapters 1 through 9 on composition have been rewritten to focus on Canadian works for analysis; Chapters 10 through 13 include Canadian poems for examination; and the discussion of character in Chapter 16 focuses on a Canadian play.

Finally, a word about our *Companion Website* included with this textbook. Icons placed in the margins throughout the text alert students to the existence of additional resources on the website that support the instruction in the text. The website includes biographical information about many of the writers featured in this text; links to the websites of writers in this text; research links, organized by author; and an interactive timeline that provides hundreds of links to contextual information on the internet. Click on any date in the timeline to learn more about the event or historical figure discussed. Alternatively, select the Politics, International Affairs, or Culture button at the bottom of the screen and then drag the green control bar across the screen to navigate through time.

Our sincere thanks go to the many reviewers who helped us craft this Canadian Edition (listed alphabetically): Marian Allen, Grant MacEwan College; Pam Bookham, Kwantlen University College; Thomas Case, University of Regina; Penny Connell, Capilano College; William Couch, Heritage College; Leda Culliford, Laurentian University; Robert Einarsson, Grant MacEwan College; Ruth Glancy, Concordian University College of Alberta; Marcia Goldberg, Vanier College; Chris Gordon-Craig, University of Alberta; Stephen Kellock, Champlain College, St-Lambert; Renée Lallier, John Abbott College; Cindy Mackenzie, University of Regina; Karen McFarlane, Mount St. Vincent; Diana Patterson, Mount Royal College; L. Douglas Reimer, University of Manitoba; Deanna Roozendaal, Camosun College; Sumana Sen-Bagchee, Grant MacEwan College; Birk Sproxton, Red Deer College; Jordan Stouck, University of Lethbridge; Jeanie Wills, University of Saskatchewan; and J. R. (Lynn) Wytenbroek, Malaspina University College.

Thanks also to the excellent Pearson Education Canada staff, who have cooperated at every step in preparing this new edition: Lise Dupont, Senior Developmental Editor; Jessica Mosher, Executive Editor; Toivo Pajo, Marketing Manager; and Söğüt Güleç, Editorial Coordinator.

To Marianne Minaker, with whom we began this project, and to Carmen Batsford, who, after accumulating so many requests for more Canadian content for this already well-crafted text, knew it could be done, our warmest appreciation for support, encouragement, and lunches. Also, we extend enormous gratitude to Karen Alliston, Barbara Czarnecki, and Sharon Kirsch, our editors, for their skill and exactitude that have refined and polished the finished product.

Elizabeth McMahan
Susan X Day
Robert Funk
Marlet Ann Ashley

PART I

Composing: An Overview

This text serves a dual purpose: to enable you to enjoy, understand, and learn from imaginative literature; and to help you write clearly, intelligently, and correctly about what you have learned. For many people, the most difficult part of the writing process is getting started. We will provide help at this stage and then show you how to follow through to the completion of a finished paper you can be proud of.

1

The Prewriting Process

Your study of writing, as we approach it in this book, will focus on the composing process: prewriting, writing, rewriting, and editing. The first section of the text takes you through each stage, explaining one way of putting together a paper on Joy Kogawa's short story "Obasan." The following sections, which include more short stories, plus poems and plays, offer further advice for understanding and writing about these various kinds of literature.

We realize, of course, that our chronological, linear (step-by-step) explanations of the writing process are not entirely true to experience; most of us juggle at least two of the steps at a time when we write. We put down half a sentence, go back and revise it, make notes of some details to include later in the essay, and then finish the sentence, perhaps crossing out and correcting a misspelled word—a combination of prewriting, writing, rewriting, and editing. We have adopted the linear, step-by-step presentation because it allows us to explain this complicated process.

READING FOR WRITING

To prepare for your study of the stages of writing an essay about a literary topic, find a comfortable spot and read the following short story, first for pleasure, then a second time for detail.

Joy Kogawa   b. 1935

Obasan

She is sitting at the kitchen table when I come in. She is so deaf now that my knocking does not rouse her and when she sees me she is startled.

'O,' she says, and the sound is short and dry as if there is no energy left to put any inflection into her voice. She begins to rise but falters and her hands, outstretched in greeting, fall to the table. She says my name as a question.

I put my shoulder bag down, remove the mud-caked boots and stand before her.

'Obasan,' I say loudly and take her hands. My aunt is not one for hugs and kisses.

She peers into my face. 'O,' she says again.

I nod in reply. We stand for a long time in silence. I open my mouth to ask, 'Did he suffer very much?' but the question feels pornographic.

'Everyone dies some day,' she says eventually. She tilts her head to the side as if it's all too heavy inside.

I hang my jacket on a coat peg and sit beside her.

The house is familiar but has shrunk over the years and is even more cluttered than I remember. The wooden table is covered with a plastic table cloth over a blue and white cloth. Along one edge are African violets in profuse bloom, salt and pepper shakers, a soya sauce bottle, an old radio, a non-automatic toaster, a small bottle full of toothpicks. She goes to the stove and turns on the gas flame under the kettle.

'Everyone dies some day,' she says again and looks in my direction, her eyes unclear and sticky with a gum-like mucus. She pours the tea. Tiny twigs and bits of popcorn circle in the cup.

When I last saw her nine years ago, she told me her tear ducts were clogged. I have never seen her cry. Her mouth is filled with a gummy saliva as well. She drinks warm water often because her tongue sticks to the roof of her false plate.

'Thank you,' I say, taking the cup in both hands.

Uncle was disoriented for weeks, my cousin's letter told me. Towards the end he got dizzier and dizzier and couldn't move without clutching things. By the time they got him to the hospital, his eyes were rolling.

'I think he was beginning to see everything upside down again,' she wrote, 'the way we see when we are born.' Perhaps for Uncle, everything had started reversing and he was growing top to bottom, his mind rooted in an upstairs attic of humus and memory, groping backwards through cracks and walls to a moist cellar. Down to water. Down to the underground sea.

Back to the fishing boat, the ocean, the skiff moored off Vancouver Island where he was born. Like Moses, he was an infant of the waves, rocked to sleep by the lap lap and *'Nen, nen, karori,'* his mother's voice singing the ancient Japanese lullaby. His father, Japanese craftsman, was also a son of the sea which had tossed and coddled his boatbuilding ancestors for centuries. And though he had crossed the ocean from one island as a stranger coming to an island of strangers, it was the sea who was his constant landlord. His fellow tenants, the

Songhee Indians of Esquimalt, and the fishermen, came from up and down the BC coast to his workshop in Victoria, to watch, to barter and to buy.

In the framed family photograph hanging above the sideboard, Grandfather sits on a chair with his short legs not quite square on the floor. A long black cape hangs from his shoulders. His left hand clutches a pair of gloves and the top of a cane. On a pedestal beside him is a top hat, open end up. Uncle stands slightly to his right, and behind, with his hand like Napoleon's in his vest. Sitting to their left is Grandmother in a lace and velvet suit with my mother in her arms. They all look in different directions, carved and rigid with their expressionless Japanese faces and their bodies pasted over with Rule Britannia. There is not a ripple out of place.

And then there is the picture, not framed, not on display, showing Uncle as a young man smiling and proud in front of an exquisitely detailed craft. Not a fishing boat, not an ordinary yacht—a creation of many years and many winter evenings—a work of art. Uncle stands, happy enough for the attention of the camera, eager to pass on the message that all is well. That forever and ever all is well.

But many things happen. There is the voice of the RCMP officer saying 'I'll keep that one,' and laughing as he cuts through the water. 'Don't worry, I'll make good use of her.' The other boats are towed away and left to rot. Hundreds of Grandfather's boats belonging to hundreds of fishermen.

The memories are drowned in a whirlpool of protective silence. 'For the sake of the children,' it is whispered over and over. *'Kodomo no tame.'*

And several years later, sitting in a shack on the edge of a sugar beet field in southern Alberta, Obasan is watching her two young daughters with their school books doing homework in the light of a coal oil lamp. Her words are the same, *'Kodomo no tame.'* For their sakes, they will survive the dust and the wind, the gumbo, the summer oven sun. For their sakes, they will work in the fields, hoeing, thinning acres of sugar beets, irrigating, topping, harvesting.

'We must go back,' Uncle would say on winter evenings, the ice thick on the windows. But later, he became more silent.

'Nen nen.' Rest, my dead uncle. The sea is severed from your veins. You have been cut loose.

They were feeding him intravenously for two days, the tubes sticking into him like grafting on a tree. But Death won against the medical artistry.

'Obasan, will you be all right?' I ask.

She clears her throat and wipes dry skin off her lips but does not speak. She rolls a bit of dried up jam off the table cloth. She isn't going to answer.

The language of grief is silence. She knows it well, its idioms, its nuances. She's had some of the best tutors available. Grief inside her body is fat and powerful. An almighty tapeworm.

Over the years, Grief has roamed like a highwayman down the channels of her body with its dynamite and its weapons blowing up every moment of relief that tried to make its way down the road. It grew rich off the unburied corpses inside her body.

Grief acted in mysterious ways, its melancholy wonders to perform. When it had claimed her kingdom fully, it admitted no enemies and no vengeance. Enemies belonged in a corridor of experience with sense and meaning, with justice and reason. Her Grief knew nothing of these and whipped her body to resignation until the kingdom was secure. But inside the fortress, Obasan's silence was that of a child bewildered.

'What will you do now?' I ask.

What choices does she have? Her daughters, unable to rescue her or bear the silent rebuke of her suffering have long since fled to the ends of the earth. Each has lived a life in perpetual flight from the density of her inner retreat—from the rays of her inverted sun sucking in their lives with the voracious appetite of a dwarf star. Approaching her, they become balls of liquid metal—mercurial—unpredictable in their moods and sudden departures. Especially for the younger daughter, departure is as necessary as breath. What metallic spider is it in her night that hammers a constant transformation, lacing open doors and windows with iron bars.

'What will you do?' I repeat.

She folds her hands together. I pour her some more tea and she bows her thanks. I take her hands in mine, feeling the silky wax texture.

'Will you come and stay with us?' Are there any other words to say? Her hands move under mine and I release them. Her face is motionless. 'We could leave in a few days and come back next month.'

'The plants . . .'

'Neighbours can water them.'

'There is trouble with the house,' she says. 'This is an old house. If I leave . . .'

'Obasan,' I say nodding, 'it is your house.'

She is an old woman. Every homemade piece of furniture, each pot holder and child's paper doily, is a link in her lifeline. She has preserved in shelves and in cupboards, under layers of clothing in closets—a daughter's rubber ball, colouring books, old hats, children's dresses. The items are endless. Every short stub pencil, every cornflake box stuffed with paper bags and old letters is of her ordering. They rest in the corners of the house like parts of her body, hair cells, skin tissue, food particles, tiny specks of memory. This house is now her blood and bones.

She is all old women in every hamlet in the world. You see her on a street corner in a village in southern France, in her black dress and her black stockings. She is squatting on stone steps in a Mexican mountain village. Everywhere she stands as the true and rightful owner of the earth, the bearer of love's keys to unknown doorways, to a network of astonishing tunnels, the possessor of life's infinite personal details.

'I am old,' she says.

These are the words my grandmother spoke that last night in the house in Victoria. Grandmother was too old then to understand political expediency, race riots, the yellow peril. I was too young.

She stands up slowly. 'Something in the attic for you,' she says.

We climb the narrow stairs one step at a time carrying a flashlight with us. Its dull beam reveals mounds of cardboard boxes, newspapers, magazines, a trunk. A dead sparrow lies in the nearest corner by the eaves.

She attempts to lift the lid of the trunk. Black fly corpses fall to the floor. Between the wooden planks, more flies fill the cracks. Old spider webs hang like blood clots, thick and black from the rough angled ceiling.

Our past is as clotted as old webs hung in dark attics, still sticky and hovering, waiting for us to adhere and submit or depart. Or like a spider with its skinny hairy legs, the past skitters out of the dark, spinning and netting the air, ready to snap us up and ensnare our thoughts in old and complex perceptions. And when its feasting is complete, it leaves its victims locked up forever, dangling like hollowed out insect skins, a fearful calligraphy, dry reminders that once there was life flitting about in the weather.

But occasionally a memory that refuses to be hollowed out, to be categorized, to be identified, to be explained away, comes thudding into the web like a giant moth. And in the daylight, what's left hanging there, ragged and shredded is a demolished fly trap, and beside it a bewildered eight-legged spinning animal.

My dead refuse to bury themselves. Each story from the past is changed and distorted, altered as much by the present as the present is shaped by the past. But potent and pervasive as a prairie dust storm, memory and dream seep and mingle through cracks, settling on furniture, into upholstery. The attic and the living room encroach onto each other, deep into their invisible places.

I sneeze and dust specks pummel across the flashlight beam. Will we all be dust in the end—a jumble of faces and lives compressed and powdered into a few lines of statistics—fading photographs in family albums, the faces no longer familiar, the clothing quaint, the anecdotes lost?

I use the flashlight to break off a web and lift the lid of the trunk. A strong whiff of mothballs assaults us. The odour of preservation. Inside, there are bits of lace and fur, a 1920s nightgown, a shoe box, red and white striped socks. She sifts through the contents, one by one.

'That's strange,' she says several times.

'What are you looking for?' I ask.

'Not here. It isn't here.'

She turns to face me in the darkness. 'That's strange,' she says and leaves her questions enclosed in silence.

I pry open the folds of a cardboard box. The thick dust slides off like chocolate icing sugar—antique pollen. Grandfather's boat building tools are wrapped in heavy cloth. These are all he brought when he came to this country wearing a western suit, western shoes, a round black hat. Here is the plane with a wooden handle which he worked by pulling it towards him. A fundamental difference in workmanship—to pull rather than push. Chisels, hammer, a mallet, a thin pointed saw, the handle extending from the blade like that of a kitchen knife.

'What will you do with these?' I ask.

'The junk in the attic', my cousin's letter said, 'should be burned. When I come there this summer, I'll have a big bonfire. It's a fire trap. I've taken the only things that are worth having.'

Beneath the box of tools is a pile of *Life* magazines dated the 1950s. A subscription maintained while the two daughters were home. Beside the pile is another box containing shoe boxes, a metal box with a disintegrating elastic band, several chocolate boxes. Inside the metal box are pictures, duplicates of some I have seen in our family albums. Obasan's wedding photo—her mid-calf dress hanging straight down from her shoulders, her smile glued on. In the next picture, Uncle is a child wearing a sailor suit.

The shoe box is full of documents.

Royal Canadian Mounted Police, Vancouver, BC, March 4, 1942. A folded mimeographed paper authorizes Uncle as the holder of a numbered Registration Card to leave a Registered Area by truck for Vernon where he is required to report to the local Registrar of Enemy Aliens, not later than the following day. It is signed by the RCMP superintendent.

Uncle's face, young and unsmiling looks up at me from the bottom right hand corner of a wallet size ID card. 'The bearer whose photograph and specimen of signature appear hereon, has been duly registered in compliance with the provisions of Order-in-Council PC 117.' A purple stamp underneath states 'Canadian Born'. His thumb print appears on the back with marks of identification specified—scar on back of right hand.

There is a letter from the Department of the Secretary of State. Office of the Custodian. Japanese Evacuation Section. 506 Royal Bank Bldg. Hastings and Granville, Vancouver, BC.

Dear Sir.

Dear Uncle. With whom were you corresponding and for what did you hope? That the enmity would cease? That you could return to your boats? I have grown tired, Uncle, of seeking the face of the enemy hiding in the thick forests of the past. You were not the enemy. The police who came to your door were not the enemy. The men who rioted against you were not the enemy. The Vancouver alderman who said 'Keep BC White' was not the enemy. The men who drafted the Order-in-Council were not the enemy. He does not wear a uniform or sit at a long meeting table. The man who read your timid letter, read your polite request, skimmed over your impossible plea, was not your enemy. He had an urgent report to complete. His wife was ill. The phone rang all the time. The senior staff was meeting in two hours. The secretary was spending too much time over coffee breaks. There were a billion problems to attend to. Injustice was the only constant in a world of flux. There were moments when expedience demanded decisions which would later be judged unjust. Uncle, he did not always know what he was doing. You too did not have an all compassionate imagination. He was just doing his job. I am just doing my work, Uncle. We are all just doing our jobs.

My dear dead Uncle. Am I come to unearth our bitterness that our buried love too may revive?

'Obasan, what shall we do with these?'

She has been waiting at the top of the stairs, holding the railing with both hands. I close the shoe box and replace the four interlocking flaps of the cardboard box. With one hand I shine the flashlight and with the other, guide her as I precede her slowly down the stairs. Near the bottom she stumbles and I hold her small body upright.

'Thank you, thank you,' she says. This is the first time my arms have held her. We walk slowly through the living room and back to the kitchen. Her lips are trembling as she sits on the wooden stool.

Outside, the sky of the prairie spring is painfully blue. The trees are shooting out their leaves in the fierce wind, the new branches elastic as whips. The sharp-edged clarity is insistent as trumpets.

But inside, the rooms are muted. Our inner trees, our veins, are involuted, cocooned, webbed. The blood cells in the trunks of our bodies, like tiny specks of light, move in a sluggish river. It is more a potential than an actual river—an electric liquid—the current flowing in and between us, between our generations. Not circular, as in a whirlpool, or climatic and tidal as in fountains or spray—but brooding. Bubbling. You expect to hear barely audible pip-pip electronic tones, a pre-concert tuning up behind the curtains in the darkness.

Towards the ends of our branches and fingertips, tiny human-shaped flames or leaves break off and leap towards the shadows. My arms are suffused with a suppressed urge to hold.

At the edges of our flesh is a hint of a spiritual osmosis, an eagerness within matter, waiting to brighten our dormant neurons, to entrust our stagnant cells with movement and dance.

Obasan drinks her tea and makes a shallow scratching sound in her throat. She shuffles to the door and squats beside the boot tray. With a putty knife, she begins to scrape off the thick clay like mud that sticks to my boots.

(1978, rev. 1984)

Now that your reading of Kogawa's story has given you material to mull over, you should consider some questions that good writers think about as they prepare to write. Granted, experienced writers might go over some of these prewriting matters almost unconsciously—and perhaps *as* they write instead of before. But in order to explain how to get the process going for you, we will present these considerations one by one.

WHO ARE MY READERS?

Unless you are writing a journal or a diary for your own satisfaction, your writing always has an audience—the person or group of people who will read it. You need to keep this audience in mind as you plan what to say and as you choose the best way to express your ideas.

ANALYZE THE AUDIENCE

No doubt you already have considerable audience awareness. You would never write a job application letter using the latest in-group slang, nor would you normally correspond with your dear Aunt Minnie in impersonal formal English. Writing for diverse groups about whom you know little is more difficult than writing for a specific audience whom you know well. In this class, for instance, you will be writing for your fellow students and for your instructor, a mixed group often thrown together by a computer. Although they are diverse, they do share some characteristics. For one thing, when you begin to write a paper about "Obasan," you know that your audience has read the story; thus, you need not summarize the plot. Also, the people in your audience are educated; therefore, you need not avoid difficult words like *epitome, eclectic,* or *protean* if they are the appropriate choices. Other shared qualities will become apparent as you get to know your classmates and your instructor. The details you include and the level of language you use in your writing are affected by the attributes of your audience.

PREWRITING EXERCISE

Compose a brief letter persuading Obasan and Uncle to speak out against the injustices inflicted upon them during World War II. Your argumentative tactics, your attitude, and even your word choice must be affected by what you know about Obasan and Uncle from reading the story—their dignity, their desire to protect their children, their determination, even their naïveté.

Then, write briefly to the Canadian government on their behalf.

Finally, adopt the persona of one of Obasan and Uncle's daughters and write a letter to a friend you left behind in Vancouver explaining what has happened.

Be prepared to discuss with the class specific ways in which your letters are different when you change your audience.

WHY AM I WRITING?

Every kind of writing, even a grocery list, has a purpose. You seldom sit down to write without some aim in mind, and this purpose affects your whole approach to writing. The immediate response to the question "Why am I writing?" may be that your teacher or your employer asked you to. But that answer will not help you understand the reasons that make writing worth doing—and worth reading—and it will not explain why you have chosen to write on a particular topic.

REASONS FOR WRITING

Sometimes you may write in order *to express* your own feelings, as in a diary or a love letter. More frequently, though, you will be writing for several other people, and the response you want from these prospective readers will determine your purpose. If, for instance, you want your audience to be amused by your writing (as in an informal essay or friendly letter), your purpose is *to entertain*. If you want your readers to gain some knowledge from your writing (say, how to get to your house from the airport), then you are writing *to inform*. If you want your readers to agree with an opinion or to accept an idea (as in a letter to the editor or an advertisement), then you are writing *to persuade*. This is, of course, the purpose of an analytical essay. Of course, these aims overlap—as do most things in the writing process—but usually one purpose predominates.

Most of the writing you do in academic settings will attempt to persuade in one way or another. Your purpose is often to convince your reader to agree with the points you are making. Logical ideas set down in clear, interesting sentences should prove convincing and keep your readers reading. As with audience, your purpose for writing will influence the language you use and the details you bring forth in your essay.

PREWRITING EXERCISE

In writing the three letters to various characters, you have already noticed how audience and purpose can change the way you think and write about "Obasan." After studying the four writing suggestions that follow, reread the story. You may discover that you have more ideas and feelings about it than you first imagined. Thinking about prospective readers and determining your purpose will help you understand your own views and reactions better.

1. If your purpose is *to express* your personal response,
    Write down your feelings about Obasan in a journal entry or in a brief note to a close friend. Do you sympathize with Obasan? Pity her? Does she irritate you or make you angry? Be as forthright as you can.
2. If your purpose is *to inform* someone else,
    Write a brief summary (less than one hundred words) of "Obasan" for a fellow student who wants to know if the story is worth reading.

Write a slightly longer summary for your instructor (or someone else who has read the story) who wants to know if you have grasped its important points.

Which summary was easier to write? What purposes besides providing information were involved in each summary?

3. If your purpose is *to entertain* yourself or your readers,

    How would you rewrite the ending of the story to make it more positive—to make it appeal to a wider audience? Would such an ending be consistent with the earlier parts of the story? Would it be true to human experience?

4. If your purpose is *to persuade* your readers,

    The narrator finds a letter from the Department of the Secretary of State, but we are not told of its contents, nor of what was in the letter from Uncle that elicited this response from the government. Write your version of one of these letters. Try to construe from evidence in the story what Uncle was trying to persuade the government to do. What details would he use as evidence? If you were the Secretary of State, what might your response be? The narrator, in an ironic voice, names a list of "non-enemies." Could any of the details provided in this list be used in either of the letters? Consider also what other purposes Uncle or the Secretary of State would try to achieve in each of these letters.

WHAT IDEAS SHOULD I USE?

Understanding literature involves learning what questions to ask yourself as you examine a literary work. To sharpen your comprehension of the story and develop ideas for writing, you need to examine the work carefully and think critically about its component parts.

THINKING CRITICALLY

Critical thinking involves analysis and evaluation. Thus, when you engage in literary *criticism*, you are not fault-finding; you are analyzing and making judgments about a work of literature. Analysis involves taking the material apart and looking at its individual parts to see how they work together. You will use critical thinking to derive meaning from the work, and you will continue to think critically as you go about discovering ideas to write about. This latter process, called *invention*, is more effective if you employ one of the following techniques designed to help you analyze literary works and generate ideas about them.

SELF-QUESTIONING

These are the kinds of questions you might ask yourself when studying a work of literature: questions about characters, their circumstances, their motives and conflicts, their fears and expectations, their relations with other characters; questions about the setting in which the story takes place; questions about any repeated details that seem significant; questions about the meaning and value of actions and events. Write out your responses to these questions about "Obasan" and keep them handy as you formulate your essay.

1. What is Obasan's home like? List all the concrete details that the narrator uses to describe it.
2. What does Obasan's daughter intend to do about Obasan's home? Why?
3. Do you think this action is warranted?
4. The word *dust* is mentioned five times in the story. What do you think is the significance of this image?
5. How old is Obasan? Is her age important for any reason?
6. What sort of person is her niece (the narrator)? What kind of person was her husband? her daughters?
7. How does Obasan feel about what has happened to her family and her husband?
8. What sort of people were the narrator's grandparents? What happened to them?
9. Does the narrator identify with Obasan in any way?
10. What do you think Obasan means when she says that "her tear ducts were clogged"?
11. Why is silence mentioned so often in the story?
12. What does the narrator mean when she says "The sea is severed from your veins" to her dead uncle?
13. What do Obasan and Uncle see as their duty to their children?
14. Have Obasan and Uncle been naive about what their silence will accomplish?
15. What is the effect of Obasan's silence on their daughters?
16. The narrator has listed those who are "not enemies." What other purpose besides irony could this list serve?
17. How does Obasan feel about leaving her home in Alberta?
18. Why is there so much clutter in Obasan's attic and the rest of her home? What do you think she searches for to give to her niece?
19. What does the narrator mean when she says "My dead refuse to bury themselves"?
20. Why does Obasan scrape the clay from her niece's boots? Does this ending support the story?

During the invention stage, you want to turn up as many ideas as possible. Later, after choosing a focus for your paper, such as characterization or theme, you will select those story details that you will be discussing when developing your ideas. Even though you narrow your focus, you still need to consider other elements of the story—imagery, symbolism, setting, point of view—as these elements serve to reveal character or theme.

DIRECTED FREEWRITING

Many people find that they can best bring ideas to the surface by writing freely, with no restrictions about correctness. When you engage in freewriting in order to "free" ideas from your subconscious mind, you should think of a pertinent question and just start writing, or, if your instructor gives you a topic, let the assigned topic direct your freewriting process.

Consider this question: "Why does Obasan use silence as a way of dealing with the injustice of her situation?" As you think, start writing. Set down everything that comes to mind. Write in complete sentences, but do not concern yourself with spelling, word choice, or punctuation. You are writing for your own benefit, attempting to discover everything about Obasan's silence that you have in mind after reading and thinking about the story.

After writing for ten minutes (or after you run out of ideas), stop and read over what you have written. Underline any idea that might serve as the focus for a paper. Put stars or asterisks in the margin beside any ideas that sound useful as support for your interpretation. Figure 1-1 provides an example of freewriting turned out by a student on this same question.

If you find freewriting a good method for generating ideas, you may want to go through the process again. This time write down a statement that you underlined in your first freewriting as a possible approach for your paper. Let's say you decide to focus (as our student did) on the idea that Obasan's silence is an ineffective response to injustice. Put that sentence at the top of a fresh sheet of paper and begin writing. Continue recording your thoughts until you either run out of ideas or run out of time (fifteen minutes is usually enough). Then read over your freewriting, underlining or putting stars by any ideas that you think would be good support to include in your paper.

Freewriting, by definition, lacks organization, focus, and cohesion, and so it should not be considered a first draft. One way to avoid thinking of it in this way is to put your freewriting in a list instead of a paragraph. Ideas that go well together are more easily marked, and those ideas that do not fit your focus are more easily crossed off your list. The ideas produced in your freewriting will then need to be organized into a unified, logical plan—a process discussed in our next chapter.

PROBLEM SOLVING

Another method of generating material for a paper involves *problem solving*. Consider some part of the work that you feel you need to understand better and pose yourself a problem, like the following:

> Why is silence mentioned so often? Obasan is deaf, which accounts for some of it. No one seems to have spoken out against the injustice done to the family — their home, Uncle's boats — all taken away. Maybe they feel they can't fight the government or the country that has betrayed them — they are Canadian born. Uncle did write a letter, but the response is less than satisfactory. Both Uncle and Obasan keep their silence in order to protect the children from bitterness and hatred, yet the daughters leave because the silence seems like a rebuke. Kogawa writes that silence is the language of grief. Obasan silently grieves many losses — her daughters, her husband, her home & livelihood, her own power.

FIGURE 1-1 DIRECTED FREEWRITING

Discuss the effectiveness of silence as a way of dealing with injustice. As you seek a solution, ask yourself more questions.

- From what do Obasan and Uncle think silence will protect their children?

- Is there anything in the description of their past that would support their need for and use of silence?
- Why would asking if her uncle had suffered seem "pornographic" to the narrator?
- Does culture have any bearing on Obasan and Uncle's decision to suffer silently?

Write down all the reasons you can find to help explain why Obasan and Uncle respond to their plight with silence. Do any of these reasons shed light on the *theme*—the overall meaning of the story? Do you now perhaps see a meaningful point you could develop that ties in with the theme of the story? (Theme is discussed further in Chapter 9.)

CLUSTERING

Another useful way of getting ideas out of your head and down on paper involves *clustering*. Begin with a blank sheet of paper. In the centre, write a crucial question about the story that you want to investigate, and circle the words. Then, draw a line out from that circle, write an idea or a question related to the central idea, and circle that. Spiralling out from that circle, add and circle any further associations that you can make. Continue drawing lines from the centre, like spokes radiating from a wheel, and record any other ideas or questions that are related. When you finish, you will have a cluster of related ideas resembling Figure 1-2, which explores the question, "Why does Obasan respond to injustice with silence?"

Clustering works just as well with statements as it does with questions. If you think you might want to write a paper focusing on the characterization of Obasan, you could simply write her name in the centre of the page and begin recording all that you know about her. Your first ring of circles might include parents, husband, daughters, niece, house, work, lifestyle, losses, grief, health, personality—and spiral out from there.

You can see that this technique works well for exploring any aspect of a work. As you progress through this course, you may decide to write in the middle of the page *point of view, setting, imagery,* or whatever element you think might serve as a meaningful focus for your paper. If you have trouble reeling out enough material, you need to try another element. If you produce too much, you can narrow your focus.

WHAT POINT SHOULD I MAKE?

Besides providing a thorough understanding of the story, these prewriting activities serve to stir up ideas for a *thesis*—the controlling idea for your paper—and to help you discover evidence to support convincingly the observations you will make in developing that thesis.

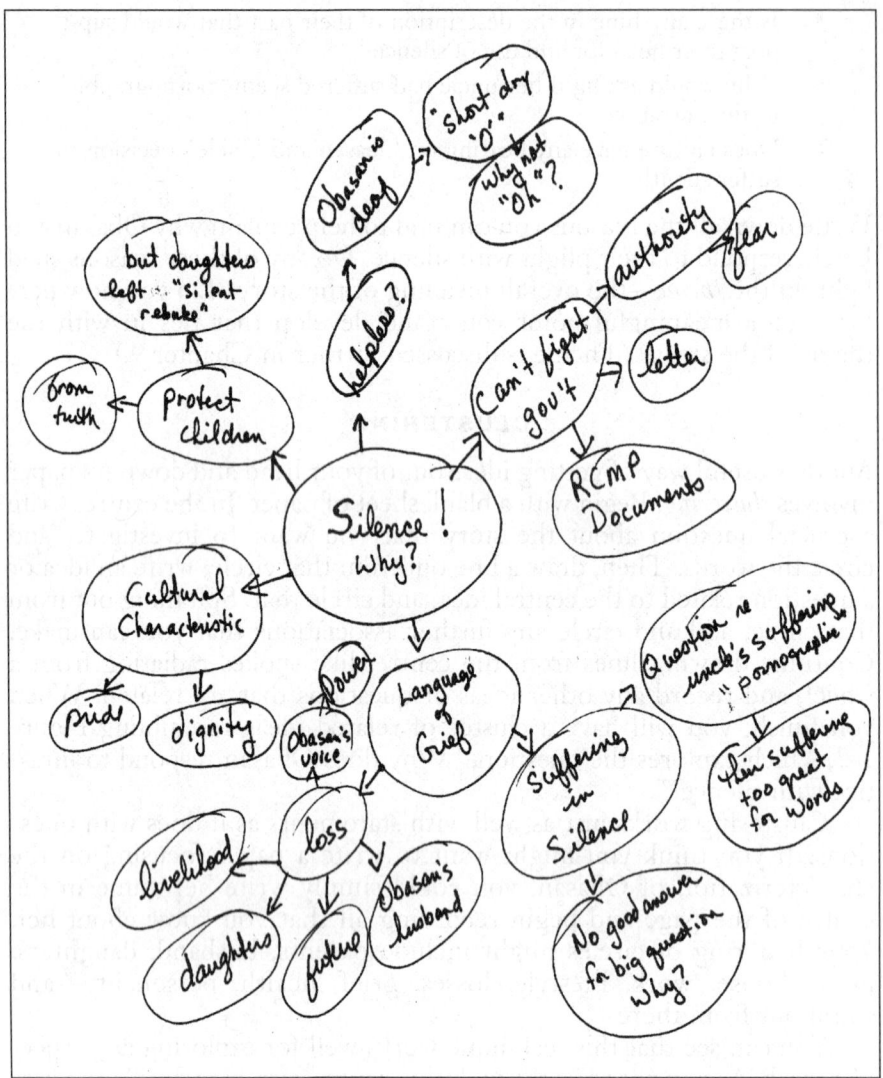

FIGURE 1-2 CLUSTERING

RELATE A PART TO THE WHOLE

One bit of advice that will help you write meaningful literary papers is the following:

> Devise a thesis that makes its point (a judgment) by relating some aspect of the work to the meaning of the whole—that is, to its theme.

Our questions so far have led you to approach Kogawa's story by analyzing character and plot. However, writing a simple character sketch (in which you discuss what sort of person Obasan is) would not produce a satisfactory critical paper. You need to go beyond that one-dimensional approach and make your essay say something about the story itself. In short, you must relate your analysis or judgment of her character to the theme.

HOW DO I FIND THE THEME?

You may have learned that the theme of a work is the moral. In a sense that is true, but a moral suggests a neatly stated, preachy comment on some vice or virtue, whereas a literary theme will seldom be so pat and should never sound preachy. In order to discover theme you need to decide what you have learned from reading the story. What did the author reveal about the behaviour of human beings, about the conduct of society? Rather than looking for a moral, look for a comment the author is making on the human condition.

Sometimes you may have a theme in mind but be unable to express it except in a cliché. You could, for instance, see the theme of "Obasan" as the following variation on an old adage: "Silence is not always golden." Although this idea may be acceptable as a theme, a clearer statement would relate the concept more closely to a judgment about the story:

> In "Obasan," Kogawa demonstrates the terrible price one may pay by remaining silent in the face of injustice.

Certainly Obasan—the kind of person she is—relates directly to this theme. If, for instance, she had been enraged to the point of protest because of the terrible injustice done to her family and other Japanese Canadians, the outcome of the story would surely be different.

The problem is thus to find a thesis that will allow you to explain in what ways Obasan's silence has affected her current life, her family, and her sense of self.

STATING THE THESIS

A good thesis statement should be a *complete sentence* that clearly conveys the point you plan to make in your paper. Notice the difference between a *topic*, which is not a complete sentence, and a *thesis*, which is:

> *Topic:* A characterization of Obasan
>
> *Thesis:* Kogawa's characterization of Obasan as a stoic and dutiful mother enables us to understand her silence in the face of outrageous injustice.
>
> *Topic:* The role of tradition in "Obasan"
>
> *Thesis:* The tradition of silence, especially the silence of women, in the face of authority helps us understand Obasan's reaction to her family's internment.
>
> *Topic:* The web as a symbol in "Obasan"
>
> *Thesis:* Kogawa's use of the web as a symbol in "Obasan" reinforces our understanding of this woman's attempts at keeping her fragmented life together.

Your thesis sentence should be broad enough to include all the ideas that are necessary as evidence but narrow enough to make a precise statement of your main point and focus your thoughts. If your thesis is too broad—like, for example, "Kogawa's characterization of Obasan is extremely well drawn"—you may end up skimming the surface, never providing a meaningful interpretation of the work. Notice that this overly broad thesis is unsatisfactory for another reason: it fails to make a real point since the words "well drawn" imply a personal opinion, not a sustainable and provable judgment.

A better thesis for a paper on "Obasan" might be stated in any of the following ways:

> Having been thoroughly betrayed by their own government, Obasan and Uncle have only silence left as their defence.

> Obasan's years of silent suffering have eroded her spirit and left her with nothing but old memories.

> Trapped in arid Alberta, far from the ocean and Uncle's livelihood, Obasan has only one means of protecting her children from the burden of hatred and bitterness—to keep silent.

Many students find writing an essay that stays focused on a thesis difficult. If comments such as "off topic" or "does not support the thesis" or even "What point are you trying to prove?" have been made on your papers in the past, a highly structured thesis statement may help you make a judgment and stick to topics that support and develop that judgment. Think of the thesis in terms of a formula:

Thesis = **Judgment** supported by Topic 1, Topic 2, and Topic 3

A structured thesis statement might be stated in the following ways:

> Obasan's overriding silence in the face of injustice has resulted in a static identification with the past, the loss of her daughters, and the lack of ability to communicate her suffering.

> The dust in Obasan's house indicates a decay of the human spirit brought about by betrayal, loss, and helplessness.

In the first example, the judgment is that Obasan's silence has cost her dearly. To prove this judgment you would discuss the specific cost to Obasan of each of the following: Topic 1, a static identification with the past; Topic 2, the loss of her daughters; and Topic 3, the lack of ability to communicate her suffering. A paragraph or two on how each of these topics supports the judgment would help you create a well-developed and highly focused analytical essay.

Most of the ideas and details needed to support any thesis statement you create will appear in the freewriting or clustering that you have already completed. In the next chapter, we will suggest some ways in which you might arrange this material in the paper itself.

WEB

For study tools to help you with your next writing assignment, please visit the Companion Website at www.pearsoned.ca/mcmahan.

The Writing Process

Now that you have examined your reactions to Joy Kogawa's "Obasan," collected your ideas, and formulated a thesis sentence, you are ready to organize this material into a workable arrangement for writing.

HOW SHOULD I ORGANIZE MY IDEAS?

A traditional but effective format includes three parts: the beginning (the introduction), the middle (the body), and the end (the conclusion). This simple plan will serve for almost any piece of writing.

The *beginning* of the paper has two main functions: to engage your readers' interest and to let them know what point you expect to make. The *middle* portion of your paper develops and supports the main point with details, examples, reasons, and explanations that make the general thesis more specific and more understandable. The *end* of the paper returns your readers to the main point by summarizing or stressing the general idea you want them to perceive from reading your essay. Later in the chapter, we will offer you more specific suggestions about how to begin and end a paper effectively. For now, we want to wrestle with the problem of organizing the body—or the middle part—of your paper about "Obasan."

THE BASIC APPROACH: DEVISING A PLAN

The thesis statements that we presented in Chapter 1 approached Kogawa's story by relating Obasan's characteristic silence to the meaning of the work. In the prewriting activities, you generated ample insights and observations about Obasan. Now you must find some arrangement for your ideas in order to present them clearly to your audience. Here is a general plan for writing a paper about a character in literature:

1. *Beginning:* Identify the character you are analyzing and state the judgment you intend to make about him or her (this point will serve as part of your thesis sentence).
2. *Middle:* Present the details of the character's personality that led you to your thesis. Pay attention to the following: what the character

says, thinks, and does; what other characters say and think about the person; and what the narrator tells about the character.
3. *End:* Conclude your interpretation and reinforce how this character's role functions to reveal theme.

The middle section of your paper can be arranged in several ways. You could organize your writing, for instance, around *central traits*, like "passivity, stoicism, dispiritedness," or around *central events* in the work that make the character's nature clear. Because "Obasan" contains so few events or incidents, you will probably choose to organize this character analysis around central traits. Here is a brief plan for a paper based on one of our sample thesis statements:

1. *Beginning:* Obasan's silent stoicism [pain] in the face of injustice has robbed her of the power to move beyond her past.
2. *Middle:* Evidence of Obasan's powerlessness can be seen in the following:
   — her static identification with a house full of long-dead memories;
   — her helplessness to prevent her daughters' escape from her impenetrable wall of mute suffering;
   — her inability to communicate the pain of her past.
3. *End:* Obasan exemplifies how a person may lose her sense of self under the weight of silent suffering.

This plan states the thesis and indicates the subpoints that will become topic sentences for several paragraphs of development and support.

The following plan organizes the middle of a paper on the same thesis by stating the topic sentences as specific forms of paralysis that contribute to Obasan's powerlessness:

2. *Middle:* Obasan's powerlessness is illustrated in these ways:
   — She is silently subsumed by the cluttered keepsakes of her past life.
   — She is unable to communicate with her daughters, and so in turn they are unable to help her.
   — She is reluctant to leave her house and speechless as to what she might do now that her husband has died.
   — In a house overflowing with mementoes of the past, she cannot find the one thing she wishes to pass on to her niece.

By writing out the subpoints, you provide yourself with a plan for writing the paragraphs that will make up the main part (the body) of your analysis.

While this example would eventually lead to a basic six-paragraph essay, the pattern of organization does not restrict you to this length. To write a longer essay, consider each topic statement as covering a topic section in which you may include two or three paragraphs instead of just one. All paragraphs in a topic section must focus on that specific topic. Remember, however, that balance is important. An essay that includes three paragraphs on one topic and only one on each of the others may not provide a balanced analysis of your subject.

ORDERING THE IDEAS

As you write the middle section of your essay, you will have to decide which point to take up first and which ones to use later in the development of your thesis. Ordinarily, you can arrange your topic sentences in two ways: logical order or chronological order.

Logical order involves arranging ideas in a way that will appeal to your readers' intelligence and good sense. Many writers begin with a less crucial idea and work up to their most important one. The logic behind this arrangement is based on the assumption that since your final point is the one your readers are most likely to remember, it should also be your strongest point.

In the second plan for writing just presented to you for a paper on "Obasan," the topic sentences about Obasan's powerlessness are arranged according to their mounting significance. The plan begins with a concrete point about Obasan's having buried her former life in a lifeless husk of stored memories, moves to the poignant effects of her silence on her relationship with her daughters, and concludes with an insight into the importance of speaking out against injustice. The last idea is particularly appropriate, as it sums up the previous two points by relating Obasan's overriding silent grief to her inability to effect change.

Chronological order, which is based on time, involves writing about events in the order in which they occur. Most narratives, such as short stories and novels, use a chronological approach. Because you will be writing about literature, your organization for a paper could simply follow the chronology of the work under consideration (although care must be taken not to fall into simple plot summary). Logical order is preferable, however, since it provides a more analytical arrangement.

HOW DO I ARGUE AN INTERPRETATION?

Is an interpretation an argument? If you want anyone to accept your interpretation, the answer is yes. You must be persuasive in your essay in order to convince your reader that your point of view on the literary work is well founded. Therefore, you may expect your readers to desire the same features in your interpretation as they would want in any argument: credibility, logic, evidence.

To be credible, your writing needs to reflect careful reading of the piece and of any other sources you bring into the argument. Logic requires that your main interpretation be consistent with the work as a whole—that it is not obviously contradicted within the work. For example, a thesis like "Obasan's silence is effective against injustice" or

"Obasan is silent because she is hard of hearing" would not meet the requirements of logic. Evidence is the most conspicuous requirement of your literary argument. Most of the evidence should come from within the reading and should directly support your point. In certain types of literary argument, some evidence can come from your own experience; for example, your observation may be that people are often speechless in the face of monumental injustice. Your own experience, however, will not provide sufficient evidence for an analytical interpretation of literature. The more unusual your interpretation, the more evidence you need, so if you go out on a limb with a thesis like "Obasan's silence is due to her Japanese heritage," you will need to show that the whole story can be viewed in this way and to provide specific details about Japanese cultural influences that support the virtues of stoicism and silence. Chart 2-1 offers a checklist for arguing an interpretation.

The balance between your interpretive points and the details you use to support them is critical. If your argument goes too far in the interpretive direction, it will sound too abstract, personal, and unconvincing. If it goes too far in listing details, it will seem as though you are summarizing the work rather than analyzing it. Let us look further into maintaining an effective balance.

DEVELOPING WITH DETAILS

Within your argument, you will make several critical generalizations (judgments focused on, but less broad than, the thesis statement) relating to your main point. These are the topic sentences that bolster the thesis.

CHART 2-1 CHECKLIST FOR ARGUING AN INTERPRETATION

1. Make sure your interpretation is reasonable and consistent.
2. Express your interpretation in a clear thesis statement.
3. Write an introduction that states your thesis and indicates briefly how you intend to support it.
4. Place the key claims of your argument in topic sentences.
5. Present your claims in a clearly defined, logical order.
6. Provide plenty of specific evidence to back up your interpretive claims.
7. Make explicit the links between your interpretation and the evidence you provide.
8. Avoid getting bogged down in mere summary.
9. Anticipate objections to your interpretation and address them in your paper.
10. Write a conclusion that recaps your argument and highlights the significance of your interpretation.

Remember to state each critical generalization clearly and to support each one with enough specific references to the story to be convincing. Sort through the observations that you made in your prewriting and select those that relate to the topic sentences in your plan. The following example shows how a writer uses specific detail and brief quotations from the story to develop the idea stated in the topic sentence:

> In the years following her family's forced relocation, Obasan's wall of silent suffering prevents her from lending a positive spirit to her husband and daughters. In order to survive, she and Uncle work tirelessly in the fields, planting and harvesting sugar beets—all "for the sake of the children." At first Uncle holds on to the hope of returning to their former life—"We must go back"—but eventually he too seems to accept his fate and "[becomes] more silent." Tragically, it is Obasan's own stoicism that ultimately drives away her daughters. After growing up in the long shadow of her mute endurance, Obasan's daughters have "fled to the ends of the earth" in order to escape from "the density of her inner retreat."

QUESTIONS FOR CONSIDERATION

In the example above, is there adequate support for the topic sentence? What story details has the writer cited to develop the main point? What other details could be used? Where does the writer bring in personal opinion or interpretation? Do you think the interpretation is reasonable?

MAINTAINING A CRITICAL FOCUS

The placement of your analytical content affects how a reader perceives your argument. Even with a solid interpretation, your paper could still sound like a plot summary if you imbed your critical insights in the middle of paragraphs. In order to achieve a sharp critical focus, the topic sentences (usually the first one of each paragraph in the body of the paper) should be critical observations supporting or relating to your thesis. In academic writing, placing the topic sentences at the beginnings of paragraphs helps your instructor follow your thinking. You should in each paragraph use the plot details to support or prove the critical generalization in the topic sentence.

DISTINGUISHING CRITICAL COMMENTS FROM PLOT DETAILS

Notice the difference between a critical comment and a plot detail:

Plot detail: Ross's story opens with the lighting of a lamp just before noon.

Critical comment: By beginning his story with the unnatural need for light at noon, Ross creates a sense of foreboding.

Plot detail: Ben Max, the youngest of three children and the only one who is beaten by their father, goes on to carry out his father's last wishes.

Critical comment: Ben Max is an ironic choice of character to perform his father's last wishes because it upsets our expectations of a child's alienation from a parent who abuses him.

If you want to use both a critical observation and a plot detail in your topic sentence, be sure that the critical comment appears in the independent (main) clause and that the plot detail is placed in a subordinate position:

Plot detail: Vanessa lies in bed listening to what she thinks might be a caught sparrow fluttering in the attic.

Critical comment: The bird in its attempt for freedom is an image of her desperation to be free from Grandmother's tyranny.

Combined: When Vanessa thinks she can hear a caught sparrow fluttering in the attic, Laurence creates an image that represents Vanessa's desperation to be free from Grandmother's tyranny.

Plot detail: Judith Templeton in "The Management of Grief" is ineffectual in her dealings with grieving Indian families.

Critical comment: Judith Templeton, a brusque social worker, serves as a character foil for Shaila, a compassionate, grieving woman, in Bharati Mukherjee's "The Management of Grief."

Combined: In "The Management of Grief" Judith Templeton, a brusque social worker who is ineffectual in assisting grieving Indian families, serves as a character foil for Shaila, a compassionate, grieving woman.

HOW SHOULD I BEGIN?

Your introduction is crucial to the effectiveness of your essay and often proves to be the most difficult to write. Try to think of this part as challenging (rather than merely hard to do), and you may find yourself rising to new heights of accomplishment.

POSTPONE IF NOTHING COMES

Remember that you do not have to write your introduction first just because it appears first in the finished essay. As long as you have your thesis clearly in mind (or clearly written out on your planning sheet), you can start right in on the body of the paper. Once you begin generating material, you may suddenly perceive an idea that will serve nicely as a beginning. Or if you postpone your introduction until the next day, your subconscious mind may provide you with the perfect opening. You may find that some of your best ideas come while you are going about your day.

WRITE AN APPEALING OPENING

Work especially hard on your opening sentence. You want to engage the interest of your readers immediately. If you begin like this,

> "Obasan" is a very interesting short story by Joy Kogawa,

no one other than your loving mother is likely to read any further unless paid to. You should mention the author and title somewhere in your introduction (even though both may appear in your title). However, try also to incorporate something specific in that first sentence. You might want to focus your readers' attention on an incident that you consider significant:

> In her short story "Obasan," Joy Kogawa portrays a woman silenced by a country's gross injustice that changes the course of her life.

Or you could start by challenging your readers' beliefs:

> As Canadians we like to think of ourselves as good and kind people, but with just one look back into our history this myth is easily dispelled.

Or you might try a shocking or disturbing fact:

> Full of fear and prejudice, many people in this country were indifferent to the plight of Japanese Canadians, whose homes and property were confiscated and who were sent far inland in the mistaken belief that they would side with Japan during the war.

STATE THE THESIS

Even more important than an arresting opening sentence is the need to let your readers know somewhere in the introductory paragraph (often the last sentence of the introduction) what the paper is going to be about, but try to avoid stating your main point too bluntly:

> I am going to show that Obasan is silent because there is nothing she can say in the face of monstrous injustice.

The phrase "I am going to show" is not stylistically effective; it is simply an announcement. Instead, subtly direct the reader to the case that you will present within your essay. Your thesis should sound more like this:

> Obasan has buried herself in silent memories of her former life, alienated her daughters, and lost her sense of self.

If you combine your thesis with a general statement or two about the story, you should have the essentials of a worthwhile introduction for a short paper:

> In Joy Kogawa's "Obasan," we see an old woman whose life is irretrievably altered when she, along with thousands of other Japanese Canadians, is forced away from her home on the Pacific coast during World War II. Over the ensuing years, Obasan has buried herself in silent memories of her former life, alienated her daughters, and lost her sense of self.

HOW SHOULD I END?

Your conclusion is just as important as your introduction—perhaps even more so. You want to leave your readers feeling satisfied that you have written something worth reading, that their time has not been wasted. Do not give them a chance to ask, "Well, so what?" at the end.

RELATE THE DISCUSSION TO THEME

Impress your readers with the value of your discussion by reinforcing in the conclusion how your analysis illuminates the theme, or meaning, of the work. This process may involve echoing your thesis statement from the introduction. Take care, however, to avoid simply repeating what you said at the beginning. Your conclusion should offer a clear expression of how your discussion relates to the theme of the story.

POSTPONE OR WRITE AHEAD

Conclusions, like introductions, do not necessarily have to be written when you come to them. If you should get some additional insight concerning the theme as you work on composing the main part of the paper, take a minute to jot down the idea so that you can later incorporate this insight into your ending. Or you could stop right then, write the final paragraph, and put it aside until you come to it. Chances are that you may change this conclusion later, but having something to work with is an enormous help—especially if you are getting tired.

If you write your way through the entire paper and still have no inspiration for the conclusion, then force yourself. Write something and keep revising it until you produce a version that pleases you. The following suggestion may help.

WRITE AN EMPHATIC FINAL SENTENCE

No matter how exhausted you are when you compose your final paragraph, do not risk ruining the effect of your entire essay by letting your conclusion trail off at the end with a limp last sentence. Regardless of the brilliance of your middle paragraphs, your readers are going to feel dejected if you end like this:

> All in all, I think "Obasan" was a fine story, and I think anyone would enjoy reading it and maybe even learn something from it.

We have advice for you in the next chapter on how to compose emphatic sentences. Study those suggestions before you rewrite your conclusion. Work *hard* on that last line. Try to come up with a final paragraph that will crystallize your meaning, something like this one:

> Kogawa makes it clear throughout the story that Obasan's voiceless suffering has only compounded her losses. Having been torn from her roots, she has in turn unwittingly forced her daughters from their own—

the "rays of her inverted sun" proving too much for them to withstand. Nevertheless, by silently scraping the mud from her niece's boots, Obasan conveys to her a mute call to action: to walk on unencumbered, to "unearth our bitterness."

COMPOSING THE FIRST DRAFT

At this point you should be ready to compose the first draft of your essay on "Obasan." You have completed the prewriting activities, devised a working thesis statement, arranged your main supporting points, and selected plenty of details to use for development. You may even have written some of your introduction and conclusion. Now is the time to move beyond these preliminary stages and write a complete draft of your paper.

PAUSING TO RESCAN

You may have been told to get your first draft down on paper as quickly as possible and then, once it is completed, to revise it. This is probably not bad advice if you suffer from writer's block, but recent studies show that most skilled writers go about it in a different way. Experienced writers tend to pause frequently as they compose—to rescan and perhaps reword what they have just written; to think about what to say next; to make additions, substitutions, or deletions; to be sure a sentence says precisely what they want it to say. After the first draft is completed, these accomplished writers revise still further, preferably several hours or even days later so that they can re-examine their writing from a reader's perspective.

If you tend to write headlong without pausing once you begin, perhaps you should try to slow down. Mina Shaughnessy, a noted composition expert, speaks of "the messy process that leads to clarity" in writing. This messy process involves pausing and thinking and reviewing and rewording in order to write well.

QUOTING FROM YOUR SOURCES

The Modern Language Association (MLA) has set a standard way to credit a source when you quote material in an essay. If you are using only a single *primary* source—the work of literature under discussion—you cite in parentheses after the quotation, the page (or pages) on which you found that material:

> The narrator comes to perceive that, although "our inner trees, our veins, are involuted, cocooned," there is nonetheless "an eagerness within matter . . . to entrust our stagnant cells with movement and dance" (7–8).

If you are using more than one primary source, you need to include the author's last name in the parentheses—with only a single blank space separating it from the page number—unless you mention the author's name in the text of your paper.

At the end of the story, Obasan does not look for resolution with words, but works silently as she "begins to scrape off the thick clay like mud that sticks to [her niece's] boots" (Kogawa 8), unlike Shaila, who waits to hear "the voices of [her] family one last time" (Mukherjee 299).

The square brackets in this quotation indicate that words in the original quotation have been altered. Essay writers often make these changes—altering pronoun references, verb tenses, and letter cases—in order to fit the quotation into the structure of the sentence.

Note that if you are using library sources, their citation becomes more complicated. Consult Chapter 17 for complete instruction in writing researched papers.

THE WORK CITED SHEET Even if you are citing only your primary source, let your readers know what it is. On a separate page at the end of your essay, centre the title ("Work Cited" or "Works Cited") at the top. Using double spacing, provide complete publication information for your source or sources. The work-cited entry for a paper on "Obasan" using the current edition of this text would look like this:

>Kogawa, Joy. "Obasan." <u>Literature and the Writing Process</u>. Elizabeth McMahan et al. Canadian ed. Toronto: Pearson, 2005. 3-8.

Notice the *hanging* indentation. Indent all lines after the first line five spaces. Space once after periods (Two spaces after a period are also acceptable, but the current practice tends strongly toward using one—as the *MLA Handbook* and this book do.) as well as after colons and commas. Use an abbreviated form of the publisher's firm—just *Pearson*, not *Pearson Education Canada*. If you are using more than one source, alphabetize the entries by their authors' last names. Double-space all lines on the Work(s) Cited page, and do not put extra space between entries. New entries are indicated when they begin at the left margin.

SAMPLE STUDENT PAPER: FIRST DRAFT

The paper that follows is the first draft of an essay on "Obasan" written by Ashley Alan, a student at Kwantlen University College, Surrey, BC. The directed freewriting for this paper appears in Figure 1-1 on page 14. The comments, suggestions, and questions in the margin were made by Ashley's instructor.

Ashley Alan 1
ENGL 1110
Kwantlen University College
November 4, 2004

A very long introduction for this short essay.

The Silent Language of Grief

As Canadians we pride ourselves on our fair-mindedness and skill at compromise; however, history reveals that we are capable of gross intolerance and injustice against our own citizens. For example, during WWII, the Canadian government interned Canadians of Japanese descent in camps far from the Pacific shores of British Columbia because it was feared that their loyalties would be with our Japanese enemies. Japanese Canadians' homes and possessions were appropriated, their livelihoods lost, and their families uprooted and sent to live in prison-like conditions, many sent as far away as Alberta where they took up new occupations such as farming in order to provide for their children. As if this injustice were not enough, the government, until recently, refused to acknowledge what it had done, using silence as a defence. However, silence proved an ineffectual defence, for every school child in British Columbia knows what happened to Canadians of Japanese heritage during the time of irrational and unchecked fear, and writers like Joy Kogawa make sure all Canadians learn from the past and do not keep silent about and ignorant of our own

Name the author and the title

Is this information necessary?

tendencies toward intolerance. Through the character of Obasan we learn that silence is not an effective tool in the face of gross injustice. In fact, through Obasan's niece, the narrator of the story, it is demonstrated that the silence of Obasan does little but express her monstrous grief. Obasan is clearly grieving terrible losses; her silence reflects the loss of her home, daughters, and husband. Most eloquently, however, Obasan's silence echoes her loss of self, including the loss of her way of life, her ability to effect change, and her voice to speak out against injustices.

Passive — Consider rewording.

Is this the best word?

Thesis is clear.

Obasan's grief reflects the loss of her former way of life; she is torn from her home beside the Pacific Ocean and forced to work the dry fields of an Alberta sugar beet farm. Canadian born, Uncle has been a boat-builder from birth, "an infant of the waves," (3) but he is forced to trade his boat-building tools for farmers' tools during the internment. Obasan has little choice but to leave her old life since she must obey government orders, follow her husband, and alter her life to protect her children. Far from the moist clean air of the ocean, she "has preserved in shelves and in cupboards, under layers of clothing in closets" (5) all of those things which provide a link in her lifeline as if her life now is so different from her life before that she might not remember who she has become.

Logic? Good use of quotation.

Does this fit?

Alan 3

[A] daughter's rubber ball, colouring
books, old hats, children's dresses . . .
[every] short stub pencil, every cornflake box stuffed with paper bags and old
letters is of her ordering. They rest in
the corners of the house like parts of
her body, hair cells, skin tissue, food
particles, tiny specks of memory. This
house is now her blood and bones. (5)

Proofread for spelling errors and typos. She has ceased to be the woman who lived with her family by the ocean and has become like a (huse) where dried and seemingly lifeless memories are stored; she reacts like a "bewildered eight-legged spinning animal" (6) to any memory that demolishes her silent order. Rather than speak out against the loss of the only way of life she has known, Obasan, in order to sur- *Verb tense?* vive, drowned memories of her past life "in a whirlpool of protective silence" (4). *Good!*

A smooth transition between topic paragraphs. After losing her way of life by the ocean, Obasan also loses the power to change what happens to her family. She cannot fight a country bent on intolerance, so the only alternative work and silence. When Obasan watches her two young daughters doing their homework in the dim light of a coal oil lamp, a far cry from how they would be living in their home in Victoria on Vancouver Island, (4) "Kodomo no tame," for the sake of the children, (4) is repeated. "For their sakes, they will survive the dust and the *Sentence structure?* *Consider rewording*

Alan 4

wind, the gumbo, the summer oven sun. For their sakes, they will work in the fields, hoeing, thinning acres of sugar beets, irrigating, topping, harvesting" (4). <u>For their sakes</u>, they will keep silent to avoid planting hatred and bitterness in their daughters. Helpless against the internment, Obasan is also helpless against what the burden of silence does to her daughters who cannot "bear the silent rebuke of [Obasan's] suffering" (5). They leave. If a punishing government cannot break the silence of the stoic, long-suffering Obasan, what chance do children have of penetrating a wall that a mother believes will protect them? Obasan's silence is as impenetrable as her suffering is palpable to her daughters, but they are "unable to rescue her" (5) <u>since she does not name her enemies</u>. Obasan remains mutely ineffectual in changing the course her life has taken.

    Finally, when her niece asks if she will be all right after the death of Uncle, "[she] clears her throat and wipes dry skin off her lips but does not speak" (4). It is as if her voice, far from the ocean and after years of ineffectual silence, has dried up. Her voice has been silenced and her "mouth . . . filled with a gummy saliva" cannot form the powerful words of accusation or revelation (3). There is something she wishes to pass on to her niece, but she has neither the voice to name

[Margin notes: "Good use of purposeful repetition"; "Personal insight is effective."; "Does this belong here?"; "Combine sentences"]

Alan 5

nor the strength to find it in the dark attic of her memory or her home. Soon, all the stored things will be lost--the pictures, details, stories, memories, and the powerful evidence they possess--since Obasan is old, near death, and silent. Obasan's daughter will burn "[the] junk in the attic," (6) but the narrator understands Obasan's obsession with passing something on to her niece. Perhaps Obasan is looking for evidence of the gross injustice done to them and wants her niece to speak out for Obasan, Uncle, and all those who have suffered. The narrator understands this when she phrases the question, "Am I come to unearth our bitterness that our buried love may too revive?" (7). Old, deaf, mute, and powerless, Obasan, "[her] lips . . . trembling," (7) uses silence to cry her grief over the loss of a voice with which to cry out against her enemies.

Quote accurately.

In the end, Obasan, "[with] a putty knife . . . begins to scrape off the thick clay like mud that sticks to [her niece's] boots" (8). The character flow, to which clay feet usually allude, may be the very silence Obasan has used all these years. Perhaps by getting rid of the clay on her niece's boots, Obasan is trying to scrape away the ineffective silence that has been employed by the family thus far. Perhaps by getting rid of the clay on her niece's boots, Obasan is freeing her niece to speak for

Good use of insight!

Alan 6

Japanese Canadians who would not or could not speak for themselves. Obasan has lost her daughters and her husband. Most important, she has lost herself since having her way of life, her self-efficacy, and her own voice taken from her. What is left is silence, "[the] language of grief," (4) a grief that has grown "rich off the unburied corpses inside [Obasan's] body" (4). This silence speaks to the heart of her niece who understands with a "sharp-edged clarity" that "is insistent as trumpets" (7) that she is the one who must give voice to her family's suffering.

Nicely reworded thesis

Is this the best quote to use here?

Focus on the main idea of loss for emphasis.

Well done, Ashley! Now, outline this draft to ensure ideas are unified.

> *Not the correct MLA format!*
>
> Alan 7
>
> Works Cited
>
> Kogawa, Joy. "Obasan." *Literature and the Writing Process*. Elizabeth McMahan, et al. 1st Canadian ed. Toronto: Pearson, 2005. (3-8).

SUGGESTIONS FOR WRITING

In order to write a paper using a short story, you first need to choose a suitable work from the anthology beginning on page 163. Kate Chopin's "The Story of an Hour" (page 172) would be a good choice for a brief paper. Read the story once for pleasure. Then turn to Chart 4-1 at the end of Chapter 4. See how many of the questions you can answer after a single reading, but do not be discouraged if you can respond to only a few. You need to read the story again—slowly and carefully, paying attention to details. After a second reading, you should be able to answer most of the questions on the list and begin arriving at an understanding of the story.

In order to come up with ideas, find a sheet of paper and perform one of the prewriting activities discussed in Chapter 1—self-questioning, directed freewriting, clustering, or whatever works for you. Look at the "Ideas for Responsive Writing" and "Ideas for Critical Writing" (page 36) if you need more help. Read the story again—and again—if you are still puzzled about its meaning. We think that the story has two distinct themes, perhaps more. When you have devised a thesis and come up with enough material to support it, write your first draft.

Next, find someone to help you get started revising, someone who will respond in writing to the peer evaluation checklist in Chart 3-1. Perhaps your instructor will provide class time for this activity. If not, find someone who has read or is willing to read the story and can thus give you thoughtful suggestions for improving your paper. In the next chapter, "The Rewriting Process," we explain in detail how you can go about making your changes.

IDEAS FOR WRITING

IDEAS FOR RESPONSIVE WRITING

1. Have you ever experienced an unexpected response to a significant event? Look at what Mrs. Mallard feels when she is alone in her room. How does it differ from what she would be expected to feel? Your own experience could be the opposite from Mrs. Mallard's—an event that should have relieved you troubled you instead. Or perhaps an event that should have evoked strong feelings left you without any feelings at all. Write a brief narrative about your experience, using plenty of specific details to make your essay believable and interesting.

2. Do you know anyone like Mrs. Mallard—someone who would feel free if his or her significant other (or others) were to disappear? Write a character sketch of this person, using plenty of specific details to make your essay plausible and appealing.

IDEAS FOR CRITICAL WRITING

1. In discussing Kate Chopin's "The Story of an Hour," focus on Mrs. Mallard's life and character to show why she reacts as she does to news of her husband's death. Why was she previously unaware of the "subtle and elusive" thoughts that come to her as she sits in her room? Why do other characters misread her reaction?

2. Focus on the imagery—the appeals to the senses—that Chopin uses to surround Mrs. Mallard. Write about how sights, sounds, smells, and sensations contribute to the reader's understanding of Mrs. Mallard's experience.

WEB

For study tools to help you with your next writing assignment, please visit the Companion Website at www.pearsoned.ca/mcmahan.

3

The Rewriting Process

You are probably relieved and pleased that you have completed the first draft of your essay. A large portion of your work is finished. But do not be in a rush to type the finished version yet. You need first to do a careful revision of your paper.

WHAT IS REVISION?

Revision involves more than just tidying your prose. The process of correcting your spelling, punctuation, and mechanics is called *editing*, but your paper is not ready for that yet. First you need *re-vision*, seeing again, to discover ways to make your writing better. Schedule your time so that you are able to lay the rough draft aside at least overnight before attempting to revise. While a draft is still warm from the writing, you cannot look at it objectively, and looking at it objectively is the basis of revision.

As you examine your essay the day after writing it, you may even see that while you were writing, your main point shifted somewhat. Sometimes writers discover what they actually want to say while trying to write something different. For example, one student made the point in the first draft of a paper on Flannery O'Connor's short story "A Good Man Is Hard to Find" that the main characters are all self-centred, deplorable individuals. As she reread her draft, she noticed that she had focused almost entirely on the grandmother and her family but had said almost nothing about The Misfit, a murderer. After some reflection—and another reading of the story—she decided to change her thesis to emphasize the point that The Misfit, the only truly evil character in the story, is the only one not punished for his behaviour. By shifting her focus to a consideration of this insight, the student discovered a number of related ideas that she had previously overlooked and thus was able to strengthen the content of her analysis.

That student was able to get some distance from her own writing, to look at it as another reader might. In revising, *look at your paper from the reader's point of view*. What questions might a reader want to ask you? These must be anticipated in the paper because you will not be around to answer them. One of the best ways to get another reader's perspective is to enlist the help of peer reviewers.

GETTING FEEDBACK: PEER REVIEW

Writers routinely seek the help of potential readers to find out what is working and what is not working in their drafts. Even professional writers ask for suggestions from editors, reviewers, teachers, and friends. Someone else can often see places where you *thought* you were being clear but were actually filling in details only in your head, not on the page.

The ideal people to help you evaluate your first draft are the members of your own writing class. They will be familiar with the assignment and will understand why you are writing the paper and for whom. Here are some guidelines to follow when asking for help with your revision:

1. *Specify the kind of help you want.* If you already know that the spelling needs to be checked, ask your readers to ignore those errors and focus on other elements in the draft. If you want suggestions about the thesis or the introduction or the tone or the organization or the examples, then ask questions about those features.
2. *Ask productive questions.* Be sure to pose questions that require more than a yes or no answer. Ask readers to tell you in detail what *they* see. You can use the questions in the Peer Evaluation Checklist (Chart 3-1, page 39) to help you solicit feedback.
3. *Don't get defensive.* Listen carefully to what your reviewers say; don't argue with them. If something confused them, it confused them. You want to see the writing through *their* eyes, not browbeat them into seeing it the way you do.
4. *Make your own decisions.* Remember that this is your paper; you are responsible for accepting or rejecting the feedback you get. If you don't agree with the suggestions, then don't follow them. However, also keep in mind that your peer reviewers are likely to be more objective about your writing than you are.

REVISING IN PEER GROUPS

In many writing classes, students work together on their papers. Meeting in small groups, they read photocopies of each other's drafts and respond to them. Sometimes students post their drafts on a class website or submit them electronically on a networked computer system (a local area network, or LAN). If your instructor doesn't arrange for peer review, try to get several readers' reactions to your drafts. You can meet together outside of class or use an internet mailing list. (You can probably get help in setting up an online review group from your school's computer centre.)

Working in peer review groups gives you a chance to write for readers other than the teacher. You increase your audience awareness, get immediate feedback on your drafts, and have a chance to discuss them with someone who doesn't have the power of a grade over you.

CHART 3-1 PEER EVALUATION CHECKLIST FOR REVISION

The following questions are designed to address the typical concerns in arguing a literary interpretation. They will help you evaluate your own or another student's first draft.

1. Does the paper meet the assignment? What is the main point? Does the whole paper relate to the main point? Is the main point interesting or too predictable?
2. Is the interpretation argued clearly and consistently? Make a note of any sentences or paragraphs that you had to reread. Make a note of any words or phrases that you found confusing.
3. Is the argument well organized? Is it logical? Is there perhaps a better order for the major points of the argument? Are there any paragraphs or points that do not seem to belong?
4. Is there enough material to make the interpretation clear and convincing? Does it need further details or examples? Make a note of places you would like to see more details or examples. Write questions to help the writer add details. For example, if the essay says "Obasan responded negatively to unpleasant memories that surfaced from time to time," you could ask, "Exactly how did she react to them?"
5. Are all the quotations from the story accurate? Do they appear within quotation marks?
6. Does the opening capture the reader's attention and make the main point of the paper clear? Does the conclusion provide an intelligent, satisfactory ending for the argument?

It takes skill to be an honest and critical reader of someone else's writing. When giving feedback, whether in groups or one-on-one, you should observe certain ground rules to ensure that your responses are productive and helpful:

- Remember that drafts are works in progress that writers intend to develop and improve. You are acting as an informed, interested reader who has questions and suggestions for improvement.
- Pay attention to *what* the other writers are saying, just as you hope they will pay attention to what you are saying. In other words, focus on content first.
- Avoid the extremes of saying that everything is wonderful or finding fault with every detail. Instead, give thoughtful, sympathetic responses—the kind of feedback that you would like to receive.
- Talk about the writing, not about the writer. If you notice errors, feel free to mention them, but concentrate on responding and suggesting rather than correcting the writer.

Once you've gathered reactions and suggestions from your peer reviewers—and perhaps from your instructor, too—you are ready to begin rewriting. The rest of this chapter will guide you through the specifics of revising and editing.

WHAT SHOULD I ADD OR TAKE OUT?

Revising is hard work, and you may wonder just where and how to start. If you have not been following a plan carefully worked out before you began writing, you should begin the revising process by outlining your first draft.

OUTLINING AFTER THE FIRST DRAFT

To be sure that your discussion is unified and complete—that is, to discover whether anything needs to be taken out or added—you should briefly outline your rough draft. It may seem odd to make an outline *after* you have written the paper, but listing your main ideas and supporting details will enable you to review your essay quickly and easily. You can examine its skeleton and decide whether everything fits together properly. This step in the revising process is *essential* if you have written the first draft without an outline or a detailed plan.

MAKING THE OUTLINE

An outline, whether done before or after the first draft, allows you to check for sufficient and logical development of ideas as well as for unity throughout the essay. Your introductory paragraph should contain your thesis, perhaps stated in a general way but stated clearly enough to let your readers know what your focus is. Here is one way to construct an after-writing outline:

1. Take a separate sheet of paper and write your thesis statement at the top.
2. Add the topic sentences stating the main ideas of your paragraphs, along with the supporting points in each one.

Your final paragraph should draw a conclusion concerning the thesis—a conclusion that relates the material in the body of the paper to the theme or purpose of the literary work.

CHECKING THE OUTLINE

Check your outline this way:

1. Make sure that the idea in every topic sentence is a significant critical observation relating directly to your thesis.
2. If not, revise the topic sentence until it clearly supports your thesis—or else delete the whole paragraph.

Just as the topic sentence of each paragraph should relate to the thesis of the paper, every piece of supporting evidence in the paragraph should relate to its topic sentence. Next, check the organization within each paragraph this way:

3. In each body paragraph, examine your supporting details to be sure that each relates directly to the topic sentence.
4. Make sure that none of your points repeats an idea included elsewhere (unless you are repeating for emphasis). Eliminate any careless repetition.
5. Decide whether your support is adequate. Think about whether you have included the most convincing details and whether you have enough of them.
6. If you decide you do not have sufficient support for a topic sentence, you need to rethink the point in order to expand it, or consider omitting the paragraph if the ideas are not essential. Sometimes you can combine the material from two paragraphs into a single new one having a broader topic sentence.

SAMPLE AFTER-WRITING OUTLINE

Since one peer reader of Ashley Alan's paper on "Obasan" noticed that a couple of examples might be out of place, Ashley outlined her first draft. Here is her after-writing outline. (Her draft appeared in Chapter 2.)

1. Intro.
    — Obasan's silence is an ineffective response to injustice (thesis)
2. She has lost her former way of life.
    — the internment has forced her and Uncle to Alberta to farm
    — preserved keepsakes from her past and become identified with her house
    — submerged old memories
3. She is unable to protect her family.
    — can't fight an intolerant country
    — survives the heat and works in the fields for her daughters' sakes
    — keeps silent to protect her daughters from becoming bitter
    — her daughters flee her suffering
    — unable to rescue her from her wall of silence
    — she's unable to name her enemies
4. Obasan can't speak out against injustice.
    — her voice has dried up from years of silence
    — can't name what she wants to pass on to her niece
    — daughter will soon burn her keepsakes
    — perhaps looking for evidence of injustice and a voice to express her suffering
5. She scrapes the clay from her niece's boots.
    — metaphorically frees her niece to speak out for Japanese Canadians
    — her silence communicates to her niece that it is she who must give voice to Obasan's suffering (conclusion)

EXAMINING THE SAMPLE OUTLINE

If you examine Ashley's outline carefully, you can see a few problems.

Topic Paragraph 1: Needs more material about Obasan's loss of her former life.

Topic Paragraph 2: The point about not being able to name her enemies is out of place in this paragraph.

Topic Paragraph 3: More focus on the topic of Obasan's loss of voice needed, especially regarding the point about her daughter burning the stored details of Obasan's life.

In the final draft of Ashley's paper, which appears at the end of this chapter on pages 55–60, you will see how she remedied the problems revealed by her outline.

OUTLINING EXERCISE

For practice in checking the relevance and organization of ideas, outline the following paragraph in the way we just described, putting the topic sentence at the top of the page and then listing each supporting idea:

> Obasan wants to pass on a meaningful memento to her niece, but she has neither the ability to find it nor the voice to name what it is. It is sadly ironic that Obasan, who is "the possessor of life's infinite personal details" (5), cannot locate the one thing she seeks amid the welter of keepsakes from a long-dead past. Her inability baffles her: "'That's strange,' she says several times" (6). Lost in her years of suffering, she cannot extract an actual object from her memories since it is only "inside the fortress" that her "kingdom was secure" (4). Furthermore, when her niece asks what she's looking for, she answers only "Not here. It isn't here" (6). Like her daughters, the object has disappeared, "unpredictable in [its] sudden [departure]" (5). Just as she cannot bring palpable evidence of her past into the beam of the flashlight, she cannot even name what it is and so give voice to her suffering.

Next, examine your outline. Do you see any irrelevant points? Can you think of any important ideas or details that have been omitted from the paragraph? Are the points arranged in an effective order? Would another arrangement be better?

Now look at the following outline and see whether it matches yours:

Topic sentence: Obasan is unable to pass on a memento from her past to her niece.

1. She can't seem to find it among all the keepsakes she stores in her house.
2. She is bewildered by this inability.
3. She is also unable to respond when her niece asks what the object is.
4. By not being able to name what it is, she can't express her suffering.

Your outline may not come out exactly like this one, but the main idea is to be sure you have included all of the supporting details.

Here are some observations to consider for a revision of the sample paragraph, based on the outline of its major points:

1. The first sentence could include a reason why Obasan might want to pass something on to her niece.
2. An earlier draft of the paragraph included a point about Obasan's daughter wanting to burn her keepsakes, but was dropped as being irrelevant to Obasan's inability to find one of these objects. Do you agree?
3. The paragraph's supporting quotations do not appear in the same order as they do in the story. Is this a valid use of supporting evidence? Have the connections been made sufficiently?

WHAT SHOULD I REARRANGE?

A crucial part of revision involves giving some thought to the order of your paragraphs and the order of the supporting details within them. The order in which they came to your mind is not necessarily the best. Luckily, rearranging is fairly easy once you have an after-writing outline.

Remember that neatness does not count at this stage. If you need to add only a sentence or two, you can perhaps squeeze the new material in between the lines or draw an arrow to the top or bottom margin and write there. If you discover the need to make major additions or to move whole paragraphs, you may want to use scissors on your rough draft. Cut your paper apart, quite literally, and tape in an added section. Or include an extra sheet of paper (numbered, for example, "p. 3A"), with a bold notation in the margin at the place on page 3 where you want to include the insert from page 3A. Revising the order of ideas is extremely easy to do if you are using a word processor, which will do your cutting and pasting electronically.

The two principles you need to use in considering how well your points are arranged are *logic* and *emphasis*. Both principles allow you to arrange ideas in a certain sequence. The following questions will help you devise an appropriate arrangement:

1. Should I arrange the paragraphs and details in my essay in the same order in which they appear in the work I am analyzing?

If you are writing a paragraph supporting the idea that Obasan is stoic, you would collect details from throughout the story. You could then put those details in the same order as they appear in the story.

2. Should I organize the descriptions in terms of space?

In a paper examining the significance of the objects in Obasan's home, you might take up these objects as though presented in a tour around the house, particularly the kitchen and the attic. Other descriptions may be arranged from near to far, from outside to inside, from small to large.

3. Should I arrange my main points along a scale of value, of power, of weight, or of forcefulness? Could I use an arrangement of
   — negative to positive?
   — universal to individual?

— most influential to least influential?
— general to specific?
— least impressive to most impressive?

You can arrange your ideas in either direction along any of these scales—negative to positive or positive to negative, for instance. It is usually effective to place the most emphatic point last in any essay. If you are writing about the several effects of Obasan's silence, and you believe that the most powerful is the inability to protest the injustice done to her and her family, you would include that idea in the last paragraph of the body of your paper, opening with a transition like this:

> Although Obasan's years of silent grief have led to her entrapment in the past and the loss of her daughters, their most powerful effect has been her inability to speak out against injustice.

The strongest-point rule is just a guideline, of course. Try to arrange your ideas in a way your readers will find effective.

DOES IT FLOW?

The best way to examine the flow (the *coherence*) of your prose is to read it aloud. Recording your essays on tape and playing them back enables you to hear with some objectivity how your writing sounds. You might also entice a friend to read your paper aloud to you. Whatever method you use, listen for choppiness or abruptness. Your ideas should be arranged in a clear sequence that is easy to follow. Will your readers experience any confusion when a new idea comes up? If so, you need stronger connections between sentences or between paragraphs—*transitions* that indicate how one idea is related to the next.

For example, when you see the words *for example*, you know what to expect. When you see *furthermore* opening a paragraph, your mind gets ready for some addition to the previous point. By contrast, when you see phrases like *on the other hand* or *by contrast*, you are prepared for something different from the previous point.

These clearly transitional phrases can be supplemented by more subtle echo transitions (in this paragraph, the words *transitional phrases* echo the main idea of the preceding paragraph), and by pronoun reference (in this paragraph, the word *these* refers to the examples in the preceding paragraph). Another technique that increases coherence in writing is the repetition of key terms and structures. In the paragraph you are reading, the key terms are forms of the words *transition*, *echo*, *refer*, and *repeat*. In the paragraph preceding this one, notice the repetition of the phrase *when you see* and, in this paragraph, the repetition of *in this paragraph* and *the word(s)*. Parallel ideas are presented in parallel ways.

In short, here are the techniques for achieving coherence:

1. A clearly sequenced flow of ideas
2. Transitional terms (see Chart 3-2 on page 45 for a handy list)

3. Echo transitions
4. Repetition of key terms
5. Repetition of parallel sentence structures.

A Revising Checklist to help you review all the important aspects of the revising process appears in Chart 3-3 on page 46.

WHAT IS EDITING?

During revision, you focused on making your paper organized, well developed, and coherent. In the editing stage, you should concentrate on improving your sentences and refining your use of language.

WHICH SENTENCES SHOULD I COMBINE?

Once you are satisfied that your ideas proceed smoothly, consider the possibility of combining sentences to avoid needless repetition of words and to eliminate choppiness. You may also decide to combine sentences to achieve emphasis and variety. Probably you can discover many ways to improve your sentences.

CHART 3-2 TRANSITIONAL TERMS FOR ALL OCCASIONS

To Continue to a New Point
next, second, third, besides, further, finally

To Make an Addition to a Point
too, moreover, in addition, for example, such as, that is, as an illustration, for instance, furthermore

To Show Cause and Effect
therefore, consequently, as a result, accordingly, then, thus, so, hence

To Show Contrast
but, still, on the other hand, nevertheless, however, conversely, notwithstanding, yet

To Show Similarity
too, similarly, in the same way, likewise, also

To Emphasize or Restate
again, namely, in other words, finally, especially, without doubt, indeed, in short, in brief, primarily, chiefly, as a matter of fact, no doubt

To Conclude a Point
finally, in conclusion, to summarize, to sum up, in sum

> **CHART 3-3 REVISING CHECKLIST**
>
> 1. Is my thesis idea intelligently and clearly stated?
> 2. Is my argument logically and effectively organized? Does the main idea of every paragraph relate directly to the thesis?
> 3. Are the paragraphs fully developed, with plenty of specific examples or illustrations to support the topic sentences?
> 4. Do the ideas flow coherently? Are the transitions easy to follow?
> 5. Have I accomplished my purpose? Does the paper make the point I set out to prove?

COMBINING FOR CONCISENESS

If you find that you are sometimes repeating the same word without meaning to, you may eliminate the problem by combining sentences. For instance, you might have written something like this:

> McNamara uses shifting narrators to narrate the story of Su Lin. The most eloquent narrator is one of the passengers.

As the repetition of the word *narrator* serves no useful purpose, the two statements can be more effectively phrased in a single sentence:

> Of all the shifting narrators that McNamara uses to tell the story of Su Lin, the most eloquent is one of the passengers.

When you combine sentences in this way, you take the main idea from one sentence and tuck it, usually as a modifier of some sort, within another sentence. We can illustrate the process in reverse to help you see more clearly what the technique involves. Notice that this sentence contains two simple statements:

> The girl, convinced that no one could know her pain, told the doctor not to judge her.

The two main ideas in that sentence are these:

> The girl was convinced that no one could know her pain.
>
> The girl told the doctor not to judge her.

You can recombine those sentences in various ways, depending on which idea you choose to emphasize:

> Convinced that no one could know her pain, the girl told the doctor not to judge her.
>
> Telling the doctor not to judge her, the girl was convinced that no one could know her pain.

Sentence combining not only eliminates wordiness but also adds variety and focus. The various combinations provide numerous stylistic choices.

SENTENCE COMBINING EXERCISE

The following sentences, all written by students, include needless repetition and wordiness that can be eliminated by sentence combining. Decide which idea in each pair of sentences should be emphasized, and put that idea in the main (independent) clause. You will, of course, need to change, add, or omit words as you work to improve these sentences, but try not to leave out any significant ideas.

1. The second common stereotype is the dark lady. Usually the dark lady stereotype symbolizes sexual temptation.
2. Alistair MacLeod wrote a short story called "The Boat." As the title of the story suggests, it is about a boat and shows how this boat influences people's lives.
3. Emily Dickinson's poetry is sometimes elliptical. It is thus sometimes difficult for readers to get even the literal meaning of her poems.
4. There are three major things to consider in understanding Grandmother MacLeod's character. These things include what the author tells us about Grandmother MacLeod, what Grandmother MacLeod says and does, and how other people respond to her.
5. In Alice Munro's "Boys and Girls," most of the incidents that inspire the girl's fantasies have humorous connotations associated with them. These can be broken down into basically two groups, the first one being her desire to be in charge of a situation.

REARRANGING FOR EMPHASIS AND VARIETY

When you rewrite to gain emphasis and variety, you will probably restructure sentences as well as combine them. In fact, you may find yourself occasionally dividing a sentence for easier reading or to produce a short, emphatic sentence. The following are some techniques to help you in polishing your sentence structure.

VARYING THE PATTERN

The usual way of forming sentences in English is to begin with the subject, follow with the verb, and add a complement (something that completes the verb), like this:

Walter Mitty is not a brave person.

Any time you depart from this expected pattern, you gain variety and some degree of emphasis. Notice the difference:

A brave person Walter Mitty is not.

Here are other variations that you may want to try:

A Dash at the End
Mark Twain found constant fault with humanity—with what he called "the damned human race."

An Interrupter Set Off by Dashes or Commas

Twain considered humanity in general—"the damned human race"—inferior to the so-called lower animals.

A Modifier at the Beginning

Although he loved individual human beings, Twain professed to loathe what he called "the damned human race."

A SHORT-SHORT SENTENCE Because most of the sentences you will write are moderately long, you gain considerable emphasis when you follow a sentence of normal length with an extremely short one:

> Plagiarizing, which means borrowing the words or ideas of another writer without giving proper credit, is a serious infraction. Do not do it.

DELIBERATE REPETITION Just a few pages ago, we cautioned you to combine sentences rather than to repeat words needlessly. That caution still holds. Repeating words for emphasis, however, is a different matter. Purposeful repetition can produce effective and emphatic sentences:

> James Joyce believed that Dublin was the centre of paralysis, a paralysis that kept the Irish people dependent.
>
> One cannot talk well, study well, or write well if one cannot think well.

That last sentence (modelled after one written by Virginia Woolf) repeats the same grammatical structure as well as the same words to achieve a powerful effect.

EXERCISE ON STYLE

Rewrite the following ordinary sentences to achieve greater emphasis, variety, and conciseness.

1. Margaret Laurence was born in the small prairie town of Neepawa, Manitoba, and she experienced the deaths of both parents before she was ten years old.
2. Her Scottish-Presbyterian grandparents instilled in her a powerful sense of a righteous and fair God, and many of Margaret Laurence's works reflect this perspective.
3. In 1943 Laurence received a scholarship to attend United College in Winnipeg, so at the age of seventeen she left her grandparents' home.
4. Jean Margaret Wemyss (Margaret Laurence's maiden name) married Jack Laurence the year she graduated (1947), and in that year she also became a reporter for the *Winnipeg Citizen*.
5. Soon after their marriage the Laurences moved to Africa, and Laurence began writing about her experiences there, but after their separation, Laurence moved to England and began her Manawaka novels.

WHICH WORDS SHOULD I CHANGE?

You may have a good thesis and convincing, detailed support for it; however, your writing style can make the difference between a dull, boring presentation and a rich, engaging one.

CHECK YOUR VERBS

After examining the construction of your sentences, look at the specific language you have used. Read through the rough draft and underline the verbs. Look for forms of these useful but well-worn words:

is (are, was, were, etc.)	go	has
get	come	move
do	make	use

Consider substituting a different verb, one that presents an image—visual or otherwise—to your readers. For example, this sentence is grammatically correct but dull:

Obasan does her work in silence.

Searching for a more precise verb than *does*, you might write:

Obasan silently executes her work.

Executes suggests a picture of Obasan working out the bitterness she refuses to express verbally.

Occasionally you can pick up a lively word from somewhere else in a limp sentence and convert it into the main verb:

Obasan is unable to leave her old house because her determination to order her clutter has trapped her there.

Trapped is an arresting word in that sentence, and you could shift it to an earlier position to good effect:

Obasan is trapped in her old house by her determination to order her clutter.

This revision also cuts unnecessary words out of the first version.

EXERCISE ON WORD CHOICE

Rewrite the following sentences about Timothy Findley's short story "Stones" using livelier verbs and fewer words:
1. The narrator's most unusual characteristic is a strong need for love from his father.
2. Ben Max's constant show of support for his father makes the readers feel sorry for Ben.
3. Readers of the story get the message that some people are unable to forgive or forget.

4. The readers come to the conclusion that Ben deserves much more than he gets.
   5. Since the narrator's memories make up the whole story, we have only his point of view.

USE THE ACTIVE VOICE MOST OF THE TIME

Although the passive voice sometimes offers the best way to construct a sentence, the habitual use of the passive sprinkles your prose with colourless helping verbs, like *is* and *was*. If a sentence is in passive voice, the subject does *not* perform the action implied by the verb:

> The paper was written by Janet, Jo's roommate.
>
> The assignment was given poorly.
>
> Her roommate's efforts were hindered by a lack of understanding.

The paper, the assignment, and the roommate's efforts did *not* carry out the writing, the giving, or the hindering. In active voice, the subjects of the sentences are the doers or the causes of the action:

> Jo's roommate, Janet, wrote the paper.
>
> The teacher gave the assignment poorly.
>
> Lack of understanding hindered her roommate's efforts.

USE THE PASSIVE VOICE IF APPROPRIATE

Sometimes, of course, you may have a good reason for writing in the passive voice. For example, you may want to give a certain word the important position of subject even though it is not the agent of the action. In the sentence

> Sensory details are emphasized in this paragraph.

the *details* are the key point. The writer of the paragraph (the agent of the action) is not important enough even to be included. In the active voice, the key term would be pushed to the middle of the sentence, a much weaker position:

> The writer emphasizes sensory details in this paragraph.

Clearly, you need not shun the passive, but if any of your sentences sound stilted or awkward, check to see if the passive voice may be the culprit.

EXERCISE ON THE PASSIVE VOICE

Change the passive voice to active in the following sentences. Feel free to add, delete, or change words.

   1. Antigone is treated brutally by Creon because of her struggle to achieve justice.

2. Creon was not convinced by her tirade against his unbending authority.
3. Conflict between male and female was portrayed in the play by the author.
4. If even a small point is won against a tyrant by society, considerable benefit may be experienced.
5. The tragedy is caused by the iron-bound authority exercised by Creon.

FEEL THE WORDS

Words have emotional meanings *(connotations)* as well as direct dictionary meanings *(denotations)*. You may be invited to a get-together, a soirée, a social gathering, a blowout, a blast, a reception, a bash, or a do, and although all are words for parties, the connotations tell you whether to wear jeans or feathers, whether to bring a case of cheap beer or a bottle of expensive wine.

In writing, take into account the emotional content of the words you use. One of our favourite essays, "The Discus Thrower," opens with this sentence:

I spy on my patients.

The word *spy* immediately captures the imagination with its connotations of intrigue and mystery and its slight flavour of deception. "I watch my patients when they don't know it" is still an interesting sentence because of its denotative content, but essayist Richard Selzer's version commands emotional as well as intellectual engagement.

We are not encouraging you to puff up your prose with strings of adverbs and adjectives; indeed, a single emotionally charged word in a simple sentence can be quite powerful.

ATTEND TO TONE

Tone—the reflection of a writer's attitude—is usually described in terms of emotion: serious, solemn, satirical, humorous, sly, mournful, expectant, and so on. Although most writing about literature calls for a plain, direct tone, other attitudes can be conveyed. Negative book reviews, for instance, sometimes have a sarcastic tone. A writer unsympathetic to Obasan might describe her as "a spineless drudge who has learned to enjoy her oppression," whereas a sympathetic reader might state that Obasan is "a pitiful victim of a brutal government." Someone who wants to remain neutral could describe Obasan as "a woman trapped by injustice and fear." These variations in tone, conveyed by word choice, reflect the writers' differing attitudes toward what is being discussed.

Once you establish a tone, you should stick with it. A humorous or sarcastic section set unexpectedly in a straightforward, direct essay will distract or disconcert your readers. Be sure to set your tone in the first paragraph; then your readers will unconsciously adjust their expectations about the rest of the paper.

USE STANDARD ENGLISH

The nature of your audience will also determine the level of usage for your writing. Essays for college and university classes usually require *standard English* and a style that takes a serious or neutral tone and avoids such informal usage as contractions, slang, and sentence fragments, even intentional ones.

Academic writing using standard English often involves a third-person approach:

One can sympathize with Obasan, at the same time regretting her silence.

The reader sympathizes with Obasan, . . .

Most instructors consider the use of first-person plural *(we, us, our, ours)* quite acceptable in formal papers:

We sympathize with Obasan, . . .

Obasan gains our sympathy, . . .

However, most consider the first-person singular *(I, me, my, mine)* to be unacceptable in academic writing:

I sympathize with Obasan, . . .

Obasan gains my sympathy, . . .

Avoid the informal second person, *you*. Do *not* write, "You can see that Obasan is caught in a terrible bind."

WHAT IS PROOFREADING?

Proofreading is the last step in preparing your final draft. After you have improved your sentences and refined your word choices, you must force yourself to read the paper one last time to pick up any careless mistakes or typographical errors. Jessica Mitford rightly says that "failure to proofread is like preparing a magnificent dinner and forgetting to set the table."

TRY READING IT BACKWARD

To avoid getting so interested in what you have written that you don't see your errors, read your sentences from the last one on the page to the first, that is, from the bottom to the top. Because your ideas will lack continuity in reverse order, you stand a better chance of keeping your attention focused on each sentence *as* a sentence. Be sure that every word is correctly spelled, that each sentence is complete and correctly punctuated. If you are using a word processor, be sure to run your spelling checker.

LOOK FOR YOUR TYPICAL ERRORS

If you know that you often have problems with certain elements of punctuation or diction, be on guard for these particular errors as you examine each sentence.

1. Make sure that each sentence really is a sentence, not a fragment—especially those beginning with *because, since, which, that, although, as, when,* or *what,* and those beginning with words ending in *ing.*
2. Make sure that independent clauses joined by *indeed, moreover, however, nevertheless, thus,* and *hence* have a semicolon before those words, not just a comma.
3. Make sure that every modifying phrase or clause is close to the word it modifies.
4. If you know you have a problem with spelling, check every word and look up all questionable ones. Run your spelling checker if you are writing on a word processor.
5. Be alert for words that you know you consistently get wrong. If you are aware that you sometimes confuse words that sound alike *(it's/its, your/you're, there/their/they're, effect/affect),* check the accuracy of your usage. Remember that your spelling checker will not help you here.

If you are not sure how to correct the errors just mentioned, you will find advice in most college and university level grammar handbooks. You will also find a handy Proofreading Checklist in Chart 3-4 on page 54.

READ THE PAPER ALOUD

In an earlier section, we recommended reading your paper aloud as a means of checking coherence. It is a good idea to read it aloud again to catch words left out or carelessly repeated.

FIND A FRIEND TO HELP

If you have a literate friend who will help you proofread your paper, you are in luck. Ask this kind person to point out errors and to let you know whether your thesis is made plain at the beginning, whether every sentence is clear, and whether the paper as a whole makes sense. You risk having to do further revising if any of your friend's responses prove negative, but try to be grateful for the help. You want to turn in a paper you can be proud of.

Relying on someone else to do your proofreading, though, is unwise. There will be writing situations in college or university that preclude your bringing a friend to help (e.g., essay examinations and in-class essays). Learn to find and correct your own errors, so you will not risk failure when you go it alone.

CHART 3-4 PROOFREADING CHECKLIST

1. Have I mixed up any of these easily confused words?

its/it's	their/they're/there	lie/lay
effect/affect	suppose/supposed	our/are
your/you're	woman/women	use/used
to/too/two	prejudice/prejudiced	then/than
who's/whose	accept/except	cite/site

2. Have I put an apostrophe appropriately in each of my possessive nouns?
3. Have I carelessly repeated any word?
4. Have I carelessly left any words out?
5. Have I omitted the first or final letter from any words?
6. Have I used the proper punctuation at the end of every sentence?
7. Have I spelled every word correctly?

SAMPLE STUDENT PAPER: FINAL DRAFT

The following is the final draft of Ashley Alan's paper on "Obasan." This finished version reflects the changes she made in organization to correct the problems revealed by her after-writing outline. The paper also includes editing changes she made to achieve precision in word choice and to increase the effectiveness of each individual sentence.

WEB   For study tools to help you with your next writing assignment, please visit the Companion Website at www.pearsoned.ca/mcmahan.

Ashley Alan 1
ENGL 1110
Kwantlen University College
November 25, 2004

The Silent Language of Grief

[margin note: Good opening] As Canadians we pride ourselves on our fair-mindedness and skill at compromise; however, history reveals that we are capable of gross intolerance and injustice against our own citizens. For example, during World War II, the Canadian government interned Canadians of Japanese descent in camps far from the Pacific shores of British Columbia because it was feared that their loyalties would be with Japan. Japanese Canadians' homes and possessions were appropriated, their livelihoods lost, and their families uprooted and sent to live in prison-like conditions, many sent as far away as Alberta where they took up new occupations such as farming in order to provide for their children. Joy Kogawa, through her short story "Obasan," makes sure we Canadians are not ignorant of our own tendencies toward intolerance. Through the character Obasan, we learn that silence, although ineffective, is sometimes the only response a victim has to gross injustice. In fact, the narrator of the story, Obasan's niece, demonstrates that Obasan's silence is only effective in expressing her monstrous grief. Obasan is clearly grieving terrible losses, most poignantly her loss of self, which involves the loss of her

[margin note: need name + story in intro]

Alan 2

way of life, her ability to effect change, and her voice to speak out against injustice. Obasan's silent grief reflects the loss of her former way of life; she is torn from her home beside the Pacific Ocean and forced to work the dry fields of an Alberta sugar beet farm. Canadian born, Uncle has been a boat-builder most of his life, "an infant of the waves" (3), but he is forced to trade his boat-building tools for farmers' implements during the internment. Obasan has little choice but to leave her old life since she must obey government orders, follow her husband, and protect her children. Far from the moist, clean air of the ocean, she "has preserved in shelves and in cupboards, under layers of clothing in closets" (5) all of those things that provide a link in her lifeline and provide a sense of order in the midst of her chaos.

> [A] daughter's rubber ball, colouring books, old hats, children's dresses . . . [every] short stub pencil, every corn-flake box stuffed with paper bags and old letters [are] of her ordering. They rest in the corners of the house like parts of her body, hair cells, skin tissue, food particles, tiny specks of memory. This house is now her blood and bones. (5)

She has ceased to be the woman who enjoyed life with her family by the ocean and has become

Alan 3

like her house where dried and seemingly lifeless memories are stored; she reacts like a "bewildered eight-legged spinning animal" (6) to any memory that demolishes her silent order. Rather than speak out against the loss of the only way of life she has known, Obasan carefully orders the clutter in her new life in order to survive, and she drowns memories of her past life "in a whirlpool of protective silence" (4). —transition

(After being forced from her life near the ocean, Obasan also loses the power to change what happens to her family.) She cannot fight a country bent on intolerance, so the only alternative is work and silence. When Obasan watches her two young daughters doing their homework in the dim light of a coal oil lamp, a far cry from how they would have lived in their home in Victoria on Vancouver Island (4), "Kodomo no tame," for the sake of the children (4), becomes Obasan and Uncle's reason for silence. "For their sakes, they will survive the dust and the wind, the gumbo, the summer oven sun. For their sakes, they will work in the fields, hoeing, thinning acres of sugar beets, irrigating, topping, harvesting" (4). For their sakes, they will keep silent to avoid planting hatred and bitterness in their daughters. Helpless against the internment, Obasan is also helpless against what the burden of her silent grief does to her daughters who cannot "bear the silent rebuke of

[margin annotations: "clear topic sentence", "generalization"]

Alan 4

[Obasan's] suffering" (5). They leave. If a punishing government cannot break the silence of the stoic, long-suffering Obasan, what chance do children have of penetrating a wall that a mother believes will protect them? Obasan's silence is as impenetrable as her suffering is palpable to her daughters, but they are "unable to rescue her" (5). Obasan remains mutely ineffectual in changing the course of events in her life.

   Finally, when her niece asks if she will be all right after the death of Uncle, "[she] clears her throat and wipes dry skin off her lips but does not speak" (4). It is as if her voice, after years of ineffectual silence, has dried up. Her voice silenced and her "mouth . . . filled with a gummy saliva," she cannot form the powerful words of accusation or revelation (3); however, she wishes to pass "something" on to her niece, but she has neither the voice to name it nor the strength to find it in the dark attics of her memory and her home. Soon, all the stored things will be lost--the pictures, details, stories, memories--and with them the powerful evidence of oppression these things possess since Obasan is old, near death, and silent. Although Obasan's daughter threatens to burn "[the] junk in the attic" (6), the narrator understands Obasan's need to pass this unnamed "something" on to her niece. Perhaps Obasan is searching for evidence of the gross injustice done to them; perhaps she searches for a voice. The narrator understands this when she phrases the question "Am I come to unearth our bitterness that our buried love too may revive?" (7). Old, deaf, mute, and powerless, Obasan, although "[her] lips are trembling" (7), uses silence to cry her grief over the loss of a voice with which to cry out against her enemies.

In the end, Obasan, "[with] a putty knife . . . begins to scrape off the thick clay-like mud that sticks to [her niece's] boots" (8). The character flaw, to which clay feet usually allude, may be the very silence Obasan has used all these years. By getting rid of the clay on her niece's boots, Obasan may be trying to scrape away the ineffective silence that has been employed by the family thus far and free her niece to speak for Japanese Canadians who would not or could not speak for themselves. Obasan has lost her daughters and her husband, and she has lost herself since having her way of life, her self-efficacy, and her own voice taken from her. What is left is silence, "[the] language of grief" (4), a grief that speaks to the heart of her niece who understands with a "sharp-edged clarity . . . insistent as trumpets" (7) that she must give voice to Obasan's loss.

Alan 6

Work Cited

Kogawa, Joy. "Obasan." *Literature and the Writing Process*. Elizabeth McMahan et al. 1st Canadian ed. Toronto: Pearson, 2005. 3-8.

PART II

Writing about Short Fiction

This section, focusing on the short story, covers the literary and rhetorical elements that you need to understand in order to write effectively about short fiction.

4

How Do I Read Short Fiction?

As noted author Joyce Carol Oates has observed, short fiction can be difficult to understand "because it demands compression; each sentence must contribute to the effect of the whole. Its strategy is not to include an excess of detail but to exclude, to select, to focus as sharply as possible." In order to grasp the full meaning of a story, you need to read it at least twice. Preferably, let some time elapse between readings so that you can mull the story over in your mind. Your initial reading can be purely for pleasure, but the second reading should involve careful and deliberate study of all the elements that combine to produce a unified whole. You should gain both pleasure and knowledge from reading short fiction. The knowledge frequently stems from understanding the *theme* that usually provides some insight into the human condition although sometimes contemporary short stories simply raise moral or ethical questions and make no pretence of providing answers.

NOTICE THE STRUCTURE

During the second reading, notice the way the story is structured. The action (i.e., what happens) is called the *plot* and is usually spurred by some conflict involving the main character (the *protagonist*). Except in some modern works, most short stories have a clear beginning, middle, and end in which the conflict producing the action becomes increasingly intense, building to a climax that sometimes resolves the conflict and sometimes simply concludes it—often in catastrophe. Do not expect many happy endings in serious fiction. A sombre conclusion is more likely.

Usually stories proceed in regular chronological order following a time sequence similar to that in real life. Occasionally, however, an author employs *flashbacks*—stopping the forward action to recount an episode that happened in the past—in order to supply necessary background material or to maintain suspense. By sorting out the numerous flashbacks in Katherine Anne Porter's "The Jilting of Granny Weatherall," readers discover that Granny has been jilted not once but twice. Conversely, the flashbacks interspersed in David Adams Richards's "A Rural Place" lead the reader chronologically to the tragic outcome of Janie's past.

SUBPLOTS

Longer works, such as novels, plays, and films, frequently include one or more *subplots*, which produce minor complications in the main action. Often, some quality of a major character is illuminated through interaction with minor characters in a subplot. In a closely unified work, the action of a subplot reinforces the theme. Again, in Richards's "A Rural Place," the subplot involving the struggles between Simon and his coworkers reflects the dynamics of the relationships between the main character, Janie, and other members of her family. Thus, the subplot strengthens Richards's theme of trust and betrayal. Occasionally, though, subplots are introduced simply to provide interest, excitement, or comic relief. As you study a work involving subplots, consider their function. Do they provide action that contributes to the meaning of the work? If so, try to decide how. You may find you can write an interesting paper by focusing on the way a subplot serves to develop character or emphasize theme.

CONSIDER POINT OF VIEW AND SETTING

Sometimes the *point of view*—the position from which an author chooses to relate a story—can be crucial to the effectiveness, even to the understanding, of short fiction. In Eugene McNamara's "Falling in Place" we are given a number of views of the death of Su Lin. In Margaret Laurence's "To Set Our House in Order" it is ten-year-old Vanessa MacLeod who traces the family dynamics of a household controlled by her overbearing grandmother. In other stories, the point of view provides access to the thoughts and feelings of more than one character. Ethel Wilson in "The Window," for example, uses an all-seeing, all-knowing *omniscient* narrator who provides access to the thoughts and actions of several characters. Ernest Hemingway, in "Hills like White Elephants," chooses to let his characters tell the story themselves through conversation. This objective (sometimes called *dramatic*) point of view is revealed by a glance at the pages, which consist primarily of dialogue. Some authors select one character to tell the story firsthand, but these first-person narrators can play quite different roles. In "Serotonin," Russell Smith creates a strong sense of believability by presenting the fine points about love that run through a young man's thoughts after he has ingested mind-altering drugs. In Bharati Mukherjee's "The Management of Grief," the first-person narrator is at once an observer of the action and a central participant in it. In James Joyce's "Araby," the narrator recounts an experience from his boyhood but from the vantage point of adulthood, employing adult perceptions.

The *setting* of a story, like the point of view, is sometimes important, sometimes not. In many of the stories included in this anthology, setting plays a role of some consequence. For instance, here is Vanessa MacLeod exploring her grandmother's house:

> I spent the morning morbidly, in seeking hidden places in the house. There were many of these—odd-shaped nooks under the stairs, small and loosely nailed-up doors at the back of clothes closets, leading to dusty tunnels and forgotten recesses in the heart of the house where the only things actually to be seen were drab oil paintings stacked upon the rafters, and trunks full of outmoded clothing and old photograph albums. But the unseen presences in these secret places I knew to be those of every person, young or old, who had ever belonged to the house and had died.

The dust, the hidden places, and the unseen presences in the house are indications of the powerful influences of the past on all who live there. As you study a short story, give some thought to the setting. Could the events just as well take place somewhere else? Or does the setting seem to play an integral part? How does its time period affect the story? Does the setting in some way add to the meaning of the work?

STUDY THE CHARACTERS

As you reread *dialogue*, pay special attention to those passages in quotation marks that characters speak to each other. You can begin to determine characterization from these exchanges, just as you come to know real people partly by what they say. As you form an understanding of a character, notice what other people in the story say about that person, how they respond to that person, as well as what the author reveals of that person's thoughts and past behaviour. Because fiction often allows us access to what the characters are thinking (as well as doing), we can sometimes know fictional persons better than we do our closest friends and family members. Sometimes, we can be certain of a character's motivation for behaving in a certain way; at other times, motivation becomes one of the elements to be determined before we can fully appreciate the work.

In Nathaniel Hawthorne's "Young Goodman Brown," in order to understand why the main character becomes an embittered and distrustful old man, we must examine his motives and his behaviour. At the beginning of the story, we see Brown as an apparently well-meaning and trusting young man who enters the forest on an errand of questionable intent, perhaps to test his faith. But we see finally that he is too easily persuaded to believe the worst of his fellow townspeople. The abundant ambiguities in the story keep us wondering what is actually happening in the forest and what is simply a figment of Brown's imagination. He is so single-minded that he does not even try to sort out illusion from reality.

Instead, he decides that everyone in the village except himself is a sinner. His loss of faith—we might even say his rejection of Faith—extends to all humanity and completely ruins his life.

FOILS

A *foil* is a minor character whose role sharpens our understanding of a major character by providing a contrast. Although far more common in drama than in the short story, foils can also prove useful in the analysis of works of fiction.

In Timothy Findley's "Stones," Cy Max understands what is meant by "Dieppe" yet grows to hate his father, whose experiences there during the war change him irrevocably for the worse. Ben, Cy's brother, is too young to know what the word signifies, yet he loves and understands his father to the end. In "A Worn Path," Eudora Welty uses minor characters to emphasize several qualities of her main character, Phoenix Jackson. The young hunter who callously points his gun at Phoenix and suggests that her trip is too long for an old woman emphasizes for us just how strong-willed and determined she is. The cold professionals who dutifully dole out the state's charity at the clinic underscore the sincerity of Phoenix's self-sacrifice.

After you have read a fictional work, ask yourself why the author included the minor characters. What role do they serve in the work as a whole? Often the role of a minor character will provide an appropriate focus for writing an analysis of a short story, a novel, or a play.

LOOK FOR SPECIALIZED LITERARY TECHNIQUES

As you study a story on second reading, you may notice irony and foreshadowing that you missed the first time through. Since *irony* involves an upsetting of expectations—having the opposite happen from what would be usual—you sometimes need to know the outcome of an action in order to detect the full extent of the irony. *Foreshadowing* works the same way: you may not be aware of these hints of future happenings until the happenings finally occur. When you go through a story again, however, both irony and foreshadowing become easily apparent and contribute to its meaning and effectiveness.

Be alert also for *images*—for words and phrases that put a picture in your mind. These images increase the enjoyment of reading fiction and, if deliberately repeated, can become *motifs* that emphasize some important element in the story and thus convey meaning. The constant images of wind in Sinclair Ross's "The Lamp at Noon" reinforce our impression of the vicious force of nature pulling and driving Ellen to madness. If a repeated image gathers significant meaning, it then becomes a *symbol*—to be clearly related to something else in the story. In this case, the wind may be understood to symbolize the power of nature over fragile human beings.

EXAMINE THE TITLE

The title may in some way point toward or be related to the meaning. Richard Wright's title "The Man Who Was Almost a Man" evokes his theme: the difficulty that black males encounter in achieving manhood in North America. Sometimes, the title identifies the controlling symbol, as in John Steinbeck's "The Chrysanthemums" and Alistair MacLeod's "The Boat." Margaret Laurence's title "To Set Our House in Order" carries a double meaning, suggesting both keeping the house presentable and preparing for death. Sheila Watson's title "Antigone" directs us to search for connections to Greek mythology.

CONTINUE QUESTIONING TO DISCOVER THEME

Your entire study of these various elements of fiction should lead to an understanding of the meaning, or *theme*, of the story. You need to ponder everything about a short story in order to discover its theme. Keep asking yourself questions until you come up with some meaningful observation about human behaviour or the conduct of society. The questions in Chart 4-1 (on page 67) will guide you in exploring any story and perhaps spark that essential insight that leads to understanding.

CHART 4-1 CRITICAL QUESTIONS FOR READING THE SHORT STORY

Before planning an analysis of any of the selections in the anthology of short stories, write out the answers to the following questions to be sure you understand the piece and to help you generate material for your paper.

1. Who is the main character? Does this person's character change during the course of the story? Do you feel sympathetic toward the main character? What sort of person is she or he? Does this character have a foil?
2. What pattern or structure is there to the development of the plot? Can you describe the way the events are organized? Is the structure significant to the meaning?
3. Does surprise play an important role in the plot? Is there foreshadowing? Does the author use flashbacks?
4. Is anything about the story ironic?
5. Is there any symbolism in the story? How does the author make you aware of symbolic actions, people, or objects?
6. What is the setting—the time and location? How important are these elements in the story? Could it be set in another time or place just as well? Is the setting significant to the meaning?
7. Describe the atmosphere of the story, if it is important. How does the author create this atmosphere?
8. Who narrates the story? Is the narrator reliable? What effect does the point of view have on your understanding of the story? What would be gained or lost if the story were told from a different point of view (for example, by another character)?
9. How does the title relate to the other elements in the story and to the overall meaning?
10. What is the theme of the story? Can you state it in a single sentence? How is this theme carried out?
11. Does the author's style of writing affect your interpretation of the story? If so, how would you describe the style? For example, is it conversational or formal? Familiar or unfamiliar? Simple or ornate? Ironic or satiric?

WEB For study tools to help you with your next writing assignment, please visit the Companion Website at www.pearsoned.ca/mcmahan.

5

Writing about Structure

When you focus on structure in discussing a literary work, you are examining the way the parts fit together to form a unified whole. Examining the structure often proves an excellent means of understanding a short story, novel, poem, or play and also provides a good way to approach a written literary analysis.

WHAT IS STRUCTURE?

Most works of literature have an underlying pattern that serves as a framework or *structure*. You are familiar with the way plays are divided into acts and scenes, identified with numerals in the script, and marked in a stage production by the opening and closing of the curtain. The structure of television drama is often marked by commercial breaks. (For a discussion of dramatic structure, see Chapter 15, "Writing about Dramatic Structure.") Poems also have a visible structure, being divided into lines and stanzas. Sometimes poetic structure is complex and arbitrary, involving a certain number of lines, an established meter, and a fixed rhyme scheme. (See Chapter 13, "Writing about Poetic Form.") Novels, as you know, are divided into chapters, usually numbered and often titled, but sometimes not. Some short stories have no visible structure at all, but many do: they have space breaks indicating the divisions. Occasionally in short stories and often in novellas, these sections are numbered.

In narrative works like novels and short stories, the plot itself is the main structural element, but these works also contain underlying structural features. Although not visible like chapter divisions or space breaks, the underlying structure serves an integral function just as a skeleton does in providing support for the body. Discovering, examining, and understanding these underlying structures involves delving beneath the surface to discover the meaning of the work.

HOW DO I DISCOVER STRUCTURE?

First, consider the *plot*. What is the central conflict and how is it resolved? Do the events in the story move in a straight line from the beginning of the conflict to its resolution? Or are there interruptions and digressions? Are there flashbacks? Is time manipulated in any other way? If so, why? For instance, without the time shifts in the plot of Richards's "A Rural Place," there would be no suspense, and we would lose the impact of Janie's final revelation about her past.

If the story has any visible structural features, like space breaks, try to figure out why they are there. Do they divide scenes? Do they indicate time shifts?

Look next for patterns, especially for contrasts and for repetitions. In "Stones," the story included in this chapter, Timothy Findley presents the conflict between the two classes of people on either side of Toronto's Yonge Street through the use of various contrasting details. He also introduces two sharply contrasting characters in the one character of David Max—David Max before the war and David Max after.

Look always at beginnings and endings. In "Stones" the opening scene reveals the social tension that is later reflected in the closing lines. How does that tension relate to the meaning of the story?

As is true when analyzing any work of literature, don't forget to consider the title. Does it have any relationship to the plot? Sometimes the title touches on the central conflict, thus focusing our attention on the structure of the story and reinforcing the theme.

LOOKING AT STRUCTURE

With our discussion of structure in mind, read Timothy Findley's "Stones," which follows, and try to determine how the parts work together to convey the meaning of the story.

Timothy Findley   1930–2002

Stones

We lived on the outskirts of Rosedale, over on the wrong side of Yonge Street. This was the impression we had, at any rate. Crossing the streetcar tracks put you in another world.

One September, my sister, Rita, asked a girl from Rosedale over to our house after school. Her name was Allison Pritchard and she lived on Cluny Drive. When my mother telephoned to see if Allison Pritchard could stay for supper, Mrs Pritchard said she didn't think it would be appropriate. That was the way they talked in Rosedale: very polite; oblique and cruel.

Over on our side—the west side—of Yonge Street, there were merchants—and this, apparently, made the difference to those whose houses were in Rosedale. People of class were not meant to live in the midst of commerce.

Our house was on Gibson Avenue, a cul-de-sac with a park across the road. My bedroom window faced a hockey rink in winter and a football field in summer. Cy, my brother, was a star in either venue. I was not. My forte, then, was the tricycle.

Up at the corner, there was an antique store on one side and a variety shop on the other. In the variety shop, you could spend your allowance on penny candy, Eskimo pies and an orange drink I favoured then called *Stubby*. *Stubby* came in short, fat bottles and aside from everything else—the thick orange flavour and the ginger in the bubbles—there was something wonderfully satisfying in the fact that it took both hands to hold it up to your lips and tip it down your throat.

Turning up Yonge Street, beyond the antique store, you came to The Women's Bakery, Adam's Grocery, Oskar Schickel, the butcher and Max's Flowers. We were Max's Flowers. My mother and my father wore green aprons when they stood behind the counter or went back into the cold room where they made up wreaths for funerals, bouquets for weddings and corsages for dances at the King Edward Hotel. Colonel Matheson, retired, would come in every morning on his way downtown and pick out a boutonnière from the jar of carnations my mother kept on the counter near the register. Once, when I was four, I caused my parents untold embarrassment by pointing out that Colonel Matheson had a large red growth on the end of his nose. The 'growth' was nothing of the sort, of course, but merely the result of Colonel Matheson's predilection for gin.

Of the pre-war years, my overall memory is one of perfect winters, heavy with snow and the smell of coal- and wood-smoke mingling with the smell of bread and cookies rising from The Women's Bakery. The coal-smoke came from our furnaces and the wood-smoke—mostly birch and maple—came to us from the chimneys of Rosedale, where it seemed that every house must have a fireplace in every room.

Summers all smelled of grass being cut in the park and burning tar from the road crews endlessly patching the potholes in Yonge Street. The heat of these summers was heroic and the cause of many legends. Mister Schickel, the butcher, I recall once cooked an egg on the sidewalk outside his store. My father, who was fond of Mister Schickel, made him a bet of roses it could not be done. I think Mister Schickel's part of the bet was pork chops trimmed of excess fat. When the egg began to sizzle, my father slapped his thigh and whistled and he sent my sister, Rita, in to get the flowers. Mister Schickel, however, was a graceful man and when he placed his winnings in the window of his butcher shop, he also placed a card that read: *Thanks to Max's Flowers one dozen roses.*

The Great Depression held us all in thrall, but its effects on those of us who were used to relative poverty—living on the west side on Yonge Street—were not so debilitating as they were on the far side in Rosedale. The people living there regarded money as something you had—as opposed to something you went out and got—and they were slower to adjust to what, for them, was the unique experience of deprivation.

I remember, too, that there always seemed to be a tramp at the door: itinerants asking if—for the price of a meal or the meal itself—they could carry out the ashes, sweep the walks or pile the baskets and pails in which my father brought his flowers from the market and the greenhouse.

Our lives continued in this way until about the time I was five—in August of 1939. Everyone's life, I suppose, has its demarcation lines—its latitudes and longitudes passing through time. Some of these lines define events that everyone shares—others are confined to personal—even to secret lives. But the end of summer 1939 is a line drawn through the memory of everyone who was then alive. We were all about to be pitched together into a melting pot of violence from which a few of us would emerge intact and the rest of us would perish.

My father joined the army even before the war had started. He went downtown one day and didn't come back till after suppertime. I noticed that he hadn't taken the truck but had ridden off on the streetcar. I asked my mother why he had worn his suit on a weekday and she replied *because today is special*. But that was all she said.

At the table, eating soufflé and salad, my brother, Cy—who was nine years old that summer—talked about the World's Fair in New York City and pictures he'd seen of the future in magazines. The Great World's Fair was a subject that had caught all our imaginations with its demonstrations of new appliances, aeroplanes and motor cars. Everything was 'streamlined' in 1939; everything designed with swept-back lines as if we were all preparing to shoot off into space. Earlier that summer, the King and Queen of England had come to Canada, riding on a streamlined train whose blue-painted engine was sleek and slim as something in a silver glove. In fact, the King and Queen had arrived in Toronto just up Yonge Street from where we lived. We got permission from the Darrow family, who lived over Max's Flowers, to stand on the roof and watch the parade with its Mounties in scarlet and its Black Watch Band and the King and Queen, all blue and white and smiling, sitting in an open Buick called a *McLaughlin—built*, according to Cy, *right here in Canada!* For one brief moment while all these symbols of who we were went marching past, the two communities—one on either side of Yonge Street—were united in a surge of cheering and applause. But after the King and Queen were gone, the ribbon of Yonge Street divided us again. It rained.

Now, Cy and Rita were arguing over the remnants in the soufflé dish. Cy held the classic belief that what was in the dish was his by virtue of his being the eldest child. He also held the classic belief that girls were meant to be second in everything. Rita, who was always hungry but never seemed to gain an ounce, held none of these beliefs and was capable of fighting Cy for hours on end when our parents weren't present. With Mother at the table, however, the argument was silenced by her announcement that the soufflé dish and all the delicious bits of cheese and egg that clung to its sides would be set aside for our father.

Then—or shortly thereafter—our father did indeed arrive, but he said he wasn't hungry and he wanted to be left alone with Mother.

In half an hour the children were called from the kitchen where we had been doing the dishes and scooping up the remains of the meal. I—the child my mother called *The Rabbit*—had been emptying the salad bowl, stuffing my mouth with lettuce, tomatoes and onion shards and nearly choking in the process. We all went into the sitting-room with food on our lips and tea towels in our hands: Father's three little Maxes—Cy and Rita and Ben. He looked at us then, as he always did, with a measure of pride he could never hide and a false composure that kept his lips from smiling, but not his eyes. I look back now on that moment with some alarm when I realize my father was only twenty-seven years old—an age I have long survived and doubled.

'Children, I have joined the army,' he said—in his formal way, as if we were his customers. 'I am going to be a soldier.'

Our mother had been weeping before we entered the room, but she had dried her eyes because she never allowed us to witness her tears. Now, she was smiling and silent. After a moment, she left the room and went out through the kitchen into the garden where, in the twilight, she found her favourite place and sat in a deck-chair amidst the flowers.

Cy, for his part, crowed with delight and yelled with excitement. He wanted to know if the war would last until he was a man and could join our father at the front.

Father, I remember, told him the war had not yet begun and the reason for his enlistment was precisely so that Cy and I could not be soldiers. 'There will be no need for that,' he said.

Cy was immensely disappointed. He begged our father to make the war go on till 1948, when he would be eighteen.

Our father only laughed at that.

'The war,' he said, 'will be over in 1940.'

I went out then and found our mother in the garden.

'What will happen to us while he's away?' I asked.

'Nothing,' she said. And then she said: 'come here.'

I went and leaned against her thigh and she put her arm around my shoulder and I could smell the roses somewhere behind us. It was getting dark.

'Look up there,' she said. 'The stars are coming out. Why don't you count them?'

This was her way of distracting me whenever my questions got out of hand. Either she told me to count the stars or go outside and dig for China. *There's a shovel in the shed*, she would tell me. *You get started and I will join you.* Just as if we would be in China and back by suppertime.

But that night in August, 1939, I wasn't prepared to bite. I didn't want to dig for China and I didn't want to count the stars. I'd dug for China so many times and had so many holes in the yard that I knew I would never arrive; it was much too far and, somehow, she was making a fool of me. As for the stars: 'I counted them last night,' I told her. 'And the night before.'

'Oh?' she said—and I felt her body tense, though she went on trying to inject a sense of ease when she spoke. 'So tell me,' she said. 'How many are there?'

'Twelve,' I said.

'Ah,' she said. And sighed. 'Just twelve. I thought there might be more than twelve.'

'I mean twelve zillion,' I said with great authority.

'Oh,' she said. 'I see. And you counted them all?'

'Unh-hunh.'

For a moment she was quiet. And then she said: 'what about that one there?'

One week later, the war began. But my father had already gone.

On the 14th of February, 1943, my father was returned. He came back home from the war. He did this on a Sunday and I recall the hush that fell upon our house, as indeed it seemed to have fallen over all the city. Only the sparrows out in the trees made sound.

We had gone downtown to the Exhibition Grounds to meet him. The journey on the streetcar took us over an hour, but Mother had splurged and hired a car and driver to take us all home. The car, I remember, embarrassed me. I was afraid some friend would see me being driven—sitting up behind a chauffeur.

A notice had come that told us the families of all returning soldiers would be permitted to witness their arrival. I suspect the building they used for this was the one now used to house the Royal Winter Fair and other equestrian events. I don't remember what it was called and I'm not inclined to inquire. It was enough that I was there that once—and once remains enough.

We sat in the bleachers, Cy and Rita and Mother and me, and there was a railing holding us back. There must have been over a thousand people waiting to catch a glimpse of someone they loved—all of them parents, children or wives of the men returning. I was eight years old that February—almost nine and feeling I would never get there. Time was like a field of clay and all the other children I knew appeared to have cleared it in a single bound while I was stuck in the mud and barely able to lift my feet. I hated being eight and dreaded being nine. I wanted to be ten—the only dignified age a child could be, it seemed to me. Cy, at ten, had found a kind of silence I admired to the point of worship. Rita, who in fact was ten that year and soon to be eleven, had also found a world of silence in which she kept her self secreted—often behind closed doors. Silence was a sign of valour.

The occasion was barely one for public rejoicing. The men who were coming home were mostly casualties whose wounds, we had been warned, could be distressing and whose spirit, we had equally been warned, had been damaged in long months of painful recuperation. Plainly, it was our job to lift their spirits and to deny the severity of their wounds. Above all else, they must not be allowed to feel they could not rejoin society at large. A man with no face must not be stared at.

Our father's wounds were greater by far than we had been told. There was not a mark on his body, but—far inside—he had been destroyed. His mind had been severely damaged and his spirit had been broken. No one had told me what this might have made of him. No one had said *he may never be kind again*. No one had said *he will never sleep again without the aid of alcohol*. No one had said *he will try to kill your mother*. No one had said *you will not be sure it's him when you see him*. Yet all these things were true.

I had never seen a military parade without a band. The effect was eerie and upsetting. Two or three officers came forward into the centre of the oval. Somebody started shouting commands and a sergeant-major, who could not yet be seen, was heard outside the building counting off the steps.

I wanted drums. I wanted bugles. Surely this ghostly, implacable sound of marching feet in the deadening sand was just a prelude to everyone standing up and cheering and the music blaring forth. But, no. We all stood up, it is true, the minute the first of the columns rounded the wooden corner of the bleachers and came into sight. But no one uttered a sound. One or two people threw their hands up over their mouths—as if to stifle cries—but most of us simply stood there—staring in disbelief.

Nurses came with some of the men, supporting them. Everyone was pale in the awful light—and the colours of their wounds and bruises were garish and quite unreal. There was a predominance of yellow flesh and dark maroon scars and of purple welts and blackened scabs. Some men wore bandages—some wore casts and slings. Others used canes and crutches to support themselves. A few had been the victims of fire, and these wore tight, blue skull-caps and collarless shirts and their faces and other areas of uncovered skin were bright with shining ointments and dressings.

It took a very great while for all these men and women—perhaps as many as two hundred of them—to arrive inside the building and make their way into the oval. They were being lined up in order of columns—several long lines, and each line punctuated here and there with attendant nurses. The voices of the sergeant-major and of the adjutant who was taking the parade were swallowed up in the dead acoustics, and—far above us—pigeons and sparrows moved among the girders and beams that supported the roof. I still had not seen Father.

At last, because my panic was spreading out of control, I tugged my mother's elbow and whispered that I couldn't see him. Had there been a mistake and he wasn't coming at all?

'No,' she told me—looking down at me sideways and turning my head with her ungloved fingers. 'There he is, there,' she said. 'But don't say anything, yet. He may not know we're here.'

My father's figure could only be told because of his remarkable height. He was six feet four and had always been, to me, a giant. But now his height seemed barely greater than the height of half a dozen other men who were gathered out in the sand. His head was bowed, though once or twice he lifted his chin when he heard the commands. His shoulders, no longer squared, were rounded forward and dipping towards his centre. His neck was so thin I thought that someone or something must have cut over half of it away. I studied him solemnly and then looked up at my mother.

She had closed her eyes against him because she could not bear to look.

Later on that night when everyone had gone to bed but none of us had gone to sleep, I said to Cy: 'what is it?'

'What?'

'That's happened to Dad . . .'

Cy didn't answer for a moment and then he said: 'Dieppe.'

I didn't understand. I thought it was a new disease.

We were told the next day not to mention at school that our father had come back home. Nothing was said about why it must be kept a secret. That was a bitter disappointment. Other children whose fathers had returned from overseas were always the centre of attention. Teachers, beaming smiles and patting heads, would congratulate them just as if they had won a prize. Classmates pestered them with questions: What does he look like? Have you seen his wounds? How many Germans did he kill? But we had none of this. All we got was: *what did you do on the weekend?*

Nothing.

All day Monday, Father remained upstairs. Our parents' bedroom was on the second floor directly over the sitting-room. Also, directly underneath the bedroom occupied by Cy and me. We had heard our mother's voice long into the night, apparently soothing him, telling him over and over again that everything was going to be all right.

We could not make out her words, but the tone of her voice was familiar. Over time, she had sat with each of us, deploying her comforts in all the same cadences and phrases, assuring us that pains and aches and sicknesses would pass.

Because we could not afford to lose the sale of even one flower—neither the single rose bought once a week by Edna Holmes to cheer her ailing sister, nor the daily boutonnière of Colonel Matheson—our mother had persuaded Mrs. Adams, the grocer's wife, to tend the store while she 'nipped home' once every hour to see to Father's needs. It was only later that we children realized what those needs entailed. He was drinking more or less constantly in every waking hour, and our mother's purpose was first to tempt him with food—which he refused—and then to make certain that his matches and cigarettes did not set fire to the house.

On the Wednesday, Father emerged from his shell around two o'clock in the afternoon. We were all at school, of course, and I have only the account of what follows from my mother. When she returned at two, Mother found that Father had come down into the hallway, fully dressed in civilian clothes. He had already donned his greatcoat when she arrived. She told me that, at first, he had seemed to be remarkably sober. He told her he wanted to go outside and walk in the street. He wanted to go and see the store, he said.

'But you can't wear your greatcoat, David,' she told him.

'Why?'

'Because you're in civilian dress. You know that's not allowed. A man was arrested just last week.'

'I wasn't here last week,' said my father.

'Nevertheless,' my mother told him, 'this man was arrested because it is not allowed.'

'But I'm a soldier!' my father yelled.

My mother had to play this scene with all the care and cunning she could muster. The man who had been arrested had been a deserter. All that winter, desertions had been increasing and there had been demonstrations of overt disloyalty. People had shouted *down with the King!* and had booed the Union Jack. There were street gangs of youths who called themselves *Zombies* and they hung around the Masonic Temple on Yonge Street and the Palais Royale at Sunnyside. Some of these young men were in uniform, members of the Home Guard: reserves who had been promised, on joining up, they would not be sent overseas. They may have disapproved of the war, but they did not disapprove of fighting. They waited outside the dancehalls, defensive of their manhood, challenging the servicemen who were dancing inside to *come out fighting and show us your guts!* Men had been killed in such encounters and the encounters had been increasing. The government was absolutely determined to stamp these incidents out before they spread across the country. These were the darkest hours of the war and morale, both in and out of the Forces, was at its lowest ebb. If my father had appeared on the street with his military greatcoat worn over his civilian clothes, it would have been assumed he was a *Zombie* or a deserter and he would have been arrested instantly. Our neighbours would have turned him in, no matter who he was. Our patriotism had come to that.

'I don't have a civilian overcoat,' my father said. 'And don't suggest that I put on my uniform, because I won't. My uniform stinks of sweat and I hate it.'

'Well, you aren't going out like that,' my mother said. 'That's all there is to it. Why not come to the kitchen and I'll fix you a sandwich . . . '

'I don't want a goddamned sandwich,' my father yelled at her. 'I want to see the store!'

At this point, he tore off his greatcoat and flung it onto the stairs. And then, before my mother could prevent him, he was out the door and running down the steps.

My mother—dressed in her green shop apron and nothing but a scarf to warm her—raced out after him.

What would the neighbours think? What would the neighbours say? How could she possibly explain?

By the time she had reached the sidewalk, my father had almost reached the corner. But, when she got to Yonge Street, her fears were somewhat allayed. My father had not gone into Max's Flowers but was standing one door shy of it, staring into the butcher's window.

'What's going on here?' he said, as my mother came abreast of him.

Mother did not know what he meant.

'Where is Mister Schickel, Lily?' he asked her.

She had forgotten that, as well.

'Mister Schickel has left,' she told him—trying to be calm—trying to steer my father wide of the butcher's window and in towards their own front stoop.

'Left?' my father shouted. 'He's only just managed to pay off his mortgage! And who the hell is this imposter, Reilly?'

'Reilly?'

'Arthur Reilly the bloody butcher!' My father pointed at and read the sign that had replaced *Oskar Schickel, Butcher* in the window.

'Mister Reilly has been there most of the winter, David. Didn't I write and tell you that?' She knew very well she hadn't.

My father blinked at the meagre cuts of rationed meat displayed beyond the glass and said: 'what happened to Oskar, Lily? Tell me.'

And so, she had to tell him, like it or not.

Mister Schickel's name was disagreeable—stuck up there on Yonge Street across from Rosedale—and someone from Park Road had thrown a stone through the window.

There. It was said.

'But Oskar wasn't a German,' my father whispered. 'He was a Canadian.'

'But his name was German, David.'

My father put his fingers against the glass and did not appear to respond to what my mother had said.

At last, my mother pulled at his arm. 'Why not come back home,' she said. 'You can come and see the shop tomorrow.'

My father, while my mother watched him, concentrated very hard and moved his finger over the dusty glass of Oskar Schickel's store.

'What are you doing, David?'

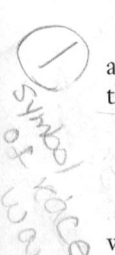

'Nothing,' said my father. 'Setting things right, that's all.'
Then he stepped back and said to her: 'now—we'll go home.'
What he had written was:
Oskar Schickel: Proprietor in absentia.
Mother said that Mrs Reilly rushed outside as soon as they had reached the corner and she washed the window clean.
This was the only remaining decent thing my father did until the day he died. The rest was all a nightmare.

I had never seen Dieppe. I had seen its face in photographs. I had read all the books and heard all the stories. The battle, of which my father had been a victim, had taken place in August of 1942—roughly six months before he was returned to us. Long since then, in my adult years, I have seen that battle, or seen its parts, through the medium of documentary film. It was only after Cy and Rita had vetted these films that I was able to watch. Till then, I had been afraid I would catch my father's image unawares—fearful that somehow our eyes would meet in that worst of moments. I couldn't bear the thought of seeing him destroyed. So, I had seen all this—the photographs, the books, the films—but I had never seen the town of Dieppe itself until that day in May of 1987 when I took my father's ashes there to scatter them.

Before I can begin this ending, I have to make it clear that the last thing I want to provoke is the sentimental image of a wind-blown stretch of rocky beach with a rainbow of ashes arching over the stones and blowing out to sea. If you want that image, let me tell you that had been the way it was when Cy, my brother, and Rita, my sister, and I went walking, wading into the ocean south of Lunenburg, Nova Scotia—where our mother had been born—to cast her ashes into the air above the Atlantic. Then there was almost music and we rejoiced because our mother had finally gained her freedom from a life that had become intolerable. But in Dieppe, when I shook my father's ashes out of their envelope, there was no rejoicing. None.

I felt, in fact, as if I had brought the body of an infidel into a holy place and laid it down amongst the true believers. Still, this was what my father had wanted—and how could I refuse him? Neither Cy nor Rita would do it for him. Gone, they had said. *Good riddance.*

And so it fell to me.

I was always the least informed. I was always the most inquisitive. During my childhood, nobody told me—aside from the single word *Dieppe*—what it was that had happened to my father. And yet, perhaps because I knew the least and because I was the youngest and seemed the most naïve and willing, it was more than often me he focused on.

His tirades would begin in silence—the silence we had been warned of when he first returned. He would sit at the head of the table, eating a piece of fish and drinking from a glass of beer. The beer was always dark in colour. Gold.

Our dining-room had a window facing west. Consequently, winter sunsets in particular got in his eyes.

Curtain, he would say at his plate—and jab his fork at me.

If I didn't understand because his mouth was full, my mother would reach my sleeve and pull it with her fingers. *The curtain, Ben,* she would say. *Your father's eyes.*

Yes, ma'am. Down I'd get and pull the curtain.

Then, no sooner would I be reseated than my father—still addressing his plate—would mumble *lights*. And I would rise and turn on the lights. Then, when I was back at last in my chair, he would look at me and say, without apparent rancour, *why don't you tell me to shove the goddamn curtain up my ass?*

You will understand my silence in response to this if you understand that—before he went away—the worst my father had ever said in our presence had been *damn* and *hell*. The ultimate worst had been *Christ!* when he'd nearly sliced his finger off with a knife. Then, however, he hadn't known that anyone was listening. And so, when he started to talk this way—and perhaps especially at table—it paralyzed me.

Cy or Mother would sometimes attempt to intervene, but he always cut them off with something worse than he'd said to me. Then he would turn his attention back in my direction and continue. He urged me to refuse his order, then to upbraid him, finally to openly defy him—call him the worst of the words he could put in my mouth and hit him. Of course, I never did any of these things, but the urging, the cajoling and ultimately the begging never ceased.

One night, he came into the bedroom where I slept in the bunk-bed over Cy and he shouted at me *why don't you fight back?* Then he dragged my covers off and threw me onto the floor against the bureau. All this was done in the dark, and after my mother had driven me down in the truck to the Emergency Ward of Wellesley Hospital, the doctors told her that my collar-bone was broken. I heard my mother saying *yes, he fell out of bed.*

Everyone—even I—conspired to protect him. The trouble was, my father had no wish to protect himself. At least, it seemed that way until a fellow veteran of Dieppe turned up one day in the shop and my father turned on him with a pair of garden shears and tried to drive him back onto Yonge Street. Far from being afraid of my father, the other man took off his jacket and threw it in my father's face and all the while he stood there, the man was yelling at my father: *Coward! Coward! Yellow Bastard!*

Then, he turned around and walked away. The victor.

Thinking for sure the police would come, my mother drew the blind and closed the shop for the rest of the day.

But that was not the end of it. She gathered us together out on the porch and Cy was told to open a can of pork and beans and to make what our mother called a *passel of toast*. He and Rita and I were to eat this meal in the kitchen, after which Cy, who'd been handed a dollar bill my mother had lifted from the till, was to take us down to the Uptown Theatre where an Abbott and Costello film was playing. All these ordinary things we did. Nonetheless, we knew that our father had gone mad.

It was summer then and when the movie was over, I remember Cy and Rita and I stood on the street and the sidewalks gave off heat and the air around us smelled of peanuts and popcorn and Cy said: 'I don't think it's safe to go home just yet.' For almost an hour, we wandered on Yonge Street, debating what we should do and, at last, we decided we would test the waters by going and looking at the house and listening to see if there was any yelling.

Gibson Avenue only has about twenty houses, most of them semi-detached—and all of them facing south and the park. The porches and the stoops that night were filled with our neighbours drinking beer from coffee cups and fanning themselves with paper plates and folded bits of the *Daily Star*. They were drinking out of cups—you could smell the beer—because the law back then forbade the public consumption, under any circumstance, of alcohol. Whatever you can hide does not exist.

Passing, we watched our neighbours watching us—the Matlocks and the Wheelers and the Conrads and the Bolts—and we knew they were thinking *there go the Max kids and David Max, their father, tried to kill a man today in his store with gardening shears* . . . .

'Hello, Cy.'
'Hello . . .'
'Ben. Rita.'
'Hi.'
'Good-night . . .'

We went and stood together on the sidewalk out in front of our house.

Inside, everything seemed to be calm and normal. The lights were turned on in their usual distribution—most of them downstairs. The radio was playing. Someone was singing *Praise the Lord and Pass the Ammunition*.

Cy went up the steps and turned the handle. He was brave—but I'd always known that. Rita and I were told to wait on the porch.

Two minutes passed—or five—or ten—and finally Cy returned. He was very white and his voice was dry, but he wasn't shaking and all he said was: 'you'd best come in. I'm calling the police.'

Our father had tried to kill our mother with a hammer. She was lying on the sofa and her hands were broken because she had used them trying to fend off the blows.

Father had disappeared. The next day, he turned himself in because, as he told the doctors, he had come to his senses. He was kept for a year and a half—almost until the war was over—at the Asylum of the Insane on Queen Street. None of us children was allowed to visit him there—but our mother went to see him six months after he had been committed. She told me they sat in a long, grey room with bars on all the windows. My father wore a dressing gown and hadn't shaved. Mother said he couldn't look her in the eyes. She told him that she forgave him for what he had done. But my father never forgave himself. My mother said she never saw his eyes again.

Two weeks after our father had tried to kill our mother, a brick was thrown through the window of Max's Flowers. On the brick, a single word was printed in yellow chalk.

Murderer.

Mother said: 'there's no way around this, now. I'm going to have to explain.'

That was how we discovered what had gone wrong with our father at Dieppe.

Our mother had known this all along, and I still have strong suspicions Cy had found it out and maybe Rita before our mother went through the formal procedure of sitting us down and telling us all together. Maybe they had thought I was just too young to understand. Maybe Cy and maybe Rita hadn't known. Maybe they had only guessed. At any rate, I had a very strong sense that I was the only one who received our mother's news in a state of shock.

Father had risen, since his enlistment in 1939, all the way up from an NCO to the rank of captain. Everyone had adored him in the army. He was what they called a natural leader. His men were particularly fond of him and they would, as the saying goes, have followed him anywhere. Then came Dieppe. All but a handful of those who went into battle there were Canadians. This was our Waterloo. Our Gettysburg.

There isn't a single history book you can read—there isn't a single man who was there who won't tell you—there isn't a single scrap of evidence in any archive to suggest that the battle of Dieppe was anything but a total and appalling disaster. Most have called it a slaughter.

Dieppe is a port and market town on the coast of Normandy in northern France. In 1942, the British High Command had chosen it to be the object of a practice raid in preparation for the invasion of Europe. The allies on every front were faltering, then. A gesture was needed, and even the smallest of victories would do.

And so, on the 19th of August, 1942, the raid on Dieppe had taken place—and the consequent carnage had cost the lives of over a thousand Canadians. Over two thousand were wounded or taken prisoner. Five thousand set out; just over one thousand came back.

My father never left his landing craft.

He was to have led his men ashore in the second wave of troops to follow the tanks—but, seeing the tanks immobilized, unable to move because the beaches were made of stone and the stones had jammed the tank tracks—and seeing the evident massacre of the first wave of troops whose attempt at storming the shore had been repulsed by machine-gun fire from the cliffs above the town—my father froze in his place and could not move. His men—it is all too apparent—did not know what to do. They had received no order to advance and yet, if they stayed, they were sitting ducks.

In the end, though a handful escaped by rushing forward into the water, the rest were blown to pieces when their landing craft was shelled. In the meantime, my father had recovered enough of his wits to crawl back over the end of the landing craft, strip off his uniform and swim out to sea where he was taken on board a British destroyer sitting offshore.

The destroyer, H.M.S. *Berkley*, was ultimately hit and everyone on board, including my father—no one knowing who he was—was transferred to another ship before the *Berkley* was scuttled where she sat. My father made it all the way back to England, where his burns and wounds were dressed and where he debated taking advantage of the chaos to disappear, hoping that, in the long run, he would be counted among the dead.

His problem was, his conscience had survived. He stayed and, as a consequence, he was confronted by survivors who knew his story. He was dishonourably discharged and sent home to us. Children don't understand such things. The only cowards they recognize are figures cut from comic books or seen on movie screens.

Fathers cannot be cowards.

It is impossible.

・・・・・

His torment and his grief were to lead my father all the way to the grave. He left our mother, in the long run, though she would not have wished him to do so and he lived out his days in little bars and back-street beer parlours, seeking whatever solace he could find with whores and derelicts whose stories might have matched his own. The phone would ring and we would dread it. Either it was him or news of him—either his drunken harangue or the name of his most recent jail.

He died in the Wellesley Hospital, the place where I was born—and when he was dying he asked to see his children. Cy and Rita 'could not be reached,' but I was found—where he'd always found me—sitting within yelling distance. Perhaps this sounds familiar to other children—of whatever age—whose parents, whether one of them or both of them, have made the mistake of losing faith too soon in their children's need to love.

I would have loved a stone.

If only he had known.

He sensed it, maybe, in the end. He told me he was sorry for everything—and meant it. He told me the names of all his men and he said he had walked with them all through hell, long since their deaths, to do them honour. He hoped they would understand him, now.

I said they might.

He asked if his ashes could be put with theirs.

Why not, I thought. *A stone among stones.*

The beaches at Dieppe can throw you off balance. The angle at which they slope into the water is both steep and dangerous. At high tide you can slide into the waves and lose your footing before you've remembered how to swim. The stones are treacherous. But they are also beautiful.

My father's ashes were contraband. You can't just walk about with someone's remains, in whatever form, in your suitcase. Stepping off the *Sealink* ferry, I carried my father in an envelope addressed to myself in Canada. This was only in case I was challenged. There was hardly more than a handful of him there. I had thrown the rest of him into the English Channel as the coast of Normandy was coming into view. It had been somewhat more than disconcerting to see the interest his ashes caused amongst the gulls and other sea birds. I had hoped to dispose of him in a private way, unnoticed. But a woman with two small children came and stood beside me at the railing and I heard her explain that *this nice man is taking care of our feathered friends*. I hoped that, if my father was watching, he could laugh. I had to look away.

The ferry arrived in the early afternoon and—once I had booked myself into La Présidence Hotel—I went for a walk along the promenade above the sea-wall. It being May, the offshore breeze was warm and filled with the faintest scent of apple trees in bloom.

I didn't want to relive the battle. I hadn't come to conjure ghosts. But the ghosts and the battle are palpable around you there, no matter what your wishes are. The sound of the tide rolling back across the stones is all the cue you need to be reminded of that summer day in 1942. I stood that evening, resting my arms along the wall and thinking *at last, my father has come ashore.*

In the morning, before the town awoke, I got up in the dark and was on the beach when the sun rose inland beyond the cliffs. I wore a thick woollen sweater, walking shorts and a pair of running shoes. The envelope was in my pocket.

The concierge must have thought I was just another crazy North American off on my morning run. He grunted as I passed and I pretended not to know that he was there. Out on the beach, I clambered over retaining walls and petrified driftwood until I felt I was safely beyond the range of prying eyes.

The stones at Dieppe are mostly flint—and their colours range from white through yellow to red. The red stones look as if they have been washed in blood and the sight of them takes your breath away. I hunkered down above them, holding all that remained of my father in my fist. He felt like a powdered stone—pummelled and broken.

I let him down between my fingers, feeling him turn to paste—watching him divide and disappear.

He is dead and he is gone.

Weekends, our parents used to take us walking under the trees on Crescent Road. This was on the Rosedale side of Yonge Street. My brother Cy and I were always dressed in dark blue suits whose rough wool shorts would chafe against our thighs. Our knee socks—also blue—were turned down over thick elastic garters. Everything itched and smelled of Sunday. Cy had cleats on his shoes because he walked in such a way as to wear his heels *to the bone*, as my mother said—and causing much expense. The cleats made a wondrous clicking noise and you could always hear him coming. I wanted cleats, but I was refused because, no matter how I tried, I couldn't walk like that.

The houses sat up neat as pins beyond their lawns—blank-eyed windows, steaming chimneys—havens of wealth and all the mysteries of wealth.

Father often walked behind us. I don't know why. Mother walked in front with Rita. Rita always wore a dress that was either red or blue beneath her princess coat and in the wintertime she wore a sort of woollen cloche that was tied with a knitted string beneath her chin. Her Mary Jane shoes were just like Shirley Temple's shoes—which, for a while, was pleasing to Rita; then it was not. Rita always had an overpowering sense of image.

After the advent of our father's return, she said from the corner of her mouth one Sunday as we walked on Crescent Road that she and Cy and I had been named as if we were manufactured products: *Cy Max Office Equipment; Rita Max Household Appliances* and *Ben Max Watches*. This, she concluded, was why our father had always walked behind us. Proudly, he was measuring our performance. Now, he had ceased to walk behind us and our mother led us forward dressed in black.

Tick. Tick. Tick. That's me. The Ben Max Watch.

I have told our story. But I think it best—and I like it best—to end with all of us moving there beneath the trees in the years before the war. Mister and Mrs. David Max out walking with their children any Sunday afternoon in any kind of weather but the rain.

Colonel Matheson, striding down his walk, is caught and forced to grunt acknowledgement that we are there. He cannot ignore us, after all. We have seen him every weekday morning choosing his boutonnière and buying it from us.

(1988)

CHAPTER 5 WRITING ABOUT STRUCTURE

PREWRITING

Before you can begin to write about structure, you must first determine the underlying patterns that serve as a framework for the story.

FINDING PATTERNS

Read the following questions; then carefully reread the story. Write down your answers to the questions.

1. How many parts of the story relate to the title "Stones"?
2. What is the major source of conflict in the story? That is, what causes tension?
3. How many different time periods are described in the story? Make a list of them in the order they appear in the story. Then organize the list in chronological (historical) order.
4. Look at the story as a series of scenes, like scenes in a play or film. Visualize the scenes. How many separate scenes are there? How can you tell when a scene begins and ends? If you were directing a film of the story, what would you emphasize in each scene?
5. Although we learn much about the lives of the family members, we don't learn everything. List some scenes that are left out of the story. Are there any you would put in if you were making a film?
6. Ben Max says, "Fathers cannot be cowards." What does he mean? Is it true? Which of the scenes in the story helps answer these questions about Ben's statement?

WRITING

Once you understand the structure of the story, you need to discover a framework within which you can effectively present your observations—that is, a structure for your own paper.

GROUPING DETAILS

Write a sentence that explains something about the author's selection of scenes to include in the story. Next, discuss which details in the story support your explanations. For example, if you mentioned that the selected scenes relate to the idea of different kinds of wars, supporting details would include the following:

- Yonge Street
- Dieppe
- the greatcoat
- Oskar Schickel and Arthur Reilly
- the hammer
- the Asylum of the Insane

RELATING DETAILS TO THEME

An accurate description of the pattern of the story and a convincing list of supporting details will be crucial to any essay about structure. However, you also need to work out a thesis—a controlling idea for your paper that relates the structure to the overall impact or meaning of the work. For example, an essay about the structure of "Stones" might have this thesis:

> The order of the episodes that occur or are remembered in "Stones" serves to deepen our understanding of David Max, reinforce our identification with Ben, and support our acceptance of Ben's final act of love for his father.

IDEAS FOR WRITING

IDEAS FOR RESPONSIVE WRITING

1. Do you perceive any "wars" in your own community? For example, are there signs of race, gender, or class hostilities? Write first about a conflict from your own point of view. Then write about the same conflict from the other side—that is, take on the opposing point of view.
2. In "Stones," things take on more importance than their simple functions—names, streets, and clothing, for example. Are there things like this in your life? Which of these things might create a dividing wall between people? Why? Write about how things may acquire special significance.
3. Have you ever walked in an area of your city or town and felt like you did not belong? Do you know anyone who has? Why did you feel unwelcome? Did someone or something in particular affect you? Write an essay about why where we live has significance for us.

IDEAS FOR CRITICAL WRITING

The following writing ideas relate structure to meaning. Adopt one of them, revise one, or create your own for a paper on "Stones."

1. The opening and the closing scenes of "Stones," which take place seemingly during the same time period, mirror each other and signify the divisions that people create and defend for themselves.
2. Timothy Findley uses a narrator, Ben Max, to chronologically tell the story of his early life; Findley also uses flashbacks to fill in details of Ben's father's Dieppe experiences but excludes any depiction of Ben's current life. There are no details about whether he is married or has children and a family of his own, or about how his unhappy childhood has affected his life as an adult. Ironically, the story closes with a flashback to a happy family outing.
3. Each discord recorded in "Stones" serves to strengthen the "social battlefield" (See "Epilogue: *Stones*" by Lorraine M. York on page 87.) that exists in the Maxes' world, a battlefield where the combatants are never at peace.

4. Certain key objects, such as stones, the greatcoat, and bricks, focus the reader's attention on the basic conflict of the story.

REWRITING

Our advice in this section focuses on problems involved in quoting when writing about a literary work.

INTEGRATING QUOTATIONS GRACEFULLY

In any literary essay you will need quotations from the text of the work you are examining. In fact, when you revise your essay, always consider adding more specific evidence straight from the text. This evidence will help your readers understand the general points you make and will show what inspired your thoughts. Quoting directly also serves as a self-check; by finding specific support in the work, you confirm that your ideas are indeed grounded in the text and not in your fancy.

Be sure that you enclose these borrowings in quotation marks as you gracefully introduce them into your own sentences. For example,

> In the opening sentence, Ben Max introduces one of the societal tensions in the story by remarking that his family lived "over on the wrong side of Yonge Street."
>
> Ben observes that it would be a war "from which a few of us would emerge intact," foreshadowing its tragic effects on his father.
>
> Ben thinks that he "was the only one [of the children] who received [their] mother's news in a state of shock."

That last example shows how you may add your own words to explain a possibly confusing word in a quotation: use square brackets. Most of the time, though, you can devise a way to avoid this awkwardness by rewriting the sentence, perhaps adding more from the source:

> Ben thinks that, although Cy and Rita might have just guessed the truth, he "was the only one who received our mother's news in a state of shock."

EXERCISE ON INTEGRATING QUOTATIONS

Below, we reprint word for word passages from "Obasan" and from "Stones." To practise integrating quotations, try your hand at using parts of the passages in sentences of your own.

1. Write a sentence that uses a phrase you quote directly as an example of a general point you make about the characters, events, or setting of the story.
2. Write a sentence that relates a detail to a theme of the story, using some exact quotation from the passage.

Use either of the following passages in writing your sentences.

From "Obasan"

Grief acted in mysterious ways, its melancholy wonders to perform. When it had claimed her kingdom fully, it admitted no enemies and no vengeance. Enemies belonged in a corridor of experience with sense and meaning, with justice and reason. Her Grief knew nothing of these and whipped her body to resignation until the kingdom was secure. But inside the fortress, Obasan's silence was that of a child bewildered.

From "Stones"

Of the pre-war years, my overall memory is one of perfect winters, heavy with snow and the smell of coal- and wood-smoke mingling with the smell of bread and cookies rising from The Women's Bakery. The coal-smoke came from our furnaces and the wood-smoke—mostly birch and maple—came to us from the chimneys of Rosedale, where it seemed that every house must have a fireplace in every room.

A CRITICAL INTERPRETATION

In order to write a persuasive analytical paper, you may find it necessary to cite the opinion of experts in the field of literary criticism. Read the following excerpt from a critical interpretation of some of Timothy Findley's writing, and see if you can find some support for an idea you have about the short story "Stones." (The short story bears the same title as the collection of Findley's short fiction *Stones*, and the page numbers in Lorraine York's "Epilogue: *Stones*" refer to the Viking Press 1988 edition of Findley's collection.)

WEB For study tools to help you with your next writing assignment, please visit the Companion Website at www.pearsoned.ca/mcmahan.

Lorraine M. York   b. 1958

Epilogue: *Stones*

I began this study of Timothy Findley's fiction with a reading of his early short story "War"; and, in a sense, I circle back to its concerns just as Findley has done in his most recent collection of short stories, *Stones* (1988). The title story is a reworking of the basic situation found in the earlier work: a child learns that his father is going to war; though his brother is exhilarated by the news, he is sickened at the thought. But now—after the writing of works such as *The Wars*, *Famous Last Words* and *Not Wanted on the Voyage*—the other variations on war which Findley has begun to explore attach themselves to this basic fictional framework.

"Stones," though it highlights military war and its effects on veterans and their families, begins and ends with class war. The setting, Toronto's Rosedale, is as much a social battlefield as the ASH and Pine Point hotels in *The Telling of Lies*; the first scene consists of a Rosedale matron's snubbing of the boy's mother (*Stones* 195), and the closing scene shows a denizen of the "better" side of Rosedale being "forced to grunt acknowledgment" of the Max family, tainted as they are by their trade of selling flowers (221).

The persistent gender wars of Findley's fiction are here too, in the father's post-war *machismo*, assumed after he himself has been accused of cowardice for not jumping to a sure death at Dieppe. Clearly, the father's harangues at the narrator, Ben, are implicit efforts to instill in his son the male-warrior ethic which Findley has been fascinated—and repelled—by before: "One night," we hear, "he came into the bedroom where I slept in the bunk-bed over Cy and he shouted at me *why don't you fight back?*" (212). Significantly, the father passes over his other son, who, like Japeth Noyes and Stuart Ross, has apparently inherited and willingly performed the male script; upon learning of his father's enlistment, Cy "crowed with delight" and "wanted to know if the war would last until he was a man and could join our father at the front" (200).

This study has revealed that in works like *The Wars* and "War," Findley's pre-war domestic worlds tend to approximate the structures of military action. Here, Findley completes this portrait of household warfare; even the post-battle world is tinged with the lingering odour of combat. Ben's father, distraught during his first few days at home after being discharged, thinks that he can go into the street with his military greatcoat over his civilian clothing. His wife's explanation that this mixture of the military and the domestic is frowned upon by local authorities only bewilders this survivor of the wars, confused as he now is about the boundaries of wars domestic and military. To Ben's father, and to a whole generation, the two conditions are as jumbled together as his ill-assorted clothing.

The domestic world also overlaps with the battlefield in its perpetuation of "sides." Ben's father cannot wear his greatcoat out of doors because he might be mistaken for a deserter or a *"Zombie,"* a street gang member—someone who would be fair game to a zealous pro-war defender (207). In effect, to appear in uniform is to take sides, whether you are on the shores of France or on a Toronto street. Sometimes, the "uniform" which designates one "friend or foe" takes a different form—nationality, for instance. Oskar Schickel's name is enough to move the warhawks to run him out of his butcher's shop; his replacement, Arthur Reilly, clearly has a first name and last name which mark him as "one of ours." For Findley, war encodes and promotes these harmful binary modes of thought; by making the domestic and military overlap as he has done throughout his career, he neatly deconstructs the binary wartime-peacetime, and encourages his readers to do the same.

Of course, the image which allies this recent story most intimately to the story written in the 1950s, at the other end of Findley's career, is the one celebrated in its title: the stone. The stones which Neil throws at his father from the hayloft in "War" prefigure the bullets of the battle to come; "Stones" shows us what happens to a society which has taken up its stones. "The stones at Dieppe are mostly flint," a mature Ben recalls, "—and their colours range from white through yellow to red. The red stones look as if they have been washed in blood . . . " (219). When he throws his father's ashes in the sea near Dieppe, he places *"A stone among stones"* (218). Like the military and civilian clothing which his father has thrown together, the remains of a dishonourably-discharged "coward" mingle with those of the men whom the prevailing warrior ethic has styled "heroes." They are no longer polar opposites but rather particles of one tragic ensemble: a death beach. A society which has turned to the stone and its primitive distinctions of hunter and hunted, crushes its own skin and bones: "I hunkered down above them [the stones], holding all that remained of my father in my fist. He felt like a powdered stone—pummelled and broken" (219).

The line of development traced by the stories "War" and "Stones," a line spanning Findley's career to date, shows him mapping out the modern world's picking up of the stones of war: military wars, gender wars, familial wars, wars of the nineteenth-century, world wars, environmental wars, and, potentially, nuclear wars. "Stones" also signals, though, the point in modern history when these stones start to crumble, when the human fabric of interconnectedness and relationship is "pummelled and broken" as never before—the holocaust of the Second World War. Ben's observations about his own life mirror intertextually, he sees, the stories of other lives, and the grand story, history itself:

> Everyone's life, I suppose, has its demarcation lines—its latitudes and longitudes passing through time. Some of these lines define events that everyone shares—others are confined to personal—even to secret lives. But the end of the summer of 1939 is a line drawn down through the memory of everyone who was then alive. We were all about to be pitched together into a melting pot of violence from which a few of us would emerge intact and the rest of us would perish. (198)

The passage could serve as a mirror, as well, for the function of war in the novels and stories of Timothy Findley; wars are the latitudes and longitudes passing through human time. Some are global, others personal or secret; and they reflect one another. Timothy Findley's fiction is not only haunted by the spectre of war; it is a compulsive testament to the infinite repetitions of war in our domestic, gender, and class conflicts. This "melting pot of violence," the ever-recurring Holocaust, is our contemporary version of Noah's Ark—a troubled vessel from which we emerge not cleansed but ready, like Mrs. Noyes, to pray for yet another bout of rain. The fiction of Timothy Findley, through its intertextual method, argues convincingly that these bouts of rain which we may prefer to call the plagues of the past, exist simultaneously in all of those texts of lived experience which we shape at every moment, through perception and art, into history.

(1991)

6

Writing about Imagery and Symbolism

Imagery and symbolism, two of the most important elements of serious imaginative literature, provide rich sources of insight. The interpretive skill necessary to detect and understand them can be developed with practice. Because the meaning or theme of a literary work is often reinforced through imagery and symbolism, you can effectively devote an entire paper to an examination of a key symbol or a pattern of imagery.

WHAT ARE IMAGES?

Images are words, sometimes phrases, which may include metaphors or similes, that appeal to the senses and often put a picture in your mind. (See Chapter 12 for a discussion of metaphors and similes.) Literary critics classify images roughly into several categories:

Visual: images of sight
("an uncultivated wilderness of white chest hair bordering on the semi-controlled stubble of his neck and chin"—Alistair MacLeod)

Auditory: images of sound
("a bird dreaming its music toward morning"—Patrick Friesen)

Gustatory: images of taste
("Seeing her again was as tart as a bite into a green windfall"—Eugene McNamara)

Kinetic: images of motion
(a memory "entered her mind like an old acquaintance"—Jane Urquhart)

Thermal: images of temperature
("the blueblack cold" of early morning—Robert Hayden)

Tactile: images of feeling
("the ache of marriage throbs in the teeth"—Denise Levertov)

Such images enrich our pleasure in reading and, if deliberately repeated, can become *motifs*, or patterns of imagery, that illuminate some element of the story. The bird images in Eudora Welty's "A Worn Path" form a significant motif—birds (which soar) are associated with the human soul (which seeks to soar). The main character is named after a mythical bird, the Phoenix, which was consumed in flames but rose from its own ashes, signifying rebirth. In Ethel Wilson's "The Window," the repeated images of light serve to reinforce Mr. Willy's need for spiritual salvation.

WHAT ARE SYMBOLS?

If a repeated image gathers significant meaning, it then becomes a *symbol*. The bird images discussed above symbolize Phoenix's stalwart soul—her fierce determination to overcome the many obstacles in her path. The dust in Sinclair Ross's "Lamp at Noon" settles in our consciousness as symbolizing the absence of hope, the defeat of sheer will in the Depression-era prairies. The young husband maintains his resolve only through the belief that "there would be rain again"; rain that would bring renewed life to the earth. In literature, we often associate water with a vigorous life force and its opposite—dryness, dust, aridity—with death of the human spirit.

ARCHETYPAL SYMBOLS

Although most symbols depend upon the time, culture, and context in which they are used, some symbols, like birds and dust, are considered *archetypal* or universal—supposedly conveying the same meaning in all cultures from the time of earliest civilization. The circle, for instance, is an ancient symbol of wholeness or perfection; the sea has for centuries symbolized the voyage through life. However, because white has long been associated with innocence and black with evil, we begin to suspect that these symbols may be "universal" only in Western culture. Be that as it may, in much of the literature you will be reading, these archetypal meanings will be conveyed.

PHALLIC AND YONIC SYMBOLS

Two important and commonly employed symbols are associated with human sexuality. A *phallic* symbol suggests the potency of the male (as does the gun in Richard Wright's "The Man Who Was Almost a Man") or the force of male dominance in a patriarchal society (as does the hammer in Timothy Findley's "Stones"). Common phallic symbols are towers, spurs, snakes, sleek cars, jet planes, motorcycles—objects resembling in shape the male sex organ. A *yonic* symbol suggests the fecundity of the female or the allure of female sexuality (as do the chrysanthemums in John Steinbeck's "The Chrysanthemums" and the green apples of McNamara's "Falling in Place"). Common yonic symbols are caves, pots, rooms, full-blown roses—round or concave objects resembling the shape of the primary sex organs of the female. If you think of fruit, then bananas are phallic and apples are yonic. Remember, though, that these objects will not always be charged with sexual significance—sometimes a pine tree is just a pine tree! You must be sure that in context the image can be reasonably associated with sexuality.

HOW WILL I RECOGNIZE SYMBOLS?

"How am I supposed to know the significance of all these things?" you may well ask. Many symbols you already understand through knowledge gathered from experience and observation. You just have to make the association. Spring signifying rebirth, for example, is a connection anyone can make who has seen the earth come alive at winter's end. Pay attention to the way objects and colours gather associations: white for brides, black for funerals, blue for sadness, red for passion or anger. Just keep making associations until you come up with a meaning that seems to fit the symbol in its context.

REFERENCE WORKS ON SYMBOLS

If you draw an absolute blank, you can consult several handy volumes that allow you to look up words to discover their symbolic implications. Your library should have copies of the following works in the humanities reference section:

- Cirlot, J. E. *A Dictionary of Symbols*
- Cooper, J. C. *An Encyclopedia of Traditional Symbols*
- Frazer, Sir James. *The Golden Bough*
- Olderr, Stephen. *Symbolism: A Comprehensive Dictionary*
- Walker, Barbara. *The Woman's Encyclopedia of Myths and Secrets*

LOOKING AT IMAGES AND SYMBOLS

Recognizing images and symbols and responding to them sensitively are requirements for an informed reading of serious fiction. Read the following story by Margaret Laurence, titled "To Set Our House in Order," and see if you are aware, on first reading, of her use of symbolic imagery.

Margaret Laurence   1926–1987

To Set Our House in Order

When the baby was almost ready to be born, something went wrong and my mother had to go into hospital two weeks before the expected time. I was wakened by her crying in the night, and then I heard my father's footsteps as he went downstairs to phone. I stood in the doorway of my room, shivering and listening, wanting to go to my mother but afraid to go lest there be some sight there more terrifying than I could bear.

'Hello—Paul?' my father said, and I knew he was talking to Dr Cates. 'It's Beth. The waters have broken, and the fetal position doesn't seem quite—well, I'm only thinking of what happened the last time, and another like that would be—I wish she were a little huskier, damn it—she's so—no, don't worry, I'm quite all right. Yes, I think that would be the best thing. Okay, make it as soon as you can, will you?'

He came back upstairs, looking bony and dishevelled in his pyjamas, and running his fingers through his sand-coloured hair. At the top of the stairs, he came face to face with Grandmother MacLeod, who was standing there in her quilted black satin dressing gown, her slight figure held straight and poised, as though she were unaware that her hair was bound grotesquely like white-feathered wings in the snare of her coarse night-time hairnet.

'What is it, Ewen?'

'It's all right, Mother. Beth's having—a little trouble. I'm going to take her into the hospital. You go back to bed.'

'I told you,' Grandmother MacLeod said in her clear voice, never loud, but distinct and ringing like the tap of a sterling teaspoon on a crystal goblet, 'I did tell you, Ewen, did I not, that you should have got a girl in to help her with the housework? She would have rested more.'

'I couldn't afford to get anyone in,' my father said. 'If you thought she should've rested more, why didn't you ever—oh God, I'm out of my mind tonight—just go back to bed, Mother, please. I must get back to Beth.'

When my father went down to the front door to let Dr Cates in, my need overcame my fear and I slipped into my parents' room. My mother's black hair, so neatly pinned up during the day, was startlingly spread across the white pillowcase. I stared at her, not speaking, and then she smiled and I rushed from the doorway and buried my head upon her.

'It's all right, honey,' she said. 'Listen, Vanessa, the baby's just going to come a little early, that's all. You'll be all right. Grandmother MacLeod will be here.'

'How can she get the meals?' I wailed, fixing on the first thing that came to mind. 'She never cooks. She doesn't know how.'

'Yes, she does,' my mother said. 'She can cook as well as anyone when she has to. She's just never had to very much, that's all. Don't worry—she'll keep everything in order, and then some.'

My father and Dr Cates came in, and I had to go, without ever saying anything I had wanted to say. I went back to my own room and lay with the shadows all around me. I listened to the night murmurings that always went on in that house, sounds which never had a source, rafters and beams contracting in the dry air, perhaps, or mice in the walls, or a sparrow that had flown into the attic through the broken skylight there. After a while, although I would not have believed it possible, I slept.

The next morning I questioned my father. I believed him to be not only the best doctor in Manawaka, but also the best doctor in the whole of Manitoba, if not in the entire world, and the fact that he was not the one who was looking after my mother seemed to have something sinister about it.

'But it's always done that way, Vanessa,' he explained. 'Doctors never attend members of their own family. It's because they care so much about them, you see, and—'

'And what?' I insisted, alarmed at the way he had broken off. But my father did not reply. He stood there, and then he put on that difficult smile with which adults seek to conceal pain from children. I felt terrified, and ran to him, and he held me tightly. 'She's going to be fine,' he said. 'Honestly she is. Nessa, don't cry—'

Grandmother MacLeod appeared beside us, steel-spined despite her apparent fragility. She was wearing a purple silk dress and her ivory pendant. She looked as though she were all ready to go out for afternoon tea.

—'Ewen, you're only encouraging the child to give way,' she said. 'Vanessa, big girls often don't make such a fuss about things. Come and get your breakfast. Now, Ewen, you're not to worry. I'll see to everything.'

Summer holidays were not quite over, but I did not feel like going out to play with any of the kids. I was very superstitious, and I had the feeling that if I left the house, even for a few hours, some disaster would overtake my mother. I did not, of course, mention this feeling to Grandmother MacLeod, for she did not believe in the existence of fear, or if she did, she never let on. I spent the morning morbidly, in seeking hidden places in the house. There were many of these—odd-shaped nooks under the stairs, small and loosely nailed-up doors at the back of clothes closets, leading to dusty tunnels and forgotten recesses in the heart of the house where the only things actually to be seen were drab oil paintings stacked upon the rafters, and trunks full of outmoded clothing and old photograph albums. But the unseen presences in these secret places I knew to be those of every person, young or old, who had ever belonged to the house and had died, including Uncle Roderick who got killed on the Somme, and the baby who would have been my sister if only she had managed to come to life. Grandfather MacLeod, who had died a year after I was born, was present in the house in more tangible form. At the top of the main stairs hung the mammoth picture of a darkly uniformed man riding upon a horse whose prancing stance and dilated nostrils suggested that the battle was not yet over, that it might indeed continue until Judgment Day. The stern man was actually the Duke of Wellington, but at the time I believed him to be my grandfather MacLeod, still keeping an eye on things.

—We had moved in with Grandmother MacLeod when the Depression got bad and she could no longer afford a housekeeper, but the MacLeod house never seemed like home to me. Its dark red brick was grown over at the front with Virginia creeper that turned crimson in the fall, until you could hardly tell brick from leaves. It boasted a small tower in which Grandmother MacLeod kept a weedy collection of anaemic ferns. The verandah was embellished with a profusion of wrought-iron scrolls, and the circular rose-window upstairs contained glass of many colours which permitted an out-looking eye to see the world as a place of absolute sapphire or emerald, or if one wished to look with a jaundiced eye, a hateful yellow. In Grandmother MacLeod's opinion, their features gave the house style.

Inside a multitude of doors led to rooms where my presence, if not actually forbidden, was not encouraged. One was Grandmother MacLeod's bedroom, with its stale and old-smelling air, the dim reek of medicines and lavender sachets. Here resided her monogrammed dresser silver, brush and mirror, nail-buffer and button hook and scissors, none of which must even be fingered by me now, for she meant to leave them to me in her will and intended to hand them over in the same flawless and unused condition in which they had always been kept. Here, too, were the silver-framed photographs of Uncle Roderick—as a child, as a boy, as a man in his Army uniform. The massive walnut spool bed had obviously been designed for queens or giants, and my tiny grandmother used to lie within it all day when she had a migraine, contriving somehow to look like a giant queen.

The living room was another alien territory where I had to tread warily, for many valuable objects sat just-so on tables and mantelpiece, and dirt must not be tracked in upon the blue Chinese carpet with its birds in eternal motionless flight and its water-lily buds caught forever just before the point of opening. My mother was always nervous when I was in this room.

'Vanessa, honey,' she would say, half apologetically, 'why don't you go and play in the den, or upstairs?'

'Can't you leave her, Beth?' my father would say. 'She's not doing any harm.'

'I'm only thinking of the rug,' my mother would say, glancing at Grandmother MacLeod, 'and yesterday she nearly knocked the Dresden shepherdess off the mantel. I mean, she can't help it, Ewen, she has to run around—'

'Goddamn it, I know she can't help it,' my father would growl, glaring at the smirking face of the Dresden shepherdess.

'I see no need to blaspheme, Ewen,' Grandmother MacLeod would say quietly, and then my father would say he was sorry, and I would leave.

The day my mother went to the hospital, Grandmother MacLeod called me at lunch-time, and when I appeared, smudged with dust from the attic, she looked at me distastefully as though I had been a cockroach that had just crawled impertinently out of the woodwork.

— 'For mercy's sake, Vanessa, what have you been doing with yourself? Run and get washed this minute. Here, not that way—you use the back stairs, young lady. Get along now. Oh—your father phoned.'

I swung around. 'What did he say? How is she? Is the baby born?'

'Curiosity killed a cat,' Grandmother MacLeod said, frowning. 'I cannot understand Beth and Ewen telling you all these things, at your age. What sort of vulgar person you'll grow up to be, I dare not think. No, it's not born yet. Your mother's just the same. No change.'

I looked at my grandmother, not wanting to appeal to her, but unable to stop myself. 'Will she—will she be all right?'

Grandmother MacLeod straightened her already-straight back. 'If I said definitely yes, Vanessa, that would be a lie, and the MacLeods do not tell lies, as I have tried to impress upon you before. What happens is God's will. The Lord giveth, and the Lord taketh away.'

Appalled, I turned away so she would not see my face and my eyes. Surprisingly, I heard her sigh and felt her papery white and perfectly manicured hand upon my shoulder.

'When your Uncle Roderick got killed,' she said, 'I thought I would die. But I didn't die, Vanessa.'

CHAPTER 6 WRITING ABOUT IMAGERY AND SYMBOLISM   95

At lunch, she chatted animatedly, and I realised she was trying to cheer me in the only way she knew.

'When I married your Grandfather MacLeod,' she related, 'he said to me, "Eleanor, don't think because we're going to the prairies that I expect you to live roughly. You're used to a proper house, and you shall have one." He was as good as his word. Before we'd been in Manawaka three years, he'd had this place built. He earned a good deal of money in his time, your grandfather. He soon had more patients than either of the other doctors. We ordered our dinner service and all our silver from Birks' in Toronto. We had resident help in those days, of course, and never had less than twelve guests for dinner parties. When I had a tea, it would always be twenty or thirty. Never any less than half a dozen different kinds of cake were ever served in this house. Well, no one seems to bother much these days. Too lazy, I suppose.'

'Too broke,' I suggested. 'That's what Dad says.'

'I can't bear slang,' Grandmother MacLeod said. 'If you mean hard up, why don't you say so? It's mainly a question of management, anyway. My accounts were always in good order, and so was my house. No unexpected expenses that couldn't be met, no fruit cellar running out of preserves before the winter was over. Do you know what my father used to say to me when I was a girl?'

'No,' I said. 'What?'

—'God loves Order,' Grandmother MacLeod replied with emphasis. 'You remember that, Vanessa. God loves Order—he wants each one of us to set our house in order. I've never forgotten those words of my father's. I was a MacInnes before I got married. The MacInnes is a very ancient clan, the lairds of Morven and constables of the Castle of Kinlochaline. Did you finish that book I gave you?'

'Yes,' I said. Then, feeling some additional comment to be called for, 'It was a swell book, Grandmother.'

This was somewhat short of the truth. I had been hoping for her cairngorm brooch on my tenth birthday, and had received instead the plaid-bound volume entitled *The Clans and Tartans of Scotland*. Most of it was too boring to read, but I had looked up the motto of my own family and those of some of my friends' families. *Be then a wall of brass. Learn to suffer. Consider the end. Go carefully.* I had not found any of these slogans reassuring. What with Mavis Duncan learning to suffer, and Laura Kennedy considering the end, and Patsy Drummond going carefully, and I spending my time in being a wall of brass, it did not seem to me that any of us were going to lead very interesting lives. I did not say this to Grandmother MacLeod.

'The MacInnes motto is *Pleasure Arises from Work*,' I said.

'Yes,' she agreed proudly. 'And an excellent motto it is, too. One to bear in mind.'

She rose from the table, rearranging on her bosom the looped ivory beads that held the pendant on which a fullblown ivory rose was stiffly carved.

'I hope Ewen will be pleased,' she said.

'What at?'

'Didn't I tell you?' Grandmother MacLeod said. 'I hired a girl this morning, for the housework. She's to start tomorrow.'

When my father got home that evening, Grandmother MacLeod told him her good news. He ran one hand distractedly across his forehead.

'I'm sorry, Mother, but you'll just have to unhire her. I can't possibly pay anyone.'

'It seems distinctly odd,' Grandmother MacLeod snapped, 'that you can afford to eat chicken four times a week.'

'Those chickens,' my father said in an exasperated voice, 'are how people are paying their bills. The same with the eggs and the milk. That scrawny turkey that arrived yesterday was for Logan MacCardney's appendix, if you must know. We probably eat better than any family in Manawaka, except Niall Cameron's. People can't entirely dispense with doctors or undertakers. That doesn't mean to say I've got any cash. Look, Mother, I don't know what's happening with Beth. Paul thinks he may have to do a Caesarean. Can't we leave all this? Just leave the house alone. Don't touch it. What does it matter?'

'I have never lived in a messy house, Ewen,' Grandmother MacLeod said, 'and I don't intend to begin now.'

'Oh Lord,' my father said. 'Well, I'll phone Edna, I guess, and see if she can give us a hand, although God knows she's got enough, with the Connor house and her parents to look after.'

'I don't fancy having Edna Connor in to help,' Grandmother MacLeod objected.

'Why not?' my father shouted. 'She's Beth's sister, isn't she?'

'She speaks in such a slangy way,' Grandmother MacLeod said. 'I have never believed she was a good influence on Vanessa. And there is no need for you to raise your voice to me, Ewen, if you please.'

I could barely control my rage. I thought my father would surely rise to Aunt Edna's defence. But he did not.

'It'll be all right,' he soothed her. 'She'd only be here for part of the day, Mother. You could stay in your room.'

Aunt Edna strode in the next morning. The sight of her bobbed black hair and her grin made me feel better at once. She hauled out the carpet sweeper and the weighted polisher and got to work. I dusted while she polished and swept, and we got through the living room and the front hall in next to no time.

'Where's her royal highness, kiddo?' she enquired.

'In her room,' I said. 'She's reading the catalogue from Robinson & Cleaver.'

'Good Glory, not again?' Aunt Edna cried. 'The last time she ordered three linen tea-cloths and two dozen serviettes. It came to fourteen dollars. Your mother was absolutely frantic. I guess I shouldn't be saying this.'

'I knew anyway,' I assured her. 'She was at the lace handkerchiefs section when I took up her coffee.'

'Let's hope she stays there. Heaven forbid she should get onto the banqueting cloths. Well, at least she believes the Irish are good for two things—manual labour and linen-making. She's never forgotten Father used to be a blacksmith, before he got the hardware store. Can you beat it? I wish it didn't bother Beth.'

'Does it?' I asked, and immediately realised this was the wrong move, for Aunt Edna was suddenly scrutinizing me.

'We're making you grow up before your time,' she said. 'Don't pay any attention to me, Nessa. I must've got up on the wrong side of the bed this morning.'

But I was unwilling to leave the subject.

'All the same,' I said thoughtfully, 'Grandmother MacLeod's family were the lairds of Morven and the constables of the Castle of Kinlochaline. I bet you didn't know that.'

Aunt Edna snorted. 'Castle, my foot. She was born in Ontario, just like your Grandfather Connor, and her father was a horse doctor. Come on, kiddo, we'd better shut up and get down to business here.'

We worked in silence for a while.

'Aunt Edna—' I said at last, 'what about Mother? Why won't they let me go and see her?'

'Kids aren't allowed to visit maternity patients. It's tough for you, I know that. Look, Nessa, don't worry. If it doesn't start tonight, they're going to do the operation. She's getting the best of care.'

I stood there, holding the feather duster like a dead bird in my hands. I was not aware that I was going to speak until the words came out.

'I'm scared,' I said.

Aunt Edna put her arms around me, and her face looked all at once stricken and empty of defences.

'Oh, honey, I'm scared, too,' she said.

It was this way that Grandmother MacLeod found us when she came stepping lightly down into the front hall with the order in her hand for two dozen lace-bordered handkerchiefs of pure Irish linen.

I could not sleep that night, and when I went downstairs, I found my father in the den. I sat down on the hassock beside his chair, and he told me about the operation my mother was to have the next morning. He kept on saying it was not serious nowadays.

'But you're worried,' I put in, as though seeking to explain why I was.

'I should at least have been able to keep from burdening you with it,' he said in a distant voice, as though to himself. 'If only the baby hadn't got itself twisted around—'

'Will it be born dead, like the little girl?'

'I don't know,' my father said. 'I hope not.'

'She'd be disappointed, wouldn't she, if it was?' I said bleakly, wondering why I was not enough for her.

'Yes, she would,' my father replied. 'She won't be able to have any more, after this. It's partly on your account that she wants this one, Nessa. She doesn't want you to grow up without a brother or sister.'

'As far as I'm concerned, she didn't need to bother,' I retorted angrily.

My father laughed. 'Well, let's talk about something else, and then maybe you'll be able to sleep. How did you and Grandmother make out today?'

'Oh, fine, I guess. What was Grandfather MacLeod like, Dad?'

'What did she tell you about him?'

'She said he made a lot of money in his time.'

'Well, he wasn't any millionaire,' my father said, 'but I suppose he did quite well. That's not what I associate with him, though.'

He reached across to the bookshelf, took out a small leather-bound volume and opened it. On the pages were mysterious marks, like doodling, only much neater and more patterned.

'What is it?' I asked.

'Greek,' my father explained. 'This is a play called *Antigone*. See, here's the title in English. There's a whole stack of them on the shelves there. *Oedipus Rex. Electra. Medea.* They belonged to your Grandfather MacLeod. He used to read them often.'

'Why?' I enquired, unable to understand why anyone would pore over those undecipherable signs.

'He was interested in them,' my father said. 'He must have been a lonely man, although it never struck me that way at the time. Sometimes a thing only hits you a long time afterwards.'

'Why would he be lonely?' I wanted to know.

'He was the only person in Manawaka who could read these plays in the original Greek,' my father said. 'I don't suppose many people, if anyone, had even read them in English translations. Maybe he would have liked to be a classical scholar—I don't know. But his father was a doctor, so that's what he was. Maybe he would have liked to talk to somebody about these plays. They must have meant a lot to him.'

It seemed to me that my father was talking oddly. There was a sadness in his voice that I had never heard before, and I longed to say something that would make him feel better, but I could not, because I did not know what was the matter.

'Can you read this kind of writing?' I asked hesitantly.

My father shook his head. 'Nope. I was never very intellectual, I guess. Rod was always brighter than I, in school, but even he wasn't interested in learning Greek. Perhaps he would've been later, if he'd lived. As a kid, all I ever wanted to do was go into the merchant marine.'

'Why didn't you, then?'

'Oh well,' my father said offhandedly, 'a kid who'd never seen the sea wouldn't have made much of a sailor. I might have turned out to be the seasick type.'

I had lost interest now that he was speaking once more like himself.

'Grandmother MacLeod was pretty cross today about the girl,' I remarked.

'I know,' my father nodded. 'Well, we must be as nice as we can to her, Nessa, and after a while she'll be all right.'

Suddenly I did not care what I said.

'Why can't she be nice to us for a change?' I burst out. 'We're always the ones who have to be nice to her.'

My father put his hand down and slowly tilted my head until I was forced to look at him.

'Vanessa,' he said, 'she's had troubles in her life which you really don't know much about. That's why she gets migraine sometimes and has to go to bed. It's not easy for her these days, either—the house is still the same, so she thinks other things should be, too. It hurts her when she finds they aren't.'

'I don't see—' I began.

'Listen,' my father said, 'you know we were talking about what people are interested in, like Grandfather MacLeod being interested in Greek plays? Well, your grandmother was interested in being a lady, Nessa, and for a long time it seemed to her that she was one.'

I thought of the Castle of Kinlochaline, and of horse doctors in Ontario.

'I didn't know—' I stammered.

'That's usually the trouble with most of us,' my father said. 'You go on up to bed now. I'll phone tomorrow from the hospital as soon as the operation's over.'

I did sleep at last, and in my dreams I could hear the caught sparrow fluttering in the attic, and the sound of my mother crying, and the voices of the dead children.

My father did not phone until afternoon. Grandmother MacLeod said I was being silly, for you could hear the phone ringing all over the house, but nevertheless I refused to move out of the den. I had never before examined my father's books, but now, at a loss for something to do, I took them out one by one and read snatches here and there. After I had been doing this for several hours, it dawned on me that most of the books were of the same kind. I looked again at the titles.

Seven-League Boots. Arabia Deserta. The Seven Pillars of Wisdom. Travels in Tibet. Count Lucknor the Sea Devil. And a hundred more. On a shelf by themselves were copies of the *National Geographic* magazine, which I looked at often enough, but never before with the puzzling compulsion which I felt now, as though I were on the verge of some discovery, something which I had to find out and yet did not want to know. I riffled through the picture-filled pages. Hibiscus and wild orchids grew in a soft-petalled confusion. The Himalayas stood lofty as gods, with the morning sun on their peaks of snow. Leopards snarled from the vined depths of a thousand jungles. Schooners buffeted their white sails like the wings of giant angels against the great sea winds.

'What on earth are you doing?' Grandmother MacLeod enquired waspishly, from the doorway. 'You've got everything scattered all over the place. Pick it all up this minute, Vanessa, do you hear?'

So I picked up the books and magazines, and put them all neatly away, as I had been told to do.

When the telephone finally rang, I was afraid to answer it. At last I picked it up. My father sounded faraway, and the relief in his voice made it unsteady.

'It's okay, honey. Everything's fine. The boy was born alive and kicking after all. Your mother's pretty weak, but she's going to be all right.'

I could hardly believe it. I did not want to talk to anyone. I wanted to be by myself, to assimilate the presence of my brother, towards whom, without ever having seen him yet, I felt such tenderness and such resentment.

That evening, Grandmother MacLeod approached my father, who, still dazed with the unexpected gift of neither life now being threatened, at first did not take her seriously when she asked what they planned to call the child.

'Oh, I don't know. Hank, maybe, or Joe. Fauntleroy, perhaps.'

She ignored his levity.

'Ewen,' she said, 'I wish you would call him Roderick.'

My father's face changed. 'I'd rather not.'

'I think you should,' Grandmother MacLeod insisted, very quietly, but in a voice as pointed and precise as her silver nail-scissors.

'Don't you think Beth ought to decide?' my father asked.

'Beth will agree if you do.'

My father did not bother to deny something that even I knew to be true. He did not say anything. Then Grandmother MacLeod's voice, astonishingly, faltered a little.

'It would mean a great deal to me,' she said.

I remembered what she had told me— *When your Uncle Roderick got killed, I thought I would die. But I didn't die.* All at once, her feeling for that unknown dead man became a reality for me. And yet I held it against her, as well, for I could see that it had enabled her to win now.

'All right,' my father said tiredly. 'We'll call him Roderick.'

Then, alarmingly, he threw back his head and laughed.

'Roderick Dhu!' he cried. 'That's what you'll call him, isn't it? Black Roderick. Like before. Don't you remember? As though he were a character out of Sir Walter Scott, instead of an ordinary kid who—'

He broke off, and looked at her with a kind of desolation in his face.

'God, I'm sorry, Mother,' he said. 'I had no right to say that.'

Grandmother MacLeod did not flinch, or tremble, or indicate that she felt anything at all.

'I accept your apology, Ewen,' she said.

My mother had to stay in bed for several weeks after she arrived home. The baby's cot was kept in my parents' room, and I could go in and look at the small creature who lay there with his tightly closed fists and his feathery black hair. Aunt Edna came in to help each morning, and when she had finished the housework, she would have coffee with my mother. They kept the door closed, but this did not prevent me from eavesdropping, for there was an air register in the floor of the spare room, which was linked somehow with the register in my parents' room. If you put your ear to the iron grille, it was almost like a radio.

'Did you mind very much, Beth?' Aunt Edna was saying.

'Oh, it's not the name I mind,' my mother replied. 'It's just the fact that Ewen felt he had to. You know that Rod had only had the sight of one eye, didn't you?'

'Sure, I knew. So what?'

'There was only a year and a half between Ewen and Rod,' my mother said, 'so they often went around together when they were youngsters. It was Ewen's air-rifle that did it.'

'Oh Lord,' Aunt Edna said heavily. 'I suppose she always blamed him?'

'No, I don't think it was so much that, really. It was how he felt himself. I think he even used to wonder sometimes if—but people shouldn't let themselves think like that, or they'd go crazy. Accidents do happen, after all. When the war came, Ewen joined up first. Rod should never have been in the Army at all, but he couldn't wait to get in. He must have lied about his eyesight. It wasn't so very noticeable unless you looked at him closely, and I don't suppose the medicals were very thorough in those days. He got in as a gunner, and Ewen applied to have him in the same company. He thought he might be able to watch out for him, I guess, Rod being—at a disadvantage. They were both only kids. Ewen was nineteen and Rod was eighteen when they went to France. And then the Somme. I don't know, Edna, I think Ewen felt that if Rod had had proper sight, or if he hadn't been in the same outfit and had been sent somewhere else—you know how people always think these things afterwards, not that it's ever a bit of use. Ewen wasn't there when Rod got hit. They'd lost each other somehow, and Ewen was looking for him, not bothering about anything else, you know, just frantically looking. Then he stumbled across him quite by chance. Rod was still alive, but—'

'Stop it, Beth,' Aunt Edna said. 'You're only upsetting yourself.'

'Ewen never spoke of it to me,' my mother went on, 'until once his mother showed me the letter he'd written to her at the time. It was a peculiar letter, almost formal, saying how gallantly Rod had died, and all that. I guess I shouldn't have, but I told him she'd shown it to me. He was very angry that she had. And then, as though for some reason he were terribly ashamed, he said—*I had to write something to her, but men don't really die like that, Beth. It wasn't that way at all.* It was only after the war that he decided to come back and study medicine and go into practice with his father.'

'Had Rod meant to?' Aunt Edna asked.

'I don't know,' my mother said slowly. 'I never felt I should ask Ewen that.'

Aunt Edna was gathering up the coffee things, for I could hear the clash of cups and saucers being stacked on the tray.

'You know what I heard her say to Vanessa once, Beth? *The MacLeods never tell lies.* Those were her exact words. Even then, I didn't know whether to laugh or cry.'

'Please, Edna—' my mother sounded worn out now. 'Don't.'

'Oh Glory,' Aunt Edna said remorsefully, 'I've got all the delicacy of a two-ton truck. I didn't mean Ewen, for heaven's sake. That wasn't what I meant at all. Here, let me plump up your pillows for you.'

Then the baby began to cry, so I could not hear anything more of interest. I took my bike and went out beyond Manawaka, riding aimlessly along the gravel highway. It was late summer, and the wheat had changed colour, but instead of being high and bronzed in the fields, it was stunted and desiccated, for there had been no rain again this year. But in the bluff where I stopped and crawled under the barbed wire fence and lay stretched out on the grass, the plentiful poplar leaves were turning to a luminous yellow and shone like church windows in the sun. I put my head down very close to the earth and looked at what was going on there. Grasshoppers with enormous eyes ticked and twitched around me, as though the dry air were perfect for their purpose. A ladybird laboured mightily to climb a blade of grass, fell off, and started all over again, seeming to be unaware that she possessed wings and could have flown up.

I thought of the accidents that might easily happen to a person—or, of course, might not happen, might happen to somebody else. I thought of the dead baby, my sister, who might as easily have been I. Would she, then, have been lying here in my place, the sharp grass making its small toothmarks on her brown arms, the sun warming her to the heart? I thought of the leatherbound volumes of Greek, and the six different kinds of iced cakes that used to be offered always in the MacLeod house, and the pictures of leopards and green seas. I thought of my brother, who had been born alive after all, and now had been given his life's name.

I could not really comprehend these things, but I sensed their strangeness, their disarray. I felt that whatever God might love in this world, it was certainly not order.

(1970)

PREWRITING

Since much of the imagery in "To Set Our House in Order" carries symbolic significance, we will focus on symbolism as the topic for writing here. Symbols in fiction are not difficult to recognize. Usually an author will give a symbol particular emphasis by mentioning it repeatedly (like the webs in "Obasan"). A crucial symbol will sometimes be placed in the story's opening or ending.

INTERPRETING SYMBOLS

Margaret Laurence directs our attention to the idea of order by making it part of the title of her story. She also gives us various images that suggest the soul-destroying consequences of order: images of trapped or static forms of life that may be found within the house or that are associated with Grandmother MacLeod herself. The ironic imperative of the title, "To Set Our House in Order," is reflected in those symbols of unruly life force caught in the stasis of overweening control.

Here are some points and questions to consider as you read the story a second time and try to work out your interpretation of its symbolism.

1. We are told a lot about Grandmother MacLeod's emphasis on order, and yet in the very heart of her house can be found "dusty tunnels and forgotten recesses." Why is this? Is it significant? Intentional?
2. The version of her history that Grandmother tells Vanessa is quite different than the one Aunt Edna tells. What is the reason for these conflicting views? What is the effect?
3. Flowers and plants are mentioned a number of times in the story. Why does the author emphasize these objects and their colours or states of health?
4. Birds and things associated with birds are also mentioned several times throughout the story. Why is their presence so important? What associations can be made with birds? Would biblical allusions be applicable?
5. Which characters seem to stand for particular ideas or views? What about Grandmother MacLeod? Look at her speeches, sayings, mottoes, and comments throughout the story. Also, look up the meaning of the characters' names, especially Vanessa, Ewen, and Edna. Are these meanings significant to the roles they play in the story?

WRITING

The key to a successful essay is a good *thesis*, or controlling idea. Before you get too far in your writing, try to state your main point in a single sentence.

PRODUCING A WORKABLE THESIS

A useful thesis should narrow the topic to an idea you can cover within your word limit. It should indicate the direction of your thinking—what you intend to *say* about that idea—in other words, your judgment about the idea. Be sure to state your thesis in a complete sentence to indicate the point you plan to make.

EXERCISE ON THESIS STATEMENTS

The numbered thesis statements are too broad to be workable. Figure out how each one can be narrowed and given direction; then write an improved version. Here is an example of the kind of revisions we hope you will produce.

Too broad: Margaret Laurence's "To Set Our House in Order" contains a number of significant symbols.

Improved: In "To Set Our House in Order" Margaret Laurence uses repeated images—trapped birds, lifeless plants, and dust—to symbolize the stagnation of overly ordered lives.

1. Margaret Laurence's "To Set Our House in Order" is a compelling story about the struggle to live.
2. The many birds serve as symbols in Margaret Laurence's story.
3. The setting of Margaret Laurence's "To Set Our House in Order" contributes to the effectiveness of the story.
4. The characters function symbolically in Margaret Laurence's "To Set Our House in Order."
5. Margaret Laurence's "To Set Our House in Order" reveals a great deal about family relationships and human nature.

IDEAS FOR WRITING

IDEAS FOR RESPONSIVE WRITING

1. What is Margaret Laurence saying about the struggle for control in families in "To Set Our House in Order"? Think of some family roles in our current society that you feel ought to be reconsidered and modified, and write an essay setting forth your views. Consider, for example, the roles that parents, grandparents, aunts, and uncles all play in the lives of children. How would you define the ideal role for each? Consider also the different styles of parenting, and which of these provide the best support for children to grow up into self-confident adults.
2. Can you think of any famous tyrants—or any who are not famous, for that matter? Write an essay discussing the role that tyrants play in society, using examples chosen from history, novels, films, or your own experience.

IDEAS FOR CRITICAL WRITING

1. Look up the word *tyrant* in a good dictionary. Then look it or its synonyms up in the *Micropaedia* of the *Encyclopaedia Britannica*, which will give you some historical examples of tyrants. Formulate a thesis that relates the symbolism of "To Set Our House in Order" to the notion of a tyrant or to the idea of order and control. Be sure, in the conclusion, to relate your remarks to the theme of the story.
2. Write an essay focusing on the symbolism of the characters in "To Set Our House in Order," especially Grandmother, Vanessa, Ewen, Roderick, and Edna. Conclude your essay by relating your observations to the story's theme.
3. In the "Anthology of Short Fiction" (a later section of this text), read Ethel Wilson's "The Window," and write a paper focused on the symbolism of the window versus the mirror, keeping in mind Wilson's theme as you devise your thesis. In your conclusion, show how these major symbols function to reveal the meaning of the story.
4. Read Eudora Welty's "A Worn Path," and show how the bird imagery contributes to the effectiveness of the story.

REWRITING

As you revise your first draft, try to improve it in every way possible. Our advice at this point involves ideas for improving your introduction.

SHARPENING THE INTRODUCTION

Look at your introductory paragraph. Does it give your readers a clear idea of the topic and purpose? Will it arouse curiosity and interest as well as lead into your subject?

One strategy for catching the attention of your readers involves using a pertinent quotation:

> "A rose is a rose is a rose," wrote Gertrude Stein, suggesting that a thing is only what it is and nothing more. However, in Margaret Laurence's "To Set Our House in Order," Grandmother MacLeod's ivory rose pendant, along with other images of ossified life, symbolizes an entrapment that transcends its literal meaning.

Another relevant quotation for this introduction might be William Blake's "O Rose, thou art sick!" (page 410). Other useful quotations are available in libraries in reference books such as *Bartlett's Familiar Quotations*.

You can also take an arresting or ironic quotation from the story itself. Vanessa's final insight that "whatever God might love in this world, it was certainly not order," or Grandmother MacLeod's heated declaration that "the MacLeods do not tell lies" might serve as an effective opening for an essay on this story.

Another strategy is to pose a question, like this:

> Why would Ewen MacLeod allow his mother to suffocate his family? This is a question that both Vanessa MacLeod and the reader are forced to consider in Margaret Laurence's symbolic story "To Set Our House in Order."

Or you can combine some suspense with a *brief* overview of the story:

> The MacLeod house is large and solid and the family therein is sheltered somewhat from the effects of the Great Depression. However, when ten-year-old Vanessa's father takes her mother into the hospital with complications from premature labour, Vanessa is left alone to endure the stern ministrations of the great house's ruling matriarch. Grandmother MacLeod presides over the family like an aloof, inflexible queen, imposing a kind of order that suffocates any hope for freedom for Vanessa, her mother, and most poignantly, her father. The story is Margaret Laurence's "To Set Our House in Order."

Another way to introduce a critical essay is to use interesting details about the author or the story's background that relate to the focus of your essay (remember, however, that fiction writers do more than simply write about their own experiences):

> Margaret Laurence was born in the small Manitoba prairie town of Neepawa, and after the death of her parents she grew up, like Vanessa MacLeod in "To Set Our House in Order," under the powerful influence of Scots-Presbyterian grandparents. Like Vanessa, she struggled for independence yet strove to understand the human conditions that allow some individuals to live with joy and freedom while others suffer under social and economic bondage. How autobiographical are Laurence's short stories? The answer reveals an often close bond between fiction and fact.

Whatever approach you choose, keep the reader in mind. Think about reading an essay yourself. What do you expect from the introduction? Remember that the reader forms an important first impression from your opening paragraph.

SAMPLE STUDENT PAPER

On the following left-hand pages appears the uncorrected second draft of an essay written by Ian Galloway from Malaspina University College in British Columbia. On the right-hand pages you will see Ian's finished version. The questions and comments in the margins of the final version ask you to consider the changes Ian made when he revised the paper.

WEB

For study tools to help you with your next writing assignment, please visit the Companion Website at www.pearsoned.ca/mcmahan.

SAMPLE STUDENT PAPER: SECOND DRAFT

Ian Galloway   1

ENG1110

January 10, 2004

The Ivory Rose

In "To Set Our House in Order" Margaret Laurence begins her story with early references to bird and flower imagery, which are images of freedom and maturity. These images are subtle and the idea of control and order that they represent doesn't become clear until a second or third reading. Other symbols such as Grandmother MacLeod's ivory rose pendant because of its strength and repetition clearly force the reader to make a deep interpretation. Sometimes, "A rose is a rose is a rose," but Margaret Laurence's use of the symbol of the rose in Grandmother MacLeod's pendant must surely reflect a lack of love and most other human emotions. Laurence's ivory rose gives us clear insight into the personality of its wearer. As a yonic symbol, this rose is concrete evidence of Grandmother MacLeod's many inabilities.

SAMPLE STUDENT PAPER: FINISHED VERSION

Ian Galloway   1
ENG1110
January 25, 2004

                        The Ivory Rose

In "To Set Our House in Order" Margaret Laurence uses many images of control and order that are subtle, and their importance doesn't become clear until a second or third reading. Other symbols, such as Grandmother MacLeod's ivory rose pendant because of its strength and repetition, clearly force the reader to make a deep interpretation. If love is usually represented as a rose, then the rose in Grandmother MacLeod's pendant must surely reflect a lack of love and most other human emotions. Laurence's ivory rose gives us clear insight into the personality of its wearer. As a yonic symbol, this rose is concrete evidence of Grandmother MacLeod's inability to be fully developed, alive, or free.

    Grandmother MacLeod's rose, "a fullblown" (95) rose, is engraved in ivory and will never develop beyond the state of peak maturity.

Why did Ian make changes in the opening sentence?

Why did he remove the quotation?

Why did Ian change the thesis statement?

Ian changed the topic statement. Why?

SECOND DRAFT

Galloway 2

Grandmother MacLeod is past her physical peak--she is a grandmother, a woman beyond childbearing years, and one whose attributes could include comfort, protection and wisdom. She is certainly beyond the "fullblown" stage of life. A rose is a living thing and will develop from bud to full-blown blossom to protective rose hip. The fullness of the ivory rose, therefore, is not an indication of Grandmother's life now, but it may indicate the stage at which her emotional development ends. Obviously, Grandmother MacLeod does not physically die when her son Roderick was killed during World War I, yet her life seems to have stopped developing emotionally at this stage of motherhood. She continues, however, to rule the household, treating all in it as if they are children in need of control and correction. When Ewen comforts his own worried child, Vanessa, Grandmother MacLeod does not relinquish her role as controlling mother, and without regard for Ewen's status as adult and father, criticizes his parenting: "Ewen, you're only encouraging the child to give way" (93). In addition, Vanessa's lively "presence . . . [is] not encouraged" (94), neither is she nurtured or protected by her grandmother. Grandmother, rather than move past the controlling admonitions that she imposes upon Vanessa, refuses to see herself.

FINISHED VERSION

Galloway 2

Grandmother MacLeod, however, is certainly beyond the "fullblown" stage of life--she is a grandmother, a woman beyond childbearing years, and one whose attributes could include being a source of comfort, protection, and wisdom. A rose is a living thing and will develop from bud to full-blown blossom to protective rose hip. The fullness of the ivory rose, therefore, is not an indication of Grandmother's life now, but it may indicate the stage at which her emotional development ends. "When your Uncle Roderick got killed," she tells her granddaughter Vanessa, "I thought I would die. But I didn't die" (94). Obviously, Grandmother MacLeod does not physically die when her son Roderick is killed during World War I, yet her life seems to have stopped developing emotionally at this stage of motherhood; she continues to rule the household, treating all in it as if they are children in need of control and correction. For instance, when Ewen comforts his own worried child, Vanessa, Grandmother MacLeod does not relinquish her role as controlling mother, and without regard for Ewen's status as adult and father, criticizes his parenting: "Ewen, you're only encouraging the child to give way" (93). In addition, Vanessa's lively "presence . . . [is] not encouraged" (94), neither is she nurtured or protected by her grandmother.

Why did he add the quotation?

What wording did he add?

Why did Ian remove some details here?

SECOND DRAFT

Galloway 3

The MacInnes' motto "Pleasure Arises from Work" (95), the proclamation "MacLeods do not tell lies" (94), and the maxim "God loves Order" (95) are falsehoods that Grandmother MacLeod cannot seem to move past in order to see what Vanessa has discovered: Grandmother MacLeod neither works nor tells the truth, and God does not seem particularly fond of order. Grandmother MacLeod's inability to develop beyond the stage of the controlling parent blinded by a false sense of herself is clearly indicated by the likeness of a rose carved permanently full-blown into an ivory pendant.

Further emphasizing her own emotional demise, Grandmother MacLeod states, "I have never lived in a messy house, Ewen . . . and I don't intend to begin now" (96). If she does not intend to live in the messiness of life, she surely intends to die. Grandmother's rose is dead, and it hangs from her neck like the proverbial albatross. The ivory, once part of a living animal, is a dead substance. The carving in this dead white ivory is a hard, permanent representation of something that is meant to be soft, fragile, and impermanent: a rose, a life. This ivory rose will never messily shed its petals, and it will never wilt nor weaken because it is not alive.

CHAPTER 6 WRITING ABOUT IMAGERY AND SYMBOLISM

FINISHED VERSION

Galloway 3

Grandmother MacLeod's inability to develop beyond the stage of the controlling parent is clearly indicated by the likeness of a rose carved permanently full-blown into an ivory pendant.

The idea of order over chaos controls every aspect of the story, and the "pendant on which a fullblown ivory rose [is] stiffly carved" (95) exemplifies Grandmother MacLeod's determination to die in her ordered existence rather than live in the chaos that is life. Further emphasizing her own emotional demise, Grandmother MacLeod states, "I have never lived in a messy house, Ewen . . . and I don't intend to begin now" (96). If she does not intend to live in the messiness of life, she surely intends to die. Grandmother's rose is dead, and it hangs from her neck like the proverbial albatross. The ivory, once part of a living animal, is a dead substance. The carving in this dead white ivory is a hard, permanent representation of something that is meant to be soft, fragile, and impermanent: a rose, a life. This ivory rose will never messily shed its petals, and it will never wilt nor weaken because it is not alive. Neither will "steel-spined" Grandmother MacLeod as represented by her ivory rose (93).

Why did Ian change the topic statement?

SECOND DRAFT

Galloway 4

Neither will "steel-spined" Grandmother MacLeod as represented by her ivory rose (93). Furthermore, she chooses death over life when she insists upon naming Vanessa's newborn baby brother after her own dead son. One may argue that she is trying to create a living memorial for Roderick through her new grandson, for when she makes her request, it is the only moment in the story when her voice falters, revealing emotion. Nevertheless, Vanessa sees through Grandmother MacLeod's manipulations: "[her feeling] had enabled her to win now" (99). Rather than support and encourage her family, Grandmother seeks to order the very life out of it.

Grandmother MacLeod's lack of freedom seems pitiable. The carved rose on the ivory pendant does, after all, represent a beautiful object caught at a magnificent moment in its life, but this perfection is like a prison for Grandmother MacLeod. Rather than express her pain over the "troubles in her life," perfectly controlled Grandmother MacLeod "gets migraine sometimes and has to go to bed" (98). Her inability to be free of her physical or emotional pain and grow with the life around her is explained by Ewen: "the house is still the same, so she thinks other things should be, too" (98).

CHAPTER 6 WRITING ABOUT IMAGERY AND SYMBOLISM 113

FINISHED VERSION

Galloway 4

Furthermore, she chooses death over life when she insists upon naming Vanessa's newborn baby brother after her own dead son: "I wish you would call him Roderick" (99). One may argue that she is trying to create a living memorial for Roderick through her new grandson, for when she makes her request, it is the only moment in the story when her voice falters, revealing emotion. Nevertheless, Vanessa sees through Grandmother MacLeod's manipulations: "[her feeling] had enabled her to win now" (99), but she has won merely the anger of her granddaughter, the guilt of her son, and the resentment of her daughter-in-law. Rather than support and encourage her family, Grandmother seeks to order the very life out of it. The rose that is permanently trapped, stiffly carved, and perfectly controlled in the ivory pendant represents Grandmother MacLeod's deadly order.

What did Ian change here? Why?

What addition did he make?

Although she appears monstrous in her control, there are also moments when Grandmother MacLeod's lack of freedom seems pitiable. The carved rose on the ivory pendant does, after all, represent a beautiful object caught at a magnificent moment in its life, but this perfection is like a prison for Grandmother MacLeod.

What changes did he make in this paragraph?

SECOND DRAFT

Galloway 5

Grandmother MacLeod has no recognition of the pain she is causing others, of the life she is ordering out of the house, of the family's present financial state, the depression in the outside world, or of her own lack of freedom to control these things. The MacLeod household is one in which physical, emotional, and spiritual deaths have touched all. Rather than face these deaths, Grandmother MacLeod retreats more deeply into her emotional prison. The full-blown rose to her represents happier moments, times when both sons and her husband were alive, when there was money and she was free to play the lady. Then, she was free to order from the Robinson and Cleaver catalogue the necessities of a comfortable life. She is criticized for ordering "two dozen lace-bordered handkerchiefs" (97). Grandmother MacLeod is a woman who, if freed from her emotional prison to feel all of her losses, would need two dozen handkerchiefs and more to dry her tears. Hardening herself against her own emotions and the life around her, she hides in her ivory and is as out of touch with life as a "giant queen" (94). The pendant with the full-blown ivory rose stiffly carved on it represents Grandmother MacLeod's lack of freedom in her emotional prison.

FINISHED VERSION

Galloway 5

For example, rather than express her pain over the "troubles in her life," perfectly controlled Grandmother MacLeod "gets migraine sometimes and has to go to bed" (98). Her inability to be free of her physical or emotional pain and grow with the life around her is further explained by Ewen: "the house is still the same, so she thinks other things should be, too" (98). Unfortunately, Grandmother MacLeod has no recognition of the pain she is causing others, the life she is ordering out of the house, the family's present financial state, the Great Depression in the outside world, or her own lack of freedom to control these things. However, rather than face these deadly realities, Grandmother MacLeod retreats more deeply into her emotional prison, for to her the full-blown rose captures happier moments, times when both sons and her husband were alive, when there was money and she was free to play the lady, and when she was free to order from the Robinson and Cleaver catalogue the necessities of a comfortable life. Now, she is criticized for ordering "two dozen lace-bordered handkerchiefs" (97). Grandmother MacLeod is a woman who, if freed from her emotional prison to feel all of her losses, would need two dozen handkerchiefs and more to dry her tears.

Why did Ian change the wording here?

SECOND DRAFT

Galloway 6

    A rose is a fragile thing with a limited life span, yet it is the epitome of beauty and grace when in its prime. Is it any wonder that Grandmother MacLeod prefers to remain at that moment, "steel-spined," refusing to freely bend with the demands of life when those demands would surely force her to acknowledge pain, her own mortality and the fragility of the lives of those close to her? A prison prevents freedom, but it also offers protection from outside forces.

FINISHED VERSION

Galloway 6

Hardening herself against her own emotions and the life around her, she hides in her ivory tower "with its stale and old-smelling air, the dim reek of medicines and lavender sachets" (94) and her "weedy collection of anaemic ferns" (93) and is as out of touch with life as a "giant queen" (94). The pendant with the full-blown ivory rose stiffly carved on it represents Grandmother MacLeod's lack of freedom in her emotional prison.

Why did Ian add quotations?

A rose is a fragile thing with a limited life span, yet it is the epitome of beauty and grace when in its prime. Is it any wonder that Grandmother MacLeod prefers to remain at that moment "steel-spined," refusing to freely bend with the demands of life when those demands would surely force her to acknowledge pain, her own mortality, and the fragility of the lives of those close to her? A prison prevents freedom, but it also offers protection from outside forces. The stiffly carved ivory rose is a symbol of stagnation, death, and imprisonment for the one around whose neck it hangs in Laurence's story.

What did Ian add to the conclusion?

SECOND DRAFT

Galloway 7

Works Cited

Laurence, Margaret. "To Set Our House in Order." From <u>A Bird in the House</u>. Toronto: McClelland and Stewart, 1989. 43-61.

FINISHED VERSION

Galloway 7

Work Cited

Laurence, Margaret. "To Set Our House in Order." <u>A Bird in the House</u>. Toronto: McClelland, 1989. 43-61.

What changes did Ian make to the Work Cited page?

7

Writing about Point of View

Learning about point of view in fiction will help you understand how the author has shaped what you know and how you feel about the events in a story. When the point of view is unusual, you may want to focus your written analysis on the narrator or on the significance of the writer's choice of narrative focus.

WHAT IS POINT OF VIEW?

In identifying point of view, you decide who tells the story—that is, whose thoughts and feelings the reader has access to. The storyteller, called the *narrator*, is a creation of the author and should not be confused with the author. In the following passage from "Boys and Girls," Alice Munro takes the reader into the private world of her narrator's fantasy:

> Now for the time that remained to me, the most perfectly private and perhaps the best time of the whole day, I arranged myself tightly under the covers and went on with one of the stories I was telling myself from night to night. These stories were about myself, when I had grown a little older; they took place in a world that was recognizably mine, yet one that presented opportunities for courage, boldness and self-sacrifice, as mine never did.

In Thomas King's "Borders," the opening lines establish not only the narrator's voice but also the direction in which the plot will move:

> When I was twelve, maybe thirteen, my mother announced that we were going to go to Salt Lake City to visit my sister who had left the reserve, moved across the line, and found a job.

However, in the opening of Ethel Wilson's "The Window," we are not conscious of a narrator at all:

> The great big window must have been at least twenty-five feet wide and ten feet high. It was constructed in sections divided by segments of something that did not interfere with the view; in fact the eye by-passed these divisions and looked only at the entrancing scenes beyond.

DESCRIBING POINT OF VIEW

There are several systems for labelling the point of view in a work of literature. They classify the stance and the identity of the person who records and reports the action—that is, the person whose eyes and mind become ours as we read the story.

In actuality, a great many points of view are possible, and you may find some overlapping among the categories we provide here, but the following should allow you to describe all of the works included in this text.

1. *Omniscient:* An all-knowing narrator freely relates many or all of the characters' thoughts, feelings, and actions. The omniscient narrator is not a character in the story and is not involved in the action. Willa Cather's "Paul's Case" is told from an omniscient point of view.

2. *Limited Omniscient:* The narration is limited to the thoughts and observations of a single character. In detective fiction, for example, we often see the plot unfold strictly from the main character's (the detective's) point of view. Sometimes our perceptions are limited to those of a minor character; in the Sherlock Holmes stories, for instance, the events are reported from the point of view of Dr. Watson, the great detective's sidekick, whose admiration and awe for Holmes's skills become ours.

3. *First-person:* The narrator recounts events in which he or she has been involved as a major or minor participant. This narrator, identified as "I" in the story, addresses the reader directly. First-person narrators usually present only their side of the story. For example, the guilt-ridden son in Alistair MacLeod's "The Boat" recounts his early life in a Cape Breton fishing family; and Shaila in Bharati Mukherjee's "The Management of Grief" gives a very moving and subjective account of coming to terms with the death of her family.

4. *Objective:* The narrator disappears and the story seems to tell itself through action and dialogue. An objective narrative does not get into the minds of the characters; it gives the reader only what could be recorded by a camera and a microphone. In reading this kind of story, we have to make judgments and draw conclusions on our own. The objective narrator may edit the tape and direct the camera, but we have to figure out why the characters behave as they do. When you read Rudy Wiebe's "Where Is the Voice Coming From?" the opening line suggests an objective point of view that will present the difficulties of making a story. Wiebe seemingly employs objective narration, but quite quickly you realize the narrator's bias. Hemingway in "Hills like White Elephants" uses dialogue almost exclusively, the result being that we are the objective eavesdroppers making inferences about the speakers as we listen in on their conversation.

SHIFTING AND UNRELIABLE NARRATORS

If a writer tells the same story, sometimes through one character and sometimes through a different character, the point of view is still limited, but *shifting*. The point of view can shift in other ways. David Adams Richards's "A Rural Place" begins with dialogue between the nursing home staff, then shifts to third-person narration as Janie Bell is helped to board the ferry:

> The man looked about, and under him she could hear the steady rumble of the engine and smell grease and car heat.

The narration shifts again as Janie tells her own story in the first person:

> *I* member we'd all our raspberries in boxes and what a time gettin them boxes and then we all wanted ta go with er every one a us and she said "Janie get yer coat on" and Isabel started cryin but when I went over ta town I diden like it anyway we hadda stand round all day waitin in the heat.

If the storyteller misrepresents or misinterprets the facts, purposely or naively, the narrator is considered *unreliable*. A child, an insane person, or a villain, for example, would sometimes be unable or unwilling to give a fully truthful presentation. Writers also sometimes use shifting narrators to emphasize the subjectivity of experience, as you will see in the following story by Eugene McNamara.

LOOKING AT POINT OF VIEW

As you read Eugene McNamara's "Falling in Place," notice how much is revealed by various narrators, for example their occupations, their relationships, and their attitudes.

Eugene McNamara   b. 1930

Falling in Place

The Chinese girl awoke in the early morning, still dark out, and found her door unlocked. The corridor was empty, silent under humming lights. The ward door was ajar. She remembered the story of the prisoner who found his cell door open and went out into the palace garden. There the poor wretch met a kindly reassuring priest who was in fact the Inquisitor. Soon the man was back in chains with the added torment of illusory freedom and false sympathy to goad him. The deepened horror.

But outside the hospital no false priest waited for her. There was only the parking lot lying there like a silent bowl of arc light. And she walked beyond it into the deeper inverted bowl of night. A deep pool starred with white water lilies. She had dreamed of rain. A school of small fish scattering in the deep. She saw them through circles on the blistered surface, thought of rain falling in a farmer's yard. Would his barn doors blow away in the wind? The hospital drains sang with rain.

Now she went up the grade to the tracks silvered in the fading moon. And she lay down across the tracks, cushioned her head on the chill steel and looked up into the slowly waking sky. Waited. Oh my iron bridegroom, she said.

On the road beside the embankment the apprentice machinist drove in early light. He had wakened to a charley horse, cursing, limping in his silent morning house. Now he drove, the night mists wipered away, the radio in cadence. His mind was already in the plant. So many there were missing fingers. The machines were hungry. He feared them. At the morning break the men will speak of women. They want full-bodied women. Somewhere else now women were breasting big waves on beaches the men will never see. The ditch beside the road was dry.

It had been a month of drought after a month of rain. He had dreamed of rain. He thought of keeping a rain journal. How many days, how many inches, what damage to property, how some drown in cars in viaducts. Good for the crops some will say. But someone else will answer no, the crop's in peril. Not enough and the lawn burns. Too much and the picnic's ruined.

Never just right, except in dreams where it falls like filmic mist in black and white movies of romance. Lovers dance in it.

Sudden there on the road in common light he heard the shudder of stopped steel on steel. Up ahead was the morning train shaking to a stop and someone there.

Oh God, he thought, and could only watch the meeting, see it happen.

Everything was falling in place as the passengers fell forward. The train had leaned into its curve, righted on the straightaway and settled down. Now, we thought. But instead we jolted from our seats in a hurtling protest of stopping. Then all was silent unmoving. We got off to see. There was blood on the sleepers. We turned to stare across the speechless fields at the still early sun. Tall weeds stood there helpless as any of us. Nothing could change now for her. The hard air stood still. It tasted like brass.

He stood in line at the supermarket, docile, thinking of nothing, and then sudden as the wreck remembered it all. His hand on the brake. Futile. Nothing doing. Throwing up afterwards into his useless hands. And now here in the supermarket line ahead of him a row of grocery carts like train cars derailed, askew. Someone back in aisle four had dropped a jar of beets. A mess for someone else to clean up. And now someone's meat on the conveyor belt red as a kiss moved on, added up, put into a bag. It cannot be called back. The young woman ahead of him tells her child again that they cannot buy the cookies, that they have plenty at home. Does the child know it's a lie?

No, he thought. I am unfair. She soothes the child at home, reads him stories. Her kitchen is orderly and everybody keeps his or her voice down. Wildly, he looked back down the checkout line. He was square in the middle of it, too late to give up or move, and more time to put in waiting. He thought, I'd like to be a private detective, save people from blackmailers, sit back in a creaking chair, stare at the smoked window, listen to the secretary type reports, wait for the phone to ring. The girl's silver voice calls to him out of the dark wire, calling for help. He could save her.

A poet once said that her eyes were the colour of sherry in the glass the guest has left. My eyes are like that. But here in the false dawn my eyes keep in them the deep shadows of night. Pillowed on the polished iron, I could see the morning glory clambering on chain-link fences facing the embankment. Someone is hanging laundry on a line. White forms rising in the wind. I hear birdsong. A faint thrum in the rail. I lay down to sleep and I am certain to rise. *[contrast]*

The weather conditions on that day: patchy morning fog thinning so that visibility was fair to good at the precise time of—and post-incident analysis indicated no mechanical fault in the braking system. From the initial locking of the brakes to the point of impact—
    The provenance of the engine: Electro-Motive Division, General Motors Company, London, Ontario, 1958.

There are several factors involved in braking: torque, brake shoe function, condition of track and gradient. The brake shoe bears against the revolving wheel with a radial force called normal brake shoe pressure. The retarding force of the brake shoe cannot be increased or prolonged indefinitely as train wheels may slide as a result of excessive braking force. (See H.J. Schrader, "Friction of Railway Brake Shoes at High Speed and High Pressure," University of Illinois Engineering Experiment Station Bulletin 301, 1938, Urbana, Illinois.)

There are other factors involved in acceleration and deceleration of course: speed, velocity (speed in a given direction), mass, air resistance or drag, acceleration and the rate of change in acceleration. Mass. The gross weight of the engine. The gross weight of the engine. The weight of the engine.

When I finished hanging the laundry, I thought of cutting the roses back. They say to cut ruthlessly so they will grow more hardy. The cadence of my steps kept to the song we danced to last night. I was humming it and then I heard the chill cry and protest of the engine and then the day was nipped in the bud.

After a long and aimless wait standing alongside the silent train, the passengers were put on buses. It was late morning. They were promised lunch in the next town. By now a kind of disaster-induced camaraderie had developed among them. A subdued cordiality ran through the buses.

I felt an odd lightheadedness, a feeling of post-excitement letdown. As the morning went on the things of our world slowly resumed their usual shapes. I smiled at my fellow voyagers. Everything seemed thick and alive and bright in the almost noon light. Just a little while ago it was all tenuous, fragile, brief and evanescent. I felt mildly hungry, on edge, jumpy, ready to burst into laughter or tears.

Then suddenly I thought of the first sight I had of the girl's foot next to the tracks as I stepped down from the car. Now all the air went just as suddenly out of the day.

Already the blue of the summer sky is turning harshly autumnal. The change has been both gradual and sudden. So also in a very brief time a man may be his actual age and simultaneously feel the swift errant emotions of childhood and youth. A man may feel grief over the loss of those periods of his life while at the same instant re-experience them. I did not know her name.

Thus I felt grief—not only for the wretched girl but for myself and my fellow passengers. Every previous experience of death came welling up. Pets, schoolmates, grandparents, friends, acquaintances, fellow workers. All crowded together in my memory in a hurly-burly of sorrow recaptured. The indifferent blue sky outside the bus window stretches on to everywhere anywhere and nowhere.

The Chinese girl had been studying music at the university. Her first piano recital had been enthusiastically received by the faculty. The recital by one of her fellow pupils, a young man from a farm in the southern part of the Province, was attended with less warmth. This did not lessen the young man's ardor. He found the girl endlessly fascinating. Her eyes were like quick fish in deep water.

She was shy, elusive, reticent, dedicated and given to long hours of practice. There was not much time left over for romance. Still the young man persevered and a kind of wary relationship developed. She told him about her loneliness, her homesickness. He spoke with confidence of a piano career for both of them.

Then came her time of retrospection, introversion, fear and collapse. She went into the hospital. The prognosis was positive. Her period of treatment would be brief, followed by outpatient therapy and a lighter academic load.

There had been a long dry spell of weather. The young man sat one afternoon in a coffee shop near campus. Some people came in and were talking to the waitress about the news. Gradually the story filtered through the damp air and the young man became aware. Rain fell that night like a breaking mirror.

The apprentice machinist dreams of counterboring holes. This procedure would be followed by milling a flat space at the bottom end of the holes. He squinted through a fine spray of coolant. Metal chips lay like sharp confetti on the grim concrete floor. Tolerances were tight—plus or minus one thousandth. Next to him an old timer ran a big Bridgeport. On the other side was another old timer running an obsolete Milwaukee V Mill. Its age was covered with many coats of grey paint.

The apprentice's hands flew from the ball crank to the reversing lever. His mind was busy with the examination he would soon take. Define running fit, push fit, force fit and shrink fit. Tables of stress conversion roll through his mind. His eyes are intent on the chips of metal curling and dropping to the floor.

And now without warning the accident flashes into his mind. Locked steel wheels grind and shear. In a grinding operation wheel and work must be kept in contact until sparks are no longer emitted. Define the function of a chucking grinder. Do not look into the shower of sparks. Do not look up into the morning sunlight. Do not look up at the tracks ahead of you.

The rain fell into the yard near the tracks. All the laundry is safely in, clean-smelling and folded. Lightning glints on the thorns of the cut-back rose bushes. The rain washes the tracks and sleepers, seeping into the roadbed gravel. Rivers flow into the lake.

The rain fell into the placid lake. The diesel horn mourned over the furrowed fields. Train going away someplace. Perhaps a bell on a wrecked ship far below is tolling. Caught in the currents off the Point, it might toll forever. Nobody there to listen. Bellsong sounds in ever-widening concentric circles.

I went back home. The apples were in. My father's orchard was full of pickers on ladders. Windfalls crushed underfoot. The air was thick and sweet. Bees hovered. We set up the old stand and sold jugs of cider to the tourists. I took my turns at the stand.
 I tried not to think of her. But a glissando of notes fell in my mind, sharp as icicles breaking off a roof.
 Su Lin at her recital. Thin, intent, as precise as the music. I saw her, not the tourists, not the bees slowly circling the cider jugs. Seeing her again was as tart as a bite into a green windfall.
 The harvest is big this year. Truckload after truckload of tomatoes go past on the road to the canneries in Leamington. The subtle curve of the road at a point just past us causes the load to shift to the right. Then there is a four-way stop. The load shifts again and the intersection is soon awash with tomato juice and loud with bee clamour. At night I dream of drowning with her. I hear a bell deep under water. The harvest is heavy this year.

I lay down on the sleepers so that I could rise again. I heard a final word spoken clearly. I told the doctor not to judge me. Nobody can know my pain. My fingers made music come from struck strings. Who could tell my fingers not to strike the chords? My love told me of his apple trees. He wanted to climb and pick the sweetest for me from the top. Oh my love, I cannot wait. I must lie down and wait to rise.

The morning train comes and goes many times. Things become usual. Journeys are undertaken. The rain sweeps the train windows, certain as the last things.
 Look mommy, says a child as he points out the train window. There's the sea.
 It's only a river, says the mother.

She does not look out the window. The train goes on, resolute, implacable as a final judgment. Its horn announces us. The river rises in the rain and flows on its certain way. We are almost home or going far from home. Everything is falling in place.

(2000)

PREWRITING

To help you examine the point of view of "Falling in Place" and to see how it affects other elements of the story, write out answers to the following questions.

IDENTIFYING POINT OF VIEW

1. Reread the story "Falling in Place," and try to identify how many different speakers there are and who each one is.
2. Why did the author choose to write the story through so many narrators?
3. After piecing together the story from the various narrations, describe what has happened. Who is the main character?
4. How do your feelings about the other characters in the story (the apprentice machinist, the passengers on the train, the brakeman, and others) affect your responses to Su Lin?
5. What has happened to lead up to Su Lin's experience?
6. How does Su Lin's boyfriend find out about what has happened to her? How does he react to the event?
7. How do the other characters in the story respond to the event, and which character seems most affected by Su Lin's death?
8. What is Su Lin's state of mind? Why is she worried about being judged?
9. Why does the child at the end of the story mistake a river for the sea? What does this final scene have to do with the rest of the story?

WRITING

Before you decide to focus your paper on point of view, you need to determine its importance in the story. An analysis of point of view may not always merit a full-length paper: a first person, *reliable* main character's narration of a personal story is such a natural and appropriate choice that there is little to say about it. But often, as in "Falling in Place," analysis of the point of view is the key to the story.

RELATING POINT OF VIEW TO THEME

Once we become aware that the narration of events is an examination of the same event from a variety of sources, we need to relate that perception to the main point or impact of the story. Why is this particular point of view effective for this particular story?

IDEAS FOR WRITING

IDEAS FOR RESPONSIVE WRITING

1. Write a description of the events in chronological order from the point of view of Su Lin's doctor or her boyfriend.
2. Imagine that you were a passenger on the train, and that you are now conducting your own research into the death of Su Lin. Write a personal journal of your findings. Be sure to include your evaluation of Su Lin's state of mind, her doctor's orders, her relationship with her boyfriend, her education and skills, and the facts about her suicide.
3. Have you ever understood an event from different people's points of view? Did each person believe he or she had the definitive information about what happened? How did your perception of the event change after getting the views of others?
4. Have you ever seen a movie, read another story, or had an experience where one event affected the lives of many people? Whose reactions to the event were strongest? Whose reactions were minimal? Why? What does this tell us about our connectedness to one another?

IDEAS FOR CRITICAL WRITING

Here are some ideas for use in thesis statements that focus on point of view. Choose one of these ideas and revise it to make up your own thesis statement.

1. That each of the unrelated narrators is affected in some way by Su Lin's death demonstrates that, without necessarily being conscious of it, we are all connected.
2. Eugene McNamara uses shifting narration to demonstrate how people respond to tragedy and, more importantly, how tragedy may bring us together.
3. The points of view used by McNamara in "Falling in Place" allow us to understand the jarring effects that shifting between limited-omniscient, first-person, third-person, and objective narration can have on a reader.
4. Written from only one point of view, the story "Falling in Place" might gain continuity, but it would lose other valuable elements.

REWRITING

When you revise, do not neglect your conclusion just because it comes last. It has a psychologically important place in your paper. It is crucial to restate (in other words) the thesis of your paper, but be sure to ask yourself, "Does my closing restate the main idea in an obvious, repetitive way? Will the readers feel let down, dropped off, cut short?" If so, consider some of these ways to make your ending livelier.

SHARPENING THE CONCLUSION

1. *Description.* After a discussion of the complexities of narration and chronology of events in "Falling in Place," in your conclusion you might write the following:

    Finally, the reader comes to terms with the finite nature of life with the image of a young child and his mother riding the train that once again has begun to operate as usual, moving on resolutely, its horn announcing arrivals and departures as a matter of course.

2. *Humour or irony (depending upon the tone of your essay).* The title "Falling in Place" seems ironic when applied to the main event in the story, and Su Lin's words "Oh my iron bridegroom" are grimly ironic in the face of her tragedy. (To refresh your memory about irony, consult the Glossary, page 825.)

3. *A quotation from the story.* Remember that it must be integrated into your own sentence, perhaps this way:

    Everyone riding on the train has been reminded of his or her mortality, and as "journeys are undertaken," passengers and readers alike realize "We are almost home."

4. *An echo from your introduction.* If in your introduction you ask the question "What difference does the death of one young woman make in this world?" you could echo these words in your conclusion with "McNamara confirms for us that one person's death affects us all."

5. *A thought-provoking question, suggestion, or statement:*

    Are we to believe, as McNamara implies in his final sentence, that everything that happens is meant to be?

    In time, we forget about the fragility of life, and things go on as usual until the next tragedy, when we are again reminded of our final destination.

 For study tools to help you with your next writing assignment, please visit the Companion Website at www.pearsoned.ca/mcmahan.

8

Writing about Setting and Atmosphere

Setting and atmosphere contribute to the effectiveness of short stories in various ways. Sometimes these elements assume enough importance to become the focus of a literary analysis.

WHAT ARE SETTING AND ATMOSPHERE?

You know, of course, the meaning of *setting* in reference to a work of literature: the setting includes the location and time of the action in a story, novel, play, or poem. Sometimes the setting conveys an *atmosphere*—the emotional effect of the setting and events—that contributes to the impact or to the meaning of the work. Atmosphere (or mood) is that feeling of chill foreboding that Sinclair Ross creates by setting "The Lamp at Noon" in a remote, isolated farmhouse in the middle of a prairie dust storm and then having the farmer and his wife engage in a fierce battle of wills. Atmosphere can also serve to increase irony, as Kate Chopin does in "The Story of an Hour" by conveying the deceptive feeling of a hopeful new springtime just before turning her tale abruptly toward death.

In deciding whether to focus on setting or atmosphere in writing a literary paper, you need to ask yourself not only how much the effect of the work would be changed if these elements were different but also how much you have to say about them—especially concerning their contribution to the power of the piece. For instance, the dance club in which Russell Smith's "Serotonin" takes place is the perfect setting for that story. We can scarcely imagine its being set as effectively anywhere else. The club, the time-honoured site of young people's ritual mating dance, is a completely believable place for Jason to experience his conflicted feelings about his girlfriend. Concerning any story, if you ask yourself, "In what other surroundings and time could this story happen?" and find it difficult to imagine an answer, probably the setting is a worthwhile topic for literary investigation.

LOOKING AT SETTING AND ATMOSPHERE

As you read the following story by Alistair MacLeod, consider how crucial setting and atmosphere are in contributing to the story's effect.

Alistair MacLeod   b. 1936

The Boat

There are times even now, when I awake at four o'clock in the morning with the terrible fear that I have overslept; when I imagine that my father is waiting for me in the room below the darkened stairs or that the shorebound men are tossing pebbles against my window while blowing their hands and stomping their feet impatiently on the frozen steadfast earth. There are times when I am half out of bed and fumbling for socks and mumbling for words before I realize that I am foolishly alone, that no one waits at the base of the stairs and no boat rides restlessly in the waters by the pier.

At such times only the grey corpses on the overflowing ashtray beside my bed bear witness to the extinction of the latest spark and silently await the crushing out of the most recent of their fellows. And then because I am afraid to be alone with death, I dress rapidly, make a great to-do about clearing my throat, turn on both faucets in the sink and proceed to make loud splashing ineffectual noises. Later I go out and walk the mile to the all-night restaurant.

In the winter it is a very cold walk and there are often tears in my eyes when I arrive. The waitress usually gives a sympathetic little shiver and says, "Boy, it must be really cold out there; you got tears in your eyes."

"Yes," I say, "it sure is; it really is."

And then the three or four of us who are always in such places at such times make uninteresting little protective chit-chat until the dawn reluctantly arrives. Then I swallow the coffee which is always bitter and leave with a great busy rush because by that time I have to worry about being late and whether I have a clean shirt and whether my car will start and about all the other countless things one must worry about when he teaches at a great Midwestern university. And I know then that that day will go by as have all the days of the past ten years, for the call and the voices and the shapes and the boat were not really there in the early morning's darkness and I have all kinds of comforting reality to prove it. They are only shadows and echoes, the animals a child's hands make on the wall by lamplight, and the voices from the rain barrel; the cuttings from an old movie made in the black and white of long ago.

I first became conscious of the boat in the same way and at almost the same time that I became aware of the people it supported. My earliest recollection of my father is a view from the floor of gigantic rubber boots and then of being suddenly elevated and having my face pressed against the stubble of his cheek, and of how it tasted of salt and of how he smelled of salt from his red-soled rubber boots to the shaggy whiteness of his hair.

When I was very small, he took me for my first ride in the boat. I rode the half-mile from our house to the wharf on his shoulders and I remember the sound of his rubber boots galumphing along the gravel beach, the tune of the indecent little song he used to sing, and the odour of the salt.

The floor of the boat was permeated with the same odour and in its constancy I was not aware of change. In the harbour we made our little circle and returned. He tied the boat by its painter, fastened the stern to its permanent anchor and lifted me high over his head to the solidity of the wharf. Then he climbed up the little iron ladder that led to the wharf's cap, placed me once more upon his shoulders and galumphed off again.

When we returned to the house everyone made a great fuss over my precocious excursion and asked, "How did you like the boat?" "Were you afraid in the boat?" "Did you cry in the boat?" They repeated "the boat" at the end of all their questions and I knew it must be very important to everyone.

My earliest recollection of my mother is of being alone with her in the mornings while my father was away in the boat. She seemed to be always repairing clothes that were "torn in the boat," preparing food "to be eaten in the boat" or looking for "the boat" through our kitchen window which faced upon the sea. When my father returned about noon, she would ask, "Well, how did things go in the boat today?" It was the first question I remember asking: "Well, how did things go in the boat today?" "Well, how did things go in the boat today?"

The boat in our lives was registered at Port Hawkesbury. She was what Nova Scotians called a Cape Island boat and was designed for the small inshore fishermen who sought the lobsters of the spring and the mackerel of summer and later the cod and haddock and hake. She was thirty-two feet long and nine wide, and was powered by an engine from a Chevrolet truck. She had a marine clutch and a high speed reverse gear and was painted light green with the name *Jenny Lynn* stencilled in black letters on her bow and painted on an oblong plate across her stern. Jenny Lynn had been my mother's maiden name and the boat was called after her as another link in the chain of tradition. Most of the boats that berthed at the wharf bore the names of some female member of their owner's household.

I say this now as if I knew it all then. All at once, all about boat dimensions and engines, and as if on the day of my first childish voyage I noticed the difference between a stencilled name and a painted name. But of course it was not that way at all, for I learned it all very slowly and there was not time enough.

I learned first about our house which was one of about fifty which marched around the horseshoe of our harbour and the wharf which was its heart. Some of them were so close to the water that during a storm the sea spray splashed against their windows while others were built farther along the beach as was the case with ours. The houses and their people, like those of the neighbouring towns and villages, were the result of Ireland's discontent and Scotland's Highland Clearances and America's War of Independence. Impulsive emotional Catholic Celts who could not bear to live with England and shrewd determined Protestant Puritans who, in the years after 1776, could not bear to live without.

The most important room in our house was one of those oblong old-fashioned kitchens heated by a wood- and coal-burning stove. Behind the stove was a box of kindlings and beside it a coal scuttle. A heavy wooden table with leaves that expanded or reduced its dimensions stood in the middle of the floor. There were five wooden homemade chairs which had been chipped and hacked by a variety of knives. Against the east wall, opposite the stove, there was a couch which sagged in the middle and had a cushion for a pillow, and above it a shelf which contained matches, tobacco, pencils, odd fish-hooks, bits of twine, and a tin can filled with bills and receipts. The south wall was dominated by a window which faced the sea and on the north there was a five-foot board which bore a variety of clothes hooks and the burdens of each. Beneath the board there was a jumble of odd footwear, mostly of rubber. There was also, on this wall, a barometer, a map of the marine area and a shelf which held a tiny radio. The kitchen was shared by all of us and was a buffer zone between the immaculate order of ten other rooms and the disruptive chaos of the single room that was my father's.

My mother ran her house as her brothers ran their boats. Everything was clean and spotless and in order. She was tall and dark and powerfully energetic. In later years she reminded me of the women of Thomas Hardy, particularly Eustacia Vye, in a physical way. She fed and clothed a family of seven children, making all of the meals and most of the clothes. She grew miraculous gardens and magnificent flowers and raised broods of hens and ducks. She would walk miles on berry-picking expeditions and hoist her skirts to dig for clams when the tide was low. She was fourteen years younger than my father, whom she had married when she was twenty-six and had been a local beauty for a period of ten years. My mother was of the sea as were all of her people, and her horizons were the very literal ones she scanned with her dark and fearless eyes.

Between the kitchen clothes rack and barometer, a door opened into my father's bedroom. It was a room of disorder and disarray. It was as if the wind which so often clamoured about the house succeeded in entering this single room and after whipping it into turmoil stole quietly away to renew its knowing laughter from without.

My father's bed was against the south wall. It always looked rumpled and unmade because he lay on top of it more than he slept within any folds it might have had. Beside it, there was a little brown table. An archaic goose-necked reading light, a battered table radio, a mound of wooden matches, one or two packages of tobacco, a deck of cigarette papers and an overflowing ashtray cluttered its surface. The brown larvae of tobacco shreds and the grey flecks of ash covered both the table and the floor beneath it. The once-varnished surface of the table was disfigured by numerous black scars and gashes inflicted by the neglected burning cigarettes of many years. They had tumbled from the ashtray unnoticed and branded their statements permanently and quietly into the wood until the odour of their burning caused the snuffing out of their lives. At the bed's foot there was a single window which looked upon the sea.

Against the adjacent wall there was a battered bureau and beside it there was a closet which held his single ill-fitting serge suit, the two or three white shirts that strangled him and the square black shoes that pinched. When he took off his more friendly clothes, the heavy woollen sweaters, mitts and socks which my mother knitted for him and the woollen and doeskin shirts, he dumped them unceremoniously on a single chair. If a visitor entered the room while he was lying on the bed, he would be told to throw the clothes on the floor and take their place upon the chair.

Magazines and books covered the bureau and competed with the clothes for domination of the chair. They further overburdened the heroic little table and lay on top of the radio. They filled a baffling and unknowable cave beneath the bed, and in the corner by the bureau they spilled from the walls and grew up from the floor.

The magazines were the most conventional: *Time, Newsweek, Life, Maclean's, Family Herald, Reader's Digest*. They were the result of various cut-rate subscriptions or of the gift subscriptions associated with Christmas, "the two whole years for only $3.50."

The books were more varied. There were a few hard-cover magnificents and bygone Book-of-the-Month wonders and some were Christmas or birthday gifts. The majority of them, however, were used paperbacks which came from those second-hand bookstores which advertise in the backs of magazines:

"Miscellaneous Used Paperbacks 10¢ Each." At first he sent for them himself, although my mother resented the expense, but in later years they came more and more often from my sisters who had moved to the cities. Especially at first they were very weird and varied. Mickey Spillane and Ernest Haycox vied with Dostoyevsky and Faulkner, and the Penguin Poets edition of Gerard Manley Hopkins arrived in the same box as a little book on sex technique called *Getting the Most Out of Love*. The former had been assiduously annotated by a very fine hand using a very blue-inked fountain pen while the latter had been studied by someone with very large thumbs, the prints of which were still visible in the margins. At the slightest provocation it would open almost automatically to particularly graphic and well-smudged pages.

When he was not in the boat, my father spent most of his time lying on the bed in his socks, the top two buttons of his trousers undone, his discarded shirt on the ever-ready chair and the sleeves of the woollen Stanfield underwear, which he wore both summer and winter, drawn half way up to his elbows. The pillows propped up the whiteness of his head and the goose-necked lamp illuminated the pages in his hands. The cigarettes smoked and smouldered on the ashtray and on the table and the radio played constantly, sometimes low and sometimes loud. At midnight and at one, two, three and four, one could sometimes hear the radio, his occasional cough, the rustling thud of a completed book being tossed to the corner heap, or the movement necessitated by his sitting on the edge of the bed to roll the thousandth cigarette. He seemed never to sleep, only to doze, and the light shone constantly from his window to the sea.

My mother despised the room and all it stood for and she had stopped sleeping in it after I was born. She despised disorder in rooms and in houses and in hours and in lives, and she had not read a book since high school. There she had read *Ivanhoe* and considered it a colossal waste of time. Still the room remained, like a solid rock of opposition in the sparkling waters of a clear deep harbour, opening off the kitchen where we really lived our lives, with its door always open and its contents visible to all.

The daughters of the room and of the house were very beautiful. They were tall and willowy like my mother and had her fine facial features set off by the reddish copper-coloured hair that had apparently once been my father's before it turned to white. All of them were very clever in school and helped my mother a great deal about the house. When they were young they sang and were very happy and very nice to me because I was the youngest and the family's only boy.

My father never approved of their playing about the wharf like the other children, and they went there only when my mother sent them on an errand. At such times they almost always overstayed, playing screaming games of tag or hide-and-seek in and about the fishing shanties, the piled traps and tubs of trawl, shouting down to the perch that swam languidly about the wharf's algae-covered piles, or jumping in and out of the boats that tugged gently at their lines. My mother was never uneasy about them at such times, and when her husband criticized her she would say, "Nothing will happen to them there," or "They could be doing worse things in worse places."

By about the ninth or tenth grade my sisters one by one discovered my father's bedroom and then the change would begin. Each would go into the room one morning when he was out. She would go with the ideal hope of imposing order or with the more practical objective of emptying the ashtray, and later she would be found spellbound by the volume in her hand. My mother's reaction was always abrupt, bordering on the angry. "Take your nose out of that trash and come and do your work," she would say, and once I saw her slap my youngest sister so hard that the print of her hand was scarletly emblazoned upon her daughter's cheek while the broken-spined paperback fluttered uselessly to the floor.

Thereafter my mother would launch a campaign against what she had discovered but could not understand. At times although she was not overly religious she would bring in God to bolster her arguments, saying, "In the next world God will see to those who waste their lives reading useless books when they should be about their work." Or without theological aid, "I would like to know how books help anyone to live a life." If my father were in, she would repeat the remarks louder than necessary, and her voice would carry into his room where he lay upon his bed. His usual reaction was to turn up the volume of the radio, although that action in itself betrayed the success of the initial thrust.

Shortly after my sisters began to read the books, they grew restless and lost interest in darning socks and baking bread, and all of them eventually went to work as summer waitresses in the Sea Food Restaurant. The restaurant was run by a big American concern from Boston and catered to the tourists that flooded the area during July and August. My mother despised the whole operation. She said the restaurant was not run by "our people," and "our people" did not eat there, and that it was run by outsiders for outsiders.

"Who are these people anyway?" she would ask, tossing back her dark hair, "and what do they, though they go about with their cameras for a hundred years, know about the way it is here, and what do they care about me and mine, and why should I care about them?"

She was angry that my sisters should even conceive of working in such a place and more angry when my father made no move to prevent it, and she was worried about herself and about her family and about her life. Sometimes she would say softly to her sisters, "I don't know what's the matter with my girls. It seems none of them are interested in any of the right things." And sometimes there would be bitter savage arguments. One afternoon I was coming in with three mackerel I'd been given at the wharf when I heard her say, "Well I hope you'll be satisfied when they come home knocked up and you'll have had your way."

It was the most savage thing I'd ever heard my mother say. Not just the words but the way she said them, and I stood there in the porch afraid to breathe for what seemed like the years from ten to fifteen, feeling the damp moist mackerel with their silver glassy eyes growing clammy against my leg.

Through the angle in the screen door I saw my father who had been walking into his room wheel around on one of his rubber-booted heels and look at her with his blue eyes flashing like clearest ice beneath the snow that was his hair. His usually ruddy face was drawn and grey, reflecting the exhaustion of a man of sixty-five who had been working in those rubber boots for eleven hours on an August day, and for a fleeting moment I wondered what I would do if he killed my mother while I stood there in the porch with those three foolish mackerel in my hand. Then he turned and went into his room and the radio blared forth the next day's weather forecast and I retreated under the noise and returned again, stamping my feet and slamming the door too loudly to signal my approach. My mother was busy at the stove when I came in, and did not raise her head when I threw the mackerel in a pan. As I looked into my father's room, I said, "Well how did things go in the boat today?" and he replied, "Oh not too badly, all things considered." He was lying on his back and lighting the first cigarette and the radio was talking about the Virginia coast.

All of my sisters made good money on tips. They bought my father an electric razor which he tried to use for a while and they took out even more magazine subscriptions. They bought my mother a great many clothes of the type she was very fond of, the wide-brimmed hats and the brocaded dresses, but she locked them all in trunks and refused to wear any of them.

On one August day my sisters prevailed upon my father to take some of their restaurant customers for an afternoon ride in the boat. The tourists with their expensive clothes and cameras and sun glasses awkwardly backed down the iron ladder at the wharf's side to where my father waited below, holding the rocking *Jenny Lynn* in snug against the wharf with one hand on the iron ladder and steadying his descending passengers with the other. They tried to look both prim and wind-blown like the girls in the Pepsi-Cola ads and did the best they could, sitting on the thwarts where the newspapers were spread to cover the splattered blood and fish entrails, crowding to one side so that they were in danger of capsizing the boat, taking the inevitable pictures or merely trailing their fingers through the water of their dreams.

All of them liked my father very much and, after he'd brought them back from their circles in the harbour, they invited him to their rented cabins which were located high on a hill overlooking the village to which they were so alien. He proceeded to get very drunk up there with the beautiful view and the strange company and the abundant liquor, and late in the afternoon he began to sing.

I was just approaching the wharf to deliver my mother's summons when he began, and the familiar yet unfamiliar voice that rolled down from the cabins made me feel as I had never felt before in my young life or perhaps as I had always felt without really knowing it, and I was ashamed yet proud, young yet old and saved yet forever lost, and there was nothing I could do to control my legs which trembled nor my eyes which wept for what they could not tell.

The tourists were equipped with tape recorders and my father sang for more than three hours. His voice boomed down the hill and bounced off the surface of the harbour, which was an unearthly blue on that hot August day, and was then reflected to the wharf and the fishing shanties where it was absorbed amidst the men who were baiting their lines for the next day's haul.

He sang all the old sea chanties which had come across from the old world and by which men like him had pulled ropes for generations, and he sang the East Coast sea songs which celebrated the sealing vessels of Northumberland Strait and the long liners of the Grand Banks, and of Anticosti, Sable Island, Grand Manan, Boston Harbor, Nantucket and Block Island. Gradually he shifted to the seemingly unending Gaelic drinking songs with their twenty or more verses and inevitable refrains, and the men in the shanties smiled at the coarseness of some of the verses and at the thought that the singer's immediate audience did not know what they were applauding nor recording to take back to staid old Boston. Later as the sun was setting he switched to the laments and the wild and haunting Gaelic war songs of those spattered Highland ancestors he had never seen, and when his voice ceased, the savage melancholy of three hundred years seemed to hang over the peaceful harbour and the quiet boats and the men leaning in the doorways of their shanties with their cigarettes glowing in the dusk and the women looking to the sea from their open windows with their children in their arms.

When he came home he threw the money he had earned on the kitchen table as he did with all his earnings but my mother refused to touch it and the next day he went with the rest of the men to bait his trawl in the shanties. The tourists came to the door that evening and my mother met them there and told them that her husband was not in although he was lying on the bed only a few feet away with the radio playing and the cigarette upon his lips. She stood in the doorway until they reluctantly went away.

In the winter they sent him a picture which had been taken on the day of the singing. On the back it said, "To Our Ernest Hemingway" and the "Our" was underlined. There was also an accompanying letter telling how much they had enjoyed themselves, how popular the tape was proving and explaining who Ernest Hemingway was. In a way it almost did look like one of those unshaven, taken-in-Cuba pictures of Hemingway. He looked both massive and incongruous in the setting. His bulky fisherman's clothes were too big for the green and white lawn chair in which he sat, and his rubber boots seemed to take up all of the well-clipped grass square. The beach umbrella jarred with his sunburned face and because he had already been singing for some time, his lips which chapped in the winds of spring and burned in the water glare of summer had already cracked in several places, producing tiny flecks of blood at their corners and on the whiteness of his teeth. The bracelets of brass chain which he wore to protect his wrists from chafing seemed abnormally large and his broad leather belt had been slackened and his heavy shirt and underwear were open at the throat revealing an uncultivated wilderness of white chest hair bordering on the semicontrolled stubble of his neck and chin. His blue eyes had looked directly into the camera and his hair was whiter than the two tiny clouds which hung over his left shoulder. The sea was behind him and its immense blue flatness stretched out to touch the arching blueness of the sky. It seemed very far away from him or else he was so much in the foreground that he seemed too big for it.

Each year another of my sisters would read the books and work in the restaurant. Sometimes they would stay out quite late on the hot summer nights and when they came up the stairs my mother would ask them many long and involved questions which they resented and tried to avoid. Before ascending the stairs they would go into my father's room and those of us who waited above could hear them throwing his clothes off the chair before sitting on it or the squeak of the bed as they sat on its edge. Sometimes they would talk to him a long time, the murmur of their voices blending with the music of the radio into a mysterious vapour-like sound which floated softly up the stairs.

I say this again as if it all happened at once and as if all of my sisters were of identical ages and like so many lemmings going into another sea and, again, it was of course not that way at all. Yet go they did, to Boston, to Montreal, to New York with the young men they met during the summers and later married in those far-away cities. The young men were very articulate and handsome and wore fine clothes and drove expensive cars and my sisters, as I said, were very tall and beautiful with their copper-coloured hair and were tired of darning socks and baking bread.

One by one they went. My mother had each of her daughters for fifteen years, then lost them for two and finally forever. None married a fisherman. My mother never accepted any of the young men, for in her eyes they seemed always a combination of the lazy, the effeminate, the dishonest and the unknown. They never seemed to do any physical work and she could not comprehend their luxurious vacations and she did not know whence they came nor who they were. And in the end she did not really care, for they were not of her people and they were not of her sea.

I say this now with a sense of wonder at my own stupidity in thinking I was somehow free and would go on doing well in school and playing and helping in the boat and passing into my early teens while streaks of grey began to appear in my mother's dark hair and my father's rubber boots dragged sometimes on the pebbles of the beach as he trudged home from the wharf. And there were but three of us in the house that had at one time been so loud.

Then during the winter that I was fifteen he seemed to grow old and ill at once. Most of January he lay upon the bed, smoking and reading and listening to the radio while the wind howled about the house and the needle-like snow blistered off the ice-covered harbour and the doors flew out of people's hands if they did not cling to them like death.

In February when the men began overhauling their lobster traps he still did not move, and my mother and I began to knit lobster trap headings in the evenings. The twine was as always very sharp and harsh, and blisters formed upon our thumbs and little paths of blood snaked quietly down between our fingers while the seals that had drifted down from distant Labrador wept and moaned like human children on the ice-floes of the Gulf.

In the daytime my mother's brother who had been my father's partner as long as I could remember also came to work upon the gear. He was a year older than my mother and was tall and dark and the father of twelve children.

By March we were very far behind and although I began to work very hard in the evenings I knew it was not hard enough and that there were but eight weeks left before the opening of the season on May first. And I knew that my mother worried and my uncle was uneasy and that all of our very lives depended on the boat being ready with her gear and two men, by the date of May the first. And I knew then that *David Copperfield* and *The Tempest* and all of those friends I had dearly come to love must really go forever. So I bade them all good-bye.

The night after my first full day at home and after my mother had gone upstairs he called me into his room where I sat upon the chair beside his bed. "You will go back tomorrow," he said simply.

I refused then, saying I had made my decision and was satisfied.

"That is no way to make a decision," he said, "and if you are satisfied I am not. It is best that you go back." I was almost angry then and told him as all children do that I wished he would leave me alone and stop telling me what to do.

He looked at me a long time then, lying there on the same bed on which he had fathered me those sixteen years before, fathered me his only son, out of who knew what emotions when he was already fifty-six and his hair had turned to snow. Then he swung his legs over the edge of the squeaking bed and sat facing me and looked into my own dark eyes with his of crystal blue and placed his hand upon my knee. "I am not telling you to do anything," he said softly, "only asking you."

The next morning I returned to school. As I left, my mother followed me to the porch and said, "I never thought a son of mine would choose useless books over the parents that gave him life."

In the weeks that followed he got up rather miraculously and the gear was ready and the *Jenny Lynn* was freshly painted by the last two weeks of April when the ice began to break up and the lonely screaming gulls returned to haunt the silver herring as they flashed within the sea.

On the first day of May the boats raced out as they had always done, laden down almost to the gunwales with their heavy cargoes of traps. They were almost like living things as they plunged through the waters of the spring and manoeuvred between the still floating icebergs of crystal-white and emerald green on their way to the traditional grounds that they sought out every May. And those of us who sat that day in the high school on the hill, discussing the water imagery of Tennyson, watched them as they passed back and forth beneath us until by afternoon the piles of traps which had been stacked upon the wharf were no longer visible but were spread about the bottoms of the sea. And the *Jenny Lynn* went too, all day, with my uncle tall and dark, like a latter-day Tashtego standing at the tiller with his legs wide apart and guiding her deftly between the floating pans of ice and my father in the stern standing in the same way with his hands upon the ropes that lashed the cargo to the deck. And at night my mother asked, "Well, how did things go in the boat today?"

And the spring wore on and the summer came and school ended in the third week of June and the lobster season on July first and I wished that the two things I loved so dearly did not exclude each other in a manner that was so blunt and too clear.

At the conclusion of the lobster season my uncle said he had been offered a berth on a deep sea dragger and had decided to accept. We all knew that he was leaving the *Jenny Lynn* forever and that before the next lobster season he would buy a boat of his own. He was expecting another child and would be supporting fifteen people by the next spring and could not chance my father against the family that he loved.

I joined my father then for the trawling season, and he made no protest and my mother was quite happy. Through the summer we baited the tubs of trawl in the afternoon and set them at sunset and revisited them in the darkness of the early morning. The men would come tramping by our house at four A.M. and we would join them and walk with them to the wharf and be on our way before the sun rose out of the ocean where it seemed to spend the night. If I was not up they would toss pebbles to my window and I would be very embarrassed and tumble downstairs to where my father lay fully clothed atop his bed, reading his book and listening to his radio and smoking his cigarette. When I appeared he would swing off his bed and put on his boots and be instantly ready and then we would take the lunches my mother had prepared the night before and walk off toward the sea. He would make no attempt to wake me himself.

It was in many ways a good summer. There were few storms and we were out almost every day and we lost a minimum of gear and seemed to land a maximum of fish and I tanned dark and brown after the manner of my uncles.

My father did not tan—he never tanned—because of his reddish complexion, and the salt water irritated his skin as it had for sixty years. He burned and reburned over and over again and his lips still cracked so that they bled when he smiled, and his arms, especially the left, still broke out into the oozing salt-water boils as they had ever since as a child I had first watched him soaking and bathing them in a variety of ineffectual solutions. The chafe-preventing bracelets of brass linked chain that all the men wore about their wrists in early spring were his the full season and he shaved but painfully and only once a week.

And I saw then, that summer, many things that I had seen all my life as if for the first time and I thought that perhaps my father had never been intended for a fisherman either physically or mentally. At least not in the manner of my uncles; he had never really loved it. And I remembered that, one evening in his room when we were talking about *David Copperfield*, he had said that he had always wanted to go to the university and I had dismissed it then in the way one dismisses his father's saying he would like to be a tight-rope walker, and we had gone on to talk about the Peggottys and how they loved the sea.

And I thought then to myself that there were many things wrong with all of us and all our lives and I wondered why my father, who was himself an only son, had not married before he was forty and then I wondered why he had. I even thought that perhaps he had had to marry my mother and checked the dates on the flyleaf of the Bible where I learned that my oldest sister had been born a prosaic eleven months after the marriage, and I felt myself then very dirty and debased for my lack of faith and for what I had thought and done.

And then there came into my heart a very great love for my father and I thought it was very much braver to spend a life doing what you really do not want rather than selfishly following forever your own dreams and inclinations. And I knew then that I could never leave him alone to suffer the iron-tipped harpoons which my mother would forever hurl into his soul because he was a failure as a husband and a father who had retained none of his own. And I felt that I had been very small in a little secret place within me and that even the completion of high school was for me a silly shallow selfish dream.

So I told him one night very resolutely and very powerfully that I would remain with him as long as he lived and we would fish the sea together. And he made no protest but only smiled through the cigarette smoke that wreathed his bed and replied, "I hope you will remember what you've said."

The room was now so filled with books as to be almost Dickensian, but he would not allow my mother to move or change them and he continued to read them, sometimes two or three a night. They came with great regularity now, and there were more hard covers, sent by my sisters who had gone so long ago and now seemed so distant and so prosperous, and sent also pictures of small red-haired grandchildren with baseball bats and dolls which he placed upon his bureau and which my mother gazed at wistfully when she thought no one would see. Red-haired grandchildren with baseball bats and dolls who would never know the sea in hatred or in love.

And so we fished through the heat of August and into the cooler days of September when the water was so clear we could almost see the bottom and the white mists rose like delicate ghosts in the early morning dawn. And one day my mother said to me, "You have given added years to his life."

And we fished on into October when it began to roughen and we could no longer risk night sets but took our gear out each morning and returned at the first sign of the squalls; and on into November when we lost three tubs of trawl and the clear blue water turned to a sullen grey and the trochoidal waves rolled rough and high and washed across our bows and decks as we ran within their troughs. We wore heavy sweaters now and the awkward rubber slickers and the heavy woollen mitts which soaked and froze into masses of ice that hung from our wrists like the limbs of gigantic monsters until we thawed them against the exhaust pipe's heat. And almost every day we would leave for home before noon, driven by the blasts of the northwest wind, coating our eyebrows with ice and freezing our eyelids closed as we leaned into a visibility that was hardly there, charting our course from the compass and the sea, running with the waves and between them but never confronting their towering might.

And I stood at the tiller now, on these homeward lunges, stood in the place and in the manner of my uncle, turning to look at my father and to shout over the roar of the engine and the slop of the sea to where he stood in the stern, drenched and dripping with the snow and the salt and the spray and his bushy eyebrows caked in ice. But on November twenty-first, when it seemed we might be making the final run of the season, I turned and he was not there and I knew even in that instant that he would never be again.

On November twenty-first the waves of the grey Atlantic are very very high and the waters are very cold and there are no signposts on the surface of the sea. You cannot tell where you have been five minutes before and in the squalls of snow you cannot see. And it takes longer than you would believe to check a boat that has been running before a gale and turn her ever so carefully in a wide and stupid circle, with timbers creaking and straining, back into the face of storm. And you know that it is useless and that your voice does not carry the length of the boat and that even if you knew the original spot, the relentless waves would carry such a burden perhaps a mile or so by the time you could return. And you know also, the final irony, that your father like your uncles and all the men that form your past, cannot swim a stroke.

The lobster beds off the Cape Breton coast are still very rich and now, from May to July, their offerings are packed in crates of ice, and thundered by the gigantic transport trucks, day and night, through New Glasgow, Amherst, Saint John and Bangor and Portland and into Boston where they are tossed still living into boiling pots of water, their final home.

And though the prices are higher and the competition tighter, the grounds to which the *Jenny Lynn* once went remain untouched and unfished as they have for the last ten years. For if there are no signposts on the sea in storm there are certain ones in calm and the lobster bottoms were distributed in calm before any of us can remember and the grounds my father fished were those his father fished before him and there were others before and before and before. Twice the big boats have come from forty and fifty miles, lured by the promise of the grounds, and strewn the bottom with their traps and twice they have returned to find their buoys cut adrift and their gear lost and destroyed. Twice the Fisheries Officer and the Mounted Police have come and asked many long and involved questions and twice they have received no answers from the men leaning in the doors of their shanties and the women standing at their windows with their children in their arms. Twice they have gone away saying: "There are no legal boundaries in the Marine area"; "No one can own the sea"; "Those grounds don't wait for anyone."

But the men and the women, with my mother dark among them, do not care for what they say, for to them the grounds are sacred and they think they wait for me.

It is not an easy thing to know that your mother lives alone on an inadequate insurance policy and that she is too proud to accept any other aid. And that she looks through her lonely window onto the ice of winter and the hot flat calm of summer and the rolling waves of fall. And that she lies awake in the early morning's darkness when the rubber boots of the men scrunch upon the gravel as they pass beside her house on their way down to the wharf. And she knows that the footsteps never stop, because no man goes from her house, and she alone of all the Lynns has neither son nor son-in-law that walks toward the boat that will take him to the sea. And it is not an easy thing to know that your mother looks upon the sea with love and on you with bitterness because the one has been so constant and the other so untrue.

But neither is it easy to know that your father was found on November twenty-eighth, ten miles to the north and wedged between two boulders at the base of the rock-strewn cliffs where he had been hurled and slammed so many many times. His hands were shredded ribbons as were his feet which had lost their boots to the suction of the sea, and his shoulders came apart in our hands when we tried to move him from the rocks. And the fish had eaten his testicles and the gulls had pecked out his eyes and the white-green stubble of his whiskers had continued to grow in death, like the grass on graves, upon the purple, bloated mass that was his face. There was not much left of my father, physically, as he lay there with the brass chains on his wrists and the seaweed in his hair.

(1976)

PREWRITING

As you read the story carefully a second time, pay particular attention to the descriptive passages that appeal to the senses—especially, in this story, images of water (in all its forms) and of the seasons. Underline any specific words or phrases that you think contribute to the atmosphere.

PREWRITING EXERCISE

1. Examine the first five paragraphs of this story, in which the narrator describes his mornings now that he, as an adult, has moved far from his Cape Breton home. What do these paragraphs reveal about the narrator? What can you say about his feelings about the past after reading only the opening of the tale?
2. What features of the setting seem essential to the way "The Boat" unfolds? In other words, how do the various settings—the kitchen, the father's room, the boat—help determine what happens in important ways?
3. Before planning your paper, write your responses to the following questions:
   a. When you think of the traditional roles of men and women, what associations come forth? Are any of these associations reflected in the story? Are any of them contradicted or undermined?
   b. How soon in the story can you distinguish the attitudes of the characters? What are some of the ways they are distinct from one another?
   c. List the scenes associated with the father and those associated with the mother. What critical events or characteristics are associated with each?
   d. What do you make of the mother's attitude toward changes in her family?
   e. In what ways does the father influence the decisions his children make? How does the decision of the son affect the father?
   f. The end of the story is rather shocking. What associations can you make with the father as he is described? In what ways does the beginning of the story prepare the reader for the ending?

WRITING

Now that you have become familiar with the story, ask yourself still more questions: How can I make a statement about the function of setting in relation to theme? What, indeed, does the setting contribute to the overall effectiveness of the story? What does the atmosphere contribute? How do both relate to the meaning of the story? Do they *heighten* the theme, do they provide a unique opportunity for the events, or do they help the reader understand what the story is about? Would a different setting change the story in important ways? As you think about answers to these questions, review your prewriting material and continue consulting the story for clues.

DISCOVERING AN ORGANIZATION

As you are trying to solve the problems posed by the questions in the preceding paragraph, write down all the likely ideas that strike you. Do not trust your memory, or some of your best inspirations may slip away. Then try to think of some point you can make about the story that will allow you to use this information. Such a point will usually make a link between the setting and something else about the story: the characters, action, plot, motivation, meaning, or emotional impact. Once you have discovered an interesting point to pursue, write out this idea in a single, clear sentence. This idea will be your thesis. Then sort through the details related to setting in the story and ask yourself: How can I organize these details in support of my thesis? You might, for instance, group your material chronologically, arranging details according to the episodes in the story as they occur from beginning to end. Or you might consider a logical arrangement, emphasizing each of the main characters in turn or focusing first on everything that happens outdoors and then on everything that happens indoors, everything that happens in the boat and then on everything that happens in the home or, more specifically, the father's room.

IDEAS FOR WRITING

IDEAS FOR RESPONSIVE WRITING

1. "The Boat" takes place in a setting where tradition, in many forms, is important. Is it important to follow traditional expectations? Is there ever a time when traditions should not be observed?
2. The narrator feels that "it [is] very much braver to spend a life doing what you really do not want rather than selfishly following forever your own dreams and inclinations." Does the father share his son's philosophy of life? Do you?

IDEAS FOR CRITICAL WRITING

1. Examine each reference to the sea and to the land or earth. What attitude toward nature is suggested by the way they are described? How are these attitudes related to the view of human nature suggested by the story?
2. The seasons are notable in the story. Relate this feature of the setting to the human arena. What season is pivotal?
3. MacLeod uses the weather to mirror situations in the story. How does the weather affect the characters, and how does it reflect their struggles?

4. Notice the diction—the word choice—MacLeod uses in describing the boat's history, the mother's housekeeping proficiency, and the father's bedroom. How does diction develop the atmosphere? How does it demonstrate their relationships? Does it foreshadow the conclusion of the story?

REWRITING: ORGANIZATION AND STYLE

Once you have written out your ideas, you will try to improve every element of that draft—from the overall organization to the individual sentences.

CHECKING YOUR ORGANIZATION

Each paragraph should have a topic, a main point that you can summarize in a sentence. On a separate sheet of paper, list the topics of your paragraphs. When you see the bare bones of your essay this way, you can ask yourself questions about your organization:

1. Do any of the topics repeat each other? If so, think about combining them or placing them close together. If there is a fine distinction between them, go back to the essay and express the distinction clearly.

2. Is each topic fully supported? Compare the topic as stated on your outline with the paragraph in your essay. Make sure that you can see how each sentence in the paragraph relates to the topic. Weed out sentences that only repeat the topic. Add specific details from the literary work instead.

3. Does the order of topics make sense? You might have originally written your paragraphs in the order the topics occurred to you, but that may not be the most reasonable organization for the final essay. Group similar topics together—for example, all the topics that relate setting to character should be close to each other, and so should all the topics that relate setting to theme. At the beginning of each paragraph, write a word, phrase, clause, or sentence that shows that paragraph's relationship to the paragraph before it. These transitions will help your readers know what to expect and prepare them for what comes next.

IMPROVING THE STYLE: BALANCED SENTENCES

Sound organization is vital to the success of your essay; graceful style is an added gift to your reader. One stylistic plus is the balanced or parallel sentence, which puts similar ideas into similar grammatical structures, like this:

> MacLeod's stories are known for their emphasis on *Cape Breton, fishermen,* and *the sea.*

> Good writers acknowledge the necessity of *thinking, planning, writing, revising, resting,* and then *thinking* and *revising* still further.

In the following sentence, though, the third item in the italicized series does not match. Compare it with the corrected version:

Unbalanced: The protagonist would willingly give up his *dreams*, his *education*, and *moving away from the trappings of home*.

Balanced: The protagonist would willingly give up his *dreams*, his *education*, and his *freedom*.

You can probably already handle such balancing in ordinary sentences; however, pay attention during revising to make sure that all items in series are indeed balanced.

If you need an emphatic sentence for your introduction or conclusion, a good way to learn to write impressive balanced sentences is through *sentence modelling*. Many expert writers—Robert Louis Stevenson, Winston Churchill, Somerset Maugham—attest that they perfected their writing by studiously copying and imitating the sentences of stylists whom they admired.

SENTENCE MODELLING EXERCISE

Examine the model sentence below to discover its structure. How is it formed? Does it use balanced phrases, clauses, or single words? Does it include any deliberate repetition of words as well as structures? Does it build to a climax at the end? If so, how? By adding ideas of increasing importance? By establishing a pattern that gathers momentum?

Once you have discovered the structure of the model sentence, write one as nearly like it as possible *using your own words and subject matter*. Then repeat this process of imitation four more times, changing your ideas with each new sentence, like this:

Model: "I regard writing not as investigation of character but as an exercise in the use of language, and with this I am obsessed."
—Evelyn Waugh

Imitation: I consider higher education not as a commodity to be purchased but as an opportunity to try for the stars, and of this I am convinced.

Imitation: I see curiosity not as an element of childhood but as a characteristic of a successful student at any age, and of this I have no doubt.

First, copy each of the numbered sentences carefully—including the exact punctuation. Then imitate each one at least five times.

1. "He knew everything about her, all in a moment: he saw the ambition, the terror, the pride."
—Mavis Gallant

2. "I want to make this texture as specific and accurate as possible, to make the surface of the fictitious world as convincing as possible, to make readers think they are actually there."
—Russell Smith (Interview with Michelle Berry in *The Notebooks*)

3. "The refrigerator was full of sulfurous scraps, dark crusts, furry oddments."

—Alice Munro

4. "It is sober without being dull; massive without being oppressive."

—Sir Kenneth Clark

5. "We peer so suspiciously at each other that we cannot see that we Canadians are standing on the mountaintop of human wealth, freedom and privilege."

—Pierre Elliott Trudeau

For study tools to help you with your next writing assignment, please visit the Companion Website at www.pearsoned.ca/mcmahan.

9

Writing about Theme

A story's theme or meaning grows out of all the elements of imaginative fiction: character, structure, symbolism, imagery, point of view, and setting. The theme is usually not an obvious moral or message, and it may be difficult to sum up succinctly. However, thinking about the theme of a story and trying to state it in your own words will help you focus your scattered reactions and to make your understanding of the author's purpose more certain. One of the pleasures of reading a good story comes from deciding what it means and why it captures your interest.

WHAT IS THEME?

Theme has been defined in many ways: the central idea or thesis; the central thought; the underlying meaning, either implied or directly stated; the general insight revealed by the entire story; the central truth; the dominating idea; the abstract concept that is made concrete through representation in person, action, and image.

Because the theme involves ideas and insights, we usually state it in general terms. "Obasan," for instance, concerns the conflicts of a specific character, but the story's main idea—its theme—relates to abstract qualities like *duty* and *fear*. If someone asks what "Obasan" is *about*, we might respond with a summary of the plot, with details about the title character's forced relocation and her subsequent life in Alberta. On the other hand, if someone asks for the story's *theme*, we would answer with a general statement of ideas or values: "Obasan" shows how people can be trapped by a respect for authority and a sense of obligation.

It is easy to confuse *subject* with *theme*. The subject is the topic or material the story examines—love, death, war, identity, prejudice, power, human relations, growing up, and so forth. The theme is the direct or implied statement that the story makes about the subject. For example, the *subject* of "The Boat" is duty versus dreams, but the *theme* emerges from what the story says about the father, the mother, and the son—and from an understanding of why these characters behave and interact as they do. The theme, then, is the insight that we gain from thinking about what we have read. If you ask "What is the author saying about the subject?" the answer should direct you to the theme.

147

LOOKING AT THEME

As you read "Boys and Girls" by Alice Munro, think about how this story of a young girl and her encounter with the confines of gender roles relates to other areas of human experience, such as relationships with others or perceptions of self.

Alice Munro b. 1931

Boys and Girls

My father was a fox farmer. That is, he raised silver foxes, in pens; and in the fall and early winter, when their fur was prime, he killed them and skinned them and sold their pelts to the Hudson's Bay Company or the Montreal Fur Traders. These companies supplied us with heroic calendars to hang, one on each side of the kitchen door. Against a background of cold blue sky and black pine forests and treacherous northern rivers, plumed adventurers planted the flags of England or of France; magnificent savages bent their backs to the portage.

For several weeks before Christmas, my father worked after supper in the cellar of our house. The cellar was whitewashed, and lit by a hundred-watt bulb over the worktable. My brother Laird and I sat on the top step and watched. My father removed the pelt inside-out from the body of the fox, which looked surprisingly small, mean and rat-like, deprived of its arrogant weight of fur. The naked, slippery bodies were collected in a sack and buried at the dump. One time the hired man, Henry Bailey, had taken a swipe at me with his sack, saying, "Christmas present!" My mother thought that was not funny. In fact she disliked the whole pelting operation—that was what the killing, skinning, and preparation of the furs was called—and wished it did not have to take place in the house. There was the smell. After the pelt had been stretched inside-out on a long board my father scraped away delicately, removing the little clotted webs of blood vessels, the bubbles of fat; the smell of blood and animal fat, with the strong primitive odour of the fox itself, penetrated all parts of the house. I found it reassuringly seasonal, like the smell of oranges and pine needles.

Henry Bailey suffered from bronchial troubles. He would cough and cough until his narrow face turned scarlet, and his light blue, derisive eyes filled up with tears; then he took the lid off the stove, and, standing well back, shot out a great clot of phlegm—hsss—straight into the heart of the flames. We admired him for this performance and for his ability to make his stomach growl at will, and for his laughter, which was full of high whistlings and gurglings and involved the whole faulty machinery of his chest. It was sometimes hard to tell what he was laughing at, and always possible that it might be us.

After we had been sent to bed we could still smell fox and still hear Henry's laugh, but these things, reminders of the warm, safe, brightly lit downstairs world, seemed lost and diminished, floating on the stale cold air upstairs. We were afraid at night in the winter. We were not afraid of *outside* though this was the time of year when snowdrifts curled around our house like sleeping whales and the wind harassed us all night, coming up from the buried fields, the frozen swamp, with its old bugbear chorus of threats and misery. We were afraid of *inside*, the room where we slept. At this time the upstairs of our house was not finished. A brick chimney went up one wall. In the middle of the floor was a square hole, with a wooden railing around it; that was where the stairs came up. On the other side of the stairwell were the things that nobody had any use for any more—a soldiery roll of linoleum, standing on end, a wicker baby carriage, a fern basket, china jugs and basins with cracks in them, a picture of the Battle of Balaclava, very sad to look at. I had told Laird, as soon as he was old enough to understand such things, that bats and skeletons lived over there; whenever a man escaped from the county jail, twenty miles away, I imagined that he had somehow let himself in the window and was hiding behind the linoleum. But we had rules to keep us safe. When the light was on, we were safe as long as we did not step off the square of worn carpet which defined our bedroom-space; when the light was off no place was safe but the beds themselves. I had to turn out the light kneeling on the end of my bed, and stretching as far as I could to reach the cord.

In the dark we lay on our beds, our narrow life rafts, and fixed our eyes on the faint light coming up the stairwell, and sang songs. Laird sang "Jingle Bells," which he would sing any time, whether it was Christmas or not, and I sang "Danny Boy." I loved the sound of my own voice, frail and supplicating, rising in the dark. We could make out the tall frosted shapes of the windows now, gloomy and white. When I came to the part, *When I am dead, as dead I well may be*—a fit of shivering caused not by the cold sheets but by pleasurable emotion almost silenced me. *You'll kneel and say, an Ave there above me*—What was an Ave? Every day I forgot to find out.

Laird went straight from singing to sleep. I could hear his long, satisfied, bubbly breaths. Now for the time that remained to me, the most perfectly private and perhaps the best time of the whole day, I arranged myself tightly under the covers and went on with one of the stories I was telling myself from night to night. These stories were about myself, when I had grown a little older; they took place in a world that was recognizably mine, yet one that presented opportunities for courage, boldness and self-sacrifice, as mine never did. I rescued people from a bombed building (it discouraged me that the real war had gone on so far away from Jubilee). I shot two rabid wolves who were menacing the schoolyard (the teachers cowered terrified at my back). I rode a fine horse spiritedly down the main street of Jubilee, acknowledging the townspeople's gratitude for some yet-to-be-worked-out piece of heroism (nobody ever rode a horse there, except King Billy in the Orangemen's Day parade). There was always riding and shooting in these stories, though I had only been on a horse twice—bareback because we did not own a saddle—and the second time I had slid right around and dropped under the horse's feet; it had stepped placidly over me. I really was learning to shoot, but I could not hit anything yet, not even tin cans on fence posts.

Alive, the foxes inhabited a world my father made for them. It was surrounded by a high guard fence, like a medieval town, with a gate that was padlocked at night. Along the streets of this town were ranged large, sturdy pens. Each of them had a real door that a man could go through, a wooden ramp along the wire, for the foxes to run up and down on, and a kennel—something like a clothes chest with airholes—where they slept and stayed in winter and had their young. There were feeding and watering dishes attached to the wire in such a way that they could be emptied and cleaned from the outside. The dishes were made of old tin cans, and the ramps and kennels of odds and ends of old lumber. Everything was tidy and ingenious; my father was tirelessly inventive and his favourite book in the world was Robinson Crusoe. He had fitted a tin drum on a wheelbarrow, for bringing water down to the pens. This was my job in summer, when the foxes had to have water twice a day. Between nine and ten o'clock in the morning, and again after supper, I filled the drum at the pump and trundled it down through the barnyard to the pens, where I parked it, and filled my watering can and went along the streets. Laird came too, with his little cream and green gardening can, filled too full and knocking against his legs and slopping water on his canvas shoes. I had the real watering can, my father's, though I could only carry it three-quarters full.

The foxes all had names, which were printed on a tin plate and hung beside their doors. They were not named when they were born, but when they survived the first year's pelting and were added to the breeding stock. Those my father had named were called names like Prince, Bob, Wally and Betty. Those I had named were called Star or Turk, or Maureen or Diana. Laird named one Maud after a hired girl we had when he was little, one Harold after a boy at school, and one Mexico, he did not say why.

Naming them did not make pets out of them, or anything like it. Nobody but my father ever went into the pens, and he had twice had blood-poisoning from bites. When I was bringing them their water they prowled up and down on the paths they had made inside their pens, barking seldom—they saved that for nighttime, when they might get up a chorus of community frenzy—but always watching me, their eyes burning, clear gold, in their pointed, malevolent faces. They were beautiful for their delicate legs and heavy, aristocratic tails and the bright fur sprinkled on dark down their backs—which gave them their name—but especially for their faces, drawn exquisitely sharp in pure hostility, and their golden eyes.

Besides carrying water I helped my father when he cut the long grass, and the lamb's quarter and flowering money-musk, that grew between the pens. He cut with the scythe and I raked into piles. Then he took a pitchfork and threw fresh-cut grass all over the top of the pens, to keep the foxes cooler and shade their coats, which were browned by too much sun. My father did not talk to me unless it was about the job we were doing. In this he was quite different from my mother, who, if she was feeling cheerful, would tell me all sorts of things— the name of a dog she had had when she was a little girl, the names of boys she had gone out with later on when she was grown up, and what certain dresses of hers had looked like—she could not imagine now what had become of them. Whatever thoughts and stories my father had were private, and I was shy of him and would never ask him questions. Nevertheless I worked willingly under his eyes, and with a feeling of pride. One time a feed salesman came down into the pens to talk to him and my father said, "Like to have you meet my new hired man." I turned away and raked furiously, red in the face with pleasure.

"Could of fooled me," said the salesman. "I thought it was only a girl."

After the grass was cut, it seemed suddenly much later in the year. I walked on stubble in the earlier evening, aware of the reddening skies, the entering silences, of fall. When I wheeled the tank out of the gate and put the padlock on, it was almost dark. One night at this time I saw my mother and father standing talking on the little rise of ground we called the gangway, in front of the barn. My father had just come from the meathouse; he had his stiff bloody apron on, and a pail of cut-up meat in his hand.

It was an odd thing to see my mother down at the barn. She did not often come out of the house unless it was to do something—hang out the wash or dig potatoes in the garden. She looked out of place, with her bare lumpy legs, not touched by the sun, her apron still on and damp across the stomach from the supper dishes. Her hair was tied up in a kerchief, wisps of it falling out. She would tie her hair up like this in the morning, saying she did not have time to do it properly, and it would stay tied up all day. It was true, too; she really did not have time. These days our back porch was piled with baskets of peaches and grapes and pears, bought in town, and onions and tomatoes and cucumbers grown at home, all waiting to be made into jelly and jam and preserves, pickles and chili sauce. In the kitchen there was a fire in the stove all day, jars clinked in boiling water, sometimes a cheesecloth bag was strung on a pole between two chairs, straining blue-black grape pulp for jelly. I was given jobs to do and I would sit at the table peeling peaches that had been soaked in the hot water, or cutting up onions, my eyes smarting and streaming. As soon as I was done I ran out of the house, trying to get out of earshot before my mother thought of what she wanted me to do next. I hated the hot dark kitchen in summer, the green blinds and the flypapers, the same old oilcloth table and wavy mirror and bumpy linoleum. My mother was too tired and preoccupied to talk to me, she had no heart to tell about the Normal School Graduation Dance; sweat trickled over her face and she was always counting under her breath, pointing at jars, dumping cups of sugar. It seemed to me that work in the house was endless, dreary and peculiarly depressing; work done out of doors, and in my father's service, was ritualistically important.

I wheeled the tank up to the barn, where it was kept, and I heard my mother saying, "Wait till Laird gets a little bigger, then you'll have a real help."

What my father said I did not hear. I was pleased by the way he stood listening, politely as he would to a salesman or a stranger, but with an air of wanting to get on with his real work. I felt my mother had no business down here and I wanted him to feel the same way. What did she mean about Laird? He was no help to anybody. Where was he now? Swinging himself sick on the swing, going around in circles, or trying to catch caterpillars. He never once stayed with me till I was finished.

"And then I can use her more in the house," I heard my mother say. She had a dead-quiet, regretful way of talking about me that always made me uneasy. "I just get my back turned and she runs off. It's not like I had a girl in the family at all."

I went and sat on a feedbag in the corner of the barn, not wanting to appear when this conversation was going on. My mother, I felt, was not to be trusted. She was kinder than my father and more easily fooled, but you could not depend on her, and the real reasons for the things she said and did were not to be known. She loved me, and she sat up late at night making a dress of the difficult style I wanted, for me to wear when school started, but she was also my enemy. She was always plotting. She was plotting now to get me to stay in the house more, although she knew I hated it (*because* she knew I hated it) and keep me from working for my father. It seemed to me she would do this simply out of perversity, and to try her power. It did not occur to me that she could be lonely, or jealous. No grown-up could be; they were too fortunate. I sat and kicked my heels monotonously against a feedbag, raising dust, and did not come out till she was gone.

At any rate, I did not expect my father to pay any attention to what she said. Who could imagine Laird doing my work—Laird remembering the padlock and cleaning out the watering-dishes with a leaf on the end of a stick, or even wheeling the tank without it tumbling over? It showed how little my mother knew about the way things really were.

I have forgotten to say what the foxes were fed. My father's bloody apron reminded me. They were fed horsemeat. At this time most farmers still kept horses, and when a horse got too old to work, or broke a leg or got down and would not get up, as they sometimes did, the owner would call my father, and he and Henry went out to the farm in the truck. Usually they shot and butchered the horse there, paying the farmer from five to twelve dollars. If they had already too much meat on hand, they would bring the horse back alive, and keep it for a few days or weeks in our stable, until the meat was needed. After the war the farmers were buying tractors and gradually getting rid of horses altogether, so it sometimes happened that we got a good healthy horse, that there was just no use for any more. If this happened in the winter we might keep the horse in our stable till spring, for we had plenty of hay and if there was a lot of snow—and the plow did not always get our road cleared—it was convenient to be able to go to town with a horse and cutter.

The winter I was eleven years old we had two horses in the stable. We did not know what names they had had before, so we called them Mack and Flora. Mack was an old black workhorse, sooty and indifferent. Flora was a sorrel mare, a driver. We took them both out in the cutter. Mack was slow and easy to handle. Flora was given to fits of violent alarm, veering at cars and even at other horses, but we loved her speed and high-stepping, her general air of gallantry and abandon. On Saturdays we went down to the stable and as soon as we opened the door on its cosy, animal-smelling darkness Flora threw up her head, rolled her eyes, whinnied despairingly and pulled herself through a crisis of nerves on the spot. It was not safe to go into her stall; she would kick.

This winter also I began to hear a great deal more on the theme my mother had sounded when she had been talking in front of the barn. I no longer felt safe. It seemed that in the minds of the people around me there was a steady undercurrent of thought, not to be deflected, on this one subject. The word *girl* had formerly seemed to me innocent and unburdened, like the word *child*; now it appeared that it was no such thing. A girl was not, as I had supposed, simply what I was; it was what I had to become. It was a definition, always touched with emphasis, with reproach and disappointment. Also it was a joke on me. Once Laird and I were fighting, and for the first time ever I had to use all my strength against him; even so, he caught and pinned my arm for a moment, really hurting me. Henry saw this, and laughed, saying, "Oh, that there Laird's gonna show you, one of these days!" Laird was getting a lot bigger. But I was getting bigger too.

My grandmother came to stay with us for a few weeks and I heard other things. "Girls don't slam doors like that." "Girls keep their knees together when they sit down." And worse still, when I asked some questions, "That's none of girls' business." I continued to slam the doors and sit as awkwardly as possible, thinking that by such measures I kept myself free.

When spring came, the horses were let out in the barnyard. Mack stood against the barn wall trying to scratch his neck and haunches, but Flora trotted up and down and reared at the fences, clattering her hooves against the rails. Snow drifts dwindled quickly, revealing the hard gray and brown earth, the familiar rise and fall of the ground, plain and bare after the fantastic landscape of winter. There was a great feeling of opening-out, of release. We just wore rubbers now, over our shoes; our feet felt ridiculously light. One Saturday we went out to the stable and found all the doors open, letting in the unaccustomed sunlight and fresh air. Henry was there, just idling around looking at his collection of calendars which were tacked up behind the stalls in a part of the stable my mother had probably never seen.

"Come to say goodbye to your old friend Mack?" Henry said. "Here, you give him a taste of oats." He poured some oats into Laird's cupped hands and Laird went to feed Mack. Mack's teeth were in bad shape. He ate very slowly, patiently shifting the oats around in his mouth, trying to find a stump of a molar to grind it on. "Poor old Mack," said Henry mournfully. "When a horse's teeth's gone, he's gone. That's about the way."

"Are you going to shoot him today?" I said. Mack and Flora had been in the stable so long I had almost forgotten they were going to be shot.

Henry didn't answer me. Instead he started to sing in a high, trembly, mocking-sorrowful voice, *Oh, there's no more work, for poor Uncle Ned, he's gone where the good darkies go.* Mack's thick, blackish tongue worked diligently at Laird's hand. I went out before the song was ended and sat down on the gangway.

I had never seen them shoot a horse, but I knew where it was done. Last summer Laird and I had come upon a horse's entrails before they were buried. We had thought it was a big black snake, coiled up in the sun. That was around in the field that ran up beside the barn. I thought that if we went inside the barn, and found a wide crack or a knothole to look through, we would be able to see them do it. It was not something I wanted to see; just the same, if a thing really happened, it was better to see it, and know.

My father came down from the house, carrying the gun.

"What are you doing here?" he said.

"Nothing."

"Go on up and play around the house."

He sent Laird out of the stable. I said to Laird, "Do you want to see them shoot Mack?" and without waiting for an answer led him around to the front door of the barn, opened it carefully, and went in. "Be quiet or they'll hear us," I said. We could hear Henry and my father talking in the stable, then the heavy, shuffling steps of Mack being backed out of his stall.

In the loft it was cold and dark. Thin, crisscrossed beams of sunlight fell through the cracks. The hay was low. It was a rolling country, hills and hollows, slipping under our feet. About four feet up was a beam going around the walls. We piled hay up in one corner and I boosted Laird up and hoisted myself. The beam was not very wide; we crept along it with our hands flat on the barn walls. There were plenty of knotholes, and I found one that gave me the view I wanted—a corner of the barnyard, the gate, part of the field. Laird did not have a knothole and began to complain.

I showed him a widened crack between two boards. "Be quiet and wait. If they hear you you'll get us in trouble."

My father came in sight carrying the gun. Henry was leading Mack by the halter. He dropped it and took out his cigarette papers and tobacco; he rolled cigarettes for my father and himself. While this was going on Mack nosed around in the old, dead grass along the fence. Then my father opened the gate and they took Mack through. Henry led Mack away from the path to a patch of ground and they talked together, not loud enough for us to hear. Mack again began searching for a mouthful of fresh grass, which was not to be found. My father walked away in a straight line, and stopped short at a distance which seemed to suit him. Henry was walking away from Mack too, but sideways, still negligently holding on to the halter. My father raised the gun and Mack looked up as if he had noticed something and my father shot him.

Mack did not collapse at once but swayed, lurched sideways and fell, first on his side; then he rolled over on his back and, amazingly, kicked his legs for a few seconds in the air. At this Henry laughed, as if Mack had done a trick for him. Laird, who had drawn a long, groaning breath of surprise when the shot was fired, said out loud, "He's not dead." And it seemed to me it might be true. But his legs stopped, he rolled on his side again, his muscles quivered and sank. The two men walked over and looked at him in a businesslike way; they bent down and examined his forehead where the bullet had gone in, and now I saw his blood on the brown grass.

"Now they just skin him and cut him up," I said. "Let's go." My legs were a little shaky and I jumped gratefully down into the hay. "Now you've seen how they shoot a horse," I said in a congratulatory way, as if I had seen it many times before. "Let's see if any barn cat's had kittens in the hay." Laird jumped. He seemed young and obedient again. Suddenly I remembered how, when he was little, I had brought him into the barn and told him to climb the ladder to the top beam. That was in the spring, too, when the hay was low. I had done it out of a need for excitement, a desire for something to happen so that I could tell about it. He was wearing a little bulky brown and white checked coat, made down from one of mine. He went all the way up, just as I told him, and sat down on the top beam with the hay far below him on one side, and the barn floor and some old machinery on the other. Then I ran screaming to my father, "Laird's up on the top beam!" My father came, my mother came, my father went up the ladder talking very quietly and brought Laird down under his arm, at which my mother leaned against the ladder and began to cry. They said to me, "Why weren't you watching him?" but nobody ever knew the truth. Laird did not know enough to tell. But whenever I saw the brown and white checked coat hanging in the closet, or at the bottom of the rag bag, which was where it ended up, I felt a weight in my stomach, the sadness of unexorcized guilt.

I looked at Laird who did not even remember this, and I did not like the look on this thin, winter-pale face. His expression was not frightened or upset, but remote, concentrating. "Listen," I said, in an unusually bright and friendly voice, "you aren't going to tell, are you?"

"No," he said absently.

"Promise."

"Promise," he said. I grabbed the hand behind his back to make sure he was not crossing his fingers. Even so, he might have a nightmare; it might come out that way. I decided I had better work hard to get all thoughts of what he had seen out of his mind—which, it seemed to me, could not hold very many things at a time. I got some money I had saved and that afternoon we went into Jubilee and saw a show, with Judy Canova, at which we both laughed a great deal. After that I thought it would be all right.

Two weeks later I knew they were going to shoot Flora. I knew from the night before, when I heard my mother ask if the hay was holding out all right, and my father said, "Well, after tomorrow there'll just be the cow, and we should be able to put her out to grass in another week." So I knew it was Flora's turn in the morning.

This time I didn't think of watching it. That was something to see just one time. I had not thought about it very often since, but sometimes when I was busy, working at school, or standing in front of the mirror combing my hair and wondering if I would be pretty when I grew up, the whole scene would flash into my mind: I would see the easy, practised way my father raised the gun, and hear Henry laughing when Mack kicked his legs in the air. I did not have any great feeling of horror and opposition, such as a city child might have had; I was too used to seeing the death of animals as a necessity by which we lived. Yet I felt a little ashamed, and there was a new wariness, a sense of holding-off, in my attitude to my father and his work.

It was a fine day, and we were going around the yard picking up tree branches that had been torn off in winter storms. This was something we had been told to do, and also we wanted to use them to make a teepee. We heard Flora whinny, and then my father's voice and Henry's shouting, and we ran down to the barnyard to see what was going on.

The stable door was open. Henry had just brought Flora out, and she had broken away from him. She was running free in the barnyard, from one end to the other. We climbed up on the fence. It was exciting to see her running, whinnying, going up on her hind legs, prancing and threatening like a horse in a Western movie, an unbroken ranch horse, though she was just an old driver, an old sorrel mare. My father and Henry ran after her and tried to grab the dangling halter. They tried to work her into a corner, and they had almost succeeded when she made a run between them, wild-eyed, and disappeared around the corner of the barn. We heard the rails clatter down as she got over the fence, and Henry yelled, "She's into the field now!"

That meant she was in the long L-shaped field that ran up by the house. If she got around the center, heading towards the lane, the gate was open; the truck had been driven into the field this morning. My father shouted to me, because I was on the other side of the fence, nearest the lane, "Go shut the gate!"

I could run very fast. I ran across the garden, past the tree where our swing was hung, and jumped across a ditch into the lane. There was the open gate. She had not got out, I could not see her up on the road; she must have run to the other end of the field. The gate was heavy. I lifted it out of the gravel and carried it across the roadway. I had it half-way across when she came in sight, galloping straight towards me. There was just time to get the chain on. Laird came scrambling through the ditch to help me.

Instead of shutting the gate, I opened it as wide as I could. I did not make any decision to do this, it was just what I did. Flora never slowed down; she galloped straight past me, and Laird jumped up and down, yelling, "Shut it, shut it!" even after it was too late. My father and Henry appeared in the field a moment too late to see what I had done. They only saw Flora heading for the township road. They would think I had not got there in time.

They did not waste any time asking about it. They went back to the barn and got the gun and the knives they used, and put these in the truck; then they turned the truck around and came bouncing up the field toward us. Laird called to them, "Let me go too, let me go too!" and Henry stopped the truck and they took him in. I shut the gate after they were all gone.

I supposed Laird would tell. I wondered what would happen to me. I had never disobeyed my father before, and I could not understand why I had done it. Flora would not really get away. They would catch up with her in the truck. Or if they did not catch her this morning somebody would see her and telephone us this afternoon or tomorrow. There was no wild country here for her to run to, only farms. What was more, my father had paid for her, we needed the meat to feed the foxes, we needed the foxes to make our living. All I had done was make more work for my father who worked hard enough already. And when my father found out about it he was not going to trust me any more; he would know that I was not entirely on his side. I was on Flora's side, and that made me no use to anybody, not even to her. Just the same, I did not regret it; when she came running at me and I held the gate open, that was the only thing I could do.

I went back to the house, and my mother said, "What's all the commotion?" I told her that Flora had kicked down the fence and got away. "Your poor father," she said, "now he'll have to go chasing over the countryside. Well, there isn't any use planning dinner before one." She put up the ironing board. I wanted to tell her, but thought better of it and went upstairs and sat on my bed.

Lately I had been trying to make my part of the room fancy, spreading the bed with old lace curtains, and fixing myself a dressing-table with some leftovers of cretonne for a skirt. I planned to put up some kind of barricade between my bed and Laird's, to keep my section separate from his. In the sunlight, the lace curtains were just dusty rags. We did not sing at night any more. One night when I was singing Laird said, "You sound silly," and I went right on but the next night I did not start. There was not so much need to anyway, we were no longer afraid. We knew it was just old furniture over there, old jumble and confusion. We did not keep to the rules. I still stayed awake after Laird was asleep and told myself stories, but even in these stories something different was happening, mysterious alterations took place. A story might start off in the old way, with a spectacular danger, a fire or wild animals, and for a while I might rescue people; then things would change around, and instead, somebody would be rescuing me. It might be a boy from our class at school, or even Mr. Campbell, our teacher, who tickled girls under the arms. And at this point the story concerned itself at great length with what I looked like—how long my hair was, and what kind of dress I had on; by the time I had these details worked out the real excitement of the story was lost.

It was later than one o'clock when the truck came back. The tarpaulin was over the back, which meant there was meat in it. My mother had to heat dinner up all over again. Henry and my father had changed from their bloody overalls into ordinary working overalls in the barn, and they washed their arms and necks and faces at the sink, and splashed water on their hair and combed it. Laird lifted his arm to show off a streak of blood. "We shot old Flora," he said, "and cut her up in fifty pieces."

"Well I don't want to hear about it," my mother said. "And don't come to my table like that."

My father made him go and wash the blood off.

We sat down and my father said grace and Henry pasted his chewing-gum on the end of his fork, the way he always did; when he took it off he would have us admire the pattern. We began to pass the bowls of steaming, overcooked vegetables. Laird looked across the table at me and said proudly, distinctly, "Anyway it was her fault Flora got away."

"What?" my father said.

"She could of shut the gate and she didn't. She just open' it up and Flora run out."

"Is that right?" my father said.

Everybody at the table was looking at me. I nodded, swallowing food with great difficulty. To my shame, tears flooded my eyes.

My father made a curt sound of disgust. "What did you do that for?"

I did not answer. I put down my fork and waited to be sent from the table, still not looking up.

But this did not happen. For some time nobody said anything, then Laird said matter-of-factly, "She's crying."

"Never mind," my father said. He spoke with resignation, even good humour, the words which absolved and dismissed me for good. "She's only a girl," he said.

I didn't protest that, even in my heart. Maybe it was true.

(1968)

PREWRITING

Understanding the theme of a piece of literature involves figuring out what the whole work means. Your prewriting task here is, as usual, to ask yourself questions that will lead to the meaning of the story you just read.

FIGURING OUT THE THEME

Reread "Boys and Girls" and formulate specific leading questions about the following elements of the story. For example, you might ask yourself, "Do the characters' names (or lack of names) seem appropriate? Do they describe the characters in any way?" or "To what extent are the characters in the story influenced by their gender roles?" Consider the following:

1. The title.
2. The setting, especially the descriptions of work in the house and outside of the house.
3. The characters in the story, especially their physical descriptions, their personality traits, and their relationships with one another.
4. Any significant elements, such as the animals and their enclosures.
5. Any changes that you notice in the characters and their feelings toward themselves or one another.
6. Any reversals or surprises that occur.
7. Any comments or observations the narrator makes about the characters and their actions.
8. The ending.

STATING THE THEME

After writing out the answers to the questions you have set for yourself, try to sum up the theme in a complete sentence, one that does not begin with the phrase "The theme of the story is . . ." since there are often several themes in a story. Make your statement a general truth about life or the human condition that is addressed in the story by Alice Munro. You may need to rewrite the sentence several times until you can express the theme satisfactorily. Then state the theme in another way, using other words. Are both statements valid? Are there any secondary themes that enrich the story and add to the primary theme? Write those down, too.

Take one of the statements of theme that you have formulated, and write it at the top of a blank sheet of paper. Fill the page with freewriting about this idea, expressing as quickly as you can your thoughts and feelings about Munro's view of human nature.

WRITING

We have emphasized that your essays should be filled with supporting details from your source. Without specific references to the literary work that you are writing about, your judgments and conclusions will be vague and unconvincing.

CHOOSING SUPPORTING DETAILS

During a close second reading of a story, pay special attention to details that have potential for symbolic meaning. Thoughtful consideration of the names, places, objects, incidents, and minor characters can guide you to a deeper understanding of the work's theme. In "Boys and Girls," for example, you may notice how often enclosures of one kind or another are mentioned. Go through the story one more time, and put a check mark next to each mention of enclosures, such as pens, stalls, and fences. During this third examination, you may also note other references to things that might imprison, such as the house, or even abstract enclosures, such as rules, customs, and traditions. Then try to come up with an insight that expresses the meaning of these details—perhaps something like, "Many of the characters seem preoccupied in one way or another with restraining the things and people around them." You now have the beginnings of a useful thesis for your paper or a topic sentence for a section of it.

A list of specific examples from the story could support your thesis statement, but a simple list would probably sound mechanical and unrevealing. So, if possible, classify the details. In this case, most of the characters seem concerned with maintaining enclosures on the farm. Quote one or two examples of each kind, and then—most important—explain their significance. In this story, the enclosures on the farm seem logical and necessary, yet as these enclosures, some physical and some emotional, extend to the narrator, they seem both cruel and unavoidable.

Approach the following writing ideas by rereading the story with your topic in mind. Jot down any details that seem relevant. Review all your notes on the story and see what general observations you can make; then select appropriate supporting details from your list and show how they support your critical generalizations.

IDEAS FOR WRITING

IDEAS FOR RESPONSIVE WRITING

1. Do you agree with the narrator's observation that "A girl was not, as I had supposed, simply what I was; it was what I had to become. It was a definition, always touched with emphasis, with reproach and disappointment"? Evaluate the validity of this assertion, especially as it relates to yourself or to someone you know.
2. Examine the character of the father and his role in the story. Do you consider him a victim or a perpetrator of society's gender role specifications? Write a character sketch (an extended description) of the father.
3. Rewrite the story from the mother's point of view. You might put your rewrite in the form of a story the mother tells to her daughter.

4. The stories the girl tells herself at night change dramatically by the end of "Boys and Girls." Is this important? How are dreams and visualizations significant in the development of a sense of self?

IDEAS FOR CRITICAL WRITING

1. At the end of the story the narrator's father says "She's only a girl," words that for her "absolved and dismissed me for good." Write an essay explaining how what is said by characters in this story both absolves and dismisses the narrator.
2. The narrator attempts to escape the gender role being imposed on her. Discuss her success or failure. Remember, you will need to prove *why* you believe she is a success or a failure, not to simply *list* her successes and failures.
3. What does "Boys and Girls" say about the development of self-perception? Write an essay examining the story's message about this subject.

REWRITING

When you revise, you should make sure that your paper *flows*—that your readers can follow your ideas easily.

ACHIEVING COHERENCE

The best way to make your writing *coherent*—to make it easy to follow—is to have a clear thesis and to make sure that all your subpoints pertain to that thesis. If you organize the development of your ideas carefully, your paragraphs should unfold in a logical, connected way. Continuity also evolves from thinking through your ideas completely and developing them adequately. Leaps in thought and shifts in meaning often result from too much generalization and too little development.

CHECKING FOR COHERENCE

Type up or print out a clean copy of the latest draft of your essay. In the margins, write a word or phrase that labels the point or describes the function of every group of related sentences. These words and phrases are called *glosses*. (You can even use short sentences.) To help write glosses for your sentences and paragraphs, ask yourself these questions: What have I said here? How many ideas are in this passage? What does this sentence/paragraph do?

When you have finished putting glosses in the margins of your essay, go back and review the glosses. Can you see a clear sequence of points? Are there any sentences or passages that you could not write a gloss for? Is there any place where you digress or introduce an unrelated idea? Using the glosses as a guide, make revisions that will improve the coherence of your essay: fill in gaps, combine repetitive sentences, cut out irrelevant material, add transitions. (See Chart 3-2, "Transitional Terms for All Occasions," on page 45.)

EDITING: IMPROVING CONNECTIONS

Here are some other ways to help you strengthen the flow and coherence of your sentences:

REPEAT WORDS AND SYNONYMS

Repeat key words for coherence as well as for emphasis:

> I do not want *to read another gothic romance*. I especially do not want *to read another long gothic romance*.

If repetition is tiresome or you want more variety, use a synonym:

> It was a rare *caper*, planned to the last second. Such elaborate *heists* seem to come right from a detective novel.

Take care when using repetition. Repeated words should be important or emphatic. Do not repeat a common, limp term because you are too tired to find a synonym. Be aware, however, that synonyms are not always interchangeable; check the meaning of any word you are not sure of. The following introduction to a student paper suffers because the writer needlessly repeats the same uninteresting verb (which we have italicized):

> Alistair MacLeod's "The Boat" is a complex story that deals with a fundamental part of human psychology, the *use* of tradition. Traditions have been *used* throughout history to justify actions. Many times traditions are *used* to conceal human errors, prejudices, and fears. Traditions are, in fact, still *used* for the same purposes today.

Notice that the repetition of the key word *tradition* emphasizes the main idea of the paper, but the ineffective repetition should be revised (our substituted verbs are italicized in the following revision):

> Alistair MacLeod's "The Boat" is a complex story that deals with a fundamental part of human psychology—the need for tradition. Traditions have been *created* throughout history to justify actions. Many times they are *employed* to conceal human errors, prejudices, and fears. In fact, traditions still *exist* for the same purposes today.

TRY PARALLEL STRUCTURE

Repeat a grammatical pattern to tie points and details together:

> In the morning Emma Bovary ate breakfast with her husband; in the afternoon she picnicked with her paramour.

> The play was about to end: the villain stalked off, the lovers kissed, the curtain fell, and the audience applauded wildly.

Be sure that your grammatical patterns actually are parallel. If your phrases or clauses do not follow the same structure, you will lose the good effect:

Not parallel: In "The Boat" these characteristics include *unwillingness to change, sticking to tradition, fear of peer pressure,* and *just plain being afraid.*

Parallel: In "The Boat" these characteristics include *unwillingness to change, enslavement to tradition, fear of peer pressure,* and *fear of outsiders.*

Not parallel: Many times traditions are invoked to conceal *human errors* or *the way people unfairly judge one another.*

Parallel: Many times traditions are invoked to conceal *human errors* and *prejudices.*

WEB

For study tools to help you with your next writing assignment, please visit the Companion Website at www.pearsoned.ca/mcmahan.

Anthology of Short Fiction

Nathaniel Hawthorne   1804–1864
Young Goodman Brown

Young Goodman[1] Brown came forth at sunset, into the street of Salem village, but put his head back, after crossing the threshold, to exchange a parting kiss with his young wife. And Faith, as the wife was aptly named, thrust her own pretty head into the street, letting the wind play with the pink ribbons of her cap, while she called to Goodman Brown.

"Dearest heart," whispered she, softly and rather sadly, when her lips were close to his ear, "prithee, put off your journey until sunrise, and sleep in your own bed to-night. A lone woman is troubled with such dreams and such thoughts, that she's afeard of herself, sometimes. Pray, tarry with me this night, dear husband, of all nights in the year!"

"My love and my Faith," replied young Goodman Brown, "of all nights in the year, this one night must I tarry away from thee. My journey, as thou callest it, forth and back again, must needs be done 'twixt now and sunrise. Why, my sweet, pretty wife, dost thou doubt me already, and we but three months married?"

"Then God bless you!" said Faith with the pink ribbons, "and may you find all well, when you come back."

"Amen!" cried Goodman Brown. "Say thy prayers, dear Faith, and go to bed at dusk, and no harm will come to thee."

So they parted; and the young man pursued his way, until, being about to turn the corner by the meeting-house, he looked back and saw the head of Faith still peeping after him, with a melancholy air, in spite of her pink ribbons.

"Poor little Faith!" thought he, for his heart smote him. "What a wretch am I, to leave her on such an errand! She talks of dreams, too. Methought, as she spoke, there was trouble in her face, as if a dream had warned her what work is to be done to-night. But no, no! 't would kill her to think it. Well she's a blessed angel on earth; and after this one night I'll cling to her skirts and follow her to Heaven."

With this excellent resolve for the future, Goodman Brown felt himself justified in making more haste on his present evil purpose. He had taken a dreary road, darkened by all the gloomiest trees of the forest, which barely stood aside to let the narrow path creep through, and closed immediately behind. It was as lonely as could be; and there is this peculiarity in such a solitude, that the traveller knows not who may be concealed by the innumerable trunks and the thick

---

[1] A title equivalent to *Mr.*, meaning a husband.

boughs overhead; so that, with lonely footsteps, he may yet be passing through an unseen multitude.

"There may be a devilish Indian behind every tree," said Goodman Brown to himself; and he glanced fearfully behind him, as he added, "What if the devil himself should be at my very elbow!"

His head being turned back, he passed a crook of the road, and looking forward again, beheld the figure of a man, in grave and decent attire, seated at the foot of an old tree. He arose at Goodman Brown's approach, and walked onward, side by side with him.

"You are late, Goodman Brown," said he. "The clock of the Old South was striking, as I came through Boston; and that is full fifteen minutes agone."

"Faith kept me back awhile," replied the young man, with a tremor in his voice, caused by the sudden appearance of his companion, though not wholly unexpected.

It was now deep dusk in the forest, and deepest in that part of it where these two were journeying. As nearly as could be discerned, the second traveller was about fifty years old, apparently in the same rank of life as Goodman Brown, and bearing a considerable resemblance to him, though perhaps more in expression than features. Still, they might have been taken for father and son. And yet, though the elder person was as simply clad as the younger, and as simple in manner too, he had an indescribable air of one who knew the world, and would not have felt abashed at the governor's dinner-table, or in King William's court, were it possible that his affairs should call him thither. But the only thing about him that could be fixed upon as remarkable, was his staff, which bore the likeness of a great black snake, so curiously wrought, that it might almost be seen to twist and wriggle itself like a living serpent. This, of course, must have been an ocular deception, assisted by the uncertain light.

"Come, Goodman Brown!" cried his fellow-traveller, "this is a dull pace for the beginning of a journey. Take my staff, if you are so soon weary."

"Friend," said the other, exchanging his slow pace for a full stop, "having kept covenant by meeting thee here, it is my purpose now to return whence I came. I have scruples, touching the matter thou wot'st of."

"Sayest thou so?" replied he of the serpent, smiling apart. "Let us walk on, nevertheless, reasoning as we go, and if I convince thee not, thou shalt turn back. We are but a little way in the forest, yet."

"Too far, too far!" exclaimed the goodman, unconsciously resuming his walk. "My father never went into the woods on such an errand, nor his father before him. We have been a race of honest men and good Christians, since the days of the martyrs. And shall I be the first of the name of Brown that ever took this path and kept—"

"Such company, thou wouldst say," observed the elder person, interrupting his pause. "Well said, Goodman Brown! I have been as well acquainted with your family as with ever a one among the Puritans; and that's no trifle to say. I helped your grandfather, the constable, when he lashed the Quaker woman so smartly through the streets of Salem. And it was I that brought your father a pitch-pine knot, kindled at my own hearth, to set fire to an Indian village, in King Philip's war. They were my good friends, both; and many a pleasant walk have we had along this path, and returned merrily after midnight. I would fain be friends with you, for their sake."

"If it be as thou sayest," replied Goodman Brown, "I marvel they never spoke of these matters. Or, verily, I marvel not, seeing that the least rumor of the sort would have driven them from New England. We are a people of prayer, and good works to boot, and abide no such wickedness."

"Wickedness or not," said the traveller with the twisted staff, "I have a very general acquaintance here in New England. The deacons of many a church have drunk the communion wine with me; the selectmen, of diverse towns, make me their chairman; and a majority of the Great and General Court are firm supporters of my interest. The governor and I, too—but these are state secrets."

"Can this be so!" cried Goodman Brown, with a stare of amazement at his undisturbed companion. "Howbeit, I have nothing to do with the governor and council; they have their own ways, and are no rule for a simple husbandman like me. But, were I to go on with thee, how should I meet the eye of that good old man, our minister, at Salem village? Oh, his voice would make me tremble, both Sabbath-day and lecture-day!"

Thus far, the elder traveller had listened with due gravity, but now burst into a fit of irrepressible mirth, shaking himself so violently, that his snakelike staff actually seemed to wriggle in sympathy.

"Ha, ha, ha!" shouted he, again and again; then composing himself, "Well, go on, Goodman Brown, go on; but, prithee, don't kill me with laughing!"

"Well, then, to end the matter at once," said Goodman Brown, considerably nettled, "there is my wife, Faith. It would break her dear little heart; and I'd rather break my own!"

"Nay, if that be the case," answered the other, "e'en go thy ways, Goodman Brown. I would not, for twenty old women like the one hobbling before us, that Faith should come to any harm."

As he spoke, he pointed his staff at a female figure on the path, in whom Goodman Brown recognized a very pious and exemplary dame, who had taught him his catechism in youth, and was still his moral and spiritual adviser, jointly with the minister and Deacon Gookin.

"A marvel, truly, that Goody[2] Cloyse should be so far in the wilderness, at nightfall!" said he. "But, with your leave, friend, I shall take a cut through the woods, until we have left this Christian woman behind. Being a stranger to you, she might ask whom I was consorting with, and whither I was going."

"Be it so," said his fellow-traveller. "Betake you to the woods, and let me keep the path."

Accordingly, the young man turned aside, but took care to watch his companion, who advanced softly along the road, until he had come within a staff's length of the old dame. She, meanwhile, was making the best of her way, with singular speed for so aged a woman, and mumbling some indistinct words, a prayer, doubtless, as she went. The traveller put forth his staff, and touched her withered neck with what seemed the serpent's tail.

"The devil!" screamed the pious old lady.

"Then Goody Cloyse knows her old friend?" observed the traveller, confronting her, and leaning on his writhing stick.

"Ah, forsooth, and is it your worship, indeed?" cried the good dame. "Yea, truly is it, and in the very image of my old gossip,[3] Goodman Brown, the grandfather of the silly fellow that now is. But, would your worship believe it? my broomstick hath strangely disappeared, stolen, as I suspect, by that unhanged

---

[2] A title meaning "good wife," usually applied to an elderly woman.
[3] Close friend.

witch, Goody Cory, and that, too, when I was all anointed with the juice of smallage and cinque-foil and wolf's-bane—"

"Mingled with fine wheat and the fat of a new-born babe," said the shape of old Goodman Brown.

"Ah, your worship knows the recipe," cried the old lady, cackling aloud. "So, as I was saying, being all ready for the meeting, and no horse to ride on, I made up my mind to foot it; for they tell me there is a nice young man to be taken into communion to-night. But now your good worship will lend me your arm, and we shall be there in a twinkling."

"That can hardly be," answered her friend. "I may not spare you my arm, Goody Cloyse, but here is my staff, if you will."

So saying, he threw it down at her feet where, perhaps, it assumed life, being one of the rods which its owner had formerly lent to the Egyptian Magi.[4] Of this fact, however, Goodman Brown could not take cognizance. He had cast up his eyes in astonishment, and looking down again, beheld neither Goody Cloyse nor the serpentine staff, but his fellow-traveller alone, who waited for him as calmly as if nothing had happened.

"That old woman taught me my catechism!" said the young man; and there was a world of meaning in this simple comment.

They continued to walk onward, while the elder traveller exhorted his companion to make good speed and persevere in the path, discoursing so aptly, that his arguments seemed rather to spring up in the bosom of his auditor, than to be suggested by himself. As they went he plucked a branch of maple, to serve for a walking-stick, and began to strip it of the twigs and little boughs, which were wet with evening dew. The moment his fingers touched them, they became strangely withered and dried up, as with a week's sunshine. Thus the pair proceeded, at a good free pace, until suddenly, in a gloomy hollow of the road, Goodman Brown sat himself down on the stump of a tree, and refused to go any farther.

"Friend," said he, stubbornly, "my mind is made up. Not another step will I budge on this errand. What if a wretched old woman do choose to go to the devil, when I thought she was going to Heaven! Is that any reason why I should quit my dear Faith, and go after her?"

"You will think better of this by and by," said his acquaintance, composedly. "Sit here and rest yourself awhile; and when you feel like moving again, there is my staff to help you along."

Without more words, he threw his companion the maple stick, and was as speedily out of sight as if he had vanished into the deepening gloom. The young man sat a few moments by the roadside, applauding himself greatly, and thinking with how clear a conscience he should meet the minister, in his morning walk, nor shrink from the eye of good old Deacon Gookin. And what calm sleep would be his, that very night, which was to have been spent so wickedly, but purely and sweetly now, in the arms of Faith! Amidst these pleasant and praiseworthy meditations, Goodman Brown heard the tramp of horses along the road, and deemed it advisable to conceal himself within the verge of the forest, conscious of the guilty purpose that had brought him thither, though now so happily turned from it.

On came the hoof-tramps and the voices of the riders, two grave old voices, conversing soberly as they drew near. These mingled sounds appeared to pass along the road, within a few yards of the young man's hiding-place; but owing,

---

[4]Priests or magicians.

doubtless, to the depth of the gloom, at that particular spot, neither the travellers nor their steeds were visible. Though their figures brushed the small boughs by the wayside, it could not be seen that they intercepted, even for a moment, the faint gleam from the strip of bright sky, athwart[5] which they must have passed. Goodman Brown alternately crouched and stood on tiptoe, pulling aside the branches, and thrusting forth his head as far as he durst,[6] without discerning so much as a shadow. It vexed him the more, because he could have sworn, were such a thing possible, that he recognized the voices of the minister and Deacon Gookin, jogging along quietly, as they were wont to do, when bound to some ordination or ecclesiastical council. While yet within hearing, one of the riders stopped to pluck a switch.

"Of the two, reverend Sir," said the voice like the deacon's, "I had rather miss an ordination dinner than to-night's meeting. They tell me that some of our community are to be here from Falmouth and beyond, and others from Connecticut and Rhode Island; besides several of the Indian powwows, who, after their fashion, know almost as much deviltry as the best of us. Moreover, there is a goodly young woman to be taken into communion."

"Mighty well, Deacon Gookin!" replied the solemn old tones of the minister. "Spur up, or we shall be late. Nothing can be done, you know, until I get on the ground."

The hoofs clattered again, and the voices, talking so strangely in the empty air, passed on through the forest, where no church had ever been gathered, nor solitary Christian prayed. Whither, then, could these holy men be journeying, so deep into the heathen wilderness? Young Goodman Brown caught hold of a tree, for support, being ready to sink down on the ground, faint and over-burthened with the heavy sickness of his heart. He looked up to the sky, doubting whether there really was a Heaven above him. Yet, there was the blue arch, and the stars brightening in it.

"With Heaven above, and Faith below, I will yet stand firm against the devil!" cried Goodman Brown.

While he still gazed upward, into the deep arch of the firmament, and had lifted his hands to pray, a cloud, though no wind was stirring, hurried across the zenith, and hid the brightening stars. The blue sky was still visible, except directly overhead, where this black mass of cloud was sweeping swiftly northward. Aloft in the air, as if from the depths of the cloud, came a confused and doubtful sound of voices. Once, the listener fancied that he could distinguish the accents of townspeople of his own, men and women, both pious and ungodly, many of whom he had met at the communion-table, and had seen others rioting at the tavern. The next moment, so indistinct were the sounds, he doubted whether he had heard aught but the murmur of the old forest, whispering without a wind. Then came a stronger swell of those familiar tones, heard daily in the sunshine, at Salem village, but never, until now, from a cloud at night. There was one voice, of a young woman, uttering lamentations, yet with an uncertain sorrow, and entreating for some favor, which, perhaps, it would grieve her to obtain. And all the unseen multitude, both saints and sinners, seemed to encourage her onward.

"Faith!" shouted Goodman Brown, in a voice of agony and desperation; and the echoes of the forest mocked him, crying—"Faith! Faith!" as if bewildered wretches were seeking her, all through the wilderness.

---

[5]Across.
[6]Dared.

The cry of grief, rage, and terror was yet piercing the night, when the unhappy husband held his breath for a response. There was a scream, drowned immediately in a louder murmur of voices fading into far-off laughter, as the dark cloud swept away, leaving the clear and silent sky above Goodman Brown. But something fluttered lightly down through the air, and caught on the branch of a tree. The young man seized it and beheld a pink ribbon.

"My Faith is gone!" cried he, after one stupefied moment. "There is no good on earth, and sin is but a name. Come, devil! for to thee is this world given."

And maddened with despair, so that he laughed loud and long, did Goodman Brown grasp his staff and set forth again, at such a rate, that he seemed to fly along the forest path, rather than to walk or run. The road grew wilder and drearier, and more faintly traced, and vanished at length, leaving him in the heart of the dark wilderness, still rushing onward, with the instinct that guides mortal man to evil. The whole forest was peopled with frightful sounds: the creaking of the trees, the howling of wild beasts, and the yell of Indians; while, sometimes, the wind tolled like a distant church bell, and sometimes gave a broad roar around the traveller, as if all Nature was laughing him to scorn. But he was himself the chief horror of the scene, and shrank not from its other horrors.

"Ha! ha! ha!" roared Goodman Brown, when the wind laughed at him. "Let us hear which will laugh loudest! Think not to frighten me with your deviltry! Come witch, come wizard, come Indian powwow, come devil himself! and here comes Goodman Brown. You may as well fear him as he fear you!"

In truth, all through the haunted forest, there could be nothing more frightful than the figure of Goodman Brown. On he flew, among the black pines, brandishing his staff with frenzied gestures, now giving vent to an inspiration of horrid blasphemy, and now shouting forth such laughter, as set all the echoes of the forest laughing like demons around him. The fiend in his own shape is less hideous, than when he rages in the breast of man. Thus sped the demoniac on his course, until, quivering among the trees, he saw a red light before him, as when the felled trunks and branches of a clearing have been set on fire, and throw up their lurid blaze against the sky, at the hour of midnight. He paused, in a lull of the tempest that had driven him onward, and heard the swell of what seemed a hymn, rolling solemnly from a distance, with the weight of many voices. He knew the tune. It was a familiar one in the choir of the village meeting-house.[7] The verse died heavily away, and was lengthened by a chorus, not of human voices, but of all the sounds of the benighted wilderness, pealing in awful harmony together. Goodman Brown cried out; and his cry was lost to his own ear, by its unison with the cry of the desert.

In the interval of silence, he stole forward, until the light glared full upon his eyes. At one extremity of an open space, hemmed in by the dark wall of the forest, arose a rock, bearing some rude, natural resemblance either to an altar or a pulpit, and surrounded by four blazing pines, their tops aflame, their stems untouched, like candles at an evening meeting. The mass of foliage, that had overgrown the summit of the rock, was all on fire, blazing high into the night, and fitfully illuminating the whole field. Each pendent twig and leafy festoon was in a blaze. As the red light arose and fell, a numerous congregation alternately shone forth, then disappeared in shadow, and again grew, as it were, out of the darkness, peopling the heart of the solitary woods at once.

---

[7]House of worship.

"A grave and dark-clad company!" quoth Goodman Brown.

In truth, they were such. Among them, quivering to-and-fro, between gloom and splendor, appeared faces that would be seen, next day, at the council-board of the province, and others which, Sabbath after Sabbath, looked devoutly heavenward, and benignantly over the crowded pews, from the holiest pulpits in the land. Some affirm, that the lady of the governor was there. At least, there were high dames well known to her, and wives of honored husbands, and widows a great multitude, and ancient maidens, all of excellent repute, and fair young girls, who trembled lest their mothers should espy them. Either the sudden gleams of light, flashing over the obscure field, bedazzled Goodman Brown, or he recognized a score of the church members of Salem village, famous for their especial sanctity. Good old Deacon Gookin had arrived, and waited at the skirts of that venerable saint, his reverend pastor. But, irreverently consorting with these grave, reputable, and pious people, these elders of the church, these chaste dames and dewy virgins, there were men of dissolute lives and women of spotted fame, wretches given over to all mean and filthy vice, and suspected even of horrid crimes. It was strange to see, that the good shrank not from the wicked, nor were the sinners abashed[8] by the saints. Scattered, also, among their pale-faced enemies, were the Indian priests, or powwows, who had often scared their native forest with more hideous incantations than any known to English witchcraft.

"But, where is Faith?" thought Goodman Brown; and, as hope came into his heart, he trembled.

Another verse of the hymn arose, a slow and mournful strain, such as the pious love, but joined to words which expressed all that our nature can conceive of sin, and darkly hinted at far more. Unfathomable to mere mortals is the lore of fiends. Verse after verse was sung, and still the chorus of the desert swelled between, like the deepest tone of a mighty organ. And, with the final peal of that dreadful anthem, there came a sound, as if the roaring wind, the rushing streams, the howling beasts, and every other voice of the unconverted wilderness were mingling and according with the voice of guilty man, in homage to the prince of all. The four blazing pines threw up a loftier flame, and obscurely discovered shapes and visages of horror on the smoke-wreaths, above the impious assembly. At the same moment, the fire on the rock shot redly forth, and formed a glowing arch above its base, where now appeared a figure. With reverence be it spoken, the apparition bore no slight similitude, both in garb and manner, to some grave divine of the New England churches.

"Bring forth the converts!" cried a voice, that echoed through the field and rolled into the forest.

At the word, Goodman Brown stepped forth from the shadow of the trees, and approached the congregation, with whom he felt a loathful[9] brotherhood, by the sympathy of all that was wicked in his heart. He could have well-nigh sworn, that the shape of his own dead father beckoned him to advance, looking downward from a smoke-wreath, while a woman, with dim features of despair, threw out her hand to warn him back. Was it his mother? But he had no power to retreat one step, nor to resist, even in thought, when the minister and good old Deacon Gookin seized his arms, and led him to the blazing rock. Thither came also the slender form of a veiled female, led between Goody Cloyse, that

---

[8]Made ill at ease.
[9]Revolting, disgusting.

pious teacher of the catechism, and Martha Carrier, who had received the devil's promise to be queen of hell. A rampant hag was she! And there stood the proselytes, beneath the canopy of fire.

"Welcome, my children," said the dark figure, "to the communion of your race! Ye have found, thus young, your nature and your destiny. My children, look behind you!"

They turned; and flashing forth, as it were, in a sheet of flame, the fiend-worshippers were seen; the smile of welcome gleamed darkly on every visage.

"There," resumed the sable form, "are all whom ye have reverenced from youth. Ye deemed them holier than yourselves, and shrank from your own sin, contrasting it with their lives of righteousness and prayerful aspirations heavenward. Yet, here are they all, in my worshipping assembly! This night it shall be granted you to know their secret deeds; how hoary-bearded[10] elders of the church have whispered wanton words to the young maids of their households; how many a woman, eager for widow's weeds, has given her husband a drink at bedtime, and let him sleep his last sleep in her bosom; how beardless youths have made haste to inherit their father's wealth; and how fair damsels—blush not, sweet ones!—have dug little graves in the garden, and bidden me, the sole guest, to an infant's funeral. By the sympathy of your human hearts for sin, ye shall scent out all the places—whether in church, bed-chamber, street, field, or forest—where crime has been committed, and shall exult to behold the whole earth one stain of guilt, one mighty blood-spot. Far more than this! It shall be yours to penetrate, in every bosom, the deep mystery of sin, the fountain of all wicked arts, and which inexhaustibly supplies more evil impulses than human power—than my power, at its utmost!—can make manifest in deeds. And now, my children, look upon each other."

They did so; and, by the blaze of the hell-kindled torches, the wretched man beheld his Faith, and the wife her husband, trembling before that unhallowed altar.

"Lo! there ye stand, my children," said the figure, in a deep and solemn tone, almost sad, with its despairing awfulness, as if his once angelic nature could yet mourn for our miserable race. "Depending upon one another's hearts, ye had still hoped that virtue were not all a dream! Now are ye undeceived!—Evil is the nature of mankind. Evil must be your only happiness. Welcome, again, my children, to the communion of your race!"

"Welcome!" repeated the fiend-worshippers, in one cry of despair and triumph.

And there they stood, the only pair, as it seemed, who were yet hesitating on the verge of wickedness, in this dark world. A basin was hollowed, naturally, in the rock. Did it contain water, reddened by the lurid light? or was it blood? or, perchance, a liquid flame? Herein did the Shape of Evil dip his hand, and prepare to lay the mark of baptism upon their foreheads, that they might be partakers of the mystery of sin, more conscious of the secret guilt of others, both in deed and thought, than they could now be of their own. The husband cast one look at his pale wife, and Faith at him. What polluted wretches would the next glance show them to each other, shuddering alike at what they disclosed and what they saw!

"Faith! Faith!" cried the husband. "Look up to Heaven, and resist the Wicked One!"

---

[10] White- or grey-bearded.

Whether Faith obeyed, he knew not. Hardly had he spoken, when he found himself amid calm night and solitude, listening to a roar of the wind, which died heavily away through the forest. He staggered against the rock, and felt it chill and damp, while a hanging twig, that had been all on fire, besprinkled his cheek with the coldest dew.

The next morning, young Goodman Brown came slowly into the street of Salem village staring around him like a bewildered man. The good old minister was taking a walk along the grave-yard, to get an appetite for breakfast and meditate his sermon, and bestowed a blessing, as he passed, on Goodman Brown. He shrank from the venerable saint, as if to avoid an anathema. Old Deacon Gookin was at domestic worship, and the holy words of his prayer were heard through the open window. "What God doth the wizard pray to?" quoth Goodman Brown. Goody Cloyse, that excellent old Christian, stood in the early sunshine, at her own lattice, catechising a little girl, who had brought her a pint of morning's milk. Goodman Brown snatched away the child, as from the grasp of the fiend himself. Turning the corner by the meeting-house, he spied the head of Faith, with the pink ribbons, gazing anxiously forth, and bursting into such joy at sight of him that she skipt along the street, and almost kissed her husband before the whole village. But Goodman Brown looked sternly and sadly into her face, and passed on without a greeting.

Had Goodman Brown fallen asleep in the forest, and only dreamed a wild dream of a witch-meeting?

Be it so, if you will. But, alas! it was a dream of evil omen for young Goodman Brown. A stern, a sad, a darkly meditative, a distrustful, if not a desperate man did he become, from the night of that fearful dream. On the Sabbath day, when the congregation were singing a holy psalm, he could not listen, because an anthem of sin rushed loudly upon his ear, and drowned all the blessed strain. When the minister spoke from the pulpit, with power and fervid eloquence, and with his hand on the open Bible, of the sacred truths of our religion, and of saint-like lives and triumphant deaths, and of future bliss or misery unutterable, then did Goodman Brown turn pale, dreading lest the roof should thunder down upon the gray blasphemer and his hearers. Often, awaking suddenly at midnight, he shrank from the bosom of Faith, and at morning or eventide, when the family knelt down at prayer, he scowled, and muttered to himself, and gazed sternly at his wife, and turned away. And when he had lived long, and was borne to his grave, a hoary corpse, followed by Faith, an aged woman, and children and grand-children, a goodly procession, besides neighbors not a few, they carved no hopeful verse upon his tombstone; for his dying hour was gloom.

(1835)

Kate Chopin   1851–1904

The Story of an Hour

Knowing that Mrs. Mallard was afflicted with a heart trouble, great care was taken to break to her as gently as possible the news of her husband's death.

It was her sister Josephine who told her, in broken sentences; veiled hints that revealed in half concealing. Her husband's friend Richards was there, too, near her. It was he who had been in the newspaper office when intelligence of the railroad disaster was received, with Brently Mallard's name leading the list of "killed." He had only taken the time to assure himself of its truth by a second telegram, and had hastened to forestall any less careful, less tender friend in bearing the sad message.

She did not hear the story as many women have heard the same, with a paralyzed inability to accept its significance. She wept at once, with sudden, wild abandonment, in her sister's arms. When the storm of grief had spent itself she went away to her room alone. She would have no one follow her.

There stood, facing the open window, a comfortable, roomy armchair. Into this she sank, pressed down by a physical exhaustion that haunted her body and seemed to reach into her soul.

She could see in the open square before her house the tops of trees that were all aquiver with the new spring life. The delicious breath of rain was in the air. In the street below a peddler was crying his wares. The notes of a distant song which some one was singing reached her faintly, and countless sparrows were twittering in the eaves.

There were patches of blue sky showing here and there through the clouds that had met and piled one above the other in the west facing her window.

She sat with her head thrown back upon the cushion of the chair, quite motionless, except when a sob came up into her throat and shook her, as a child who has cried itself to sleep continues to sob in its dreams.

She was young, with a fair, calm face, whose lines bespoke repression and even a certain strength. But now there was a dull stare in her eyes, whose gaze was fixed away off yonder on one of those patches of blue sky. It was not a glance of reflection, but rather indicated a suspension of intelligent thought.

There was something coming to her and she was waiting for it, fearfully. What was it? She did not know; it was too subtle and elusive to name. But she felt it, creeping out of the sky, reaching toward her through the sounds, the scents, the color that filled the air.

Now her bosom rose and fell tumultuously. She was beginning to recognize this thing that was approaching to possess her, and she was striving to beat it back with her will—as powerless as her two white slender hands would have been.

When she abandoned herself a little whispered word escaped her slightly parted lips. She said it over and over under her breath: "free, free, free!" The vacant stare and the look of terror that had followed it went from her eyes. They stayed keen and bright. Her pulses beat fast, and the coursing blood warmed and relaxed every inch of her body.

She did not stop to ask if it were or were not a monstrous joy that held her. A clear and exalted perception enabled her to dismiss the suggestion as trivial.

She knew that she would weep again when she saw the kind, tender hands folded in death; the face that had never looked save with love upon her, fixed and gray and dead. But she saw beyond that bitter moment a long procession of years to come that would belong to her absolutely. And she opened and spread her arms out to them in welcome.

There would be no one to live for her during those coming years; she would live for herself. There would be no powerful will bending hers in that blind persistence with which men and women believe they have a right to impose a private will upon a fellow-creature. A kind intention or a cruel intention made the act seem no less a crime as she looked upon it in that brief moment of illumination.

And yet she had loved him—sometimes. Often she had not. What did it matter! What could love, the unsolved mystery, count for in face of this possession of self-assertion which she suddenly recognized as the strongest impulse of her being!

"Free! Body and soul free!" she kept whispering.

Josephine was kneeling before the closed door with her lips to the keyhole, imploring for admission. "Louise, open the door! I beg; open the door—you will make yourself ill. What are you doing, Louise? For heaven's sake open the door."

"Go away. I am not making myself ill." No; she was drinking in a very elixir of life through that open window.

Her fancy was running riot along those days ahead of her. Spring days, and summer days, and all sorts of days that would be her own. She breathed a quick prayer that life might be long. It was only yesterday she had thought with a shudder that life might be long.

She arose at length and opened the door to her sister's importunities. There was a feverish triumph in her eyes, and she carried herself unwittingly like a goddess of Victory. She clasped her sister's waist, and together they descended the stairs. Richards stood waiting for them at the bottom.

Some one was opening the front door with a latchkey. It was Brently Mallard who entered, a little travel-stained, composedly carrying his grip-sack and umbrella. He had been far from the scene of accident, and did not even know there had been one. He stood amazed at Josephine's piercing cry; at Richards' quick motion to screen him from the view of his wife.

But Richards was too late.

When the doctors came they said she had died of heart disease—of joy that kills.

(1894)

Willa Cather   1873–1947

Paul's Case

It was Paul's afternoon to appear before the faculty of the Pittsburgh High School to account for his various misdemeanors. He had been suspended a week ago, and his father had called at the Principal's office and confessed his perplexity about his son. Paul entered the faculty room suave and smiling. His clothes were a trifle outgrown and the tan velvet on the collar of his open overcoat was frayed and worn; but for all that there was something of the dandy about him, and he wore an opal pin in his neatly knotted black four-in-hand, and a red carnation in his buttonhole. This latter adornment the faculty somehow felt was not properly significant of the contrite spirit befitting a boy under the ban of suspension.

Paul was tall for his age and very thin, with high, cramped shoulders and a narrow chest. His eyes were remarkable for a certain hysterical brilliancy and he continually used them in a conscious, theatrical sort of way, peculiarly offensive in a boy. The pupils were abnormally large, as though he were addicted to belladonna,[1] but there was a glassy glitter about them which that drug does not produce.

When questioned by the Principal as to why he was there, Paul stated, politely enough, that he wanted to come back to school. This was a lie, but Paul was quite accustomed to lying; found it, indeed, indispensable for overcoming friction. His teachers were asked to state their respective charges against him, which they did with such a rancor and aggrievedness as evinced that this was not a usual case. Disorder and impertinence were among the offences named, yet each of his instructors felt that it was scarcely possible to put into words the real cause of the trouble, which lay in a sort of hysterically defiant manner of the boy's; in the contempt which they all knew he felt for them, and which he seemingly made not the least effort to conceal. Once, when he had been making a synopsis of a paragraph at the blackboard, his English teacher had stepped to his side and attempted to guide his hand. Paul had started back with a shudder and thrust his hands violently behind him. The astonished woman could scarcely have been more hurt and embarrassed had he struck at her. The insult was so involuntary and definitely personal as to be unforgettable. In one way and another, he had made all his teachers, men and women alike, conscious of the same feeling of physical aversion. In one class he habitually sat with his hand shading his eyes; in another he always looked out of the window during the recitation; in another he made a running commentary on the lecture, with humorous intention.

His teachers felt this afternoon that his whole attitude was symbolized by his shrug and his flippantly red carnation flower, and they fell upon him without mercy, his English teacher leading the pack. He stood through it smiling, his pale lips parted over his white teeth. (His lips were continually twitching, and he had a habit of raising his eyebrows that was contemptuous and irritating to the last degree.) Older boys than Paul had broken down and shed tears under that baptism of fire, but his set smile did not once desert him, and his only sign of discomfort was the nervous trembling of the fingers that toyed with the buttons of his overcoat, and an occasional jerking of the other hand which held his hat.

---

[1] Atropine, a drug that dilates the pupils.

Paul was always smiling, always glancing about him, seeming to feel that people might be watching him and trying to detect something. This conscious expression, since it was as far as possible from boyish mirthfulness, was usually attributed to insolence or "smartness."

As the inquisition proceeded, one of his instructors repeated an impertinent remark of the boy's, and the Principal asked him whether he thought that a courteous speech to have made to a woman. Paul shrugged his shoulders slightly and his eyebrows twitched.

"I don't know," he replied. "I didn't mean to be polite or impolite, either. I guess it's a sort of way I have of saying things regardless."

The Principal, who was a sympathetic man, asked him whether he didn't think that a way it would be well to get rid of. Paul grinned and said he guessed so. When he was told that he could go, he bowed gracefully and went out. His bow was like a repetition of the scandalous red carnation.

His teachers were in despair, and his drawing master voiced the feeling of them all when he declared there was something about the boy which none of them understood. He added: "I don't really believe that smile of his comes altogether from insolence; there's something sort of haunted about it. I happen to know that he was born in Colorado, only a few months before his mother died out there of a long illness. The boy is not strong, for one thing. There is something wrong about the fellow."

The drawing master had come to realize that, in looking at Paul, one saw only his white teeth and the forced animation of his eyes. One warm afternoon the boy had gone to sleep at his drawing-board, and his master had noted with amazement what a white, blue-veined face it was; drawn and wrinkled like an old man's about the eyes, the lips twitching even in his sleep, and stiff with a nervous tension that drew them back from his teeth.

His teachers left the building dissatisfied and unhappy; humiliated to have felt so vindictive toward a mere boy, to have uttered this feeling in cutting terms, and to have set each other on, as it were, in the gruesome game of intemperate reproach. Some of them remembered having seen a miserable street cat set at bay by a ring of tormentors.

As for Paul, he ran down the hill whistling the Soldiers' Chorus from *Faust* looking wildly behind him now and then to see whether some of his teachers were not there to writhe under this light-heartedness. As it was now late in the afternoon and Paul was on duty that evening as usher at Carnegie Hall, he decided that he would not go home to supper. When he reached the concert hall the doors were not yet open. It was chilly outside, and he decided to go up into the picture gallery—always deserted at this hour—where there were some of Raffelli's gay studies of Paris streets and an airy blue Venetian scene or two that always exhilarated him. He was delighted to find no one in the gallery but the old guard, who sat in the corner, a newspaper on his knee, a black patch over one eye and the other closed. Paul possessed himself of the place and walked confidently up and down, whistling under his breath. After a while he sat down before a blue Rico and lost himself. When he bethought him to look at his watch, it was after seven o'clock, and he rose with a start and ran downstairs, making a face at Augustus, peering out from the cast-room, and an evil gesture at the Venus of Milo as he passed her on the stairway.

When Paul reached the ushers' dressing-room half-a-dozen boys were there already, and he began excitedly to tumble into his uniform. It was one of the few that at all approached fitting, and Paul thought it very becoming—

though he knew the tight, straight coat accentuated his narrow chest, about which he was exceedingly sensitive. He was always considerably excited while he dressed, twanging all over to the tuning of the strings and the preliminary flourishes of the horns in the music-room; but to-night he seemed quite beside himself, and he teased and plagued the boys until, telling him that he was crazy, they put him down on the floor and sat on him.

Somewhat calmed by his suppression, Paul dashed out to the front of the house to seat the early comers. He was a model usher; gracious and smiling he ran up and down the aisles; nothing was too much trouble for him; he carried messages and brought programs as though it were his greatest pleasure in life, and all the people in his section thought him a charming boy, feeling that he remembered and admired them. As the house filled, he grew more and more vivacious and animated, and the color came to his cheeks and lips. It was very much as though this were a great reception and Paul were the host. Just as the musicians came out to take their places, his English teacher arrived with checks for the seats which a prominent manufacturer had taken for the season. She betrayed some embarrassment when she handed Paul the tickets, and a *hauteur*[2] which subsequently made her feel very foolish. Paul was startled for a moment, and had the feeling of wanting to put her out; what business had she here among all these fine people and gay colors? He looked her over and decided that she was not appropriately dressed and must be a fool to sit downstairs in such togs. The tickets had probably been sent her out of kindness, he reflected as he put down a seat for her, and she had about as much right to sit there as he had.

When the symphony began Paul sank into one of the rear seats with a long sigh of relief, and lost himself as he had done before the Rico. It was not that symphonies, as such, meant anything in particular to Paul, but the first sigh of the instruments seemed to free some hilarious and potent spirit within him; something that struggled there like the Geni in the bottle found by the Arab fisherman. He felt a sudden zest of life; the lights danced before his eyes and the concert hall blazed into unimaginable splendor. When the soprano soloist came on, Paul forgot even the nastiness of his teacher's being there and gave himself up to the peculiar stimulus such personages always had for him. The soloist chanced to be a German woman, by no means in her first youth, and the mother of many children; but she wore an elaborate gown and a tiara, and above all she had that indefinable air of achievement, that world-shine upon her, which, in Paul's eyes, made her a veritable queen of Romance.

After a concert was over Paul was often irritable and wretched until he got to sleep, and tonight he was even more than usually restless. He had the feeling of not being able to let down, of its being impossible to give up this delicious excitement which was the only thing that could be called living at all. During the last number he withdrew and, after hastily changing his clothes in the dressing-room, slipped out to the side door where the soprano's carriage stood. Here he began pacing rapidly up and down the walk, waiting to see her come out.

Over yonder the Schenley, in its vacant stretch, loomed big and square through the fine rain, the windows of its twelve stories glowing like those of a lighted cardboard house under a Christmas tree. All the actors and singers of any better class stayed there when they were in the city, and a number of the big

---

[2]Haughtiness, disdain.

manufacturers of the place lived there in the winter. Paul had often hung about the hotel, watching the people go in and out, longing to enter and leave schoolmasters and dull care behind him forever.

At last the singer came out, accompanied by the conductor, who helped her into her carriage and closed the door with a cordial *auf wiedersehen*,[3] which set Paul to wondering whether she were not an old sweetheart of his. Paul followed the carriage over to the hotel, walking so rapidly as not to be far from the entrance when the singer alighted and disappeared behind the swinging glass doors which were opened by a negro in a tall hat and a long coat. In the moment that the door was ajar it seemed to Paul that he, too, entered. He seemed to feel himself go after her up the steps, into the warm, lighted building, into an exotic, a tropical world of shiny, glistening surfaces and basking ease. He reflected upon the mysterious dishes that were brought into the dining-room, the green bottles in buckets of ice, as he had seen them in the supper party pictures of the *Sunday World* supplement. A quick gust of wind brought the rain down with sudden vehemence, and Paul was startled to find that he was still outside in the slush of the gravel driveway; that his boots were letting in the water and his scanty overcoat was clinging wet about him; that the lights in front of the concert hall were out, and that the rain was driving in sheets between him and the orange glow of the windows above him. There it was, what he wanted—tangibly before him, like the fairy world of a Christmas pantomime, but mocking spirits stood guard at the doors, and, as the rain beat in his face, Paul wondered whether he were destined always to shiver in the black night outside, looking up at it.

He turned and walked reluctantly toward the car tracks. The end had to come sometime; his father in his night-clothes at the top of the stairs, explanations that did not explain, hastily improvised fictions that were forever tripping him up, his upstairs room and its horrible yellow wall-paper, the creaking bureau with the greasy plush collar-box, and over his painted wooden bed the pictures of George Washington and John Calvin, and the framed motto, "Feed my Lambs," which had been worked in red worsted by his mother.

Half an hour later, Paul alighted from his car and went slowly down one of the side streets off the main thoroughfare. It was a highly respectable street, where all the houses were exactly alike, and where businessmen of moderate means begot and reared large families of children, all of whom went to Sabbath-school and learned the shorter catechism, and were interested in arithmetic; all of whom were as exactly alike as their homes, and of a piece with the monotony in which they lived. Paul never went up Cordelia Street without a shudder of loathing. His home was next to the house of the Cumberland minister. He approached it tonight with the nerveless sense of defeat, the hopeless feeling of sinking back forever into ugliness and commonness that he had always had when he came home. The moment he turned into Cordelia Street he felt the waters close above his head. After each of these orgies of living, he experienced all the physical depression which follows a debauch; the loathing of respectable beds, of common food, of a house permeated by kitchen odors; a shuddering repulsion for the flavorless, colorless mass of everyday existence; a morbid desire for cool things and soft lights and fresh flowers.

The nearer he approached the house, the more absolutely unequal Paul felt to the sight of it all; his ugly sleeping chamber; the cold bathroom with the

---

[3] "Goodbye" in German.

grimy zinc tub, the cracked mirror, the dripping spiggots;[4] his father, at the top of the stairs, his hairy legs sticking out from his night-shirt, his feet thrust into carpet slippers. He was so much later than usual that there would certainly be inquiries and reproaches. Paul stopped short before the door. He felt that he could not be accosted by his father tonight; that he could not toss again on that miserable bed. He would not go in. He would tell his father that he had no car fare, and it was raining so hard he had gone home with one of the boys and stayed all night.

Meanwhile, he was wet and cold. He went around to the back of the house and tried one of the basement windows, found it open, raised it cautiously, and scrambled down the cellar wall to the floor. There he stood, holding his breath, terrified by the noise he had made, but the floor above him was silent, and there was no creak on the stairs. He found a soap-box, and carried it over to the soft ring of light that streamed from the furnace door, and sat down. He was horribly afraid of rats, so he did not try to sleep, but sat looking distrustfully at the dark, still terrified lest he might have awakened his father. In such reactions, after one of the experiences which made days and nights out of the dreary blanks of the calendar, when his senses were deadened, Paul's head was always singularly clear. Suppose his father had heard him getting in at the window and had come down and shot him for a burglar? Then, again, suppose his father had come down, pistol in hand, and he had cried out in time to save himself, and his father had been horrified to think how nearly he had killed him? Then, again, suppose a day should come when his father would remember that night, and wish there had been no warning cry to stay his hand? With this last supposition Paul entertained himself until daybreak.

The following Sunday was fine; the sodden November chill was broken by the last flash of autumnal summer. In the morning Paul had to go to church and Sabbath-school, as always. On seasonable Sunday afternoons the burghers of Cordelia Street usually sat out on their front "stoops," and talked to their neighbors on the next stoop, or called to those across the street in neighborly fashion. The men sat placidly on gay cushions placed upon the steps that led down to the sidewalk, while the women, in their Sunday "waists," sat in rockers on the cramped porches, pretending to be greatly at their ease. The children played in the streets; there were so many of them that the place resembled the recreation grounds of a kindergarten. The men on the steps—all in their shirt sleeves, their vests unbuttoned—sat with their legs well apart, their stomachs comfortably protruding, and talked of the prices of things, or told anecdotes of the sagacity of their various chiefs and overlords. They occasionally looked over the multitude of squabbling children, listened affectionately to their high-pitched, nasal voices, smiling to see their own proclivities reproduced in their offspring, and interspersed their legends of the iron kings[5] with remarks about their sons' progress at school, their grades in arithmetic, and the amounts they had saved in their toy banks.

On this last Sunday of November, Paul sat all the afternoon on the lowest step of his "stoop," staring into the street, while his sisters, in their rockers, were talking to the minister's daughters next door about how many shirt-waists they had made in the last week, and how many waffles someone had eaten at the last church supper. When the weather was warm, and his father was in a particu-

---

[4]Faucets.
[5]Men who made huge fortunes in iron and steel.

larly jovial frame of mind, the girls made lemonade, which was always brought out in a red-glass pitcher, ornamented with forget-me-nots in blue enamel. This the girls thought very fine, and the neighbors joked about the suspicious color of the pitcher.

Today Paul's father sat on the top step, talking to a young man who shifted a restless baby from knee to knee. He happened to be the young man who was daily held up to Paul as a model, and after whom it was his father's dearest hope that he would pattern. This young man was of a ruddy complexion, with a compressed, red mouth, and faded, near-sighted eyes, over which he wore thick spectacles, with gold bows that curved about his ears. He was clerk to one of the magnates of a great steel corporation, and was looked upon in Cordelia Street as a young man with a future. There was a story that, some five years ago—he was now barely twenty-six—he had been a trifle dissipated but in order to curb his appetites and save the loss of time and strength that a sowing of wild oats might have entailed, he had taken his chief's advice, oft reiterated to his employees, and at twenty-one had married the first woman whom he could persuade to share his fortunes. She happened to be an angular school-mistress, much older than he, who also wore thick glasses, and who had now borne him four children, all near-sighted, like herself.

The young man was relating how his chief, now cruising in the Mediterranean, kept in touch with all the details of the business; arranging his office hours on his yacht just as though he were at home, and "knocking off work enough to keep two stenographers busy." His father told, in turn, the plan his corporation was considering, of putting in an electric railway plant at Cairo. Paul snapped his teeth; he had an awful apprehension that they might spoil it all before he got there. Yet he rather liked to hear these legends of the iron kings, that were told and retold on Sundays and holidays; these stories of palaces in Venice, yachts on the Mediterranean, and high play[6] at Monte Carlo appealed to his fancy, and he was interested in the triumphs of cash boys who had become famous, though he had no mind for the cash-boy stage.

After supper was over, and he had helped to dry the dishes, Paul nervously asked his father whether he could go to George's to get some help in his geometry, and still more nervously asked for car fare. This latter request he had to repeat, as his father, on principle, did not like to hear requests for money, whether much or little. He asked Paul whether he could not go to some boy who lived nearer, and told him that he ought not to leave his school work until Sunday; but he gave him the dime. He was not a poor man, but he had a worthy ambition to come up in the world. His only reason for allowing Paul to usher was, that he thought a boy ought to be earning a little.

Paul bounded upstairs, scrubbed the greasy odor of the dish-water from his hands with the ill-smelling soap he hated, and then shook over his fingers a few drops of violet water from the bottle he kept hidden in his drawer. He left the house with his geometry conspicuously under his arm, and the moment he got out of Cordelia Street and boarded a downtown car, he shook off the lethargy of two deadening days, and began to live again.

The leading juvenile[7] of the permanent stock company which played at one of the downtown theatres was an acquaintance of Paul's, and the boy had been invited to drop in at the Sunday-night rehearsals whenever he could. For more

---

[6]Gambling in the casinos.
[7]Youthful actor.

than a year Paul had spent every available moment loitering about Charley Edwards's dressing-room. He had won a place among Edwards's following not only because the young actor, who could not afford to employ a dresser, often found him useful, but because he recognized in Paul something akin to what churchmen term "vocation."

It was at the theatre and at Carnegie Hall that Paul really lived; the rest was but a sleep and a forgetting. This was Paul's fairy tale, and it had for him all the allurement of a secret love. The moment he inhaled the gassy, painty, dusty odor behind the scenes, he breathed like a prisoner set free, and felt within him the possibility of doing or saying splendid, brilliant, poetic things. The moment the cracked orchestra beat out the overture from *Martha*, or jerked at the serenade from *Rigoletto*, all stupid and ugly things slid from him, and his senses were deliciously, yet delicately fired.

Perhaps it was because, in Paul's world, the natural nearly always wore the guise of ugliness, that a certain element of artificiality seemed to him necessary in beauty. Perhaps it was because his experience of life elsewhere was so full of Sabbath-school picnics, petty economies, wholesome advice as to how to succeed in life, and the unescapable odors of cooking, that he found this existence so alluring, these smartly-clad men and women so attractive, that he was so moved by these starry apple orchards that bloomed perennially under the lime-light.

It would be difficult to put it strongly enough how convincingly the stage entrance of that theatre was for Paul the actual portal of Romance. Certainly none of the company ever suspected it, least of all Charley Edwards. It was very like the old stories that used to float about London of fabulously rich Jews, who had subterranean halls there, with palms, and fountains, and soft lamps and richly apparelled women who never saw the disenchanting light of London day. So, in the midst of that smoke-palled city, enamoured of figures and grimy toil, Paul had his secret temple, his wishing carpet, his bit of blue-and-white Mediterranean shore bathed in perpetual sunshine.

Several of Paul's teachers had a theory that his imagination had been perverted by garish fiction, but the truth was that he scarcely ever read at all. The books at home were not such as would either tempt or corrupt a youthful mind, and as for reading the novels that some of his friends urged upon him—well, he got what he wanted much more quickly from music; any sort of music, from an orchestra to a barrel organ. He needed only the spark, the indescribable thrill that made his imagination master of his senses, and he could make plots and pictures enough of his own. It was equally true that he was not stage-struck—not, at any rate, in the usual acceptation of that expression. He had no desire to become an actor, any more than he had to become a musician. He felt no necessity to do any of these things; what he wanted was to see, to be in the atmosphere, float on the wave of it, to be carried out, blue league[8] after blue league, away from everything.

After a night behind the scenes, Paul found the school-room more than ever repulsive; the bare floors and naked walls; the prosy men who never wore frock coats, or violets in their buttonholes; the women with their dull gowns, shrill voices, and pitiful seriousness about prepositions that govern the dative. He could not bear to have the other pupils think, for a moment, that he took these people seriously; he must convey to them that he considered it all trivial, and was there only by way of a jest, anyway. He had autographed pictures of all the mem-

---

[8]About three nautical miles.

bers of the stock company which he showed his classmates, telling them the most incredible stories of his familiarity with these people, of his acquaintance with the soloists who came to Carnegie Hall, his suppers with them and the flowers he sent them. When these stories lost their effect, and his audience grew listless, he became desperate and would bid all the boys good-bye, announcing that he was going to travel for a while; going to Naples, to Venice, to Egypt. Then, next Monday, he would slip back, conscious and nervously smiling; his sister was ill, and he would have to defer his voyage until spring.

Matters went steadily worse with Paul at school. In the itch to let his instructors know how heartily he despised them and their homilies, and how thoroughly he was appreciated elsewhere, he mentioned once or twice that he had no time to fool with theorems; adding—with a twitch of the eyebrows and a touch of that nervous bravado which so perplexed them—that he was helping the people down at the stock company; they were old friends of his.

The upshot of the matter was that the Principal went to Paul's father, and Paul was taken out of school and put to work. The manager at Carnegie Hall was told to get another usher in his stead; the door-keeper at the theatre was warned not to admit him to the house; and Charley Edwards remorsefully promised the boy's father not to see him again.

The members of the stock company were vastly amused when some of Paul's stories reached them—especially the women. They were hard-working women, most of them supporting indigent husbands or brothers, and they laughed rather bitterly at having stirred the boy to such fervid and florid inventions. They agreed with the faculty and with his father that Paul's was a bad case.

The east-bound train was ploughing through a January snow-storm; the dull dawn was beginning to show grey when the engine whistled a mile out of Newark. Paul started up from the seat where he had lain curled in uneasy slumber, rubbed the breath-misted window glass with his hand, and peered out. The snow was whirling in curling eddies above the white bottom lands, and the drifts lay already deep in the fields and along the fences, while here and there the long dead grass and dried weed stalks protruded black above it. Lights shone from the scattered houses, and a gang of laborers who stood beside the track waved their lanterns.

Paul had slept very little, and he felt grimy and uncomfortable. He had made the all-night journey in a day coach, partly because he was ashamed, dressed as he was, to go into a Pullman, and partly because he was afraid of being seen by some Pittsburgh businessman, who might have noticed him in Denny & Carson's office. When the whistle woke him, he clutched quickly at his breast pocket, glancing about him with an uncertain smile. But the little, clay-bespattered Italians were still sleeping, the slatternly women across the aisle were in open-mouthed oblivion, and even the crumby, crying babies were for the nonce stilled. Paul settled back to struggle with his impatience as best he could.

When he arrived at the Jersey City station, he hurried through his breakfast, manifestly ill at ease and keeping a sharp eye about him. After he reached the Twenty-third Street station, he consulted a cabman, and had himself driven to a men's furnishing establishment which was just opening for the day. He spent upward of two hours there, buying with endless reconsidering and great care. His new street suit he put on in the fitting-room; the frock coat and dress clothes he had bundled into the cab with his linen. Then he drove to a hatter's and a shoe house. His next errand was at Tiffany's, where he selected his silver and a new scarf-pin. He would not wait to have his silver mounted brushes marked, he said.

Lastly, he stopped at a trunk shop on Broadway, and had his purchases packed into various traveling bags.

It was a little after one o'clock when he drove up to the Waldorf, and, after settling with the cabman, went into the office. He registered from Washington; said his mother and father had been abroad, and that he had come down to await the arrival of their steamer. He told his story plausibly and had no trouble, since he volunteered to pay for them in advance, in engaging his rooms; a sleeping-room, sitting-room and bath.

Not once, but a hundred times Paul had planned this entry into New York. He had gone over every detail of it with Charley Edwards, and in his scrap book at home there were pages of description about New York hotels, cut from the Sunday papers. When he was shown to his sitting-room on the eighth floor, he saw at a glance that everything was as it should be; there was but one detail in his mental picture that the place did not realize, so he rang for the bell boy and sent him down for flowers. He moved about nervously until the boy returned, putting away his new linen and fingering it delightedly as he did so. When the flowers came, he put them hastily into water, and then tumbled into a hot bath. Presently he came out of his white bath-room, resplendent in his new silk underwear, and playing with the tassels of his red robe. The snow was whirling so fiercely outside his windows that he could scarcely see across the street; but within, the air was deliciously soft and fragrant. He put the violets and jonquils on the tabouret[9] beside the couch, and threw himself down, with a long sigh, covering himself with a Roman blanket. He was thoroughly tired; he had been in such haste, he had stood up to such a strain, covered so much ground in the last twenty-four hours, that he wanted to think how it had all come about. Lulled by the sound of the wind, the warm air, and the cool fragrance of the flowers, he sank into deep, drowsy retrospection.

It had been wonderfully simple; when they had shut him out of the theatre and concert hall, when they had taken away his bone, the whole thing was virtually determined. The rest was a mere matter of opportunity. The only thing that at all surprised him was his own courage—for he realized well enough that he had always been tormented by fear, a sort of apprehensive dread that, of late years, as the meshes of the lies he had told closed about him, had been pulling the muscles of his body tighter and tighter. Until now, he could not remember a time when he had not been dreading something. Even when he was a little boy, it was always there—behind him, or before, or on either side. There had always been the shadowed corner, the dark place into which he dared not look, but from which something seemed always to be watching him—and Paul had done things that were not pretty to watch, he knew.

But now he had a curious sense of relief, as though he had at last thrown down the gauntlet to the thing in the corner.

Yet it was but a day since he had been sulking in the traces; but yesterday afternoon that he had been sent to the bank with Denny & Carson's deposit, as usual—but this time he was instructed to leave the book to be balanced. There was above two thousand dollars in checks, and nearly a thousand in the bank notes which he had taken from the book and quietly transferred to his pocket. At the bank he had made out a new deposit slip. His nerves had been steady enough to permit of his returning to the office, where he had finished his work and asked for a full day's holiday tomorrow, Saturday, giving a perfectly reason-

---

[9]A small table.

able pretext. The bank book, he knew, would not be returned before Monday or Tuesday, and his father would be out of town for the next week. From the time he slipped the bank notes into his pocket until he boarded the night train for New York, he had not known a moment's hesitation. It was not the first time Paul had steered through treacherous waters.

How astonishingly easy it had all been; here he was, the thing done; and this time there would be no awakening, no figure at the top of the stairs. He watched the snow flakes whirling by his window until he fell asleep.

When he awoke, it was four o'clock in the afternoon. He bounded up with a start; one of his precious days gone already! He spent nearly an hour in dressing, watching every stage of his toilet carefully in the mirror. Everything was quite perfect; he was exactly the kind of boy he had always wanted to be.

When he went downstairs, Paul took a carriage and drove up Fifth Avenue toward the Park. The snow had somewhat abated; carriages and tradesmen's wagons were hurrying soundlessly to and fro in the winter twilight; boys in woollen mufflers were shoveling off the doorsteps; the avenue stages made fine spots of color against the white street. Here and there on the corners were stands, with whole flower gardens blooming under glass cases, against the sides of which the snow flakes stuck and melted; violets, roses, carnations, lilies of the valley—somewhat vastly more lovely and alluring that they blossomed thus unnaturally in the snow. The Park itself was a wonderful stage winterpiece.

When he returned, the pause of the twilight had ceased, and the tune of the streets had changed. The snow was falling faster, lights streamed from the hotels that reared their dozen stories fearlessly up into the storm, defying the raging Atlantic winds. A long, black stream of carriages poured down the avenue, intersected here and there by other streams, tending horizontally. There were a score of cabs about the entrance of his hotel, and his driver had to wait. Boys in livery were running in and out of the awning stretched across the sidewalk, up and down the red velvet carpet laid from the door to the street. Above, about, within it all was the rumble and roar, the hurry and toss of thousands of human beings as hot for pleasure as himself, and on every side of him towered the glaring affirmation of the omnipotence of wealth.

The boy set his teeth and drew his shoulders together in a spasm of realization; the plot of all dramas, the text of all romances, the nerve-stuff of all sensations was whirling about him like the snow flakes. He burnt like a faggot in a tempest.

When Paul came down to dinner, the music of the orchestra floated up the elevator shaft to greet him. His head whirled as he stepped into the thronged corridor, he sank back into one of the chairs against the wall to get his breath. The lights, the chatter, the perfumes, the bewildering medley of color—he had, for a moment, the feeling of not being able to stand it. But only for a moment; these were his own people, he told himself. He went slowly about the corridors, through the writing-rooms, smoking-rooms, reception-rooms, as though he were exploring the chambers of an enchanted palace, built and peopled for him alone.

When he reached the dining-room he sat down at a table near a window. The flowers, the white linen, the many-colored wine glasses, the gay toilettes of the women, the low popping of corks, the undulating repetitions of the *Blue Danube* from the orchestra, all flooded Paul's dream with bewildering radiance. When the roseate tinge of his champagne was added—that cold, precious, bubbling stuff that creamed and foamed in his glass—Paul wondered that there were honest men in the world at all. This was what all the world was fighting for, he reflected; this was what all the struggle was about. He doubted the reality of his past. Had he ever known a place called Cordelia Street, a place where fagged-looking businessmen got on the early car; mere rivets in a machine they seemed to Paul—sickening men, with combings of children's hair always hanging to their coats, and the smell of cooking in their clothes. Cordelia Street—Ah! that belonged to another time and country; had he not always been thus, had he not sat here night after night, from as far back as he could remember, looking pensively over just such shimmering textures, and slowly twirling the stem of a glass like this one between his thumb and middle finger? He rather thought he had.

He was not in the least abashed or lonely. He had no especial desire to meet or to know any of these people; all he demanded was the right to look on and conjecture, to watch the pageant. The mere stage properties were all he contended for. Nor was he lonely later in the evening, in his loge at the Metropolitan. He was entirely rid of his nervous misgivings, of his forced aggressiveness, of the imperative desire to show himself different from his surroundings. He felt now that his surroundings explained him. Nobody questioned the purple; he had only to wear it passively. He had only to glance down at his attire to reassure himself that here it would be impossible for anyone to humiliate him.

He found it hard to leave his beautiful sitting-room to go to bed that night, and sat long watching the raging storm from his turret window. When he went to sleep it was with the lights turned on in his bedroom; partly because of his old timidity, and partly so that, if he should wake in the night, there would be no wretched moment of doubt, no horrible suspicion of yellow wall-paper, or of Washington and Calvin above his bed.

Sunday morning the city was practically snow-bound. Paul breakfasted late, and in the afternoon he fell in with a wild San Francisco boy, a freshman at Yale, who said he had run down for a "little flyer" over Sunday. The young man offered to show Paul the night side of the town, and the two boys went off together after dinner, not returning to the hotel until seven o'clock the next morning. They had started out in the confiding warmth of a champagne friendship, but their parting in the elevator was singularly cool. The freshman pulled himself together to make his train, and Paul went to bed. He awoke at two o'clock in the afternoon, very thirsty and dizzy, and rang for ice-water, coffee, and the Pittsburgh papers.

On the part of the hotel management, Paul excited no suspicion. There was this to be said for him, that he wore his spoils with dignity and in no way made himself conspicuous. Even under the glow of his wine he was never boisterous, though he found the stuff like a magician's wand for wonder-building. His chief greediness lay in his ears and eyes, and his excesses were not offensive ones. His dearest pleasures were the grey winter twilights in his sitting-room; his quiet enjoyment of his flowers, his clothes, his wide divan, his cigarette, and his sense of power. He could not remember a time when he had felt so at peace with himself. The mere release from the necessity of petty lying, lying every day and every day, restored his self-respect. He had never lied for pleasure, even at school; but to be noticed and admired, to assert his difference from other Cordelia Street boys; and he felt a good deal more manly, more honest, even, now that he had no need for boastful pretensions, now that he could, as his actor friends used to say, "dress the part." It was characteristic that remorse did not occur to him. His golden days went by without a shadow, and he made each as perfect as he could.

On the eighth day after his arrival in New York, he found the whole affair exploited in the Pittsburgh papers, exploited with a wealth of detail which indicated that local news of a sensational nature was at a low ebb. The firm of Denny & Carson announced that the boy's father had refunded the full amount of his theft, and that they had no intention of prosecuting. The Cumberland minister had been interviewed, and expressed his hope of yet reclaiming the motherless lad, and his Sabbath-school teacher declared that she would spare no effort to that end. The rumor had reached Pittsburgh that the boy had been seen in a New York hotel, and his father had gone East to find him and bring him home.

Paul had just come in to dress for dinner; he sank into a chair, weak in the knees, and clasped his head in his hands. It was to be worse than jail, even; the tepid waters of Cordelia Street were to close over him finally and forever. The grey monotony stretched before him in hopeless, unrelieved years; Sabbath-school, Young People's Meeting, the yellow-papered room, the damp dish-towels; it all rushed back upon him with a sickening vividness. He had the old feeling that the orchestra had suddenly stopped, the sinking sensation that the play was over. The sweat broke out on his face, and he sprang to his feet, looked about him with his white, conscious smile, and winked at himself in the mirror. With something of the childish belief in miracles with which he had so often gone to class, all his lessons unlearned, Paul dressed and dashed whistling down the corridor to the elevator.

He had no sooner entered the dining-room and caught the measure of the music than his remembrance was lightened by his old elastic power of claiming the moment, mounting with it, and finding it all sufficient. The glare and glitter about him, the mere scenic accessories had again, and for the last time, their old potency. He would show himself that he was game, he would finish the thing splendidly. He doubted, more than ever, the existence of Cordelia Street, and for the first time he drank his wine recklessly. Was he not, after all, one of these fortunate beings born to the purple, was he not still himself and in his own place? He drummed a nervous accompaniment to the Pagliacci music and looked about him, telling himself over and over that it had paid.

He reflected drowsily, to the swell of the violin and the chill sweetness of his wine, that he might have done it more wisely. He might have caught an outbound steamer and been well out of their clutches before now. But the other side of the world had seemed too far away and too uncertain then; he could not have waited for it; his need had been too sharp. If he had to choose over again, he would do the same thing tomorrow. He looked affectionately about the dining-room, now gilded with a soft mist. Ah, it had paid indeed!

Paul was awakened next morning by a painful throbbing in his head and feet. He had thrown himself across the bed without undressing, and had slept with his shoes on. His limbs and hands were lead heavy, and his tongue and throat were parched and burnt. There came upon him one of those fateful attacks of clear-headedness that never occurred except when he was physically exhausted and his nerves hung loose. He lay still and closed his eyes and let the tide of realities wash over him.

His father was in New York; "stopping at some joint or other," he told himself. The memory of successive summers on the front stoop fell upon him like a weight of black water. He had not a hundred dollars left; and he knew now, more than ever, that money was everything, the wall that stood between all he loathed and all he wanted. The thing was winding itself up; he had thought of that on his first glorious day in New York, and had even provided a way to snap the thread.

It lay on his dressing-table now; he had got it out last night when he came blindly up from dinner, but the shiny metal hurt his eyes, and he disliked the look of it.

He rose and moved about with a painful effort, succumbing now and again to attacks of nausea. It was the old depression exaggerated; all the world had become Cordelia Street. Yet somehow he was not afraid of anything, was absolutely calm; perhaps because he had looked into the dark corner at last and knew. It was bad enough, what he saw there, but somehow not so bad as his long fear of it had been. He saw everything clearly now. He had a feeling that he had made the best of it, that he had lived the sort of life he was meant to live, and for half an hour he sat staring at the revolver. But he told himself that was not the way, so he went downstairs and took a cab to the ferry.

When Paul arrived at Newark, he got off the train and took another cab, directing the driver to follow the Pennsylvania tracks out of the town. The snow lay heavy on the roadways and had drifted deep in the open fields. Only here and there the dead grass or dried weed stalks projected, singularly black, above it. Once well into the country, Paul dismissed the carriage and walked, floundering along the tracks, his mind a medley of irrelevant things. He seemed to hold in his brain an actual picture of everything he had seen that morning. He remembered every feature of both his drivers, of the toothless old woman from whom he had bought the red flowers in his coat, the agent from whom he had got his ticket, and all of his fellow-passengers on the ferry. His mind, unable to cope with vital matters near at hand, worked feverishly and deftly at sorting and grouping these images. They made for him a part of the ugliness of the world, of the ache in his head, and the bitter burning on his tongue. He stooped and put a handful of snow into his mouth as he walked, but that, too, seemed hot. When he reached a little hillside, where the tracks ran through a cut some twenty feet below him, he stopped and sat down.

The carnations in his coat were drooping with the cold, he noticed; all their red glory over. It occurred to him that all the flowers he had seen in the glass cases that first night must have gone the same way, long before this. It was only one splendid breath they had, in spite of their brave mockery at the winter outside the glass; and it was a losing game in the end, it seemed, this revolt against the homilies by which the world is run. Paul took one of the blossoms carefully from his coat and scooped a little hole in the snow, where he covered it up. Then he dozed a while, from his weak condition, seeming insensible to the cold.

The sound of an approaching train awoke him, and he started to his feet, remembering only his resolution, and afraid lest he should be too late. He stood watching the approaching locomotive, his teeth chattering, his lips drawn away from them in a frightened smile; once or twice he glanced nervously sidewise, as though he were being watched. When the right moment came, he jumped. As he fell, the folly of his haste occurred to him with merciless clearness, the vastness of what he had left undone. There flashed through his brain, clearer than ever before, the blue of Adriatic water, the yellow of Algerian sands.

He felt something strike his chest, and that his body was being thrown swiftly through the air, on and on, immeasurably far and fast, while his limbs gently relaxed. Then, because the picture making mechanism was crushed, the disturbing visions flashed into black, and Paul dropped back into the immense design of things.

(1905)

James Joyce   1882–1941

Araby

North Richmond Street, being blind,[1] was a quiet street except at the hour when the Christian Brothers' School set the boys free. An uninhabited house of two storeys stood at the blind end, detached from its neighbours in a square ground. The other houses of the street, conscious of decent lives within them, gazed at one another with brown imperturbable faces.

The former tenant of our house, a priest, had died in the back drawing-room. Air, musty from having been long enclosed, hung in all the rooms, and the waste room behind the kitchen was littered with old useless papers. Among these I found a few paper-covered books, the pages of which were curled and damp: *The Abbot*, by Walter Scott, *The Devout Communicant* and *The Memoirs of Vidocq*. I liked the last best because its leaves were yellow. The wild garden behind the house contained a central apple-tree and a few straggling bushes under one of which I found the late tenant's rusty bicycle-pump. He had been a very charitable priest; in his will he had left all his money to institutions and the furniture of his house to his sister.

When the short days of winter came dusk fell before we had well eaten our dinners. When we met in the street the houses had grown sombre. The space of sky above us was the colour of ever-changing violet and towards it the lamps of the street lifted their feeble lanterns. The cold air stung us and we played till our bodies glowed. Our shouts echoed in the silent street. The career of our play brought us through the dark muddy lanes behind the houses where we ran the gauntlet of the rough tribes from the cottages, to the back doors of the dark dripping gardens where odours arose from the ashpits, to the dark odorous stables where a coachman smoothed and combed the horse or shook music from the buckled harness. When we returned to the street light from the kitchen windows had filled the areas. If my uncle was seen turning the corner we hid in the shadow until we had seen him safely housed. Or if Mangan's sister came out on the doorstep to call her brother in to his tea we watched her from our shadow peer up and down the street. We waited to see whether she would remain or go in and, if she remained, we left our shadow and walked up to Mangan's steps resignedly. She was waiting for us, her figure defined by the light from the half-opened door. Her brother always teased her before he obeyed and I stood by the railings looking at her. Her dress swung as she moved her body and the soft rope of her hair tossed from side to side.

Every morning I lay on the floor in the front parlour watching her door. The blind was pulled down to within an inch of the sash so that I could not be seen. When she came out on the doorstep my heart leaped. I ran to the hall, seized my books and followed her. I kept her brown figure always in my eye and, when we came near the point at which our ways diverged, I quickened my pace and passed her. This happened morning after morning. I had never spoken to her, except for a few casual words, and yet her name was like a summons to all my foolish blood.

Her image accompanied me even in places the most hostile to romance. On Saturday evenings when my aunt went marketing I had to go to carry some of

---

[1] Dead end.

the parcels. We walked through the flaring[2] streets, jostled by drunken men and bargaining women, amid the curse of labourers, the shrill litanies of shop-boys who stood on guard by the barrels of pigs' cheeks, the nasal chanting of street-singers, who sang a *come-all-you* about O'Donovan Rossa,[3] or a ballad about the troubles in our native land. These noises converged in a single sensation of life for me: I imagined that I bore my chalice safely through a throng of foes. Her name sprang to my lips at moments in strange prayers and praises which I myself did not understand. My eyes were often full of tears (I could not tell why) and at times a flood from my heart seemed to pour itself out into my bosom. I thought little of the future. I did not know whether I would ever speak to her or not or, if I spoke to her, how I could tell her of my confused adoration. But my body was like a harp and her words and gestures were like fingers running upon the wires.

One evening I went into the back drawing-room in which the priest had died. It was a dark rainy evening and there was no sound in the house. Through one of the broken panes I heard the rain impinge upon the earth, the fine incessant needles of water playing in the sodden beds. Some distant lamp or lighted window gleamed below me. I was thankful that I could see so little. All my senses seemed to desire to veil themselves and, feeling that I was about to slip from them, I pressed the palms of my hands together until they trembled, murmuring: "*O love! O love!*" many times.

At last she spoke to me. When she addressed the first words to me I was so confused that I did not know what to answer. She asked me was I going to *Araby*.[4] I forgot whether I answered yes or no. It would be a splendid bazaar, she said; she would love to go.

"And why can't you?" I asked.

While she spoke she turned a silver bracelet round and round her wrist. She could not go, she said, because there would be a retreat that week in her convent. Her brother and two other boys were fighting for their caps and I was alone at the railings. She held one of the spikes, bowing her head towards me. The light from the lamp opposite our door caught the white curve of her neck, lit up her hair that rested there and, falling, lit up the hand upon the railing. It fell over one side of her dress and caught the white border of a petticoat just visible as she stood at ease.

"It's well for you," she said.

"If I go," I said, "I will bring you something."

What innumerable follies laid waste my waking and sleeping thoughts after that evening! I wished to annihilate the tedious intervening days. I chafed against the work of school. At night in my bedroom and by day in the classroom her image came between me and the page I strove to read. The syllables of the word *Araby* were called to me through the silence in which my soul luxuriated and cast an Eastern enchantment over me. I asked for leave to go to the bazaar on Saturday night. My aunt was surprised and hoped it was not some Freemason affair. I answered few questions in class. I watched my master's face pass from amiability to sternness; he hoped I was not beginning to idle. I could not call my wandering thoughts together. I had hardly any patience with the

---

[2]Branching.
[3]A rousing song about Irish patriot Jeremiah O'Donovan, in which each verse begins, "Come, all you Irishmen."
[4]A bazaar, held in Dublin in the spring of 1894, featuring an oriental theme.

serious work of life which, now that it stood between me and my desire, seemed to me child's play, ugly monotonous child's play.

On Saturday morning I reminded my uncle that I wished to go to the bazaar in the evening. He was fussing at the hall stand, looking for the hatbrush, and answered me curtly:

"Yes, boy, I know."

As he was in the hall I could not go into the front parlour and lie at the window. I left the house in bad humour and walked slowly towards the school. The air was pitilessly raw and already my heart misgave me.

When I came home to dinner my uncle had not yet been home. Still it was early. I sat staring at the clock for some time and, when its ticking began to irritate me, I left the room. I mounted the staircase and gained the upper part of the house. The high cold empty gloomy rooms liberated me and I went from room to room singing. From the front window I saw my companions playing below in the street. Their cries reached me weakened and indistinct and, leaning my forehead against the cool glass, I looked over at the dark house where she lived. I may have stood there for an hour, seeing nothing but the brown-clad figure cast by my imagination, touched discreetly by the lamplight at the curved neck, at the hand upon the railings and at the border below the dress.

When I came downstairs again I found Mrs. Mercer sitting at the fire. She was an old garrulous woman, a pawnbroker's widow, who collected used stamps for some pious purpose. I had to endure the gossip of the tea-table. The meal was prolonged beyond an hour and still my uncle did not come. Mrs. Mercer stood up to go: she was very sorry she couldn't wait any longer, but it was after eight o'clock and she did not like to be out late, as the night air was bad for her. When she had gone I began to walk up and down the room, clenching my fists. My aunt said:

"I'm afraid you may put off your bazaar for this night of Our Lord."

At nine o'clock I heard my uncle's latchkey in the halldoor. I heard him talking to himself and heard the hallstand rocking when it had received the weight of his overcoat. I could interpret these signs. When he was midway through his dinner I asked him to give me the money to go to the bazaar. He had forgotten.

"The people are in bed and after their first sleep now," he said.

I did not smile. My aunt said to him energetically:

"Can't you give him the money and let him go? You've kept him late enough as it is."

My uncle said he was very sorry he had forgotten. He said he believed in the old saying: "All work and no play makes Jack a dull boy." He asked me where I was going and, when I had told him a second time he asked me did I know *The Arab's Farewell to his Steed*.[5] When I left the kitchen he was about to recite the opening lines of the piece to my aunt.

I held a florin tightly in my hand as I strode down Buckingham Street towards the station. The sight of the streets thronged with buyers and glaring with gas[6] recalled to me the purpose of my journey. I took my seat in a third-class carriage of a deserted train. After an intolerable delay the train moved out of the station slowly. It crept onward among ruinous houses and over the twinkling river. At Westland Row Station a crowd of people pressed to the carriage

---

[5] A sentimental poem popular at the time.
[6] Gas lamps.

doors; but the porters moved them back, saying that it was a special train for the bazaar. I remained alone in the bare carriage. In a few minutes the train drew up beside an improvised wooden platform. I passed out on to the road and saw by the lighted dial of a clock that it was ten minutes to ten. In front of me was a large building which displayed the magical name.

I could not find any sixpenny entrance and, fearing that the bazaar would be closed, I passed quickly through a turnstile, handing a shilling to a weary-looking man. I found myself in a big hall girdled at half its height by a gallery. Nearly all the stalls were closed and the greater part of the hall was in darkness. I recognized a silence like that which pervades a church after a service. I walked into the centre of the bazaar timidly. A few people were gathered about the stalls which were still open. Before a curtain, over which the words *Café Chantant*[7] were written in coloured lamps, two men were counting money on a salver.[8] I listened to the fall of the coins.

Remembering with difficulty why I had come I went over to one of the stalls and examined porcelain vases and flowered tea-sets. At the door of the stall a young lady was talking and laughing with two young gentlemen. I remarked their English accents and listened vaguely to their conversation.

"O, I never said such a thing!"

"O, but you did!"

"O, but I didn't!"

"Didn't she say that?"

"Yes. I heard her."

"O, there's a . . . fib!"

Observing me the young lady came over and asked me did I wish to buy anything. The tone of her voice was not encouraging; she seemed to have spoken to me out of a sense of duty. I looked humbly at the great jars that stood like eastern guards at either side of the dark entrance to the stall and murmured:

"No, thank you."

The young lady changed the position of one of the vases and went back to the two young men. They began to talk of the same subject. Once or twice the young lady glanced at me over her shoulder.

I lingered before her stall, though I knew my stay was useless, to make my interest in her wares seem the more real. Then I turned away slowly and walked down the middle of the bazaar. I allowed the two pennies to fall against the sixpence in my pocket. I heard a voice call from one end of the gallery that the light was out. The upper part of the hall was now completely dark.

Gazing up into the darkness I saw myself as a creature driven and derided by vanity; and my eyes burned with anguish and anger.

(1914)

---

[7] A café featuring music.
[8] A serving tray.

Eveline

She sat at the window watching the evening invade the avenue. Her head was leaned against the window curtains and in her nostrils was the odour of dusty cretonne. She was tired.

Few people passed. The man out of the last house passed on his way home; she heard his footsteps clacking along the concrete pavement and afterwards crunching on the cinder path before the new red houses. One time there used to be a field there in which they used to play every evening with other people's children. Then a man from Belfast bought the field and built houses in it—not like their little brown houses but bright brick houses with shining roofs. The children of the avenue used to play together in that field—the Devines, the Waters, the Dunns, little Keogh the cripple, she and her brothers and sisters. Ernest, however, never played: he was too grown up. Her father used often to hunt them in out of the field with his blackthorn stick; but usually little Keogh used to keep nix and call out when he saw her father coming. Still they seemed to have been rather happy then. Her father was not so bad then; and besides, her mother was alive. That was a long time ago; she and her brothers and sisters were all grown up; her mother was dead. Tizzie Dunn was dead, too, and the Waters had gone back to England. Everything changes. Now she was going to go away like the others, to leave her home.

Home! She looked round the room, reviewing all its familiar objects which she had dusted once a week for so many years, wondering where on earth all the dust came from. Perhaps she would never see again those familiar objects from which she had never dreamed of being divided. And yet during all those years she had never found out the name of the priest whose yellowing photograph hung on the wall above the broken harmonium beside the coloured print of the promises made to Blessed Margaret Mary Alacoque. He had been a school friend of her father. Whenever he showed the photograph to a visitor her father used to pass it with a casual word:

"He is in Melbourne now."

She had consented to go away, to leave her home. Was that wise? She tried to weigh each side of the question. In her home anyway she had shelter and food; she had those whom she had known all her life about her. Of course she had to work hard, both in the house and at business. What would they say of her in the Stores when they found out that she had run away with a fellow? Say she was a fool, perhaps; and her place would be filled up by advertisement. Miss Gavan would be glad. She had always had an edge on her, especially whenever there were people listening.

"Miss Hill, don't you see these ladies are waiting?"

"Look lively, Miss Hill, please."

She would not cry many tears at leaving the Stores.

But in her new home, in a distant unknown country, it would not be like that. Then she would be married—she, Eveline. People would treat her with respect then. She would not be treated as her mother had been. Even now, though she was over nineteen, she sometimes felt herself in danger of her father's violence. She knew it was that that had given her the palpitations. When they were growing up he had never gone for her, like he used to go for Harry and Ernest, because she was a girl; but latterly he had begun to threaten her and say what he would do to her only for her dead mother's sake. And now she had nobody to protect her. Ernest was dead and Harry, who was in the church decorating business, was nearly always down somewhere in the country. Besides, the invariable squabble for money on Saturday nights had begun to weary her unspeakably. She always gave her entire wages—seven shillings—and Harry always sent up what he could but the trouble was to get any money from her father. He said she used to squander the money, that she had no head, that he wasn't going to give her his hard-earned money to throw about the streets, and much more, for he was usually fairly bad on Saturday night. In the end he would give her the money and ask her had she any intention of buying Sunday's dinner. Then she had to rush out as quickly as she could and do her marketing, holding her black leather purse tightly in her hand as she elbowed her way through the crowds and returning home late under her load of provisions. She had hard work to keep the house together and to see that the two young children who had been left to her charge went to school regularly and got their meals regularly. It was hard work—a hard life—but now that she was about to leave it she did not find it a wholly undesirable life.

She was about to explore another life with Frank. Frank was very kind, manly, open-hearted. She was to go away with him by the night-boat to be his wife and to live with him in Buenos Ayres where he had a home waiting for her. How well she remembered the first time she had seen him; he was lodging in a house on the main road where she used to visit. It seemed a few weeks ago. He was standing at the gate, his peaked cap pushed back on his head and his hair tumbled forward over a face of bronze. Then they had come to know each other. He used to meet her outside the Stores every evening and see her home. He took her to see *The Bohemian Girl* and she felt elated as she sat in an unaccustomed part of the theatre with him. He was awfully fond of music and sang a little. People knew that they were courting and, when he sang about the lass that loves a sailor, she always felt pleasantly confused. He used to call her Poppens out of fun. First of all it had been an excitement for her to have a fellow and then she had begun to like him. He had tales of distant countries. He had started as a deck boy at a pound a month on a ship of the Allan Line going out to Canada. He told her the names of the ships he had been on and the names of the different services. He had sailed through the Straits of Magellan and he told her stories of the terrible Patagonians. He had fallen on his feet in Buenos Ayres, he said, and had come over to the old country just for a holiday. Of course, her father had found out the affair and had forbidden her to have anything to say to him.

"I know these sailor chaps," he said.

One day he had quarrelled with Frank and after that she had to meet her lover secretly.

The evening deepened in the avenue. The white of two letters in her lap grew indistinct. One was to Harry; the other was to her father. Ernest had been her favourite but she liked Harry too. Her father was becoming old lately, she noticed; he would miss her. Sometimes he could be very nice. Not long before, when she had been laid up for a day, he had read her out a ghost story and made toast for her at the fire. Another day, when their mother was alive, they had all gone for a picnic to the Hill of Howth. She remembered her father putting on her mother's bonnet to make the children laugh.

Her time was running out but she continued to sit by the window, leaning her head against the window curtain, inhaling the odour of dusty cretonne. Down far in the avenue she could hear a street organ playing. She knew the air.

Strange that it should come that very night to remind her of the promise to her mother, her promise to keep the home together as long as she could. She remembered the last night of her mother's illness; she was again in the close dark room at the other side of the hall and outside she heard a melancholy air of Italy. The organ-player had been ordered to go away and given sixpence. She remembered her father strutting back into the sickroom saying:

"Damned Italians! coming over here!"

As she mused the pitiful vision of her mother's life laid its spell on the very quick of her being—that life of commonplace sacrifices closing in final craziness. She trembled as she heard again her mother's voice saying constantly with foolish insistence:

"Derevaun Seraun! Derevaun Seraun!"[1]

She stood up in a sudden impulse of terror. Escape! She must escape! Frank would save her. He would give her life, perhaps love, too. But she wanted to live. Why should she be unhappy? She had a right to happiness. Frank would take her in his arms, fold her in his arms. He would save her.

She stood among the swaying crowd in the station at the North Wall. He held her hand and she knew that he was speaking to her, saying something about the passage over and over again. The station was full of soldiers with brown baggages. Through the wide doors of the sheds she caught a glimpse of the black mass of the boat, lying in beside the quay wall, with illumined portholes. She answered nothing. She felt her cheek pale and cold and, out of a maze of distress, she prayed to God to direct her, to show her what was her duty. The boat blew a long mournful whistle into the mist. If she went, tomorrow she would be on the sea with Frank, steaming towards Buenos Ayres. This passage had been booked. Could she still draw back after all he had done for her? Her distress awoke a nausea in her body and she kept moving her lips in silent fervent prayer.

A bell clanged upon her heart. She felt him seize her hand:

"Come!"

All the seas of the world tumbled about her heart. He was drawing her into them: he would drown her. She gripped with both hands at the iron railing.

"Come!"

No! No! No! It was impossible. Her hands clutched the iron in frenzy. Amid the seas she sent a cry of anguish.

"Eveline! Evvy!"

He rushed beyond the barrier and called to her to follow. He was shouted at to go on but he still called to her. She set her white face to him, passive, like a helpless animal. Her eyes gave him no sign of love or farewell or recognition.

(1914)

---

[1] "The end of pleasure is pain!"

Ethel Wilson   1888–1980

The Window

The great big window must have been at least twenty-five feet wide and ten feet high. It was constructed in sections divided by segments of something that did not interfere with the view; in fact the eye by-passed these divisions and looked only at the entrancing scenes beyond. The window, together with a glass door at the western end, composed a bland shallow curve and formed the entire transparent north-west (but chiefly north) wall of Mr Willy's living-room.

Upon his arrival from England Mr Willy had surveyed the various prospects of living in the quickly growing city of Vancouver with the selective and discarding characteristics which had enabled him to make a fortune and retire all of a sudden from business and his country in his advanced middle age. He settled immediately upon the very house. It was a small old house overlooking the sea between Spanish Banks and English Bay. He knocked out the north wall and made the window. There was nothing particular to commend the house except that it faced immediately on the sea-shore and the view. Mr Willy had left his wife and her three sisters to play bridge together until death should overtake them in England. He now paced from end to end of his living-room, that is to say from east to west, with his hands in his pockets, admiring the northern view. Sometimes he stood with his hands behind him looking through the great glass window, seeing the wrinkled or placid sea and the ships almost at his feet and beyond the sea the mountains, and seeing sometimes his emancipation. His emancipation drove him into a dream, and sea sky mountains swam before him, vanished, and he saw with immense release his wife in still another more repulsive hat. He did not know, nor would he have cared, that much discussion went on in her world, chiefly in the afternoons, and that he was there alleged to have deserted her. So he had, after providing well for her physical needs which were all the needs of which she was capable. Mrs Willy went on saying ' . . . and he would come home my dear and never speak a word I can't tell you my dear how *frightful* it was night after night I might say for *years* I simply can't tell you . . .' No, she could not tell but she did, by day and night. Here he was at peace, seeing out of the window the crimped and wrinkled sea and the ships which passed and passed each other, the seabirds and the dream-inducing sky.

At the extreme left curve of the window an island appeared to slope into the sea. Behind this island and to the north, the mountains rose very high. In the summer time the mountains were soft, deceptive in their innocency, full of crags and crevasses and arêtes and danger. In the winter they lay magnificent, white and much higher, it seemed, than in the summer time. They tossed, static, in almost visible motion against the sky, inhabited only by eagles and—so a man had told Mr Willy, but he didn't believe the man—by mountain sheep and some cougars, bears, wild cats and, certainly, on the lower slopes, deer, and now a ski camp far out of sight. Mr Willy looked at the mountains and regretted his past youth and his present wealth. How could he endure to be old and rich and able only to look at these mountains which in his youth he had not known and did not climb. Nothing, now, no remnant of his youth would come and enable him to climb these mountains. This he found hard to believe, as old people do. He was shocked at the newly realized decline of his physical powers which had proved good enough on the whole for his years of success, and by the fact that now he had, at last, time and could not swim (heart), climb mountains (heart and legs), row a boat in a rough enticing sea (call that old age). These things have happened to other people, thought Mr Willy, but not to us, now, who have been so young, and yet it will happen to those who now are young.

Immediately across the water were less spectacular mountains, pleasant slopes which in winter time were covered with invisible skiers. Up the dark mountain at night sprang the lights of the ski-lift, and ceased. The shores of these mountains were strung with lights, littered with lights, spangled with lights, necklaces, bracelets, constellations, far more beautiful as seen through this window across the dark water than if Mr Willy had driven his car across the Lions' Gate Bridge and westwards among those constellations which would have disclosed only a shopping centre, people walking in the streets, street lights, innumerable cars and car lights like anywhere else and, up the slopes, people's houses. Then, looking back to the south across the dark water towards his own home and the great lighted window which he would not have been able to distinguish so far away, Mr Willy would have seen lights again, a carpet of glitter thrown over the slopes of the city.

Fly from one shore to the other, fly and fly back again, fly to a continent or to an island, but you are no better off than if you stayed all day at your own window (and such a window), thought Mr Willy pacing back and forth, then into the kitchen to put the kettle on for a cup of tea which he will drink beside the window, back for a glass of whisky, returning in time to see a cormorant flying level with the water, not an inch too high not an inch too low, flying out of sight. See the small ducks lying on the water, one behind the other, like beads on a string. In the mornings Mr Willy drove into town to see his investment broker and perhaps to the bank or round the park. He lunched, but not at a club. He then drove home. On certain days a woman called Mrs Ogden came in to 'do' for him. This was his daily life, very simple, and a routine was formed whose pattern could at last be discerned by an interested observer outside the window.

One night Mr Willy beheld a vast glow arise behind the mountains. The Arctic world was obviously on fire—but no, the glow was not fire glow, flame glow. The great invasion of colour that spread up and up the sky was not red, was not rose, but of a synthetic cyclamen colour. This cyclamen glow remained steady from mountain to zenith and caused Mr Willy, who had never seen the Northern Lights, to believe that these were not Northern Lights but that something had occurred for which one must be prepared. After about an hour, flanges of green as of putrefaction, and a melodious yellow arose and spread. An hour later the Northern Lights faded, leaving Mr Willy small and alone.

Sometimes as, sitting beside the window, he drank his tea, Mr Willy thought that nevertheless it is given to few people to be as happy (or contented, he would say), as he was, at his age, too. In his life of decisions, men, pressures, more men, antagonisms, fusions, fissions and Mrs Willy, in his life of hard success, that is, he had sometimes looked forward but so vaguely and rarely to a time when he would not only put this life down; he would leave it. Now he had left it and here he was by his window. As time went on, though, he had to make an effort to summon this happiness, for it seemed to elude him. Sometimes a thought or a shape (was it?), gray, like wood ash that falls in pieces when it is touched, seemed to be behind his chair, and this shape teased him and communicated to him that he had left humanity behind, that a man needs humanity and that if he ceases to be in touch with man and is not in touch with

God, he does not matter. 'You do not matter any more,' said the spectre like wood ash before it fell to pieces, 'because you are no longer in touch with any one and so you do not exist. You are in a vacuum and so you are nothing.' Then Mr Willy, at first uneasy, became satisfied again for a time after being made uneasy by the spectre. A storm would get up and the wind, howling well, would lash the window sometimes carrying the salt spray from a very high tide which it flung against the great panes of glass. That was a satisfaction to Mr Willy and within him something stirred and rose and met the storm and effaced the spectre and other phantoms which were really vague regrets. But the worst that happened against the window was that from time to time a little bird, sometimes but not often a seabird, flung itself like a stone against the strong glass of the window and fell, killed by the passion of its flight. This grieved Mr Willy, and he could not sit unmoved when the bird flew at the clear glass and was met by death. When this happened, he arose from his chair, opened the glass door at the far end of the window, descended three or four steps and sought in the grasses for the body of the bird. But the bird was dead, or it was dying, its small bones were smashed, its head was broken, its beak split, it was killed by the rapture of its flight. Only once Mr Willy found the bird a little stunned and picked it up. He cupped the bird's body in his hands and carried it into the house.

Looking up through the grasses at the edge of the rough terrace that descended to the beach, a man watched him return into the house, carrying the bird. Still looking obliquely through the grasses the man watched Mr Willy enter the room and vanish from view. Then Mr Willy came again to the door, pushed it open, and released the bird which flew away, who knows where. He closed the door, locked it, and sat down on the chair facing east beside the window and began to read his newspaper. Looking over his paper he saw, to the east, the city of Vancouver deployed over rising ground with low roofs and high buildings and at the apex the tall Electric Building which at night shone like a broad shaft of golden light.

This time, as evening drew on, the man outside went away because he had other business.

Mr Willy's investment broker was named Gerald Wardho. After a time he said to Mr Willy in a friendly but respectful way, 'Will you have lunch with me at the Club tomorrow?' and Mr Willy said he would. Some time later Gerald Wardho said, 'Would you like me to put you up at the Club?'

Mr Willy considered a little the life which he had left and did not want to re-enter and also the fact that he had only last year resigned his membership in three clubs, so he said, 'That's very good of you, Wardho, but I think not. I'm enjoying things as they are. It's a novelty, living in a vacuum . . . I like it, for a time anyway.'

'Yes, but,' said Gerald Wardho, 'you'd be some time on the waiting list. It wouldn't hurt—'

'No,' said Mr Willy, 'no.'

Mr Willy had, Wardho thought, a distinguished appearance or perhaps it was an affable accustomed air, and so he had. When Mrs Wardho said to her husband, 'Gerry, there's not an extra man in this town and I need a man for Saturday,' Gerald Wardho said, 'I know a man. There's Willy.'

Mrs Wardho said doubtfully, 'Willy? Willy who? Who's Willy?'

Her husband said, 'He's fine, he's okay, I'll ask Willy.'

'How old is he?'

'About a hundred . . . but he's okay.'

'Oh-h-h,' said Mrs Wardho, 'isn't there anyone anywhere unattached young any more? Does he play bridge?'

'I'll invite him, I'll find out,' said her husband, and Mr Willy said he'd like to come to dinner.

'Do you care for a game of bridge, Mr Willy?' asked Gerald Wardho.

'I'm afraid not,' said Mr Willy kindly but firmly. He played a good game of bridge but had no intention of entering servitude again just yet, losing his freedom, and being enrolled as what is called a fourth. Perhaps later; not yet. 'If you're having bridge I'll come another time. Very kind of you, Wardho.'

'No no no,' said Gerald Wardho, 'there'll only be maybe a table of bridge for anyone who wants to play. My wife would be disappointed.'

'Well thank you very much. Black tie?'

'Yes. Black tie,' said Gerald Wardho.

And so, whether he would or no, Mr Willy found himself invited to the kind of evening parties to which he had been accustomed and which he had left behind, given by people younger and more animated than himself, and he realized that he was on his way to becoming old odd man out. There was a good deal of wood ash at these parties—that is, behind him the spectre arose, falling to pieces when he looked at it, and said 'So this is what you came to find out on this coast, so far from home, is it, or is there something else. What else is there?' The spectre was not always present at these parties but sometimes awaited him at home and said these things.

One night Mr Willy came home from an evening spent at Gerald Wardho's brother-in-law's house, a very fine house indeed. He had left lights burning and began to turn out the lights before he went upstairs. He went into the living-room and before turning out the last light gave a glance at the window which had in the course of the evening behaved in its accustomed manner. During the day the view through the window was clear or cloudy, according to the weather or the light or absence of light in the sky; but there it was—the view—never quite the same though, and that is owing to the character of oceans or of any water, great or small, and of light. Both water and light have so great an effect on land observed on any scene, rural, urban or wilderness, that one begins to think that life, that a scene, is an illusion produced by influences such as water and light. At all events, by day the window held this fine view as in a frame, and the view was enhanced by ships at sea of all kinds, but never was the sea crowded, and by birds, clouds, and even aeroplanes in the sky—no people to spoil this fine view. But as evening approached, and moonless night, all the view (illusion again) vanished slowly. The window, which was not illusion, only the purveyor of illusion, did not vanish, but became a mirror which reflected against the blackness every detail of the shallow living-room. Through this clear reflection of the whole room, distant lights from across the water intruded, and so chains of light were thrown across the reflected mantel-piece, or a picture, or a human face, enhancing it. When Mr Willy had left his house to dine at Gerald Wardho's brother-in-law's house the view through the window was placidly clear, but when he returned at 11:30 the window was dark and the room was reflected from floor to ceiling against the blackness. Mr Willy saw himself entering the room like a stranger, looking at first debonair with such a gleaming shirt front and then—as he approached himself—a little shabby, his hair perhaps. He advanced to the window and stood looking at himself with the room in all its detail behind him.

Mr Willy was too often alone, and spent far too much time in that space which lies between the last page of the paper or the turning-off of the radio in surfeit, and sleep. Now as he stood at the end of the evening and the beginning of the night, looking at himself and the room behind him, he admitted that the arid feeling which he had so often experienced lately was probably what is called loneliness. And yet he did not want another woman in his life. It was a long time since he had seen a woman whom he wanted to take home or even to see again. Too much smiling. Men were all right, you talked to them about the market, the emergence of the Liberal Party, the impossibility of arriving anywhere with those people while that fellow was in office, nuclear war (instant hells opened deep in everyone's mind and closed again), South Africa where Mr Willy was born, the Argentine where Mr Wardho's brother-in-law had spent many years—and then everyone went home.

Mr Willy, as the months passed by, was dismayed to find that he had entered an area of depression unknown before, like a tundra, and he was a little frightened of this tundra. Returning from the dinner party he did not at once turn out the single last light and go upstairs. He sat down on a chair beside the window and at last bowed his head upon his hands. As he sat there, bowed, his thoughts went very stiffly (for they had not had much exercise in that direction throughout his life), to some area that was not tundra but that area where there might be some meaning in creation which Mr Willy supposed must be the place where some people seemed to find a God, and perhaps a personal God at that. Such theories, or ideas, or passions had never been of interest to him, and if he had thought of such theories, or ideas, or passions he would have dismissed them as invalid and having no bearing on life as it is lived, especially when one is too busy. He had formed the general opinion that people who hold such beliefs were either slaves to an inherited convention, hypocrites, or nit-wits. He regarded such people without interest, or at least he thought them negligible as he returned to the exacting life in hand. On the whole, though, he did not like them. It is not easy to say why Mr Willy thought these people were hypocrites or nit-wits because some of them, not all, had a strong religious faith, and why he was not a hypocrite or nit-wit because he had not a strong religious faith; but there it was.

As he sat on and on looking down at the carpet with his head in his hands he did not think of these people, but he underwent a strong shock of recognition. He found himself looking this way and that way out of his aridity for some explanation or belief beyond the non-explanation and non-belief that had always been sufficient and had always been his, but in doing this he came up against a high and solid almost visible wall of concrete or granite, set up between him and a religious belief. This wall had, he thought, been built by him through the period of his long life, or perhaps he was congenitally unable to have a belief; in that case it was no fault of his and there was no religious belief possible to him. As he sat there he came to have the conviction that the absence of a belief which extended beyond the visible world had something to do with his malaise; yet the malaise might possibly be cirrhosis of the liver or a sort of delayed male menopause. He recognized calmly that death was as inevitable as tomorrow morning or even tonight and he had a rational absence of fear of death. Nevertheless his death (he knew) had begun, and had begun—what with his awareness of age and this malaise of his—to assume a certainty that it had not had before. His death did not trouble him as much as the increasing tastelessness of living in this tundra of mind into which a belief did not enter.

The man outside the window had crept up through the grasses and was now watching Mr Willy from a point rather behind him. He was a morose man and strong. He had served two terms for robbery with violence. When he worked, he worked up the coast. Then he came to town and if he did not get into trouble it was through no fault of his own. Last summer he had lain there and, rolling over, had looked up through the grasses and into—only just into—the room where this guy was who seemed to live alone. He seemed to be a rich guy because he wore good clothes and hadn't he got this great big window and—later, he discovered—a high-price car. He had lain in the grasses and because his thoughts always turned that way, he tried to figger out how he could get in there. Money was the only thing that was any good to him and maybe the old guy didn't keep money or even carry it but he likely did. The man thought quite a bit about Mr Willy and then went up the coast and when he came down again he remembered the great big window and one or two nights he went around and about the place and figgered how he'd work it. The doors was all locked, even that glass door. That was easy enough to break but he guessed he'd go in without warning when the old guy was there so's he'd have a better chance of getting something off of him as well. Anyways he wouldn't break in, not that night, but if nothing else offered he'd do it some time soon.

Suddenly Mr Willy got up, turned the light out, and went upstairs to bed. That was Wednesday.

On Sunday he had his first small party. It seemed inevitable if only for politeness. Later he would have a dinner party if he still felt sociable and inclined. He invited the Wardhos and their in-laws and some other couples. A Mrs Lessways asked if she might bring her aunt and he said yes. Mrs Wardho said might she bring her niece who was arriving on Saturday to meet her fiancé who was due next week from Hong Kong, and the Wardhos were going to give the two young people a quiet wedding, and Mr Willy said 'Please do.' Another couple asked if they could bring another couple.

Mr Willy, surveying his table, thought that Mrs Ogden had done well. 'Oh I'm so glad you think so,' said Mrs Ogden, pleased. People began to arrive. 'Oh!' they exclaimed without fail, as they arrived, 'what a beautiful view!' Mrs Lessways' aunt who had blue hair fell delightedly into the room, turning this way and that way, acknowledging smiles and tripping to the window. 'Oh,' she cried turning to Mr Willy in a fascinating manner, 'isn't that just lovely! Edna says you're quite a recluse! I'm sure I don't blame you! Don't you think that's the loveliest view Edna . . . oh how d'you do how d'you do, isn't that the loveliest view? . . .' Having paid her tribute to the view she turned away from the window and did not see it again. The Aunt twirled a little bag covered with iridescent beads on her wrist. 'Oh!' and 'Oh!' she exclaimed, turning, 'My dear how *lovely* to see you! I didn't even know you were back! Did you have a good time?' She reminded Mr Willy uneasily of his wife. Mr and Mrs Wardho arrived accompanied by their niece Sylvia.

A golden girl, thought Mr Willy taking her hand, but her young face surrounded by sunny curls was stern. She stood, looking from one to another, not speaking, for people spoke busily to each other and the young girl stood apart, smiling only when need be and wishing that she had not had to come to the party. She drifted to the window and seemed (and was) forgotten. She looked at the view as at something seen for the first and last time. She inscribed those notable hills on her mind because had she not arrived only yesterday? And in two days Ian would be here and she would not see them again.

A freighter very low laden emerged from behind a forest and moved slowly into the scene. So low it was that it lay like an elegant black line upon the water with great bulkheads below. Like an iceberg, thought Sylvia, and her mind moved along with the freighter bound for foreign parts. Someone spoke to her and she turned. 'Oh thank you!' she said for her cup of tea.

Mr Willy opened the glass door and took with him some of the men who had expressed a desire to see how far his property ran. 'You see, just a few feet, no distance,' he said.

After a while day receded and night came imperceptibly on. There was not any violence of reflected sunset tonight and mist settled down on the view with only distant dim lights aligning the north shore. Sylvia, stopping to respond to ones and twos, went to the back of the shallow room and sat down behind the out-jut of the fireplace where a wood fire was burning. Her mind was on two levels. One was all Ian and the week coming, and one—no thicker than a crust on the surface—was this party and all these people talking, the Aunt talking so busily that one might think there was a race on, or news to tell. Sylvia, sitting in the shadow of the corner and thinking about her approaching lover, lost herself in this reverie, and her lips, which had been so stern, opened slightly in a tender smile. Mr Willy who was serving drinks from the dining-room where Mrs Ogden had left things ready, came upon her and, struck by her beauty, saw a different sunny girl. She looked up at him. She took her drink from him with a soft and tender smile that was grateful and happy and was only partly for him. He left her, with a feeling of beauty seen.

Sylvia held her glass and looked towards the window. She saw, to her surprise, so quickly had black night come, that the end of the room which had been a view was now a large black mirror which reflected the glowing fire, the few lights, and the people unaware of the view, its departure, and its replacement by their own reflections behaving to each other like people at a party. Sylvia watched Mr Willy who moved amongst them, taking a glass and bringing a glass. He was removed from the necessities, now, of conversation, and looked very sad. Why does he look sad, she wondered and was young enough to think, he shouldn't look sad, he is well off. She took time off to like Mr Willy and to feel sorry that he seemed melancholy.

People began to look at their watches and say good-bye. The Aunt redoubled her vivacity. The women all thanked Mr Willy for his tea party and for the beautiful beautiful view. They gave glances at the window but there was no view.

When all his guests had gone, Mr Willy, who was an orderly man, began to collect glasses and take them into the kitchen. In an armchair lay the bag covered with iridescent beads belonging to the Aunt. Mr Willy picked it up and put it on a table, seeing the blue hair of the Aunt. He would sit down and smoke for awhile. But he found that when, lately, he sat down in the evening beside the window and fixed his eyes upon the golden shaft of the Electric Building, in spite of his intention of reading or smoking, his thoughts turned towards this subject of belief which now teased him, eluded, yet compelled him. He was brought up, every time, against the great stone wall, how high, how wide he knew, but not how thick. If he could, in some way, break through the wall which bounded the area of his aridity and his comprehension, he knew without question that there was a light (not darkness) beyond, and that this light could in some way come through to him and alleviate the sterility and lead him, lead him. If there were some way, even some conventional way—although he did not care for convention—he would take it in order to break the wall down and reach the light so that it would enter his life; but he did not know the way. So fixed did Mr Willy become in contemplation that he looked as though he were graven in stone.

Throughout the darkened latter part of the tea party, the man outside had lain or crouched near the window. From the sands, earlier, he had seen Mr Willy open the glass door and go outside, followed by two or three men. They looked down talking, and soon went inside again together. The door was closed. From anything the watcher knew, it was not likely that the old guy would turn and lock the door when he took the other guys in. He'd just close it, see.

As night came on the man watched the increased animation of the guests preparing for departure. Like departing birds they moved here and there in the room before taking flight. The man was impatient but patient because when five were left, then three, then no one but the old guy who lived in the house, he knew his time was near. (How gay and how meaningless the scene had been, of these well-dressed persons talking and talking, like some kind of a show where nothing happened—or so it might seem, on the stage of the lighted room from the pit of the dark shore.)

The watcher saw the old guy pick up glasses and take them away. Then he came back into the room and looked around. He took something out of a chair and put it on a table. He stood still for a bit, and then he found some kind of a paper and sat down in the chair facing eastward. But the paper drooped in his hand and then it dropped to the floor as the old guy bent his head and then he put his elbows on his knees and rested his head in his hands as if he was thinking, or had some kind of a headache.

The watcher, with a sort of joy and a feeling of confidence that the moment had come, moved strongly and quietly to the glass door. He turned the handle expertly, slid inside, and slowly closed the door so that no draught should warn his victim. He moved cat-like to the back of Mr Willy's chair and quickly raised his arm. At the selfsame moment that he raised his arm with a short blunt weapon in his hand, he was aware of the swift movement of another person in the room. The man stopped still, his arm remained high, every fear was aroused. He turned instantly and saw a scene clearly enacted beside him in the dark mirror of the window. At the moment and shock of turning, he drew a sharp intake of breath and it was this that Mr Willy heard and that caused him to look up and around and see in the dark mirror the intruder, the danger, and the victim who was himself. At that still moment, the telephone rang shrilly, twice as loud in that still moment, on a small table near him.

It was not the movement of that figure in the dark mirror, it was not the bell ringing close at hand and insistently. It was an irrational and stupid fear lest his action, reproduced visibly beside him in the mirror, was being faithfully registered in some impossible way that filled the intruder with fright. The telephone ringing shrilly, Mr Willy now facing him, the play enacted beside him, and this irrational momentary fear caused him to turn and bound towards the door, to escape into the dark, banging the glass door with a clash behind him. When he got well away from the place he was angry—everything was always against him, he never had no luck, and if he hadn'ta lost his head it was a cinch he coulda done it easy.

'Damn you!' shouted Mr Willy in a rage, with his hand on the telephone, 'you might have broken it! Yes?' he said into the telephone, moderating the anger that possessed him and continuing within himself a conversation that said It was eighteen inches away, I was within a minute of it and I didn't know, it's no use telephoning the police but I'd better do that, it was just above me and I'd have died not knowing. 'Yes? Yes?' he said impatiently, trembling a little.

'Oh,' said a surprised voice, 'it *is* Mr Willy, isn't it? Just for a minute it didn't sound like you Mr Willy that was the *loveliest* party and what a lovely view and I'm sorry to be such a nuisance I kept on ringing and ringing because I thought you couldn't have gone out so soon' (tinkle tinkle) 'and you couldn't have gone to bed so soon but I do believe I must have left my little bead bag it's not the *value* but . . .' Mr Willy found himself shaking more violently now, not only with death averted and the rage of the slammed glass door but with the powerful thoughts that had usurped him and were interrupted by the dangerous moment which was now receding, and the tinkling voice on the telephone.

'I have it here. I'll bring it tomorrow,' he said shortly. He hung up the telephone and at the other end the Aunt turned and exclaimed, 'Well if he isn't the rudest man I never was treated like that in my whole life d'you know what he . . .'

Mr Willy was in a state of abstraction.

He went to the glass door and examined it. It was intact. He turned the key and drew the shutter down. Then he went back to the telephone in this state of abstraction. Death or near-death was still very close, though receding. It seemed to him at that moment that a crack had been coming in the great wall that shut him off from the light but perhaps he was wrong. He dialled the police, perfunctorily not urgently. He knew that before him lay the hardest work of his life—in his life but out of his country. He must in some way and very soon break the great wall that shut him off from whatever light there might be. Not for fear of death oh God not for fear of death but for fear of something else.

(1961)

Katherine Anne Porter   1890–1980

The Jilting of Granny Weatherall

She flicked her wrist neatly out of Doctor Harry's pudgy careful fingers and pulled the sheet up to her chin. The brat ought to be in knee breeches.[1] Doctoring around the country with spectacles on his nose! "Get along now, take your schoolbooks and go. There's nothing wrong with me."

Doctor Harry spread a warm paw like a cushion on her forehead where the forked green vein danced and made her eyelids twitch. "Now, now, be a good girl, and we'll have you up in no time."

"That's no way to speak to a woman nearly eighty years old just because she's down. I'd have you respect your elders, young man."

"Well, Missy, excuse me." Doctor Harry patted her cheek. "But I've got to warn you, haven't I? You're a marvel, but you must be careful or you're going to be good and sorry."

"Don't tell me what I'm going to be. I'm on my feet now, morally speaking. It's Cornelia. I had to go to bed to get rid of her."

Her bones felt loose, and floated around in her skin, and Doctor Harry floated like a balloon around the foot of the bed. He floated and pulled down his waistcoat and swung his glasses on a cord. "Well, stay where you are, it certainly can't hurt you."

"Get along and doctor your sick," said Granny Weatherall. "Leave a well woman alone. I'll call for you when I want you. . . . Where were you forty years ago when I pulled through milk-leg[2] and double pneumonia? You weren't even born. Don't let Cornelia lead you on," she shouted, because Doctor Harry appeared to float up to the ceiling and out. "I pay my own bills, and I don't throw my money away on nonsense!"

She meant to wave good-by, but it was too much trouble. Her eyes closed of themselves, it was like a dark curtain drawn around the bed. The pillow rose and floated under her, pleasant as a hammock in a light wind. She listened to the leaves rustling outside the window. No, somebody was swishing newspapers: no, Cornelia and Doctor Harry were whispering together. She leaped broad awake, thinking they whispered in her ear.

"She was never like this, *never* like this!" "Well, what can we expect?" "Yes, eighty years old. . . ."

Well, and what if she was? She still had ears. It was like Cornelia to whisper around doors. She always kept things secret in such a public way. She was always being tactful and kind. Cornelia was dutiful; that was the trouble with her. Dutiful and good: "So good and dutiful," said Granny, "that I'd like to spank her." She saw herself spanking Cornelia and making a fine job of it.

"What'd you say, Mother?"

Granny felt her face tying up in hard knots.

"Can't a body think, I'd like to know?"

"I thought you might want something."

"I do. I want a lot of things. First off, go away and don't whisper."

---

[1] Knee-length pants worn by little boys.
[2] Phlebitis following childbirth.

She lay and drowsed, hoping in her sleep that the children would keep out and let her rest a minute. It had been a long day. Not that she was tired. It was always pleasant to snatch a minute now and then. There was always so much to be done, let me see: tomorrow.

Tomorrow was far away and there was nothing to trouble about. Things were finished somehow when the time came; thank God there was always a little margin over for peace: then a person could spread out the plan of life and tuck in the edges orderly. It was good to have everything clean and folded away, with the hair brushes and tonic bottles sitting straight on the white embroidered linen: the day started without fuss and the pantry shelves laid out with rows of jelly glasses and brown jugs and white stone-china jars with blue whirligigs and words painted on them: coffee, tea, sugar, ginger, cinnamon, allspice: and the bronze clock with the lion on top nicely dusted off. The dust that lion could collect in twenty-four hours! The box in the attic with all those letters tied up, well she'd have to go through that tomorrow. All those letters—George's letters and John's letters and her letters to them both—lying around for the children to find afterwards made her uneasy. Yes, that would be tomorrow's business. No use to let them know how silly she had been once.

While she was rummaging around she found death in her mind and it felt clammy and unfamiliar. She had spent so much time preparing for death there was no need for bringing it up again. Let it take care of itself now. When she was sixty she had felt very old, finished, and went around making farewell trips to see her children and grandchildren, with a secret in her mind: This is the very last of your mother, children! Then she made her will and came down with a long fever. That was all just a notion like a lot of other things, but it was lucky too, for she had once for all got over the idea of dying for a long time. Now she couldn't be worried. She hoped she had better sense now. Her father had lived to be one hundred and two years old and had drunk a noggin[3] of strong hot toddy on his last birthday. He told the reporters it was his daily habit, and he owed his long life to that. He had made quite a scandal and was very pleased about it. She believed she'd just plague Cornelia a little.

"Cornelia! Cornelia!" No footsteps, but a sudden hand on her cheek. "Bless you, where have you been?"

"Here, mother."

"Well, Cornelia, I want a noggin of hot toddy."

"Are you cold, darling?"

"I'm chilly, Cornelia. Lying in bed stops the circulation. I must have told you that a thousand times."

Well, she could just hear Cornelia telling her husband that Mother was getting childish and they'd have to humor her. The thing that most annoyed her was that Cornelia thought she was deaf, dumb, and blind. Little hasty glances and tiny gestures tossed around her and over her head saying, "Don't cross her, let her have her way, she's eighty years old," and she sitting there as if she lived in a thin glass cage. Sometimes Granny almost made up her mind to pack up and move back to her own house where nobody could remind her every minute that she was old. Wait, wait, Cornelia, till your own children whisper behind your back!

In her day she had kept a better house and had got more work done. She wasn't too old yet for Lydia to be driving eighty miles for advice when one of

---

[3] A small mug.

the children jumped the track, and Jimmy still dropped in and talked things over: "Now, Mammy, you've a good business head, I want to know what you think of this? . . ." Old Cornelia couldn't change the furniture around without asking. Little things, little things! They had been so sweet when they were little. Granny wished the old days were back again with the children young and everything to be done over. It had been a hard pull, but not too much for her. When she thought of all the food she had cooked, and all the clothes she had cut and sewed, and all the gardens she had made—well, the children showed it. There they were, made out of her, and they couldn't get away from that. Sometimes she wanted to see John again and point to them and say, Well, I didn't do so badly, did I? But that would have to wait. That was for tomorrow. She used to think of him as a man, but now all the children were older than their father, and he would be a child beside her if she saw him now. It seemed strange and there was something wrong in the idea. Why, he couldn't possibly recognize her. She had fenced in a hundred acres once, digging the post holes herself and clamping the wires with just a negro boy to help. That changed a woman. John would be looking for a young woman with the peaked Spanish comb in her hair and the painted fan. Digging post holes changed a woman. Riding country roads in the winter when women had their babies was another thing: sitting up nights with sick horses and sick negroes and sick children and hardly ever losing one. John, I hardly ever lost one of them! John would see that in a minute, that would be something he could understand, she wouldn't have to explain anything!

It made her feel like rolling up her sleeves and putting the whole place to rights again. No matter if Cornelia was determined to be everywhere at once, there were a great many things left undone on this place. She would start tomorrow and do them. It was good to be strong enough for everything, even if all you made melted and changed and slipped under your hands, so that by the time you finished you almost forgot what you were working for. What was it I set out to do? she asked herself intently, but she could not remember. A fog rose over the valley, she saw it marching across the creek swallowing the trees and moving up the hill like an army of ghosts. Soon it would be at the near edge of the orchard, and then it was time to go in and light the lamps. Come in, children, don't stay out in the night air.

Lighting the lamps had been beautiful. The children huddled up to her and breathed like little calves waiting at the bars in the twilight. Their eyes followed the match and watched the flame rise and settle in a blue curve, then they moved away from her. The lamp was lit, they didn't have to be scared and hang on to mother any more. Never, never, never more. God, for all my life I thank Thee. Without Thee, my God, I could never have done it. Hail, Mary, full of grace.

I want you to pick all the fruit this year and see that nothing is wasted. There's always someone who can use it. Don't let good things rot for want of using. You waste life when you waste good food. Don't let things get lost. It's bitter to lose things. Now, don't let me get to thinking, not when I am tired and taking a little nap before supper. . . .

The pillow rose about her shoulders and pressed against her heart and the memory was being squeezed out of it: oh, push down the pillow, somebody: it would smother her if she tried to hold it. Such a fresh breeze blowing and such a green day with no threats in it. But he had not come, just the same. What does a woman do when she has put on the white veil and set out the white cake for a man and he doesn't come? She tried to remember. No, I swear he never harmed me but in that. He never harmed me but in that . . . and what if he did? There was the day, the day, but a whirl of dark smoke rose and covered it, crept up and over into the bright field where everything was planted so carefully in orderly rows. That was hell, she knew hell when she saw it. For sixty years she had prayed against remembering him and against losing her soul in the deep pit of hell, and now the two things were mingled in one and the thought of him was a smoky cloud from hell that moved and crept in her head when she had just got rid of Doctor Harry and was trying to rest a minute: Wounded vanity, Ellen, said a sharp voice in the top of her mind. Don't let your wounded vanity get the upper hand of you. Plenty of girls get jilted. You were jilted, weren't you? Then stand up to it. Her eyelids wavered and let in streamers of blue-gray light like tissue paper over her eyes. She must get up and pull the shades down or she'd never sleep. She was in bed again and the shades were not down. How could that happen? Better turn over, hide from the light, sleeping in the light gave you nightmares. "Mother, how do you feel now?" and a stinging wetness on her forehead. But I don't like having my face washed in cold water!

Hapsy? George? Lydia? Jimmy? No, Cornelia, and her features were swollen and full of little puddles. "They're coming, darling, they'll all be here soon." Go wash your face, child, you look funny.

Instead of obeying, Cornelia knelt down and put her head on the pillow. She seemed to be talking but there was no sound. "Well, are you tongue-tied? Whose birthday is it? Are you going to give a party?"

Cornelia's mouth moved urgently in strange shapes. "Don't do that, you bother me, daughter."

"Oh, no, Mother, Oh, no. . . ."

Nonsense. It was strange about children. They disputed your every word. "No what, Cornelia?"

"Here's Doctor Harry."

"I won't see that boy again. He just left five minutes ago."

"That was this morning, Mother. It's night now. Here's the nurse."

"This is Doctor Harry, Mrs. Weatherall. I never saw you look so young and happy!"

"Ah, I'll never be young again—but I'd be happy if they'd let me be in peace and get rested."

She thought she spoke up loudly, but no one answered. A warm weight on her forehead, a warm bracelet on her wrist, and a breeze went on whispering, trying to tell her something. A shuffle of leaves in the everlasting hand of God. He blew on them and they danced and rattled. "Mother, don't mind, we're going to give you a little hypodermic." "Look here, daughter, how do ants get in this bed? I saw sugar ants yesterday." Did you send for Hapsy too?

It was Hapsy she really wanted. She had to go a long way back through a great many rooms to find Hapsy standing with a baby on her arm. She seemed to herself to be Hapsy also, and the baby on Hapsy's arm was Hapsy and himself and herself, all at once, and there was no surprise in the meeting. Then Hapsy melted from within and turned flimsy as gray gauze and the baby was a gauzy shadow, and Hapsy came up close and said, "I thought you'd never come," and looked at her very searchingly and said, "You haven't changed a bit!" They leaned forward to kiss, when Cornelia began whispering from a long way off, "Oh, is there anything you want to tell me? Is there anything I can do for you?"

Yes, she had changed her mind after sixty years and she would like to see George. I want you to find George. Find him and be sure to tell him I forgot him. I want him to know I had my husband just the same and my children and my house like any other woman. A good house too and a good husband that I loved and fine children out of him. Better than I hoped for even. Tell him I was given back everything he took away and more. Oh, no, oh, God, no, there was something else besides the house and the man and the children. Oh, surely they were not all? What was it? Something not given back. . . . Her breath crowded down under her ribs and grew into a monstrous frightening shape with cutting edges; it bored up into her head, and the agony was unbelievable: Yes, John, get the doctor now, no more talk, my time has come.

When this one was born it should be the last. The last. It should have been born first, for it was the one she had truly wanted. Everything came in good time. Nothing left out, left over. She was strong, in three days she would be as well as ever. Better. A woman needed milk in her to have her full health.

"Mother, do you hear me?"

"I've been telling you—"

"Mother, Father Connolly's here."

"I went to Holy Communion only last week. Tell him I'm not so sinful as all that."

"Father just wants to speak to you."

He could speak as much as he pleased. It was like him to drop in and inquire about her soul as if it were a teething baby, and then stay on for a cup of tea and a round of cards and gossip. He always had a funny story of some sort, usually about an Irishman who made his little mistakes and confessed them, and the point lay in some absurd thing he would blurt out in the confessional showing his struggles between native piety and original sin. Granny felt easy about her soul. Cornelia, where are your manners? Give Father Connolly a chair. She had her secret, comfortable understanding with a few favorite saints who cleared a straight road to God for her. All as surely signed and sealed as the papers for the new Forty Acres. Forever . . . heirs and assigns forever. Since the day the wedding cake was not cut, but thrown out and wasted. The whole bottom dropped out of the world, and there she was blind and sweating with nothing under her feet and the walls falling away. His hand had caught her under the breast, she had not fallen, there was the freshly polished floor with the green rug on it, just as before. He had cursed like a sailor's parrot and said, "I'll kill him for you." Don't lay a hand on him, for my sake leave something to God. "Now, Ellen, you must believe what I tell you. . . ."

So there was nothing, nothing to worry about any more, except sometimes in the night one of the children screamed in a nightmare, and they both hustled out shaking and hunting for the matches and calling, "There, wait a minute, here we are!" John, get the doctor now. Hapsy's time has come. But there was Hapsy standing by the bed in a white cap. "Cornelia, tell Hapsy to take off her cap. I can't see her plain."

Her eyes opened very wide and the room stood out like a picture she had seen somewhere. Dark colors with the shadows rising towards the ceiling in long angles. The tall black dresser gleamed with nothing on it but John's picture, enlarged from a little one, with John's eyes very black when they should have been blue. You never saw him, so how do you know how he looked? But the man insisted the copy was perfect, it was very rich and handsome. For a picture, yes, but it's not my husband. The table by the bed had a linen cover and a candle and a crucifix. The light was blue from Cornelia's silk lampshades. No sort of light at all, just frippery.[4] You had to live forty years with kerosene lamps to appreciate honest electricity. She felt very strong and she saw Doctor Harry with a rosy nimbus around him.

"You look like a saint, Doctor Harry, and I vow that's as near as you'll ever come to it."

"She's saying something."

"I heard you, Cornelia. What's all this carrying-on?"

"Father Connolly's saying—"

Cornelia's voice staggered and bumped like a cart in a bad road. It rounded corners and turned back again and arrived nowhere. Granny stepped up in the cart very lightly and reached for the reins, but a man sat beside her and she knew him by his hands, driving the cart. She did not look in his face, for she knew without seeing, but looked instead down the road where the trees leaned over and bowed to each other and a thousand birds were singing a Mass. She felt like singing too, but she put her hand in the bosom of her dress and pulled out a rosary, and Father Connolly murmured Latin in a very solemn voice and tickled her feet. My God, will you stop that nonsense? I'm a married woman. What if he did run away and leave me to face the priest by myself? I found another a whole world better. I wouldn't have exchanged my husband for anybody except St. Michael himself, and you may tell him that for me with a thank you in the bargain.

Light flashed on her closed eyelids, and a deep roaring shook her. Cornelia, is that lightning? I hear thunder. There's going to be a storm. Close all the windows. Call the children in. . . . "Mother, here we are, all of us." "Is that you, Hapsy?" "Oh, no, I'm Lydia. We drove as fast as we could." Their faces drifted above her, drifted away. The rosary fell out of her hands and Lydia put it back. Jimmy tried to help, their hands fumbled together, and Granny closed two fingers around Jimmy's thumb. Beads[5] wouldn't do it, it must be something alive. She was so amazed her thoughts ran round and round. So, my dear Lord, this is my death and I wasn't even thinking about it. My children have come to see me die. But I can't, it's not time. Oh, I always hated surprises. I wanted to give Cornelia the amethyst set—Cornelia, you're to have the amethyst set, but Hapsy's to wear it when she wants, and, Doctor Harry, do shut up. Nobody sent for you. Oh, my dear Lord, do wait a minute. I meant to do something about the Forty Acres, Jimmy doesn't need it and Lydia will later on, with that worthless husband of hers. I meant to finish the altar cloth and send six bottles of wine to Sister Borgia for her dyspepsia. I want to send six bottles of wine to Sister Borgia, Father Connolly, now don't let me forget.

Cornelia's voice made short turns and tilted over and crashed. "Oh, Mother, oh, Mother, oh, Mother. . . ."

"I'm not going Cornelia. I'm taken by surprise. I can't go."

You'll see Hapsy again. What about her? "I thought you'd never come." Granny made a long journey outward, looking for Hapsy. What if I don't find her? What then? Her heart sank down and down, there was no bottom to death, she couldn't come to the end of it. The blue light from Cornelia's lampshade drew into a tiny point in the center of her brain, it flickered and winked like an eye, quietly it fluttered and dwindled. Granny lay curled down within herself,

---

[4] Showy foolishness.
[5] Rosary beads.

amazed and watchful, staring at the point of light that was herself; her body was now only a deeper mass of shadow in an endless darkness and this darkness would curl around the light and swallow it up. God, give a sign!

For the second time there was no sign. Again no bridegroom and the priest in the house. She could not remember any other sorrow because this grief wiped them all away. Oh, no, there's nothing more cruel than this—I'll never forgive it. She stretched herself with a deep breath and blew out the light.

(1930)

Ernest Hemingway   1899–1961

Hills like White Elephants

The hills across the valley of the Ebro[1] were long and white. On this side there was no shade and no trees and the station was between two lines of rails in the sun. Close against the side of the station there was the warm shadow of the building and a curtain, made of strings of bamboo beads, hung across the open door into the bar, to keep out flies. The American and the girl with him sat at a table in the shade, outside the building. It was very hot and the express from Barcelona would come in forty minutes. It stopped at this junction for two minutes and went on to Madrid.

"What should we drink?" the girl asked. She had taken off her hat and put it on the table.

"It's pretty hot," the man said.

"Let's drink beer."

"Dos cervezas," the man said into the curtain.

"Big ones?" a woman asked from the doorway.

"Yes. Two big ones."

The woman brought two glasses of beer and two felt pads. She put the felt pads and the beer glasses on the table and looked at the man and the girl. The girl was looking off at the line of hills. They were white in the sun and the country was brown and dry.

"They look like white elephants," she said.

"I've never seen one," the man drank his beer.

"No, you wouldn't have."

"I might have," the man said. "Just because you say I wouldn't have doesn't prove anything."

The girl looked at the bead curtain. "They've painted something on it," she said. "What does it say?"

"Anis del Toro. It's a drink."

"Could we try it?"

The man called "Listen" through the curtain. The woman came out from the bar.

"Four reales."[2]

"We want two Anis del Toro."

"With water?"

"Do you want it with water?"

"I don't know," the girl said. "Is it good with water?"

"It's all right."

"You want them with water?" asked the woman.

"Yes, with water."

"It tastes like licorice," the girl said and put the glass down.

"That's the way with everything."

"Yes," said the girl. "Everything tastes of licorice. Especially all the things you've waited so long for, like absinthe."

"Oh, cut it out."

---

[1] A river in Spain.
[2] Spanish coins.

"You started it," the girl said. "I was being amused. I was having a fine time."

"Well, let's try and have a fine time."

"All right. I was trying. I said the mountains looked like white elephants. Wasn't that bright?"

"That was bright."

"I wanted to try this new drink. That's all we do, isn't it—look at things and try new drinks?"

"I guess so."

The girl looked across at the hills.

"They're lovely hills," she said. "They don't really look like white elephants. I just meant the coloring of their skin through the trees."

"Should we have another drink?"

"All right."

The warm wind blew the bead curtain against the table.

"The beer's nice and cool," the man said.

"It's lovely," the girl said.

"It's really an awfully simple operation, Jig," the man said. "It's not really an operation at all."

The girl looked at the ground the table legs rested on.

"I know you wouldn't mind it, Jig. It's really not anything. It's just to let the air in."

The girl did not say anything.

"I'll go with you and I'll stay with you all the time. They just let the air in and then it's all perfectly natural."

"Then what will we do afterward?"

"We'll be fine afterward. Just like we were before."

"What makes you think so?"

"That's the only thing that bothers us. It's the only thing that's made us unhappy."

The girl looked at the bead curtain, put her hand out and took hold of two of the strings of beads.

"And you think then we'll be all right and be happy."

"I know we will. You don't have to be afraid. I've known lots of people that have done it."

"So have I," said the girl. "And afterward they were all so happy."

"Well," the man said, "if you don't want to you don't have to. I wouldn't have you do it if you didn't want to. But I know it's perfectly simple."

"And you really want to?"

"I think it's the best thing to do. But I don't want you to do it if you don't really want to."

"And if I do it you'll be happy and things will be like they were and you'll love me?"

"I love you now. You know I love you."

"I know. But if I do it, then it will be nice again if I say things are like white elephants, and you'll like it?"

"I'll love it. I love it now but I just can't think about it. You know how I get when I worry."

"If I do it you won't ever worry?"

"I won't worry about that because it's perfectly simple."

"Then I'll do it. Because I don't care about me."

"What do you mean?"

"I don't care about me."

"Well, I care about you."

"Oh, yes. But I don't care about me. And I'll do it and then everything will be fine."

"I don't want you to do it if you feel that way."

The girl stood up and walked to the end of the station. Across, on the other side, were fields of grain and trees along the banks of the Ebro. Far away, beyond the river, were mountains. The shadow of a cloud moved across the field of grain and she saw the river through the trees.

"And we could have all this," she said. "And we could have everything and every day we make it more impossible."

"What did you say?"

"I said we could have everything."

"We can have everything."

"No, we can't."

"We can have the whole world."

"No, we can't."

"We can go everywhere."

"No, we can't. It isn't ours any more."

"It's ours."

"No, it isn't. And once they take it away, you never get it back."

"But they haven't taken it away."

"We'll wait and see."

"Come on back in the shade," he said. "You mustn't feel that way."

"I don't feel any way," the girl said. "I just know things."

"I don't want you to do anything that you don't want to do—"

"Nor that isn't good for me," she said. "I know. Could we have another beer?"

"All right. But you've got to realize—"

"I realize," the girl said. "Can't we maybe stop talking?"

They sat down at the table and the girl looked across at the hills on the dry side of the valley and the man looked at her and at the table.

"You've got to realize," he said, "that I don't want you to do it if you don't want to. I'm perfectly willing to go through with it if it means anything to you."

"Doesn't it mean anything to you? We could get along."

"Of course it does. But I don't want anybody but you. I don't want anyone else. And I know it's perfectly simple."

"Yes, you know it's perfectly simple."

"It's all right for you to say that, but I do know it."

"Would you do something for me now?"

"I'd do anything for you."

"Would you please please please please please please please stop talking?"

He did not say anything but looked at the bags against the wall of the station. There were labels on them from all the hotels where they had spent nights.

"But I don't want you to," he said. "I don't care anything about it."

"I'll scream," the girl said.

The woman came out through the curtains with two glasses of beer and put them down on the damp felt pads. "The train comes in five minutes," she said.

"What did she say?" asked the girl.

"That the train is coming in five minutes."

The girl smiled brightly at the woman, to thank her.

"I'd better take the bags over to the other side of the station," the man said. She smiled at him.

"All right. Then come back and we'll finish the beer."

He picked up the two heavy bags and carried them around the station to the other tracks. He looked up the tracks but could not see the train. Coming back, he walked through the barroom, where people waiting for the train were drinking. He drank an Anis at the bar and looked at the people. They were all waiting reasonably for the train. He went out through the bead curtain. She was sitting at the table and smiled at him.

"Do you feel better?" he asked.

"I feel fine," she said. "There's nothing wrong with me. I feel fine."

(1927)

John Steinbeck   1902–1968

The Chrysanthemums

The high gray-flannel fog of winter closed off the Salinas Valley from the sky and from all the rest of the world. On every side it sat like a lid on the mountains and made of the great valley a closed pot. On the broad, level land floor the gang plows bit deep and left the black earth shining like metal where the shares had cut. On the foothill ranches across the Salinas River, the yellow stubble fields seemed to be bathed in pale cold sunshine, but there was no sunshine in the valley now in December. The thick willow scrub along the river flamed with sharp and positive yellow leaves.

It was a time of quiet and of waiting. The air was cold and tender. A light wind blew up from the southwest so that the farmers were mildly hopeful of a good rain before long; but fog and rain do not go together.

Across the river, on Henry Allen's foothill ranch there was little work to be done, for the hay was cut and stored and the orchards were plowed up to receive the rain deeply when it should come. The cattle on the higher slopes were becoming shaggy and rough-coated.

Elisa Allen, working in her flower garden, looked down across the yard and saw Henry, her husband, talking to two men in business suits. The three of them stood by the tractor shed, each man with one foot on the side of the little Fordson. They smoked cigarettes and studied the machine as they talked.

Elisa watched them for a moment and then went back to her work. She was thirty-five. Her face was lean and strong and her eyes were as clear as water. Her figure looked blocked and heavy in her gardening costume, a man's black hat pulled down over her eyes, clodhopper shoes, a figured print dress almost completely covered by a big corduroy apron with four big pockets to hold the snips, the trowel and scratcher, the seeds and the knife she worked with. She wore heavy leather gloves to protect her hands while she worked.

She was cutting down the old year's chrysanthemum stalks with a pair of short and powerful scissors. She looked down toward the men by the tractor shed now and then. Her face was eager and mature and handsome; even her work with the scissors was over-eager, over-powerful. The chrysanthemum stems seemed too small and easy for her energy.

She brushed a cloud of hair out of her eyes with the back of her glove, and left a smudge of earth on her cheek in doing it. Behind her stood the neat white farm house with red geraniums close-banked around it as high as the windows. It was a hard-swept looking little house, with hard-polished windows, and a clean mud-mat on the front steps.

Elisa cast another glance toward the tractor shed. The strangers were getting into their Ford coupe. She took off a glove and put her strong fingers down into the forest of new green chrysanthemum sprouts that were growing around the old roots. She spread the leaves and looked down among the close-growing stems. No aphids were there, no sowbugs or snails or cutworms. Her terrier fingers destroyed such pests before they could get started.

Elisa started at the sound of her husband's voice. He had come near quietly, and he leaned over the wire fence that protected her flower garden from cattle and dogs and chickens.

"At it again," he said. "You've got a strong new crop coming."

Elisa straightened her back and pulled on the gardening glove again. "Yes. They'll be strong this coming year." In her tone and on her face there was a little smugness.

"You've got a gift with things," Henry observed. "Some of those yellow chrysanthemums you had this year were ten inches across. I wish you'd work out in the orchard and raise some apples that big."

Her eyes sharpened. "Maybe I could do it, too. I've a gift with things, all right. My mother had it. She could stick anything in the ground and make it grow. She said it was having planters' hands that knew how to do it."

"Well, it sure works with flowers," he said.

"Henry, who were those men you were talking to?"

"Why, sure, that's what I came to tell you. They were from the Western Meat Company. I sold them those thirty head of three-year-old steers. Got nearly my own price, too."

"Good," she said. "Good for you."

"And I thought," he continued, "I thought how it's Saturday afternoon, and we might go into Salinas for dinner at a restaurant, and then to a picture show—to celebrate, you see."

"Good," she repeated. "Oh, yes. That will be good."

Henry put on his joking tone. "There's fights tonight. How'd you like to go to the fights?"

"Oh, no," she said breathlessly. "No, I wouldn't like fights."

"Just fooling, Elisa. We'll go to a movie. Let's see. It's two now. I'm going to take Scotty and bring down those steers from the hill. It'll take us maybe two hours. We'll go in town about five and have dinner at the Cominos Hotel. Like that?"

"Of course I'll like it. It's good to eat away from home."

"All right, then. I'll go get up a couple of horses."

She said, "I'll have plenty of time to transplant some of these sets, I guess."

She heard her husband calling Scotty down by the barn. And a little later she saw the two men ride up the pale yellow hillside in search of the steers.

There was a little square sandy bed kept for rooting the chrysanthemums. With her trowel she turned the soil over and over, and smoothed it and patted it firm. Then she dug ten parallel trenches to receive the sets. Back at the chrysanthemum bed she pulled out the little crisp shoots, trimmed off the leaves of each one with her scissors and laid it on a small orderly pile.

A squeak of wheels and plod of hoofs came from the road. Elisa looked up. The country road ran along the dense bank of willows and cottonwoods that bordered the river, and up this road came a curious vehicle, curiously drawn. It was an old spring-wagon, with a round canvas top on it like the cover of a prairie schooner. It was drawn by an old bay horse and a little gray-and-white burro. A big stubble-bearded man sat between the cover flaps and drove the crawling team. Underneath the wagon, between the hind wheels, a lean and rangy mongrel dog walked sedately. Words were painted on the canvas, in clumsy, crooked letters. "Pots, pans, knives, sisors, lawn mores, Fixed." Two rows of articles, and the triumphantly definitive "Fixed" below. The black paint had run down in little sharp points beneath each letter.

Elisa, squatting on the ground, watched to see the crazy, loose-jointed wagon pass by. But it didn't pass. It turned into the farm road in front of her house, crooked old wheels skirling and squeaking. The rangy dog darted from between the wheels and ran ahead. Instantly the two ranch shepherds flew out at him. Then all three stopped, and with stiff and quivering tails, with taut straight legs, with ambassadorial dignity, they slowly circled, sniffing daintily. The caravan pulled up to Elisa's wire fence and stopped. Now the newcomer dog, feeling out-numbered, lowered his tail and retired under the wagon with raised hackles and bared teeth.

The man on the wagon seat called out, "That's a bad dog in a fight when he gets started."

Elisa laughed. "I see he is. How soon does he generally get started?"

The man caught up her laughter and echoed it heartily. "Sometimes not for weeks and weeks," he said. He climbed stiffly down, over the wheel. The horse and the donkey drooped like unwatered flowers.

Elisa saw that he was a very big man. Although his hair and beard were graying, he did not look old. His worn black suit was wrinkled and spotted with grease. The laughter had disappeared from his face and eyes the moment his laughing voice ceased. His eyes were dark, and they were full of the brooding that gets in the eyes of teamsters and of sailors. The calloused hands he rested on the wire fence were cracked, and every crack was a black line. He took off his battered hat.

"I'm off my general road, ma'am," he said. "Does this dirt road cut over across the river to the Los Angeles highway?"

Elisa stood up and shoved the thick scissors in her apron pocket. "Well, yes, it does, but it winds around and then fords the river. I don't think your team could pull through the sand."

He replied with some asperity, "It might surprise you what them beasts can pull through."

"When they get started?" she asked.

He smiled for a second. "Yes. When they get started."

"Well," said Elisa, "I think you'll save time if you go back to the Salinas road and pick up the highway there."

He drew a big finger down the chicken wire and made it sing. "I ain't in any hurry, ma'am. I go from Seattle to San Diego and back every year. Takes all my time. About six months each way. I aim to follow nice weather."

Elisa took off her gloves and stuffed them in the apron pocket with the scissors. She touched the under edge of her man's hat, searching for fugitive hairs. "That sounds like a nice kind of way to live," she said.

He leaned confidentially over the fence. "Maybe you noticed the writing on my wagon. I mend pots and sharpen knives and scissors. You got any of them things to do?"

"Oh, no," she said quickly. "Nothing like that." Her eyes hardened with resistance.

"Scissors is the worst thing," he explained. "Most people just ruin scissors trying to sharpen 'em, but I know how. I got a special tool. It's a little bobbit kind of thing, and patented. But it sure does the trick."

"No. My scissors are all sharp."

"All right, then. Take a pot," he continued earnestly, "a bent pot, or a pot with a hole. I can make it like new so you don't have to buy no new ones. That's a saving for you."

"No," she said shortly. "I tell you I have nothing like that for you to do."

His face fell to an exaggerated sadness. His voice took on a whining undertone. "I ain't had a thing to do today. Maybe I won't have no supper tonight. You see I'm off my regular road. I know folks on the highway clear from Seattle to San Diego. They save their things for me to sharpen up because they know I do it so good and save them money."

"I'm sorry," Elisa said irritably. "I haven't anything for you to do."

His eyes left her face and fell to searching the ground. They roamed about until they came to the chrysanthemum bed where she had been working. "What's them plants, ma'am?"

The irritation and resistance melted from Elisa's face. "Oh, those are chrysanthemums, giant whites and yellows. I raise them every year, bigger than anybody around here."

"Kind of a long-stemmed flower? Looks like a quick puff of colored smoke?" he asked.

"That's it. What a nice way to describe them."

"They smell kind of nasty till you get used to them," he said.

"It's a good bitter smell," she retorted, "not nasty at all."

He changed his tone quickly. "I like the smell myself."

"I had ten-inch blooms this year," she said.

The man leaned farther over the fence. "Look. I know a lady down the road a piece, has got the nicest garden you ever seen. Got nearly every kind of flower but no chrysanthemums. Last time I was mending a copper-bottom washtub for her (that's a hard job but I do it good), she said to me, 'If you ever run acrost some nice chrysanthemums I wish you'd try to get me a few seeds.' That's what she told me."

Elisa's eyes grew alert and eager. "She couldn't have known much about chrysanthemums. You *can* raise them from seed, but it's much easier to root the little sprouts you see there."

"Oh," he said. "I s'pose I can't take none to her, then."

"Why yes you can," Elisa cried. "I can put some in damp sand, and you can carry them right along with you. They'll take root in the pot if you keep them damp. And then she can transplant them."

"She'd sure like to have some, ma'am. You say they're nice ones?"

"Beautiful," she said. "Oh, beautiful." Her eyes shone. She tore off the battered hat and shook out her dark pretty hair. "I'll put them in a flower pot, and you can take them right with you. Come into the yard."

While the man came through the picket gate Elisa ran excitedly along the geranium-bordered path to the back of the house. And she returned carrying a big red flower pot. The gloves were forgotten now. She kneeled on the ground by the starting bed and dug up the sandy soil with her fingers and scooped it into the bright new flower pot. Then she picked up the little pile of shoots she had prepared. With her strong fingers she pressed them into the sand and tamped around them with her knuckles. The man stood over her. "I'll tell you what to do," she said. "You remember so you can tell the lady."

"Yes, I'll try to remember."

"Well, look. These will take root in about a month. Then she must set them out, about a foot apart in good rich earth like this, see?" She lifted a handful of dark soil for him to look at. "They'll grow fast and tall. Now remember this: In July tell her to cut them down, about eight inches from the ground."

"Before they bloom?" he asked.

"Yes, before they bloom." Her face was tight with eagerness. "They'll grow right up again. About the last of September the buds will start."

She stopped and seemed perplexed. "It's the budding that takes the most care," she said hesitantly. "I don't know how to tell you." She looked deep into his eyes, searchingly. Her mouth opened a little, and she seemed to be listening. "I'll try to tell you," she said. "Did you ever hear of planting hands?"

"Can't say I have, ma'am."

"Well, I can only tell you what it feels like. It's when you're picking off the buds you don't want. Everything goes right down into your fingertips. You watch your fingers work. They do it themselves. You can feel how it is. They pick and pick the buds. They never make a mistake. They're with the plant. Do you see? Your fingers and the plant. You can feel that, right up your arm. They know. They never make a mistake. You can feel it. When you're like that you can't do anything wrong. Do you see that? Can you understand that?"

She was kneeling on the ground looking up at him. Her breast swelled passionately.

The man's eyes narrowed. He looked away self-consciously. "Maybe I know," he said. "Sometimes in the night in the wagon there—"

Elisa's voice grew husky. She broke in on him, "I've never lived as you do, but I know what you mean. When the night is dark—why, the stars are sharp-pointed, and there's quiet. Why, you rise up and up! Every pointed star gets driven into your body. It's like that. Hot and sharp and—lovely."

Kneeling there, her hand went out toward his legs in the greasy black trousers. Her hesitant fingers almost touched the cloth. Then her hand dropped to the ground. She crouched low like a fawning dog.

He said, "It's nice, just like you say. Only when you don't have no dinner, it ain't."

She stood up then, very straight, and her face was ashamed. She held the flower pot out to him and placed it gently in his arms. "Here. Put it in your wagon, on the seat, where you can watch it. Maybe I can find something for you to do."

At the back of the house she dug in the can pile and found two old and battered aluminum saucepans. She carried them back and gave them to him. "Here, maybe you can fix these."

His manner changed. He became professional. "Good as new I can fix them." At the back of his wagon he set a little anvil, and out of an oily tool box dug a small machine hammer. Elisa came through the gate to watch him while he pounded out the dents in the kettles. His mouth grew sure and knowing. At a difficult part of the work he sucked his underlip.

"You sleep right in the wagon?" Elisa asked.

"Right in the wagon, ma'am. Rain or shine I'm dry as a cow in there."

"It must be nice," she said. "It must be very nice. I wish women could do such things."

"It ain't the right kind of life for a woman."

Her upper lip raised a little, showing her teeth. "How do you know? How can you tell?" she said.

"I don't know, ma'am," he protested. "Of course I don't know. Now here's your kettles, done. You don't have to buy no new ones."

"How much?"

"Oh, fifty cents'll do. I keep my prices down and my work good. That's why I have all them satisfied customers up and down the highway."

Elisa brought him a fifty-cent piece from the house and dropped it in his hand. "You might be surprised to have a rival some time. I can sharpen scissors, too. And I can beat the dents out of little pots. I could show you what a woman might do."

He put his hammer back in the oily box and shoved the little anvil out of sight. "It would be a lonely life for a woman, ma'am, and a scary life, too, with animals creeping under the wagon all night." He climbed over the singletree, steadying himself with a hand on the burro's white rump. He settled himself in the seat, picked up the lines. "Thank you kindly, ma'am," he said. "I'll do like you told me; I'll go back and catch the Salinas road."

"Mind," she called, "if you're long in getting there, keep the sand damp."

"Sand, ma'am? . . . Sand? Oh, sure. You mean around the chrysanthemums. Sure I will." He clucked his tongue. The beasts leaned luxuriously into their collars. The mongrel dog took his place between the back wheels. The wagon turned and crawled out the entrance road and back the way it had come, along the river.

Elisa stood in front of her wire fence watching the slow progress of the caravan. Her shoulders were straight, her head thrown back, her eyes half-closed, so that the scene came vaguely into them. Her lips moved silently, forming the words "Good-bye—good-bye." Then she whispered, "That's a bright direction. There's a glowing there." The sound of her whisper startled her. She shook herself free and looked about to see whether anyone had been listening. Only the dogs had heard. They lifted their heads toward her from their sleeping in the dust, and then stretched out their chins and settled asleep again. Elisa turned and ran hurriedly into the house.

In the kitchen she reached behind the stove and felt the water tank. It was full of hot water from the noonday cooking. In the bathroom she tore off her soiled clothes and flung them into the corner. And then she scrubbed herself with a little block of pumice, legs and thighs, loins and chest and arms, until her skin was scratched and red. When she had dried herself she stood in front of a mirror in her bedroom and looked at her body. She tightened her stomach and threw out her chest. She turned and looked over her shoulder at her back.

After a while she began to dress slowly. She put on her newest underclothing and her nicest stockings and the dress which was the symbol of her prettiness. She worked carefully on her hair, penciled her eyebrows and rouged her lips.

Before she was finished she heard the little thunder of hoofs and the shouts of Henry and his helper as they drove the red steers into the corral. She heard the gate bang shut and set herself for Henry's arrival.

His steps sounded on the porch. He entered the house calling, "Elisa, where are you?"

"In my room, dressing. I'm not ready. There's hot water for your bath. Hurry up. It's getting late."

When she heard him splashing in the tub, Elisa laid his dark suit on the bed, and shirt and socks and tie beside it. She stood his polished shoes on the floor beside the bed. Then she went to the porch and sat primly and stiffly down. She looked toward the river road where the willow-line was still yellow with frosted leaves so that under the high gray fog they seemed a thin band of sunshine. This was the only color in the gray afternoon. She sat unmoving for a long time. Her eyes blinked rarely.

Henry came banging out of the door, shoving his tie inside his vest as he came. Elisa stiffened and her face grew tight. Henry stopped short and looked at her. "Why—why, Elisa. You look so nice!"

"Nice? You think I look nice? What do you mean by 'nice'?"

Henry blundered on. "I don't know. I mean you look different, strong and happy."

"I am strong? Yes, strong. What do you mean 'strong'?"

He looked bewildered. "You're playing some kind of a game," he said helplessly. "It's a kind of a play. You look strong enough to break a calf over your knee, happy enough to eat it like a watermelon."

For a second she lost her rigidity. "Henry! Don't talk like that. You didn't know what you said." She grew complete again. "I'm strong," she boasted. "I never knew before how strong."

Henry looked down toward the tractor shed, and when he brought his eyes back to her, they were his own again. "I'll get out the car. You can put on your coat while I'm starting."

Elisa went into the house. She heard him drive to the gate and idle down his motor, and then she took a long time to put on her hat. She pulled it here and pressed it there. When Henry turned the motor off she slipped into her coat and went out.

The little roadster bounced along on the dirt road by the river, raising the birds and driving the rabbits into the brush. Two cranes flapped heavily over the willow-line and dropped into the riverbed.

Far ahead on the road Elisa saw a dark speck. She knew.

She tried not to look as they passed it, but her eyes would not obey. She whispered to herself sadly, "He might have thrown them off the road. That wouldn't have been much trouble, not very much. But he kept the pot," she explained. "He had to keep the pot. That's why he couldn't get them off the road."

The roadster turned a bend and she saw the caravan ahead. She swung full around toward her husband so she could not see the little covered wagon and the mismatched team as the car passed them.

In a moment it was over. The thing was done. She did not look back.

She said loudly, to be heard above the motor, "It will be good, tonight, a good dinner."

"Now you're changed again," Henry complained. He took one hand from the wheel and patted her knee. "I ought to take you in to dinner oftener. It would be good for both of us. We get so heavy out on the ranch."

"Henry," she asked, "could we have wine at dinner?"

"Sure we could. Say! That will be fine."

She was silent for a while; then she said, "Henry, at those prize fights, do the men hurt each other very much?"

"Sometimes a little, not often. Why?"

"Well, I've read how they break noses, and blood runs down their chests. I've read how the fighting gloves get heavy and soggy with blood."

He looked around at her. "What's the matter, Elisa? I didn't know you read things like that." He brought the car to a stop, then turned to the right over the Salinas River bridge.

"Do any women ever go to the fights?" she asked.

"Oh, sure, some. What's the matter, Elisa? Do you want to go? I don't think you'd like it, but I'll take you if you really want to go."

She relaxed limply in the seat. "Oh, no. No. I don't want to go. I'm sure I don't." Her face was turned away from him. "It will be enough if we can have wine. It will be plenty." She turned up her coat collar so he could not see that she was crying weakly—like an old woman.

(1938)

Richard Wright   1908–1960

The Man Who Was Almost a Man

Dave struck out across the fields, looking homeward through paling light. Whut's the use of talkin wid em niggers in the field? Anyhow, his mother was putting supper on the table. Them niggers can't understan nothing. One of these days he was going to get a gun and practice shooting, then they couldn't talk to him as though he were a little boy. He slowed, looking at the ground. Shucks, Ah ain scareda them even ef they are biggern me! Aw, Ah know whut Ahma do. Ahm going by ol Joe's sto n git that Sears Roebuck catlog n look at them guns. Mebbe Ma will lemme buy one when she gits mah pay from ol man Hawkins. Ahma beg her t gimme some money. Ahm ol ernough to hava gun. Ahm seventeen. Almost a man. He strode, feeling his long loose-jointed limbs. Shucks, a man oughta hava little gun aftah he done worked hard all day.

He came in sight of Joe's store. A yellow lantern glowed on the front porch. He mounted steps and went through the screen door, hearing it bang behind him. There was a strong smell of coal oil and mackerel fish. He felt very confident until he saw fat Joe walk in through the rear door, then his courage began to ooze.

"Howdy, Dave! Whutcha want?"

"How yuh, Mistah Joe? Aw, Ah don wanna buy nothing. Ah jus wanted t see ef yuhd lemme look at tha catlog erwhile."

"Sure! You wanna see it here?"

"Nawsuh. Ah wans t take it home wid me. Ah'll bring it back termorrow when Ah come in from the fiels."

"You plannin on buying something?"

"Yessuh."

"Your ma lettin you have your own money now?"

"Shucks. Mistah Joe, Ahm gittin t be a man like anybody else!"

Joe laughed and wiped his greasy white face with a red bandanna.

"Whut you plannin on buyin?"

Dave looked at the floor, scratched his head, scratched his thigh, and smiled. Then he looked up shyly.

"Ah'll tell yuh, Mistah Joe, ef yuh promise yuh won't tell."

"I promise."

"Waal, Ahma buy a gun."

"A gun? Whut you want with a gun?"

"Ah wanna keep it."

"You ain't nothing but a boy. You don't need a gun."

"Aw, lemme have the catlog, Mistah Joe. Ah'll bring it back."

Joe walked through the rear door. Dave was elated. He looked around at barrels of sugar and flour. He heard Joe coming back. He craned his neck to see if he were bringing the book. Yeah, he's got it. Gawddog, he's got it!

"Here, but be sure you bring it back. It's the only one I got."

"Sho, Mistah Joe."

"Say, if you wanna buy a gun, why don't you buy one from me? I gotta gun to sell."

"Will it shoot?"

"Sure it'll shoot."

"Whut kind is it?"
"Oh, it's kinda old . . . a left-hand Wheeler. A pistol. A big one."
"Is it got bullets in it?"
"It's loaded."
"Kin Ah see it?"
"Where's your money?"
"Whut yuh wan fer it?"
"I'll let you have it for two dollars."
"Just two dollahs? Shucks, Ah could buy tha when Ah git mah pay."
"I'll have it here when you want it."
"Awright, suh. Ah be in fer it."

He went through the door, hearing it slam again behind him. Ahma git some money from Ma n buy me a gun! Only two dollahs! He tucked the thick catalogue under his arm and hurried.

"Where yuh been, boy?" His mother held a steaming dish of black-eyed peas.

"Aw, Ma, Ah jus stopped down the road t talk wid the boys."

"Yuh know bettah t keep suppah waitin."

He sat down, resting the catalogue on the edge of the table.

"Yuh git up from there and git to the well n wash yoself! Ah ain feedin no hogs in mah house!"

She grabbed his shoulder and pushed him. He stumbled out of the room, then came back to get the catalogue.

"Whut this?"
"Aw, Ma, it's jusa catlog."
"Who yuh git it from?"
"From Joe, down at the sto."
"Waal, thas good. We kin use it in the outhouse."
"Naw, Ma." He grabbed for it. "Gimme ma catlog, Ma."

She held onto it and glared at him.

"Quit hollerin at me! Whut's wrong wid yuh? Yuh crazy?"

"But Ma, please. It ain mine! It's Joe's! He tol me t bring it back t im termorrow."

She gave up the book. He stumbled down the back steps, hugging the thick book under his arm. When he had splashed water on his face and hands, he groped back to the kitchen and fumbled in a corner for the towel. He bumped into a chair; it clattered to the floor. The catalogue sprawled at his feet. When he had dried his eyes he snatched up the book and held it again under his arm. His mother stood watching him.

"Now, ef yuh gonna act a fool over that ol book, Ah'll take it n burn it up."

"Naw, Ma, please."

"Waal, set down n be still!"

He sat down and drew the oil lamp close. He thumbed page after page, unaware of the food his mother set on the table. His father came in. Then his small brother.

"Whutcha got there, Dave?" his father asked.

"Jusa catlog," he answered, not looking up.

"Yeah, here they is!" His eyes glowed at blue-and-black revolvers. He glanced up, feeling sudden guilt. His father was watching him. He eased the book under the table and rested it on his knees. After the blessing was asked, he ate. He scooped up peas and swallowed fat meat without chewing. Buttermilk helped to wash it down. He did not want to mention money before his father. He would do much better by cornering his mother when she was alone. He looked at his father uneasily out of the edge of his eye.

"Boy, how come yuh don quit foolin wid tha book n eat yo suppah?"

"Yessuh."

"How you n ol man Hawkins gitten erlong?"

"Suh?"

"Can't yuh hear? Why don yuh lissen? Ah ast yu how wuz yuh n ol man Hawkins gittin erlong?"

"Oh, swell, Pa. Ah plows mo lan than anybody over there."

"Waal, yuh oughta keep yo mind on whut yuh doin."

"Yessuh."

He poured his plate full of molasses and sopped it up slowly with a chunk of cornbread. When his father and brother had left the kitchen, he still sat and looked again at the guns in the catalogue, longing to muster courage enough to present his case to his mother. Lawd, ef Ah only had tha pretty one! He could almost feel the slickness of the weapon with his fingers. If he had a gun like that he would polish it and keep it shining so it would never rust. N Ah'd keep it loaded, by Gawd!

"Ma?" His voice was hesitant.

"Hunh?"

"Ol man Hawkins give yuh mah money yit?"

"Yeah, but ain no usa yuh thinking bout throwin nona it erway. Ahm keepin tha money sos yuh kin have cloes t go to school this winter."

He rose and went to her side with the open catalogue in his palms. She was washing dishes, her head bent low over a pan. Shyly he raised the book. When he spoke, his voice was husky, faint.

"Ma, Gawd knows Ah wans one of these."

"One of whut?" she asked, not raising her eyes.

"One of these," he said again, not daring even to point. She glanced up at the page, then at him with wide eyes.

"Nigger, is yuh gone plumb crazy?"

"Aw, Ma—"

"Git outta here! Don yuh talk t me bout no gun! Yuh a fool!"

"Ma, Ah kin buy one fer two dollahs."

"Not ef Ah knows it, yuh ain!"

"But yuh promised me one—"

"Ah don care whut Ah promised! Yuh ain nothing but a boy yit!"

"Ma, ef yuh lemme buy one Ah'll *never* ast yuh fer nothing no mo."

"Ah tol yuh t git outta here! Yuh ain gonna toucha penny of tha money fer no gun! Thas how come Ah has Mistah Hawkins t pay yo wages t me, cause Ah knows yuh ain got no sense."

"But, Ma, we needa gun. Pa ain got no gun. We needa gun in the house. Yuh kin never tell whut might happen."

"Now don yuh try to maka fool outta me, boy! Ef we did hava gun, yuh wouldn't have it!"

He laid the catalogue down and slipped his arm around her waist.

"Aw, Ma, Ah done worked hard alla summer n ain ast yuh fer nothin, is Ah, now?"

"Thas whut yuh spose t do!"

"But Ma, Ah wans a gun. Yuh kin lemme have two dollahs outta mah money. Please, Ma. I kin give it to Pa . . . . Please, Ma! Ah loves yuh, Ma."

When she spoke her voice came soft and low.

"Whut yu wan wida gun, Dave? Yuh don need no gun. Yuh'll git in trouble. N ef yo pa jus thought Ah let yuh have money t buy a gun he'd hava fit."

"Ah'll hide it, Ma. It ain but two dollahs."

"Lawd, chil, whut's wrong wid yuh?"

"Ain nothin wrong, Ma. Ahm almos a man now. Ah wans a gun."

"Who gonna sell yuh a gun?"

"Ol Joe at the sto."

"N it don cos but two dollahs?"

"Thas all, Ma. Jus two dollahs. Please, Ma."

She was stacking the plates away; her hands moved slowly, reflectively. Dave kept an anxious silence. Finally, she turned to him.

"Ah'll let yuh git tha gun ef yuh promise me one thing."

"Whut's tha, Ma?"

"Yuh bring it straight back t me, yuh hear? It be fer Pa."

"Yessum! Lemme go now, Ma."

She stopped, turned slightly to one side, raised the hem of her dress, rolled down the top of her stocking, and came up with a slender wad of bills.

"Here," she said. "Lawd knows yuh don need no gun. But yer pa does. Yuh bring it right back t me, yuh hear? Ahma put it up. Now ef yuh don, Ahma have yuh pa lick yuh so hard yuh won fergit it."

"Yessum."

He took the money, ran down the steps, and across the yard.

"Dave! Yuuuuuh Daaaaave!"

He heard, but he was not going to stop now. "Naw, Lawd!"

The first movement he made the following morning was to reach under his pillow for the gun. In the gray light of dawn he held it loosely, feeling a sense of power. Could kill a man with a gun like this. Kill anybody, black or white. And if he were holding his gun in his hand, nobody could run over him; they would have to respect him. It was a big gun, with a long barrel and a heavy handle. He raised and lowered it in his hand, marveling at its weight.

He had not come straight home with it as his mother had asked; instead he had stayed out in the fields, holding the weapon in his hand, aiming it now and then at some imaginary foe. But he had not fired it; he had been afraid that his father might hear. Also he was not sure he knew how to fire it.

To avoid surrendering the pistol he had not come into the house until he knew that they were all asleep. When his mother had tiptoed to his bedside late that night and demanded the gun, he had first played possum; then he had told her that the gun was hidden outdoors, that he would bring it to her in the morning. Now he lay turning it slowly in his hands. He broke it, took out the cartridges, felt them, and then put them back.

He slid out of bed, got a long strip of old flannel from a trunk, wrapped the gun in it, and tied it to his naked thigh while it was still loaded. He did not go in to breakfast. Even though it was not yet daylight, he started for Jim Hawkins' plantation. Just as the sun was rising he reached the barns where the mules and plows were kept.

"Hey! That you, Dave?"

He turned. Jim Hawkins stood eying him suspiciously.

"What're yuh doing here so early?"

"Ah didn't know Ah wuz gittin up so early, Mistah Hawkins. Ah wuz fixin t hitch up ol Jenny n take her t the fiels."

"Good. Since you're so early, how about plowing that stretch down by the woods?"

"Suits me, Mistah Hawkins."

"O.K. Go to it!"

He hitched Jenny to a plow and started across the fields. Hot dog! This was just what he wanted. If he could get down by the woods, he could shoot his gun and nobody would hear. He walked behind the plow, hearing the traces creaking, feeling the gun tied tight to his thigh.

When he reached the woods, he plowed two whole rows before he decided to take out the gun. Finally, he stopped, looked in all directions, then untied the gun and held it in his hand. He turned to the mule and smiled.

"Know whut this is, Jenny? Naw, yuh wouldn know! Yuhs jusa ol mule! Anyhow, this is a gun, n it kin shoot, by Gawd!"

He held the gun at arm's length. Whut t hell, Ahma shoot this thing! He looked at Jenny again.

"Lissen here, Jenny! When Ah pull this ol trigger, Ah don wan yuh t run n acka fool now!"

Jenny stood with head down, her short ears pricked straight. Dave walked off about twenty feet, held the gun far out from him at arm's length, and turned his head. Hell, he told himself, Ah ain afraid. The gun felt loose in his fingers; he waved it wildly for a moment. Then he shut his eyes and tightened his forefinger. Bloom! A report half deafened him and he thought his right hand was torn from his arm. He heard Jenny whinnying and galloping over the field, and he found himself on his knees, squeezing his fingers hard between his legs. His hand was numb; he jammed it into his mouth, trying to warm it, trying to stop the pain. The gun lay at his feet. He did not quite know what had happened. He stood up and stared at the gun as though it were a living thing. He gritted his teeth and kicked the gun. Yuh almos broke mah arm! He turned to look for Jenny; she was far over the fields, tossing her head and kicking wildly.

"Hol on there, ol mule!"

When he caught up with her she stood trembling, walling her big white eyes at him. The plow was far away; the traces had broken. Then Dave stopped short, looking, not believing. Jenny was bleeding. Her left side was red and wet with blood. He went closer. Lawd, have mercy! Wondah did Ah shoot this mule? He grabbed for Jenny's mane. She flinched, snorted, whirled, tossing her head.

"Hol on now! Hol on."

Then he saw the hole in Jenny's side, right between the ribs. It was round, wet, red. A crimson stream streaked down the front leg, flowing fast. Good Gawd! Ah wuzn't shootin at tha mule. He felt panic. He knew he had to stop that blood, or Jenny would bleed to death. He had never seen so much blood in all his life. He chased the mule for half a mile, trying to catch her. Finally she stopped, breathing hard, stumpy tail half arched. He caught her mane and led her back to where the plow and gun lay. Then he stooped and grabbed handfuls of damp black earth and tried to plug the bullet hole. Jenny shuddered, whinnied, and broke from him.

"Hol on! Hol on now!"

He tried to plug it again, but blood came anyhow. His fingers were hot and sticky. He rubbed dirt into his palms, trying to dry them. Then again he attempted to plug the bullet hole, but Jenny shied away, kicking her heels high. He stood helpless. He had to do something. He ran at Jenny; she dodged him. He watched a red stream of blood flow down Jenny's leg and form a bright pool at her feet.

"Jenny . . . Jenny," he called weakly.

His lips trembled. She's bleeding t death! He looked in the direction of home, wanting to go back, wanting to get help. But he saw the pistol lying in the damp black clay. He had a queer feeling that if he only did something, this would not be; Jenny would not be there bleeding to death.

When he went to her this time, she did not move. She stood with sleepy, dreamy eyes; and when he touched her she gave a low-pitched whinny and knelt to the ground, her front knees slopping in blood.

"Jenny . . . Jenny . . . " he whispered.

For a long time she held her neck erect; then her head sank, slowly. Her ribs swelled with a mighty heave and she went over.

Dave's stomach felt empty, very empty. He picked up the gun and held it gingerly between his thumb and forefinger. He buried it at the foot of a tree. He took a stick and tried to cover the pool of blood with dirt—but what was the use? There was Jenny lying with her mouth open and her eyes walled and glassy. He could not tell Jim Hawkins he had shot his mule. But he had to tell something. Yeah, Ah'll tell em Jenny started gittin wil n fell on the joint of the plow. . . . But that would hardly happen to a mule. He walked across the field slowly, head down.

It was sunset. Two of Jim Hawkins' men were over near the edge of the woods digging a hole in which to bury Jenny. Dave was surrounded by a knot of people, all of whom were looking down at the dead mule.

"I don't see how in the world it happened," said Jim Hawkins for the tenth time.

The crowd parted and Dave's mother, father, and small brother pushed into the center.

"Where Dave?" his mother called.

"There he is," said Jim Hawkins.

His mother grabbed him.

"Whut happened, Dave? Whut yuh done?"

"Nothin."

"C'mon, boy, talk," his father said.

Dave took a deep breath and told the story he knew nobody believed.

"Waal," he drawled. "Ah brung ol Jenny down here sos Ah could do mah plowin. Ah plowed bout two rows, just like yuh see." He stopped and pointed at the long rows of upturned earth. "Then somethin musta been wrong wid ol Jenny. She wouldn ack right a-tall. She started snortin n kickin her heels. Ah tried t hol her, but she pulled erway, rearin n goin in. Then when the point of the plow was stickin up in the air, she swung erroun n twisted herself back on it. . . . She stuck herself n started t bleed. N fo Ah could do anything, she wuz dead."

"Did you ever hear of anything like that in all your life?" asked Jim Hawkins.

There were white and black standing in the crowd. They murmured. Dave's mother came close to him and looked hard into his face. "Tell the truth, Dave," she said.

"Looks like a bullet hole to me," said one man.

"Dave, whut yuh do wid tha gun?" his mother asked.

The crowd surged in, looking at him. He jammed his hands into his pockets, shook his head slowly from left to right, and backed away. His eyes were wide and painful.

"Did he hava gun?" asked Jim Hawkins.

"By Gawd, Ah tol yuh tha wuz a gun wound," said a man, slapping his thigh.

His father caught his shoulders and shook him till his teeth rattled.

"Tell whut happened, yuh rascal! Tell whut . . ."

Dave looked at Jenny's stiff legs and began to cry.

"Whut yuh do wid tha gun?" his mother asked.

"Whut wuz he doin wida gun?" his father asked.

"Come on and tell the truth," said Hawkins. "Ain't nobody going to hurt you. . . ."

His mother crowded close to him.

"Did yuh shoot tha mule, Dave?"

Dave cried, seeing blurred white and black faces.

"Ahh ddinn gggo tt sshooot hher. . . . Ah ssswear ffo Gawd Ahh ddin. . . . Ah wuz a-tryin t sssee ef the old gggun would sshoot—"

"Where yuh git the gun from?" his father asked.

"Ah got it from Joe, at the sto."

"Where yuh git the money?"

"Ma give it t me."

"He kept worryin me, Bob. Ah had t. Ah tol im t bring the gun right back t me. . . . It was fer yuh, the gun."

"But how yuh happen to shoot that mule?" asked Jim Hawkins.

"Ah wuzn shootin at the mule, Mistah Hawkins. The gun jumped when Ah pulled the trigger. . . . N fo Ah knowed anythin Jenny was there a-bleedin."

Somebody in the crowd laughed. Jim Hawkins walked close to Dave and looked into his face.

"Well, looks like you have bought you a mule, Dave."

"Ah swear fo Gawd, Ah didn go t kill the mule, Mistah Hawkins!"

"But you killed her!"

All the crowd was laughing now. They stood on tiptoe and poked heads over one another's shoulders.

"Well, boy, looks like yuh done bought a dead mule! Hahaha!"

"Ain tha ershame."

"Hohohohoho."

Dave stood, head down, twisting his feet in the dirt.

"Well, you needn't worry about it, Bob," said Jim Hawkins to Dave's father. "Just let the boy keep on working and pay me two dollars a month."

"Whut yuh wan fer yo mule, Mistah Hawkins?"

Jim Hawkins screwed up his eyes.

"Fifty dollars."

"Whut yuh do wid tha gun?" Dave's father demanded.

Dave said nothing.

"Yuh wan me t take a tree n beat yuh till yuh talk!"

"Nawsuh!"

"Whut yuh do wid it?"

"Ah throwed it erway."

"Where?"

"Ah . . . Ah throwed it in the creek."

"Waal, c'mon home. N firs thing in the mawnin git to tha creek n fin tha gun."

"Yessuh."

"Whut yuh pay fer it?"

"Two dollahs."

"Take tha gun n git yo money back n carry it t Mistah Hawkins, yuh hear? N don fergit Ahma lam you black bottom good fer this! Now march yosef on home, suh!"

Dave turned and walked slowly. He heard people laughing. Dave glared, his eyes welling with tears. Hot anger bubbled in him. Then he swallowed and stumbled on.

That night Dave did not sleep. He was glad that he had gotten out of killing the mule so easily, but he was hurt. Something hot seemed to turn over inside him each time he remembered how they had laughed. He tossed on his bed, feeling his hard pillow. N Pa says he's gonna beat me. . . . He remembered other beatings, and his back quivered. Naw, naw, Ah sho don wan im t beat me tha way no mo. Dam em all! Nobody ever gave him anything. All he did was work. They treat me like a mule, n then they beat me. He gritted his teeth. N Ma had t tell on me.

Well, if he had to, he would take old man Hawkins that two dollars. But that meant selling the gun. And he wanted to keep that gun. Fifty dollars for a dead mule.

He turned over, thinking how he had fired the gun. He had an itch to fire it again. Ef other men kin shoota gun, by Gawd, Ah kin! He was still, listening. Mebbe they all sleepin now. The house was still. He heard the soft breathing of his brother. Yes, now! He would go down and get that gun and see if he could fire it! He eased out of bed and slipped into overalls.

The moon was bright. He ran almost all the way to the edge of the woods. He stumbled over the ground, looking for the spot where he had buried the gun. Yeah, here it is. Like a hungry dog scratching for a bone, he pawed it up. He puffed his black cheeks and blew dirt from the trigger and barrel. He broke it and found four cartridges unshot. He looked around; the fields were filled with silence and moonlight. He clutched the gun stiff and hard in his fingers. But, as soon as he wanted to pull the trigger, he shut his eyes and turned his head. Naw, Ah can't shoot wid mah eyes closed n mah head turned. With effort he held his eyes open; then he squeezed. *Blooooom!* He was stiff, not breathing. The gun was still in his hands. Dammit, he'd done it! He fired again. *Blooooom!* He smiled. *Blooooom! Blooooom! Click, click*. There! It was empty. If anybody could shoot a gun, he could. He put the gun into his hip pocket and started across the fields.

When he reached the top of a ridge he stood straight and proud in the moonlight, looking at Jim Hawkins' big white house, feeling the gun sagging in his pocket. Lawd, ef Ah had just one mo bullet Ah'd taka shot at tha house. Ah'd like t scare ol man Hawkins jusa little. . . . Jusa enough t let im know Dave Saunders is a man.

To his left the road curved, running to the tracks of the Illinois Central. He jerked his head, listening. From far off came a faint *hoooof-hoooof; hoooof-hoooof; hoooof-hoooof*. . . . He stood rigid. Two dollahs a mont. Les see now. . . . Tha means it'll take bout two years. Shucks! Ah'll be dam!

He started down the road, toward the tracks. Yeah, here she comes! He stood beside the track and held himself stiffly. Here she comes, erroun the ben. . . . C mon, yuh slow poke! C mon! He had his hand on his gun; something quivered in his stomach. Then the train thundered past, the gray and brown box cars rumbling and clinking. He gripped the gun tightly; then he jerked his hand out of his pocket. Ah betcha Bill wouldn't do it! Ah betcha. . . . The cars slid past, steel grinding upon steel. Ahm ridin yuh ternight, so hep me Gawd! He was hot all over. He hesitated just a moment; then he grabbed, pulled atop of a car, and lay flat. He felt his pocket; the gun was still there. Ahead the long rails were glinting in the moonlight, stretching away, away to somewhere, somewhere where he could be a man. . . .

(1940)

Sinclair Ross   1908–1996

The Lamp at Noon

A little before noon she lit the lamp. Demented wind fled keening past the house: a wail through the eaves that died every minute or two. Three days now without respite it had held. The dust was thickening to an impenetrable fog.

She lit the lamp, then for a long time stood at the window motionless. In dim, fitful outline the stable and oat granary still were visible; beyond, obscuring fields and landmarks, the lower of dust clouds made the farmyard seem an isolated acre, poised aloft above a sombre void. At each blast of wind it shook, as if to topple and spin hurtling with the dust-reel into space.

From the window she went to the door, opening it a little, and peering towards the stable again. He was not coming yet. As she watched there was a sudden rift overhead, and for a moment through the tattered clouds the sun raced like a wizened orange. It shed a soft, diffused light, dim and yellow as if it were the light from the lamp reaching out through the open door.

She closed the door, and going to the stove tried the potatoes with a fork. Her eyes all the while were fixed and wide with a curious immobility. It was the window. Standing at it she had let her forehead press against the pane until the eyes were strained apart and rigid. Wide like that they had looked out to the deepening ruin of the storm. Now she could not close them.

The baby started to cry. He was lying in a home-made crib over which she had arranged a tent of muslin. Careful not to disturb the folds of it she knelt and tried to still him, whispering huskily in a sing-song voice that he must hush and go to sleep again. She would have liked to rock him, to feel the comfort of his little body in her arms, but a fear had obsessed her that in the dust-filled air he might contract pneumonia. There was dust sifting everywhere. Her own throat was parched with it. The table had been set less than ten minutes, and already a film was gathering on the dishes. The little cry continued, and with wincing, frightened lips she glanced around as if to find a corner where the air was less oppressive. But while the lips winced the eyes maintained their wide, immobile stare. "Sleep," she whispered again. "It's too soon for you to be hungry. Daddy's coming for his dinner."

He seemed a long time. Even the clock, still a few minutes off noon, could not dispel a foreboding sense that he was longer than he should be. She went to the door again—then recoiled slowly to stand white and breathless in the middle of the room. She mustn't. He would only despise her if she ran to the stable looking for him. There was too much grim endurance in his nature ever to let him understand the fear and weakness of a woman. She must stay quiet and wait. Nothing was wrong. At noon he would come—and perhaps after dinner stay with her a while.

Yesterday, and again at breakfast this morning, they had quarrelled bitterly. She wanted him now, the assurance of his strength and nearness, but he would stand aloof, wary, remembering the words she had flung at him in her anger, unable to understand it was only the dust and wind that had driven her.

Tense she fixed her eyes upon the clock, listening. There were two winds: the wind in flight, and the wind that pursued. The one sought refuge in the eaves, whimpering, in fear; the other assailed it there, and shook the eaves apart to make it flee again. Once as she listened this first wind sprang into the room, distraught like a bird that has felt the graze of talons on its wing; while furious the other wind shook the walls, and thudded tumbleweeds against the window till its quarry glanced away again in flight. But only to return—to return and quake among the feeble eaves, as if in all this dust-mad wilderness it knew no other sanctuary.

Then Paul came. At his step she hurried to the stove, intent upon the pots and frying-pan. "The worst wind yet," he ventured, hanging up his cap and smock. "I had to light the lantern in the tool shed too."

They looked at each other, then away. She wanted to go to him, to feel his arms supporting her, to cry a little just that he might soothe her, but because his presence made the menace of the wind seem less, she gripped herself and thought, "I'm in the right. I won't give in. For his sake too I won't."

He washed, hurriedly, so that a few dark welts of dust remained to indent upon his face a haggard strength. It was all she could see as she wiped the dishes and set the food before him: the strength, the grimness, the young Paul growing old and hard, buckled against a desert even grimmer than his will. "Hungry?" she asked, touched to a twinge of pity she had not intended. "There's dust in everything. It keeps coming faster than I can clean it up."

He nodded. "To-night though you'll see it go down. This is the third day." She looked at him in silence a moment, and then as if to herself muttered broodingly, "Until the next time. Until it starts again."

There was a dark timbre of resentment in her voice now that boded another quarrel. He waited, his eyes on her dubiously as she mashed a potato with her fork. The lamp between them threw strong lights and shadows on their faces. Dust and drouth, earth that betrayed alike his labor and his faith, to him the struggle had given sternness, an impassive courage. Beneath the whip of sand his youth had been effaced. Youth, zest, exuberance—there remained only a harsh and clenched virility that yet became him, that seemed at the cost of more engaging qualities to be fulfilment of his inmost and essential nature. Whereas to her the same debts and poverty had brought in a plaintive indignation, a nervous dread of what was still to come. The eyes were hollowed, the lips pinched dry and colorless. It was the face of a woman that had aged without maturing, that had loved the little vanities of life, and lost them wistfully.

"I'm afraid, Paul," she said suddenly. "I can't stand it any longer. He cries all the time. You will go, Paul—say you will. We aren't living here—not really living—"

The pleading in her voice now after its shrill bitterness yesterday made him think that this was only another way to persuade him. Evenly he answered, "I told you this morning, Ellen: we keep on right where we are. At least I do. It's yourself you're thinking about, not the baby."

This morning such an accusation would have stung her to rage; now, her voice swift and panting, she pressed on, "Listen, Paul—I'm thinking of all of us—you, too. Look at the sky—and your fields. Are you blind? Thistles and tumbleweeds—it's a desert, Paul. You won't have a straw this fall. You won't be able to feed a cow or a chicken. Please, Paul—say that we'll go away—"

"No Ellen—" His voice as he answered was still remote and even, inflexibly in unison with the narrowed eyes, and the great hunch of muscle-knotted shoulder. "Even as a desert it's better than sweeping out your father's store and running his errands. That's all I've got ahead of me if I do what you want."

"And here—" she flared. "What's ahead of you here? At least we'll get enough to eat and wear when you're sweeping out his store. Look at it—look at it, you fool. Desert—the lamp lit at noon—"

"You'll see it come back," he said quietly. "There's good wheat in it yet."

"But in the meantime—year after year—can't you understand, Paul? We'll never get them back—"

He put down his knife and fork and leaned towards her across the table. "I can't go, Ellen. Living off your people—charity—stop and think of it. This is where I belong. I've no trade or education. I can't do anything else."

"Charity!" she repeated him, letting her voice rise in derision. "And this—you call this independence! Borrowed money you can't even pay the interest on—seed from the government—grocery bills—doctor bills—"

"We'll have crops again," he persisted. "Good crops—the land will come back. It's worth waiting for."

"And while we're waiting, Paul!" It was not anger now, but a kind of sob. "Think of me—and him. It's not fair. We have our lives too to live."

"And you think that going home to your family—taking your husband with you—"

"I don't care—anything would be better than this. Look at the air he's breathing. He cries all the time. For his sake, Paul. What's ahead of him here, even if you do get crops?"

He clenched his lips a minute, then with his eyes hard and contemptuous struck back, "As much as in town, growing up a pauper. You're the one who wants to go, Ellen—it's not for his sake. You think that in town you'd have a better time—not so much work—more clothes—"

"Maybe—" She dropped her head defencelessly. "I'm young still. I like pretty things."

There was silence now—a deep fastness of it enclosed by rushing wind and creaking walls. It seemed the yellow lamplight cast a hush upon them. Through the haze of dusty air the walls receded, dimmed, and came again. Listlessly at last she said, "Go on—your dinner's getting cold. Don't sit and stare at me. I've said it all."

The spent quietness in her voice was harder even than her anger to endure. It reproached him, against his will insisted that he see and understand her lot. To justify himself he tried, "I was a poor man when you married me. You said you didn't mind. Farming's never been easy, and never will be."

"I wouldn't mind the work or the scrimping if there was something to look forward to. It's the hopelessness—going on—watching the land blow away."

"The land's all right," he repeated. "The dry years won't last forever."

"But it's not just dry years, Paul!" The little sob in her voice gave way suddenly to a ring of exasperation. "Will you never see? It's the land itself—the soil. You've plowed and harrowed it until there's not a root or fibre left to hold it down. That's why the soil drifts—that's why in a year or two there'll be nothing left but the bare clay. If in the first place you farmers had taken care of your land—if you hadn't been so greedy for wheat every year—"

She had taught school before she married him, and of late in her anger there had been a kind of disdain, an attitude almost of condescension, as if she no longer looked upon the farmers as her equals. He sat still, his eyes fixed on the yellow lampflame, and seeming to know how her words had hurt him she went on softly, "I want to help you Paul. That's why I won't sit quiet while you go on wasting your life. You're only thirty—you owe it to yourself as well as me."

Still he sat with his lips drawn white and his eyes on the lampflame. It seemed indifference now, as if he were ignoring her, and stung to anger again she cried, "Do you ever think what my life is? Two rooms to live in—once a month to town, and nothing to spend when I get there. I'm still young—I wasn't brought up this way."

Stolidly he answered, "You're a farmer's wife now. It doesn't matter what you used to be, or how you were brought up. You get enough to eat and wear. Just now that's all that I can do. I'm not to blame that we've been dried out five years."

"Enough to eat!" she laughed back shrilly, her eyes all the while fixed expressionless and wide. "Enough salt pork—enough potatoes and eggs. And look—" Springing to the middle of the room she thrust out a foot for him to see the scuffed old slipper. "When they're completely gone I suppose you'll tell me I can go barefoot—that I'm a farmer's wife—that it's not your fault we're dried out—"

"And look at these—" He pushed his chair away from the table now to let her see what he was wearing. "Cowhide—hard as boards—but my feet are so calloused I don't feel them anymore."

Then hurriedly he stood up, ashamed of having tried to match her hardships with his own. But frightened now as he reached for his smock she pressed close to him. "Don't go yet. I brood and worry when I'm left alone. Please, Paul—you can't work on the land anyway."

"And keep on like this?" Grimly he buttoned his smock right up to his throat. "You start before I'm through the door. Week in and week out—I've troubles enough of my own."

"Paul—please stay—" The eyes were glazed now, distended a little as if with the intensity of her dread and pleading. "We won't quarrel any more. Hear it! I can't work—just stand still and listen—"

The eyes frightened him, but responding to a kind of instinct that he must withstand her, that it was his self-respect and manhood against the fretful weakness of a woman, he answered unfeelingly, "In here safe and quiet—you don't know how well off you are. If you were out in it—fighting it—swallowing it—"

"Sometimes, Paul, I wish I were. I'm so caged—if I could only break away and run. See—I stand like this all day. I can't relax. My throat's so tight it aches—"

Firmly he loosened his smock from the clutch of her hands. "If I stay we'll only keep on like this all afternoon. To-morrow when the wind's down we can talk things over quietly."

Then without meeting her eyes again he swung outside, and doubled low against the buffets of the wind, fought his way slowly towards the stable. There was a deep hollow calm within, a vast darkness engulfed beneath the tides of moaning wind. He stood breathless a moment, hushed almost to a stupor by the sudden extinction of the storm and the incredible stillness that enfolded him. It was a long, far-reaching stillness. The first dim stalls and rafters led the way into cavernlike obscurity, into vaults and recesses that extended far beyond the stable walls. Nor in these first quiet moments did he forbid the illusion, the sense of release from a harsh, familiar world into one of immeasurable peace and darkness. The contentious mood that his stand against Ellen had roused him to, his tenacity and clenched despair before the ravages of wind, it was ebbing now, losing itself in the cover of darkness. Ellen and the wheat seemed remote, unimportant. At a whinney from the bay mare Bess he went forward and into her stall. She seemed grateful for his presence, and thrust her nose deep between his arm and body. They stood a long time thus, comforting and assuring each other.

For soon again the first deep sense of quiet and peace was shrunken to the battered shelter of the stable. Instead of release or escape from the assaulting wind, the walls were but a feeble stand against it. They creaked and sawed as if the fingers of a giant hand were tightening to collapse them; the empty loft sustained a pipelike cry that rose and fell but never ended. He saw the dust-black sky again, and his fields blown smooth with drifted soil.

But always, even while listening to the storm outside, he could feel the tense and apprehensive stillness of the stable. There was not a hoof that clumped or shifted, not a rub of halter against manger. And yet, though it had been a strange stable, into which he had never set foot before, he would have known, despite the darkness, that every stall was filled. They too were all listening.

From Bess he went to the big grey gelding Prince. Prince was twenty years old, with rib-grooved sides, and high, protruding hipbones. Paul ran his hand over the ribs, and felt a sudden shame, a sting of fear that Ellen might be right in what she said. For wasn't it true—nine years a farmer now on his own land, and still he couldn't even feed his horses? What then could he hope to do for his wife and son?

There was much he planned. And so vivid was the future of his planning, so real and constant, that often the actual present was but half-felt, but half-endured. Its difficulties were lessened by a confidence in what lay beyond them. A new house for Ellen, new furniture, new clothes. Land for the boy—land and still more land—or education, whatever he might want.

But all the time was he only a blind and stubborn fool? Was Ellen right? Was he trampling on her life, and throwing away his own? The five years since he married her, were they to go on repeating themselves, five, ten, twenty, until all the brave future he looked forward to was but a stark and futile past?

She looked forward to no future. She had no faith or dream with which to make the dust and poverty less real. He understood suddenly. He saw her face again as only a few minutes ago it had begged him not to leave her. The darkness round him now was as a slate on which her lonely terror limned itself. He went from Prince to the other horses, combing their manes and forelocks with his fingers, but always still it was her face he saw, its staring eyes and twisted suffering. "See Paul—I stand like this all day. I just stand still—My throat's so tight it aches—"

And always the wind, the creak of walls, the wild lipless wailing through the loft. Until at last as he stood there, staring into the livid face before him, it seemed that this scream of wind was a cry from her parched and frantic lips. He knew it couldn't be, he knew that she was safe within the house, but still the wind persisted as a woman's cry. The cry of a woman with eyes like those that watched him through the dark. Eyes that were mad now—lips that even as they cried still pleaded, "See, Paul—I stand like this all day. I just stand still—so caged! If I could only run!"

He saw her running, pulled and driven headlong by the wind, but when at last he returned to the house, compelled by his anxiety, she was walking quietly back and forwards with the baby in her arms. Careful, despite his concern, not to reveal a fear or weakness that she might think capitulation to her wishes, he watched a moment through the window, and then went off to the tool shed to mend old harness. All afternoon he stitched and rivetted. It was easier with the lantern lit and his hands occupied. There was wind whining high past the tool shed too, but it was only wind. He remembered the arguments with which Ellen had tried to persuade him away from the farm, and one by one he defeated them. There would be rain again—next year, or the next. Maybe she was right. Maybe in his ignorance he had farmed his land the wrong way, seeding wheat every year, working the soil till it was lifeless dust—but he would do better now. He would plant clover and alfalfa, breed cattle, acre by acre and year by year restore to his land its fibre and fertility. That was something to work for, a way to prove himself. It was ruthless wind, blackening the sky with his earth, screaming in derision of his labour, but it was not his master. Out of his land it had made a wilderness. He now, out of the wilderness, would make a farm and home again.

To-night he must talk with Ellen. Patiently, when the wind was down, and they were both quiet again. It was she who had told him to grow fibrous crops, who had called him an ignorant fool because he kept on with summer fallow and wheat. Now she might be gratified to find him acknowledging her wisdom. Perhaps she would begin to feel the power and steadfastness of the land, to take a pride in it, to understand that he was not a fool, but working for her future and their son's.

And already the wind was slackening. At four o'clock he could sense a lull. At five, straining his eyes from the tool shed doorway, he could make out a neighbour's buildings half a mile away. It was over—three days of blight and havoc like a scourge—three days so bitter and so long that for a moment he stood still, unseeing, his senses idle with a numbness of relief.

But only for a moment. Suddenly he emerged from the numbness; suddenly the fields before him struck his eyes to comprehension. They lay black, naked. Beaten and mounded smooth with dust as if a sea in gentle swell had turned to stone. And though he had tried to prepare himself for such a scene, though he had known since yesterday that not a blade would last the storm, still now, before the utter waste confronting him, he sickened and stood cold. Suddenly like the fields he was naked. Everything that had sheathed him a little from the realities of existence: vision and purpose, faith in the land, in the future, in himself—it was all rent now, all stripped away. "Desert," he heard her voice begin to sob. "Desert, you fool—the lamp lit at noon!"

In the stable again, measuring out their feed to the horses, he wondered what he would say to her to-night. For so deep were his instincts of loyalty to the land that still, even with the images of its betrayal stark upon his mind, his concern was how to withstand her, how to go on again and justify himself. It had not occurred to him yet that he might or should abandon the land. He had lived with it too long. Rather was his impulse to defend it still—as a man defends against the scorn of strangers even his most worthless kin.

He fed his horses, then waited. She too would be waiting, ready to cry at him, "Look now—that crop that was to feed and clothe us! And you'll still keep on! You'll still say 'Next year—there'll be rain next year'!"

But she was gone when he reached the house. The door was open, the lamp blown out, the crib empty. The dishes from their meal at noon were still on the table. She had perhaps begun to sweep, for the broom was lying in the middle of the floor. He tried to call, but a terror clamped upon his throat. In the wan, returning light it seemed that even the deserted kitchen was straining to whisper what it had seen. The tatters of the storm still whimpered through the eaves, and in their moaning told the desolation of the miles they had traversed. On tiptoe at last he crossed to the adjoining room; then at the threshold, without even a glance inside to satisfy himself that she was really gone, he wheeled again and plunged outside.

He ran a long time—distraught and headlong as a few hours ago he had seemed to watch her run—around the farmyard, a little distance into the pasture, back again blindly to the house to see whether she had returned—and then at a stumble down the road for help.

They joined him in the search, rode away for others, spread calling across the fields in the direction she might have been carried by the wind—but nearly two hours later it was himself who came upon her. Crouched down against a drift of sand as if for shelter, her hair in matted strands around her neck and face, the child tightly in her arms.

The child was quite cold. It had been her arms, perhaps, too frantic to protect him, or the smother of dust upon his throat and lungs. "Hold him," she said as he knelt beside her. "So—with his face away from the wind. Hold him until I tidy my hair."

Her eyes were still wide in an immobile stare, but with her lips she smiled at him. For a long time he knelt transfixed, trying to speak to her, touching fearfully with his fingertip the dust-grimed cheeks and eyelids of the child. At last she said, "I'll take him again. Such clumsy hands—you don't know how to hold a baby yet. See how his head falls forward on your arms."

Yet it all seemed familiar—a confirmation of what he had known since noon. He gave her the child, then, gathering them both up in his arms, struggled to his feet and turned towards home.

It was evening now. Across the fields a few spent clouds of dust still shook and fled. Beyond, as if through smoke, the sunset smouldered like a distant fire.

He walked with a long dull stride, his eyes before him, heedless of her weight. Once he glanced down and with her eyes she still was smiling. "Such strong arms, Paul—and I was so tired with carrying just him . . . "

He tried to answer, but it seemed that now the dusk was drawn apart in breathless wailing, a finger on its lips until they passed. "You were right, Paul—" Her voice came whispering, as if she too could feel the hush. "You said to-night we'd see the storm go down. So still now, and the sky burning—it means to-morrow will be fine."

(1938)

Sheila Watson   1909–1998

Antigone

My father ruled a kingdom on the right bank of the river. He ruled it with a firm hand and a stout heart though he was often more troubled than Moses, who was simply trying to bring a stubborn and moody people under God's yoke. My father ruled men who thought they were gods or the instruments of gods or, at very least, god-afflicted and god-pursued. He ruled Atlas who held up the sky, and Hermes who went on endless messages, and Helen who'd been hatched from an egg, and Pan the gardener, and Kallisto the bear, and too many others to mention by name. Yet my father had no thunderbolt, no trident, no helmet of darkness. His subjects were delivered bound into his hands. He merely watched over them as the hundred-handed ones watched over the dethroned Titans so that they wouldn't bother Hellas again.

Despite the care which my father took to maintain an atmosphere of sober common sense in his whole establishment, there were occasional outbursts of self-indulgence which he could not control. For instance, I have seen Helen walking naked down the narrow cement path under the chestnut trees for no better reason, I suppose, than that the day was hot and the white flowers themselves lay naked and expectant in the sunlight. And I have seen Atlas forget the sky while he sat eating the dirt which held him up. These were things which I was not supposed to see.

If my father had been as sensible through and through as he was thought to be, he would have packed me off to boarding school when I was old enough to be disciplined by men. Instead he kept me at home with my two cousins who, except for the accident of birth, might as well have been my sisters. Today I imagine people concerned with our welfare would take such an environment into account. At the time I speak of most people thought us fortunate—especially the girls whose father's affairs had come to an unhappy issue. I don't like to revive old scandal and I wouldn't except to deny it; but it takes only a few impertinent newcomers in any community to force open cupboards which have been decently sealed by time. However, my father was so busy setting his kingdom to rights that he let weeds grow up in his own garden.

As I said, if my father had had all his wits about him he would have sent me to boarding school—and Antigone and Ismene too. I might have fallen in love with the headmaster's daughter and Antigone might have learned that no human being can be right always. She might have found out besides that from the seeds of eternal justice grow madder flowers than any which Pan grew in the gardens of my father's kingdom.

Between the kingdom which my father ruled and the wilderness flows a river. It is this river which I am crossing now. Antigone is with me.

How often can we cross the same river, Antigone asks.

Her persistence annoys me. Besides, Heraklitos made nonsense of her question years ago. He saw a river too—the Inachos, the Kephissos, the Lethaios. The name doesn't matter. He said: See how quickly the water flows. However agile a man is, however nimbly he swims, or runs, or flies, the water slips away before him. See, even as he sets down his foot the water is displaced by the stream which crowds along in the shadow of its flight.

But after all, Antigone says, one must admit that it is the same kind of water. The oolichans run in it as they ran last year and the year before. The gulls cry above the same banks. Boats drift towards the Delta and circle back against the current to gather up the catch.

At any rate, I tell her, we're standing on a new bridge. We are standing so high that the smell of mud and river weeds passes under us out to the straits. The unbroken curve of the bridge protects the eye from details of river life. The bridge is foolproof as a clinic's passport to happiness.

The old bridge still spans the river, but the cat-walk with its cracks and knot-holes, with its gap between planking and handrail has been torn down. The centre arch still grinds open to let boats up and down the river, but a child can no longer be walked on it or swung out on it beyond the water-gauge at the very centre of the flood.

I've known men who scorned any kind of bridge, Antigone says. Men have walked into the water, she says, or, impatient, have jumped from the bridge into the river below.

But these, I say, didn't really want to cross the river. They went Persephone's way, cradled in the current's arms, down the long halls under the pink feet of the gulls, under the booms and towlines, under the soft bellies of the fish.

Antigone looks at me.

There's no coming back, she says, if one goes far enough.

I know she's going to speak of her own misery and I won't listen. Only a god has the right to say: Look what I suffer. Only a god should say: What more ought I to have done for you that I have not done?

Once in winter, she says, a man walked over the river.

Taking advantage of nature, I remind her, since the river had never frozen before.

Yet he escaped from the penitentiary, she says. He escaped from the guards walking round the walls or standing with their guns in the sentry-boxes at the four corners of the enclosure. He escaped.

Not without risk, I say. He had to test the strength of the ice himself. Yet safer perhaps than if he had crossed by the old bridge where he might have slipped through a knot-hole or tumbled out through the railing.

He did escape, she persists, and lived forever on the far side of the river in the Alaska tea and bulrushes. For where, she asks, can a man go farther than to the outermost edge of the world?

The habitable world, as I've said, is on the right bank of the river. Here is the market with its market stalls—the coops of hens, the long-tongued geese, the haltered calf, the bearded goat, the shoving pigs, and the empty bodies of cows and sheep and rabbits hanging on iron hooks. My father's kingdom provides asylum in the suburbs. Near it are the convent, the churches, and the penitentiary. Above these on the hill the cemetery looks down on the people and on the river itself.

It is a world spread flat, tipped up into the sky so that men and women bend forward, walking as men walk when they board a ship at high tide. This is the world I feel with my feet. It is the world I see with my eyes.

I remember standing once with Antigone and Ismene in the square just outside the gates of my father's kingdom. Here from a bust set high on a cairn the stone eyes of Simon Fraser look from his stone face over the river that he found.

It is the head that counts, Ismene said.

It's no better than an urn, Antigone said, one of the urns we see when we climb to the cemetery above.

And all I could think was that I didn't want an urn, only a flat green grave with a chain about it.

A chain won't keep out the dogs, Antigone said.

But his soul could swing on it, Ismene said, like a bird blown on a branch in the wind.

And I remember Antigone's saying: The cat drags its belly on the ground and the rat sharpens its tooth in the ivy.

I should have loved Ismene, but I didn't. It was Antigone I loved. I should have loved Ismene because, although she walked the flat world with us, she managed somehow to see it round.

The earth is an oblate spheroid, she'd say. And I knew that she saw it there before her comprehensible and whole like a tangerine spiked through and held in place while it rotated on the axis of one of Nurse's steel sock needles. The earth was a tangerine and she saw the skin peeled off and the world parcelled out into neat segments, each segment sweet and fragrant in its own skin.

It's the head that counts, she said.

In her own head she made diagrams to live by, cut and fashioned after the eternal patterns spied out by Plato as he rummaged about in the sewing basket of the gods.

I should have loved Ismene. She would live now in some prefabricated and perfect chrysolite by some paradigm which made love round and whole. She would simply live and leave destruction in the purgatorial ditches outside her own walled paradise.

Antigone is different. She sees the world flat as I do and feels it tip beneath her feet. She has walked in the market and seen the living animals penned and the dead hanging stiff on their hooks. Yet she defies what she sees with a defiance which is almost denial. Like Atlas she tries to keep the vaulted sky from crushing the flat earth. Like Hermes she brings a message that there is life if one can escape to it in the brush and the bulrushes in some dim Hades beyond the river. It is defiance not belief and I tell her that this time we walk the bridge to a walled cave where we can deny death no longer.

Yet she asks her question still. And standing there I tell her that Heraklitos has made nonsense of her question. I should have loved Ismene for she would have taught me what Plato meant when he said in all earnest that the union of the soul with the body is in no way better than dissolution. I expect that she understood things which Antigone is too proud to see.

I turn away from her and flatten my elbows on the high wall of the bridge. I look back at my father's kingdom. I see the terraces rolling down from the red-brick buildings with their barred windows. I remember hands shaking the bars and hear fingers tearing up paper and stuffing it through the meshes. Diktynna, mother of nets and high leaping fear. O Artemis, mistress of wild beasts and wild men.

The inmates are beginning to come out on the screened verandas. They pace up and down in straight lines or stand silent like figures which appear at the same time each day from some depths inside a clock.

On the upper terrace Pan the gardener is shifting sprinklers with a hooked stick. His face is shadowed by the brim of his hat. He moves as economically as an animal between the beds of lobelia and geranium. It is high noon.

Antigone has cut out a piece of sod and has scooped out a grave. The body lies in a coffin in the shade of the magnolia tree. Antigone and I are standing. Ismene is sitting between two low angled branches of the monkey puzzle tree. Her lap is filled with daisies. She slits the stem of one daisy and pulls the stem of another through it. She is making a chain for her neck and a crown for her hair.

Antigone reaches for a branch of the magnolia. It is almost beyond her grip. The buds flame above her. She stands on a small fire of daisies which smoulder in the roots of the grass.

I see the magnolia buds. They brood above me, whiteness feathered on whiteness. I see Antigone's face turned to the light. I hear the living birds call to the sun. I speak private poetry to myself: Between four trumpeting angels at the four corners of the earth a bride stands before the altar in a gown as white as snow.

Yet I must have been speaking aloud because Antigone challenges me: You're mistaken. It's the winds the angels hold, the four winds of the earth. After the just are taken to paradise the winds will destroy the earth. It's a funeral, she says, not a wedding.

She looks towards the building.

Someone is coming down the path from the matron's house, she says.

I notice that she has pulled one of the magnolia blossoms from the branch. I take it from her. It is streaked with brown where her hands have bruised it. The sparrow which she has decided to bury lies on its back. Its feet are clenched tight against the feathers of its breast. I put the flower in the box with it.

Someone is coming down the path. She is wearing a blue cotton dress. Her cropped head is bent. She walks slowly carrying something in a napkin.

It's Kallisto the bear, I say. Let's hurry. What will my father say if he sees us talking to one of his patients?

If we live here with him, Antigone says, what can he expect? If he spends his life trying to tame people he can't complain if you behave as if they were tame. What would your father think, she says, if he saw us digging in the Institution lawn?

Pan comes closer. I glower at him. There's no speaking to him. He's deaf and dumb.

Listen, I say to Antigone, my father's not unreasonable. Kallisto thinks she's a bear and he thinks he's a bear tamer, that's all. As for the lawn, I say quoting my father without conviction, a man must have order among his own if he is to keep order in the state.

Kallisto has come up to us. She is smiling and laughing to herself. She gives me her bundle.

Fish, she says.

I open the napkin.

Pink fish sandwiches, I say.

For the party, she says.

But it isn't a party, Antigone says. It's a funeral.

For the funeral breakfast, I say.

Ismene is twisting two chains of daisies into a rope. Pan has stopped pulling the sprinkler about. He is standing beside Ismene resting himself on his hooked stick. Kallisto squats down beside her. Ismene turns away, preoccupied, but she can't turn far because of Pan's legs.

Father said we never should
Play with madmen in the wood.

I look at Antigone.

It's my funeral, she says.

I go over to Ismene and gather up a handful of loose daisies from her lap. The sun reaches through the shadow of the magnolia tree.

It's my funeral, Antigone says. She moves possessively toward the body.

An ant is crawling into the bundle of sandwiches which I've put on the ground. A file of ants is marching on the sparrow's box.

I go over and drop daisies on the bird's stiff body. My voice speaks ritual words: Deliver me, O Lord, from everlasting death on this dreadful day. I tremble and am afraid.

The voice of a people comforts me. I look at Antigone. I look her in the eye.

It had better be a proper funeral then, I say.

Kallisto is crouched forward on her hands. Tears are running down her cheeks and she is licking them away with her tongue.

My voice rises again: I said in the midst of my days, I shall not see—

Antigone just stands there. She looks frightened, but her eyes defy me with their assertion.

It's my funeral, she says. It's my bird. I was the one who wanted to bury it.

She is looking for a reason. She will say something which sounds eternally right.

Things have to be buried, she says. They can't be left lying around anyhow for people to see.

Birds shouldn't die, I tell her. They have wings. Cats and rats haven't wings.

Stop crying, she says to Kallisto. It's only a bird.

It has a bride's flower in its hand, Kallisto says.

We shall rise again, I mutter, but we shall not all be changed.

Antigone does not seem to hear me.

Behold, I say in a voice she must hear, in a moment, in the twinkling of an eye, the trumpet shall sound.

Ismene turns to Kallisto and throws the daisy chain about her neck.

Shall a virgin forget her adorning or a bride the ornament of her breast?

Kallisto is lifting her arms towards the tree.

The bridegroom has come, she says, white as a fall of snow. He stands above me in a great ring of fire.

Antigone looks at me now.

Let's cover the bird up, she says. Your father will punish us all for making a disturbance.

He has on his garment, Kallisto says, and on his thigh is written King of Kings.

I look at the tree. If I could see with Kallisto's eyes I wouldn't be afraid of death, or punishment, or the penitentiary guards. I wouldn't be afraid of my father's belt or his honing strap or his bedroom slipper. I wouldn't be afraid of falling into the river through a knot-hole in the bridge.

But, as I look, I see the buds falling like burning lamps and I hear the sparrow twittering in its box: Woe, woe, woe because of the three trumpets which are yet to sound.

Kallisto is on her knees. She is growling like a bear. She lumbers over to the sandwiches and mauls them with her paw.

Ismene stands alone for Pan the gardener has gone.

Antigone is fitting a turf in place above the coffin. I go over and press the edge of the turf with my feet. Ismene has caught me by the hand.

Go away, Antigone says.

I see my father coming down the path. He has an attendant with him. In front of them walks Pan holding the sprinkler hook like a spear.

What are you doing here? my father asks.

Burying a bird, Antigone says.

Here? my father asks again.

Where else could I bury it? Antigone says.

My father looks at her.

This ground is public property, he says. No single person has any right to an inch of it.

I've taken six inches, Antigone says. Will you dig up the bird again?

Some of his subjects my father restrained since they were moved to throw themselves from high places or to tear one another to bits from jealousy or rage. Others who disturbed the public peace he taught to walk in the airing courts or to work in the kitchen or in the garden.

If men live at all, my father said, it is because discipline saves their life for them.

From Antigone he simply turned away.

(1984)

Eudora Welty 1909–2001

A Worn Path

It was December—a bright frozen day in the early morning. Far out in the country there was an old Negro woman with her head tied in a red rag, coming along a path through the pinewoods. Her name was Phoenix Jackson. She was very old and small and she walked slowly in the dark pine shadows, moving a little from side to side in her steps, with the balanced heaviness and lightness of a pendulum in a grandfather clock. She carried a thin, small cane made from an umbrella, and with this she kept tapping the frozen earth in front of her. This made a grave and persistent noise in the still air, that seemed meditative like the chirping of a solitary little bird.

She wore a dark striped dress reaching down to her shoe tops, and an equally long apron of bleached sugar sacks, with a full pocket: all neat and tidy, but every time she took a step she might have fallen over her shoelaces, which dragged from her unlaced shoes. She looked straight ahead. Her eyes were blue with age. Her skin had a pattern all its own of numberless branching wrinkles and as though a whole little tree stood in the middle of her forehead, but a golden color ran underneath, and the two knobs of her cheeks were illumined by a yellow burning under the dark. Under the red rag her hair came down on her neck in the frailest of ringlets, still black, and with an odor like copper.

Now and then there was a quivering in the thicket. Old Phoenix said, "Out of my way, all you foxes, owls, beetles, jack rabbits, coons and wild animals! . . . Keep out from under these feet, little bob-whites. . . . Keep the big wild hogs out of my path. Don't let none of those come running my direction. I got a long way." Under her small black-freckled hand her cane, limber as a buggy whip, would switch at the brush as if to rouse up any hiding things.

On she went. The woods were deep and still. The sun made the pine needles almost too bright to look at, up where the wind rocked. The cones dropped as light as feathers. Down in the hollow was the mourning dove—it was not too late for him.

The path ran up a hill. "Seem like there is chains about my feet, time I get this far," she said, in the voice of argument old people keep to use with themselves. "Something always take a hold of me on this hill—pleads I should stay."

After she got to the top she turned and gave a full, severe look behind her where she had come. "Up through pines," she said at length. "Now down through oaks."

Her eyes opened their widest, and she started down gently. But before she got to the bottom of the hill a bush caught her dress.

Her fingers were busy and intent, but her skirts were full and long, so that before she could pull them free in one place they were caught in another. It was not possible to allow the dress to tear. "I in the thorny bush," she said. "Thorns, you doing your appointed work. Never want to let folks pass, no sir. Old eyes thought you was a pretty little *green* bush."

Finally, trembling all over, she stood free, and after a moment dared to stoop for her cane.

"Sun so high!" she cried, leaning back and looking, while the thick tears went over her eyes. "The time getting all gone here."

At the foot of this hill was a place where a log was laid across the creek.

"Now comes the trial," said Phoenix.

Putting her right foot out, she mounted the log and shut her eyes. Lifting her skirt, leveling her cane fiercely before her, like a festival figure in some parade, she began to march across. Then she opened her eyes and she was safe on the other side.

"I wasn't as old as I thought," she said.

But she sat down to rest. She spread her skirts on the bank around her and folded her hands over her knees. Up above her was a tree in a pearly cloud of mistletoe. She did not dare to close her eyes, and when a little boy brought her a plate with a slice of marble-cake on it she spoke to him. "That would be acceptable," she said. But when she went to take it there was just her own hand in the air.

So she left that tree, and had to go through a barbed-wire fence. There she had to creep and crawl, spreading her knees and stretching her fingers like a baby trying to climb the steps. But she talked loudly to herself: she could not let her dress be torn now, so late in the day, and she could not pay for having her arm or her leg sawed off if she got caught fast where she was.

At last she was safe through the fence and risen up out in the clearing. Big dead trees, like black men with one arm, were standing in the purple stalks of the withered cotton field. There sat a buzzard.

"Who you watching?"

In the furrow she made her way along.

"Glad this not the season for bulls," she said, looking sideways, "and the good Lord made his snakes to curl up and sleep in the winter. A pleasure I don't see no two-headed snake coming around that tree, where it come once. It took a while to get by him, back in the summer."

She passed through the old cotton and went into a field of dead corn. It whispered and shook and was taller than her head. "Through the maze now," she said, for there was no path.

Then there was something tall, black, and skinny there, moving before her.

At first she took it for a man. It could have been a man dancing in the field. But she stood still and listened, and it did not make a sound. It was as silent as a ghost.

"Ghost," she said sharply, "who be you the ghost of? For I have heard of nary death close by."

But there was no answer—only the ragged dancing in the wind.

She shut her eyes, reached out her hand, and touched a sleeve. She found a coat and inside that an emptiness, cold as ice.

"You scarecrow," she said. Her face lighted. "I ought to be shut up for good," she said with laughter. "My senses is gone. I too old. I the oldest people I ever know. Dance, old scarecrow," she said, "while I dancing with you."

She kicked her foot over the furrow and, with mouth drawn down, shook her head once or twice in a little strutting way. Some husks blew down and whirled in streamers about her skirts.

Then she went on, parting her way from side to side with the cane, through the whispering field. At last she came to the end, to a wagon track where the silver grass blew between the red ruts. The quail were walking around like pullets, seeming all dainty and unseen.

"Walk pretty," she said. "This the easy place. This the easy going."

She followed the track, swaying through the quiet bare fields, through the little strings of trees silver in their dead leaves, past cabins silver from weather, with the doors and windows boarded shut, all like old women under a spell sitting there. "I walking in their sleep," she said, nodding her head vigorously.

In a ravine she went where a spring was silently flowing through a hollow log. Old Phoenix bent and drank. "Sweet-gum makes the water sweet," she said, and drank more. "Nobody know who made this well, for it was here when I was born."

The track crossed a swampy part where the moss hung as white as lace from every limb. "Sleep on, alligators, and blow your bubbles." Then the track went into the road.

Deep, deep the road went down between the high green-colored banks. Overhead the live-oaks met, and it was as dark as a cave.

A black dog with a lolling tongue came up out of the weeds by the ditch. She was meditating, and not ready, and when he came at her she only hit him a little with her cane. Over she went in the ditch, like a little puff of milkweed.

Down there, her senses drifted away. A dream visited her, and she reached her hand up, but nothing reached down and gave her a pull. So she lay there and presently went to talking. "Old woman," she said to herself, "that black dog come up out of the weeds to stall you off, and now there he sitting on his fine tail, smiling at you."

A white man finally came along and found her—a hunter, a young man, with his dog on a chain.

"Well, Granny!" he laughed. "What are you doing there?"

"Lying on my back like a June-bug waiting to be turned over, mister," she said, reaching up her hand.

He lifted her up, gave her a swing in the air, and set her down. "Anything broken, Granny?"

"No sir, them old dead weeds is springy enough," said Phoenix, when she had got her breath. "I thank you for your trouble."

"Where do you live, Granny?" he asked, while the two dogs were growling at each other.

"Away back yonder, sir, behind the ridge. You can't even see it from here."

"On your way home?"

"No sir, I going to town."

"Why, that's too far! That's as far as I walk when I come out myself, and I get something for my trouble." He patted the stuffed bag he carried, and there hung down a little closed claw. It was one of the bob-whites, with its beak hooked bitterly to show it was dead. "Now you go on home, Granny!"

"I bound to go to town, mister," said Phoenix. "The time come around."

He gave another laugh, filling the whole landscape. "I know you old colored people! Wouldn't miss going to town to see Santa Claus!"

But something held old Phoenix very still. The deep lines in her face went into a fierce and different radiation. Without warning, she had seen with her own eyes a flashing nickel fall out of the man's pocket onto the ground.

"How old are you, Granny?" he was saying.

"There is no telling, mister," she said, "no telling."

Then she gave a little cry and clapped her hands and said, "Git on away from here, dog! Look! Look at that dog!" She laughed as if in admiration. "He ain't scared of nobody. He a big black dog." She whispered, "Sic him!"

"Watch me get rid of that cur," said the man. "Sic him, Pete! Sic him!"

Phoenix heard the dogs fighting, and heard the man running and throwing sticks. She even heard a gunshot. But she was slowly bending forward by that time, further and further forward, the lids stretched down over her eyes, as if she were doing this in her sleep. Her chin was lowered almost to her knees. The yellow palm of her hand came out from the fold of her apron. Her fingers slid down and along the ground under the piece of money with the grace and care they would have in lifting an egg from under a setting hen. Then she slowly straightened up, she stood erect, and the nickel was in her apron pocket. A bird flew by. Her lips moved. "God watching me the whole time. I come to stealing."

The man came back, and his own dog panted about them. "Well, I scared him off that time," he said, and then he laughed and lifted his gun and pointed it at Phoenix.

She stood straight and faced him.

"Doesn't the gun scare you?" he said, still pointing it.

"No, sir, I seen plenty go off closer by, in my day, and for less than what I done," she said, holding utterly still.

He smiled, and shouldered the gun. "Well, Granny," he said, "you must be a hundred years old, and scared of nothing. I'd give you a dime if I had any money with me. But you take my advice and stay home, and nothing will happen to you."

"I bound to go on my way, mister," said Phoenix. She inclined her head in the red rag. Then they went in different directions, but she could hear the gun shooting again and again over the hill.

She walked on. The shadows hung from the oak trees to the road like curtains. Then she smelled wood-smoke, and smelled the river, and she saw a steeple and the cabins on their steep steps. Dozens of little black children whirled around her. There ahead was Natchez shining. Bells were ringing. She walked on.

In the paved city it was Christmas time. There were red and green electric lights strung and criss-crossed everywhere, and all turned on in the daytime. Old Phoenix would have been lost if she had not distrusted her eyesight and depended on her feet to know where to take her.

She paused quietly on the sidewalk where people were passing by. A lady came along in the crowd, carrying an armful of red-, green- and silver-wrapped presents; she gave off perfume like the red roses in hot summer, and Phoenix stopped her.

"Please, missy, will you lace up my shoe?" She held up her foot.

"What do you want, Grandma?"

"See my shoe," said Phoenix. "Do all right for out in the country, but wouldn't look right to go in a big building."

"Stand still then, Grandma," said the lady. She put her packages down on the sidewalk beside her and laced and tied both shoes tightly.

"Can't lace 'em with a cane," said Phoenix. "Thank you, missy. I doesn't mind asking a nice lady to tie up my shoe, when I gets out on the street."

Moving slowly and from side to side, she went into the big building, and into a tower of steps, where she walked up and around and around until her feet knew to stop.

She entered a door, and there she saw nailed up on the wall the document that had been stamped with the gold seal and framed in the gold frame, which matched the dream that was hung up in her head.

"Here I be," she said. There was a fixed and ceremonial stiffness over her body.

"A charity case, I suppose," said an attendant who sat at the desk before her.

But Phoenix only looked above her head. There was sweat on her face, the wrinkles in her skin shone like a bright net.

"Speak up, Grandma," the woman said. "What's your name? We must have your history, you know. Have you been here before? What seems to be the trouble with you?"

Old Phoenix only gave a twitch to her face as if a fly were bothering her.

"Are you deaf?" cried the attendant.

But then the nurse came in.

"Oh, that's just old Aunt Phoenix," she said. "She doesn't come for herself—she has a little grandson. She makes these trips just as regular as clockwork. She lives away back off the Old Natchez Trace." She bent down. "Well, Aunt Phoenix, why don't you just take a seat? We won't keep you standing after your long trip." She pointed.

The old woman sat down, bolt upright in the chair.

"Now, how is the boy?" asked the nurse.

Old Phoenix did not speak.

"I said, how is the boy?"

But Phoenix only waited and stared straight ahead, her face very solemn and withdrawn into rigidity.

"Is his throat any better?" asked the nurse. "Aunt Phoenix, don't you hear me? Is your grandson's throat any better since the last time you came for the medicine?"

With her hands on her knees, the old woman waited, silent, erect and motionless, just as if she were in armor.

"You mustn't take up our time this way, Aunt Phoenix," the nurse said. "Tell us quickly about your grandson, and get it over. He isn't dead, is he?"

At last there came a flicker and then a flame of comprehension across her face, and she spoke.

"My grandson. It was my memory had left me. There I sat and forgot why I made my long trip."

"Forgot?" The nurse frowned. "After you came so far?"

Then Phoenix was like an old woman begging a dignified forgiveness for waking up frightened in the night. "I never did go to school, I was too old at the Surrender," she said in a soft voice. "I'm an old woman without an education. It was my memory fail me. My little grandson, he is just the same, and I forgot it in the coming."

"Throat never heals, does it?" said the nurse, speaking in a loud, sure voice to old Phoenix. By now she had a card with something written on it, a little list. "Yes. Swallowed lye. When was it?—January—two, three years ago—"

Phoenix spoke unasked now. "No, missy, he not dead, he just the same. Every little while his throat begin to close up again, and he not able to swallow. He not get his breath. He not able to help himself. So the time come around, and I go on another trip for the soothing medicine."

"All right. The doctor said as long as you came to get it, you could have it," said the nurse. "But it's an obstinate case."

"My little grandson, he sit up there in the house all wrapped up, waiting by himself," Phoenix went on. "We is the only two left in the world. He suffer and it don't seem to put him back at all. He got a sweet look. He going to last. He wear a little patch quilt and peep out holding his mouth open like a little bird. I remembers so plain now. I not going to forget him again, no, the whole enduring time. I could tell him from all the others in creation."

"All right." The nurse was trying to hush her now. She brought her a bottle of medicine. "Charity," she said, making a checkmark in a book.

Old Phoenix held the bottle close to her eyes, and then carefully put it into her pocket.

"I thank you," she said.

"It's Christmas time, Grandma," said the attendant. "Could I give you a few pennies out of my purse?"

"Five pennies is a nickel," said Phoenix stiffly.

"Here's a nickel," said the attendant.

Phoenix rose carefully and held out her hand. She received the nickel and then fished the other nickel out of her pocket and laid it beside the new one. She stared at her palm closely, with her head on one side.

Then she gave a tap with her cane on the floor.

"This is what come to me to do," she said. "I going to the store and buy my child a little windmill they sells, made out of paper. He going to find it hard to believe there such a thing in the world. I'll march myself back where he waiting, holding it straight up in this hand."

She lifted her free hand, gave a little nod, turned around, and walked out of the doctor's office. Then her slow step began on the stairs, going down.

(1941)

Hisaye Yamamoto   b. 1921

Seventeen Syllables

The first Rosie knew that her mother had taken to writing poems was one evening when she finished one and read it aloud for her daughter's approval. It was about cats, and Rosie pretended to understand it thoroughly and appreciate it no end, partly because she hesitated to disillusion her mother about the quantity and quality of Japanese she had learned in all the years now that she had been going to Japanese school every Saturday (and Wednesday, too, in the summer). Even so, her mother must have been skeptical about the depth of Rosie's understanding, because she explained afterwards about the kind of poem she was trying to write.

See, Rosie, she said, it was a *haiku*, a poem in which she must pack all her meaning into seventeen syllables only, which were divided into three lines of five, seven, and five syllables. In the one she had just read, she had tried to capture the charm of a kitten, as well as comment on the superstition that owning a cat of three colors meant good luck.

"Yes, yes, I understand. How utterly lovely," Rosie said, and her mother, either satisfied or seeing through the deception and resigned, went back to composing.

The truth was that Rosie was lazy; English lay ready on the tongue but Japanese had to be searched for and examined, and even then put forth tentatively (probably to meet with laughter). It was so much easier to say yes, yes, even when one meant no, no. Besides, this was what was in her mind to say: I was looking through one of your magazines from Japan last night, Mother, and towards the back I found some *haiku* in English that delighted me. There was one that made me giggle off and on until I fell asleep—

> It is morning, and lo!
> I lie awake, comme il faut,[1]
> sighing for some dough.

Now, how to reach her mother, how to communicate the melancholy song? Rosie knew formal Japanese by fits and starts, her mother had even less English, no French. It was much more possible to say yes, yes.

It developed that her mother was writing the *haiku* for a daily newspaper, the *Mainichi Shimbun*, that was published in San Francisco. Los Angeles, to be sure, was closer to the farming community in which the Hayashi family lived and several Japanese vernaculars were printed there, but Rosie's parents said they preferred the tone of the northern paper. Once a week, the *Mainichi* would have a section devoted to *haiku*, and her mother became an extravagant contributor, taking for herself the blossoming pen name, Ume Hanazono.

So Rosie and her father lived for awhile with two women, her mother and Ume Hanazono. Her mother (Tome Hayashi by name) kept house, cooked, washed, and, along with her husband and the Carrascos, the Mexican family hired for the harvest, did her ample share of picking tomatoes out in the sweltering fields and boxing them in tidy strata in the cool packing shed. Ume

---
[1] In good form; proper. Pronounced *come il fō*.

Hanazono, who came to life after the dinner dishes were done, was an earnest, muttering stranger who often neglected speaking when spoken to and stayed busy at the parlor table as late as midnight scribbling with pencil on scratch paper or carefully copying characters on good paper with her fat, pale green Parker.

The new interest had some repercussions on the household routine. Before, Rosie had been accustomed to her parents and herself taking their hot baths early and going to bed almost immediately afterwards, unless her parents challenged each other to a game of flower cards or unless company dropped in. Now if her father wanted to play cards, he had to resort to solitaire (at which he always cheated fearlessly), and if a group of friends came over, it was bound to contain someone who was also writing *haiku*, and the small assemblage would be split in two, her father entertaining the non-literary members and her mother comparing ecstatic notes with the visiting poet.

If they went out, it was more of the same thing. But Ume Hanazono's life span, even for a poet's, was very brief—perhaps three months at most.

One night they went over to see the Hayano family in the neighboring town to the west, an adventure both painful and attractive to Rosie. It was attractive because there were four Hayano girls, all lovely and each one named after a season of the year (Haru, Natsu, Aki, Fuyu), painful because something had been wrong with Mrs. Hayano ever since the birth of her first child. Rosie would sometimes watch Mrs. Hayano, reputed to have been the belle of her native village, making her way about a room, stooped, slowly shuffling, violently trembling (*always* trembling), and she would be reminded that this woman, in this same condition, had carried and given issue to three babies. She would look wonderingly at Mr. Hayano, handsome, tall, and strong, and she would look at her four pretty friends. But it was not a matter she could come to any decision about.

On this visit, however, Mrs. Hayano sat all evening in the rocker, as motionless and unobtrusive as it was possible for her to be, and Rosie found the greater part of the evening practically anaesthetic. Too, Rosie spent most of it in the girls' room, because Haru, the garrulous one, said almost as soon as the bows and other greetings were over, "Oh, you must see my new coat!"

It was a pale plaid of grey, sand, and blue, with an enormous collar, and Rosie, seeing nothing special in it, said, "Gee, how nice."

"Nice?" said Haru, indignantly. "Is that all you can say about it? It's gorgeous! And so cheap, too. Only seventeen-ninety-eight, because it was a sale. The saleslady said it was twenty-five dollars regular."

"Gee," said Rosie. Natsu, who never said much and when she said anything said it shyly, fingered the coat covetously and Haru pulled it away.

"Mine," she said, putting it on. She minced in the aisle between the two large beds and smiled happily. "Let's see how your mother likes it."

She broke into the front room and the adult conversation and went to stand in front of Rosie's mother, while the rest watched from the door. Rosie's mother was properly envious. "May I inherit it when you're through with it?"

Haru, pleased, giggled and said yes, she could, but Natsu reminded gravely from the door, "You promised me, Haru."

Everyone laughed but Natsu, who shamefacedly retreated into the bedroom. Haru came in laughing, taking off the coat. "We were only kidding, Natsu," she said. "Here, you try it on now."

After Natsu buttoned herself into the coat, inspected herself solemnly in the bureau mirror, and reluctantly shed it, Rosie, Aki, and Fuyu got their turns, and Fuyu, who was eight, drowned in it while her sisters and Rosie doubled up in amusement. They all went into the front room later, because Haru's mother quaveringly called to her to fix the tea and rice cakes and open a can of sliced peaches for everybody. Rosie noticed that her mother and Mr. Hayano were talking together at the little table—they were discussing a *haiku* that Mr. Hayano was planning to send to the *Mainichi*, while her father was sitting at one end of the sofa looking through a copy of *Life*, the new picture magazine. Occasionally, her father would comment on a photograph, holding it toward Mrs. Hayano and speaking to her as he always did—loudly, as though he thought someone such as she must surely be at least a trifle deaf also.

The five girls had their refreshments at the kitchen table, and it was while Rosie was showing the sisters her trick of swallowing peach slices without chewing (she chased each slippery crescent down with a swig of tea) that her father brought his empty teacup and untouched saucer to the sink and said, "Come on, Rosie, we're going home now."

"Already?" asked Rosie.

"Work tomorrow," he said.

He sounded irritated, and Rosie, puzzled, gulped one last yellow slice and stood up to go, while the sisters began protesting, as was their wont.

"We have to get up at five-thirty," he told them, going into the front room quickly, so that they did not have their usual chance to hang onto his hands and plead for an extension of time.

Rosie, following, saw that her mother and Mr. Hayano were sipping tea and still talking together, while Mrs. Hayano concentrated, quivering, on raising the handleless Japanese cup to her lips with both her hands and lowering it back to her lap. Her father, saying nothing, went out the door, onto the bright porch, and down the steps. Her mother looked up and asked, "Where is he going?"

"Where is he going?" Rosie said. "He said we were going home now."

"Going home?" Her mother looked with embarrassment at Mr. Hayano and his absorbed wife and then forced a smile. "He must be tired," she said.

Haru was not giving up yet. "May Rosie stay overnight?" she asked, and Natsu, Aki, and Fuyu came to reinforce their sister's plea by helping her make a circle around Rosie's mother. Rosie, for once having no desire to stay, was relieved when her mother, apologizing to the perturbed Mr. and Mrs. Hayano for her father's abruptness at the same time, managed to shake her head no at the quartet, kindly but adamant, so that they broke their circle and let her go.

Rosie's father looked ahead into the windshield as the two joined him. "I'm sorry," her mother said. "You must be tired." Her father, stepping on the starter, said nothing. "You know how I get when it's *haiku*," she continued, "I forget what time it is." He only grunted.

As they rode homeward silently, Rosie, sitting between, felt a rush of hate for both—for her mother for begging, for her father for denying her mother. I wish this old Ford would crash, right now, she thought, then immediately, no, no, I wish my father would laugh, but it was too late: already the vision had passed through her mind of the green pick-up crumpled in the dark against one of the mighty eucalyptus trees they were just riding past, of the three contorted, bleeding bodies, one of them hers.

Rosie ran between two patches of tomatoes, her heart working more rambunctiously than she had ever known it to. How lucky it was that Aunt Taka and Uncle Gimpachi had come tonight, though, how very lucky. Otherwise she might not have really kept her half-promise to meet Jesus Carrasco. Jesus was going to be a senior in September at the same school she went to, and his parents were the ones helping with the tomatoes this year. She and Jesus, who hardly remembered seeing each other at Cleveland High where there were so many other people and two whole grades between them, had become great friends this summer—he always had a joke for her when he periodically drove the loaded pick-up up from the fields to the shed where she was usually sorting while her mother and father did the packing, and they laughed a great deal together over infinitesimal repartee during the afternoon break for chilled watermelon or ice cream in the shade of the shed.

What she enjoyed most was racing him to see which could finish picking a double row first. He, who could work faster, would tease her by slowing down until she thought she would surely pass him this time, then speeding up furiously to leave her several sprawling vines behind. Once he had made her screech hideously by crossing over, while her back was turned, to place atop the tomatoes in her green-stained bucket a truly monstrous, pale green worm (it had looked more like an infant snake). And it was when they had finished a contest this morning, after she had pantingly pointed a green finger at the immature tomatoes evident in the lugs at the end of his row and he had returned the accusation (with justice), that he had startlingly brought up the matter of their possibly meeting outside the range of both their parents' dubious eyes.

"What for?" she had asked.

"I've got a secret I want to tell you," he said.

"Tell me now," she demanded.

"It won't be ready till tonight," he said.

She laughed. "Tell me tomorrow then."

"It'll be gone tomorrow," he threatened.

"Well, for seven hakes, what is it?" she had asked, more than twice, and when he had suggested that the packing shed would be an appropriate place to find out, she had cautiously answered maybe. She had not been certain she was going to keep the appointment until the arrival of mother's sister and her husband. Their coming seemed a sort of signal of permission, of grace, and she had definitely made up her mind to lie and leave as she was bowing them welcome.

So as soon as everyone appeared settled back for the evening, she announced loudly that she was going to the privy outside. "I'm going to the *benjo*!" and slipped out the door. And now that she was actually on her way, her heart pumped in such an undisciplined way that she could hear it with her ears. It's because I'm running, she told herself, slowing to a walk. The shed was up ahead, one more patch away, in the middle of the fields. Its bulk, looming in the dimness, took on a sinisterness that was funny when Rosie reminded herself that it was only a wooden frame with a canvas roof and three canvas walls that made a slapping noise on breezy days.

Jesus was sitting on the narrow plank that was the sorting platform and she went around to the other side and jumped backwards to seat herself on the rim of a packing stand. "Well, tell me," she said without greeting, thinking her voice sounded reassuringly familiar.

"I saw you coming out the door," Jesus said. "I heard you running part of the way, too."

"Uh-huh," Rosie said. "Now tell me the secret."

"I was afraid you wouldn't come," he said.

Rosie delved around on the chicken-wire bottom of the stall for number two tomatoes, ripe, which she was sitting beside, and came up with a left-over that felt edible. She bit into it and began sucking out the pulp and seeds. "I'm here," she pointed out.

"Rosie, are you sorry you came?"

"Sorry? What for?" she said. "You said you were going to tell me something."

"I will, I will," Jesus said, but his voice contained disappointment, and Rosie fleetingly felt the older of the two, realizing a brand-new power which vanished without category under her recognition.

"I have to go back in a minute," she said. "My aunt and uncle are here from Wintersburg. I told them I was going to the privy."

Jesus laughed. "You funny thing," he said. "You slay me!"

"Just because you have a bathroom *inside*," Rosie said. "Come on, tell me."

Chuckling, Jesus came around to lean on the stand facing her. They still could not see each other very clearly, but Rosie noticed that Jesus became very sober again as he took the hollow tomato from her hand and dropped it back into the stall. When he took hold of her empty hand, she could find no words to protest; her vocabulary had become distressingly constricted and she thought desperately that all that remained intact now was yes and no and oh, and even these few sounds would not easily out. Thus, kissed by Jesus, Rosie fell for the first time entirely victim to a helplessness delectable beyond speech. But the terrible, beautiful sensation lasted no more than a second, and the reality of Jesus' lips and tongue and teeth and hands made her pull away with such strength that she nearly tumbled.

Rosie stopped running as she approached the lights from the windows of home. How long since she had left? She could not guess, but gasping yet, she went to the privy in back and locked herself in. Her own breathing deafened her in the dark, close space, and she sat and waited until she could hear at last the nightly calling of the frogs and crickets. Even then, all she could think to say was oh, my, and the pressure of Jesus' face against her face would not leave.

No one had missed her in the parlor, however, and Rosie walked in and through quickly, announcing that she was next going to take a bath. "Your father's in the bathhouse," her mother said, and Rosie, in her room, recalled that she had not seen him when she entered. There had been only Aunt Taka and Uncle Gimpachi with her mother at the table, drinking tea. She got her robe and straw sandals and crossed the parlor again to go outside. Her mother was telling them about the *haiku* competition in the *Mainichi* and the poem she had entered.

Rosie met her father coming out of the bathhouse. "Are you through, Father?" she asked. "I was going to ask you to scrub my back."

"Scrub your own back," he said shortly, going toward the main house.

"What have I done now?" she yelled after him. She suddenly felt like doing a lot of yelling. But he did not answer, and she went into the bathhouse. Turning on the dangling light, she removed her denims and T-shirt and threw them in the big carton for dirty clothes standing next to the washing machine. Her other things she took with her into the bath compartment to wash after her bath.

After she had scooped a basin of hot water from the square wooden tub, she sat on the grey cement of the floor and soaped herself at exaggerated leisure, singing "Red Sails in the Sunset" at the top of her voice and using da-da-da where she suspected her words. Then, standing up, still singing, for she was possessed by the notion that any attempt now to analyze would result in spoilage and she believed that the larger her volume the less she would be able to hear herself think, she obtained more hot water and poured it on until she was free of lather. Only then did she allow herself to step into the steaming vat, one leg first, then the remainder of her body inch by inch until the water no longer stung and she could move around at will.

She took a long time soaking, afterwards remembering to go around outside to stoke the embers of the tin-lined fireplace beneath the tub and to throw on a few more sticks so that the water might keep its heat for her mother, and when she finally returned to the parlor, she found her mother still talking *haiku* with her aunt and uncle, the three of them on another round of tea. Her father was nowhere in sight.

At Japanese school the next day (Wednesday, it was), Rosie was grave and giddy by turns. Preoccupied at her desk in the row for students on Book Eight, she made up for it at recess by performing wild mimicry for the benefit of her friend Chizuko. She held her nose and whined a witticism or two in what she considered was the manner of Fred Allen; she assumed intoxication and a British accent to go over the climax of the Rudy Vallee recording of the pub conversation about William Ewart Gladstone; she was the child Shirley Temple piping, "On the Good Ship Lollipop"; she was the gentleman soprano of the Four Inkspots trilling, "If I Didn't Care." And she felt reasonably satisfied when Chizuko wept and gasped, "Oh, Rosie, you ought to be in the movies!"

Her father came after her at noon, bringing her sandwiches of minced ham and two nectarines to eat while she rode, so that she could pitch right into the sorting when they got home. The lugs were piling up, he said, and the ripe tomatoes in them would probably have to be taken to the cannery tomorrow if they were not ready for the produce haulers tonight. "This heat's not doing them any good. And we've got no time for a break today."

It *was* hot, probably the hottest day of the year, and Rosie's blouse stuck damply to her back even under the protection of the canvas. But she worked as efficiently as a flawless machine and kept the stalls heaped, with one part of her mind listening in to the parental murmuring about the heat and the tomatoes and with another part planning the exact words she would say to Jesus when he drove up with the first load of the afternoon. But when at last she saw that the pick-up was coming, her hands went berserk and the tomatoes started falling in the wrong stalls, and her father said, "Hey, hey! Rosie, watch what you're doing!"

"Well, I have to go to the *benjo*," she said, hiding panic.

"Go in the weeds over there," he said, only half-joking.

"Oh, Father!" she protested.

"Oh, go on home," her mother said. "We'll make out for awhile."

In the privy Rosie peered through a knothole toward the fields, watching as much as she could of Jesus. Happily she thought she saw him look in the direction of the house from time to time before he finished unloading and went back toward the patch where his mother and father worked. As she was heading for the shed, a very presentable black car purred up the dirt driveway to the house and its driver motioned to her. Was this the Hayashi home, he wanted to know.

She nodded. Was she a Hayashi? Yes, she said, thinking that he was a good-looking man. He got out of the car with a huge, flat package and she saw that he warmly wore a business suit. "I have something here for your mother then," he said, in a more elegant Japanese than she was used to.

She told him where her mother was and he came along with her, patting his face with an immaculate white handkerchief and saying something about the coolness of San Francisco. To her surprised mother and father, he bowed and introduced himself as, among other things, the *haiku* editor of the *Mainichi Shimbun*, saying that since he had been coming as far as Los Angeles anyway, he had decided to bring her the first prize she had won in the recent contest.

"First prize?" her mother echoed, believing and not believing, pleased and overwhelmed. Handed the package with a bow, she bobbed her head up and down numerous times to express her utter gratitude.

"It is nothing much," he added, "but I hope it will serve as a token of our great appreciation for your contributions and our great admiration of your considerable talent."

"I am not worthy," she said, falling easily into his style. "It is I who should make some sign of my humble thanks for being permitted to contribute."

"No, no, to the contrary," he said, bowing again.

But Rosie's mother insisted, and then saying that she knew she was being unorthodox, she asked if she might open the package because her curiosity was so great. Certainly she might. In fact, he would like her reaction to it, for personally, it was one of his favorite *Hiroshiges*.

Rosie thought it was a pleasant picture, which looked to have been sketched with delicate quickness. There were pink clouds, containing some graceful calligraphy, and a sea that was a pale blue except at the edges, containing four sampans with indications of people in them. Pines edged the water and on the far-off beach there was a cluster of thatched huts towered over by pine-dotted mountains of grey and blue. The frame was scalloped and gilt.

After Rosie's mother pronounced it without peer and somewhat prodded her father into nodding agreement, she said Mr. Kuroda must at least have a cup of tea after coming all this way, and although Mr. Kuroda did not want to impose, he soon agreed that a cup of tea would be refreshing and went along with her to the house, carrying the picture for her.

"Ha, your mother's crazy!" Rosie's father said, and Rosie laughed uneasily as she resumed judgment on the tomatoes. She had emptied six lugs when he broke into an imaginary conversation with Jesus to tell her to go and remind her mother of the tomatoes, and she went slowly.

Mr. Kuroda was in his shirtsleeves expounding some *haiku* theory as he munched a rice cake, and her mother was rapt. Abashed in the great man's presence, Rosie stood next to her mother's chair until her mother looked up inquiringly, and then she started to whisper the message, but her mother pushed her gently away and reproached, "You are not being very polite to our guest."

"Father says the tomatoes . . . " Rosie said aloud, smiling foolishly.

"Tell him I shall only be a minute," her mother said, speaking the language of Mr. Kuroda.

When Rosie carried the reply to her father, he did not seem to hear and she said again, "Mother says she'll be back in a minute."

"All right, all right," he nodded, and they worked again in silence. But suddenly, her father uttered an incredible noise, exactly like the cork of a bottle popping, and the next Rosie knew, he was stalking angrily toward the house, almost running in fact, and she chased after him crying, "Father! Father! What are you going to do?"

He stopped long enough to order her back to the shed. "Never mind!" he shouted. "Get on with the sorting!"

And from the place in the fields where she stood, frightened and vacillating, Rosie saw her father enter the house. Soon Mr. Kuroda came out alone, putting on his coat. Mr. Kuroda got into his car and backed out down the driveway onto the highway. Next her father emerged, also alone, something in his arms (it was the picture, she realized), and, going over to the bathhouse woodpile, he threw the picture on the ground and picked up the axe. Smashing the picture, glass and all (she heard the explosion faintly), he reached over for the kerosene that was used to encourage the bath fire and poured it over the wreckage. I am dreaming, Rosie said to herself, I am dreaming, but her father, having made sure that his act of cremation was irrevocable, was even then returning to the fields.

Rosie ran past him and toward the house. What had become of her mother? She burst into the parlor and found her mother at the back window watching the dying fire. They watched together until there remained only a feeble smoke under the blazing sun. Her mother was very calm.

"Do you know why I married your father?" she said without turning.

"No," said Rosie. It was the most frightening question she had ever been called upon to answer. Don't tell me now, she wanted to say, tell me tomorrow, tell me next week, don't tell me today. But she knew she would be told now, that the telling would combine with the other violence of the hot afternoon to level her life, her world to the very ground.

It was like a story out of the magazines illustrated in sepia, which she had consumed so greedily for a period until the information had somehow reached her that those wretchedly unhappy autobiographies, offered to her as the testimonials of living men and women, were largely inventions: Her mother, at nineteen, had come to America and married her father as an alternative to suicide.

At eighteen she had been in love with the first son of one of the well-to-do families in her village. The two had met whenever and wherever they could, secretly, because it would not have done for his family to see him favor her—her father had no money; he was a drunkard and a gambler besides. She had learned she was with child; an excellent match had already been arranged for her lover. Despised by her family, she had given premature birth to a stillborn son, who would be seventeen now. Her family did not turn her out, but she could no longer project herself in any direction without refreshing in them the memory of her indiscretion. She wrote to Aunt Taka, her favorite sister in America, threatening to kill herself if Aunt Taka would not send for her. Aunt Taka hastily arranged a marriage with a young man of whom she knew, but lately arrived from Japan, a young man of simple mind, it was said, but of kindly heart. The young man was never told why his unseen betrothed was so eager to hasten the day of meeting.

The story was told perfectly, with neither groping for words nor untoward passion. It was as though her mother had memorized it by heart, reciting it to herself so many times over that its nagging vileness had long since gone.

"I had a brother then?" Rosie asked, for this was what seemed to matter now; she would think about the other later, she assured herself, pushing back the illumination which threatened all that darkness that had hitherto been merely mysterious or even glamorous. "A half-brother?"

"Yes."

"I would have liked a brother," she said.

Suddenly, her mother knelt on the floor and took her by the wrists. "Rosie," she said urgently, "Promise me you will never marry!" Shocked more by the request than the revelation, Rosie stared at her mother's face. Jesus, Jesus, she called silently, not certain whether she was invoking the help of the son of the Carrascos or of God, until there returned sweetly the memory of Jesus' hand, how it had touched her and where. Still her mother waited for an answer, holding her wrists so tightly that her hands were going numb. She tried to pull free. Promise, her mother whispered fiercely, promise. Yes, yes, I promise, Rosie said. But for an instant she turned away, and her mother, hearing the familiar glib agreement, released her. Oh, you, you, you, her eyes and twisted mouth said, you fool. Rosie, covering her face, began at last to cry, and the embrace and consoling hand came much later than she expected.

(1949)

Flannery O'Connor   1925–1964

A Good Man Is Hard to Find

The dragon is by the side of the road, watching those who pass. Beware lest he devour you. We go to the Father of Souls, but it is necessary to pass by the dragon.

—St. Cyril of Jerusalem

The grandmother didn't want to go to Florida. She wanted to visit some of her connections in east Tennessee and she was seizing at every chance to change Bailey's mind. Bailey was the son she lived with, her only boy. He was sitting on the edge of his chair at the table, bent over the orange sports section of the *Journal*. "Now look here, Bailey," she said, "see here, read this," and she stood with one hand on her thin hip and the other rattling the newspaper at his bald head. "Here this fellow that calls himself The Misfit is aloose from the Federal Pen and headed toward Florida and you read here what it says he did to these people. Just you read it. I wouldn't take my children in any direction with a criminal like that aloose in it. I couldn't answer to my conscience if I did."

Bailey didn't look up from his reading so she wheeled around then and faced the children's mother, a young woman in slacks, whose face was as broad and innocent as a cabbage and was tied around with a green headkerchief that had two points on the top like a rabbit's ears. She was sitting on the sofa, feeding the baby his apricots out of a jar. "The children have been to Florida before," the old lady said. "You all ought to take them somewhere else for a change so they would see different parts of the world and be broad. They never have been to east Tennessee."

The children's mother didn't seem to hear her but the eight-year-old boy, John Wesley, a stocky child with glasses, said, "If you don't want to go to Florida, why dontcha stay at home?" He and the little girl, June Star, were reading the funny papers on the floor.

"She wouldn't stay at home to be queen for a day," June Star said without raising her yellow head.

"Yes and what would you do if this fellow, The Misfit, caught you?" the grandmother asked.

"I'd smack his face," John Wesley said.

"She wouldn't stay at home for a million bucks," June Star said. "Afraid she'd miss something. She has to go everywhere we go."

"All right, Miss," the grandmother said. "Just remember that the next time you want me to curl your hair."

June Star said her hair was naturally curly.

The next morning the grandmother was the first one in the car, ready to go. She had her big black valise that looked like the head of a hippopotamus in one corner, and underneath it she was hiding a basket with Pitty Sing, the cat, in it. She didn't intend for the cat to be left alone in the house for three days because he would miss her too much and she was afraid he might brush against one of the gas burners and accidentally asphyxiate himself. Her son, Bailey, didn't like to arrive at a motel with a cat.

She sat in the middle of the back seat with John Wesley and June Star on either side of her. Bailey and the children's mother and the baby sat in front and they left Atlanta at eight forty-five with the mileage on the car at 55890. The grandmother wrote this down because she thought it would be interesting to say how many miles they had been when they got back. It took them twenty minutes to reach the outskirts of the city.

The old lady settled herself comfortably, removing her white cotton gloves and putting them up with her purse on the shelf in front of the back window. The children's mother still had on slacks and still had her head tied up in a green kerchief, but the grandmother had on a navy blue straw sailor hat with a bunch of white violets on the brim and a navy blue dress with a small white dot in the print. Her collars and cuffs were white organdy trimmed with lace and at her neckline she had pinned a purple spray of cloth violets containing a sachet. In case of an accident, anyone seeing her dead on the highway would know at once that she was a lady.

She said she thought it was going to be a good day for driving, neither too hot nor too cold, and she cautioned Bailey that the speed limit was fifty-five miles an hour and that the patrolmen hid themselves behind billboards and small clumps of trees and sped out after you before you had a chance to slow down. She pointed out interesting details of the scenery: Stone Mountain; the blue granite that in some places came up to both sides of the highway; the brilliant red clay banks slightly streaked with purple; and the various crops that made rows of green lace-work on the ground. The trees were full of silver-white sunlight and the meanest of them sparkled. The children were reading comic magazines and their mother had gone back to sleep.

"Let's go through Georgia fast so we won't have to look at it much," John Wesley said.

"If I were a little boy," said the grandmother, "I wouldn't talk about my native state that way. Tennessee has the mountains and Georgia has the hills."

"Tennessee is just a hillbilly dumping ground," John Wesley said, "and Georgia is a lousy state too."

"You said it," June Star said.

"In my time," said the grandmother, folding her thin veined fingers, "children were more respectful of their native states and their parents and everything else. People did right then. Oh look at the cute little pickaninny!" she said and pointed to a Negro child standing in the door of a shack. "Wouldn't that make a picture, now?" she asked and they all turned and looked at the little Negro out of the back window. He waved.

"He didn't have any britches on," June Star said.

"He probably didn't have any," the grandmother explained. "Little niggers in the country don't have things like we do. If I could paint, I'd paint that picture," she said.

The children exchanged comic books.

The grandmother offered to hold the baby and the children's mother passed him over the front seat to her. She set him on her knee and bounced him and told him about the things they were passing. She rolled her eyes and screwed up her mouth and stuck her leathery thin face into his smooth bland one. Occasionally he gave her a faraway smile. They passed a large cotton field with five or six graves fenced in the middle of it, like a small island. "Look at the graveyard!" the grandmother said, pointing it out. "That was the old family burying ground. That belonged to the plantation."

"Where's the plantation?" John Wesley asked.

"Gone with the Wind," said the grandmother. "Ha. Ha."

When the children finished all the comic books they had brought, they opened the lunch and ate it. The grandmother ate a peanut butter sandwich and an olive and would not let the children throw the box and the paper napkins out the window. When there was nothing else to do they played a game by choosing a cloud and making the other two guess what shape it suggested. John Wesley took one the shape of a cow and June Star guessed a cow and John Wesley said, no, an automobile, and June Star said he didn't play fair, and they began to slap each other over the grandmother.

The grandmother said she would tell them a story if they would keep quiet. When she told a story, she rolled her eyes and waved her head and was very dramatic. She said once when she was a maiden lady she had been courted by a Mr. Edgar Atkins Teagarden from Jasper, Georgia. She said he was a very good-looking man and a gentleman and that he brought her a watermelon every Saturday afternoon with his initials cut in it, E. A. T. Well, one Saturday, she said, Mr. Teagarden brought the watermelon and there was nobody at home and he left it on the front porch and returned in his buggy to Jasper, but she never got the watermelon, she said, because a nigger boy ate it when he saw the initials, E. A. T.! This story tickled John Wesley's funny bone and he giggled and giggled but June Star didn't think it was any good. She said she wouldn't marry a man that just brought her a watermelon on Saturday. The grandmother said she would have done well to marry Mr. Teagarden because he was a gentleman and had bought Coca-Cola stock when it first came out and that he had died only a few years ago, a very wealthy man.

They stopped at The Tower for barbecued sandwiches. The Tower was a part stucco and part wood filling station and dance hall set in a clearing outside of Timothy. A fat man named Red Sammy Butts ran it and there were signs stuck here and there on the building and for miles up and down the highway saying, TRY RED SAMMY'S FAMOUS BARBECUE. NONE LIKE FAMOUS RED SAMMY'S! RED SAM! THE FAT BOY WITH THE HAPPY LAUGH! A VETERAN! RED SAMMY'S YOUR MAN!

Red Sammy was lying on the bare ground outside The Tower with his head under a truck while a gray monkey about a foot high, chained to a small chinaberry tree, chattered nearby. The monkey sprang back into the tree and got on the highest limb as soon as he saw the children jump out of the car and run toward him.

Inside, The Tower was a long dark room with a counter at one end and tables at the other and dancing space in the middle. They all sat down at a board table next to the nickelodeon and Red Sam's wife, a tall burnt-brown woman with hair and eyes lighter than her skin, came and took their order. The children's mother put a dime in the machine and played "The Tennessee Waltz," and the grandmother said that tune always made her want to dance. She asked Bailey if he would like to dance but he only glared at her. He didn't have a naturally sunny disposition like she did and trips made him nervous. The grandmother's brown eyes were very bright. She swayed her head from side to side and pretended she was dancing in her chair. June Star said play something she could tap to so the children's mother put in another dime and played a fast number and June Star stepped out onto the dance floor and did her tap routine.

"Ain't she cute?" Red Sam's wife said, leaning over the counter. "Would you like to come be my little girl?"

"No I certainly wouldn't," June Star said. "I wouldn't live in a broken-down place like this for a million bucks!" and she ran back to the table.

"Ain't she cute?" the woman repeated, stretching her mouth politely.

"Aren't you ashamed?" hissed the grandmother.

Red Sam came in and told his wife to quit lounging on the counter and hurry up with these people's order. His khaki trousers reached just to his hip bones and his stomach hung over them like a sack of meal swaying under his shirt. He came over and sat down at a table nearby and let out a combination sigh and yodel. "You can't win," he said. "You can't win," and he wiped his sweating red face off with a gray handkerchief. "These days you don't know who to trust," he said. "Ain't that the truth?"

"People are certainly not nice like they used to be," said the grandmother.

"Two fellers come in here last week," Red Sammy said, "driving a Chrysler. It was a old beat-up car but it was a good one and these boys looked all right to me. Said they worked at the mill and you know I let them fellers charge the gas they bought? Now why did I do that?"

"Because you're a good man!" the grandmother said at once.

"Yes'm, I suppose so," Red Sam said as if he were struck with this answer.

His wife brought the orders, carrying the five plates all at once without a tray, two in each hand and one balanced on her arm. "It isn't a soul in this green world of God's that you can trust," she said. "And I don't count nobody out of that, not nobody," she repeated, looking at Red Sammy.

"Did you read about that criminal, The Misfit, that's escaped?" asked the grandmother.

"I wouldn't be a bit surprised if he didn't attack this place right here," said the woman. "If he hears about it being here, I wouldn't be none surprised to see him. If he hears it's two cent in the cash register, I wouldn't be a tall surprised if he...."

"That'll do," Red Sam said. "Go bring these people their Co'-Colas," and the woman went off to get the rest of the order.

"A good man is hard to find," Red Sammy said. "Everything is getting terrible. I remember the day you could go off and leave your screen door unlatched. Not no more."

He and the grandmother discussed better times. The old lady said that in her opinion Europe was entirely to blame for the way things were now. She said the way Europe acted you would think we were made of money and Red Sam said it was no use talking about it, she was exactly right. The children ran outside into the white sunlight and looked at the monkey in the lacy chinaberry tree. He was busy catching fleas on himself and biting each one carefully between his teeth as if it were a delicacy.

They drove off again into the hot afternoon. The grandmother took cat naps and woke up every few minutes with her own snoring. Outside of Toombsboro she woke up and recalled an old plantation that she had visited in this neighborhood once when she was a young lady. She said the house had six white columns across the front and that there was an avenue of oaks leading up to it and two little wooden trellis arbors on either side in front where you sat down with your suitor after a stroll in the garden. She recalled exactly which road to turn off to get to it. She knew that Bailey would not be willing to lose any time looking at an old house, but the more she talked about it, the more she wanted to see it once again and find out if the little twin arbors were still standing. "There was a secret panel in this house," she said craftily, not telling the truth but wishing that she were, "and the story went that all the family silver was hidden in it when Sherman came through but it was never found...."

"Hey!" John Wesley said. "Let's go see it! We'll find it! We'll poke all the woodwork and find it! Who lives there? Where do you turn off at? Hey Pop, can't we turn off there?"

"We never have seen a house with a secret panel!" June Star shrieked. "Let's go to the house with the secret panel! Hey Pop, can't we go see the house with the secret panel!"

"It's not far from here, I know," the grandmother said. "It won't take over twenty minutes."

Bailey was looking straight ahead. His jaw was as rigid as a horseshoe. "No," he said.

The children began to yell and scream that they wanted to see the house with the secret panel. John Wesley kicked the back of the front seat and June Star hung over her mother's shoulder and whined desperately into her ear that they never had any fun even on their vacation, that they could never do what THEY wanted to do. The baby began to scream and John Wesley kicked the back of the seat so hard that his father could feel the blows in his kidney.

"All right!" he shouted and drew the car to a stop at the side of the road. "Will you all shut up? Will you all just shut up for one second? If you don't shut up, we won't go anywhere."

"It would be very educational for them," the grandmother murmured.

"All right," Bailey said, "but get this: this is the only time we're going to stop for anything like this. This is the one and only time."

"The dirt road that you have to turn down is about a mile back," the grandmother directed. "I marked it when we passed."

"A dirt road," Bailey groaned.

After they had turned around and were headed toward the dirt road, the grandmother recalled other points about the house, the beautiful glass over the front doorway and the candle-lamp in the hall. John Wesley said that the secret panel was probably in the fireplace.

"You can't go inside this house," Bailey said. "You don't know who lives there."

"While you all talk to the people in front, I'll run around behind and get in a window," John Wesley suggested.

"We'll all stay in the car," his mother said.

They turned onto the dirt road and the car raced roughly along in a swirl of pink dust. The grandmother recalled the times when there were no paved roads and thirty miles was a day's journey. The dirt road was hilly and there were sudden washes in it and sharp curves on dangerous embankments. All at once they would be on a hill, looking down over the blue tops of trees for miles around, then the next minute, they would be in a red depression with the dust-coated trees looking down on them.

"This place had better turn up in a minute," Bailey said, "or I'm going to turn around."

The road looked as if no one had traveled on it for months.

"It's not much farther," the grandmother said and just as she said it, a horrible thought came to her. The thought was so embarrassing that she turned red in the face and her eyes dilated and her feet jumped up, upsetting her valise in the corner. The instant the valise moved, the newspaper top she had over the basket under it rose with a snarl and Pitty Sing, the cat, sprang onto Bailey's shoulder.

The children were thrown to the floor and their mother, clutching the baby, was thrown out the door onto the ground; the old lady was thrown into the front seat. The car turned over once and landed right-side-up in a gulch off the side of the road. Bailey remained in the driver's seat with the cat—gray-striped with a broad white face and an orange nose—clinging to his neck like a caterpillar.

As soon as the children saw they could move their arms and legs, they scrambled out of the car, shouting, "We've had an ACCIDENT!" The grandmother was curled up under the dashboard, hoping she was injured so that Bailey's wrath would not come down on her all at once. The horrible thought she had before the accident was that the house she had remembered so vividly was not in Georgia but in Tennessee.

Bailey removed the cat from his neck with both hands and flung it out the window against the side of a pine tree. Then he got out of the car and started looking for the children's mother. She was sitting against the side of the red gutted ditch, holding the screaming baby, but she only had a cut down her face and a broken shoulder. "We've had an ACCIDENT!" the children screamed in a frenzy of delight.

"But nobody's killed," June Star said with disappointment as the grandmother limped out of the car, her hat still pinned to her head but the broken front brim standing up at a jaunty angle and the violet spray hanging off the side. They all sat down in the ditch, except the children, to recover from the shock. They were all shaking.

"Maybe a car will come along," said the children's mother hoarsely.

"I believe I have injured an organ," said the grandmother, pressing her side, but no one answered her. Bailey's teeth were clattering. He had on a yellow sport shirt with bright blue parrots designed in it and his face was as yellow as the shirt. The grandmother decided that she would not mention that the house was in Tennessee.

The road was about ten feet above and they could see only the tops of the trees on the other side of it. Behind the ditch they were sitting in there were more woods, tall and dark and deep. In a few minutes they saw a car some distance away on top of a hill, coming slowly as if the occupants were watching them. The grandmother stood up and waved both arms dramatically to attract their attention. The car continued to come on slowly, disappeared around a bend and appeared again, moving even slower, on top of the hill they had gone over. It was a big black battered hearse-like automobile. There were three men in it.

It came to a stop just over them and for some minutes, the driver looked down with a steady expressionless gaze to where they were sitting, and didn't speak. Then he turned his head and muttered something to the other two and they got out. One was a fat boy in black trousers and a red sweat shirt with a silver stallion embossed on the front of it. He moved around on the right side of them and stood staring, his mouth partly open in a kind of loose grin. The other had on khaki pants and a blue striped coat and a gray hat pulled down very low, hiding most of his face. He came around slowly on the left side. Neither spoke.

The driver got out of the car and stood by the side of it, looking down at them. He was an older man than the other two. His hair was just beginning to gray and he wore silver-rimmed spectacles that gave him a scholarly look. He had a long creased face and didn't have on any shirt or undershirt. He had on blue jeans that were too tight for him and was holding a black hat and a gun. The two boys also had guns.

"We've had an ACCIDENT!" the children screamed.

The grandmother had the peculiar feeling that the bespectacled man was someone she knew. His face was as familiar to her as if she had known him all her life but she could not recall who he was. He moved away from the car and began to come down the embankment, placing his feet carefully so that he wouldn't slip. He had on tan and white shoes and no socks, and his ankles were red and thin. "Good afternoon," he said. "I see you all had you a little spill."

"We turned over twice!" said the grandmother.

"Oncet," he corrected. "We seen it happen. Try their car and see will it run, Hiram," he said quietly to the boy with the gray hat.

"What you got that gun for?" John Wesley asked. "Whatcha gonna do with that gun?"

"Lady," the man said to the children's mother, "would you mind calling them children to sit down by you? Children make me nervous. I want all you all to sit down right together there where you're at."

"What are you telling US what to do for?" June Star asked.

Behind them the line of woods gaped like a dark open mouth. "Come here," said their mother.

"Look here now," Bailey said suddenly, "we're in a predicament! We're in. . . ."

The grandmother shrieked. She scrambled to her feet and stood staring. "You're The Misfit!" she said. "I recognized you at once!"

"Yes'm," the man said, smiling slightly as if he were pleased in spite of himself to be known, "but it would have been better for all of you, lady, if you hadn't of reckernized me."

Bailey turned his head sharply and said something to his mother that shocked even the children. The old lady began to cry and The Misfit reddened.

"Lady," he said, "don't you get upset. Sometimes a man says things he don't mean. I don't reckon he meant to talk to you thataway."

"You wouldn't shoot a lady, would you?" the grandmother said and removed a clean handkerchief from her cuff and began to slap at her eyes with it.

The Misfit pointed the toe of his shoe into the ground and made a little hole and then covered it up again. "I would hate to have to," he said.

"Listen," the grandmother almost screamed, "I know you're a good man. You don't look a bit like you have common blood. I know you must come from nice people!"

"Yes mam," he said, "finest people in the world." When he smiled he showed a row of strong white teeth. "God never made a finer woman than my mother and my daddy's heart was pure gold," he said. The boy with the red sweat shirt had come around behind them and was standing with his gun at his hip. The Misfit squatted down on the ground. "Watch them children, Bobby Lee," he said. "You know they make me nervous." He looked at the six of them huddled together in front of him and he seemed to be embarrassed as if he couldn't think of anything to say. "Ain't a cloud in the sky," he remarked, looking up at it. "Don't see no sun but don't see no cloud neither."

"Yes, it's a beautiful day," said the grandmother. "Listen," she said, "you shouldn't call yourself The Misfit because I know you're a good man at heart. I can just look at you and tell."

"Hush!" Bailey yelled. "Hush! Everybody shut up and let me handle this!" He was squatting in the position of a runner about to sprint forward but he didn't move.

"I pre-chate that, lady," The Misfit said and drew a little circle in the ground with the butt of his gun.

"It'll take a half a hour to fix this here car," Hiram called, looking over the raised hood of it.

"Well, first you and Bobby Lee get him and that little boy to step over yonder with you," The Misfit said, pointing to Bailey and John Wesley. "The boys want to ast you something," he said to Bailey. "Would you mind stepping back in them woods there with them?"

"Listen," Bailey began, "we're in a terrible predicament! Nobody realizes what this is," and his voice cracked. His eyes were as blue and intense as the parrots in his shirt and he remained perfectly still.

The grandmother reached up to adjust her hat brim as if she were going to the woods with him but it came off in her hand. She stood staring at it and after a second she let it fall to the ground. Hiram pulled Bailey up by the arm as if he were assisting an old man. John Wesley caught hold of his father's hand and Bobby Lee followed. They went off toward the woods and just as they reached the dark edge, Bailey turned and supporting himself against a gray naked pine trunk, he shouted, "I'll be back in a minute, Mamma, wait on me!"

"Come back this instant!" his mother shrilled but they all disappeared into the woods.

"Bailey Boy!" the grandmother called in a tragic voice but she found she was looking at The Misfit squatting on the ground in front of her. "I just know you're a good man," she said desperately. "You're not a bit common!"

"Nome, I ain't a good man," The Misfit said after a second as if he had considered her statement carefully, "but I ain't the worst in the world neither. My daddy said I was a different breed of dog from my brothers and sisters. 'You know,' Daddy said, 'it's some that can live their whole life out without asking about it and it's others has to know why it is, and this boy is one of the latters. He's going to be into everything!'" He put on his black hat and looked up suddenly and then away deep into the woods as if he were embarrassed again. "I'm sorry I don't have on a shirt before you ladies," he said, hunching his shoulders slightly. "We buried our clothes that we had on when we escaped and we're just making do until we can get better. We borrowed these from some folks we met," he explained.

"That's perfectly all right," the grandmother said. "Maybe Bailey has an extra shirt in his suitcase."

"I'll look and see terrectly," The Misfit said.

"Where are they taking him?" the children's mother screamed.

"Daddy was a card himself," The Misfit said. "You couldn't put anything over on him. He never got in trouble with the Authorities though. Just had the knack of handling them."

"You could be honest too if you'd only try," said the grandmother. "Think how wonderful it would be to settle down and live a comfortable life and not have to think about somebody chasing you all the time."

The Misfit kept scratching in the ground with the butt of his gun as if he were thinking about it. "Yes'm, somebody is always after you," he murmured.

The grandmother noticed how thin his shoulder blades were just behind his hat because she was standing up looking down on him. "Do you ever pray?" she asked.

He shook his head. All she saw was the black hat wiggle between his shoulder blades. "Nome," he said.

There was a pistol shot from the woods, followed closely by another. Then silence. The old lady's head jerked around. She could hear the wind move through the tree tops like a long satisfied insuck of breath. "Bailey Boy!" she called.

"I was a gospel singer for a while," The Misfit said. "I been most everything. Been in the arm service, both land and sea, at home and abroad, been twict married, been an undertaker, been with the railroads, plowed Mother Earth, been in a tornado, seen a man burnt alive oncet," and he looked up at the children's mother and the little girl who were sitting close together, their faces white and their eyes glassy; "I even seen a woman flogged," he said.

"Pray, pray," the grandmother began, "pray, pray. . . ."

"I never was a bad boy that I remember of," The Misfit said in an almost dreamy voice, "but somewheres along the line I done something wrong and got sent to the penitentiary. I was buried alive," and he looked up and held her attention to him by a steady stare.

"That's when you should have started to pray," she said. "What did you do to get sent to the penitentiary that first time?"

"Turn to the right, it was a wall," The Misfit said, looking up again at the cloudless sky. "Turn to the left, it was a wall. Look up it was a ceiling, look down it was a floor. I forget what I done, lady. I set there and set there, trying to remember what it was I done and I ain't recalled it to this day. Oncet in a while, I would think it was coming to me, but it never come."

"Maybe they put you in by mistake," the old lady said vaguely.

"Nome," he said. "It wasn't no mistake. They had the papers on me."

"You must have stolen something," she said.

The Misfit sneered slightly. "Nobody had nothing I wanted," he said. "It was a head-doctor at the penitentiary said what I had done was kill my daddy but I known that for a lie. My daddy died in nineteen ought nineteen of the epidemic flu and I never had a thing to do with it. He was buried in the Mount Hopewell Baptist churchyard and you can see for yourself."

"If you would pray," the old lady said, "Jesus would help you."

"That's right," The Misfit said.

"Well then, why don't you pray?" she asked trembling with delight suddenly.

"I don't want no hep," he said. "I'm doing all right by myself."

Bobby Lee and Hiram came ambling back from the woods. Bobby Lee was dragging a yellow shirt with bright blue parrots in it.

"Thow me that shirt, Bobby Lee," The Misfit said. The shirt came flying at him and landed on his shoulder and he put it on. The grandmother couldn't name what the shirt reminded her of. "No, lady," The Misfit said while he was buttoning it up, "I found out the crime don't matter. You can do one thing or you can do another, kill a man or take a tire off his car, because sooner or later you're going to forget what it was you done and just be punished for it."

The children's mother had begun to make heaving noises as if she couldn't get her breath. "Lady," he asked, "would you and that little girl like to step off yonder with Bobby Lee and Hiram and join your husband?"

"Yes, thank you," the mother said faintly. Her left arm dangled helplessly and she was holding the baby, who had gone to sleep, in the other. "Hep that lady up, Hiram," The Misfit said as she struggled to climb out of the ditch, "and Bobby Lee, you hold onto that little girl's hand."

"I don't want to hold hands with him," June Star said. "He reminds me of a pig."

The fat boy blushed and laughed and caught her by the arm and pulled her off into the woods after Hiram and her mother.

Alone with The Misfit, the grandmother found that she had lost her voice. There was not a cloud in the sky nor any sun. There was nothing around her but woods. She wanted to tell him that he must pray. She opened and closed her mouth several times before anything came out. Finally she found herself saying, "Jesus, Jesus," meaning Jesus will help you, but the way she was saying it, it sounded as if she might be cursing.

"Yes'm," The Misfit said as if he agreed. "Jesus thown everything off balance. It was the same case with Him as with me except He hadn't committed any crime and they could prove I had committed one because they had the papers on me. Of course," he said, "they never shown me my papers. That's why I sign myself now. I said long ago, you get your signature and sign everything you do and keep a copy of it. Then you'll know what you done and you can hold up the crime to the punishment and see do they match and in the end you'll have something to prove you ain't been treated right. I call myself The Misfit," he said, "because I can't make what all I done wrong fit what all I gone through in punishment."

There was a piercing scream from the woods, followed closely by a pistol report. "Does it seem right to you, lady, that one is punished a heap and another ain't punished at all?"

"Jesus!" the old lady cried. "You've got good blood! I know you wouldn't shoot a lady! I know you come from nice people! Pray! Jesus, you ought not to shoot a lady. I'll give you all the money I've got!"

"Lady," The Misfit said, looking beyond her far into the woods, "there never was a body that give the undertaker a tip."

There were two more pistol reports and the grandmother raised her head like a parched old turkey hen crying for water and called, "Bailey Boy, Bailey Boy!" as if her heart would break.

"Jesus was the only One that ever raised the dead," The Misfit continued, "and He shouldn't have done it. He thown everything off balance. If He did what He said, then it's nothing for you to do but thow away everything and follow Him, and if He didn't, then it's nothing for you to do but enjoy the few minutes you got left the best way you can—by killing somebody or burning down his house or doing some other meanness to him. No pleasure but meanness," he said and his voice had become almost a snarl.

"Maybe He didn't raise the dead," the old lady mumbled, not knowing what she was saying and feeling so dizzy that she sank down in the ditch with her legs twisted under her.

"I wasn't there so I can't say He didn't," The Misfit said. "I wisht I had of been there," he said, hitting the ground with his fist. "It ain't right I wasn't there because if I had of been there I would of known. Listen lady," he said in a high voice, "if I had of been there I would of known and I wouldn't be like I am now." His voice seemed about to crack and the grandmother's head cleared for an instant. She saw the man's face twisted close to her own as if he were going to cry and she murmured, "Why you're one of my babies. You're one of my own children!" She reached out and touched him on the shoulder. The Misfit sprang back as if a snake had bitten him and shot her three times through the chest. Then he put his gun down on the ground and took off his glasses and began to clean them.

Hiram and Bobby Lee returned from the woods and stood over the ditch, looking down at the grandmother who half sat and half lay in a puddle of blood with her legs crossed under her like a child's and her face smiling up at the cloudless sky.

Without his glasses, The Misfit's eyes were red-rimmed and pale and defenseless-looking. "Take her off and thow her where you thown the others," he said, picking up the cat that was rubbing itself against his leg.

"She was a talker, wasn't she?" Bobby Lee said, sliding down the ditch with a yodel.

"She would of been a good woman," The Misfit said, "if it had been somebody there to shoot her every minute of her life."

"Some fun!" Bobby Lee said.

"Shut up, Bobby Lee," The Misfit said. "It's no real pleasure in life."

(1953)

Chinua Achebe   b. 1930

Dead Men's Path

Michael Obi's hopes were fulfilled much earlier than he expected. He was appointed headmaster of Ndume Central School in January 1949. It had always been an unprogressive school, so the Mission authorities decided to send a young and energetic man to run it. Obi accepted this responsibility with enthusiasm. He had many wonderful ideas and this was an opportunity to put them into practice. He had had sound secondary school education which designated him a "pivotal teacher" in the official records and set him apart from the other headmasters in the mission field. He was outspoken in his condemnation of the narrow views of these older and often less-educated ones.

"We shall make a good job of it, shan't we?" he asked his young wife when they first heard the joyful news of his promotion.

"We shall do our best," she replied. "We shall have such beautiful gardens and everything will be just *modern* and delightful . . ." In their two years of married life she had become completely infected by his passion for "modern methods" and his denigration of "these old and superannuated people in the teaching field who would be better employed as traders in the Onitsha market." She began to see herself already as the admired wife of the young headmaster, the queen of the school.

The wives of the other teachers would envy her position. She would set the fashion in everything . . . Then, suddenly, it occurred to her that there might not be other wives. Wavering between hope and fear, she asked her husband, looking anxiously at him.

"All our colleagues are young and unmarried," he said with enthusiasm which for once she did not share. "Which is a good thing," he continued.

"Why?"

"Why? They will give all their time and energy to the school."

Nancy was downcast. For a few minutes she became sceptical about the new school; but it was only for a few minutes. Her little personal misfortune could not blind her to her husband's happy prospects. She looked at him as he sat folded up in a chair. He was stoop-shouldered and looked frail. But he sometimes surprised people with sudden bursts of physical energy. In his present posture, however, all his bodily strength seemed to have retired behind his deep-set eyes, giving them an extraordinary power of penetration. He was only twenty-six, but looked thirty or more. On the whole, he was not unhandsome.

"A penny for your thoughts, Mike," said Nancy after a while, imitating the woman's magazine she read.

"I was thinking what a grand opportunity we've got at last to show these people how a school should be run."

Ndume school was backward in every sense of the word. Mr. Obi put his whole life into the work, and his wife hers too. He had two aims. A high standard of teaching was insisted upon, and the school compound was to be turned into a place of beauty. Nancy's dream-gardens came to life with the coming of the rains, and blossomed. Beautiful hibiscus and allamanda hedges in brilliant red and yellow marked out the carefully tended school compound from the rank neighbourhood bushes.

One evening as Obi was admiring his work he was scandalized to see an old woman from the village hobble right across the compound, through a marigold flower-bed and the hedges. On going up there he found faint signs of an almost disused path from the village across the school compound to the bush on the other side.

"It amazes me," said Obi to one of his teachers who had been three years in the school, "that you people allowed the villagers to make use of this footpath. It is simply incredible." He shook his head.

"The path," said the teacher apologetically, "appears to be very important to them. Although it is hardly used, it connects the village shrine with their place of burial."

"And what has that got to do with the school?" asked the headmaster.

"Well, I don't know," replied the other with a shrug of the shoulders. "But I remember there was a big row some time ago when we attempted to close it."

"That was some time ago. But it will not be used now," said Obi as he walked away. "What will the Government Education Officer think of this when he comes to inspect the school next week? The villagers might, for all I know, decide to use the schoolroom for a pagan ritual during the inspection."

Heavy sticks were planted closely across the path at the two places where it entered and left the school premises. These were further strengthened with barbed wire.

Three days later the village priest of *Ani* called on the headmaster. He was an old man and walked with a slight stoop. He carried a stout walking-stick which he usually tapped on the floor, by way of emphasis, each time he made a new point in his argument.

"I have heard," he said after the usual exchange of cordialities, "that our ancestral footpath has recently been closed . . . "

"Yes," replied Mr. Obi. "We cannot allow people to make a highway of our school compound."

"Look here, my son," said the priest bringing down his walking-stick, "this path was here before you were born and before your father was born. The whole life of this village depends on it. Our dead relatives depart by it and our ancestors visit us by it. But most important, it is the path of children coming in to be born . . . "

Mr. Obi listened with a satisfied smile on his face.

"The whole purpose of our school," he said finally, "is to eradicate just such beliefs as that. Dead men do not require footpaths. The whole idea is just fantastic. Our duty is to teach your children to laugh at such ideas."

"What you say may be true," replied the priest, "but we follow the practices of our fathers. If you re-open the path we shall have nothing to quarrel about. What I always say is: let the hawk perch and let the eagle perch." He rose to go.

"I am sorry," said the young headmaster. "But the school compound cannot be a thoroughfare. It is against our regulations. I would suggest your constructing another path, skirting our premises. We can even get our boys to help in building it. I don't suppose the ancestors will find the little detour too burdensome."

"I have no more words to say," said the old priest, already outside.

Two days later, a young woman in the village died in childbed. A diviner was immediately consulted and he prescribed heavy sacrifices to propitiate ancestors insulted by the fence.

Obi woke up next morning among the ruins of his work. The beautiful hedges were torn up not just near the path but right round the school, the flowers trampled to death and one of the school buildings pulled down . . . That day, the white Supervisor came to inspect the school and wrote a nasty report on the state of the premises but more seriously about the "tribal-war situation developing between the school and the village, arising in part from the misguided zeal of the new headmaster."

(1972)

Rudy Wiebe   b. 1934
Where Is the Voice Coming From?

The problem is to make the story.

One difficulty of this making may have been excellently stated by Teilhard de Chardin: 'We are continually inclined to isolate ourselves from the things and events which surround us . . . as though we were spectators, not elements, in what goes on.' Arnold Toynbee does venture, 'For all that we know, Reality is the undifferentiated unity of the mystical experience,' but that need not here be considered. This story ended long ago; it is one of finite acts, of orders, of elemental feelings and reactions, of obvious legal restrictions and requirements.

Presumably all the parts of the story are themselves available. A difficulty is that they are, as always, available only in bits and pieces. Though the acts themselves seem quite clear, some written reports of the acts contradict each other. As if these acts were, at one time, too well known; as if the original nodule of each particular fact had from somewhere received non-factual accretions; or even more, as if, since the basic facts were so clear perhaps there were a larger number of facts than any one reporter, or several, or even any reporter had ever attempted to record. About facts that are still simply told by this mouth to that ear, of course, even less can be expected.

An affair seventy-five years old should acquire some of the shiny transparency of an old man's skin. It should.

Sometimes it would seem that it would be enough—perhaps more than enough—to hear the names only. The grandfather One Arrow; the mother Spotted Calf; the father Sounding Sky; the wife (wives rather, but only one of them seems to have a name, though their fathers are Napaise, Kapahoo, Old Dust, The Rump)—the one wife named, of all things, Pale Face; the cousin of Going-Up-To-Sky; the brother-in-law (again, of all things) Dublin. The names of the police sound very much alike; they all begin with Constable or Corporal or Sergeant, but here and there an Inspector, then a Superintendent and eventually all the resonance of an Assistant Commissioner echoes down. More. Herself: Victoria, by the Grace of God, etc., etc., QUEEN, defender of the Faith, etc., etc.; and witness 'Our Right Trusty and Right Well-beloved Cousin and Councillor the Right Honorable Sir John Campbell Hamilton-Gordon, Earl of Aberdeen; Viscount Formartine, Baron Haddo, Methlic, Tarves and Kellie, in the Peerage of Scotland; Viscount Gordon of Aberdeen, County of Aberdeen, in the peerage of the United Kingdom; Baronet of Nova Scotia, Knight Grand Cross of Our Most Distinguished Order of Saint Michael and Saint George, etc., Governor General of Canada'. And of course himself: in the award proclamation named 'Jean-Baptiste' but otherwise known only as Almighty Voice.

But hearing cannot be enough; not even hearing all the thunder of A Proclamation: 'Now Hear Ye that a reward of FIVE HUNDRED DOLLARS will be paid to any person or persons who will give such information as will lead . . . (etc., etc.) the Twentieth day of April, in the year of Our Lord one thousand eight hundred and ninety-six, and the Fifty-ninth year of Our Reign . . . ' etc. and etc.

Such hearing cannot be enough. The first item to be seen is the piece of white bone. It is almost triangular, slightly convex—concave actually as it is positioned at this moment with its corners slightly raised—graduating from perhaps a strong eighth to a weak quarter of an inch in thickness, its scattered pore structure varying between larger and smaller on its perhaps polished, certainly shiny surface. Precision is difficult since the glass showcase is at least thirteen inches deep and therefore an eye cannot be brought as close as the minute inspection of such a small, though certainly quite adequate, sample of skull would normally require. Also, because of the position it cannot be determined whether the several hairs, well over a foot long, are still in some manner attached or not.

The seven-pounder cannon can be seen standing almost shyly between the showcase and the interior wall. Officially it is known as a gun, not a cannon, and clearly its bore is not large enough to admit a large man's fist. Even if it can be believed that this gun was used in the 1885 Rebellion and that on the evening of Saturday, May 29, 1897 (while the nine-pounder, now unidentified, was in the process of arriving with the police on the special train from Regina), seven shells (all that were available in Prince Albert at that time) from it were sent shrieking into the poplar bluffs as night fell, clearly such shelling could not and would not disembowel the whole earth. Its carriage is now nicely lacquered, the perhaps oak spokes of its petite wheels (little higher than a knee) have been recently scraped, puttied and varnished; the brilliant burnish of its brass breeching testifies with what meticulous care charmen and women have used nationally-advertised cleaners and restorers.

Though it can also be seen, even a careless glance reveals that the same concern has not been expended on the one (of two) .44 calibre 1866 model Winchesters apparently found at the last in the pit with Almighty Voice. It also is preserved in a glass case; the number 1536735 is still, though barely, distinguishable on the brass cartridge section just below the brass saddle ring. However, perhaps because the case was imperfectly sealed at one time (though sealed enough not to warrant disturbance now), or because of simple neglect, the rifle is obviously spotted here and there with blotches of rust and the brass itself reveals discolorations almost like mildew. The rifle bore, the three long strands of hair themselves, actually bristle with clots of dust. It may be that this museum cannot afford to be as concerned as the other; conversely, the disfiguration may be something inherent in the items themselves.

The small building which was the police guardroom at Duck Lake, Saskatchewan Territory, in 1895 may also be seen. It had subsequently been moved from its original place and used to house small animals, chickens perhaps, or pigs—such as a woman might be expected to have under her responsibility. It is, of course, now perfectly empty, and clean so that the public may enter with no more discomfort than a bend under the doorway and a heavy encounter with disinfectant. The door-jamb has obviously been replaced; the bar network at one window is, however, said to be original; smooth still, very smooth. The logs inside have been smeared again and again with whitewash, perhaps paint, to an insistent point of identity-defying characterlessness. Within the small rectangular box of these logs not a sound can be heard from the streets of the, probably dead, town.

> *Hey Injun you'll get hung for stealing that steer*
> *Hey Injun for killing that government cow you'll get three*
> *weeks on the woodpile Hey Injun*

The place named Kinistino seems to have disappeared from the map but the Minnechinass Hills have not. Whether they have ever been on a map is doubtful but they will, of course, not disappear from the landscape as long as the grass grows and the rivers run. Contrary to general report and belief, the Canadian prairies are rarely, if ever, flat and the Minnechinass (spelled five different ways and translated sometimes as 'The Outside Hill', sometimes as 'Beautiful Bare Hills') are dissimilar from any other of the numberless hills that everywhere block out the prairie horizon. They are bare; poplars lie tattered along their tops, almost black against the straw-pale grass and sharp green against the grey soil of the plowing laid in half-mile rectangular blocks upon their western slopes. Poles holding various wires stick out of the fields, back down the bend of the valley; what was once a farmhouse is weathering into the cultivated earth. The poplar bluff where Almighty Voice made his stand has, of course, disappeared.

The policemen he shot and killed (not the ones he wounded, of course) are easily located. Six miles east, thirty-nine miles north in Prince Albert, the English Cemetery. Sergeant Colin Campbell Colebrook, North West Mounted Police Registration Number 605, lies presumably under a gravestone there. His name is seventeenth in a very long 'list of non-commissioned officers and men who have died in the service since the inception of the force.' The date is October 29, 1895, and the cause of death is anonymous: 'Shot by escaping Indian prisoner near Prince Albert.' At the foot of this grave are two others: Constable John R. Kerr, No. 3040, and Corporal C. H. S. Hockin. No. 3106. Their cause of death on May 28, 1897 is even more anonymous, but the place is relatively precise: 'Shot by Indians at Min-etch-inass Hills, Prince Albert District.'

The gravestone, if he has one, of the fourth man Almighty Voice killed is more difficult to locate. Mr Ernest Grundy, postmaster at Duck Lake in 1897, apparently shut his window the afternoon of Friday, May 28, armed himself, rode east twenty miles, participated in the second charge into the bluff at about 6:30 p.m., and on the third sweep of that charge was shot dead at the edge of the pit. It would seem that he thereby contributed substantially not only to the Indians' bullet supply, but his clothing warmed them as well.

The burial place of Dublin and Going-Up-To-Sky is unknown, as is the grave of Almighty Voice. It is said that a Métis named Henry Smith lifted the latter's body from the pit in the bluff and gave it to Spotted Calf. The place of burial is not, of course, of ultimate significance. A gravestone is always less evidence than a triangular piece of skull, provided it is large enough.

Whatever further evidence there is to be gathered may rest on pictures. There are, presumably, almost numberless pictures of the policemen in the case, but the only one with direct bearing is one of Sergeant Colebrook who apparently insisted on advancing to complete an arrest after being warned three times that if he took another step he would be shot. The picture must have been taken before he joined the force; it reveals him a large-eared man, hair brush-cut and ascot tie, his eyelids slightly drooping, almost hooded under thick brows. Unfortunately a picture of Constable R. C. Dickson, into whose charge Almighty Voice was apparently committed in that guardroom and who after Colebrook's death was convicted of negligence, sentenced to two months hard labour and discharged, does not seem to be available.

There are no pictures to be found of either Dublin (killed early by rifle fire) or Going-Up-To-Sky (killed in the pit), the two teenage boys who gave their ultimate fealty to Almighty Voice. There is, however, one said to be of Almighty Voice, Junior. He may have been born to Pale Face during the year, two hundred and twenty-one days that his father was a fugitive. In the picture he is kneeling before what could be a tent, he wears striped denim overalls and displays twin babies whose sex cannot be determined from the double-laced dark bonnets they wear. In the supposed picture of Spotted Calf and Sounding Sky, Sounding Sky stands slightly before his wife; he wears a white shirt and a striped blanket folded over his left shoulder in such a manner that the arm in which he cradles a long rifle cannot be seen. His head is thrown back; the rim of his hat appears as a black half-moon above eyes that are pressed shut in, as it were, profound concentration; above a mouth clenched thin in a downward curve. Spotted Calf wears a long dress, a sweater which could also be a man's dress coat, and a large fringed and embroidered shawl which would appear distinctly Doukhobor in origin if the scroll patterns on it were more irregular. Her head is small and turned slightly towards her husband so as to reveal her right ear. There is what can only be called a quizzical expression on her crumpled face; it may be she does not understand what is happening and that she would have asked a question, perhaps of her husband, perhaps of the photographers, perhaps even of anyone, anywhere in the world if such questioning were possible for an Indian lady.

There is one final picture. That is one of Almighty Voice himself. At least it is purported to be of Almighty Voice himself. In the Royal Canadian Mounted Police Museum on the Barracks Grounds just off Dewdney Avenue in Regina, Saskatchewan, it lies in the same showcase, as a matter of fact immediately beside, that triangular piece of skull. Both are unequivocally labelled, and it must be assumed that a police force with a world-wide reputation would not label *such* evidence incorrectly. But here emerges an ultimate problem in making the story.

There are two official descriptions of Almighty Voice. The first reads: 'Height about five feet, ten inches, slight build, rather good looking, a sharp hooked nose with a remarkably flat point. Has a bullet scar on the left side of his face about 1 ½ inches long running from near corner of mouth towards ear. The scar cannot be noticed when his face is painted but otherwise is plain. Skin fair for an Indian.' The second description is on the Award Proclamation: 'About twenty-two years old, five feet ten inches in height, weight about eleven stone, slightly erect, neat small feet and hands; complexion inclined to be fair, wavy dark hair to shoulders, large dark eyes, broad forehead, sharp features and parrot nose with flat tip, scar on left cheek running from mouth towards ear, feminine appearance.'

So run the descriptions that were, presumably, to identify a well-known fugitive in so precise a manner that an informant could collect five hundred dollars—a considerable sum when a police constable earned between one and two dollars a day. The nexus of the problems appears when these supposed official descriptions are compared to the supposed official picture. The man in the picture is standing on a small rug. The fingers of his left hand touch a curved Victorian settee, behind him a photographer's backdrop of scrolled patterns merges to vaguely paradisiacal trees and perhaps a sky. The moccasins he wears makes it impossible to deduce whether his feet are 'neat small'. He may be five feet, ten inches tall, may weigh eleven stone, he certainly is 'rather good looking' and, though it is a frontal view, it may be that the point of his long and flaring nose could be 'remarkably flat'. The photograph is slightly over-illuminated and so the unpainted complexion could be 'inclined to be fair'; however, nothing can be seen of a scar, the hair is not wavy and shoulder-length but hangs almost to the waist in two thick straight braids worked through with beads, fur, ribbons and cords. The right hand that holds the corner of the blanket-like coat in position is large and, even in the high illumination, heavily veined. The neck is concealed under coiled beads and the forehead seems more low than 'broad'.

Perhaps, somehow, these picture details could be reconciled with the official description if the face as a whole were not so devastating.

On a cloth-backed sheet two feet by two and one-half feet in size, under the Great Seal of the Lion and the Unicorn, dignified by the names of the Deputy of the Minister of Justice, the Secretary of State, the Queen herself and all the heaped detail of her 'Right Trusty and Right Well Beloved Cousin', this description concludes: 'feminine appearance'. But the pictures: any face of history, any believed face that the world acknowledges as *man*—Socrates, Jesus, Attila, Genghis Khan, Mahatma Gandhi, Joseph Stalin—no believed face is more *man* than this face. The mouth, the nose, the clenched brows, the eyes— the eyes are large, yes, and dark, but even in this watered-down reproduction of unending reproductions of that original, a steady look into those eyes cannot be endured. It is a face like an ax.

It is now evident that the de Chardin statement quoted at the beginning has relevance only as it proves itself inadequate to explain what has happened. At the same time, the inadequacy of Aristotle's much more famous statement becomes evident: 'The true difference [between the historian and the poet] is that one relates what *has* happened, the other what *may* happen.' These statements cannot explain the storyteller's activity since, despite the most rigid application of impersonal investigation, the elements of the story have now run me aground. If ever I could, I can no longer pretend to objective, omnipotent disinterestedness. I am no longer *spectator* of what *has* happened or what *may* happen: I am become *element* in what is happening at this very moment.

For it is, of course, I myself who cannot endure the shadows on that paper which are those eyes. It is I who stand beside this broken veranda post where two corner shingles have been torn away, where barbed wire tangles the dead weeds on the edge of this field. The bluff that sheltered Almighty Voice and his two friends has not disappeared from the slope of the Minnechinass, no more than the sound of Constable Dickson's voice in that guardhouse is silent. The sound of his speaking is there even if it has never been recorded in an official report:

> *hey injun you'll get*
> *hung*
> *for stealing that steer*
> *hey injun for killing that government*
> *cow you'll get three*
> *weeks on the woodpile hey injun*

The unknown contradictory words about an unprovable act that move a boy to defiance, an implacable Cree warrior long after the three-hundred-and-fifty-year war is ended, a war already lost the day the Cree watch Cartier hoist his gun ashore at Hochelaga and they begin the long retreat west; these words of incomprehension, of threatened incomprehensible law are there to be heard just as the unmoving tableau of the three-day siege is there to be seen on the slopes of the Minnechinass. Sounding Sky is somewhere not there, under arrest, but Spotted Calf stands on a shoulder of the Hills a little to the left, her arms upraised to the setting sun. Her mouth is open. A horse rears, riderless, above the scrub willow at the edge of the bluff, smoke puffs, screams tangle in rifle barrage, there are wounds, somewhere. The bluff is so green this spring, it will not burn and the ragged line of seven police and two civilians is staggering through, faces twisted in rage, terror, and rifles sputter. Nothing moves. There is no sound of frogs in the night; twenty-seven policemen and five civilians stand in cordon at thirty-yard intervals and a body also lies in the shelter of a gully. Only a voice rises from the bluff:

> *We have fought well*
> *You have died like braves*
> *I have worked hard and am hungry*
> *Give me food*

but nothing moves. The bluff lies, a bright green island on the grassy slope surrounded by men hunched forward rigid over their long rifles, men clumped out of rifle-range, thirty-five men dressed as for fall hunting on a sharp spring day, a small gun positioned on a ridge above. A crow is falling out of the sky into the bluff, its feathers sprayed as by an explosion. The first gun and the second gun are in position, the beginning and end of the bristling surround of thirty-five Prince Albert Volunteers, thirteen civilians and fifty-six policemen in position relative to the bluff and relative to the unnumbered whites astride their horses, standing up in their carts, staring and pointing across the valley, in position relative to the bluff and the unnumbered Indians squatting silent along the higher ridges of the Hills, motionless mounds, faceless against the Sunday morning sunlight edging between and over them down along the tree tips, down into the shadows of the bluff. Nothing moves. Beside the second gun the red-coated officer has flung a handful of grass into the motionless air, almost to the rim of the red sun.

And there is a voice. It is an incredible voice that rises from among the young poplars ripped of their spring bark, from among the dead somewhere lying there, out of the arm-deep pit shorter than a man; a voice rises over the exploding smoke and thunder of guns that reel back in their positions, worked over, serviced by the grimed motionless men in bright coats and glinting buttons, a voice so high and clear, so unbelievably high and strong in its unending wordless cry.

The voice of 'Gitchie-Manitou Wayo'—interpreted as 'voice of the Great Spirit'—that is, The Almighty Voice. His death chant no less incredible in its beauty than in its incomprehensible happiness.

I say 'wordless cry' because that is the way it sounds to me. I could be more accurate if I had a reliable interpreter who would make a reliable interpretation. For I do not, of course, understand the Cree myself.

(1982)

Joyce Carol Oates   b. 1938

Where Are You Going, Where Have You Been?

For Bob Dylan[1]

Her name was Connie. She was fifteen and she had a quick, nervous giggling habit of craning her neck to glance into mirrors or checking other people's faces to make sure her own was all right. Her mother, who noticed everything and knew everything and who hadn't much reason any longer to look at her own face, always scolded Connie about it. "Stop gawking at yourself. Who are you? You think you're so pretty?" she would say. Connie would raise her eyebrows at these familiar old complaints and look right through her mother, into a shadowy vision of herself as she was right at that moment: she knew she was pretty and that was everything. Her mother had been pretty once too, if you could believe those old snapshots in the album, but now her looks were gone and that was why she was always after Connie.

"Why don't you keep your room clean like your sister? How've you got your hair fixed—what the hell stinks? Hair spray? You don't see your sister using that junk."

Her sister June was twenty-four and still lived at home. She was a secretary in the high school Connie attended, and if that wasn't bad enough—with her in the same building—she was so plain and chunky and steady that Connie had to hear her praised all the time by her mother and her mother's sisters. June did this, June did that, she saved money and helped clean the house and cooked and Connie couldn't do a thing, her mind was all filled with trashy daydreams. Their father was away at work most of the time and when he came home he wanted supper and he read the newspaper at supper and after supper he went to bed. He didn't bother talking much to them, but around his bent head Connie's mother kept picking at her until Connie wished her mother was dead and she herself was dead and it was all over. "She makes me want to throw up sometimes," she complained to her friends. She had a high, breathless, amused voice that made everything she said sound a little forced, whether it was sincere or not.

There was one good thing: June went places with girl friends of hers, girls who were just as plain and steady as she, and so when Connie wanted to do that her mother had no objections. The father of Connie's best girl friend drove the girls the three miles to town and left them at a shopping plaza so they could walk through the stores or go to a movie, and when he came to pick them up again at eleven he never bothered to ask what they had done.

They must have been familiar sights, walking around the shopping plaza in their shorts and flat ballerina slippers that always scuffed the sidewalk, with charm bracelets jingling on their thin wrists; they would lean together to whisper and laugh secretly if someone passed who amused or interested them. Connie had long dark blond hair that drew anyone's eye to it, and she wore part of it pulled up on her head and puffed out and the rest of it she let fall down her back. She wore a pull-over jersey blouse that looked one way when she was at home and

---

[1] Bob Dylan (b. 1941) is the composer, author, and singer who devised and popularized folk rock during the 1960s.

another way when she was away from home. Everything about her had two sides to it, one for home and one for anywhere that was not home: her walk, which could be childlike and bobbing, or languid enough to make anyone think she was hearing music in her head; her mouth, which was pale and smirking most of the time, but bright and pink on these evenings out; her laugh, which was cynical and drawling at home—"Ha, ha, very funny,"—but high-pitched and nervous anywhere else, like the jingling of the charms on her bracelet.

Sometimes they did go shopping or to a movie, but sometimes they went across the highway, ducking fast across the busy road, to a drive-in restaurant where older kids hung out. The restaurant was shaped like a big bottle, though squatter than a real bottle, and on its cap was a revolving figure of a grinning boy holding a hamburger aloft. One night in midsummer they ran across, breathless with daring, and right away someone leaned out a car window and invited them over, but it was just a boy from high school they didn't like. It made them feel good to be able to ignore him. They went up through the maze of parked and cruising cars to the bright-lit, fly-infested restaurant, their faces pleased and expectant as if they were entering a sacred building that loomed up out of the night to give them what haven and blessing they yearned for. They sat at the counter and crossed their legs at the ankles, their thin shoulders rigid with excitement, and listened to the music that made everything so good: the music was always in the background, like music at a church service; it was something to depend upon.

A boy named Eddie came in to talk with them. He sat backwards on his stool, turning himself jerkily around in semi-circles and then stopping and turning back again, and after a while he asked Connie if she would like something to eat. She said she would and so she tapped her friend's arm on her way out—her friend pulled her face up into a brave, droll look—and Connie said she would meet her at eleven, across the way. "I just hate to leave her like that," Connie said earnestly, but the boy said that she wouldn't be alone for long. So they went out to his car, and on the way Connie couldn't help but let her eyes wander over the windshields and faces all around her, her face gleaming with a joy that had nothing to do with Eddie or even this place; it might have been the music. She drew her shoulders up and sucked in her breath with the pure pleasure of being alive, and just at that moment she happened to glance at a face just a few feet from hers. It was a boy with shaggy black hair, in a convertible jalopy painted gold. He stared at her and then his lips widened into a grin. Connie slit her eyes at him and turned away, but she couldn't help glancing back and there he was, still watching her. He wagged a finger and laughed and said, "Gonna get you, baby," and Connie turned away again without Eddie noticing anything.

She spent three hours with him, at the restaurant where they ate hamburgers and drank Cokes in wax cups that were always sweating, and then down an alley a mile or so away, and when he left her off at five to eleven only the movie house was still open at the plaza. Her girl friend was there, talking with a boy. When Connie came up, the two girls smiled at each other and Connie said, "How was the movie?" and the girl said, "*You* should know." They rode off with the girl's father, sleepy and pleased, and Connie couldn't help but look back at the darkened shopping plaza with its big empty parking lot and its signs that were faded and ghostly now, and over at the drive-in restaurant where cars were still circling tirelessly. She couldn't hear the music at this distance.

Next morning June asked her how the movie was and Connie said, "So-so."

She and that girl and occasionally another girl went out several times a week, and the rest of the time Connie spent around the house—it was summer vacation—getting in her mother's way and thinking, dreaming about the boys she met. But all the boys fell back and dissolved into a single face that was not even a face but an idea, a feeling, mixed up with the urgent insistent pounding of the music and the humid night air of July. Connie's mother kept dragging her back to the daylight by finding things for her to do or saying suddenly, "What's this about the Pettinger girl?"

And Connie would say nervously, "Oh, her. That dope." She always drew thick clear lines between herself and such girls, and her mother was simple and kind enough to believe it. Her mother was so simple, Connie thought, that it was maybe cruel to fool her so much. Her mother went scuffling around the house in old bedroom slippers and complained over the telephone to one sister about the other, then the other called up and the two of them complained about the third one. If June's name was mentioned her mother's tone was approving, and if Connie's name was mentioned it was disapproving. This did not really mean she disliked Connie, and actually Connie thought that her mother preferred her to June just because she was prettier, but the two of them kept up a pretense of exasperation, a sense that they were tugging and struggling over something of little value to either of them. Sometimes, over coffee, they were almost friends, but something would come up—some vexation that was like a fly buzzing suddenly around their heads—and their faces went hard with contempt.

One Sunday Connie got up at eleven—none of them bothered with church—and washed her hair so that it could dry all day long in the sun. Her parents and sister were going to a barbecue at an aunt's house and Connie said no, she wasn't interested, rolling her eyes to let her mother know just what she thought of it. "Stay home alone then," her mother said sharply. Connie sat out back in a lawn chair and watched them drive away, her father quiet and bald, hunched around so that he could back the car out, her mother with a look that was still angry and not at all softened through the windshield, and in the back seat poor old June, all dressed up as if she didn't know what a barbecue was, with all the running yelling kids and the flies. Connie sat with her eyes closed in the sun, dreaming and dazed with the warmth about her as if this were a kind of love, the caresses of love, and her mind slipped over onto thoughts of the boy she had been with the night before and how nice he had been, how sweet it always was, not the way someone like June would suppose but sweet, gentle, the way it was in movies and promised in songs; and when she opened her eyes she hardly knew where she was, the back yard ran off into weeds and a fence-like line of trees and behind it the sky was perfectly blue and still. The asbestos "ranch house" that was now three years old startled her—it looked small. She shook her head as if to get awake.

It was too hot. She went inside the house and turned on the radio to drown out the quiet. She sat on the edge of her bed, barefoot, and listened for an hour and a half to a program called XYZ Sunday Jamboree, record after record of hard, fast, shrieking songs she sang along with, interspersed by exclamations from "Bobby King": "An' look here, you girls at Napoleon's—Son and Charley want you to pay real close attention to this song coming up!"

And Connie paid close attention herself, bathed in a glow of slow-pulsed joy that seemed to rise mysteriously out of the music itself and lay languidly about the airless little room, breathed in and breathed out with each gentle rise and fall of her chest.

After a while she heard a car coming up the drive. She sat up at once, startled, because it couldn't be her father so soon. The gravel kept crunching all the way in from the road—the driveway was long—and Connie ran to the window. It was a car she didn't know. It was an open jalopy, painted a bright gold that caught the sunlight opaquely. Her heart began to pound and her fingers snatched at her hair, checking it, and she whispered, "Christ. Christ," wondering how bad she looked. The car came to a stop at the side door and the horn sounded four short taps, as if this were a signal Connie knew.

She went into the kitchen and approached the door slowly, then hung out the screen door, her bare toes curling down off the step. There were two boys in the car and now she recognized the driver: he had shaggy, shabby black hair that looked crazy as a wig and he was grinning at her.

"I ain't late, am I?" he said.

"Who the hell do you think you are?" Connie said.

"Toldja I'd be out, didn't I?"

"I don't even know who you are."

She spoke sullenly, careful to show no interest or pleasure, and he spoke in a fast, bright monotone. Connie looked past him to the other boy, taking her time. He had fair brown hair, with a lock that fell onto his forehead. His sideburns gave him a fierce, embarrassed look, but so far he hadn't even bothered to glance at her. Both boys wore sunglasses. The driver's glasses were metallic and mirrored everything in miniature.

"You wanna come for a ride?" he said.

Connie smirked and let her hair fall loose over one shoulder.

"Don'tcha like my car? New paint job," he said. "Hey."

"What?"

"You're cute."

She pretended to fidget, chasing flies away from the door.

"Don'tcha believe me, or what?" he said.

"Look, I don't even know who you are," Connie said in disgust.

"Hey, Ellie's got a radio, see. Mine broke down." He lifted his friend's arm and showed her the little transistor radio the boy was holding, and now Connie began to hear the music. It was the same program that was playing inside the house.

"Bobby King?" she said.

"I listen to him all the time. I think he's great."

"He's kind of great," Connie said reluctantly.

"Listen, that guy's *great*. He knows where the action is."

Connie blushed a little, because the glasses made it impossible for her to see just what this boy was looking at. She couldn't decide if she liked him or if he was just a jerk, and so she dawdled in the doorway and wouldn't come down or go back inside. She said, "What's all that stuff painted on your car?"

"Can'tcha read it?" He opened the door very carefully, as if he were afraid it might fall off. He slid out just as carefully, planting his feet firmly on the ground, the tiny metallic world in his glasses slowing down like gelatine hardening, and in the midst of it Connie's bright green blouse. "This here is my name, to begin with," he said. ARNOLD FRIEND was written in tarlike black letters on the side, with a drawing of a round, grinning face that reminded Connie of a pumpkin, except it wore sunglasses. "I wanta introduce myself. I'm Arnold Friend and that's my real name and I'm gonna be your friend, honey, and inside the car's Ellie Oscar, he's kinda shy." Ellie brought his transistor radio up to his shoulder and balanced it there. "Now, these numbers are a secret code, honey," Arnold Friend explained. He read off the numbers 33, 19, 17 and raised his eyebrows at her to see what she thought of that, but she didn't think much of it. The left rear fender had been smashed and around it was written, on the gleaming gold background: DONE BY CRAZY WOMAN DRIVER. Connie had to laugh at that. Arnold Friend was pleased at her laughter and looked up at her. "Around the other side's a lot more— you wanta come and see them?"

"No."

"Why not?"

"Why should I?"

"Don'tcha wanta see what's on the car? Don'tcha wanta go for a ride?"

"I don't know."

"Why not?"

"I got things to do."

"Like what?"

"Things."

He laughed as if she had said something funny. He slapped his thigh. He was standing in a strange way, leaning back against the car as if he were balancing himself. He wasn't tall, only an inch or so taller than she would be if she came down to him. Connie liked the way he was dressed, which was the way all of them dressed: tight faded jeans stuffed into black, scuffed boots, a belt that pulled his waist in and showed how lean he was, and a white pull-over shirt that was a little soiled and showed the hard small muscles of his arms and shoulders. He looked as if he probably did hard work, lifting and carrying things. Even his neck looked muscular. And his face was a familiar face, somehow: the jaw and chin and cheeks slightly darkened because he hadn't shaved for a day or two, and the nose long and hawk-like, sniffing as if she were a treat he was going to gobble up and it was all a joke.

"Connie, you ain't telling the truth. This is your day set aside for a ride with me and you know it," he said, still laughing. The way he straightened and recovered from his fit of laughing showed that it had been all fake.

"How do you know what my name is?" she said suspiciously.

"It's Connie."

"Maybe and maybe not."

"I know my Connie," he said, wagging his finger. Now she remembered him even better, back at the restaurant, and her cheeks warmed at the thought of how she had sucked in her breath just at the moment she passed him—how she must have looked to him. And he had remembered her. "Ellie and I come out here especially for you," he said. "Ellie can sit in back. How about it?"

"Where?"

"Where what?"

"Where're we going?"

He looked at her. He took off the sunglasses and she saw how pale the skin around his eyes was, like holes that were not in shadow but instead in light. His eyes were like chips of broken glass that catch the light in an amiable way. He smiled. It was as if the idea of going for a ride somewhere, to someplace, was a new idea to him.

"Just for a ride, Connie sweetheart."

"I never said my name was Connie," she said.

"But I know what it is. I know your name and all about you, lots of things," Arnold Friend said. He had not moved yet but stood still leaning back against the side of his jalopy. "I took a special interest in you, such a pretty girl, and found out all about you—like I know your parents and sister are gone somewheres and I know where and how long they're going to be gone, and I know who you were with last night, and your best girl friend's name is Betty. Right?"

He spoke in a simple lilting voice, exactly as if he were reciting the words to a song. His smile assured her that everything was fine. In the car Ellie turned up the volume on his radio and did not bother to look around at them.

"Ellie can sit in the back seat," Arnold Friend said. He indicated his friend with a casual jerk of his chin, as if Ellie did not count and she should not bother with him.

"How'd you find out all that stuff?" Connie said.

"Listen: Betty Schultz and Tony Fitch and Jimmy Pettinger and Nancy Pettinger," he said in a chant. "Raymond Stanley and Bob Hutter—"

"Do you know all those kids?"

"I know everybody."

"Look, you're kidding. You're not from around here."

"Sure."

"But—how come we never saw you before?"

"Sure you saw me before," he said. He looked down at his boots, as if he were a little offended. "You just don't remember."

"I guess I'd remember you," Connie said.

"Yeah?" He looked up at this, beaming. He was pleased. He began to mark time with the music from Ellie's radio, tapping his fists lightly together. Connie looked away from his smile to the car, which was painted so bright it almost hurt her eyes to look at it. She looked at that name, ARNOLD FRIEND. And up at the front fender was an expression that was familiar—MAN THE FLYING SAUCERS. It was an expression kids had used the year before but didn't use this year. She looked at it for a while as if the words meant something to her that she did not yet know.

"What're you thinking about? Huh?" Arnold Friend demanded. "Not worried about your hair blowing around in the car, are you?"

"No."

"Think I maybe can't drive good?"

"How do I know?"

"You're a hard girl to handle. How come?" he said. "Don't you know I'm your friend? Didn't you see me put my sign in the air when you walked by?"

"What sign?"

"My sign." And he drew an X in the air, leaning out toward her. They were maybe ten feet apart. After his hand fell back to his side the X was still in the air, almost visible. Connie let the screen door close and stood perfectly still inside it, listening to the music from her radio and the boy's blend together. She stared at Arnold Friend. He stood there so stiffly relaxed, pretending to be relaxed, with one hand idly on the door handle as if he were keeping himself up that way and had no intention of ever moving again. She recognized most things about him, the tight jeans that showed his thighs and buttocks and the greasy leather boots and the tight shirt, and even that slippery friendly smile of his, that sleepy dreamy smile that all the boys used to get across ideas they didn't want to put into words. She recognized all this and also the singsong way he talked, slightly mocking, kidding, but serious and a little melancholy, and she recognized the way he tapped one fist against the other in homage to the perpetual music behind him. But all these things did not come together.

She said suddenly, "Hey, how old are you?"

His smile faded. She could see then that he wasn't a kid, he was much older—thirty, maybe more. At this knowledge her heart began to pound faster.

"That's a crazy thing to ask. Can'tcha see I'm your own age?"

"Like hell you are."

"Or maybe a coupla years older. I'm eighteen."

"Eighteen?" she said doubtfully.

He grinned to reassure her and lines appeared at the corners of his mouth. His teeth were big and white. He grinned so broadly his eyes became slits and she saw how thick the lashes were, thick and black as if painted with a black tarlike material. Then, abruptly, he seemed to become embarrassed and looked over his shoulder at Ellie. "*Him*, he's crazy," he said. "Ain't he a riot? He's a nut, a real character." Ellie was still listening to the music. His sunglasses told nothing about what he was thinking. He wore a bright orange shirt unbuttoned halfway to show his chest, which was a pale, bluish chest and not muscular like Arnold Friend's. His shirt collar was turned up all around and the very tips of the collar pointed out past his chin as if they were protecting him. He was pressing the transistor radio up against his ear and sat there in a kind of daze, right in the sun.

"He's kinda strange," Connie said.

"Hey, she says you're kinda strange! Kinda strange!" Arnold Friend cried. He pounded on the car to get Ellie's attention. Ellie turned for the first time and Connie saw with shock that he wasn't a kid either—he had a fair, hairless face, cheeks reddened slightly as if the veins grew too close to the surface of his skin, the face of a forty-year-old baby. Connie felt a wave of dizziness rise in her at this sight and she stared at him as if waiting for something to change the shock of the moment, make it all right again. Ellie's lips kept shaping words, mumbling along with the words blasting in his ear.

"Maybe you two better go away," Connie said faintly.

"What? How come?" Arnold Friend cried. "We come out here to take you for a ride. It's Sunday." He had the voice of the man on the radio now. It was the same voice, Connie thought. "Don'tcha know it's Sunday all day? And honey, no matter who you were with last night, today you're with Arnold Friend and don't you forget it! Maybe you better step out here," he said, and this last was in a different voice. It was a little flatter, as if the heat was finally getting to him.

"No. I got things to do."

"Hey."

"You two better leave."

"We ain't leaving until you come with us."

"Like hell I am—"

"Connie, don't fool around with me. I mean—I mean, don't fool *around*," he said, shaking his head. He laughed incredulously. He placed his sunglasses on top of his head, carefully, as if he were indeed wearing a wig, and brought the stems down behind his ears. Connie stared at him, another wave of dizziness and fear rising in her so that for a moment he wasn't even in focus but was just a blur standing there against his gold car, and she had the idea that he had driven up the driveway all right but had come from nowhere before that and belonged nowhere and that everything about him and even about the music that was so familiar to her was only half real.

"If my father comes and sees you—"

"He ain't coming. He's at a barbecue."

"How do you know that?"

"Aunt Tillie's. Right now they're—uh—they're drinking. Sitting around," he said vaguely, squinting as if he were staring all the way to town and over to Aunt Tillie's back yard. Then the vision seemed to get clear and he nodded energetically. "Yeah. Sitting around. There's your sister in a blue dress, huh? And high heels, the poor sad bitch—nothing like you, sweetheart! And your mother's helping some fat woman with the corn, they're cleaning the corn—husking the corn—"

"What fat woman?" Connie cried.

"How do I know what fat woman, I don't know every goddamn fat woman in the world!" Arnold Friend laughed.

"Oh, that's Mrs. Hornsby. . . . Who invited her?" Connie said. She felt a little lightheaded. Her breath was coming quickly.

"She's too fat. I don't like them fat. I like them the way you are, honey," he said, smiling sleepily at her. They stared at each other for a while through the screen door. He said softly, "Now, what you're going to do is this: you're going to come out that door. You're going to sit up front with me and Ellie's going to sit in the back, the hell with Ellie, right? This isn't Ellie's date. You're my date. I'm your lover, honey."

"What? You're crazy—"

"Yes, I'm your lover. You don't know what that is but you will," he said. "I know that too. I know all about you. But look: it's real nice and you couldn't ask for nobody better than me, or more polite. I always keep my word. I'll tell you how it is, I'm always nice at first, the first time. I'll hold you so tight you won't think you have to try to get away or pretend anything because you'll know you can't. And I'll come inside you where it's all secret and you'll give in to me and you'll love me—"

"Shut up! You're crazy!" Connie said. She backed away from the door. She put her hands up against her ears as if she'd heard something terrible, something not meant for her. "People don't talk like that, you're crazy," she muttered. Her heart was almost too big now for her chest and its pumping made sweat break out all over her. She looked out to see Arnold Friend pause and then take a step toward the porch, lurching. He almost fell. But, like a clever drunken man, he managed to catch his balance. He wobbled in his high boots and grabbed hold of one of the porch posts.

"Honey?" he said. "You still listening?"

"Get the hell out of here!"

"Be nice, honey. Listen."

"I'm going to call the police—"

He wobbled again and out of the side of his mouth came a fast spat curse, an aside not meant for her to hear. But even this "Christ!" sounded forced. Then he began to smile again. She watched this smile come, awkward as if he were smiling from inside a mask. His whole face was a mask, she thought wildly, tanned down to his throat but then running out as if he had plastered makeup on his face but had forgotten about his throat.

"Honey—? Listen, here's how it is. I always tell the truth and I promise you this: I ain't coming in that house after you."

"You better not! I'm going to call the police if you—if you don't—"

"Honey," he said, talking right through her voice, "honey, I'm not coming in there but you are coming out here. You know why?"

She was panting. The kitchen looked like a place she had never seen before, some room she had run inside but that wasn't good enough, wasn't going to help her. The kitchen window had never had a curtain, after three years, and there were dishes in the sink for her to do—probably—and if you ran your hand across the table you'd probably feel something sticky there.

"You listening honey? Hey?"

"—going to call the police—"

"Soon as you touch the phone I don't need to keep my promise and can come inside. You won't want that."

She rushed forward and tried to lock the door. Her fingers were shaking. "But why lock it," Arnold Friend said gently, talking right into her face. "It's just a screen door. It's just nothing." One of his boots was at a strange angle, as if his foot wasn't in it. It pointed out to the left, bent at the ankle. "I mean, anybody can break through a screen door and glass and wood and iron or anything else if he needs to, anybody at all, and especially Arnold Friend. If the place got lit up with a fire, honey, you'd come runnin' out into my arms, right into my arms an' safe at home—like you knew I was your lover and'd stopped fooling around. I don't mind a nice shy girl but I don't like no fooling around." Part of those words were spoken with a slight rhythmic lilt, and Connie somehow recognized them—the echo of a song from last year, about a girl rushing into her boy friend's arms and coming home again—

Connie stood barefoot on the linoleum floor, staring at him. "What do you want?" she whispered.

"I want you," he said.

"What?"

"Seen you that night and thought, that's the one, yes sir. I never needed to look anymore."

"But my father's coming back. He's coming to get me. I had to wash my hair first—" She spoke in a dry, rapid voice, hardly raising it for him to hear.

"No, your daddy is not coming and yes, you had to wash your hair and you washed it for me. It's nice and shining and all for me. I thank you sweetheart," he said with a mock bow, but again he almost lost his balance. He had to bend and adjust his boots. Evidently his feet did not go all the way down; the boots must have been stuffed with something so that he would seem taller. Connie stared out at him and behind him at Ellie in the car, who seemed to be looking off toward Connie's right, into nothing. This Ellie said, pulling the words out of the air one after another as if he were just discovering them, "You want me to pull out the phone?"

"Shut your mouth and keep it shut," Arnold Friend said, his face red from bending over or maybe from embarrassment because Connie had seen his boots. "This ain't none of your business."

"What—what are you doing? What do you want?" Connie said. "If I call the police they'll get you, they'll arrest you—"

"Promise was not to come in unless you touch that phone, and I'll keep that promise," he said. He resumed his erect position and tried to force his shoulders back. He sounded like a hero in a movie, declaring something important. But he spoke too loudly and it was as if he were speaking to someone behind Connie. "I ain't made plans for coming in that house where I don't belong but just for you to come out to me, the way you should. Don't you know who I am?"

"You're crazy," she whispered. She backed away from the door but did not want to go into another part of the house, as if this would give him permission to come through the door. "What do you . . . you're crazy, you . . . ."

"Huh? What're you saying, honey?"

Her eyes darted everywhere in the kitchen. She could not remember what it was, this room.

"This is how it is, honey: you come out and we'll drive away, have a nice ride. But if you don't come out we're gonna wait till your people come home and then they're all going to get it."

"You want that telephone pulled out?" Ellie said. He held the radio away from his ear and grimaced, as if without the radio the air was too much for him.

"I toldja shut up, Ellie," Arnold Friend said, "you're deaf, get a hearing aid, right? Fix yourself up. This little girl's no trouble and's gonna be nice to me, so Ellie keep to yourself, this ain't your date—right? Don't hem in on me, don't hog, don't crush, don't bird dog, don't trail me," he said in a rapid, meaningless voice, as if he were running through all the expressions he'd learned but was no longer sure which of them was in style, then rushing on to new ones, making them up with his eyes closed. "Don't crawl under my fence, don't squeeze in my chipmunk hole, don't sniff my glue, suck my popsicle, keep your own greasy fingers on yourself!" He shaded his eyes and peered in at Connie, who was backed against the kitchen table. "Don't mind him, honey, he's just a creep. He's a dope. Right? I'm the boy for you and like I said, you come out here nice like a lady and give me your hand, and nobody else gets hurt, I mean, your nice old bald-headed daddy and your mummy and your sister in her high heels. Because listen: why bring them in this?"

"Leave me alone," Connie whispered.

"Hey, you know that old woman down the road, the one with the chickens and stuff—you know her?"

"She's dead!"

"Dead? What? You know her?" Arnold Friend said.

"She's dead—"

"Don't you like her?"

"She's dead—she's—she isn't here any more—"

"But don't you like her, I mean, you got something against her? Some grudge or something?" Then his voice dipped as if he were conscious of a rudeness. He touched the sunglasses perched up on top of his head as if to make sure they were still there. "Now, you be a good girl."

"What are you going to do?"

"Just two things, or maybe three," Arnold Friend said. "But I promise it won't last long and you'll like me the way you get to like people you're close to. You will. It's all over for you here, so come on out. You don't want your people in any trouble, do you?"

She turned and bumped against a chair or something, hurting her leg, but she ran into the back room and picked up the telephone. Something roared in her ear, a tiny roaring, and she was so sick with fear that she could do nothing but listen to it—the telephone was clammy and very heavy and her fingers groped down to the dial but were too weak to touch it. She began to scream into the phone, into the roaring. She cried out, she cried for her mother, she felt her breath start jerking back and forth in her lungs as if it were something Arnold Friend was stabbing her with again and again with no tenderness. A noisy sorrowful wailing rose all about her and she was locked inside it the way she was locked inside this house.

After a while she could hear again. She was sitting on the floor with her wet back against the wall.

Arnold Friend was saying from the door, "That's a good girl. Put the phone back."

She kicked the phone away from her.

"No, honey. Pick it up. Put it back right."

She picked it up and put it back. The dial tone stopped.

"That's a good girl. Now, you come outside."

She was hollow with what had been fear but what was now just an emptiness. All that screaming had blasted it out of her. She sat, one leg cramped under her, and deep inside her brain was something like a pinpoint of light that kept going and would not let her relax. She thought, I'm not going to see my mother again. She thought, I'm not going to sleep in my bed again. Her bright green blouse was all wet.

Arnold Friend said, in a gentle-loud voice that was like a stage voice, "The place where you came from ain't there any more, and where you had in mind to go is cancelled out. This place you are now—inside your daddy's house—is nothing but a cardboard box I can knock down any time. You know that and always did know it. You hear me?"

She thought, I have got to think. I have got to know what to do.

"We'll go out to a nice field, out in the country here where it smells so nice and it's sunny," Arnold Friend said. "I'll have my arms tight around you so you won't need to try to get away and I'll show you what love is like, what it does. The hell with this house! It looks solid all right," he said. He ran a fingernail down the screen and the noise did not make Connie shiver, as it would have the day before. "Now, put your hand on your heart, honey. Feel that? That feels solid too but we know better. Be nice to me, be sweet like you can because what else is there for a girl like you but to be sweet and pretty and give in?—and get away before her people come back?"

She felt her pounding heart. Her hand seemed to enclose it. She thought for the first time in her life that it was nothing that was hers, that belonged to her, but just a pounding, living thing inside this body that wasn't really hers either.

"You don't want them to get hurt," Arnold Friend went on. "Now, get up, honey. Get up all by yourself."

She stood.

"Now, turn this way. That's right. Come over here to me.—Ellie, put that away, didn't I tell you? You dope. You miserable creepy dope," Arnold Friend said. His words were not angry but only part of an incantation. The incantation was kindly. "Now, come out through the kitchen to me, honey, and let's see a smile, try it, you're a brave, sweet little girl and now they're eating corn and hot dogs cooked to bursting over an outdoor fire, and they don't know one thing about you and never did and honey, you're better than them because not a one of them would have done this for you."

Connie felt the linoleum under her feet; it was cool. She brushed her hair back out of her eyes. Arnold Friend let go of the post tentatively and opened his arms for her, his elbows pointing in toward each other and his wrists limp, to show that this was an embarrassed embrace and a little mocking, he didn't want to make her self-conscious.

She put out her hand against the screen. She watched herself push the door slowly open as if she were back safe somewhere in the other doorway, watching this body and this head of long hair moving out into the sunlight where Arnold Friend waited.

"My sweet little blue-eyed girl," he said in a half-sung sigh that had nothing to do with her brown eyes but was taken up just the same by the vast sunlit reaches of the land behind him and on all sides of him—so much land that Connie had never seen before and did not recognize except to know that she was going to it.

(1966)

Bharati Mukherjee   b. 1940

The Management of Grief

A woman I don't know is boiling tea the Indian way in my kitchen. There are a lot of women I don't know in my kitchen, whispering and moving tactfully. They open doors, rummage through the pantry, and try not to ask me where things are kept. They remind me of when my sons were small, on Mother's Day or when Vikram and I were tired, and they would make big, sloppy omelets. I would lie in bed pretending I didn't hear them.

Dr. Sharma, the treasurer of the Indo-Canada Society, pulls me into the hallway. He wants to know if I am worried about money. His wife, who has just come up from the basement with a tray of empty cups and glasses, scolds him. "Don't bother Mrs. Bhave with mundane details." She looks so monstrously pregnant her baby must be days overdue. I tell her she shouldn't be carrying heavy things. "Shaila," she says, smiling, "this is the fifth." Then she grabs a teenager by his shirttails. He slips his Walkman off his head. He has to be one of her four children; they have the same domed and dented foreheads. "What's the official word now?" she demands. The boy slips the headphones back on. "They're acting evasive, Ma. They're saying it could be an accident or a terrorist bomb."

All morning, the boys have been muttering, Sikh bomb, Sikh bomb. The men, not using the word, bow their heads in agreement. Mrs. Sharma touches her forehead at such a word. At least they've stopped talking about space debris and Russian lasers.

Two radios are going in the dining room. They are tuned to different stations. Someone must have brought the radios down from my boys' bedrooms. I haven't gone into their rooms since Kusum came running across the front lawn in her bathrobe. She looked so funny, I was laughing when I opened the door.

The big TV in the den is being whizzed through American networks and cable channels.

"Damn!" some man swears bitterly. "How can these preachers carry on like nothing's happened?" I want to tell him we're not that important. You look at the audience, and at the preacher in his blue robe with his beautiful white hair, and potted palm trees under a blue sky, and you know they care about nothing.

The phone rings and rings. Dr. Sharma's taken charge. "We're with her," he keeps saying. "Yes, yes, the doctor has given calming pills. Yes, yes, pills are having necessary effect." I wonder if pills alone explain this calm. Not peace, just a deadening quiet. I was always controlled, but never repressed. Sound can reach me, but my body is tensed, ready to scream. I hear their voices all around me. I hear my boys and Vikram cry, "Mommy, Shaila!" and their screams insulate me, like headphones.

The woman boiling water tells her story again and again. "I got the news first. My cousin called from Halifax before six A.M., can you imagine? He'd gotten up for prayers and his son was studying for medical exams and heard on a rock channel that something had happened to a plane. They said first it had disappeared from the radar, like a giant eraser just reached out. His father called me, so I said to him, what do you mean, 'something bad'? You mean a hijacking? And he said, *Behn*, there is no confirmation of anything yet, but check with your neighbors because a lot of them must be on that plane. So I called poor Kusum straight away. I knew Kusum's husband and daughter were booked to go yesterday."

Kusum lives across the street from me. She and Satish had moved in less than a month ago. They said they needed a bigger place. All these people, the Sharmas and friends from the Indo-Canada Society, had been there for the housewarming. Satish and Kusum made tandoori on their big gas grill and even the white neighbors piled their plates high with that luridly red, charred, juicy chicken. Their younger daughter had danced, and even our boys had broken away from the Stanley Cup telecast to put in a reluctant appearance. Everyone took pictures for their albums and for the community newspapers—another of our families had made it big in Toronto—and now I wonder how many of those happy faces are gone. "Why does God give us so much if all along He intends to take it away?" Kusum asks me.

I nod. We sit on carpeted stairs, holding hands like children. "I never once told him that I loved him," I say. I was too much the well-brought-up woman. I was so well brought up I never felt comfortable calling my husband by his first name.

"It's all right," Kusum says. "He knew. My husband knew. They felt it. Modern young girls have to say it because what they feel is fake."

Kusum's daughter Pam runs in with an overnight case. Pam's in her McDonald's uniform. "Mummy! You have to get dressed!" Panic makes her cranky. "A reporter's on his way here."

"Why?"

"You want to talk to him in your bathrobe?" She starts to brush her mother's long hair. She's the daughter who's always in trouble. She dates Canadian boys and hangs out in the mall, shopping for tight sweaters. The younger one, the goody-goody one according to Pam, the one with a voice so sweet that when she sang *bhajans* for Ethiopian relief even a frugal man like my husband wrote out a hundred-dollar check, *she* was on that plane. *She* was going to spend July and August with grandparents because Pam wouldn't go. Pam said she'd rather waitress at McDonald's. "If it's a choice between Bombay and Wonderland, I'm picking Wonderland," she said.

"Leave me alone," Kusum yells. "You know what I want to do? If I didn't have to look after you now, I'd hang myself."

Pam's young face goes blotchy with pain. "Thanks," she says, "don't let me stop you."

"Hush," pregnant Mrs. Sharma scolds Pam. "Leave your mother alone. Mr. Sharma will tackle the reporters and fill out the forms. He'll say what has to be said."

Pam stands her ground. "You think I don't know what Mummy's thinking? *Why her?* That's what. That's sick! Mummy wishes my little sister were alive and I were dead."

Kusum's hand in mine is trembly hot. We continue to sit on the stairs.

She calls before she arrives, wondering if there's anything I need. Her name is Judith Templeton and she's an appointee of the provincial government. "Multiculturalism?" I ask, and she says "partially," but that her mandate is bigger. "I've been told you knew many of the people on the flight," she says. "Perhaps if you'd agree to help us reach the others . . . ?"

She gives me time at least to put on tea water and pick up the mess in the front room. I have a few *samosas* from Kusum's housewarming that I could fry up, but then I think, why prolong this visit?

Judith Templeton is much younger than she sounded. She wears a blue suit with a white blouse and a polka-dot tie. Her blond hair is cut short, her only jewelry is pearl-drop earrings. Her briefcase is new and expensive looking, a gleaming cordovan leather. She sits with it across her lap. When she looks out the front windows onto the street, her contact lenses seem to float in front of her light blue eyes.

"What sort of help do you want from me?" I ask. She has refused the tea, out of politeness, but I insist, along with some slightly stale biscuits.

"I have no experience," she admits. "That is, I have an M.S.W. and I've worked in liaison with accident victims, but I mean I have no experience with a tragedy of this scale—"

"Who could?" I ask.

"—and with the complications of culture, language, and customs. Someone mentioned that Mrs. Bhave is a pillar—because you've taken it more calmly."

At this, perhaps, I frown, for she reaches forward, almost to take my hand. "I hope you understand my meaning, Mrs. Bhave. There are hundreds of people in Metro directly affected, like you, and some of them speak no English. There are some widows who've never handled money or gone on a bus, and there are old parents who still haven't eaten or gone outside their bedrooms. Some houses and apartments have been looted. Some wives are still hysterical. Some husbands are in shock and profound depression. We want to help, but our hands are tied in so many ways. We have to distribute money to some people, and there are legal documents—these things can be done. We have interpreters, but we don't always have the human touch, or maybe the right human touch. We don't want to make mistakes, Mrs. Bhave, and that's why we'd like to ask you to help us."

"More mistakes, you mean," I say.

"Police matters are not in my hands," she answers.

"Nothing I can do will make any difference," I say. "We must all grieve in our own way."

"But you are coping very well. All the people said, Mrs. Bhave is the strongest person of all. Perhaps if the others could see you, talk with you, it would help them."

"By the standards of the people you call hysterical, I am behaving very oddly and very badly, Miss Templeton." I want to say to her, *I wish I could scream, starve, walk into Lake Ontario, jump from a bridge.* "They would not see me as a model. I do not see myself as a model."

I am a freak. No one who has ever known me would think of me reacting this way. This terrible calm will not go away.

She asks me if she may call again, after I get back from a long trip that we all must make. "Of course," I say. "Feel free to call, anytime."

Four days later, I find Kusum squatting on a rock overlooking a bay in Ireland. It isn't a big rock, but it juts sharply out over water. This is as close as we'll ever get to them. June breezes balloon out her sari and unpin her knee-length hair. She has the bewildered look of a sea creature whom the tides have stranded.

It's been one hundred hours since Kusum came stumbling and screaming across my lawn. Waiting around the hospital, we've heard many stories. The police, the diplomats, they tell us things thinking that we're strong, that knowledge is helpful to the grieving, and maybe it is. Some, I know, prefer ignorance, or their own versions. The plane broke into two, they say. Unconsciousness was instantaneous. No one suffered. My boys must have just finished their breakfasts. They loved eating on planes, they loved the smallness of plates, knives, and forks. Last year they saved the airline salt and pepper shakers. Half an hour more and they would have made it to Heathrow.

Kusum says that we can't escape our fate. She says that all those people—our husbands, my boys, her girl with the nightingale voice, all those Hindus, Christians, Sikhs, Muslims, Parsis, and atheists on that plane—were fated to die together off this beautiful bay. She learned this from a swami in Toronto.

I have my Valium.

Six of us "relatives"—two widows and four widowers—choose to spend the day today by the waters instead of sitting in a hospital room and scanning photographs of the dead. That's what they call us now: relatives. I've looked through twenty-seven photos in two days. They're very kind to us, the Irish are very understanding. Sometimes understanding means freeing a tourist bus for this trip to the bay, so we can pretend to spy our loved ones through the glassiness of waves or in sun-speckled cloud shapes.

I could die here, too, and be content.

"What is that, out there?" She's standing and flapping her hands, and for a moment I see a head shape bobbing in the waves. She's standing in the water, I, on the boulder. The tide is low, and a round, black, head-sized rock has just risen from the waves. She returns, her sari end dripping and ruined and her face is a twisted remnant of hope, the way mine was a hundred hours ago, still laughing but inwardly knowing that nothing but the ultimate tragedy could bring two women together at six o'clock on a Sunday morning. I watch her face sag into blankness.

"That water felt warm, Shaila," she says at length.

"You can't," I say. "We have to wait for our turn to come."

I haven't eaten in four days, haven't brushed my teeth.

"I know," she says. "I tell myself I have no right to grieve. They are in a better place than we are. My swami says I should be thrilled for them. My swami says depression is a sign of our selfishness."

Maybe I'm selfish. Selfishly I break away from Kusum and run, sandals slapping against stones, to the water's edge. What if my boys aren't lying pinned under the debris? What if they aren't stuck a mile below that innocent blue chop? What if, given the strong currents. . . .

Now I've ruined my sari, one of my best. Kusum has joined me, knee-deep in water that feels to me like a swimming pool. I could settle in the water, and my husband would take my hand and the boys would slap water in my face just to see me scream.

"Do you remember what good swimmers my boys were, Kusum?"

"I saw the medals," she says.

One of the widowers, Dr. Ranganathan from Montreal, walks out to us, carrying his shoes in one hand. He's an electrical engineer. Someone at the hotel mentioned his work is famous around the world, something about the place where physics and electricity come together. He has lost a huge family, something indescribable. "With some good luck," Dr. Ranganathan suggests to me, "a good swimmer could make it safely to some island. It is quite possible that there may be many, many microscopic islets scattered around."

"You're not just saying that?" I tell Dr. Ranganathan about Vinod, my elder son. Last year he took diving as well.

"It's a parent's duty to hope," he says. "It is foolish to rule out possibilities that have not been tested. I myself have not surrendered hope."

Kusum is sobbing once again. "Dear lady," he says, laying his free hand on her arm, and she calms down.

"Vinod is how old?" he asks me. He's very careful, as we all are. *Is*, not was.

"Fourteen. Yesterday he was fourteen. His father and uncle were going to take him down to the Taj and give him a big birthday party. I couldn't go with them because I couldn't get two weeks off from my stupid job in June." I process bills for a travel agent. June is a big travel month.

Dr. Ranganathan whips the pockets of his suit jacket inside out. Squashed roses, in darkening shades of pink, float on the water. He tore the roses off creepers in somebody's garden. He didn't ask anyone if he could pluck the roses, but now there's been an article about it in the local papers. When you see an Indian person, it says, please give him or her flowers.

"A strong youth of fourteen," he says, "can very likely pull to safety a younger one."

My sons, though four years apart, were very close. Vinod wouldn't let Mithun drown. *Electrical engineering*, I think, foolishly perhaps: this man knows important secrets of the universe, things closed to me. Relief spins me light-headed. No wonder my boys' photographs haven't turned up in the gallery of photos of the recovered dead. "Such pretty roses," I say.

"My wife loved pink roses. Every Friday I had to bring a bunch home. I used to say, Why? After twenty-odd years of marriage you're still needing proof positive of my love?" He has identified his wife and three of his children. Then others from Montreal, the lucky ones, intact families with no survivors. He chuckles as he wades back to shore. Then he swings around to ask me a question. "Mrs. Bhave, you are wanting to throw in some roses for your loved ones? I have two big ones left."

But I have other things to float: Vinod's pocket calculator; a half-painted model B-52 for my Mithun. They'd want them on their island. And for my husband? For him I let fall into the calm, glassy waters a poem I wrote in the hospital yesterday. Finally he'll know my feelings for him.

"Don't tumble, the rocks are slippery," Dr. Ranganathan cautions. He holds out a hand for me to grab.

Then it's time to get back on the bus, time to rush back to our waiting posts on hospital benches.

Kusum is one of the lucky ones. The lucky ones flew here, identified in multiplicate their loved ones, then will fly to India with the bodies for proper ceremonies. Satish is one of the few males who surfaced. The photos of faces we saw on the walls in an office at Heathrow and here in the hospital are mostly of women. Women have more body fat, a nun said to me matter-of-factly. They float better.

Today I was stopped by a young sailor on the street. He had loaded bodies, he'd gone into the water when—he checks my face for signs of strength—when the sharks were first spotted. I don't blush, and he breaks down. "It's all right," I say. "Thank you." I heard about the sharks from Dr. Ranganathan. In his orderly mind, science brings understanding, it holds no terror. It is the shark's duty. For every deer there is a hunter, for every fish a fisherman.

The Irish are not shy; they rush to me and give me hugs and some are crying. I cannot imagine reactions like that on the streets of Toronto. Just strangers, and I am touched. Some carry flowers with them and give them to any Indian they see.

After lunch, a policeman I have gotten to know quite well catches hold of me. He says he thinks he has a match for Vinod. I explain what a good swimmer Vinod is.

"You want me with you when you look at photos?" Dr. Ranganathan walks ahead of me into the picture gallery. In these matters, he is a scientist, and I am grateful. It is a new perspective. "They have performed miracles," he says. "We are indebted to them."

The first day or two the policemen showed us relatives only one picture at a time; now they're in a hurry, they're eager to lay out the possibles, and even the probables.

The face on the photo is of a boy much like Vinod; the same intelligent eyes, the same thick brows dipping into a V. But this boy's features, even his cheeks, are puffier, wider, mushier.

"No." My gaze is pulled by other pictures. There are five other boys who look like Vinod.

The nun assigned to console me rubs the first picture with a fingertip. "When they've been in the water for a while, love, they look a little heavier." The bones under the skin are broken, they said on the first day—try to adjust your memories. It's important.

"It's not him. I'm his mother. I'd know."

"I know this one!" Dr. Ranganathan cries out, and suddenly from the back of the gallery. "And this one!" I think he senses that I don't want to find my boys. "They are the Kutty brothers. They were also from Montreal." I don't mean to be crying. On the contrary, I am ecstatic. My suitcase in the hotel is packed heavy with dry clothes for my boys.

The policeman starts to cry. "I am so sorry, I am so sorry, ma'am. I really thought we had a match."

With the nun ahead of us and the policeman behind, we, the unlucky ones without our children's bodies, file out of the makeshift gallery.

From Ireland most of us go on to India. Kusum and I take the same direct flight to Bombay, so I can help her clear customs quickly. But we have to argue with a man in uniform. He has large boils on his face. The boils swell and glow with sweat as we argue with him. He wants Kusum to wait in line and he refuses to take authority because his boss is on a tea break. But Kusum won't let her coffins out of sight, and I shan't desert her though I know that my parents, elderly and diabetic, must be waiting in a stuffy car in a scorching lot.

"You bastard!" I scream at the man with the popping boils. Other passengers press closer. "You think we're smuggling contraband in those coffins!"

Once upon a time we were well-brought-up women; we were dutiful wives who kept our heads veiled, our voices shy and sweet.

In India, I become, once again, an only child of rich, ailing parents. Old friends of the family come to pay their respects. Some are Sikh, and inwardly, involuntarily, I cringe. My parents are progressive people; they do not blame communities for a few individuals.

In Canada it is a different story now.

"Stay longer," my mother pleads. "Canada is a cold place. Why would you want to be all by yourself?" I stay.

Three months pass. Then another.

"Vikram wouldn't have wanted you to give up things!" they protest. They call my husband by the name he was born with. In Toronto he'd changed to Vik so the men he worked with at his office would find his name as easy as Rod or Chris. "You know, the dead aren't cut off from us!"

My grandmother, the spoiled daughter of a rich zamindar,[1] shaved her head with rusty razor blades when she was widowed at sixteen. My grandfather died of childhood diabetes when he was nineteen, and she saw herself as the harbinger of bad luck. My mother grew up without parents, raised indifferently by an uncle, while her true mother slept in a hut behind the main estate house and took her food with the servants. She grew up a rationalist. My parents abhor mindless mortification.

The zamindar's daughter kept stubborn faith in Vedic rituals; my parents rebelled. I am trapped between two modes of knowledge. At thirty-six, I am too old to start over and too young to give up. Like my husband's spirit, I flutter between worlds.

Courting aphasia, we travel. We travel with our phalanx of servants and poor relatives. To hill stations and to beach resorts. We play contract bridge in dusty gymkhana clubs. We ride stubby ponies up crumbly mountain trails. At tea dances, we let ourselves be twirled twice round the ballroom. We hit the holy spots we hadn't made time for before. In Varanasi, Kalighat, Rishikesh, Hardwar, astrologers and palmists seek me out and for a fee offer me cosmic consolations.

Already the widowers among us are being shown new bride candidates. They cannot resist the call of custom, the authority of their parents and older brothers. They must marry; it is the duty of a man to look after a wife. The new wives will be young widows with children, destitute but of good family. They will make loving wives, but the men will shun them. I've had calls from the men over crackling Indian telephone lines. "Save me," they say, these substantial, educated, successful men of forty. "My parents are arranging a marriage for me." In a month they will have buried one family and returned to Canada with a new bride and partial family.

I am comparatively lucky. No one here thinks of arranging a husband for an unlucky widow.

Then, on the third day of the sixth month into this odyssey, in an abandoned temple in a tiny Himalayan village, as I make my offering of flowers and sweetmeats to the god of a tribe of animists, my husband descends to me. He is squatting next to a scrawny sadhu[2] in moth-eaten robes. Vikram wears the vanilla suit he wore the last time I hugged him. The sadhu tosses petals on a butter-fed flame, reciting Sanskrit mantras, and sweeps his face of flies. My husband takes my hands in his.

You're beautiful, he starts. Then, *What are you doing here?*

Shall I stay? I ask. He only smiles, but already the image is fading. *You must finish alone what we started together.* No seaweed wreathes his mouth. He speaks too fast, just as he used to when we were an envied family in our pink split-level. He is gone.

In the windowless altar room, smoky with joss sticks and clarified butter lamps, a sweaty hand gropes for my blouse. I do not shriek. The sadhu arranges his robe. The lamps hiss and sputter out.

When we come out of the temple, my mother says, "Did you feel something weird in there?"

---

[1] Landlord.
[2] Holy man.

My mother has no patience with ghosts, prophetic dreams, holy men, and cults.

"No," I lie. "Nothing."

But she knows that she's lost me. She knows that in days I shall be leaving.

Kusum's put up her house for sale. She wants to live in an ashram in Hardwar. Moving to Hardwar was her swami's idea. Her swami runs two ashrams, the one in Hardwar and another here in Toronto.

"Don't run away," I tell her.

"I'm not running away," she says. "I'm pursuing inner peace. You think you or that Ranganathan fellow are better off?"

Pam's left for California. She wants to do some modeling, she says. She says when she comes into her share of the insurance money she'll open a yoga-cum-aerobics studio in Hollywood. She sends me postcards so naughty I daren't leave them on the coffee table. Her mother has withdrawn from her and the world.

The rest of us don't lose touch, that's the point. Talk is all we have, says Dr. Ranganathan, who has also resisted his relatives and returned to Montreal and to his job, alone. He says, Whom better to talk with than other relatives? We've been melted down and recast as a new tribe.

He calls me twice a week from Montreal. Every Wednesday night and every Saturday afternoon. He is changing jobs, going to Ottawa. But Ottawa is over a hundred miles away, and he is forced to drive two hundred and twenty miles a day from his home in Montreal. He can't bring himself to sell his house. The house is a temple, he says; the king-sized bed in the master bedroom is a shrine. He sleeps on a folding cot. A devotee.

There are still some hysterical relatives. Judith Templeton's list of those needing help and those who've "accepted" is in nearly perfect balance. Acceptance means you speak of your family in the past tense and you make active plans for moving ahead with your life. There are courses at Seneca and Ryerson we could be taking. Her gleaming leather briefcase is full of college catalogues and lists of cultural societies that need our help. She has done impressive work, I tell her.

"In the textbooks on grief management," she replies—I am her confidante, I realize, one of the few whose grief has not sprung bizarre obsessions—"there are stages to pass through: rejection, depression, acceptance, reconstruction." She has compiled a chart and finds that six months after the tragedy, none of us still rejects reality, but only a handful are reconstructing. "Depressed acceptance" is the plateau we've reached. Remarriage is a major step in reconstruction (though she's a little surprised, even shocked, over *how* quickly some of the men have taken on new families). Selling one's house and changing jobs and cities is healthy.

How to tell Judith Templeton that my family surrounds me, and that like creatures in epics, they've changed shapes? She sees me as calm and accepting but worries that I have no job, no career. My closest friends are worse off than I. I cannot tell her my days, even my nights, are thrilling.

She asks me to help with families she can't reach at all. An elderly couple in Agincourt whose sons were killed just weeks after they had brought their parents over from a village in Punjab. From their names, I know they are Sikh. Judith Templeton and a translator have visited them twice with offers of money for airfare to Ireland, with bank forms, power-of-attorney forms, but they have refused to sign, or to leave their tiny apartment. Their sons' money is frozen in the bank. Their sons' investment apartments have been trashed by tenants, the furnishings sold off. The parents fear that anything they sign or any money they receive will end the company's or the country's obligations to them. They fear they are selling their sons for two airline tickets to a place they've never seen.

The high-rise apartment is a tower of Indians and West Indians, with a sprinkling of Orientals. The nearest bus-stop kiosk is lined with women in saris. Boys practice cricket in the parking lot. Inside the building, even I wince a bit from the ferocity of onion fumes, the distinctive and immediate Indianness of frying ghee, but Judith Templeton maintains a steady flow of information. These poor old people are in imminent danger of losing their place and all their services.

I say to her, "They are Sikh. They will not open up to a Hindu woman." And what I want to add is, as much as I try not to, I stiffen now at the sight of beards and turbans. I remember a time when we all trusted each other in this new country, it was only the new country we worried about.

The two rooms are dark and stuffy. The lights are off, and an oil lamp sputters on the coffee table. The bent old lady has let us in, and her husband is wrapping a white turban over his oiled, hip-length hair. She immediately goes to the kitchen, and I hear the most familiar sound of an Indian home, tap water hitting and filling a teapot.

They have not paid their utility bills, out of fear and inability to write a check. The telephone is gone, electricity and gas and water are soon to follow. They have told Judith their sons will provide. They are good boys, and they have always earned and looked after their parents.

We converse a bit in Hindi. They do not ask about the crash and I wonder if I should bring it up. If they think I am here merely as a translator, then they may feel insulted. There are thousands of Punjabi speakers, Sikhs, in Toronto to do a better job. And so I say to the old lady, "I too have lost my sons, and my husband, in the crash."

Her eyes immediately fill with tears. The man mutters a few words which sound like a blessing. "God provides and God takes away," he says.

I want to say, But only men destroy and give back nothing. "My boys and my husband are not coming back," I say. "We have to understand that."

Now the old woman responds. "But who is to say? Man alone does not decide these things." To this her husband adds his agreement.

Judith asks about the bank papers, the release forms. With a stroke of the pen, they will have a provincial trustee to pay their bills, invest their money, send them a monthly pension.

"Do you know this woman?" I ask them.

The man raises his hand from the table, turns it over, and seems to regard each finger separately before he answers. "This young lady is always coming here, we make tea for her, and she leaves papers for us to sign." His eyes scan a pile of papers in the corner of the room. "Soon we will be out of tea, then will she go away?"

The old lady adds, "I have asked my neighbors and no one else gets *angrezi*[3] visitors. What have we done?"

"It's her job," I try to explain. "The government is worried. Soon you will have no place to stay, no lights, no gas, no water."

---

[3]English.

"Government will get its money. Tell her not to worry, we are honorable people."

I try to explain the government wishes to give money, not take. He raises his hand. "Let them take," he says. "We are accustomed to that. That is no problem."

"We are strong people," says the wife. "Tell her that."

"Who needs all this machinery?" demands the husband. "It is unhealthy, the bright lights, the cold air on a hot day, the cold food, the four gas rings. God will provide, not government."

"When our boys return," the mother says.

Her husband sucks his teeth. "Enough talk," he says.

Judith breaks in. "Have you convinced them?" The snaps on her cordovan briefcase go off like firecrackers in that quiet apartment. She lays the sheaf of legal papers on the coffee table. "If they can't write their names, an X will do—I've told them that."

Now the old lady has shuffled to the kitchen and soon emerges with a pot of tea and two cups. "I think my bladder will go first on a job like this," Judith says to me, smiling. "If only there was some way of reaching them. Please thank her for the tea. Tell her she's very kind."

I nod in Judith's direction and tell them in Hindi, "She thanks you for the tea. She thinks you are being very hospitable but she doesn't have the slightest idea what it means."

I want to say, Humor her. I want to say, My boys and my husband are with me too, more than ever. I look in the old man's eyes and I can read his stubborn, peasant's message: *I have protected this woman as best I can. She is the only person I have left. Give to me or take from me what you will, but I will not sign for it. I will not pretend that I accept.*

In the car, Judith says, "You see what I'm up against? I'm sure they're lovely people, but their stubbornness and ignorance are driving me crazy. They think signing a paper is signing their sons' death warrants, don't they?"

I am looking out the window. I want to say, *In our culture, it is a parent's duty to hope.*

"Now Shaila, this next woman is a real mess. She cries day and night, and she refuses all medical help. We may have to—"

"Let me out at the subway," I say.

"I beg your pardon?" I can feel those blue eyes staring at me.

It would not be like her to disobey. She merely disapproves, and slows at a corner to let me out. Her voice is plaintive. "Is there anything I said? Anything I did?"

I could answer her suddenly in a dozen ways, but I choose not to. "Shaila? Let's talk about it," I hear, then slam the door.

A wife and mother begins her life in a new country, and that life is cut short. Yet her husband tells her: Complete what we have started. We, who stayed out of politics and came half way around the world to avoid religious and political feuding, have been the first in the New World to die from it. I no longer know what we started, nor how to complete it. I write letters to the editors of local papers and to members of Parliament. Now at least they admit it was a bomb. One MP answers back, with sympathy, but with a challenge. You want to make a difference? Work on a campaign. Work on mine. Politicize the Indian voter.

My husband's old lawyer helps me set up a trust. Vikram was a saver and a careful investor. He had saved the boys' boarding school and college fees. I sell the pink house at four times what we paid for it and take a small apartment downtown. I am looking for a charity to support.

We are deep in the Toronto winter, gray skies, icy pavements. I stay indoors, watching television. I have tried to assess my situation, how best to live my life, to complete what we began so many years ago. Kusum has written me from Hardwar that her life is now serene. She has seen Satish and has heard her daughter sing again. Kusum was on a pilgrimage, passing through a village, when she heard a young girl's voice, singing one of her daughter's favorite *bhajans*. She followed the music through the squalor of a Himalayan village, to a hut where a young girl, an exact replica of her daughter, was fanning coals under the kitchen fire. When she appeared, the girl cried out, "Ma!" and ran away. What did I think of that?

I think I can only envy her.

Pam didn't make it to California, but writes me from Vancouver. She works in a department store, giving makeup hints to Indian and Oriental girls. Dr. Ranganathan has given up his commute, given up his house and job, and accepted an academic position in Texas, where no one knows his story and he has vowed not to tell it. He calls now once a week.

I wait, I listen and I pray, but Vikram has not returned to me. The voices and the shapes and the nights filled with visions ended abruptly several weeks ago.

I take it as a sign.

One rare, beautiful, sunny day last week, returning from a small errand on Yonge Street, I was walking through the park from the subway to my apartment. I live equidistant from the Ontario Houses of Parliament and the University of Toronto. The day was not cold, but something in the bare trees caught my attention. I looked up from the gravel, into the branches and the clear blue sky beyond. I thought I heard the rustling of larger forms, and I waited a moment for voices. Nothing.

"What?" I asked.

Then as I stood in the path looking north to Queen's Park and west to the university, I heard the voices of my family one last time. *Your time has come*, they said. *Go, be brave.*

I do not know where this voyage I have begun will end. I do not know which direction I will take. I dropped the package on a park bench and started walking.

(1988)

Sandra Birdsell   b. 1942
The Wednesday Circle

Betty crosses the double planks that span the ditch in front of Joys' yard. Most people have only one plank. But Mrs Joy needs two. Mrs Joy is a possible candidate for the circus. Like sleeping with an elephant, Betty's father says often. But Mr and Mrs Joy, the egg people, don't sleep together. Betty knows this even though she's never gone further than inside their stale smelling kitchen.

The highway is a smeltering strip of gunmetal grey at her back. It leads to another town like the one she lives in. If you kept on going south, you would get to a place called Pembina in the States and a small dark tavern where a woman will serve under-age kids beer. Laurence, Betty's friend, knows about this. But if you turn from the highway and go west, there are dozens of villages and then the Pembina Hills which Betty has seen on one occasion, a school trip to the man-made lake at Morden. Home of the rich and the godly, Betty's father calls these villages. Wish the godly would stay home. Can't get a seat in the parlour on Friday nights.

Beyond her lies a field in summer fallow and a dirt road rising to a slight incline and then falling as it meets the highway. Before her is the Joys' crumbling yellow cottage, flanked on all sides by greying bales of straw which have swollen and broken free from their bindings and are scattered about the yard. Behind the cottage is the machine shed. Behind the machine shed and bumping up against the prairie is the chicken coop.

Because Mika, Betty's mother, sends her for the eggs instead of having them delivered by Mr Joy, she gets them cheaper.

Betty balances the egg cartons beneath her chin and pushes open the gate. It shrieks on its rusty hinges. The noise doesn't affect her as it usually does. Usually, the noise is like a door opening into a dark room and she is filled with dread. Today, she is prepared for it. Today is the day for the Wednesday Circle. The church ladies are meeting at her home. Even now, they're there in the dining room, sitting in a circle with their Bibles in their laps. It's like women and children in the centre. And arrows flying. Wagons are going up in flames and smoke. The goodness and matronly wisdom of the Wednesday Circle is a newly discovered thing. She belongs with them now. They can reach out to protect her even here, by just being what they are. And although she wants nothing to happen today, she is prepared for the worst.

'Come on in,' Mrs Joy calls from the kitchen.

Betty sets the egg cartons down on the steps and enters the house. Mrs Joy's kitchen resembles a Woolworth store. There are porcelain dogs and cats in every corner on knick-knack shelves. Once upon a time, she used to love looking at those figurines but now she thinks they're ugly.

The woman sits in her specially made chair which is two chairs wired together. Her legs are stretched out in front resting up on another chair. Out of habit, Betty's heart constricts because she knows the signs. Mrs Joy is not up to walking back to the chicken coop with her. And that's how it all began.

'Lo, I am with you always even unto the end of the world,' her mind recites.

These verses rise unbidden. She has memorized one hundred of them and won a trip to a summer Bible camp at Lake Winnipeg. She has for the first time seen the ocean on the prairie and tried to walk on water. The waves have lifted and pulled her out where her feet couldn't touch the sandy bottom and she has been swept beneath that mighty sea and heard the roaring of the waves in her head and felt the sting of fish water in her nostrils. Like a bubble of froth she is swept beneath the water, back and forth by the motion of the waves. She is drowning. What happens is just as she's heard. Her whole life flashes by. Her head becomes a movie screen playing back every lie and swearing, malicious and unkind deeds, thoughts, words. There is not one thing that makes her look justified for having done or said them. And then her foot touches a rock and she pushes herself forward in desperation, hoping it's the right direction.

Miraculously, it is. She bounces forward from the depths to where she can tiptoe to safety, keeping her nose above the waves. She runs panting with fear to her cabin. She pulls the blankets over her. She tells no one. But that evening in the chapel during devotions, the rustling wind in the poplars against the screen causes her to think of God. When they all sing, 'Love Lifted Me,' the sunset parts the clouds above the water so there is a crack of gold where angels hover, watching. So she goes forward to the altar with several others and has her name written in the Book of Life. They tell her the angels are clapping and she thinks she can hear them there at that crack of gold which is the door to heaven. She confesses every sin she's been shown in the water except for one. For some reason, it wasn't there in the movie. And they are such gentle, smiling nice people who have never done what she's done. So she can't bring herself to tell them that Mr Joy puts his hands in her pants.

'Rainin' today, ain't it child?' Mrs Joy asks.

'No, not yet,' Betty says. 'It's very muggy.'

'Don't I know it,' she says.

'Are your legs sore?' Betty asks.

'Oh lord, yes, how they ache,' Mrs Joy says and rolls her eyes back into her head. Her jersey dress is a tent stretched across her knees. She cradles a cookie tin in her lap.

'That's too bad,' Betty says.

A chuckle comes from deep inside her mammoth chest. 'You sound just like your mother,' she says. 'And you're looking more and more like her each time I see you. You're just like an opal, always changing.'

God's precious jewels, Mrs Joy calls them when she visits Mika. She lines them up verbally, Betty and her sisters and brothers, comparing chins, noses. This one here, she says about Betty, she's an opal. You oughta keep a watch over that one. Always changing. But it just goes to show, His mysteries does He perform. Not one of them the same.

'Thank you,' Betty says, but she hates being told she looks like her mother. Mika has hazel eyes and brown hair. She is blonde and blue-eyed like her Aunt Elizabeth.

'Well, you know where the egg pail is,' Mrs Joy says, dismissing her with a flutter of her pudgy hand.

'Aren't you coming?' Betty asks.

'Not today, girl. It aches me so to walk. You collect the eggs and then you jest find Mr Joy and you pay him. He gets it in the end anyhow.'

Betty looks around the kitchen. His jacket is missing from its hook on the wall. She goes over to the corner by the window and feigns interest in the porcelain figures. She picks one up, sets it down. His truck is not in the yard.

'Where is he?'

'Went to town for something,' Mrs Joy says. 'But I thought he'd be back by now. Doesn't matter though, jest leave the money in the back porch.'

The egg pail thumps against her leg as she crosses the yard to the chicken coop. She walks towards the cluttered wire enclosure, past the machine shed. The doors are open wide. The hens scratch and dip their heads in her direction as she approaches. Hope rises like an erratic kite as she passes the shed and there are no sounds coming from it. She stamps her feet and the hens scatter before her, then circle around and approach her from behind, silently. She quickly gathers three dozen of the warm, straw-flecked eggs, and then steps free of the stifling smelly coop out into the fresh moist air. She is almost home-free. She won't have to face anything today. It has begun to rain. Large spatters spot her white blouse, feel cool on her back. She sets the pail down on the ground beside the egg cartons and begins to transfer the eggs.

'Here, you don't have to do that outside.' His sudden voice, as she fills the egg cartons, brings blood to her face, threatens to pitch her forward over the pail.

He strides across the yard from the shed. 'Haven't got enough sense to come in out of the rain,' he says. 'Don't you know you'll melt? Be nothing left of you but a puddle.'

He carries the pail, she carries the cartons. He has told her: Mrs Joy is fat and lazy, you are my sunshine, my only sunshine. I would like six little ones running around my place too, but Mrs Joy is fat and lazy. His thin hand has gone from patting her on the head with affection, to playfully slapping her on the behind, graduated then to tickling her armpits and ribs and twice now, his hands have been inside her underpants.

'Be not afraid,' a verse leaps into her head. 'For I am with you.' She will put her plan into action. The Wednesday Circle women are strong and mighty. She knows them all, they're her mother's friends. She'll just go to them and say, Mr Joy feels me up, and that will be the end of it.

She walks behind him, her heart pounding. He has an oil rag hanging from his pocket and his boots are caked with clay, adding inches to his height.

'I'm waiting for my parts,' he says over his shoulder. 'Can't do anything until I get that truck fixed.' Sometimes he talks to her as though she were an adult. Sometimes as though she were ten again and just coming for the eggs for the first time. How old are you, he'd asked the last time and was surprised when she said, fourteen. My sunshine has grown up.

They enter the machine shed and he slides the doors closed behind them, first one and then the other, leaving a sliver of daylight beaming through where the doors join. A single light bulb dangles from a wire, shedding a circle of weak yellow light above the truck, not enough to clear the darkness from the corners.

'Okay-dokey,' he says and puts the pail of eggs on the workbench. 'You can work here. I've got things to do.' He goes over to the truck, disappears beneath its raised hood.

Then he's back at the workbench, searching through his tool-box. 'Seen you with your boyfriend the other day,' he says. 'That Anderson boy.'

'He's not my boyfriend,' she says.

'I saw you,' he says. His usual bantering tone is missing. 'The two of you were in the coulee.' Then his breath is warm on the side of her face as he reaches across her. His arm knocks against her breast, sending pain shooting through her chest. I need a bra, she has told Mika. Whatever for? Wear an undershirt if you think you really need to.

'Do you think it's a good idea to hang around in the coulee with your boyfriend?'

'He's not my boyfriend,' she says. 'I told you.'

He sees her flushed cheeks, senses her discomfort. 'Aha,' he says. 'So he is. You can't fool me.'

She moves away from him. Begins to stack the cartons up against her chest, protection against his nudgings. Why is it that everyone but her own mother notices that she has breasts now?

'Don't rush off,' he says. 'Wait until the rain passes.' The sound of it on the tin roof is like small pebbles being dropped one by one.

He takes the cartons from her and sets them back on the workbench. He smiles and she can see that perfect decayed circle between his front teeth. His hair is completely grey even though he's not as old as her father. He starts to walk past her, back towards the truck and then suddenly he grasps her about the waist and begins to tickle her ribs. She is slammed up against him and gasping for breath. His whiskers prickle against her neck. She tastes the bitterness of his flannel shirt.

She pushes away. 'Stop.'

He holds her tighter. 'You're so pretty,' he says. 'No wonder the boys are chasing you. When I'm working in here, know what I'm thinking all the time?'

'Let me go.' She continues to push against his bony arms.

'I'm thinking about all the things I could do to you.'

Against her will, she has been curious to know. She feels desire rising when he speaks of what he would like to do. He has drawn vivid word-pictures that she likes to reconstruct until her face burns. Only it isn't Mr Joy in the pictures, it's Laurence. It's what made her pull aside her underpants so he could fumble inside her moist crevice with his grease-stained fingers.

'Show me your tits,' he whispers into her neck. 'I'll give you a dollar if you do.'

She knows the only way out of this is to tell. When the whole thing is laid out before the Wednesday Circle, she will become whiter than snow. 'No,' she says.

'What do you mean, no,' he says, jabbing her in the ribs once again.

'I'm going to tell,' she says. 'You can't make me do anything anymore because I'm going to tell on you.' She feels as though a rock has been taken from her stomach. He is ugly. He is like a salamander dropping from the sky after a rainstorm into a mincemeat pail. She doesn't know how she could ever have liked him.

'Make you?' he says. 'Make you? Listen here, girlie, I've only done what you wanted me to do.'

She knows this to be true and not true. She isn't certain how she has come to accept and even expect his fondling. It has happened over a course of four years, gradually, like growing.

She walks to the double doors where the light shines through. 'Open them, please,' she says.

'Open them yourself,' he says. She can feel the presence of the Wednesday Circle. The promise of their womanly strength is like a lamp unto her feet. They will surround her and protect her. Freedom from his word-pictures will make her a new person.

'You say anything,' he says. 'You say one thing and I'll have some pretty stories to tell about you. You betcha.'

'That woman,' Mika is saying to the Wednesday Circle as Betty enters the dining room. 'That woman. She has absolutely no knowledge of the scriptures. She takes everything out of context.' Mika is standing at the buffet with a china teacup in her hand. Betty steps into the circle of chairs and sits down in Mika's empty one. Mika stops talking, throws her a look of surprise and question. The other women greet her with smiles, nods.

'Did you get the eggs?' Mika asks.

Betty feels her mouth stretching, moving of its own accord into a silly smile. She knows the smile irritates Mika but she can't help it. At times like these, her face moves on its own. She can hear her own heartbeat in her ears, like the ocean, roaring.

'What now?' Mika asks, worried.

'What do you mean, she takes everything out of context?' Mrs Brawn asks, ignoring Betty. It's her circle. She started it off, arranging for the church women to meet in each others' homes twice a month to read scripture and sew things which they send to a place in the city where they are distributed to the poor. The women are like the smell of coffee to Betty and at the same time, they are like the cool opaque squares of Mika's lemon slice which is arranged on bread and butter plates on the table. They are also like the sturdy varnished chairs they sit on. To be with them now is the same as when she was a child and thought that if you could always be near an adult when you were ill, you wouldn't die.

'My, my,' Mika mimics someone to demonstrate to Mrs Brawn what she means. She places her free hand against her chest in a dramatic gesture. 'They are different, ain't they? God's precious jewels. Just goes to show, His mysteries does He perform.'

Betty realizes with a sudden shock that her mother is imitating Mrs Joy.

Mrs Brawn takes in Mika's pose with a stern expression and immediately Mika looks guilty, drops her hand from her breast and begins to fill cups with coffee.

'I suppose that we really can't expect much from Mrs Joy,' Mika says with her back to them. Betty hears the slight mocking tone in her voice that passes them by.

Heads bent over needlework nod their understanding. The women's stitches form thumbs, forest-green fingers; except for the woman who sits beside Betty. With a hook she shapes intricate spidery patterns to lay across varnished surfaces, the backs of chairs. What the poor would want with those, I'll never know, Mika has said privately. But they include the doilies in their parcels anyway because they have an understanding. They whisper that this white-haired woman has known suffering.

She works swiftly. It seems to Betty as though the threads come from the ends of her fingers, white strings with a spot of red every few inches. It looks as though she's cut her finger and secretly bleeds the colour into the lacy scallops. The women all unravel and knit and check closely for evenness of tension.

Mika enters the circle of chairs then, carrying the tray of coffee, and begins to make her way around it. She continues to speak of Mrs Joy.

'Are you looking forward to school?' the white-haired woman asks Betty. Her voice is almost a whisper, a knife peeling skin from a taut apple. Betty senses that it has been difficult for her to speak, feels privileged that she has.

'Yes, I miss school.'

The woman blinks as she examines a knot in her yarn. She scrapes at it with her large square thumbnail which is flecked oddly with white fish-hook-shaped marks. 'Your mother tells us you were at camp,' she says. 'What did you do there?'

Mika approaches them with the tray of coffee. 'I just wish she hadn't picked me out, that's all,' Mika says. 'She insists on coming over here in the morning and it's impossible to work with her here. And Mr Joy is just as bad. I send Betty for the eggs now because he used to keep me at the door talking.'

Mr Joy is just as bad. Mr Joy makes me ashamed of myself and I let him do it. The woman shakes loose the doily; it unfolds into the shape of a star as she holds it up.

'You like it?' the white-haired woman asks Betty.

'It's pretty.'

'Maybe I give it to you.'

'Ah, Mika,' a woman across the circle says, 'she just knows where she can find the best baking in town.'

Then they all laugh; even the quiet woman beside Betty has a dry chuckle over the comment, only Mrs Brawn doesn't smile. She stirs her coffee with more force than necessary and sets the spoon alongside it with a clang.

'Obesity is no laughing matter,' she says. 'Mrs Joy is a glutton and that's to be pitied. We don't laugh at sin, the wages of sin is death.'

'But the gift of God is eternal life through Jesus Christ our Lord,' the woman says so softly, the words are nail filings dropping into her lap. If Betty hadn't seen her lips moving, she wouldn't have heard it. 'God forgives,' the woman says then, louder. She is an odd combination of young and old. Her voice and breasts are young but her hair is white.

Mika stands before them with the tray of coffee. 'Not always,' Mika says. 'There's the unpardonable sin, don't forget about that.' She seems pleased to have remembered this.

'Which is?' the woman asks.

'Well, suicide,' Mika says. 'It has to be, because when you think of it, it's something you can't repent of once the deed is done.' Mika smiles around the circle as if to say to them, see, I'm being patient with this woman who has known suffering.

'Perhaps there is no need to repent,' the woman says.

'Pardon?'

'In Russia,' the woman begins and then stops to set her thread down into her lap. She folds her hands one on top of the other and closes her eyes. The others, sensing a story, fall silent.

'During the revolution in Russia, there was once a young girl who was caught by nine soldiers and was their prisoner for two weeks. She was only thirteen. These men had their way with her many times, each one taking their turn, every single night. In the end, she shot herself. What about her?'

'I've never heard of such a case,' Mika says. She sounds as though she resents hearing of it now.

'There are always such cases,' the woman says. 'If God knows the falling of a single sparrow, He is also merciful. He knows we're only human.'

Mrs Brawn sets her knitting down on the floor in front of her chair, leans forward slightly. 'Oh, He knows,' she says. 'But he never gives us more than we can bear. When temptation arises, He gives us the strength to resist.' She closes her statement with her hands, like a conductor pinching closed the last sound.

Betty watches as the white-haired woman twists and untwists her yarn into a tight ring around her finger. 'I don't believe for one moment,' she says finally, 'that God would condemn such a person to hell. Jesus walked the earth and so He knows.'

'No, no,' Mika says from the buffet. 'He doesn't condemn us, don't you see? That's where you're wrong. We condemn ourselves. We make that choice.'

'And what choice did that young girl have?' the woman asks. 'It was her means of escape. God provided the gun.'

Mika holds the tray of lemon squares up before her as though she were offering them to the sun. She looks stricken. Deep lines cut a sharp V above her nose. 'You don't mean that,' she says. 'Suicide is unpardonable. I'm sure of it. Knowing that keeps me going. Otherwise, I would have done it myself long ago.'

There is shocked silence and a rapid exchange of glances around the circle, at Betty, to see if she's heard.

'You shouldn't say such things,' Mrs Brawn says quietly. 'For shame. You have no reason to say that.'

The white-haired woman speaks with a gaunt smile. 'Occasionally,' she says, 'in this room, someone dares to speak the truth.'

'What do you mean?' asks Mrs Brawn.

'Look at us,' the woman says. 'We're like filthy rags to Him in our self-righteousness. We obey because we fear punishment, not because we love.'

Betty sees the grease spot on her blouse where his arm has brushed against her breast. Her whole body is covered in handprints. The stone is back in her stomach. She feels betrayed. For a moment the women are lost inside their own thoughts and they don't notice as she rises from her chair and sidles over to the door. Then, as if on some signal, their conversation resumes its usual level, each one waiting impatiently for the other to be finished so they can speak their words. Their laughter and goodwill have a feeling of urgency, of desperation. Betty stands at the door; a backward glance and she sees the white-haired woman bending over her work once again, eyes blinking rapidly, her fingers moving swiftly and the doily, its flecked pattern spreading like a web across her lap.

(1982)

Thomas King   b. 1943

Borders

When I was twelve, maybe thirteen, my mother announced that we were going to go to Salt Lake City to visit my sister who had left the reserve, moved across the line, and found a job. Laetitia had not left home with my mother's blessing, but over time my mother had come to be proud of the fact that Laetitia had done all of this on her own.

"She did real good," my mother would say.

Then there were the fine points to Laetitia's going. She had not, as my mother liked to tell Mrs. Manyfingers, gone floating after some man like a balloon on a string. She hadn't snuck out of the house, either, and gone to Vancouver or Edmonton or Toronto to chase rainbows down alleys. And she hadn't been pregnant.

"She did real good."

I was seven or eight when Laetitia left home. She was seventeen. Our father was from Rocky Boy on the American side.

"Dad's American," Laetitia told my mother, "so I can go and come as I please."

"Send us a postcard."

Laetitia packed her things, and we headed for the border. Just outside of Milk River, Laetitia told us to watch for the water tower.

"Over the next rise. It's the first thing you see."

"We got a water tower on the reserve," my mother said. "There's a big one in Lethbridge, too."

"You'll be able to see the tops of the flagpoles, too. That's where the border is."

When we got to Coutts, my mother stopped at the convenience store and bought her and Laetitia a cup of coffee. I got an Orange Crush.

"This is real lousy coffee."

"You're just angry because I want to see the world."

"It's the water. From here on down, they got lousy water."

"I can catch the bus from Sweetgrass. You don't have to lift a finger."

"You're going to have to buy your water in bottles if you want good coffee."

There was an old wooden building about a block away, with a tall sign in the yard that said "Museum." Most of the roof had been blown away. Mom told me to go and see when the place was open. There were boards over the windows and doors. You could tell that the place was closed, and I told Mom so, but she said to go and check anyway. Mom and Laetitia stayed by the car. Neither one of them moved. I sat down on the steps of the museum and watched them, and I don't know that they ever said anything to each other. Finally, Laetitia got her bag out of the trunk and gave Mom a hug.

I wandered back to the car. The wind had come up, and it blew Laetitia's hair across her face. Mom reached out and pulled the strands out of Laetitia's eyes, and Laetitia let her.

"You can still see the mountain from here,' my mother told Laetitia in Blackfoot.

"Lots of mountains in Salt Lake," Laetitia told her in English.

"The place is closed," I said. "Just like I told you."

Laetitia tucked her hair into her jacket and dragged her bag down the road to the brick building with the American flag flapping on a pole. When she got to where the guards were waiting, she turned, put the bag down, and waved to us. We waved back. Then my mother turned the car around, and we came home.

We got postcards from Laetitia regular, and, if she wasn't spreading jelly on the truth, she was happy. She found a good job and rented an apartment with a pool.

"And she can't even swim," my mother told Mrs. Manyfingers.

Most of the postcards said we should come down and see the city, but whenever I mentioned this, my mother would stiffen up.

So I was surprised when she bought two new tires for the car and put on her blue dress with the green and yellow flowers. I had to dress up, too, for my mother did not want us crossing the border looking like Americans. We made sandwiches and put them in a big box with pop and potato chips and some apples and bananas and a big jar of water.

"But we can stop at one of those restaurants, too, right?"

"We maybe should take some blankets in case you get sleepy."

"But we can stop at one of those restaurants, too, right?"

The border was actually two towns, though neither one was big enough to amount to anything. Coutts was on the Canadian side and consisted of the convenience store and gas station, the museum that was closed and boarded up, and a motel. Sweetgrass was on the American side, but all you could see was an overpass that arched across the highway and disappeared into the prairies. Just hearing the names of these towns, you would expect that Sweetgrass, which is a nice name and sounds like it is related to other places such as Medicine Hat and Moose Jaw and Kicking Horse Pass, would be on the Canadian side, and that Coutts, which sounds abrupt and rude, would be on the American side. But this was not the case.

Between the two borders was a duty-free shop where you could buy cigarettes and liquor and flags. Stuff like that.

We left the reserve in the morning and drove until we got to Coutts.

"Last time we stopped here," my mother said, "you had an Orange Crush. You remember that?"

"Sure," I said. "That was when Laetitia took off."

"You want another Orange Crush?"

"That means we're not going to stop at a restaurant, right?"

My mother got a coffee at the convenience store, and we stood around and watched the prairies move in the sunlight. Then we climbed back in the car. My mother straightened the dress across her thighs, leaned against the wheel, and drove all the way to the border in first gear, slowly, as if she were trying to see through a bad storm or riding high on black ice.

The border guard was an old guy. As he walked to the car, he swayed from side to side, his feet set wide apart, the holster on his hip pitching up and down. He leaned into the window, looked into the back seat, and looked at my mother and me.

"Morning ma'am."

"Good morning."

"Where you heading?"

"Salt Lake City."

"Purpose of your visit?"

"Visit my daughter."

"Citizenship."

"Blackfoot," my mother told him.

"Ma'am?"

"Blackfoot," my mother repeated.

"Canadian?"

"Blackfoot."

It would have been easier if my mother had just said "Canadian" and been done with it, but I could see she wasn't going to do that. The guard wasn't angry or anything. He smiled and looked towards the building. Then he turned back and nodded.

"Morning, ma'am."

"Good morning."

"Any firearms or tobacco?"

"No."

"Citizenship?"

"Blackfoot."

He told us to sit in the car and wait, and we did. In about five minutes, another guard came out with the first man. They were talking as they came, both men swaying back and forth like two cowboys headed for a bar or a gunfight.

"Morning, ma'am."

"Good morning."

"Cecil tells me you and the boy are Blackfoot."

"That's right."

"Now, I know that we got Blackfeet on the American side and the Canadians got Blackfeet on their side. Just so we can keep our records straight, what side do you come from?"

I knew exactly what my mother was going to say, and I could have told them if they had asked me.

"Canadian side or American side?" asked the guard.

"Blackfoot side," she said.

It didn't take them long to lose their sense of humour, I can tell you that. The one guard stopped smiling altogether and told us to park our car at the side of the building and come in.

We sat on a wood bench for about an hour before anyone came over to talk to us. This time it was a woman. She had a gun, too.

"Hi," she said. "I'm Inspector Pratt. I understand there is a little misunderstanding."

"I'm going to visit my daughter in Salt Lake City," my mother told her. "We don't have any guns or beer."

"It's a legal technicality, that's all."

"My daughter's Blackfoot, too."

The woman opened a briefcase and took out a couple of forms and began to write on one of them. "Everyone who crosses our border has to declare their citizenship. Even Americans. It helps us keep track of the visitors we get from the various countries."

She went on like that for maybe fifteen minutes, and a lot of the stuff she told us was interesting.

"I can understand how you feel about having to tell us your citizenship, and here's what I'll do. You tell me, and I won't put it down on the form. No-one will know but you and me."

Her gun was silver. There were several chips in the wood handle and the name "Stella" was scratched into the metal butt.

We were in the border office for about four hours, and we talked to almost everyone there. One of the men bought me a Coke. My mother brought a couple of sandwiches in from the car. I offered a part of mine to Stella, but she said she wasn't hungry.

I told Stella that we were Blackfoot and Canadian, but she said that didn't count because I was a minor. In the end, she told us that if my mother didn't declare our citizenship, we would have to go back where we came from. My mother stood up and thanked Stella for her time. Then we got back in the car and drove to the Canadian border, which was only about a hundred yards away.

I was disappointed. I hadn't seen Laetitia for a long time, and I had never been to Salt Lake City. When she was still at home, Laetitia would go on and on about Salt Lake City. She had never been there, but her boyfriend Lester Tallbull had spent a year in Salt Lake at a technical school.

"It's a great place," Lester would say. 'Nothing but blondes in the whole state."

Whenever he said that, Laetitia would slug him on his shoulder hard enough to make him flinch. He had some brochures on Salt Lake and some maps, and every so often the two of them would spread them out on the table.

"That's the temple. It's right downtown. You got to have a pass to get in."

"Charlotte says anyone can go in and look around."

"When was Charlotte in Salt Lake? Just when the hell was Charlotte in Salt Lake?"

"Last year."

"This is Liberty Park. It's got a zoo. There's good skiing in the mountains."

"Got all the skiing we can use," my mother would say. "People come from all over the world to ski at Banff. Cardston's got a temple, if you like those kinds of things."

"Oh, this one is real big," Lester would say. "They got armed guards and everything."

"Not what Charlotte says."

"What does she know?"

Lester and Laetitia broke up, but I guess the idea of Salt Lake stuck in her mind.

The Canadian border guard was a young woman, and she seemed happy to see us.

"Hi," she said. "You folks sure have a great day for a trip. Where are you coming from?"

"Standoff."

"Is that in Montana?"

"No."

"Where are you going?"

"Standoff."

The woman's name was Carol and I don't guess she was any older than Laetitia. "Wow, you both Canadians?"

"Blackfoot."

"Really? I have a friend I went to school with who is Blackfoot. Do you know Mike Harley?"

"No."

"He went to school in Lethbridge, but he's really from Browning."

It was a nice conversation and there were no cars behind us, so there was no rush.

"You're not bringing any liquor back, are you?"

"No."

"Any cigarettes or plants or stuff like that?"

"No."

"Citizenship?"

"Blackfoot."

"I know," said the woman, "and I'd be proud of being Blackfoot if I were Blackfoot. But you have to be American or Canadian."

When Laetitia and Lester broke up, Lester took his brochures and maps with him, so Laetitia wrote to someone in Salt Lake City, and, about a month later, she got a big envelope of stuff. We sat at the table and opened up all the brochures, and Laetitia read each one out loud.

"Salt Lake City is the gateway to some of the world's most magnificent skiing."

"Salt Lake City is the home of one of the newest professional basketball franchises, the Utah Jazz."

"The Great Salt Lake is one of the natural wonders of the world."

It was kind of exciting seeing all those colour brochures on the table and listening to Laetitia read all about how Salt Lake City was one of the best places in the entire world.

"That Salt Lake City place sounds too good to be true," my mother told her.

"It has everything."

"We got everything right here."

"It's boring here."

"People in Salt Lake City are probably sending away for brochures of Calgary and Lethbridge and Pincher Creek right now."

In the end, my mother would say that maybe Laetitia should go to Salt Lake City, and Laetitia would say that maybe she would.

We parked the car to the side of the building and Carol led us into a small room on the second floor. I found a comfortable spot on the couch and flipped through some back issues of *Saturday Night* and *Alberta Report*.

When I woke up, my mother was just coming out of another office. She didn't say a word to me. I followed her down the stairs and out to the car. I thought we were going home, but she turned the car around and drove back towards the American border, which made me think we were going to visit Laetitia in Salt Lake City after all. Instead she pulled into the parking lot of the duty-free store and stopped.

"We going to see Laetitia?"

"No."

"We going home?"

Pride is a good thing to have, you know. Laetitia had a lot of pride, and so did my mother. I figured that someday, I'd have it, too.

"So where are we going?"

Most of that day, we wandered around the duty-free store, which wasn't very large. The manager had a name tag with a tiny American flag on one side and tiny Canadian flag on the other. His name was Mel. Towards evening, he began suggesting that we should be on our way. I told him we had nowhere to go, that neither the Americans nor the Canadians would let us in. He laughed at that and told us that we should buy something or leave.

The car was not very comfortable, but we did have all that food and it was April, so even if it did snow as it sometimes does on the prairies, we wouldn't freeze. The next morning my mother drove to the American border.

It was a different guard this time, but the questions were the same. We didn't spend as much time in the office as we had the day before. By noon, we were back at the Canadian border. By two we were back in the duty-free shop parking lot.

The second night in the car was not as much fun as the first, but my mother seemed in good spirits, and, all in all, it was as much an adventure as an inconvenience. There wasn't much food left and that was a problem, but we had lots of water as there was a faucet at the side of the duty-free shop.

One Sunday, Laetitia and I were watching television. Mom was over at Mrs. Manyfingers's. Right in the middle of the programme, Laetitia turned off the set and said she was going to Salt Lake City, that life around here was too boring. I had wanted to see the rest of the programme and really didn't care if Laetitia went to Salt Lake City or not. When Mom got home, I told her what Laetitia had said.

What surprised me was how angry Laetitia got when she found out that I had told Mom.

"You got a big mouth."

"That's what you said."

"What I said is none of your business."

"I didn't say anything."

"Well, I'm going for sure, now."

That weekend, Laetitia packed her bags, and we drove her to the border.

Mel turned out to be friendly. When he closed up for the night and found us still parked in the lot, he came over and asked us if our car was broken down or something. My mother thanked him for his concern and told him that we were fine, that things would get straightened out in the morning.

"You're kidding," said Mel. "You'd think they could handle the simple things."

"We got some apples and a banana," I said, "but we're all out of ham sandwiches."

"You know, you read about these things, but you just don't believe it. You just don't believe it."

"Hamburgers would be even better because they got more stuff for energy."

My mother slept in the back seat. I slept in the front because I was smaller and could lie under the steering wheel. Late that night, I heard my mother open the car door. I found her sitting on her blanket leaning against the bumper of the car.

"You see all those stars," she said. "When I was a little girl, my grandmother used to take me and my sisters out on the prairies and tell us stories about all the stars."

"Do you think Mel is going to bring us any hamburgers?"

"Every one of those stars has a story. You see that bunch of stars over there that look like a fish?"

"He didn't say no."

"Coyote went fishing, one day. That's how it all started." We sat out under the stars that night, and my mother told me all sorts of stories. She was serious about it, too. She'd tell them slow, repeating parts as she went, as if she expected me to remember each one.

Early the next morning, the television vans began to arrive, and guys in suits and women in dresses came trotting over to us, dragging microphones and cameras and lights behind them. One of the vans had a table set up with orange juice and sandwiches and fruit. It was for the crew, but when I told them we hadn't eaten for a while, a really skinny blonde woman told us we could eat as much as we wanted.

They mostly talked to my mother. Every so often one of the reporters would come over and ask me questions about how it felt to be an Indian without a country. I told them we had a nice house on the reserve and that my cousins had a couple of horses we rode when we went fishing. Some of the television people went over to the American border, and then they went to the Canadian border.

Around noon, a good-looking guy in a dark blue suit and an orange tie with little ducks on it drove up in a fancy car. He talked to my mother for a while, and, after they were done talking, my mother called me over, and we got into our car. Just as my mother started the engine, Mel came over and gave us a bag of peanut brittle and told us that justice was a damn hard thing to get, but that we shouldn't give up.

I would have preferred lemon drops, but it was nice of Mel anyway.

"Where are we going now?"

"Going to visit Laetitia."

The guard who came out to our car was all smiles. The television lights were so bright they hurt my eyes, and, if you tried to look through the windshield in certain directions, you couldn't see a thing.

"Morning, ma'am."

"Good morning."

"Where you heading?"

"Salt Lake City."

"Purpose of your visit?"

"Visit my daughter"

"Any tobacco, liquor, or firearms?"

"Don't smoke."

"Any plants or fruit?"

"Not any more."

"Citizenship?"

"Blackfoot."

The guard rocked back on his heels and jammed his thumbs into his gun belt. "Thank you," he said, his fingers patting the butt of the revolver. "Have a pleasant trip."

My mother rolled the car forward, and the television people had to scramble out of the way. They ran alongside the car as we pulled away from the border, and, when they couldn't run any farther, they stood in the middle of the highway and waved and waved and waved.

We got to Salt Lake City the next day. Laetitia was happy to see us, and, that first night, she took us out to a restaurant that made really good soups. The list of pies took up a whole page. I had cherry. Mom had chocolate. Laetitia said that she saw us on television the night before and, during the meal, she had us tell her the story over and over again.

Laetitia took us everywhere. We went to a fancy ski resort. We went to the temple. We got to go shopping in a couple of large malls, but they weren't as large as the one in Edmonton, and Mom said so.

After a week or so, I got bored and wasn't at all sad when my mother said we should be heading back home. Laetitia wanted us to stay longer, but Mom said no, that she had things to do back home and that, next time, Laetitia should come up and visit. Laetitia said she was thinking about moving back, and Mom told her to do as she pleased, and Laetitia said that she would.

On the way home we stopped at the duty-free shop, and my mother gave Mel a green hat that said "Salt Lake" across the front. Mel was a funny guy. He took the hat and blew his nose and told my mother that she was an inspiration to us all. He gave us some more peanut brittle and came out into the parking lot and waved at us all the way to the Canadian border.

It was almost evening when we left Coutts. I watched the border through the rear window until all you could see were the tops of the flagpoles and the blue water tower, and then they rolled over a hill and disappeared.

(1993)

David Adams Richards b. 1950
A Rural Place

'Maybe so,' said the man, 'I didn't say she weren't here an hour ago, I didn't say nothin, all I said is she's gone now, look ya see her in 'er room, ya see her in 'er bed?'

'No,' the woman said.

'Well she's gone.'

'She's 96 years old,' said the woman. 'She didn't just walk out onto the street and disappear—she has to be somewhere.'

'I don't care she's gone, I'm not talkin ta ya, botherin standin here arguin about it—I ain't gonna argue about it while she goes drowns herself and you stand here and argue about it!'

'I'm not arguing about it,' said the woman.

'Ya are arguin ya are,' said the man under his breath, but by this time the woman had moved along the hallway to see the administrator, and the man stood there alone in the sun that came through the high window.

'She's gone?' said the administrator.

'Yes.'

'Where to?'

'I don't know where to, we've looked just about everyplace—think we should call the police?'

'Did you look in her closet?'

'In her closet?' said the woman.

'I bet anything she's locked herself in a closet.'

'Maybe,' said the woman slowly.

'No maybe about it—I'll bet anything.'

'She's in nobody's closet around here,' said the man.

'Have you looked in them all—I mean on the third floor?'

'I looked in them all. I ain't seen her in no closet, she's in nobody's closet.'

The woman said nothing.

'How the hell would she get up on the third floor anyways?' said the man.

'I don't know.'

'Well I don't have the foggiest what's goin on round here anyways,' said the man. 'Why would she wanta hide in a closet, tell me that?'

But by this time the woman had turned and started down the hallway again.

'Just tell me that,' said the man.

'Well,' the administrator said, flicking his pencil back and forth on the desk.

'I think we should look for her,' said the woman.

'Yes perhaps—where, you mean downtown?'

'Yes perhaps,' said the woman, 'Think we should phone the police?'

'Yes perhaps.'

'Now that's just what I been standin here an sayin for over an hour,' said the man.

'Do you know what she was wearing?'

'Clothes is all—I never looked at her.'

'Probably the brown dress,' the woman said. 'She won't let anyone dress her.'

'Could possibly be,' the man said, snapping a match with his finger to light a cigarette and shaking his head.

'Yes.'

'I don't have the foggiest what's goin on round here at all,' said the man.

Janie Bell crossed the railway tracks and stood at the wharf. It was a bright September day and a wind came off the water. *The first time I crossed this river was me and my mother we came on the paddle boat to this side of the river I member we comin ta sell raspberries in the summer.* Though there were whitecaps and spray the water looked gently warm and in the fresh September heat was the taste of salt and boards and leaves changing colour. And children passed her as she waited driving their bicycles over the boarded sidewalk.

The children laughed and yelled at one another and the sound of their voices echoed along the bank and down across the water. She leaned against the timbers. When the ferry docked there were three cars to go on and she waited until the last one started across the ramp because the man in the hat had watched her ever since the ferry entered. She walked slowly down the sidewalk onto the ferry, her black boots scraping and shuffling down its stained cement floor.

'Hello,' the man said coming out of his narrow box and standing in front of her. He stared at her small greying face where her eyes protruded, and her brown hat was pinched against her head with pins. She stood silently.

'Where ya going Mam?'

'Across the river.'

The man looked about, and under him she could hear the steady rumble of the engine and smell grease and car heat. There was sweat dribbling from the man's face when he looked about, and his fingers were smudged and dirty.

'You're from the Senior Citizens Home are you?'

'I'm 100 years old right now—I got a message from the government.'

'Oh,' the man said. He stepped back a little and rubbed his left shoulder against the small narrow box. 'You're not from the Home are you?'

'A message from the government,' she said. Her eyes protruded and as she spoke her lips moved without her mouth opening. 'I live by meself.'

'Oh,' he said. He stepped into the box and sat on the stool still watching her.

She sat on a bench at the stern as they crossed the river. For a moment everything was cold and distant. The children with the bicycles sat across from her laughing and yelling. Then the man came to them and said:

'This is yer last trip today boys.'

'It's free,' one of them said. 'We don't havta pay nothin—ya can't kick us off for not payin.'

'I'm not kickin ya off for not payin—I'm tellin ya ta stay off the ferry, ya been back and forth all day.'

'It's a free country,' one of the boys said. 'Ya don't own the ferry.'

'Ya, you don't own the ferry—what d'ya think you own the ferry?'

'Try ta get on again and you'll see who owns it.'

'Ah go sit down,' the first boy said. He was smoking a cigarette and looked around nervously when the others laughed. The man turned red and scratched his arms and below her she could hear the waves churning and see gulls climbing in the air.

'Just anyaya try ta get on 'er again and you'll see who owns the ferry—ya should be in school.' He turned and started back, nodding to her quickly.

'We're smarter than you,' the boy yelled. 'Go ta school yerself and see who owns the ferry.'

'Ya,' another boy laughed. 'Try ta figure out who owns the ferry.'

The first boy spit and butted his cigarette. 'Old fucker,' he said.

I member we'd all our raspberries in boxes and what a time gettin them boxes and then we all wanted ta go with er every one a us and she said 'Janie get yer coat on' and Isabel started cryin but when I went over ta town I diden like it anyway we hadda stand round all day waitin in the heat—it weren't no fun and when we came back Isabel said 'How's it like?' and I first said ta Isabel 'You wait until you havta start sellin raspberries' and then I handed her seven peppermints I member there was seven.

The ferry docked and she waited until the cars left and the boys screaming and yelling to each other went down the boardwalk on their bicycles. The man came out of his office and took her arm,

'You must remember the old paddleboats they had here,' he said to her.

'Yes, I member them,' she said.

'I member them,' she mumbled as he helped her along, she feeling the strength of his hand under her arm and smelling him, and the tar on the tying poles. She crooked her neck to look at him and he was smiling at her, as if she was his grandmother or some old lady he'd known for a long time. She didn't like that.

'Are you visiting relatives over here Mam?'

'Yes—*Isabel's* daughter—I'm visiting *Isabel's* daughter.'

'Are they here to meet you?'

They were at the front again, and she scraped along on the cement with her black boots while the man still held her steady and smiled. She could smell warm tar off the tying poles in the air and could see swarms of dirt in the water, and cardboard boxes looking like rags floating. The water was black in the shadows of the timbers. People watched her as he helped her across the boardwalk. His arm stiffened when he saw people watching and he no longer looked at her. Again for a moment it was distant and cold.

'Are they here to meet you Mam?'

He let go of her arm and she kept walking small and hunched as people watched her. She went to a pole and leaned against it for a moment not turning to look in case he was still there. The sun was warm again and everything sounded quiet in the September heat. The boys were at the top of the lane running their bicycles against one another and as the cars passed dust rose from their tires. She moved over the pebbles on the side of the lane, watching her feet and a car had to stop behind her when she moved onto the lane.

'Can we give you a lift somewhere?' a woman asked.

'Can we take you somewhere?' the man said. They'd pulled alongside her in their car.

'Isabel's daughter's,' she said.

'What?' the man said.

'Isabel's daughter's—Deborah's place.'

The man looked at the woman and smiled and she nudged him in the ribs with her arm, her arm looking purple in the darkness of the car.

'Well, we can take ya there I suppose,' the man said. He got out of the car and opened the back door for her and helped her into the back seat.

'Warm today ain't it,' she said.

'Yes,' he said.

'I'm goin for a visit—I'm 100 years old right now—I got a message from the government.'

'Really,' the woman said.

'The Queen sent me flowers.'

'Don't call me stupid,' the man from the ferry said.

'Ya are I can't help it if ya are.'

'I called ya didn't I soon as I got back ta town I called ya.'

'Don't matter ta me ya musta known where she was from ya musta known that, we havin everyone in the world out lookin for her—and it bein on the radio about a million times.'

'Jesus,' the man from the ferry said.

'And she isn't 100 either she's only 96.'

'Well she told me she was—she told me she had a phone call from the Prime Minister about it.'

'Well she didn't.'

'She told me.'

'And her relatives are all dead—she doesn't have a relative in the world to visit.'

'Well where in hell is she off to?'

'If we knew that we'd catch her. So she got in a car—did they know her?'

The man from the ferry shrugged and bit his lower lip, breathed deeply between his closed teeth.

'Do you know them?'

'They cross for groceries bout once a week but I don't know them.'

'Fine mess now—fine mess now.'

'Ya'd think ta Christ it was my fault—who the hell let her escape in the first place?'

'Not me.'

'Bet anything it was.'

'Run yer ferry.'

'Run yer old age place.'

The man from the Home shook his head and spit. A breeze came off the water and dried the sweat on his forehead.

'We'll haveta get the police down here,' he said.

'She couldn't be goin ta no relatives?'

'Not unless she wanted ta hitchhike to Toronto—she's got someone there.'

The man from the ferry laughed.

The man from the Home walked back along the main street as dust rose in the noon hour September air and children dressed pale and bright came running from the schools. Everything was smelling fresh and quiet and the ferry whistle sounded, its rounded bulk moving slowly on the waves. He crossed the street and went into the corner store.

'Nice day for a change.'

'Very best of a day—pack a Players there will ya?'

'I hear on the radio ya let one out.'

'Sometime this morning I think,' he said opening the package immediately. He looked at the man behind the counter, who was grinning at him, and shrugged. 'Ya'd think the people downtown'd be a little bit smarter than that.'
'Than what?'
'Than letten an old woman like she is wander about without catchin her—like the guy in the ferry there letten her slip right through his fingers like that.'
'Call the police is what'cha gotta do.'
'We did we did,' he said, leaving the store.
'Ya should get yerself a wife an stop worrying about the old ones,' the other man yelled. Then he laughed.
He walked along the sidewalk close to the water and saw in the alley two men sitting on dried, broken bait barrels drinking wine. He lit his cigarette and felt the breeze again, gentle and sweet smelling. Above him, on the opposite street, he could hear a hammer ringing dully under the blue sky. 'I wish they'd leave me the hell alone bout gettin married,' he thought. 'It's none of their business about me gettin married.'

'How much farther is it?' the man asked. She didn't answer so he turned to look at her. 'I think she's asleep.'
'Poor old soul,' the woman said.
'I'm not cartin her all over, I wanta get back home and finish those cabinets.'
'Tcch,' the woman said moving her tongue against her teeth.
'Look ya been after me for days to do them, I couldn't breathe and you'd be yellin at me so now I wanta do them!'
'Well, I can't help it—we can't put her out in the middle of the road.'
'Christ.'
'Stop swearing.'
'I'm not swearing.'
'If you live to be 100 you'd like people to treat you kind.'
'What in hell am I doin to her?'
'What's that?' the old woman said suddenly, opening her eyes and raising her head. 'What's that?'
'You must have fell asleep,' the woman said. 'We were just wondering where you wanted to go—is it close to here?'
Janie Bell looked out one window and then the other. On her right the fields sloped to the river and cows lazed in them, and on her left the woods started again where spruce and alders and maples tangled together. She rested her head on her hand once more.
'Deborah's place,' she said.
'Yes, but where is Deborah's place?'
'Along aways—ya haven't reached it yet.'
'Down further?'
'Yes—and then back where I was brought up.'
'Back where?'
'Just hang on.'
'Okay,' the man said laughing, scratching the side of his face and shifting the gears suddenly.
'Watch yourself how you drive,' his wife said.
They drove down another five miles and the man cursed under his breath. He saw clouds forming over the bay water and he'd wanted to bring the cabinets outside to finish them. And every house he came to he'd slow down and say:

'This it?'

'No it ain't.'

Until they were down another five miles and the old woman told him to turn up a side road.

'So it's back here then?'

'Yes,' she said.

The paved road ended and a dirt road began. He geared the car down, and started up the long hill thinking 'This'll be the end of it,' but when they came to the top of the hill and he saw the road on the other side, defaced with ruts and boulders his stomach became knotted and sick.

'No-one in the world can live back here anymore,' he said looking at his wife for some explanation. 'No-one coulda lived here for at least 100 or 200 years.'

'Now Ralph, take her down the hill.'

'I'm not takin my car down that hill.'

'Now Ralph.'

'Never mind it then I'll walk,' Janie Bell said.

'No you won't walk,' the woman said, 'How much further is it?'

'Not too much further dear just down the hill where the bridge is.'

'What bridge?' Ralph said. His face looked white and sick. They could smell fall in the trees and the leaves tinged and golden were bathed in light. The boulders themselves were rich brown and far below the small river rounded a bend, its water green. 'They're tearin that old bridge down!' he said.

'How do you know?' his wife said.

'Because I know,' he yelled.

'Stop yelling with a stranger in the car.'

'Never mind I'll walk,' the old woman said. 'That's where I get out.'

'That's where yer gettin out?' the man asked clutching the steering wheel. 'What are you getting out there for—you can't get out there—no-one lives there—no-one lives down there.' He looked around at her and tried to smile, 'Look now, ya can't go gettin out there.'

'Yes,' she said.

'Now Ralph she must know more about it than you.'

'I don't care,' he said. 'No-one in the world lives back here in a thousand years.'

'Maybe ya should come back to town,' the woman said.

'No, now I'm goin for a visit,' Janie Bell said.

'That's the bridge they were talking about tearin apart,' he said, still trying to smile, 'I betcha they're workin on it right now.'

'Ralph,' she said, nudging him, 'Ralph.'

'Across the ferry,' said the administrator. 'Why would she do that—why didn't they stop her either?'

'I don't know—I suppose they just didn't think to,' said the woman.

'Who's running the ferry, a bunch of morons?' he said.

'I don't know,' said the woman, 'But surely to heavens they'll catch on and bring her back.'

'I'd better phone the police.'

'I've already done that,' said the woman.

'Well, I can't have a thing like this happening, it's bad enough as it is with all the trouble around here.'

'Yes,' she said.
'I'd love to know how she got out of the yard in the first place without you checking.'
'I was at lunch,' said the woman.
'I'd just love to know what's going on around here—a bunch of morons.'
'Yes.'
'What are the police doing—sleeping I suppose?'
'They've two cars out, and volunteers.'
'A bunch of morons.'

She sat by a tree above the bridge and all day men came and went, passing her with hooks and pevies, and all day she watched them going without a sound sitting on the fallen leaves. And now and then the grass stirred in the afternoon wind and clouds blocked the light so that the river changed from green to dusk colour, and the men's shouts sounded faint and far off.

Her hat was crooked on her head, the pins bothered her scalp and her eyes watered when the wind blew. She moved constantly in trying to be comfortable, but then her eyes stopped watering, became dry and sore, and she closed them.

'Do ya know who the hell she is?'
'Who who is?'
'That woman over there, she must be 80.'
'Where?'
'Over there.'
'Where?'
'There—there look.'
'She looks like a scarecrow don't she?'
'Should talk to her see what she's doin?'
'Fuck you.'
'Should take her home and use her for a scarecrow.'

The men's shouts sounded faint and far off, the timbers cracked and split on the underbelly of the bridge. The men on the bridge roof danced in the afternoon light jumping from timber to timber as the sills groaned under weight and commotion—and laughter. Always laughter.

'Try 'er.'
'The hell with you I'm not that steady on me Jesus feet.'
'She's only 40 feet down whatcha worried about?'
'Ha.'
'She's a mere 40 feet.'
'Jump 'er.'

And she thought: *This is a nice place when Isabel was goin courtin with Bennie I came down the first time and sat here and all of a sudden Bennie comes struttin across big as life balancin himself, the bridge werent a quarter finished: 'Ya'll fall fer sure.' 'Betcha I won't.' 'What'll Isabel say now if you fall?' He hopped on one foot and then the other, his cork boots hoppin: 'Who cares what Isabel says anyway,' he laughed. 'I know who cares.' 'No sirree.' 'Ha.' 'No sirree!'*

'Go over and talk ta her Simon.'
'No.'
'Go on and see what she's doin.'
'No, you go.'
'Yer not doin any work here anyway—ya mays well go over, ya little bastard.'

'Go ta hell I work as much as you.'
'Jerkin off.'
'I work as much as you.'
'Go on over Simon see what she's fuckin doin.'
'No.'
'Hey maybe she come ta blow us.'
Simon said nothing.
'Boy what a filthy mind eh Simon?'
Simon said nothing.
'Ha.'

He came over and sat with me right here though it was different from this—there were dark pools in the water and the trees on the other side were crooked and smelt like a magic forest, their dirt and roots. Off the path to the left from me was the old mill. 'Goin ta see Isabel?' 'Nope.' 'Why not?' 'Don't want to.' I could feel him breathin moving my hair back on my neck. 'What's Isabel gonna say ta you?' 'We go ta that mill I'll show ya around.' 'What's Isabel gonna say ta that?' 'Stop mentionin her will ya?' 'Why?' 'Just will ya stop mentionin Isabel.'

Shoved by the men the timbers cracked, the braces split where they were pressed and the men yelled and hollered as the wood splashed and echoed in the river. And then the men like goats shoved and laughed at one another.

'Watch 'er,' Simon said, 'Someone'll kill themselves doin that.'
'Sookie—go see what she's doin.'
'You go see.'
'Yer no help ta us anyway—we mays well have someone on er that knows what he's doin.'
'I work as hard as you.'
'Jerkin off.'
'Go ta hell.'
'We shoulda got Orville MacDurmot for this job—he's half there anyways.'
'Go ta hell.'
'He's half there anyways.'

Simon said nothing, and the men laughing challenged one another against the open face of the bridge and the woman sat under the tree, as much to them as the black wood that acted as scarecrows in the fields. The water changed from green to brown when the clouds covered the sun, and a wind came badgering the limbs of pine and maples so that she could smell from the wind the darkening screen of autumn.

She knew the young boy on the bridge, who'd gone down to the stream for water and brought a bucket up to the men, watched her though she kept her eyes closed because of the soreness. The pins on her hat pressed into her scalp and the dress was filled with the smell of leaves.

And then after I went home that night I was scared cause poor Isabel was thinkin it was alright with Bennie, he havin a job buildin the bridge so that they'd get married. I watched her pickin raspberries in the field and I thought 'poor Isabel, poor little Isabel' but didn't care I felt so good. And then I said ta Bennie the next day. 'Ya know I'm older than you by five years.' 'Stop talkin about it,' he said. 'About what?' 'About last night—I don't wanta talk about last night—about—' 'About what Bennie, about what?' 'Nothin,' he said. He walked on the limbed sills that spanned the river. The air was close to us that day and my head was sweatin, and I felt weak as anything in my legs and head. He went down under the bridge and I knew he was drinkin. 'Ya wanta trout,' he said. 'No.' 'I'll getcha a trout,' he said. 'I don't want no friggin trout,' I said. 'What—swearin are ya; what'll yer old man say you swearin?' 'I don't want no friggin trout,' I said again. 'Whatdya mean ya don't wanta talk about last night.' He didn't answer. I said it again and he wouldn't answer. Then he came up from the pool, his eyes glassy from drinkin and on the baited pin the trout was jiggling. 'Here ya go,' he said. 'You leave me alone,' I said and then he patted me. I knew my face was ready for cryin and yet he stood there pattin me all over. I didn't do nothin. 'Here ya go,' he said, 'here ya go,' the trout still jigglin on the baited pin.

The boy came off the last timbers that spanned the river, and as the men stood working with their pevies he walked up the hillside to where she was sitting. They had said to the boy:

'Ya'd better get off now or ya'll get hurt.'

'I won't get hurt anymore than you,' he said.

'What'll yer old man say you gettin killed on the bridge.'

'My old man's got nothin ta do with it,' he said.

'No, then who got ya on the fuckin bridge in the first place, just tell me that?'

Simon said nothing.

'Just tell me that—yer useless as tits on a bull.'

'Go ta hell.'

'Didja ever use yer hands?'

Simon said nothing.

'Jerkin off maybe,' one of them said.

'Shoulda got Orville MacDurmot for this here job.'

'Go ta hell.'

So the boy stood beside the old woman and watched her breathing, her sunken chest heaving in the September air—the air that smelt clean with the bright trout running from the pools, going to the sea.

'Whatcha doin?' he asked suddenly, so that his own voice sounded strange.

'Restin,' she said, and smiled. It was an almost frightened smile. Simon watched her chest and when just a moment ago he'd thought it was heaving now it seemed it wasn't moving at all. When she put her eyes on him he turned and looked toward the bridge. The men stood, silhouetted against the embattled framework, and he could see them taking water from the bucket he'd lugged up the hill, even though the water striders still skimmed the surface of the dark water and clung against the sides of the aluminum bucket.

'What in hell da ya think she's doin?'

'Ol Simon'll find out.'

'Betcha he's already tryin ta rip off a piece.'

'A piece a what is the question.'

'Ha.'

'A piece a what is the question.'

'I wonder where in hell she come from—there a house round here?'

'Not unless ya wanta walk through to the Settlement—four mile.'

'She didn't come no four mile.'

'I didn't say she did ya fucker.'

'She got outta a car awhile ago.'

There were rocks below the bridge that suggested at one time there was a mountain, and they clung in the earth so that even the roots of trees emerged and buckled against them, and the strands of roots almost touched the water where at one time salmon lay submerged at the bottom. Simon turned back to the woman. She had sat up now to face him and was straightening the pins in her hat and smoothing her dress. A wind badgered the limbs of spruce above her.

'Whatcha doin—I mean are ya sick?' he said.

'Oh no,' she said, and smiled, 'I'm just restin—I just live over there—in Deborah's place.'

'Oh,' he said, 'Over where?'

But the woman said nothing more, and again Simon could hear the men laughing and cursing so that it embarrassed him to be standing beside the woman and listening to them, yet his face betrayed nothing. In the back of his mind was acceptance of what they'd said to him, what he imagined they were saying—and he felt that he didn't hate what they said or them for saying it; that it was nothing more than a game. And when he watched them ply the timbers on the bridge, he was ashamed for hating. Actually he was laughing with them, he thought. And now he couldn't imagine that a moment ago when they were shoving and jostling one another, he'd wanted them to fall.

The boy turned and went back down the path, over the slanting flint and shale and onto the framework again. The river was gorged and shallow in the afternoon. The woman watched as the boy moved onto the bridge, amidst the yells and hollering of the others, becoming finally indistinguishable.

Yes, Janie Bell thought, that's where 'e was standin puttin sheetin on. It was what, only about two weeks after their marriage and I come down to him and called him over, the men laughin and goin on. When he came up the path I said: 'I'm pregnant.' He didn't answer and I said it again. I said: 'I'm pregnant ta you.' 'No ya are not,' he said. 'I am.' 'Well, ya can't be.' His voice was weak and scared, and he rubbed the top of his head with his hand. I turned and walked away from him and I could almost hear him shakin. Then I went home and Isabel said: 'When ya gonna find yerself someone Janie—yer gettin on,' she laughed.

When it came time ta tell them—goin on my fourth month I couldn't hide it no longer—everyone one was at me to tell them who done it, so that they'd make him marry'd ta me. The bridge was finished and Bennie was just getting ready ta go into the woods. I didn't say nothin, except stare at him—and he'd never stay in a room with me more than a second.

'I guess Bennie'n I'll bring up the child for ya,' Isabel said one day, 'Unless yer gonna tell us who it was.' 'Yes,' Bennie said looking to my father who was sittin by the wood stove near the box, and wasn't speakin ta me at all saying 'I thought I brought them up better'n that and look what happens.' He was fixin his bucksaw and Mom always saying, 'Can'tcha take that outta the house ta do?' 'Yes,' Bennie said still lookin at Papa, his eyes almost closed: 'Isabel and I decided we'd take the kid off yer hands—I mean a single woman bringin it up and everythin—I don't mind at all; it'll be just like me own. But I wish ya'd tell everybody who did it.' He still didn't look at me but I and no-one else could see his face turnin white. I just shook my head the same as always. Then he said, 'If I ever got holda the bugger who did it I'd break his neck—to an innocent girl.' 'I don't wantcha swearin in this house,' Papa said. 'Well, it makes me so mad,' Bennie said, his voice as loud as anything.

Simon received the first drops of rain with indifference and strode across the braced timbers, except that the men still laughed at his clumsiness. And as soon as they laughed he became aware of himself again, of those watching him. The air had turned thick and muggy, polluted with the scent of drizzle and wood. Below them a crow called and along the riverbank the exposed roots of trees turned grey. There was the hollow thumping of a woodpecker when the men stopped working.

'How'd ya liked ta have taken this road inta town?'

'Take ya a time wouldn't it?'

'The old horse and buggy, Jesus—wouldn't a wanted ta come through in the spring.'

'Ask Simon what she's doin?'

'You.'

'Ask Simon what she's doin?'

'Waitin for us ta hop her.'

'Ha.'

Simon scooped some water from the bucket and putting a sugar cube in his mouth sucked on it as he drank. He wanted the woman to go away, so that he wouldn't *feel* her presence yet he couldn't understand why he felt that. The rain fell on the shallow water below with widening circles, there was no longer any wind and the birds were quiet. The men worked solemnly now, laughter gone the rain pressed them into grey shapes on the slanting structure as the sound of mallets hitting wood reverberated dull and lonely. He picked up his pevie and went to join them jabbing it into the sill before him to keep his balance. When he reached them the youngest one said:

'Here ya want me ta show ya how ta do it?'

'I can do it,' Simon said, 'as well as you.' He rammed his pevie against the rotted sheeting, cracking and splitting the wood yet each time he thrust forward he thought he'd lose his balance and jerked back desperately.

'I'm just tryin ta give ya a hand.'

Simon didn't answer.

'Suit yerself—I'm just tryin ta help ya out—if yer gonna be goddamn pigheaded about it it's yer fault.'

'Ha.'

'Here then,' Simon said, reddening, 'show me how ta do it.'

Simon handed his pevie to the other boy who stood just above him on one of the half-rotted braces, his left boot dangling over the edge. When Simon handed him the pevie he held it for a moment as if inspecting it and then yelling hurled it into the air. 'That's how ya use a pevie.'

'That's how ya use a fuckin pevie—right boys?'

'S'pose.'

'S'pose.'

'Ha.'

It hit the water below them, and was gone.

There were sounds all that night of the wind blowing snow through the cracks in the porch and each little while Papa'd come to the door an say: 'Is he born yet?' 'No,' ol Mrs Dunstan'd say. 'Well, I thought I heard somethin like a baby or something like that,' Papa'd say from behind the door that looked far away and pink though it was always white as long as I could remember. 'No,' she'd say again, everytime and I member me tellin her to stop sayin 'No,' and then Momma tellin Isabel ta leave the room cause she was nothin but a fuss. 'I wanta stay,' Isabel said. 'Go on wait in the kitchen, it'll be your turn someday.' 'I'll make sure the doctor gets here for sure for me,' she said. 'Yes, yes,' Momma said. 'Yes I will,' Isabel said. 'Yer nothin but a fuss,' Momma said. 'Damn,' I said, 'leave me alone everyone a ya—damn.' 'She's swearin,' Isabel said, 'she's swearin.'

Deborah was an ugly baby, I never liked her because of Bennie until I felt somethin for her when they started making her call Isabel Momma, then I got mad, and after Momma died Papa got callin her Isabel's too; there's nothin like takin someone away from ya ta make ya start lovin them. All the men around guessin who it was that made me pregnant, even saying it was Dwight Everett who was bout ten at the time. I know it wasn't ta hurt me, but ta hurt Papa who figured he had it all hid. He'd go out to the shed and saw wood all day alone.

When Simon went off the bridge to look for his pevie the rain was coning so hard he felt that it didn't matter if he waded the river. But he couldn't find it, and now and then the men would shout at him, giving him directions. He paid no attention to them, the one who'd thrown it yelling and shouting louder than the rest, as if he must be heard. Then he thought that it didn't matter if he found it—it wouldn't be his fault if he didn't, and he left the river again.

'I'll just tell Pete is all,' he yelled.

'Ho, ho,' the boy yelled back, 'What're ya still in school squealin to the teacher?'

He didn't answer.

'Still in school squealin to the teacher—yer old man tellin everyone not ta pick on ya.'

'Go to hell.'

He'd not go on the bridge again, he thought, and so he remained below them on the side of the shale banking for a long while staring at the vague cross-sections above him. The men, it seemed, had forgotten him already and rain beat the water in thousands of tiny shots. He shivered, turned and climbed the shale banking where myriads of streams flowed in the reddish clay saturating and being absorbed all at once. He was wet from the waist down with river water and the sweet cold rain that drove against his face and laced his coat with smudges and streaks of red mud.

He reached the top of the bank after a long while, and in the stillness (for a rain like this in the middle of the woods brought a stillness to the ground and trees standing in the ground) his heart thumped so that he could hear it in his ears—a warm wet driving sound, almost he thought, as if something mysterious inside the heart (life itself he thought) was trying to break forward into the trees and mud along the shale banking. What the men had said to him had faded again—all except for their laughter. He tried not to think of one of them falling into the water.

'My it's gettin cold now, ain't it?' the woman said to him.

'Yes,' he said. 'You should go home now.' He looked at the brown laced frills at the neck of her dress and at the coarse wrinkled folds of skin, 'I'll take you home.'

The woman's dress was soaking and beginning to smell. He took off his coat and put it over her, clumsily trying to adjust it, though he felt she didn't really know or care what he did, suddenly looking about him for assistance.

'You know I'm 100 years old right now,' Janie Bell said.

'Oh,' he said.

'The Queen sent me flowers.'

The men had decided to quit for the day. The boy who'd thrown the pevie balanced himself on struts and then came down from the bridge, while the men followed him. And the boy said.

'What in Jesus is she doin over there is what I wanta know.'

'How much she's chargin for it is what I wanta know meself.'

'Maybe she needs some help,' the boy said.

'Ol Simon'll find out; why, you goin over?'

'I think she probably don't even know where she is,' the boy said, his face pensive and streaked with rain.

The men lit cigarettes and said nothing, each of them spitting now and then, and now and then looking toward the old woman and Simon who was standing beside her.

So Bennie come inta me, with Isabel right behind him—and Papa not even cold and Bennie the big man now that Papa's gone all mouth on him says: 'I don't wantcha saying yer her mother, it ain't natural for a little girl like that ta have ta know those things.' 'Know what things?' I said. 'Bennie's right,' Isabel said. 'Know what things Bennie?' I said. He looked away, and walked across the room. I started laughin hysterical and screaming and picked up my commode and threw it against the walls. 'Yer not right in the head,' Isabel said. 'First havin a baby like ya did and then makin life miserable for the people tryin to help ya—yer not right in the head; yer not fit ta live here either, and me and Bennie bearin the brunt of all the talk about ya.' 'What talk eh Bennie—what talk?' I couldn't stop laughing. 'I never thought I'd hate me own sister, flesh and blood—Dad brought us up better'n that there but I hate you,' she said. 'Yes I hate you,' Deborah said, running up to kick me. And then Isabel sat down on the chair and cried. Bennie said nothing else. I just stared and stared. 'And ya ain't coming ta church with us no more either,' Isabel said, cryin and shakin, her nose red. So after that whenever they had someone around, I sat in me room. I wouldn't bother them at all, even at Christmas cept ta take a bit of food at the table. And ya could tell Deborah thought I was crazy livin in the room off of her parents—especially as she got older, so I hated her again. And then I got pains in me head and never felt good and couldn't talk ta no-one. I could hear them in their bedroom at night too, don'tcha think I couldn't.

'Here,' the boy said, 'Ya think she needs my coat too?'

'I don't know,' Simon said.

The boy placed his coat over her also and stood beside Simon, and one by one the men came back to the truck parked in the overgrown road that led to the mill, carrying mallets and axes and pevies.

'How are you?' one of the men said. 'Where do you live?'

She didn't answer.

'I think she's crazier than a loon,' another said.

'Betcha she ain't even there—betcha she's a ghost or something.'

'Ha.'

'Shutup now.'

'Yes, shutup,' Simon said. 'Someone should phone the police.'

'I'll run out and phone the police,' the boy said, 'I think she's dyin or somethin right here.'

'She can't have too much left in 'er—she must be 80 anyways.'

'I ain't standin round here all day so hurry up.'

'Go home if ya want to—I'm not stoppin ya,' the boy said.

'Don't yap at me.'

'Well, go home if ya want to—we don't need a ton a people here.'

'Don't yap at me flap mouth—I ain't Simon.'

Simon said nothing.

'I ain't Simon for fuck's sake,' he said again.

'Everyone just shutup,' another man said.

Isabel couldn't stomach ta nurse Bennie when he was sick—so I did it, not because I wanted to, but because I had to. It was hate, not love or kindness that made me wash and scrub him, and clean the mess from the bed each and every day, with Isabel so much of a fuss she couldn't go inta the room at all. Yet even when I saw that he knew in his eyes he was dyin—would he talk? Would he speak out once and tell them, and let me rest, carrying his bucket a mess out each and every day—with Isabel and Deborah as useless and whiny as could be. And every time I'd clean him and change him about I'd look and see he couldn't say nothin—that he'd lied to himself all his life anyways. Yet I still could member him dancin with his cork boots on.

Keepin a garden till I was 88 each and every season and then my granddaughter—my own granddaughter comin ta tell me they were puttin me over there cause George had a job in Toronto and they couldn't bring me. 'I'll keep me own self,' I said. 'No now you'll be better over there Aunt Janie; it'd be like a new home with new friends.' 'I'll keep me own self,' I said again, gettin scared and lookin about the room, first the latch on the door and then the flowers I had and my commode where I glued it together. I didn't want to go. 'I keep a garden right here now,' I said. 'Aunt Janie,' she said, 'Aunt Janie.' 'I ain't yer aunt,' I said, 'at all.' 'Why, of course you're my aunt,' she said smiling, 'my great aunt,' as if I was again a child or already dead. Already dead when I kept me own garden was more than her mother or her could ever once do. I couldn't say nothing. She smiled at me. I didn't want to go.

The men swung into the box of the truck and it creaked and groaned over the washed-out road the men silent and wet, the air above them filled with the smoke of cigarettes.

'Where'd they say she's from?'

'The old folks home across the river.'

'I knew she was some sorta old just lookin at her—what was she doin over here anyway?'

'How the hell should I know?'

'Crazy old fucker probably lookin for us ta hop on her.'

'Filthy mind, eh Simon?'

Simon said nothing.

'Boy, what a filthy mind eh Simon?'

'I betcha Simon was on and off her.'

'Ha.'

'So that's whatcha were doin.'

'Go ta hell,' Simon said.

'Ha.'

'Just go to hell.'

The man walked along the wet and littered streets just before dark, in the quiet alleys rain still dripped across the tin barrels making an inconsistent drumming sound. Now and then there were the shouts and cries of children playing, the almost squalid noise of a dog barking. He crossed to the smaller street and went into the tavern where he ordered a beer and sat at an end table.

'I hear ya lost one,' the waiter said.

'We found her again,' he said. 'She probably won't make 'er though.'

'How's that?'

'Cause there's a bunch a morons around who let her get unconscious—at her age an everything.'

'Oh,' the waiter said smiling, 'You should get married anyway, and stop worrying about the old ones.'

'Shit,' he said. He stood up and left the tavern, went onto the street again. Across the water the ferry sounded in the darkness. 'I wish everyone'd just mind their own business about me getting married,' he thought. 'It's my own business if I'm gonna get married.'

(1978)

Louise Erdrich   b. 1954

The Red Convertible

Lyman Lamartine

I was the first one to drive a convertible on my reservation. And of course it was red, a red Olds. I owned that car along with my brother Henry Junior. We owned it together until his boots filled with water on a windy night and he bought out my share. Now Henry owns the whole car, and his youngest brother Lyman (that's myself), Lyman walks everywhere he goes.

How did I earn enough money to buy my share in the first place? My own talent was I could always make money. I had a touch for it, unusual in a Chippewa. From the first I was different that way, and everyone recognized it. I was the only kid they let in the American Legion Hall to shine shoes, for example, and one Christmas I sold spiritual bouquets for the mission door to door. The nuns let me keep a percentage. Once I started, it seemed the more money I made the easier the money came. Everyone encouraged it. When I was fifteen I got a job washing dishes at the Joliet Cafe, and that was where my first big break happened.

It wasn't long before I was promoted to busing tables, and then the short-order cook quit and I was hired to take her place. No sooner than you know it I was managing the Joliet. The rest is history. I went on managing. I soon became part owner, and of course there was no stopping me then. It wasn't long before the whole thing was mine.

After I'd owned the Joliet for one year, it blew over in the worst tornado ever seen around here. The whole operation was smashed to bits. A total loss. The fryalator was up in a tree, the grill torn in half like it was paper. I was only sixteen. I had it all in my mother's name, and I lost it quick, but before I lost it I had every one of my relatives, and their relatives, to dinner, and I also bought that red Olds I mentioned, along with Henry.

The first time we saw it! I'll tell you when we first saw it. We had gotten a ride to Winnipeg, and both of us had money. Don't ask me why, because we never mentioned a car or anything, we just had all our money. Mine was cash, a big bankroll from the Joliet's insurance. Henry had two checks—a week's extra pay for being laid off, and his regular check from the Jewel Bearing Plant.

We were walking down Portage anyway, seeing the sights, when we saw it. There it was, parked, large as life. Really as *if* it was alive. I thought of the word *repose*, because the car wasn't simply stopped, parked, or whatever. That car reposed, calm and gleaming, a FOR SALE sign in its left front window. Then, before we had thought it over at all, the car belonged to us and our pockets were empty. We had just enough money for gas back home.

We went places in that car, me and Henry. We took off driving all one whole summer. We started off toward the Little Knife River and Mandaree in Fort Berthold and then we found ourselves down in Wakpala somehow, and then suddenly we were over in Montana on the Rocky Boy, and yet the summer was not even half over. Some people hang on to details when they travel, but we didn't let them bother us and just lived our everyday lives here to there.

I do remember this place with willows. I remember I laid under those trees and it was comfortable. So comfortable. The branches bent down all around me like a tent or a stable. And quiet, it was quiet, even though there was a powwow close enough so I could see it going on. The air was not too still, not too windy either. When the dust rises up and hangs in the air around dancers like that, I feel good. Henry was asleep with his arms thrown wide. Later on, he woke up and we started driving again. We were somewhere in Montana, or maybe on the Blood Reserve—it could have been anywhere. Anyway it was where we met the girl.

All her hair was in buns around her ears, that's the first thing I noticed about her. She was posed alongside the road with her arm out, so we stopped. That girl was short, so short her lumber shirt looked comical on her, like a nightgown. She had jeans on and fancy moccasins and she carried a little suitcase.

"Hop on in," says Henry. So she climbs in between us.
"We'll take you home," I says. "Where do you live?"
"Chicken," she says.
"Where the hell's that?" I ask her.
"Alaska."
"Okay," says Henry, and we drive.

We got up there and never wanted to leave. The sun doesn't truly set there in summer, and the night is more a soft dusk. You might doze off, sometimes, but before you know it you're up again, like an animal in nature. You never feel like you have to sleep hard or put away the world. And things would grow up there. One day just dirt or moss, the next day flowers and long grass. The girl's name was Susy. Her family really took to us. They fed us and put us up. We had our own tent to live in by their house, and the kids would be in and out of there all day and night. They couldn't get over me and Henry being brothers, we looked so different. We told them we knew we had the same mother, anyway.

One night Susy came in to visit us. We sat around in the tent talking of this and that. The season was changing. It was getting darker by that time, and the cold was even getting just a little mean. I told her it was time for us to go. She stood up on a chair.

"You never seen my hair," Susy said.

That was true. She was standing on a chair, but still, when she unclipped her buns the hair reached all the way to the ground. Our eyes opened. You couldn't tell how much hair she had when it was rolled up so neatly. Then my brother Henry did something funny. He went up to the chair and said, "Jump on my shoulders." So she did that, and her hair reached down past his waist, and he started twirling, this way and that, so her hair was flung out from side to side.

"I always wondered what it was like to have long pretty hair," Henry says. Well, we laughed. It was a funny sight, the way he did it. The next morning we got up and took leave of those people.

On to greener pastures, as they say. It was down through Spokane and across Idaho then Montana and very soon we were racing the weather right along under the Canadian border through Columbus, Des Lacs, and then were in Bottineau County and soon home. We'd made most of the trip, that summer, without putting up the car hood at all. We got home just in time.

I don't wonder that the army was so glad to get my brother that they turned him into a Marine. He was built like a brick outhouse anyway. We liked to tease him that they really wanted him for his Indian nose. He had a nose big and sharp as a hatchet, like the nose on Red Tomahawk, the Indian who killed

Sitting Bull, whose profile is on signs all along the North Dakota highways. Henry went off to training camp, came home once during Christmas, then the next thing you know we got an overseas letter from him. It was 1970, and he said he was stationed up in the northern hill country. Whereabouts I did not know. He wasn't such a hot letter writer, and only got off two before the enemy caught him. I could never keep it straight, which direction those good Vietnam soldiers were from.

I wrote him back several times, even though I didn't know if those letters would get through. I kept him informed all about the car. Most of the time I had it up on blocks in the yard or half taken apart, because that long trip did a hard job on it under the hood.

I always had good luck with numbers, and never worried about the draft myself. I never even had to think about what my number was. But Henry was never lucky in the same way as me. It was at least three years before Henry came home. By then I guess the whole war was solved in the government's mind, but for him it would keep on going. In those years I'd put his car into almost perfect shape. I always thought of it as his car while he was gone, even though when he left he said, "Now it's yours," and threw me his key.

"Thanks for the extra key," I'd said. "I'll put it in your drawer just in case I need it." He laughed.

When he came home, though, Henry was very different, and I'll say this: the change was no good. You could hardly expect him to change for the better, I know. But he was quiet, so quiet, and never comfortable sitting still anywhere but always up and moving around. I thought back to times we'd sat still for whole afternoons, never moving a muscle, just shifting our weight along the ground, talking to whoever sat with us, watching things. He'd always had a joke, then, too, and now you couldn't get him to laugh, or when he did it was more the sound of a man choking, a sound that stopped up the throats of other people around him. They got to leaving him alone most of the time, and I didn't blame them. It was a fact: Henry was jumpy and mean.

I'd bought a color TV set for my mom and the rest of us while Henry was away. Money still came very easy. I was sorry I'd ever bought it though, because of Henry. I was also sorry I'd bought color, because with black-and-white the pictures seem older and farther away. But what are you going to do? He sat in front of it, watching it, and that was the only time he was completely still. But it was the kind of stillness that you see in a rabbit when it freezes and before it will bolt. He was not easy. He sat in his chair gripping the armrests with all his might, as if the chair itself was moving at a high speed and if he let go at all he would rocket forward and maybe crash right through the set.

Once I was in the room watching TV with Henry and I heard his teeth click at something. I looked over, and he'd bitten through his lip. Blood was going down his chin. I tell you right then I wanted to smash that tube to pieces. I went over to it but Henry must have known what I was up to. He rushed from his chair and shoved me out of the way, against the wall. I told myself he didn't know what he was doing.

My mom came in, turned the set off real quiet, and told us she had made something for supper. So we went and sat down. There was still blood going down Henry's chin, but he didn't notice it and no one said anything, even though every time he took a bite of his bread his blood fell onto it until he was eating his own blood mixed in with the food.

While Henry was not around we talked about what was going to happen to him. There were no Indian doctors on the reservation, and my mom couldn't come around to trusting the old man, Moses Pillager, because he courted her long ago and was jealous of her husbands. He might take revenge through her son. We were afraid that if we brought Henry to a regular hospital they would keep him.

"They don't fix them in those places," Mom said; "they just give them drugs."

"We wouldn't get him there in the first place," I agreed, "so let's just forget about it."

Then I thought about the car.

Henry had not even looked at the car since he'd gotten home, though like I said, it was in tip-top condition and ready to drive. I thought the car might bring the old Henry back somehow. So I bided my time and waited for my chance to interest him in the vehicle.

One night Henry was off somewhere. I took myself a hammer. I went out to that car and I did a number on its underside. Whacked it up. Bent the tail pipe double. Ripped the muffler loose. By the time I was done with the car it looked worse than any typical Indian car that has been driven all its life on reservation roads, which they always say are like government promises—full of holes. It just about hurt me, I'll tell you that! I threw dirt in the carburetor and I ripped all the electric tape off the seats. I made it look just as beat up as I could. Then I sat back and waited for Henry to find it.

Still, it took him over a month. That was all right, because it was just getting warm enough, not melting, but warm enough to work outside.

"Lyman," he says, walking in one day, "that red car looks like shit."

"Well, it's old," I says. "You got to expect that."

"No way!" says Henry. "That car's a classic! But you went and ran the piss right out of it, Lyman, and you know it don't deserve that. I kept that car in A-one shape. You don't remember. You're too young. But when I left, that car was running like a watch. Now I don't even know if I can get it to start again, let alone get it anywhere near its old condition."

"Well you try," I said, like I was getting mad, "but I say it's a piece of junk."

Then I walked out before he could realize I knew he'd strung together more than six words at once.

After that I thought he'd freeze himself to death working on that car. He was out there all day, and at night he rigged up a little lamp, ran a cord out the window, and had himself some light to see by while he worked. He was better than he had been before, but that's still not saying much. It was easier for him to do the things the rest of us did. He ate more slowly and didn't jump up and down during the meal to get this or that or look out the window. I put my hand in the back of the TV set, I admit, and fiddled around with it good, so that it was almost impossible now to get a clear picture. He didn't look at it very often anyway. He was always out with that car or going off to get parts for it. By the time it was really melting outside, he had it fixed.

I had been feeling down in the dumps about Henry around this time. We had always been together before. Henry and Lyman. But he was such a loner now that I didn't know how to take it. So I jumped at the chance one day when Henry seemed friendly. It's not that he smiled or anything. He just said, "Let's take that old shitbox for a spin." Just the way he said it made me think he could be coming around.

We went out to the car. It was spring. The sun was shining very bright. My only sister, Bonita, who was just eleven years old, came out and made us stand together for a picture. Henry leaned his elbow on the red car's windshield, and he took his other arm and put it over my shoulder, very carefully, as though it was heavy for him to lift and he didn't want to bring the weight down all at once.

"Smile," Bonita said, and he did.

That picture. I never look at it anymore. A few months ago, I don't know why, I got his picture out and tacked it on the wall. I felt good about Henry at the time, close to him. I felt good having his picture on the wall, until one night when I was looking at television. I was a little drunk and stoned. I looked up at the wall and Henry was staring at me. I don't know what it was, but his smile had changed, or maybe it was gone. All I know is I couldn't stay in the same room with that picture. I was shaking. I got up, closed the door, and went into the kitchen. A little later my friend Ray came over and we both went back into that room. We put the picture in a brown bag, folded the bag over and over tightly, then put it way back in a closet.

I still see that picture now, as if it tugs at me, whenever I pass that closet door. The picture is very clear in my mind. It was so sunny that day Henry had to squint against the glare. Or maybe the camera Bonita held flashed like a mirror, blinding him, before she snapped the picture. My face is right out in the sun, big and round. But he might have drawn back, because the shadows on his face are deep as holes. There are two shadows curved like little hooks around the ends of his smile, as if to frame it and try to keep it there—that one, first smile that looked like it might have hurt his face. He has his field jacket on and the worn-in clothes he'd come back in and kept wearing ever since. After Bonita took the picture, she went into the house and we got into the car. There was a full cooler in the trunk. We started off, east, toward Pembina and the Red River because Henry said he wanted to see the high water.

The trip over there was beautiful. When everything starts changing, drying up, clearing off, you feel like your whole life is starting. Henry felt it, too. The top was down and the car hummed like a top. He'd really put it back in shape, even the tape on the seats was very carefully put down and glued back in layers. It's not that he smiled again or even joked, but his face looked to me as if it was clear, more peaceful. It looked as though he wasn't thinking of anything in particular except the bare fields and windbreaks and houses we were passing.

The river was high and full of winter trash when we got there. The sun was still out, but it was colder by the river. There were still little clumps of dirty snow here and there on the banks. The water hadn't gone over the banks yet, but it would, you could tell. It was just at its limit, hard swollen, glossy like an old gray scar. We made ourselves a fire, and we sat down and watched the current go. As I watched it I felt something squeezing inside me and tightening and trying to let go all at the same time. I knew I was not just feeling it myself; I knew I was feeling what Henry was going through at that moment. Except that I couldn't stand it, the closing and opening. I jumped to my feet. I took Henry by the shoulders and I started shaking him. "Wake up," I says, "wake up, wake up, wake up!" I didn't know what had come over me. I sat down beside him again.

His face was totally white and hard. Then it broke, like stones break all of a sudden when water boils up inside them.

"I know it," he says. "I know it. I can't help it. It's no use."

We start talking. He said he knew what I'd done with the car. It was obvious it had been whacked out of shape and not just neglected. He said he wanted to give the car to me for good now, it was no use. He said he'd fixed it just to give it back and I should take it.

"No way," I says. "I don't want it."

"That's okay," he says, "you take it."

"I don't want it, though," I says back to him, and then to emphasize, just to emphasize, you understand, I touch his shoulder. He slaps my hand off.

"Take that car," he says.

"No," I say. "Make me," I say, and then he grabs my jacket and rips the arm loose. That jacket is a class act, suede with tags and zippers. I push Henry backwards, off the log. He jumps up and bowls me over. We go down in a clinch and come up swinging hard, for all we're worth, with our fists. He socks my jaw so hard I feel like it swings loose. Then I'm at his rib cage and land a good one under his chin so his head snaps back. He's dazzled. He looks at me and I look at him and then his eyes are full of tears and blood and at first I think he's crying. But no, he's laughing. "Ha, ha!" he says. "Ha! Ha! Take good care of it."

"Okay," I says. "Okay, no problem. Ha! Ha!"

I can't help it, and I start laughing, too. My face feels fat and strange, and after a while I get a beer from the cooler in the trunk, and when I hand it to Henry he takes his shirt and wipes my germs off. "Hoof-and-mouth disease," he says. For some reason this cracks me up, and so we're really laughing for a while, and then we drink all the rest of the beers one by one and throw them in the river and see how far, how fast, the current takes them before they fill up and sink.

"You want to go on back?" I ask after a while. "Maybe we could snag a couple nice Kashpaw girls."

He says nothing. But I can tell his mood is turning again.

"They're all crazy, the girls up here, every damn one of them."

"You're crazy too," I say, to jolly him up. "Crazy Lamartine boys!"

He looks as though he will take this wrong at first. His face twists, then clears, and he jumps up on his feet. "That's right!" he says. "Crazier 'n hell. Crazy Indians!"

I think it's the old Henry again. He throws off his jacket and starts springing his legs up from the knees like a fancy dancer. He's down doing something between a grass dance and a bunny hop, no kind of dance I ever saw before, but neither has anyone else on all this green growing earth. He's wild. He wants to pitch whoopee! He's up and at me and all over. All this time I'm laughing so hard, so hard my belly is getting tied up in a knot.

"Got to cool me off!" he shouts all of a sudden. Then he runs over to the river and jumps in.

There's boards and other things in the current. It's so high. No sound comes from the river after the splash he makes, so I run right over. I look around. It's getting dark. I see he's halfway across the water already, and I know he didn't swim there but the current took him. It's far. I hear his voice, though, very clearly across it.

"My boots are filling," he says.

He says this in a normal voice, like he just noticed and he doesn't know what to think of it. Then he's gone. A branch comes by. Another branch. And I go in.

By the time I get out of the river, off the snag I pulled myself onto, the sun is down. I walk back to the car, turn on the high beams, and drive it up the bank. I put it in first gear and then I take my foot off the clutch. I get out, close the door, and watch it plough softly into the water. The headlights reach in as they go down, searching, still lighted even after the water swirls over the back end. I wait. The wires short out. It is all finally dark. And then there is only the water, the sound of it going and running and going and running and running.

(1984)

Russell Smith   b. 1963

Serotonin

The first guy up was a local guy, so Jason and Doke and Rajiv hung back, near the door, where the murky space with the sofas merged into the hard floor near the speakers. They were waiting for the Detroit guy to come on, and that would probably be in an hour, at about one, maybe two. They all lit cigarettes and nodded their heads, listening, but not dancing. Emily and Sherry were already dancing, at the back of the dance floor where it wasn't too crowded, just about ten, fifteen feet away. The boys watched them with their eyes narrowed, watched their bare shoulders and backs in their tie-tops, watched their little sneakers flash, picking up the black light. They watched how other guys turned their heads as they walked past them, how close they came to them. They knew that Sherry and Emily knew they were watching them. Sherry liked to wave her hands all over like a windmill. Emily liked to swivel her hips. Jason felt clean and cool and alert. He didn't feel like drinking. He felt healthy. He didn't feel like dancing yet. He said, "Who is this guy?"

Doke shook his head. He sucked on a beer. He had a plastic bracelet because he had ID and could go into the licensed area. He wasn't supposed to have his beer in here. The bracelet glowed green in the air. It made him look as if he had just come out of hospital.

"Guy called Hardflow," said Rajiv. "He's from here."

"He's not bad," said Jason. "Stompy."

Rajiv shrugged. "Not bad. Clean. Clean and stompy. It's not too cheesy."

"You wait though," said Doke. He tottered a little, taller than either of them. His eyes seemed a little too wide already. "This is nothing. This is cheesy in comparison to Helmet."

"I know," said Jason. "I know. I've seen Helmet before. He's the best. But I don't mind this guy. It's housey, but it's a clean house. No breakbeats, no cheesy samples."

"It's a bleepy house," said Rajiv.

"This is nothing," said Doke. "This is fucking nothing. This is cheeseball house stuff. Helmet is going to blow this guy away."

"Okay, dude. I know he is. I was just saying this guy—"

"He's right though, man," said Rajiv. "It's going to be awesome. It's going to be fucking awesome."

"I know. I know it is. All I was saying—"

"You get ready," said Doke, poking Jason in the chest with a long finger. "You get ready for something hard. Fucking hard."

"Okay." Jason blew out his cheeks. "Awesome." He kept his eye on Emily. She had her hair in two short pigtails and they were whipping around. Her shoulders were bare except for two tiny straps, and her skin seemed to be glowing.

Sherry's hips were wide and her long skirt was too tight. It had been too tight for several months now but still she wore it. You could see lines under it.

Jason's throat tensed a little as he looked at the two of them and he felt something painful and hot shoot though him, just looking at Emily's arms and little shoulders. And then he felt a little guilty about that and a little sorry for Sherry, who was already dancing even though she hadn't really wanted to come, and he tried to catch her eye and smile at her but she was too far away. "Love you," he said to no one, and then quickly glanced over to Doke and Rajiv to see if they had heard. Doke was staring straight ahead, not even nodding.

He still wasn't ready to go over there. He would talk to her when she came back for a rest.

He looked at her and smiled and then said, to no one, "Okay. This is chemicals. This is just serotonin."

On the long subway ride downtown Sherry was quiet. Jason said, "Well, he has the tickets."

"What?"

"Doke has the tickets. So we have to go there anyway."

"He could meet us there.'

Jason bit on his lip. He said, "Well, if you want to go without doing anything first."

"He could bring it. We could meet him there."

"They'll search us going in. You know that."

"Oh come on." She said this without energy, as if already tired. It was only ten. "We've done it a million times. They don't look in bras."

Jason sighed. "I don't know why you hate Doke so much."

"I don't hate him.'

"Well what's the big deal?"

"I don't get you. You hate that place too. It weirds you out. I don't know why you keep going back there."

"He has good music."

"Good music." She squished her lips together and looked out the black window.

"Don't come if you don't want to."

The train rattled. Black women with shopping bags and Indian men with moustaches were looking at them with their eyes narrowed and the corners of their mouths turned down, their skin bleached green by the lights.

"Hey pal," said Jason to a shopkeeper in a suit jacket and V-neck sweater. "You want to search my bag or what?"

The man turned away. Everyone turned away.

"Shut up," said Sherry.

The doors opened with a hiss and slammed shut. There was an echo of the slamming all the way down the train, as if someone had tweaked the reverb.

"I won't come if you don't want me to," she said.

Jason looked at her hand lying small and puffy on her cargo skirt and knew this would be the right moment to pick it up and stroke it and everything would be okay. He wished he could. Instead he said, "We're fucking fifteen stops from home now. You would have to wake your dad up anyway."

"That's my problem." Her voice wavered. She was staring doggedly out the window.

Jason clenched his jaw, briefly. Then he took her hand. "We'll just drop in and do the stuff and leave. I want to be there early anyway."

She let him squeeze her hand. She leaned her head on his shoulder. "You know, if you think I'd like you more if you were more like Doke, you're wrong. I'm not impressed he has his own apartment or has his own decks or anything. I don't think he's any cooler than you are." She paused for a second and said, "I don't get at all why Emily is with him. It doesn't make sense to me. He doesn't deserve her."

Jason said nothing. He watched the lamps in the tunnel flicker past like strobes.

Helmet came on at two. He was a little bald-headed guy, barely visible over the mixing board. There was a roar from the crowd and a lot of hands in the air and the lights went down low when he came up. He didn't look at the crowd, didn't look up at all, just put his head down and started the beat up.

Jason was standing as close as he could to the front, in the hot mass. He had been dancing for about an hour and a half and was finally feeling it. He found himself in a group of Vietnamese guys with their shirts off, all serious, their heads down, kicking at the floor, panting. Their chests were shiny. They all had dragons on one shoulder. Jason worked his way in among them, his head nodding hard. He was at the point where he couldn't control it. He looked up at the DJ platform, where the little bald-headed guy was working, his head bobbing, in a red glow. He was building the beat up faster, layering in a lot of crystalline smashes like glass needles.

Jason remembers thinking, this is getting fucking intense.

In Doke's apartment there was a collapsed sofa and a beanbag chair, where Emily lay coiled. Jason and Sherry sat in the sloping middle of the sofa. The overhead light was too bright. There was a Confederate flag covering the one small window. Doke walked in and out of the kitchenette with no shirt on. He liked to do this to show off the tattoos on his shoulders, the furious scar on his back. He seemed to be looking for something. His roommate Head was kneeling in a pile of vinyl discs and sleeves. The two decks were set up on milk crates between the speakers. There was only one disc spinning, some angry hip hop that was already slicing at Jason's ears. Jason had been picking up records at random and looking at them but he had felt Head's eyes on him every time, waiting for him to put each record down as soon as he picked it up, so he had given up and gone over beside Sherry and sat down.

There were limp clothes on the arms and back of the sofa. There was an empty pizza box on the broken coffee table. Jason glimpsed a popper cartridge peeking out from under the sofa.

Emily was trying to talk to Sherry. "I like your skirt." She leaned over to stroke it. Jason watched her thin fingers. She wore a plastic daisy ring.

"Thanks."

"Where you get it?"

Sherry shrugged. "Don't know."

"It's nice. You're looking really good."

Sherry smoothed the bulky skirt over her thick thighs as if to flatten them out, smush them into the sofa.

"So how's your mom doing?"

"Okay," said Sherry.

"She's living downtown?"

"Yup."

"That's good." Emily smiled at her and her face glowed. Emily was wearing a head scarf over her pigtails and looked like a little girl. She had her legs drawn up on the beanbag chair, and as she leaned forward to hug them her little collarbones moved forward, the little points at the tops of her shoulders gliding under the thin straps of her top. She said, "Do you ever think of moving in with your mom? So that you could live downtown?"

Sherry sighed. "I've thought about it." She seemed about to say something else but stopped.

Jason looked across at her with his eyes wide enough to say *she's trying to be nice*, but Sherry wouldn't look at him. He inched away from her on the sofa. He didn't know why she had come. He didn't know why she had to blame Emily just because she didn't like Doke. Besides, even Doke wasn't so bad.

Doke came in with a foaming beer. He looked at Head and nodded his head to the music. "If you *really* want to rock the funky beat," he shouted, firing a finger in the air like a gun, "some*body* in the house say *yeah*."

"Do we get beers?" said Emily.

"I asked you ten minutes ago if you wanted a beer."

"Well that's very hospitable." Emily stood up and stretched like a rubber band. Jason eyed the hard little bumps in her top and looked away.

"I *am* what I *am*," chanted Doke, pointing at Emily. "If I *waddnt*, why would I *say* I am? Chill out, my bitch."

Emily was not smiling as she slid into the kitchenette to get beers. Jason felt a sudden fury at her for being with Doke, at Doke for not realizing what he had, and at Sherry. He didn't know why he was mad at Sherry, but he was. He closed his eyes and breathed deeply. "It's time to take some drugs, I think," he said.

"Jason," said Emily, reappearing with three beers, "do you remember those yellow butterflies you had last winter at the Turbo 2000 thing? You gave me one? I kept it all this time and I just took it last week, just one night at Nasa. And may I just say oh my fucking god?" She sank into her bag of beans. "I think they were the strongest I'd ever had. And there was this reporter guy there with us—do you remember this, Dokey, that older guy who came with Jeffie who took one and—" Emily began to giggle, wiping beer from her mouth. "And this guy, this guy thought he was so cool, his first time high, and he goes into the washroom and some guy asks him are you spinning?" Emily laughed high and clear.

"Oh yeah," said Jason, "and he thinks he means—"

"And he's like, oh yeah man, I'm spinning, and the guy goes, what are you spinning?"

"What are you spinning? And he's like what?" Jason laughed. He was aware that Sherry was not laughing and hated her for it. He turned to her. "And he realizes the guy thinks he's deejaying and he's like, oh, excuse me, gotta go."

Sherry said, "Why don't we go?"

"That was hilarious."

"What are we waiting for?"

Jason took her hand. "Doke, man," he called. "Where's Rajiv and Priti?"

Doke yelled from another room, "Meeting us here."

"I know, but where are they."

Doke yelled, "Play that fucking Snakemen track."

Head stood behind the decks and started mixing in some jungle with a screaming MC. He wasn't going with them; he was going to stay in all night in this bright box, mixing, alone.

Jason was trying not to look at Emily, who was hugging her knees with her skinny arms and was stroking her forearms with her fingertips. He watched Head instead. Head was a little guy, and was already losing his hair. He had a dark beard that he could never shave enough. He was like a little ball of testosterone, which was funny because he was so small. He was a little penis-man. Cock Man. Jason made a hiccuping sound to stop from laughing. Head frowned as he stroked the knobs on the mixer.

Doke came in with a black T-shirt on with the Moonshine logo on it. He had got it free at the Buffalo Dance Earth Project Festival and now he wore it every time he went out. He kneeled by the coffee table and took out three clear plastic packets. He poured four pink pills on the table and pushed one toward Emily, one toward Sherry, one toward Jason. Jason looked closely at the pink disc stamped with the three flattened diamonds that they called Mitsubishi, and his stomach fluttered a little, as it always did. He wasn't sure why they called that symbol Mitsubishi, but everyone did. He leaned forward, his elbows on his knees, eager to swallow. The beat that Head was spinning was tough and earthy in him. He had the two rolled twenties ready in his back pocket and handed the wad over to Doke, who took it without comment.

Doke said, "This is supposed to be really fucking good."

"You did it."

"Head did."

Head did not look up from the decks.

"He said it was fucking plutonium." Doke was bouncing other pills on the shiny surface of the coffee table. He made a little pile of three pills in front of him. The round pink Mitsubishi, an oblong white caplet, and a triangular green thing. He made a little mountain of them in front of him and looked up and grinned. Jason glanced at Emily, who raised her eyebrows and said nothing.

They downed their pills with their beers. Sherry took hers too, without saying anything. When Jason looked back at the table all Doke's pills were gone.

"Let's do this," said Doke, standing, suddenly massive in the tiny room.

The Vietnamese guys were spinning their feet around him like street sweepers. Heads down, fists clenched, punching the air in front of them. Helmet had his head angled to his shoulder, pinning one side of his headphones like a telephone receiver, and had one hand down on one deck, scratching. If Jason stood to one side he could see in a gap between two speaker columns the guy's other hand on the mixer, flipping rhythmically between decks, alternating between a scratch beat he was making with one record and the spinning beat on the other deck. "Yeah," yelled Jason. He punched his fists into the air and beat the space in front of him. "Whoa." The Tiger Balm that Emily had slathered on his neck stung sweetly; it burned his upper lip. He felt the air rushing smooth and cool into his nostrils, his open lungs. His body felt as open and light as the outdoors. He didn't know where Sherry was.

Two girls had climbed onto the DJ platform and were facing the crowd, their hands high, waving glow-sticks. They had big smiles, their eyes closed. This DJ was cool: not too much sound, not too many tunes, just this nice clean beat, a thumping that was deep, pure, cold. It was like something that drove pistons, a propulsion.

The girls held both hands high, painting traces of pink and green in the air, and swung their hips in circles. Jason watched their bare underarms, their little breasts jiggling under spandex, their navel rings. Their shoulders shone. He could see one girl's nipples clearly. His eyes stuck to them as if they were darting cursors.

Helmet cut out the kick drum all of a sudden and the lights went down low. There was just the ringing smash and rattle of the snare and high-hat patterns, and the crowd subsided into nodding, waiting for the kick drum to come back. He brought in a siren from underneath, low and rising, and Jason felt excited, waiting for it to come up high. There was no light but a big police car thing, flashing up by the DJ platform, sweeping red beams in arcs. It was low and in everyone's eyes; when it hit you it blinded you with red, and then passed on, sweeping like radar. The siren began its climb into hysteria, and the sea of shoulders began to vibrate again, willing it upwards and wanting the booming back, the big driving bass and the thump. Jason felt his shoulders begin to jump up and down; the approaching climax was bringing him up onto his toes. He began to yell. "Come on," he yelled. "Whooo."

But the bald guy played with them, waiting. He kept it spare. The police light flashed faster and wilder, and then the smoke machines hissed. The sweet smell filled the floor. The smoke rose around his knees. Jason waved his hands in it. He wanted the strobe light back, too. There was a guy all in black next to him with both hands outstretched, palms lifting the air in front of him. The guy was frowning, trying to get the beat back up, pushing it upwards. The siren came back suddenly, and a throbbing with it, rising. Jason knew this would be it, it was going to go off. The siren rose, rose, piercing, and the drum roll began, faster and faster, and at the top the big beat was going to come back in, the pounding, and everyone knew it and began to yell.

When the deep big pounding kicked in, there was a communal whoop like release, and a blanket of hands in the air, punching. The bass boomed, the kick drum pounded, the siren wailed, the drums rattled like a train, like a helicopter taking off. The strobe flicked on and Jason was spinning and soaring. He snapped his body about like a snipped wire, whipping and spitting sparks. "Oh yes," he said, dancing. "Oh yes." He felt the beat in his veins like light. There were needles in his ears. His rib cage vibrated, the air sucked in and out.

It may have lasted a few minutes or half an hour. He just all of a sudden realized his jaw was sore from clenching and he wondered if Doke had any gum. He felt outside the beat again, as if it had dropped him. He stopped dancing and watched the sweaty shoulders. He remembered Sherry, and the wisp of a thought came to him, as if from a great distance, that she would be mad at him for not checking on her, and that he should do that now, but then it vanished again. He was not going to feel guilty about anything just then. He thought of getting his water bottle refilled. He started pushing through to the washroom.

He saw Doke standing by himself in a corner. He wasn't dancing, but he was waving his hands in patterns in front of his face and his lips were moving. His eyes were moving too, following his hands as if they were something complicated. Jason slid through arms and shoulders to get to him. "Hey," he shouted in his ear. "I was rushing." He had to angle his head up because Doke was so tall. Doke didn't say anything.

"Hey dude," yelled Jason. "How's it going?" He laid a hand on Doke's shoulder.

Doke nodded quickly, his eyes darting sideways and away.

"You seen Sherry?"

Doke's mouth was open.

"You okay?" Jason tried massaging his shoulder a little.

Doke didn't seem to notice. He jerked his head in the rapid nod again, sending a tiny fleck of foam into the air from his lips.

"Okay man," said Jason. He slapped him on the back again and looked around for Emily. The lights went through another dark phase and the smoke was hissing out all over again. Everyone looked the same. There was more space between bodies here at the back. Jason wove sideways through them, looking for Emily's big grey skirt and her tennis hat. He grabbed a girl's bare arm as she twisted by him and she turned and looked at him with no reaction at all, no surprise, just dull bare eyes. "Sorry," said Jason, "Look like someone else." She blinked and moved away into the smoke.

Emily was about halfway toward the front, in a sound of shotguns. They were caught in the crossfire between two banks of speakers. Jason felt the hair trembling on his neck and arms as the treble snaps caught him. He grabbed Emily's arm. "Hey," he yelled. She turned to face him with a wet smile, full of love, her eyes all black and wide, and wrapped her bare arms around his neck. He hugged her for a second, feeling the bare skin of her back amazingly smooth under his fingertips. Her neck was wet against him. "How are you?" he yelled.

She said nothing, holding him tighter.

For a second he thought that that was the moment to tell her what he felt about her, to say something that would take them outside the moment and stay with her the next day, something that would tell her how he wanted to peel the straps off her shoulders and kiss her shallow breasts with their upturned nipples, something that would make her eyes open wider and begin or end something, probably end it, have it all out in the open and end it, and even then he knew he shouldn't, that he had to clamp his jaw down hard and hold the heat in, because it was just a chemical in his brain that he could ride but shouldn't trust, and that's what it was in her brain, too, just serotonin, and it was going to fade. He had to let it burn away.

"Listen," he shouted, "Doke is a little sketchy."

She pulled back. "Where?"

Jason gestured. He took Emily's hand and led her to her boyfriend.

Doke was still stuck to the same spot, sweat running down his forehead, flapping his arms as if drawing on a big blackboard. "Oh, fuck," said Emily. "It's that crystal. Fucking crystal." She reached up to his face and took it in both hands and made him look at her, and when he did he focused.

"Hey baby," she said. "Are you sketching?"

"I'm fine," he said. "I'm great."

"Come on back to the quiet room with us," she shouted in his ear.

He shook his head. His knees were flexing, jerking.

"Let's just stay here awhile then," said Jason to Emily. He didn't want Doke to punch anyone. Emily could keep him calm.

She nodded. She stood beside Doke and took his hand. He kept nodding his head. She just stood there beside him, dancing a little, holding his hand. Jason stood behind him and started massaging his shoulders. He smiled at Emily, who smiled back. He felt nothing but an ache of love for Emily, a painful love like the first time you feel it in childhood. She was so small and smooth. But he loved Doke too, and didn't want him to sketch out any more and get kicked out again. He leaned toward Emily's ear. "Let's just keep him away from the crowd up front," he said. He was thinking of the knot of Vietnamese guys, the dragon tattoos.

She nodded, pulling Doke backwards slightly.

The DJ was being nasty now. He had stopped with the respites: there were no down moments now, the kick drum was hysterical. He was getting into the helicopter and chainsaw sounds. Someone had turned the volume up and it was getting painful. He added a high uninterrupted bleep like a household smoke alarm and Jason stuck his fingers in his ears. He gestured to Emily, and slid backwards toward the chill-out.

He looked for an empty sofa. He sat next to a Chinese girl with her eyes closed. He asked her if she was okay but she didn't answer. She didn't seem to have any friends around. He pushed the light button on his watch and it said 5:45. It would be getting light outside. There were two white guys in long shorts and tennis hats standing in a corner with coloured blobs swirling over them. They were standing in the psychedelic projection and their skins were crawling with snakes. They were just talking quietly. Jason saw one pull something small out of his pocket and hand it over, and it unleashed a wave of movement around them, a sudden parting of the crowd, and there were three big bouncers pushing through toward them in black T-shirts and black pants with black headsets. They were all around the two guys in the corner, and blocking Jason's way out.

He had to duck under one bouncer's arm to get away. He looked behind him to see the guys both emptying their pockets, the bouncers' arms folded like walls. The Chinese girl still had her eyes closed.

He found Doke and Emily where they were.

"We should go," he said to Emily's ear. "We should get him out of here."

"Why?" she yelled.

Jason jerked his thumb over his shoulder. "The bouncers are being tough. They're looking for trouble. I don't want them to see him."

Emily peered through the crowd at the clump of bouncers, now pulling the two guys toward the exit. There was a wide space around them as they moved.

"Let's get our stuff," she yelled up at Doke.

"Are we going?" he said quite reasonably, as if he was just waking up.

Jason found Sherry on the sofas with Pritika. She did not move over to let him sit down.

"Hey," he said.

"Hey," said Pritika. "Have you seen my brother?"

Jason shook his head. Sherry was looking away.

Helmet was doing something that sounded like a lawnmower and an old Carpenter's song. The dance floor was emptying out. "He's getting weird," said Jason.

Sherry looked up at him. "I hope you've been having a good time."

"I thought you'd be okay. I knew you weren't far."

She shrugged.

"We have to get Doke out of here. You ready to go?"

"I was about to go anyway."

Jason felt the energy seeping from him. Now would be a really fun time to have a fight with Sherry. A really perfect time, right now, at 5:45 a.m. He opened his mouth wide to stretch his jaw, massaged his temples. His mouth was dry. He just said, "Are you coming with us?"

She got up and he took her hand and led her toward the door.

They got Doke out okay, although he started shouting "Rock the house, rock the house!" in a scratchy voice and punching the air while they waited at the coat check. The bouncers watched him, their arms folded. Jason kept a hand on his shoulder.

They split up from Rajiv and Priti at the door because they had to get the first subway to be home before their parents were up. The air was cold and glowing. Jason felt the sweat on his body turn to shivers. The streetlights were spiky crystals. They walked down to Wellington and Spadina because Emily said she knew a park there that would be quiet. Doke kicked at parking metres the whole way, shouting.

When Jason looked at the edges of buildings or trees they shifted slightly, slid sideways a half an inch and then were still and solid. They walked very slowly and deliberately into the park.

They sat on a picnic table. Doke ran around and around the table like a dog. Jason was shivering and sweating. There was a hiss in his ears like the sound speakers make when you turn them up really loud with no music. He wrapped his jacket around him. Emily began rolling a joint. The sky was turning a metallic blue. He watched Emily's face and saw it was white and pinched. She frowned and flattened her lips together. She had grey circles under her eyes.

He needed a drink of water and a pee. He pushed the light button on his watch and it said 6:23. The subway would be running. He closed his eyes at the thought of taking it home. Sherry's mother would be getting up at seven, so they could go there. There would be a streetcar. He put his arm around Sherry, who was sitting next to him on the picnic table, and she let him. He tried to get as tight to her as he could, to get warm. She put a hand on his knee. She said softly, "You okay?"

He nodded and squeezed the soft flesh at her waist.

His hand was shaking as he took the joint from Emily. Sherry didn't want it, but she didn't say anything about him taking it. Jason was thinking it would help him sleep. They got Doke to stand still long enough to take a long toke, and then he sat down on the picnic bench, breathing heavily. His lips were flecked with spittle.

Jason was tired, looking at him, and realized he was bored, bored with Doke, bored with Emily, who was sitting there rolling another joint with determination, who was going to stay with Doke forever. Emily looked to him like a girl from Sir Stanley Spencer who had never finished high school and who was going to smoke an awful lot of joints between now and the time she was going to have babies with someone like Doke and be one of those lined skinny women who work in roadside diners, and he was relieved, intensely relieved, to not be in love with her anymore.

"Whoo," he sighed. "I'm down." He felt like shit but knew he was smiling. He squeezed Sherry's waistband again, the soft flesh she couldn't contain in her cargo skirts and her baby Ts although she wrapped herself in strict cotton and nylon, flesh that he wanted to be expansive and soft then, not taut like Emily's, warm and safe and known and forgiving. It was a relief not to feel love like a pain for Sherry, but something else, a comfort. Comfort was better. He kissed her on the cheek as you would kiss a sister, and she pulled away and he realized she would have every reason to be mad at him, to be furious and sad for not paying enough attention to her and taking her to Doke's which she hated and not explaining to her that it was about Emily, it was always about Emily, which he didn't need to explain now, since it was over, it had never been about anything but serotonin in his brain. He couldn't explain this to her, but he could feel grateful that she was still there, incredibly, dumbly letting him hold her and waiting till he was down and not in love with Emily anymore, which she probably realized, he had to admit, she had probably understood all along, and so he was lucky that she was still there, just waiting for him. He could at least feel grateful.

She looked at him with worried eyes. He smiled at her but she still looked worried.

"Do you guys want to come over to our place and chill?" said Emily. "I can't sleep yet."

Jason felt Sherry's hand stiffening in his and he said, quietly, to her, "Can we go to your mom's?"

She whispered, "I thought you hated it there."

"No. I never said that."

She was silent.

"I just want us two to be alone and, and normal."

"Okay," she said, still in her small voice. "If you don't mind."

"If I don't *mind!*" He laughed, brought her hand to his face and kissed it. "Thanks. Thank you."

"You want?" said Emily.

"No, thanks," said Jason, standing. He helped Sherry down from the bench and kept his arm wrapped around her shoulder as if protecting her from a fire or a riot. "We better crash. We're going to Sherry's mom's."

Emily shrugged.

"We can help you get Doke home, if you like."

"I'm fine," said Doke soberly. He was staring straight ahead. "See you guys."

"You sure?" said Jason.

"We'll be fine." Emily smiled at them with tired eyes. She stubbed out the joint and got up to hug them both. She held on to Sherry for a long time. She kissed Jason's cheek. He slapped Doke's back and shook his hand and thanked him. "That was awesome," he said.

"Okay man," said Doke. "Have a good one."

On the sidewalk it seemed to be daylight. The sky was fluorescent. Jason squinted. His skull vibrated. His ears were still humming.

"What did you say thank you for?"

"I don't know. I was glad you were there."

It was only then that she turned to him and hugged him and he felt her relax against him and open to him, her little breasts and wide hips against him, familiar as clothing. It was a great relief not to have love in his brain anymore. A streetcar came thumping toward them, wheels grating like feedback. Over it he could hear the rhythmic beeping of a dumpster truck backing up. When he closed his eyes he saw the beeps as bars of green light on a mixing board, flashing.

(2002)

PART III
Writing about Poetry

The language of poetry is even more compressed than the language of the short story. You need to give yourself willingly to the understanding of poetry. The pleasure of reading it derives from the beauty of the language—the delight of the sounds and the images—as well as the power of the emotion and the depth of the insights conveyed. Poetry may seem difficult, but it can also be intensely rewarding.

10

How Do I Read Poetry?

In order to enjoy discovering the meaning of poetry, you must approach it with a positive attitude—a willingness to understand. Poetry invites your creative participation. More than any other form of literature, poetry allows you as reader to inform its meaning as you bring your own knowledge and experience to bear in interpreting images, motifs, and symbols.

Begin by reading the poem aloud—or at least by sounding the words aloud in your mind. Rhyme and rhythm work in subtle ways to emphasize key words and clarify meaning. As you reread, go slowly, paying careful attention to every word, looking up in a good dictionary any words that are unclear, and examining again and again any difficult lines.

GET THE LITERAL MEANING FIRST: PARAPHRASE

Before you begin interpreting a poem, you must be sure that you understand the literal meaning. Because one of the delights of poetry stems from the unusual ways in which poets put words together, you may sometimes need to straighten out the syntax. For instance, Thomas Hardy writes,

> And why unblooms the best hope ever sown?

The usual way of expressing that question would be something like this:

> And why does the best hope ever sown not bloom?

Occasionally you may need to fill in words that the poet has deliberately omitted through ellipsis. When Walt Whitman writes,

> But I with mournful tread,
> Walk the deck my Captain lies,
> Fallen cold and dead,

we can tell that he means "the deck on which my Captain lies, / Fallen cold and dead."

Pay close attention to punctuation; it can provide clues to meaning, but do not be distressed if you discover that poets (like Emily Dickinson and Phyllis Webb) sometimes use punctuation in strange ways or (like bp Nichol in some poems) not at all. Along with the deliberate fracturing of syntax, this unusual use of punctuation comes under the heading of poetic licence.

You must always look up any words that you do not know—as well as any familiar words that fail to make complete sense in the context. When you read this line from Whitman,

> Passing the apple-tree blows of white and pink in the orchards,

the word "blows" seems a strange choice. If you consult your dictionary, you will discover an unusual definition of blows: "masses of blossoms," a meaning which fits exactly.

MAKE ASSOCIATIONS FOR MEANING

Once you understand the literal meaning of a poem, you can begin to expand that meaning into an interpretation. As you do so, keep asking yourself questions: Who is the speaker? Who is being addressed? What is the message? What do the images contribute? What do the symbols suggest? How does it all fit together?

When, for instance, Emily Dickinson in the following lines envisions "Rowing in Eden," how do you respond to this image?

> Rowing in Eden—
> Ah, the Sea!
> Might I but moor—Tonight—
> In Thee!

Can she mean *literally* rowing in Eden? Not unless you picture a lake in the Garden, which is, of course, a possibility. What do you associate with Eden? Complete bliss? Surely. Innocence, perhaps—the innocence of Adam and Eve before the Fall? Or their lustful sensuality after the Fall? Given the opening lines of the poem,

> Wild Nights—Wild Nights!
> Were I with thee
> Wild Nights should be
> Our luxury!

one fitting response might be that "Rowing in Eden" suggests paddling through sexual innocence in a far from chaste anticipation of reaching the port of ecstasy: to "moor—Tonight— / In Thee!"

Sometimes poems, like stories and plays, contain *allusions* (indirect references to famous persons, events, or places, or to other works of literature) that add to the meaning. Some allusions are fairly easy to perceive. When Eliot's Prufrock, in his famous love song, observes,

> No! I am not Prince Hamlet, nor was meant to be,

we know that he declines to compare himself to Shakespeare's Hamlet, a character who also had difficulty taking decisive action. Some allusions, though, are more subtle. You need to know these lines from Ernest Dowson,

> Last night, ah, yesternight, betwixt her lips and mine,
> There fell thy shadow, Cynara!

in order to catch the allusion to them in Eliot's "The Hollow Men":

> Between the motion
> And the act
> Falls the shadow.

Many allusions you can simply look up. If you are puzzled by Swinburne's line

> Thou has conquered, O pale Galilean,

your dictionary will identify the Galilean as Jesus Christ. For less well-known figures or events, you may need to consult a dictionary of biblical characters, a dictionary of classical mythology, or a good encyclopedia.

CHART 10-1 CRITICAL QUESTIONS FOR READING POETRY

Before planning an analysis of any selection in the anthology of poetry, write out your answers to the following questions to confirm your understanding of the poem and to generate material for the paper.

1. Can you paraphrase the poem if necessary?
2. Who is the speaker in the poem? How would you describe this persona?
3. What is the speaker's tone? Which words reveal this tone? Is the poem perhaps ironic?
4. What heavily connotative words are used? What words have unusual or special meanings? Are any words or phrases repeated? If so, why? Which words do you need to look up?
5. What images does the poet use? How do the images relate to one another? Do these images form a unified pattern (a motif) throughout the poem? Is there a central, controlling image?
6. What figures of speech are used? How do they contribute to the tone and meaning of the poem?
7. Are there any symbols? What do they mean? Are they universal symbols, or do they arise from the particular context of this poem?
8. Is the occasion for or the setting of the poem important in understanding its meaning? If so, why?
9. What is the theme (the central idea) of this poem? Can you state it in a single sentence?
10. How important is the role of metrics (sound effects), such as rhyme and rhythm? How do they affect tone and meaning?
11. How important is the contribution of form, such as rhyme scheme and line arrangement? How does the form influence the overall effect of the poem?

Other valuable reference tools are Sir James Frazer's *The Golden Bough*, which discusses preclassical myth, magic, and religion, and Cirlot's *A Dictionary of Symbols*, which traces through mythology and world literature the significance of various *archetypal* (i.e., universal) symbols—the sea, the seasons, colours, numbers, islands, serpents, and a host of others.

Thus, learning to understand poetry—like learning to understand any imaginative literature—involves asking yourself questions, then speculating and researching until you come up with satisfying answers.

For study tools to help you with your next writing assignment, please visit the Companion Website at www.pearsoned.ca/mcmahan.

11

Writing about Persona and Tone

Tone, which can be important in analyzing a short story, is crucial to the interpretation of poetry. Persona is closely related to tone. In order to identify persona and determine tone, you need (as usual) to ask yourself questions about the poem.

WHO IS SPEAKING?

A good question to begin with is this: Who is the speaker in the poem? Often the most obvious answer seems to be "The poet," especially if the poem is written in the first person. When Emily Dickinson begins,

> This is my letter to the world
> That never wrote to me—

we can be fairly sure that she is writing in her own voice—that the poem itself is her "letter to the world." But poets often adopt a *persona;* that is, they speak through the voice of a character they have created. Stevie Smith, herself a middle-aged woman, adopts a persona of a different age and of the opposite sex in these lines:

> An old man of seventy-three
> I lay with my young bride in my arms....

Thomas Hardy in "The Ruined Maid" (on page 354) composes a dramatic monologue with dual personae (or two personas), two young women who converse throughout the poem. The speaker in Margaret Atwood's "Death of a Young Son by Drowning" (page 456) is a mother but most certainly is not Atwood herself. Thus, in order to be strictly accurate, you should avoid "The poet says . . ." and use instead, "The speaker in the poem says . . ." or "The persona in the poem says. . . ."

WHAT IS TONE?

After deciding who the speaker is, your next question might be "What is the tone of this poetic voice?" *Tone* in poetry is essentially the same as in fiction, drama, or expository prose: the attitude of the writer toward the subject matter of the work—the poem, story, play, or essay. Tone in a piece of writing is always similar to tone of voice in speaking. If a friend finds you on the verge of tears and comments, "You certainly look cheerful today," her tone of voice—as well as the absurdity of the statement—lets you know that your friend is using *verbal irony;* that is, she means the opposite of what she says.

RECOGNIZING VERBAL IRONY

Since verbal irony involves a reversal of meaning, it is the most important tone to recognize. To miss the irony is to miss the meaning in many cases. When Stephen Crane begins a poem,

> Do not weep, maiden, for war is kind,

an alert reader will catch the ironic tone at once from the word *kind,* which war definitely is not. However, irony can at times be much more subtle. Sometimes you need to put together a number of verbal clues in order to perceive the irony. James Reaney's "The School Globe" (page 447) is such a poem. As you read, you might become aware that within the images of a remembered happy childhood are embedded words faintly suggesting something quite otherwise ("fists" of roses; "irregular" mirrors; "pluperfect" things). The abrupt violence of the last line will send you back through the poem to ferret out these subtle clues. (For a discussion of other types of irony that appear in drama and fiction but not often in poetry, look up *irony* in the glossary.)

DESCRIBING TONE

One of the chief problems in identifying tone involves finding exactly the right word or words to describe it. Even after you have detected that a work's tone is ironic, you may need to decide whether the irony is gentle or bitter, or whether it is light or scathing in tone. Remember that you are trying to identify the tone of the poetic voice, just as you would identify the tone of anyone speaking to you.

You need a number of adjectives at your command to pinpoint tone. As you analyze poetic tone, keep the following terms in mind to see whether any may prove useful: *humorous, joyous, playful, light, hopeful, brisk, lyrical, admiring, celebratory, laudatory, expectant, wistful, sad, mournful, dreary, tragic, elegiac, solemn, sombre, poignant, earnest, blasé, disillusioned, straightforward, curt, hostile, sarcastic, cynical, ambivalent, ambiguous.*

LOOKING AT PERSONA AND TONE

Read the following five poems for pleasure. Then, as you read through them again slowly and carefully, pay attention to the persona and try to identify the tone of this speaker's voice. Is the speaker angry, frightened, astonished, admiring? Or perhaps sincere, sarcastic, humorous, or deceptive?

Theodore Roethke   1908–1963

My Papa's Waltz

The whiskey on your breath
Could make a small boy dizzy;
But I hung on like death:
Such waltzing was not easy.

We romped until the pans
Slid from the kitchen shelf;
My mother's countenance
Could not unfrown itself.

The hand that held my wrist
Was battered on one knuckle;   10
At every step you missed
My right ear scraped a buckle.

You beat time on my head
With a palm caked hard by dirt,
Then waltzed me off to bed
Still clinging to your shirt.

(1948)

Thomas Hardy   1840–1928

The Ruined Maid

"O 'Melia, my dear, this does everything crown!
Who could have supposed I should meet you in Town?
And whence such fair garments, such prosperi-ty?"—
"O didn't you know I'd been ruined?" said she.

—"You left us in tatters, without shoes or socks,
Tired of digging potatoes, and spudding up docks;
And now you've gay bracelets and bright feathers three!"—
"Yes: that's how we dress when we're ruined," said she.

—"At home in the barton[1] you said 'thee' and 'thou,'
And 'thik oon,' and 'theas oon,' and 't'other'; but now   10
Your talking quite fits 'ee for high compa-ny!"—
"Some polish is gained with one's ruin," said she.

—"Your hands were like paws then, your face blue and bleak,
But now I'm bewitched by your delicate cheek,
And your little gloves fit as on any la-dy!"—
"We never do work when we're ruined," said she.

---

[1] Farmyard.

—"You used to call home-life a hag-ridden dream,
And you'd sigh, and you'd sock;[2] but at present you seem
To know not of megrims[3] or melancho-ly!"—
"True. One's pretty lively when ruined," said she.   20

—"I wish I had feathers, a fine sweeping gown,
And a delicate face, and could strut about Town!"—
"My dear—a raw country girl, such as you be,
Cannot quite expect that. You ain't ruined," said she.

(1866)

Pauline Johnson   1861–1913

A Cry from an Indian Wife

My Forest Brave, my Red-skin love, farewell;
We may not meet to-morrow; who can tell
What mighty ills befall our little band.
Or what you'll suffer from the white man's hand?
Here is your knife! I thought 'twas sheathed for aye.
No roaming bison calls for it to-day;
No hide of prairie cattle will it maim;
The plains are bare, it seeks a nobler game:
'Twill drink the life-blood of a soldier host.
Go; rise and strike, no matter what the cost.   10
Yet stay. Revolt not at the Union Jack,
Nor raise Thy hand against this stripling pack
Of white-faced warriors, marching West to quell
Our fallen tribe that rises to rebel.
They all are young and beautiful and good;
Curse to the war that drinks their harmless blood.
Curse to the fate that brought them from the East
To be our chiefs—to make our nation least
That breathes the air of this vast continent.
Still their new rule and council is well meant.   20
They but forget we Indians owned the land
From ocean unto ocean; that they stand
Upon a soil that centuries agone
Was our sole kingdom and our right alone.
They never think how they would feel to-day,
If some great nation came from far away,
Wresting their country from their hapless braves,
Giving what they gave us—but wars and graves.
Then go and strike for liberty and life,
And bring back honour to your Indian wife.   30
Your wife? Ah, what of that, who cares for me?
Who pities my poor love and agony?
What white-robed priest prays for your safety here,

---
[2] Moan.
[3] Sadness.

As prayer is said for every volunteer
That swells the ranks that Canada sends out?
Who prays for vict'ry for the Indian scout?
Who prays for our poor nation lying low?
None—therefore take your tomahawk and go.
My heart may break and burn into its core,
But I am strong to bid you go to war.   40
Yet stay, my heart is not the only one
That grieves the loss of husband and of son;
Think of the mothers o'er the inland seas;
Think of the pale-faced maiden on her knees;
One pleads her God to guard some sweet-faced child
That marches on toward the North-West wild.
The other prays to shield her love from harm,
To strengthen his young, proud uplifted arm.
Ah, how her white face quivers thus to think,
Your tomahawk his life's best blood will drink.   50
She never thinks of my wild aching breast,
Nor prays for your dark face and eagle crest
Endangered by a thousand rifle balls,
My heart the target if my warrior falls.
O! coward self I hesitate no more;
Go forth, and win the glories of the war.
Go forth, nor bend to greed of white men's hands,
By right, by birth we Indians own these lands,
Though starved, crushed, plundered, lies our nation low . . .
Perhaps the white man's God has willed it so.   60

(1895)

Edmund Waller   1606–1687

Go, Lovely Rose

Go, lovely Rose,
Tell her that wastes her time and me,
   that now she knows,
When I resemble her to thee,
How sweet and fair she seems to be.

Tell her that's young,
And shuns to have her graces spied,
   that had'st thou sprung
In deserts where no men abide,
Thou must have uncommended died.   10

Small is the worth
Of beauty from the light retir'd:
   Bid her come forth,
Suffer herself to be desir'd,
And not blush so to be admir'd.

Then die, that she
The common fate of all things rare
    May read in thee,
How small a part of time they share,
That are so wondrous sweet and fair.   20

(1645)

Dorothy Parker   1893–1967

One Perfect Rose

A single flow'r he sent me, since we met.
    All tenderly his messenger he chose;
Deep-hearted, pure, with scented dew still wet—
    One perfect rose.

I knew the language of the floweret;
    "My fragile leaves," it said, "his heart enclose."
Love long has taken for his amulet
    One perfect rose.

Why is it no one ever sent me yet
    One perfect limousine, do you suppose?   10
Ah no, it's always just my luck to get
    One perfect rose.

(1926)

PREWRITING

As you search for a fuller understanding of a poem and for a possible writing thesis, remember to keep rereading the poem (or at least pertinent parts of it). The questions you pose for yourself will become easier to answer and your responses more enlightened.

ASKING QUESTIONS ABOUT THE SPEAKER IN "MY PAPA'S WALTZ"

If a poem lends itself to an approach through persona or tone, you will, of course, find something unusual or perhaps puzzling about the speaker or the poetic voice. Consider Theodore Roethke's "My Papa's Waltz," which you just read. Ask yourself first, "Who is the speaker?" You know from line 2: "a small boy." But the past-tense verbs suggest that the boy may be grown now, remembering a childhood experience. Sometimes this adult perspective requires additional consideration.

Next, ask yourself, "What is the speaker's attitude toward his father?" The boy's feelings about his father become the crucial issue in determining the tone of the poem. You need to look carefully at details and word choice to discover your answer. Consider, for instance, these questions:

1. Is it pleasant or unpleasant to be made dizzy from the smell of whiskey on someone's breath?
2. Does it sound like fun to hang on "like death"?
3. How does it change the usually pleasant experience of waltzing to call it "not easy"?
4. What sort of "romping" would be necessary to cause pans to slide from a shelf?
5. Is it unusual to hold your dancing partner by the wrist? How is this different from being held by the hand?
6. Would it be enjoyable or painful to have your ear scraped repeatedly by a buckle?
7. Would you like or resent having someone "beat time" on your head with a hard, dirty hand?
8. If the father is gripping the boy's wrist with one hand and thumping his head with the other, does this explain why the boy must hang on for dear life?
9. What other line in the poem does the last line echo?

If your answers to these questions lead you to conclude that this waltzing was not fun for the boy, then you could describe the tone as ironic (because of the discrepancy between the pleasant idea of the waltz and the boy's unpleasant experience). You could, possibly, describe the tone as detached, because the boy gives no clear indication of his feelings. We have to deduce them from details in the poem. You could even describe the tone as reminiscent, but this term is too general to indicate the meaning carried by the tone.

We all bring our own experience to bear in interpreting a poem. What you should be careful about is allowing your personal experience to carry too much weight in your response. If, for instance, you had an abusive father, you might so strongly identify with the boy's discomfort that you would call the tone resentful. On the other hand, if you enjoyed a loving relationship with your father, you might well find, as does X. J. Kennedy, "the speaker's attitude toward his father warmly affectionate," and take this recollection of childhood to be a happy one. Kennedy cites as evidence "the rollicking rhythms of the poem; the playfulness of a rhyme like *dizzy* and *easy*; the joyful suggestions of the words *waltz*, *waltzing*, and *romped*." He suggests that a reader who sees the tone as resentful fails "to visualize this scene in all its comedy, with kitchen pans falling and the father happily using his son's head for a drum." Kennedy also feels in the last line the suggestion of "the boy *still clinging* with persistent love."[1]

DEVISING A THESIS

Since your prewriting questioning has been directed toward discovering the attitude of the speaker in the poem, you could formulate a thesis that

---
[1] *An Introduction to Poetry*, 4th ed. (Boston, MA: Little, Brown, 1971), 10.

allows you to focus on the importance of understanding the persona in order to perceive the tone of the poem. Of course, the way you interpret the poem will determine the way you state your thesis. You could write a convincing paper after developing any one of the following thesis statements:

> The attitude of the boy toward his father in Roethke's "My Papa's Waltz" conveys to us the poet's ambivalent tone.
>
> The attitude of the boy toward his father in Roethke's "My Papa's Waltz" allows us to perceive the poet's ironic tone.
>
> The attitude of the boy toward his father in Roethke's "My Papa's Waltz" reinforces the poet's loving, nostalgic tone.

If you wrote on the first thesis, you would focus on the conflicting evidence suggesting that the boy is delighted by his father's attention but frightened by the coercion of the dance. If you wrote on the second thesis, you would cite evidence of the boy's discomfort and argue that the "waltz" in the title and the rollicking meter are thus clearly ironic. If you wrote on the last thesis, you would emphasize the sprightly meter and playful rhymes, which present the dance as a frisky romp and show that the boy is having a splendid time.

DESCRIBING THE TONE IN "THE RUINED MAID"

You can see by now that speaker and tone are all but impossible to separate. In order to get at the tone of Hardy's poem, write out responses to the following questions and be prepared to discuss the tone in class.

1. Who are the two speakers in this poem?
2. What does the term *maid* mean in the title? Look it up in your dictionary if you are not sure.
3. What different meanings does your dictionary give for *ruined*? Which one applies in the poem?
4. How does the ruined maid probably make her living? What details suggest this?
5. Describe how the tone of the country maid's speeches changes during the course of the poem.
6. What tone does the ruined maid use in addressing her former friend?
7. How does the final line undercut the ruined maid's boast that she gained "polish" with her ruin?
8. What is Hardy's tone—that is, the tone of the poem itself?

DISCOVERING A THESIS

If you are going to write on tone in "The Ruined Maid," you might devise a statement focusing on the way we, as readers, discover the irony in the poem. Your thesis could read something like this:

In Hardy's poem the discrepancy between the supposedly "ruined" woman's present condition and her previous wretched state reveals the ironic tone.

If you wanted, instead, to write about the dual personas in the poem, you might think about how they function—to figure out why Hardy chose to present the poem through two speakers instead of the usual one. Perhaps he chose this technique because the two voices enable him to convey his theme convincingly. You might invent a thesis along these lines:

> Hardy employs dual personas in "The Ruined Maid" to convince us that prostitution, long considered "a fate worse than death," is actually much preferable to grinding poverty.

In each paper, although your focus would be different, the evidence you use in presenting the contrast would be essentially the same.

DESCRIBING THE TONE IN "A CRY FROM AN INDIAN WIFE"

1. How would you describe the different emotions the speaker experiences as her husband prepares for war?
2. Identify those lines in the poem that mark each time the speaker shifts her position. Do these junctures also mark a change in the tone?
3. Examine each group of lines that put forth one of the speaker's alternating attitudes. How does the poet gradually intensify the tone within each section?
4. Given that Pauline Johnson is a Confederation-era poet of Mohawk and English descent, how might the historical times and Johnson's dual heritage influence the tone of this poem?
5. What is the attitude of the poetic voice toward the Native and the white warriors, respectively? How do the images in the poem help convey these views?
6. What is meant by the last line: "Perhaps the white man's God has willed it so"? Could this be irony? Is it acceptance or simply acknowledgment of what has already occurred?
7. What, then, is the overall tone of the poem?

DISCOVERING A THESIS

If you were going to write on tone in Johnson's "A Cry from an Indian Wife," you would focus on the features of the poem that reveal that tone—beginning or ending perhaps with the idea of the speaker's mixed emotions as her husband heads off for war. You might frame a thesis something like this:

> Johnson's shifts in tone reveal the speaker's conflicting emotions as she alternately bids her husband to go and fight for their nation and urges him to stay back out of sympathy for the white warriors and their loved ones.

As you develop this thesis, you can focus on the discrepancies you recognize between the speaker's attitudes toward her people and her ability to see things from the point of view of the enemy. You might even do some research on Pauline Johnson to see how her own dual heritage might contribute to the tension in her poem. If when writing an essay you include information other than that from the poem itself, be sure to document all sources. See Chapter 17 regarding correct documentation of primary and secondary sources.

DISCOVERING THE TONE IN "GO, LOVELY ROSE"

1. What has happened between the speaker and the woman before the poem was written?
2. Why does he choose a rose to carry his message?
3. What does *uncommended* mean in line 10?
4. Can you detect a tone slightly different in lines 2 and 7 from the speaker's admiring tone in the poem as a whole?
5. How do you respond to his telling the rose to die so that the woman may be reminded of how quickly her beauty will also die?
6. Does the title "Song," as the poem is sometimes called, convey any hint about the tone?
7. How would you describe the tone of this poem?

DISCOVERING THE TONE IN "ONE PERFECT ROSE"

1. What are the similarities between Parker's poem and Waller's?
2. What are the major differences?
3. Why does Parker put an apostrophe in *flow'r*?
4. What is an amulet?
5. How does the tone of the poem change in the last stanza? Can you explain why this happens?
6. What is the tone of the entire poem?

WRITING

Because you may find poetry more difficult to write about than short stories, first be sure that you understand the poem. If the poem is difficult, write a complete *paraphrase* in which you straighten out the word order and replace any unfamiliar words or phrases with everyday language. Yes, you damage the poem when you paraphrase it, but the poem will survive.

After you are sure you have a firm grasp on the literal level, you can then begin to examine the images, make associations, and flesh out the meanings that will eventually lead you to an interpretation of the poem. By this time, you should have generated sufficient material to write about the work. The writing process is essentially the same as it is for analyzing a short story.

EXPLICATING AND ANALYZING

In explicating a poem, you proceed carefully through the text, interpreting it, usually, line by line. Because of the attention to detail, explication is best suited to writing about a short poem or a key section of a longer work. As an explicator you may look at any or all elements of the poem—tone, persona, images, symbolism, metrics—as you discuss the way these elements function together to form the poem. Although you may paraphrase an occasional line, your explication will be concerned mainly with revealing hidden meanings in the poem. Probably most of your class discussions involve a kind of informal explication of poems, stories, or plays.

A written explication is easy to organize: you start with the first line and work straight through the poem. But explicating well requires a discerning eye. You have to make numerous decisions about what to comment on and how far to pursue a point, and you also have to pull various strands together in the end to arrive at a conclusion involving a statement of the theme or purpose of the poem. This approach, if poorly handled, can be a mechanical task, but if well done, explication can prove a rewarding way to examine a rich and complex work.

A written analysis involves explication but differs by focusing on some element of the poem and examining how that element (tone, persona, imagery, symbolism, metrics) contributes to an understanding of the meaning or purpose of the whole. You can see that an analysis is more challenging to write because you must exercise more options in selecting and organizing your material. Your instructor will let you know if it matters which type of paper you compose.

IDEAS FOR WRITING

IDEAS FOR RESPONSIVE WRITING

1. Were you ever frightened or hurt as a child, like the boy in Roethke's poem, by being handled too roughly by an adult? Describe the experience, explaining not only how you felt but also what you now think the adult's motives might have been.
2. Using Dorothy Parker's "One Perfect Rose" as a guide, write an ironic or humorous response to Lord Byron's "She Walks in Beauty" or rewrite the poem from a woman's point of view describing a man she admires.
3. Have you ever felt conflicted about the prospect of someone close to you confronting an opponent, much as Johnson's Indian Wife does? If so, write an updated cry that delineates your conflicting feelings of anger and sympathy toward this enemy. Using "A Cry from an Indian Wife" as a model, write your impassioned cry as a speech, an essay, or a poem.

IDEAS FOR CRITICAL WRITING

1. Develop one of the sample thesis statements included in the "Prewriting" section of this chapter and write an essay exploring that thesis.
2. Both "My Papa's Waltz" by Theodore Roethke and "pa poem 4: naked and nailed" by Patrick Friesen (page 467) concern the childhood experience of a young boy. Study both poems until you are sure you understand them; then compare or contrast their tones.
3. Compare Waller's "Go, Lovely Rose" with Parker's parody "One Perfect Rose" by focusing on the differences in tone. You might add William Blake's "The Sick Rose" to make an analysis of the tone or persona of all three poems. (See the Sample Comparison Paper in Chapter 12.)
4. Stevie Smith's "Not Waving but Drowning" seems difficult until you realize that two voices are speaking—the "I" of the first and third stanzas and the "they" of the second. Once you understand the implications of this dual perspective, write an explication of the poem.
5. Discuss the effectiveness of the speaker's anguished voice in "A Cry from an Indian Wife."

EDITING

In this section we will explain a few conventions that you should observe in writing about poetry. If you have often written papers analyzing poetry, you probably incorporate these small but useful bits of mechanical usage automatically. If not, take time during the revising or editing stage to get them right.

QUOTING POETRY IN ESSAYS

The following are the main conventions to observe when quoting poetry in writing.

INSERTING SLASH MARKS When quoting only a couple of lines, use a slash mark to indicate the end of each line (except the last):

> Whitman similarly describes the soul's position in the universe in these lines: "And you O my soul where you stand, / Surrounded, detached, in measureless oceans of space" (6–7).

CITING LINE NUMBERS Cite line numbers in parentheses after the quotation marks and before the period when quoting complete lines, as in the previous example. When quoting only a phrase, cite the line number immediately after closing the quotation marks, even if your sentence continues:

> In the italicized portion of the poem, the bird sings a carol in praise of "lovely and soothing death" (135) to help the persona overcome his grief.

Note, however, that according to the Modern Language Association's (MLA) *Handbook for Writers of Research Papers*, 6th ed., the first reference in an essay to a line or lines of poetry should include the word *line* or *lines* before the number(s):

> Lampman's persona in "A Summer Dream" is closer to death than life: "On my cold hand you laid your fingertips" (line 5).

ADJUSTING END PUNCTUATION Since you are using the lines you quote in a different context from that in the poem, adjust the punctuation of the last line you quote to make it fit your sentence. Here is a line from Whitman's "When Lilacs Last in the Dooryard Bloom'd":

> To adorn the burial-house of him I love?

Notice how the end punctuation is dropped in order to suit the writer's sentence:

> The persona brings visions of the varying beauty of the entire country, as he says, "To adorn the burial-house of him I love" (80).

USING ELLIPSIS DOTS To show omissions when quoting poetry, use three dots, just as you would if quoting prose:

> The poet's sympathies are not for the living but for the dead: "They themselves were fully at rest. . . . / The living remain'd and suffer'd . . ." (181–82).

USING SQUARE BRACKETS If you need to change a word, a capital letter, or some punctuation *within* the line or lines you quote, enclose the changed letter or mark of punctuation in square brackets (not parentheses):

> The persona brings visions of the varying beauty of the entire country "[t]o adorn the burial-house of him [he] love[s]" (80).

Remember that you do not have to quote complete lines. Rather than clutter your sentence with three sets of brackets, you could quote only the telling phrase in that line:

> The persona brings visions of the varying beauty of the entire country to "adorn the burial-house" (80) of the one he loves.

QUOTING MULTIPLE LINES If you are quoting more than two or three lines, indent ten spaces and omit the quotation marks (since the indention tells your readers that the material is quoted):

> After describing the carnage of war dead, the persona realizes that his sympathies have been misplaced:
>
> > They themselves were fully at rest, they suffer'd not,
> > The living remain'd and suffer'd, the mother suffer'd,
> > And the wife and the child and the musing comrade suffer'd
> > And the armies that remain'd suffer'd. (181–84)

The indented material should still be double-spaced (unless your instructor asks you to single-space the lines).

SAMPLE STUDENT PAPER

The following student paper was written in response to A. E. Housman's poem "To an Athlete Dying Young" and is included here not as a model but to generate class discussion. Read the poem, which appears in the Anthology of Poetry section, and then decide if you agree with the student's views about the tone and persona of Housman's poem.

Kenric L. Bond
English 1100
October 2, 2003

Death at an Early Age

It would be great to die in the prime of life, not to be remembered as old and feeble but as still strong and vibrant. This is the idea proposed in A. E. Housman's poem "To an Athlete Dying Young" in which he tells of an athlete who died a hero not too long after winning a record-setting race.

The first stanza describes a celebrated athlete coming home after winning a race: "The time you won your town the race / We chaired you through the market-place" (lines 1-2). Abruptly in the next stanza a different kind of reception is held: "To-day, the road all runners come, / Shoulder-high we bring you home" (5-6). The similarity between these two scenes is shocking. Ordinarily, the image of pallbearers carrying the deceased home in a casket is not linked with a hero being carried on the shoulders of his cheering fans. These first two stanzas set up the comparison between glory and death that continues through the rest of the poem.

The third stanza reveals the persona's attitude toward dying in one's prime by using the image of "the laurel," which grows "early" but "withers quicker than the rose" (11-12). The laurel has long been used as a crown of victory

Bond 2

for winning a race, but fame is forgotten sooner than the brief life of a rose.

This point about the brevity of fame is repeated in the last stanza:

>   And round that early-laurelled head
>   Will flock to gaze the strengthless dead,
>   And find unwithered on its curls
>   The garland briefer than a girl's. (25-28)

The dead athlete's victory garland is still green with life; the fame of winning the race is shorter than a girl's innocence and purity. Thus, Housman implies that the time to die is while the recent victory is fresh, as fresh as the garland, and still being discussed among the living.

During the poem, A. E. Housman tries to convince us that it is best to die young: "Smart lad, to slip betimes away / From fields where glory does not stay" (9-10). Housman calls the athlete smart for dying while the memory of victory is still fresh in the minds of a society where positive accomplishments are easily forgotten. The poet also applauds the athlete's death because then the runner won't have to face the disheartening sight of a new runner breaking his records and stealing the glory he once enjoyed: "Eyes the shady night has shut / Cannot see the record cut" (13-14).

As an athlete myself, I know that I will someday see all the records that I set in high school broken. I have already witnessed a few of my marks reset by other runners. If I had died right after my high school years, I could have missed these superficial disappointments. An athlete, however, shouldn't be so shallow that he or she can't bear to live and see such trivial things as records broken. They are just names on a wall or trophies in a case. I hope that somebody does break my records because that's why I made them--to be broken.

A. E. Housman seems to think that setting records and living in the limelight are all that athletes live for. The poet suggests that it would be too difficult for an athlete to live and see the record books rewritten and that a victorious athlete would be vain enough to worry about what other people think of his or her physical state after death. Well, I think the poet is wrong. I'm one athlete who has more than records and glory to live for.

ANALYZING THE STUDENT ESSAY

After rereading Housman's poem, write an analysis of the above student response. (Or, if you prefer, write your own analysis of "To an Athlete Dying Young.") The following questions may help you:

1. Does the student have a clear understanding of the poem's main theme? Where does he state the theme? Do you agree with his statement of the theme?
2. Does the student identify the speaker in the poem? Are the speaker and the poet the same person? How do you know?
3. Does the student identify the poem's tone? Could the speaker's attitude toward death be ironic? Does the student see any irony in the poem? Does the student ever use any irony himself?
4. Do you agree with the student's statement of Housman's purpose (first sentence of paragraph 4)? How does this statement of purpose relate to the student's understanding of the poem's tone?
5. How do the student's own experiences influence his responses to the poem? How does the student feel about the poet's attitude toward athletes? Do you agree with the reactions expressed in the last two paragraphs?
6. Consider the strength and format of the thesis statement, the development of the paragraphs, and the overall organization of the essay. How could the structure and focus of this paper be changed to create a critical analysis of the poem instead of a reader response?

For study tools to help you with your next writing assignment, please visit the Companion Website at www.pearsoned.ca/mcmahan.

12

Writing about Poetic Language

In no other form of literature are words so important as in poetry. As you study the language of poetry—its freshness, precision, and beauty—you can learn ways in which to use words effectively in your own prose writing.

WHAT DO THE WORDS SUGGEST?

Your sensitivity to poetic language will be enhanced if you learn the meaning of a few terms in literary criticism. (The important term *allusion* is defined in Chapter 10, page 349.)

CONNOTATION AND DENOTATION

Many single words carry a rich load of meaning, both denotative and connotative. The *denotation* of a word is the definition you will find in the dictionary. The *connotation* of a word is the emotional overtones you may feel when encountering the term. Consider the word *mother*. Most people would respond positively with feelings of warmth, security, and love associated with bedtime stories, a warm lap, and fresh apple pies. So, when Stephen Crane includes the word in these moving lines,

> Mother whose heart hung humble as a button
> On the bright splendid shroud of your son,
> Do not weep.
> War is kind,

the connotations of the word *mother* probably account for part of our emotional response.

FIGURES OF SPEECH

The most common figures of speech—metaphor, simile, and personification—appear in our everyday language. You might say, if you keep forgetting things, "My mind is a sieve," creating a metaphor. Or you might note, "That dog looks like a dust mop without a handle," making a simile. Or you might complain, "My typewriter can't spell worth a darn," using personification. Of course, poets use figures of speech that are much fresher and more imaginative than the kind most of us employ—one of the cardinal reasons for considering them poets.

METAPHOR AND SIMILE

A *metaphor* is an imaginative comparison that makes use of the connotative values of words. When Shakespeare writes to a young lover, "[T]hy eternal summer shall not fade," he is comparing youth to the joys of summertime. In "Dulce et Decorum Est" (page 431), a compelling antiwar poem, Wilfred Owen uses the metaphors "[d]runk with fatigue," "blood-shod," "like old beggars under sacks," "coughing like hags," "flound'ring like a man in fire or lime," and "[h]is hanging face, like a devil's sick of sin." The last four of these singularly grim comparisons would usually be called *similes* because they include the connective *like*, but you can also find similes that use *as* and other explicitly comparative words. In fact, you may use the broader term *metaphor* to refer to a figure of speech that is either a metaphor or a simile.

A metaphor goes beyond descriptive detail by making an association that can *only* be imaginary, one that is impossible in reality. A person's life does not have seasons except in a metaphorical way; nor do people really become intoxicated with fatigue. However, the mental stretch these comparisons demand is part of their power. "Drunk with fatigue" makes many imaginative associations: the tired soldiers have lost their ability to think straight; they are staggering along about to fall over; they are not physiologically alert. In the poem, it is this state that makes one of them unable to don his mask quickly when a chlorine gas bomb strikes. His reaction time is fatally impaired, just like a drunk's. You can see how the metaphor packs in meaning and guides our response to the poem's narrative.

These metaphorical ideas—life having seasons or people feeling drunk with fatigue—are not difficult to grasp, since they resonate with our own experiences. Some critics would say that the best metaphors demand a more intellectual leap, having a shocking or puzzling aspect. An example from "Dulce et Decorum Est" might be the description of the soldiers' hurry to grab their gas masks as "[a]n ecstasy of fumbling." We usually associate "ecstasy" with happiness, yet this cannot be the meaning here. We are forced to think beyond the obvious, to the features of ecstasy that do apply—intensity, overpowering emotion, lack of thought, lack of conscious control.

In this chapter, the poem "Shall I Compare Thee to a Summer's Day?" provides an example of an *extended metaphor*. An extended metaphor is exactly what it sounds like: an imaginative comparison worked out through several lines or perhaps even an entire poem, accruing meaning as it goes along. In this case, your understanding of the poem hinges on your understanding of the metaphor it develops.

PERSONIFICATION

"Daylight is nobody's friend," writes Anne Sexton in a metaphor that compares daylight to a friend, but more exactly it is a *personification* because it makes a non-human thing sound like a human being. Archibald Lampman uses personification when he writes "Stern creeping frosts, and winds that touch like steel," as does Andrew Marvell in "Fate with jealous eyes does see." Lisel Mueller's poem "Things" (page 445) offers an explanation for our extensive use and enjoyment of personification.

IMAGERY

Perhaps personification is so widely used in poetry because it gives us a clear image of something otherwise vague or abstract, like daylight or fate. *Imagery* is the term we use to speak of these sensory impressions literature gives us. Robert Frost, in a famous poem, describes a sleigh driver "stopping here / To watch his woods fill up with snow," providing a visual image that most readers find easy to picture. Don McKay in "Glenn Gould, Humming" gives us an apt auditory and tactile image: " . . . humming / he furs the air." Similarly, anyone who has spent time in a big airport surely agrees with Yvor Winters's image of one: "the light gives perfect vision, false and hard; / The metal glitters, deep and bright."

SYMBOL

As you learned in Chapter 6, a *symbol* is an image that becomes so suggestive that it takes on much more meaning than its descriptive value. The connotations of the words, the repetition, the placement, and the meaning it may gather from the rest of the poem help identify an image as a symbol. Blue skies and fresh spring breezes can certainly be just that, but they can also symbolize freedom. Look at the first four lines of "The Swimmer's Moment" by Margaret Avison (page 441):

> For everyone
> The swimmer's moment at the whirlpool comes,
> But many will not say
> "This is the whirlpool, then."

The image in line 2 is descriptive: you can envision the dangerous, downward-spiralling waters of a whirlpool. The observation is also symbolic because once in these waters, their captives are drawn into unforeseeable depths; the rest of the poem endorses the courage of those who brave whirlpools and thereby gain a wider understanding of life.

PARADOX

In a W. H. Auden poem are the lines "You shall love your crooked neighbor / With your crooked heart." An inexperienced reader might say, "Now, that doesn't make any sense! *Crooked heart* and *love* seem contradictory." Others, though, would be sensitive to the paradox in those lines.

A *paradox* is a phrase or statement that on the surface seems contradictory but makes some kind of emotional sense. Looking back at Yvor Winters's description of the San Francisco airport at night, you will find the phrase "perfect vision, false and hard." How can perfect vision be false instead of true? Only as a paradox. Paradoxical also are the "sounds of silence," which is the title of a Paul Simon song. Also, popular singer Carly Simon tells her lover paradoxically that "Nobody does it better / Makes me feel bad so good." The standard Christian paradox is stated in the motto of Mary, Queen of Scots: "In my end is my beginning." In order to make sense of that statement, all we need to know is the customary Christian belief that after death begins a better life in heaven.

OXYMORON

Another figure of speech that appears occasionally in both poetry and prose is an *oxymoron*, an extreme paradox in which two words having opposite meanings are juxtaposed, as in "deafening silence" or "elaborately simple."

OTHER FIGURES OF SPEECH

Many other figures of speech are used in poetry, including apostrophe, conceit, hyperbole, metonymy, onomatopoeia, synecdoche, and synesthesia. These and other types of figurative language are discussed in the Glossary of Literary and Rhetorical Terms at the back of the book.

LOOKING AT POETIC LANGUAGE

The six poems you are about to study exemplify elements of poetic language. As you read them over several times, identify figures of speech, imagery, symbol, and paradox.

Walt Whitman   1819–1892

A Noiseless Patient Spider

A noiseless patient spider,
I mark'd where on a little promontory it stood isolated,
Mark'd how to explore the vacant vast surrounding,
It launched forth filament, filament, filament, out of itself,
Ever unreeling them, ever tirelessly speeding them.

And you O my soul where you stand,
Surrounded, detached, in measureless oceans of space,
Ceaselessly musing, venturing, throwing, seeking the spheres
    to connect them,
Till the bridge you will need be form'd, till the ductile anchor hold,
Till the gossamer thread you fling catch somewhere, O my soul.   10

(1881)

William Shakespeare 1564–1616

Shall I Compare Thee to a Summer's Day?

Shall I compare thee to a summer's day?
Thou art more lovely and more temperate:
Rough winds do shake the darling buds of May,
And summer's lease hath all too short a date:
Sometimes too hot the eye of heaven shines,
And often is his gold complexion dimmed;
And every fair from fair sometimes declines,
By chance or nature's changing course untrimmed;
But thy eternal summer shall not fade,
Nor lose possession of that fair thou ow'st;   10
Nor shall death brag thou wander'st in his shade,
When in eternal lines to time thou grow'st:
So long as men can breathe, or eyes can see,
So long lives this, and this gives life to thee.

(1609)

Archibald Lampman 1861–1899

Voices of Earth

We have not heard the music of the spheres,[1]
The song of star to star, but there are sounds
More deep than human joy and human tears,
That Nature uses in her common rounds;
The fall of streams, the cry of winds that strain
The oak, the roaring of the sea's surge, might
Of thunder breaking afar off, or rain
That falls by minutes in the summer night.
These are the voices of earth's secret soul,
Uttering the mystery from which she came.   10
To him who hears them grief beyond control,
Or joy inscrutable without a name,
Wakes in his heart thoughts bedded there, impearled,
Before the birth and making of the world.

(1899)

---

[1] Melodic sounds created by the movement of the stars and planets.

Dorothy Livesay   1909–1996

Bartok[1] and the Geranium

She lifts her green umbrellas
Towards the pane
Seeking her fill of sunlight
Or of rain;
Whatever falls
She has no commentary
Accepts, extends,
Blows out her furbelows,[2]
Her bustling boughs;

And all the while he whirls   10
Explodes in space,
Never content with this small room:
Not even can he be
Confined to sky
But must speed high and higher still
From galaxy to galaxy,
Wrench from the stars their momentary notes
Steal music from the moon.

She's daylight
He is dark
She's heaven-held breath
He storms and crackles   20
Spits with hell's own spark.

Yet in this room, this moment now
These together breathe and be:
She, essence of serenity,
He in a mad intensity
Soars beyond sight
Then hurls, lost Lucifer,
From heaven's height.

And when he's done, he's out   30
She leans a lip against the glass
And preens herself in light.

(1955)

---

[1] A Hungarian composer (1881–1945). Béla Bartók's music was influenced by ethnic folk traditions; his works reflect strong emotion and often part from the diatonic scale.
[2] Elaborate frills or trims; here the inference is that the plant's petals are like flounces or ruffles of a dress.

Lorna Crozier   b. 1948

Poem about Nothing

Zero is the one we didn't understand
at school. Multiplied by anything
it remains nothing.

When I ask my friend
the mathematician who studies rhetoric
if zero is a number, he says *yes*
and I feel great relief.

If it were a landscape
it would be a desert.
If it had anything to do   10

with anatomy, it would be
a mouth, a missing limb,
a lost organ.

ø

Zero worms its way
               between one and one
and changes everything.
It slips inside the alphabet.
It is the vowel on a mute tongue,
the pupil in a blind man's eye,
the image   20
         of the face
he holds on his fingertips.

ø

When you look up
from the bottom of a dry well
zero is what you see,
the terrible blue of it.

It is the rope
you knot around your throat
when your heels itch for wings.

Icarus understood zero   30
as he caught the smell
of burning feathers
and fell into the sea.

Ø

If you roll zero down a hill
it will grow,
swallow the towns, the farms,
the people at their tables
playing tic-tac-toe.

Ø

When the Cree chiefs
signed the treaties on the plains	40
they wrote X
beside their names.

In English, X equals zero.

Ø

I ask my friend
the rhetorician who studies mathematics
What does zero mean and keep it simple.

He says *Zip*.

Ø

Zero is the pornographer's number.
He orders it through the mail
under a false name. It is the number	50
of the last man on death row,
the number of the girl who jumps
three stories to abort.

Zero starts and ends
at the same place. Some compare it
to driving across the Prairies all day
and feeling you've gone nowhere.

Ø Ø Ø

In the beginning God made zero.

(1985)

Donald Hall   b. 1928

My Son My Executioner

My son, my executioner,
    I take you in my arms,
Quiet and small and just astir,
    And whom my body warms.

Sweet death, small son, our instrument
    Of immortality,
Your cries and hungers document
    Our bodily decay.

We twenty-five and twenty-two,
    Who seemed to live forever,   10
Observe enduring life in you
    And start to die together.

(1955)

PREWRITING

The following exercises will help you analyze the use of language in the poems that you just read in preparation for writing a paper focusing on that approach.

EXAMINING POETIC LANGUAGE

1. Why could one say that "Shall I Compare Thee to a Summer's Day?" presents contrast rather than comparison?
2. In a group of classmates, attempt to write a companion poem to "Shall I Compare Thee to a Summer's Day?" only with the extended metaphor being, "Shall I compare thee to a winter's day?" Try to use connotative language.
3. What is the main comparison made in "A Noiseless Patient Spider"? What is personified? Using a thesaurus, paraphrase the poem, substituting near synonyms for some of the original words. Comment on the differences in meaning and tone you create. (Imagine, for example, if the spider "launched forth string, string, string, out of itself.")
4. What is the predominant type of imagery used in Lampman's "Voices of Earth"? What is being personified? In a group of classmates, write a companion poem to "Voices of Earth" using another type of sensory imagery, for example, touch, taste, sight, or smell.
5. Dorothy Livesay in "Bartok and the Geranium" effectively uses personification as a means of comparing two subjects. How is tone affected through this comparison? To expand your understanding of the poem's tone, do a little research to discover more about the Hungarian composer Béla Bartók.

6. Lorna Crozier's "Poem about Nothing" depends on paradox almost exclusively. List the paradoxes, and discuss how each one contributes to the effect of the final line.
7. Explain the paradox that is central to "My Son My Executioner."

WRITING

Poetic language is one of the richest veins of material for writing. You could, for example, analyze the role of nature imagery in "Voices of Earth," in "Shall I Compare Thee to a Summer's Day?" or in "A Noiseless Patient Spider." Or you could examine the cumulative effect of the extended metaphor in "Poem about Nothing."

COMPARING AND CONTRASTING

Noticing similarities and differences between poems will sharpen your sensitivity to each of them. If you listed all the words in the short poem "Voices of Earth" and scrambled them, then listed all the words in "Poem about Nothing" and scrambled them, putting the two lists side by side, you might see for the first time that "Poem about Nothing" has surprisingly few abstract terms, and that in contrast with "Voices of Earth" it has few words that convey emotion. Taking the comparison further, you might say that "Voices of Earth" focuses on creating strong, sensuous images to enhance feeling while "Poem about Nothing" focuses on expression of ideas to enhance tone.

The following writing assignments suggest some meaningful comparisons to explore.

IDEAS FOR WRITING

IDEAS FOR RESPONSIVE WRITING

1. Whitman's poem comparing the explorations of the spider to the searchings of his soul makes the totally abstract idea of the soul's search for meaning clear and concrete. Think of some abstraction that you might want to explain to a five-year-old child—something like gentleness, aggression, wisdom, slyness, or perseverance. Then think of an appropriate animal or insect to illustrate the quality, and write a poem or a fable to show the child why the quality is good or bad. Remember to keep your vocabulary simple and your lines or sentences short.
2. Livesay's poem "Bartok and the Geranium" contrasts two very dissimilar subjects. Using the poem as a guide, write a comparison or a contrast of two subjects, one a person, the other an object requiring personification.
3. Write a description of an abstract concept, using personification and metaphors the way Crozier does in her poem "Poem about Nothing."

IDEAS FOR CRITICAL WRITING

1. In your study of literature and in your everyday life, you have come across many metaphors and similes for the last stage of life. Examine the imagery and tone of Archibald Lampman's "Winter Evening" (page 420 of the anthology) in terms of similarities to and differences from other figures of speech that describe the approach of death.
2. Focusing on the imagery, the personas, and/or the tone of each, compare the poems "We Real Cool" by Gwendolyn Brooks and A. E. Housman's "To an Athlete Dying Young" (pages 392 and 418). Be sure you thoroughly read and understand each poem.
3. Discuss the symbol of the spider in Robert Frost's "Design" (page 423 in the anthology) and Whitman's "A Noiseless Patient Spider" (in this chapter).
4. Compare and contrast the tone in Shakespeare's Sonnet 18 ("Shall I Compare Thee to a Summer's Day?" on page 374) and "My Mistress' Eyes Are Nothing Like the Sun" (page 405). Remember that it is almost impossible to separate the persona from the tone, so you may have to discuss both.

REWRITING: STYLE

After looking so closely at poetic language, you should have a grasp of how important every word is to the total effect of a piece of writing.

CHOOSING VIVID, DESCRIPTIVE TERMS

George Elliott Clarke's "Blank Sonnet" (page 473) draws its strength almost exclusively from the vividness of its language. For the poem's speaker, "[t]he air smells of rhubarb, occasional / Roses, or first birth of blossoms, a fresh, / Undulant hurt, so body snaps and curls / Like flower." While your expository prose should not be quite so packed with arresting terminology, it can probably be improved by some attention to descriptive wording. Look at several of your back papers from this class. See whether you can identify your pet vacant words. Do you always express positive evaluations with *nice* or *beautiful*? Do you usually intensify an adjective with the word *very*? Do you refer to everything from ideas to irises as *things*? Furthermore, do you describe anything that causes a faint stir in your being as *interesting*, causing you to come up with vapid sentences like "This beautiful poem is full of very interesting things"? If so, you need to find livelier, more exact terms.

FINDING LIVELY WORDS

Two quite different sources of help can work together in your quest for a more descriptive style. The first is your imagination: when you see that word *interesting* crop up as you write your rough draft, put a check in the margin; later, as you rewrite, ask yourself what you really meant.

Sometimes you mean *significant* or *meaningful*; sometimes you mean *unusual* or *odd*; sometimes you even mean *perplexing* or *disturbing*.

If you are not completely pleased with your efforts, try using a thesaurus to jog your memory. Under *interesting* in our Roget's *Thesaurus*, we find "racy, spicy, breezy, salty; succulent, piquant, appealing, zestful, glamorous, colorful, picturesque; absorbing, enthralling, engrossing, fascinating, entertaining, ageless, dateless," as well as cross-references to more lists at *amusement, attention, attraction,* and *right*. Somewhere in this large selection you should be able to find a word that conveys a clearer image than *interesting* does. Never choose an unfamiliar word, though, without first looking it up in a college- or university-level dictionary to be sure it conveys the exact meaning you want.

EXERCISE ON DICTION

Find five to ten sentences in your back papers (from this class or others) that can be improved by the use of livelier, more descriptive words. Write down the original, using every other line on your page. Then revise each sentence, crossing out expressionless words and writing in the new ones on the blank lines.

SAMPLE COMPARISON PAPER

The following is a sample paper written for a first-year university English course. In her paper, Martha McKnight compares the personas and the tones of three poems that rely almost exclusively on the symbol of the rose. (Note Martha's Works Cited page: she uses cross-referencing in her list of poems to avoid repeating the title of the same anthology.)

If you wish to write a comparison or contrast essay, try to identify poems in the anthology section that use common themes or poetic devices. As well, take note of the poems grouped together in the Thematic Contents at the beginning of the book.

 For study tools to help you with your next writing assignment, please visit the Companion Website at www.pearsoned.ca/mcmahan.

Martha McKnight
English 1110
September 23, 2003

Persona and Tone in Three "Rose" Poems

The rose has long been a symbol of love, as the Scottish poet Robbie Burns expresses in one of the world's best known similes: "O My Luve's like a red, red rose" (line 1). Readers come to expect the symbol to express love's most positive attributes, such as beauty, constancy, sweetness, purity, and perfection. Not all poems in which the symbol is used focus on love's positive aspects, however. Edmund Waller's "Go, Lovely Rose," Dorothy Parker's "One Perfect Rose," and William Blake's "The Sick Rose" attend more to the thorns of love than to the delicate petals. While these poems certainly speak of love through the symbol of the rose, the persona in each poem expresses a different attitude toward love and toward the symbol of the rose itself. One persona is a seducer, one is a cynic, and one is a weary soul.

The persona of Edmund Waller's "Go, Lovely Rose" is an impatient individual intent upon the seduction of a beautiful woman, and he uses the rose as a symbol of the perishable nature of beauty. The rose he sends is supposed to "Tell her that wastes her time and [his], / that now she knows" (2-3) just how short a time she has to be young and beautiful, and, therefore, in his eyes, lovable. The more subtle message the reader is able to deduce is that this persona's love is also as perishable as the rose itself. As explained in the third stanza, the persona sees no worth in beauty unless it is exposed to or desired by him:

> Small is the worth
> Of beauty from the light retir'd
> Bid her come forth,
> Suffer herself to be desir'd. (11-14)

There is no message of faithfulness or any other positive characteristic of love sent with this rose. In fact, the persona, shallow and self-serving individual that he is, instructs the rose to "die, that she / The common fate of all things rare / May read in thee" (16-18): her own mortality. It seems a thinly veiled threat that if this beautiful woman does not allow herself to be seduced by the persona, she will wither and die like the rose. What seems implicit is that from this persona's perspective it would be a fate worse than death for the object of his shallow affection to die unloved by him. Impatience, superficiality, and inconstancy are descriptors applicable to the seducer-persona of Waller's "Go, Lovely Rose."

While Waller's persona is self-serving, Parker's persona is cynical regarding the effectiveness of the rose as a messenger of love. "One Perfect Rose" establishes the persona as one who is familiar with "the language of the floweret" (5) and sensitive to the positive qualities of love, as the words "Deephearted, pure" (3) imply. Throughout the first two stanzas, we are convinced that the rose is doing its job as love's messenger until we read the final stanza. Here the persona reveals the suspicion she has that the rose may not be the best symbol of love after all. Instead, she questions, "Why is it no one ever sent me yet / One perfect limousine, do you suppose?" (9-10). The cynicism of the persona may be made clearer through a comparison between the rose as a symbol of love and a limousine as love's messenger. A rose is corruptible; a limousine is corruptible, but it certainly lasts longer than a flower. A rose is relatively inexpensive; a limousine requires more of an investment on behalf of the giver. A rose is fragile; a limousine is powerful. If the rose of Edmund Waller is to be believed, the message is that the receiver will inevitably die as does the rose; the truth of this message is not altered by having a limousine as messenger, but it would surely get the receiver to her inevitable end in style! Therefore, is the limousine with its characteristics of longevity, reliability, sturdiness, and beauty not a better representative of love than the flimsy rose? The persona of Parker's "One Perfect Rose" certainly thinks so. She is an unromantic cynic, but she is one who is asking more of an overused symbol than is the seducer in "Go, Lovely Rose."

Given the shallowness and the cynicism of the previous personas, it is little wonder, then, that the persona of Blake's "The Sick Rose," weary of the ill use the symbol has received, sees the rose as a dying representative of love: "O Rose, thou art sick!" (1). Blake's poem, written in 1794, was constructed before the derisive Parker poem; however, the symbol of the rose had been in use for centuries before Blake's time, and cynicism is not exclusive to the twentieth century. It is plausible that Blake capitalizes the word "Rose" in order to focus attention on the rose as a symbol. As such, "The invisible worm / That flies in the night" (2-3) could be anything that casts aspersions on the rose as a pure symbol of love: the cynicism of some or the seductiveness of others. "[T]he howling storm" (4) may refer to the strife and stress of lust or to the convoluted twists and turns of cynicism, and the "bed / Of crimson joy" (5-6) may refer to the passion of the love-bed or the former delight in a well-used symbol such as the rose. When the symbol of the rose is misused for purposes of "dark secret love," (7) then the purity, nobility, and directness of the symbol are destroyed. The dark seductiveness and secret duplicity have destroyed the usefulness of the symbol. Blake's persona seems weary of the misused symbol and seems to be putting the rose as symbol to rest not because he does not understand its worth, but because he all too well understands its misuse.

    Waller, Parker, and Blake develop personas to reveal different attitudes concerning the symbol of the rose in their respective poems "Go, Lovely Rose," "One Perfect Rose," and "The Sick Rose." The rose has long been used as a symbol for love, and there is little chance that it will be dropped from the lexicon of love even if it carries with it a few more thorns.

McKnight 6

Works Cited

Blake, William. "The Sick Rose." <u>Literature and the Writing Process</u>. Eds. Elizabeth McMahan, Susan X. Day, and Robert Funk. 6th ed. Upper Saddle River, NJ: Prentice Hall, 2002. 497.

Burns, Robert. "A Red, Red Rose." <u>Norton Anthology of English Literature</u>. Ed. M. H. Abrams et al. 4th ed. Vol. 2. New York: Norton, 1979. 106-07.

Parker, Dorothy. "One Perfect Rose." McMahan, Day, and Funk. 438.

Waller, Edmund. "Go, Lovely Rose." McMahan, Day, and Funk. 437.

13

Writing about Poetic Form

When we say that poetry has *form*, we mean it has design or structure. All poems have some kind of form. Many elements go into making the forms of poetry, but they all involve arranging the words in patterns. Sometimes sound controls the pattern; sometimes the number of words or the length of the lines determines the form.

WHAT ARE THE FORMS OF POETRY?

Poetic forms can be divided into those that use sound effects (rhythm, rhyme), those that involve the length and organization of lines (stanza), and those that artistically manipulate word order (syntax).

RHYTHM AND RHYME

Sound effects are produced by organized repetition. Stressing or accenting words and syllables produces *rhythm*; repeating similar sounds in an effective scheme produces *rhyme*. Both effects intensify the meaning of a poem, arouse interest, and give pleasure. Once we notice a pattern of sound we expect it to continue, and this expectation makes us more attentive to subtleties in the entire poem.

Rhythm can affect us powerfully. We respond almost automatically to the beat of a drum, the thumping of our heart, the pulsing of an engine. Poetic rhythm, usually more subtle, is created by repeating stresses and pauses. Rhythm conveys no verbal meaning itself, but when used skilfully it reinforces the meaning and tone of a poem. Consider how Theodore Roethke captures the raucous spirit of "My Papa's Waltz" in the recurring three-stress rhythm of these lines:

> We romped until the pans
> Slid from the kitchen shelf; . . .
> Then waltzed me off to bed
> Still clinging to your shirt.

For more details about the rhythms of poetry, see Chart 13-1 on meter.

> **CHART 13-1 RHYTHM AND METER IN POETRY**
>
> When the rhythm has a regular pattern—that is, when the stress recurs at regular intervals—the result is *meter*. Not all poems are metered, but many are written in one dominant pattern.
>
> **NUMBER OF FEET** Poetic meter is measured in *feet*, units of stressed and unstressed syllables. A line of poetry may be written in monometer (having one foot), dimeter (two feet), trimeter (three feet), tetrameter (four feet), pentameter (five feet), hexameter (six feet), and so on.
>
> **KINDS OF FEET** The syllables in a line can occur in regular patterns. The most common pattern for poetry written in English is *iambic*, an unstressed syllable (˘) followed by a stressed one (´). This line is written in iambic pentameter; it has five iambic feet:
>
> Mў mis | trĕss' ҆eyes | ăre nó | thĭng líke | thĕ sún
>
> Three other meters are of some importance in English poetry:
>
> *trochaic* (a stressed syllable followed by an unstressed one):
> Téll mĕ | nót ĭn | móurn fŭl | núm bĕrs
>
> *anapestic* (two unstressed syllables followed by a stressed one):
> 'Twăs thĕ níght | bĕ fŏre Chríst | măs ănd áll | thrŏugh thĕ hóuse
>
> *dactylic* (a stressed syllable followed by two unstressed ones):
> Wóman much missed, how you call to me, call to me

Rhyme, a recurring pattern of similar sounds, also enhances tone and meaning. Because rhymed language is special language, it helps set poetry apart from ordinary expression and calls attention to the sense, feeling, and tone of the words. Rhyme also gives a certain pleasure to the reader by fulfilling the expectation of the sound patterns. Rhyme, which usually depends on sound, not spelling, occurs when accented syllables contain the same or a similar vowel sound with identical consonants following the vowel: *right* and *bite*, *knuckle* and *buckle*. Rhymes are commonly used at regular intervals within a poem, often at the ends of lines:

> West wind, blow from your prairie nest,
> Blow from the mountains, blow from the west

ALLITERATION, ASSONANCE, AND CONSONANCE

Closely allied to rhyme are other verbal devices that depend on the correspondence of sounds. *Alliteration* is the repetition of consonant sounds either at the beginning of words or in stressed syllables: "The Soul selects her own Society—" or "Nature's first green is gold, / Her hardest hue to hold." *Assonance* is the repetition of similar vowel sounds that are not followed by identical consonant sounds: *grave* and *gain*, *shine* and *bright*. *Consonance* is a kind of half-rhyme in which the consonants are parallel but the vowels change: *blade* and *blood*, *flash* and *flesh*. Alliteration, assonance, and consonance are likely to be used occasionally and not in regular, recurring patterns; but these devices of sound do focus our attention and affect the tone, melody, and tempo of poetic expression.

EXERCISE ON POETIC FORM

Listen to a favourite popular song and copy down the lyrics (you may have to listen several times). Now arrange the lines on the page as you think they would be printed. What patterns of rhythm and sound do you see? Did you notice them before you wrote the words down and arranged the lines? Does the lineation (the arrangement into lines of poetry) help make the meaning any clearer? If possible, compare your written version with a printed one (on the CD cover or album liner or in a magazine that publishes song lyrics).

STANZAS: CLOSED AND OPEN FORMS

In the past, almost all poems were written in *closed form*: poetry with lines of equal length arranged in fixed patterns of stress and rhyme. Although these elements of form are still much in evidence today, modern poets prefer the greater freedom of *open form poetry*, which uses lines of varying length and avoids prescribed patterns of rhyme or rhythm.

Closed forms give definition and shape to poetic expression. *Rhyme schemes* and *stanza patterns* demand the careful arrangement of words and lines into units of meaning that guide both writer and reader in understanding poetry.

COUPLETS AND QUATRAINS Stanzas can be created on the basis of the number of lines, the length of the lines, the pattern of stressed syllables (the meter), and the rhyme scheme (the order in which rhymed words recur). The simplest stanza form is the *couplet*: two rhymed lines, usually of equal length and similar meter. Pauline Johnson's "The Song My Paddle Sings" (page 419) is written in rhyming couplets although the lines vary in length and sometimes in rhythm. The most common stanza in English poetry is the *quatrain*, a group of four lines with any number of rhyme schemes. "The Ruined Maid" (page 354) is composed of six quatrains in which the lines rhyme as couplets (critics indicate this pattern of rhyme with letters: *a a b b*). While this rhyme scheme and stanza form are used in "The Ruined Maid," the quatrains of "My Papa's Waltz" (page 354) employ an alternating rhyme pattern (*a b a b*). Longer stanza patterns are used, of course, but the quatrain and the couplet remain the basic components of closed-form poetry.

SONNETS The fixed form that has been used most frequently by the greatest variety of notable poets in England and North America is the *sonnet*. Originating in Italy in the fourteenth century, the sonnet became a staple of English poetry in the sixteenth century and has continued to attract practitioners ever since.

The form of the sonnet is firmly fixed: fourteen lines, with ten syllables per line, arranged in a set rhyme scheme. The *Shakespearean sonnet* uses the rhyme scheme most common for sonnets in English: *a b a b, c d c d, e f e f, g g*. You will notice the rhyme scheme falls into three quatrains and an ending couplet, with a total of seven rhymes. "Shall I Compare Thee to a Summer's Day?" (page 374) is a splendid example of Shakespeare's mastery of the sonnet (he wrote 154 of them) and illustrates why this traditional verse form continues to entice and stir both poets and readers. George Elliott Clarke wrote a modern sonnet that adheres to the ten syllables per line structure, but as the title "Blank Sonnet" implies, it has no rhyme scheme (page 473). The Italian sonnet, not very common in English poetry, uses fewer rhymes (five) and has only two groupings of lines, the first eight called the *octave*, and the last six the *sestet*. Robert Frost created a chilling Italian sonnet in "Design" (page 423).

FREE VERSE A poem written in *open form* generally has no rhyme scheme and no basic meter for the entire selection. Rhyme and rhythm do occur, of course, but not in the fixed patterns that are required of stanzas and sonnets. Many readers think that open-form poetry is easy to write, but that is not the case. Only careless poetry is easy to write, and even closed forms can be sloppily written. Open forms demand their own special arrangements; without the fixed patterns of traditional forms to guide them, modern poets must discover these structures on their own. Walt Whitman's "A Noiseless Patient Spider" (page 373) demonstrates how open form still uses sound and rhythm to create tone, enhance meaning, and guide the responses of the reader.

POETIC SYNTAX

Rhyme, rhythm, and stanza are not the only resources of form available to poets. Writers can also manipulate the way the words are arranged into sentences. For instance, the short, staccato sentences of "We Real Cool" (page 392) impress us in a way entirely different from the effect of the intricate expression of "Nuns Fret Not" (page 394), which is a single sentence stretching over fourteen lines. Words in English sentences must be arranged in fairly standard patterns. If we reverse the order of "John struck the ball" to "The ball struck John," the words take on a new meaning altogether. As with stanza form and rhyme scheme, poets can either stick with the rigidity of English sentence structure (syntax) or try to achieve unusual effects through inversion. E. E. Cummings, for example, forces his readers to pay close attention to the line "anyone lived in a pretty how town" by rearranging the words in an unexpected way. (In the standard pattern of an exclamation, the line would read "How pretty a town anyone lived in!")

LOOKING AT THE FORMS OF POETRY

The following poems illustrate many of the variations of sound and organization that we have just discussed. As you read these poems, be alert for the special effects that the poets create with rhythm, rhyme, stanza form, and syntax. You may have to read some selections several times to appreciate how thoroughly form and meaning work together.

Gwendolyn Brooks 1917–2000

We Real Cool

The Pool Players
Seven at the Golden Shovel

We real cool. We
Left school. We

Lurk late. We
Strike straight. We

Sing sin. We
Thin gin. We

Jazz June. We
Die soon.

(1960)

bp Nichol 1944–1988

landscape: 1

for thomas a. clark

alongthehorizongrewanunbrokenlineoftrees
_____

(1986)

E. E. Cummings   1894–1962

anyone lived in a pretty how town

    anyone lived in a pretty how town
    (with up so floating many bells down)
    spring summer autumn winter
    he sang his didn't he danced his did.

    Women and men (both little and small)
    cared for anyone not at all
    they sowed their isn't they reaped their same
    sun moon stars rain

    children guessed (but only a few
    and down they forgot as up they grew   10
    autumn winter spring summer)
    that noone loved him more by more

    when by now and tree by leaf
    she laughed his joy she cried his grief
    bird by snow and stir by still
    anyone's any was all to her

    someones married their everyones
    laughed their cryings and did their dance
    (sleep wake hope and then) they
    said their nevers they slept their dream   20

    stars rain sun moon
    (and only the snow can begin to explain
    how children are apt to forget to remember
    with up so floating many bells down)

    one day anyone died i guess
    (and noone stooped to kiss his face)
    busy folk buried them side by side
    little by little and was by was

    all by all and deep by deep
    and more by more they dream their sleep   30
    noone and anyone earth by april
    wish by spirit and if by yes.

    Women and men (both dong and ding)
    summer autumn winter spring
    reaped their sowing and went their came
    sun moon stars rain

    (1940)

Phyllis Webb   b. 1927

Treblinka Gas Chamber

*'Klostermayer ordered another count of the children.
Then their stars were snipped off and thrown into
the center of the courtyard. It looked like a field of buttercups.'*
—A FIELD OF BUTTERCUPS *by* JOSEPH HYAMS

```
fallingstars
           'a field of
                    buttercups'
           yellow stars
                    of David
                           falling
the prisoners
           the children
                    falling
           in heaps                                              10
                on one another
                           they go down

Thanatos
      showers
           his dirty breath
                           they must breathe
                                         him in

           they see stars
                    behind their
                              eyes                               20
David's
      'a field of
                buttercups'
                a metaphor
                         where all that's
                                      left lies down
                                                           (1978)
```

WEB

William Wordsworth   1770–1850

Nuns Fret Not

Nuns fret not at their convent's narrow room;
And hermits are contented with their cells;
And students with their pensive citadels;
Maids at the wheel, the weaver at his loom,

Sit blithe and happy; bees that soar for bloom,
High as the highest Peak of Furness-fells,[1]
Will murmur by the hour in foxglove bells:[2]
In truth the prison, unto which we doom
Ourselves, no prison is: and hence for me,
In sundry moods, 'twas pastime to be bound   10
Within the sonnet's scanty plot of ground;
Pleased if some souls (for such there needs must be)
Who have felt the weight of too much liberty,
Should find brief solace there, as I have found.

(1807)

PREWRITING

Writing about poetic form is challenging. Because it is impossible to separate form from meaning, you must be sure that you understand what a poem says before you try to analyze how its formal characteristics contribute to your understanding and appreciation. In completing the following exercises, you should read the poems aloud, if possible, and reread the difficult passages a number of times before you decide upon your answers.

EXPERIMENTING WITH POETIC FORMS

1. Write out the following poem, filling in the blanks with one of the choices given in parentheses to the right of each line. Use sound, rhyme, and context to determine your choices.

The Death of the Ball Turret Gunner

From my mother's ____ I fell into the State,	(womb, sleep)
And I ____ in its belly till my wet	(hunched, crouched)
____ froze.	(skin, fur)
Six miles from earth, ____ from its dream of life,	(freed, loosed)
I woke to black flak and the ____ fighters.	(loud, nightmare)
When I died they ____ me out of the turret with a ____.	(washed, flushed) (mop, hose)

Now turn to page 438 and compare your choices with the poet's. Can you explain why each word was chosen?

2. Examine "We Real Cool" by Gwendolyn Brooks (page 392). How would you describe the rhythm of this poem? How does the rhythm

---
[1] Mountains near Wordsworth's home.
[2] Wildflowers.

affect your perception of the speakers (the "We" of the poem)? Why are all the sentences in the last four stanzas only three words long? What is the effect of placing the subject of those sentences ("We") at the ends of the lines?

3. Look at bp Nichol's concrete poem "landscape: 1," and notice how the form reflects the content. Who is Thomas A. Clark, the individual to whom the poem is dedicated? Does his occupation add to the meaning of the poem? Why are all the words jammed together without spacing? What effect does this have? Is the long line underscoring and extending beyond the beginning and the end of the words important to the poem? Why? Is it important that the word "grew" is the middle syllable in the poem? "Grew" is the only verb in the poem; why is it written in the past tense? If you rewrite the poem with line breaks, how is the effect altered? Does this poem adhere to a rhythmic pattern?

4. Study the rhyme schemes and line variations of the following poems, all of which are written in quatrains:

    — "My Son My Executioner" (page 378)
    — "anyone lived in a pretty how town" (page 393)
    — "The Tyger" (page 409)
    — "Because I Could Not Stop for Death" (page 416)
    — "The Ruined Maid" (page 354)
    — "One Perfect Rose" (page 357)

    In which of the poems do the stanza divisions indicate a change of time or a shift in thought? Do any of the poets disregard the stanza patterns? Try to decide why all of these poets used quatrains.

5. Complete as many of the following quatrains as you can by supplying a last line. Try to write a line that puts a picture in the reader's mind.

    Tell me not, sweet, I am unkind,
        That from the nunnery
    Of thy chaste breast and quiet mind
    _____.

    Because I could not stop for Death—
    He kindly stopped for me—
    The Carriage held but just Ourselves—
    _____.

    The time you won your town the race
    We chaired you through the market-place;
    Man and boy stood cheering by,
    _____.

    Aunt Jennifer's tigers prance across a screen,
    Bright topaz denizens of a world of green.
    They do not fear the men beneath the tree;
    _____.

Compare your creations with the originals, which can be found in the Anthology of Poetry. Look up the first line of each poem in the Index of Authors, Titles, and First Lines of Poems.

6. Rewrite the following lines—from W. H. Auden's "Musée des Beaux Arts" (page 436) and "anyone lived in a pretty how town" (page 393)— putting them in the word order you would expect them to follow in ordinary speech:

>About suffering they were never wrong, The Old Masters

>In Brueghel's *Icarus*, for instance: how everything turns away
>Quite leisurely from the disaster

>anyone lived in a pretty how town
>(with up so floating many bells down)

>Women and men (both little and small)
>cared for anyone not at all

7. Ogden Nash was the whimsical master of outrageous rhymes and comical couplets. Often playful and nonsensical, Nash's verse can also be pointed and critical. Read the following rhymed couplets by Ogden Nash and then try to imitate them. In writing your own couplets, you will probably want to follow Nash's practice of using a title to set up the theme of your two-line commentaries.

>*Common Sense*
>Why did the Lord give us agility
>If not to evade responsibility?

>*The Cow*
>The cow is of the bovine ilk;
>One end is moo, the other, milk.

>*Reflection on Ingenuity*
>Here's a good rule of thumb:
>Too clever is dumb.

>*The Parent*
>Children aren't happy with nothing to ignore,
>And that's what parents were created for.

>*Grandpa Is Ashamed*
>A child need not be very clever
>To learn that "Later, dear" means "Never."

WRITING

Since rhythm, rhyme, syntax, and stanza convey no meaning in themselves, you probably will not write an entire essay on form alone. Instead you can use what you have learned about poetic form to help you analyze and interpret a poem (or poems) with greater understanding and confidence.

RELATING FORM TO MEANING

You can use observations about form to confirm and develop your ideas about the meaning or theme of a poem. Looking at a poem's formal characteristics will help you answer such important questions as these: What is the tone? Is the speaker being ironic? What are the key words and images? And how does the main idea advance through the poem?

Specifically, elements of form offer clues like these:

1. Close, obvious rhyme often indicates a comic or ironic tone. Subtle rhymes support more serious tones.
2. Heavy stress can be humorous, but it can also suggest anger, defiance, strength, or fear.
3. Alliteration can be humorous, but it can also be chillingly serious; it serves to provide emphasis by slowing the reading of the line.
4. Assonance can provide a rich, solemn effect, a certain grandeur perhaps, or even a sensuous effect.
5. Rhythm and repetition emphasize key words.
6. Stanzas and rhyme schemes mark out patterns of thought and can serve as guides to development of theme.
7. Important images are often underscored with rhyme and stress.
8. Inverted or unusual syntax calls attention to complex ideas.
9. Various elements of form can be used to indicate a change in speaker or a shift in thought or tone.
10. Typographical effects can call attention to significant feelings or ideas.

This list does not exhaust the possibilities, but it should alert you to the various ways that form relates to thought and meaning in poetry.

IDEAS FOR WRITING

IDEAS FOR EXPRESSIVE WRITING

1. Write an original haiku. A *haiku* is a rhymeless Japanese poem. Its form is based on syllables: seventeen syllables usually arranged in three lines, often following a pattern of five, seven, and five. Haiku written in English, however, do not always follow the original Japanese syllable pattern and may even be rhymed. Because of their brevity, haiku compress their expression by focusing on images and letting the closely observed details suggest the feelings and meanings. The following haiku, translated from Japanese originals and some written in English, provide a variety of models for you to follow:

> The piercing chill I feel:
>   my dead wife's comb, in our bedroom,
>   under my heel . . .
>   —Taniguchi Buson (trans. Harold G. Henderson)

> Affiliated
> with puddles, a small boy drowns
> new red rubber boots.
>
> —Mildred A. Rose

> Rain in night London
> umbrellas black tulips
>   in aerial ballet.
>
> —Mildred A. Rose

> Heat-lightning streak—
>   through darkness pierces
> the heron's shriek.
>
> —Matsuo Basho

Notice that the images in these haiku convey strong sensory experiences implying a great deal more than a mere description would suggest.

2. Write an original limerick. The *limerick* is a form of humorous verse popularized in the nineteenth century by Englishman Edward Lear. Its form is fairly simple—a five-line stanza built on two rhymes (*a a b b a*) with the third and fourth lines one beat shorter than the other three. The meter (or rhythm pattern) usually involves two unstressed syllables followed by an accented syllable, giving the lines a kind of playful skipping or jogging sound when they are recited or read aloud. Lear's limericks depended on a curious or fantastic "plot" for their effects:

> There was a Young Lady whose chin
> Resembled the point of a pin;
>   So she had it made sharp
>   And purchased a harp,
> And played several tunes with her chin.

More contemporary limericks take delight in giving the last line an extra twist with a surprise rhyme or an absurd idea. Some modern limericks make their point by using outrageous spellings or tricks of typography:

> There was a young fellow named Tate
> Who dined with his girl at 8.8,
>   But I'd hate to relate
>   What that person named Tate
> And his tête-à-tête ate at 8.8.
>
> —Carolyn Wells

> There was a young lady of Warwick,
> Who lived in a castle histarwick,
>   On the damp castle mould
>   She contracted a could,
> And the doctor prescribed paregarwick.
>
> —Anonymous

These often ingenious and slightly mad little verses continue to entertain readers and writers alike.

Wear and Tear

There was an old man of the Cape,
Who made himself garments of crêpe.
   When asked, "Do they tear?"
   He replied, "Here and there,
But they're perfectly splendid for shape!"

—Robert Louis Stevenson

There was a young virgin named Wilde,
Who kept herself quite undefiled,
   By thinking of Jesus,
   Contagious diseases,
And the bother of having a child.

—Anonymous

IDEAS FOR CRITICAL WRITING

1. Show how rhythm, repetition, rhyme, and the simplicity of language affect the tone and meaning in "We Real Cool" (page 392) and William Blake's "The Tyger" (page 409). Are the effects the same in both poems?

2. Write an interpretation of "anyone lived in a pretty how town" or Earle Birney's "Anglosaxon Street" (page 433). Give particular attention to the way that meter, rhyme, alliteration, syntax, and stanza form contribute to your understanding of the poem.

3. Explain the humorous use of language and poetic form in Thomas Hardy's "The Ruined Maid" (page 354).

4. Analyze the series of metaphors in "Nuns Fret Not" (page 394). What is Wordsworth saying about writing sonnets and using traditional closed forms of poetry?

5. Compare one of Shakespeare's sonnets (page 374 or page 405) with a modern sonnet, such as Frost's "Design" (page 423) or George Elliott Clarke's "Blank Sonnet" (page 473). Why do the modern poems *not* seem like sonnets? Pay close attention to the syntax and the way each poem is subdivided.

6. Look up the term *concrete poetry*. Examine bp Nichol's "landscape: 1" (page 392) and discuss how the form of this concrete poem is also its content.

7. Phyllis Webb's "Treblinka Gas Chamber" (page 394) is structured in a distinctive pattern. Once you have read and understood the poem, consider the effect that such a structure has on the content.

REWRITING: STYLE

As a writer, you must choose your words carefully. Many English words are to some extent synonymous, even interchangeable, but often the distinctions between synonyms are as important as their similarities. "The difference between the right word and the almost right word," said Mark Twain, "is the difference between lightning and the lightning bug." When you revise your essay, focus on the accuracy and precision of the words you use.

FINDING THE EXACT WORD

You must take care that both the denotations and connotations of the words you use are the ones you intend. You do not want to write *heroics* when you really mean *heroism*. You do not want to "*expose* three main topics" when you really intend to *explore* them. The following are some problem areas to consider as you look at the words you have used in your essay.

1. **Distinguish among synonyms.**

    Exact writing demands that you choose among different shades of meaning. Although *feeling* and *sensation* are synonyms, they are certainly not interchangeable. Neither are *funny* and *laughable* or *famous* and *notorious*. Consult your dictionary for help in choosing the word that says exactly what you mean.

    Explain the differences in meaning among the following groups of words and phrases:
    a. a *renowned* politician, a *famous* politician, a *notorious* politician
    b. an *indifferent* parent, a *detached* parent, an *unconcerned* parent
    c. to *condone* an action, to *excuse* an action, to *forgive* an action
    d. *pilfer, steal, rob, burglarize, loot, ransack*
    e. an *apparent* error, a *visible* error, an *egregious* error
    f. a *proud* person, a *pompous* person, an *arrogant* person

2. **Watch out for words with similar sound or spelling.**

    Homonyms (words that have the *same* pronunciation but different meanings and different spellings) are sometimes a source of confusion. The student who wrote that a song conveyed the composer's "piece of mind" let the sound of the word override her knowledge of spelling and meaning. Words that are *similar* in sound and spelling (homophones) can also be confusing. If you are not careful, you can easily confuse *eminent* with *imminent* or write *quiet* when you mean *quite*. Explain the difference in meaning in the following pairs of words:

    a. *apprise, appraise*
    b. *anecdote, antidote*
    c. *chord, cord*
    d. *elicit, illicit*
    e. *martial, marital*
    f. *statue, statute*
    g. *human, humane*
    h. *lose, loose*
    i. *idol, idle*
    j. *accept, except*
    k. *simple, simplistic*
    l. *beside, besides*
    m. *isle, aisle*
    n. *weather, whether*
    o. *incidence, incident*
    p. *angle, angel*

3. **Choose the precise adjective form.**

    Many words have two or more adjective forms: a *questioning* remark is not the same as a *questionable* remark. As with homonyms and other words that sound alike, do not let the similarity in spelling and pronunciation mislead you.

Point out the connotative differences in meaning in the following pairs of adjectives:

a. an *intelligible* essay, an *intelligent* essay
b. a *hateful* sibling, a *hated* sibling
c. a *likely* roommate, a *likeable* roommate
d. an *informed* speaker, an *informative* speaker
e. a *workable* thesis, a *working* thesis
f. a *liberal* man, a *liberated* man

4. **Watch out for malapropisms.**

Misused words are often unintentionally funny. These humorous confusions and near-misses are called *malapropisms*. You may get a laugh from your readers if you write "My car insurance collapsed last week," but you will not be impressing them with your command of the language.

In the following sentences, what do you think the writer probably meant to say?

a. He has only a *supercilious* knowledge of the subject.
b. She was the *pineapple* of perfection.
c. They burned the *refuge*.
d. He passed his civil service *eliminations*.
e. They are in for a *shrewd* awakening.
f. It is a *doggy dog* world out there.
g. That sculpture seems but a *hare's breath* from life.

5. **Be sure the words fit the context.**

Sentences can be disconcerting if all the words do not have the same emotional associations. For instance, "The thief brandished his gun and angrily requested the money" is confusing because *brandished* and *angrily* suggest a different emotion from *requested*. A better word choice would be "*demanded* the money."

Explain why the italicized words are inappropriate in the following sentences. What words would you use as replacements?

a. Her *stubbornness* in the face of danger saved our lives.
b. The use of violence to obtain a goal is too *poignantly* barbaric for most people to *sympathize* with.
c. The mob shouted in *displeasure*.
d. The cop *screeched* for the *pilferer* to drop the stolen *articles*.

SAMPLE PUBLISHED ESSAY ON POETIC FORM

David Huddle's essay—"The 'Banked Fire' of Robert Hayden's 'Those Winter Sundays'"—on the following pages is an example of a published essay on poetic form. (The Robert Hayden poem appears on page 437.)

David Huddle

The "Banked Fire" of Robert Hayden's "Those Winter Sundays"

For twenty years I've been teaching Robert Hayden's most frequently anthologized poem to undergraduate poetry-writing students. By "teach," I mean that from our textbook I read the poem aloud in the classroom, I ask one of the students to read it aloud, I make some observations about it, I invite the students to make some observations about it, then we talk about it a while longer. Usually to wrap up the discussion, I'll read the poem through once more. Occasions for such teaching come up about half a dozen times a year, and so let's say that during my life I've been privileged to read this poem aloud approximately 240 times. "Those Winter Sundays" has withstood my assault upon it. It remains a poem I look forward to reading and discussing in my classroom. The poem remains alive to me, so that for hours and sometimes days after it visits my classroom, I'm hearing its lines in my mind's ear.

Though a fourteen-liner, "Those Winter Sundays" is only loosely a sonnet. Its stanzas are five, four, and five lines long. There are rhymes and near-rhymes, but no rhyme scheme. The poem's lines probably average about eight syllables. There are only three strictly iambic lines: the fourth, the eighth, and (significantly) the fourteenth. It's a poem that's powerfully informed by the sonnet form; it's a poem that "feels like" a sonnet—it has the density and gravity of a sonnet—which is to say that in its appearance on the page, in its diction and syntax, in its tone, cadence, and argumentative strategy, "Those Winter Sundays" presents the credentials of a work of literary art in the tradition of English letters. But it's also a poem that has gone its own way, a definite departure from that most conventional of all the poetic forms of English and American verse.

The abstract issue of this poem's sonnethood is of less value to my beginning poets than the tangible matter of the sounds the poem makes, especially those *k*-sounding words of the first eleven lines that one comes to associate with discomfort: "clothes . . . blueback cold . . . cracked . . . ached . . . weekday . . . banked . . . thanked . . . wake . . . cold . . . breaking . . . call . . . chronic . . . cold." What's missing from the final three lines? The *k* sounds have been driven from the poem, as the father has "driven out the cold" from the house. The sounds that have replaced those *k* sounds are the *o* sounds of "good . . . shoes . . . know . . . know . . . love . . . lonely offices." The poem lets us associate the *o* sounds with love and loneliness. Sonically the poem tells the same story the poem narrates for us. The noise of this poem moves us through its emotional journey from discomfort to lonely love. If ever there was a poem that could teach a beginning poet the viability of the element of sound-crafting, it is "Those Winter Sundays."

Quote its first two words, and a great many poets and English teachers will be able to finish the first line (if not the whole poem) from memory. Somewhat remarkably, the poem's thesis—that the office of love can be relentless, thankless, and more than a little mysterious—resides in that initially odd-sounding two-word beginning, "Sundays too." The rest of the line—the rest of the independent clause—is ordinary. Nowhere else in Anglo-American literature does the word *too* carry the weight it carries in "Those Winter Sundays."

Not as immediately apparent as its opening words but very nearly as important to the poem's overall strategy is the two-sentence engineering of the first stanza. Because they will appreciate it more if they discover it for themselves, I often maneuver Socratically to have my students describe the poem's first two sentences: long and complex, followed by short and simple. It almost always seems to me worthwhile to ask, "Why didn't Hayden begin his poem this way: 'No one ever thanked my father for getting up early on Sundays, too'? Wouldn't that be a more direct and hospitable way to bring the reader into the poem?" After I've taken my students that far, they are quick to see how that ordinary five-word unit, "No one ever thanked him," gains meaning and emotion, weight, and force, from the elaborate preparation given it by the thirty-two-word "Sundays too" first sentence.

So much depends on "No one ever thanked him" that it requires the narrative enhancement of the first four and a half lines. It is the crux of the poem. What is this poem about? It is about a son's remorse over never thanking his father not only for what he did for him but also for how (he now realizes) he felt about him. And what is the poem if not an elegantly fashioned, permanent expression of gratitude?

"Those Winter Sundays" tells a story, or it describes a circumstance, of father-son conflict, and it even makes some excuses for the son's "Speaking indifferently" to the father: there was a good deal of anger between them; "chronic angers of that house" suggests that the circumstances were complicated somewhat beyond the usual and ordinary conflict between fathers and sons. Of the father, we know that he labored outdoors with his hands. Of the son, we know that he was, in the classic manner of youth, heedless of the ways in which his father served him.

Though the evidence of his "labor" is visible in every stanza of this poem, the father himself is somewhere else. We don't see him. He is in some other room of the house than the one where our speaker is. That absence suggests the emotional distance between the father and the son as well as the current absence, through death, of the father on the occasion of this utterance. It's easy enough to imagine this poem as a graveside meditation, an elegy, and a rather impassioned one at that, "What did I know, what did I know?"

The grinding of past against present gives the poem its urgency. The story is being told with such clarity, thoughtfulness, and apparent calm that we are surprised by the outburst of the repeated question of the thirteenth line. The fourteenth line returns to a tone of tranquillity. Its diction is formal, even arch, and its phrasing suggests an extremely considered conclusion; the fourteenth line is the answer to a drastic rephrasing of the original question: *What is the precise name of what as a youth I was incapable of perceiving but that as a life-examining adult, I now suddenly understand?*

I tell my students that they may someday need this poem, they may someday be walking along downtown and find themselves asking aloud, "What did I know, what did I know?" But what I mean to suggest to them is that Hayden has made them the gift of this final phrase like a package that in ten years' time they may open and find immensely valuable: "love's austere and lonely offices." Like "the banked fires" his father made, Hayden has made a poem that will be of value to readers often years after they've first read it.

(1996)

For study tools to help you with your next writing assignment, please visit the Companion Website at www.pearsoned.ca/mcmahan.

Anthology of Poetry

William Shakespeare   1564–1616

Let Me Not to the Marriage of True Minds

Let me not to the marriage of true minds
Admit impediments. Love is not love
Which alters when it alteration finds,
Or bends with the remover to remove:
O, no! it is an ever-fixéd mark
That looks on tempests and is never shaken;
It is the star to every wandering bark,
Whose worth's unknown, although his height be taken.
Love's not Time's fool, though rosy lips and cheeks
Within his bending sickle's compass come;   10
Love alters not with his brief hours and weeks,
But bears it out even to the edge of doom.
If this be error and upon me proved,
I never writ, nor no man ever loved.

(1609)

My Mistress' Eyes Are Nothing Like the Sun

My mistress' eyes are nothing like the sun;
Coral is far more red than her lips' red;
If snow be white, why then her breasts are dun;
If hairs be wires, black wires grow on her head.
I have seen roses damask'd, red and white,
But no such roses see I in her cheeks,
And in some perfumes there is more delight
Than in the breath that from my mistress reeks.
I love to hear her speak, yet well I know
That music hath a far more pleasing sound.   10
I grant I never saw a goddess go;
My mistress, when she walks, treads on the ground:
And yet, by heaven, I think my love as rare
As any she belied with false compare.

(1609)

John Donne   1572–1631

The Flea

Mark but this flea, and mark in this
How little that which thou deny'st me is;
Me it sucked first, and now sucks thee,
And in this flea our two bloods mingled be;
Thou know'st that this cannot be said
A sin, or shame, or loss of maidenhead,
    Yet this enjoys before it woo,
      And pampered swells with one blood made of two,
    And this, alas, is more than we would do.

Oh stay, three lives in one flea spare,   10
Where we almost, nay more than married, are.
This flea is you and I, and this
Our marriage bed and marriage temple is;
Though parents grudge, and you, we're met
And cloistered in these living walls of jet.
    Though use[1] make you apt to kill me,
    Let not to that, self-murder added be,
    And sacrilege, three sins in killing three.

Cruel and sudden, has thou since
Purpled thy nail in blood of innocence?   20
Wherein could this flea guilty be,
Except in that drop which it sucked from thee?
Yet thou triumph'st, and say'st that thou
Find'st not thyself, nor me, the weaker now;
    'Tis true; then learn how false fears be;
    Just so much honor, when thou yield'st to me,
    Will waste, as this flea's death took life from thee.

(1633)

Death, Be Not Proud

Death, be not proud, though some have callèd thee
Mighty and dreadful, for thou art not so,
For those whom thou think'st thou dost overthrow
Die not, poor Death, nor yet canst thou kill me.
From rest and sleep, which but thy pictures be,
Much pleasure, then from thee much more must flow;
And soonest our best men with thee do go—
Rest of their bones and souls' delivery!
Thou'rt slave to fate, chance, kings, and desperate men,
And dost with poison, war, and sickness dwell,   10
And poppy or charms can make us sleep as well,
And better than thy stroke; why swell'st thou then?

---

[1] Habit.

One short sleep past, we wake eternally,
And death shall be no more: Death, thou shalt die!

(1633)

Ben Jonson 1572–1637
On My First Son

Farewell, thou child of my right hand and joy;
   My sin was too much hope of thee, loved boy.
Seven years thou wert lent to me, and I thee pay,
   Exacted by thy fate, on the just day.
O, could I lose all father now! For why
   Will man lament the state he should envy?
To have so soon 'scaped world's and flesh's rage,
   And, if no other misery, yet age?
Rest in soft peace, and asked, say here doth lie
   Ben Jonson, his best piece of poetry: 10
For whose sake, henceforth, all his vows be such,
   As what he loves may never like too much.

(1616)

Richard Lovelace 1618–1657
To Lucasta, on Going to the Wars

   Tell me not, sweet, I am unkind,
      That from the nunnery
   Of thy chaste breast and quiet mind
      To war and arms I fly.

   True, a new mistress now I chase,
      The first foe in the field;
   And with a stronger faith embrace
      A sword, a horse, a shield.

   Yet this inconstancy is such
      As thou too shalt adore;   10
   I could not love thee, dear, so much,
      Loved I not honor more.

(1649)

Andrew Marvell 1621–1678
To His Coy Mistress

Had we but world enough, and time,
This coyness,[1] lady, were no crime.

---

[1] Modesty, reluctance.

We would sit down, and think which way
To walk, and pass our long love's day.
Thou by the Indian Ganges' side
Shouldst rubies find: I by the tide
Of Humber[2] would complain. I would
Love you ten years before the Flood:
And you should if you please refuse
Till the conversion of the Jews.   10
My vegetable love should grow
Vaster than empires, and more slow.
An hundred years should go to praise
Thine eyes, and on thy forehead gaze.
Two hundred to adore each breast:
But thirty thousand to the rest.
An age at least to every part,
And the last age should show your heart.
For, lady, you deserve this state;
Nor would I love at lower rate.   20
    But at my back I always hear
Time's wingéd chariot hurrying near:
And yonder all before us lie
Deserts of vast eternity.
Thy beauty shall no more be found,
Nor, in thy marble vault, shall sound
My echoing song; then worms shall try
That long preserved virginity:
And your quaint honour turn to dust;
And into ashes all my lust.   30
The grave's a fine and private place,
But none, I think, do there embrace.
    Now therefore, while the youthful hue
Sits on thy skin like morning dew,
And while thy willing soul transpires
At every pore with instant fires,
Now let us sport us while we may;
And now, like am'rous birds of prey,
Rather at once our time devour,
Than languish in his slow-chapped[3] pow'r.   40
Let us roll all our strength, and all
Our sweetness, up into one ball:
And tear our pleasures with rough strife,
Through the iron gates of life.
Thus, though we cannot make our sun
Stand still, yet we will make him run.

(1681)

---

[2] A river in northern England.
[3] Slow-chewing.

William Blake   1757–1827

The Lamb

From *Songs of Innocence*

    Little Lamb, who made thee?
    Dost thou know who made thee?
Gave thee life, and bid thee feed
By the stream and o'er the mead;
Gave thee clothing of delight,
Softest clothing, wooly, bright;
Gave thee such a tender voice,
Making all the vales rejoice?
    Little Lamb, who made thee?
    Dost thou know who made thee?   10

    Little Lamb, I'll tell thee,
    Little Lamb, I'll tell thee:
He is calléd by thy name,
For he calls himself a Lamb.
He is meek, and he is mild;
He became a little child.
I a child, and thou a lamb,
We are calléd by his name.
    Little Lamb, God bless thee!
    Little Lamb, God bless thee!   20

(1789)

The Tyger

From *Songs of Experience*

Tyger, Tyger, burning bright
In the forests of the night,
What immortal hand or eye
Could frame thy fearful symmetry?

In what distant deeps or skies
Burnt the fire of thine eyes?
On what wings dare he aspire?
What the hand dare seize the fire?

And what shoulder and what art
Could twist the sinews of thy heart?   10
And, when thy heart began to beat,
What dread hand? and what dread feet?

What the hammer? What the chain?
In what furnace was thy brain?
What the anvil? What dread grasp
Dare its deadly terrors clasp?

When the stars threw down their spears,
And watered heaven with their tears,
Did He smile his work to see?
Did He who made the lamb make thee?   20

Tyger, Tyger, burning bright
In the forests of the night,
What immortal hand or eye
Dare frame thy fearful symmetry?

(1794)

The Sick Rose

O Rose, thou art sick!
The invisible worm
That flies in the night,
In the howling storm,

Has found out thy bed
Of crimson joy,
And his dark secret love
Does thy life destroy.

(1794)

William Wordsworth   1770–1850

The World Is Too Much with Us

The world is too much with us; late and soon,
Getting and spending, we lay waste our powers;
Little we see in Nature that is ours;
We have given our hearts away, a sordid boon![1]
This Sea that bares her bosom to the moon,
The winds that will be howling at all hours,
And are up-gathered now like sleeping flowers,
For this, for everything, we are out of tune;
It moves us not.—Great God! I'd rather be
A Pagan suckled in a creed outworn;   10
So might I, standing on this pleasant lea,[2]
Have glimpses that would make me less forlorn;
Have sight of Proteus[3] rising from the sea;
Or hear old Triton[4] blow his wreathéd horn.

(1807)

---

[1] Blessing.
[2] Meadow.
[3] A sea god who could change shape.
[4] A sea god whose top half was man and bottom half was fish.

George Gordon, Lord Byron   1788–1824

She Walks in Beauty

She walks in beauty, like the night
   Of cloudless climes and starry skies;
And all that's best of dark and bright
   Meet in her aspect and her eyes:
Thus mellowed to that tender light
   Which Heaven to gaudy day denies.

One shade the more, one ray the less,
   Had half impaired the nameless grace
Which waves in every raven tress,
   Or softly lightens o'er her face;   10
Where thoughts serenely sweet express,
   How pure, how dear their dwelling-place.

And on that cheek, and o'er that brow,
   So soft, so calm, yet eloquent,
The smiles that win, the tints that glow,
   But tell of days in goodness spent,
A mind at peace with all below,
   A heart whose love is innocent!

(1814)

Percy Bysshe Shelley   1792–1822

Ozymandias

I met a traveller from an antique land
Who said: "Two vast and trunkless legs of stone
Stand in the desert.... Near them, on the sand,
Half sunk, a shattered visage lies, whose frown,
And wrinkled lip, and sneer of cold command,
Tell that its sculptor well those passions read
Which yet survive, stamped on these lifeless things,
The hand that mocked them, and the heart that fed:
And on the pedestal these words appear:
My name is Ozymandias, king of kings: 10
Look on my works, ye Mighty, and despair!"
Nothing beside remains. Round the decay
Of that colossal wreck, boundless and bare
The lone and level sands stretch far away.

(1817)

John Keats   1795–1821

Ode on a Grecian Urn

Thou still unravished bride of quietness,
   Thou foster-child of silence and slow time,

    Sylvan historian, who canst thus express
     A flowery tale more sweetly than our rhyme:
    What leaf-fringed legend haunts about thy shape
    Of deities or mortals, or of both,
      In Tempe[1] or the dales of Arcady?[2]
    What men or gods are these? What maidens loth?
      What mad pursuit? What struggle to escape?
       What pipes and timbrels? What wild ecstasy?   10

    Heard melodies are sweet, but those unheard
     Are sweeter; therefore, ye soft pipes, play on;
    Not to the sensual ear, but, more endeared,
     Pipe to the spirit ditties of no tone:
    Fair youth, beneath the trees, thou canst not leave
     Thy song, nor ever can those trees be bare;
      Bold Lover, never, never canst thou kiss,
    Though winning near the goal—yet, do not grieve;
     She cannot fade, though thou hast not thy bliss,
      For ever wilt thou love, and she be fair!   20

    Ah, happy, happy boughs! that cannot shed
     Your leaves, nor ever bid the spring adieu;
    And, happy melodist, unwearièd,
     For ever piping songs for ever new;
    More happy love! more happy, happy love!
    For ever warm and still to be enjoyed,
     For ever panting, and for ever young;
      All breathing human passion far above,
      That leaves a heart high-sorrowful and cloyed,
      A burning forehead, and a parching tongue.   30

    Who are these coming to the sacrifice?
     To what green altar, O mysterious priest,
    Lead'st thou that heifer lowing at the skies,
     And all her silken flanks with garlands dressed?
    What little town by river or sea shore,
     Or mountain-built with peaceful citadel,
      Is emptied of this folk, this pious morn?
    And, little town, thy streets for evermore
     Will silent be; and not a soul to tell
      Why thou art desolate, can e'er return.   40

    O Attic[3] shape! Fair attitude! with brede[4]
     Of marble men and maidens overwrought,
    With forest branches and the trodden weed;
     Thou, silent form, dost tease us out of thought

---

[1] Valley in Thessaly, noted for its natural beauty.
[2] Region in Greece, a traditional setting for pastoral poetry.
[3] Of Attica, thus, classic in grace and simplicity.
[4] Design, decoration.

As doth eternity: Cold Pastoral!
    When old age shall this generation waste,
      Thou shalt remain, in midst of other woe
Than ours, a friend to man, to whom thou say'st,
    "Beauty is truth, truth beauty,"—that is all
      Ye know on earth, and all ye need to know.   50

(1819)

Susanna Moodie   1803–1885

XI. Brian, the Still-Hunter

O'er memory's glass I see his shadow flit,
Though he was gathered to the silent dust
Long years ago. A strange and wayward man,
That shunn'd companionship, and lived apart;
The leafy covert of the dark brown woods,
The gleamy lakes, hid in their gloomy depths,
Whose still, deep waters never knew the stroke
Of cleaving oar, or echoed to the sound
Of social life, contained for him the sum
Of human happiness. With dog and gun
Day after day he track'd the nimble deer
Through all the tangled mazes of the forest.

(1852)

Alfred, Lord Tennyson   1809–1892

The Eagle

He clasps the crag with crooked hands;
Close to the sun in lonely lands,
Ringed with the azure world, he stands.

The wrinkled sea beneath him crawls;
He watches from his mountain walls,
And like a thunderbolt he falls.

(1851)

Robert Browning   1812–1889

My Last Duchess

Ferrara

That's my last Duchess painted on the wall,
Looking as if she were alive; I call

That piece a wonder, now: Frà Pandolf's[1] hands
Worked busily a day, and there she stands.
Will't please you sit and look at her? I said
"Frà Pandolf" by design, for never read
Strangers like you that pictured countenance,
The depth and passion of its earnest glance,
But to myself they turned (since none puts by
The curtain I have drawn for you, but I)   10
And seemed as they would ask me, if they durst,
How such a glance came there; so, not the first
Are you to turn and ask thus. Sir, 'twas not
Her husband's presence only, called that spot
Of joy into the Duchess' cheek: perhaps
Frà Pandolf chanced to say "Her mantle laps
Over my Lady's wrist too much," or "Paint
Must never hope to reproduce the faint
Half-flush that dies along her throat": such stuff
Was courtesy, she thought, and cause enough   20
For calling up that spot of joy. She had
A heart—how shall I say?—too soon made glad,
Too easily impressed; she liked whate'er
She looked on, and her looks went everywhere.
Sir, 'twas all one! My favor at her breast,
The dropping of the daylight in the West,
The bough of cherries some officious fool
Broke in the orchard for her, the white mule
She rode with round the terrace—all and each
Would draw from her alike the approving speech,   30
Or blush, at least. She thanked men,—good; but thanked
Somehow—I know not how—as if she ranked
My gift of a nine-hundred-years-old name
With anybody's gift. Who'd stoop to blame
This sort of trifling? Even had you skill
In speech—(which I have not)—to make your will
Quite clear to such an one, and say, "Just this
Or that in you disgusts me; here you miss,
Or there exceed the mark"—and if she let
Herself be lessoned so, nor plainly set   40
Her wits to yours, forsooth, and made excuse,
—E'en then would be some stooping, and I choose
Never to stoop. Oh, Sir, she smiled, no doubt,
Whene'er I passed her; but who passed without
Much the same smile? This grew; I gave commands;
Then all smiles stopped together. There she stands
As if alive. Will't please you rise? We'll meet
The company below, then. I repeat,
The Count your Master's known munificence
Is ample warrant that no just pretence   50
Of mine for dowry will be disallowed;

---
[1] A fictitious artist.

Though his fair daughter's self, as I avowed
At starting, is my object. Nay, we'll go
Together down, Sir! Notice Neptune, though,
Taming a sea-horse, thought a rarity,
Which Claus of Innsbruck[2] cast in bronze for me.

(1842)

Matthew Arnold 1822–1888

Dover Beach

The sea is calm to-night,
The tide is full, the moon lies fair
Upon the Straits;—on the French coast, the light
Gleams, and is gone; the cliffs of England stand,
Glimmering and vast, out in the tranquil bay.
Come to the window, sweet is the night air!
Only, from the long line of spray
Where the sea meets the moon-blanched sand,
Listen! you hear the grating roar
Of pebbles which the waves draw back, and fling,   10
At their return, up the high strand,
Begin, and cease, and then again begin,
With tremulous cadence slow, and bring
The eternal note of sadness in.
Sophocles[1] long ago
Heard it on the Aegean, and it brought
Into his mind the turbid ebb and flow
Of human misery; we
Find also in the sound a thought,
Hearing it by this distant northern sea.   20

The Sea of Faith
Was once, too, at the full, and round earth's shore
Lay like the folds of a bright girdle furled;
But now I only hear
Its melancholy, long, withdrawing roar,
Retreating to the breath
Of the night-wind down the vast edges drear
And naked shingles[2] of the world.

Ah, love, let us be true
To one another! for the world, which seems   30
To lie before us like a land of dreams,
So various, so beautiful, so new,
Hath really neither joy, nor love, nor light,

---

[2]Another fictitious artist.
[1]In *Antigone* the Greek dramatist Sophocles likens the curse of heaven to the ebb and flow of the sea.
[2]Gravel beaches.

Nor certitude, nor peace, nor help for pain;
And we are here as on a darkling³ plain
Swept with confused alarms of struggle and flight,
Where ignorant armies clash by night.

(1867)

Emily Dickinson   1830–1886

Safe in Their Alabaster Chambers

Safe in their Alabaster Chambers—
Untouched by Morning—
And untouched by Noon—
Lie the meek members of the Resurrection—
Rafter of Satin—and Roof of Stone!

Grand go the Years—in the Crescent—above them—
Worlds scoop their Arcs—
And Firmaments—row¹—
Diadems—drop—and Doges²—surrender—
Soundless as dots—on a Disc of Snow—   10

(ca. 1861)

Because I Could Not Stop for Death

Because I could not stop for Death—
He kindly stopped for me—
The Carriage held but just Ourselves—
And Immortality—

We slowly drove—He knew no haste
And I had put away
My labor and my leisure too,
For His Civility—

We passed the School, where Children strove
At Recess—in the Ring—   10
We passed the Fields of Gazing Grain—
We passed the Setting Sun—

Or rather—He passed Us—
The Dews drew quivering and chill—
For only Gossamer,¹ my Gown—
My Tippet²—only Tulle³—

---

³Darkened.
¹Cast down heavenly light.
²Early rulers in Venice.
¹Thin, sheer.
²Short cape covering just the shoulders.
³Soft net fabric.

We paused before a House that seemed
A Swelling of the Ground—
The Roof was scarcely visible—
The Cornice—in the Ground— 20

Since then—'tis Centuries—and yet
Feels shorter than the Day
I first surmised the Horses' Heads
Were toward Eternity—

(ca. 1863)

Gerard Manley Hopkins 1844–1889

Pied Beauty

Glory be to God for dappled things—
   For skies of couple-colour as a brinded[1] cow;
     For rose-moles all in stipple[2] upon trout that swim;
Fresh-firecoal chestnut-falls;[3] finches' wings;
   Landscape plotted and pieced—fold, fallow, and plow;
     And áll trádes, their gear and tackle and trim.[4]

All things counter, original, spare, strange;
   Whatever is fickle, freckled (who knows how?)
     With swift, slow; sweet, sour; adazzle, dim;
He fathers-forth whose beauty is past change: 10
     Praise him.

(1877)

Spring and Fall

To a Young Child

Márgarét áre you gríeving
Over Goldengrove unleaving?
Leáves, líke the things of man, you
With your fresh thoughts care for, can you?
Áh! ás the heart grows older
It will come to such sights colder
By and by, nor spare a sigh
Though worlds of wanwood[1] leafmeal[2] lie;
And yet you *will* weep and know why.
Now no matter, child, the name: 10
Sórrow's spríngs áre the same.

---

[1] Striped.
[2] Small dots.
[3] Chestnuts fresh from the fire with their hulls off.
[4] Tools.
[1] Pale woods, as though bloodless.
[2] Fallen leaf by leaf.

Nor mouth had, no nor mind, expressed
What heart heard of, ghost[3] guessed:
It ís the blight man was born for,
It is Margaret you mourn for.

(1880)

A. E. Housman   1859–1936

To an Athlete Dying Young

The time you won your town the race
We chaired you through the market-place;
Man and boy stood cheering by,
And home we brought you shoulder-high.

To-day, the road all runners come,
Shoulder-high we bring you home,
And set you at your threshold down,
Townsman of a stiller town.

Smart lad, to slip betimes away
From fields where glory does not stay,   10
And early though the laurel grows
It withers quicker than the rose.

Eyes the shady night has shut
Cannot see the record cut,
And silence sounds no worse than cheers
After earth has stopped the ears.

Now you will not swell the rout
Of lads that wore their honors out,
Runners whom renown outran
And the name died before the man.   20

So set, before its echoes fade,
The fleet foot on the sill of shade,
And hold to the low lintel[1] up
The still-defended challenge-cup.

And round that early-laurelled[2] head
Will flock to gaze the strengthless dead,
And find unwithered on its curls
The garland briefer than a girl's.

(1896)

---

[3]Spirit, soul.
[1]Horizontal support above a door.
[2]In ancient times victors were crowned with laurel wreaths.

Sir Charles G. D. Roberts   1860–1943

The Flight of the Geese

I hear the low wind wash the softening snow,
    The low tide loiter down the shore. The night,
    Full filled with April forecast, hath no light.
The salt wave on the sedge-flat[1] pulses slow.
Through the hid furrows lisp in murmurous flow
    The thaw's shy ministers; and hark! The height
    Of heaven grows weird and loud with unseen flight
Of strong hosts prophesying as they go!

High through the drenched and hollow night their wings
    Beat northward hard on Winter's trail. The sound   10
Of their confused and solemn voices, borne
Athwart the dark to their long Arctic morn,
    Comes with a sanction and an awe profound,
A boding of unknown, foreshadowed things.

(1893)

Pauline Johnson   1861–1913

The Song My Paddle Sings

West wind, blow from your prairie nest,
Blow from the mountains, blow from the west
The sail is idle, the sailor too ;
O ! wind of the west, we wait for you.
Blow, blow !
I have wooed you so,
But never a favour you bestow.
You rock your cradle the hills between,
But scorn to notice my white lateen.

I stow the sail, unship the mast :   10
I wooed you long but my wooing's past ;
My paddle will lull you into rest.
O ! drowsy wind of the drowsy west,
Sleep, sleep,
By your mountain steep,
Or down where the prairie grasses sweep !
Now fold in slumber your laggard wings,
For soft is the song my paddle sings.

August is laughing across the sky,
Laughing while paddle, canoe and I,   20
Drift, drift,
Where the hills uplift
On either side of the current swift.

---

[1]Grasslike plants on flat marshlands or bogs.

The river rolls in its rocky bed;
My paddle is plying its way ahead;
Dip, dip,
While the waters flip
In foam as over their breast we slip.

And oh, the river runs swifter now;
The eddies circle about my bow. 30
Swirl, swirl!
How the ripples curl
In many a dangerous pool awhirl!

And forward far the rapids roar,
Fretting their margin for evermore.
Dash, dash,
With a mighty crash,
They seethe, and boil, and bound, and splash.

Be strong, O paddle! be brave, canoe!
The reckless waves you must plunge into. 40
Reel, reel,
On your trembling keel,
But never a fear my craft will feel.

We've raced the rapid, we're far ahead!
The river slips through its silent bed.
Sway, sway,
As the bubbles spray
And fall in tinkling tunes away.

And up on the hills against the sky,
A fir tree rocking its lullaby, 50
Swings, swings,
Its emerald wings,
Swelling the song that my paddle sings.

(1891–1892, rev. 1895)

Archibald Lampman   1861–1899

Winter Evening

Tonight the very horses springing by
Toss gold from whitened nostrils. In a dream
The streets that narrow to the westward gleam
Like rows of golden palaces; and high
From all the crowded chimneys tower and die
A thousand aureoles. Down in the west
The brimming plains beneath the sunset rest,
One burning sea of gold. Soon, soon shall fly
The glorious vision, and the hours shall feel

A mightier master, soon from height to height,   10
With silence and the sharp unpitying stars,
Stern creeping frosts, and winds that touch like steel,
Out of the depth beyond the eastern bars,
Glittering and still shall come the awful night.

(1899)

William Butler Yeats   1865–1939

The Second Coming

Turning and turning in the widening gyre[1]
The falcon cannot hear the falconer;
Things fall apart; the centre cannot hold;
Mere anarchy is loosed upon the world,
The blood-dimmed tide is loosed, and everywhere
The ceremony of innocence is drowned;
The best lack all conviction, while the worst
Are full of passionate intensity.

Surely some revelation is at hand;
Surely the Second Coming is at hand.   10
The Second Coming! Hardly are those words out
When a vast image out of *Spiritus Mundi*[2]
Troubles my sight: somewhere in sands of the desert
A shape with lion body and the head of a man,
A gaze blank and pitiless as the sun,
Is moving its slow thighs, while all about it
Reel shadows of the indignant desert birds.
The darkness drops again; but now I know
That twenty centuries of stony sleep
Were vexed to nightmare by a rocking cradle,   20
And what rough beast, its hour come round at last,
Slouches towards Bethlehem to be born?

(1921)

Sailing to Byzantium[1]

That is no country for old men. The young
In one another's arms, birds in the trees
—Those dying generations—at their song,
The salmon-falls, the mackerel-crowded seas,
Fish, flesh, or fowl, commend all summer long
Whatever is begotten, born, and dies.

---

[1]A spiral motion, used by Yeats to suggest the cycles of history.
[2]The Soul of the World, a collective unconscious from which humans draw memories, symbols, dreams.
[1]The capital of the Byzantine Empire, the city now called Istanbul in Turkey; for Yeats, a symbol of life perfected by art.

Caught in that sensual music all neglect
Monuments of unaging intellect.

An agéd man is but a paltry thing,
A tattered coat upon a stick, unless
Soul clap its hands and sing, and louder sing
For every tatter in its mortal dress,
Nor is there singing school but studying
Monuments of its own magnificence;
And therefore I have sailed the seas and come
To the holy city of Byzantium.

O sages standing in God's holy fire
As in the gold mosaic of a wall,
Come from the holy fire, perne in a gyre,[2]
And be the singing-masters of my soul.
Consume my heart away; sick with desire
And fastened to a dying animal
It knows not what it is; and gather me
Into the artifice of eternity.

Once out of nature I shall never take
My bodily form from any natural thing,
But such a form as Grecian goldsmiths make
Of hammered gold and gold enamelling
To keep a drowsy Emperor awake;
Or set upon a golden bough to sing
To lords and ladies of Byzantium
Of what is past, or passing, or to come.

(1928)

Stephen Crane   1871–1900

War Is Kind

Do not weep, maiden, for war is kind.
Because your lover threw wild hands toward the sky
And the affrighted steed ran on alone,
Do not weep.
War is kind.

    Hoarse, booming drums of the regiment,
    Little souls who thirst for fight,
    These men were born to drill and die.
    The unexplained glory flies above them,
    Great is the Battle-God, great, and his Kingdom—
    A field where a thousand corpses lie.

---

[2]The spiralling motion that Yeats associates with the whirling of fate; see "The Second Coming."

Do not weep, babe, for war is kind.
Because your father tumbled in the yellow trenches,
Raged at his breast, gulped and died,
Do not weep.
War is kind.

    Swift blazing flag of the regiment,
    Eagle with crest of red and gold,
    These men were born to drill and die.
    Point for them the virtue of slaughter,   20
    Make plain to them the excellence of killing
    And a field where a thousand corpses lie.

Mother whose heart hung humble as a button
On the bright spendid shroud of your son,
Do not weep.
War is kind.

                                                   (1899)

Paul Laurence Dunbar   *1872–1906*

We Wear the Mask

We wear the mask that grins and lies,
It hides our cheeks and shades our eyes,—
This debt we pay to human guile;
With torn and bleeding hearts we smile,
And mouth with myriad subtleties.

Why should the world be overwise,
In counting all our tears and sighs?
Nay, let them only see us, while
    We wear the mask.

We smile, but, O great Christ, our cries   10
To thee from tortured souls arise.
We sing, but oh the clay is vile
Beneath our feet, and long the mile;
But let the world dream otherwise,
    We wear the mask!

                                                   (1895)

Robert Frost   *1874–1963*

Design

I found a dimpled spider, fat and white,
On a white heal-all,[1] holding up a moth

---

[1] A low-growing plant, usually having violet-blue flowers.

Like a white piece of rigid satin cloth—
Assorted characters of death and blight
Mixed ready to begin the morning right,
Like the ingredients of a witches' broth—
A snow-drop spider, a flower like a froth,
And dead wings carried like a paper kite.

What had that flower to do with being white,
The wayside blue and innocent heal-all?   10
What brought the kindred spider to that height,
Then steered the white moth thither in the night?
What but design of darkness to appall?—
If design govern in a thing so small.

(1936)

Carl Sandburg   1878–1967

Fog

The fog comes
on little cat feet.

It sits looking
over harbor and city
on silent haunches
and then moves on.

(1916)

Grass

Pile the bodies high at Austerlitz and Waterloo.[1]
Shovel them under and let me work—
   I am the grass; I cover all.

And pile them high at Gettysburg[2]
And pile them high at Ypres and Verdun.[3]
Shovel them under and let me work.
Two years, ten years, and passengers ask the conductor:
   What place is this?
   Where are we now?

   I am the grass.   10
   Let me work.

(1918)

---

[1] Battlefields of the Napoleonic Wars.
[2] American Civil War battlefield.
[3] Battlefields in World War I.

Wallace Stevens   1879–1955

The Emperor of Ice-Cream

Call the roller of big cigars,
The muscular one, and bid him whip
In kitchen cups concupiscent curds.
Let the wenches dawdle in such dress
As they are used to wear, and let the boys
Bring flowers in last month's newspapers.
Let be be finale of seem.
The only emperor is the emperor of ice-cream.

Take from the dresser of deal,[1]
Lacking the three glass knobs, that sheet   10
On which she embroidered fantails once
And spread it so as to cover her face.
If her horny feet protrude, they come
To show how cold she is, and dumb.
Let the lamp affix its beam.
The only emperor is the emperor of ice-cream.

(1923)

E. J. Pratt   1882–1964

From Stone to Steel

From stone to bronze, from bronze to steel
Along the road-dust of the sun,
Two revolutions of the wheel
From Java[1] to Geneva run.

The snarl Neanderthal[2] is worn
Close to the smiling Aryan lips,
The civil polish of the horn
Gleams from our praying finger tips.

The evolution of desire
Has but matured a toxic wine,   10
Drunk long before its heady fire
Reddened Euphrates or the Rhine.

Between the temple and the cave
The boundary lies tissue-thin:
The yearlings still the altars crave
As satisfaction for a sin.

---

[1] Fir or pine wood.
[1] Refers to Java man, a very early form of human being inferred from fossil remains found in Java, an Indonesian island.
[2] An extinct people of Europe, Africa, and Asia in the early Stone Age; evidence of these people was found in West Germany.

The road goes up, the road goes down—
Let Java or Geneva be—
But whether to the cross or crown,
The path lies through Gethsemane.[3]

(1932)

Marjorie Pickthall 1883–1922

The Bird in the Room

Last autumn when they aired the house
A bird got in, and died in this room.
Here it fluttered
Close to the shuttered
Window, and beat in the airless gloom,
No space for its wing, no drop for its mouth,—
A swallow, flying south.

And the velvet-creeping unsleeping mouse
Trampled that swiftness where it fell
On the dusty border   10
Pattern'd in order
With a citron flower and a golden shell,—
But it might not fly and it might not drink,
On the carpet's sunless brink.

A thought of you beat into my mind,
Empty and shuttered, dark, and spread
With dusty sheeting
To hide the beating
Tread of the hours. But the thought was dead
When I opened the door of that room, to find   20
If the Spring
Had left me anything—

(1936)

William Carlos Williams 1883–1963

The Red Wheelbarrow

    so much depends
    upon

    a red wheel
    barrow

---

[3] A garden near Jerusalem where Jesus was betrayed and arrested.

> glazed with rain
> water
>
> beside the white
> chickens.

(1923)

Ezra Pound   1885–1972

In a Station of the Metro[1]

The apparition of these faces in the crowd;
Petals on a wet, black bough.

(1913)

T. S. Eliot   1888–1965

The Love Song of J. Alfred Prufrock

> *S'io credesse che mia risposta fosse*
> *A persona che mai tornasse al mondo,*
> *Questa fiamma staria senza piu scosse.*
> *Ma perciocche giammai di questo fondo*
> *Non torno vivo alcun, s'i'odo il vero,*
> *Senze tema d'infamia ti rispondo.*[1]

Let us go then, you and I,
When the evening is spread out against the sky
Like a patient etherised upon a table;
Let us go, through certain half-deserted streets,
The muttering retreats
Of restless nights in one-night cheap hotels
And sawdust restaurants with oyster-shells:
Streets that follow like a tedious argument
Of insidious intent
To lead you to an overwhelming question . . .   10
Oh, do not ask, "What is it?"
Let us go and make our visit.

In the room the women come and go
Talking of Michelangelo.

The yellow fog that rubs its back upon the window-panes,
The yellow smoke that rubs its muzzle on the window-panes

---

[1] Subway in Paris.
[1] The epigraph is from Dante's *Inferno*—the speech of one dead and damned, Count Guido da Montefeltro, who thinks his hearer is also going to remain in hell; he offers to tell Dante his story: "If I thought my reply were to someone who could ever return to the world, this flame would waver no more. But since, I'm told, nobody ever escapes from this pit, I'll tell you without fear of ill fame."

Licked its tongue into the corners of the evening,
Lingered upon the pools that stand in drains,
Let fall upon its back the soot that falls from chimneys,
Slipped by the terrace, made a sudden leap,   20
And seeing that it was a soft October night,
Curled once about the house, and fell asleep.

And indeed there will be time
For the yellow smoke that slides along the street
Rubbing its back upon the window-panes;
There will be time, there will be time
To prepare a face to meet the faces that you meet;
There will be time to murder and create,
And time for all the works and days of hands
That lift and drop a question on your plate;   30
Time for you and time for me,
And time yet for a hundred indecisions,
And for a hundred visions and revisions,
Before the taking of a toast and tea.

In the room the women come and go
Talking of Michelangelo.

And indeed there will be time
To wonder, "Do I dare?" and, "Do I dare?"
Time to turn back and descend the stair,
With a bald spot in the middle of my hair—   40
(They will say: "How his hair is growing thin!")
My morning coat, my collar mounting firmly to the chin,
My necktie rich and modest, but asserted by a simple pin—
(They will say: "But how his arms and legs are thin!")
Do I dare
Disturb the universe?
In a minute there is time
For decisions and revisions which a minute will reverse.

For I have known them all already, known them all—
Have known the evenings, mornings, afternoons,   50
I have measured out my life with coffee spoons;
I know the voices dying with a dying fall
Beneath the music from a farther room.
       So how should I presume?

And I have known the eyes already, known them all—
The eyes that fix you in a formulated phrase,
And when I am formulated, sprawling on a pin,
When I am pinned and wriggling on the wall,
Then how should I begin
To spit out all the butt-ends of my days and ways?   60
       And how should I presume?

And I have known the arms already, known them all—
Arms that are braceleted and white and bare
(But in the lamplight, downed with light brown hair!)
Is it perfume from a dress
That makes me so digress?
Arms that lie along a table, or wrap about a shawl.
    And should I then presume?
    And how should I begin?

       . . . . .

Shall I say, I have gone at dusk through narrow streets   70
And watched the smoke that rises from the pipes
Of lonely men in shirt-sleeves, leaning out of windows? . . .

I should have been a pair of ragged claws
Scuttling across the floors of silent seas.

       . . . . .

And the afternoon, the evening, sleeps so peacefully!
Smoothed by long fingers,
Asleep . . . tired . . . or it malingers,
Stretched on the floor, here beside you and me.
Should I, after tea and cakes and ices,
Have the strength to force the moment to its crisis?   80
But though I have wept and fasted, wept and prayed,
Though I have seen my head (grown slightly bald) brought in upon a
    platter,[2]
I am no prophet—and here's no great matter;
I have seen the moment of my greatness flicker,
And I have seen the eternal Footman hold my coat, and snicker,
And in short, I was afraid.

And would it have been worth it, after all,
After the cups, the marmalade, the tea,
Among the porcelain, among some talk of you and me,
Would it have been worth while,   90
To have bitten off the matter with a smile,
To have squeezed the universe into a ball
To roll it toward some overwhelming question,
To say: "I am Lazarus,[3] come from the dead,
Come back to tell you all, I shall tell you all"—
If one, settling a pillow by her head,
    Should say: "That is not what I meant at all;
    That is not it, at all."

And would it have been worth it, after all,
Would it have been worth while,   100

---

[2]The head of John the Baptist was presented to Salome on a platter. See Matthew 14:1–11.
[3]Jesus raised Lazarus from the dead. See John 11:1–44.

After the sunsets and the dooryards and the sprinkled streets,
After the novels, after the teacups, after the skirts that trail along the
    floor—
And this, and so much more?—
It is impossible to say just what I mean!
But as if a magic lantern threw the nerves in patterns on a screen:
Would it have been worth while
If one, settling a pillow or throwing off a shawl,
And turning toward the window, should say:
"That is not it at all,
That is not what I meant, at all."   110

· · · · ·

No! I am not Prince Hamlet, nor was meant to be;
Am an attendant lord, one that will do
To swell a progress, start a scene or two,
Advise the prince; no doubt, an easy tool,
Deferential, glad to be of use,
Politic, cautious, and meticulous;
Full of high sentence, but a bit obtuse;
At times, indeed, almost ridiculous—
Almost, at times, the Fool.

I grow old . . . I grow old . . .   120
I shall wear the bottoms of my trousers rolled.

Shall I part my hair behind? Do I dare to eat a peach?
I shall wear white flannel trousers, and walk upon the beach.
I have heard the mermaids singing, each to each.

I do not think that they will sing to me.

I have seen them riding seaward on the waves
Combing the white hair of the waves blown back
When the wind blows the water white and black.

We have lingered in the chambers of the sea
By sea-girls wreathed with seaweed red and brown   130
Till human voices wake us, and we drown.

(1917)

Edna St. Vincent Millay   1892–1950

First Fig

My candle burns at both ends;
It will not last the night;
But ah, my foes, and oh, my friends—
It gives a lovely light!

(1920)

Wilfred Owen   1893–1918

Dulce et Decorum Est

Bent double, like old beggars under sacks,
Knock-kneed, coughing like hags, we cursed through sludge,
Till on the haunting flares we turned our backs
And towards our distant rest began to trudge.
Men marched asleep. Many had lost their boots
But limped on, blood-shod. All went lame; all blind;
Drunk with fatigue; deaf even to the hoots
Of tired, outstripped Five-Nines[1] that dropped behind.

Gas! Gas! Quick, boys!—An ecstasy of fumbling,
Fitting the clumsy helmets just in time;   10
But someone still was yelling out and stumbling
And flound'ring like a man in fire or lime . . .
Dim, through the misty panes and thick green light,
As under a green sea, I saw him drowning.
In all my dreams before my helpless sight,
He plunges at me, guttering, choking, drowning.

If in some smothering dreams you too could pace
Behind the wagon that we flung him in,
And watch the white eyes writhing in his face,
His hanging face, like a devil's sick of sin;   20
If you could hear, at every jolt, the blood
Come gargling from the froth-corrupted lungs,
Obscene as cancer, bitter as the cud
Of vile, incurable sores on innocent tongues,—
My friend, you would not tell with such high zest
To children ardent for some desperate glory,
The old Lie: Dulce et decorum est
Pro patria mori.[2]

(1920)

F. R. Scott   1899–1985

Laurentian Shield

Hidden in wonder and snow, or sudden with summer,
This land stares at the sun in a huge silence
Endlessly repeating something we cannot hear.
Inarticulate, arctic,
Not written on by history, empty as paper,
It leans away from the world with songs in its lakes
Older than love, and lost in the miles.

---

[1] Poison gas shells.
[2] The quotation is from the Latin poet Horace, meaning, "It is sweet and fitting to die for one's country."

This waiting is wanting.
It will choose its language
When it has chosen its technic,   10
A tongue to shape the vowels of its productivity.

A language of flesh and of roses.[1]

Now there are pre-words,
Cabin syllables,
Nouns of settlement
Slowly forming, with steel syntax,
The long sentence of its exploitation.

The first cry was the hunter, hungry for fur,
And the digger for gold, nomad, no-man, a particle;
Then the bold commands of monopoly, big with machines,   20
Carving its kingdoms out of the public wealth;
And now the drone of the plane, scouting the ice,
Fills all the emptiness with neighbourhood
And links our future over the vanished pole.

But a deeper note is sounding, heard in the mines,
The scattered camps and the mills, a language of life,
And what will be written in the full culture of occupation
Will come, presently, tomorrow,
From millions whose hands can turn this rock into children.

(1954)

Langston Hughes   1902–1967

Harlem (A Dream Deferred)

What happens to a dream deferred?

    Does it dry up
    like a raisin in the sun?
    Or fester like a sore—
    And then run?
    Does it stink like rotten meat?
    Or crust and sugar over—
    like a syrupy sweet?

    Maybe it just sags
    like a heavy load.   10

    Or does it explode?

(1951)

---

[1] In his essay "The Making of a Poem," Stephen Spender views the effects that people have on the landscape and the effects of the landscape on people, as a kind of language. Scott uses Spender's theories here to express his own similar ideas on the creation of poetry.

A. J. M. Smith   1902–1980

The Wisdom of Old Jelly Roll[1]

How all men wrongly death to dignify
Conspire, I tell. Parson, poetaster, pimp,
Each acts or acquiesces. They prettify,
Dress up, deodorize, embellish, primp,
And make a show of Nothing. Ah, but met-
aphysics laughs; she touches, tastes, and smells
—Hence knows—the diamond holes that make a net.
Silence resettled testifies to bells.
'Nothing' depends on 'Thing', which is or was:
So death makes life or makes life's worth, a worth   10
Beyond all highfalutin' woes or shows
To publish and confess, 'Cry at the birth,
Rejoice at the death,' old Jelly Roll said,
Being on whiskey, ragtime, chicken, and the scriptures fed.

(1962)

Stevie Smith   1902–1971

Not Waving but Drowning

Nobody heard him, the dead man,
But still he lay moaning:
I was much further out than you thought
And not waving but drowning.

Poor chap, he always loved larking
And now he's dead
It must have been too cold for him his heart gave way,
They said.

Oh, no no no, it was too cold always
(Still the dead one lay moaning)   10
I was much too far out all my life
And not waving but drowning.

(1957)

Earle Birney   1904–1995

Anglosaxon Street[1]

Dawn drizzle ended   dampness steams from
blotching brick and   blank plasterwaste

---

[1]Ferdinand Joseph La Menthe ("Jelly Roll") Morton (1885–1941), American jazz composer and pianist.
[1]This poem uses the figurative language and devices of Anglo-Saxon verse, including caesura (a break in each line) with alliteration joining both halves of a line, kennings (metaphoric names or compound words used to replace ordinary words—e.g., plasterwaste for stucco, worldrise for dawn), and litotes (understatement achieved when expressing an affirmative by negating its contrary—e.g., unstinks, not humbly).

Faded housepatterns   hoary and finicky
unfold stuttering   stick like a phonograph

Here is a ghetto   gotten for goyim
O with care denuded   of nigger and kike
No coonsmell rankles   reeks only cellarrot
Ottar² of carexhaust   catcorpse and cookinggrease
Imperial hearts   heave in this haven
Cracks across windows   are welded with slogans
There'll Always Be An England   enhances geraniums   10
and V's for Victory   vanquish the housefly

Ho! with climbing sun   march the bleached beldames
festooned with shopping bags   farded³ flatarched
bigthewed Saxonwives   stepping over buttrivers
waddling back wienerladen   to suckle smallfry

Hoy! with sunslope   shrieking over hydrants
flood from learninghall   the lean fingerlings
Nordic nobblecheeked⁴   not all clean of nose
leaping Commandowise   into leprous lanes   20

What! after whistleblow!   spewed from wheelboat
after daylight doughtiness   dire handplay
in sewertrench or sandpit   come Saxonthegns⁵
Junebrown Jutekings⁶   jawslack for meat

Sit after supper   on smeared doorsteps
not humbly swearing   hatedeeds on Huns⁷
profiteers politicians   pacifists Jews

Then by twobit magic   to muse in movie
unlock picturehoard   or lope to alehall
soaking bleakly   in beer skittleless   30

Home again to hotbox   and humid husbandhood
in slumbertough adding   sleepily to Anglekin
Alongside in lanenooks   carling and leman⁸
caterwaul and clip⁹   careless of Saxonry
with moonglow and haste   and a higher heartbeat

---

²Attar—perfume made from rose petals or other flowers.
³Farde or fardel—burdened.
⁴Pimpled, blemished.
⁵Thane; in Anglo-Saxon England, one who ranked between an earl and a freeman and served in the military in return for land.
⁶A Jute was a member of an early Germanic tribe that invaded and settled in Southeast England in the fifth century BCE.
⁷The Huns were an aggressive Asiatic people who in the fourth century invaded Europe. Since World War I the term has also been used as a derogatory reference to Germans.
⁸"Carling," a boorish peasant; "leman," sweetheart or lover.
⁹Hold tightly, fasten.

> Slumbers now slumtrack   unstinks cooling
> waiting brief for milkmaid   mornstar and worldrise

(1942, rev. 1966)

Pablo Neruda   1904–1973

The United Fruit Co.[1]

Translated by Robert Bly

When the trumpet sounded, it was
all prepared on the earth,
and Jehovah parceled out the earth
to Coca-Cola, Inc., Anaconda,[2]
Ford Motors, and other entities:
The Fruit Company, Inc.
reserved for itself the most succulent,
the central coast of my own land,
the delicate waist of America.
It rechristened its territories   10
as the "Banana Republics"
and over the sleeping dead,
over the restless heroes
who brought about the greatness,
the liberty and the flags,
it established the comic opera:
abolished the independencies,
presented crowns of Caesar,
unsheathed envy, attracted
the dictatorship of the flies,   20
Trujillo flies, Tacho flies,
Carias flies, Martinez flies,
Ubico flies,[3] damp flies
of modest blood and marmalade,
drunken flies who zoom
over the ordinary graves,
circus flies, wise flies
well trained in tyranny.
Among the bloodthirsty flies
the Fruit Company lands its ships,   30
taking off the coffee and the fruit;
the treasure of our submerged

---

[1]"The Betrayed Sand" (a long poem by Neruda) concentrates on the men who allowed South American nations to fall back on colonialism of the United States, and on the men who support United States interests today. He mentions the pressure from U.S. companies to keep wages low. He describes especially events in the year 1946, while he was senator in Chile. We have chosen one of the poems in the centre of the section, on the United Fruit Company. (*Translator's note*)
[2]Anaconda Mining Company.
[3]Political dictators of Central and South America.

territories flows as though
on plates into the ships.
Meanwhile Indians are falling
into the sugared chasms
of the harbors, wrapped
for burial in the mist of the dawn:
a body rolls, a thing
that has no name, a fallen cipher,   40
a cluster of dead fruit
thrown down on the dump.
                                                    (1971)

W. H. Auden   1907–1973

Musée des Beaux Arts[1]

About suffering they were never wrong,
The Old Masters: how well they understood
Its human position; how it takes place
While someone else is eating or opening a window or just
    walking dully along;
How, when the aged are reverently, passionately waiting
For the miraculous birth, there always must be
Children who did not specially want it to happen, skating
On a pond at the edge of the wood:

They never forgot
That even the dreadful martyrdom must run its course   10
Anyhow in a corner, some untidy spot
Where the dogs go on with their doggy life and the torturer's
    horse
Scratches its innocent behind on a tree.

In Brueghel's *Icarus*,[2] for instance: how everything turns away
Quite leisurely from the disaster; the ploughman may
Have heard the splash, the forsaken cry,
But for him it was not an important failure; the sun shone
As it had to on the white legs disappearing into the green
Water; and the expensive delicate ship that must have seen
Something amazing, a boy falling out of the sky,   20
Had somewhere to get to and sailed calmly on.
                                                        (1940)

---

[1]Museum of Fine Arts.
[2]Painting by Pieter Brueghel the Elder (1520–1569) that depicts the fall of Icarus, who in Greek mythology had flown too close to the sun on wings made of feathers and wax. Only the legs of Icarus are visible below the ship, as he slips beneath the waves.

Irving Layton   b. 1912

The Bull Calf

The thing could barely stand. Yet taken
from his mother and the barn smells
he still impressed with his pride,
with the promise of sovereignty in the way
his head moved to take us in.
The fierce sunlight tugging the maize from the ground
licked at his shapely flanks.
He was too young for all that pride.
I thought of the deposed Richard II.

'No money in bull calves,' Freeman had said.   10
The visiting clergyman rubbed the nostrils
now snuffing pathetically at the windless day.
'A pity,' he sighed.
My gaze slipped off his hat toward the empty sky
that circled over the black knot of men,
over us and the calf waiting for the first blow

Struck,
the bull calf drew in his thin forelegs
as if gathering strength for a mad rush . . .
tottered . . . raised his darkening eyes to us,   20
and I saw we were at the far end
of his frightened look, growing smaller and smaller
till we were only the ponderous mallet
that flicked his bleeding ear
and pushed him over on his side, stiffly,
like a block of wood.

Below the hill's crest
the river snuffled on the improvised beach.
We dug a deep pit and threw the dead calf into it.
It made a wet sound, a sepulchral gurgle,   30
as the warm sides bulged and flattened.
Settled, the bull calf lay as if asleep,
one foreleg over the other,
bereft of pride and so beautiful now,
without movement, perfectly still in the cool pit,
I turned away and wept.

(1956)

Robert Hayden   1913–1980

Those Winter Sundays

Sundays too my father got up early
and put his clothes on in the blueblack cold,
then with cracked hands that ached

from labor in the weekday weather made
banked fires blaze. No one ever thanked him.

I'd wake and hear the cold splintering, breaking.
When the rooms were warm, he'd call,
and slowly I would rise and dress,
fearing the chronic angers of that house,

Speaking indifferently to him,   10
who had driven out the cold
and polished my good shoes as well.
What did I know, what did I know
of love's austere and lonely offices[1]?

(1966)

Randall Jarrell   1914–1965

The Death of the Ball Turret Gunner

From my mother's sleep I fell into the State,
And I hunched in its belly till my wet fur froze.
Six miles from earth, loosed from its dream of life,
I woke to black flak and the nightmare fighters.
When I died they washed me out of the turret with a hose.

(1945)

Dylan Thomas   1914–1953

Do Not Go Gentle into That Good Night

Do not go gentle into that good night,
Old age should burn and rave at close of day;
Rage, rage against the dying of the light.

Though wise men at their end know dark is right,
Because their words had forked no lightning they
Do not go gentle into that good night.

Good men, the last wave by, crying how bright
Their frail deeds might have danced in a green bay,
Rage, rage against the dying of the light.

Wild men who caught and sang the sun in flight,   10
And learn, too late, they grieved it on its way,
Do not go gentle into that good night.

---

[1] Duties.

Grave men, near death, who see with blinding sight
Blind eyes could blaze like meteors and be gay,
Rage, rage against the dying of the light.

And you, my father, there on the sad height,
Curse, bless, me now with your fierce tears, I pray.
Do not go gentle into that good night.
Rage, rage against the dying of the light.

(1952)

P. K. Page   b. 1916
Stories of Snow

Those in the vegetable rain retain
an area behind their sprouting eyes
held soft and rounded with the dream of snow
precious and reminiscent as those globes—
souvenir of some never-nether land—
which hold their snow-storms circular, complete,
high in a tall and teakwood cabinet.

In countries where the leaves are large as hands
where flowers protrude their fleshy chins
and call their colours,   10
an imaginary snow-storm sometimes falls
among the lilies.
And in the early morning one will waken
to think the glowing linen of his pillow
a northern drift, will find himself mistaken
and lie back weeping.
And there the story shifts from head to head,
of how in Holland, from their feather beds
hunters arise and part the flakes and go
forth to the frozen lakes in search of swans—   20
the snow-light falling white along their guns,
their breath in plumes.
While tethered in the wind like sleeping gulls
ice-boats wait the raising of their wings
to skim the electric ice at such a speed
they leap jet strips of naked water,
and how these flying, sailing hunters feel
air in their mouths as terrible as ether.
And on the story runs that even drinks
in that white landscape dare to be no colour;   30
how flasked and water clear, the liquor slips
silver against the hunters' moving hips.
And of the swan in death these dreamers tell
of its last flight and how it falls, a plummet,

pierced by the freezing bullet
and how three feathers, loosened by the shot,
descend like snow upon it.
While hunters plunge their fingers in its down
deep as a drift, and dive their hands
up to the neck of the wrist   40
in that warm metamorphosis of snow
as gentle as the sort that woodsmen know
who, lost in the white circle, fall at last
and dream their way to death.

And stories of this kind are often told
in countries where great flowers bar the roads
with reds and blues which seal the route to snow—
as if, in telling, raconteurs unlock
the colour with its complement and go
through to the area behind the eyes   50
where silent, unrefractive whiteness lies.

(1946)

Miriam Waddington   1917–2004

Ten Years and More

When my husband
lay dying a mountain
a lake three
cities ten years
and more
lay between us:

There were our
sons my wounds
and theirs,
despair loneliness,   10
handfuls of un-
hammered nails
pictures never
hung all

The uneaten
meals and unslept
sleep; there was
retirement, and
worst of all
a green umbrella   20
he can never
take back.

I wrote him a
letter but all

I could think of
to say was: do you
remember Severn
River, the red canoe
with the sail
and lee-boards?   30

I was really saying
for the sake of our
youth and our love
I forgave him for
everything
and I was asking him
to forgive me too.
                                                          (1976)

Margaret Avison   b. 1918

The Swimmer's Moment

For everyone
The swimmer's moment at the whirlpool comes,
But many at that moment will not say,
"This is the whirlpool, then."
By their refusal they are saved
From the black pit, and also from contesting
The deadly rapids, and emerging in
The mysterious, and more ample, further waters.
And so their bland-blank faces turn and turn
Pale and forever on the rim of suction   10
They will not recognize.
Of those who dare the knowledge
Many are whirled into the ominous centre
That, gaping vertical, seals up
For them an eternal boon of privacy,
So that we turn away from their defeat
With a despair, not for their deaths, but for
Ourselves, who cannot penetrate their secret
Nor even guess at the anonymous breadth
Where one or two have won: 20
(The silver reaches of the estuary).
                                                          (1960)

Al Purdy   1918–2000

The Dead Poet

I was altered in the placenta
by the dead brother before me

who built a place in the womb
knowing I was coming:
he wrote words on the walls of flesh
painting a woman inside a woman
whispering a faint lullaby
that sings in my blind heart still

The others were lumberjacks
backwoods wrestlers and farmers
their women were meek and mild
nothing of them survives
but an image inside an image
of a cookstove and the kettle boiling
—how else explain myself to myself
where does the song come from?

Now on my wanderings:
at the Alhambra's lyric dazzle
where the Moors built stone poems
a wan white face peering out
—and the shadow in Plato's cave
remembers the small dead one
—at Samarkand in pale blue light
the words came slowly from him
—I recall the music of blood
on the Street of the Silversmiths

Sleep softly spirit of earth
as the days and nights join hands
when everything becomes one thing
wait softly brother
but do not expect it to happen
that great whoop announcing resurrection
expect only a small whisper
of birds nesting and green things growing
and a brief saying of them
and know where the words came from

(1986)

Lawrence Ferlinghetti   b. 1919

Constantly Risking Absurdity

Constantly risking absurdity
                      and death
  whenever he performs
              above the heads
                      of his audience
the poet like an acrobat
         climbs on rime
                 to a high wire of his own making

               and balancing on eyebeams
                              above a sea of faces   10
         paces his way
                    to the other side of day
              performing entrechats¹
                            and sleight-of-foot tricks
         and other high theatrics
                             and all without mistaking
                   any thing
                            for what it may not be
         For he's the super realist
                             who must perforce perceive   20
                taut truth
                           before the taking of each stance or step
         in his supposed advance
                              toward that still higher perch
         where Beauty stands and waits
                              with gravity
                                      to start her death-defying leap
         And he
              a little charleychaplin man
                              who may or may not catch   30
                her fair eternal form
                              spreadeagled in the empty air
                 of existence
                                                                 (1958)

Howard Nemerov   1920–1991

The Goose Fish

On the long shore, lit by the moon
To show them properly alone,
Two lovers suddenly embraced
So that their shadows were as one.
The ordinary night was graced
For them by the swift tide of blood
That silently they took at flood,
And for a little time they prized
    Themselves emparadised.

Then, as if shaken by stage-fright   10
Beneath the hard moon's bony light,
They stood together on the sand
Embarrassed in each other's sight
But still conspiring hand in hand,
Until they saw, there underfoot,
As though the world had found them out,

---

¹Difficult ballet leaps.

The goose fish turning up, though dead,
   His hugely grinning head.

There in the china light he lay,
Most ancient and corrupt and gray   20
They hesitated at his smile,
Wondering what it seemed to say
To lovers who a little while
Before had thought to understand,
By violence upon the sand,
The only way that could be known
   To make a world their own.

It was a wide and moony grin
Together peaceful and obscene;
They knew not what he would express,   30
So finished a comedian
He might mean failure or success,
But took it for an emblem of
Their sudden, new and guilty love
To be observed by, when they kissed,
   That rigid optimist.

So he became their patriarch,
Dreadfully mild in the half-dark.
His throat that the sand seemed to choke,
His picket teeth, these left their mark   40
But never did explain the joke
That so amused him, lying there
While the moon went down to disappear
Along the still and tilted track
   That bears the zodiac.

                                                    (1960)

Philip Larkin   1922–1985

Home Is So Sad

Home is so sad. It stays as it was left,
Shaped to the comfort of the last to go
As if to win them back. Instead, bereft
Of anyone to please, it withers so,
Having no heart to put aside the theft

And turn again to what it started as,
A joyous shot at how things ought to be,
Long fallen wide. You can see how it was:
Look at the pictures and the cutlery.
The music in the piano stool. That vase.   10

                                                    (1964)

Denise Levertov   1923–1997

O Taste and See

The world is
not with us enough.
O taste and see

the subway Bible poster said,
meaning The Lord, meaning
if anything all that lives
to the imagination's tongue,

grief, mercy, language,
tangerine, weather, to
breathe them, bite,   10
savor, chew, swallow, transform
into our flesh our
deaths, crossing the street, plum, quince,
living in the orchard and being

hungry, and plucking
the fruit

(1962)

Lisel Mueller   b. 1924

Things

What happened is, we grew lonely
living among the things,
so we gave the clock a face,
the chair a back,
the table four stout legs
which will never suffer fatigue.

We fitted our shoes with tongues
as smooth as our own
and hung tongues inside bells
so we could listen   10
to their emotional language,

and because we loved graceful profiles
the pitcher received a lip,
the bottle a long, slender neck.

Even what was beyond us
was recast in our image;
we gave the country a heart,
the storm an eye,

            the cave a mouth
            so we could pass into safety.   20
                                                          (1992)

                    Allen Ginsberg   1926–1997

                    A Supermarket in California

   What thoughts I have of you tonight, Walt Whitman, for I walked down the sidestreets under the trees with a headache self-conscious looking at the full moon.
   In my hungry fatigue, and shopping for images, I went into the neon fruit supermarket, dreaming of your enumerations!
   What peaches and what penumbras![1] Whole families shopping at night! Aisles full of husbands! Wives in the avocados, babies in the tomatoes!—and you, García Lorca,[2] what were you doing down by the watermelons?

   I saw you, Walt Whitman, childless, lonely old grubber, poking among the meats in the refrigerator and eyeing the grocery boys.
   I heard you asking questions of each: Who killed the pork chops? What price bananas? Are you my Angel?
   I wandered in and out of the brilliant stacks of cans following you, and followed in my imagination by the store detective.
   We strode down the open corridors together in our solitary fancy tasting artichokes, possessing every frozen delicacy, and never passing the cashier.

   Where are we going, Walt Whitman? The doors close in an hour. Which way does your beard point tonight?
   (I touch your book and dream of our odyssey in the supermarket and feel absurd.)
   Will we walk all night through solitary streets? The trees add   10
shade to shade, lights out in the houses, we'll both be lonely.

   Will we stroll dreaming of the lost America of love past blue automobiles in driveways, home to our silent cottage?
   Ah, dear father, graybeard, lonely old courage-teacher, what America did you have when Charon[3] quit poling his ferry and you got out on a smoking bank and stood watching the boat disappear on the black waters of Lethe?[4]

                                                          (1956)

---

[1]Partial shadows.
[2]Spanish poet who wrote an ode to Whitman.
[3]Ferryman who conveyed the dead across the river Styx to Hades.
[4]River of Forgetfulness in Hades.

James Reaney   b. 1926

The School Globe

Sometimes when I hold
Our faded old globe
That we used at school
To see where oceans were
And the five continents,
The lines of latitude and longitude,
The North Pole, the Equator and the South Pole—
Sometimes when I hold this
Wrecked blue cardboard pumpkin
I think: here in my hands   10
Rest the fair fields and lands
Of my childhood
Where still lie or still wander
Old games, tops and pets;
A house where I was little
And afraid to swear
Because God might hear and
Send a bear
To eat me up;
Rooms where I was as old   20
As I was high;
Where I loved the pink clenches,
The white, red and pink fists
Of roses; where I watched the rain
That Heaven's clouds threw down
In puddles and rutfuls
And irregular mirrors
Of soft brown glass upon the ground.
This school globe is a parcel of my past,
A basket of pluperfect[1] things.   30
And here I stand with it
Sometime in the summertime
All alone in an empty schoolroom
Where about me hang
Old maps, an abacus, pictures,
Blackboards, empty desks.
If I raise my hand
No tall teacher will demand
What I want.
But if someone in authority   40
Were here, I'd say
Give me this old world back
Whose husk I clasp
And I'll give you in exchange
The great sad real one

---

[1] More than perfect. In grammar it is the past perfect tense.

That's filled
Not with a child's remembered and pleasant skies
But with blood, pus, horror, death, stepmothers, and lies.

(1949)

Phyllis Webb   b. 1927

Sitting

The degree of nothingness
is important:
to sit emptily
in the sun
receiving fire
that is the way
to mend
an extraordinary world,
sitting perfectly
still
and only
remotely human.

(1965)

Adrienne Rich   b. 1929

Aunt Jennifer's Tigers

Aunt Jennifer's tigers prance across a screen,
Bright topaz denizens of a world of green.
They do not fear the men beneath the tree;
They pace in sleek chivalric certainty.

Aunt Jennifer's fingers fluttering through her wool
Find even the ivory needle hard to pull.
The massive weight of Uncle's wedding band
Sits heavily upon Aunt Jennifer's hand.

When Aunt is dead, her terrified hands will lie
Still ringed with ordeals she was mastered by.   10
The tigers in the panel that she made
Will go on prancing, proud and unafraid.

(1951)

Sylvia Plath   1932–1963

Daddy

You do not do, you do not do
Any more, black shoe

In which I have lived like a foot
For thirty years, poor and white,
Barely daring to breathe or Achoo.

Daddy, I have had to kill you.
You died before I had time—
Marble-heavy, a bag full of God,
Ghastly statue with one grey toe
Big as a Frisco seal   10

And a head in the freakish Atlantic
Where it pours bean green over blue
In the waters off beautiful Nauset.[1]
I used to pray to recover you.
Ach, du.[2]

In the German tongue, in the Polish town
Scraped flat by the roller
Of wars, wars, wars.
But the name of the town is common.
My Polack friend   20

Says there are a dozen or two.
So I never could tell where you
Put your foot, your root,
I never could talk to you.
The tongue stuck in my jaw.

It stuck in a barb wire snare.
Ich, ich, ich, ich,[3]
I could hardly speak.
I thought every German was you.
And the language obscene   30

An engine, an engine
Chuffing me off like a Jew.
A Jew to Dachau, Auschwitz, Belsen.[4]
I began to talk like a Jew.
I think I may well be a Jew.

The snows of the Tyrol, the clear beer of Vienna
Are not very pure or true.
With my gypsy ancestress and my weird luck
And my Taroc pack[5] and my Taroc pack
I may be a bit of a Jew.   40

---

[1] Beach and harbour on Cape Cod.
[2] German for "Ah, you."
[3] German for "I, I, I, I."
[4] Nazi concentration camps.
[5] Tarot cards, used in fortune telling.

I have always been scared of *you*,
With your Luftwaffe,[6] your gobbledygoo.
And your neat moustache
And your Aryan eye, bright blue.
Panzer[7]-man, panzer-man, O You—

Not God but a swastika
So black no sky could squeak through.
Every woman adores a Fascist,
The boot in the face, the brute
Brute heart of a brute like you.   50

You stand at the blackboard, daddy,
In the picture I have of you,
A cleft in your chin instead of your foot
But no less a devil for that, no not
Any less the black man who

Bit my pretty red heart in two.
I was ten when they buried you.
At twenty I tried to die
And get back, back, back to you.
I thought even the bones would do.   60

But they pulled me out of the sack,
And they stuck me together with glue.
And then I knew what to do.
I made a model of you,
A man in black with a Meinkampf[8] look

And a love of the rack and the screw.
And I said I do, I do.
So daddy, I'm finally through.
The black telephone's off at the root,
The voices just can't worm through.   70

If I've killed one man, I've killed two—
The vampire who said he was you
And drank my blood for a year,
Seven years, if you want to know.
Daddy, you can lie back now.

There's a stake in your fat black heart
And the villagers never liked you.
They are dancing and stamping on you.
They always *knew* it was you.
Daddy, daddy, you bastard, I'm through.   80

(1963)

---

[6]The German air force in World War II.
[7]Referring to a German tank unit in World War II.
[8]*My Struggle*, the title of Adolf Hitler's political autobiography.

Alden Nowlan   1933–1983

I, Icarus

There was a time when I could fly. I swear it.
Perhaps, if I think hard for a moment, I can even tell you the
   year.
My room was on the ground floor at the rear of the house.
My bed faced a window.
Night after night I lay on my bed and willed myself to fly.
It was hard work, I can tell you.
Sometimes I lay perfectly still for an hour before I felt
   my body rising from the bed.
I rose slowly, slowly until I floated three or four feet
   above the floor.
Then, with a kind of swimming motion, I propelled myself
   toward the window.
Outside, I rose higher and higher, above the pasture fence,
   above the clothesline, above the dark, haunted trees
   beyond the pasture. 10
And, all the time, I heard the music of flutes.
It seemed the wind made this music.
And sometimes there were voices singing.

(1967)

The Middle-Aged Man in the Supermarket

I'm pretending to test the avocadoes for ripeness
while gaping obliquely at the bare brown legs
of the girl in the orange skirt selecting mushrooms
when she says, 'Hi, there, let's make love.'
At first I think that she must have caught me
and is being sarcastic and then I decide
she's joking with someone she knows, perhaps the boy
   weighing green beans
or the young man with the watercress, so I try to act
as if I hadn't heard her, walk away at what I hope
is the right speed, without looking back, 10
and don't stop until I come to
the frozen-food bins, where I'm still standing,
gazing down at things I almost never buy, when
   I become aware
she's near me again, although I see only
a few square inches of brown thigh, a bit of
   orange cloth
and two symmetrical bare feet. I wish I could know
her body so well I could ever afterwards identify her
by taste alone. I rattle a carton
of frozen peas, read both French and English
   directions

on a package of frozen bread dough. She still   20
    stands there.
I wait for her to say to me:
'I fell in love the moment I saw you.
I want us to spend our first week together
in bed. We'll have our meals sent up. I'm even
    prettier
when I'm bare and I promise I'll keep my eyes shut
while you're naked, so that you'll never worry
that I might be comparing your body with that
of a previous lover, none of whom was older
than twenty, although the truth is I like
fat hips and big bellies—it's a kink   30
    that I have:
my nipples harden when I envision
those mountainous moons of flesh above me.'

(1974)

Leonard Cohen   b. 1934

A Kite Is a Victim

A kite is a victim you are sure of.
You love it because it pulls
gentle enough to call you master,
strong enough to call you fool;
because it lives
like a desperate trained falcon
in the high sweet air,
and you can always haul it down
to tame it in your drawer.

A kite is a fish you have already caught   10
in a pool where no fish come,
so you play him carefully and long,
and hope he won't give up,
or the wind die down.

A kite is the last poem you've written,
so you give it to the wind,
but you don't let it go
until someone finds you
something else to do.

A kite is a contract of glory   20
that must be made with the sun,
so you make friends with the field
the river and the wind,
then you pray the whole cold night before,
under the travelling cordless moon,
to make you worthy and lyric and pure.

(1961)

Joy Kogawa   b. 1935

Where There's a Wall

Where there's a wall
there's a way through a
gate or door. There's even
a ladder perhaps and a
sentinel who sometimes sleeps.
There are secret passwords you
can overhear. There are methods
of torture for extracting clues
to maps of underground passages.
There are zeppelins, helicopters,   10
rockets, bombs, battering rams,
armies with trumpets whose
all at once blast shatters
the foundations.

Where there's a wall there are
words to whisper by loose bricks,
wailing prayers to utter, birds
to carry messages taped to their feet
There are letters to be written—   20
poems even.

Faint as in a dream
is the voice that calls
from the belly
of the wall.

(1985)

Michele Lalonde   b. 1937

Speak White

Translated by D. G. Jones

Speak white
it is so lovely to listen to you
speaking of Paradise Lost
or the anonymous, graceful profile trembling in the sonnets of
   Shakespeare

We are a rude and stammering people
but we are not deaf to the genius of a language
speak with the accent of Milton and Byron and Shelley and Keats
speak white
and please excuse us if in return
we've only our rough ancestral songs   10
and the chagrin of Nelligan[1]

---
[1]Émile Nelligan (1879–1941), an exceptionally sensitive poet whom many consider the national poet of Quebec.

speak white
speak of places, this and that
speak to us of the Magna Carta
of the Lincoln Monument
of the cloudy charm of the Thames
or blossom-time on the Potomac
speak to us of your traditions
We are a people who are none too bright
but we are quick to sense   20
the great significance of crumpets
or the Boston Tea Party

But when you really speak white
when you get down to brass tacks
to speak of Better Homes and Gardens
and the high standard of living
and the Great Society
a little louder then speak white

raise your foremen's voices
we are a little hard of hearing   30
we live too close to the machines
and only hear our heavy breathing over the tools
speak white and loud
so we can hear you clearly
from Saint Henri to Santo Domingo
yes, what a marvellous language
for hiring and firing
for giving the orders
for fixing the hour to be worked to death
and that pause that refreshes   40
and bucks up the dollar

Speak white
tell us that God is a great big shot
and that we're paid to trust him
speak white
speak to us of production, profits and percentages
speak white
it's a rich language
for buying
but for selling oneself   50
but for selling one's soul
but for selling oneself

Ah
speak white
big deal
but for telling about
the eternity of a day on strike
for telling the whole

life-story of a nation of caretakers
for coming back home in the evening
at the hour when the sun's gone bust in the alleys
for telling you yes the sun does set yes
every day of our lives to the east of your empires
Nothing's as good as a language of oaths
our mode of expression none too clean
dirtied with oil and with axle grease

Speak white
feel at home with your words
we are a bitter people
but we'd never reproach a soul
for having a monopoly
on how to improve one's speech

In the sweet tongue of Shakespeare
with the accent of Longfellow
speak a French purely and atrociously white
as in Viet Nam, in the Congo
speak impeccable German
a yellow star between your teeth
speak Russian speak of the right to rule speak of repression
speak white
it's a universal language
we were born to understand it
with its tear-gas phrases
with its billy-club words

Speak white
tell us again about freedom and democracy
We know that liberty is a Black word
as misery is Black
as blood is muddied with the dust of Algiers[2] or of Little Rock[3]

Speak white
from Westminster to Washington take turns
speak white as on Wall Street
white as in Watts
Be civilized
and understand our conventional answer
when you ask us politely
how do you do
and we mean to reply
we're doing all right
we're doing fine

---

[2]Algeria's capital city. Algeria gained independence from France in 1962 after seven years of war.
[3]Little Rock, Arkansas, where demonstrations and rioting occurred following 1958 desegregation decisions by the U.S. Supreme Court.

we
are not alone

We know now
that we are not alone

(1969)

Margaret Atwood   b. 1939

Death of a Young Son by Drowning

He, who navigated with success
the dangerous river of his own birth
once more set forth

on a voyage of discovery
into the land I floated on
but could not touch to claim.

His feet slid on the bank,
the currents took him;
he swirled with ice and trees in the swollen water

and plunged into distant regions,   10
his head a bathysphere;
through his eyes' thin glass bubbles

he looked out, reckless adventurer
on a landscape stranger than Uranus
we have all been to and some remember.

There was an accident; the air locked,
he was hung in the river like a heart.
They retrieved the swamped body,

cairn of my plans and future charts,
with poles and hooks   20
from among the nudging logs.

It was spring, the sun kept shining, the new grass
leapt to solidity;
my hands glistened with details.

After the long trip I was tired of waves.
My foot hit rock. The dreamed sails
collapsed, ragged.

    I planted him in this country
    like a flag.

(1970)

Dream 2: Brian the Still-Hunter[1]

The man I saw in the forest
used to come to our house
every morning, never said anything;
I learned from the neighbours later
he once tried to cut his throat.

I found him at the end of the path
sitting on a fallen tree
cleaning his gun.

There was no wind;
around us the leaves rustled.   10

He said to me:
I kill because I have to

but every time I aim, I feel
my skin grow fur
my head heavy with antlers
and during the stretched instant
the bullet glides on its thread of speed
my soul runs innocent as hooves.

Is God just to his creatures?

I die more often than many.   20

He looked up and I saw
the white scar made by the hunting knife
around his neck.

When I woke
I remembered: he has been gone
twenty years and not heard from.

(1970)

Seamus Heaney   b. 1939

Digging

Between my finger and my thumb
The squat pen rests; snug as a gun.

Under my window, a clean rasping sound
When the spade sinks into gravelly ground:
My father, digging. I look down

---

[1] A sly and quiet hunter who travels on foot. See Susanna Moodie's "XI. Brian the Still-Hunter" on page 413. Susanna Moodie had a friendship with Brian, a depressed man who felt much admiration and affinity for the animals he hunted. See Chapter 10 of Moodie's *Roughing It in the Bush*. Margaret Atwood elaborates upon Moodie's life and writing in her collection *The Journals of Susanna Moodie*.

Till his straining rump among the flowerbeds
Bends low, comes up twenty years away
Stooping in rhythm through potato drills
Where he was digging.

The coarse boot nestled on the lug, the shaft   10
Against the inside knee was levered firmly.
He rooted out tall tops, buried the bright edge deep
To scatter new potatoes that we picked
Loving their cool hardness in our hands.

By God, the old man could handle a spade.
Just like his old man.
My grandfather cut more turf[1] in a day
Than any other man on Toner's bog.
Once I carried him milk in a bottle
Corked sloppily with paper. He straightened up   20
To drink it, then fell to right away
Nicking and slicing neatly, heaving sods
Over his shoulder, going down and down
For the good turf. Digging.

The cold smell of potato mould, the squelch and slap
Of soggy peat, the curt cuts of an edge
Through living roots awaken in my head.
But I've no spade to follow men like them.

Between my finger and my thumb
The squat pen rests.   30
I'll dig with it.

(1966)

Patrick Lane   b. 1939

The Bird

The bird you captured is dead.
I told you it would die
but you would not learn
from my telling. You wanted
to cage a bird in your hands
and learn to fly.

Listen again.
You must not handle birds.
They cannot fly through your fingers.
You are not a nest   10
and a feather is
not made of blood and bone.

---

[1] Peat, used for fuel in Ireland.

Only words
can fly for you like birds
on the wall of the sun.
A bird is a poem
that talks of the end of cages.

(1974)

John Lennon   1940–1980
Paul McCartney   b. 1942

Eleanor Rigby

Ah, look at all the lonely people!
Ah, look at all the lonely people!

Eleanor Rigby
Picks up the rice in the church where a wedding has been,
Lives in a dream,
Waits at the window
Wearing the face that she keeps in a jar by the door.
Who is it for?

All the lonely people,
Where do they all come from?   10
All the lonely people,
Where do they all belong?

Father McKenzie,
Writing the words of a sermon that no one will hear,
No one comes near.
Look at him working,
Darning his socks in the night when there's nobody there.
What does he care?

All the lonely people,
Where do they all come from?   20
All the lonely people,
Where do they all belong?

Eleanor Rigby
Died in the church and was buried along with her name.
Nobody came.
Father McKenzie,
Wiping the dirt from his hands as he walks from the grave,
No one was saved.

All the lonely people,
Where do they all come from?   30
All the lonely people,
Where do they all belong?

Ah, look at all the lonely people!
Ah, look at all the lonely people!

(1966)

Gwendolyn MacEwen   1941–1987

Icarus

Feather and wax, the artful wings
bridge a blue gulf between
the stiff stone tower
and its languid god, fat sky.

The boy, bent to the whim of wind,
the blue, and the snarling sun
form a brief triumvirate
—flesh, feather, light—
locked in the jaws of the noon
they rule with fleeting liberty.

>These are the wings, then,
>a legacy of hollow light—
>feathers, a quill to write
>white poetry across the sky.

Through the mouth of the air, the boy
sees his far father, whose muscled flight
is somehow severed from his own.
Two blinking worlds, and Daedalus'
unbound self is a thing apart.

>You, bound for that other area
>know that this legacy of mindflight
>is all you have to leave me.

The boy, Icarus, twists the threads of his throat
and his eyes argue with the sun
on a flimsy parallel, and
the mouth of the sun eager, eager,
smuggles a hot word to the boy's ear.

>But flying, locked in dark dream,
>I see Queen Dream, Queen Flight,
>The last station of the poet
>years above my brow, and

Something, something in the air,
in the light's flight, in the vaguely
voluptuous arc of the wings
drives a foreign rhythm into his arms,
his arms which are lean, white willows.

Icarus feels his blood race to his wrist
in a marathon of red light. Swifter,
swift, he tears away the slow veil
from his tendons; the playful biceps   40
sing; they wish new power to the beautiful
false wings
and the boy loops up into tall cobalt.
His hair is a swirl of drunken light,
his arms are wet blades; wings wed with arms.

> You knew
> I would get drunk on beauty.
> The famous phantom quill
> would write me, pull me
> through the eye   50
> of needle noon.

Crete is a huge hump of a black whore beneath him.
Her breasts, two wretched mountains
tremble under his eye.
All is black, except the sun in slow explosion;
a great war strangles his vision
and knots his flying nerve.
Black, and fire, and the boy.

> You and your legacy!
> You knew I would try to   60
> slay the sunlight.

Look, Icarus has kissed the sun
and it sucks the wax,
feathers and wax.
The wings are melting!

The boy Icarus is lean and beautiful.
His body grows limp and falls.
It is cruel poetry set
to the tempo of lightning; it is too swift,
this thin descent.   70

On the lips of the Aegean:
globules of wax,
strands of wet light,

> the lean poem's flesh
> tattered and torn
> by a hook
> of vengeful fire . . .

Combustion of brief feathers

(1961)

Daphne Marlatt   b. 1942

retrieving madrone[1]

take, take the

        arbutus, crazy-woman tree, she said, does
everything at the wrong time, sheds last year's leaves midsummer, yellow, out of new green, sheds ochre bark at the
end of summer when

      you'd think she'd hang onto it

              the way
light catches in the curled edges of her

           skin, it's only
paper, thin enough to let light, as the words of this world   10
impinge, turn me out of mine. i throw off words, leave outgrown images of myself

      crazy-waving-in-air ma-
drone this murmur you make, a stir of bright
leaves hitting home, the sound of *geta*, his
name for the thongs he wears against sharp
things on his path underfoot: a name, a use

overhead, over my head, i listen to slippery
woman, word peeler, leaf weaver, hear the slur
of a different being approach   20

        leaf lingua love-
                tongue
                      turning me
inside out

                            (2001)

Don McKay   b. 1942

Glenn Gould, Humming

not along with the music, which isn't listening,
but to the animal inside the instrument,
muffling the perfections of hammer, pedal,
wire, the whole
tool-kit, humming
he furs the air,
paints an exquisite velvet painting of a far-off country

---

[1] Arbutus tree, an evergreen tree unique to the Pacific coast from northern California to British Columbia.

where the rain falls
contrapuntally the wind lies on the land
like a hand caressing a cat's back, humming 10
"this is your death, which is but a membrane away
which is but a leaf, turning,
which is falling in these delicate
explicit fingers, as you have always known,
and worn, though only we,
the instrumentalists,
have found a way to sing it for you.
Sleep."

(1997)

Icarus

isn't sorry. We do not find him
doing penance, writing out the golden mean for all
eternity, or touring its high schools to tell student bodies
not to do what he done
done. Over and over he rehearses flight
and fall, tuning his moves, entering
with fresh rush into the mingling of the air
with spirit. This is his practice
and his prayer: to be translated into air, as air
with each breath enters lungs, 10
then blood. He feels resistance gather in his stiff
strange wings, angles his arms to shuck the sweet lift
from the drag, runs the full length
of a nameless corridor, his feet striking the paving stones
less and less heavily, then
they're bicycling above the ground,
a few shallow beats and he's up,
he's out of the story and into the song.

At the melting point of wax, which now he knows
the way Doug Harvey knows the blue line, 20
he will back-beat to create a pause, hover for maybe fifty
hummingbird heartbeats and then
lose it, tumbling into freefall, shedding feathers
like a lover shedding clothes. He may glide
in the long arc of a Tundra Swan or pull up sharp
to Kingfisher into the sea which bears his name. Then,
giving it the full Ophelia, drown.

On the shore
the farmer ploughs his field, the dull ship
sails away, the poets moralize about our 30
unsignificance. But Icarus is thinking tremolo and
backflip, is thinking
next time with a half-twist
and a tuck and isn't
sorry.

(2000)

Michael Ondaatje b. 1943

The Cinnamon Peeler

If I were a cinnamon peeler
I would ride your bed
and leave the yellow bark dust
on your pillow.

Your breasts and shoulders would reek
you could never walk through markets
without the profession of my fingers
floating over you. The blind would
stumble certain of whom they approached
though you might bathe
under rain gutters, monsoon.

Here on the upper thigh
at this smooth pasture
neighbour to your hair
or the crease
that cuts your back. This ankle.
You will be known among strangers
as the cinnamon peeler's wife.

I could hardly glance at you
before marriage
never touch you
—your keen nosed mother, your rough brothers.
I buried my hands
in saffron, disguised them
over smoking tar,
helped the honey gatherers . . .

*

When we swam once
I touched you in water
and our bodies remained free,
you could hold me and be blind of smell.
You climbed the bank and said

   this is how you touch other women
the grass cutter's wife, the lime burner's daughter.
And you searched your arms
for the missing perfume
    and knew

   what good is it
to be the lime burner's daughter
left with no trace
as if not spoken to in the act of love
as if wounded without the pleasure of a scar.

You touched
your belly to my hands
in the dry air and said
I am the cinnamon
peeler's wife. Smell me.

(1981)

bp Nichol   1944–1988

Blues

```
          l   e

          o   e

          l o v e

          o   e v o l

       l o v e   o

          e v o l

          e   o

          e   l
```

(1974)

Bronwen Wallace   1945–1989

The Woman in This Poem

The woman in this poem
lives in the suburbs
with her husband and two children
each day she waits for the mail and
once a week receives
a letter from her lover
who lives in another city
writes of roses   warm patches
of sunlight on his bed
Come to me he pleads   10
I need you and the woman
reaches for the phone
to dial the airport
she will leave this afternoon
her suitcase packed
with a few light clothes

But as she is dialing
the woman in this poem
remembers the pot-roast
and the fact that it is Thursday
she thinks of how her husband's face
will look when he reads her note
his body curling sadly toward
the empty side of the bed

She stops dialing and begins
to chop onions for the pot-roast
but behind her back the phone
shapes itself insistently
the number for airline reservations
chants in her head
in an hour her children will be
home from school and after that
her husband will arrive
to kiss the back of her neck
while she thickens the gravy
and she knows that
all through dinner
her mouth will laugh and chatter
while she walks with her lover
on a beach somewhere

She puts the onions in the pot
and turns toward the phone
but even as she reaches
she is thinking of
her daughter's piano lessons
her son's dental appointment

Her arms fall to her side
and as she stands there
in the middle of her spotless kitchen
we can see her growing
old like this
and wish for something   anything
to happen   we could have her go
mad perhaps and lock herself
in the closet   crouch there
for days her dresses withering
around her like cast-off skins
or maybe she could take
to cruising the streets at night
in her husband's car
picking up teenage boys
and fucking them in the back seat
we can even imagine
finding her body
dumped in a ditch somewhere
on the edge of town

The woman in this poem offends us
with her useless phone and the persistent
smell of onions   we regard her as we do
the poorly calculated overdose
who lies in a bed somewhere
not knowing how her life drips
through her drop by measured drop
we want to think of death
as something sudden
stroke or the leap
that carries us over the railing
of the bridge in one determined arc
the pistol aimed precisely
at the right part of the brain
we want to hate this woman

but mostly we hate knowing
that for us too it is
moments like this
our thoughts   stiff fingers
tear at again and again
when we stop in the middle
of an ordinary day and
like the woman in this poem
begin to feel
our own deaths
rising slow within us

(1987)

Patrick Friesen   b. 1946

pa poem 4: naked and nailed

I remember those carpenter's hands
thick fingers drumming the table
fingers that tightened around my biceps
lifted me right off the kitchen floor
down basement steps
and there we were in front of the furnace
me pleading across your knee   both of us wishing we were
                                         someplace else

but you not spoiling the child
and you swung that leather high
me twisting to look up   your arm flung out
seeing you naked and nailed like a child to a tree

how could there be so much love?

I wish I could have seen you sidestep
or shout the words of your hurt

    even better I would have loved to see you leaping
    on your long narrow feet   howling
    and sweat flying from that fine muscled chest

    what's a father if he doesn't let out
    the whirling dervish the gypsy or the juggler?   20

    you one-eyed monster
    you saw more than you let on
    maybe more than you ever knew
    but you couldn't find the words for me

    you rowing that boat into mother's dreams
    someplace out there   maybe still looking for the words
    and one night with me sleeping creepy
    you'll find them and you'll find me
    sitting in bed shivering
    maybe before I find you   30
    you'll tap me on the shoulder
    I'll turn
    I'll recognize you

    and see   you old dead man
    how I start with my grievance
    and always end up with this Goddamned love
    but I tell you that won't happen everytime
    or it'll kill me

                                                      (1994)

Jim Wong-Chu   b. 1949

old chinese cemetery kamloops

        like a child lost
        wandering about
        touching   feeling
        tattered grounds
        touching   seeing
        wooden boards

        etched in ink
        etched in weather
        etched in fading memories
        etched   10
        faded
        forgotten

        I walk
        on earth
        above the bones
        of a multitude

    of golden mountain men
    searching for scraps
    of memory

    like a child unloved   20
    his face pressed hard
    against the wet window
    peering in
    for a desperate moment
    I touch my past

                                                             (1977)

Anne Carson   b. 1950

God's Work

Moonlight in the kitchen is a sign of God.
The kind of sadness that is a black suction pipe extracting you
from your own navel and which the Buddhists call

'no mindcover' is a sign of God.
The blind alleys that run alongside human conversation
like lashes are a sign of God.

God's own calmness is a sign of God.
The surprisingly cold smell of potatoes or money.
Solid pieces of silence.

From these diverse signs you can see   10
how much work remains to do.
Put away your sadness, it is a mantle of work

                                                               (1995)

Dionne Brand   b. 1953

Land to Light On

V i

Maybe this wide country just stretches your life to a thinness
just trying to take it in, trying to calculate in it what you must
do, the airy bay at its head scatters your thoughts like someone
going mad from science and birds pulling your hair, ice invades
your nostrils in chunks, land fills your throat, you are so busy
with collecting the north, scrambling to the Arctic so wilfully, so
busy getting a handle to steady you to this place you get blown
into bays and lakes and fissures you have yet to see, except

on a map in a schoolroom long ago but you have a sense that
whole parts of you are floating in heavy lake water heading for
what you suspect is some other life that lives there, and you, you
only trust moving water and water that reveals itself in colour. It
always takes long to come to what you have to say, you have to
sweep this stretch of land up around your feet and point to the
signs, pleat whole histories with pins in your mouth and guess
at the fall of words

V ii

But the sight of land has always baffled you,
there is dirt somewhere older than any exile
and try as you might, your eyes only compose
the muddy drain in front of the humid almond
tree, the unsettling concrete sprawl of the housing
scheme, the stone your uncle used to smash his name
into another uncle's face, your planet is your hands,
your house behind your eyebrows and the tracing
paper over the bead of islands of indifferent and
reversible shapes, now Guadeloupe is a crab pinched
at the waist, now Nevis' borders change by mistake
and the carelessness of history, now sitting in Standard
Five,[1] the paper shifting papery in the sweat of your
fingers you come to be convinced that these lines will
not matter, your land is a forced march on the bottom
of the Sargasso,[2] your way tangled in life

V iii

I am giving up on land to light on, it's only true, it is only
something someone tells you, someone you should not trust
anyway. Days away, years before, a beer at your lips and the view
from Castara,[3] the ocean as always pulling you towards its bone
and much later, in between, learning to drive the long drive
to Burnt River, where the land is not beautiful, braised
like the back of an animal, burnt in coolness, but the sky is,
like the ocean pulling you toward its bone, skin falling away
from your eyes, you see it without its history of harm, without
its damage, or everywhere you walk on the earth there's harm,
everywhere resounds. This is the only way you will know
the names of cities, not charmed or overwhelmed, all you see is
museums of harm and metros full, in Paris, walls inspected
crudely for dates, and Amsterdam, street corners full of
druggists, ashen with it, all the way from Suriname, Curaçao,
Dutch and German inking their lips, pen nibs of harm blued in
the mouth, not to say London's squares, blackened in statues,

---

[1] A grade level of the British school system, in this case in the Caribbean.
[2] A sea between the Azores and the Caribbean in the West Atlantic region. Its name comes from the dense masses of floating sargasso seaweed that were dangerous for sailing ships.
[3] A fishing village on the northwest coast of Tobago.

Zeebrugge,[4] searching the belly of fish, Kinshasa,[5] through an 50
airplane window the dictator cutting up bodies grips the plane
to the tarmac and I can't get out to kiss the ground

V iv

This those slaves must have known who were my mothers, skin
falling from their eyes, they moving toward their own bone,
'so thank god for the ocean and the sky all implicated, all
unconcerned,' they must have said, 'or there'd be nothing to
love.' How they spent a whole lifetime undoing the knot
of a word and as fast it would twirl up again, spent
whole minutes inching their eyes above sea level only
for latitude to shift, only for a horrible horizon to list, thank god 60
for the degrees of the chin, the fooling plane of a doorway, only
the mind, the not just simple business of return and turning,
that is for scholars and indecisive frigates, circling and circling,
stripped in their life, naked as seaweed, they would have sat
and sunk but no, the sky was a doorway, a famine and a jacket,
the sea a definite post

V v

I'm giving up on land to light on, slowly, it isn't land,
it is the same as fog and mist and figures and lines
and erasable thoughts, it is buildings and governments
and toilets and front door mats and typewriter shops, 70
cards with your name and clothing that comes undone,
skin that doesn't fasten and spills and shoes. It's paper,
paper, maps. Maps that get wet and rinse out, in my hand
anyway. I'm giving up what was always shifting, mutable
cities' fluorescences, limbs, chalk curdled blackboards
and carbon copies, wretching water, cunning walls. Books
to set it right. Look. What I know is this. I'm giving up.
No offence. I was never committed. Not ever, to offices
or islands, continents, graphs, whole cloth, these sequences
or even footsteps 80

V vi

Light passes through me lightless, sound soundless,
smoking nowhere, groaning with sudden birds. Paper
dies, flesh melts, leaving stockings and their useless vanity
in graves, bodies lie still across foolish borders.
I'm going my way, going my way gleaning shade, burnt
meridians, dropping carets,[6] flung latitudes, inattention,

---

[4] A Belgian seaport.
[5] The capital of the Democratic Republic of Congo, where Mobutu Sese Seko was dictator from 1965 to 1997.
[6] A caret mark (^) is an indication that something should be inserted in this spot. On maps, routes are marked by a line of carets.

screeching looks. I'm trying to put my tongue on dawns
now, I'm busy licking dusk away, tracking deep twittering
silences. You come to this, here's the marrow of it, not
moving, not standing, it's too much to hold up, what I 90
really want to say is, I don't want no fucking country, here
or there and all the way back, I don't like it, none of it,
easy as that. I'm giving up on land to light on, and why not,
I can't perfect my own shadow, my violent sorrow, my
individual wrists.

(1997)

Louise Erdrich   b. 1954

Indian Boarding School: The Runaways

Home's the place we head for in our sleep.
Boxcars stumbling north in dreams
don't wait for us. We catch them on the run.
The rails, old lacerations that we love,
shoot parallel across the face and break
just under Turtle Mountains. Riding scars
you can't get lost. Home is the place they cross.

The lame guard strikes a match and makes the dark
less tolerant. We watch through cracks in boards
as the land starts rolling, rolling till it hurts 10
to be here, cold in regulation clothes.
We know the sheriff's waiting at midrun
to take us back. His car is dumb and warm.
The highway doesn't rock, it only hums
like a wing of long insults. The worn-down welts
of ancient punishments lead back and forth.

All runaways wear dresses, long green ones,
the color you would think shame was. We scrub
the sidewalks down because it's shameful work.
Our brushes cut the stone in watered arcs 20
and in the soak frail outlines shiver clear
a moment, things us kids pressed on the dark
face before it hardened, pale, remembering
delicate old injuries, the spines of names and leaves.

(1984)

Jan Zwicky   b. 1955

Musicians

I pass a bunch of musicians in the street.
It's about 12:30, rehearsal just over, they're

standing around outside the side door of the church.
A good rehearsal; and it's April. They're laughing,
horsing around, talking about shoes, or taxes, where
to go for lunch, anything
except what their heads are full of.

It's a kind of helplessness, you can see
they're still breathing almost in unison, like people
the searchlight has passed over   10
and spared, their attention
lifts, swerves, settles; even
the gravel dust stuttering at their feet
is coherent.

(1998)

Anne Michaels   b. 1958

There Is No City That Does Not Dream

There is no city that does not dream
from its foundations. The lost lake
crumbling in the hands of brickmakers,
the floor of the ravine where light lies broken
with the memory of rivers. All the winters
stored in that geologic
garden. Dinosaurs sleep in the subway
at Bloor and Shaw, a bed of bones
under the rumbling track. The storm
that lit the city with the voltage   10
of spring, when we were eighteen
on the clean earth. The ferry ride in the rain,
wind wet with wedding music and everything that
sings in the carbon of stone and bone
like a page of love, wind-lost from a hand, unread.

(1999)

George Elliott Clarke   b. 1960

Blank Sonnet

The air smells of rhubarb, occasional
Roses, or first birth of blossoms, a fresh,
Undulant hurt, so body snaps and curls
Like flower. I step through snow as thin as script,
Watch white stars spin dizzy as drunks, and yearn
To sleep beneath a patchwork quilt of rum,
I want the slow, sure collapse of language
Washed out by alcohol. Lovely Shelley,
I have no use for measured, cadenced verse

If you won't read. Icarus-like, I'll fall　　　　　　　　　　　10
Against this page of snow, tumble blackly
Across vision to drown in the white sea
That closes every poem—the white reverse
That cancels the blackness of each image.

(1990)

Billie Livingston　　b. 1965

Paperweight

As I come loose, I realize
that you can't do the job I need done
These papery limbs—
these onion skins of mine
need pinning by someone weighty

Look how rattled I am,
afraid the thinnest cough
will prove tornado-strength,
pull space between the earth and me

Sucked into its twists with such force,　　　　　　　　　　10
I wouldn't hear my own screeches

Nothing personal—
you're just too flimsy
to lie heavy down the length of me
keep the edges from curling
and hold my origami heart
under the fold

(2001)

PART IV

Writing about Drama

This section, focusing on drama and including brief discussions of its beginnings and more recent developments in contemporary theatre, completes our literary and rhetorical instruction.

14

How Do I Read a Play?

A play is written to be performed. Although most drama begins with a written script, the author of a play counts on the collaboration of others—actors, directors, set designers, costumers, makeup artists, lighting and sound engineers—to translate the written words into a performance on stage or film or videotape. Unlike novelists and poets, playwrights do not necessarily expect their words to be read by the audience.

The performance goal of drama does not mean, however, that you cannot read and study a play as you would a story or a poem. Plays share many literary qualities with other types of creative writing: character, plot, structure, atmosphere, theme, symbolism, and point of view. But it is important to recognize the differences between reading a play and seeing one performed.

LISTEN TO THE LINES

The major difference between reading and watching a play is that, as reader, you do not have the actors' voices and gestures to interpret the lines and establish the characters for you. Because playwrights rely almost entirely on speeches or conversations (called *dialogue*) to define character, develop plot, and convey theme, it will be your task as a reader to listen to the lines in your mind. Read the dialogue as you would expect to hear it spoken. For example, when you read Antigone's response to Creon,

> So for me, at least, to meet this doom of yours
> is precious little pain. But if I had allowed
> my own mother's son to rot, an unburied corpse—
> that would have been an agony!

do you hear the assurance and defiance in her voice? Or when you read Morgan's explanation of the great lie he tells Angus in Michael Healey's *The Drawer Boy*, can you detect the mixture of tenderness and sorrow in his words?

> Finally, when you were racing up the stairs to start over again, I tackled you. I hauled you down, and we sat on the stairs, and I told you the lie. I told you the story of the black car crashing for the first time. I told it again, and you

stopped crying. I told it again, and you fell asleep. I kept telling it 'cause it made you feel better. Goddamn it, it made me feel better.

Of course, the tone of these lines is not as clear when they are taken out of context, but even these brief quotations illustrate the charged nature of language you should expect when you read a play.

You can actually read the lines out loud to yourself or enlist some fellow students to act out some scenes with you. These oral readings will force you to decide how to interpret the words. Most of the time, however, you will have to use your imagination to re-create the sound of the spoken medium. If you do get to see a performance of a play you are reading or to hear a recording of it, you will appreciate the extraordinary liveliness of dramatic literature when it is lifted from the page and provided with sound and action.

Reading a play does have some advantage over viewing a live performance. Unlike a theatregoer, a reader can stop and return to lines or speeches that seem especially complicated or meaningful. Close reading gives you the opportunity to examine and consider the playwright's exact words, which often fly by quickly, sometimes in altered form, in an actual performance.

VISUALIZE THE SCENE

In addition to imagining the sound of the dialogue, you will also want to picture in your mind what the stage looks like. In a traditional theatre the audience sits out front while the actors perform on a raised stage separated from the viewers by a curtain and perhaps an orchestra. The arch from which the curtain hangs is called the *proscenium*; the space extending from the bottom of the curtain to the footlights is the *apron*. The stage directions (printed in italics) indicate where the playwright wants the actors to move. *Upstage* means toward the back; *downstage* means toward the apron. A traditional set, made of canvas-covered frames called *flats*, will look like a room—with one wall removed for the audience to see through. Sometimes the set will be constructed to resemble the battlements of a castle, an opening in a forest, or a lifeboat on the ocean. Occasionally the setting is only suggested: a character climbs a ladder to deliver lines supposedly from a balcony or from an upstairs room. In one modern play, the two protagonists are presented on a bare stage speaking throughout the production (with only their heads visible) from inside garbage cans.

Another kind of stage, called *theatre in the round* or an *arena stage*, puts the audience in raised seats on all sides with the players performing in the round space in the middle. After the audience is seated, the lights are extinguished, and the actors enter through the same aisles used earlier by the audience. When the actors are in position, the lights come up, illuminating only the stage, and the play begins. At the end of a scene or an act, the lights go down again, signifying the fall of the curtain and allowing the actors to leave. Stagehands come on between acts or scenes, if needed, to rearrange the setting. Not all plays are suited to this intimate staging, of course, but the audience at an arena production gains an immediacy, a feeling almost of being involved in the action, that cannot be achieved in a traditional theatre.

ENVISION THE ACTION

Poet and playwright Ezra Pound pointed out that the "medium of drama is not words, but persons moving about on a stage using words." This observation underlines the importance of movement, gesture, and setting in the performance of a play. These nonverbal elements of the language of drama are sometimes described in the author's stage directions. Often, though, you will find the cues for gestures, movements, and facial expressions in the words themselves, just as the director and the actors do when they are preparing a script for production. For example, these lines of Othello, spoken when he has been roused from his bed by a fight among his men, suggest the physical performance that would accompany the words:

> Why, how now, ho! from whence ariseth this?
> Are we turn'd Turks and to ourselves do that
> Which heaven hath forbid the Ottomites?
> For Christian shame, put by this barbarous brawl:
> He that stirs next to carve for his own rage
> Holds his soul light; he dies upon his motion.
> Silence that dreadful bell.

Reading this speech with an actor's or director's imagination, you can see in your mind the character stride angrily into the fight scene, gesture threateningly at the men who are poised to continue the fight, and then point suddenly offstage in the direction of the clamouring alarm bell. Such a detailed reading will take time, but you will be rewarded by the fun and satisfaction of catching the full dramatic quality of the play.

In more recent years, playwrights like Daniel David Moses have tried to keep artistic control over the interpretations of their works by including detailed stage directions in the scripts. The extensive production notes for Moses' *Almighty Voice and His Wife* sometimes read like descriptions from a novel or poem. In the following case, the stage directions are an entire scene:

> A projected title: "Scene Nine: His Vision". The drum beats in the night. The moon is low in the sky, pulsing. *Almighty Voice* lies by the dead fire, his leg badly wounded. The spectral tipi appears and the drum goes silent. Inside the tipi are *White Girl* and her baby, mother and child, a destination. *Almighty Voice* rises and uses his Winchester as a crutch to come to the tipi. *White Girl* comes out and shows him the baby and the baby cries. The moon turns white. *Almighty Voice* dies.

With or without notes like this, your imagination will be working full time when you read a play. You will not be at the mercy of some designer's taste or the personal interpretation of a director or actor. You will be free to produce the play in the theatre of your mind.

DRAMA ON FILM

Many plays are available on videotape or digital videodiscs. These include filmed versions of stage performances, such as the Laurence Olivier production of Shakespeare's *Othello*, or movies adapted from plays, such as the screen version of David Hwang's *M. Butterfly* starring Jeremy Irons. You will find that many plays in this book are on video.

You can often gain insight and special pleasure from seeing a dramatic work on film. A video production provides you with an opportunity to compare your responses to the play as you read it with your responses as you watch the video. You will also be able to think about the decisions that the film director has made. Here are some points to consider when comparing a film with the written text of a play:

- What scenes or characters, if any, have been cut? What, if anything, has been added? Why do you think these changes were made? What is their effect?
- Are the characters portrayed as you imagined they would be? Has the film changed your perception of the characters or your understanding of the plot?
- Would you have cast the same actors in these roles? If not, whom would you have chosen? What difference do you think your choices would make?
- Does the film focus your attention on certain characters or actions through such techniques as close-ups or reaction shots? What are the results of these uses of the camera?
- How is the setting different from what you imagined as you read the play? Did the filmmaker take liberties with the setting suggested by the playwright? (For example, were indoor play scenes transferred outdoors in the film?)
- Does the play transfer effectively from the page to the screen? Do you think the play is better suited to the stage?
- Does the film version clarify the play for you? Does it enhance your appreciation of the play? Can you explain why or why not?
- Do you think the playwright would be pleased with the film version? Why or why not?
- Imagine that you are directing a film version of a play that you have read. What important decisions about character, setting, and pacing of the action would you have to make? Would you cut any scenes? Would you add any new scenes? What advice would you give to the performers about their roles?

Before writing about a play or a film, be sure to respond to the critical questions in Chart 14–1.

CHART 14–1 CRITICAL QUESTIONS FOR READING PLAYS

Before planning an analysis of any of the plays in this text, write out your answers to the following questions to be sure you understand the play and to help you generate material for your paper.

1. What is the central conflict in the play? How is it resolved?
2. Does the play contain any secondary conflicts (subplots)? How do they relate to the main conflict?
3. Does the play follow a traditional dramatic structure (see Chapter 15)? What is the climax? Is there a denouement?
4. Who is the main character or protagonist (see Chapter 15)? What sort of person is he or she? Does this protagonist have a fatal flaw? Is the protagonist a hero (see Chapter 16)?
5. Is the antagonist (the one who opposes the protagonist) a person, an environment, or a social force (see Chapter 15)? If a person, does the antagonist cause conflict intentionally?
6. Do the other characters provide exposition (background information)? Are they used as *foils* to oppose, contrast, criticize, and thus help develop the main characters?
7. What are the time and setting of the play? How important are these elements? Could the play be set just as effectively in another time or place?
8. Does the title provide any clues to an understanding of the play? If you had to give the play another title, what would it be?
9. What is the theme of the play? Can you state it in a single sentence?
10. Is the play a tragedy, a comedy, or a mixture (see Chapter 16)? Is this classification important?
11. Is the presentation realistic? Does the playwright use any special theatrical devices (such as lighting, music, costumes, distinctive or surreal settings)? If so, what effect do they have on your impression of the play?

WEB For study tools to help you with your next writing assignment, please visit the Companion Website at www.pearsoned.ca/mcmahan.

15

Writing about Dramatic Structure

Drama is not as flexible as other forms of literature. A writer of fiction can take as much time as needed to inform the reader about character, setting, motivation, or theme. The dramatist must do everything quickly and clearly. Audiences will not sit through a tedious first act; neither can they stop the play, pick it up tomorrow, or go back to Act I to refresh their memories. Even with the technology of video recording, most plays, including film and television drama, are seen in a single, relatively brief sitting.

WHAT IS DRAMATIC STRUCTURE?

More than two thousand years ago the Greek philosopher Aristotle pointed out that the most important element of drama is the *fable*, what we call the *story*, or *plot*. The fable, said Aristotle, has to have a beginning, a middle, and an end. As obvious as this observation seems, it emphasizes the dramatist's special need to engage an audience early and keep it engaged until the conclusion of the play.

Recognizing the drama's strict time limits, Aristotle set down a number of conditions for developing the fable, or plot, in a clear and interesting way. According to Aristotle, the heart of the dramatic story is the *agon*, or *argument*, and the conflict surrounding this argument creates tension and incites interest. The two sides of the conflict, the pros and cons of the argument, are represented on stage by the *protagonist* and the *antagonist*. The protagonist may be one person or many, and the antagonist may be a person, a group, a thing, or a force (supernatural or natural). We often call the protagonist of a play its *hero* or *heroine*, and sometimes the antagonist is also the *villain*.

The fundamental struggle between the protagonist and the antagonist is developed according to a set pattern that theatre audiences have come to recognize and expect. This conventional structure can be varied, of course, but most dramatic literature contains the following components:

1. *Point of attack*—the starting point from which the dramatist leads the audience into the plot. A playwright can begin at the story's beginning and allow the audience to discover what is going on at the same time the characters do; or the writer can begin in the middle of things (*in medias res*), or even near the end, and gradually reveal the events that have already taken place.

2. *Exposition*—the revelation of facts, circumstances, and past events. Establishing the essential facts about the characters and the conflict can be accomplished in a number of ways: from having minor characters reveal information through conversation to plunging the audience right into the action.

3. *Rising action*—the building of interest through complication of the conflict. In this stage, the protagonist and antagonist move steadily toward a confrontation.

4. *Climax*—the play's high point, the decisive showdown between protagonist and antagonist. The climax—the play's turning point—can be a single moment or a series of events, but once reached, it becomes a point of no return.

5. *Falling action*—the unravelling of the plot, where events fall into place and the conflict moves toward final resolution.

6. *Denouement*—the play's conclusion; the explanation or outcome of the action. The term *denouement* (literally an "untying") may be applied to both comedy and tragedy, but the Greeks used the word *catastrophe* for a tragic denouement, probably because it involved the death of the hero or heroine. Comedies, of course, end happily, often with a wedding.

Whatever it is called, the denouement marks the end of the play: the lovers kiss, the bodies are carried off the stage, and the audience goes home. Most dramatists employ this traditional pattern. Even when they mix in other devices, rearrange elements, and invent new ways to exhibit their materials, dramatists still establish a conflict, develop both sides of the argument, and reach a credible conclusion. After centuries of theatre history, the basic structure of drama has changed very little.

LOOKING AT DRAMATIC STRUCTURE

As you read *Antigone*, written in 442 BCE, notice that the play's central conflict is introduced, developed, and resolved according to the pattern we have just described.

Although written first, *Antigone* is the third and last play in the chronology of events constituting Sophocles' Oedipus cycle; the first two plays are *Oedipus the King* and *Oedipus at Colonus*.

According to Greek legend, King Laius of Thebes and his descendants were doomed by the god Apollo. Warned by the Oracle of Delphi that his own son would kill him, Laius leaves the son, Oedipus, to die in the mountains. But Oedipus survives and unknowingly kills his father, whom he encounters on the road to Thebes. Oedipus solves the riddle of the Sphinx for the Thebans and becomes their king, marrying his mother, Jocasta, the widow of Laius. Several years later, when he learns what he has done, Oedipus blinds himself and leaves Thebes. Creon, brother of Jocasta, becomes the ruler of Thebes and is entrusted with caring for Oedipus' two daughters, Antigone and Ismene. Oedipus' two sons, Polynices and Eteocles, reject their father and struggle for power in Thebes. Polynices is driven from the city but returns with an army; in the ensuing battle he and Eteocles kill each other, while Creon succeeds to the throne. As the play opens, Antigone and Ismene are discussing Creon's first official decree.

Sophocles   ca. 496–ca. 405 BCE

Antigone

Translated by Robert Fagles

CHARACTERS

ANTIGONE, *daughter of Oedipus and Jocasta*
ISMENE, *sister of Antigone*
A CHORUS *of old Theban citizens and their* LEADER
CREON, *king of Thebes, uncle of Antigone and Ismene*
A SENTRY
HAEMON, *son of Creon and Eurydice*
TIRESIAS, *a blind prophet*
A MESSENGER
EURYDICE, *wife of Creon*
GUARDS, ATTENDANTS, *and* A BOY

TIME AND SCENE

The royal house of Thebes. It is still night, and invading armies have just been driven from the city. Fighting on opposite sides, the sons of Oedipus, Eteocles and Polynices, have killed each other in combat. Their uncle, CREON, *is now king of Thebes.*

Enter ANTIGONE, *slipping through the central doors of the palace. She motions to her sister,* ISMENE, *who follows her cautiously toward an altar at the center of the stage.*

ANTIGONE. My own flesh and blood—dear sister, dear Ismene,
how many griefs our father Oedipus handed down!
Do you know one, I ask you, one grief
that Zeus[1] will not perfect for the two of us
while we still live and breathe? There's nothing,
no pain—our lives are pain—no private shame,
no public disgrace, nothing I haven't seen
in your griefs and mine. And now this:
an emergency decree, they say, the Commander
has just declared for all of Thebes.   10
What, haven't you heard? Don't you see?
The doom reserved for enemies
marches on the ones we love the most.

ISMENE. Not I, I haven't heard a word, Antigone.
Nothing of loved ones,
no joy or pain has come my way, not since
the two of us were robbed of our two brothers,
both gone in a day, a double blow—
not since the armies of Argos vanished,
just this very night. I know nothing more,   20
whether our luck's improved or ruin's still to come.

---

[1] **Zeus:** The highest Olympian deity.

ANTIGONE. I thought so. That's why I brought you out here,
    past the gates, so you could hear in private.
ISMENE. What's the matter? Trouble, clearly . . .
    you sound so dark, so grim.
ANTIGONE. Why not? Our own brothers' burial!
    Hasn't Creon graced one with all the rites,
    disgraced the other? Eteocles, they say,
    has been given full military honors,
    rightly so—Creon's laid him in the earth   30
    and he goes with glory down among the dead.
    But the body of Polynices, who died miserably—
    why, a city-wide proclamation, rumor has it,
    forbids anyone to bury him, even mourn him.
    He's to be left unwept, unburied, a lovely treasure
    for birds that scan the field and feast to their heart's content.

    Such, I hear, is the martial law our good Creon
    lays down for you and me—yes, me, I tell you—
    and he's coming here to alert the uninformed
    in no uncertain terms,   40
    and he won't treat the matter lightly. Whoever
    disobeys in the least will die, his doom is sealed:
    stoning to death inside the city walls!

    There you have it. You'll soon show what you are,
    worth your breeding, Ismene, or a coward—
    for all your royal blood.
ISMENE. My poor sister, if things have come to this,
    who am I to make or mend them, tell me,
    what good am I to you?
ANTIGONE.   Decide.
    Will you share the labor, share the work?   50
ISMENE. What work, what's the risk? What do you mean?
ANTIGONE.
Raising her hands.
    Will you lift up his body with these bare hands
    and lower it with me?
ISMENE.   What? You'd bury him—
    when a law forbids the city?
ANTIGONE.   Yes!
    He is my brother and—deny it as you will—
    your brother too.
    No one will ever convict me for a traitor.
ISMENE. So desperate, and Creon has expressly—
ANTIGONE.   No,
    he has no right to keep me from my own.
ISMENE. Oh my sister, think—   60

think how our own father died, hated,
his reputation in ruins, driven on
by the crimes he brought to light himself
to gouge out his eyes with his own hands—
then mother . . . his mother and wife, both in one,
mutilating her life in the twisted noose—
and last, our two brothers dead in a single day,
both shedding their own blood, poor suffering boys,
battling out their common destiny hand-to-hand.

Now look at the two of us, left so alone . . . 70
think what a death we'll die, the worst of all
if we violate the laws and override
the fixed decree of the throne, its power—
we must be sensible. Remember we are women,
we're not born to contend with men. Then too,
we're underlings, ruled by much stronger hands,
so we must submit in this, and things still worse.

I, for one, I'll beg the dead to forgive me—
I'm forced, I have no choice—I must obey
the ones who stand in power. Why rush to extremes? 80
It's madness, madness.

ANTIGONE.   I won't insist,
no, even if you should have a change of heart,
I'd never welcome you in the labor, not with me.
So, do as you like, whatever suits you best—
I'll bury him myself.
And even if I die in the act, that death will be a glory.
I'll lie with the one I love and loved by him—
an outrage sacred to the gods! I have longer
to please the dead than please the living here:
in the kingdom down below I'll lie forever. 90
Do as you like, dishonor the laws
the gods hold in honor.

ISMENE.   I'd do them no dishonor . . .
but defy the city? I have no strength for that.

ANTIGONE. You have your excuses. I am on my way,
I'll raise a mound for him, for my dear brother.

ISMENE. Oh Antigone, you're so rash—I'm so afraid for you!

ANTIGONE. Don't fear for me. Set your own life in order.

ISMENE. Then don't, at least, blurt this out to anyone.
Keep it a secret. I'll join you in that, I promise.

ANTIGONE. Dear god, shout it from the rooftops. I'll hate you 100
all the more for silence—tell the world!

ISMENE. So fiery—and it ought to chill your heart.

ANTIGONE. I know I please where I must please the most.

ISMENE. Yes, if you can, but you're in love with impossibility.

ANTIGONE. Very well then, once my strength gives out
   I will be done at last.

ISMENE.   You're wrong from the start.
   You're off on a hopeless quest.

ANTIGONE. If you say so, you will make me hate you,
   and the hatred of the dead, by all rights,
   will haunt you night and day.   110
   But leave me to my own absurdity, leave me
   to suffer this—dreadful thing. I'll suffer
   nothing as great as death without glory.

Exit to the side.

ISMENE. Then go if you must, but rest assured,
   wild, irrational as you are, my sister,
   you are truly dear to the ones who love you.

Withdrawing to the palace. Enter a CHORUS, *the old citizens of Thebes, chanting as the sun begins to rise.*

CHORUS. Glory!—great beam of sun, brightest of all
   that ever rose on the seven gates of Thebes,
      you burn through night at last!
         Great eye of the golden day,   120
   mounting the Dirce's[2] banks you throw him back—
   the enemy out of Argos, the white shield, the man of bronze—
   he's flying headlong now
      the bridle of fate stampeding him with pain!

   And he had driven against our borders,
   launched by the warring claims of Polynices—
   like an eagle screaming, winging havoc
   over the land, wings of armor
   shielded white as snow,
   a huge army massing,   130
   crested helmets bristling for assault.

   He hovered above our roofs, his vast maw gaping
   closing down around our seven gates,
      his spears thirsting for the kill
         but now he's gone, look,
   before he could glut his jaws with Theban blood
   or the god of fire put our crown of towers to the torch.
   He grappled the Dragon none can master—Thebes—
      the clang of our arms like thunder at his back!

   Zeus hates with a vengeance all bravado,   140
   the mighty boasts of men. He watched them
   coming on in a rising flood, the pride

---

[2]**Dirce:** A river near Thebes.

>   of their golden armor ringing shrill—
>   and brandishing his lightning
>   blasted the fighter just at the goal,
>   rushing to shout his triumph from our walls.
>
> Down from the heights he crashed, pounding down on the earth!
> And a moment ago, blazing torch in hand—
>   mad for attack, ecstatic
> he breathed his rage, the storm   150
>   of his fury hurling at our heads!
> But now his high hopes have laid him low
> and down the enemy ranks the iron god of war
>   deals his rewards, his stunning blows—Ares[3]
>   rapture of battle, our right arm in the crisis.
>
>   Seven captains marshaled at seven gates
>   seven against their equals, gave
>   their brazen trophies up to Zeus,
>   god of the breaking rout of battle,
>   all but two: those blood brothers,   160
>   one father, one mother—matched in rage,
>   spears matched for the twin conquest—
>   clashed and won the common prize of death.
>
> But now for Victory! Glorious in the morning,
> joy in her eyes to meet our joy
>   she is winging down to Thebes,
> our fleets of chariots wheeling in her wake—
>   Now let us win oblivion from the wars,
> thronging the temples of the gods
> in singing, dancing choirs through the night!   170
>   Lord Dionysus,[4] god of the dance
>   that shakes the land of Thebes, now lead the way!

Enter CREON *from the palace, attended by his guard.*

>   But look, the king of the realm is coming,
>   Creon, the new man for the new day,
>   whatever the gods are sending now . . .
>   what new plan will he launch?
>   Why this, this special session?
>   Why this sudden call to the old men
>   summoned at one command?

CREON.   My countrymen,
>   the ship of state is safe. The gods who rocked her,   180
>   after a long, merciless pounding in the storm,
>   have righted her once more.
>   Out of the whole city
>   I have called you here alone. Well I know,
>   first, your undeviating respect

---

[3]**Ares:** God of war.
[4]**Dionysus:** God of fertility and wine.

for the throne and royal power of King Laius.
Next, while Oedipus steered the land of Thebes,
and even after he died, your loyalty was unshakable,
you still stood by their children. Now then,
since the two sons are dead—two blows of fate
in the same day, cut down by each other's hands,   190
both killers, both brothers stained with blood—
as I am next in kin to the dead,
I now possess the throne and all its powers.

Of course you cannot know a man completely,
his character, his principles, sense of judgment,
not till he's shown his colors, ruling the people,
making laws. Experience, there's the test.
As I see it, whoever assumes the task,
the awesome task of setting the city's course,
and refuses to adopt the soundest policies   200
but fearing someone, keeps his lips locked tight,
he's utterly worthless. So I rate him now,
I always have. And whoever places a friend
above the good of his own country, he is nothing:
I have no use for him. Zeus my witness,
Zeus who sees all things, always—
I could never stand by silent, watching destruction
march against our city, putting safety to rout,
nor could I ever make that man a friend of mine
who menaces our country. Remember this: 210
our country *is* our safety.
Only while she voyages true on course
can we establish friendships, truer than blood itself.
Such are my standards. They make our city great.

Closely akin to them I have proclaimed,
just now, the following decree to our people
concerning the two sons of Oedipus.
Eteocles, who died fighting for Thebes,
excelling all in arms: he shall be buried,
crowned with a hero's honors, the cups we pour   220
to soak the earth and reach the famous dead.

But as for his blood brother, Polynices,
who returned from exile, home to his father-city
and the gods of his race, consumed with one desire—
to burn them roof to roots—who thirsted to drink
his kinsmen's blood and sell the rest to slavery:
that man—a proclamation has forbidden the city
to dignify him with burial, mourn him at all.
No, he must be left unburied, his corpse
carrion for the birds and dogs to tear,   230
an obscenity for the citizens to behold!

> These are my principles. Never at my hands
> will the traitor be honored above the patriot.
> But whoever proves his loyalty to the state:
> I'll prize that man in death as well as life.

LEADER. If this is your pleasure, Creon, treating
our city's enemy and our friend this way . . .
The power is yours, I suppose, to enforce it
with the laws, both for the dead and all of us,
the living.

CREON.   Follow my orders closely then,   240
be on your guard.

LEADER.   We're too old.
Lay that burden on younger shoulders.

CREON.   No, no,
I don't mean the body—I've posted guards already.

LEADER. What commands for us then? What other service?

CREON. See that you never side with those who break my orders.

LEADER. Never. Only a fool could be in love with death.

CREON. Death is the price—you're right. But all too often
the mere hope of money has ruined many men.

A SENTRY *enters from the side.*

SENTRY.   My lord,
I can't say I'm winded from running, or set out
with any spring in my legs either—no sir,   250
I was lost in thought, and it made me stop, often,
dead in my tracks, wheeling, turning back,
and all the time a voice inside me muttering,
"Idiot, why? You're going straight to your death."
Then muttering, "Stopped again, poor fool?
If somebody gets the news to Creon first,
what's to save your neck?"

                 And so,
mulling it over, on I trudged, dragging my feet,
you can make a short road take forever . . .
but at last, common sense won out,   260
I'm here, and I'm all yours,
and even though I come empty-handed
I'll tell my story just the same, because
I've come with a good grip on one hope,
what will come will come, whatever fate—

CREON. Come to the point!
What's wrong—why so afraid?

SENTRY. First, myself, I've got to tell you,
I didn't do it, didn't see who did—
Be fair, don't take it out on me.   270

CREON. You're playing it safe, soldier,
    barricading yourself from any trouble.
    It's obvious, you've something strange to tell.

SENTRY. Dangerous too, and danger makes you delay
    for all you're worth.

CREON. Out with it—then dismiss!

SENTRY. All right, here it comes. The body—
    someone's just buried it, then run off . . .
    sprinkled some dry dust on the flesh,
    given it proper rites.

CREON.   What?   280
    What man alive would dare—

SENTRY.   I've no idea, I swear it.
    There was no mark of a spade, no pickaxe there,
    no earth turned up, the ground packed hard and dry,
    unbroken, no tracks, no wheelruts, nothing,
    the workman left no trace. Just at sunup
    the first watch of the day points it out—
    it was a wonder! We were stunned . . .
    a terrific burden too, for all of us, listen:
    you can't see the corpse, not that it's buried,
    really, just a light cover of road-dust on it,   290
    as if someone meant to lay the dead to rest
    and keep from getting cursed.
    Not a sign in sight that dogs or wild beasts
    had worried the body, even torn the skin.

    But what came next! Rough talk flew thick and fast,
    guard grilling guard—we'd have come to blows
    at last, nothing to stop it; each man for himself
    and each the culprit, no one caught red-handed,
    all of us pleading ignorance, dodging the charges,
    ready to take up red-hot iron in our fists,   300
    go through fire, swear oaths to the gods—
    "I didn't do it, I had no hand in it either,
    not in the plotting, not in the work itself!"

    Finally, after all this wrangling came to nothing,
    one man spoke out and made us stare at the ground,
    hanging our heads in fear. No way to counter him,
    no way to take his advice and come through
    safe and sound. Here's what he said:
    "Look, we've got to report the facts to Creon,
    we can't keep this hidden." Well, that won out,   310
    and the lot fell on me, condemned me,
    unlucky as ever, I got the prize. So here I am,
    against my will and yours too, well I know—
    no one wants the man who brings bad news.

LEADER.   My king,
    ever since he began I've been debating in my mind,
    could this possibly be the work of the gods?
CREON.   Stop—
    before you make me choke with anger—the gods!
    You, you're senile, must you be insane?
    You say—why it's intolerable—say the gods
    could have the slightest concern for that corpse?   320
    Tell me, was it for meritorious service
    they proceeded to bury him, prized him so? The hero
    who came to burn their temples ringed with pillars,
    their golden treasures—scorch their hallowed earth
    and fling their laws to the winds.
    Exactly when did you last see the gods
    celebrating traitors? Inconceivable!

    No, from the first there were certain citizens
    who could hardly stand the spirit of my regime,
    grumbling against me in the dark, heads together,   330
    tossing wildly, never keeping their necks beneath
    the yoke, loyally submitting to their king.
    These are the instigators, I'm convinced—
    they've perverted my own guard, bribed them
    to do their work.
                    Money! Nothing worse
    in our lives, so current, rampant, so corrupting.
    Money—you demolish cities, root men from their homes,
    you train and twist good minds and set them on
    to the most atrocious schemes. No limit,
    you make them adept at every kind of outrage,   340
    every godless crime—money!
                              Everyone—
    the whole crew bribed to commit this crime,
    they've made one thing sure at least:
    sooner or later they will pay the price.

Wheeling on the SENTRY.
                                        You—
    I swear to Zeus as I still believe in Zeus,
    if you don't find the man who buried that corpse,
    the very man, and produce him before my eyes,
    simple death won't be enough for you,
    not till we string you up alive
    and wring the immorality out of you.   350
    Then you can steal the rest of your days,
    better informed about where to make a killing.
    You'll have learned, at last, it doesn't pay
    to itch for rewards from every hand that beckons.
    Filthy profits wreck most men, you'll see—
    they'll never save your life.

SENTRY.   Please,
   may I say a word or two, or just turn and go?
CREON. Can't you tell? Everything you say offends me.
SENTRY. Where does it hurt you, in the ears or in the heart?
CREON. And who are you to pinpoint my displeasure?   360
SENTRY. The culprit grates on your feelings,
   I just annoy your ears.
CREON.   Still talking?
   You talk too much! A born nuisance—
SENTRY.   Maybe so,
   but I never did this thing, so help me!
CREON.   Yes, you did—
   what's more, you squandered your life for silver!
SENTRY. Oh it's terrible when the one who does the judging
   judges things all wrong.
CREON.   Well now,
   you just be clever about your judgments—
   if you fail to produce the criminals for me,
   you'll swear your dirty money brought you pain.   370

Turning sharply, reentering the palace.

SENTRY. I hope he's found. Best thing by far.
   But caught or not, that's in the lap of fortune;
   I'll never come back, you've seen the last of me.
   I'm saved, even now, and I never thought,
   I never hoped—
   dear gods, I owe you all my thanks!

Rushing out.

CHORUS.   Numberless wonders
   terrible wonders walk the world but none the match for man—
   that great wonder crossing the heaving gray sea,
            driven on by the blasts of winter
   on through breakers crashing left and right,   380
         holds his steady course
   and the oldest of the gods he wears away—
   the Earth, the immortal, the inexhaustible—
   as his plows go back and forth, year in, year out
      with the breed of stallions turning up the furrows.

   And the blithe, lightheaded race of birds he snares,
   the tribes of savage beasts, the life that swarms the depths—
         with one fling of his nets
   woven and coiled tight, he takes them all,
      man the skilled, the brilliant!   390
   He conquers all, taming with his techniques
   the prey that roams the cliffs and wild lairs,
   training the stallion, clamping the yoke across
      his shaggy neck, and the tireless mountain bull.

And speech and thought, quick as the wind
and the mood and mind for law that rules the city—
    all these he has taught himself
and shelter from the arrows of the frost
when there's rough lodging under the cold clear sky
and the shafts of lashing rain—   400
        ready, resourceful man!
                Never without resources
never an impasse as he marches on the future—
only Death, from Death alone he will find no rescue
but from desperate plagues he has plotted his escapes.

Man the master, ingenious past all measure
past all dreams, the skills within his grasp—
    he forges on, now to destruction
now again to greatness. When he weaves in
the laws of the land, and the justice of the gods   410
that binds his oaths together
    he and his city rise high—
        but the city casts out
that man who weds himself to inhumanity
thanks to reckless daring. Never share my hearth
never think my thoughts, whoever does such things.

Enter ANTIGONE *from the side, accompanied by the* SENTRY.

    Here is a dark sign from the gods—
    what to make of this? I know her,
    how can I deny it? That young girl's Antigone!
    Wretched, child of a wretched father,   420
    Oedipus. Look, is it possible?
    They bring you in like a prisoner—
    why? did you break the king's laws?
    Did they take you in some act of mad defiance?

SENTRY. She's the one, she did it single-handed—
    we caught her burying the body. Where's Creon?

Enter CREON *from the palace.*

LEADER. Back again, just in time when you need him.

CREON. In time for what? What is it?

SENTRY.   My king,
    there's nothing you can swear you'll never do—
    second thoughts make liars of us all.   430
    I could have sworn I wouldn't hurry back
    (what with your threats, the buffeting I just took),
    but a stroke of luck beyond our wildest hopes,
    what a joy, there's nothing like it. So,
    back I've come, breaking my oath, who cares?
    I'm bringing in our prisoner—this young girl—
    we took her giving the dead the last rites.
    But no casting lots this time; this is *my* luck,
    my prize, no one else's.

                    Now, my lord,
    here she is. Take her, question her,   440
    cross-examine her to your heart's content.
    But set me free, it's only right—
    I'm rid of this dreadful business once for all.

CREON. Prisoner! Her? You took her—where, doing what?

SENTRY. Burying the man. That's the whole story.

CREON.   What?
    You mean what you say, you're telling me the truth?

SENTRY. She's the one. With my own eyes I saw her
    bury the body, just what you've forbidden.
    There. Is that plain and clear?

CREON. What did you see? Did you catch her in the act?   450

SENTRY. Here's what happened. We went back to our post,
    those threats of yours breathing down our necks—
    we brushed the corpse clean of the dust that covered it,
    stripped it bare . . . it was slimy, going soft,
    and we took to high ground, backs to the wind
    so the stink of him couldn't hit us;
    jostling, baiting each other to keep awake,
    shouting back and forth—no napping on the job,
    not this time. And so the hours dragged by
    until the sun stood dead above our heads,   460
    a huge white ball in the noon sky, beating,
    blazing down, and then it happened—
    suddenly, a whirlwind!
    Twisting a great dust-storm up from the earth,
    a black plague of the heavens, filling the plain,
    ripping the leaves off every tree in sight,
    choking the air and sky. We squinted hard
    and took our whipping from the gods.

    And after the storm passed—it seemed endless—
    there, we saw the girl!   470
    And she cried out a sharp, piercing cry,
    like a bird come back to an empty nest,
    peering into its bed, and all the babies gone . . .
    Just so, when she sees the corpse bare
    she bursts into a long, shattering wail
    and calls down withering curses on the heads
    of all who did the work. And she scoops up dry dust,
    handfuls, quickly, and lifting a fine bronze urn,
    lifting it high and pouring, she crowns the dead
    with three full libations.
                            Soon as we saw   480
    we rushed her, closed on the kill like hunters,
    and she, she didn't flinch. We interrogated her,
    charging her with offenses past and present—
    she stood up to it all, denied nothing. I tell you,

it made me ache and laugh in the same breath.
It's pure joy to escape the worst yourself,
it hurts a man to bring down his friends.
But all that, I'm afraid, means less to me
than my own skin. That's the way I'm made.

CREON.
Wheeling on ANTIGONE.
                                                You.
  with your eyes fixed on the ground—speak up.   490
  Do you deny you did this, yes or no?

ANTIGONE. I did it. I don't deny a thing.

CREON.
To the SENTRY.
  You, get out, wherever you please—
  you're clear of a very heavy charge.
He leaves; CREON *turns back to* ANTIGONE.
  You, tell me briefly, no long speeches—
  were you aware a decree had forbidden this?

ANTIGONE. Well aware. How could I avoid it? It was public.

CREON. And still you had the gall to break this law?

ANTIGONE. Of course I did. It wasn't Zeus, not in the least,
  who made this proclamation—not to me.   500
  Nor did that Justice, dwelling with the gods
  beneath the earth, ordain such laws for men.
  Nor did I think your edict had such force
  that you, a mere mortal, could override the gods,
  the great unwritten, unshakable traditions.
  They are alive, not just today or yesterday:
  they live forever, from the first of time,
  and no one knows when they first saw the light.

  These laws—I was not about to break them,
  not out of fear of some man's wounded pride,   510
  and face the retribution of the gods.
  Die I must, I've known it all my life—
  how could I keep from knowing?—even without
  your death-sentence ringing in my ears.
  And if I am to die before my time
  I consider that a gain. Who on earth,
  alive in the midst of so much grief as I,
  could fail to find his death a rich reward?
  So for me, at least, to meet this doom of yours
  is precious little pain. But if I had allowed   520
  my own mother's son to rot, an unburied corpse—
  that would have been an agony! This is nothing.
  And if my present actions strike you as foolish,
  let's just say I've been accused of folly
  by a fool.

LEADER.   Like father like daughter,
    passionate, wild . . .
    she hasn't learned to bend before adversity.

CREON. No? Believe me, the stiffest stubborn wills
    fall the hardest; the toughest iron,
    tempered strong in the white-hot fire,   530
    you'll see it crack and shatter first of all.
    And I've known spirited horses you can break
    with a light bit—proud, rebellious horses.
    There's no room for pride, not in a slave,
    not with the lord and master standing by.

    This girl was an old hand at insolence
    when she overrode the edicts we made public.
    But once she'd done it—the insolence,
    twice over—to glory in it, laughing,
    mocking us to our face with what she'd done.   540
    I'm not the man, not now: she is the man
    if this victory goes to her and she goes free.

    Never! Sister's child or closer in blood
    than all my family clustered at my altar
    worshipping Guardian Zeus—she'll never escape,
    she and her blood sister, the most barbaric death.
    Yes, I accuse her sister of an equal part
    in scheming this, this burial.

To his ATTENDANTS.

                                Bring her here!
    I just saw her inside, hysterical, gone to pieces.
    It never fails: the mind convicts itself   550
    in advance, when scoundrels are up to no good,
    plotting in the dark. Oh but I hate it more
    when a traitor, caught red-handed,
    tries to glorify his crimes.

ANTIGONE. Creon, what more do you want
    than my arrest and execution?

CREON. Nothing. Then I have it all.

ANTIGONE. Then why delay? Your moralizing repels me,
    every word you say—pray god it always will.
    So naturally all I say repels you too.

                                Enough.   560
    Give me glory! What greater glory could I win
    than to give my own brother decent burial?
    These citizens here would all agree,

To the CHORUS.

    they'd praise me too
    if their lips weren't locked in fear.

Pointing to CREON.

        Lucky tyrants—the perquisites of power!
        Ruthless power to do and say whatever pleases *them*.
CREON. You alone, of all the people in Thebes,
    see things that way.
ANTIGONE.   They see it just that way
    but defer to you and keep their tongues in leash.   570
CREON. And you, aren't you ashamed to differ so from them?
    So disloyal!
ANTIGONE.   Not ashamed for a moment,
    not to honor my brother, my own flesh and blood.
CREON. Wasn't Eteocles a brother too—cut down, facing him?
ANTIGONE. Brother, yes, by the same mother, the same father.
CREON. Then how can you render his enemy such honors,
    such impieties in his eyes?
ANTIGONE. He'll never testify to that,
    Eteocles dead and buried.
CREON.   He will—
    if you honor the traitor just as much as him.   580
ANTIGONE. But it was his brother, not some slave that died—
CREON. Ravaging our country!—
    but Eteocles died fighting in our behalf.
ANTIGONE. No matter—Death longs for the same rites for all.
CREON. Never the same for the patriot and the traitor.
ANTIGONE. Who, Creon, who on earth can say the ones below
    don't find this pure and uncorrupt?
CREON. Never. Once an enemy, never a friend,
    not even after death.
ANTIGONE. I was born to join in love, not hate—   590
    that is my nature.
CREON.   Go down below and love,
    if love you must—love the dead! While I'm alive,
    no woman is going to lord it over me.

Enter ISMENE *from the palace, under guard.*

CHORUS.   Look,
    Ismene's coming, weeping a sister's tears,
    loving sister, under a cloud . . .
    her face is flushed, her cheeks streaming.
    Sorrow puts her lovely radiance in the dark.
CREON.   You—
    in my house, you viper, slinking undetected,
    sucking my life-blood! I never knew
    I was breeding twin disasters, the two of you   600
    rising up against my throne. Come, tell me,
    will you confess your part in the crime or not?

Answer me. Swear to me.

ISMENE.   I did it, yes—
    if only she consents—I share the guilt,
    the consequences too.

ANTIGONE.   No,
    Justice will never suffer that—not you,
    you were unwilling. I never brought you in.

ISMENE. But now you face such dangers . . . I'm not ashamed
    to sail through trouble with you,
    make your troubles mine.

ANTIGONE.   Who did the work?   610
    Let the dead and the god of death bear witness!
    I've no love for a friend who loves in words alone.

ISMENE. Oh no, my sister, don't reject me, please,
    let me die beside you, consecrating
    the dead together.

ANTIGONE.   Never share my dying,
    don't lay claim to what you never touched.
    My death will be enough.

ISMENE. What do I care for life, cut off from you?

ANTIGONE. Ask Creon. Your concern is all for him.

ISMENE. Why abuse me so? It doesn't help you now.

ANTIGONE.   You're right—   620
    if I mock you, I get no pleasure from it,
    only pain.

ISMENE.   Tell me, dear one,
    what can I do to help you, even now?

ANTIGONE. Save yourself. I don't grudge you your survival.

ISMENE. Oh no, no, denied my portion in your death?

ANTIGONE. You chose to live, I chose to die.

ISMENE.   Not, at least,
    without every kind of caution I could voice.

ANTIGONE. Your wisdom appealed to one world—mine, another.

ISMENE. But look, we're both guilty, both condemned to death.

ANTIGONE. Courage! Live your life. I gave myself to death,   630
    long ago, so I might serve the dead.

CREON. They're both mad, I tell you, the two of them.
    One's just shown it, the other's been that way
    since she was born.

ISMENE.   True, my king,
    the sense we were born with cannot last forever . . .
    commit cruelty on a person long enough
    and the mind begins to go.

CREON.   Yours did,
   when you chose to commit your crimes with her.
ISMENE. How can I live alone, without her?
CREON.   Her?
   Don't even mention her—she no longer exists.   640
ISMENE. What? You'd kill your own son's bride?
CREON.   Absolutely:
   there are other fields for him to plow.
ISMENE.   Perhaps,
   but never as true, as close a bond as theirs.
CREON. A worthless woman for my son? It repels me.
ISMENE. Dearest Haemon, your father wrongs you so!
CREON. Enough, enough—you and your talk of marriage!
ISMENE. Creon—you're really going to rob your son of Antigone?
CREON. Death will do it for me—break their marriage off.
LEADER. So, it's settled then? Antigone must die?
CREON. Settled, yes—we both know that.   650

To the GUARDS.

   Stop wasting time. Take them in.
   From now on they'll act like women.
   Tie them up, no more running loose;
   even the bravest will cut and run,
   once they see Death coming for their lives.

The GUARDS *escort* ANTIGONE *and* ISMENE *into the palace.* CREON *remains while the old citizens form their* CHORUS.

CHORUS. Blest, they are the truly blest who all their lives
   have never tasted devastation. For others, once
   the gods have rocked a house to its foundations
      the ruin will never cease, cresting on and on
   from one generation on throughout the race—   660
   like a great mounting tide
   driven on by savage northern gales,
      surging over the dead black depths
   roiling up from the bottom dark heaves of sand
   and the headlands, taking the storm's onslaught full-force,
   roar, and the low moaning
                 echoes on and on
                              and now
   as in ancient times I see the sorrows of the house,
   the living heirs of the old ancestral kings,
   piling on the sorrows of the dead
      and one generation cannot free the next—   670
   some god will bring them crashing down,
   the race finds no release.
   And now the light, the hope
      springing up from the late last root

    in the house of Oedipus, that hope's cut down in turn
by the long, bloody knife swung by the gods of death
by a senseless word
                  by fury at the heart.
                                  Zeus,
yours is the power, Zeus, what man on earth
can override it, who can hold it back?
Power that neither Sleep, the all-ensnaring   680
    no, nor the tireless months of heaven
can ever overmaster—young through all time,
mighty lord of power, you hold fast
    the dazzling crystal mansions of Olympus.
And throughout the future, late and soon
as through the past, your law prevails:
no towering form of greatness
    enters into the lives of mortals
        free and clear of ruin.
                            True,
our dreams, our high hopes voyaging far and wide   690
bring sheer delight to many, to many others
    delusion, blithe, mindless lusts
and the fraud steals on one slowly . . . unaware
till he trips and puts his foot into the fire.
    He was a wise old man who coined
the famous saying: "Sooner or later
foul is fair, fair is foul
to the man the gods will ruin"—
    He goes his way for a moment only
        free of blinding ruin.   700

Enter HAEMON *from the palace.*

    Here's Haemon now, the last of all your sons.
Does he come in tears for his bride,
his doomed bride, Antigone—
bitter at being cheated of their marriage?

CREON. We'll soon know, better than seers could tell us.

Turning to HAEMON.

    Son, you've heard the final verdict on your bride?
Are you coming now, raving against your father?
Or do you love me, no matter what I do?

HAEMON. Father, I'm your *son* . . . you in your wisdom
    set my bearings for me—I obey you.   710
No marriage could ever mean more to me than you,
whatever good direction you may offer.

CREON.   Fine, Haemon.
    That's how you ought to feel within your heart,
subordinate to your father's will in every way.
That's what a man prays for: to produce good sons—
households full of them, dutiful and attentive,
so they can pay his enemy back with interest
and match the respect their father shows his friend.

But the man who rears a brood of useless children,
what has he brought into the world, I ask you? 720
Nothing but trouble for himself, and mockery
from his enemies laughing in his face.
                        Oh Haemon,
never lose your sense of judgment over a woman.
The warmth, the rush of pleasure, it all goes cold
in your arms, I warn you . . . a worthless woman
in your house, a misery in your bed.
What wound cuts deeper than a loved one
turned against you? Spit her out,
like a mortal enemy—let the girl go.
Let her find a husband down among the dead. 730

Imagine it: I caught her in naked rebellion,
the traitor, the only one in the whole city.
I'm not about to prove myself a liar,
not to my people, no, I'm going to kill her!
That's right—so let her cry for mercy, sing her hymns
to Zeus who defends all bonds of kindred blood.
Why, if I bring up my own kin to be rebels,
think what I'd suffer from the world at large.
Show me the man who rules his household well:
I'll show you someone fit to rule the state. 740
That good man, my son,
I have every confidence he and he alone
can give commands and take them too. Staunch
in the storm of spears he'll stand his ground,
a loyal, unflinching comrade at your side.

But whoever steps out of line, violates the laws
or presumes to hand out orders to his superiors,
he'll win no praise from me. But that man
the city places in authority, his orders
must be obeyed, large and small 750
right and wrong.
            Anarchy—
show me a greater crime in all the earth!
She, she destroys cities, rips up houses,
breaks the ranks of spearmen into headlong rout.
But the ones who last it out, the great mass of them
owe their lives to discipline. Therefore
we must defend the men who live by law,
never let some woman triumph over us.
Better to fall from power, if fall we must,
at the hands of a man—never be rated 760
inferior to a woman, never.

LEADER.   To us,
unless old age has robbed us of our wits,
you seem to say what you have to say with sense.

HAEMON. Father, only the gods endow a man with reason,
    the finest of all their gifts, a treasure.
    Far be it from me—I haven't the skill,
    and certainly no desire, to tell you when,
    if ever, you make a slip in speech . . . though
    someone else might have a good suggestion.

    Of course it's not for you, 770
    in the normal run of things, to watch
    whatever men say or do, or find to criticize.
    The man in the street, you know, dreads your glance,
    he'd never say anything displeasing to your face.
    But it's for me to catch the murmurs in the dark,
    the way the city mourns for this young girl.
    "No woman," they say, "ever deserved death less,
    and such a brutal death for such a glorious action.
    She, with her own dear brother lying in his blood—
    she couldn't bear to leave him dead, unburied, 780
    food for the wild dogs or wheeling vultures.
    Death? She deserves a glowing crown of gold!"
    So they say, and the rumor spreads in secret,
    darkly . . .
            I rejoice in your success, father—
    nothing more precious to me in the world.
    What medal of honor brighter to his children
    than a father's growing glory? Or a child's
    to his proud father? Now don't, please,
    be quite so single-minded, self-involved
    or assume the world is wrong and you are right. 790
    Whoever thinks that he alone possesses intelligence,
    the gift of eloquence, he and no one else,
    and character too . . . such men, I tell you,
    spread them open—and you will find them empty.
                                     No,
    it's no disgrace for a man, even a wise man,
    to learn many things and not to be too rigid.
    You've seen trees by a raging winter torrent,
    how many sway with the flood and salvage every twig,
    but not the stubborn—they're ripped out, roots and all.
    Bend or break. The same when a man is sailing: 800
    haul your sheets too taut, never give an inch,
    you'll capsize, go the rest of the voyage
    keel up and the rowing-benches under.

    Oh give way. Relax your anger—change!
    I'm young, I know, but let me offer this:
    it would be best by far, I admit,
    if a man were born infallible, right by nature.
    If not—and things don't often go that way,
    it's best to learn from those with good advice.

LEADER. You'd do well, my lord, if he's speaking to the point, 810
    to learn from him,
Turning to HAEMON.
                            and you, my boy, from him.
    You both are talking sense.
CREON.   So,
    men our age, we're to be lectured, are we?—
    schooled by a boy his age?
HAEMON. Only in what is right. But if I seem young,
    look less to my years and more to what I do.
CREON. Do? Is admiring rebels an achievement?
HAEMON. I'd never suggest that you admire treason.
CREON.   Oh?—
    isn't that just the sickness that's attacked her?
HAEMON. The whole city of Thebes denies it, to a man. 820
CREON. And is Thebes about to tell me how to rule?
HAEMON. Now, you see? Who's talking like a child?
CREON. Am I to rule this land for others—or myself?
HAEMON. It's no city at all, owned by one man alone.
CREON. What? The city *is* the king's—that's the law!
HAEMON. What a splendid king you'd make of a desert island—
    you and you alone.
CREON.
To the CHORUS.
                    This boy, I do believe,
    is fighting on her side, the woman's side.
HAEMON. If you are a woman, yes;
    my concern is all for you. 830
CREON. Why, you degenerate—bandying accusations,
    threatening me with justice, your own father!
HAEMON. I see my father offending justice—wrong.
CREON.   Wrong?
    To protect my royal rights?
HAEMON.   Protect your rights?
    When you trample down the honors of the gods?
CREON. You, you soul of corruption, rotten through—
    woman's accomplice!
HAEMON.   That may be,
    but you'll never find me accomplice to a criminal.
CREON. That's what *she* is,
    and every word you say is a blatant appeal for her— 840
HAEMON. And you, and me, and the gods beneath the earth.
CREON. You'll never marry her, not while she's alive.

HAEMON. Then she'll die . . . but her death will kill another.

CREON. What, brazen threats? You go too far!

HAEMON.   What threat?
   Combatting your empty, mindless judgments with a word?

CREON. You'll suffer for your sermons, you and your empty wisdom!

HAEMON. If you weren't my father, I'd say you were insane.

CREON. Don't flatter me with Father—you woman's slave!

HAEMON. You really expect to fling abuse at me
   and not receive the same?

CREON.   Is that so!   850
   Now, by heaven, I promise you, you'll pay—
   taunting, insulting me! Bring her out,
   that hateful—she'll die now, here,
   in front of his eyes, beside her groom!

HAEMON. No, no, she will never die beside me—
   don't delude yourself. And you will never
   see me, never set eyes on my face again.
   Rage your heart out, rage with friends
   who can stand the sight of you.

Rushing out.

LEADER. Gone, my king, in a burst of anger.   860
   A temper young as his . . . hurt him once,
   he may do something violent.

CREON.   Let him do—
   dream up something desperate, past all human limit!
   Good riddance. Rest assured,
   he'll never save those two young girls from death.

LEADER. Both of them, you really intend to kill them both?

CREON. No, not her, the one whose hands are clean;
   you're quite right.

LEADER.   But Antigone—
   what sort of death do you have in mind for her?

CREON. I'll take her down some wild, desolate path   870
   never trod by men, and wall her up alive
   in a rocky vault, and set out short rations,
   just a gesture of piety
   to keep the entire city free of defilement.
   There let her pray to the one god she worships:
   Death—who knows?—may just reprieve her from death.
   Or she may learn at last, better late than never,
   what a waste of breath it is to worship Death.

Exit to the palace.

CHORUS. Love, never conquered in battle
   Love the plunderer laying waste the rich!   880
   Love standing the night-watch

                    guarding a girl's soft cheek,
you range the seas, the shepherds' steadings off in the wilds—
not even the deathless gods can flee your onset,
nothing human born for a day—
whoever feels your grip is driven mad.
                                        Love
you wrench the minds of the righteous into outrage,
swerve them to their ruin—you have ignited this,
this kindred strife, father and son at war
                    and Love alone the victor—   890
warm glance of the bride triumphant, burning with desire!
Throned in power, side-by-side with the mighty laws!
Irresistible Aphrodite,[5] never conquered—
Love, you mock us for your sport.

ANTIGONE *is brought from the palace under guard.*

        But now, even I'd rebel against the king,
        I'd break all bounds when I see this—
        I fill with tears, can't hold them back,
        not any more . . . I see Antigone make her way
        to the bridal vault where all are laid to rest.

ANTIGONE. Look at me, men of my fatherland,   900
        setting out on the last road
looking into the last light of day
the last I'll ever see . . .
the god of death who puts us all to bed
takes me down to the banks of Acheron[6] alive—
        denied my part in the wedding-songs,
no wedding-song in the dusk has crowned my marriage—
I go to wed the lord of the dark waters.

CHORUS. Not crowned with glory, crowned with a dirge,
        you leave for the deep pit of the dead.   910
        No withering illness laid you low,
        no strokes of the sword—no law to yourself,
        alone, no mortal like you, ever, you go down
        to the halls of Death alive and breathing.

ANTIGONE. But think of Niobe[7]—well I know her story—
        think what a living death she died,
Tantalus' daughter, stranger queen from the east:
there on the mountain heights, growing stone
binding as ivy, slowly walled her round
and the rains will never cease, the legends say   920
the snows will never leave her . . .
        wasting away, under her brows the tears

---

[5]**Aphrodite:** Goddess of love.
[6]**Acheron:** A river in the underworld, to which the dead go.
[7]**Niobe:** A queen of Thebes who was punished by the gods for her pride and was turned into stone.

showering down her breasting ridge and slopes—
a rocky death like hers puts me to sleep.

CHORUS. But she was a god, born of gods,
and we are only mortals born to die.
And yet, of course, it's a great thing
for a dying girl to hear, just hear
she shares a destiny equal to the gods,
during life and later, once she's dead.

ANTIGONE.   O you mock me!   930
Why, in the name of all my fathers' gods
why can't you wait till I am gone—
must you abuse me to my face?
O my city, all your fine rich sons!
And you, you springs of the Dirce,
holy grove of Thebes where the chariots gather,
you at least, you'll bear me witness, look,
unmourned by friends and forced by such crude laws
I go to my rockbound prison, strange new tomb—
always a stranger, O dear god,   940
I have no home on earth and none below,
not with the living, not with the breathless dead.

CHORUS. You went too far, the last limits of daring—
smashing against the high throne of Justice!
Your life's in ruins, child—I wonder . . .
do you pay for your father's terrible ordeal?

ANTIGONE. There—at last you've touched it, the worst pain
the worst anguish! Raking up the grief for father
three times over, for all the doom
that's struck us down, the brilliant house of Laius.   950
O mother, your marriage-bed
the coiling horrors, the coupling there—
you with your own son, my father—doomstruck mother!
Such, such were my parents, and I their wretched child.
I go to them now, cursed, unwed, to share their home—
I am a stranger! O dear brother, doomed
in your marriage—your marriage murders mine,
your dying drags me down to death alive!

Enter CREON.

CHORUS. Reverence asks some reverence in return—
but attacks on power never go unchecked,   960
not by the man who holds the reins of power.
Your own blind will, your passion has destroyed you.

ANTIGONE. No one to weep for me, my friends,
no wedding-song—they take me away
in all my pain . . . the road lies open, waiting.
Never again, the law forbids me to see
the sacred eye of day. I am agony!
No tears for the destiny that's mine,
no loved one mourns my death.

CREON.   Can't you see?
  If a man could wail his own dirge *before* he dies,   970
  he'd never finish.
To the GUARDS.
                        Take her away, quickly!
  Wall her up in the tomb, you have your orders.
  Abandon her there, alone, and let her choose—
  death or a buried life with a good roof for shelter.
  As for myself, my hands are clean. This young girl—
  dead or alive, she will be stripped of her rights,
  her stranger's rights, here in the world above.

ANTIGONE. O tomb, my bridal-bed—my house, my prison
  cut in the solid rock, my everlasting watch!
  I'll soon be there, soon embrace my own,   980
  the great growing family of our dead
  Persephone[8] has received among her ghosts.
                                                    I,
  the last of them all, the most reviled by far,
  go down before my destined time's run out.
  But still I go, cherishing one good hope:
  my arrival may be dear to father,
  dear to you, my mother,
  dear to you, my loving brother, Eteocles—
  When you died I washed you with my hands,
  I dressed you all, I poured the cups   990
  across your tombs. But now, Polynices,
  because I laid your body out as well,
  this, this is my reward. Nevertheless
  I honored you—the decent will admit it—
  well and wisely too.
                        Never, I tell you,
  if I had been the mother of children
  or if my husband died, exposed and rotting—
  I'd never have taken this ordeal upon myself,
  never defied our people's will. What law,
  you ask, do I satisfy with what I say?   1000
  A husband dead, there might have been another.
  A child by another too, if I had lost the first.
  But mother and father both lost in the halls of Death,
  no brother could ever spring to light again.

  For this law alone I held you first in honor.
  For this, Creon, the king, judges me a criminal
  guilty of dreadful outrage, my dear brother!
  And now he leads me off, a captive in his hands,
  with no part in the bridal-song, the bridal-bed,
  denied all joy of marriage, raising children—   1010
  deserted so by loved ones, struck by fate,
  I descend alive to the caverns of the dead.

---
[8]**Persephone:** Queen of the underworld.

What law of the mighty gods have I transgressed?
Why look to the heavens any more, tormented as I am?
Whom to call, what comrades now? Just think,
my reverence only brands me for irreverence!
Very well: if this is the pleasure of the gods,
once I suffer I will know that I was wrong.
But if these men are wrong, let them suffer
nothing worse than they mete out to me— 1020
these masters of injustice!

LEADER. Still the same rough winds, the wild passion
raging through the girl.

CREON.

To the GUARDS.

                    Take her away.
You're wasting time—you'll pay for it too.

ANTIGONE. Oh god, the voice of death. It's come, it's here.

CREON. True. Not a word of hope— your doom is sealed.

ANTIGONE. Land of Thebes, city of all my fathers—
    O you gods, the first gods of the race!
    They drag me away, now, no more delay.
    Look on me, you noble sons of Thebes— 1030
    the last of a great line of kings,
    I alone, see what I suffer now
    at the hands of what breed of men—
    all for reverence, my reverence for the gods!

She leaves under guard; the CHORUS *gathers.*

CHORUS. Danaë, Danaë[9]—
    even she endured a fate like yours,
        in all her lovely strength she traded
    the light of day for the bolted brazen vault—
    buried within her tomb, her bridal-chamber,
    wed to the yoke and broken. 1040
        But she was of glorious birth
            my child, my child
    and treasured the seed of Zeus within her womb,
    the cloudburst streaming gold!
        The power of fate is a wonder,
        dark, terrible wonder—
    neither wealth nor armies
    towered walls nor ships
    black hulls lashed by the salt
    can save us from that force. 1050

    The yoke tamed him too
        young Lycurgus[10] flaming in anger

---

[9]**Danaë:** Locked in a cell by her father because it was prophesied that her son would kill him, but visited by Zeus in the form of a shower of gold. Their son was Perseus.
[10]**Lycurgus:** Punished by Dionysus because he would not worship him.

> king of Edonia, all for his mad taunts
> Dionysus clamped him down, encased
> in the chain-mail of rock
> > and there his rage
> > > his terrible flowering rage burst—
> sobbing, dying away . . . at last that madman
> came to know his god—
> > the power he mocked, the power
> > he taunted in all his frenzy
> > trying to stamp out
> > the women strong with the god—
> > the torch, the raving sacred cries—
> > enraging the Muses[11] who adore the flute.
> And far north where the Black Rocks
> > cut the sea in half
> and murderous straits
> split the coast of Thrace
> > a forbidding city stands
> where once, hard by the walls
> the savage Ares thrilled to watch
> a king's new queen, a Fury rearing in rage
> against his two royal sons—
> > her bloody hands, her dagger-shuttle
> stabbing out their eyes—cursed, blinding wounds—
> their eyes blind sockets screaming for revenge!
>
> They wailed in agony, cries echoing cries
> > the princes doomed at birth . . .
> and their mother doomed to chains,
> walled off in a tomb of stone—
> > but she traced her own birth back
> to a proud Athenian line and the high gods
> and off in caverns half the world away,
> born of the wild North Wind
> > she sprang on her father's gales,
> > > racing stallions up the leaping cliffs—
> child of the heavens. But even on her the Fates
> the gray everlasting Fates rode hard
> my child, my child.

Enter TIRESIAS, *the blind prophet, led by a* BOY.

TIRESIAS.   Lords of Thebes,
  I and the boy have come together,
  hand in hand. Two see with the eyes of one . . .
  so the blind must go, with a guide to lead the way.

CREON. What is it, old Tiresias? What news now?

TIRESIAS. I will teach you. And you obey the seer.

---

[11]**Muses:** Goddesses of the arts.

CREON.   I will,
   I've never wavered from your advice before.

TIRESIAS. And so you kept the city straight on course.

CREON. I owe you a great deal, I swear to that.

TIRESIAS. Then reflect, my son: you are poised,
   once more, on the razor-edge of fate.   1100

CREON. What is it? I shudder to hear you.

TIRESIAS.   You will learn
   when you listen to the warnings of my craft.
   As I sat on the ancient seat of augury,[12]
   in the sanctuary where every bird I know
   will hover at my hands—suddenly I heard it,
   a strange voice in the wingbeats, unintelligible,
   barbaric, a mad scream! Talons flashing, ripping,
   they were killing each other—that much I knew—
   the murderous fury whirring in those wings
   made that much clear!
                           I was afraid,   1110
   I turned quickly, tested the burnt-sacrifice,
   ignited the altar at all points—but no fire,
   the god in the fire never blazed.
   Not from those offerings . . . over the embers
   slid a heavy ooze from the long thighbones,
   smoking, sputtering out, and the bladder
   puffed and burst—spraying gall into the air—
   and the fat wrapping the bones slithered off
   and left them glistening white. No fire!
   The rites failed that might have blazed the future   1120
   with a sign. So I learned from the boy here;
   he is my guide, as I am guide to others.
                                And it's you—
   your high resolve that sets this plague on Thebes.
   The public altars and sacred hearths are fouled,
   one and all, by the birds and dogs with carrion
   torn from the corpse, the doomstruck son of Oedipus!
   And so the gods are deaf to our prayers, they spurn
   the offerings in our hands, the flame of holy flesh.
   No birds cry out an omen clear and true—
   they're gorged with the murdered victim's blood and fat.   1130
   Take these things to heart, my son, I warn you.
   All men make mistakes, it is only human.
   But once the wrong is done, a man
   can turn his back on folly, misfortune too,
   if he tries to make amends, however low he's fallen,
   and stops his bullnecked ways. Stubbornness
   brands you for stupidity—pride is a crime.
   No, yield to the dead!

---

[12]**Seat of augury:** Where Tiresias looked for omens among birds.

>   Never stab the fighter when he's down.
>   Where's the glory, killing the dead twice over?   1140
>
>   I mean you well. I give you sound advice.
>   It's best to learn from a good adviser
>   when he speaks for your own good:
>   it's pure gain.
>
> CREON.   Old man—all of you! So,
>   you shoot your arrows at my head like archers at the target—
>   I even have *him* loosed on me, this fortune-teller.
>   Oh his ilk has tried to sell me short
>   and ship me off for years. Well,
>   drive your bargains, traffic—much as you like—
>   in the gold of India, silver-gold of Sardis.   1150
>   You'll never bury that body in the grave,
>   not even if Zeus's eagles rip the corpse
>   and wing their rotten pickings off to the throne of god!
>   Never, not even in fear of such defilement
>   will I tolerate his burial, that traitor.
>   Well I know, we can't defile the gods—
>   no mortal has the power.
>   No,
>   reverend old Tiresias, all men fall,
>   it's only human, but the wisest fall obscenely
>   when they glorify obscene advice with rhetoric—   1160
>   all for their own gain.
>
> TIRESIAS. Oh god, is there a man alive
>   who knows, who actually believes . . .
>
> CREON.   What now?
>   What earth-shattering truth are you about to utter?
>
> TIRESIAS. . . . just how much a sense of judgment, wisdom
>   is the greatest gift we have?
>
> CREON.   Just as much, I'd say,
>   as a twisted mind is the worst affliction going.
>
> TIRESIAS. You are the one who's sick, Creon, sick to death.
>
> CREON. I am in no mood to trade insults with a seer.
>
> TIRESIAS. You have already, calling my prophecies a lie.
>
> CREON.   Why not?   1170
>   You and the whole breed of seers are mad for money!
>
> TIRESIAS. And the whole race of tyrants lusts to rake it in.
>
> CREON. This slander of yours—
>   are you aware you're speaking to the king?
>
> TIRESIAS. Well aware. Who helped you save the city?
>
> CREON.   You—
>   you have your skills, old seer, but you lust for injustice!
>
> TIRESIAS. You will drive me to utter the dreadful secret in my heart.

CREON. Spit it out! Just don't speak it for profit.

TIRESIAS. Profit? No, not a bit of profit, not for you.

CREON. Know full well, you'll never buy off my resolve. 1180

TIRESIAS. Then know this too, learn this by heart!
　　The chariot of the sun will not race through
　　so many circuits more, before you have surrendered
　　one born of your own loins, your own flesh and blood,
　　a corpse for corpses given in return, since you have thrust
　　to the world below a child sprung for the world above,
　　ruthlessly lodged a living soul within the grave—
　　then you've robbed the gods below the earth,
　　keeping a dead body here in the bright air,
　　unburied, unsung, unhallowed by the rites. 1190

　　You, you have no business with the dead,
　　nor do the gods above—this is violence
　　you have forced upon the heavens.
　　And so the avengers, the dark destroyers late
　　but true to the mark, now lie in wait for you,
　　the Furies sent by the gods and the god of death
　　to strike you down with the pains that you perfected!
　　There. Reflect on that, tell me I've been bribed.
　　The day comes soon, no long test of time, not now,
　　that wakes the wails for men and women in your halls. 1200
　　Great hatred rises against you—
　　cities in tumult, all whose mutilated sons
　　the dogs have graced with burial, or the wild beasts,
　　some wheeling crow that wings the ungodly stench of carrion
　　back to each city, each warrior's hearth and home.

　　These arrows for your heart! Since you've raked me
　　I loose them like an archer in my anger,
　　arrows deadly true. You'll never escape
　　their burning, searing force.

Motioning to his escort.

　　Come, boy, take me home. 1210
　　So he can vent his rage on younger men,
　　and learn to keep a gentler tongue in his head
　　and better sense than what he carries now.

Exit to the side.

LEADER. The old man's gone, my king—
　　terrible prophecies. Well I know,
　　since the hair on this old head went gray,
　　he's never lied to Thebes.

CREON. I know it myself—I'm shaken, torn.
　　It's a dreadful thing to yield . . . but resist now?
　　Lay my pride bare to the blows of ruin? 1220
　　That's dreadful too.

LEADER. But good advice,
Creon, take it now, you must.

CREON. What should I do? Tell me . . . I'll obey.

LEADER. Go! Free the girl from the rocky vault
and raise a mound for the body you exposed.

CREON. That's your advice? You think I should give in?

LEADER. Yes, my king, quickly. Disasters sent by the gods
cut short our follies in a flash.

CREON. Oh it's hard,
giving up the heart's desire . . . but I will do it—
no more fighting a losing battle with necessity. 1230

LEADER. Do it now, go, don't leave it to others.

CREON. Now—I'm on my way! Come, each of you,
take up axes, make for the high ground,
over there, quickly! I and my better judgment
have come round to this—I shackled her,
I'll set her free myself. I am afraid . . .
it's best to keep the established laws
to the very day we die.

Rushing out, followed by his entourage. The CHORUS *clusters around the altar.*

CHORUS. God of a hundred names!
Great Dionysus—
Son and glory of Semele! Pride of Thebes— 1240
Child of Zeus whose thunder rocks the clouds—
Lord of the famous lands of evening—
King of the Mysteries!
King of Eleusis, Demeter's plain[13]
her breasting hills that welcome in the world—
Great Dionysus!
Bacchus,[14] living in Thebes
the mother-city of all your frenzied women—
Bacchus
living along the Ismenus'[15] rippling waters
standing over the field sown with the Dragon's teeth!

You—we have seen you through the flaring smoky fires,
your torches blazing over the twin peaks 1250
where nymphs of the hallowed cave climb onward
fired with you, your sacred rage—
we have seen you at Castalia's running spring[16]
and down from the heights of Nysa[17] crowned with ivy
the greening shore rioting vines and grapes

---

[13]**Demeter's plain:** The goddess of grain was worshipped at Eleusis, near Athens.
[14]**Bacchus:** Another name for Dionysus.
[15]**Ismenus:** A river near Thebes where the founders of the city were said to have sprung from a dragon's teeth.
[16]**Castalia's running spring:** The sacred spring of Apollo's oracle at Delphi.
[17]**Nysa:** A mountain where Dionysus was worshipped.

                    down you come in your storm of wild women
                            ecstatic, mystic cries—
                                            Dionysus—
down to watch and ward the roads of Thebes!

First of all cities, Thebes you honor first
you and your mother, bride of the lightning—   1260
come, Dionysus! now your people lie
in the iron grip of plague,
come in your racing, healing stride
                    down Parnassus' slopes[18]
or across the moaning straits.
                            Lord of the dancing—
dance, dance the constellations breathing fire!
Great master of the voices of the night!
Child of Zeus, God's offspring, come, come forth!
Lord, king, dance with your nymphs, swirling, raving
arm-in-arm in frenzy through the night   1270
        they dance you, Iacchus[19]—
                    Dance, Dionysus
giver of all good things!

Enter a MESSENGER *from the side.*

MESSENGER.   Neighbors,
    friends of the house of Cadmus[20] and the kings,
    there's not a thing in this life of ours
    I'd praise or blame as settled once for all.
    Fortune lifts and Fortune fells the lucky
    and unlucky every day. No prophet on earth
    can tell a man his fate. Take Creon:
    there was a man to rouse your envy once,
    as I see it. He saved the realm from enemies;   1280
    taking power, he alone, the lord of the fatherland,
    he set us true on course—flourished like a tree
    with the noble line of sons he bred and reared . . .
    and now it's lost, all gone.
                        Believe me,
    when a man has squandered his true joys,
    he's good as dead, I tell you, a living corpse.
    Pile up riches in your house, as much as you like—
    live like a king with a huge show of pomp,
    but if real delight is missing from the lot,
    I wouldn't give you a wisp of smoke for it,   1290
    not compared with joy.

LEADER.   What now?
    What new grief do you bring the house of kings?

---

[18]**Parnassus:** A mountain in Greece that was sacred to Dionysus as well as other gods and goddesses.
[19]**Iacchus:** Dionysus.
[20]**Cadmus:** The legendary founder of Thebes.

MESSENGER. Dead, dead—and the living are guilty of their death!

LEADER. Who's the murderer? Who is dead? Tell us.

MESSENGER. Haemon's gone, his blood spilled by the very hand—

LEADER. His father's or his own?

MESSENGER.   His own . . .
   raging mad with his father for the death—

LEADER.   Oh great seer,
   you saw it all, you brought your word to birth!

MESSENGER. Those are the facts. Deal with them as you will.

As he turns to go, EURYDICE *enters from the palace.*

LEADER. Look, Eurydice. Poor woman, Creon's wife,   1300
   so close at hand. By chance perhaps,
   unless she's heard the news about her son.

EURYDICE.   My countrymen,
   all of you—I caught the sound of your words
   as I was leaving to do my part,
   to appeal to queen Athena[21] with my prayers.
   I was just loosing the bolts, opening the doors,
   when a voice filled with sorrow, family sorrow,
   struck my ears, and I fell back, terrified,
   into the women's arms—everything went black.
   Tell me the news, again, whatever it is . . .   1310
   sorrow and I are hardly strangers;
   I can bear the worst.

MESSENGER.   I—dear lady,
   I'll speak as an eye-witness. I was there.
   And I won't pass over one word of the truth.
   Why should I try to soothe you with a story,
   only to prove a liar in a moment?
   Truth is always best.
                       So,
   I escorted your lord, I guided him
   to the edge of the plain where the body lay,
   Polynices, torn by the dogs and still unmourned.   1320
   And saying a prayer to Hecate of the Crossroads,
   Pluto[22] too, to hold their anger and be kind,
   we washed the dead in a bath of holy water
   and plucking some fresh branches, gathering . . .
   what was left of him, we burned them all together
   and raised a high mound of native earth, and then
   we turned and made for that rocky vault of hers,
   the hollow, empty bed of the bride of Death.
   And far off, one of us heard a voice,
   a long wail rising, echoing   1330
   out of that unhallowed wedding-chamber;

---

[21]**Athena:** Goddess of wisdom and protector of Greek cities.
[22]**Hecate, Pluto:** Gods of the underworld.

he ran to alert the master and Creon pressed on,
closer—the strange, inscrutable cry came sharper,
throbbing around him now, and he let loose
a cry of his own, enough to wrench the heart,
"Oh god, am I the prophet now? going down
the darkest road I've ever gone? My son—
it's *his* dear voice, he greets me! Go, men,
closer, quickly! Go through the gap,
the rocks are dragged back— 1340
right to the tomb's very mouth—and look,
see if it's Haemon's voice I think I hear,
or the gods have robbed me of my senses."

The king was shattered. We took his orders,
went and searched, and there in the deepest,
dark recesses of the tomb we found her . . .
hanged by the neck in a fine linen noose,
strangled in her veils—and the boy,
his arms flung around her waist,
clinging to her, wailing for his bride, 1350
dead and down below, for his father's crimes
and the bed of his marriage blighted by misfortune.
When Creon saw him, he gave a deep sob,
he ran in, shouting, crying out to him,
"Oh my child—what have you done? what seized you,
what insanity? what disaster drove you mad?
Come out, my son! I beg you on my knees!"
But the boy gave him a wild burning glance,
spat in his face, not a word in reply,
he drew his sword—his father rushed out, 1360
running as Haemon lunged and missed!—
and then, doomed, desperate with himself,
suddenly leaning his full weight on the blade,
he buried it in his body, halfway to the hilt.
And still in his senses, pouring his arms around her,
he embraced the girl and breathing hard,
released a quick rush of blood,
bright red on her cheek glistening white.
And there he lies, body enfolding body . . .
he has won his bride at last, poor boy, 1370
not here but in the houses of the dead.

Creon shows the world that of all the ills
afflicting men the worst is lack of judgment.

EURYDICE *turns and reenters the palace.*

LEADER. What do you make of that? The lady's gone,
without a word, good or bad.

MESSENGER. I'm alarmed too
but here's my hope—faced with her son's death,
she finds it unbecoming to mourn in public.

            Inside, under her roof, she'll set her women
            to the task and wail the sorrow of the house.
            She's too discreet. She won't do something rash.   1380
LEADER. I'm not so sure. To me, at least,
    a long heavy silence promises danger,
    just as much as a lot of empty outcries.
MESSENGER. We'll see if she's holding something back,
    hiding some passion in her heart.
    I'm going in. You may be right—who knows?
    Even too much silence has its dangers.

Exit to the palace. Enter CREON *from the side, escorted by* ATTENDANTS *carrying* HAEMON's *body on a bier.*

LEADER. The king himself! Coming toward us,
            look, holding the boy's head in his hands.
            Clear, damning proof, if it's right to say so—   1390
            proof of his own madness, no one else's,
                no, his own blind wrongs.
CREON.   Ohhh,
        so senseless, so insane . . . my crimes,
        my stubborn, deadly—
        Look at us, the killer, the killed,
        father and son, the same blood—the misery!
        My plans, my mad fanatic heart,
        my son, cut off so young!
        Ai, dead, lost to the world,
        not through your stupidity, no, my own.
LEADER.   Too late,   1400
    too late, you see what justice means.
CREON.   Oh I've learned
        through blood and tears! Then, it was then,
        when the god came down and struck me—a great weight
        shattering, driving me down that wild savage path,
        ruining, trampling down my joy. Oh the agony!
            the heartbreaking agonies of our lives.

Enter the MESSENGER *from the palace.*

MESSENGER.   Master,
    what a hoard of grief you have, and you'll have more.
    The grief that lies to hand you've brought yourself—

Pointing to HAEMON's *body.*

    the rest, in the house, you'll see it all too soon.
CREON. What now? What's worse than this?
MESSENGER.   The queen is dead.   1410
    The mother of this dead boy . . . mother to the end—
    poor thing, her wounds are fresh.
CREON.   No, no,
        harbor of Death, so choked, so hard to cleanse!—
        why me? why are you killing me?

      Herald of pain, more words, more grief?
      I died once, you kill me again and again!
      What's the report, boy . . . some news for me?
      My wife dead? O dear god!
      Slaughter heaped on slaughter?

The doors open; the body of EURYDICE *is brought out on her bier.*

MESSENGER.   See for yourself:
    now they bring her body from the palace.

CREON.   Oh no,   1420
      another, a second loss to break the heart.
      What next, what fate still waits for me?
      I just held my son in my arms and now,
      look, a new corpse rising before my eyes—
          wretched, helpless mother—O my son!

MESSENGER. She stabbed herself at the altar,
    then her eyes went dark, after she'd raised
    a cry for the noble fate of Megareus,[23] the hero
    killed in the first assault, then for Haemon,
    then with her dying breath she called down   1430
    torments on your head—you killed her sons.

CREON.   Oh the dread,
      I shudder with dread! Why not kill me too?—
      run me through with a good sharp sword?
      Oh god, the misery, anguish—
      I, I'm churning with it, going under.

MESSENGER. Yes, and the dead, the woman lying there,
    piles the guilt of all their deaths on you.

CREON. How did she end her life, what bloody stroke?

MESSENGER. She drove home to the heart with her own hand,
    once she learned her son was dead . . . that agony.   1440

CREON. And the guilt is all mine—
      can never be fixed on another man,
      no escape for me. I killed you,
      I, god help me, I admit it all!

To his ATTENDANTS.
      Take me away, quickly, out of sight.
      I don't even exist—I'm no one. Nothing.

LEADER. Good advice, if there's any good in suffering.
    Quickest is best when troubles block the way.

CREON.
Kneeling in prayer.
      Come, let it come!—that best of fates for me
      that brings the final day, best fate of all.   1450
      Oh quickly, now—
      so I never have to see another sunrise.

---

[23]**Megareus:** A son of Creon and Eurydice; he died when Thebes was attacked.

LEADER. That will come when it comes;
   we must deal with all that lies before us.
   The future rests with the ones who tend the future.

CREON. That prayer—I poured my heart into that prayer!

LEADER. No more prayers now. For mortal men
   there is no escape from the doom we must endure.

CREON. Take me away, I beg you, out of sight.
      A rash, indiscriminate fool!   1460
      I murdered you, my son, against my will—
      you too, my wife . . .
                  Wailing wreck of a man,
      whom to look to? where to lean for support?

Desperately turning from HAEMON *to* EURYDICE *on their biers.*

      Whatever I touch goes wrong—once more
      a crushing fate's come down upon my head.

The MESSENGER *and* ATTENDANTS *lead* CREON *into the palace.*

CHORUS. Wisdom is by far the greatest part of joy,
      and reverence toward the gods must be safeguarded.
      The mighty words of the proud are paid in full
      with mighty blows of fate, and at long last
         those blows will teach us wisdom.   1470

The old citizens exit to the side.

                                                   (ca. 442 BCE)

CHAPTER 15 WRITING ABOUT DRAMATIC STRUCTURE 521

PREWRITING

Now that you have read *Antigone* and have some sense of its basic structure, read the play again carefully and write out the answers to the questions below. Your responses will not only help you sharpen your understanding of dramatic structure; they will also lead you to clarify your reactions to *Antigone*'s characters and themes.

ANALYZING DRAMATIC STRUCTURE

1. What background are we given in the opening scene (lines 1–116)? List the main points of information that this exchange between Antigone and Ismene reveals.
2. What exposition does the Chorus give in lines 117–72?
3. How does Sophocles use the Sentry (lines 249 and following)? Does this character provide more than factual exposition?
4. What do you think the main conflict is? State it as specifically as you can in a single sentence.
5. Identify the protagonist and the antagonist. Is it fair to apply the labels *heroine* or *villain* to them?
6. Where does the climax occur? Identify the scene and describe what happens. Why do you think this is the play's turning point?
7. Does the climax seem to come early in the play? How does Sophocles maintain interest after the turning point? Did you expect such dramatic developments after the climax? Do you think Creon expected them?
8. When does the catastrophe occur? Was this outcome inevitable? Were your feelings about the outcome different the second time you read the play?
9. State what you consider the play's theme to be.
10. A *foil* is a contrasting character who sets off or helps define another character. How is Ismene a foil to Antigone? Are there any foils to Creon?
11. Why is Eurydice included in the plot? How do you feel about her fate?

Having answered these questions about the structure of *Antigone*, devise a graph or chart that illustrates the pattern of events in the play. Make sure your graph shows the six structural components discussed on page 482.

WRITING

Your understanding of the structure of *Antigone* will enable you to write more easily about the play's arguments. As you watched the conflict develop between Antigone and Creon, you undoubtedly became aware of the opposing values that these two characters represent. As one critic has observed about *Antigone*, "The characters *are* the issues, and the issues the characters."[1] It is now your turn to examine these issues and decide where you stand.

DISCOVERING A WORKABLE ARGUMENTATIVE THESIS

Argument means dispute; it implies that there are opposing sides. Any matter worth arguing will involve at least one "issue"—that is, an essential point in question or disagreement. You need not always take sides, but once you have decided what issues are involved in an argument, you can write an effective paper by taking a stand and explaining why you have chosen one side over the other.

Your approach to *Antigone* will have to take into account the controversial nature of the play's conflict. Review your responses to the prewriting questions about the disagreement and about the antagonist and protagonist. Can you identify an issue that you think is central to the play's meaning? Are there other issues involved in the conflict? Try to get the main issues stated as clearly and specifically as you can before you begin to write. The ideas for writing that follow should help you work out the important issues of the play.

You can argue an issue in two ways. You can take an affirmative position on one side of the question and present reasons and evidence to support your stand. Or you can anticipate the arguments of the opposing side and show how the evidence does not support this side, indicating where the fallacies or errors lie in the opposition's reasoning. You will probably want to combine both techniques in writing about *Antigone*.

Whatever your approach, you need to study the evidence and examine the ideas on both sides for flaws in logical thinking. One way to make this examination involves listing the main arguments, pro and con, in two columns on a sheet of paper:

Creon	**Antigone**
Public interest outweighs private loyalties.	Eternal unwritten laws take precedence.
Polynices made war on his own country.	All the dead deserve honour.

You can make a similar listing of speeches or lines from the play that serve as evidence for the two sides of the argument. For instance, you may want to note such revealing statements by Creon as these:

> whoever places a friend / above the good of his own country, he is nothing (203–04)

> that man / the city places in authority, his orders / must be obeyed, large and small, / right and wrong (748–51)

---

[1] Charles Paul Segal, "Sophocles' Praise of Man and the Conflicts of *Antigone*," *Sophocles: A Collection of Critical Essays*, ed. T. Woodward (Englewood Cliffs, NJ: Prentice-Hall, 1966), 63.

Compare these lists and see which side has the stronger arguments and the greater amount of evidence. You can then decide which side you are going to support; you also have a convenient listing of specific ideas and quotations to use in developing your essay.

QUOTING FROM A PLAY

When writing a paper on a single play, instead of citing page numbers, you need to give act and scene numbers in parentheses at the end of the quoted material; for verse plays give act, scene, and line numbers. Because *Antigone* is not divided into acts and scenes, give the line numbers for the quotations you use. Long quotations (more than three lines) should be indented with *no* quotation marks. Also, indicate the speaker when quoting a passage in which more than one character speaks. Here are some samples:

> It is up to Ismene, then, to point out the obvious: "Remember we are women, / we're not born to contend with men" (74–75).

(Only two lines quoted—separated with a slash and enclosed in quotation marks)

> During her defence, Antigone declares her defiance:
>
> > This is nothing.
> > And if my present actions strike you as foolish,
> > let's just say I've been accused of folly
> > by a fool. (522–25)

(Long quotation—indented, no quotation marks)

For plays *not* written in verse, give act and scene or page numbers in parentheses at the end of the quoted material.

IDEAS FOR WRITING

IDEAS FOR RESPONSIVE WRITING

1. Do you see yourself as approving of or opposing the rules and norms of the society you live in? How do you support, change, or disobey these rules and norms? Write about one rule or group of related rules (for example, sex roles or parent–child relationships) that you accept or reject.
2. In modern society, what might Creon and Antigone disagree about? Write an essay explaining where the two characters would probably stand on one of today's issues.

IDEAS FOR CRITICAL WRITING

1. Is Creon a politician concerned with imposing and maintaining order? Is Antigone an anarchist whose action will destroy that

order? Or is she a private citizen determined to follow the dictates of her personal beliefs? Write about the issues in *Antigone* as a struggle between public policy and individual conscience, supporting the side that you think is "right."

2. Can you analyze the conflict between Antigone and Creon as a psychological clash between a woman and a man? Write an essay that focuses on the male–female opposition in the play. You may want to work Ismene, Haemon, and Eurydice into your scheme of opposing values.

REWRITING

You will want to be certain that your arguments about *Antigone* are perfectly clear. Take some time to ensure that what you have written cannot be misunderstood. If you can, coax a friend or classmate into reading your first draft; ask your reader to point out sentences that do not make sense or that are unclear.

AVOIDING UNCLEAR LANGUAGE

Multisyllabic words and long, involved sentences may dazzle your readers, but they can also hinder clear communication. Your first goal in writing should be to convey ideas and information. Trying to impress your readers with big words and fancy phrases may lead to one or more forms of unclear expression:

1. *Engfish:* Writing specialist Ken Macrorie uses this term to call attention to artificial language that does not represent a writer's own experience and education. Engfish is phony, pretentious, stuffy, and often impossible to decode. Writers use Engfish, it seems, when they are unsure of which attitude to take toward their subject and their audience. The student who wrote,

    Antigone's unacceptable posture toward the designated governmental powers inevitably entailed the termination of her existence,

    no doubt thought that this inflated diction was appropriate for a serious paper on a classical play. But most readers probably would prefer to see that sentence revised to read more clearly, like this one:

    Antigone's defiance led to her death.

    In the long run, clarity will impress your readers more than Engfish ever can.

2. *Jargon:* This term applies to the specialized language used by a particular group of people. Computer operators, sociologists, teenagers, architects, hockey players, mobsters—all sorts of interest groups and professions—employ words and terms that relate only to their particular activities. The problem with jargon is that outsiders do not understand it. Writing about a "love game" or the "ad court" will be all right for an audience of tennis buffs, but you will have to

change your language for more general readers. Jargon may not come up in your essay about *Antigone*, but it can creep in from other sources. For instance, the student who wrote,

> Antigone's behaviour is marked by regressive reaction formation toward authoritarian figures,

was apparently influenced by the jargon of her psychology class. Unless you are writing for an audience of fellow psychoanalysts, you would do better to say the following:

> Antigone sometimes acted like a disobedient daughter.

3. *Abstract words:* Abstract terms and general expressions do not automatically make your writing intellectual and impressive. Although it is true that writing an argumentative essay requires using abstract ideas, your paper will be more persuasive if it is factual, concrete, and clear. Abstractions tend to be hazy and difficult to define. Words like *duty*, *anarchy*, *patriotism*, and *truth* have different meanings to different people. When writing about an abstract concept, make certain that you have a definite meaning in your own mind. If, for instance, you write that

> Antigone is a woman of honour,

it is a good idea to check the dictionary to see if your understanding of the word *honour* coincides with a standard definition. *The Canadian Oxford Dictionary* gives eleven entries for *honour* as a noun and four more entries for the verb *honour*. Which one does the above sentence convey? Would "a woman's chastity" be accurate in this context? It might be more meaningful to say,

> Antigone is a woman of principle and integrity,

although those words are also abstract. Try, if possible, to specify the meaning you want when using an abstract term:

> Above all, Creon is a master politician—a man of ambition intent on holding his power.

SAMPLE STUDENT PAPER

In the following sample paper, Lynda Melnik argues that the chief conflict in *Antigone* involves a power struggle between male and female. Notice how she uses and documents quoted material from the play to support her argument.

Lynda Melnik   1
English 1110
July 16, 2003

                Gender Conflict in <u>Antigone</u>

   Just beneath the obvious conflict of the
individual versus societal laws in Sophocles'
<u>Antigone</u> lies the ancient struggle of male ver-
sus female. The protagonist, Antigone, chooses
to break the law, and in doing so becomes a
criminal. However, she has not deliberately
created the gender struggle with the antagonist
Creon. The gender struggle is set in motion
nevertheless, but it is Creon who sees the conflict as such, and it is Creon who fights to
retain control over Antigone, not only as king
over subject but also as man over woman.
Antigone's fight, unlike Creon's, is a noble
one that allows her to surpass gender-specific
behaviour, to limit the scope of her battle,
and to clearly identify her enemy.

   Antigone knows that she has violated the
king's order not to bury her brother Polynices,
but she seems not to notice that she has also
violated the social code by stepping outside
the boundaries of acceptable feminine behaviour. Her act of defiance is courageous, displays self-reliance, and is completely contrary
to the obedience expected of women in her society. She fearlessly assures her sister, Ismene,

that Creon "has no right to keep me from my
own" (59). It is up to Ismene to point out the
obvious: "Remember we are women, / we're not
born to contend with men" (74-75). Eventually,
Ismene is rewarded for her passivity when Creon
spares her life. Antigone, in her struggle for
justice, cannot be limited by gender-behaviour
restrictions.

When Antigone is arrested, King Creon
expresses shock that a woman in his court has
committed the ultimate crime, and it is at this
moment that the struggle is transformed from
one of ruler versus disobedient subject to one
of man versus woman. His disbelief regarding
the criminal's gender soon turns to perverse
pleasure at the opportunity to punish this
woman for her audacity. While Antigone's crime
against the state is clear, Creon sees the
subterfuge of women as the real issue to be
dealt with. The focus of his original lofty (if
erroneous) and purposeful conflict is distorted,
and the struggle becomes personal and petty.
Creon's threatening speeches to Antigone bring
out his overall contempt for women: "Go down
below and love, / if love you must--love the
dead! While I'm alive, / no woman is going to
lord it over me" (591-93).

Melnik 3

Antigone, however, rises above the pettiness of gender rivalry focusing her battle strategy against an unjust law and responding only to the conflict between king and subject. Unlike Creon, Antigone acts out of a heartfelt moral obligation, proclaiming that she is "Not ashamed for a moment, / not to honor [her] brother, [her] own flesh and blood" (572-73). As Antigone calmly and eloquently argues the righteousness of her action, instead of quivering with fear under Creon's threats, the king's sense of triumph slowly turns to rage. During her defence, Antigone very specifically declares her defiance against a ruler who would make unjust laws: "And if my present actions strike you as foolish, / let's just say I've been accused of folly / by a fool" (523-25), to which Creon angrily replies:

> This girl was an old hand at insolence
> when she overrode the edicts we made public.
> But once she'd done it--the insolence,
> twice over--to glory in it, laughing,
> mocking us to our face with what she'd done
> I'm not the man, not now: she is the man
> if this victory goes to her and she goes
> free. (536-42)

Antigone has committed a criminal act, but it is the fact that a mere woman has defied him that enrages Creon. Her death alone will not

Melnik 4

satisfy him. He needs to master her wilfulness and make her regret her very gender. Creon is waging war against all women while Antigone, refusing to be drawn into a gender war, focuses on her war against an unjust law and king.

As well as being specific about the battle she is fighting, Antigone knows who and what her enemy is, but Creon seeks victory and dominance over women; by losing sight of the real conflict, he has lost his stateliness as king, becoming bitter and petty. In his wild attempt to control women rather than focus on his disobedient subject alone, Creon sees enemies everywhere. His paranoia is evident as he rejects his son's pleas for Antigone:

> we must defend the men who live by law,
> never let some woman triumph over us.
> Better to fall from power, if we must,
> at the hands of a man--never be rated
> inferior to a woman, never. (757-61)

Haemon, disgusted by his father's cruelty, rejects him. This rejection makes the king even more bitter. Since the focus of Creon's conflict is distorted, he sees his own son as an enemy and has come to suspect that anyone who disagrees with him is involved in a plot against him as these words to the loyal Ismene reveal: "You-- / in my house, you viper, slinking undetected, / sucking my life-blood!" (597-99)

Antigone all the while clearly identifies her one and only enemy--an unjust law. Antigone's prediction of the fate of unjust lawmakers is not an act of unreasonable outrage against all men: "But if these men are wrong, let them suffer / nothing worse than they mete out to me-- / these masters of injustice!" (1019-21). Creon fulfills the prediction while Antigone remains clearly focused on eradicating injustice--her enemy.

   Creon has mistaken Antigone's act of piety for a wild attempt by a power-hungry woman to undermine his rule. Out of his own fear of being beaten by a woman, Creon begins a chain of events that results in his own demise. All along, however, Antigone has risen above gender-specific behaviour, has sought victory over only an unjust law, and has clearly identified her enemy.

Melnik 6

Work Cited

Sophocles. <u>Antigone</u>. Trans. Robert Fagles. <u>Literature and the Writing Process</u>. Elizabeth McMahan, Susan X. Day, and Robert Funk. 6th ed. Upper Saddle River: Prentice Hall, 2002. 605-640.

QUESTIONS FOR DISCUSSION

1. Do you think this essay overemphasizes the gender issue in analyzing the conflict between Creon and Antigone? Has the author slighted or ignored more important issues?
2. Can you find any additional evidence that the author of the essay overlooked or chose not to use? Would the case be strengthened by including Eurydice in the analysis?
3. The author says that Antigone rises above sexual rivalry in her defiant behaviour. Is this view entirely true? Can you find any evidence to suggest that Antigone is also caught up in the power struggle between male and female?
4. In carrying out her approach, the author of the essay analyzes Creon more than Antigone. Why is that? Is this strategy productive? Do you agree with the conclusion about Creon's character development?

For study tools to help you with your next writing assignment, please visit the Companion Website at www.pearsoned.ca/mcmahan.

16

Writing about Character

Pondering people's characters comes quite naturally and easily. You will remember that we began our approach to literature with the study of character in the short story. Drama also provides us with carefully drawn examples of human speech and behaviour. Whether the presentation is realistic or not, the characters are at the heart of the play.

WHAT IS THE MODERN HERO?

In everyday life, we use the word *heroic* to describe people who save others' lives while risking their own, acts of great self-sacrifice or self-control, feats that we hold in awe. Before you read on, think of the last time you remember calling something heroic or referring to someone as a hero. Note the situation, and think about what you meant by the word. We often use it lightly—the person who supplies a much-needed extension cord or an emergency ten-dollar loan may temporarily be a hero. Drama, however, practically forces us into deeper consideration of what a hero is.

THE CLASSICAL TRAGIC HERO

In the fourth century BCE, Aristotle described the classic concept of the tragic hero. He wrote that the hero must be someone "who is highly renowned and prosperous." Classical tragedy involves the inevitable destruction of a noble person by means of a character flaw, usually a disproportionate measure of a specific human attribute such as pride or jealousy or indecision. The Aristotelian definition implies this basic premise: there is a natural, right ordering and proportion of traits within the human being that, if violated, produces calamity. Many critics cite Antigone's "difficult wilfulness" as the explanation of her fate. Charles Segal claims that "she can assert what she is only by staking her entire being, her life. It is by this extreme defence of her beliefs that she rises to heroic and deeply tragic stature."[1]

---

[1] Charles Paul Segal, "Sophocles' Praise of Man and the Conflicts of *Antigone*." *Sophocles: A Collection of Critical Essays*, ed. T. Woodward (Englewood Cliffs, NJ: Prentice-Hall, 1966): 65.

THE MODERN TRAGIC HERO

In 1949, the famous playwright Arthur Miller described what he considered a new kind of hero. In an article called "Tragedy and the Common Man" (*New York Times*, 27 Feb. 1949: 3.1.3.), he challenged Aristotle's idea that the hero must be a "highly renowned and prosperous" figure who has a tragic flaw. In contrast to a disorder exclusively within the personal traits of the hero, Miller's idea of the modern hero emphasizes a clash between the character and the environment, especially the social environment. He says that each person has a chosen image of self and position and that tragedy results when the character's environment denies the fulfillment of this self-concept. The hero no longer must be born into the nobility but gains stature in the action of pitting self against cosmos. The tragedy is "the disaster inherent in being torn away from our chosen image of what and who we are in this world." Feelings of displacement and indignity, then, are the driving forces for Miller's modern tragic hero. In his own play *Death of a Salesman*, the character Willy Loman imagines himself as a well-liked, successful, worldly businessman. Tragically, he is really an object of ridicule and contempt, always on the edge of poverty. Such conflicts between ideal self-image and reality occur over and over in the modern world, and the tragic hero, therefore, may be found living among us.

Although the play you are about to read may not meet the criteria of a classical tragedy, some elements of tragedy are evident. For instance, the hero at first seems to be fully aware of himself and the environment in which he operates, more so than any other character, yet his self-deception and the reasons for it are made apparent to the audience.

LOOKING AT THE MODERN HERO

As you read for pleasure *The Drawer Boy* by Michael Healey, take special note of the characters. Who is the hero? the antagonist?—or are there none? Which characters do you respond positively to? Are there any to whom you respond negatively?

Michael Healey   b. 1963

The Drawer Boy

CHARACTERS

MORGAN, *in his fifties*
ANGUS, *also in his fifties*
MILES, *in his twenties*

ACT I

SCENE I

The kitchen of a central Ontario farm house, in the summer of 1972. It is dominated by a large, old oak table; there is a wood stove for heat and a rather modern oven in some ghastly colour. The decorating touches are either from the forties, or are non-existent. There is a back door stage-left, with a small, unheated mud room. Downstage is a yard (with chickens? small vegetable garden?), and off stage-right is the barn.

Lights up. ANGUS *is alone in the kitchen. There is a long moment where he sits, then eventually gets up and starts making sandwiches. Just as he finishes one,* MORGAN *comes into the kitchen.*

ANGUS. Morgan! Hello!

MORGAN *takes the sandwich, eats a couple of bites, and then leaves, taking the sandwich.* ANGUS *starts to make another sandwich. Meanwhile,* MILES *wanders into the yard. He looks at the farmhouse, leaves, then comes back and knocks on the door.* ANGUS *opens the door.*

ANGUS. Hello!

MILES. Good morning, sir. My name's—

ANGUS. Hey! Who're you?

MILES. I'm . . . My name's Miles.

ANGUS. Miles! Hello!

MILES. Hi. I'm from Toronto.

ANGUS. Oh. That's too bad.

MILES. Yes. Uh, I'm here with a group of actors. We're making up a play about farmers.

ANGUS. Oh.

MILES. Yes. I was wondering—could I help out here in any way? We want to spend time with—

ANGUS. We're farmers.

MILES. I . . . Yes. Could you use some help around the farm for the next couple of weeks? Free of charge. I just need a place to stay and the chance to watch you.

ANGUS. Watch me.

MILES. Uh, yes.

ANGUS. Watch me what?

MILES. Well, whatever you do all day. As a farmer.

ANGUS. As a farmer.

MILES. Yes.

ANGUS. I better ask Morgan.

MILES. Okay.

ANGUS. Okay.

> ANGUS *goes inside.* MILES *waits.* ANGUS *heads across the room. He notices the sandwiches and this stops him. He returns to the counter and continues making sandwiches. As he finishes one,* MORGAN *comes in and takes it.*

ANGUS. Morgan! Hello!

MORGAN. Angus. Did I hear you talking?

ANGUS. Talking?

MORGAN. Forget it. Thanks.

> MORGAN *goes.* ANGUS *makes a sandwich and starts to eat.* MILES *waits patiently outside. Slow fade out of lights, as* ANGUS *eats and* MILES *waits.*

SCENE II

> *In the blackout, there is noise off right: a tractor engine being gunned. The following dialogue should be only partially audible over the tractor.*

MORGAN. Alright, now. Alright. Give 'er. Little more . . . little more.

ANGUS. Give 'er. Give 'er. Give 'er.

MILES. Okay. . . .

MORGAN. You got to line up those parts—

MILES. Right.

MORGAN. —so I can connect them.

ANGUS. Give 'er. Give 'er. Give 'er.

MORGAN. That's it, son. That's it. Now back it up into place. You want it to go left, so turn the wheel right, yeah? Back it up. Reverse! REVERSE!

MILES. Right on, okay. How do I—where's the— *(the gears grind terribly)* Oh, shit.

ANGUS. Give 'er. GIVE 'ER! GIVE 'ER!

MILES. Alright. I got it. I got it. Okay! *(the motor dies: there's a pause)* Wow. Sorry.

ANGUS. Uh oh. Oh, shit.

MORGAN. Alright, son. Just—start 'er up again.

> *He starts the engine up again.*

MORGAN. Now. Just back it up slow. Just a few feet's all. Just a few more. . . .

ANGUS. Give 'er!

MILES. Oooookay. Ooooooookaaaaaay. . . .

Suddenly the engine roars, then dies. After the briefest of pauses, the following occurs all at once.

MORGAN. Eeeezuz Rice! Sonnova . . . ! Arrrgh!

MILES. Oh, no. Oh, Jesus.

ANGUS. Oh boy. Oh boy, Morgan. OH BOY. Morgan?

MILES. Are you okay? Sir? Are you—?

MORGAN. Goddamn it.

ANGUS. Oh boy, oh boy, oh boy. Oh my.

Lights have come up by now. ANGUS *runs on, and into the kitchen; as soon as he gets there, he forgets why.* MORGAN *enters, sits on the stoop, examining his wounded arm.* MILES *comes in, writing in a small notebook.*

MORGAN. Farm's a dangerous place. Put that in yer . . . play.

MILES. You okay?

MORGAN. Eyuh.

MILES. *(writing)* I'm really, really sorry.

MORGAN. Thought you said you knew how to drive a tractor.

MILES. Just a sec. *(finishes writing)* I really, really thought I did.

ANGUS *wanders out to the stoop and sees* MORGAN.

ANGUS. Christ! Morgan! What happened to you?

MORGAN. Angus. You were there! He backed the tractor over me.

ANGUS. Who did?

MORGAN. He did.

ANGUS. *(noticing Miles)* Hello!

MILES. Hi.

ANGUS. Morgan. Who's that?

MORGAN. Angus. Get me a wet towel, will yeh?

ANGUS. Sure.

ANGUS *goes inside, to the sink. He pauses, and during the following gets a tablespoon out of a drawer, puts water in it from the tap, and carefully walks it out to the stoop.*

MILES. There's no little "R" on your knob.

MORGAN. 'Scuse me?

MILES. And your clutch goes, I think, abnormally far in. I think I should probably not do anything but watch you guys from now on, and take notes. If I just do that, rather than actually help you guys around the farm, I think it'd be better for everyone.

MORGAN. If you want to stay here, you'll help out. Don't mind you being here and doing your playwriting, but I can't see having a pair of hands around here that don't do nothing.

MILES. Alright, I guess I could. . . .

ANGUS *comes out with the spoonful of water.*

ANGUS. Morgan. Here.

    ANGUS *shoves the spoon in* MORGAN'*s mouth.*

MORGAN. Thanks. A towel?

ANGUS. You bet.

    ANGUS *goes back indoors.*

MILES. I think I might be better off if I stick to the animals. Animals like me.

MORGAN. Uh huh.

MILES. Could you tell me about the milking operation?

MORGAN. Cows are milked twice a day, milk goes to the dairy, dairy gives us money.

MILES. Okay, but what's it like? Do the cows mind being milked continually?

MORGAN. Do they mind?

MILES. Yeah, well, you know—how does a cow feel about getting interfered with twice a day?

    ANGUS *returns with another spoonful of water.*

MORGAN. *(to* ANGUS*)* Thanks. A towel?

ANGUS. You bet.

    ANGUS *goes back inside, and gets another spoonful of water.*

MORGAN. How does the cow feel. About getting milked.

MILES. Yeah. Do they find it traumatic at all?

MORGAN. Well, even though you're from the city, you must know that your cow is the laziest of God's creatures.

MILES. Right.

MORGAN. And I'm sure you realize that we slaughter some of the cows we got. For eatin'.

MILES. Right.

MORGAN. 'Bout one a week we slaughter. Keeps the deep freeze full. Maybe you can help with the next one. Well, the way we choose which cow to kill for meat is related to their milk output. Lowest producer gets the axe. The cows know this, and they produce as much milk as they can, to keep from— you know—being chosen.

MILES. I see.

MORGAN. Otherwise, the dang things would stand around all day.

MILES. Really.

MORGAN. Here's what I suggest you do. Go into the barn, sit down with the cows. At first, they'll seem real casual. But just watch them for a while, and before long you'll see just how much pressure they're labouring under. They're all tense as cats.

MILES. Right. Okay! Thanks. *(he starts to leave, then comes back)* Morgan? I'm sorry I hit you with the tractor.

MORGAN. Think nothing of it. Hardly a day goes by on most farms when something or somebody doesn't get run over. I expect you'll find that out firsthand.

MILES. Thanks.

MILES exits. ANGUS returns with the water, and shoves the spoon in MORGAN's mouth.

MORGAN. Thanks. A towel?

ANGUS. Morgan, I'm tired.

MORGAN. Okay.

ANGUS. Morgan? What happened. I smell bread. Oh boy.

MORGAN goes to ANGUS and feels his head.

MORGAN. Okay, Angus. Get upstairs and get to bed. I'll come up and close the curtains. Go now.

ANGUS. Okay. Oh my. The smell . . . I wonder, I wish . . . I. . . .

MORGAN. Angus? Upstairs now.

SCENE III

Later. MORGAN is in the kitchen, making a sandwich. MILES wanders into the yard. He is staring at his notebook, talking softly.

MILES. Mooo. Mooo—low. Loooow. Lowing. Loooow. Soooooo. Sooooo scared. Don't want to get eaaaten. Muuuust maaaake miiiilk.

MILES practises bovine look and movements. Satisfied, he makes a final notation and goes into the house.

Morgan. You were right. All those cows are absolutely terrified.

MORGAN. Sandwich?

MILES. Sure. What kind?

MORGAN. Spleen. Beef Spleen.

MILES. Sure. Great. A small one. How's your hand?

MORGAN. Numb. Some of the nerves are crushed, I expect.

MILES. Oh, my God. . . .

MORGAN. Well, at least the throbbing's stopped. If it's not right in a week or so, I'll get it removed.

MILES. You'll . . . ?

MORGAN. Government'll pay for a hook or something. How'er things in the barn?

MILES. Uhh, well, I sat there for a long time, watching your cows. One of them, a brown one—

MORGAN. Which brown one?

MILES. Uh. . . .

MORGAN. Bow-legged brown one, or the brown one that smells like vanilla beans?

MILES. The bow-legged one. I guess.

MORGAN. Daisy.

MILES. She kept trying to turn around to look at me. I think she thought I was coming to choose the next one to get—you know. She looked me in the eye, she—Daisy has these eyes that are like brown tennis balls. She stared and stared right at me. For a long time. It felt like we . . . exchanged something. Daisy's not . . . next, is she?

    MORGAN *comes to the table with the sandwiches.*

MORGAN. 'Fraid so.

MILES. Jeez. *(eating)* You said this was beef? Tastes like ham.

MORGAN. That's because we feed the pigs to the cows.

MILES. Really?

MORGAN. Well, not the whole pig.

MILES. *(takes notebook out)* What's it like, being around death and rebirth all the time? To grow things and kill things for a living, year in and year out? You've been here how long?

MORGAN. We bought the place in '42.

MILES. So, for thirty years you've been doing this. Planting, nurturing, nourishing, building up; then harvesting, reaping, destroying, eviscerating.

MORGAN. Uh huh.

MILES. Must be . . . difficult. I mean, you grow wheat and corn out of the dirt, out of literally nothing, then you cut it down and sell it. You raise animals, feed them and house them for years, name them; and then you kill them and eat them.

MORGAN. Uh huh.

MILES. What is that like? How does that make you feel?

MORGAN. Miles, it's an emotional rollercoaster.

MILES. I bet. Is Angus going to have lunch?

MORGAN. Angus is upstairs asleep. He's got one of his headaches.

MILES. Is there something wrong with him? I mean, apart from his being. . . .

MORGAN. Being what?

MILES. Well, uh, you know. . . .

MORGAN. Simple?

MILES. Yeah, I guess.

MORGAN. 'The hell do you mean by that?

MILES. Uuuuhh. . . .

MORGAN. He gets headaches. Says he sees lights flashing, sometimes he smells bread baking. Lasts for a day, then he's fine. Sometimes, just before a headache comes on, he'll get giddy. Excited. Then I know to put him to bed.

MILES. Was he always like this?

MORGAN. Angus got knocked down by the front door of a house, in London in '41, during the bombing. He's got a plate in his skull that keeps the two broken parts of it from rubbing together. Before that, he was just like you or me. We went over together, and came back together. We grew up.

MILES. And you've taken care of him since the war?

MORGAN. He doesn't need much taking care of. Angus's no invalid. I show him how to do things, remind him. He can run the tractor, he can use the stove. Knits. Does the accounts. You should see him with a bunch of figures. Only thing that makes Angus different is he can't remember from one minute to the next. He only knows right now. He won't remember you.

MILES. Ever?

MORGAN. Nope. You'll have to tell him who you are, what you're doing here, probably every morning.

MILES. What do the doctors say?

MORGAN. They say he's normal, for someone who's had done to him what he's had.

MILES. Will he ever—I mean, is he. . . .

MORGAN. Angus's fine. He stays here, does what I've taught him—we're just fine.

MILES. You've lived here alone since the war?

MORGAN. Yup. We bought this land right after. Finish up. Plenty to do this afternoon.

MILES. *(wolfing sandwich and rising)* Right. Nothing dangerous, I hope.

MORGAN. Nah. Ever gutted anything?

MILES. You mean—what—like, cut the guts out of something?

MORGAN. Uh huh. Do you know how to use a chainsaw?

MILES. I, uhh. *(remembers the tractor)* No. No sir, I don't.

MORGAN. Nothing to it. Just put on the welder's mask and the raincoat, and hold on tight when things get slippery.

MILES. Think it's a good idea? After the tractor?

MORGAN. Probably not. But there'll be no mollycoddling on this farm while there's work to do. Plus, I'll stand well back.

MILES. They're not going to believe this at rehearsal.

ANGUS *enters, disoriented and in pain. The light hurts him. He's looking for something.*

ANGUS. Morgan? Hello. The car got scratched. Right?

MORGAN. You need to be lying down. You know, Angus.

ANGUS. Right. *(pointing to* MILES*)* Who'r . . . you?

MILES. My name's Miles. I'm staying here with you while I put on a play about farmers.

ANGUS. Tall. You look like . . . standing there, beside the . . . the girl.

MORGAN. (*to* MILES) You go ahead, meet you in the barn.

MILES. Sure.

MILES *exits*.

MORGAN. Angus. Come now. Come up.

ANGUS. (*softly, as* MORGAN *leads him out*) You bet.

SCENE IV

Lights up. ANGUS *enters the kitchen. He's looking for something, and begins his search by examining a wall. Eventually he starts to look around, opening cupboard doors and looking under things. He's on his hands and knees when* MILES *limps into the farm house, his hands and thighs raw from moving hay bales. He has some trouble getting the door open.*

MILES. Wow. Ow, Jeez.

ANGUS. Hullo. Hey. Get outta here.

MILES. Hello, Angus. My name is Miles and I'm staying with you and Morgan to learn about farming so I can write a play about it.

ANGUS. (*throws a hand up in the air*) Hello, Miles. Okay.

MILES *limps to the sink, starts to tend to his wounds.*

ANGUS. Are yuh hurt? Yuh want some Freshie?

MILES. I was just out helping Morgan with the hay bales. I musta hauled six hundred of the damn things off the wagon and on to the . . . escalator thing. . . .

ANGUS. The what?

MILES. The—you know—the thing that takes the bales up to the top of the barn.

ANGUS. Oh yeah, that thing's called the . . . uh.

ANGUS *goes to the sink during the following, gets* MILES *a spoonful of water.*

MILES. The only way to do that's to drag them off the wagon and sorta throw the bale onto the escalator using your leg. Look at my leg.

ANGUS. It's called the, uh. . . .

MILES. Morgan looks at me and says: "Folks wear long pants around a farm." I bet this is infected. (ANGUS *shoves the water into* MILES' *mouth*) Thanks.

ANGUS. Uh huh. Help yourself.

MILES. Then I go up into the barn to stack the bales, and that's even worse, 'cause there's no air up there—lots of dust, but no air—and I have to pick the damn things up, lift them over my head, and pile them up.

ANGUS. Hey. We got Freshie.

MILES. I wrestled in high school. I've done hard things, Angus. I was a hedgehog in a show last year about a group of dead animals. That show was three hours long. *I didn't move.* I've done hard things. And I wasn't about to quit, not with Morgan watching. I just picked them up, (*demonstrating*) one by one, hauled them over to the side of the barn, built a wall of hay. Look at my hands. Splinters inside of exploded blisters. "The twine, city boy, pick them up by the twine!" For God's sake. I'm not supposed to be doing this. I'm supposed to be writing a play.

ANGUS. Was it hay or straw you were loadin'?

MILES. I dunno. What's the difference?

ANGUS. Between hay and straw?

MILES. Yeah.

ANGUS. Hmmmmm. Nope. Don't know. Wouldn't eat no straw, though.

MILES. Do you think that Morgan's still upset with me over the thing with the tractor?

ANGUS. Thing with the. . . ?

MILES. Running him over with the tractor. I ran him down two mornings ago, remember?

ANGUS. Uuuhhhh. Nope. Tractor, eh?

MILES. Yes. Never mind.

ANGUS. Someone got hit by the tractor?

MILES. Yes, it's okay, Angus. Forget it.

ANGUS. You bet.

MILES. *(points to fridge)* Angus, what's that called?

ANGUS. That's the uuuhhh. Nope.

MILES. Is that the refrigerator?

ANGUS. Sure it is.

MILES. Or the stove?

ANGUS. Morgan. We better ask Morgan that.

MILES. It's okay. *(points to table)* That's the chair, right?

ANGUS. Chair.

MILES. Angus. What's my name?

ANGUS. Don't you know?

MILES. Do you?

ANGUS. Ha ha.

MILES. Okay.

ANGUS. Okay then.

MILES. My name's Miles.

ANGUS. Hello, Miles, okay.

MILES. Angus? Twelve, fifty-six, one-oh-seven, twelve again, and six seventy-nine.

ANGUS. Uh huh.

MILES. What's my name?

ANGUS. Oh. Uuuuhhh. Ha ha.

MILES. Okay, Angus. What about those numbers I said. Can you add them up?

ANGUS. Eight hundred, sixty-six.

MILES. Right! I think that's right. . . .

ANGUS. Oh, yes.

MILES. How old are you?

ANGUS. 'Bout your age.

MILES. Oh yeah? Is Morgan our age, too?

ANGUS. Naw. He's an old feller.

MILES. Did you ever fight in the war?

ANGUS. Yes, I did. Sure. Prince's Pats. Went to France, went to England. With Morgan.

MILES. What did you have for breakfast this morning?

ANGUS. Ha ha. Sure.

MILES. And what's my name?

> ANGUS *looks at* MILES. *This is starting to upset him.*

MILES. My name's Miles. Angus. Tell me about your head.

ANGUS. Hurts . . . sometimes . . . always. . . .

MILES. How'd you hurt it? Do you know?

ANGUS. Morgan says . . . they were waiting for . . . hey. What's your name?

MILES. You tell me.

ANGUS. Don't know. Didn't tell me.

MILES. Angus—

ANGUS. Me too! My name's Angus too! Ha ha ha!

MILES. No, Angus. Listen. Your head. In London, did you get hit by a—

ANGUS. Noo, no. No.

MILES. In the bombing—by a, a front door.

ANGUS. Front . . . ? No no no no. I did not.

MILES. Is that what happened, or do you just not remember? Morgan said.

ANGUS. Morgan knows. He knows. He tells me. I . . . the drawer boy. The tall girls. You see . . . Morgan . . . he knows. He knows. He . . . oh boy. (ANGUS *holds his head and starts to weep*) Ohhh boy. . . .

MILES. Angus. What is it? Are you— *(runs to the door)* Morgan! Morgan! Come quick! Angus, I'm sorry. . . . Morgan!

> MORGAN *enters.*

MORGAN. Jesus. Alright now, Angus. Alright.

> MORGAN *goes to the sink and gets a tablespoon of water.*

ANGUS. Morgan? Hello. How did I get hurt?

> MORGAN *shoves the spoon into* ANGUS' *mouth.* ANGUS *calms down somewhat.*

Thanks. Okay. But.

MORGAN. Hush now.

ANGUS. Was it the front door? Was it?

MORGAN. Hush.

ANGUS. He says. . . .

MORGAN. *(suddenly)* Angus! Make me a sandwich.

ANGUS. Eyuh.

> ANGUS *gets up, goes to the fridge, and gets out sandwich materials. He is almost instantaneously distracted by this task, and stops crying.*

MORGAN. 'The hell have you been doing?

MILES. I didn't mean to upset him. I asked him a few questions about the war. His accident. . . .

MORGAN. I thought you were here to find out *about farming.*

MILES. Yes, I—

MORGAN. You don't know what you're doing, asking him about that. I told you, his memory's faulty. You upset him, he spends the day in bed, and I have to do everything by myself. You got questions, ask me. I said I'd tell you everything you need to know about farming. Stick to the cows and the chickens. If you can't do that, you'd better leave. Can you do that?

MILES. Yes.

MORGAN. Miles? You better.

MILES. Yes, sir. I'm sorry. *(to* ANGUS*)* Angus? I'm sorry I . . . I'm sorry about what just happened.

> ANGUS *has no idea what* MILES *is talking about.*

ANGUS. Oh. Well, uh . . . no, no. That's fine. Hey! Who wants Freshie?

SCENE V

> *Night.* MILES *and* MORGAN *are seated at the table. Dinner is over.* ANGUS *has finished washing up and starts to make bread. He gets out the ingredients and makes dough throughout the scene.* MILES *makes notes furiously through the following.*

MORGAN. *(to* MILES*)* You know what a steak costs? Per pound?

ANGUS. Dollar forty-seven.

MILES. Dollar forty-seven?

MORGAN. One dollar forty-seven cents. People scream over a price like that. Drop down dead in the meat aisle when they see that price, but let me tell you something: if the price of that steak had increased in the last ten years as much as the price of a postage stamp, that steak would be a dollar fifty-seven per pound.

ANGUS. Eight point oh-two percent.

MORGAN. If that steak had gone up like the price of a newspaper, it'd cost a dollar seventy-five.

ANGUS. Ten point three percent.

MILES. Per pound.

MORGAN. Per pound. If that pound of steak had gone up like wages have in the last ten years, it'd cost two-oh-eight a pound.

ANGUS. Thirty-nine percent.

MORGAN. And if it'd gone up like the income tax has, that steak would be three-eighty a pound.

ANGUS. Fifty-eight point three three three three three. Percent.

MORGAN. And wouldn't that make people scream blue murder in the grocery store. We get nothing for what we do. An egg costs nine cents in the store, there's practically an armed uprising in the city over how expensive an egg is. Know how much it costs me to produce that egg? Nine point one three cents. Care to guess what my profit margin is on that egg?

ANGUS. Negative eighteen point seven-two cents per gross of eggs.

MORGAN. And if I drop one or two, it gets even worse.

MILES. How can you afford to run a losing business, year in, year out?

MORGAN. I make a little on the milk, and that almost evens things out with the eggs. The rest of the debt I put over to next year, until the year when my crops finally go for what they're actually worth. That year, of course, will never come. Government gets wind of that, they'll start doin' business that way. Then, God help us all.

Public complains about us, they believe all us farmers are making a killing. Politicians complain about us, tired of giving us subsidies that just get us to next year—maybe. Kids are leaving the farms, moving to Toronto; nobody wants to do this anymore. Soon nobody will.

ANGUS. Morgan? Why're you shouting?

MORGAN. Farms in a strip from Windsor to Montreal provide forty percent of the food for the country, and soon they'll all just stop. You'll get your food imported from God knows where, then see how much a pound of steak goes for. You go to university?

MILES. Yeah.

MORGAN. What'd you study?

MILES. English and drama. And political science, and geology, and law, and French. Phys Ed and a little Latin.

MORGAN. Uh huh. Graduate?

MILES. Well, I was living at this place called Rochdale College, and we really didn't believe that the point was to graduate; we thought that we should be able to—

MORGAN. How big a student-loan debt didja run up?

MILES. That's a little personal, Morgan, I—

MORGAN. More than two thousand dollars?

MILES. Oh, yeah.

MORGAN. More than three?

MILES. Well, I sort of missed a term in there—a whole year, really, once the customs thing got cleared up—never mind—so, actually I went for five years, on and off. So it wound up being around thirty-six hundred dollars. All together.

MORGAN. The government gave you more than I paid myself for the last four years.

ANGUS. 1968: eight sixty-one. 1969: nine hundred and five. 1970: seven hundred, seventy-four. And 1971: seven hundred and ninety.

MORGAN. Don't you write that down. I make about the same as everyone else out here, but nobody needs to hear the exact figures from your stage.

MILES. Can I use the figures about the pound of steak?

MORGAN. Wish you would.

MILES. This is going to blow people's minds in rehearsal. You know, we all just go to the store, buy some fruit or a steak, and never think about where it comes from. Did you ever think of starting up a communal farm?

MORGAN. Eh?

MILES. Have you ever studied the Soviet model? They've been farming communally for decades in Russia, and the results are incredible.

ANGUS. Goddamn communists.

MILES. Productivity is up, the people all have enough to eat, money's not a—

ANGUS. *Goddamn communists.*

MILES. —worry. Anybody who looks at it sees it's the wave of the future. Who are your neighbours to the north?

MORGAN. Lobbs. Don and Alison Lobb.

MILES. What if the fence came down between your two places. What if you and the Lobbs agreed—

ANGUS. *Goddamn communists.*

MILES. —agreed that from now on you'd both work the fields, take turns, maybe even sell one of the tractors—you'd only need the one, one barn for all the animals, an equal division of labour, materials, and profits—

ANGUS. GOD. DAMN. COMMUNISTS!

MORGAN. Angus! Why're *you* shouting?

ANGUS. Was I?

MORGAN. How's that bread corning?

ANGUS *puts the bread in the oven.*

ANGUS. Done!

During the following, ANGUS *goes outside and stands in the yard. He stares up at the stars and becomes transfixed.*

MORGAN. Good. Miles. Let me ask you a question. Now, your answer to this question may have a direct bearing on where you sleep tonight, on how comfortable a place it is you're sleeping in. A place where the humans normally sleep, or a place where furred and feathered animals generally lay their heads. A place that smells a bit. Miles? How would you describe yourself, politically?

MILES. *(after a pause)* Oh. Well, I'm an actor. We don't have politics.

MORGAN. I think that's best. Angus. Don't you let that bread burn.

ANGUS. Bread?

MORGAN. He's ruined more bread. . . . Where will you be putting on this play of yours?

MILES. Ray Bird is lending us his barn for the first show. Eventually, we hope to do it all over the county. Hope you'll come and see it, both of you. In fact, we're inviting some people to a rehearsal day after tomorrow, just so they can tell us if we're on the right track. Maybe you'd come to that?

MORGAN. Prob'ly will, seeing as how you're going to give your rendition of our cow Daisy.

MILES. Well, maybe not. I did the monologue for the others in the show—you know, "Have to make milk, don't want to get eaten"—and nobody believed it. I couldn't convince anybody that cows are petrified all the time. They want to do the stereotypical cow—you know, placid, dumb, cud-chewing. Bourgeois theatrical cow; that cow that we've seen onstage for years and years. And which of course I now know is a lie. I said, if you want to do a scene about a cow that's a lie, we could have stayed in Toronto and made it up out of our heads. I said I wasn't going to insult Daisy by portraying her without exploring her pain, her anxiety. Her reality. The director said okay, fair enough. And then he cut the scene.

MORGAN. Tough break.

MILES. Yeah. So far they aren't using anything I've brought to rehearsal. Remember the day we piled up all those hay bales? I made up a dance, the dance of the hay-bale stacker. It got cut too.

MORGAN. *(to* MILES*)* Lemme ask you something. *(goes to the door)* Lie down, Angus.

ANGUS. Morgan. Hello.

MORGAN. Lie down if you want to look at them stars. You'll hurt your neck again.

ANGUS. Okay, sure.

   ANGUS *lies down.*

MORGAN. *(to* MILES*)* What happens if none of the . . . things you make up get put in the show?

MILES. Jeez. I don't know. I guess they'd probably have to kick me out of the collective.

MORGAN. So, if you don't produce, you die—is that it?

MILES. . . . I guess so.

MORGAN. Well, there you go. You have something in common with my cows there.

MILES. You're right.

MORGAN. You got that in common with me, too. I don't produce, I go as sure as you or the cows do.

MILES. Right on. That's good. Mind if I use that?

MORGAN. Guess not.

MILES. Thanks. Think I'll take this upstairs and try to put it into some kind of shape for rehearsal tomorrow.

MORGAN. Right. You'd better get some sleep. We're rotating the crops tomorrow.

MILES. Is that right? That a big job?

MORGAN. Uh huh. We have to dig up all the hay growing on the east side of the field, the hay that gets all the morning sun, and move it to the west side, to get the afternoon sun. Big job. And we have to do it in the dark. Set your alarm for three.

MILES. Three? A.M.??

MORGAN. That's right. And I don't want to have to call you.

MILES. I'll be ready.

MORGAN. See that you are.

MILES. Yes, sir.

    MILES *exits.* MORGAN *goes outside and sits on the back step. Silence, as he looks at the sky and at* ANGUS.

MORGAN. Angus? Bread in the oven.

ANGUS. Uh huh.

MORGAN. Don't forget.

ANGUS. Aww.

MORGAN. How many?

ANGUS. Nineteen thousand, four hundred and forty-four. Total.

MORGAN. That's a lot.

    Silence.

ANGUS. Tell it.

MORGAN. Naw. . . . Not tonight, Angus.

ANGUS. Sure, tonight. You never tell it.

MORGAN. I tell it daily, you just don't. . . . Alright. Just . . . listen.

    A couple of boys played shinney and went to school and grew up. One drew pictures of a cabin—fine pictures of the inside and the outside—until finally they built the cabin together. Stole nails, played hookey until it was done.

    They finished school. One just barely. The other finished easily, but never got his diploma because he wouldn't give back the poetry book. That one almost went off to school, to keep drawing. The other one never would of. He was all set to work for his father, to start in on the farm. And then they both got called up, both went off to Europe. No school for the one, no farm for the other. They managed to stick together.

MILES *comes into the kitchen to retrieve his pen, and overhears the following.*

They fired their guns straight up in the air, and yelled to each other the louder things got. When it got so loud they couldn't hear, they sang. They had three boots between them.

In England they met two girls, one tall and one taller. The taller one liked the drawer; the tall one, the farmer. They talked, they made plans. The girls talked together, the boys talked together.

The tall girl and the farmer would talk all night. The taller girl and the drawer would walk and talk all night. One girl would talk to the other boy about the boy she liked; so would the other girl to the other boy about the first boy.

Also, they talked in threes. Drawer boy, two tall girls; farmer boy, two tall girls; tall girl and two boys; taller girl and two boys. They talked to themselves, too.

The plans they made were like something the one boy would draw: Inside and out, all the details mixed, and when they were done talking, all four got ready to come home.

One night, in an air raid, the drawer boy was outside. The tall English girls and his friend were together and safe, in the butler's pantry of a large and empty house. They lit candles and made jokes about where the other one might be.

Well, he was down the street, looking at another large house. Probably staring at the wrought iron, or memorizing the slope of the roof. The front door of the house flew off when the shell hit, and the drawer boy watched it come for him.

A doctor took two inches of copper plate out of the boy's head, from the front-door door-knocker. The doctor put in twenty-six millimeters of stainless steel. Before the doctor could close up the wound, the boy's memory escaped.

His hair grew back and the boy's three friends slowly put his memory back, too. One day he woke up and remembered right and left, and up and down. One day he woke up and remembered he loved the taller English girl. They got ready to go home again, talked about their plans again. They showed the drawer boy pictures he made of the house all four would live in, pictures he had made before the front door came. He could not remember making the pictures, but he agreed to the plan: They would come home. There would be a double wedding. There was money enough for one piece of land. The house would be built on a farm they would share, and it would be two houses joined. Two families would be started, life would begin for the four friends.

They came home. There was a double wedding. The drawer boy recited a poem from the stolen book. They bought one piece of land. They started to build the house. They bought a car. They bought an old black car.

ANGUS. Right.

MORGAN. The taller English girl loved to drive, and one day she and the tall English girl went in the old black car to a berry bush the farmer boy had shown them. Coming home, there were two pails of raspberries between them on the seats. They knew what side of the road to be on. They did. An old army transport came over the hill on their side, coming toward them;

the transport was passing a horse. The taller English girl turned, turned her side of the old black car into the transport, because she knew they could not miss. Her side of the old car was just ruined. Not a scratch on the tall girl's side. But the tall girl died too.

ANGUS. Right. My Sally. My . . . Sally. Your?

MORGAN. My Frances. Then the two tall English girls went to a hill, both in the same carriage, pulled by a horse. The hill is the highest point in the county. That's where they are now. And then, it was the two friends again. And the drawer makes bread and adds rows of numbers in his head, and the farmer farms and tends to the place on the hill and keeps their memories safe, like a pail of raspberries between them.

ANGUS. Right. Morgan. I smell bread.

MORGAN. You do? How do you feel? How's your head?

ANGUS. No. I smell bread.

MORGAN. *(jumping up)* Jesus.

MORGAN runs into the kitchen to rescue the bread. MILES escapes without being seen.

MORGAN. *(pulling the burnt bread out of oven)* Jesus! Angus! Goddamn it!

ANGUS. Nineteen thousand, four hundred and forty . . . five.

SCENE VI

Late that night. MILES comes into the kitchen. He pulls out his notebook.

MILES. Two friends built a cabin with nails they stole from. . . . Two friends grew up together; one was a farmer, one drew pictures. They made plans, they went to school. They went off to war. They shot their guns in the air and sang war songs. They had three boots between them. They met two English girls, one tall and one taller.

ANGUS enters in his pyjamas. He's searching for something. As MILES watches, he goes carefully through the kitchen, beginning again with the blank space on the wall. Eventually, he sees MILES.

ANGUS. Hey! Who are you??

MILES. My name's Miles. I'm staying with you and Morgan to learn about farming so I can write a play about it.

ANGUS. *(waves)* Okay. Hello, Miles.

ANGUS sits down at the table. He looks at MILES.

MILES. Did you come down for something? It's a couple of hours until we have to rotate the crops.

ANGUS. Eh?

MILES. Were you looking for something?

ANGUS. Sure.

MILES. What?

ANGUS. No idea.

MILES. . . . Should you go to bed then?

ANGUS. You bet.

> ANGUS *gets up, hesitates, then heads outside.* MILES *follows, and watches as* ANGUS *stands, looking at the stars.*

MILES. Angus?

ANGUS. You bet.

MILES. Nice night.

ANGUS. That's right. *(silence)* You organize it into sections. The whole sky. It's just pieces. No bigger than you. Then you count it. *(silence, then* ANGUS *turns to* MILES*)* See?

MILES. Uh huh.

> ANGUS *goes inside. He repeats exactly the same moves from earlier, looking for something.* MILES *watches him for a while.*

MILES. Can I help you find it?

ANGUS. Jeez. I couldn't tell ya. You hungry?

MILES. Not really.

ANGUS. Me neither.

> ANGUS *leaves. After a moment,* MILES *returns to his notebook.*

SCENE VII

An afternoon, a couple of days later. MORGAN *and* ANGUS *enter,* ANGUS *is excited.*

ANGUS. That was exactly right, wasn't it? The tractor? Them two girls were the tires, and the one fella on the other's shoulders, and he was driving the fella and the two girls, because they were the tractor. And telling about the tractor breaking down when the harvest hasta come in, and how you gotta be awake when you go over hills and the like. The fella sitting on top of the fella's shoulders, talking away to us while he's driving the tractor. That was exactly right.

MORGAN. Uh huh.

ANGUS. And that girl who came out and said she was . . . was. . . .

MORGAN. Alison Lobb.

ANGUS. That's right. D'you know for a long while there I thought she was Alison Lobb? I thought, good Lord, Alison Lobb's lost her senses and gone up there on the stage and was talking to us. It wasn't, you know. That was an actress. Acting.

MORGAN. I know.

ANGUS. *I laughed.* And then . . . Miles comes out and starts with that story about the two tall English girls, and the war and all, in that funny voice, and all of a sudden I realized—it's you! He's pretending to be you and that's why I knew the story just before he said each word. He told it just the way you do! I remembered all of it as he said it, I could have said it along with him. . . . Hey! Shit! That other fella! The simple-looking fella he was telling the story to! That was me! The one fella was you and the other one was supposed to be me! Jesus, that was something. That was us.

MORGAN. That was us.

ANGUS. He got us, didn't he? Miles. He got us.

MORGAN. He did.

ANGUS. He did. I'll never forget that. I can't wait until everyone—

MORGAN. Angus? Want a sandwich?

ANGUS. Sure. *(gets sandwich materials out of fridge, starts to make two)* I'll tell yuh, Morgan, that was just . . . I never seen. . . .

MORGAN. Angus? How many stars you count last night?

ANGUS. Six-hundred and eighteen I never counted before. One thousand and seventy-nine I already did.

MORGAN. Got a new total?

ANGUS. Sure. Twenty-two thousand, seven-hundred and fifty-seven. New total.

MORGAN. Good. What did we do today?

ANGUS. Aaww. We just got back.

MORGAN. From where.

ANGUS. From . . . town?

MORGAN. What on earth were we doing in town?

ANGUS. Well, Morgan, I don't know. We were . . . I don't . . . I'm hungry, though. Sandwich?

MORGAN. Okay.

MORGAN *sees* MILES *coming into the yard, and goes out to intercept him.*

MILES. What'd you think of the rehearsal? A lot of it's pretty rough, but I thought some of it went—

MORGAN. You get out of here.

MILES. . . . I'm sorry?

MORGAN. You heard. Get out. You can't stay here.

MILES. Morgan, hold it. You're upset I used that story and didn't tell you—I wanted that to be a surprise.

MORGAN. It was. You put that in your play and I'll see to it you never put it on.

MILES. Look, if I didn't get the story exactly right, it's because I only heard it once. You can give me the details, we can work on it together. It's important. We're here to get your history and give it back to you.

MORGAN. It ain't—you can't use that. It's private between Angus and me, and I don't want people to hear it.

MILES. Everyone around here must know the story already. I just want to tell it to them in the play, so they can see how important it is.

MORGAN. Just get out of here. You can't stay. You lied.

MILES. What does Angus say about it?

MORGAN. Angus's already forgotten it, thank God. You oughta be ashamed, coming here, stealing. . . .

MILES. Morgan, listen to me. It's the only thing I've got in the show right now. If I cut this scene—which the director loves, by the way—I'm out of the show. Produce or die, remember?

ANGUS *comes outside, sees* MILES.

ANGUS. Hey!!!

MILES. Hello, Angus. My name's—

ANGUS. Miles! We saw you! You were Morgan and that other fella was me! You got us!

MILES. *(pause)* That's right. You remember the play?

MORGAN. You know who that is?

ANGUS. Sure. You're Miles, and you're staying with Morgan and me while you learn about farming and write that play! You were Morgan. You told about us. God! I'll never forget it. Come in and have a sandwich, Miles.

MILES. *(to* MORGAN*)* Has he ever . . . ?

MORGAN. Never recognized anyone but me.

ANGUS. You were him. You sounded just like Morgan. Come in and have a sandwich.

MORGAN. He has to go now. He's gonna get his things and leave.

ANGUS. Why?

MILES. I don't know, exactly.

ANGUS. Well, that's just silly. You can't go. Just got here.

MORGAN. He's leaving.

ANGUS. Why?

MILES. Because of what I did on stage.

ANGUS. Whatareyuh . . . ?

MILES. Your story. About the two tall English girls. Morgan says I can't use it.

ANGUS. Oh. Well. Shit. That's not a story. That's us. You have to use that.

ANGUS *goes back inside.* MILES *and* MORGAN *stare at each other.*

He has to use that. He's here because he's. . . . Miles! Get in here! 'Kinda sandwich you want?

MILES *goes inside and sits with* ANGUS.

End of Act One.

ACT II

SCENE I

The next day. MILES *sits on the ground outdoors, talking to* ANGUS. *There are two piles of gravel beside him: a big pile and a little pile. He takes a stone from the big pile, dunks it in a bucket of soapy water, scrubs it with a vegetable brush, and dries it carefully with a small towel. Then he puts it onto the small pile.* ANGUS *sits on the back step, listening.*

MILES. . . . and I have these two friends. From university. They're funny. They talk alike, and they sort of dress alike, and they're always together. And because I'm sad, my stepfather calls them up and says, "He mopes around wearing black all day, come and visit and cheer him up"—and so they do. Except what my stepfather really wants them to do is spy on me, in case I get it into my head that I want to kill him.

ANGUS. Why would you . . . ?

MILES. Because, like I said, he killed my father and married my mum, and my father told me to. Sort of. His ghost sort of told me to.

ANGUS. Right.

MILES. Their names are Rosencrantz and Guildenstern.

ANGUS. You're kidding.

MILES. I am not.

ANGUS. Hee hee.

MILES. So they show up, and I know right off that they're here to spy on me for my stepfather. So I put on an antic disposition. I pretend to go mad. I threaten them, and call them names, and kick them out. Except you start to wonder—am I acting mad, or am I really going mad? I'm all sad and angry, I keep hearing voices, and I can't decide what to do, so I do nothing, and that makes me even worse. I start treating my girlfriend really badly. I yell at her and call her bad names. I just treat her terribly, until she goes mad for sure and drowns herself in a pond.

ANGUS. Miles. You went mad.

MILES. And then I yell at my mother. And—Angus, you aren't baking, are you?

ANGUS. Who knows. You yelled at your mum?

MILES. And then I kill this nice old guy who talked all the time. I stabbed him through the arras.

ANGUS. The arras. Ouch. Were you mad then? Or just pretending?

MILES. Well, you still weren't sure. You still couldn't tell.

ANGUS. But—could you?

MILES. I. . . . Yes. I think I was a little mad then. I think stabbing a guy makes you go even more mad.

ANGUS. Oh, I know.

MILES. Anyway, by the time I finish talking to my mum and stabbing the old guy, I decide I have to kill my stepfather.

ANGUS. 'Cause of hearing your dad's voice?

MILES. Yes.

ANGUS. But, Miles! What if the voice in your head is just some voice? You can't go killing people because of that.

MILES. That's right. . . .

ANGUS. I mean—Jesus!—what if everybody acted that way?

MILES. I know.

ANGUS. Killing people just 'cause of something they heard in their head once or twice.

MILES. I know.

ANGUS. Everybody did that, there'd be no one left. S'not right.

MILES. You're right. That's what I'm so worried about. That's why I went mad.

MORGAN comes in from the barn, and speaks to MILES as he passes.

MORGAN. Hurry up. I'll need that gravel by after lunch.

ANGUS. Morgan! Hello.

MORGAN goes inside.

ANGUS. That's a tough job you've got.

MILES. Yeah, the actor's life's a difficult one.

ANGUS. No. The.... *(points at what MILES is doing)*

MILES. Have you ever done this?

ANGUS. Well, I guess I must of, some time. Tough job. So ... what ... where ... Oh! Your stepfather. Didja kill him?

MILES. Well, not right away. My girlfriend's brother comes home. He's mad at me because she killed herself, so we have a couple of sword fights, everybody takes some drugs sort of by accident, and then everybody dies.

ANGUS. Everybody dies by accident?

MILES. Sort of.

ANGUS. Helluvan accident.

MILES. And then I die too.

ANGUS. I should hope so. Did people clap?

MILES. Oh, yeah. People loved it. The people that saw it. The critics hated it.

ANGUS. Why?

MILES. I don't know. They said I was too Canadian.

ANGUS. Well, that makes sense.

MORGAN comes back outside with a dessert fork.

ANGUS. Morgan. Hello. He went mad.

MORGAN. *(to MILES)* Here. Know what this is? This is a short-handled insilage fork. After the gravel's washed, I want you to muck out the cow stalls. Using this. Cows have been eating corn lately, and not all of it gets digested. You use this to retrieve the undigested corn and put it into a bucket. We feed the chickens that fortified corn. You understand me?

MILES. Yes. *(MORGAN exits)* He must think I'm so stupid.

ANGUS. Oh, he does.

MILES. As if I'd go through all the cow crap with this. With a stupid little fork.

ANGUS. It's crazy.

MILES. It sure is.

ANGUS. I'll get you a spoon. Tell me another.

MILES. Let's see. Did one about a family from out around here, called the Donnellys. Bad bunch. They were so nasty to so many people, that one night a mob came and burned down their house.

ANGUS. Jeez. Who made that up? That Shakespeare?

MILES. No, a Canadian wrote it, but it's not made up. It's a true story. It really happened.

ANGUS. Whadda ya mean! It was on stage, wasn't it? It was a play.

MILES. It was a play from a true story. Like the one that we're making up now. It's a play about farmers, but the stories we tell in it are true ones. Like the story I heard Morgan tell you.

ANGUS. The two tall English girls.

MILES. Right.

ANGUS. Tell it.

MILES. I don't think so, Angus.

ANGUS. Go on.

MILES. No, I don't think Morgan would like it.

ANGUS. 'Course he would. Why wouldn't he?

MILES. Well, because it's his story. His and yours. And he should tell it to you, not me.

ANGUS. Okay.

MILES. Sorry.

ANGUS. No. *(pause)* What if you pretended you were him. You be Morgan, and I'll pretend I'm Angus, and you tell it that way.

MILES. I can't do that.

ANGUS. Can too.

MILES. No, I can't.

ANGUS. Sure, just pretend you're Morgan sitting there washing rocks, and you think to yourself, "Geez, I'd better tell Angus that there tall-girl story before I do another thing." And then say "Angus," and I'll say "What?," and you say the story of the two English tall-girls now hurry up.

MILES. No, look, I can't. It's Morgan's story to tell. It's not right that I start telling it to you.

ANGUS. Oh. Unless you're up on stage telling everybody, right?

MILES. Uhh. Right.

ANGUS. Oh.

MILES. Right, so. . . .

ANGUS. It'd be okay for me, though? To tell it?

MILES. Of course. Yes. I'd love to hear it.

ANGUS. Okay. I'll pretend to be you pretending to be Morgan telling the story. *(he looks around)* Now, would I be on a stage, or. . . .

MILES. No. You're just sitting on the back step.

ANGUS. Oh. Right. Okay then. *(he contorts himself, raises his voice an octave)* Now I'm you. *(he hunches over, drops his voice two octaves)* And now I'm you being Morgan. Any good?

MILES. Perfect.

ANGUS. Perfect. *(pause)* How's it start?

MILES. *(pulls out his notebook)* Once there were two friends. . . .

ANGUS. Once there were two friends. . . .

> As MILES *leads* ANGUS *through the story,* MILES *falls into his "Morgan" persona, until there are two slightly grotesque "Morgans" telling the story back and forth.*

MILES. Two boys. They played hockey together, they did everything together.

ANGUS. Boys who played hockey. And everything.

MILES. The one boy drew pictures.

ANGUS. The one boy drew pictures. The drawer boy.

MILES. Yes. He drew pictures of a cabin. Inside and out, lots of pictures. Then they built the cabin.

ANGUS. Drawer boy drew a cabin, inside and out. Then they stole nails, and played hookey, and built the cabin.

MILES. And then they went off to war together.

ANGUS. And then they went off to war together.

MILES. They fought together, and hid together, and sang when it was loudest. They had three boots between them.

ANGUS. They fired up in the air together, and hid, and sang together when it got too loud, and . . . three boots.

MILES. In England they met two girls. . . .

ANGUS. One tall and one taller.

MILES. The taller one liked the drawer.

ANGUS. And the tall one liked Morgan. Liked me.

MILES. The tall girl and the farmer would talk all night; the taller girl and the drawer would walk all night and talk. One girl would talk to the other boy about the boy she liked, so would the other girl to the other boy. . . .

ANGUS. They talked. . . .

MILES. When they were done talking, their plans were as complete as something the boy would draw.

ANGUS. When they were done talking, they had a picture of the next thing they would make together, the four of them. They came home and had a double wedding. . . .

MILES. No, Angus. Next is the air raid. The front door flying. Remember?

ANGUS. Uh huh. But. I don't want to.

MILES. Okay.

ANGUS. They went home. There was a double wedding, he said the stolen poem. They started the house, the two houses joined.

MILES. Right.

ANGUS. Where?

MILES. Where what.

ANGUS. Where's the houses joined and separate?

MILES. I don't know.

ANGUS. He said—you said, "They started to build the house."

MILES. You're right.

ANGUS. Where?

MILES. Let's ask him later.

ANGUS. Okay.

MILES. They bought a car.

ANGUS. They bought a black car. Now, Angus, you say "My Sally."

MILES. My Sally. Your . . . ?

ANGUS. My Frances. Your Sally loved to drive the car, the black car. To where raspberries grew wild. A horse came the other way, and the army headed straight for my Frances, but my Sally—your Sally—Sally. . . .

MILES. She turned her side into the truck, to save her friend, Angus. Your Sally tried to save Frances.

ANGUS. She . . . yes.

MILES. And now it's the two friends again.

ANGUS. And now it's the. . . . No. They got taken in a cart to the highest point in the county. Buried there.

MILES. Yes. That's right. And now it's the two friends again.

ANGUS. And now it's. . . . I've never been there. The highest point in the county. Hey.

He's being led by a memory so faint, he behaves as though he's smelling something. ANGUS *walks inside, drops to his knees, and pulls up a floorboard. He pulls out a beat-up metal tube, khaki green, about three feet long. He opens the tube, pulls out several architectural drawings, and spreads them out on the table.*

The houses joined. Together and separate.

MORGAN *enters.* ANGUS *greets him without looking up.*

Morgan! Hello! The houses joined. They never got started. Did they? You said they did. I want to go to them.

MORGAN. *(to* MILES*)* How did you find these?

MILES. I didn't.

MORGAN. How did you find these?

ANGUS. You hid them. I saw you. You didn't see me.

MORGAN. You remember that?

ANGUS. I . . . I guess I do. . . .

MILES. You made these?

ANGUS. The two houses joined up. I drew these. Separate and joined. I was the drawer boy.

MORGAN. You did. You were.

ANGUS. I am. I want to see her, Morgan. Take me to where they are. Up on that hill. The tallest point. *(to* MILES*)* You should come, too. You did this. Let's go right now.

ANGUS *goes outside.*

MORGAN. No, Angus. You're baking.

ANGUS. Well, just—turn off the damn . . . whatever that is! I want to go now. My Sally.

MORGAN. *(following* ANGUS *out)* Listen to me. We can't go, Angus. Now, just stop this.

ANGUS. Can too. I have to.

MORGAN. Angus! Make me a sandwich. I'm hungry.

ANGUS. Make you. . . . ? Make your own damn sandwich, old fella! I got to. . . . Damn it! I WANT TO GO!

MILES *comes outside.*

I been waiting so long. I never—why'd you not ever take me? That's my Sally. That's my WIFE.

MILES. Angus. I'm sure he must of. You don't remember things, you know.

ANGUS. I want to go to them. I'll remember them now.

MORGAN. I'm hungry. I want to eat something.

ANGUS. I'll cook once we get back. Let's go. Why'd you never take me there before?

MORGAN. No.

ANGUS. Yes.

MORGAN. No.

ANGUS/MILES. *(together)* Yes!

MORGAN. *(to* MILES*)* I beg your pardon?

MILES. Well, I mean, he seems to want to go. I just thought—

MORGAN. Would you excuse us, please? Wait inside.

MILES. Sure.

ANGUS. He'll come too!

MILES. Yes, but, I'm just going to go inside for a while.

MILES *goes inside.*

ANGUS. I'll get the truck—or, you should get the truck, you know where we're going. Plus, do I know how to drive?

MORGAN. Angus, I'm tired. I want my lunch. There's so much I need to do this afternoon.

ANGUS. Not more important than this! There's a picture of the place in my head—the tallest spot—I want to go and match it. Now.

MORGAN. Feed came this morning. Usual amount, and I wrote Wally a cheque. Can we cover it?

ANGUS. Leaves forty-four dollars and sixteen cents. Dairy give us ninety-one twenty-one in the next three days, we can cover the loan and have sixteen-oh-eight to spare—now, let's go.

MORGAN. Angus. No. We aren't going.

ANGUS. *(after a pause)* You eat lunch first. *Then.*

MORGAN. No. Not then.

ANGUS. Yes then. Go now and quick—there's some, there's some . . . something for a sandwich in the . . . thing. Quick. Go. I'll wait out here.

MORGAN. Listen to me.

ANGUS. You go! I'll wait patiently for you to come out, and we'll go see—

MORGAN. Listen.

ANGUS. —SEE MY SALLY.

> ANGUS *holds his head, has to sit.*

MORGAN. Angus, are you—

ANGUS. GO IN! Go in and come out.

> MORGAN *goes inside. He starts to make a sandwich.*

MILES. I believe he will remember this time, if you take him.

MORGAN. I'm not taking him.

ANGUS. Morgan. Done yet?

MILES. But why?

ANGUS. Morgan.

MORGAN. That's between him and me.

MILES. Fine, I don't want to interfere—

ANGUS. Morgan! Time's up!

MILES. —but he's better now, he seems better. Since rehearsal. He's remembering things. And he wants to go.

MORGAN. I told him no, and I'm telling you no.

ANGUS. *(holding his head)* Aw, God. Moorgan!

> Silence while MORGAN *finishes making the sandwich, sits, and begins to eat.*

Morgan! Let's go! Morgan! Mooorgan! You got to drive!

> ANGUS *is in more and more pain.*

Moooorgan!!

MILES. Morgan, Jesus. . . .

MORGAN. How's the gravel coming?

MILES. I'll take him myself. Just tell me where it is.

ANGUS. Mooorgan! Get the . . . truck!

MORGAN. You got too much to do. Gravel and then the muckin' out.

ANGUS. Aaaaahhh. Morgan! Morgan.

MILES. This is, just, cruel.

ANGUS. *(suddenly no longer in pain)* Morgan! Get the jeep!

MILES. Morgan, for God's sake.

ANGUS. Get a, we need a jeep! Don't tell anyone! Morgan!

MORGAN. *(goes to the door)* Angus! Come indoors.

ANGUS. Morgan! Hello! We need a ride. We can't tell anyone. We got to go.

MORGAN. Come inside.

They go inside.

ANGUS. What did you do to get us passes? Sergeant says don't tell anyone, and be back by oh-six-hundred. Jesus, Morgan! Miles. You can't come.

MORGAN. Angus, listen—

ANGUS. Sally will just—let's go now. Surprise them.

MORGAN. Angus? You need to go upstairs. To bed, now.

ANGUS. To hell with that! They're waiting for us. Did you call? Did you?

MORGAN. I. . . . Yes. I did.

ANGUS. I knew it! Jesus, you did. Goddamn it! You set it all up.

MORGAN. That's right. I did.

ANGUS. Yuh clever bastard! Let's go. Miles. You can't go. The girls are waiting, but we got just the two passes. Morgan set it up.

MILES. Angus. I'm sorry. I don't understand you.

MORGAN. This happened.

MILES. What?

MORGAN. I got leave for the two of us overnight. It was his birthday. It was a surprise.

MILES. He remembers!

MORGAN. This is your fault.

ANGUS. You've got to lend me some shoes, mine are still wet from the ditch. Sergeant says we have to . . . we have to be back . . . *(his headache resumes)* Morgan? It's too bright.

MORGAN. Let's go, Angus. Upstairs.

ANGUS. No! She's waiting with . . . to give me . . . cufflinks.

MORGAN. You can't go like that. Can you.

ANGUS. No. Not like this.

MORGAN. Let's go up and get your uniform on.

ANGUS. Okay.

MORGAN. Get you that shoe.

ANGUS. Let's . . . hurry. *(looks at MILES)* Hey. Who're you?

MORGAN. That's the man who did this to you.

MORGAN leads ANGUS upstairs.

SCENE II

Late that night. ANGUS *walks into the kitchen. As in Act One, he's looking for something. He comes across the architectural drawings, and stares at them for a while.*

ANGUS. "God with honour hang your head,[1]
    Groom, and grace your bride, your bed,
    With lissome scions, sweet scions,
    Out of hallowed bodies bred.

    "Each be other's comfort kind:
    Deep, deeper than divined—"

He looks up.

Morgan?

He gets no response, and goes back to the blueprints.

I want to. . . .

He looks out the door, then looks back toward the stairs.

I'll go. I'll go now.

He goes out the back door and off into the night. After a moment, MORGAN *comes into the kitchen.*

MORGAN. Angus? *(sees the open back door and goes out)* Angus? Angus!!

He walks off. MILES *comes into the kitchen.*

MILES. Morgan? What is it.

MORGAN *comes back into the house. He pulls on his boots, puts on a jacket.*

MORGAN. He's gone.

MILES. Oh, no. He went to the graveyard, I'll go. . . .

MORGAN. You stay here.

MILES. Look—I'm "the man who did this." I want to help.

MORGAN. *You stay here.*

MORGAN *exits.*

SCENE III

Dawn. MILES *is sitting in the kitchen, waiting impatiently. He gets up and goes outside. He sees the two piles of rocks left over from the day before; picks up a rock, dunks it in the pail of water, dries it with the cloth, and sets it on the small pile. He does this again, distractedly. Then he looks around, surreptitiously; picks up the bucket of water, dumps the water on the larger pile of rocks, pats the pile dry a couple of times, and then pushes the big pile and the little pile together.* MORGAN *enters.*

MORGAN. Anybody call?

MILES. No. Any luck?

MORGAN. No.

---

[1]From "At the Wedding March," a poem by Gerard Manley Hopkins.

Morgan goes inside. He doesn't know what to do with himself. He makes a sandwich. Miles goes in. Angus walks through the yard unseen, his arm bleeding, and then goes off again.

MILES. He'll turn up. *(pause)* Finished the gravel.

MORGAN. Huh? Oh. Goes in the culvert.

MILES. Sure. Is the culvert that shed thing out behind the barn?

MORGAN. No, it's . . . never mind. I'll do it. *(goes to the phone and dials)* Tom? Morgan. Any sign of him? Okay. Thanks. *(hangs up)*

MILES. What about the graveyard?

MORGAN. What about it.

MILES. Did you look there.

MORGAN. No.

MILES. But that's where he wanted to go.

MORGAN. I'm gonna say this once, as nice as I can under the circumstances: You are not being helpful.

MILES. Fine. I'm sorry. Tell me how I can help.

MORGAN. Go to the henhouse. Shuffle the eggs.

MILES. Morgan—

MORGAN. Take the eggs out from underneath each chicken, put them under a different chicken.

MILES. Look—

MORGAN. That way, they don't raise a fuss when we take their eggs away for good.

MILES. Stop it.

MORGAN. And no chicken has to suffer.

MILES. Tell me why you wouldn't take him to the graveyard. Why you won't look for him there now.

MORGAN. Why? Your play not long enough yet?

MILES. Because I did something to Angus, and I hurt you, and I don't know how I did that. And I want to fix it.

MORGAN. I'll fix it.

MILES. Tremendous. Fix it. Go to the graveyard and get him. Go now.

MORGAN. Cows need to be milked.

MILES. I'll milk the goddamn cows!

MORGAN. Oh, you will, will you? Think you could figure out the milking machine on your own?

MILES. Yes. I do.

Angus walks into the yard again.

MORGAN. You can't recognize the useful end of a shovel. You go out there, the barn'll fall over.

MILES. I'll do it. Go. Or I'll call the cops and send them up there for him.

MORGAN. You'll what?

MILES. And I'll tell them that you knew he was out wandering around, and you wouldn't go to get him.

MORGAN. You're gonna call the police?

MILES. I. . . . No, of course not. I just—I don't understand it. We both know where he is, we both know why he went there, and I can't figure out why you won't—

MORGAN. Stop trying.

MILES. —why you won't go and get him. He could be hurt, he could be God knows what. Jesus, Morgan. Don't you care?

MORGAN. You watch your step, young man.

MILES. Tell me why you won't go. Tell me why you're just standing there.

MORGAN. *(tosses his truck keys to* MILES*)* You go.

MILES. Okay. Thank you. I will.

> MILES *turns to go. But before he gets outside, he stops suddenly and turns to* MORGAN.

MILES. It's not true. What you tell him isn't true. That's why you won't go. Isn't it.

MORGAN. You get out of here.

> MILES *leaves; he sees* ANGUS.

MILES. Morgan!

ANGUS. *(to* MILES*)* What did you. . . ?

> MORGAN *comes outdoors.*

MORGAN. Angus! Are you alright? What happened to you? Where did you get to?

ANGUS. *(to* MORGAN*)* What did he mean?

MORGAN. *(to* MILES*)* You leave us alone?

MILES. Sure.

> *He goes.*

MORGAN. Angus? You alright? Come inside.

> ANGUS *goes in.*

MORGAN. Sit down. Lemme look at that arm. How did this happen?

ANGUS. What did . . . he mean?

MORGAN. You hungry? Want a sandwich?

ANGUS. No, I heard, I . . . what—

MORGAN. Jesus, Angus. You haven't walked off for some time. Once I found you up in the mow, looked all day, and your one leg had gone through a hole and you were just stuck there. You didn't care. Looking off, like you were waiting for a train or something. Do you know, I pulled you out, carried you down and it took you till the next day to come back to yourself. You scared me. What were you thinking about? You'd do it when we were kids. I'd find you up on a tree somewhere, you'd be staring off, I'd be yelling "Angus, Angus", and you'd come back to yourself, climb back down, ask what day it was. It was funny when we were kids.

I'm gonna make you something to eat and I want you to eat it.

ANGUS. No. Please.

> MORGAN *goes to the fridge, starts sandwich-making. He stops and then goes to the sink, gets a spoonful of water, and gives it to* ANGUS.

ANGUS. Okay, but. I don't . . .

MORGAN. Hush now.

> MORGAN *then goes back to the sandwich.* ANGUS *looks down at the blueprints.*

ANGUS. The houses joined. Together and separate.

MORGAN. Yes.

ANGUS. I drew these.

MORGAN. Yes.

ANGUS. Don't remember doing that. Remember him hiding them, though. I saw him hide them.

MORGAN. Saw who?

ANGUS. Him. He didn't see me.

MORGAN. Angus. Look at me. Who am I?

ANGUS. You're the man who did this to me.

MORGAN. What's my name.

ANGUS. Don't you know?

MORGAN. Look at me.

ANGUS. You played the farmer boy. You got us.

MORGAN. No Angus.

ANGUS. Sure.

MORGAN. No, Angus. Please. Tell me who I am.

ANGUS. Why should I?

MORGAN. I want to know if you're okay.

ANGUS. I don't care. I was in the dark, walking, and I got stopped. I heard a voice. It was a ghost, stopped me, it warned me against you.

MORGAN. What?

ANGUS. It told me what you did. It told me I should be afraid of you. It said: HE KILLED YOUR FATHER. HE MARRIED YOUR MUM.

MORGAN. Angus, you're scaring me.

ANGUS. *(a pause. He finally looks at* MORGAN*)* Good. Okay. I was just pretending. I was pretending I was mad. There was no voice. It was my antic disposition. Morgan. I'm scared. Listen, I was out there, and I heard. He said, Miles said "It's not true. What you tell him isn't true." I heard.

MORGAN. You did.

ANGUS. Yes. Miles said "It's not true. What you tell him isn't true." Did he mean me?

MORGAN. Yes.

ANGUS. Oh. What did he mean?

MORGAN. He means I lied. I lied to you.

ANGUS. Is that true?

MORGAN. Yes.

ANGUS. Oh. Okay. You lied. You're a bastard. God. Look. The houses joined. Where's Miles. I want him to tell it.

MORGAN. Not now.

ANGUS. Yes. Now. I want—Miles to. He, what did he do? Oh God, Morgan.

MORGAN. What's wrong?

ANGUS. What'd he do to me? I have, in my head. . . .

MORGAN. What. Tell me.

ANGUS. Just everything. Just . . . everything. It came all night. Listen: I'm a boy, and I have a cough and a nosebleed on my shirt. On my short pants. I remembered that. Then, another time, I'm writing a test, and the smell of you sittin' beside me, smell of you failing it. I remember France, that boy running away. You would not shoot the boy running away. Sally, the first sight of her from behind in that church. Oh, God, oh no, I remember that. Her hair, my finger trapped in the pages of the hymn book. And, then, I got hurt—God, the noise, I'm lying on the ground. . . . I remember when my head didn't hurt, I think. I remember the double wedding.

MORGAN. You remember the double wedding?

ANGUS. I do. I stood up, I said: "God with honour hang your head, groom—"

MORGAN. You remember getting hurt?

ANGUS. I do. I remember the door flying. At me. The three of you safe, and me on my way to you, and I got stopped by the architecture.

MORGAN. No, that's—oh, Jesus.

ANGUS. I remember everything.

MORGAN. No, you don't.

ANGUS. Yes. Yes, I do! It came all night. I walked. I was looking for them.

MORGAN. You remember the story. What he said on stage.

ANGUS. No. I remember *it*.

MORGAN. What was in your hand?

ANGUS. My hand?

MORGAN. What were you carrying?

ANGUS. Nothing. I don't think. . . .

MORGAN. What you just told me is what I've told you all these years. That's our story. What you had in your hand was a bottle of cheap brandy, given to me in a card game. I sent you to fetch it. Remember? *We laughed*, and I made you get it. You were safe, and I sent you out—you understand? Angus? I did that. I did that to you. That's the first thing.

ANGUS. That's the first thing? See. You're a bastard. What do I remember?

MORGAN. You remember the story.

ANGUS. Aw, God.

MORGAN. Angus. What'd I get for that car?

ANGUS. Car?

MORGAN. The black car.

ANGUS. It got wrecked. The army truck.

MORGAN. Did it? If you can remember, then remember.

ANGUS. Don't.

MORGAN. What'd I get for that car.

ANGUS. It got wrecked, my Sally was driving, and she turned it into the truck—

MORGAN. No. It's a number.

ANGUS. I don't want to. I want him—I want the story.

MORGAN. How much'd I get for that car?

ANGUS. Hundred and ten dollars.

MORGAN. That's right.

ANGUS. Hundred and ten dollars. Oh. From Doug Hamm. It didn't crash.

MORGAN. That's right. We sold it. You do remember.

ANGUS. No, I don't.

MORGAN. Angus, listen—

ANGUS. No. It's not true. "What you tell him isn't true." I heard.

MORGAN. It is true.

ANGUS. Where's Miles? Hey! Get in here!

MORGAN. No, Angus, wait.

ANGUS. I want him. Miles!

   MILES *runs on.*

   (*to* MILES) You said, "What you tell him isn't true." He said, "I lied." He lied. He's a bastard. Now he says something ... else. You have to tell it.

MILES. Morgan'll tell you.

ANGUS. No, he won't. He's a bastard. You will. You know.

MILES. Angus. Do you know what I am? I'm an actor. I play at things. I was playing Morgan when you saw me. But he's here. He's right there, and he can tell you.

ANGUS. He lied. I remember you.

MILES. Listen to me. Do you know what I did? Just now? I was out in the barn, pretending to be a farmer. All those cows were in agony, they were all begging to be milked, and do you know what I did? I broke the milking machine. I hooked it up to Daisy and switched it on, and she groaned, and then the whole thing stopped. I broke it. I don't know what I'm doing, Angus. Let Morgan tell you.

ANGUS. You broke the milking machine?

MILES. Yes.

ANGUS. Oh boy.

MORGAN. *(simultaneous with the above)* Aw, Jesus.

MILES. Sorry. You were right. But you don't need to rush out there. Daisy's okay. They're all okay. I milked them by hand.

MORGAN. You milked nine cows by hand?

MILES. Well, a little bit each. Just to take the pressure off. I was standing there amid all these weeping cows. I had to do something. I just sat down, grabbed hold, and got the hang of it pretty fast. I just went from cow to cow, one after another—grab, milk, grab, milk, grab, milk, grab, milk. . . . Suddenly, I looked up, and it was done.

MORGAN. What'd you do when the bucket got full?

MILES. You're supposed to use a bucket?

ANGUS. Oh boy.

MILES. I've got to go. I've got rehearsal. . . .

ANGUS. No! Tell it.

MORGAN. I am. I will.

ANGUS. No. Him.

MILES. Angus, no.

ANGUS. Okay. Both of you. Tell it.

MORGAN. I will, but not with him here.

ANGUS. Yes, with him here. I'm scared. You're scaring me, yuh bastard. From the start. Both of you.

MORGAN. Angus, don't—

ANGUS. BOTH OF YOU. Please. So I can match them. Find me in them. I'm starved to know.

MORGAN. Alright.

ANGUS. Right. Go. You start.

MILES. Okay.

ANGUS. But, as him.

MILES. Right.

ANGUS. Like you did, on the . . . thing.

MILES. I got it. *(as* MORGAN*)* A couple of boys played shinney, and went to school, and grew up.

ANGUS. Now you.

MORGAN. They built—

ANGUS. But, as you.

MORGAN. . . . We built a cabin together. You dreamed it up, I did all the work.

MILES. Stole nails, and played hookey, and built a cabin. From the drawer boy's pictures.

MORGAN. You were about to go to university. I talked you out of it. The war started, and I talked you into volunteering with me. It was going to be an adventure. We were so excited. No. I was excited, and you were—you were my friend. We joined up. As soon as we got over there, we were at an air field, and we saw something. A stupid accident during training. Do you remember?

ANGUS. I. . . .

MORGAN. We watched three men burn to death. We couldn't help. It was awful. And then the only thing we did was survive. We never volunteered for anything, we hid when things got bad. We'd use up ammunition by shooting straight up.

MILES. Then, they met two girls. One tall, and one taller. The taller one liked the drawer, the tall one, the farmer.

MORGAN. They agreed to marry us. They agreed to come home with us. They were friends, like we were friends. The four of us were together as much as possible. We would spend whole nights talking, the four of us. You and Sally would take long walks and count the stars. She taught you how. She knew the names of stars, and how to cut the sky up into manageable pieces for counting. It was the first thing she gave you.

MILES. They made plans. By the time they were done talking, they had a picture of what they would do, like something the one boy would draw.

MORGAN. All we had to do was wait out our tour. All we had to do was keep hiding. Then, one night in an air raid, I sent you out, to get a bottle of brandy I left in Sally's car. We decided we wanted a drink. We were all together, we felt indestructible, because of—because of each other. Like the war was just a dream or something. You took a long time to come back. We made jokes about where you might be. I said to Sally, "He's found someone else."

MILES. The drawer boy was standing down the street, looking at a large house.

MORGAN. You were running like hell down the street, trying to get back. Jesus. You were laughing.

MILES. The front door of the house flew off when the shell hit, and the drawer boy watched it come for him.

MORGAN. A piece of shrapnel caught you from behind. I watched you get carried through the air. You flew right at me. You nearly died. But you didn't. You woke up. But your memory was . . . gone.
  We came home. They came with us. There was no double wedding. Sally wanted to wait until you were better.

ANGUS. But—the stolen poem. . . .

MORGAN. You never said it. You've been waiting to say it.

    We bought this land. We lived here, in the house that came with the land, English girls in one room, us in the other. The house you designed was never started. We tacked the plans up over there *(indicates the spot where* ANGUS *looks first when he's searching)*, so that we could see every day what we intended to do. Eventually, they became just a . . . reminder. So, one day when you were asleep, when I thought you were asleep, I took them down and I hid them. We did buy an old car, so they could go into town. They were lonely. The car didn't help much.

    Sally looked after you. She stayed by you all the time, every minute. She watched you wander off, she'd follow behind, hiding behind trees so you wouldn't see. You'd get lost, she'd be there, and she'd bring you back home. She'd clean you. She'd feed you. She gave you medicine from a spoon.

    You kept having headaches. They made you different, Angus. They made you mean. Because she was always there, you'd get mean at Sally.

ANGUS. *(to himself)* At Sally.

MORGAN. One day, she was very tired. It was hot, hot like they'd never felt at home. You had another headache. Sally was cooking, baking bread, and you came up to her, and without saying a thing, you hit her. She cried and cried; she wasn't hurt much, but she was tired. You looked at her, and then you had to ask me who that crying girl was. And it was then that Sally decided to leave.

ANGUS. Your Frances . . . ?

MORGAN. They were friends. They were here alone.

    The day they went, they called a taxi from town. You were asleep. I was here *(in the kitchen doorway)*, I couldn't move. The taxi came, and I went to help Frances with her suitcase, and she said, "This is the worst thing I could do to you. Don't you dare help me do it." She dragged it outside and snarled at the taxi driver when he tried to help her. She was crying from the effort of it. The suitcase made a little trench across the driveway where she dragged it. They got in the taxi. They left. I've not heard a word from her in all this time.

    When you woke up—

ANGUS. No.

MORGAN. When you woke up, you knew something was wrong. You went into their room. Looked in the closet, looked under the bed. Tore the room apart. You didn't know what you were looking for. You went through all the rooms, looking, and when you had searched the whole house, you started again. You tore through the house, faster and faster—you wouldn't stop, Angus, and you couldn't say what you were looking for. Finally, when you were racing up the stairs to start over again, I tackled you. I hauled you down, and we sat on the stairs, and I told you the lie. I told you the story of the black car crashing for the first time. I told it again, and you stopped crying. I told it again, and you fell asleep. I kept telling it 'cause it made you feel better. Goddamn it, it made me feel better.

Pause.

ANGUS. I hit my Sally, and you lost your. . . .

MORGAN. Yes.

ANGUS. That's what I did to you. God, you must hate me.

MORGAN. I guess I did, Angus.

ANGUS. So. That's me. I'm scared I'll forget *that* now.

MORGAN. We'll tell it to each other. Daily.

ANGUS. Okay. Thank you.

MORGAN. We'll fill it all in. If you can remember, we'll do that.

ANGUS. Even if I don't. Let's do that.

MORGAN. Okay.

ANGUS. *(to* MILES*)* He was right. You are the man who did this to me.

MILES. I'm late. I should go.

ANGUS. Go?

MILES. I have to go to work. To rehearse.

ANGUS. Yes. You're making a. . . .

MILES. That's right.

ANGUS. Miles? That was just a story.

MILES. I know.

ANGUS. No, I mean—you can use it if you want.

MILES. Thanks. But—thanks.

MILES *takes his notebook out of his pocket, hands it to* MORGAN, *then leaves.*

ANGUS. That was Miles. He's here staying with you and me while he puts on a play about farming. You told him awful stories.

MORGAN. Yes.

ANGUS. And you're Morgan.

MORGAN. Yes. And you're Angus.

ANGUS. You carried me—and all that—around all this time? Since the taxi went?

MORGAN. Yes.

ANGUS. Must be tired. I'll make you a sandwich. Or—here—someone made this one already.

MORGAN. Thanks. I'd better go outside and see what he's done to the barn.

MORGAN *exits.*

ANGUS. "God with honour hang your head,
    Groom, and grace you bride, your bed
    With lissome scions, sweet scions,
    Out of hallowed bodies bred.

"Each be other's comfort kind:
    Deep, deeper than divined . . . "

MORGAN. *(from off)* Angus! The bulk cooler's full of milk! He used the milking machine after all. He was—he was lying to us, the silly bugger!

ANGUS. " . . . Divine charity, dear charity,
    Fast you ever, fast bind.

    "Then let the march tread our ears:
    I to him turn with tears
    Who to wedlock, his wonder wedlock,
    Deals triumph and immortal years."

As the lights fade, ANGUS *takes the drawings and holds them up where they used to live.*

The End.

(1999)

PREWRITING

Begin your study of *The Drawer Boy* by writing about and discussing the following six ideas.

ANALYZING THE CHARACTERS

1. One way to look at this play is as a layering of deceptions. List five deceptions or self-deceptions that occur in the play. Compare your list with those of others in your class. Discuss how you would rank the seriousness or harmlessness of the deceptions you have identified.
2. Reread the opening two scenes involving Angus, Miles, and Morgan. With two other people, prepare an oral reading of the scenes, choosing one quality to emphasize in each of the characters. Present the scenes to your class, asking them to identify the qualities you chose. Listen to the other students' interpretations of the scenes.
3. In Act I, Scene V, Morgan repeats a story to Angus, one that he has clearly told many times. Who would you say is the hero of this story? Does this hero correspond to Miller's concept of tragic heroism? In other words, is there any indication of displacement or indignity? How is the heroism of Antigone different?
4. How is tradition important to the characters in both *Antigone* and *The Drawer Boy*?
5. Reread the latter part of Act II, Scene III, where Miles, Angus, and Morgan recount the true events of Angus and Morgan's lives. Why has Morgan lied all these years? Why does he, when speaking to Angus, refer to Miles as "the man who did this to you"?
6. Choose a character from *The Drawer Boy* and argue that he is the hero. Can you argue for more than one character as a hero?

WRITING

In your prewriting, you gathered a list of deceptions that you found in *The Drawer Boy*. Looking at that list, you may come up with a thesis for an essay on the play. "Deception is an important element in *The Drawer Boy*" is not enough, even though that may be your first reaction to such a long list. You must say *why* deception is important. Here are some possible thesis ideas:

> Though Morgan deceives both Angus and himself, his falsehoods were born out of great pain. This tempers our attitude toward him.

> One of the moral questions addressed in *The Drawer Boy* is this: Which is more damaging to the spirit, deception of others or self-deception?

> In *The Drawer Boy*, Healey presents deception on all levels of seriousness, seeming to encourage a view of humanity as suffused with lies and illusions.

CHOOSING A STRUCTURE

Your choice of thesis should determine how you organize your raw material—in this case, your list of examples from the prewriting activity. Perhaps your list looks something like this:

Deception

— Cows produce milk to avoid being slaughtered
— Beef sandwich actually ham
— Feed pigs to cows
— Actors don't have politics
— Crop rotation
— Story about Angus's accident, the double wedding, and the death of Sally and Frances
— The play—by omission, Miles deceives Morgan about what would be included in the play
— Is Morgan as rational as he seems?
— Miles says he broke the milking machine

This unorganized jumble can be structured in several ways. For the first thesis we mentioned, you would probably sort the deceptions character by character, perhaps presenting Morgan's first and then those of the others. For the second thesis, you would separate deceptions of others from self-deceptions and devote a section of your essay to each type, closing with an evaluation of the spiritual damage done by each. For the last thesis, you would have the challenging work of arranging the list from the most trivial to the most serious so that your readers appreciate the full spectrum.

IDEAS FOR WRITING

IDEAS FOR RESPONSIVE WRITING

1. Devise a scale for ranking your responses to the three characters: Angus, Miles, and Morgan. It could be something like "least admirable to most admirable" or "most like me to most unlike me." Write a brief paragraph to explain your placement of each character on your scale.
2. Morgan's stories about his and Angus's boyhood are strong and positive. How has this positive view affected Angus's outlook as an adult? Write a first-person narrative in which an older Angus might look back on his life if his memory were intact. How does he remember his boyhood, his war experience, and his relationship with Sally? What are his feelings toward Morgan—would Morgan still be a hero to Angus?

IDEAS FOR CRITICAL WRITING

1. Examine the role of truth and lies in each character's life.
2. Expand the comment that Morgan makes in Act I, Scene II: "Farm's a dangerous place. Put that in yer . . . play."

3. Consider the character of Miles. Is he, as Morgan tells Angus, "the man who did this to you"?
4. Investigate the ideas of oddness and normality in the play.
5. Explain how the two English women, Sally and Frances, are important characters even though they never appear in person.
6. Character development and change are key elements in drama and fiction. Does Miles change Angus or Morgan? How?

REWRITING

The more specifically you support your statements about the work, the more credible you will be to your readers. Another crucial advantage of forcing yourself to be specific is that you will prevent yourself from straying from the printed page into the fields of your own mind, which may be rich and green but not relevant.

DEVELOPING PARAGRAPHS SPECIFICALLY

The following paragraph makes several good observations but lacks specifics:

> In many ways, Morgan fulfills Arthur Miller's characterization of the modern tragic hero. His ideal image of himself is frustrated at home, at work on the farm, and at the play. He fears he will be misunderstood, a victim of indignity. He is clearly at odds with his environment.

Although these statements are true, the writer has given the reader no particular cause to believe them. The paragraph should have additional details from the play. Compare the following:

> In many ways, Morgan fulfills Arthur Miller's characterization of the modern tragic hero. Of the three characters, Morgan is the rational one who takes care of the farm and his friend, Angus. His ideal image of himself is that of long-suffering hero, sardonic realist, and capable farmer. However, after seeing Miles's play, it is clear even to Morgan that he perpetuates the lie about the deaths of Sally and Frances, in part to protect Angus but in truth to protect himself from the reality of causing his friend's injury and thereby falling from grace as a hero. When Morgan finally confesses, "You were safe, and I sent you out—you understand? Angus? I did that. I did that to you," what he fears surfaces. Angus, in the anguish of remembering, shouts, "You're a bastard." He then makes Morgan and Miles recount the truth, with Morgan playing himself as both the hero and "the man that did this." This is clearly a man at odds with his environment.

The references to the text of the play specifically support the writer's contentions. The exercise that follows will give you practice in finding such support.

EXERCISE ON PROVIDING QUOTATIONS

For each general statement, provide appropriate quotations from the play. Some of these generalizations may give you further ideas for papers.

1. Morgan is never deeply and completely self-deceived.
2. The truth disturbs all three characters.
3. Morgan and Miles take both realistic and unrealistic action toward their goals.
4. Allusion is a powerful device in the play.
5. Morgan has been living as much in unreality as have Angus and Miles.

QUESTIONS FOR DISCUSSION

1. What effect does humour have on such a deeply tender play?
2. Identify the allusions made in the play. What do these allusions add?
3. Examine Healey's use of the play within the play. How does this format increase the work's effectiveness?
4. What is Michael Healey saying about the role of art in the lives of ordinary people?

WEB
For study tools to help you with your next writing assignment, please visit the Companion Website at www.pearsoned.ca/mcmahan.

17

Drama for Writing: The Research Paper

Until now, we have been discussing and illustrating how to write papers supported with material mainly from *primary sources* (from the literary works under consideration). In this chapter, we consider the process of writing a paper supported with primary material but also drawn from *secondary sources* (critical material from the library or the internet). As we explain how to incorporate other people's ideas into your own writing, we also introduce you to a special way of reading and responding to literary works: *cultural analysis*. You thus have two avenues to explore in your writing for this chapter. You may try a cultural analysis of a play or you may examine critical opinions about that play. You may, if you wish, combine the two approaches.

As you study this chapter, keep in mind that the process described for writing about drama is the same procedure employed for any documented paper on any work—a short story, a poem, a novel, or a play.

WHAT IS CULTURAL ANALYSIS?

Human beings survive by struggling with their surroundings. In time, the elements of this struggle become established as traditions that people rely on to conduct their lives and direct their social interactions. This body of elements—customs, habits, beliefs, practices, and values—becomes known as culture. Because culture changes from time to time and place to place, we can speak individually about Canadian culture, Japanese culture, Victorian culture, middle-class culture, and so forth. A cultural approach to literature assumes that a work is part of its social context—both a product of its culture and a contribution to that culture. For example, we may read *Antigone* as a way of understanding ancient Greek culture, or we may study the culture of ancient Greece as a way of understanding *Antigone*. Because drama and fiction tend to present accounts of social and cultural problems, they are likely subjects for cultural analyses. Works that are specifically designed to attack or support some cultural value or practice (such as racism or monogamy) are especially appropriate to such an approach. Many works, too, unwittingly embody elements of the culture that engendered them. The worlds of Anton Chekhov, Ernest Hemingway, Susanna Moodie, and Pauline Johnson were not like ours, and cultural analysis can throw light on the values and beliefs underlying their writings.

LOOKING AT CULTURAL ISSUES

In his play *M. Butterfly*, David Henry Hwang takes the cultural stereotype of the submissive Asian female and turns it inside out. By combining elements of the opera *Madama Butterfly* with the true story of a French diplomat who carried on a lengthy affair with a Chinese actress without realizing that "she" was a man, the playwright has fashioned a complex drama about politics, race, gender, and sexuality.

WEB

David Henry Hwang   b. 1957

M. Butterfly

CHARACTERS

RENE GALLIMARD
SONG LILING
MARC / MAN NO. 2 / CONSUL
   SHARPLESS
RENEE / WOMAN AT PARTY /
   PINUP GIRL

COMRADE CHIN / SUZUKI / SHU-
   FANG
HELGA
TOULON / MAN NO. 1 / JUDGE
DANCERS

Playwright's Note:
This play was suggested by international newspaper accounts of a recent espionage trial. For purposes of dramatization, names have been changed, characters created, and incidents devised or altered, and this play does not purport to be a factual record of real events or real people.

A former French diplomat and a Chinese opera singer have been sentenced to six years in jail for spying for China after a two-day trial that traced a story of clandestine love and mistaken sexual identity....

Mr. Bouriscot was accused of passing information to China after he fell in love with Mr. Shi, whom he believed for twenty years to be a woman.

—*The New York Times*, May 11, 1986

I could escape this feeling
With my China girl ...

—David Bowie & Iggy Pop

TIME AND PLACE

The action of the play takes place in a Paris prison in the present, and, in recall, during the decade 1960–1970 in Beijing, and from 1966 to the present in Paris.

ACT I

SCENE I

M. GALLIMARD's *prison cell. Paris. 1988.*

Lights fade up to reveal RENE GALLIMARD, *sixty-five, in a prison cell. He wears a comfortable bathrobe, and looks old and tired. The sparsely furnished cell contains a wooden crate, upon which sits a hot plate with a kettle, and a portable tape recorder.* GALLIMARD *sits on the crate staring at the recorder, a sad smile on his face.*

Upstage SONG, *who appears as a beautiful woman in traditional Chinese garb, dances a traditional piece from the Peking Opera, surrounded by the percussive clatter of Chinese music.*

Then, slowly, lights and sound cross-fade; the Chinese opera music dissolves into a Western opera, the "Love Duet" from Puccini's Madame Butterfly. SONG *continues dancing, now to the Western accompaniment. Though her movements are the same, the difference in music now gives them a balletic quality.*

GALLIMARD *rises, and turns upstage towards the figure of* SONG, *who dances without acknowledging him.*

GALLIMARD. Butterfly, Butterfly . . .

[*He forces himself to turn away, as the image of* SONG *fades out, and talks to us.*]

GALLIMARD. The limits of my cell are as such: four-and-a-half meters by five. There's one window against the far wall; a door, very strong, to protect me from autograph hounds. I'm responsible for the tape recorder, the hot plate, and this charming coffee table.

When I want to eat, I'm marched off to the dining room—hot, steaming slop appears on my plate. When I want to sleep, the light bulb turns itself off—the work of fairies. It's an enchanted space I occupy. The French—we know how to run a prison.

But, to be honest, I'm not treated like an ordinary prisoner. Why? Because I'm a celebrity. You see, I make people laugh.

I never dreamed this day would arrive. I've never been considered witty or clever. In fact, as a young boy, in an informal poll among my grammar school classmates, I was voted "least likely to be invited to a party." It's a title I managed to hold on to for many years. Despite some stiff competition.

But now, how the tables turn! Look at me: the life of every social function in Paris. Paris? Why be modest: My fame has spread to Amsterdam, London, New York. Listen to them! In the world's smartest parlors, I'm the one who lifts their spirits!

[*With a flourish,* GALLIMARD *directs our attention to another part of the stage.*]

SCENE II

A party. 1988.

Lights go up on a chic-looking parlor, where a well-dressed trio, two men and one woman, make conversation. GALLIMARD *also remains lit; he observes them from his cell.*

WOMAN. And what of Gallimard?

MAN 1. Gallimard?

MAN 2. Gallimard!

GALLIMARD [*to us*]. You see? They're all determined to say my name, as if it were some new dance.

WOMAN. He still claims not to believe the truth.

MAN 1. What? Still? Even since the trial?

WOMAN. Yes. Isn't it mad?

MAN 2 [*laughing*]. He says . . . it was dark . . . and she was very modest!

[*The trio break into laughter.*]

MAN 1. So—what? He never touched her with his hands?

MAN 2. Perhaps he did, and simply misidentified the equipment. A compelling case for sex education in the schools.

WOMAN. To protect the National Security—the Church can't argue with that.

MAN 1. That's impossible! How could he not know?

MAN 2. Simple ignorance.

MAN 1. For twenty years?

MAN 2. Time flies when you're being stupid.

WOMAN. Well, I thought the French were ladies' men.

MAN 2. It seems Monsieur Gallimard was overly anxious to live up to his national reputation.

WOMAN. Well, he's not very good-looking.

MAN 1. No, he's not.

MAN 2. Certainly not.

WOMAN. Actually, I feel sorry for him.

MAN 2. A toast! To Monsieur Gallimard!

WOMAN. Yes! To Gallimard!

MAN 1. To Gallimard!

MAN 2. *Vive la différence!*

[*They toast, laughing. Lights down on them.*]

SCENE III

M. GALLIMARD's cell.

GALLIMARD [*smiling*]. You see? They toast me. I've become a patron saint of the socially inept. Can they really be so foolish? Men like that—they should be scratching at my door, begging to learn my secrets! For I, Rene Gallimard, you see, I have known, and been loved by . . . the Perfect Woman.

    Alone in this cell, I sit night after night, watching our story play through my head, always searching for a new ending, one which redeems my honor, where she returns at last to my arms. And I imagine you—my ideal audience—who come to understand and even, perhaps just a little, to envy me.

[*He turns on his tape recorder. Over the house speakers, we hear the opening phrases of* Madame Butterfly.]

GALLIMARD. In order for you to understand what I did and why, I must introduce you to my favorite opera: *Madame Butterfly*. By Giacomo Puccini. First produced at La Scala, Milan, in 1904, it is now beloved throughout the Western world.

[*As* GALLIMARD *describes the opera, the tape segues in and out to sections he may be describing.*]

GALLIMARD. And why not? Its heroine, Cio-Cio-San, also known as Butterfly, is a feminine ideal, beautiful and brave. And its hero, the man for whom she gives up everything, is— [*He pulls out a naval officer's cap from under his crate, pops it on his head, and struts about*] —not very good-looking, not too bright, and pretty much a wimp: Benjamin Franklin Pinkerton of the U.S. Navy. As the curtain rises, he's just closed on two great bargains: one on a house, the other on a woman—call it a package deal.

Pinkerton purchased the rights to Butterfly for one hundred yen—in modern currency, equivalent to about . . . sixty-six cents. So, he's feeling pretty pleased with himself as Sharpless, the American consul, arrives to witness the marriage.

[MARC, *wearing an official cap to designate* SHARPLESS, *enters and plays the character.*]

SHARPLESS/MARC. Pinkerton!

PINKERTON/GALLIMARD. Sharpless! How's it hangin'? It's a great day, just great. Between my house, my wife, and the rickshaw ride in from town, I've saved nineteen cents just this morning.

SHARPLESS. Wonderful. I can see the inscription on your tombstone already: "I saved a dollar, here I lie." [*He looks around.*] Nice house.

PINKERTON. It's artistic. Artistic, don't you think? Like the way the shoji screens slide open to reveal the wet bar and disco mirror ball? Classy, huh? Great for impressing the chicks.

SHARPLESS. "Chicks"? Pinkerton, you're going to be a married man!

PINKERTON. Well, sort of.

SHARPLESS. What do you mean?

PINKERTON. This country—Sharpless, it is okay. You got all these geisha girls running around—

SHARPLESS. I know! I live here!

PINKERTON. Then, you know the marriage laws, right? I split for one month, it's annulled!

SHARPLESS. Leave it to you to read the fine print. Who's the lucky girl?

PINKERTON. Cio-Cio-San. Her friends call her Butterfly. Sharpless, she eats out of my hand!

SHARPLESS. She's probably very hungry.

PINKERTON. Not like American girls. It's true what they say about Oriental girls. They want to be treated bad!

SHARPLESS. Oh, please!

PINKERTON. It's true!

SHARPLESS. Are you serious about this girl?

PINKERTON. I'm marrying her, aren't I?

SHARPLESS. Yes—with generous trade-in terms.

PINKERTON. When I leave, she'll know what it's like to have loved a real man. And I'll even buy her a few nylons.

SHARPLESS. You aren't planning to take her with you?

PINKERTON. Huh? Where?

SHARPLESS. Home!

PINKERTON. You mean, America? Are you crazy? Can you see her trying to buy rice in St. Louis?

SHARPLESS. So, you're not serious.

[*Pause*]

PINKERTON/GALLIMARD [*as* PINKERTON]. Consul, I am a sailor in port. [*As* GALLIMARD.] They then proceed to sing the famous duet, "The Whole World Over."

[*The duet plays on the speakers.* GALLIMARD, *as* PINKERTON, *lip-syncs his lines from the opera.*]

GALLIMARD. To give a rough translation: "The whole world over, the Yankee travels, casting his anchor wherever he wants. Life's not worth living unless he can win the hearts of the fairest maidens, then hotfoot it off the premises ASAP." [*He turns towards* MARC.] In the preceding scene, I played Pinkerton, the womanizing cad, and my friend Marc from school . . . [MARC *bows grandly for our benefit.*] played Sharpless, the sensitive soul of reason. In life, however, our positions were usually—no, always—reversed.

SCENE IV

École Nationale.[1] Aix-en-Provence. 1947.

GALLIMARD. No, Marc, I think I'd rather stay home.

MARC. Are you crazy?! We are going to Dad's condo in Marseilles! You know what happened last time?

GALLIMARD. Of course I do.

MARC. Of course you don't! You never know. . . . They stripped, Rene!

GALLIMARD. Who stripped?

MARC. The girls!

GALLIMARD. Girls? Who said anything about girls?

MARC. Rene, we're a buncha university guys goin' up to the woods. What are we gonna do—talk philosophy?

GALLIMARD. What girls? Where do you get them?

MARC. Who cares? The point is, they come. On trucks. Packed in like sardines. The back flips open, babes hop out, we're ready to roll.

GALLIMARD. You mean, they just—?

MARC. Before you know it, every last one of them—they're stripped and splashing around my pool. There's no moon out, they can't see what's going on, their boobs are flapping, right? You close your eyes, reach out—it's grab

---

[1]National School.

bag, get it? Doesn't matter whose ass is between whose legs, whose teeth are sinking into who. You're just in there, going at it, eyes closed, on and on for as long as you can stand. [*Pause.*] Some fun, huh?

GALLIMARD. What happens in the morning?

MARC. In the morning, you're ready to talk some philosophy. [*Beat.*] So how 'bout it?

GALLIMARD. Marc, I can't... I'm afraid they'll say no—the girls. So I never ask.

MARC. You don't have to ask! That's the beauty—don't you see? They don't have to say yes. It's perfect for a guy like you, really.

GALLIMARD. You go ahead... I may come later.

MARC. Hey, Rene—it doesn't matter that you're clumsy and got zits—they're not looking!

GALLIMARD. Thank you very much.

MARC. Wimp.

[MARC *walks over to the other side of the stage, and starts waving and smiling at women in the audience.*]

GALLIMARD [*to us*]. We now return to my version of *Madame Butterfly* and the events leading to my recent conviction for treason.

[GALLIMARD *notices* MARC *making lewd gestures.*]

GALLIMARD. Marc, what are you doing?

MARC. Huh? [*Sotto voce.*] Rene, there're a lotta great babes out there. They're probably lookin' at me and thinking, "What a dangerous guy."

GALLIMARD. Yes—how could they help but be impressed by your cool sophistication?

[GALLIMARD *pops the* SHARPLESS *cap on* MARC's *head, and points him offstage.* MARC *exits, leering.*]

SCENE V

M. GALLIMARD's cell.

GALLIMARD. Next, Butterfly makes her entrance. We learn her age—fifteen... but very mature for her years.

[*Lights come up on the area where we saw* SONG *dancing at the top of the play. She appears there again, now dressed as Madame Butterfly, moving to the "Love Duet."* GALLIMARD *turns upstage slightly to watch, transfixed.*]

GALLIMARD. But as she glides past him, beautiful, laughing softly behind her fan, don't we who are men sigh with hope? We, who are not handsome, nor brave, nor powerful, yet somehow believe, like Pinkerton, that we deserve a Butterfly. She arrives with all her possessions in the folds of her sleeves, lays them all out, for her man to do with as he pleases. Even her life itself— she bows her head as she whispers that she's not even worth the hundred yen he paid for her. He's already given too much, when we know he's really had to give nothing at all.

[*Music and lights on* SONG *out.* GALLIMARD *sits at his crate.*]

GALLIMARD. In real life, women who put their total worth at less than sixty-six cents are quite hard to find. The closest we come is in the pages of these magazines. [*He reaches into his crate, pulls out a stack of girlie magazines, and begins flipping through them.*] Quite a necessity in prison. For three or four dollars, you get seven or eight women.

I first discovered these magazines at my uncle's house. One day, as a boy of twelve. The first time I saw them in his closet . . . all lined up—my body shook. Not with lust—no, with power. Here were women—a shelfful—who would do exactly as I wanted.

[*The "Love Duet" creeps in over the speakers. Special comes up, revealing, not* SONG *this time, but a* PINUP GIRL *in a sexy negligee, her back to us.* GALLIMARD *turns upstage and looks at her.*]

GIRL. I know you're watching me.

GALLIMARD. My throat . . . it's dry.

GIRL. I leave my blinds open every night before I go to bed.

GALLIMARD. I can't move.

GIRL. I leave my blinds open and the lights on.

GALLIMARD. I'm shaking. My skin is hot, but my penis is soft. Why?

GIRL. I stand in front of the window.

GALLIMARD. What is she going to do?

GIRL. I toss my hair, and I let my lips part . . . barely.

GALLIMARD. I shouldn't be seeing this. It's so dirty. I'm so bad.

GIRL. Then, slowly, I lift off my nightdress.

GALLIMARD. Oh, god. I can't believe it. I can't—

GIRL. I toss it to the ground.

GALLIMARD. Now, she's going to walk away. She's going to—

GIRL. I stand there, in the light, displaying myself.

GALLIMARD. No. She's—why is she naked?

GIRL. To you.

GALLIMARD. In front of a window? This is wrong. No—

GIRL. Without shame.

GALLIMARD. No, she must . . . like it.

GIRL. I like it.

GALLIMARD. She . . . she wants me to see.

GIRL. I want you to see.

GALLIMARD. I can't believe it! She's getting excited!

GIRL. I can't see you. You can do whatever you want.

GALLIMARD. I can't do a thing. Why?

GIRL. What would you like me to do . . . next?

[*Lights go down on her. Music off. Silence, as* GALLIMARD *puts away his magazines. Then he resumes talking to us.*]

GALLIMARD. Act Two begins with Butterfly staring at the ocean. Pinkerton's been called back to the U.S., and he's given his wife a detailed schedule of his plans. In the column marked "return date," he's written "when the robins nest." This failed to ignite her suspicions. Now, three years have passed without a peep from him. Which brings a response from her faithful servant, Suzuki.

[*Comrade* CHIN *enters, playing* SUZUKI.]

SUZUKI. Girl, he's a loser. What'd he ever give you? Nineteen cents and those ugly Day-Glo stockings? Look, it's finished! Kaput! Done! And you should be glad! I mean, the guy was a woofer! He tried before, you know—before he met you, he went down to geisha central and plunked down his spare change in front of the usual candidates—everyone else gagged! These are hungry prostitutes, and they were not interested, get the picture? Now, stop slathering when an American ship sails in, and let's make some bucks—I mean, yen! We are broke!

Now, what about Yamadori? Hey, hey—don't look away—the man is a prince—figuratively, and, what's even better, literally. He's rich, he's handsome, he says he'll die if you don't marry him—and he's even willing to overlook the little fact that you've been deflowered all over the place by a foreign devil. What do you mean, "But he's Japanese"? What do you think you are? You think you've been touched by the whitey god? He was a sailor with dirty hands!

[SUZUKI *stalks offstage.*]

GALLIMARD. She's also visited by Consul Sharpless, sent by Pinkerton on a minor errand.

[MARC *enters, as* SHARPLESS.]

SHARPLESS. I hate this job.

GALLIMARD. This Pinkerton—he doesn't show up personally to tell his wife he's abandoning her. No, he sends a government diplomat . . . at taxpayers' expense.

SHARPLESS. Butterfly? Butterfly? I have some bad—I'm going to be ill. Butterfly, I came to tell you—

GALLIMARD. Butterfly says she knows he'll return and if he doesn't she'll kill herself rather than go back to her own people. [*Beat.*] This causes a lull in the conversation.

SHARPLESS. Let's put it this way . . .

GALLIMARD. Butterfly runs into the next room, and returns holding—

[*Sound cue: a baby crying.* SHARPLESS, *"seeing" this, backs away.*]

SHARPLESS. Well, good. Happy to see things going so well. I suppose I'll be going now. Ta ta. Ciao. [*He turns away. Sound cue out.*] I hate this job. [*He exits.*]

GALLIMARD. At that moment, Butterfly spots in the harbor an American ship—the *Abramo Lincoln!*

[*Music cue: "The Flower Duet."* SONG, *still dressed as Butterfly, changes into a wedding kimono, moving to the music.*]

GALLIMARD. This is the moment that redeems her years of waiting. With Suzuki's help, they cover the room with flowers—

[CHIN, *as* SUZUKI, *trudges onstage and drops a lone flower without much enthusiasm.*]

GALLIMARD. —and she changes into her wedding dress to prepare for Pinkerton's arrival.

[SUZUKI *helps Butterfly change.* HELGA *enters, and helps* GALLIMARD *change into a tuxedo.*]

GALLIMARD. I married a woman older than myself—Helga.

HELGA. My father was ambassador to Australia. I grew up among criminals and kangaroos.

GALLIMARD. Hearing that brought me to the altar—

[HELGA *exits.*]

GALLIMARD. —where I took a vow renouncing love. No fantasy woman would ever want me, so, yes, I would settle for a quick leap up the career ladder. Passion, I banish, and in its place—practicality!

But my vows had long since lost their charm by the time we arrived in China. The sad truth is that all men want a beautiful woman, and the uglier the man, the greater the want.

[SUZUKI *makes final adjustments of Butterfly's costume, as does* GALLIMARD *of his tuxedo.*]

GALLIMARD. I married late, at age thirty-one. I was faithful to my marriage for eight years. Until the day when, as a junior-level diplomat in puritanical Peking, in a parlor at the German ambassador's house, during the "Reign of a Hundred Flowers,"[2] I first saw her . . . singing the death scene from *Madame Butterfly*.

[SUZUKI *runs offstage.*]

SCENE VI

German ambassador's house. Beijing. 1960.

*The upstage special area now becomes a stage. Several chairs face upstage, representing seating for some twenty guests in the parlor. A few "diplomats"—*RENEE, MARC, TOULON—*in formal dress enter and take seats.*

GALLIMARD *also sits down, but turns towards us and continues to talk. Orchestral accompaniment on the tape is now replaced by a simple piano. Song picks up the death scene from the point where Butterfly uncovers the hara-kiri knife.*

GALLIMARD. The ending is pitiful. Pinkerton, in an act of great courage, stays home and sends his American wife to pick up Butterfly's child. The truth, long deferred, has come up to her door.

---

[2]Name given to a brief period of free expression in China.

[SONG, *playing Butterfly, sings the lines from the opera in her own voice—which, though not classical, should be decent.*]

SONG. *"Con onor muore / chi non puo serbar / vita con onore."*

GALLIMARD [*simultaneously*]. "Death with honor / Is better than life / Life with dishonor."

[*The stage is illuminated; we are now completely within an elegant diplomat's residence.* SONG *proceeds to play out an abbreviated death scene. Everyone in the room applauds.* SONG, *shyly, takes her bows. Others in the room rush to congratulate her.* GALLIMARD *remains with us.*]

GALLIMARD. They say in opera the voice is everything. That's probably why I'd never before enjoyed opera. Here . . . here was a Butterfly with little or no voice—but she had the grace, the delicacy . . . I believed this girl. I believed her suffering. I wanted to take her in my arms—so delicate, even I could protect her, take her home, pamper her until she smiled.

[*Over the course of the preceding speech,* SONG *has broken from the upstage crowd and moved directly upstage of* GALLIMARD.]

SONG. Excuse me. Monsieur . . . ?

[GALLIMARD *turns upstage, shocked.*]

GALLIMARD. Oh! Gallimard. Mademoiselle . . . ? A beautiful . . .

SONG. Song Liling.

GALLIMARD. A beautiful performance.

SONG. Oh, please.

GALLIMARD. I usually—

SONG. You make me blush. I'm no opera singer at all.

GALLIMARD. I usually don't like *Butterfly*.

SONG. I can't blame you in the least.

GALLIMARD. I mean, the story—

SONG. Ridiculous.

GALLIMARD. I like the story, but . . . what?

SONG. Oh, you like it?

GALLIMARD. I . . . what I mean is, I've always seen it played by huge women in so much bad makeup.

SONG. Bad makeup is not unique to the West.

GALLIMARD. But, who can believe them?

SONG. And you believe me?

GALLIMARD. Absolutely. You were utterly convincing. It's the first time—

SONG. Convincing? As a Japanese woman? The Japanese used hundreds of our people for medical experiments during the war, you know. But I gather such an irony is lost on you.

GALLIMARD. No! I was about to say, it's the first time I've seen the beauty of the story.

SONG. Really?

GALLIMARD. Of her death. It's a . . . a pure sacrifice. He's unworthy, but what can she do? She loves him . . . so much. It's a very beautiful story.

SONG. Well, yes, to a Westerner.

GALLIMARD. Excuse me?

SONG. It's one of your favorite fantasies, isn't it? The submissive Oriental woman and the cruel white man.

GALLIMARD. Well, I didn't quite mean . . .

SONG. Consider it this way: what would you say if a blonde homecoming queen fell in love with a short Japanese businessman? He treats her cruelly, then goes home for three years, during which time she prays to his picture and turns down marriage from a young Kennedy. Then, when she learns he has remarried, she kills herself. Now, I believe you would consider this girl to be a deranged idiot, correct? But because it's an Oriental who kills herself for a Westerner—ah!—you find it beautiful.

[*Silence.*]

GALLIMARD. Yes . . . well . . . I see your point . . .

SONG. I will never do Butterfly again, Monsieur Gallimard. If you wish to see some real theater, come to the Peking Opera sometime. Expand your mind.
[SONG *walks offstage. Other guests exit with her.*]

GALLIMARD [*to us*]. So much for protecting her in my big Western arms.

SCENE VII

M. GALLIMARD'S apartment. Beijing. 1960.

GALLIMARD *changes from his tux into a casual suit.* HELGA *enters.*

GALLIMARD. The Chinese are an incredibly arrogant people.

HELGA. They warned us about that in Paris, remember?

GALLIMARD. Even Parisians consider them arrogant. That's a switch.

HELGA. What is it that Madame Su says? "We are a very old civilization." I never know if she's talking about her country or herself.

GALLIMARD. I walk around here, all I hear every day, everywhere is how *old* this culture is. The fact that "old" may be synonymous with "senile" doesn't occur to them.

HELGA. You're not going to change them. "East is east, west is west, and . . ." whatever that guy said.

GALLIMARD. It's just that—silly. I met . . . at Ambassador Koening's tonight—you should've been there.

HELGA. Koening? Oh god, no. Did he enchant you all again with the history of Bavaria?

GALLIMARD. No. I met, I suppose, the Chinese equivalent of a diva. She's a singer in the Chinese opera.

HELGA. They have an opera, too? Do they sing in Chinese? Or maybe—in Italian?

GALLIMARD. Tonight, she did sing in Italian.

HELGA. How'd she manage that?

GALLIMARD. She must've been educated in the West before the Revolution. Her French is very good also. Anyway, she sang the death scene from *Madame Butterfly.*

HELGA. *Madame Butterfly!* Then I should have come. [*She begins humming, floating around the room as if dragging long kimono sleeves.*] Did she have a nice costume? I think it's a classic piece of music.

GALLIMARD. That's what *I* thought, too. Don't let her hear you say that.

HELGA. What's wrong?

GALLIMARD. Evidently the Chinese hate it.

HELGA. She hated it, but she performed it anyway? Is she perverse?

GALLIMARD. They hate it because the white man gets the girl. Sour grapes if you ask me.

HELGA. Politics again? Why can't they just hear it as a piece of beautiful music? So, what's in their opera?

GALLIMARD. I don't know. But, whatever it is, I'm sure it must be *old.*

[HELGA *exits.*]

SCENE VIII

Chinese opera house and the streets of Beijing. 1960.

The sound of gongs clanging fills the stage.

GALLIMARD. My wife's innocent question kept ringing in my ears. I asked around, but no one knew anything about the Chinese opera. It took four weeks, but my curiosity overcame my cowardice. This Chinese diva—this unwilling Butterfly—what did she do to make her so proud?

The room was hot, and full of smoke. Wrinkled faces, old women, teeth missing—a man with a growth on his neck, like a human toad. All smiling, pipes falling from their mouths, cracking nuts between their teeth, a live chicken pecking at my foot—all looking, screaming, gawking . . . at her.

[*The upstage area is suddenly hit with a harsh white light. It has become the stage for the Chinese opera performance. Two dancers enter, along with* SONG. GALLIMARD *stands apart, watching.* SONG *glides gracefully amidst the two dancers. Drums suddenly slam to a halt.* SONG *strikes a pose, looking straight at* GALLIMARD. *Dancers exit. Light change. Pause, then* SONG *walks right off the stage and straight up to* GALLIMARD.]

SONG. Yes. You. White man. I'm looking straight at you.

GALLIMARD. Me?

SONG. You see any other white men? It was too easy to spot you. How often does a man in my audience come in a tie?

[SONG *starts to remove her costume. Underneath, she wears simple baggy clothes. They are now backstage. The show is over.*]

SONG. So, you are an adventurous imperialist?

GALLIMARD. I . . . thought it would further my education.

SONG. It took you four weeks. Why?

GALLIMARD. I've been busy.

SONG. Well, education has always been undervalued in the West, hasn't it?

GALLIMARD [*laughing*]. I don't think that's true.

SONG. No, you wouldn't. You're a Westerner. How can you objectively judge your own values?

GALLIMARD. I think it's possible to achieve some distance.

SONG. Do you? [*Pause.*] It stinks in here. Let's go.

GALLIMARD. These are the smells of your loyal fans.

SONG. I love them for being my fans, I hate the smell they leave behind. I too can distance myself from my people. [*She looks around, then whispers in his ear.*] "Art for the masses" is a shitty excuse to keep artists poor. [*She pops a cigarette in her mouth.*] Be a gentleman, will you? And light my cigarette.

[GALLIMARD *fumbles for a match.*]

GALLIMARD. I don't . . . smoke.

SONG [*lighting her own*]. Your loss. Had you lit my cigarette, I might have blown a puff of smoke right between your eyes. Come.

[*They start to walk about the stage. It is a summer night on the Beijing streets. Sounds of the city play on the house speakers.*]

SONG. How I wish there were even a tiny café to sit in. With cappuccinos, and men in tuxedos and bad expatriate jazz.

GALLIMARD. If my history serves me correctly, you weren't even allowed into the clubs in Shanghai before the Revolution.

SONG. Your history serves you poorly, Monsieur Gallimard. True, there were signs reading "No dogs and Chinamen." But a woman, especially a delicate Oriental woman—we always go where we please. Could you imagine it otherwise? Clubs in China filled with pasty, big-thighed white women, while thousands of slender lotus blossoms wait just outside the door? Never. The clubs would be empty. [*Beat.*] We have always held a certain fascination for you Caucasian men, have we not?

GALLIMARD. But . . . that fascination is imperialist, or so you tell me.

SONG. Do you believe everything I tell you? Yes. It is always imperialist. But sometimes . . . sometimes, it is also mutual. Oh—this is my flat.

GALLIMARD. I didn't even—

SONG. Thank you. Come another time and we will further expand your mind.

[SONG *exits.* GALLIMARD *continues roaming the streets as he speaks to us.*]

GALLIMARD. What was that? What did she mean, "Sometimes . . . it is mutual"? Women do not flirt with me. And I normally can't talk to them. But tonight, I held up my end of the conversation.

SCENE IX

GALLIMARD'S bedroom. Beijing. 1960.

[HELGA *enters.*]

HELGA. You didn't tell me you'd be home late.

GALLIMARD. I didn't intend to. Something came up.

HELGA. Oh? Like what?

GALLIMARD. I went to the . . . to the Dutch ambassador's home.

HELGA. Again?

GALLIMARD. There was a reception for a visiting scholar. He's writing a six-volume treatise on the Chinese revolution. We all gathered that meant he'd have to live here long enough to actually write six volumes, and we all expressed our deepest sympathies.

HELGA. Well, I had a good night too. I went with the ladies to a martial arts demonstration. Some of those men—when they break those thick boards—[*She mimes fanning herself.*] whoo-whoo!

[HELGA *exits. Lights dim.*]

GALLIMARD. I lied to my wife. Why? I've never had any reason to lie before. But what reason did I have tonight? I didn't do anything wrong. That night, I had a dream. Other people, I've been told, have dreams when angels appear. Or dragons, or Sophia Loren in a towel. In my dream, Marc from school appeared.

[MARC *enters, in a nightshirt and cap.*]

MARC. Rene! You met a girl!

[GALLIMARD *and* MARC *stumble down the Beijing streets. Night sounds over the speakers.*]

GALLIMARD. It's not that amazing, thank you.

MARC. No! It's so monumental, I heard about it halfway around the world in my sleep!

GALLIMARD. I've met girls before, you know.

MARC. Name one. I've come across time and space to congratulate you. [*He hands* GALLIMARD *a bottle of wine.*]

GALLIMARD. Marc, this is expensive.

MARC. On those rare occasions when you become a formless spirit, why not steal the best?

[MARC *pops open the bottle, begins to share it with* GALLIMARD.]

GALLIMARD. You embarrass me. She . . . there's no reason to think she likes me.

MARC. "Sometimes, it is mutual"?

GALLIMARD. Oh.

MARC. "Mutual"? "Mutual"? What does that mean?

GALLIMARD. You heard?

MARC. It means the money is in the bank, you only have to write the check!

GALLIMARD. I am a married man!

MARC. And an excellent one too. I cheated after . . . six months. Then again and again, until now—three hundred girls in twelve years.

GALLIMARD. I don't think we should hold that up as a model.

MARC. Of course not! My life—it is disgusting! Phooey! Phooey! But, you—you are the model husband.

GALLIMARD. Anyway, it's impossible. I'm a foreigner.

MARC. Ah, yes. She cannot love you, it is taboo, but something deep inside her heart . . . she cannot help herself . . . she must surrender to you. It is her destiny.

GALLIMARD. How do you imagine all this?

MARC. The same way you do. It's an old story. It's in our blood. They fear us, Rene. Their women fear us. And their men—their men hate us. And, you know something? They are all correct.

[*They spot a light in a window.*]

MARC. There! There, Rene!

GALLIMARD. It's her window.

MARC. Late at night—it burns. The light—it burns for you.

GALLIMARD. I won't look. It's not respectful.

MARC. We don't have to be respectful. We're foreign devils.

[Enter SONG, *in a sheer robe, her face completely swathed in black cloth. The "One Fine Day" aria creeps in over the speakers. With her back to us,* SONG *mimes attending to her toilette. Her robe comes loose, revealing her white shoulders.*]

MARC. All your life you've waited for a beautiful girl who would lay down for you. All your life you've smiled like a saint when it's happened to every other man you know. And you see them in magazines and you see them in movies. And you wonder, what's wrong with me? Will anyone beautiful ever want me? As the years pass, your hair thins and you struggle to hold on to even your hopes. Stop struggling, Rene. The wait is over. [*He exits.*]

GALLIMARD. Marc? Marc?

[*At that moment,* SONG, *her back still towards us, drops her robe. A second of her naked back, then a sound cue: a phone ringing, very loud. Blackout, followed in the next beat by a special up on the bedroom area, where a phone now sits.* GALLIMARD *stumbles across the stage and picks up the phone. Sound cue out. Over the course of his conversation, area lights fill in the vicinity of his bed. It is the following morning.*]

GALLIMARD. Yes? Hello?

SONG [*offstage*]. Is it very early?

GALLIMARD. Why, yes.

SONG [*offstage*]. How early?

GALLIMARD. It's . . . it's 5:30. Why are you—?

SONG [*offstage*]. But it's light outside. Already.

GALLIMARD. It is. The sun must be in confusion today.

[*Over the course of* SONG's *next speech, her upstage special comes up again. She sits in a chair, legs crossed, in a robe, telephone to her ear.*]

SONG. I waited until I saw the sun. That was as much discipline as I could manage for one night. Do you forgive me?

GALLIMARD. Of course . . . for what?

SONG. Then I'll ask you quickly. Are you really interested in the opera?

GALLIMARD. Why, yes. Yes I am.

SONG. Then come again next Thursday. I am playing *The Drunken Beauty*. May I count on you?

GALLIMARD. Yes. You may.

SONG. Perfect. Well, I must be getting to bed. I'm exhausted. It's been a very long night for me.

[SONG *hangs up; special on her goes off.* GALLIMARD *begins to dress for work.*]

SCENE X

SONG LILING's apartment. Beijing. 1960.

GALLIMARD. I returned to the opera that next week, and the week after that . . . she keeps our meetings so short—perhaps fifteen, twenty minutes at most. So I am left each week with a thirst which is intensified. In this way, fifteen weeks have gone by. I am starting to doubt the words of my friend Marc. But no, not really. In my heart, I know she has . . . an interest in me. I suspect this is her way. She is outwardly bold and outspoken, yet her heart is shy and afraid. It is the Oriental in her at war with her Western education.

SONG [*offstage*]. I will be out in an instant. Ask the servant for anything you want.

GALLIMARD. Tonight, I have finally been invited to enter her apartment. Though the idea is almost beyond belief, I believe she is afraid of me.

[GALLIMARD *looks around the room. He picks up a picture in a frame, studies it. Without his noticing,* SONG *enters, dressed elegantly in a black gown from the twenties. She stands in the doorway looking like Anna May Wong.*[3]]

SONG. That is my father.

GALLIMARD [*surprised*]. Mademoiselle Song . . .

[*She glides up to him, snatches away the picture.*]

SONG. It is very good that he did not live to see the Revolution. They would, no doubt, have made him kneel on broken glass. Not that he didn't deserve such a punishment. But he is my father. I would've hated to see it happen.

GALLIMARD. I'm very honored that you've allowed me to visit your home.

[SONG *curtseys.*]

SONG. Thank you. Oh! Haven't you been poured any tea?

GALLIMARD. I'm really not—

---

[3]Chinese-American actress (1905–1961).

SONG [*to her offstage servant*]. Shu-Fang! Cha! Kwai-lah! [*To* GALLIMARD.] I'm sorry. You want everything to be perfect—

GALLIMARD. Please.

SONG. —and before the evening even begins—

GALLIMARD. I'm really not thirsty.

SONG. —it's ruined.

GALLIMARD [*sharply*]. Mademoiselle Song!

[SONG *sits down*.]

SONG. I'm sorry.

GALLIMARD. What are you apologizing for now?

[*Pause;* SONG *starts to giggle*.]

SONG. I don't know!

[GALLIMARD *laughs*.]

GALLIMARD. Exactly my point.

SONG. Oh, I am silly. Light-headed. I promise not to apologize for anything else tonight, do you hear me?

GALLIMARD. That's a good girl.

[SHU-FANG, *a servant girl, comes out with a tea tray and starts to pour*.]

SONG [*to* SHU-FANG]. No! I'll pour myself for the gentleman!

[SHU-FANG, *staring at* GALLIMARD, *exits*.]

GALLIMARD. You have a beautiful home.

SONG. No, I . . . I don't even know why I invited you up.

GALLIMARD. Well, I'm glad you did.

[SONG *looks around the room*.]

SONG. There is an element of danger to your presence.

GALLIMARD. Oh?

SONG. You must know.

GALLIMARD. It doesn't concern me. We both know why I'm here.

SONG. It doesn't concern me either. No . . . well perhaps . . .

GALLIMARD. What?

SONG. Perhaps I am slightly afraid of scandal.

GALLIMARD. What are we doing?

SONG. I'm entertaining you. In my parlor.

GALLIMARD. In France, that would hardly—

SONG. France. France is a country living in the modern era. Perhaps even ahead of it. China is a nation whose soul is firmly rooted two thousand years in the past. What I do, even pouring the tea for you now . . . it has . . . implications. The walls and windows say so. Even my own heart, strapped inside this Western dress . . . even it says things—things I don't care to hear.

[SONG *hands* GALLIMARD *a cup of tea.* GALLIMARD *puts his hand over both the teacup and* SONG's *hand.*]

GALLIMARD. This is a beautiful dress.

SONG. Don't.

GALLIMARD. What?

SONG. I don't even know if it looks right on me.

GALLIMARD. Believe me—

SONG. You are from France. You see so many beautiful women.

GALLIMARD. France? Since when are the European women—?

SONG. Oh! What am I trying to do, anyway?!

[SONG *runs to the door, composes herself, then turns towards* GALLIMARD.]

SONG. Monsieur Gallimard, perhaps you should go.

GALLIMARD. But . . . why?

SONG. There's something wrong about this.

GALLIMARD. I don't see what.

SONG. I feel . . . I am not myself.

GALLIMARD. No. You're nervous.

SONG. Please. Hard as I try to be modern, to speak like a man, to hold a Western woman's strong face up to my own . . . in the end, I fail. A small, frightened heart beats too quickly and gives me away. Monsieur Gallimard, I'm a Chinese girl. I've never . . . never invited a man up to my flat before. The forwardness of my actions makes my skin burn.

GALLIMARD. What are you afraid of? Certainly not me, I hope.

SONG. I'm a modest girl.

GALLIMARD. I know. And very beautiful. [*He touches her hair.*]

SONG. Please—go now. The next time you see me, I shall again be myself.

GALLIMARD. I like you the way you are right now.

SONG. You are a cad.

GALLIMARD. What do you expect? I'm a foreign devil.

[GALLIMARD *walks downstage.* SONG *exits.*]

GALLIMARD [*to us*]. Did you hear the way she talked about Western women? Much differently than the first night. She does—she feels inferior to them—and to me.

SCENE XI

The French embassy. Beijing. 1960.

GALLIMARD *moves towards a desk.*

GALLIMARD. I determined to try an experiment. In *Madame Butterfly*, Cio-Cio-San fears that the Western man who catches a butterfly will pierce its heart with a needle, then leave it to perish. I began to wonder: had I, too, caught a butterfly who would writhe on a needle?

[MARC *enters, dressed as a bureaucrat, holding a stack of papers. As* GALLIMARD *speaks,* MARC *hands papers to him. He peruses, then signs, stamps, or rejects them.*]

GALLIMARD. Over the next five weeks, I worked like a dynamo. I stopped going to the opera, I didn't phone or write her. I knew this little flower was waiting for me to call, and, as I wickedly refused to do so, I felt for the first time that rush of power—the absolute power of a man.

[MARC *continues acting as the bureaucrat, but he now speaks as himself.*]

MARC. Rene! It's me.

GALLIMARD. Marc—I hear your voice everywhere now. Even in the midst of work.

MARC. That's because I'm watching you—all the time.

GALLIMARD. You were always the most popular guy in school.

MARC. Well, there's no guarantee of failure in life like happiness in high school. Somehow I knew I'd end up in the suburbs working for Renault and you'd be in the Orient picking exotic women off the trees. And they say there's no justice.

GALLIMARD. That's why you were my friend?

MARC. I gave you a little of my life, so that now you can give me some of yours. [*Pause.*] Remember Isabelle?

GALLIMARD. Of course I remember! She was my first experience.

MARC. We all wanted to ball her. But she only wanted me.

GALLIMARD. I had her.

MARC. Right. You balled her.

GALLIMARD. You were the only one who ever believed me.

MARC. Well, there's a good reason for that. [*Beat.*] C'mon. You must've guessed.

GALLIMARD. You told me to wait in the bushes by the cafeteria that night. The next thing I knew, she was on me. Dress up in the air.

MARC. She never wore underwear.

GALLIMARD. My arms were pinned to the dirt.

MARC. She loved the superior position. A girl ahead of her time.

GALLIMARD. I looked up, and there was this woman . . . bouncing up and down on my loins.

MARC. Screaming, right?

GALLIMARD. Screaming, and breaking off the branches all around me, and pounding my butt up and down into the dirt.

MARC. Huffing and puffing like a locomotive.

GALLIMARD. And in the middle of all this, the leaves were getting into my mouth, my legs were losing circulation, I thought, "God. So this is *it*?"

MARC. You thought that?

GALLIMARD. Well, I was worried about my legs falling off.

MARC. You didn't have a good time?

GALLIMARD. No, that's not what I—I had a great time!

MARC. You're sure?

GALLIMARD. Yeah. Really.

MARC. 'Cuz I wanted you to have a good time.

GALLIMARD. I did.

[*Pause.*]

MARC. Shit. [*Pause.*] When all is said and done, she was kind of a lousy lay, wasn't she? I mean, there was a lot of energy there, but you never knew what she was doing with it. Like when she yelled "I'm coming!"—hell, it was so loud, you wanted to go, "Look, it's not that big a deal."

GALLIMARD. I got scared. I thought she meant someone was actually coming. [*Pause.*] But, Marc?

MARC. What?

GALLIMARD. Thanks.

MARC. Oh, don't mention it.

GALLIMARD. It was my first experience.

MARC. Yeah. You got her.

GALLIMARD. I got her.

MARC. Wait! Look at that letter again!

[GALLIMARD *picks up one of the papers he's been stamping, and rereads it.*]

GALLIMARD [*to us*]. After six weeks, they began to arrive. The letters.

[*Upstage special on* SONG, *as Madame Butterfly. The scene is underscored by the "Love Duet."*]

SONG. Did we fight? I do not know. Is the opera no longer of interest to you? Please come—my audiences miss the white devil in their midst.

[GALLIMARD *looks up from the letter, towards us.*]

GALLIMARD [*to us*]. A concession, but much too dignified. [*Beat; he discards the letter.*] I skipped the opera again that week to complete a position paper on trade.

[*The bureaucrat hands him another letter.*]

SONG. Six weeks have passed since last we met. Is this your practice—to leave friends in the lurch? Sometimes I hate you, sometimes I hate myself, but always I miss you.

GALLIMARD [*to us*]. Better, but I don't like the way she calls me "friend." When a woman calls a man her "friend," she's calling him a eunuch or a homosexual. [*Beat; he discards the letter.*] I was absent from the opera for the seventh week, feeling a sudden urge to clean out my files.

[*Bureaucrat hands him another letter.*]

SONG. Your rudeness is beyond belief. I don't deserve this cruelty. Don't bother to call. I'll have you turned away at the door.

GALLIMARD [*to us*]. I didn't. [*He discards the letter; bureaucrat hands him another.*] And then finally, the letter that concluded my experiment.

SONG. I am out of words. I can hide behind dignity no longer. What do you want? I have already given you my shame.

[GALLIMARD *gives the letter back to* MARC, *slowly. Special on* SONG *fades out.*]

GALLIMARD [*to us*]. Reading it, I became suddenly ashamed. Yes, my experiment had been a success. She was turning on my needle. But the victory seemed hollow.

MARC. Hollow?! Are you crazy?

GALLIMARD. Nothing, Marc. Please go away.

MARC [*exiting, with papers*]. Haven't I taught you anything?

GALLIMARD. "I have already given you my shame." I had to attend a reception that evening. On the way, I felt sick. If there is a God, surely he would punish me now. I had finally gained power over a beautiful woman, only to abuse it cruelly. There must be justice in the world. I had the strange feeling that the axe would fall this very evening.

SCENE XII

Ambassador Toulon's residence. Beijing. 1960.

Sound cue: party noises. Light change. We are now in a spacious residence. TOULON, *the French ambassador, enters and taps* GALLIMARD *on the shoulder.*

TOULON. Gallimard? Can I have a word? Over here.

GALLIMARD [*to us*]. Manuel Toulon. French ambassador to China. He likes to think of us all as his children. Rather like God.

TOULON. Look, Gallimard, there's not much to say. I've liked you. From the day you walked in. You were no leader, but you were tidy and efficient.

GALLIMARD. Thank you, sir.

TOULON. Don't jump the gun. Okay, our needs in China are changing. It's embarrassing that we lost Indochina. Someone just wasn't on the ball there. I don't mean you personally, of course.

GALLIMARD. Thank you, sir.

TOULON. We're going to be doing a lot more information-gathering in the future. The nature of our work here is changing. Some people are just going to have to go. It's nothing personal.

GALLIMARD. Oh.

TOULON. Want to know a secret? Vice-Consul LeBon is being transferred.

GALLIMARD [*to us*]. My immediate superior!

TOULON. And most of his department.

GALLIMARD [*to us*]. Just as I feared! God has seen my evil heart—

TOULON. But not you.

GALLIMARD [*to us*]. —and he's taking her away just as . . . [*To* TOULON.] Excuse me, sir?

TOULON. Scare you? I think I did. Cheer up, Gallimard. I want you to replace LeBon as vice-consul.

GALLIMARD. You—? Yes, well, thank you, sir.

TOULON. Anytime.

GALLIMARD. I . . . accept with great humility.

TOULON. Humility won't be part of the job. You're going to coordinate the revamped intelligence division. Want to know a secret? A year ago, you would've been out. But the past few months, I don't know how it happened, you've become this new aggressive confident . . . thing. And they also tell me you get along with the Chinese. So I think you're a lucky man, Gallimard. Congratulations.

[*They shake hands.* TOULON *exits. Party noises out.* GALLIMARD *stumbles across a darkened stage.*]

GALLIMARD. Vice-consul? Impossible! As I stumbled out of the party, I saw it written across the sky: There is no God. Or, no—say that there is a God. But that God . . . understands. Of course! God who creates Eve to serve Adam, who blesses Solomon with his harem but ties Jezebel to a burning bed[4]—that God is a man. And he understands! At age thirty-nine, I was suddenly initiated into the way of the world.

SCENE XIII

SONG LILING's apartment. Beijing. 1960.

[SONG *enters, in a sheer dressing gown.*]

SONG. Are you crazy?

GALLIMARD. Mademoiselle Song—

SONG. To come here—at this hour? After . . . after eight weeks?

GALLIMARD. It's the most amazing—

SONG. You bang on my door? Scare my servants, scandalize the neighbors?

GALLIMARD. I've been promoted. To vice-consul.

[*Pause.*]

SONG. And what is that supposed to mean to me?

GALLIMARD. Are you my Butterfly?

SONG. What are you saying?

GALLIMARD. I've come tonight for an answer: are you my Butterfly?

SONG. Don't you know already?

GALLIMARD. I want you to say it.

SONG. I don't want to say it.

GALLIMARD. So, that is your answer?

SONG. You know how I feel about—

GALLIMARD. I do remember one thing.

---

[4]Biblical allusions; see Genesis 2:18–25, I Kings 11:1–8, and II Kings 9:30–37.

SONG. What?

GALLIMARD. In the letter I received today.

SONG. Don't.

GALLIMARD. "I have already given you my shame."

SONG. It's enough that I even wrote it.

GALLIMARD. Well, then—

SONG. I shouldn't have it splashed across my face.

GALLIMARD. —if that's all true—

SONG. Stop!

GALLIMARD. Then what is one more short answer?

SONG. I don't want to!

GALLIMARD. Are you my Butterfly? [*Silence; he crosses the room and begins to touch her hair.*] I want from you honesty. There should be nothing false between us. No false pride.

[*Pause.*]

SONG. Yes, I am. I am your Butterfly.

GALLIMARD. Then let me be honest with you. It is because of you that I was promoted tonight. You have changed my life forever. My little Butterfly, there should be no more secrets: I love you.

[*He starts to kiss her roughly. She resists slightly.*]

SONG. No . . . no . . . gently . . . please, I've never . . .

GALLIMARD. No?

SONG. I've tried to appear experienced, but . . . the truth is . . . no.

GALLIMARD. Are you cold?

SONG. Yes. Cold.

GALLIMARD. Then we will go very, very slowly.

[*He starts to caress her; her gown begins to open.*]

SONG. No . . . let me . . . keep my clothes . . . .

GALLIMARD. But . . .

SONG. Please . . . it all frightens me. I'm a modest Chinese girl.

GALLIMARD. My poor little treasure.

SONG. I am your treasure. Though inexperienced, I am not . . . ignorant. They teach us things, our mothers, about pleasing a man.

GALLIMARD. Yes?

SONG. I'll do my best to make you happy. Turn off the lights.

[GALLIMARD *gets up and heads for a lamp.* SONG, *propped up on one elbow, tosses her hair back and smiles.*]

SONG. Monsieur Gallimard?

GALLIMARD. Yes, Butterfly?

SONG. *"Vieni, vieni!"*

GALLIMARD. "Come, darling."

SONG. *"Ah! Dolce notte!"*

GALLIMARD. "Beautiful night."

SONG. *"Tutto estatico d'amor ride il ciel!"*

GALLIMARD. "All ecstatic with love, the heavens are filled with laughter."

[*He turns off the lamp. Blackout.*]

ACT II
SCENE I

M. GALLIMARD's cell. Paris. 1988.

Lights up on GALLIMARD. *He sits in his cell, reading from a leaflet.*

GALLIMARD. This, from a contemporary critic's commentary on *Madame Butterfly*: "Pinkerton suffers from . . . being an obnoxious bounder whom every man in the audience itches to kick." Bully for us men in the audience! Then, in the same note: "Butterfly is the most irresistibly appealing of Puccini's 'Little Women.' Watching the succession of her humiliations is like watching a child under torture." [*He tosses the pamphlet over his shoulder.*] I suggest that, while we men may all want to kick Pinkerton, very few of us would pass up the opportunity to *be* Pinkerton.

[GALLIMARD *moves out of his cell.*]

SCENE II

GALLIMARD and Butterfly's flat. Beijing. 1960.

We are in a simple but well-decorated parlor. GALLIMARD *moves to sit on a sofa, while* SONG, *dressed in a chong sam,*[5] *enters and curls up at his feet.*

GALLIMARD [*to us*]. We secured a flat on the outskirts of Peking. Butterfly, as I was calling her now, decorated our "home" with Western furniture and Chinese antiques. And there, on a few stolen afternoons or evenings each week, Butterfly commenced her education.

SONG. The Chinese men—they keep us down.

GALLIMARD. Even in the "New Society"?

SONG. In the "New Society," we are all kept ignorant equally. That's one of the exciting things about loving a Western man. I know you are not threatened by a woman's education.

GALLIMARD. I'm no saint, Butterfly.

SONG. But you come from a progressive society.

GALLIMARD. We're not always reminding each other how "old" we are, if that's what you mean.

SONG. Exactly. We Chinese—once, I suppose, it is true, we ruled the world. But so what? How much more exciting to be part of the society ruling the world today. Tell me—what's happening in Vietnam?

---

[5]Tight-fitting dress with slits in the sides of the skirt.

GALLIMARD. Oh, Butterfly—you want me to bring my work home?

SONG. I want to know what you know. To be impressed by my man. It's not the particulars so much as the fact that you're making decisions which change the shape of the world.

GALLIMARD. Not the world. At best, a small corner.

[TOULON *enters, and sits at a desk upstage.*]

SCENE III

French embassy. Beijing. 1961.

GALLIMARD *moves downstage, to* TOULON's *desk.* SONG *remains upstage, watching.*

TOULON. And a more troublesome corner is hard to imagine.

GALLIMARD. So, the Americans plan to begin bombing?

TOULON. This is very secret, Gallimard: yes. The Americans don't have an embassy here. They're asking us to be their eyes and ears. Say Jack Kennedy signed an order to bomb North Vietnam, Laos. How would the Chinese react?

GALLIMARD. I think the Chinese will squawk—

TOULON. Uh-huh.

GALLIMARD. —but, in their hearts, they don't even like Ho Chi Minh.[6]

[*Pause.*]

TOULON. What a bunch of jerks. Vietnam was *our* colony. Not only didn't the Americans help us fight to keep them, but now, seven years later, they've come back to grab the territory for themselves. It's very irritating.

GALLIMARD. With all due respect, sir, why should the Americans have won our war for us back in 'fifty-four if we didn't have the will to win it ourselves?

TOULON. You're kidding, aren't you?

[*Pause.*]

GALLIMARD. The Orientals simply want to be associated with whoever shows the most strength and power. You live with the Chinese, sir. Do you think they like Communism?

TOULON. I live in China. Not with the Chinese.

GALLIMARD. Well, I—

TOULON. *You* live with the Chinese.

GALLIMARD. Excuse me?

TOULON. I can't keep a secret.

GALLIMARD. What are you saying?

TOULON. Only that I'm not immune to gossip. So, you're keeping a native mistress? Don't answer. It's none of my business. [*Pause.*] I'm sure she must be gorgeous.

---

[6]President of North Vietnam, 1945–1969.

GALLIMARD. Well . . .

TOULON. I'm impressed. You had the stamina to go out into the streets and hunt one down. Some of us have to be content with the wives of the expatriate community.

GALLIMARD. I do feel . . . fortunate.

TOULON. So, Gallimard, you've got the inside knowledge—what *do* the Chinese think?

GALLIMARD. Deep down, they miss the old days. You know, cappuccinos, men in tuxedos—

TOULON. So what do we tell the Americans about Vietnam?

GALLIMARD. Tell them there's a natural affinity between the West and the Orient.

TOULON. And that you speak from experience?

GALLIMARD. The Orientals are people too. They want the good things we can give them. If the Americans demonstrate the will to win, the Vietnamese will welcome them into a mutually beneficial union.

TOULON. I don't see how the Vietnamese can stand up to American firepower.

GALLIMARD. Orientals will always submit to a greater force.

TOULON. I'll note your opinions in my report. The Americans always love to hear how "welcome" they'll be. [*He starts to exit.*]

GALLIMARD. Sir?

TOULON. Mmmm?

GALLIMARD. This . . . rumor you've heard.

TOULON. Uh-huh?

GALLIMARD. How . . . widespread do you think it is?

TOULON. It's only widespread within this embassy. Where nobody talks because everybody is guilty. We were worried about you, Gallimard. We thought you were the only one here without a secret. Now you go and find a lotus blossom . . . and top us all. [*He exits.*]

GALLIMARD [*to us*]. Toulon knows! And he approves! I was learning the benefits of being a man. We form our own clubs, sit behind thick doors, smoke— and celebrate the fact that we're still boys. [*He starts to move downstage, towards* SONG.] So, over the—

[*Suddenly* COMRADE CHIN *enters.* GALLIMARD *backs away.*]

GALLIMARD [*to* SONG]. No! Why does she have to come in?

SONG. Rene, be sensible. How can they understand the story without her? Now, don't embarrass yourself.

[GALLIMARD *moves down center.*]

GALLIMARD [*to us*]. Now, you will see why my story is so amusing to so many people. Why they snicker at parties in disbelief. Please—try to understand it from my point of view. We are all prisoners of our time and place. [*He exits.*]

SCENE IV

Gallimard and Butterfly's flat. Beijing. 1961.

Song [*to us*]. 1961. The flat Monsieur Gallimard rented for us. An evening after he has gone.

Chin. Okay, see if you can find out when the Americans plan to start bombing Vietnam. If you can find out what cities, even better.

Song. I'll do my best, but I don't want to arouse his suspicions.

Chin. Yeah, sure, of course. So, what else?

Song. The Americans will increase troops in Vietnam to 170,000 soldiers with 120,000 militia and 11,000 American advisors.

Chin [*writing*]. Wait, wait, 120,000 militia and—

Song. —11,000 American—

Chin. —American advisors. [*Beat.*] How do you remember so much?

Song. I'm an actor.

Chin. Yeah. [*Beat.*] Is that how come you dress like that?

Song. Like what, Miss Chin?

Chin. Like that dress! You're wearing a dress. And every time I come here, you're wearing a dress. Is that because you're an actor? Or what?

Song. It's a . . . disguise, Miss Chin.

Chin. Actors, I think they're all weirdos. My mother tells me actors are like gamblers or prostitutes or—

Song. It helps me in my assignment.

[*Pause.*]

Chin. You're not gathering information in any way that violates Communist Party principles, are you?

Song. Why would I do that?

Chin. Just checking. Remember: when working for the Great Proletarian State, you represent our Chairman Mao in every position you take.

Song. I'll try to imagine the Chairman taking my positions.

Chin. We all think of him this way. Good-bye, comrade. [*She starts to exit.*] Comrade?

Song. Yes?

Chin. Don't forget: there is no homosexuality in China!

Song. Yes, I've heard.

Chin. Just checking. [*She exits.*]

Song [*to us*]. What passes for a woman in modern China.

[Gallimard *sticks his head out from the wings.*]

Gallimard. Is she gone?

Song. Yes, Rene. Please continue in your own fashion.

SCENE V

Beijing. 1961–1963.

GALLIMARD *moves to the couch where* SONG *still sits. He lies down in her lap, and she strokes his forehead.*

GALLIMARD [*to us*]. And so, over the years 1961, '62, '63, we settled into our routine, Butterfly and I. She would always have prepared a light snack and then, ever so delicately, and only if I agreed, she would start to pleasure me. With her hands, her mouth . . . too many ways to explain, and too sad, given my present situation. But mostly we would talk. About my life. Perhaps there is nothing more rare than to find a woman who passionately listens.

[SONG *remains upstage, listening, as* HELGA *enters and plays a scene downstage with* GALLIMARD.]

HELGA. Rene, I visited Dr. Bolleart this morning.

GALLIMARD. Why? Are you ill?

HELGA. No, no. You see, I wanted to ask him . . . that question we've been discussing.

GALLIMARD. And I told you, it's only a matter of time. Why did you bring a doctor into this? We just have to keep trying—like a crapshoot, actually.

HELGA. I went, I'm sorry. But listen: he says there's nothing wrong with me.

GALLIMARD. You see? Now, will you stop—?

HELGA. Rene, he says he'd like you to go in and take some tests.

GALLIMARD. Why? So he can find there's nothing wrong with both of us?

HELGA. Rene, I don't ask for much. One trip! One visit! And then, whatever you want to do about it—you decide.

GALLIMARD. You're assuming he'll find something defective!

HELGA. No! Of course not! Whatever he finds—if he finds nothing, we decide what to do about nothing! But go!

GALLIMARD. If he finds nothing, we keep trying. Just like we do now.

HELGA. But at least we'll know! [*Pause.*] I'm sorry. [*She starts to exit.*]

GALLIMARD. Do you really want me to see Dr. Bolleart?

HELGA. Only if you want a child, Rene. We have to face the fact that time is running out. Only if you want a child. [*She exits.*]

GALLIMARD [*to* SONG]. I'm a modern man, Butterfly. And yet, I don't want to go. It's the same old voodoo. I feel like God himself is laughing at me if I can't produce a child.

SONG. You men of the West—you're obsessed by your odd desire for equality. Your wife can't give you a child, and *you're* going to the doctor?

GALLIMARD. Well, you see, she's already gone.

SONG. And because this incompetent can't find the defect, you now have to subject yourself to him? It's unnatural.

GALLIMARD. Well, what is the "natural" solution?

SONG. In Imperial China, when a man found that one wife was inadequate, he turned to another—to give him his son.

GALLIMARD. What do you—? I can't . . . marry you, yet.

SONG. Please. I'm not asking you to be my husband. But I am already your wife.

GALLIMARD. Do you want to . . . have my child?

SONG. I thought you'd never ask.

GALLIMARD. But, your career . . . your—

SONG. Phooey on my career! That's your Western mind, twisting itself into strange shapes again. Of course I love my career. But what would I love most of all? To feel something inside me—day and night—something I know is yours. [*Pause.*] Promise me . . . you won't go to this doctor. Who is this Western quack to set himself as judge over the man I love? I know who is a man, and who is not. [*She exits.*]

GALLIMARD [*to us*]. Dr. Bolleart? Of course I didn't go. What man would?

SCENE VI

Beijing. 1963.

Party noises over the house speakers. RENEE *enters, wearing a revealing gown.*

GALLIMARD. 1963. A party at the Austrian embassy. None of us could remember the Austrian ambassador's name, which seemed somehow appropriate. [*To Renee.*] So, I tell the Americans, Diem[7] must go. The U.S. wants to be respected by the Vietnamese, and yet they're propping up this nobody seminarian as her president. A man whose claim to fame is his sister-in-law imposing fanatic "moral order" campaigns? Oriental women—when they're good, they're very good, but when they're bad, they're Christians.

RENEE. Yeah.

GALLIMARD. And what do you do?

RENEE. I'm a student. My father exports a lot of useless stuff to the Third World.

GALLIMARD. How useless?

RENEE. You know. Squirt guns, confectioner's sugar, Hula Hoops . . .

GALLIMARD. I'm sure they appreciate the sugar.

RENEE. I'm here for two years to study Chinese.

GALLIMARD. Two years!

RENEE. That's what everybody says.

GALLIMARD. When did you arrive?

RENEE. Three weeks ago.

GALLIMARD. And?

---

[7]Ngo Dinh Diem (1901–1963), president of South Vietnam, 1955–1963; assassinated in a U.S.-supported coup.

RENEE. I like it. It's primitive, but . . . well, this is the place to learn Chinese, so here I am.

GALLIMARD. Why Chinese?

RENEE. I think it'll be important someday.

GALLIMARD. You do?

RENEE. Don't ask me when, but . . . that's what I think.

GALLIMARD. Well, I agree with you. One hundred percent. That's very far-sighted.

RENEE. Yeah. Well of course, my father thinks I'm a complete weirdo.

GALLIMARD. He'll thank you someday.

RENEE. Like when the Chinese start buying Hula Hoops?

GALLIMARD. There're a billion bellies out there.

RENEE. And if they end up taking over the world—well, then I'll be lucky to know Chinese too, right?

[*Pause.*]

GALLIMARD. At this point, I don't see how the Chinese can possibly take—

RENEE. You know what I *don't* like about China?

GALLIMARD. Excuse me? No—what?

RENEE. Nothing to do at night.

GALLIMARD. You come to parties at embassies like everyone else.

RENEE. Yeah, but they get out at ten. And then what?

GALLIMARD. I'm afraid the Chinese idea of a dance hall is a dirt floor and a man with a flute.

RENEE. Are you married?

GALLIMARD. Yes. Why?

RENEE. You wanna . . . fool around?

[*Pause.*]

GALLIMARD. Sure.

RENEE. I'll wait for you outside. What's your name?

GALLIMARD. Gallimard. Rene.

RENEE. Weird. I'm Renee too. [*She exits.*]

GALLIMARD [*to us*]. And so, I embarked on my first extra-extramarital affair. Renee was picture perfect. With a body like those girls in the magazines. If I put a tissue paper over my eyes, I wouldn't have been able to tell the difference. And it was exciting to be with someone who wasn't afraid to be seen completely naked. But is it possible for a woman to be *too* uninhibited, *too* willing, so as to seem almost too . . . masculine?

[*Chuck Berry blares from the house speakers, then comes down in volume as* RENEE *enters, toweling her hair.*]

RENEE. You have a nice weenie.

GALLIMARD. What?

RENEE. Penis. You have a nice penis.

GALLIMARD. Oh. Well, thank you. That's very . . .

RENEE. What—can't take a compliment?

GALLIMARD. No, it's very . . . reassuring.

RENEE. But most girls don't come out and say it, huh?

GALLIMARD. And also . . . what did you call it?

RENEE. Oh. Most girls don't call it a "weenie," huh?

GALLIMARD. It sounds very—

RENEE. Small, I know.

GALLIMARD. I was going to say, "young."

RENEE. Yeah. Young, small, same thing. Most guys are pretty, uh, sensitive about that. Like, you know, I had a boyfriend back home in Denmark. I got mad at him once and called him a little weeniehead. He got so mad! He said at least I should call him a great big weeniehead.

GALLIMARD. I suppose I just say "penis."

RENEE. Yeah. That's pretty clinical. There's "cock," but that sounds like a chicken. And "prick" is painful, and "dick" is like you're talking about someone who's not in the room.

GALLIMARD. Yes. It's a . . . bigger problem than I imagined.

RENEE. I—I think maybe it's because I really don't know what to do with them—that's why I call them "weenies."

GALLIMARD. Well, you did quite well with . . . mine.

RENEE. Thanks, but I mean, really *do* with them. Like, okay, have you ever looked at one? I mean, really?

GALLIMARD. No, I suppose when it's part of you, you sort of take it for granted.

RENEE. I guess. But, like, it just hangs there. This little . . . flap of flesh. And there's so much fuss that we make about it. Like, I think the reason we fight wars is because we wear clothes. Because no one knows—between the men, I mean—who has the biggest . . . weenie. So, if I'm a guy with a small one, I'm going to build a really big building or take over a really big piece of land or write a really long book so the other men don't know, right? But, see, it never really works, that's the problem. I mean, you conquer the country, or whatever, but you're still wearing clothes, so there's no way to prove absolutely whose is bigger or smaller. And that's what we call a civilized society. The whole world run by a bunch of men with pricks the size of pins. [*She exits.*]

GALLIMARD [*to us*]. This was simply not acceptable.

[*A high-pitched chime rings through the air.* SONG, *dressed as Butterfly, appears in the upstage special. She is obviously distressed. Her body swoons as she attempts to clip the stems of flowers she's arranging in a vase.*]

GALLIMARD. But I kept up our affair, wildly, for several months. Why? I believe because of Butterfly. She knew the secret I was trying to hide. But, unlike a

Western woman, she didn't confront me, threaten, even pout. I remembered the words of Puccini's *Butterfly*:

SONG. *"Noi siamo gente avvezza / alle piccole cose / umili e silenziose."*

GALLIMARD. "I come from a people / Who are accustomed to little / Humble and silent." I saw Pinkerton and Butterfly, and what she would say if he were unfaithful . . . nothing. She would cry, alone, into those wildly soft sleeves, once full of possessions, now empty to collect her tears. It was her tears and her silence that excited me, every time I visited Renee.

TOULON [*offstage*]. Gallimard!

[TOULON *enters.* GALLIMARD *turns towards him. During the next section,* SONG, *up center, begins to dance with the flowers. It is a drunken, reckless dance, where she breaks small pieces off the stems.*]

TOULON. They're killing him.

GALLIMARD. Who? I'm sorry? What?

TOULON. Bother you to come over at this late hour?

GALLIMARD. No . . . of course not.

TOULON. Not after you hear my secret. Champagne?

GALLIMARD. Um . . . thank you.

TOULON. You're surprised. There's something that you've wanted, Gallimard. No, not a promotion. Next time. Something in the world. You're not aware of this, but there's an informal gossip circle among intelligence agents. And some of ours heard from some of the Americans—

GALLIMARD. Yes?

TOULON. That the U.S. will allow the Vietnamese generals to stage a coup . . . and assassinate President Diem.

[*The chime rings again.* TOULON *freezes.* GALLIMARD *turns upstage and looks at Butterfly, who slowly and deliberately clips a flower off its stem.* GALLIMARD *turns back towards* TOULON.]

GALLIMARD. I think . . . that's a very wise move!

[TOULON *unfreezes.*]

TOULON. It's what you've been advocating. A toast?

GALLIMARD. Sure. I consider this a vindication.

TOULON. Not exactly. "To the test. Let's hope you pass."

[*They drink. The chime rings again.* TOULON *freezes.* GALLIMARD *turns upstage, and* SONG *clips another flower.*]

GALLIMARD [*to* TOULON]. The test?

TOULON [*unfreezing*]. It's a test of everything you've been saying. I personally think the generals probably will stop the Communists. And you'll be a hero. But if anything goes wrong, then your opinions won't be worth a pig's ear. I'm sure that won't happen. But sometimes it's easier when they don't listen to you.

GALLIMARD. They're your opinions too, aren't they?

TOULON. Personally, yes.

GALLIMARD. So we agree.

TOULON. But my opinions aren't on that report. Yours are. Cheers.

[TOULON *turns away from* GALLIMARD *and raises his glass. At that instant* SONG *picks up the vase and hurls it to the ground. It shatters.* SONG *sinks down amidst the shards of the vase, in a calm, childlike trance. She sings softly, as if reciting a child's nursery rhyme.*]

SONG [*repeat as necessary*]. "The whole world over, the white man travels, setting anchor, wherever he likes. Life's not worth living, unless he finds, the finest maidens, of every land . . . ."

[GALLIMARD *turns downstage towards us.* SONG *continues singing.*]

GALLIMARD. I shook as I left his house. That coward! That worm! To put the burden for his decisions on my shoulders!

I started for Renee's. But no, that was all I needed. A schoolgirl who would question the role of the penis in modern society. What I wanted was revenge. A vessel to contain my humiliation. Though I hadn't seen her in several weeks, I headed for Butterfly's.

[GALLIMARD *enters* SONG's *apartment.*]

SONG. Oh! Rene . . . I was dreaming!

GALLIMARD. You've been drinking?

SONG. If I can't sleep, then yes, I drink. But then, it gives me these dreams which—Rene, it's been almost three weeks since you visited me last.

GALLIMARD. I know. There's been a lot going on in the world.

SONG. Fortunately I am drunk. So I can speak freely. It's not the world, it's you and me. And an old problem. Even the softest skin becomes like leather to a man who's touched it too often. I confess I don't know how to stop it. I don't know how to become another woman.

GALLIMARD. I have a request.

SONG. Is this a solution? Or are you ready to give up the flat?

GALLIMARD. It may be a solution. But I'm sure you won't like it.

SONG. Oh well, that's very important. "Like it?" Do you think I "like" lying here alone, waiting, always waiting for your return? Please—don't worry about what I may not "like."

GALLIMARD. I want to see you . . . naked.

[*Silence.*]

SONG. I thought you understood my modesty. So you want me to—what—strip? Like a big cowboy girl? Shiny pasties on my breasts? Shall I fling my kimono over my head and yell "ya-hoo" in the process? I thought you respected my shame!

GALLIMARD. I believe you gave me your shame many years ago.

SONG. Yes—and it is just like a white devil to use it against me. I can't believe it. I thought myself so repulsed by the passive Oriental and the cruel white man. Now I see—we are always most revolted by the things hidden within us.

GALLIMARD. I just mean—

SONG. Yes?

GALLIMARD. —that it will remove the only barrier left between us.

SONG. No, Rene. Don't couch your request in sweet words. Be yourself—a cad—and know that my love is enough, that I submit—submit to the worst you can give me. [*Pause.*] Well, come. Strip me. Whatever happens, know that you have willed it. Our love, in your hands. I'm helpless before my man.

[GALLIMARD *starts to cross the room.*]

GALLIMARD. Did I not undress her because I knew, somewhere deep down, what I would find? Perhaps. Happiness is so rare that our mind can turn somersaults to protect it.

At the time, I only knew that I was seeing Pinkerton stalking towards his Butterfly, ready to reward her love with his lecherous hands. The image sickened me, pulled me to my knees, so I was crawling towards her like a worm. By the time I reached her, Pinkerton . . . had vanished from my heart. To be replaced by something new, something unnatural, that flew in the face of all I'd learned in the world—something very close to love.

[*He grabs her around the waist; she strokes his hair.*]

GALLIMARD. Butterfly, forgive me.

SONG. Rene . . .

GALLIMARD. For everything. From the start.

SONG. I'm . . .

GALLIMARD. I want to—

SONG. I'm pregnant. [*Beat.*] I'm pregnant. [*Beat.*] I'm pregnant.

[*Beat.*]

GALLIMARD. I want to marry you!

SCENE VII

GALLIMARD and Butterfly's flat. Beijing. 1963.

Downstage, SONG *paces as* COMRADE CHIN *reads from her notepad. Upstage,* GALLIMARD *is still kneeling. He remains on his knees throughout the scene, watching it.*

SONG. I need a baby.

CHIN [*from pad*]. He's been spotted going to a dorm.

SONG. I need a baby.

CHIN. At the Foreign Language Institute.

SONG. I need a baby.

CHIN. The room of a Danish girl. . . . What do you mean, you need a baby?!

SONG. Tell Comrade Kang—last night, the entire mission, it could've ended.

CHIN. What do you mean?

SONG. Tell Kang—he told me to strip.

CHIN. Strip?!

SONG. Write!

CHIN. I tell you, I don't understand nothing about this case anymore. Nothing.

SONG. He told me to strip, and I took a chance. Oh, we Chinese, we know how to gamble.

CHIN [*writing*]. ". . . told him to strip."

SONG. My palms were wet, I had to make a split-second decision.

CHIN. Hey! Can you slow down?!

[*Pause.*]

SONG. You write faster, I'm the artist here. Suddenly, it hit me—"All he wants is for her to submit. Once a woman submits, a man is always ready to become 'generous.'"

CHIN. You're just gonna end up with rough notes.

SONG. And it worked! He gave in! Now, if I can just present him with a baby. A Chinese baby with blond hair—he'll be mine for life!

CHIN. Kang will never agree! The trading of babies has to be a counterrevolutionary act!

SONG. Sometimes, a counterrevolutionary act is necessary to counter a counter-revolutionary act.

[*Pause.*]

CHIN. Wait.

SONG. I need one . . . in seven months. Make sure it's a boy.

CHIN. This doesn't sound like something the Chairman would do. Maybe you'd better talk to Comrade Kang yourself.

SONG. Good. I will.

[CHIN *gets up to leave.*]

SONG. Miss Chin? Why, in the Peking Opera, are women's roles played by men?

CHIN. I don't know. Maybe, a reactionary remnant of male—

SONG. No. [*Beat.*] Because only a man knows how a woman is supposed to act.

[CHIN *exits.* SONG *turns upstage, towards* GALLIMARD.]

GALLIMARD [*calling after* CHIN]. Good riddance! [*To* SONG.] I could forget all that betrayal in an instant, you know. If you'd just come back and become Butterfly again.

SONG. Fat chance. You're here in prison, rotting in a cell. And I'm on a plane, winging my way back to China. Your President pardoned me of our treason, you know.

GALLIMARD. Yes, I read about that.

SONG. Must make you feel . . . lower than shit.

GALLIMARD. But don't you, even a little bit, wish you were here with me?

SONG. I'm an artist, Rene. You were my greatest . . . acting challenge. [*She laughs.*] It doesn't matter how rotten I answer, does it? You still adore me. That's why I love you, Rene. [*She points to us.*] So—you were telling your audience about the night I announced I was pregnant.

[GALLIMARD *puts his arms around* SONG'S *waist. He and* SONG *are in the positions they were in at the end of Scene VI.*]

SCENE VIII

Same.

GALLIMARD. I'll divorce my wife. We'll live together here, and then later in France.

SONG. I feel so . . . ashamed.

GALLIMARD. Why?

SONG. I had begun to lose faith. And now, you shame me with your generosity.

GALLIMARD. Generosity? No, I'm proposing for very selfish reasons.

SONG. Your apologies only make me feel more ashamed. My outburst a moment ago!

GALLIMARD. Your outburst? What about my request?!

SONG. You've been very patient dealing with my . . . eccentricities. A Western man, used to women freer with their bodies—

GALLIMARD. It was sick! Don't make excuses for me.

SONG. I have to. You don't seem willing to make them for yourself.

[*Pause.*]

GALLIMARD. You're crazy.

SONG. I'm happy. Which often looks like crazy.

GALLIMARD. Then make me crazy. Marry me.

[*Pause.*]

SONG. No.

GALLIMARD. What?

SONG. Do I sound silly, a slave, if I say I'm not worthy?

GALLIMARD. Yes. In fact you do. No one has loved me like you.

SONG. Thank you. And no one ever will. I'll see to that.

GALLIMARD. So what is the problem?

SONG. Rene, we Chinese are realists. We understand rice, gold, and guns. You are a diplomat. Your career is skyrocketing. Now, what would happen if you divorced your wife to marry a Communist Chinese actress?

GALLIMARD. That's not being realistic. That's defeating yourself before you begin.

SONG. We conserve our strength for the battles we can win.

GALLIMARD. That sounds like a fortune cookie!

SONG. Where do you think fortune cookies come from!

GALLIMARD. I don't care.

SONG. You do. So do I. And we should. That is why I say I'm not worthy. I'm worthy to love and even to be loved by you. But I am not worthy to end the career of one of the West's most promising diplomats.

GALLIMARD. It's not that great a career! I made it sound like more than it is!

SONG. Modesty will get you nowhere. Flatter yourself, and you flatter me. I'm flattered to decline your offer. [*She exits.*]

GALLIMARD [*to us*]. Butterfly and I argued all night. And, in the end, I left, knowing I would never be her husband. She went away for several months—to the countryside, like a small animal. Until the night I received her call.

[*A baby's cry from offstage.* SONG *enters, carrying a child.*]

SONG. He looks like you.

GALLIMARD. Oh! [*Beat; he approaches the baby.*] Well, babies are never very attractive at birth.

SONG. Stop!

GALLIMARD. I'm sure he'll grow more beautiful with age. More like his mother.

SONG. "*Chi vide mai / a bimbo del Giappon . . .*"

GALLIMARD. "What baby, I wonder, was ever born in Japan"—or China, for that matter—

SONG. " *. . . occhi azzurrini?*"

GALLIMARD. "With azure eyes"—they're actually sort of brown, wouldn't you say?

SONG. "*E il labbro.*"

GALLIMARD. "And such lips!" [*He kisses* SONG.] And such lips.

SONG. "*E i ricciolini d'oro schietto?*"

GALLIMARD. "And such a head of golden"—if slightly patchy—"curls?"

SONG. I'm going to call him "Peepee."

GALLIMARD. Darling, could you repeat that because I'm sure a rickshaw just flew by overhead.

SONG. You heard me.

GALLIMARD. "Song Peepee"? May I suggest Michael, or Stephan, or Adolph?

SONG. You may, but I won't listen.

GALLIMARD. You can't be serious. Can you imagine the time this child will have in school?

SONG. In the West, yes.

GALLIMARD. It's worse than naming him Ping Pong or Long Dong or—

SONG. But he's never going to live in the West, is he?

[*Pause.*]

GALLIMARD. That wasn't my choice.

SONG. It is mine. And this is my promise to you: I will raise him, he will be our child, but he will never burden you outside of China.

GALLIMARD. Why do you make these promises? I want to be burdened! I want a scandal to cover the papers!

SONG [*to us*]. Prophetic.

GALLIMARD. I'm serious.

SONG. So am I. His name is as I registered it. And he will never live in the West.
[SONG *exits with the child.*]

GALLIMARD [*to us*]. It is possible that her stubbornness only made me want her more. That drawing back at the moment of my capitulation was the most brilliant strategy she could have chosen. It is possible. But it is also possible that by this point she could have said, could have done . . . anything, and I would have adored her still.

SCENE IX

Beijing. 1966.
A driving rhythm of Chinese percussion fills the stage.

GALLIMARD. And then, China began to change. Mao became very old, and his cult became very strong. And, like many old men, he entered his second childhood. So he handed over the reins of state to those with minds like his own. And children ruled the Middle Kingdom[8] with complete caprice. The doctrine of the Cultural Revolution[9] implied continuous anarchy. Contact between Chinese and foreigners became impossible. Our flat was confiscated. Her fame and my money now counted against us.

[*Two dancers in Mao suits and red-starred caps enter, and begin crudely mimicking revolutionary violence, in an agitprop fashion.*]

GALLIMARD. And somehow the American war went wrong too. Four hundred thousand dollars were being spent for every Viet Cong[10] killed; so General Westmoreland's[11] remark that the Oriental does not value life the way Americans do was oddly accurate. Why weren't the Vietnamese people giving in? Why were they content instead to die and die and die again?

[TOULON *enters. Percussion and dancers continue upstage.*]

TOULON. Congratulations, Gallimard.

GALLIMARD. Excuse me, sir?

TOULON. Not a promotion. That was last time. You're going home.

GALLIMARD. What?

TOULON. Don't say I didn't warn you.

---

[8]From earliest history, the Chinese have called their country the Middle Kingdom.
[9]Name given to the era of fierce suppression of ideologies contrary to the ideas of Chinese leader Mao Tse-tung, 1965–1967.
[10]Vietnamese communists who sought to overthrow the South Vietnam government.
[11]William Westmoreland, commander of U.S. military forces in Vietnam, 1964–1968.

GALLIMARD. I'm being transferred . . . because I was wrong about the American war?

TOULON. Of course not. We don't care about the Americans. We care about your mind. The quality of your analysis. In general, everything you've predicted here in the Orient . . . just hasn't happened.

GALLIMARD. I think that's premature.

TOULON. Don't force me to be blunt. Okay, you said China was ready to open to Western trade. The only thing they're trading out there are Western heads. And, yes, you said the Americans would succeed in Indochina. You were kidding, right?

GALLIMARD. I think the end is in sight.

TOULON. Don't be pathetic. And don't take this personally. You were wrong. It's not your fault.

GALLIMARD. But I'm going home.

TOULON. Right. Could I have the number of your mistress? [*Beat.*] Joke! Joke! Eat a croissant for me.

> [TOULON *exits.* SONG, *wearing a Mao suit, is dragged in from the wings as part of the upstage dance. They "beat" her, then lampoon the acrobatics of the Chinese opera, as she is made to kneel onstage.*]

GALLIMARD [*simultaneously*]. I don't care to recall how Butterfly and I said our hurried farewell. Perhaps it was better to end our affair before it killed her.

> [GALLIMARD *exits. Percussion rises in volume. The lampooning becomes faster, more frenetic. At its height,* COMRADE CHIN *walks across the stage with a banner reading:* "The Actor Renounces His Decadent Profession!" *She reaches the kneeling* SONG. *At the moment* CHIN *touches* SONG's *chin, percussion stops with a thud. Dancers strike poses.*]

CHIN. Actor-oppressor, for years you have lived above the common people and looked down on their labor. While the farmer ate millet—

SONG. I ate pastries from France and sweetmeats from silver trays.

CHIN. And how did you come to live in such an exalted position?

SONG. I was a plaything for the imperialists!

CHIN. What did you do?

SONG. I shamed China by allowing myself to be corrupted by a foreigner. . . .

CHIN. What does this mean? The People demand a full confession!

SONG. I engaged in the lowest perversions with China's enemies!

CHIN. What perversions? Be more clear!

SONG. I let him put it up my ass!

[*Dancers look over, disgusted.*]

CHIN. Aaaa-ya! How can you use such sickening language?!

SONG. My language . . . is only as foul as the crimes I committed. . . .

CHIN. Yeah. That's better. So—what do you want to do . . . now?

SONG. I want to serve the people

[*Percussion starts up, with Chinese strings.*]

CHIN. What?

SONG. I want to serve the people!

[*Dancers regain their revolutionary smiles, and begin a dance of victory.*]

CHIN. What?!

SONG. I want to serve the people!!

[*Dancers unveil a banner: "The Actor Is Re-Habilitated!"* SONG *remains kneeling before* CHIN, *as the dancers bounce around them, then exit. Music out.*]

SCENE X

A commune. Hunan Province. 1970.

CHIN. How you planning to do that?

SONG. I've already worked four years in the fields of Hunan, Comrade Chin.

CHIN. So? Farmers work all their lives. Let me see your hands.

[SONG *holds them out for her inspection.*]

CHIN. Goddamn! Still so smooth! How long does it take to turn you actors into good anythings? Hunh. You've just spent too many years in luxury to be any good to the Revolution.

SONG. I served the Revolution.

CHIN. Served the Revolution? Bullshit! You wore dresses! Don't tell me—I was there. I saw you! You and your white vice-consul! Stuck up there in your flat, living off the People's Treasury! Yeah, I knew what was going on! You two . . . homos! Homos! Homos! [*Pause; she composes herself.*] Ah! Well . . . you will serve the people, all right. But not with the Revolution's money. This time, you use your own money.

SONG. I have no money.

CHIN. Shut up! And you won't stink up China anymore with your pervert stuff. You'll pollute the place where pollution begins—the West.

SONG. What do you mean?

CHIN. Shut up! You're going to France. Without a cent in your pocket. You find your consul's house, you make him pay your expenses—

SONG. No.

CHIN. And you give us weekly reports! Useful information!

SONG. That's crazy. It's been four years.

CHIN. Either that, or back to the rehabilitation center!

SONG. Comrade Chin, he's not going to support me! Not in France! He's a white man! I was just his plaything—

CHIN. Oh yuck! Again with the sickening language? Where's my stick?

SONG. You don't understand the mind of a man.

[*Pause.*]

CHIN. Oh no? No I don't? Then how come I'm married, huh? How come I got a man? Five, six years ago, you always tell me those kind of things, I felt very bad. But not now! Because what does the Chairman say? He tells us *I'm* now the smart one, you're now the nincompoop! *You're* the blockhead, the harebrain, the nitwit! You think you're so smart? You understand "The Mind of a Man"? Good! Then *you* go to France and be a pervert for Chairman Mao!

[CHIN *and* SONG *exit in opposite directions.*]

SCENE XI

Paris. 1968–1970.

[GALLIMARD *enters.*]

GALLIMARD. And what was waiting for me back in Paris? Well, better Chinese food than I'd eaten in China. Friends and relatives. A little accounting, regular schedule, keeping track of traffic violations in the suburbs. . . . And the indignity of students shouting the slogans of Chairman Mao at me—in French.

HELGA. Rene? Rene? [*She enters, soaking wet.*] I've had a . . . problem. [*She sneezes.*]

GALLIMARD. You're wet.

HELGA. Yes, I . . . coming back from the grocer's. A group of students, waving red flags, they—

[GALLIMARD *fetches a towel.*]

HELGA. —they ran by, I was caught up along with them. Before I knew what was happening—

[GALLIMARD *gives her the towel.*]

HELGA. Thank you. The police started firing water cannons at us. I tried to shout, to tell them I was the wife of a diplomat, but—you know how it is . . . [*Pause.*] Needless to say, I lost the groceries. Rene, what's happening to France?

GALLIMARD. What's—? Well, nothing, really.

HELGA. Nothing?! The storefronts are in flames, there's glass in the streets, buildings are toppling—and I'm wet!

GALLIMARD. Nothing! . . . that I care to think about.

HELGA. And is that why you stay in this room?

GALLIMARD. Yes, in fact.

HELGA. With the incense burning? You know something? I hate incense. It smells so sickly sweet.

GALLIMARD. Well, I hate the French. Who just smell—period!

HELGA. And the Chinese were better?

GALLIMARD. Please—don't start.

HELGA. When we left, this exact same thing, the riots—

GALLIMARD. No, no . . .

HELGA. Students screaming slogans, smashing down doors—

GALLIMARD. Helga—

HELGA. It was all going on in China, too. Don't you remember?!

GALLIMARD. Helga! Please! [*Pause.*] You have never understood China, have you? You walk in here with these ridiculous ideas, that the West is falling apart, that China was spitting in our faces. You come in, dripping of the streets, and you leave water all over my floor. [*He grabs* HELGA's *towel, begins mopping up the floor.*]

HELGA. But it's the truth!

GALLIMARD. Helga, I want a divorce.

[*Pause;* GALLIMARD *continues mopping the floor.*]

HELGA. I take it back. China is . . . beautiful. Incense, I like incense.

GALLIMARD. I've had a mistress.

HELGA. So?

GALLIMARD. For eight years.

HELGA. I knew you would. I knew you would the day I married you. And now what? You want to marry her?

GALLIMARD. I can't. She's in China.

HELGA. I see. You know that no one else is ever going to marry me, right?

GALLIMARD. I'm sorry.

HELGA. And you want to leave. For someone who's not here, is that right?

GALLIMARD. That's right.

HELGA. You can't live with her, but still you don't want to live with me.

GALLIMARD. That's right.

[*Pause.*]

HELGA. Shit. How terrible that I can figure that out. [*Pause.*] I never thought I'd say it. But, in China, I was happy. I knew, in my own way, I knew that you were not everything you pretended to be. But the pretense—going on your arm to the embassy ball, visiting your office and the guards saying, "Good morning, good morning, Madame Gallimard"—the pretense . . . was very good indeed. [*Pause.*] I hope everyone is mean to you for the rest of your life. [*She exits.*]

GALLIMARD [*to us*]. Prophetic.

[MARC *enters with two drinks.*]

GALLIMARD [*to* MARC]. In China, I was different from all other men.

MARC. Sure. You were white. Here's your drink.

GALLIMARD. I felt . . . touched.

MARC. In the head? Rene, I don't want to hear about the Oriental goddess. Okay? One night—can we just drink and throw up without a lot of conversation?

GALLIMARD. You still don't believe me, do you?

MARC. Sure I do. She was the most beautiful, et cetera, et cetera, blasé, blasé.

[*Pause.*]

GALLIMARD. My life in the West has been such a disappointment.

MARC. Life in the West is like that. You'll get used to it. Look, you're driving me away. I'm leaving. Happy, now? [*He exits, then returns.*] Look, I have a date tomorrow night. You wanna come? I can fix you up with—

GALLIMARD. Of course. I would love to come.

[*Pause.*]

MARC. Uh—on second thought, no. You'd better get ahold of yourself first.
[*He exits;* GALLIMARD *nurses his drink.*]

GALLIMARD [*to us*]. This is the ultimate cruelty, isn't it? That I can talk and talk and to anyone listening, it's only air—too rich a diet to be swallowed by a mundane world. Why can't anyone understand? That in China, I once loved, and was loved by, very simply, the Perfect Woman.

[SONG *enters, dressed as Butterfly in wedding dress.*]

GALLIMARD [*to* SONG]. Not again. My imagination is hell. Am I asleep this time? Or did I drink too much?

SONG. Rene!

GALLIMARD. God, it's too painful! That you speak?

SONG. What are you talking about? Rene—touch me.

GALLIMARD. Why?

SONG. I'm real. Take my hand.

GALLIMARD. Why? So you can disappear again and leave me clutching at the air? For the entertainment of my neighbors who—?

[SONG *touches* GALLIMARD.]

SONG. Rene?

[GALLIMARD *takes* SONG's *hand. Silence.*]

GALLIMARD. Butterfly? I never doubted you'd return.

SONG. You hadn't . . . forgotten—?

GALLIMARD. Yes, actually, I've forgotten everything. My mind, you see—there wasn't enough room in this hard head—not for the world *and* for you. No, there was only room for one. [*Beat.*] Come, look. See? Your bed has been waiting, with the Klimt[12] poster you like, and—see? The *xiang lu*[13] you gave me?

SONG. I . . . I don't know what to say.

GALLIMARD. There's nothing to say. Not at the end of a long trip. Can I make you some tea?

SONG. But where's your wife?

---

[12]Gustav Klimt (1862–1918), an Austrian painter.
[13]Incense burner.

GALLIMARD. She's by my side. She's by my side at last.

[GALLIMARD *reaches to embrace* SONG. SONG *sidesteps, dodging him.*]

GALLIMARD. Why?!

SONG [*to us*]. So I did return to Rene in Paris. Where I found—

GALLIMARD. Why do you run away? Can't we show them how we embraced that evening?

SONG. Please. I'm talking.

GALLIMARD. You have to do what I say! I'm conjuring you up in *my* mind!

SONG. Rene, I've never done what you've said. Why should it be any different in your mind? Now split—the story moves on, and I must change.

GALLIMARD. I welcomed you into my home! I didn't have to, you know! I could've left you penniless on the streets of Paris! But I took you in!

SONG. Thank you.

GALLIMARD. So . . . please . . . don't change.

SONG. You know I have to. You know I will. And anyway, what difference does it make? No matter what your eyes tell you, you can't ignore the truth. You already know too much.

[GALLIMARD *exits.* SONG *turns to us.*]

SONG. The change I'm going to make requires about five minutes. So I thought you might want to take this opportunity to stretch your legs, enjoy a drink, or listen to the musicians. I'll be here, when you return, right where you left me.

[SONG *goes to a mirror in front of which is a washbasin of water. She starts to remove her makeup as stagelights go to half and houselights come up.*]

ACT III

SCENE I

A courthouse in Paris. 1986.

As he promised, SONG *has completed the bulk of his transformation onstage by the time the houselights go down and the stagelights come up full. As he speaks to us, he removes his wig and kimono, leaving them on the floor. Underneath, he wears a well-cut suit.*

SONG. So I'd done my job better than I had a right to expect. Well, give him some credit, too. He's right—I was in a fix when I arrived in Paris. I walked from the airport into town, then I located, by blind groping, the Chinatown district. Let me make one thing clear: whatever else may be said about the Chinese, they are stingy! I slept in doorways three days until I could find a tailor who would make me this kimono on credit. As it turns out, maybe I didn't even need it. Maybe he would've been happy to see me in a simple shift and mascara. But . . . better safe than sorry.

That was 1970, when I arrived in Paris. For the next fifteen years, yes, I lived a very comfy life. Some relief, believe me, after four years on a fucking commune in Nowheresville, China. Rene supported the boy and me, and I did some demonstrations around the country as part of my "cultural exchange" cover. And then there was the spying.

[SONG *moves upstage, to a chair.* TOULON *enters as a judge, wearing the appropriate wig and robes. He sits near* SONG. *It's 1986, and* SONG *is testifying in a courtroom.*]

SONG. Not much at first. Rene had lost all his high-level contacts. Comrade Chin wasn't very interested in parking-ticket statistics. But finally, at my urging, Rene got a job as a courier, handling sensitive documents. He'd photograph them for me, and I'd pass them on to the Chinese embassy.

JUDGE. Did he understand the extent of his activity?

SONG. He didn't ask. He knew that I needed those documents, and that was enough.

JUDGE. But he must've known he was passing classified information.

SONG. I can't say.

JUDGE. He never asked what you were going to do with them?

SONG. Nope.

[*Pause.*]

JUDGE. There is one thing that the court—indeed, that all of France—would like to know.

SONG. Fire away.

JUDGE. Did Monsieur Gallimard know you were a man?

SONG. Well, he never saw me completely naked. Ever.

JUDGE. But surely, he must've . . . how can I put this?

SONG. Put it however you like. I'm not shy. He must've felt around?

JUDGE. Mmmmm.

SONG. Not really. I did all the work. He just laid back. Of course we did enjoy more . . . complete union, and I suppose he *might* have wondered why I was always on my stomach, but . . . But what you're thinking is, "Of course a wrist must've brushed . . . a hand hit . . . over twenty years!" Yeah. Well, Your Honor, it was my job to make him think I was a Woman. And chew on this: it wasn't all that hard. See, my mother was a prostitute along the Bundt before the Revolution. And, uh, I think it's fair to say she learned a few things about Western men. So I borrowed her knowledge. In service to my country.

JUDGE. Would you care to enlighten the court with this secret knowledge? I'm sure we're all very curious.

SONG. I'm sure you are. [*Pause.*] Okay, Rule One is: Men always believe what they want to hear. So a girl can tell the most obnoxious lies and the guys will believe them every time—"This is my first time"—"That's the biggest I've ever seen"—or *both*, which, if you really think about it, is not possible in a single lifetime. You've maybe heard those phrases a few times in your own life, yes, Your Honor?

JUDGE. It's not my life, Monsieur Song, which is on trial today.

SONG. Okay, okay, just trying to lighten up the proceedings. Tough room.

JUDGE. Go on.

SONG. Rule Two: As soon as a Western man comes into contact with the East—he's already confused. The West has sort of an international rape mentality towards the East. Do you know rape mentality?

JUDGE. Give us your definition, please.

SONG. Basically, "Her mouth says no, but her eyes say yes."

    The West thinks of itself as masculine—big guns, big industry, big money—so the East is feminine—weak, delicate, poor . . . but good at art, and full of inscrutable wisdom—the feminine mystique.

    Her mouth says no, but her eyes say yes. The West believes the East, deep down, *wants* to be dominated—because a woman can't think for herself.

JUDGE. What does this have to do with my question?

SONG. You expect Oriental countries to submit to your guns, and you expect Oriental women to be submissive to your men. That's why you say they make the best wives.

JUDGE. But why would that make it possible for you to fool Monsieur Gallimard? Please—get to the point.

SONG. One, because when he finally met his fantasy woman, he wanted more than anything to believe that she was, in fact, a woman. And second, I am an Oriental. And being an Oriental, I could never be completely a man.

[*Pause.*]

JUDGE. Your armchair political theory is tenuous, Monsieur Song.

SONG. You think so? That's why you'll lose in all your dealings with the East.

JUDGE. Just answer my question: did he know you were a man?

[*Pause.*]

SONG. You know, Your Honor, I never asked.

SCENE II

Same.

Music from the "Death Scene" from Butterfly *blares over the house speakers. It is the loudest thing we've heard in this play.*

    [GALLIMARD *enters, crawling towards* SONG's *wig and kimono.*]

GALLIMARD. Butterfly? Butterfly?

[SONG *remains a man, in the witness box, delivering a testimony we do not hear.*]

GALLIMARD [*to us*]. In my moment of greatest shame, here, in this courtroom—with that . . . person up there, telling the world. . . . What strikes me especially is how shallow he is, how glib and obsequious . . . completely . . . without substance! The type that prowls around discos with a gold medallion stinking of garlic. So little like my Butterfly.

    Yet even in this moment my mind remains agile, flip-flopping like a man on a trampoline. Even now, my picture dissolves, and I see that . . . witness . . . talking to me.

[SONG *suddenly stands straight up in his witness box, and looks at* GALLIMARD.]

SONG. Yes. You. White man.

[SONG *steps out of the witness box, and moves downstage towards* GALLIMARD. *Light change.*]

GALLIMARD [*to* SONG]. Who? Me?

SONG. Do you see any other white men?

GALLIMARD. Yes. There're white men all around. This is a French courtroom.

SONG. So you are an adventurous imperialist. Tell me, why did it take you so long? To come back to this place?

GALLIMARD. What place?

SONG. This theater in China. Where we met many years ago.

GALLIMARD [*to us*]. And once again, against my will, I am transported.

[*Chinese opera music comes up on the speakers.* SONG *begins to do opera moves, as he did the night they met.*]

SONG. Do you remember? The night you gave your heart?

GALLIMARD. It was a long time ago.

SONG. Not long enough. A night that turned your world upside down.

GALLIMARD. Perhaps.

SONG. Oh, be honest with me. What's another bit of flattery when you've already given me twenty years' worth? It's a wonder my head hasn't swollen to the size of China.

GALLIMARD. Who's to say it hasn't?

SONG. Who's to say? And what's the shame? In pride? You think I could've pulled this off if I wasn't already full of pride when we met? No, not just pride. Arrogance. It takes arrogance, really—to believe you can will, with your eyes and your lips, the destiny of another. [*He dances.*] C'mon. Admit it. You still want me. Even in slacks and a button-down collar.

GALLIMARD. I don't see what the point of—

SONG. You don't? Well maybe, Rene, just maybe—I want you.

GALLIMARD. You do?

SONG. Then again, maybe I'm just playing with you. How can you tell? [*Reprising his feminine character, he sidles up to* GALLIMARD.] "How I wish there were even a small café to sit in. With men in tuxedos, and cappuccinos, and bad expatriate jazz." Now you want to kiss me, don't you?

GALLIMARD [*pulling away*]. What makes you—?

SONG. —so sure? See? I take the words from your mouth. Then I wait for you to come and retrieve them. [*He reclines on the floor.*]

GALLIMARD. Why?! Why do you treat me so cruelly?

SONG. Perhaps I *was* treating you cruelly. But now—I'm being nice. Come here, my little one.

GALLIMARD. I'm not your little one!

SONG. My mistake. It's I who am *your* little one, right?

GALLIMARD. Yes, I—

SONG. So come get your little one. If you like, I may even let you strip me.

GALLIMARD. I mean, you were! Before . . . but not like this!

SONG. I was? Then perhaps I still am. If you look hard enough. [*He starts to remove his clothes.*]

GALLIMARD. What—what are you doing?

SONG. Helping you to see through my act.

GALLIMARD. Stop that! I don't want to! I don't—

SONG. Oh, but you asked me to strip, remember?

GALLIMARD. What? That was years ago! And I took it back!

SONG. No. You postponed it. Postponed the inevitable. Today, the inevitable has come calling.

[*From the speakers, cacophony: Butterfly mixed in with Chinese gongs.*]

GALLIMARD. No! Stop! I don't want to see!

SONG. Then look away.

GALLIMARD. You're only in my mind! All this is in my mind! I order you! To stop!

SONG. To what? To strip? That's just what I'm—

GALLIMARD. No! Stop! I want you—!

SONG. You want me?

GALLIMARD. To stop!

SONG. You know something, Rene? Your mouth says no, but your eyes say yes. Turn them away. I dare you.

GALLIMARD. I don't have to! Every night, you say you're going to strip, but then I beg you and you stop!

SONG. I guess tonight is different.

GALLIMARD. Why? Why should that be?

SONG. Maybe I've become frustrated. Maybe I'm saying "Look at me, you fool!" Or maybe I'm just feeling . . . sexy. [*He is down to his briefs.*]

GALLIMARD. Please. This is unnecessary. I know what you are.

SONG. You do? What am I?

GALLIMARD. A—a man.

SONG. You don't really believe that.

GALLIMARD. Yes I do! I knew all the time somewhere that my happiness was temporary, my love a deception. But my mind kept the knowledge at bay. To make the wait bearable.

SONG. Monsieur Gallimard—the wait is over.

[SONG *drops his briefs. He is naked. Sound cue out. Slowly, we and* SONG *come to the realization that what we had thought to be* GALLIMARD'*s sobbing is actually his laughter.*]

GALLIMARD. Oh god! What an idiot! Of course!

SONG. Rene—what?

GALLIMARD. Look at you! You're a man! [*He bursts into laughter again.*]

SONG. I fail to see what's so funny!

GALLIMARD. "You fail to see—!" I mean, you never did have much of a sense of humor, did you? I just think it's ridiculously funny that I've wasted so much time on just a man!

SONG. Wait. I'm not "just a man."

GALLIMARD. No? Isn't that what you've been trying to convince me of?

SONG. Yes, but what I mean—

GALLIMARD. And now, I finally believe you, and you tell me it's not true? I think you must have some kind of identity problem.

SONG. Will you listen to me?

GALLIMARD. Why?! I've been listening to you for twenty years. Don't I deserve a vacation?

SONG. I'm not just any man!

GALLIMARD. Then, what exactly are you?

SONG. Rene, how can you ask—? Okay, what about this?

[*He picks up Butterfly's robes, starts to dance around. No music.*]

GALLIMARD. Yes, that's very nice. I have to admit.

[SONG *holds out his arm to* GALLIMARD.]

SONG. It's the same skin you've worshipped for years. Touch it.

GALLIMARD. Yes, it does feel the same.

SONG. Now—close your eyes.

[SONG *covers* GALLIMARD's *eyes with one hand. With the other,* SONG *draws* GALLIMARD's *hand up to his face.* GALLIMARD, *like a blind man, lets his hands run over* SONG's *face.*]

GALLIMARD. This skin, I remember. The curve of her face, the softness of her cheek, her hair against the back of my hand . . .

SONG. I'm your Butterfly. Under the robes, beneath everything, it was always me. Now, open your eyes and admit it—you adore me. [*He removes his hand from* GALLIMARD's *eyes.*]

GALLIMARD. You, who knew every inch of my desires—how could you, of all people, have made such a mistake?

SONG. What?

GALLIMARD. You showed me your true self. When all I loved was the lie. A perfect lie, which you let fall to the ground—and now, it's old and soiled.

SONG. So—you never really loved me? Only when I was playing a part?

GALLIMARD. I'm a man who loved a woman created by a man. Everything else—simply falls short.

[*Pause.*]

SONG. What am I supposed to do now?

GALLIMARD. You were a fine spy, Monsieur Song, with an even finer accomplice. But now I believe you should go. Get out of my life!

SONG. Go where? Rene, you can't live without me. Not after twenty years.

GALLIMARD. I certainly can't live with you—not after twenty years of betrayal.

SONG. Don't be stubborn! Where will you go?

GALLIMARD. I have a date . . . with my Butterfly.

SONG. So, throw away your pride. And come. . . .

GALLIMARD. Get away from me! Tonight, I've finally learned to tell fantasy from reality. And, knowing the difference, I choose fantasy.

SONG. *I'm* your fantasy!

GALLIMARD. You? You're as real as hamburger. Now get out! I have a date with my Butterfly and I don't want your body polluting the room! [*He tosses* SONG's *suit at him.*] Look at these—you dress like a pimp.

SONG. Hey! These are Armani slacks and—! [*He puts on his briefs and slacks.*] Let's just say . . . I'm disappointed in you, Rene. In the crush of your adoration, I thought you'd become something more. More like . . . a woman.

But no. Men. You're like the rest of them. It's all in the way we dress, and make up our faces, and bat our eyelashes. You really have so little imagination!

GALLIMARD. You, Monsieur Song? Accuse me of too little imagination? You, if anyone, should know—I am pure imagination. And in imagination I will remain. Now get out!

[GALLIMARD *bodily removes* SONG *from the stage, taking his kimono.*]

SONG. Rene! I'll never put on those robes again! You'll be sorry!

GALLIMARD [*to* SONG]. I'm already sorry! [*Looking at the kimono in his hands.*] Exactly as sorry . . . as a Butterfly.

SCENE III

M. GALLIMARD's prison cell. Paris. 1988.

GALLIMARD. I've played out the events of my life night after night, always searching for a new ending to my story, one where I leave this cell and return forever to my Butterfly's arms.

Tonight I realize my search is over. That I've looked all along in the wrong place. And now, to you, I will prove that my love was not in vain— by returning to the world of fantasy where I first met her.

[*He picks up the kimono; dancers enter.*]

GALLIMARD. There is a vision of the Orient that I have. Of slender women in chong sams and kimonos who die for the love of unworthy foreign devils. Who are born and raised to be the perfect women. Who take whatever punishment we give them, and bounce back, strengthened by love, unconditionally. It is a vision that has become my life.

[*Dancers bring the washbasin to him and help him make up his face.*]

GALLIMARD. In public, I have continued to deny that Song Liling is a man. This brings me headlines, and is a source of great embarrassment to my French colleagues, who can now be sent into a coughing fit by the mere mention of Chinese food. But alone, in my cell, I have long since faced the truth.

And the truth demands a sacrifice. For mistakes made over the course of a lifetime. My mistakes were simple and absolute—the man I loved was a cad, a bounder. He deserved nothing but a kick in the behind, and instead I gave him . . . all my love.

Yes—love. Why not admit it all? That was my undoing, wasn't it? Love warped my judgment, blinded my eyes, rearranged the very lines on my face . . . until I could look in the mirror and see nothing but . . . a woman.

[*Dancers help him put on the Butterfly wig.*]

GALLIMARD. I have a vision. Of the Orient. That, deep within its almond eyes, there are still women. Women willing to sacrifice themselves for the love of a man. Even a man whose love is completely without worth.

[*Dancers assist* GALLIMARD *in donning the kimono. They hand him a knife.*]

GALLIMARD. Death with honor is better than life . . . life with dishonor. [*He sets himself center stage, in a seppuku position.*[14]] The love of a Butterfly can withstand many things—unfaithfulness, loss, even abandonment. But how can it face the one sin that implies all others? The devastating knowledge that, underneath it all, the object of her love was nothing more, nothing less than . . . a man. [*He sets the tip of the knife against his body.*] It is 1988. And I have found her at last. In a prison on the outskirts of Paris. My name is Rene Gallimard—also known as Madame Butterfly.

[GALLIMARD *turns upstage and plunges the knife into his body, as music from the "Love Duet" blares over the speakers. He collapses into the arms of the dancers, who lay him reverently on the floor. The image holds for several beats. Then a tight special up on* SONG, *who stands as a man, staring at the dead* GALLIMARD. *He smokes a cigarette; the smoke filters up through the lights. Two words leave his lips.*]

SONG. Butterfly? Butterfly?

[*Smoke rises as lights fade slowly to black.*]

(1988)

---

[14]The position assumed in committing *hara kiri* (ritual suicide).

CHAPTER 17 DRAMA FOR WRITING 631

USING LIBRARY SOURCES IN YOUR WRITING

The ability to locate sources of information on a given subject and then incorporate the new ideas you find into your own writing is a valuable skill that every well-educated person needs to learn. To begin a documented paper about a literary work, carefully read—at least twice—the primary source (the piece of literature you intend to write about). Our advice uses examples related to Hwang's *M. Butterfly*, but remember that the process is the same for writing a secondary source paper on any piece of literature.

A STUDENT RESEARCHER'S PROCESS

Here is the process reported by our student writer, Linda Samuel. She constructed the sample research paper that appears later in this chapter. After summarizing what she did, we go through the process step by step.

1. *Reading*—As Linda read the play, she took notes on a piece of scratch paper—"anything I noticed as original, unusual, or amusing," she said.
2. *Research*—Linda went to the library and used computer databases to find articles about *M. Butterfly*. She also got a copy of Hwang's own Afterword to the play from a friend. While she read, she jotted down ideas from the articles, even copying some sentences directly, using quotation marks.
3. *Thesis idea*—When Linda reread her reading and research notes, she generated a few ideas for theses, and finally she decided that fantasy versus reality was a good subject to start with, considering the desired length of the paper and what her research could support.
4. *Rereading sources*—Next, Linda reread her articles and the play with the subject of fantasy versus reality in mind. This time, she highlighted sections she could use in her essay.
5. *Drafting the essay and refining the focus*—As Linda began to write her paper, she realized that the questions of how and why Gallimard and other characters fooled themselves were important. She noticed that she had to go back and cross out sections where she wandered off into a discussion of the strange love affair instead of focusing on the subject of illusion.
6. *Sleep*—The night before Linda planned to complete the paper, she did not work on it. She let it "cool off" overnight so she could see it freshly the next day.
7. *Final draft*—On rereading her essay, Linda found and revised more areas where she wandered away from support for her thesis. She added refinements such as making a distinction between Gallimard's and other characters' fantasies.
8. *Editing*—Linda ran her computer's spelling checker. Then she printed the paper and proofread by hand. Finally, she asked a friend to read it carefully. The friend made suggestions about how to reiterate the thesis in the conclusion and helped Linda think of a title. She also

pointed out that Linda used the word *rationale* when she meant *rationality* and *transcends* when she meant *transfixes*.

PREWRITING

The prewriting stage for a documented paper is necessarily more complex than simply gathering ideas for writing only from your own thoughts. You still need to completely understand the literary work before you begin, and your task is complicated by the need to find, read, and assimilate the works of others, being careful to credit these ideas when you incorporate them into your own writing. Figure 17-1 shows a page of Linda's notes from her first reading of the play.

FINDING A THESIS

To write a good paper involving research, begin with a thesis question, which you can eventually turn into a thesis statement once you have discovered the information needed to provide the answer. You might want to approach the matter as a problem to be solved.

POSE YOURSELF A PROBLEM You will write with greater engagement if you can discover some problem concerning your chosen literary work that genuinely interests you and then set out to solve that problem. Do you wonder, as most readers do, whether Gallimard was *really* ignorant of his lover's biological sex for twenty years? By reading about *M. Butterfly*, you can probably find the answer to that question and arrive at a more thorough understanding of the play. The problem you would then work on solving as you write your paper would be this:

> Is Gallimard thoroughly deceived about Song's biological sex, and if so, how and why?

Your thesis statement involves your solution of that problem and might read something like this:

> Gallimard's thorough commitment to the illusion of heterosexual romance with Song allows him to feel that he is finally a real man in several ways.

Perhaps you find yourself more interested in the literary techniques used by Hwang. If so, you might conceive your problem this way:

> How is the opera *Madame Butterfly* used in the play *M. Butterfly*?

An interest in cultural analysis might lead to a question like this:

> How are sexual and racial stereotypes active in Gallimard's life story?

LOCATING SOURCES

At some stage in the writing of a documented paper, you need to visit the library and find out what other people have said about the literary work you have chosen as your subject. In the old days, the first things you

> *Rene* - extra-marital affair -
>   "Body like those girls in magazines"
>   But not a 66¢
>   Women - Rene -   mind
>   too uninhibited/
>   masculine role?
>   • It was "her tears and her
>   silence that excited me every
>   time I visited Rene."
>
> *Butterfly* - "a <u>vessel</u> to contain my humiliation."
>
>   Women waiting
>   for men - I | Contrast Song
>   personally!!! | (him) to
>   despise | Butterfly.
>
> SONG: "only a man knows how a woman
>   is supposed to act" (operative word -
>   "supposed to" based on socialization)
> LOVE - Disinterest breeds interest
>
> Illusion ← wife - no one else will marry
>   me - knew when she married
>   him
>   Wife loved pretence of "faithful" husband
>   in China → Both lived in fantasy world.

FIGURE 17-1 READING NOTES

were likely to see upon entering a library were imposing rows of polished wood cabinets with small drawers: the card catalogue. In most libraries those cabinets have been replaced with row upon row of computers. More than likely you will conduct your search for sources on a computer.

Computer searches, online databases, and internet search engines vary in the way you can use them; they are being expanded and improved all the time. We can offer here some general instructions to help you find your way around the modern library.

THE ONLINE CATALOGUE

The computer version of the card catalogue is called a *public access catalogue* (PAC) or an *online catalogue* (OC). The PAC or OC terminal itself will tell you how to use it. The opening screen of the OC at the library Linda Samuel used shows that she could search by subject, title, and author, as well as by call number, shelf position, and international standard book number (ISBN). She could search for books, titles of journals, and other items owned by her library or by other libraries in the province.

INDEXES AND DATABASES

Even though you might find material in books to use in documenting your ideas and critical judgments, your paper will not be well researched unless you also discover available articles and reviews by consulting bibliographies, indexes, and databases. The library terminal that Linda was using allowed her to switch from the online catalogue to search four data systems: Wilson Indexes, ERIC databases, PsychINFO, CARL Uncover, and Infotrac SearchBank. Each of these targets a different set of sources.

Linda chose the Infotrac SearchBank because she wanted academic articles and reviews about David Henry Hwang and *M. Butterfly*. After typing in Hwang's name for her search term, she discovered that there were sixty-two references. She was able to narrow that list to twenty-eight items by typing in a second search term, "M. Butterfly." Linda could then view these entries one at a time or print out the entire list. Each citation included the article title, the name of the magazine, the volume, date, and page number; it also supplied the call number of the magazine if her library owned it. Some of the entries contained a brief summary of the article's contents, and a few supplied the full text of the article for her to read or print out. She could also send the data to her home computer via email.

These are just the first few steps in the search for possible sources. Numerous periodicals and periodically published reference works, such as annual bibliographies and indexes, are published on compact disc files (CD-ROM). Some of these are accessible through the online catalogue; others are stored in computers close to the areas where the books, periodicals, and reference works in the field are shelved. One source that Linda consulted online was *The MLA International Bibliography*, which lists (year by year) articles from leading periodicals devoted to literary criticism and theory.

USING THE INTERNET

The internet is a vast storehouse of information and can be accessed in a number of ways. It is relatively easy to get on the net. All you need is a computer, a modem (which connects your computer to phone lines) or a digital connection, and a browser (software that helps you find places on the internet). If you don't have a computer at home, your college or university library probably has a bank of computers that are hooked up to the net.

On the net you can find government documents and archives, news groups, online publications, texts of published materials, and databases provided by commercial servers such as America Online and Prodigy. You can browse the noncommercial contents of the net through the World Wide Web or by using what is called a Gopher Service. While internet sources can be informative and valuable, there are few, if any, standards for what is published there. There is no editorial board to screen internet publications, and not all material on a literary work is considered scholarly. Non-scholarly sources do not provide convincing support for academic writing.

It is not possible for us to give you instructions for using the net—it would simply take up too much space. If you are interested in finding out more, consult a book like *The Harcourt Guide to the Internet* by Carol Lea Clark (Harcourt Brace, 2001) or *Dave Sperling's Internet Guide*, 2nd ed. (Prentice Hall, 1998).

REFERENCE WORKS IN PRINT

As you can see, the library's computers provide an overwhelming number of sources and service options. You will have to spend some time with these data systems to find out how they work and how useful they are for your work.

On the other hand, if you are bewildered or intimidated by all these electronic resources, you can take solace in the fact that most libraries still hold almost all this material in old-fashioned print. The *MLA Bibliography*, for example, is still issued in book form. Your library probably has in print several other indexes and guides to articles on literature divided according to genre. Some of the most useful ones are listed in Chart 17-1 (page 636). So if the computer terminals are crowded or not working—or if you simply want some peace and quiet while researching—your librarian can tell you where on the shelves the reference books you seek are kept.

TAKING NOTES

Once you have found titles of articles and reviews that sound pertinent, locate the journal and see whether the actual article or review lives up to the promise of its title. If the material proves useful, take notes. Be sure to record the name of the journal, the volume number, date, and pages. If the article spreads over several pages, write down which exact page you used for each note. You will need this information later in order to credit your sources.

WRITING

Before you begin writing your first draft, turn the thesis question you were investigating into a thesis statement—a sentence that conveys the

> **CHART 17-1 GUIDES TO CRITICISM OF POETRY, DRAMA, AND FICTION**
>
> ### Guides to Criticism of Poetry
>
> *Index to Criticism of British and American Poetry*
> *Poetry Explication: A Checklist of Interpretation Since 1925 of British and American Poems, Past and Present*
> *McGill's Critical Survey of Poetry*
>
> ### Guides to Criticism of Drama
>
> *New York Theater Critics' Reviews*
> *New York Times Theater Reviews*
> *Dramatic Criticism Index*
> *A Guide to Critical Reviews*
>
> ### Guides to Criticism of Fiction
>
> *Canadian Forum*
> *Essays on Canadian Writing*
> *Quill and Quire*
> *Twentieth-Century Short Story Explication*
>
> ### Guides to Authors and Their Works
>
> *Contemporary Literary Criticism*
> *Contemporary Canadian Authors*
> *Dictionary of Literary Biography*
>
> Some of these reference works may also be computerized and available on CD-ROM. Check with your school's librarian. Many universities offer published reviews of drama, poetry, and short stories; for example, the *University of Windsor Review*.

point you want to make after studying your primary source and reading your secondary sources. If, for instance, you begin by investigating this question:

> Why are Hwang's characters, especially Gallimard, so prone to illusion?

you might, after doing your research, end up with a thesis statement something like this:

> Characters in *M. Butterfly* use illusion for purposes of self-aggrandizement; Gallimard is an extreme case of creating identity through illusion.

Your thesis may change as you work with your material, but you need a fairly clear idea of what you want to say and how you will go about saying it before you begin.

A highly structured thesis statement provides a pattern for organizing the research material you have already collected and gives you an organized way to go about doing more research. If you have a sense that issues of morality, gender, and culture are important factors in how Gallimard could remain unaware of Song's gender for so long, you may structure a thesis statement as follows:

> Gallimard must cling to the illusion of his heterosexual relationship with Song in order to maintain a sense of moral, gender, and cultural superiority.

You would then do further research focusing specifically on the three ideas of morality, gender, and culture.

DEVELOPING A PLAN

Many people strongly recommend taking notes on three-by-five-inch or five-by-seven-inch notecards during the researching stage of writing a documented paper. These small cards make the material easy to organize. If you have, instead, pages of notes, you may find yourself wasting time as you shuffle through dozens of sheets trying to locate the note you need.

USING NOTECARDS After completing your note taking, read each card and try to select a word or two that summarize the meaning of the passage on each card. Write that heading in the upper right-hand corner of the card. You can do this as you take notes, if you prefer. After all the cards have headings, read through these headings and group the cards with similar ideas together in stacks.

That's the easy part. Next, put your mind to work and decide on some reasonable order in which to present these ideas. Then, arrange the stacks according to your plan. As you write, following this plan, the necessary information will be in front of you ready to be incorporated into the first draft of your paper. If you have developed a highly structured thesis, one that offers a judgment about your subject and then divides your discussion about that subject into three (or more) topics, the pattern will be clear to you as researcher and as writer.

USING PHOTOCOPIES Linda used a two-stage process, using copies of articles. First, she took notes while reading. Then, after firming up her topic, she highlighted her articles so she could easily find relevant passages.

On longer projects, you might stack highlighted photocopies in piles according to headings. After using an article for one section of your paper, you may have to move it to another stack, where it serves as a source under another heading.

WRITING BEFORE RESEARCHING

If you are fired with enthusiasm for the literary work, and if you have a number of significant observations that you want to express, you should devise a thesis, marshall your evidence, order your ideas, and write a first draft. Then go to the library, locate and read a number of pertinent *secondary sources* (articles, reviews, sections of books, perhaps even whole books if your research needs to be thorough), and incorporate ideas from this reading into your paper at the appropriate places. You may find—especially if you are writing about a popular work by a well-known author—that most of your cogent insights have already appeared in print. Try not to be disheartened. Grit your teeth and give credit to the person who published first.

Say, for example, you had made this comment in your first draft:

> Gender confusion is almost unbelievable in the play.

After reading the secondary sources, you discover that virtually every writer makes this same observation. Thus, you would need to alter your statement to read something like this:

> Critics and reviewers agree that gender confusion is almost unbelievable in the play.

If a critic has made the point more effectively than you did, you might decide to scrap your sentence and quote the secondary source directly:

> As Corliss observes, "The gender lines are so tangled that it's hard to tell yin from yang" (85).

After crediting your sources throughout your paper, you may want to emphasize—if you can do so gracefully—the remaining ideas that are entirely yours, but it is best to check with your instructor since many prefer a more objective approach to academic writing than the following:

> The compelling issue that transfixed the opening night audience when I saw *M. Butterfly* is Gallimard's admitted ignorance of his lover's gender after twenty years of intimacy.

Some people find this method of plugging in ideas from their research the easiest way to handle a documented paper. If you are knowledgeable and enthusiastic about your topic, it may be the best way to proceed. Remember, however, that any ideas you have not credited to someone else are assumed to be your own.

On the other hand, if after reading the primary source you find yourself devoid of ideas, perhaps confused about the work, a better method is the one we described first: go to the library, locate the pertinent secondary sources, and study them carefully. Then, after having gained a thorough understanding of the primary source, you devise a thesis, choose your supporting material (both from the literary work and from the critics), arrange your ideas in an orderly way, and write your first draft.

AVOIDING PLAGIARISM

Whenever you write a paper after consulting secondary sources, you must take scrupulous care to give credit to those sources for any ideas or phrasings that you borrow. *Plagiarism* involves carelessly—or, far worse, deliberately—presenting the words or ideas of another writer as your own.

You must be careful in taking notes to put quotation marks around any passages—or even phrases—that you copy word for word. Changing an occasional word here and there will not do: such close paraphrasing is still considered plagiarism. The following examples may help you see the difference between plagiarism and paraphrasing (stating another's ideas in your own words):

Original Passage

"Hwang has spun a phantasm of multiple myopia: a man preposterously blinded by love." (Richard Corliss, "Betrayal in Beijing," *Time*, October 4, 1994: 85.)

Plagiarism

Corliss notes that Hwang has spun a fantasy of extreme myopia about a man foolishly blinded by love.

Plagiarism

Hwang has spun a myopic fantasy about a man foolishly blinded by love.

Combined Paraphrase and Direct Quotation

Corliss notes that Hwang presents "a phantasm of multiple myopia" involving "a man preposterously blinded by love" (85).

Paraphrase

Corliss notes that the playwright presents the tale of a man blinded by a fantasy of love (85).

Direct Quotation

"Hwang has spun," according to Corliss, "a phantasm of multiple myopia: a man preposterously blinded by love" (85).

INTRODUCING QUOTATIONS

Whether you are quoting directly or simply paraphrasing someone else's ideas, you should always give credit in the text of your paper to the person from whom you are borrowing. The MLA documentary style now requires you to do so. No longer will you be able to toss in a quotation, put a note number at the end, and trust your reader to fumble for the note page to discover your source. Because you now have to cite all sources within the paper, you need to exercise great skill in varying the way you introduce quotations and borrow ideas.

As you read your secondary sources, pay attention to the various ways that these writers credit their sources. If you read widely enough, this graceful introducing of other people's ideas will become second nature to you. However, in case you still have to work at introducing your quotations and paraphrases, here are a few models for you to go by:

As critic Lawrence Stone explains, daughters in Shakespeare's England were "often unwanted and might be regarded as no more than a tiresome drain on the economic resources of the family" (112).

Northrop Frye maintains that "poetry is the product, not only of a deliberate and voluntary act of consciousness, . . . but of processes which are subconscious or preconscious or half-conscious or unconscious as well" (88).

Kettle declares *Middlemarch* to be "the most impressive novel in our language" (1:160).

According to biographer Joan Givner, the failure of Porter's personal relationship with Josephson caused a temporary inability to write (221).

In his preface to *Contemporary Canadian Drama*, Joseph Shaver admits "The drama of this country is the most neglected form of art" (1).

As Rachel Brownstein points out, "A beautiful virgin walled off from an imperfect real world is the central figure in romance" (35).

"With the tremendous success of *Les Belles Soeurs*," observes Jerry Wasserman, "Tremblay changed the face of theatre in Quebec, becoming an icon of Québécois nationalism and launching a career that would make him Quebec's—and Canada's—foremost dramatist" (97).

IDEAS FOR RESEARCHED WRITING

ABOUT SHORT STORIES

1. Discuss the "power of blackness" in Hawthorne's "Young Goodman Brown."
2. Use library sources to discover the cultural values of young Goodman Brown's puritan society. What, for instance, was a "black mass"? What was the Calvinist attitude toward evil? How do the social codes of that society influence the behaviour of the major characters?
3. Consult several sources focusing on sex roles in marriage in late nineteenth-century society. Then discuss the influence of sex roles in the changing attitude of Louise Mallard in "The Story of an Hour."
4. Examine library sources to discover major differences in behaviour patterns and values between North American males and females. Relate your findings to the behaviour of male and female characters in "The Chrysanthemums."
5. Discuss the retelling of the quest myth in Welty's "A Worn Path."
6. Investigate attitudes toward out-of-wedlock pregnancy and sex roles in Japanese society. How do those cultural attitudes influence the lives of the family in Yamamoto's "Seventeen Syllables"?
7. Discuss the role of popular music in Oates's "Where Are You Going, Where Have You Been?"
8. Find information in the library concerning attitudes in our culture toward Aboriginal people. Relate your findings to Thomas King's "Borders" or Louise Erdrich's "The Red Convertible."
9. Consult several sources regarding the effects of alcohol and of the drug ecstasy on human emotion, and discuss these effects in relation to Russell Smith's "Serotonin."

ABOUT POETRY

1. Compare the cultural assumptions underlying the excerpt from Susanna Moodie's "Brian, the Still-Hunter" and Margaret Atwood's "Dream 2: Brian the Still-Hunter."
2. Look at the biographical information on Stephen Crane, Wilfred Owen, and Phyllis Webb to discover how the milieu in which each author lived influenced his or her attitude toward war.
3. Look up the history of Byzantium, the capital of the Eastern Roman Empire and the holy city of Greek Orthodoxy, and discuss what the city represents symbolically in Yeats's poem "Sailing to Byzantium."
4. Discuss E. E. Cummings's disregard for traditional form in his poetry.
5. Investigate the allusions in William Blake's "The Lamb" and "The Tyger," and relate that information to Blake's poems.
6. Find some details about Glenn Gould, and show how Don McKay makes use of and develops these details in his poem "Glenn Gould, Humming."
7. Compare the form and content of William Wordsworth's "Nuns Fret Not."
8. Investigate Pauline Johnson's dual heritage, and discuss the resulting tension in her poem "The Song My Paddle Sings."

ABOUT DRAMA

1. Othello is called "the Moor of Venice." Find out what the label means, and write an analysis of racial issues in *Othello*.
2. Analyze the images of women in *Othello* from the viewpoint of social class and the position women occupied in Venetian society. Use library sources to find supporting material about the position of women in sixteenth-century European society.
3. In Greek plays such as *Antigone*, women's roles were originally played by men. How might a modern audience respond to an all-male production of these plays?
4. Gather information about Theatre Passe Muraille and *The Farm Show*. Use this material to develop and support an analysis of *The Drawer Boy* as a comment on the coming together of the community and the often distant theatrical world.
5. Compare Natásha from *The Proposal* with Song from *M. Butterfly*. How do these "female" characters deal with cultural stereotypes?
6. Does *Almighty Voice and His Wife* advocate "assimilation" for Aboriginal people? Find out what critics and writers think about the way racial and social issues are treated in this play.
7. Consult several reference works about literature and drama to find out how *comedy* is defined and what its goals usually are. Relate your findings to the various ways that Anton Chekhov and Michael Healey use comedy.

REWRITING

Many people who do researched writing make no attempt to provide complete, accurate documentation of sources in the first draft because pausing to do so interrupts the flow of ideas. You need, of course, to include at least the last name of the person whose words are quoted or paraphrased (or the title of an anonymous source), but you can fill in from your notes the remaining information as part of the revising process.

CITING SOURCES

Various academic disciplines use different documentation styles. Because you are writing about literature, the appropriate one for you to follow is the Modern Language Association style. Sample entries illustrating the MLA format appear at the end of this chapter. You may also use as a model the documentation included in the two sample student research papers in the next section.

Be sure that you follow the models accurately. You should have all the necessary information recorded on your notecards. If you neglected to write down a page number or a date or a publisher, you must now trudge back to the library and track down the book or periodical again. You can see that taking care during the information-gathering stage will save you frustration later during the documenting stage.

INCLUDING INFORMATIONAL NOTES

With the MLA style you no longer use footnotes or endnotes to credit your sources. Any numbered notes will be informational notes. Any brief comment that is important enough to include but that is not precisely to the point of your discussion can be placed in a note. When you type these informational notes, you should entitle them simply "Notes" and place them on a separate page at the end of the paper, just before the Works Cited page.

EDITING

You must be particularly careful in proofreading and correcting a documented paper. Careless errors in typing will ruin your credibility—as well as your grade. Careless errors in crediting your sources could result in plagiarism, thus threatening your credibility—and your grade. A checklist for accurate documentation appears in Chart 17-2.

SAMPLE DOCUMENTED PAPERS BY STUDENTS

PAPER ON DRAMA

The paper beginning on page 644 was written by a university student. A complete guide to using the MLA system appears at the end of this chapter.

CHART 17-2 CHECKLIST FOR ACCURATE DOCUMENTATION

Besides following your usual procedures for proofreading and editing, take time to read through the paper one extra time, checking nothing but the way you have incorporated your sources. Ask yourself these questions:

1. Did I put quotation marks around all sentences and phrases borrowed from my reading?
2. Did I give credit in the text for all ideas borrowed from my reading, whether quoted directly or not?
3. Did I always put periods and commas before the quotation marks except when documentation in parentheses follows the quotation? Here's an example:

   "Arrabal's world," Esslin believes, "derives its absurdity [. . .] from the fact that his characters see the human situation with uncomprehending eyes of childlike simplicity" (217).

4. Did I include all the required information in the citations?
5. Did I use accurate paraphrases that are not too close to the original wording?

Then, take a few extra minutes to check carefully your Works Cited page. Ask yourself these questions:

1. Did I alphabetize correctly? (*A*, *an*, and *the* do not count when alphabetizing the title of an anonymous article.)
2. Did I use hanging indention (indent all lines of an entry five spaces or one-half inch, except for the first line)?
3. Did I use colons where colons are needed, periods where periods are needed, parentheses where parentheses are needed?
4. Did I underline the titles of all books and the names of all magazines and scholarly journals?
5. Did I use quotation marks around the titles of articles and chapters from books?
6. Did I convert all Roman numerals to Arabic?
7. Did I include all the necessary data?

Linda Samuel   1
English 102
September 28, 2003

   The Choice for Illusion in M. Butterfly

   David Henry Hwang's M. Butterfly captivates
the audience through a tense, cynical interplay
of racial, sexual, and cultural stereotypes in
a barely believable plot. The most compelling
challenge to belief that transfixes Hwang's
audience is Gallimard's admitted ignorance of
his lover's sex after twenty years of intimacy.
   James S. Moy, associate professor of theatre
and drama at the University of Wisconsin,
reflects upon the audience's reservation regarding Gallimard's lack of intimate knowledge
about his lover: "As audiences leave the theater, then, racial/sexual identity is not an
issue; rather, most are simply incredulous at
how for twenty years Gallimard could have confused Song's rectum for a woman's vagina" (54).
Moy further remarks that "the audience is left
to ponder how a sophisticated western diplomat
could fall victim to so amusing a case of gender confusion" (49).
   Even the judge, at the play's culmination,
dares to ask Song what every reader begs to
know: "There is one thing that the court--
indeed, that all of France--would like to know.
[. . .] Did Monsieur Gallimard know you were
a man?" (780). Readers of M. Butterfly silently

Samuel 2

repeat the judge's question. Did Gallimard know that Song was a man, or did ignorance somehow supplant intelligence, illusion supplant reality? These questions play havoc with rationality. How could Gallimard not know? How dare he not know? Readers scoff at the implausible concept that Gallimard could not know his lover's true sex.

  Might Gallimard be guilty of a greater flaw than ignorance? Might his greater offence be that of knowingly placing fantasy over reality? John Simon, theatre critic for New York magazine, questions Gallimard's supposed ignorance when he asks, "Can love be <u>that</u> blind? Can wish-fulfillment fantasy be <u>that</u> strong?" (117). Gallimard's actions from the play's genesis to its conclusion not only suggest his choice of fantasy over reality but confirm that it is a choice most of the characters make. Gallimard is more whole-heartedly involved in his illusion and is ennobled by his total immersion.

  David Henry Hwang, writer of <u>M. Butterfly</u>, gives credibility to this conclusion in an Afterword, asserting that racial as well as sexual fantasy held Gallimard in its grip: Gallimard's "assumption was consistent with a certain stereotyped view of Asians as bowing, blushing flowers. I therefore concluded that the diplomat must have fallen in love, not with a person, but with a fantasy stereotype" (Hwang 95). Theatre critic Richard Corliss provides further insight into Gallimard's world of illusion, insisting that "the heart sees what it sees" (85). What does Gallimard's heart see? In Song Liling, Gallimard sees a beautiful butterfly, despite initial evidence to the contrary. Her westernized words and tone combined with equal amounts of brass and sass stand in stark contrast to the Oriental butterfly that Gallimard seeks. Notice how Song questions Gallimard: "It's one of your favorite fantasies, isn't it? The submissive Oriental woman and the cruel white man" (750). Any evidence of a gentle butterfly here?

Although Song's harsh statements clearly do not reflect the submissive Oriental butterfly that consumes Gallimard's fantasies, his heart nevertheless "sees what it sees." He chooses fantasy over reality by rationalizing her attitude. "She is outwardly bold and outspoken, yet her heart is shy and afraid" (755). Fact or fantasy? Gallimard convinces himself, despite evidence to the contrary, that Song is a butterfly.

Why is Gallimard driven toward illusion over reality? For Gallimard, up to the time of meeting Song, reality was disappointing in both his professional and personal worlds. By his own admission, he was not a "true man." Recall

Gallimard's statement, "The sad truth is that all men want a beautiful woman, and the uglier the man, the greater the want" (749). He acknowledges his status by concluding, "We, who are not handsome, nor brave, nor powerful, yet somehow believe, like Pinkerton, that we deserve a Butterfly" (747).

In Gallimard's world of fantasy, here finally is beautiful Song, who not only is attracted to Gallimard but has also conceded that "I have already given you my shame" (759). Song is not only beautiful but under Gallimard's power as well. His response to Song's concession is "I had finally gained power over a beautiful woman" (759). It is a dual fantasy come true. First, he gains power over a woman, apparently for the first time in his life. Second, he gains power over a <u>beautiful</u> woman. This fantasy come true is worth clinging to and defending even in the face of clues about gender deception. The illusion of heterosexual romance with Song makes room for dreams of political power and paternity to come true. <u>New York Times</u> critic Frank Rich emphasizes this point: "Gallimard believes he can become a real man only if he can exercise power over a beautiful and submissive women, which is why he's so ripe to be duped by Song Liling's impersonation of a shrinking butterfly" (C13).

However, is Song solely responsible for duping Gallimard? Song does her part in making the fantasy real; as playwright Hwang comments, "The Chinese spy encouraged these misperceptions" (95). However, the principal weight of the fantasy rests with Gallimard's willingness to be duped and refusal to betray his own illusion. Although he states quite emphatically in the concluding act, "Tonight, I've finally learned to tell fantasy from reality. And, knowing the difference, I choose fantasy" (784), the truth is that Gallimard fully chooses fantasy over reality throughout the play, in the only authentic choice of his life.

Gallimard's wife, Helga, cannot conceive a child by Gallimard through intercourse. That Song can conceive a child by Gallimard is the illusion. Which "truth" would Gallimard believe? Leo Sauvage, theatre critic, mentions the absurdity of the situation. "As for the baby Song convinces him s/he has had (surely the most preposterous unexplained item in the actual news story)[1] the play shows Chinese intelligence officers supplying it to their agent" (22). Gallimard once again chooses fantasy by accepting the Eurasian child as his own, never having witnessed its development within Song's body.

Samuel 6

    Gallimard is not the only character in the play who endorses illusion. Other characters likewise choose illusion in the face of reality. Recall what Comrade Chin says to Song, "Don't forget: there is no homosexuality in China" (765). In reality, however, does Chin really believe that Song could procure political secrets from Gallimard over a twenty-year period without engaging in homosexual acts? Chin is well aware that Song is a man; however, like Gallimard, she promotes the illusion.

    Even Gallimard's wife, upon hearing Gallimard's request for a divorce, responds:

> I knew, in my own way, I knew that you were not everything you pretended to be. But the pretense--going on your arm to the embassy ball, visiting your office and the guards saying, "Good morning, good morning, Madame Gallimard"--the pretense . . . was very good indeed. (778)

The greatest distinction between Helga's and Chin's fantasy and Gallimard's is that Helga and Chin recognize the illusion for what it is--and isn't--more clearly.

    Ambassador Toulon, Gallimard's superior, also chooses fantasy over reality by promoting Gallimard to vice-counsel and accepting his ideas on international policy, knowing at the same time that Gallimard is inexperienced in international affairs (outside his affair with the Butterfly). Toulon accepts Gallimard's political fantasizing based on his personal stereotype that "Orientals will always submit to a greater force" (764). Moy notes, "This, of course, was the mistake of the Vietnam War" (50). In the end, Toulon's illusion proves to be as costly and tragic as Gallimard's.

   The question raised by the judge still begs for an answer. At what level does Gallimard know that Song is a man? Gallimard incriminates himself at the play's conclusion in his efforts to prevent Song from displaying evidence beyond all shadow of a doubt that he indeed is a man. At this point, Gallimard announces, "I know what you are . . . a man" (783).

   Gallimard comes face to face with fact and fantasy. For the first time throughout the entire play, he acknowledges fact. However, he wastes no time in moving from this uncomfortable reality to a position closer to home. Gallimard exchanges his old fantasy of making his Butterfly "writhe on a needle" (757) for a new fantasy where he is the butterfly, as he places the wig on his head and wraps himself in the kimono. Now, clothed within this new fantasy, Gallimard proudly announces, "My name is Rene Gallimard--also known as Madame Butterfly"

Samuel 8

(785). Like Chin and Helga, he now is able to sustain two contradictory beliefs at once.

As with his previous illusions, Gallimard pushes this fatal fantasy of being Madame Butterfly to the limit. He mimics the dying words and actions of Madame Butterfly, "Death with honor is better than life . . . life with dishonor" (785), as he pierces his heart with the knife. We must conclude that the dishonour equals an existence where fantasy and reality know each other's face.

Note

[1]Hwang based this play on a brief story that appeared in the <u>New York Times</u> ("France Jails 2 in Odd Case of Espionage": 11 May 1986), but he did not do any further research into the incident.

Samuel 10

Works Cited

Corliss, Richard. "Cinema: Betrayal in Beijing."
    Time 4 Oct. 1993: 85. *InfoTrac Expanded*
    Academic Index ASAP. OCLC FirstSearch.
    Illinois State U Lib. 8 Sept. 2001.

Hwang, David H. Afterword. *M. Butterfly*. New
    York: New American Library, 1988.

---. *M. Butterfly*. *Literature and the Writing*
    Process. 5th ed. Eds. Elizabeth McMahan,
    Susan X. Day, and Robert Funk. Upper Saddle
    River: Prentice-Hall, 1999. 706-50.

Moy, James S. "David Henry Hwang's *M. Butterfly*
    and Philip Kan Gotanda's *Yankee Dawg You*
    Die: Repositioning Chinese American
    Marginality on the American Stage." *Theatre*
    Journal 42 (1990): 48-56.

Rich, Frank. "*M. Butterfly*: A Story of a
    Strange Love, Conflict and Betrayal." *New*
    York Times 21 March 1988: C13.

Sauvage, Leo. "On Stage: Spring Salad." *The New*
    Leader 11 April 1988: 22-23. *InfoTrac*
    Expanded Academic Index ASAP. OCLC
    FirstSearch. Illinois State U Lib. 8 Sept.
    2001.

Simon, John. "Finding Your Song." *New York* 11
    April 1988: 117.

PAPER ON A SHORT STORY

The following essay analyzes a story that appears in the anthology section.

Richard Lee 1
English 1110
September 2003

A Room, a Door, and a Window: Metaphors for Change in
       Chopin's "The Story of an Hour"

    When Mrs. Mallard of Kate Chopin's "The Story of an Hour" learns of her husband's death, she weeps then goes to her room, allowing no one to follow her. Here, behind a closed door, Louise Mallard experiences an all too brief moment of self-realization. Initially, the exhaustion she feels haunts "her body and [seems] to reach into her soul" (Chopin 182), yet within the course of less than one hour, Louise experiences a transformation: she is converted into "a goddess of Victory" (183). In this room Chopin's protagonist is reborn, and her transformation comes as a result of the insight she gains after closing the door and looking through the open window. Once free, Louise would rather die than become Mrs. Brently Mallard again. The room, door, and window are metaphors used by Chopin to reveal the introspection, separation, and opportunity necessary for the development of autonomy.

    "[She] went away to her room alone" (182). In such a short story Chopin's specific reference to Louise Mallard's room as *her* room is significant

Lee 2

enough to render it a symbol. Common yonic symbols such as rooms and caves have the metaphoric value, as McMahan asserts, of "the fecundity of the female" (76), yet Louise Mallard is a character who seems devoid of creativity. Initially, while Mrs. Mallard is in her room, her face reveals a certain "repression" and her eyes "a dull stare" (182). Ultimately, we are shown a woman whose "intelligent thought" is suspended (182). However, critic Emily Toth states that Chopin herself acknowledged the duality of a woman's life: "the 'outward existence which conforms, the inward life which questions'" (115). It is in her room that Louise Mallard questions her outward life and inwardly is reborn. "Every woman," as Gilbert and Gubar explain, "might seem to have metaphorical access to the dark knowledge buried in caves" (95). Through introspection into her life while in her room/womb/cave, Louise Mallard begins to recognize that a change is coming over her, and with both fear and joy she allows the change to begin. While in her room, Louise finally understands she is "Free! Body and soul free!" (183), and that "this possession of self-assertion [is] the strongest impulse of her being" (183).

It takes the solitude of her own room for Louise Mallard to understand herself, and it certainly requires her to close the door on and separate herself from those who could not possibly understand her new-found self and would seek to draw her back into a traditional way of life. Behind the closed door of her room, Louise Mallard is "drinking in a very elixir of life" (183), yet uncomprehending the absurdity of her words, Josephine calls out, "I beg; open the door--you will make yourself ill" (183). Perhaps in 19th century America a woman who decided to live alone (much less enjoy it!), as Mary Anne Ferguson in her book *Images of Women in Literature* suggests, decided, in effect, not to live at all (346). Josephine might well worry about her sister, for Louise "'dies to the world' as a nun does upon taking her vows" (Ferguson 346). Josephine would, in her unenlightened state, see Louise's future as a lone woman "a diminishment of life" (346) and would certainly see Louise's "monstrous joy" (Chopin 182) at the prospect, sheer madness. Chopin uses Josephine to represent women who have not experienced "that brief moment of illumination" (182) and who blindly follow the societal role set out for them.

However, Louise has closed the door on the limitations imposed by society. As Sylvia

Lee 4

Bailey Shurbutt explains, "Chopin presents revised portraits of women achieving fulfillment in roles other than marriage and of women evincing a passionate nature considered inappropriate by conventional, patriarchal standards of 'Victorian' America" (15). Behind Louise's closed door a metamorphosis is taking place, one that anyone on the other side must see as "inappropriate." Josephine kneels before the closed door in a posture of supplication, begging for her sister to return to her former life, not realizing that Louise has, for the first time in her adult life, separated herself from tradition and has just begun to live. Doors are barriers between people, and while they shut some people, ideas, and influences out, they also preserve the much needed retreat for others. Perhaps if Louise had had more time behind her closed door, she could have summoned the strength to withstand the shock of her husband's existence and gone on to create the life she had imagined for herself.

 A variation on an old saying states that when one door closes, a window opens. In Louise's case, the open window in her room is the window to her soul. Louise is exhausted by her initial "storm of grief" (182) and sits staring blankly through the open window, yet she is not entirely withdrawn because somewhere in her subconscious she is able to recognize "patches of blue sky," "tops of trees," and "new spring life" (182). Chopin's choice of images conjures up an as of yet unspoken idea. Through this window to her soul creeps the "elusive" and "subtle" knowledge Louise cannot name (182). Why is the idea of freedom so frightening to Louise that she fights it off, "striving to beat it back with her will"? (182). To many readers, Louise's "monstrous joy" at the death of her husband seems disloyal at least and, according to Ferguson, "inhuman and unnatural" (347), so is it any wonder that Louise herself is repulsed by the idea that she should find joy and freedom at the cost of her husband's life? This window into a woman's soul gives the reader the opportunity to understand just how life-destroying the traditional role for women in the 19th century was. She has loved her husband, and she will certainly feel grief "again when she [sees] the kind, tender hands folded in death" (182), but through this window, she sees "beyond that bitter moment" (182) into the future. Louise Mallard, however, has no idea that the only way she will achieve this opportunity for freedom is not through her husband's death but through her own. "Till death us do part" become ominous words to one who has no opportunity for freedom in an unfulfilling marriage, so when she discovers her husband is alive, and since she has

Lee 6

seen her potential through the window to her soul, death is the only opportunity for freedom left to Louise.

Louise Mallard's room is a womb for the development of self-discovery. The closed door protects Louise as she learns more about herself and her new-found freedom, and the open window in Kate Chopin's "The Story of an Hour" is a metaphor for the briefly freed soul of Louise Mallard. We may see these things simply as descriptions of places and things necessary to the setting of a short, sad tale, or we may understand that metaphors allow us, as Northrop Frye advises, to

> "realize that there's a difference between the world [we're] living in and the world [we] want to live in. The world [we] want to live in is . . . not an environment but a home; it's not the world [we] see but the world [we] build out of what [we] see" (4).

Louise Mallard builds a future for herself in her room, closed off from outside influences and open to opportunities to which she finally abandons herself, briefly, at least in her imagination.

Works Cited

Chopin, Kate. "The Story of an Hour." *Literature and the Writing Process*. Eds. Elizabeth McMahan, Susan X Day, and Robert Funk. Upper Saddle River, NJ: Prentice Hall, 2002.

Ferguson, Mary Anne. *Images of Women in Literature*. Boston: Houghton Mifflin, 1981.

Frye, Northrop. *The Educated Imagination*. Toronto: Anansi, 1993.

Gilbert, Sandra M., and Susan Gubar. *The Madwoman in the Attic: The Woman Writer and the Nineteenth-Century Literary Imagination*. Boston: Yale UP, 1984.

McMahan, Elizabeth, Susan X Day, and Robert Funk. Eds. *Literature and the Writing Process*. Upper Saddle River, NJ: Prentice Hall, 2002.

Shurbutt, Sylvia Bailey. "The Cane River Characters and Revisionist Mythmaking in the Work of Kate Chopin." *Southern Literary Journal* 25.2 (1993): 14-24.

Toth, Emily. "Kate Chopin on Divine Love and Suicide: Two Rediscovered Articles." *American Literature* 63.1 (1991): 115-21.

EXPLANATION OF THE MLA DOCUMENTATION STYLE

1. Your paper will end with an alphabetized list of Works Cited that includes all sources mentioned in your essay.
2. In citing primary sources (i.e., short stories, poems, novels, or plays), include author's name and page number (or line number, if a poem) in the text for the first entry. Thereafter, page number alone will suffice, unless your list of Works Cited includes more than one work by that author and if in your essay the author of a quote is at all ambiguous. You should include a shortened title if you have several works by the same author, like this: (Gissing, *Grub Street* 37).

   a. **Quotation from a novel or short story:**

   Rhonda Nunn emphasizes the importance of role models as she declares to Monica, "Your mistake was in looking only at the weak women" (Gissing 316).

   We are told that Dorie "loved that woman's husband with a fierce love that was itself a little ugly" (Oates 112).

   The Works Cited entries are

   Gissing, George. <u>The Odd Women</u>. 1893. Rpt. New York: Norton, 1977.

   Oates, Joyce Carol. "Accomplished Desires." <u>The Wheel of Love and Other Stories</u>. New York: Fawcett, 1972. 111-47.

   b. **Quotation from a poem:**

   Coleridge's assertion that poetic life is a "miracle of rare device / A sunny pleasure dome with caves of ice" (35-36) proves paradoxical.

   Do not include the abbreviations for *line* or *lines* since the letter *l* may be confused with the number one. For the first reference of a line or lines of poetry, write the word *line* or *lines*, but use only the line number(s) after the first reference.

   The Works Cited entry is

   Coleridge, S. T. "Kubla Khan." <u>Coleridge: Poetical Works</u>. Ed. Ernest H. Coleridge. London: Oxford UP, 1973. 277-98.

c. Quotation from a play:

In *Othello*, Iago's striking comment, "What you know, you know. / From this time forth I will never speak a word" (5.2.299-300), serves as a philosophic closure.

The ontological level of discourse can be seen in the words of Emilia, who exclaims, "O, the more angel she, / And you the blacker devil!" (*Othello* 5.1.129-30).

The numbers separated by periods mean: Act 5, scene 1, lines 129 through 130. In some modern plays such as those with only one act, you may simply cite page numbers, as you would with a quotation from a novel or short story.

The Works Cited entry is

Shakespeare, William. *Othello*. *Literature: An Introduction to Fiction, Poetry, and Drama*. Ed. X. J. Kennedy. 3rd ed. Boston: Little Brown, 1983. 875-958.

d. Quotations from essays are cited the same way as a novel.

3. Individual citations of secondary sources (books or articles considering the work under discussion) are inserted in the paper by author and page number (or by author, shortened title, and page number if your list of Works Cited includes more than one work by that person).

a. Quotation from a work in more than one volume:

Kettle declares *Middlemarch* to be "the most impressive novel in our language" (1:160).

The Works Cited entry is

Kettle, Arnold. *An Introduction to the English Novel*. 2 vols. New York: Harper, 1951.

b. Quotation from a book with a single author:

As Lawrence Stone explains, daughters in Shakespeare's England were "often unwanted and might be regarded as no more than a tiresome drain on the economic resources of the family" (112).

The Works Cited entry is

Stone, Lawrence. *The Family, Sex and Marriage in England: 1500-1800*. New York: Harper, 1977.

c. **Quotation from an article:**

As Michael Holzman reports, many of his students felt that "Expression and communication were reserved for speech" (235).

The Works Cited entry is

Holzman, Michael. "Teaching Is Remembering." <u>College English</u> 46 (184): 229-38.

4. Any notes in your paper will be informational; that is, they will contain material of interest that is not essential to your discussion. These content notes are included as Notes just before your list of Works Cited.
5. Always use Arabic numbers, except when citing pages from a preface, introduction, or table of contents (vi) or when mentioning monarchs (James I, Elizabeth II).
6. If the place of publication of a book is a foreign city, cite the original name and add the English version in brackets: München [Munich].
7. Always omit the abbreviations *p.* and *pp.* (for page and pages).
8. In general, use lower case for *vol., no., chap., trans.* in citations.
9. If you cite two or more entries by the same author, do not repeat the author's name. Instead use three hyphens, followed by a period. Then give the remaining information as usual.
10. One space after periods is now acceptable in Works Cited lists.

SAMPLE ENTRIES FOR A WORKS CITED LIST

Remember, you must alphabetize your list and use hanging indention; that is, after the first line, indent subsequent lines five spaces or one-half inch.

1. **Book with one author:**

   Fowke, Edith. <u>Canadian Folklore</u>. Toronto: Oxford UP, 1988.

2. **Reprint of an earlier edition:**

   Traill, Catharine Parr. <u>The Backwoods of Canada: Letters from the Wife of an Emigrant Officer</u>. 1836. Toronto: Prospero, 2000.

3. **Revised edition:**

   Bonnycastle, Stephen. <u>In Search of Authority</u>. 2nd ed. Peterborough: Broadview P, 1998.

4. **Book with two authors:**

   Gilbert, Sandra, and Susan Gubar. <u>The Madwoman in the Attic: The Woman Writer and the Nineteenth-Century Literary Imagination</u>. New Haven: Yale UP, 1979.

5. **Book with more than three authors or editors:**

   Spiller, Robert E., et al. <u>LHUS</u>. 3rd ed. London: Macmillan, 1969.

   LHUS means *Literary History of the United States* and is abbreviated in citations, as is *PMLA* (*Publication of the Modern Language Association*) and *TLS* (*London Times Literary Supplement*).

6. **Work in several volumes:**

   Kettle, Arnold. <u>An Introduction to the English Novel</u>. 2 vols. New York: Harper, 1951.

7. **Essay in a collection, casebook, or critical edition:**

   Geist, Stanley. "Portraits from a Family Album: <u>Daisy Miller</u>." <u>Hudson Review</u> 5 (Summer 1952): 203-06. Rpt. in <u>James's</u> Daisy Miller. Ed. William T. Stafford. New York: Scribner's, 1963. 131-33.

   If an underlined title contains another title that should be underlined, leave the second title without underlining.

   Matthews, James H. "Frank O'Connor." Lewisburg: Bucknell UP, 1976. Rpt. in <u>Contemporary Literary Criticism</u>. Ed. Dedria Bryfonski and Laurie Harris. Vol. 14. Detroit: Gale, 1983. 399-402.

8. **Work in an anthology:**

   Smith, Russell. "Serotonin." <u>The Notebooks: Interviews and New Fiction from Contemporary Writers</u>. Eds. Michelle Berry and Natalee Caple. Toronto: Anchor, 2002. 341-57.

9. **Work in translation:**

   Cirlot, J. E. <u>A Dictionary of Symbols</u>. Trans. Jack Sage. 2nd ed. New York: Philosophical Lib., 1976.

10. **Anonymous book:**

    <u>The Statutes of the Realm</u>. London: Record Commissions, 1820-28; facsim. ed. 1968.

    Facsim is the abbreviation for *facsimile*.

11. **Anonymous article (magazine with no volume number):**

    "Speaking Softly, Carrying No Stick." Newsweek 11 Nov. 1991: 66.

12. **Signed article (newspaper):**

    Harding, D. W. "Father and Daughter in Shakespeare's Last Plays." TLS 30 Nov. 1979: 59-61.

    TLS means the London *Times Literary Supplement.*

13. **Unsigned article (newspaper):**

    "College Grads Better Consumers." Chicago Tribune 3 May 1976: 2.3.

    2.3 means section 2, page 3.

14. **Signed article (periodical with no volume number):**

    Heilbrun, Carolyn. "The Masculine Wilderness of the American Novel." Saturday Review 29 Jan. 1962: 41-44.

15. **Signed article (periodical with continuous pagination):**

    Mason, John B. "Whitman's Catalogues: Rhetorical Means for Two Journeys in 'Song of Myself.'" American Literature 45 (1973): 34-49.

16. **Signed article (periodical with each issue separately paged):**

    Frey, John R. "America and Her Literature Reviewed by Postwar Germany." American-German Review 10.5 (1954): 4-7.

    10.5 means vol. 10, issue 5.

17. **Unsigned encyclopedia article:**

    "Abolitionists." Encyclopedia Americana. 1974 ed.

18. **Signed encyclopedia article:**

    P[ar]k, T[homas]. "Ecology." Encyclopaedia Britannica. 1968 ed.

19. **Article from *Dictionary of American Biography*:**

    N[evins], A[llan]. "Warren Gamaliel Harding." DAB (1932).

    The article is signed with initials. The corresponding name is listed at the beginning of the volume.

20. Anonymous pamphlet:

<u>Preparing Your Dissertation for Microfilming</u>. Ann Arbor: UMI, n.d.

UMI means *University Microfilms International;* n.d. means *no date given.*

21. Reference to the Bible:

<u>The Bible</u>. Trans. J. M. P. Smith, et al. Chicago: U of Chicago P, 1939.

<u>The Geneva Bible</u>. 1560. Facsim. Rpt. Madison: U of Wisconsin P, 1961.

In your paper, do not underline the King James version of the Bible, and do not include the Bible in your Works Cited list unless you have used a version other than the King James. Cite chapter and verse in parentheses in the text of your paper this way: (Dan. 9.25–27).

22. Reference to a letter (in a published collection):

Roy, Gabrielle. <u>Letters to Bernadette</u>. Trans. Patricia Claxton. Toronto: Lester & Orpen Dennys, 1990.

23. Reference to a letter (unpublished or personal):

Wharton, Edith. Letter to William Brownell. 6 Nov. 1907. Wharton Archives. Amherst College, Amherst, MA.

Vidal, Gore. Letter to author. 2 June 1984.

24. Personal or telephone interview:

Friesen, Patrick. Personal interview. 26 Feb. 2004.

McNamara, Eugene. Telephone interview. 29 Dec. 2003.

25. Review (signed or unsigned):

Rothman, Claire. "Forgotten Novelist Gwethalyn Graham Makes a Comeback." Rev. of <u>Earth and High Heaven</u>. <u>The Vancouver Sun</u> 20 March. 2004: D20.

Rev. of <u>Ring</u>, by Jonathan Yardley. <u>The New Yorker</u> 12 Sept. 1977: 159-60.

26. Lecture:

Axelrod, Rise. "Who Did What with Whom?" MLA Convention. Chicago. 30 Dec. 1977.

27. **Film:**

> <u>Modern Times</u>. Dir. Charles Chaplin. With Chaplin and
> Paulette Goddard. United Artists, 1936.

If you are discussing the contribution of an individual, begin with that person's name.

28. **Document from ERIC (Education Resources Information Center):**

> Cooper, Grace C. "The Teaching of Composition and
> Different Cognitive Styles." Mar. 1980. Ed 186 915.

CITING WORKS IN ELECTRONIC FORM

If you use material from a computer database or online source, you need to indicate that you read it in electronic form. You will probably use a service that your school library subscribes to. In literary research, most of the items you read have also appeared in print. Give the print information first, and complete the citation by giving the name of the database (underlined), the name of the online service (in this case, OCLC FirstSearch), the library you used, and the date of access:

> Wells, Walter. "John Updike's 'A & P': A Return Visit to
> Araby." <u>Studies in Short Fiction</u> 32.2 (1993): 127-34.
> <u>InfoTrac: Expanded Academic Index ASAP</u>. OCLC
> FirstSearch. Eastern Illinois. U Lib., 6 Mar. 1999.

If no printed source or printed analogue is indicated for the material you cite, your entry in the Works Cited list would look like this:

> "Expressionism." <u>Microsoft Encarta '95: Multimedia
> Encyclopedia</u>. CD-ROM. Funk & Wagnalls, 1994.

CITING SOURCES FROM THE INTERNET

Sources on the internet that you are likely to use for a literary research paper include reference databases and articles in periodicals.

1. **Article in a reference database:**

> "Fresco." <u>Britannica Online</u>. Vers. 97.1.1. Mar. 1997.
> <u>Encyclopaedia Britannica</u>. 29 Mar. 1997
> <http://www.eb.com:180>.

Vers. stands for the *version* number of the source. That is followed by the date of the electronic posting, the name of the institution or organization sponsoring the website, the date when you accessed the source, and the electronic address, or URL (Uniform Resource Location), in angle brackets.

2. Article in a periodical:

```
Flannagan, Roy. "Reflections on Milton and Ariosto."
    Early Modern Literary Studies 2.3 (1996): 16 pars.
    22 Feb. 1997 <http://unixg.ubc.ca:7001/0/
    e-source/emls/02-3/flanmilt.html>.
```

Cite the author, title, and publication information of the printed source as usual. Then give the number of pages, paragraphs, or other sections of the electronic version—followed by the date of access and the electronic address in angle brackets. *Pars.* stands for *paragraphs.*

Material from personal sites and discussion lists should be used with care. Consult with your instructor about using information from these internet sources.

For more detailed information about citing electronic and Internet sources, consult *The MLA Handbook for Writers of Research Papers*, 6th ed. (2003) or the MLA's website, <http://www.mla.org>.

WEB For study tools to help you with your next writing assignment, please visit the Companion Website at www.pearsoned.ca/mcmahan.

Anthology of Drama

William Shakespeare   1564–1616

Othello, the Moor of Venice

THE NAMES OF THE ACTORS

OTHELLO, *the Moor.*
BRABANTIO, *a senator, father to Desdemona.*
CASSIO, *an honourable lieutenant to Othello.*
IAGO, *Othello's ancient, a villain.*
RODERIGO, *a gulled gentleman.*
DUKE OF VENICE.
SENATORS *of Venice.*
MONTANO, *governor of Cyprus.*
LODOVICO *and* GRATIANO, *kinsmen to Brabantio, two noble Venetians.*

SAILORS.
CLOWN.
DESDEMONA, *daughter to Brabantio and wife to Othello.*
EMILIA, *wife to Iago.*
BIANCA, *a courtezan and mistress to Cassio.*
MESSENGER, HERALD, OFFICERS, GENTLEMEN, MUSICIANS, *and* ATTENDANTS.

[SCENE: VENICE; A SEA-PORT IN CYPRUS]

ACT I

SCENE I   *Venice. A street.*

[*Enter* RODERIGO *and* IAGO.]

ROD. Tush! never tell me; I take it much unkindly
That thou, Iago, who hast had my purse
As if the strings were thine, shouldst know of this.

IAGO. 'Sblood,[1] but you'll not hear me:
If ever I did dream of such a matter,
Abhor me.

ROD. Thou told'st me thou didst hold him in thy hate.

IAGO. Despise me, if I do not. Three great ones of the city,[2]
In personal suit to make me his lieutenant,
Off-capp'd to him:[3] and, by the faith of man,   10

---

[1]**'Sblood** an oath, "by God's blood."
[2]**great ones of the city** Iago means to indicate his importance in the community; this is suggested also by his use of the word *worth* in line 11.
[3]**him** Othello.

I know my price, I am worth no worse a place:
But he, as loving his own pride and purposes,
Evades them, with a bombast circumstance
Horribly stuff'd with epithets of war;
And, in conclusion,
Nonsuits[4] my mediators; for, "Certes," says he,
"I have already chose my officer."
And what was he?
Forsooth, a great arithmetician,[5]
One Michael Cassio, a Florentine,   20
A fellow almost damn'd in a fair wife;[6]
That never set a squadron in the field,
Nor the division[7] of a battle knows
More than a spinster; unless the bookish theoric,[8]
Wherein the toged[9] consuls can propose[10]
As masterly as he: mere prattle, without practice,
Is all his soldiership. But he, sir, had th' election:
And I, of whom his eyes had seen the proof
At Rhodes, at Cyprus[11] and on other grounds
Christian and heathen, must be be-lee'd and calm'd   30
By debitor and creditor: this counter-caster,[12]
He, in good time,[13] must his lieutenant be,
And I—God bless the mark![14]—his Moorship's ancient.[15]

ROD. By heaven, I rather would have been his hangman.

IAGO. Why, there's no remedy; 'tis the curse of service,
Preferment goes by letter and affection,
And not by old gradation,[16] where each second
Stood heir to th' first. Now, sir, be judge yourself,
Whether I in any just term am affin'd[17]
To love the Moor.

ROD.   I would not follow then.   40

IAGO. O, sir, content you;
I follow him to serve my turn upon him:

---

[4]**Nonsuits** rejects.
[5]**arithmetician** a man whose military knowledge was merely theoretical, based on books of tactics.
[6]**A . . . wife** Cassio does not seem to be married, but his counterpart in Shakespeare's source did have a wife.
[7]**division** disposition of a battle line.
[8]**theoric** theory.
[9]**toged** wearing the toga.
[10]**propose** discuss.
[11]**Rhodes, Cyprus** islands in the Mediterranean south of Asia Minor, long subject to contention between the Venetians and the Turks.
[12]**counter-caster** a sort of bookkeeper; contemptuous term.
[13]**in good time** forsooth.
[14]**God bless the mark** anciently, a pious interjection to avert evil omens.
[15]**ancient** standardbearer, ensign.
[16]**old gradation** seniority; Iago here expresses a characteristic prejudice of professional soldiers.
[17]**affin'd** bound.

We cannot all be masters, nor all masters
Cannot be truly follow'd. You shall mark
Many a duteous and knee-crooking knave,
That, doting on his own obsequious bondage,
Wears out his time, much like his master's ass,
For nought but provender, and when he's old, cashier'd:
Whip me such honest knaves. Others there are
Who, trimm'd in forms and visages of duty, 50
Keep yet their hearts attending on themselves,
And, throwing but shows of service on their lords,
Do well thrive by them and when they have lin'd their coats
Do themselves homage: these fellows have some soul;
And such a one do I profess myself. For, sir,
It is as sure as you are Roderigo,
Were I the Moor, I would not be Iago:[18]
In following him, I follow but myself;
Heaven is my judge, not I for love and duty,
But seeming so, for my peculiar end: 60
For when my outward action doth demonstrate
The native act and figure of my heart
In compliment extern,[19] 'tis not long after
But I will wear my heart upon my sleeve
For daws to peck at: I am not what I am.

ROD. What a full fortune does the thick-lips[20] owe,
    If he can carry 't thus!

IAGO.   Call up her father,
    Rouse him: make after him, poison his delight,
    Proclaim him in the streets, incense her kinsmen,
    And, though he in a fertile climate dwell, 70
    Plague him with flies: though that his joy be joy,
    Yet throw such changes of vexation on 't,
    As it may lose some colour.

ROD. Here is her father's house; I'll call aloud.

IAGO. Do, with like timorous[21] accent and dire yell
    As when, by night and negligence, the fire
    Is spied in populous cities.

ROD. What, ho, Brabantio! Signior Brabantio, ho!

IAGO. Awake! what, ho, Brabantio! thieves! thieves! thieves!
    Look to your house, your daughter and your bags! 80
    Thieves! thieves!

[BRABANTIO *appears above at a window.*]

BRA. What is the reason of this terrible summons?
    What is the matter there?

---

[18]**Were . . . Iago** Were I in the position of the Moor, I should not feel as Iago feels.
[19]**compliment extern** outward civility.
[20]**thick-lips** Elizabethans often applied the term *Moor* to Negroes.
[21]**timorous** frightening.

ROD. Signior, is all your family within?

IAGO. Are your doors lock'd?

BRA. Why, wherefore ask you this?

IAGO. 'Zounds, sir, y' are robb'd; for shame, put on your gown;
Your heart is burst, you have lost half your soul;
Even now, now, very now, an old black ram
Is tupping your white ewe. Arise, arise:
Awake the snorting[22] citizens with the bell, 90
Or else the devil will make a grandsire of you:
Arise, I say.

BRA. What, have you lost your wits?

ROD. Most reverend signior, do you know my voice?

BRA. Not I: what are you?

ROD. My name is Roderigo.

BRA. The worser welcome:
I have charg'd thee not to haunt about my doors:
In honest plainness thou has heard me say
My daughter is not for thee; and now, in madness,
Being full of supper and distemp'ring draughts,
Upon malicious bravery,[23] doest thou come 100
To start[24] my quiet.

ROD. Sir, sir, sir,—

BRA. But thou must needs be sure
My spirit and my place have in them power
To make this bitter to thee.

ROD. Patience, good sir.

BRA. What tell'st thou me of robbing? this is Venice;
My house is not a grange.[25]

ROD. Most grave Brabantio,
In simple and pure soul I come to you.

IAGO. 'Zounds, sir, you are one of those that will not serve God, if the devil bid you. Because we come to do you service and you think we are ruffians, you'll have your daughter covered with a Barbary horse; you'll have your nephews[26] neigh to you; you'll have coursers for cousins and gennets[27] for germans.[28] 110

BRA. What profane wretch are thou?

IAGO. I am one, sir, that comes to tell you your daughter and the Moor are now making the beast with two backs.

---

[22]**snorting** snoring.
[23]**bravery** defiance, bravado.
[24]**start** disrupt.
[25]**grange** isolated farmhouse.
[26]**nephews** grandsons.
[27]**gennets** small Spanish horses.
[28]**germans** near relatives.

BRA. Thou art a villain.

IAGO. You are—a senator.

BRA. This thou shalt answer; I know thee, Roderigo.

ROD. Sir, I will answer any thing. But, I beseech you,
   If 't be your pleasure and most wise consent,
   As partly I find it is, that your fair daughter, 120
   At this odd-even[29] and dull watch o' th' night,
   Transported, with no worse nor better guard
   But with a knave of common hire, a gondolier,
   To the gross clasps of a lascivious Moor,—
   If this be known to you and your allowance,[30]
   We then have done you bold and saucy wrongs;
   But if you know not this, my manners tell me
   We have your wrong rebuke. Do not believe
   That, from[31] the sense of all civility,
   I thus would play and trifle with your reverence: 130
   Your daughter, if you have not given her leave,
   I say again, hath made a gross revolt;
   Tying her duty, beauty, wit and fortunes
   In an extravagant[32] and wheeling[33] stranger
   Of here and every where. Straight satisfy yourself:
   If she be in her chamber or your house,
   Let loose on me the justice of the state
   For thus deluding you.

BRA.   Strike on the tinder,[34] ho!
   Give me a taper! call up all my people!
   This accident[35] is not unlike my dream: 140
   Belief of it oppresses me already.
   Light, I say! light!   [*Exit above.*]

IAGO.   Farewell; for I must leave you:
   It seems not meet, nor wholesome to my place,
   To be produc'd—as, if I stay, I shall—
   Against the Moor: for, I do know, the state,
   However this may gall him with some check,[36]
   Cannot with safety cast[37] him, for he's embark'd
   With such loud reason to the Cyprus wars,
   Which even now stand in act,[38] that, for their souls,
   Another of his fathom[39] they have none, 150
   To lead their business: in which regard,

---

[29]**odd-even** between night and morning.
[30]**allowance** permission.
[31]**from** contrary to.
[32]**extravagant** wandering.
[33]**wheeling** vagabond.
[34]**tinder** charred linen kept in a metal box, and ignited by a spark from flint and steel.
[35]**accident** occurrence, event.
[36]**check** rebuke.
[37]**cast** dismiss.
[38]**stand in act** are going on.
[39]**fathom** ability.

Though I do hate him as I do hell-pains,
Yet, for necessity of present life,
I must show out a flag and sign of love,
Which is indeed but sign. That you shall surely find him,
Lead to the Sagittary[40] the raised search:
And there will I be with him. So, farewell. [*Exit.*]

[*Enter below* BRABANTIO, *with* SERVANTS *and torches.*]

BRA. It is too true an evil: gone she is;
And what's to come of my despised time
Is nought but bitterness. Now, Roderigo, 160
Where didst thou see her? O unhappy girl!
With the Moor, say'st thou? Who would be a father!
How didst thou know 'twas she? O, she deceives me
Past thought! What said she to you? Get moe[41] tapers:
Raise all my kindred. Are they married, think you?

ROD. Truly, I think they are.

BRA. O heaven! How got she out? O treason of the blood!
Fathers, from hence trust not your daughters' minds
By what you see them act. Is[42] there not charms
By which the property[43] of youth and maidhood 170
May be abus'd? Have you not read, Roderigo,
Of some such thing?

ROD.   Yes, sir, I have indeed.

BRA. Call up my brother. O, would you[44] had had her!
Some one way, some another. Do you know
Where we may apprehend her and the Moor?

ROD. I think I can discover him, if you please
To get good guard and go along with me.

BRA. Pray you, lead on. At every house I'll call;
I may command at most. Get weapons, ho!
And raise some special officers of night.[45] 180
On, good Roderigo: I will deserve your pains.

[*Exeunt.*]

SCENE II   *Another street.*

[*Enter* OTHELLO, IAGO, ATTENDANTS *with torches.*]

IAGO. Though in the trade of war I have slain men,
Yet do I hold it very stuff o' th' conscience
To do no contriv'd murder: I lack iniquity
Sometime to do me service: nine or ten times
I had thought t' have yerk'd[46] him here under the ribs.

---

[40]**Sagitarry** probably an inn.
[41]**moe** more.
[42]**Is** are.
[43]**property** special quality.
[44]**you** Roderigo.
[45]**officers of night** police.
[46]**yerk'd** stabbed.

OTH. 'Tis better as it is.

IAGO. Nay, but he prated,
And spoke such scurvy and provoking terms
Against your honour
That, with the little godliness I have,
I did full hard forbear him. But, I pray you, sir, 10
Are you fast married? Be assur'd of this,
That the magnifico[47] is much belov'd,
And hath in his effect[48] a voice potential[49]
As double[50] as the duke's: he will divorce you;
Or put upon you what restraint and grievance
The law, with all his might to enforce it on,
Will give him cable.

OTH. Let him do his spite;
My services, which I have done the signiory[51]
Shall out-tongue his complaints. 'Tis yet to know—
Which, when I know that boasting is an honour, 20
I shall promulgate—I fetch my life and being
From men of royal siege,[52] and my demerits[53]
May speak unbonneted[54] to as proud a fortune
As this that I have reach'd: for know, Iago,
But that I love the gentle Desdemona,
I would not my unhoused free condition
Put into circumscription and confine
For the sea's worth. But, look! what lights come yond?

IAGO. Those are the raised father and his friends:
You were best go in.

OTH. Not I; I must be found: 30
My parts, my title and my perfect soul[55]
Shall manifest me rightly. Is it they?

IAGO. By Janus, I think no.

[*Enter* CASSIO *and certain* OFFICERS *with torches.*]

OTH. The servants of the duke, and my lieutenant.
The goodness of the night upon you, friends!
What is the news?

CAS. The duke does greet you, general,
And he requires your haste-post-haste appearance,
Even on the instant.

OTH. What is the matter, think you?

---

[47]**magnifico** Venetian grandee (i.e., Brabantio).
[48]**effect** influence.
[49]**potential** powerful.
[50]**double** twice as influential as most men's.
[51]**signiory** Venetian government.
[52]**siege** rank.
[53]**demerits** deserts.
[54]**unbonneted** on equal terms.
[55]**perfect soul** unflawed conscience.

CAS. Something from Cyprus, as I may divine:
It is a business of some heat: the galleys 40
Have sent a dozen sequent[56] messengers
This very night at one another's heels,
And many of the consuls,[57] rais'd and met,
Are at the duke's already: you have been hotly call'd for;
When, being not at your lodging to be found,
The senate hath sent about three several[58] quests
To search you out.

OTH. 'Tis well I am found by you.
I will but spend a word here in the house,
And go with you.
[Exit.]

CAS. Ancient, what makes he here?

IAGO. 'Faith, he to-night hath boarded a land carack:[59] 50
If it prove lawful prize, he's made for ever.

CAS. I do not understand.

IAGO. He's married.

CAS. To who?

[Enter OTHELLO.]

IAGO. Marry, to—Come, captain will you?

OTH. Have with you.

CAS. Here comes another troop to seek for you.

[Enter BRABANTIO, RODERIGO, with OFFICERS and torches.]

IAGO. It is Brabantio. General, be advis'd;
He comes to bad intent.

OTH. Holla! stand there!

ROD. Signior, it is the Moor.

BRA. Down with him, thief!
[They draw on both sides.]

IAGO. You, Roderigo! come, sir, I am for you.

OTH. Keep up your bright swords, for the dew will rust them.
Good Signior, you shall more command with years 60
Than with your weapons.

BRA. O thou foul thief, where hast thou stow'd my daughter?
Damn'd as thou art, thou has enchanted her;
For I'll refer me to all things of sense,[60]
If she in chains of magic were not bound,
Whether a maid so tender, fair and happy,

---

[56]**sequent** successive.
[57]**consuls** senators.
[58]**several** separate.
[59]**carack** large merchant ship.
[60]**things of sense** commonsense understandings of the natural order.

> So opposite to marriage that she shunn'd
> The wealthy curled darlings of our nation,
> Would ever have, t' incur a general mock,
> Run from her guardage[61] to the sooty bosom   70
> Of such a thing as thou, to fear, not to delight.
> Judge me the world, if 'tis not gross in sense[62]
> That thou has practis'd on her with foul charms,
> Abus'd her delicate youth with drugs or minerals[63]
> That weaken motion:[64] I'll have't disputed on;[65]
> 'Tis probable and palpable to thinking.
> I therefore apprehend and do attach thee
> For an abuser of the world,[66] a practiser
> Of arts inhibited[67] and out of warrant.
> Lay hold upon him: if he do resist,   80
> Subdue him at his peril.

OTH.   Hold your hands,
> Both you of my inclining,[68] and the rest:
> Were it my cue to fight, I should have known it
> Without a prompter. Whither will you that I go
> To answer this charge?

BRA.   To prison, till fit time
> Of law and course of direct session[69]
> Call thee to answer.

OTH.   What if I do obey?
> How may the duke be therewith satisfied,
> Whose messengers are here about my side,
> Upon some present business of the state   90
> To bring me to him?

FIRST OFF.   'Tis true, most worthy signior;
> The duke's in council, and your noble self,
> I am sure, is sent for.

BRA.   How! the duke in council!
> In this time of night! Bring him away:
> Mine's not an idle cause: the duke himself,
> Or any of my brothers of the state,
> Cannot but feel this wrong as 'twere their own;
> For if such actions may have passage free,
> Bond-slaves and pagans[70] shall our statesmen be.

                                                      [Exeunt.]

---

[61] **guardage** guardianship.
[62] **gross in sense** easily discernible in apprehension or perception.
[63] **minerals** medicine, poison.
[64] **motion** thought, reason.
[65] **disputed on** argued in court by professional counsel.
[66] **abuser of the world** corrupter of society.
[67] **inhibited** prohibited.
[68] **inclining** following, party.
[69] **course of direct session** regular legal proceedings.
[70] **Bond-slaves and pagans** contemptuous reference to Othello's past history.

SCENE III *A council-chamber.*

[*Enter* DUKE, SENATORS *and* OFFICERS *set at a table, with lights and* ATTENDANTS.]

DUKE. There is no composition in these news
  That gives them credit.
FIRST SEN.   Indeed, they are disproportion'd;[71]
  My letters say a hundred and seven galleys.
DUKE. And mine, a hundred forty.
SEC. SEN.   And mine, two hundred:
  But though they jump[72] not on a just account,—
  As in these cases, where the aim[73] reports,
  'Tis oft with difference—yet do they all confirm
  A Turkish fleet, and bearing up to Cyprus.
DUKE. Nay, it is possible enough to judgment:
  I do not so secure me[74] in the error,   10
  But the main article[75] I do approve
  In fearful sense.
SAILOR.   [*Within*] What, ho! what, ho! what, ho!
FIRST OFF. A messenger from the galleys.

[*Enter* SAILOR.]

DUKE.   Now, what's the business?
SAIL. The Turkish preparation makes for Rhodes;
  So was I bid report here to the state
  By Signior Angelo.
DUKE. How say you by this change?
FIRST SEN.   This cannot be,
  By no assay[76] of reason: 'tis a pageant,
  To keep us in false gaze. When we consider
  Th' importancy of Cyprus to the Turk,   20
  And let ourselves again but understand,
  That as it more concerns the Turk than Rhodes,
  So may he with more facile question[77] bear it,
  For that it stands not in such warlike brace,[78]
  But altogether lacks th' abilities
  That Rhodes is dress'd in: if we make thought of this,
  We must not think the Turk is so unskilful
  To leave that latest which concerns him first,
  Neglecting an attempt of ease and gain,
  To wake and wage a danger profitless.   30

---

[71]**disporportion'd** inconsistent.
[72]**jump** agree.
[73]**aim** conjecture.
[74]**secure me** feel myself secure.
[75]**main article** i.e., that the Turkish fleet is threatening.
[76]**assay** test.
[77]**more facile question** greater facility of effort.
[78]**brace** state of defence.

DUKE. Nay, in all confidence, he's not for Rhodes.
FIRST OFF. Here is more news.
  [*Enter a* MESSENGER.]
MESS. The Ottomites, reverend and gracious,
  Steering with due course toward the isle of Rhodes,
  Have there injointed them with an after fleet.
FIRST SEN. Ay, so I thought. How many, as you guess?
MESS. Of thirty sail: and now they do re-stem[79]
  Their backward course, bearing with frank appearance
  Their purposes toward Cyprus. Signior Montano,
  Your trusty and most valiant servitor,   40
  With his free duty recommends you thus,
  And prays you to believe him.
DUKE. 'Tis certain, then, for Cyprus.
  Marcus Luccicos, is not he in town?
FIRST SEN. He's now in Florence.
DUKE. Write from us to him; post-post-haste dispatch.
FIRST SEN. Here comes Brabantio and the valiant Moor.
  [*Enter* BRABANTIO, OTHELLO, CASSIO, IAGO, RODERIGO, *and* OFFICERS.]
DUKE. Valiant Othello, we must straight employ you
  Against the general enemy Ottoman.
  [*To* BRABANTIO] I did not see you; welcome, gentle signior;   50
  We lack'd your counsel and your help to-night.
BRA. So did I yours. Good your grace, pardon me;
  Neither my place nor aught I heard of business
  Hath rais'd me from my bed, nor doth the general care
  Take hold on me, for my particular grief
  Is of so flood-gate and o'erbearing nature
  That it engluts[80] and swallows other sorrows
  And it is still itself.
DUKE.   Why, what's the matter?
BRA. My daughter! O, my daughter!
DUKE *and* SEN.   Dead?
BRA.   Ay, to me;
  She is abus'd, stol'n from me, and corrupted   60
  By spells and medicines bought of mountebanks;
  For nature so preposterously to err,
  Being not deficient, blind, or lame of sense,
  Sans witchcraft could not.
DUKE. Whoe'er he be that in this foul proceeding
  Hath thus beguil'd your daughter of herself
  And you of her, the bloody book of law

---
[79]**re-stem** steer again.
[80]**engluts** engulfs.

You shall yourself read in the bitter letter
After your own sense, yea, though our proper son
Stood in your action.[81]

BRA. Humbly I thank your grace. 70
Here is the man, this Moor, whom now, it seems,
Your special mandate for the state-affairs
Hath hither brought.

DUKE *and* SEN. We are very sorry for 't.

DUKE [*To* OTHELLO]. What, in your own part, can you say to this?

BRA. Nothing, but this is so.

OTH. Most potent, grave, and reverend signiors,
My very noble and approv'd good masters,
That I have ta'en away this old man's daughter,
It is most true; true, I have married her:
The very head and front of my offending 80
Hath this extent, no more. Rude am I in my speech,
And little bless'd with the soft phrase of peace;
For since these arms of mine had seven years' pith,[82]
Till now some nine moons wasted, they have us'd
Their dearest action in the tented field,
And little of this great world can I speak,
More than pertains to feats of broil and battle,
And therefore little shall I grace my cause
In speaking for myself. Yet, by your gracious patience,[83]
I will a round unvarnish'd tale deliver 90
Of my whole course of love; what drugs, what charms,
What conjuration and what mighty magic,
For such proceeding I am charg'd withal,
I won his daughter.

BRA. A maiden never bold;
Of spirit so still and quiet, that her motion
Blush'd at herself,[84] and she, in spite of nature,
Of years, of country, credit, every thing,
To fall in love with what she fear'd to look on!
It is a judgment maim'd and most imperfect
That will confess perfection so could err 100
Against all rules of nature, and must be driven
To find our practices of cunning hell,
Why this should be. I therefore vouch[85] again
That with some mixtures pow'rful o'er the blood,
Or with some dram conjur'd to this effect,
He wrought upon her.

---

[81]**Stood . . . action** was under your accusation.
[82]**pith** strength, vigour.
[83]**patience** suffering, permission.
[84]**motion . . . herself** inward impulses blushed at themselves.
[85]**vouch** assert.

DUKE.   To vouch this, is no proof,
    Without more wider and more overt test
    Than these thin habits and poor likelihoods
    Of modern seeming do prefer against him.

FIRST SEN. But, Othello, speak: 110
    Did you by indirect and forced courses
    Subdue and poison this young maid's affections?
    Or came it by request and such fair question
    As soul to soul affordeth?

OTH.   I do beseech you,
    Send for the lady to the Sagittary,
    And let her speak of me before her father:
    If you do find me foul in her report,
    The trust, the office I do hold of you,
    Not only take away, but let your sentence
    Even fall upon my life.

DUKE.   Fetch Desdemona hither.   120

OTH. Ancient, conduct them; you best know the place.
                        [*Exeunt* IAGO *and* ATTENDANTS.]
    And, till she come, as truly as to heaven
    I do confess the vices of my blood,
    So justly to your grave ear I'll present
    How I did thrive in this fair lady's love,
    And she in mine.

DUKE. Say it, Othello.

OTH. Her father lov'd me; oft invited me;
    Still question'd me the story of my life,
    From year to year, the battles, sieges, fortunes,   130
    That I have pass'd.
    I ran it through, even from my boyish days,
    To th' very moment that he bade me tell it;
    Wherein I spake of most disastrous chances,
    Of moving accidents by flood and field,
    Of hair-breadth scapes i' th' imminent[86] deadly breach,
    Of being taken by the insolent foe
    And sold to slavery, of my redemption thence
    And portance[87] in my travels' history:
    Wherein of antres[88] vast and deserts idle,[89]   140
    Rough quarries, rocks and hills whose heads touch heaven,
    It was my hint[90] to speak,—such was the process;
    And of the Cannibals that each other eat,[91]
    The Anthropophagi[92] and men whose heads

---

[86]**imminent** i.e., impending parts when a gap has been made in a fortification.
[87]**portance** conduct.
[88]**antres** caverns.
[89]**idle** barren, unprofitable.
[90]**hint** occasion.
[91]**eat** ate.
[92]**Anthropophagi** man-eaters.

Do grow beneath their shoulders. This to hear
Would Desdemona seriously incline:
But still the house-affairs would draw her thence:
Which ever as she could with haste dispatch,
She'd come again, and with a greedy ear
Devour up my discourse: which I observing, 150
Took once a pliant hour, and found good means
To draw from her a prayer of earnest heart
That I would all my pilgrimage dilate,[93]
Whereof by parcels she had something heard,
But not intentively:[94] I did consent,
And often did beguile her of her tears,
When I did speak of some distressful stroke
That my youth suffer'd. My story being done,
She gave me for my pains a world of sighs:
She swore, in faith, 'twas strange, 'twas passing strange, 160
'Twas pitiful, 'twas wondrous pitiful:
She wish'd she had not heard it, yet she wish'd
That heaven had made her such a man: she thank'd me,
And bade me, if I had a friend that lov'd her,
I should but teach him how to tell my story,
And that would woo her. Upon this hint I spake:
She lov'd me for the dangers I had pass'd,
And I lov'd her that she did pity them.
This only is the witchcraft I have us'd:
Here comes the lady; let her witness it. 170

[*Enter* DESDEMONA, IAGO, *and* ATTENDANTS.]

DUKE. I think this tale would win my daughter too.
  Good Brabantio,
  Take up this mangled matter at the best:
  Men do their broken weapons rather use
  Than their bare hands.

BRA.   I pray you, hear her speak:
  If she confess that she was half the wooer,
  Destruction on my head, if my bad blame
  Light on the man! Come hither, gentle mistress:
  Do you perceive in all this noble company
  Where most you owe obedience?

DES.   My noble father, 180
  I do perceive here a divided duty:[95]
  To you I am bound for life and education;
  My life and education both do learn me
  How to respect you; you are the lord of duty;
  I am hitherto your daughter: but here's my husband,
  And so much duty as my mother show'd

---

[93] **dilate** relate in detail.
[94] **intentively** with full attention.
[95] **divided duty** Desdemona recognizes that she still owes a duty to her father even after marriage.

To you, preferring you before her father,
So much I challenge that I may profess
Due to the Moor my lord.

BRA. God be with you! I have done.
Please it your grace, on to[96] the state-affairs:
I had rather to adopt a child than get[97] it.
Come hither, Moor:
I here do give thee that with all my heart
Which, but thou hast already, with all my heart
I would keep from thee. For your sake,[98] jewel,
I am glad at soul I have no other child;
For thy escape would teach me tyranny,
To hang clogs on them. I have done, my lord.

DUKE. Let me speak like yourself,[99] and lay a sentence,[100]
Which, as a grise[101] or step, may help these lovers
Into your favour.
When remedies are past, the griefs are ended
By seeing the worst, which late on hopes depended.
To mourn a mischief that is past and gone
Is the next[102] way to draw new mischief on.
What cannot be preserv'd when fortune takes,
Patience her injury a mock'ry makes.
The robb'd that smiles steals something from the thief;
He robs himself that spends a bootless grief.

BRA. So let the Turk of Cyprus us beguile;
We lost it not, so long as we can smile.
He bears the sentence well that nothing bears
But the free comfort[103] which from thence he hears,
But he bears both the sentence and the sorrow
That, to pay grief, must of poor patience borrow.
These sentences, to sugar, or to gall,
Being strong on both sides, are equivocal:
But words are words; I never yet did hear
That the bruis'd heart was pierced through the ear.
I humbly beseech you, proceed to th' affairs of state.

DUKE. The Turk with a most mighty preparation makes for Cyprus. Othello, the fortitude[104] of the place is best known to you; and though we have there a substitute of most allowed[105] sufficiency, yet opinion, a sovereign mistress of effects, throws a more safer

---

[96]**on to** i.e., proceed with.
[97]**get** beget.
[98]**For your sake** on your account.
[99]**like yourself** i.e., as you would, in your proper temper.
[100]**sentence** maxim.
[101]**grise** step.
[102]**next** nearest.
[103]**comfort** i.e., the consolation that it may be borne with patience.
[104]**fortitude** strength.
[105]**allowed** acknowledged.

voice on you:[106] you must therefore be content to slubber[107] the gloss of your new fortunes with this more stubborn and boisterous expedition.

OTH. The tyrant custom, most grave senators,
Hath made the flinty and steel couch of war
My thrice-driven[108] bed of down: I do agnize[109]   230
A natural and prompt alacrity
I find in hardness[110] and do undertake
These present wars against the Ottomites.
Most humbly therefore bending to your state,
I crave fit disposition for my wife,
Due reference of place and exhibition,[111]
With such accommodation and besort[112]
As levels with her breeding.

DUKE.   If you please,
Be 't at her father's.

BRA.   I'll not have it so.

OTH. Nor I.

DES.   Nor I; I would not there reside,   240
To put my father in impatient thoughts
By being in his eye. Most gracious duke,
To my unfolding lend your prosperous[113] ear;
And let me find a charter[114] in your voice,
T' assist my simpleness.[115]

DUKE. What would you, Desdemona?

DES. That I did love the Moor to live with him,
My downright violence and storm of fortunes,
May trumpet to the world: my heart's subdu'd
Even to the very quality of my lord: 250
I saw Othello's visage in his mind,
And to his honours and his valiant parts
Did I my soul and fortunes consecrate.
So that, dear lords, if I be left behind,
A moth of peace, and he go to the war,
The rites for why I love him are bereft me,
And I a heavy interim shall support
By his dear absence. Let me go with him.

---

[106]**opinion . . . on you** public opinion, an important determiner of affairs, chooses you as the best man.
[107]**slubber** soil, sully.
[108]**thrice-driven** thrice sifted.
[109]**agnize** know in myself.
[110]**hardness** hardship.
[111]**exhibition** allowance.
[112]**besort** suitable company.
[113]**prosperous** propitious.
[114]**charter** privilege.
[115]**simpleness** simplicity.

OTH. Let her have your voices.
    Vouch with me, heaven, I therefore beg it not, 260
    To please the palate of my appetite,
    Nor to comply with heat—the young affects[116]
    In me defunct—and proper satisfaction,
    But to be free and bounteous to her mind:
    And heaven defend your good souls, that you think
    I will your serious and great business scant
    When she is with me: no, when light-wing'd toys
    Of feather'd Cupid seel[117] with wanton dullness
    My speculative and offic'd instruments,[118]
    That[119] my disports[120] corrupt and taint[121] my business, 270
    Let housewives make a skillet of my helm,
    And all indign[122] and base adversities
    Make head against my estimation![123]

DUKE. Be it as you shall privately determine,
    Either for her stay or going: th' affair cries haste,
    And speed must answer it.

FIRST SEN. You must away to-night.

OTH.   With all my heart.

DUKE. At nine i' th' morning here we'll meet again.
    Othello, leave some officer behind,
    And he shall our commission bring to you; 280
    With such things else of quality and respect
    As doth import[124] you.

OTH.   So please your grace, my ancient;
    A man he is of honesty and trust:
    To his conveyance I assign my wife,
    With what else needful your good grace shall think
    To be sent after me.

DUKE.   Let it be so.
    Good night to every one. [*To* BRABANTIO.] And, noble signior,
    If virtue no delighted[125] beauty lack,
    Your son-in-law is far more fair than black.

FIRST SEN. Adieu, brave Moor; use Desdemona well. 290

BRA. Look to her, Moor, if thou hast eyes to see;
    She has deceiv'd her father, and may thee.
                           [*Exeunt* DUKE, SENATORS, OFFICERS, *&c.*]

---

[116]**affects** inclinations, desires.
[117]**seel** in falconry, to make blind by sewing up the eyes of the hawk in training.
[118]**speculative . . . instruments** ability to see and reason clearly.
[119]**That** so that.
[120]**disports** pastimes.
[121]**taint** impair.
[122]**indign** unworthy, shameful.
[123]**estimation** reputation.
[124]**import** concern.
[125]**delighted** delightful.

OTH. My life upon her faith! Honest Iago,[126]
My Desdemona must I leave to thee:
I prithee, let thy wife attend on her;
And bring them after in the best advantage.
Come, Desdemona; I have but an hour
Of love, of worldly matters and direction,
To spend with thee: we must obey the time.

[*Exit with* DESDEMONA.]

ROD. Iago—   300

IAGO. What say'st thou, noble heart?

ROD. What will I do, thinkest thou?

IAGO. Why, go to bed, and sleep.

ROD. I will incontinently[127] drown myself.

IAGO. If thou dost, I shall never love thee after. Why, thou silly gentleman!

ROD. It is silliness to live when to live is torment; and then have we a prescription to die when death is our physician.

IAGO. O villainous! I have looked upon the world for four times seven years; and since I could distinguish betwixt a benefit and an injury, I never found man that knew how to love himself. Ere I would say, I would drown myself for the love of a guinea-hen, I would change my humanity with a baboon.   310

ROD. What should I do? I confess it is my shame to be so fond; but it is not in my virtue[128] to amend it.

IAGO. Virtue! a fig! 'tis in ourselves that we are thus or thus. Our bodies are our gardens, to the which our wills are gardeners; so that if we will plant nettles, or sow lettuce, set hyssop[129] and weed up thyme, supply it with one gender[130] of herbs, or distract it with many, either to have it sterile with idleness,[131] or manured with industry, why, the power and corrigible authority[132] of this lies in our wills. If the balance of our lives had not one scale of reason to poise another of sensuality, the blood and baseness of our natures would conduct us to most preposterous conclusions:[133] but we have reason to cool our raging motions,[134] our carnal stings, our unbitted[135] lusts, whereof I take this that you call love to be a sect[136] or scion.   320

---

[126]**Honest Iago** an evidence of Iago's carefully built reputation.
[127]**incontinently** immediately.
[128]**virtue** strength.
[129]**hyssop** an herb of the mint family.
[130]**gender** kind.
[131]**idleness** want of cultivation.
[132]**corrigible authority** the power to correct.
[133]**reason . . . conclusions** Iago understands the warfare between reason and sensuality, but his ethics are totally inverted; reason works in him not good, as it should according to natural law, but evil, which he has chosen for his good.
[134]**motions** appetites.
[135]**unbitted** uncontrolled.
[136]**sect** cutting.

ROD. It cannot be.

IAGO. It is merely a lust of the blood and a permission of the will. Come, be a man. Drown thyself! drown cats and blind puppies. I have professed me thy friend and I confess me knit to thy deserving with cables of perdurable[137] toughness; I could never better stead thee than now. Put money in thy purse; follow thou the wars; defeat thy favour[138] with an usurped beard; I say, put money in thy purse. It cannot be that Desdemona should long continue her love to the Moor,—put money in thy purse,—nor he his to her: it was a violent commencement in her, and thou shalt see an answerable sequestration:[139]—put but money in thy purse. These Moors are changeable in their wills:—fill thy purse with money:—the food that to him now is as luscious as locusts,[140] shall be to him shortly as bitter as coloquintida.[141] She must change for youth: when she is sated with his body, she will find the error of her choice: she must have change, she must: therefore put money in thy purse. If thou wilt needs damn thyself, do it a more delicate way than drowning. Make all the money thou canst: if sanctimony and a frail vow betwixt an erring[142] barbarian and a super-subtle Venetian be not too hard for my wits and all the tribe of hell, thou shalt enjoy her; therefore make money. A pox of drowning thyself! it is clean out of the way: seek thou rather to be hanged in compassing the joy than to be drowned and go without her.

ROD. Wilt thou be fast to my hopes, if I depend on the issue?

IAGO. Thou art sure of me:—go, make money:—I have told thee often, and I re-tell thee again and again, I hate the Moor: my cause is hearted;[143] thine hath no less reason. Let us be conjunctive[144] in our revenge against him; if thou canst cuckold him, thou dost thyself a pleasure, me a sport. There are many events in the womb of time which will be delivered. Traverse![145] go, provide thy money. We will have more of this to-morrow. Adieu.

ROD. Where shall we meet i' the morning?

IAGO. At my lodging.

ROD. I'll be with thee betimes.

IAGO. Go to; farewell. Do you hear, Roderigo?

ROD. What say you?

IAGO. No more of drowning, do you hear?

ROD. I am changed: I'll go sell all my land. [*Exit*]

---

[137]**perdurable** very durable.
[138]**defeat thy favour** disguise and disfigure thy face.
[139]**answerable sequestration** a corresponding separation or estrangement.
[140]**locusts** of doubtful meaning; defined as fruit of the carob tree, as honeysuckle, and as lollipops or sugar sticks.
[141]**coloquintida** colocynth, or bitter apple, a purgative.
[142]**erring** wandering.
[143]**hearted** fixed in the heart.
[144]**conjunctive** united.
[145]**Traverse** go (military term).

IAGO. Thus do I ever make my fool my purse;
    For I mine own gain'd knowledge should profane,
    If I would time expend with such a snipe,[146]
    But for my sport and profit. I hate the Moor;
    And it is thought abroad, that 'twixt my sheets 370
    H' as done my office: I know not if 't be true;
    But I, for mere suspicion in that kind,
    Will do as if for surety. He holds me well;
    The better shall my purpose work on him.
    Cassio's a proper man: let me see now:
    To get his place and to plume up[147] my will
    In double knavery—How, how?—Let's see:—
    After some time, to abuse Othello's ears
    That he[148] is too familiar with his wife.
    He hath a person and a smooth dispose[149] 380
    To be suspected, fram'd to make women false.
    The Moor is of a free[150] and open nature,
    That thinks men honest that but seem to be so,
    And will as tenderly be led by th' nose
    As asses are.
    I have 't. It is engend'red. Hell and night
    Must bring this monstrous birth to the world's light.
                                                               [*Exit.*]

ACT II

    SCENE I   *A Sea-port in Cyprus. An open place near the quay.*

[*Enter* MONTANO *and two* GENTLEMEN.]

MON. What from the cape can you discern at sea?

FIRST GENT. Nothing at all: it is a high-wrought flood;
    I cannot, 'twixt the heaven and the main,
    Descry a sail.

MON. Methinks the wind hath spoke aloud at land;
    A fuller blast ne'er shook our battlements:
    If it hath ruffian'd[1] so upon the sea,
    What ribs of oak, when mountains melt on them,
    Can hold the mortise?[2] What shall we hear of this?

SEC. GENT. A segregation[3] of the Turkish fleet: 10
    For do but stand upon the foaming shore,
    The chidden billow seems to pelt the clouds:
    The wind-shak'd surge, with high and monstrous mane,

---

[146]**snipe** gull, fool.
[147]**plume up** glorify, gratify.
[148]**he** i.e., Cassio.
[149]**dispose** external manner.
[150]**free** frank.
[1]**ruffian'd** raged.
[2]**mortise** the socket hollowed out in fitting timbers.
[3]**segregation** dispersion.

    Seems to cast water on the burning bear,[4]
    And quench the guards[5] of th' ever-fixed pole:
    I never did like molestation view
    On the enchafed[6] flood.

MON.   If that the Turkish fleet
    Be not enshelter'd and embay'd, they are drown'd;
    It is impossible they bear it out.

[*Enter a third* GENTLEMAN.]

THIRD GENT. News, lads! our wars are done.   20
    The desperate tempest hath so bang'd the Turks,
    That their designment[7] halts: a noble ship of Venice
    Hath seen a grievous wrack and sufferance[8]
    On most part of their fleet.

MON. How! is this true?

THIRD GENT.   The ship is here put in,
    A Veronesa; Michael Cassio,
    Lieutenant to the warlike Moor Othello,
    Is come on shore: the Moor himself at sea,
    And is in full commission here for Cyprus.

MON. I am glad on 't; 'tis a worthy governor.   30

THIRD GENT. But this same Cassio, though he speak of comfort
    Touching the Turkish loss, yet he looks sadly,
    And prays the Moor be safe; for they were parted
    With foul and violent tempest.

MON.   Pray heavens he be;
    For I have serv'd him, and the man commands
    Like a full[9] soldier. Let's to the seaside, ho!
    As well to see the vessel that's come in
    As to throw out our eyes for brave Othello,
    Even till we make the main and th' aerial blue
    And indistinct regard.[10]

THIRD GENT.   Come, let's do so;   40
    For every minute is expectancy
    Of more arrivance.[11]

[*Enter* CASSIO.]

CAS. Thanks, you the valiant of this warlike isle,
    That so approve the Moor! O, let the heavens
    Give him defence against the elements,
    For I have lost him on a dangerous sea.

---

[4]**bear** a constellation.
[5]**quench the guards** overwhelm the stars near the polestar.
[6]**enchafed** angry.
[7]**designment** enterprise.
[8]**sufferance** disaster.
[9]**full** perfect.
[10]**make . . . regard** cause the blue of the sea and the air to grow indistinguishable in our view.
[11]**arrivance** arrival.

MON. Is he well shipp'd?

CAS. His bark is stoutly timber'd, and his pilot
  Of very expert and approv'd allowance;¹²
  Therefore my hopes, not surfeited to death, 50
  Stand in bold cure. [*A cry within.*] "A sail, a sail, a sail!"

[*Enter a fourth* GENTLEMAN.]

CAS. What noise?

FOURTH GENT. The town is empty; on the brow o' th' sea
  Stand ranks of people, and they cry "A sail!"

CAS. My hopes do shape him for the governor. [*Guns heard.*]

SEC. GENT. They do discharge their shot of courtesy:
  Our friends at least.

CAS.   I pray you, sir, go forth,
  And give us truth who 'tis that is arriv'd.

SEC. GENT. I shall.

[*Exit.*]

MON. But, good lieutenant, is your general wiv'd? 60

CAS. Most fortunately: he hath achiev'd a maid
  That paragons¹³ description and wild fame;
  One that excels the quirks¹⁴ of blazoning¹⁵ pens,
  And in th' essential vesture of creation¹⁶
  Does tire the ingener.¹⁷

[*Enter second* GENTLEMAN.]

           How now! who has put in?

SEC. GENT. 'Tis one Iago, ancient to the general.

CAS. Has had most favourable and happy speed:
  Tempests themselves, high seas and howling winds,
  The gutter'd¹⁸ rocks and congregated sands,—
  Traitors ensteep'd¹⁹ to clog the guiltless keel,— 70
  As having sense of beauty, do omit
  Their mortal²⁰ natures, letting go safely by
  The divine Desdemona.

MON.   What is she?

CAS. She that I spake of, our great captain's captain,
  Left in the conduct of the bold Iago,
  Whose footing here anticipates our thoughts

---

¹²**allowance** reputation.
¹³**paragons** surpasses.
¹⁴**quirks** witty conceits.
¹⁵**blazoning** setting forth honourably in words.
¹⁶**vesture of creation** the real qualities with which creation has invested her.
¹⁷**ingener** inventor, praiser.
¹⁸**gutter'd** jagged, trenched.
¹⁹**ensteep'd** lying under water.
²⁰**mortal** deadly.

          A se'nnight's[21] speed. Great Jove, Othello guard,
          And swell his sail with thine own powr'ful breath,
          That he may bless this bay with his tall ship,
          Make love's quick pants in Desdemona's arms,   80
          Give renew'd fire to our extinguish'd spirits,
          And bring all Cyprus comfort!
          [Enter DESDEMONA, IAGO, RODERIGO, and EMILIA with ATTENDANTS.]
                              O, behold,
          The riches of the ship is come on shore!
          You men of Cyprus, let her have your knees.
          Hail to thee, lady! and the grace of heaven,
          Before, behind thee and on every hand,
          Enwheel thee round!
DES.   I thank you, valiant Cassio.
          What tidings can you tell me of my lord?
CAS. He is not yet arriv'd: nor know I aught
          But that he's well and will be shortly here.   90
DES. O, but I fear—How lost you company?
CAS. The great contention of the sea and skies
          Parted our fellowship—But, hark! a sail.
          [Within] "A sail, a sail!" [Guns heard.]
SEC. GENT. They give their greeting to the citadel:
          This likewise is a friend.
CAS.   See for the news.   [Exit GENTLEMAN.]
          Good ancient, you are welcome. [To EMILIA] Welcome, mistress:
          Let it not gall your patience, good Iago,
          That I extend my manners; 'tis my breeding
          That gives me this bold show of courtesy.   [Kissing her.] 100
IAGO. Sir, would she give you so much of her lips
          As of her tongue she oft bestows on me,
          You would have enough.
DES.   Alas, she has no speech.
IAGO. In faith, too much;
          I find it still, when I have list to sleep:
          Marry, before your ladyship, I grant,
          She puts her tongue a little in her heart,
          And chides with thinking.
EMIL. You have little cause to say so.
IAGO. Come on, come on; you are pictures out of doors,   110
          Bells in your parlours, wild-cats in your kitchens,
          Saints in your injuries, devils being offended,
          Players in your housewifery, and housewives[22] in your beds.
DES. O, fie upon thee, slanderer!

---
[21]**se'nnight's** week's.
[22]**housewives** hussies.

IAGO. Nay, it is true, or else I am a Turk:
   You rise to play and go to bed to work.
EMIL. You shall not write my praise.
IAGO.   No, let me not.
DES. What wouldst thou write of me, if thou shouldst praise me?
IAGO. O gentle lady, do not put me to 't;
   For I am nothing, if not critical.²³   120
DES. Come on, assay. There's one gone to the harbour?
IAGO. Ay, madam.
DES. I am not merry; but I do beguile
   The thing I am, by seeming otherwise.
   Come, how wouldst thou praise me?
IAGO. I am about it; but indeed my invention
   Comes from my pate as birdlime²⁴ does from frieze;²⁵
   It plucks out brains and all: but my Muse labours,
   And thus she is deliver'd.
   If she be fair and wise, fairness and wit,   130
   The one's for use, the other useth it.
DES. Well praised! How if she be black and witty?
IAGO. If she be black, and thereto have a wit,
   She'll find a white²⁶ that shall her blackness fit.
DES. Worse and worse.
EMIL. How if fair and foolish?
IAGO. She never yet was foolish that was fair;
   For even her folly help'd her to an heir.
DES. These are old fond²⁷ paradoxes to make fools laugh i' the
   alehouse.   140
   What miserable praise hast thou for her that's foul and foolish?
IAGO. There's none so foul and foolish thereunto,
   But does foul pranks which fair and wise ones do.
DES. O heavy ignorance! thou praisest the worst best. But what
   praise couldst thou bestow on a deserving woman indeed, one
   that, in the authority of her merit, did justly put on the vouch²⁸
   of her malice itself?
IAGO. She that was ever fair and never proud,
   Had tongue at will and yet was never loud,
   Never lack'd gold and yet went never gay,   150
   Fled from her wish and yet said "Now I may,"
   She that being ang'red, her revenge being nigh,

---
²³**critical** censorious.
²⁴**birdlime** sticky substance smeared on twigs to catch small birds.
²⁵**frieze** coarse woolen cloth.
²⁶**white** a fair person, with a wordplay on *wight*.
²⁷**fond** foolish.
²⁸**put on the vouch** compel the approval.

Bade her wrong stay and her displeasure fly,
She that in wisdom never was so frail
To change the cod's head for the salmon's tail,[29]
She that could think and ne'er disclose her mind,
See suitors following and not look behind,
She was a wight, if ever such wight were,—

DES. To do what?

IAGO. To suckle fools and chronicle small beer.[30]

DES. O most lame and impotent conclusion! Do not learn of him, Emilia, though he be thy husband. How say you, Cassio? is he not a most profane and liberal[31] counsellor?

CAS. He speaks home,[32] madam: you may relish him more in the soldier than in the scholar.

IAGO [*Aside*]. He takes her by the palm: ay, well said, whisper: with as little a web as this will I ensnare as great a fly as Cassio. Ay, smile upon her, do; I will gyve[33] thee in thine own courtship.[34] You say true; 'tis so, indeed: if such tricks as these strip you out of your lieutenantry, it had been better you had not kissed your three fingers[35] so oft, which now again you are most apt to play the sir[36] in. Very good; well kissed! an excellent courtesy! 'tis so, indeed. Yet again your fingers to your lips? would they were clyster-pipes[37] for your sake. [*Trumpet within.*] The Moor! I know his trumpet.

CAS. 'Tis truly so.

DES. Let's meet him and receive him.

CAS. Lo, where he comes!

[*Enter* OTHELLO *and* ATTENDANTS.]

OTH. O my fair warrior!

DES.   My dear Othello!

OTH. It gives me wonder great as my content
To see you here before me. O my soul's joy!
If after every tempest comes such calms,
May the winds blow till they have waken'd death!
And let the labouring bark climb hills of seas
Olympus-high and duck again as low
As hell 's from heaven! If it were now to die,
'Twere now to be most happy; for, I fear,
My soul hath her content so absolute
That not another comfort like to this
Succeeds in unknown fate.

---

[29]**To change . . . tail** to exchange a delicacy for mere refuse.
[30]**chronicle small beer** keep petty household accounts.
[31]**liberal** licentious.
[32]**speaks home** i.e., without reserve.
[33]**gyve** fetter, shackle.
[34]**courtship** courtesy.
[35]**kissed your three fingers** he kisses his own hand as a token of reverence.
[36]**the sir** i.e., the fine gentleman.
[37]**clyster-pipes** tubes used for enemas.

DES.   The heavens forbid
    But that our loves and comforts should increase,   190
    Even as our days do grow!

OTH.   Amen to that, sweet powers!
    I cannot speak enough of this content;
    It stops me here; it is too much of joy:
    And this, and this, the greatest discords be [*Kissing her*]
    That e'er our hearts shall make!

IAGO.   [*Aside.*] O, you are well tun'd now!
    But I'll set down the pegs[38] that make this music,
    As honest as I am.

OTH.   Come, let us to the castle.
    News, friends; our wars are done, the Turks are drowned.
    How does my old acquaintance of this isle?
    Honey, you shall be well desir'd in Cyprus;   200
    I have found great love amongst them. O my sweet,
    I prattle out of fashion, and I dote
    In mine own comforts. I prithee, good Iago,
    Go to the bay and disembark my coffers:
    Bring thou the master to the citadel;
    He is a good one, and his worthiness
    Does challenge much respect. Come, Desdemona,
    Once more, well met at Cyprus.

                              [*Exeunt* OTHELLO *and* DESDEMONA *and all but*
                              IAGO *and* RODERIGO.]

IAGO [*to an* ATTENDANT]. Do thou meet me presently at the harbour.
    [*To* RODERIGO.] Come hither. If thou be'st valiant,—as, they say,   210
    base men being in love have then a nobility in their natures more
    than is native to them,—list me. The lieutenant tonight watches on
    the court of guard.[39]—First, I must tell thee this—Desdemona is
    directly in love with him.

ROD. With him! why 'tis not possible.

IAGO. Lay thy finger thus, and let thy soul be instructed. Mark me with
    what violence she first loved the Moor, but for bragging and telling
    her fantastical lies: and will she love him still for prating? let not thy
    discreet heart think it. Her eye must be fed; and what delight shall
    she have to look on the devil? When the blood is made dull with the   220
    act of sport, there should be, again to inflame it and to give satiety
    a fresh appetite, loveliness in favour, sympathy in years, manners
    and beauties; all which the Moor is defective in: now, for want of
    these required conveniences, her delicate tenderness will find itself
    abused, begin to heave the gorge, disrelish and abhor the Moor;
    very nature will instruct her in it and compel her to some second
    choice. Now, sir, this granted,—as it is a most pregnant and unforced
    position—who stands so eminent in the degree of this fortune as

---

[38]**set down the pegs** lower the pitch of the strings, i.e., disturb the harmony.
[39]**court of guard** guardhouse.

Cassio does? a knave very voluble; no further conscionable⁴⁰ than in putting on the mere form of civil and humane seeming, for the better compassing of his salt⁴¹ and most hidden loose affection? why, none; why, none: a slipper⁴² and subtle knave, a finder of occasions, that has an eye can stamp and counterfeit advantages, though true advantage never present itself; a devilish knave. Besides, the knave is handsome, young, and hath all those requisites in him that folly and green minds look after: a pestilent complete knave; and the woman hath found him already.

ROD. I cannot believe that in her; she's full of most blessed condition.

IAGO. Blessed fig's-end! the wine she drinks is made of grapes: if she had been blessed, she would never have loved the Moor. Blessed pudding! Didst thou not see her paddle with the palm of his hand? didst not mark that?

ROD. Yes, that I did; but that was but courtesy.

IAGO. Lechery, by his hand; an index and obscure prologue to the history of lust and foul thoughts. They met so near with their lips that their breaths embraced together. Villainous thoughts, Roderigo! when these mutualities so marshall the way, hard at hand comes the master and main exercise, the incorporate conclusion. Pish! But, sir, be you ruled by me: I have brought you from Venice. Watch you to-night; for the command, I'll lay't upon you. Cassio knows you not. I'll not be far from you: do you find some occasion to anger Cassio, either by speaking too loud, or tainting⁴³ his discipline; or from what other course you please, which the time shall more favourably minister.

ROD. Well.

IAGO. Sir, he is rash and very sudden in choler, and haply may strike at you: provoke him, that he may; for even out of that will I cause these of Cyprus to mutiny; whose qualification⁴⁴ shall come into no true taste again but by the displanting of Cassio. So shall you have a shorter journey to your desires by the means I shall then have to prefer them; and the impediment most profitably removed, without the which there were no expectation of our prosperity.

ROD. I will do this, if I can bring it to any opportunity.

IAGO. I warrant thee. Meet me by and by⁴⁵ at the citadel: I must fetch his necessaries ashore. Farewell.

ROD. Adieu.

[*Exit.*]

IAGO. That Cassio loves her, I do well believe 't;

---

⁴⁰**conscionable** conscientious.
⁴¹**salt** licentious.
⁴²**slipper** slippery.
⁴³**tainting** disparaging.
⁴⁴**qualification** appeasement.
⁴⁵**by and by** immediately.

That she loves him, 'tis apt⁴⁶ and of great credit:⁴⁷
The Moor, howbeit that I endure him not,
Is of a constant, loving, noble nature,   270
And I dare think he'll prove to Desdemona
A most dear husband. Now, I do love her too;
Not out of absolute lust, though peradventure
I stand accountant for as great a sin,
But partly led to diet my revenge,
For that I do suspect the lusty Moor
Hath leap'd into my seat; the thought whereof
Doth, like a poisonous mineral, gnaw my inwards;
And nothing can or shall content my soul
Till I am even'd with him, wife for wife,   280
Or failing so, yet that I put the Moor
At least into a jealousy so strong
That judgment cannot cure. Which thing to do,
If this poor trash⁴⁸ of Venice, whom I trash⁴⁹
For his quick hunting, stand the putting on,⁵⁰
I'll have our Michael Cassio on the hip,⁵¹
Abuse him to the Moor in the rank garb—
For I fear Cassio with my night-cap too—
Make the Moor thank me, love me and reward me,
For making him egregiously an ass   290
And practising upon his peace and quiet
Even to madness. 'Tis here, but yet confus'd:
Knavery's plain face is never seen till us'd.

[*Exit.*]

SCENE II *A street.*

[*Enter Othello's* HERALD *with a proclamation.*]

HER. It is Othello's pleasure, our noble and valiant general, that, upon certain tidings now arrived, importing the mere perdition⁵² of the Turkish fleet, every man put himself into triumph; some to dance, some to make bonfires, each man to what sport and revels his addiction leads him: for, besides these beneficial news, it is the celebration of his nuptial. So much was his pleasure should be proclaimed. All offices⁵³ are open, and there is full liberty of feasting from this present hour of five till the bell have told eleven. Heaven bless the isle of Cyprus and our general Othello!

[*Exit.*]

---

⁴⁶**apt** probable.
⁴⁷**credit** credibility.
⁴⁸**trash** worthless thing (Roderigo).
⁴⁹**trash** hold in check.
⁵⁰**putting on** incitement to quarrel.
⁵¹**on the hip** at my mercy (wrestling term).
⁵²**mere perdition** complete destruction.
⁵³**offices** rooms where food and drink were kept.

SCENE III *A hall in the castle.*

[*Enter* OTHELLO, DESDEMONA, CASSIO, *and* ATTENDANTS.]

OTH. Good Michael, look you to the guard to-night:
Let's teach ourselves that honourable stop,[54]
Not to outsport discretion.

CAS. Iago hath direction what to do;
But, notwithstanding, with my personal eye
Will I look to 't.

OTH.   Iago is most honest.
Michael, goodnight: to-morrow with your earliest
Let me have speech with you. [*To* DESDEMONA] Come, my dear love,
The purchase made, the fruits are to ensue;
That profit's yet to come 'tween me and you.   10
Good night.

                    [*Exit* OTHELLO, *with* DESDEMONA *and*
                    ATTENDANTS.]

[*Enter* IAGO.]

CAS. Welcome, Iago; we must to the watch.

IAGO. Not this hour, lieutenant; 'tis not yet ten o' the clock. Our general cast[55] us thus early for the love of his Desdemona; who let us not therefore blame: he hath not yet made wanton the night with her; and she is sport for Jove.

CAS. She's a most exquisite lady.

IAGO. And, I'll warrant her, full of game.

CAS. Indeed, she's a most fresh and delicate creature.

IAGO. What an eye she has! methinks it sounds a parley of provocation.   20

CAS. An inviting eye; and yet methinks right modest.

IAGO. And when she speaks, is it not an alarum to love?

CAS. She is indeed perfection.

IAGO. Well, happiness to their sheets! Come, lieutenant, I have a stoup[56] of wine; and here without are a brace of Cyprus gallants that would fain have a measure to the health of black Othello.

CAS. Not to-night, good Iago: I have very poor and unhappy brains for drinking: I could well wish courtesy would invent some other custom of entertainment.

IAGO. O, they are our friends, but one cup: I'll drink for you.   30

CAS. I have drunk but one cup to-night, and that was craftily qualified[57] too, and, behold, what innovation[58] it makes here:[59] I am

---

[54] **stop** restraint.
[55] **cast** dismissed.
[56] **stoup** measure of liquor, two quarts.
[57] **qualified** diluted.
[58] **innovation** disturbance.
[59] **here** i.e., in Cassio's head.

unfortunate in the infirmity, and dare not task my weakness with any more.

IAGO. What, man! 'tis a night of revels: the gallants desire it.

CAS. Where are they?

IAGO. Here at the door; I pray you, call them in.

CAS. I'll do 't; but it dislikes me. [*Exit.*]

IAGO. If I can fasten but one cup upon him,
With that which he hath drunk to-night already, 40
He'll be as full of quarrel and offence
As my young mistress' dog. Now, my sick fool Roderigo,
Whom love hath turn'd almost the wrong side out,
To Desdemona hath to-night carous'd
Potations pottle-deep;[60] and he's to watch:
Three lads of Cyprus, noble swelling spirits,
That hold their honours in a wary distance,[61]
The very elements[62] of this warlike isle,
Have I to-night fluster'd with flowing cups,
And they watch[63] too. Now, 'mongst this flock of drunkards, 50
Am I to put our Cassio in some action
That may offend the isle.—But here they come:

[*Enter* CASSIO, MONTANO, *and* GENTLEMEN; SERVANTS *following with wine.*]

If consequence do but approve[64] my dream,
My boat sails freely, both with wind and stream.

CAS. 'Fore God, they have given me a rouse[65] already.

MON. Good faith, a little one; not past a pint, as I am a soldier.

IAGO. Some wine, ho!
[*Sings*] And let me the canakin[66] clink, clink;
    And let me the canakin clink:
        A soldier's a man; 60
        A life 's but a span;
    Why, then, let a soldier drink.
Some wine, boys!

CAS. 'Fore God, an excellent song.

IAGO. I learned it in England, where, indeed, they are most potent in potting: your Dane, your German, and your swag-bellied Hollander—Drink, ho!—are nothing to your English.

CAS. Is your Englishman so expert in his drinking?

---

[60]**pottle-deep** to the bottom of the tankard.
[61]**hold . . . distance** i.e., are extremely sensitive of their honour.
[62]**very elements** true representatives.
[63]**watch** are members of the guard.
[64]**approve** confirm.
[65]**rouse** full draft of liquor.
[66]**canakin** small drinking vessel.

IAGO. Why, he drinks you, with facility, your Dane dead drunk; he sweats not to overthrow your Almain;⁶⁷ he gives your Hollander a vomit, ere the next pottle can be filled.

CAS. To the health of our general!

MON. I am for it, lieutenant; and I'll do you justice.⁶⁸

IAGO. O sweet England! [*Sings.*]
    King Stephen was a worthy peer,
        His breeches cost him but a crown;
    He held them sixpence all too dear,
        With that he call'd the tailor lown.⁶⁹

    He was a wight of high renown,
        And thou art but of low degree:
    'Tis pride that pulls the country down;
        Then take thine auld cloak about thee.
Some wine, ho!

CAS. Why, this is a more exquisite song than the other.

IAGO. Will you hear 't again?

CAS. No; for I hold him to be unworthy of his place that does those things. Well, God's above all; and there be souls must be saved, and there be souls must not be saved.

IAGO. It's true, good lieutenant.

CAS. For mine own part,—no offence to the general, nor any man of quality,—I hope to be saved.

IAGO. And so do I too, lieutenant.

CAS. Ay, but, by your leave, not before me; the lieutenant is to be saved before the ancient. Let 's have no more of this; let 's to our affairs.—God forgive us our sins!—Gentlemen, let 's look to our business. Do not think, gentlemen, I am drunk: this is my ancient; this is my right hand, and this is my left: I am not drunk now: I can stand well enough, and speak well enough.

ALL. Excellent well.

CAS. Why, very well then; you must not think then that I am drunk. [*Exit.*]

MON. To th' platform, masters; come, let's set the watch.

IAGO. You see this fellow that is gone before;
    He's soldier fit to stand by Caesar
And give direction: and do but see his vice;
'Tis to his virtue a just equinox,⁷⁰
The one as long as th' other: 'tis pity of him.
I fear the trust Othello puts him in,
On some odd time of his infirmity,
Will shake this island.

---

⁶⁷**Almain** German.
⁶⁸**I'll . . . justice** i.e., drink as much as you.
⁶⁹**lown** lout, loon.
⁷⁰**equinox** equal length of days and nights; used figuratively to mean "counterpart."

MON. But is he often thus?

IAGO. 'Tis evermore the prologue to his sleep: 110
    He'll watch the horologe[71] a double set,[72]
    If drink rock not his cradle.

MON.   It were well
    The general were put in mind of it.
    Perhaps he sees it not; or his good nature
    Prizes the virtue that appears in Cassio,
    And looks not on his evils: is not this true?

[*Enter* RODERIGO.]

IAGO [*Aside to him*]. How now, Roderigo!
    I pray you, after the lieutenant; go.

                                                            [*Exit* RODERIGO.]

MON. And 'tis great pity that the noble Moor
    Should hazard such a place as his own second 120
    With one of an ingraft[73] infirmity:
    It were an honest action to say
    So to the Moor.

IAGO.   Not I, for this fair island:
    I do love Cassio well; and would do much
    To cure him of this evil—But, hark! what noise?

[*Cry within:* "Help! help!"]

              [*Enter* CASSIO, *pursuing* RODERIGO.]

CAS. 'Zounds, you rogue! you rascal!

MON.   What's the matter, lieutenant?

CAS. A knave teach me my duty!
    I'll beat the knave into a twiggen[74] bottle.

ROD. Beat me!

CAS.   Dost thou prate, rogue?   [*Striking* RODERIGO.]

MON.   Nay, good lieutenant; [*Staying him.*] 130
    I pray you, sir, hold your hand.

CAS.   Let me go, sir,
    Or I'll knock you o'er the mazzard.[75]

MON.   Come, come, you're drunk.

CAS. Drunk!   [*They fight.*]

IAGO [*aside to* RODERIGO]. Away, I say; go out, and cry a mutiny.
                                                          [*Exit* RODERIGO.]
    Nay, good lieutenant,—God's will, gentlemen;—
    Help, ho!—Lieutenant,—sir,—Montano,—sir,—

---

[71]**horologe** clock.
[72]**double set** twice around.
[73]**ingraft** ingrafted, inveterate.
[74]**twiggen** covered with woven twigs.
[75]**mazzard** head.

Help, masters!—Here's a goodly watch indeed!   [*Bell rings.*]
Who's that which rings the bell?—Diablo,[76] ho!
The town will rise:[77] God's will, lieutenant, hold!
You'll be asham'd for ever.

[*Enter* OTHELLO *and* ATTENDANTS.]

OTH.   What is the matter here?   140

MON. 'Zounds, I bleed still; I am hurt to th' death.
    He dies!   [*Thrusts at* CASSIO.]

OTH. Hold, for your lives!

IAGO. Hold, ho! Lieutenant,—sir,—Montano,—gentlemen,—
    Have you forgot all sense of place and duty?
    Hold! the general speaks to you; hold, for shame!

OTH. Why, how now, ho! from whence ariseth this?
    Are we turn'd Turks[78] and to ourselves do that
    Which heaven hath forbid the Ottomites?
    For Christian shame, put by this barbarous brawl: 150
    He that stirs next to carve for[79] his own rage
    Holds his soul light; he dies upon his motion.
    Silence that dreadful bell: it frights the isle
    From her propriety.[80] What is the matter, masters?
    Honest Iago, that looks dead with grieving,
    Speak, who began this? on thy love, I charge thee.

IAGO. I do not know: friends all but now, even now,
    In quarter,[81] and in terms like bride and groom
    Devesting them for bed; and then, but now—
    As if some planet had unwitted men—   160
    Swords out, and tilting one at other's breast,
    In opposition bloody. I cannot speak
    Any beginning to this peevish odds;[82]
    And would in action glorious I had lost
    Those legs that brought me to a part of it!

OTH. How comes it, Michael, you are thus forgot?

CAS. I pray you, pardon me; I cannot speak.

OTH. Worthy Montano, you were wont be civil;
    The gravity and stillness of your youth
    The world hath noted, and your name is great   170
    In mouths of wisest censure.[83] What's the matter,
    That you unlace[84] your reputation thus

---

[76]**Diablo** the devil.
[77]**rise** grow riotous.
[78]**turn'd Turks** changed completely for the worse; proverbial.
[79]**carve for** indulge.
[80]**propriety** proper state or condition.
[81]**In quarter** on terms.
[82]**peevish odds** childish quarrel.
[83]**censure** judgment.
[84]**unlace** degrade.

　　　　　And spend your rich opinion for the name
　　　　　Of a night-brawler? Give me answer to it.
Mon. Worthy Othello, I am hurt to danger:
　　　　　Your officer, Iago, can inform you,—
　　　　　While I spare speech, which something now offends me,—
　　　　　Of all that I do know: nor know I aught
　　　　　By me that's said or done amiss this night;
　　　　　Unless self-charity be sometimes a vice,　　　　　　　　　　180
　　　　　And to defend ourselves it be a sin
　　　　　When violence assails us.
Oth.　　　　　　　　　　Now, by heaven,
　　　　　My blood begins my safer guides to rule;
　　　　　And passion, having my best judgment collied,[85]
　　　　　Assays to lead the way: if I once stir,
　　　　　Or do but lift this arm, the best of you
　　　　　Shall sink in my rebuke. Give me to know
　　　　　How this foul rout began, who set it on;
　　　　　And he that is approv'd in[86] this offence,
　　　　　Though he had twinn'd with me, both at a birth,　　　　190
　　　　　Shall lose me. What! in a town of war,
　　　　　Yet wild, the people's hearts brimful of fear,
　　　　　To manage private and domestic quarrel,
　　　　　In night, and on the court and guard[87] of safety!
　　　　　'Tis monstrous. Iago, who began 't?
Mon. If partially affin'd,[88] or leagu'd in office,
　　　　　Thou dost deliver more or less than truth,
　　　　　Thou art no soldier.
Iago.　　　　　　　　　　Touch me not so near:
　　　　　I had rather have this tongue cut from my mouth
　　　　　Than it should do offence to Michael Cassio;　　　　　200
　　　　　Yet, I persuade myself, to speak the truth
　　　　　Shall nothing wrong him. Thus it is, general.
　　　　　Montano and myself being in speech,
　　　　　There comes a fellow crying out for help;
　　　　　And Cassio following him with determin'd sword,
　　　　　To execute[89] upon him. Sir, this gentleman
　　　　　Steps in to Cassio, and entreats his pause:
　　　　　Myself the crying fellow did pursue,
　　　　　Lest by his clamour—as it so fell out—
　　　　　The town might fall in fright: he, swift of foot,　　　　210
　　　　　Outran my purpose; and I return'd the rather
　　　　　For that I heard the clink and fall of swords,
　　　　　And Cassio high in oath; which till to-night
　　　　　I ne'er might say before. When I came back—

---

[85]**collied** darkened.
[86]**approv'd in** found guilty of.
[87]**court and guard** spot and guarding place, i.e., the main guardhouse.
[88]**affin'd** bound by a tie.
[89]**execute** give effect to (his anger).

> For this was brief—I found them close together,
> At blow and thrust; even as again they were
> When you yourself did part them.
> More of this matter cannot I report:
> But men are men; the best sometimes forget:
> Though Cassio did some little wrong to him, 220
> As men in rage strike those that wish them best,
> Yet surely, Cassio, I believe, receiv'd
> From him that fled some strange indignity,
> Which patience could not pass.

OTH.   I know, Iago,
> Thy honesty and love doth mince this matter,
> Making it light to Cassio. Cassio, I love thee;
> But never more be officer of mine.

[*Enter* DESDEMONA, *attended.*]

> Look, if my gentle love be not rais'd up!
> I'll make thee an example.

DES.   What's the matter?

OTH. All's well now, sweeting; come away to bed. 230
> Sir, for your hurts, myself will be your surgeon:
> Lead him off.   [*To* MONTANO, *who is led off.*]
> Iago, look with care about the town,
> And silence those whom this vile brawl distracted.
> Come, Desdemona: 'tis the soldiers' life
> To have their balmy slumbers wak'd with strife.
>   [*Exit with all but* IAGO *and* CASSIO.]

IAGO. What, are you hurt, lieutenant?

CAS. Ay, past all surgery.

IAGO. Marry, God forbid!

CAS. Reputation, reputation, reputation! O, I have lost my reputa- 240
tion! I have lost the immortal part of myself, and what remains is
bestial. My reputation, Iago, my reputation!

IAGO. As I am an honest man, I thought you had received some bodily
wound; there is more sense in that than in reputation. Reputation is an idle and most false imposition; oft got without merit,
and lost without deserving: you have lost no reputation at all,
unless you repute yourself such a loser. What, man! there are ways
to recover the general again: you are but now cast in his mood, a
punishment more in policy than in malice; even so as one would
beat his offenceless dog to affright an imperious lion: sue to him 250
again, and he 's yours.

CAS. I will rather sue to be despised than to deceive so good a commander with so slight, so drunken, and so indiscreet an officer.
Drunk? and speak parrot?[90] and squabble? swagger? swear? and discourse fustian[91] with one's own shadow? O thou invisible spirit of
wine, if thou hast no name to be known by, let us call thee devil!

---

[90]**speak parrot** talk nonsense.
[91]**discourse fustian** talk nonsense.

IAGO. What was he that you followed with your sword? What had he done to you?

CAS. I know not.

IAGO. Is 't possible?

CAS. I remember a mass of things, but nothing distinctly; a quarrel, but nothing wherefore. O God, that men should put an enemy in their mouths to steal away their brains! that we should, with joy, pleasance, revel and applause, transform ourselves into beasts!

IAGO. Why, but you are now well enough: how came you thus recovered?

CAS. It hath pleased the devil drunkenness to give place to the devil wrath: one unperfectness[92] shows me another, to make me frankly despise myself.

IAGO. Come, you are too severe a moraler: as the time, the place, and the condition of this country stands, I could heartily wish this had not befallen; but, since it is as it is, mend it for your own good.

CAS. I will ask him for my place again; he shall tell me I am a drunkard! Had I as many mouths as Hydra,[93] such an answer would stop them all. To be now a sensible man, by and by a fool, and presently a beast! O strange! Every inordinate cup is unblessed and the ingredient is a devil.

IAGO. Come, come, good wine is a good familiar creature, if it be well used: exclaim no more against it. And, good lieutenant, I think you think I love you.

CAS. I have well approved[94] it, sir. I drunk!

IAGO. You or any man living may be a drunk at a time, man. I'll tell you what you shall do. Our general's wife is now the general: I may say so in this respect, for that he hath devoted and given up himself to the contemplation, mark, and denotement[95] of her parts and graces: confess yourself freely to her; importune her help to put you in your place again: she is of so free, so kind, so apt, so blessed a disposition, she holds it a vice in her goodness not to do more than she is requested: this broken joint between you and her husband entreat her to splinter;[96] and, my fortunes against any lay[97] worth naming, this crack of your love shall grow stronger than it was before.

CAS. You advise me well.

IAGO. I protest, in the sincerity of love and honest kindness.

CAS. I think it freely; and betimes in the morning I will beseech the virtuous Desdemona to undertake for me: I am desperate of my fortunes if they check[98] me here.

---

[92]**unperfectness** imperfection.
[93]**Hydra** a monster with many heads, slain by Hercules as the second of his twelve labours.
[94]**approved** proved.
[95]**denotement** observation.
[96]**splinter** bind with splints.
[97]**lay** stake, wager.
[98]**check** repulse.

IAGO. You are in the right. Good night, lieutenant; I must to the watch.

CAS. Good night, honest Iago. [*Exit* CASSIO.]

IAGO. And what's he then that says I play the villain? 300
When this advice is free I give and honest,
Probal[99] to thinking and indeed the course
To win the Moor again? For 'tis most easy
Th' inclining[100] Desdemona to subdue[101]
In any honest suit: she's fram'd as fruitful
As the free elements. And then for her
To win the Moor—were 't to renounce his baptism,
All seals and symbols of redeemed sin,
His soul is so enfetter'd to her love,
That she may make, unmake, do what she list, 310
Even as her appetite shall play the god
With his weak function. How am I then a villain
To counsel Cassio to this parallel[102] course,
Directly to his good? Divinity of hell!
When devils will the blackest sins put on,[103]
They do suggest[104] at first with heavenly shows,
As I do now: for whiles this honest fool
Plies Desdemona to repair his fortunes
And she for him pleads strongly to the Moor,
I'll pour this pestilence into his ear, 320
That she repeals him[105] for her body's lust;
And by how much she strives to do him good,
She shall undo her credit with the Moor.
So will I turn her virtue into pitch,
And out of her own goodness make the net
That shall enmesh them all.

[*Enter* RODERIGO.]

How now, Roderigo!

ROD. I do not follow here in the chase, not like a hound that hunts, but one that fills up the cry.[106] My money is almost spent; I have been tonight exceedingly well cudgellèd; and I think the issue will be, I shall have so much experience for my pains, and so, with no 330 money at all and a little more wit, return again to Venice.

IAGO. How poor are they that have not patience!
What wound did ever heal but by degrees?
Thou know'st we work by wit, and not by witchcraft;
And wit depends on dilatory time.
Does 't not go well? Cassio hath beaten thee,

---

[99]**Probal** probable.
[100]**inclining** favourably disposed.
[101]**subdue** persuade.
[102]**parallel** probably, corresponding to his best interest.
[103]**put on** further.
[104]**suggest** tempt.
[105]**repeals him** i.e., attempts to get him restored.
[106]**cry** pack.

And thou, by that small hurt, hast cashier'd[107] Cassio:
Though other things grow fair against the sun,
Yet fruits that blossom first will first be ripe:
Content thyself awhile. By th' mass, 'tis morning;   340
Pleasure and action make the hours seem short.
Retire thee; go where thou art billeted:
Away, I say; thou shalt know more hereafter:
Nay, get thee gone.   [*Exit* RODERIGO.]
            Two things are to be done:
My wife must move for Cassio to her mistress;
I'll set her on;
Myself the while to draw the Moor apart,
And bring him jump[108] when he may Cassio find
Soliciting his wife: ay, that's the way:
Dull not device by coldness and delay.   [*Exit.*]   350

ACT III

SCENE I   *Before the castle.*

[*Enter* CASSIO *and* MUSICIANS.]

CAS. Masters, play here; I will content[1] your pains;
   Something that's brief; and bid "Good morrow, general."   [*They play.*]

[*Enter* CLOWN.]

CLO. Why, masters, have your instruments been in Naples, that they speak i' the nose[2] thus?

FIRST MUS. How, sir, how!

CLO. Are these, I pray you, wind-instruments?

FIRST MUS. Ay, marry, are they, sir.

CLO. O, thereby hangs a tail.

FIRST MUS. Whereby hangs a tale,[3] sir?

CLO. Marry, sir, by many a wind-instrument that I know. But, mas-   10
   ters, here's money for you: and the general so likes your music,
   that he desires you, for love's sake, to make no more noise with it.

FIRST MUS. Well, sir, we will not.

CLO. If you have any music that may not be heard, to't again: but, as they say, to hear music the general does not greatly care.

FIRST MUS. We have none such, sir.

CLO. Then put up your pipes in your bag, for I'll away: go; vanish into air; away!   [*Exeunt* MUSICIANS.]

---

[107] **cashier'd** dismissed from service.
[108] **jump** precisely.
[1] **content** reward.
[2] **speak i' the nose** i.e., like Neapolitans, who spoke a nasal dialect (with a joke on syphilis, which attacks the nose).
[3] **tale** pun on *tail*, a wind instrument of sorts.

CAS. Dost thou hear, my honest friend?

CLO. No, I hear not your honest friend; I hear you. 20

CAS. Prithee, keep up thy quillets. There 's a poor piece of gold for thee: if the gentlewoman that attends the general's wife be stirring, tell her there 's one Cassio entreats her a little favour of speech; wilt thou do this?

CLO. She is stirring, sir: if she will stir hither, I shall seem to notify unto her.

CAS. Do, good my friend.   [*Exit* CLOWN.]
    [*Enter* IAGO.]
                        In happy time, Iago.

IAGO. You have not been a-bed, then?

CAS. Why, no; the day had broke
    Before we parted. I have made bold, Iago,   30
    To send in to your wife: my suit to her
    Is, that she will to virtuous Desdemona
    Procure me some access.

IAGO.   I'll send her to you presently;
    And I'll devise a means to draw the Moor
    Out of the way, that your converse and business
    May be more free.

CAS. I humbly thank you for 't.   [*Exit* IAGO.]
                        I never knew
    A Florentine more kind and honest.
    [*Enter* EMILIA.]

EMIL. Good morrow, good lieutenant: I am sorry
    For your displeasure; but all will sure be well.   40
    The general and his wife are talking of it;
    And she speaks for you stoutly: the Moor replies,
    That he you hurt is of great fame in Cyprus
    And great affinity⁴ and that in wholesome wisdom
    He might not but refuse you, but he protests he loves you
    And needs no other suitor but his likings
    To take the safest occasion by the front⁵
    To bring you in again.

CAS.   Yet, I beseech you,
    If you think fit, or that it may be done,
    Give me advantage of some brief discourse   50
    With Desdemona alone.

EMIL.   Pray you, come in:
    I will bestow you where you shall have time
    To speak your bosom freely.

CAS. I am much bound to you.   [*Exeunt.*]

---
⁴**affinity** kindred, family connection.
⁵**by the front** i.e., by the forelock.

SCENE II *A room in the castle.*

[*Enter* OTHELLO, IAGO, *and* GENTLEMEN.]

OTH. These letters give, Iago, to the pilot;
  And by him do my duties to the senate:
  That done, I will be walking on the works:[6]
  Repair there to me.

IAGO.   Well, my good lord, I'll do 't.

OTH. This fortification, gentlemen, shall we see't?

GENT. We'll wait upon your lordship.   [*Exeunt.*]

SCENE III *The garden of the castle.*

[*Enter* DESDEMONA, CASSIO, *and* EMILIA.]

DES. Be thou assur'd, good Cassio, I will do
  All my abilities in thy behalf.

EMIL. Good madam, do: I warrant it grieves my husband,
  As if the case were his.

DES. O, that's an honest fellow. Do not doubt, Cassio,
  But I will have my lord and you again
  As friendly as you were.

CAS.   Bounteous madam,
  Whatever shall become of Michael Cassio,
  He's never any thing but your true servant.

DES. I know 't; I thank you. You do love my lord: 10
  You have known him long; and be you well assur'd
  He shall in strangeness[7] stand no farther off
  Than in a politic distance.

CAS.   Ay, but lady,
  That policy may either last so long
  Or feed upon such nice and waterish diet,
  Or breed itself so out of circumstance,[8]
  That, I being absent and my place supplied,
  My general will forget my love and service.

DES. Do not doubt[9] that; before Emilia here
  I give thee warrant of thy place: assure thee,   20
  If I do vow a friendship, I'll perform it
  To the last article: my lord shall never rest;
  I'll watch him tame[10] and talk him out of patience;
  His bed shall seem a school, his board a shrift;[11]
  I'll intermingle every thing he does
  With Cassio's suit: therefore be merry, Cassio;

---
[6]**works** earthworks, fortifications.
[7]**strangeness** distant behaviour.
[8]**breed . . . circumstance** increase itself so on account of accidents.
[9]**doubt** fear.
[10]**watch him tame** tame him by keeping him from sleeping (a term from falconry).
[11]**shrift** confessional.

      For thy solicitor shall rather die
      Than give thy cause away.[12]

[*Enter* OTHELLO *and* IAGO *at a distance.*]

EMIL. Madam, here comes my lord.

CAS. Madam, I'll take my leave.   30

DES. Why, stay, and hear me speak.

CAS. Madam, not now: I am very ill at ease,
      Unfit for mine own purposes.

DES. Well, do your discretion.   [*Exit* CASSIO.]

IAGO. Ha! I like not that.

OTH.   What dost thou say?

IAGO. Nothing, my lord: or if—I know not what.

OTH. Was not that Cassio parted from my wife?

IAGO. Cassio, my lord! No, sure, I cannot think it,
      That he would steal away so guilty-like,
      Seeing you coming.

OTH.   I do believe 'twas he.   40

DES. How now, my lord!
      I have been talking with a suitor here,
      A man that languishes in your displeasure.

OTH. Who is 't you mean?

DES. Why, your lieutenant, Cassio. Good my lord,
      If I have any grace or power to move you,
      His present reconciliation take;
      For if he be not one that truly loves you,
      That errs in ignorance and not in cunning,
      I have no judgment in an honest face: 50
      I prithee, call him back.

OTH.   Went he hence now?

DES. Ay, sooth; so humbled
      That he hath left part of his grief with me,
      To suffer with him. Good love, call him back.

OTH. Not now, sweet Desdemon; some other time.

DES. But shall 't be shortly?

OTH.   The sooner, sweet, for you.

DES. Shall 't be to-night at supper?

OTH.   No, not to-night.

DES. To-morrow dinner, then?

OTH.   I shall not dine at home;
      I meet the captain at the citadel.

---

[12] **away** up.

DES. Why, then, to-morrow night; or Tuesday morn; 60
  On Tuesday noon, or night; on Wednesday morn:
  I prithee, name the time, but let it not
  Exceed three days: in faith, he's penitent;
  And yet his trespass, in our common reason[13]—
  Save that, they say, the wars must make examples
  Out of their best—is not almost a fault
  T' incur a private check. When shall he come?
  Tell me, Othello: I wonder in my soul,
  What you would ask me, that I should deny,
  Or stand so mamm'ring on.[14] What! Michael Cassio, 70
  That came a-wooing with you, and so many a time,
  When I have spoke of you dispraisingly,
  Hath ta'en your part; to have so much to do
  To bring him in! Trust me, I could do much,—

OTH. Prithee, no more: let him come when he will;
  I will deny thee nothing.

DES.   Why, this is not a boon;
  'Tis as I should entreat you wear your gloves,
  Or feed on nourishing dishes, or keep you warm,
  Or sue to you to do a peculiar profit
  To your own person: nay, when I have a suit 80
  Wherein I mean to touch your love indeed,
  It shall be full of poise[15] and difficult weight
  And fearful to be granted.

OTH.   I will deny thee nothing:
  Whereon, I do beseech thee, grant me this,
  To leave me but a little to myself.

DES. Shall I deny you? No: farewell, my lord.

OTH. Farewell, my Desdemona: I'll come to thee straight.

DES. Emilia, come. Be as your fancies teach you;
  Whate'er you be, I am obedient.   [*Exit with* EMILIA.]

OTH. Excellent wretch![16] Perdition catch my soul, 90
  But I do love thee! And when I love thee not,
  Chaos is come again.

IAGO. My noble lord—

OTH.   What dost thou say, Iago?

IAGO. Did Michael Cassio, when you woo'd my lady,
  Know of your love?

OTH. He did, from first to last: why dost thou ask?

IAGO. But for a satisfaction of my thought;
  No further harm.

---

[13]**common reason** everyday judgments.
[14]**mamm'ring on** wavering.
[15]**poise** weight, heaviness.
[16]**wretch** term of affectionate endearment with a connotation of pity.

OTH.   Why of thy thought, Iago?

IAGO. I did not think he had been acquainted with her.

OTH. O, yes; and went between us very oft.   100

IAGO. Indeed!

OTH. Indeed! Ay, indeed: discern'st thou aught in that?
  Is he not honest?

IAGO.   Honest, my lord!

OTH.   Honest! ay, honest.

IAGO. My lord, for aught I know.

OTH. What dost thou think?

IAGO.   Think, my lord!

OTH.   Think, my lord!
  By heaven, he echoes me,
  As if there were some monster in his thought
  Too hideous to be shown. Thou dost mean something:
  I heard thee say even now, thou lik'st not that,
  When Cassio left my wife: what didst not like?   110
  And when I told thee he was of my counsel
  In my whole course of wooing, thou criedst "Indeed!"
  And didst contract and purse thy brow together,
  As if thou then hadst shut up in thy brain
  Some horrible conceit: if thou dost love me,
  Show me thy thought.

IAGO. My lord, you know I love you.

OTH.   I think thou dost;
  And, for I know thou 'rt full of love and honesty,
  And weigh'st thy words before thou giv'st them breath,
  Therefore these stops of thine fright me the more: 120
  For such things in a false disloyal knave
  Are tricks of custom, but in a man that's just
  They 're close delations,[17] working from the heart
  That passion cannot rule.

IAGO.   For Michael Cassio,
  I dare be sworn I think that he is honest.

OTH. I think so too.

IAGO.   Men should be what they seem;
  Or those that be not, would they might seem none!

OTH. Certain, men should be what they seem.

IAGO. Why, then, I think Cassio 's an honest man.

OTH. Nay, yet there 's more in this: 130
  I prithee, speak to me as to thy thinkings,
  As thou dost ruminate, and give thy worst of thoughts
  The worst of words.

---

[17] **close delations** secret or involuntary accusations.

IAGO. Good my lord, pardon me:
  Though I am bound to every act of duty,
  I am not bound to that all slaves are free to.
  Utter my thoughts? Why, say they are vile and false;
  As where's that palace whereinto foul things
  Sometimes intrude not? Who has a breast so pure,
  But some uncleanly apprehensions
  Keep leets[18] and law-days[19] and in sessions sit   140
  With meditations lawful?

OTH. Thou dost conspire against thy friend, Iago,
  If thou but think'st him wrong'd and mak'st his ear
  A stranger to thy thoughts.

IAGO.   I do beseech you—
  Though I perchance am vicious[20] in my guess,
  As, I confess, it is my nature's plague
  To spy into abuses, and oft my jealousy[21]
  Shapes faults that are not—that your wisdom yet,
  From one that so imperfectly conceits,[22]
  Would take no notice, nor build yourself a trouble   150
  Out of his scattering and unsure observance.
  It were not for your quiet nor your good,
  Nor for my manhood, honesty, or wisdom,
  To let you know my thoughts.

OTH.   What dost thou mean?

IAGO. Good name in man and woman, dear my lord,
  Is the immediate jewel of their souls:
  Who steals my purse steals trash: 'tis something, nothing;
  'Twas mine, 'tis his, and has been slave to thousands;
  But he that filches from me my good name
  Robs me of that which not enriches him   160
  And makes me poor indeed.

OTH. By heaven, I'll know thy thoughts.

IAGO. You cannot, if my heart were in your hand;
  Nor shall not, whilst 'tis in my custody.

OTH. Ha!

IAGO.   Oh, beware, my lord, of jealousy;
  It is the green-ey'd monster which doth mock
  The meat it feeds on: that cuckold lives in bliss
  Who, certain of his fate, loves not his wronger;
  But, O, what damned minutes tells he o'er
  Who dotes, yet doubts, suspects, yet strongly loves!   170

OTH. O misery!

---

[18]**Keep leets** hold courts.
[19]**law-days** court days.
[20]**vicious** wrong.
[21]**jealousy** suspicion of evil.
[22]**conceits** judges.

IAGO. Poor and content is rich and rich enough,
    But riches fineless[23] is as poor as winter
    To him that ever fears he shall be poor.
    Good God, the souls of all my tribe defend
    From jealousy!

OTH.   Why, why is this?
    Think'st thou I'd make a life of jealousy,
    To follow still the changes of the moon
    With fresh suspicions? No; to be once in doubt
    Is once to be resolv'd: exchange me for a goat,   180
    When I shall turn the business of my soul
    To such exsufflicate and blown[24] surmises,
    Matching thy inference. 'Tis not to make me jealous
    To say my wife is fair, feeds well, loves company,
    Is free of speech, sings, plays and dances well;
    Where virtue is, these are more virtuous;
    Nor from mine own weak merits will I draw
    The smallest fear or doubt of her revolt:
    For she had eyes, and chose me. No, Iago;
    I'll see before I doubt; when I doubt, prove;   190
    And on the proof, there is no more but this,—
    Away at once with love or jealousy!

IAGO. I am glad of this; for now I shall have reason
    To show the love and duty that I bear you
    With franker spirit: therefore, as I am bound,
    Receive it from me. I speak not yet of proof.
    Look to your wife; observe her well with Cassio;
    Wear your eye thus, not jealous nor secure:[25]
    I would not have your free and noble nature,
    Out of self-bounty,[26] be abus'd; look to 't: 200
    I know our country disposition well;
    In Venice they do let heaven see the pranks
    They dare not show their husbands; their best conscience
    Is not to leave 't undone, but keep 't unknown.

OTH. Dost thou say so?

IAGO. She did deceive her father, marrying you;
    And when she seem'd to shake and fear your looks,
    She lov'd them most.

OTH.   And so she did.

IAGO.   Why, go to then;
    She that, so young, could give out such a seeming,[27]
    To seel[28] her father's eyes up close as oak—   210
    He thought 'twas witchcraft—but I am much to blame;

---

[23] **fineless** boundless.
[24] **exsufflicate and blown** unsubstantial and inflated, flyblown.
[25] **secure** free from uneasiness.
[26] **self-bounty** inherent or natural goodness.
[27] **seeming** false appearance.
[28] **seel** blind (a term from falconry).

>   I humbly do beseech you of your pardon
>   For too much loving you.

OTH.   I am bound to thee for ever.

IAGO. I see this hath a little dash'd your spirits.

OTH. Not a jot, not a jot.

IAGO.   I' faith, I fear it has.
>   I hope you will consider what is spoke
>   Comes from my love. But I do see y' are mov'd:
>   I am to pray you not to strain my speech
>   To grosser issues nor to larger reach[29]
>   Than to suspicion.   220

OTH. I will not.

IAGO.   Should you do so, my lord,
>   My speech should fall into such vile success
>   As my thoughts aim not at. Cassio 's my worthy friend—
>   My lord, I see y' are mov'd.

OTH.   No, not much mov'd:
>   I do not think but Desdemona's honest.

IAGO. Long live she so! and long live you to think so!

OTH. And yet, how nature erring from itself,—

IAGO. Ay, there's the point: as—to be bold with you—
>   Not to affect many proposed matches
>   Of her own clime, complexion, and degree,   230
>   Whereto we see in all things nature tends—
>   Foh! one may smell in such a will[30] most rank,
>   Foul disproportion,[31] thoughts unnatural.
>   But pardon me; I do not in position[32]
>   Distinctly speak of her; though I may fear
>   Her will, recoiling to[33] her better judgment,
>   May fall to match you with her country forms[34]
>   And happily repent.[35]

OTH.   Farewell, farewell:
>   If more thou dost perceive, let me know more;
>   Set on thy wife to observe: leave me, Iago.   240

IAGO [*going*]. My lord, I take my leave.

OTH. Why did I marry? This honest creature doubtless
>   Sees and knows more, much more, than he unfolds.

IAGO [*returning*]. My Lord, I would I might entreat your honour
>   To scan this thing no farther; leave it to time:

---

[29]**reach** meaning.
[30]**will** sensuality.
[31]**disproportion** abnormality.
[32]**position** general argument.
[33]**recoiling to** falling back upon, or recoiling against.
[34]**fall . . . forms** happen to compare you with Venetian norms of handsomeness.
[35]**repent** i.e., of her marriage.

Although 'tis fit that Cassio have his place,
For, sure, he fills it up with great ability,
Yet, if you please to hold him off awhile,
You shall by that perceive him and his means:
Note, if your lady strain his entertainment[36]   250
With any strong or vehement importunity;
Much will be seen in that. In the mean time,
Let me be thought too busy in my fears—
As worthy cause I have to fear I am—
And hold her free,[37] I do beseech your honour.

OTH. Fear not my government.[38]

IAGO. I once more take my leave.   [*Exit.*]

OTH. This fellow 's of exceeding honesty,
And knows all qualities, with a learned spirit,
Of human dealings. If I do prove her haggard,[39]   260
Though that her jesses[40] were my dear heartstrings,
I 'ld whistle her off and let her down the wind,
To prey at fortune.[41] Haply, for I am black
And have not those soft parts of conversation
That chamberers[42] have, or for I am declin'd
Into the vale of years,—yet that 's not much—
She 's gone. I am abus'd: and my relief
Must be to loathe her. O curse of marriage,
That we can call these delicate creatures ours,
And not their appetites! I had rather be a toad,   270
And live upon the vapour of a dungeon,
Than keep a corner in the thing I love
For others' uses. Yet, 'tis the plague of great ones;
Prerogativ'd[43] are they less than the base;
'Tis destiny unshunnable, like death:
Even then this forked[44] plague is fated to us
When we do quicken.[45] Look where she comes:

[*Enter* DESDEMONA *and* EMILIA.]

If she be false, O, then heaven mocks itself!
I'll not believe 't.

DES.   How now, my dear Othello!
Your dinner, and the generous[46] islanders   280
By you invited, do attend your presence.

---

[36]**strain his entertainment** urge his reinstatement.
[37]**hold her free** regard her as innocent.
[38]**government** self-control.
[39]**haggard** a wild female duck.
[40]**jesses** straps fastened around the legs of a trained hawk.
[41]**at fortune** at random.
[42]**chamberers** gallants.
[43]**Prerogativ'd** privileged.
[44]**forked** an allusion to the horns of the cuckold.
[45]**quicken** receive life.
[46]**generous** noble.

OTH. I am to blame.

DES. Why do you speak so faintly?
Are you not well?

OTH. I have a pain upon my forehead here.

DES. 'Faith, that 's with watching;[47] 'twill away again:
Let me but bind it hard, within this hour
It will be well.

OTH. Your napkin is too little:

[*He puts the handkerchief from him; and it drops.*]

Let it alone. Come, I'll go in with you.

DES. I am very sorry that you are not well. [*Exit with* OTHELLO.]

EMIL. I am glad I have found this napkin: 290
This was her first remembrance from the Moor:
My wayward husband hath a hundred times
Woo'd me to steal it; but she so loves the token,
For he conjur'd her she should ever keep it,
That she reserves it evermore about her
To kiss and talk to. I'll have the work ta'en out,[48]
And give 't Iago: what he will do with it
Heaven knows, not I;
I nothing but to please his fantasy.

[*Enter* IAGO.]

IAGO. How now! what do you here alone? 300

EMIL. Do not you chide; I have a thing for you.

IAGO. A thing for me? it is a common thing[49]—

EMIL. Ha!

IAGO. To have a foolish wife.

EMIL. O, is that all? What will you give me now
For that same handkerchief?

IAGO. What handkerchief?

EMIL. What handkerchief!
Why, that the Moor first gave to Desdemona;
That which so often you did bid me steal.

IAGO. Hast stol'n it from her? 310

EMIL. No, 'faith; she let it drop by negligence,
And, to th' advantage, I, being here, took 't up.
Look, here it is.

IAGO. A good wench; give it me.

---

[47]**watching** working late.
[48]**work ta'en out** design copied.
[49]**common thing** *common* suggests coarseness and availability to all, and *thing* is slang for female sexual organs.

EMIL. What will you do with 't, that you have been so earnest
  To have me filch it?

IAGO.   [*Snatching it*] Why, what is that to you?

EMIL. If it be not for some purpose of import,
  Give 't me again: poor lady, she'll run mad
  When she shall lack it.

IAGO. Be not acknown on 't;[50] I have use for it.
  Go, leave me.   [*Exit* EMILIA.]   320

  I will in Cassio's lodging lose this napkin,
  And let him find it. Trifles light as air
  Are to the jealous confirmations strong
  As proofs of holy writ: this may do something.
  The Moor already changes with my poison:
  Dangerous conceits are, in their natures, poisons,
  Which at the first are scarce found to distaste,
  But with a little act[51] upon the blood,
  Burn like the mines of sulphur. I did say so:

  [*Enter* OTHELLO.]

  Look, where he comes! Not poppy, nor mandragora,   330
  Nor all the drowsy syrups of the world,
  Shall ever medicine thee to that sweet sleep
  Which thou owedst yesterday.

OTH.   Ha! ha! false to me?

IAGO. Why, how now, general! no more of that.

OTH. Avaunt! be gone! thou has set me on the rack;
  I swear 'tis better to be much abus'd
  Than but to know 't a little.

IAGO.   How now, my lord!

OTH. What sense had I of her stol'n hours of lust?
  I saw 't not, thought it not, it harm'd not me:
  I slept the next night well, fed well, was free and merry;   340
  I found not Cassio's kisses on her lips:
  He that is robb'd, not wanting what is stol'n,
  Let him not know 't, and he 's not robb'd at all.

IAGO. I am sorry to hear this.

OTH. I had been happy, if the general camp,
  Pioners[52] and all, had tasted her sweet body,
  So I had nothing known. O, now, for ever
  Farewell the tranquil mind! farewell content!
  Farewell the plumed troop, and the big wars,
  That make ambition virtue! O, farewell!   350
  Farewell the neighing steed, and the shrill trump,

---

[50]**Be . . . on't** do not confess knowledge of it.
[51]**act** action, working.
[52]**Pioners** sappers, a low grade of soldiers.

> The spirit-stirring drum, th' ear-piercing fife,
> The royal banner, and all quality,
> Pride, pomp and circumstance[53] of glorious war!
> And, O you mortal engines,[54] whose rude throats
> Th' immortal Jove's dread clamours counterfeit,
> Farewell! Othello's occupation 's gone!

IAGO. Is 't possible, my lord?

OTH. Villain, be sure thou prove my love a whore,
    Be sure of it; give me the ocular proof;   360
    Or, by the worth of mine eternal soul,
    Thou hadst been better have been born a dog
    Than answer my wak'd wrath!

IAGO.   Is 't come to this?

OTH. Make me see 't; or, at the least, so prove it,
    That the probation bear no hinge nor loop
    To hang a doubt on; or woe upon thy life!

IAGO. My noble lord,—

OTH. If thou dost slander her and torture me,
    Never pray more; abandon all remorse;
    On horror's head horrors[55] accumulate;   370
    Do deeds to make heaven weep, all earth amaz'd;
    For nothing canst thou to damnation add
    Greater than that.

IAGO.   O grace! O heaven forgive me!
    Are you a man? have you a soul or sense?
    God be wi' you; take mine office. O wretched fool,
    That liv'st to make thine honesty a vice!
    O monstrous world! Take note, take note, O world,
    To be direct and honest is not safe.
    I thank you for this profit; and from hence
    I'll love no friend, sith love breeds such offence.   380

OTH. Nay, stay: thou shouldst be honest.

IAGO. I should be wise, for honesty 's a fool
    And loses that it works for.

OTH.   By the world,
    I think my wife be honest and think she is not;
    I think that thou are just and think thou art not.
    I'll have some proof. Her name, that was as fresh
    As Dian's visage, is now begrim'd and black
    As mine own face. If there be cords, or knives,
    Poison, or fire, or suffocating streams,
    I'll not endure it. Would I were satisfied!   390

IAGO. I see, sir, you are eaten up with passion:

---

[53] **circumstance** attendant fact; here, formal display.
[54] **mortal engines** i.e., cannon.
[55] **horrors** object of *accumulate*.

I do repent me that I put it to you.
You would be satisfied?

OTH.   Would! nay, I will.

IAGO. And may: but, how? how satisfied, my lord?
Would you, the supervisor, grossly gape on—
Behold her topp'd?

OTH.   Death and damnation! O!

IAGO. It were a tedious difficulty, I think,
To bring them to that prospect: damn them then,
If ever mortal eyes do see them bolster[56]
More than their own! What then? how then?
What shall I say? Where's satisfaction?
It is impossible you should see this,
Were they as prime as goats, as hot as monkeys,
As salt[57] as wolves in pride, and fools as gross
As ignorance made drunk. But yet, I say,
If imputation[58] and strong circumstances,
Which lead directly to the door of truth,
Will give you satisfaction, you may have 't.

OTH. Give me a living reason she's disloyal.

IAGO. I do not like the office:
But, sith I am ent'red in this cause so far,
Prick'd to 't by foolish honesty and love,
I will go on. I lay with Cassio lately;
And, being troubled with a raging tooth,
I could not sleep.
There are a kind of men so loose of soul,
That in their sleeps will mutter their affairs:
One of this kind is Cassio:
In sleep I heard him say "Sweet Desdemona,
Let us be wary, let us hide our loves";
And then, sir, would he grip and wring my hand,
Cry "O sweet creature!" and then kiss me hard,
As if he pluck'd up kisses by the roots
That grew upon my lips: then laid his leg
Over my thigh, and sigh'd and kiss'd; and then
Cried "Cursed fate that gave thee to the Moor!"

OTH. O monstrous! monstrous!

IAGO.   Nay, this was but his dream.

OTH. But this denoted a foregone conclusion:[59]
'Tis a shrewd doubt, though it be but a dream.

IAGO. And this may help to thicken other proofs
That do demonstrate thinly.

---

[56]**bolster** lie together.
[57]**salt** wanton, sensual.
[58]**imputation** i.e., opinion founded on strong circumstantial evidence.
[59]**foregone conclusion** previous trial or experience (not used in our sense).

OTH.   I'll tear her all to pieces.

IAGO. Nay, but be wise: yet we see nothing done;
  She may be honest yet. Tell me but this,
  Have you not sometimes seen a handkerchief
  Spotted with strawberries in your wife's hand?

OTH. I gave her such a one; 'twas my first gift.

IAGO. I know not that: but such a handkerchief—
  I am sure it was your wife's—did I to-day
  See Cassio wipe his beard with.

OTH.   If it be that,—

IAGO. If it be that, or any that was hers,   440
  It speaks against her with the other proofs.

OTH. O, that the slave had forty thousand lives!
  One is too poor, too weak for my revenge.
  Now do I see 'tis true. Look here, Iago;
  All my fond love thus do I blow to heaven.
  'Tis gone.
  Arise, black vengeance, from the hollow hell!
  Yield up, O love, thy crown and hearted[60] throne
  To tyrannous hate! Swell, bosom, with thy fraught,[61]
  For 'tis of aspics'[62] tongues!

IAGO.   Yet be content.   450

OTH. O, blood, blood, blood!

IAGO. Patience, I say; your mind perhaps may change.

OTH. Never, Iago. Like to the Pontic sea,
  Whose icy current and compulsive course
  Ne'er feels retiring ebb, but keeps due on
  To the Propontic and the Hellespont,
  Even so my bloody thoughts, with violent pace,
  Shall ne'er look back, ne'er ebb to humble love,
  Till that a capable and wide revenge
  Swallow them up. Now, by yond marble[63] heaven,   460
  [*Kneels*] In the due reverence of a sacred vow
  I here engage my words.

IAGO.   Do not rise yet.
  [*Kneels*] Witness, you ever-burning lights above,
  You elements that clip us round about,
  Witness that here Iago doth give up
  The execution[64] of his wit, hands, heart,
  To wrong'd Othello's service! Let him command,
  And to obey shall be in me remorse,[65]

---

[60]**hearted** fixed in the heart.
[61]**fraught** freight, burden.
[62]**aspics'** venomous serpents'.
[63]**marble** i.e., gleaming like marble.
[64]**execution** exercise.
[65]**remorse** pity for Othello's wrongs.

    What bloody business ever. [*They rise.*]

OTH.   I greet thy love,
    Not with vain thanks, but with acceptance bounteous,   470
    And will upon the instant put thee to 't:
    Within these three days let me hear thee say
    That Cassio 's not alive.

IAGO. My friend is dead; 'tis done at your request:
    But let her live.

OTH. Damn her, lewd minx! O, damn her! damn her!
    Come, go with me apart; I will withdraw,
    To furnish me with some swift means of death
    For the fair devil. Now art thou my lieutenant.

IAGO. I am your own for ever.   [*Exeunt.*]   480

SCENE IV   *Before the castle.*

[*Enter* DESDEMONA, EMILIA, *and* CLOWN.]

DES. Do you know, sirrah, where Lieutenant Cassio lies?

CLO. I dare not say he lies any where.

DES. Why, man?

CLO. He's a soldier, and for one to say a soldier lies, is stabbing.

DES. Go to: where lodges he?

CLO. To tell you where he lodges, is to tell you where I lie.

DES. Can any thing be made of this?

CLO. I know not where he lodges, and for me to devise a lodging and
    say he lies here or he lies there, were to lie in mine own throat.

DES. Can you inquire him out, and be edified by report?   10

CLO. I will catechize the world for him; that is, make questions, and
    by them answer.

DES. Seek him, bid him come hither: tell him I have moved my lord
    on his behalf, and hope all will be well.

CLO. To do this is within the compass of man's wit; and therefore I
    will attempt the doing it.   [*Exit* CLOWN.]

DES. Where should I lose that handkerchief, Emilia?

EMIL. I know not, madam.

DES. Believe me, I had rather have lost my purse
    Full of crusadoes:[66] and, but my noble Moor   20
    Is true of mind and made of no such baseness
    As jealous creatures are, it were enough
    To put him to ill thinking.

EMIL.   Is he not jealous?

---

[66]**crusadoes** Portuguese gold coins.

DES. Who, he? I think the sun where he was born
Drew all such humours from him.

EMIL. Look, where he comes.

[*Enter* OTHELLO.]

DES. I will not leave him now till Cassio
Be call'd to him.—How is 't with you, my lord?

OTH. Well, my good lady. [*Aside*] O, hardness to dissemble!—
How do you, Desdemona?

DES. Well, my good lord.

OTH. Give me your hand: this hand is moist, my lady. 30

DES. It yet hath felt no age nor known no sorrow.

OTH. This argues fruitfulness and liberal heart:
Hot, hot, and moist: this hand of yours requires
A sequester[67] from liberty, fasting and prayer,
Much castigation, exercise devout;
For here 's a young and sweating devil here,
That commonly rebels. 'Tis a good hand,
A frank one.

DES. You may, indeed, say so:
For 'twas that hand that gave away my heart.

OTH. A liberal hand: the hearts of old gave hands; 40
But our new heraldry is hands, not hearts.[68]

DES. I cannot speak of this. Come now, your promise.

OTH. What promise, chuck?

DES. I have sent to bid Cassio come speak with you.

OTH. I have a salt and sorry rheum[69] offends me;
Lend my thy handkerchief.

DES. Here, my lord.

OTH. That which I gave you.

DES. I have it not about me.

OTH. Not?

DES. No, indeed, my lord.

OTH. That 's a fault.
That handkerchief
Did an Egyptian[70] to my mother give; 50
She was a charmer, and could almost read
The thoughts of people: she told her, while she kept it,
'Twould make her amiable and subdue my father

---

[67]**sequester** separation, sequestration.
[68]**new . . . hearts** a current expression referring to marriages in which there is a joining of hands without the giving of hearts.
[69]**sorry rheum** distressful head cold.
[70]**Egyptian** gypsy.

Entirely to her love, but if she lost it
Or made a gift of it, my father's eye
Should hold her loathed and his spirits should hunt
After new fancies: she, dying, gave it me;
And bid me, when my fate would have me wive,
To give it her. I did so: and take heed on 't;
Make it a darling like your precious eye; 60
To lose 't or give 't away were such perdition
As nothing else could match.

DES.   Is 't possible?

OTH. 'Tis true: there 's magic in the web of it:
A sibyl, that had numb'red in the world
The sun to course two hundred compasses,
In her prophetic fury sew'd the work;
The worms were hallow'd that did breed the silk;
And it was dy'd in mummy[71] which the skilful
Conserv'd of[72] maidens' hearts.

DES.   Indeed! is 't true?

OTH. Most veritable; therefore look to 't well. 70

DES. Then would to God that I had never seen 't!

OTH. Ha! wherefore?

DES. Why do you speak so startingly and rash?

OTH. Is 't lost? is 't gone? speak, is it out o' th' way?

DES. Heaven bless us!

OTH. Say you?

DES. It is not lost; but what an if it were?

OTH. How!

DES. I say, it is not lost.

OTH.   Fetch 't, let me see 't.

DES. Why, so I can, sir, but I will not now. 80
    This is a trick to put me from my suit:
    Pray you, let Cassio be receiv'd again.

OTH. Fetch me the handkerchief: my mind misgives.

DES. Come, come;
    You'll never meet a more sufficient man.

OTH. The handkerchief!

DES.   I pray, talk me of Cassio.

OTH. The handkerchief!

DES.   A man that all his time
    Hath founded his good fortunes on your love,
    Shar'd dangers with you,—

---

[71]**mummy** medicinal or magical preparation drained from the flesh of mummified bodies.
[72]**Conserv'd of** preserved out of.

OTH. The handkerchief!   90

DES. In sooth, you are to blame.

OTH. Away!   [*Exit* OTHELLO.]

EMIL. Is not this man jealous?

DES. I ne'er saw this before.
  Sure, there's some wonder in this handkerchief:
  I am most unhappy in the loss of it.

EMIL. 'Tis not a year or two shows us a man:
  They are all but stomachs, and we all but food;
  They eat us hungerly, and when they are full,
  They belch us.
  [*Enter* IAGO *and* CASSIO.]
                    Look you, Cassio and my husband!   100

IAGO. There is no other way; 'tis she must do 't:
  And, lo, the happiness! go, and importune her.

DES. How now, good Cassio! what's the news with you?

CAS. Madam, my former suit: I do beseech you
  That by your virtuous means I may again
  Exist, and be a member of his love
  Whom I with all the office of my heart
  Entirely honour: I would not be delay'd.
  If my offence be of such mortal kind
  That nor my service past, nor present sorrows,   110
  Nor purpos'd merit in futurity,
  Can ransom me into his love again,
  But to know so much be my benefit;[73]
  So shall I clothe me in a forc'd content,
  And shut myself up in some other course,
  To fortune's alms.

DES.   Alas, thrice-gentle Cassio!
  My advocation[74] is not now in tune;
  My lord is not my lord; nor should I know him,
  Were he in favour as in humour alter'd.
  So help me every spirit sanctified   120
  As I have spoken for you all my best
  And stood within the blank[75] of his displeasure
  For my free speech! You must awhile be patient:
  What I can do I will; and more I will
  Than for myself I dare: let that suffice you.

IAGO. Is my lord angry?

EMIL.   He went hence but now,
  And certainly in strange unquietness.

---

[73]**to know . . . benefit** to know that my case is hopeless will end my vain endeavour.
[74]**advocation** advocacy.
[75]**blank** white spot in the centre of a target; here, range.

IAGO. Can he be angry? I have seen the cannon,
   When it hath blown his ranks into the air,
   And, like the devil, from his very arm   130
   Puff'd his own brother:—and can he be angry?
   Something of moment then: I will go meet him:
   There's matter in 't indeed, if he be angry.

DES. I prithee, do so.   [*Exit* IAGO.]
               Something, sure, of state,
   Either from Venice, or some unhatch'd practice
   Made demonstrable here in Cyprus to him,
   Hath puddled[76] his clear spirit; and in such cases
   Men's natures wrangle with inferior things,
   Though great ones are their object. 'Tis even so;
   For let our finger ache, and it indues[77]   140
   Our other healthful members even to a sense
   Of pain: nay, we must think men are not gods,
   Nor of them look for such observancy
   As fits the bridal. Beshrew me much, Emilia,
   I was, unhandsome[78] warrior as I am,
   Arraigning his unkindness with my soul;
   But now I find I had suborn'd the witness,
   And he's indicted falsely.

EMIL. Pray heaven it be state-matters, as you think,
   And no conception[79] nor no jealous toy   150
   Concerning you.

DES. Alas the day! I never gave him cause.

EMIL. But jealous souls will not be answer'd so;
   They are not ever jealous for the cause,
   But jealous for they are jealous: 'tis a monster
   Begot upon itself, born on itself.

DES. Heaven keep that monster from Othello's mind!

EMIL. Lady, amen.

DES. I will go seek him. Cassio, walk here about:
   If I do find him fit, I'll move your suit   160
   And seek to effect it to my uttermost.

CAS. I humbly thank your ladyship.
                              [*Exit* DESDEMONA *with* EMILIA.]

[*Enter* BIANCA.]

BIAN. Save you, friend Cassio!

CAS.   What make you from home?
   How is 't with you, my most fair Bianca?
   I' faith, sweet love, I was coming to your house.

---
[76]**puddled** sullied the purity of.
[77]**indues** brings to the same condition.
[78]**unhandsome** unfair.
[79]**conception** mere fancy.

BIAN. And I was going to your lodging, Cassio.
What, keep a week away? seven days and nights?
Eight score eight hours? and lovers' absent hours,
More tedious than the dial eight score times?
O weary reck'ning!

CAS.   Pardon me, Bianca.   170
I have this while with leaden thoughts been press'd;
But I shall, in a more continuate[80] time,
Strike off this score of absence. Sweet Bianca,

[*Giving her* DESDEMONA'S *handkerchief.*]

Take me this work out.[81]

BIAN.   O Cassio, whence came this?
This is some token from a newer friend:
To the felt absence now I feel a cause:
Is 't come to this? Well, well.

CAS.   Go to, woman!
Throw your vile guesses in the devil's teeth,
From whence you have them. You are jealous now
That this is from some mistress, some remembrance: 180
No, in good troth, Bianca.

BIAN.   Why, whose is it?

CAS. I know not, sweet: I found it in my chamber.
I like the work well: ere it be demanded—
As like enough it will—I would have it copied:
Take it, and do 't; and leave me for this time.

BIAN. Leave you! wherefore?

CAS. I do attend here on the general;
And think it no addition, nor my wish,
To have him see me woman'd.

BIAN.   Why, I pray you?

CAS. Not that I love you not.

BIAN.   But that you do not love me.   190
I pray you, bring me on the way a little,
And say if I shall see you soon at night.

CAS. 'Tis but a little way that I can bring you;
For I attend here: but I'll see you soon.

BIAN. 'Tis very good; I must be circumstance'd.[82]   [*Exeunt omnes.*]

---

[80]**continuate** uninterrupted.
[81]**Take . . . out** i.e., copy this embroidery for me.
[82]**circumstance'd** governed by circumstances.

ACT IV

SCENE I *Cyprus. Before the castle.*

[*Enter* OTHELLO *and* IAGO.]

IAGO. Will you think so?

OTH.   Think so, Iago!

IAGO.   What,
To kiss in private?

OTH.   An unauthoriz'd kiss.

IAGO. Or to be naked with her friend in bed
An hour or more, not meaning any harm?

OTH. Naked in bed, Iago, and not mean harm!
It is hypocrisy against the devil:
They that mean virtuously, and yet do so,
The devil their virtue tempts, and they tempt heaven.

IAGO. So[1] they do nothing, 'tis a venial slip:
But if I give my wife a handkerchief,—   10

OTH. What then?

IAGO. Why, then, 'tis hers, my lord: and, being hers,
She may, I think, bestow 't on any man.

OTH. She is protectress of her honour too:
May she give that?

IAGO. Her honour is an essence that's not seen;
They have it very oft that have it not:
But, for the handkerchief,—

OTH. By heaven, I would most gladly have forgot it.
Thou said'st—O, it comes o'er my memory,   20
As doth the raven o'er the infected house,[2]
Boding to all—he had my handkerchief.

IAGO. Ay, what of that?

OTH.   That's not so good now.

IAGO.   What,
If I had said I had seen him do you wrong?
Or heard him say,—as knaves be such abroad,
Who having, by their own importunate suit,
Or voluntary dotage of some mistress,
Convinced or supplied[3] them, cannot choose
But they must blab—

OTH.   Hath he said any thing?

---

[1] **So** so long as.
[2] **raven . . . house** allusion to the belief that the raven hovered over a house of sickness or infection.
[3] **Convinced or supplied** i.e., mistresses gained by importunity and those who doted voluntarily.

IAGO. He hath, my lord; but be you well assur'd, 30
  No more than he'll unswear.

OTH. What hath he said?

IAGO. 'Faith, that he did—I know not what he did.

OTH. What? what?

IAGO. Lie—

OTH. With her?

IAGO. With her, on her; what you will.

OTH. Lie with her! lie on her! We say lie on her, when they belie her. Lie with her! that's fulsome.—Handkerchief—confessions—handkerchief—To confess, and be hanged for his labour;—first, to be hanged, and then to confess.—I tremble at it. Nature would not invest herself in such shadowing passion without some instruction.[4] It is not words that shakes me thus. Pish! Noses, ears, and lips.— 40
Is 't possible?—Confess—handkerchief—O devil! [*Falls in a trance.*]

IAGO. Work on,
  My medicine, work! Thus credulous fools are caught;
  And many worthy and chaste dames even thus,
  All guiltless, meet reproach. What, ho! my lord!
  My lord, I say! Othello!
  [*Enter* CASSIO.]
                    How now, Cassio!

CAS. What 's the matter?

IAGO. My lord is fall'n into an epilepsy:
  This is his second fit; he had one yesterday.

CAS. Rub him about the temples.

IAGO. No, forbear; 50
  The lethargy[5] must have his quiet course:
  If not, he foams at mouth and by and by
  Breaks out to savage madness. Look, he stirs:
  Do you withdraw yourself a little while,
  He will recover straight: when he is gone,
  I would on great occasion speak with you.
                              [*Exit* CASSIO.]
  How is it, general? have you not hurt your head?

OTH. Dost thou mock me?

IAGO. I mock you! no, by heaven.
  Would you would bear your fortune like a man!

OTH. A horned man 's a monster and a beast. 60

IAGO. There 's many a beast then in a populous city,
  And many a civil[6] monster.

---

[4]**Nature . . . instruction** i.e., my jealousy cannot be merely the result of natural imagination, but must have some foundation in fact.
[5]**lethargy** unconscious condition.
[6]**civil** i.e., in civilized society.

OTH. Did he confess it?

IAGO.   Good sir, be a man;
   Think every bearded fellow that 's but yok'd
   May draw with you:[7] there's millions now alive
   That nightly lie in those unproper[8] beds
   Which they dare swear peculiar:[9] your case is better.
   O, 'tis the spite of hell, the fiend's arch-mock,
   To lip a wanton in a secure couch,
   And to suppose her chaste! No, let me know;   70
   And knowing what I am, I know what she shall be.

OTH. O, thou are wise; 'tis certain.

IAGO.   Stand you awhile apart;
   Confine yourself but in a patient list.[10]
   Whilst you were here o'erwhelmed with your grief—
   A passion most unsuiting such a man—
   Cassio came hither: I shifted him away,
   And laid good 'scuse upon your ecstasy,
   Bade him anon return and here speak with me;
   The which he promis'd. Do but encave[11] yourself,
   And mark the fleers,[12] the gibes, and notable scorns,   80
   That dwell in every region of his face;
   For I will make him tell the tale anew,
   Where, how, how oft, how long ago, and when
   He hath, and is again to cope your wife:
   I say, but mark his gesture. Marry, patience;
   Or I shall say y' are all in all in spleen,
   And nothing of a man.

OTH.   Dost thou hear, Iago?
   I will be found most cunning in my patience;
   But—dost thou hear?—most bloody.

IAGO.   That 's not amiss;
   But yet keep time[13] in all. Will you withdraw?   [OTHELLO *retires*.]   90
   Now will I question Cassio of Bianca,
   A housewife that by selling her desires
   Buys herself bread and clothes: it is a creature
   That dotes on Cassio; as 'tis the strumpet's plague
   To beguile many and be beguil'd by one:
   He, when he hears of her, cannot refrain
   From the excess of laughter. Here he comes:

[*Enter* CASSIO.]

   As he shall smile, Othello shall go mad;

---

[7]**draw with you** i.e, share your fate as cuckold.
[8]**unproper** not belonging exclusively to an individual.
[9]**peculiar** private, one's own.
[10]**patient list** within the bounds of patience.
[11]**encave** conceal.
[12]**fleers** sneers.
[13]**keep time** use judgment and order.

And his unbookish[14] jealousy must conster[15]
Poor Cassio's smiles, gestures and light behaviour,   100
Quite in the wrong. How do you know, lieutenant?

CAS. The worser that you give me the addition[16]
Whose want even kills me.

IAGO. Ply Desdemona well, and you are sure on 't.
[*Speaking lower*] Now, if this suit lay in Bianca's power,
How quickly should you speed!

CAS.   Alas, poor caitiff!

OTH. Look, how he laughs already!

IAGO. I never knew woman love man so.

CAS. Alas, poor rogue! I think, i' faith, she loves me.

OTH. Now he denies it faintly, and laughs it out.   110

IAGO. Do you hear, Cassio?

OTH.   Now he importunes him
To tell o'er: go to; well said, well said.

IAGO. She gives it out that you shall marry her:
Do you intend it?

CAS. Ha, ha, ha!

OTH. Do you triumph, Roman?[17] do you triumph?

CAS. I marry her! what? a customer![18] Prithee, bear some charity to
my wit; do not think it so unwholesome. Ha, ha, ha!

OTH. So, so, so, so: they laugh that win.

IAGO. 'Faith, the cry goes that you shall marry her.   120

CAS. Prithee, say true.

IAGO. I am a very villain else.

OTH. Have you scored me?[19] Well.

CAS. This is the monkey's own giving out: she is persuaded I will marry
her, out of her own love and flattery, not out of my promise.

OTH. Iago beckons me; now he begins the story.

CAS. She was here even now; she haunts me in every place. I was the
other day talking on the seabank with certain Venetians; and
thither comes the bauble,[20] and, by this hand, she falls me thus
about my neck—   130

OTH. Crying, 'O dear Cassio!' as it were: his gesture imports it.

---

[14]**unbookish** uninstructed.
[15]**conster** construe.
[16]**addition** title.
[17]**Roman** epithet arising from the association of the Romans with the idea of triumph.
[18]**customer** prostitute.
[19]**scored me** made up my reckoning, or branded me.
[20]**bauble** plaything.

CAS. So hangs, and lolls, and weeps upon me; so shakes, and pulls me: ha, ha, ha!

OTH. Now he tells how she plucked him to my chamber. O, I see that nose of yours, but not that dog I shall throw it to.

CAS. Well, I must leave her company.

IAGO. Before me!²¹ look, where she comes.

[*Enter* BIANCA.]

CAS. 'Tis such another fitchew!²² marry, a perfumed one.— What do you mean by this haunting of me?

BIAN. Let the devil and his dam haunt you! What did you mean by that same handkerchief you gave me even now? I was a fine fool to take it. I must take out the work?—A likely piece of work, that you should find it in your chamber, and not know who left it there! This is some minx's token, and I must take out the work? There; give it your hobby-horse.²³ Wheresoever you had it, I'll take out no work on 't. 140

CAS. How now, my sweet Bianca! how now! how now!

OTH. By heaven, that should be my handkerchief!

BIAN. An you'll come to supper to-night, you may; an you will not, come when you are next prepared for. [*Exit.*] 150

IAGO. After her, after her.

CAS. 'Faith, I must; she'll rail in the street else.

IAGO. Will you sup there?

CAS. Yes, I intend so.

IAGO. Well, I may chance to see you; for I would very fain speak with you.

CAS. Prithee, come; will you?

IAGO. Go to; say no more. [*Exit* CASSIO.]

OTH [*advancing*]. How shall I murder him, Iago?

IAGO. Did you perceive how he laughed at his vice? 160

OTH. O Iago!

IAGO. And did you see the handkerchief?

OTH. Was that mine?

IAGO. Yours, by this hand: and to see how he prizes the foolish woman your wife! She gave it him, and he hath given it his whore.

OTH. I would have him nine years a-killing. A fine woman! a fair woman! a sweet woman!

---

²¹**Before me!** On my soul!
²²**fitchew** polecat (because of her strong perfume; also, slang word for a prostitute).
²³**hobby-horse** harlot.

IAGO. Nay, you must forget that.

OTH. Ay, let her rot, and perish, and be damned to-night; for she shall not live: no, my heart is turned to stone; I strike it, and it hurts my hand. O, the world hath not a sweeter creature: she might lie by an emperor's side and command him tasks. 170

IAGO. Nay, that's not your way.[24]

OTH. Hang her! I do but say what she is: so delicate with her needle: an admirable musician: O! she will sing the savageness out of a bear: of so high and plenteous wit and invention:—

IAGO. She's the worse for all this.

OTH. O, a thousand thousand times: and then, of so gentle a condition!

IAGO. Ay, too gentle.

OTH. Nay, that's certain: but yet the pity of it, Iago! O Iago, the pity of it, Iago! 180

IAGO. If you are so fond over her iniquity, give her patent[25] to offend; for, if it touch not you, it comes near nobody.

OTH. I will chop her into messes;[26] cuckold me!

IAGO. O, 'tis foul in her.

OTH. With mine officer!

IAGO. That's fouler.

OTH. Get me some poison, Iago; this night: I'll not expostulate with her, lest her body and beauty unprovide[27] my mind again: this night, Iago. 190

IAGO. Do it not with poison, strangle her in her bed, even the bed she hath contaminated.

OTH. Good, good: the justice of it pleases: very good.

IAGO. And for Cassio, let me be his undertaker:[28] you shall hear more by midnight.

OTH. Excellent good. [*A trumpet within.*] What trumpet is that same?

IAGO. I warrant something from Venice.

[*Enter* LODOVICO, DESDEMONA, *and* ATTENDANTS.]

                            'Tis Lodovico.
This comes from the duke: and, see, your wife's with him.

LOD. God save you, worthy general!

OTH.   With all my heart, sir.

LOD. The duke and the senators of Venice greet you. [*Gives him a letter.*] 200

OTH. I kiss the instrument of their pleasures.   [*Opens the letter, and reads.*]

---

[24]**your way** i.e., the way you should think of her.
[25]**patent** licence.
[26]**messes** dishes of food.
[27]**unprovide** weaken, unfit.
[28]**let . . . undertaker** i.e., let me settle with him.

DES. And what's the news, good cousin Lodovico?

IAGO. I am very glad to see you, signior;
   Welcome to Cyprus.

LOD. I thank you. How does Lieutenant Cassio?

IAGO. Lives, sir.

DES. Cousin, there's fall'n between him and my lord
   An unkind breach: but you shall make all well.

OTH. Are you sure of that?

DES. My lord? 210

OTH [*reads*]. "This fail you not to do, as you will—"

LOD. He did not call; he's busy in the paper.
   Is there division 'twixt my lord and Cassio?

DES. A most unhappy one: I would do much
   T' atone them, for the love I bear to Cassio.

OTH. Fire and brimstone!

DES.   My lord?

OTH.   Are you wise?

DES. What, is he angry?

LOD.   May be the letter mov'd him:
   For, as I think, they do command him home,
   Deputing Cassio in his government.²⁹

DES. Trust me, I am glad on 't.

OTH.   Indeed!

DES.   My lord? 220

OTH. I am glad to see you mad.

DES.   Why, sweet Othello,—

OTH [*striking her*]. Devil!

DES. I have not deserv'd this.

LOD. My lord, this would not be believ'd in Venice,
   Though I should swear I saw 't; 'tis very much:
   Make her amends; she weeps.

OTH.   O devil, devil!
   If that the earth could teem with woman's tears,
   Each drop she falls would prove a crocodile.³⁰
   Out of my sight!

DES.   I will not stay to offend you.   [*Going.*]

LOD. Truly, an obedient lady: 230
   I do beseech your lordship, call her back.

---

²⁹**government** office.
³⁰**prove a crocodile** i.e., by weeping crocodile tears; it was believed the crocodile shed tears over the body of the person it was eating.

OTH. Mistress!

DES. My lord?

OTH. What would you with her, sir?

LOD. Who, I, my lord?

OTH. Ay; you did wish that I would make her turn:
    Sir, she can turn, and turn, and yet go on,
    And turn again; and she can weep, sir, weep;
    And she's obedient, as you say, obedient,
    Very obedient. Proceed you in your tears.
    Concerning this, sir,—O well-painted passion!—[31]
    I am commanded home. Get you away;   240
    I'll send for you anon. Sir, I obey the mandate,
    And will return to Venice. Hence, avaunt!
                                          [*Exit* DESDEMONA.]
    Cassio shall have my place. And, sir, to-night,
    I do entreat that we may sup together:
    You are welcome, sir, to Cyprus.—Goats and monkeys!   [*Exit.*]

LOD. Is this the noble Moor whom our full senate
    Call all in all sufficient? Is this the nature
    Whom passion could not shake? whose solid virtue
    The shot of accident, nor dart of chance,
    Could neither graze nor pierce?

IAGO. He is much chang'd.   250

LOD. Are his wits safe? is he not light of brain?

IAGO. He's that he is: I may not breathe my censure
    What he might be: if what he might he is not,
    I would to heaven he were!

LOD. What, strike his wife!

IAGO. 'Faith, that was not so well; yet would I knew
    That stroke would prove the worst!

LOD. Is it his use?
    Or did the letters work upon his blood,
    And new-create this fault?

IAGO. Alas, alas!
    It is not honesty in me to speak
    What I have seen and known. You shall observe him,   260
    And his own courses will denote him so
    That I may save my speech: do but go after,
    And mark how he continues.

LOD. I am sorry that I am deceiv'd in him.   [*Exeunt.*]

---

[31] **well-painted passion** well-simulated emotion.

SCENE II *A room in the castle.*

[*Enter* OTHELLO *and* EMILIA.]

OTH. You have seen nothing then?

EMIL. Nor ever heard, nor ever did suspect.

OTH. Yes, you have seen Cassio and she together.

EMIL. But then I saw no harm, and then I heard
Each syllable that breath made up between them.

OTH. What, did they never whisper?

EMIL.   Never, my lord.

OTH. Nor send you out 'o th' way?

EMIL. Never.

OTH. To fetch her fan, her gloves, her mask, nor nothing?

EMIL. Never, my lord.   10

OTH. That 's strange.

EMIL. I durst, my lord, to wager she is honest,
Lay down my soul at stake: if you think other,
Remove your thought; it doth abuse your bosom.
If any wretch have put this in your head,
Let heaven requite it with the serpent's curse!
For, if she be not honest, chaste, and true,
There 's no man happy; the purest of their wives
Is foul as slander.

OTH.   Bid her come hither: go.

[*Exit* EMILIA.]

She says enough; yet she 's a simple bawd   20
That cannot say as much. This is a subtle whore,
A closet lock and key[32] of villainous secrets:
And yet she'll kneel and pray; I have seen her do 't.

[*Enter* DESDEMONA *and* EMILIA.]

DES. My lord, what is your will?

OTH.   Pray, chuck, come hither.

DES. What is your pleasure?

OTH.   Let me see your eyes;
Look in my face.

DES.   What horrible fancy 's this?

OTH [*to* EMILIA]. Some of your function,[33] mistress;
Leave procreants[34] alone and shut the door;
Cough, or cry "hem," if any body come:
Your mystery, your mystery:[35] nay, dispatch.   [*Exit* EMILIA.]   30

---

[32]**closet lock and key** complete storeroom.
[33]**Some . . . function** i.e., set to work in your chosen profession, that of bawd.
[34]**procreants** mating couples.
[35]**mystery** trade, occupation.

DES. Upon my knees, what doth your speech import?
  I understand a fury in your words,
  But not the words.

OTH. Why, what art thou?

DES.   Your wife, my lord; your true
  And loyal wife.

OTH.   Come, swear it, damn thyself;
  Lest, being like one of heaven, the devils themselves
  Should fear to seize thee: therefore be double damn'd:
  Swear thou are honest.

DES.   Heaven doth truly know it.

OTH. Heaven truly knows that thou are false as hell.

DES. To whom, my lord? with whom? how am I false? 40

OTH. O Desdemon! away! away! away!

DES. Alas the heavy day! Why do you weep?
  Am I the motive of these tears, my lord?
  If haply you my father do suspect
  An instrument of this your calling back,
  Lay not your blame on me: if you have lost him,
  Why, I have lost him too.

OTH.   Had it pleas'd heaven
  To try me with affliction; had they[36] rain'd
  All kinds of sores and shames on my bare head,
  Steep'd me in poverty to the very lips,   50
  Given to captivity me and my utmost hopes,
  I should have found in some place of my soul
  A drop of patience: but, alas, to make me
  A fixed figure for the time of scorn
  To point his slow unmoving finger at![37]
  Yet could I bear that too; well, very well:
  But there, where I have garner'd up my heart,
  Where either I must live, or bear no life;
  The fountain from the which my current runs,
  Or else dries up; to be discarded thence!   60
  Or keep it as a cistern for foul toads
  To knot and gender[38] in! Turn thy complexion[39] there,
  Patience, thou young and rose-lipp'd cherubin,—
  Ay, there, look grim as hell!

DES. I hope my noble lord esteems me honest.

OTH. O, ay; as summer flies are in the shambles,[40]

---

[36]**they** heavenly powers.
[37]**A . . . at** Othello possibly thinks of himself as a man set in a pillory at whom the scornful world points in mockery. There seems to be a comparison with the sundial, whose gnomon, or indicator, becomes the finger of scornful time.
[38]**gender** engender.
[39]**Turn thy complexion** grow pale.
[40]**shambles** slaughterhouse.

      That quicken⁴¹ even with blowing. O thou weed,
      Who are so lovely fair and smell'st so sweet
      That the sense aches at thee, would thou hads't ne'er been born!

DES. Alas, what ignorant sin have I committed?   70

OTH. Was this fair paper, this most goodly book,
      Made to write "whore" upon? What committed!
      Committed! O thou public commoner!⁴²
      I should make very forges of my cheeks,
      That would to cinders burn up modesty,
      Did I but speak thy deeds. What committed!
      Heaven stops the nose at it and the moon winks,
      The bawdy wind that kisses all it meets
      Is hush'd within the hollow mine of earth,
      And will not hear it. What committed!   80
      Impudent strumpet!

DES.   By heaven, you do me wrong.

OTH. Are not you a strumpet?

DES.   No, as I am a Christian:
      If to preserve this vessel⁴³ for my lord
      From any other foul unlawful touch
      Be not to be a strumpet, I am none.

OTH. What, not a whore?

DES.   No, as I shall be sav'd.

OTH. Is 't possible?

DES. O, heaven forgive us!

OTH.   I cry you mercy, then:
      I took you for the cunning whore of Venice
      That married with Othello. [*Raising his voice*] You, mistress,   90
      That have the office opposite to Saint Peter,
      And keep the gate of hell!

      [*Enter* EMILIA.]

                        You, you, ay, you!
      We have done our course; there 's money for your pains:
      I pray you, turn the key and keep our counsel.   [*Exit.*]

EMIL. Alas, what does this gentleman conceive?
      How do you, madam? how do you, my good lady?

DES. 'Faith, half asleep.

EMIL. Good madam, what 's the matter with my lord?

DES. With who?

EMIL. Why, with my lord, madam.   100

DES. Who is thy lord?

---

⁴¹**quicken** come to life.
⁴²**commoner** prostitute.
⁴³**vessel** body.

EMIL. He that is yours, sweet lady.

DES. I have none: do not talk to me, Emilia;
I cannot weep; nor answers have I none,
But what should go by water.[44] Prithee, tonight
Lay on my bed my wedding sheets: remember;
And call thy husband hither.

EMIL. Here's a change indeed! [*Exit.*]

DES. 'Tis meet I should be us'd so, very meet.
How have I been behav'd, that he might stick
The small'st opinion on my least misuse?[45]

[*Enter* IAGO *and* EMILIA.]

IAGO. What is your pleasure, madam? How is 't with you? 110

DES. I cannot tell. Those that do teach young babes
Do it with gentle means and easy tasks:
He might have chid me so; for, in good faith,
I am a child to chiding.

IAGO. What is the matter, lady?

EMIL. Alas, Iago, my lord hath so bewhor'd her,
Thrown such despite[46] and heavy terms upon her,
As true hearts cannot bear.

DES. Am I that name, Iago?

IAGO. What name, fair lady?

DES. Such as she said my lord did say I was.

EMIL. He call'd her whore: a beggar in his drink 120
Could not have laid such terms upon his callet.[47]

IAGO. Why did he so?

DES. I do not know; I am sure I am none such.

IAGO. Do not weep, do not weep. Alas the day!

EMIL. Hath she forsook so many noble matches,
Her father and her country and her friends,
To be call'd whore? would it not make one weep?

DES. It is my wretched fortune.

IAGO. Beshrew him for 't!
How comes this trick upon him?

DES. Nay, heaven doth know.

EMIL. I will be hang'd, if some eternal villain, 130
Some busy and insinuating rogue,
Some cogging,[48] cozening slave, to get some office,
Have not devis'd this slander; I will be hang'd else.

---

[44] **go by water** be expressed by tears.
[45] **misuse** evil conduct.
[46] **despite** contempt, scorn.
[47] **callet** lewd woman.
[48] **cogging** cheating.

IAGO. Fie, there is no such man; it is impossible.

DES. If any such there be, heaven pardon him!

EMIL. A halter pardon him! and hell gnaw his bones!
    Why should he call her whore? who keeps her company?
    What place? what time? what form? what likelihood?
    The Moor's abus'd by some most villainous knave,
    Some base notorious knave, some scurvy fellow.   140
    O heaven, that such companions thou 'ldst unfold,
    And put in every honest hand a whip
    To lash the rascals naked through the world
    Even from the east to th' west!

IAGO.   Speak within door.[49]

EMIL. O, fie upon them! Some such squire he was
    That turn'd your wit the seamy side without,
    And made you to suspect me with the Moor.

IAGO. You are a fool; go to.

DES.   Alas, Iago.
    What shall I do to win my lord again?
    Good friend, go to him; for, by this light of heaven,   150
    I know not how I lost him. Here I kneel:
    If e'er my will did trespass 'gainst his love,
    Either in discourse of thought or actual deed,
    Or that mine eyes, mine ears, or any sense,
    Delighted them in any other form;
    Or that I do not yet, and ever did,
    And ever will—though he do shake me off
    To beggarly divorcement—love him dearly,
    Comfort forswear me! Unkindness may do much;
    And his unkindness may defeat my life,   160
    But never taint my love. I cannot say "whore":
    It doth abhor me now I speak the word;
    To do the act that might the addition[50] earn
    Not the world's mass of vanity could make me.

IAGO. I pray you, be content; 'tis but his humour:
    The business of the state does him offence,
    And he does chide with you.

DES. If 'twere no other,—

IAGO.   'Tis but so, I warrant.   [*Trumpets within.*]
    Hark, how these instruments summon to supper!
    The messengers of Venice stay the meat;[51]   170
    Go in, and weep not; all things shall be well.

                     [*Exeunt* DESDEMONA *and* EMILIA.]

[*Enter* RODERIGO.]
How now, Roderigo!

---

[49]**Speak . . . door** i.e., not so loud.
[50]**addition** title.
[51]**stay the meat** are waiting for supper.

ROD. I do not find that thou dealest justly with me.

IAGO. What in the contrary?

ROD. Everyday thou daffest me[52] with some device, Iago; and rather, as it seems to me now, keepest from me all conveniency[53] than suppliest me with the least advantage of hope. I will indeed no longer endure it, nor am I yet persuaded to put up[54] in peace what already I have foolishly suffered.

IAGO. Will you hear me, Roderigo?

ROD. 'Faith, I have heard too much, for your words and performances are no kin together.

IAGO. You charge me most unjustly.

ROD. With nought but truth. I have wasted myself out of my means. The jewels you have had from me to deliver to Desdemona would half have corrupted a votarist:[55] you have told me she hath received them and returned me expectations and comforts of sudden respect and acquaintance, but I find none.

IAGO. Well; go to; very well.

ROD. Very well! go to! I cannot go to, man; nor 'tis not very well: nay, I think it is scurvy, and begin to find myself fopped[56] in it.

IAGO. Very well.

ROD. I tell you 'tis not very well. I will make myself known to Desdemona: if she will return me my jewels, I will give over my suit and repent my unlawful solicitation; if not, assure yourself I will seek satisfaction of you.

IAGO. You have said now.[57]

ROD. Ay, and said nothing but what I protest intendment[58] of doing.

IAGO. Why, now I see there's mettle in thee, and even from this instance do build on thee a better opinion than ever before. Give my thy hand, Roderigo: thou hast taken against me a most just exception; but yet, I protest, I have dealt most directly in thy affair.

ROD. It hath not appeared.

IAGO. I grant indeed it hath not appeared, and your suspicion is not without wit and judgment. But, Roderigo, if thou hast that in thee indeed, which I have greater reason to believe now than ever, I mean purpose, courage and valour, this night show it; if thou the next night following enjoy not Desdemona, take me from this world with treachery and devise engines for[59] my life.

ROD. Well, what is it? is it within reason and compass?

---

[52]**daffest me** puts me off with an excuse.
[53]**conveniency** advantage, opportunity.
[54]**put up** submit to.
[55]**votarist** nun.
[56]**fopped** fooled.
[57]**You . . . now** well said, quite right.
[58]**intendment** purpose, intention.
[59]**engines for** plots against.

IAGO. Sir, there is especial commission come from Venice to depute Cassio in Othello's place.

ROD. Is that true? why, then Othello and Desdemona return again to Venice.

IAGO. O, no; he goes into Mauritania[60] and takes away with him the fair Desdemona, unless his abode be lingered here by some accident: wherein none can be so determinate[61] as the removing of Cassio.

ROD. How do you mean, removing of him?

IAGO. Why, by making him uncapable of Othello's place; knocking out his brains. 220

ROD. And that you would have me to do?

IAGO. Ay, if you dare do yourself a profit and a right. He sups to-night with a harlotry,[62] and thither will I go to him: he knows not yet of his honourable fortune. If you will watch his going thence, which I will fashion to fall out between twelve and one, you may take him at your pleasure: I will be near to second your attempt, and he shall fall between us. Come, stand not amazed at it, but go along with me; I will show you such a necessity in his death that you shall think yourself bound to put it on him. It is now high[63] 230 suppertime, and the night grows to waste: about it.

ROD. I will hear further reason for this.

IAGO. And you shall be satisfied. *[Exeunt.]*

SCENE III *Another room in the castle.*

[*Enter* OTHELLO, LODOVICO, DESDEMONA, EMILIA, *and* ATTENDANTS.]

LOD. I do beseech you, sir, trouble yourself no further.

OTH. O, pardon me; 'twill do me good to walk.

LOD. Madam, good night: I humbly thank your ladyship.

DES. Your honour is most welcome.

OTH.   Will you walk, sir?
   O,—Desdemona,—

DES. My lord?

OTH. Get you to bed on th' instant; I will be returned forthwith: dismiss your attendant there: look 't be done.

DES. I will, my lord.

[*Exit* OTHELLO, *with* LODOVICO *and* ATTENDANTS.]

EMIL. How goes it now? he looks gentler than he did. 10

DES. He says he will return incontinent:[64]

---

[60]**Mauritania** Roman name of northwest Africa, supposed land of the Moors.
[61]**determinate** decisive.
[62]**harlotry** courtesan.
[63]**high** quite.
[64]**incontinent** immediately.

He hath commanded me to go to bed,
And bade me to dismiss you.

EMIL.   Dismiss me!

DES. It was his bidding; therefore, good Emilia,
Give me my nightly wearing, and adieu:
We must not now displease him.

EMIL. I would you had never seen him!

DES. So would not I: my love doth so approve him,
That even his stubbornness,[65] his checks,[66] his frowns,—
Prithee, unpin me,—have grace and favour in them.   20

EMIL. I have laid those sheets you bade me on the bed.

DES. All 's one. Good faith, how foolish are our minds!
If I do die before thee, prithee, shroud me
In one of those same sheets.

EMIL.   Come, come, you talk.

DES. My mother had a maid call'd Barbary:
She was in love, and he she lov'd prov'd mad
And did forsake her: she had a song of 'willow';
An old thing 'twas, but it express'd her fortune,
And she died singing it: that song to-night
Will not go from my mind; I have much to do,   30
But to[67] go hang my head all at one side,
And sing it like poor Barbary. Prithee, dispatch.

EMIL. Shall I go fetch your night-gown?[68]

DES.   No, unpin me here.
This Lodovico is a proper man.

EMIL. A very handsome man.

DES. He speaks well.

EMIL. I know a lady in Venice would have walked barefoot to Palestine for a touch of his nether lip.

DES [*Singing*]. The poor soul sat sighing by a sycamore tree,
    Sing all a green willow;   40
  Her hand on her bosom, her head on her knee,
    Sing willow, willow, willow:
  The fresh streams ran by her, and murmur'd her moans;
    Sing willow, willow, willow;
  Her salt tears fell from her, and soft'ned the stones;—
Lay by these:—
[*Singing*] Sing willow, willow, willow;
Prithee, hie thee; he'll come anon:—
[*Singing*] Sing all a green willow must be my garland.

---

[65]**stubbornness** harshness.
[66]**checks** rebukes.
[67]**But to** not to.
[68]**night-gown** dressing gown.

> Let nobody blame him; his scorn I approve,— 50
> Nay, that's not next.—Hark! who is't that knocks?

EMIL. It's the wind.

DES [*Singing*]. I call'd my love false love; but what said he then?
> Sing willow, willow, willow:
> If I court moe women, you'll couch with moe men.—
So, get thee gone; good night. Mine eyes do itch;
Doth that bode weeping?

EMIL.   'Tis neither here nor there.

DES. I have heard it said so. O, these men, these men!
Doet thou in conscience think,—tell me, Emilia,—
That there be women do abuse their husbands 60
In such gross kind?

EMIL.   There be some such, no question.

DES. Wouldst thou do such a deed for all the world?

EMIL. Why, would not you?

DES.   No, by this heavenly light!

EMIL. Nor I neither by this heavenly light; I might do 't as well i'
the dark.

DES. Wouldst thou do such a deed for all the world?

EMIL. The world's a huge thing: it is a great price
For a small vice.

DES. In troth, I think thou wouldst not.

EMIL. In troth, I think I should; and undo 't when I had done. Marry, 70
I would not do such a thing for a joint-ring,[69] nor for measures of lawn, nor for gowns, petticoats, nor caps, nor any petty exhibition;[70] but, for all the whole world,—why, who would not make her husband a cuckold to make him a monarch? I should venture purgatory for 't.

DES. Beshrew me, if I would do such a wrong
For the whole world.

EMIL. Why, the wrong is but a wrong i' the world; and having the
world for your labour, 'tis a wrong in your own world, and you
might quickly make it right. 80

DES. I do not think there is any such woman.

EMIL. Yes, a dozen; and as many to the vantage[71] as would store the
world they played for.
But I do think it is their husbands' faults
If wives do fall: say that they slack their duties,
And pour our treasures into foreign laps,[72]

---

[69]**joint-ring** a ring made in separable halves as a lover's token.
[70]**exhibition** gift, present.
[71]**to the vantage** in addition.
[72]**pour . . . laps** i.e., are unfaithful.

>   Or else break out in peevish jealousies,
>   Throwing restraint upon us; or say they strike us,
>   Or scant our former having in despite;⁷³
>   Why, we have galls,⁷⁴ and though we have some grace,⁷⁵ 90
>   Yet have we some revenge. Let husbands know
>   Their wives have sense like them: they see and smell
>   And have their palates both for sweet and sour,
>   As husbands have. What is it that they do
>   When they change us for others? Is it sport?
>   I think it is: and doth affection breed it?
>   I think it doth: is 't frailty that thus errs?
>   It is so too: and have not we affections,
>   Desires for sport, and frailty, as men have?
>   Then let them use us well: else let them know, 100
>   The ills we do, their ills instruct us so.
>
> DES. Good night, good night: heaven me such uses send,
>   Not to pick bad from bad, but by bad mend!   [*Exeunt.*]

ACT V

SCENE I *Cyprus. A street.*

[*Enter* IAGO *and* RODERIGO.]

IAGO. Here stand behind this bulk;¹ straight will he come:
    Wear thy good rapier bare, and put it home:
    Quick, quick; fear nothing; I'll be at thy elbow:
    It makes us, or it mars us; think on that,
    And fix most firm thy resolution.

ROD. Be near at hand; I may miscarry in 't.

IAGO. Here, at thy hand: be bold, and take thy stand.   [*Retires.*]

ROD. I have no great devotion to the deed;
    And yet he hath given me satisfying reasons:
    'Tis but a man gone. Forth, my sword: he dies.   10

IAGO. I have rubb'd this young quat² almost to the sense,³
    And he grows angry. Now, whether he kill Cassio,
    Or Cassio him, or each do kill the other,
    Every way makes my gain: live Roderigo,
    He calls me to a restitution large
    Of gold and jewels that I bobb'd⁴ from him,
    As gifts to Desdemona;
    It must not be: if Cassio do remain,
    He hath a daily beauty in his life

---

⁷³**scant . . . despite** reduce our allowance to spite us.
⁷⁴**have galls** are capable of resenting injury and insult.
⁷⁵**grace** i.e., to forgive.
¹**bulk** framework projecting from the front of a shop.
²**quat** pimple, pustule; used contemptuously.
³**to the sense** to the quick.
⁴**bobb'd** filched cunningly.

That makes me ugly; and, besides, the Moor 20
May unfold me to him; there stand I in much peril:
No, he must die. But so: I hear him coming.

[*Enter* CASSIO.]

ROD. I know his gait, 'tis he.—Villain, thou diest! [*Makes a pass at* CASSIO.]

CAS. That thrust had been mine enemy indeed,
But that my coat[5] is better than thou know'st:
I will make proof of thine. [*Draws, and wounds* RODERIGO.]

ROD.   O, I am slain!
[IAGO *from behind wounds* CASSIO *in the leg, and exits.*]

CAS. I am maim'd for ever. Help, ho! murder! murder! [*Falls.*]

[*Enter* OTHELLO.]

OTH. The voice of Cassio: Iago keeps his word.

ROD. O, villain that I am!

OTH.   It is even so.

CAS. O, help, ho! light! a surgeon! 30

OTH. 'Tis he:—O brave Iago, honest and just,
That hast such noble sense of thy friend's wrong!
Thou teachest me. Minion, your dear lies dead,
And your unblest fate hies: strumpet, I come.
Forth of my heart those charms, thine eyes, are blotted;
Thy bed, lust-stain'd, shall with lust's blood be spotted.
                                  [*Exit* OTHELLO.]

[*Enter* LODOVICO *and* GRATIANO.]

CAS. What, ho! no watch? no passage?[6] murder! murder!

GRA. 'Tis some mischance; the cry is very direful.

CAS. O, help!

LOD. Hark! 40

ROD. O wretched villain!

LOD. Two or three groan: it is a heavy[7] night;
These may be counterfeits: let 's think 't unsafe
To come in to the cry without more help.

ROD. Nobody come? then shall I bleed to death.

LOD. Hark!

[*Enter* IAGO *with a light.*]

GRA. Here 's one comes in his shirt, with light and weapons.

IAGO. Who 's there? whose noise is this that cries on[8] murder?

---

[5] **coat** coat of mail.
[6] **passage** people passing.
[7] **heavy** thick, cloudy.
[8] **cries on** cries out.

LOD. We do not know.

IAGO. Did not you hear a cry?

CAS. Here, here! for heaven's sake, help me!

IAGO. What 's the matter? 50

GRA. This is Othello's ancient, as I take it.

LOD. The same indeed; a very valiant fellow.

IAGO. What are you here that cry so grievously?

CAS. Iago? O, I am spoil'd, undone by villains!
Give me some help.

IAGO. O me, lieutenant! what villains have done this?

CAS. I think that one of them is hereabout,
And cannot make away.

IAGO. O treacherous villains!
What are you there? come in, and give some help.
[*To* LODOVICO *and* GRATIANO.]

ROD. O, help me here! 60

CAS. That's one of them.

IAGO. O murd'rous slave! O villain! [*Stabs* RODERIGO.]

ROD. O damn'd Iago! O inhuman dog!

IAGO. Kill men i' th' dark!—Where be these bloody thieves?—
How silent in this town!—Ho! murder! murder!—
What[9] may you be? are you of good or evil?

LOD. As you shall prove us, praise us.

IAGO. Signior Lodovico?

LOD. He, sir.

IAGO. I cry you mercy. Here 's Cassio hurt by villains.

GRA. Cassio! 70

IAGO. How is 't, brother!

CAS. My leg is cut in two.

IAGO. Marry, heaven forbid!
Light, gentlemen: I'll bind it with my shirt.
[*Enter* BIANCA.]

BIAN. What is the matter, ho? who is 't that cried?

IAGO. Who is 't that cried?

BIAN. O my dear Cassio! my sweet Cassio!
O Cassio, Cassio, Cassio!

IAGO. O notable strumpet! Cassio, may you suspect
Who they should be that have thus mangled you?

---

[9]**What** who.

CAS. No.   80

GRA. I am sorry to find you thus: I have been to seek you.

IAGO. Lend me a garter. So. O, for a chair,[10]
  To bear him easily hence!

BIAN. Alas, he faints! O Cassio, Cassio, Cassio!

IAGO. Gentlemen all, I do suspect this trash[11]
  To be a party in this injury.
  Patience awhile, good Cassio. Come, come;
  Lend me a light. Know we this face or no?
  Alas, my friend and my dear countryman
  Roderigo! no:—yes, sure:—O heaven! Roderigo.   90

GRA. What, of Venice?

IAGO. Even he, sir: did you know him?

GRA.   Know him! ay.

IAGO. Signior Gratiano? I cry your gentle pardon;
  These bloody accidents must excuse my manners,
  That so neglected you.

GRA.   I am so glad to see you.

IAGO. How do you, Cassio? O, a chair, a chair!

GRA. Roderigo!

IAGO. He, he, 'tis he. [*A chair brought in.*] O, that's well said; the chair.
  Some good man bear him carefully from hence;
  I'll fetch the general's surgeon. [*To* BIANCA] For you, mistress,   100
  Save you your labour. He that lies slain here, Cassio,
  Was my dear friend: what malice was between you?

CAS. None in the world; nor do I know the man.

IAGO [*To* BIANCA.]. What, look you pale? O, bear him out o' th' air.
                    [CASSIO *and* RODERIGO *are borne off.*]
  Stay you, good gentlemen. Look you pale, mistress?
  Do you perceive the gastness[12] of her eye?
  Nay, if you stare, we shall hear more anon.
  Behold her well; I pray you, look upon her:
  Do you see, gentlemen? nay, guiltiness will speak,
  Though tongues were out of use.   110

  [*Enter* EMILIA.]

EMIL. 'Las, what's the matter? what's the matter, husband?

IAGO. Cassio hath here been set on in the dark
  By Roderigo and fellows that are scap'd:
  He's almost slain, and Roderigo dead.

EMIL. Alas, good gentlemen! alas, good Cassio!

---

[10]**chair** sedan chair.
[11]**trash** worthless thing—i.e., Bianca.
[12]**gastness** terror, ghastliness.

IAGO. This is the fruit of whoring. Prithee, Emilia,
   Go know of Cassio where he supp'd to-night.
   [*To* BIANCA] What, do you shake at that?

BIAN. He supp'd at my house; but I therefore shake not.

IAGO. O, did he so? I charge you, go with me.   120

EMIL. Fie, fie upon thee, strumpet!

BIAN. I am no strumpet; but of life as honest
   As you that thus abuse me.

EMIL.   As I! foh! fie upon thee!

IAGO. Kind gentlemen, let 's go see poor Cassio dress'd.
   Come, mistress, you must tell 's another tale.
   Emilia, run you to the citadel,
   And tell my lord and lady what hath happ'd.
   Will you go on afore? [*Aside*] This is the night
   That either makes me or fordoes[13] me quite.   [*Exeunt.*]

SCENE II   *A bedchamber in the castle.*

[*Enter* OTHELLO *with a light;* DESDEMONA *in her bed.*]

OTH. It is the cause, it is the cause,[14] my soul,—
   Let me not name it to you, you chaste stars!—
   It is the cause. Yet I'll not shed her blood;
   Nor scar that whiter skin of hers than snow,
   And smooth as monumental alabaster.
   Yet she must die, else she'll betray more men.
   Put out the light, and then put out the light:
   If I quench thee, thou flaming minister,
   I can again thy former light restore,
   Should I repent me: but once put out thy light,   10
   Thou cunning'st pattern of excelling nature,
   I know not where is that Promethean heat[15]
   That can thy light relume.[16] When I have pluck'd the rose,
   I cannot give it vital growth again,
   It needs must wither: I'll smell thee on the tree.   [*Kissing her.*]
   O balmy breath, that dost almost persuade
   Justice to break her sword! One more, one more.
   Be thus when thou art dead, and I will kill thee,
   And love thee after. One more, and that 's the last:
   So sweet was ne'er so fatal. I must weep,   20
   But they are cruel tears: this sorrow 's heavenly;[17]
   It strikes where it doth love. She wakes.

---

[13]**fordoes** undoes, ruins.

[14]**It is the cause** i.e., the cause of justice on which Othello must act, Desdemona's deed, which is too unmentionable to be named to the chaste stars.

[15]**Promethean heat** divine fire; allusion to the theft of fire from heaven by Prometheus.

[16]**relume** rekindle.

[17]**this . . . heavenly** this tenderness, with which I lament the punishment which justice compels me to inflict, is a holy passion.

DES. Who's there? Othello?

OTH. Ay, Desdemona.

DES. Will you come to bed, my lord?

OTH. Have you pray'd to-night, Desdemon?

DES. Ay, my lord.

OTH. If you bethink yourself of any crime
Unreconcil'd as yet to heaven and grace,
Solicit for it straight.

DES. Alack, my lord, what may you mean by that?

OTH. Well, do it, and be brief; I will walk by: 30
I would not kill thy unprepared spirit;
No; heaven forfend! I would not kill thy soul.

DES. Talk you of killing?

OTH. Ay, I do.

DES. Then heaven
Have mercy on me!

OTH. Amen, with all my heart!

DES. If you say so, I hope you will not kill me.

OTH. Hum!

DES. And yet I fear you; for you 're fatal then
When your eyes roll so: why I should fear I know not,
Since guiltiness I know not; but yet I feel I fear.

OTH. Think on thy sins.

DES. They are loves I bear to you. 40

OTH. Ay, and for that thou diest.

DES. That death's unnatural that kills for loving.
Alas, why gnaw you so your nether lip?
Some bloody passion shakes your very frame:
These are portents; but yet I hope, I hope,
They do not point on me.

OTH. Peace, and be still!

DES. I will so. What's the matter?

OTH. That handkerchief which I so lov'd and gave thee
Thou gav'st to Cassio.

DES. No, by my life and soul!
Send for the man, and ask him.

OTH. Sweet soul, take heed, 50
Take heed of perjury; thou are on thy deathbed.

DES. Ay, but not yet to die.

OTH. Yes, presently:
Therefore confess thee freely of thy sin;
For to deny each article with oath

Cannot remove nor choke the strong conception[18]
That I do groan withal. Thou art to die.

DES. Then Lord have mercy on me!

OTH.   I say, amen.

DES. And have you mercy too! I never did
Offend you in my life; never lov'd Cassio
But with such general warranty of heaven   60
As I might love; I never gave him token.

OTH. By heaven, I saw my handkerchief in 's hand.
O perjur'd woman! thou dost stone[19] my heart,
And makes me call what I intend to do
A murder, which I thought a sacrifice:
I saw the handkerchief.

DES.   He found it then;
I never gave it him: send for him hither;
Let him confess a truth.

OTH.   He hath confess'd.

DES. What, my Lord?

OTH. That he hath us'd thee.

DES.   How? unlawfully?

OTH.   Ay.   70

DES. He will not say so.

OTH.   No, his mouth is stopp'd;
Honest Iago hath ta'en order[20] for 't.

DES. O! my fear interprets: what, is he dead?

OTH. Had all his hairs been lives, my great revenge
Had stomach for them all.

DES. Alas! he is betray'd and I undone.

OTH. Out, strumpet! weep'st thou for him to my face?

DES. O, banish me, my lord, but kill me not!

OTH. Down, strumpet!

DES. Kill me to-morrow: let me live to-night!   80

OTH. Nay, if you strive,—

DES. But half an hour!

OTH.   Being done, there is no pause.[21]

DES. But while I say one prayer!

OTH.   It is too late.   [*Smothers her.*]

---

[18]**conception** plan, intention.
[19]**stone** turn to stone, harden; Othello means that he will be tempted to kill her in sheer anger because of her perjury.
[20]**ta'en order** taken measures.
[21]**Being . . . pause** i.e., when the execution of the deed has once begun, there is no stopping.

EMIL [*at the door*]. My lord, my lord! what, ho! my lord, my lord!

OTH. What noise is this? Not dead? not yet quite dead?
  I that am cruel am yet merciful;
  I would not have thee linger in thy pain:
  So, so.

EMIL [*within.*] What, ho! my lord, my lord!

OTH.   Who's there?

EMIL [*within*]. O, good my lord, I would speak a word with you!   90

OTH. Yes: 'tis Emilia. By and by. She 's dead.
  'Tis like she comes to speak of Cassio's death.—
  The noise was here. Ha! no more moving?
  Still as the grave. Shall she come in? were 't good?—
  I think she stirs again:—no. What 's best to do?
  If she come in, she'll sure speak to my wife.
  My wife! my wife! what wife? I have no wife.
  O, insupportable! O heavy hour!
  Methinks it should be now a huge eclipse
  Of sun and moon, and that th' affrighted globe   100
  Should yawn[22] at alteration.[23]

EMIL.   [*Within*] I do beseech you
  That I may speak with you, O, good my lord!

OTH. I had forgot thee: O, come in, Emilia:
  Soft; by and by. Let me the curtains draw.
  Where art thou?   [*Closes bed-curtains and opens door.*]
  [*Enter* EMILIA.]
              What 's the matter with thee now?

EMIL. O, my good lord, yonder's foul murders done!

OTH. What, now?

EMIL. But now, my lord.

OTH. It is the very error[24] of the moon;
  She comes more nearer earth than she was wont,   110
  And makes men mad.

EMIL. Cassio, my lord, hath kill'd a young Venetian
  Call'd Roderigo.

OTH.   Roderigo kill'd!
  And Cassio kill'd!

EMIL.   No, Cassio is not kill'd.

OTH. Not Cassio kill'd! then murder 's out of tune,
  And sweet revenge grows harsh.

DES. O, falsely, falsely murder'd!

---

[22]**yawn** gape in amazement.
[23]**at alteration** at the change.
[24]**error** irregularity.

EMIL. Alas, what cry is that?

OTH. That! what?

EMIL. Out, and alas! that was my lady's voice.
    Help, help, ho! help. O lady, speak again! 120
    Sweet Desdemona! O sweet mistress, speak!

DES. A guiltless death I die.

EMIL. O, who hath done this deed?

DES. Nobody; I myself. Farewell:
    Commend me to my kind lord: O, farewell! [*Dies.*]

OTH. Why, how should she be murd'red?

EMIL. Alas, who knows?

OTH. You heard her say herself, it was not I.

EMIL. She said so: I must needs report the truth.

OTH. She's, like a liar, gone to burning hell:
    'Twas I that kill'd her.

EMIL. O, the more angel she, 130
    And you the blacker devil!

OTH. She turn'd to folly,[25] and she was a whore.

EMIL. Thou dost belie her, and thou art a devil.

OTH. She was false as water.

EMIL. Thou art rash as fire, to say
    That she was false: O, she was heavenly true!

OTH. Cassio did top her; ask thy husband else.
    O, I were damned beneath all depth in hell,
    But that I did proceed upon just grounds
    To this extremity. Thy husband knew it all.

EMIL. My husband! 140

OTH. Thy husband.

EMIL. That she was false to wedlock?

OTH. Ay, with Cassio. Nay, had she been true,
    If heaven would make me such another world
    Of one entire and perfect chrysolite,[26]
    I'd not have sold her for it.

EMIL. My husband!

OTH. Ay, 'twas he that told me first:
    An honest man he is, and hates the slime
    That sticks on filthy deeds.

EMIL. My husband!

---

[25]**folly** unchastity.
[26]**chrysolite** the golden stone; a name given to various precious stones of green colour.

OTH. What needs this iterance,[27] woman? I say thy husband.   150

EMIL. O mistress, villainy hath made mocks with[28] love!
    My husband say that she was false!

OTH.   He, woman;
    I say thy husband: dost understand the word?
    My friend, thy husband, honest, honest Iago.

EMIL. If he say so, may his pernicious soul
    Rot half a grain a day! he lies to th' heart:
    She was too fond of her most filthy bargain.

OTH. Ha!

EMIL. Do thy worst:
    This deed of thine is no more worthy heaven   160
    Than thou wast worthy her.

OTH.   Peace, you were best.

EMIL. Thou hast not half that power to do me harm
    As I have to be hurt.[29] O gull! O dolt!
    As ignorant as dirt! thou has done a deed—
    I care not for thy sword; I'll make thee known,
    Though I lost twenty lives.—Help! help, ho! help!
    The Moor hath kill'd my mistress! Murder! murder!

[*Enter* MONTANO, GRATIANO, *and* IAGO *with others.*]

MON. What is the matter? How now, general!

EMIL. O, are you come, Iago? you have done well,
    That men must lay their murders on your neck.   170

GRA. What is the matter?

EMIL. Disprove this villain, if thou be'st a man:
    He says thou told'st him that his wife was false:
    I know thou didst not, thou 'rt not such a villain:
    Speak, for my heart is full.

IAGO. I told him what I thought, and told no more
    Than what he found himself was apt[30] and true.

EMIL. But did you ever tell him she was false?

IAGO. I did.

EMIL. You told a lie; an odious, damned lie;   180
    Upon my soul, a lie, a wicked lie.
    She false with Cassio!—did you say with Cassio?

IAGO. With Cassio, mistress. Go to, charm[31] your tongue.

EMIL. I will not charm my tongue; I am bound to speak:
    My mistress here lies murdered in her bed,—

ALL. O heavens forfend!

---

[27]**iterance** iteration, repetition.
[28]**made mocks with** derided, made sport of.
[29]**to be hurt** i.e., to endure hurting.
[30]**apt** natural, likely.
[31]**charm** keep silent.

EMIL. And your reports have set the murder on.

OTH. Nay, stare not, masters: it is true, indeed.

GRA. 'Tis a strange truth.

MON. O monstrous act!

EMIL.   Villainy, villainy, villainy!
   I think upon 't, I think: I smell 't: O villainy—
   I thought so then:[32] I'll kill myself for grief:—
   O villainy, villainy!

IAGO. What, are you mad? I charge you, get you home.

EMIL. Good gentlemen, let me have leave to speak:
   'Tis proper I obey him, but not now.
   Perchance, Iago, I will ne'er go home.

OTH. O! O! O!   [*He falls on the bed.*]

EMIL.   Nay, lay thee down and roar;
   For thou hast kill'd the sweetest innocent
   That e'er did lift up eye.

OTH.   [*Rising*] O, she was foul!
   I scarce did know you, uncle: there lies your niece,
   Whose breath, indeed, these hands have newly stopp'd:
   I know this act shows horrible and grim.

GRA. Poor Desdemon! I am glad thy father 's dead:
   Thy match was mortal to him, and pure grief
   Shore[33] his old thread in twain: did he live now,
   This sight would make him do a desperate turn,
   Yea, curse his better angel from his side,
   And fall to reprobation.[34]

OTH. 'Tis pitiful; but yet Iago knows
   That she with Cassio hath the act of shame
   A thousand times committed; Cassio confess'd it:
   And she did gratify his amorous works
   With that recognizance[35] and pledge of love
   Which I first gave her; I saw it in his hand:
   It was a handkerchief, an antique token
   My father gave my mother.

EMIL. O heaven! O heavenly pow'rs!

IAGO. Come, hold your peace.

EMIL.   'Twill out, 'twill out: I peace!
   No, I will speak as liberal as the north:[36]
   Let heaven and men and devils, let them all,
   All, all, cry shame against me, yet I'll speak.

---

[32]**then** i.e., at some earlier time, probably IV, ii, when she suspected the machinations of *some eternal villain*; she did not, however, know that villain to be Iago until this moment.
[33]**Shore** cut.
[34]**reprobation** damnation, rejection by God.
[35]**recognizance** token.
[36]**liberal as the north** freely as the north wind.

IAGO. Be wise, and get you home.

EMIL.   I will not!   [IAGO *offers to stab* EMILIA.]

GRA.   Fie!
   Your sword upon a woman?

EMIL. O thou dull Moor! that handkerchief thou speak'st of
   I found by fortune[37] and did give my husband;
   For often, with solemn earnestness,
   More than indeed belong'd to such a trifle,
   He begg'd me to steal it.

IAGO.   Villainous whore!

EMIL. She give it Cassio! no, alas! I found it,   230
   And I did give 't my husband.

IAGO.   Filth, thou liest!

EMIL. By heaven, I do not, I do not, gentlemen.
   O murd'rous coxcomb![38] what should such a fool
   Do with so good a wife!

OTH.   Are there no stones in heaven[39]
   But what serves for the thunder?—Precious villain!
              [*He runs at* IAGO: IAGO, *from behind, stabs* EMILIA, *and exits.*]

GRA. The woman falls; sure, he hath kill'd his wife.

EMIL. Ay, ay: O, lay me by my mistress' side.

GRA. He's gone, but his wife's kill'd.

MON. 'Tis a notorious villain. Take you this weapon,
   Which I have here recover'd from the Moor: 240
   Come, guard the door without; let him not pass,
   But kill him rather. I'll after that same villain,
   For 'tis a damned slave.
              [*Exit with all but* OTHELLO *and* EMILIA.]

OTH.   I am not valiant neither,
   But every puny whipster[40] gets my sword:
   But why should honour outlive honesty?[41]
   Let it go all.

EMIL.   What did thy song bode, lady?
   Hark, canst thou hear me? I will play the swan,
   And die in music. [*Singing*] Willow, willow, willow.—
   Moor, she was chaste; she lov'd thee, cruel Moor;
   So come my soul to bliss, as I speak true;   250
   So speaking as I think, I die, I die.   [*Dies.*]

---

[37]**fortune** chance.
[38]**coxcomb** fool; addressed to Othello.
[39]**stones in heaven** thunderbolts. It was supposed that real stones fell with the thunder and caused the damage.
[40]**whipster** contemptible fellow.
[41]**honour outlive honesty** Othello realizes that he has done a shameful deed; he asks why his reputation for valour should endure.

OTH. I have another weapon in this chamber;
   It is a sword of Spain, the ice-brook's temper[42]:—
   O, here it is. Uncle, I must come forth.

GRA [*within*]. If thou attempt it, it will cost thee dear:
   Thou hast no weapon, and perforce must suffer.

OTH. Look in upon me then and speak with me,
   Or, naked[43] as I am, I will assault thee.

[*Enter* GRATIANO.]

GRA. What is the matter?

OTH.   Behold, I have a weapon;
   A better never did itself sustain   260
   Upon a soldier's thigh: I have seen the day,
   That, with this little arm and this good sword,
   I have made my way through more impediments
   Than twenty times your stop:[44] but, O vain boast!
   Who can control his fate? 'tis not so now.
   Be not afraid, though you do see me weapon'd;
   Here is my journey's end, here is my butt,[45]
   And very sea-mark[46] of my utmost sail.
   Do you go back dismay'd? 'tis a lost fear;
   Man[47] but a rush[48] against Othello's breast,   270
   And he retires. Where should Othello go?
   Now, how dost thou look now? O ill-starr'd wench!
   Pale as thy smock! when we shall meet at compt,[49]
   This look of thine will hurl my soul from heaven,
   And fiends will snatch at it. Cold, cold, my girl!
   Even like thy chastity. O cursed, cursed slave!
   Whip me, ye devils,
   From the possession of this heavenly sight!
   Blow me about in winds! roast me in sulphur!
   Wash me in steep-down gulfs of liquid fire!   280
   O Desdemona! Desdemona! dead!
   Oh! Oh!

[*Enter* LODOVICO, CASSIO *carried in a chair*, MONTANO, *and* IAGO, *prisoner, with* OFFICERS.]

LOD. Where is this rash and most unfortunate man?

OTH. That's he that was Othello: here I am.

LOD. Where is that viper? bring the villain forth.

OTH. I look down towards his feet;[50] but that's a fable.

---

[42]**ice-brook's temper** usually defined as "tempered in ice-cold water."
[43]**naked** unarmed.
[44]**stop** power.
[45]**butt** mark for archery, goal, limit.
[46]**sea-mark** beacon (marking his destination or limit).
[47]**Man** provide, as in manning a gun.
[48]**rush** reed.
[49]**compt** account, judgment day.
[50]**towards his feet** i.e., to see if they were cloven like a devil's.

If that thou be'st a devil, I cannot kill thee. [*Wounds* IAGO.]

LOD. Wrench his sword from him.

IAGO. I bleed sir; but not kill'd.

OTH. I am not sorry neither: I 'ld have thee live;
For, in my sense, 'tis happiness to die. 290

LOD. O thou Othello, that wert once so good,
Fall'n in the practice of a damned slave,
What shall be said to thee?

OTH. Why, any thing:
An honourable murderer, if you will;
For nought I did in hate, but all in honour.

LOD. This wretch hath part confess'd his villainy:
Did you and he consent in Cassio's death?

OTH. Ay.

CAS. Dear general, I never gave you cause.

OTH. I do believe it, and I ask your pardon. 300
Will you, I pray, demand that demi-devil
Why he hath thus ensnar'd my soul and body?

IAGO. Demand me nothing: what you know, you know:
From this time forth I never will speak word.

LOD. What, not to pray?

GRA. Torments will ope your lips.

OTH. Well, thou dost best.

LOD. Sir, you shall understand what hath befall'n,
Which, as I think, you know not. Here is a letter
Found in the pocket of the slain Roderigo;
And here another: the one of them imports 310
The death of Cassio to be undertook
By Roderigo.

OTH. O villain!

CAS. Most heathenish and most gross!

LOD. Now here 's another discontented[51] paper,
Found in his pocket too; and this, it seems,
Roderigo meant t' have sent this damned villain;
But that belike Iago in the interim
Came in and satisfied him.

OTH. O thou pernicious caitiff[52]!—
How came you, Cassio, by that handkerchief
That was my wife's?

CAS. I found it in my chamber: 320
And he himself confess'd but even now

---

[51]**discontented** expressing dissatisfaction.
[52]**caitiff** wretch.

> That there he dropp'd it for a special purpose
> Which wrought to his desire.

OTH.   O fool! O fool! fool!

CAS. There is besides in Roderigo's letter,
> How he upbraids Iago, that he made him
> Brave[53] me upon the watch; whereon it came
> That I was cast:[54] and even but now he spake,
> After long seeming dead, Iago hurt him,
> Iago set him on.

LOD. You must forsake this room, and go with us: 330
> Your power and your command is taken off,[55]
> And Cassio rules in Cyprus. For this slave,
> If there be any cunning cruelty
> That can torment him much and hold him long,
> It shall be his. You shall close prisoner rest,
> Till that the nature of your fault be known
> To the Venetian state. Come, bring him away.

OTH. Soft you; a word or two before you go.
> I have done the state some service, and they know 't.
> No more of that. I pray you, in your letters,   340
> When you shall these unlucky deeds relate,
> Speak of me as I am; nothing extenuate,[56]
> Nor set down aught in malice: then must you speak
> Of one that lov'd not wisely but too well;
> Of one not easily jealous, but being wrought,
> Perplex'd[57] in the extreme; of one whose hand,
> Like the base Judean,[58] threw a pearl away
> Richer than all his tribe; of one whose subdu'd eyes,
> Albeit unused to the melting mood,
> Drop tears as fast as the Arabian trees   350
> Their medicinable gum. Set you down this;
> And say besides, that in Aleppo[59] once,
> Where a malignant and a turban'd Turk
> Beat a Venetian and traduc'd the state,
> I took by th' throat the circumcised dog,
> And smote him, thus.   [*Stabs himself.*]

LOD. O bloody period![60]

GRA.   All that is spoke is marr'd.

---

[53]**Brave** defy.
[54]**cast** dismissed.
[55]**taken off** taken away.
[56]**extenuate** diminish, depreciate; the idea is contrasted with the thought of *malice* in the following line.
[57]**Perplex'd** confounded, distracted.
[58]**Judean** infidel or disbeliever.
[59]**Aleppo** a Turkish city where the Venetians had special trading privileges. It is stated that it was immediate death for a Christian to strike a Turk in Aleppo; Othello risked his life for the honour of Venice.
[60]**period** termination, conclusion.

OTH. I kiss'd thee ere I kill'd thee: no way but this;
   Killing myself, to die upon a kiss.   [*Falls on the bed, and dies.*]
CAS. This did I fear, but thought he had no weapon;   360
   For he was great of heart.
LOD.   [*To* IAGO] O Spartan dog,[61]
   More fell than anguish, hunger, or the sea!
   Look on the tragic loading of this bed;
   This is thy work: the object poisons sight;
   Let it be hid. Gratiano, keep the house,
   And seize upon the fortunes of the Moor,
   For they succeed on you. To you, lord governor,
   Remains the censure of this hellish villain;
   The time, the place, the torture: O, enforce it!
   Myself will straight abroad; and to the state   370
   This heavy act with heavy heart relate.   [*Exeunt.*]

                                              (1604)

---

[61]**Spartan dog** Spartan dogs were noted for their savagery.

Anton Chekhov   1860–1904

The Proposal

Translated by Paul Schmidt

CHARACTERS

STEPÁN STEPÁNICH CHUBUKÓV, *a landowner*
NATÁLIA STEPÁNOVNA (NATÁSHA), *his daughter*
IVÁN VASSÍLIEVICH LÓMOV, *their neighbor*

The action takes place in CHUBUKÓV's *farmhouse.*

A room in CHUBUKÓV's *farmhouse. Enter* LÓMOV, *wearing a tailcoat and white gloves.* CHUBUKÓV *goes to meet him.*

CHUBUKÓV. By God, if it isn't my old friend Iván Vassílievich! Glad to see you, boy, glad to see you. (*Shakes his hand*) This is certainly a surprise, and that's a fact. How are you doing?

LÓMOV. Oh, thanks a lot. And how are you? Doing, I mean?

CHUBUKÓV. We get by, my boy, we get by. Glad to know you think of us occasionally and all the rest of it. Have a seat, boy, be my guest, glad you're here, and that's a fact. Don't want to forget your old friends and neighbors, you know. But why so formal, boy? What's the occasion? You're all dressed up and everything—you on your way to a party, or what?

LÓMOV. No, I only came to see you, Stepán Stepánich.

CHUBUKÓV. But why the fancy clothes, boy? You look like you're still celebrating New Year's Eve!

LÓMOV. Well, I'll tell you. (*Takes his arm*) You see, Stepán Stepánich, I hope I'm not disturbing you, but I came to ask you a little favor. This isn't the first time I've, uh, had occasion, as they say, to ask you for help, and I want you to know that I really admire you when I do it. . . . Er, what I mean is . . . Look, you have to excuse me, Stepán Stepánich, this is making me very nervous. I'll just take a little drink of water, if it's all right with you. (*Takes a drink of water*)

CHUBUKÓV (*Aside*). He wants me to lend him some money. I won't. (*To him*) So! What exactly are you here for, hm? A big strong boy like you.

LÓMOV. You see, I really have the greatest respect for you, Stepán Respéctovich—excuse me, I mean Stepán Excúsemevich. What I mean is— I'm really nervous, as you can plainly see. . . . Well, what it all comes down to is this: you're the only person who can give me what I want and I know I don't deserve it of course that goes without saying and I haven't any real right to it either—

CHUBUKÓV. Now, my boy, you don't have to beat about the bush with me. Speak right up. What do you want?

LÓMOV. All right, I will. I will. Well, what I came for is, I came to ask for the hand of your daughter Natásha.

CHUBUKÓV (*Overjoyed*). Oh, mama! Iván Vassílievich, say it again! I don't think I caught that last part!

LÓMOV. I came to ask—

CHUBUKÓV. Lover boy! Buddy boy! I can't tell you how happy I am and everything. And that's a fact. And all the rest of it. (*Gives him a bear hug*) I've always hoped this would happen. It's a longtime dream come true. (*Sheds a tear*) I have always loved you, boy, just like you were my own son, and you know it. God bless you both and all the rest of it. This is a dream come true. But why am I standing here like a big dummy? Happiness has got my tongue, that's what's happened, happiness has got my tongue. Oh, from the bottom of my heart . . . You wait right here, I'll go get Natásha and whatever.

LÓMOV (*Intense concern*). What do you think, Stepán Stepánich? Do you think she'll say yes?

CHUBUKÓV. Big, good-looking fellow like you—how could she help herself? Of course she'll say yes, and that's a fact. She's like a cat in heat. And all the rest of it. Don't go away, I'll be right back. (*Exit*)

LÓMOV. It must be cold in here. I'm starting to shiver, just like I was going to take an exam. The main thing is, you have to make up your mind. You just keep thinking about it, you argue back and forth and talk a lot and wait for the ideal woman or for true love, you'll never get married. Brr . . . it's cold in here. Natásha is a very good housekeeper, she's kind of good-looking, she's been to school . . . What more do I need? I'm starting to get that hum in my ears again; it must be my nerves. (*Drinks some water*) And I can't just *not* get married. First of all, I'm already thirty-five, and that's about what they call the turning point. Second of all, I have to start leading a regular, normal life. There's something wrong with my heart—I've got a *murmur*; I'm always nervous as a tick, and the least little thing can drive me crazy. Like right now, for instance. My lips are starting to shudder, and this little whatsit keeps twitching in my right eyelid. But the worst thing about me is sleep. I mean, I don't. I go to bed, and as soon as I start falling asleep, all of a sudden something in my left side goes *drrrk!* and it pounds right up into my shoulder and my head. . . . I jump out of bed like crazy and walk around for a while and then I lie down again and as soon as I start falling asleep all of a sudden something in my left side goes *drrrk!* And that happens twenty times a night—

(*Enter* NATÁSHA.)

NATÁSHA. Oh, it's you. It's just you, and Papa said go take a look in the other room, somebody wants to sell you something. Oh, well. How are you anyway?

LÓMOV. How do you do, Natásha?

NATÁSHA. You'll have to excuse me, I'm still in my apron. We were shelling peas. How come you haven't been by to see us for so long? Sit down. . . .

(*They both sit.*)

You feel like something to eat?

LÓMOV. No, thanks. I ate already.

NATÁSHA. You smoke? Go ahead if you want to; here's some matches. Beautiful day today, isn't it? And yesterday it was raining so hard the men in the hayfields couldn't do a thing. How many stacks you people got cut so far? You know what happened to me? I got so carried away I had them cut the whole meadow, and now I'm sorry I did—the hay's going to rot. Oh, my! Look at you! What've you got on those fancy clothes for? Well, if you aren't something! You going to a party, or what? You know, you're looking kind of cute these days. . . . Anyway, what are you all dressed up for?

LÓMOV (*A bit nervous*). Well, you see, Natásha . . . well, the fact is I decided to come ask you to . . . to listen to what I have to say. Of course, you'll probably be sort of surprised and maybe get mad, but I . . . (*Aside*) It's awful cold in here.

NATÁSHA. So . . . so what did you come for, huh? (*Pause*) Huh?

LÓMOV. I'll try to make this brief. Now, Natásha, you know, we've known each other for a long time, ever since we were children, and I've had the pleasure of knowing your entire family. My poor dead aunt and her husband—and as you know, I inherited my land from them—they always had the greatest respect for your father and your poor dead mother. The Lómovs and the Chubukóvs have always been on very friendly terms, almost like we were related. And besides—well, you already know this—and besides, your land and mine are right next door to each other. Take my Meadowland, for instance. It lies right alongside of your birch grove.

NATÁSHA. Excuse me. I don't mean to interrupt you, but I think you said "my Meadowland." Are you saying that Meadowland belongs to you?

LÓMOV. Well, yes; as a matter of fact, I am.

NATÁSHA. Well, I never! Meadowland belongs to us, not you!

LÓMOV. No, Natásha. Meadowland is mine.

NATÁSHA. Well, that's news to me. Since when is it yours?

LÓMOV. What do you mean, since when? I'm talking about the little pasture they call Meadowland, the one that makes a wedge between your birch grove and Burnt Swamp.

NATÁSHA. Yes, I know the one you mean. But it's ours.

LÓMOV. Natásha, I think you're making a mistake. That field belongs to me.

NATÁSHA. Iván Vassílich, do you realize what you're saying? And just how long has it belonged to you?

LÓMOV. What do you mean, how long? As far as I know, it's always been mine.

NATÁSHA. Now wait just a minute. Excuse me, but—

LÓMOV. It's all very clearly marked on the deeds, Natásha. Now, it's true there was some argument about it back a ways, but nowadays everybody knows it belongs to me. So there's no use arguing about it. You see, what happened was, my aunt's grandmother let your grandfather's tenants have that field free of charge for an indefinite time in exchange for their making bricks for her. So your grandfather's people used that land for free for about forty years and they started to think it was theirs, but then, when it turned out what the real situation was—

NATÁSHA. My grandfather and my great-grandfather both always said that the land went as far as Burnt Swamp, which means Meadowland belongs to us. So what's the point of arguing about it? I think you're just being rude.

LÓMOV. I can show you the papers, Natálya Stepánovna!

NATÁSHA. Oh, you're just teasing! You're trying to pull my leg! This is all a big joke, isn't it? We've owned that land for going on three hundred years, and all of a sudden you say it doesn't belong to us. Excuse me, Iván Vassílich, excuse me, but I can't believe you said that. And believe me, I don't care one bit about that old meadow: it's only twelve acres, it's not worth three hundred rubles, even, but that's not the point. It's the injustice of it that hurts. And I don't care what anybody says—injustice is something I just can't put up with.

LÓMOV. But you didn't listen to what I was saying! Please! Your grandfather's tenants, as I was trying very politely to point out to you, made bricks for my aunt's grandmother. Now, my aunt's grandmother just wanted to make things easier and—

NATÁSHA. Grandmother, grandfather, father—what difference does it all make? The field belongs to us, and that's that.

LÓMOV. That field belongs to me!

NATÁSHA. That field belongs to us! You can go on about your grandmother until you're blue in the face, you can wear fifteen fancy coats—it still belongs to us! It's ours, ours, ours! I don't want anything that belongs to you, but I do want to keep what's my own, thank you very much!

LÓMOV. Natálya Stepánovna, I don't care about that field either; I don't need that field; I'm talking about the principle of the thing. If you want the field, you can have it. I'll give it to you.

NATÁSHA. If there's any giving to be done, I'll do it! That field belongs to me! Iván Vassílich, I have never gone through anything this crazy in all my life! Up till now I've always thought of you as a good neighbor, a real friend—last year we even lent you our threshing machine, which meant that we were threshing *our* wheat in November—and now all of a sudden you start treating us like Gypsies. *You*'ll give *me* my own field? Excuse me, but that is a pretty unneighborly thing to do. In fact, in my opinion, it's downright insulting!

LÓMOV. So in your opinion I'm some kind of claim jumper, you mean? Look, lady, I have never tried to take anybody else's land, and I'm not going to let anybody try to tell me I did, not even you. (*Runs to the table and takes a drink of water*) Meadowland is mine!

NATÁSHA. You lie! It's ours!

LÓMOV. It's mine!

NATÁSHA. You lie! I'll show you! I'll send my mowers out there today!

LÓMOV. You'll what?

NATÁSHA. I said I'll have my mowers out there today, and they'll hay that field flat!

LÓMOV. You do, and I'll break their necks!

NATÁSHA. You wouldn't dare!

LÓMOV (*Clutches his chest*). Meadowland is mine! You understand? Mine!

NATÁSHA. Please don't shout. You can scream and carry on all you want in your own house, but as long as you're in mine, try to behave like a gentleman.

LÓMOV. I tell you, if I didn't have these murmurs, these awful pains, these veins throbbing in my temples, I wouldn't be talking like this. (*Shouts*) Meadowland is mine!

NATÁSHA. Ours!

LÓMOV. Mine!

NATÁSHA. Ours!

LÓMOV. Mine!

(*Enter* CHUBUKÓV.)

CHUBUKÓV. What's going on? What are you both yelling for?

NATÁSHA. Papa, will you please explain to this gentleman just who owns Meadowland, him or us?

CHUBUKÓV. Lover boy, Meadowland belongs to us.

LÓMOV. I beg your pardon, Stepán Stepánich, how can it belong to you? Think what you're saying! My aunt's grandmother let your grandfather's people have that land to use free of charge, temporarily, and they used that land for forty years and started thinking it was theirs, but it turned out what the problem was—

CHUBUKÓV. Allow me, sweetheart. You're forgetting that the reason those people didn't pay your granny and all the rest of it was because there was *already* a real problem about just who *did* own the meadow. And everything. But nowadays every dog in the village knows it belongs to us, and that's a fact. I don't think you've ever seen the survey map—

LÓMOV. Look, I can prove to you that Meadowland belongs to me!

CHUBUKÓV. No you can't, lover boy.

LÓMOV. I can too!

CHUBUKÓV. Oh, for crying out loud! What are you shouting for? You can't prove anything by shouting, and that's a fact! Look, I am not interested in taking any of your land, and neither am I interested in giving away any of my own. Why should I? And if it comes down to it, lover boy, if you want to make a case out of this, or anything like that, I'd just as soon give it to the peasants as give it to you. So there!

LÓMOV. You're not making any sense. What gives you the right to give away someone else's land?

CHUBUKÓV. I'll be the judge of whether I have the right or not! The fact is, boy, I am not used to being talked to in that tone of voice and all the rest of it. I am twice your age, boy, and I'll ask you to talk to me without getting so excited and whatever.

LÓMOV. No! You think I'm just stupid, and you're making fun of me! You stand there and tell me my own land belongs to you, and then you expect me to be calm about it and talk as if nothing had happened! That's not the way good neighbors behave, Stepán Stepánich! You are not a neighbor, you are a *usurper*!

CHUBUKÓV. I'm a *what*? What did you call me?

NATÁSHA. Papa, you send our mowers out to Meadowland right this very minute!

CHUBUKÓV. You, boy! What did you just call me?

NATÁSHA. Meadowland belongs to us, and I'll never give it up—never, never, never!

LÓMOV. We'll see about that! I'll take you to court, and then we'll see who it belongs to!

CHUBUKÓV. To court! Well, you just go right ahead, boy, you take us to court! I dare you! Oh, now I get it, you were just waiting for a chance to take us to court and all the rest of it! And whatever! It's inbred, isn't it? Your whole family was like that—they couldn't wait to start suing. They were always in court! And that's a fact!

LÓMOV. You leave my family out of this! The Lómovs were all decent, law-abiding citizens, every one of them, not like some people I could name, who were arrested for embezzlement—your uncle, for instance!

CHUBUKÓV. Every single one of the Lómovs was crazy! All of them!

NATÁSHA. All of them! Every single one!

CHUBUKÓV. Your uncle was a falling-down drunk, and that's a fact! And your aunt, the youngest one, she used to run around with an architect! An architect! And that's a fact!

LÓMOV. And your mother was a hunchback! (*Clutches his chest*) Oh, my God, I've got a pain in my side . . . my head's beginning to pound! Oh, my God, give me some water!

CHUBUKÓV. And your father was a gambler and a glutton!

NATÁSHA. And your aunt was a tattletale; she was the worst gossip in town!

LÓMOV. My left leg is paralyzed. . . . And you're a sneak! Oh, my heart! And everybody knows that during the elections, you people . . . I've got spots in front of my eyes. . . . Where's my hat?

NATÁSHA. You're low! And lousy! And cheap!

CHUBUKÓV. You are a lowdown two-faced snake in the grass, and that's a fact! An absolute fact!

LÓMOV. Here's my hat! My heart! How do I get out of here . . . where's the door? I think I'm dying . . . I can't move my leg. (*Heads for the door*)

CHUBUKÓV (*Following him*). And don't you ever set foot in this house again!

NATÁSHA. And you just take us to court! Go ahead, and see what happens!

(*Exit* LÓMOV, *staggering.*)

CHUBUKÓV (*Walks up and down in agitation*). He can go to hell!

NATÁSHA. What a creep! See if I ever trust a neighbor again after this!

CHUBUKÓV. Crook!

NATÁSHA. Creep! He takes over somebody else's land and then has the nerve to threaten them!

CHUBUKÓV. And would you believe that wig-worm, that chicken-brain, had the nerve to come here and propose? Hah? He proposed!

NATÁSHA. He proposed what?

CHUBUKÓV. What? He came here to propose to you!

NATÁSHA. To propose? To me? Why didn't you tell me that before!

CHUBUKÓV. That's why he was all dressed up in that stupid coat! What a silly sausage!

NATÁSHA. Me? He came to propose to me? Oh, my God, my God! (*Collapses into a chair and wails*) Oh, make him come back! Make him come back! Oh, please, make him come back! (*She has hysterics*)

CHUBUKÓV. What's the matter? What's the matter with you? (*Smacks his head*) Oh, my God, what have I done! I ought to shoot myself! I ought to be hanged! I ought to be tortured to death!

NATÁSHA. I think I'm going to die! Make him come back!

CHUBUKÓV. All right! Just stop screaming! Please! (*Runs out*)

NATÁSHA (*Alone, wailing*). What have we done? Oh, make him come back! Make him come back!

CHUBUKÓV (*Reenters*). He's coming, he's coming back and everything, goddamn it! You talk to him yourself this time; I can't. . . . And that's a fact!

NATÁSHA (*Wailing*). Make him come back!

CHUBUKÓV. I just told you, he *is* coming back. Oh, God almighty, what an ungrateful assignment, being the father of a grown-up girl! I'll slit my throat, I swear I'll slit my throat! We yell at the man, we insult him, we chase him away . . . and it's all your fault. It's your fault!

NATÁSHA. No, it's your fault!

CHUBUKÓV. All right, I'm sorry, it's my fault. Or whatever.

(LÓMOV *appears in the doorway.*)

This time you do the talking yourself! (*Exit*)

LÓMOV (*Entering, exhausted*). I'm having a heart murmur, it's awful, my leg is paralyzed . . . my left side is going *drrrk*!

NATÁSHA. You'll have to excuse us, Iván Vassílich—we got a little bit carried away. . . . Anyway, I just remembered, Meadowland belongs to you after all.

LÓMOV. There's something wrong with my heart—it's beating too loud. . . . Meadowland is mine? These little whatsits are twitching in both my eyelids. . . .

NATÁSHA. It's yours—Meadowland is all yours. Here, sit down.

(*They both sit.*)

We made a mistake.

LÓMOV. It was always just the principle of the thing. I don't care about the land, but I do care about the principle of the thing.

NATÁSHA. I know, the principle of the thing. . . . Why don't we talk about something else?

LÓMOV. And besides, I really can prove it. My aunt's grandmother let your grandfather's tenants have that field—

NATÁSHA. That's enough! I think we should change the subject. (*Aside*) I don't know where to start. . . . (*To* LÓMOV) How's the hunting? Are you going hunting any time soon?

LÓMOV. Oh, yes, geese and grouse hunting, Natásha, geese and grouse. I was thinking of going after the harvest is in. Oh, by the way, did I tell you? The worst thing happened to me! You know my old hound Guesser? Well, he went lame on me.

NATÁSHA. Oh, that's terrible! What happened?

LÓMOV. I don't know; he must have dislocated his hip, or maybe he got into a fight with some other dogs and got bit. (*Sighs*) And he was the best hound dog, not to mention how much he cost. I got him from Mirónov, and I paid a hundred and twenty-five for him.

NATÁSHA (*Beat*). Iván Vassílich, you paid too much.

LÓMOV (*Beat*). I thought I got him pretty cheap. He's a real good dog.

NATÁSHA. Papa paid only eighty-five for his hound dog Messer, and Messer is a lot better than your old Guesser!

LÓMOV. Messer is better than Guesser? What do you mean? (*Laughs*) Messer is better than Guesser!

NATÁSHA. Of course he's better! I mean, he's not full grown yet, he's still a pup, but when it comes to a bark and a bite, nobody has a better dog.

LÓMOV. Excuse me, Natásha, but I think you're forgetting something. He's got an underslung jaw, and a dog with an underslung jaw can never be a good retriever.

NATÁSHA. An underslung jaw? That's the first I ever heard of it!

LÓMOV. I'm telling you, his lower jaw is shorter than his upper.

NATÁSHA. What did you do, measure it?

LÓMOV. Of course I measured it! I grant you he's not so bad on point, but you tell him to go fetch, and he can barely—

NATÁSHA. In the first place, our Messer is a purebred from a very good line—he's the son of Pusher and Pisser, so that limp-foot mutt of yours couldn't touch him for breeding. Besides which, your dog is old and ratty and full of fleas—

LÓMOV. He may be old, but I wouldn't take five of your Messers for him. How can you even say that? Guesser is a real hound, and that Messer is a joke, he's not even worth worrying about. Every old fart in the country's got a dog just like your Messer—there's a mess of them everywhere you look! You paid twenty rubles, you paid too much!

NATÁSHA. Iván Vassílich, for some reason you are being perverse on purpose. First you think Meadowland belongs to you, now you think Guesser is better than Messer. I don't think much of a man who doesn't say what he knows to be a fact. You know perfectly well that Messer is a hundred times better than that . . . that dumb Guesser of yours. So why do you keep saying the opposite?

LÓMOV. You must think I'm either blind or stupid! Can't you understand that your Messer has an underslung jaw?

NATÁSHA. It's not true!

LÓMOV. He has an underslung jaw!

NATÁSHA (*Shouting*). It's not true!

LÓMOV. What are you shouting for?

NATÁSHA. What are you lying for? I can't stand any more of this. You ought to be getting ready to put your old Guesser out of his misery, and here you are comparing him to our Messer!

LÓMOV. You'll have to excuse me, I can't go on with this conversation. I'm having a heart murmur.

NATÁSHA. This just goes to prove what I've always known: the hunters who talk the most are the ones who know the least.

LÓMOV. Will you please do me a favor and just shut up. . . . My heart is starting to pound. . . . (*Shouts*) Shut up!

NATÁSHA. I will not shut up until you admit that Messer is a hundred times better than Guesser!

LÓMOV. He's a hundred times worse! I hope he croaks, your Messer. . . . My head . . . my eyes . . . my shoulders . . .

NATÁSHA. And your dumb old Guesser doesn't need to croak—he's dead already!

LÓMOV. Shut up! (*Starts to cry*) I'm having a heart attack!

NATÁSHA. I will not shut up!

(*Enter* CHUBUKÓV.)

CHUBUKÓV. Now what's the matter?

NATÁSHA. Papa, will you please tell us frankly, on your honor, who's a better dog: Guesser or Messer?

LÓMOV. Stepán Stepánich, I just want to know one thing: does your Messer have an underslung jaw or doesn't he? Yes or no?

CHUBUKÓV. Well? So what if he does? What difference does it make? Anyway, there isn't a better dog in the whole county, and that's a fact.

LÓMOV. But don't you think my Guesser is better? On your honor!

CHUBUKÓV. Now, loverboy, don't get all upset; just wait a minute. Please. Your Guesser has his good points and whatever. He's a thoroughbred, got a good stance, nice round hindquarters, all the rest of it. But that dog, if you really want to know, boy, has got two vital defects: he's old and he's got a short bite.

LÓMOV. You'll have to excuse me, I'm having another heart murmur. Let's just look at the facts, shall we? All I'd like you to do is just think back to that time at the field trials when my Guesser kept up with the count's dog Fresser. They were going ear to ear, and your Messer was a whole half mile behind.

CHUBUKÓV. He was behind because one of the count's men whopped him with his whip!

LÓMOV. That's not the point! All the other dogs were after the fox, and your Messer was chasing a sheep!

CHUBUKÓV. That's not true! Now listen, boy, I have a very quick temper, as you very well know, and that's a fact, so I think we should keep this discussion very short. He whopped him because none of the rest of you can stand watching other people's dogs perform! You're all rotten with envy! Even you, buddy boy, even you! The fact is, all somebody has to do is point out that somebody's dog is better than your Guesser, and right away you start in with this and that and all the rest of it. I happen to remember exactly what happened!

LÓMOV. And I remember too!

CHUBUKÓV (*Mimics him*). "And I remember too!" What do you remember?

LÓMOV. My heart murmur . . . My leg is paralyzed . . . I can't move . . .

NATÁSHA (*Mimics him*). "My heart murmur!" What kind of hunter are you? You'd do better in the kitchen catching cockroaches instead of out hunting foxes! A heart murmur!

CHUBUKÓV. She's right—what kind of hunter are you? You and your heart murmur should stay home instead of galloping cross-country, and that's a fact. You say you like to hunt; all you really want to do is ride around arguing and interfering with other people's dogs and whatever. You are *not*, and that's a fact, a hunter.

LÓMOV. And what makes you think you're a hunter? The only reason you go hunting is so you can get in good with the count! My heart! You're a sneak!

CHUBUKÓV. I'm a what? A sneak! (*Shouts*) Shut up!

LÓMOV. A sneak!

CHUBUKÓV. You young whippersnapper! You puppy!

LÓMOV. You rat! You rickety old rat!

CHUBUKÓV. You shut up, or I'll give you a tailful of buckshot! You snoop!

LÓMOV. Everybody knows your poor dead wife—oh, my heart!—used to beat you. My legs . . . my head . . . I see spots . . . I'm going to faint, I'm going to faint!

CHUBUKÓV. And everyone knows your housekeeper has you tied to her apron strings!

LÓMOV. Wait wait wait . . . here it comes! A heart attack! My shoulder just came undone—where's my shoulder? I'm going to die! (*Collapses into a chair*) Get a doctor! (*Faints*)

CHUBUKÓV. Whippersnapper! Milk sucker! Snoop! You make me sick! (*Drinks some water*) Sick!

NATÁSHA. What kind of a hunter are you? You can't even ride a horse! (*To* CHUBUKÓV) Papa! What's the matter with him? Papa! Look at him, Papa! (*Screeching*) Iván Vassílich! He's dead!

LÓMOV. I'm sick! I can't breathe . . . give me some air!

NATÁSHA. He's dead! (*Shakes* LÓMOV's *shoulders*) Iván Vassílich! Iván Vassílich! What have we done? He's dead! (*Collapses into the other chair*) Get a doctor! Get a doctor! (*She has hysterics*)

CHUBUKÓV. Oh, now what? What's the matter with you?

NATÁSHA (*Wailing*). He's dead! He's dead!

CHUBUKÓV. Who's dead? (*Looks at* LÓMOV) Oh, my God, he *is* dead! Oh, my God! Get some water! Get a doctor! (*Puts glass to* LÓMOV's *mouth*) Here, drink this.... He's not drinking it.... That means he's really dead ... and everything! Oh, what a mess! I'll kill myself! I'll kill myself! Why did I wait so long to kill myself? What am I waiting for right now? Give me a knife! Lend me a gun! (LÓMOV *stirs*) I think he's going to live! Here, drink some water. That's the way.

LÓMOV. Spots ... everything is all spots ... it's all cloudy.... Where am I?

CHUBUKÓV. Just get married as soon as you can and then get out of here! She says yes! (*Joins* LÓMOV's *and* NATÁSHA's *hands*) She says yes and all the rest of it. I give you both my blessing and whatever. Only please just leave me in peace!

LÓMOV. Huh? Wha'? (*Starts to get up*) Who?

CHUBUKÓV. She says yes! All right? go ahead and kiss her.... And then get the hell out of here!

NATÁSHA (*Moaning*). He's alive.... Yes, yes, I say yes....

CHUBUKÓV. Go ahead, give him a kiss.

LÓMOV. Huh? Who?

(NATÁSHA *kisses him.*)

Oh, that's very nice.... Excuse me, but what's happening? Oh, yes, I remember now.... My heart ... those spots ... I'm so happy, Natásha! (*Kisses her hand*) My leg is still paralyzed....

NATÁSHA. I'm ... I'm very happy too.

CHUBUKÓV. And I'm getting a weight off my shoulders. Oof!

NATÁSHA. But all the same—you can admit it now, can't you?—Messer is better than Guesser.

LÓMOV. He's worse!

NATÁSHA. He's better!

CHUBUKÓV. And they lived happily ever after! Bring on the champagne!

LÓMOV. He's worse!

NATÁSHA. Better! Better! Better!

CHUBUKÓV (*Tries to make himself heard*). Champagne! Bring on the champagne!

CURTAIN.

(1889)

Daniel David Moses   b. 1952

Almighty Voice and His Wife

CHARACTERS

ALMIGHTY VOICE *At first a young Cree man, early twenties, Kisse-Manitou-Wayou, also known as Jean Baptiste, later his own playful* GHOST.

WHITE GIRL *At first a young Cree woman, early teens, the daughter of Old Dust and the wife of Almighty Voice, later the* INTERLOCUTOR.

The action of Act One incorporates historic events and happens between the end of October 1895 and May of 1897 on the Saskatchewan prairie at, and between, the One Arrow and Fort A La Corne reserves. Act Two occurs on the auditorium stage of the abandoned industrial school at Duck Lake.

ACT I

A projected title: "Act One: Running with the Moon".

SCENE I

The projected title: "Scene One: Her Vision". A drum beats in night's blue darkness. The full moon sweeps down from the sky like a spotlight to show and surround WHITE GIRL *asleep, in a fetal position on the ground. The drum begins a sneak-up beat, the moon pulses in a similar rhythm.* WHITE GIRL *wakes at the quake, gets to her feet, and takes a step. The drum hesitates. A gun shot and a slanting bolt of light stop her and block out the moon. Three more shots and slanting bolts of light come in quick succession, confining her in a spectral tipi. She peers out through its skin of light at* ALMIGHTY VOICE, *a silhouette against the moon. He collapses to the beats of the drum, echoes of the gun shots.* WHITE GIRL *falls to her knees as the tipi fades and the moon bleeds.*

SCENE II

The projected title: "Scene Two: The Proposal". WHITE GIRL *is by the fire, stripping meat for drying.* ALMIGHTY VOICE *loiters at a distance.*

VOICE. Hiya. Hiya. Hey girl, I said "Hiya."

GIRL. I heard you the first time. I'm working here.

VOICE. Oh ya?

GIRL. I am. And my Dad doesn't like it, you talking to me.

VOICE. Old Dust? What's he got to worry about? He's winning over there. I'm just talking.

GIRL. It's not your talking he's worried about.

VOICE. What you talking about?

GIRL. You never mind.

VOICE. What you talking about, girl? Hey White Girl, what you talking about?

GIRL. My Dad says you already got a wife.

VOICE. What's that got to do with anything?

GIRL. I hear you already had two others.

VOICE. You don't have to believe everything you hear. White Girl, you know something? I think you got pretty eyes.

GIRL. I got no time to be told my eyes are pretty.

VOICE. You're pretty fierce for a little girl.

GIRL. You should leave little girls alone, Almighty Voice.

VOICE. You're not that little, little girl.

GIRL. I'm working here.

VOICE. You're big enough.

GIRL. Go away.

VOICE. Is that the way they do it at that school? That's not the way my mother does it.

GIRL. Spotted Calf doesn't know every thing.

VOICE. She knows how to strip meat. Here let me—

GIRL. You could get cut.

VOICE. You're pretty fierce all right, little girl. You are like Spotted Calf.

GIRL. What?

VOICE. My mother's not as pretty as you.

GIRL. Go bother my brother for a while.

VOICE. But he's not as pretty as you.

GIRL. Sure he is. He's my brother. You know what?

VOICE. What is it, White Girl?

GIRL. My brother, Young Dust, he likes you.

VOICE. He's my friend.

GIRL. No, Almighty Voice, he likes you. He thinks you are the pretty one. Your wife won't kiss you? Well, my brother will.

VOICE. You're a crazy one.

GIRL. You're right. I am a crazy one. As long as you know. But my brother does want to kiss—

VOICE. I don't want to talk about your brother.

GIRL. Look, he's coming this way.

VOICE. What? No he's not.

GIRL. But Young Dust does like you.

VOICE. And I like you.

GIRL. I'm just a little girl, Almighty Voice.

VOICE. A little girl working away.

GIRL. You could get cut.

VOICE. I want to kiss you, White Girl.

GIRL. My father's looking at you. He sees you talking to me.

VOICE. Let him.

GIRL. You got to talk to him first, you know.

VOICE. I don't want to break that hand game up. All right, I'll go talk to him first.

GIRL. Then we'll talk.

VOICE. Just talk? What will we talk about?

GIRL. The wife you have now.

VOICE. What wife?

GIRL. The Rump's Daughter.

VOICE. Oh ya.

GIRL. You're going to send her home to her father.

VOICE. She won't go.

GIRL. She will go. I'm going to be your wife now. Your only wife. You can't feed us both. Well then, my father's waiting to talk to you. Go on.

VOICE. Crazy.

SCENE III

A projected title: "Scene Three: The Wedding Night". A second fire in night's blue. A gunshot and a slanting bolt of light. The reverberations become a social dance beat on a drum and bring up the rest of the tipi of light. WHITE GIRL *enters it and sits. Then* ALMIGHTY VOICE *enters. The drum and tipi fade.*

VOICE. Hiya, wife. I said "Hiya, wife."

GIRL. What can I do for my husband?

VOICE. Come here. Look at me. Leave that be.

GIRL. Does my husband want some tea?

VOICE. Your husband wants his blanket.

GIRL. There. Your blanket's ready for you. It's snowing out. Shall I go for wood to build the fire up?

VOICE. Can't you be quiet, girl?

GIRL. Shall I tell your friends to be quiet? Shall I tell them to go away?

VOICE. They'll go when they're full.

GIRL. Do you want more to eat, husband? I'll go get some more.

VOICE. Stay here with me. Look at me, White Girl.

GIRL. That was a wonderful cow you brought for the feast. It was so fat.

VOICE. You didn't eat much.

GIRL. I'm stuffed full. I have never eaten so well before, husband. Now my father will have to admit his daughter is well fed. You are such a hunter.

VOICE. It was only a stupid cow. What's wrong, White Girl?

GIRL. I was thinking about my mother. She would have made him come. And your father. How could the Mounties take him? The day before our wedding.

VOICE. They're stupid. Look at me, wife.

GIRL. I don't want to be a wife. I don't want to be a woman. That school—I don't know how. I'm only thirteen. I'm crazy.

VOICE. You're not crazy.

GIRL. I am. I am.

VOICE. Come here. Let me hold you.

GIRL. No, it's too dangerous.

VOICE. It's not dangerous. Hey come on, pretend I'm your brother.

GIRL. No, you're my husband. I don't want you to die.

VOICE. You're not going to kill me. You're going to kiss me.

GIRL. I have bad medicine in me. I went to that school. The treaty agent took me.

VOICE. But you got away, girl.

GIRL. School's a strange place. All made out of stone. The wind tries to get in, and can't, and cries. It's so hot and dry, your throat gets sore. You cough a lot, too. I used to even cough blood. And they won't let you talk. They try to make you talk like they do. It's like stones in your mouth.

VOICE. You're here now.

GIRL. I liked it there.

VOICE. How could you like that?

GIRL. They said I could live there forever.

VOICE. What are you talking about?

GIRL. They said everybody at home had died of the small pox. They said I could live forever but I had to marry their God.

VOICE. Hey, you're my wife now and I'm alive. Everybody's alive.

GIRL. He's going to kill you. He's a jealous god.

VOICE. He's another one of their lies.

GIRL. They say he's everywhere. He can see everything.

VOICE. He's got nothing better to do than watch us?

GIRL. They say he's like a ghost.

VOICE. Hey little girl, even your Dad didn't know for sure about us and he watched you like a hawk.

GIRL. Or a white bird. They say he's like a white bird.

VOICE. A white bird? A white bird in here?

GIRL. He made the small pox.
VOICE. Let's get that bird out of here! Where is it?
GIRL. You crazy, he'll kill you.
VOICE. Hey, little girl, I found it! (*he mocks flatulence*)
GIRL. Stop that. You're crazy.
VOICE. Oh ya? Both of us? Made for each other. (*he kisses and caresses her*) Little girl, my White Girl.
GIRL. Wait husband, wait. I'm afraid.
VOICE. Don't be. I'm brave now I got you for my wife.
GIRL. But I'm afraid.
VOICE. What is it now, girl?
GIRL. It's the bad medicine. They gave me another name when I married their god.
VOICE. Shut up about their god! I don't want to hear it!
GIRL. They called me Marrie. It's the name of their god's mother.
VOICE. What's wrong with White Girl? White Girl's a good name. They're so stupid. That agent has to call me John Baptist so I can get my treaty money.
GIRL. John Baptist. That's the name of one of their ghosts.
VOICE. I'm no ghost. I'm Almighty Voice. Why can't they say Almighty Voice?
GIRL. I'll call you John Baptist too.
VOICE. You're not the agent! You're my wife.
GIRL. It's so he'll kill the ghost instead of you, husband. That god won't know it's us if we use their names.
VOICE. So I have to call my wife Marrie?
GIRL. Yes. Their god won't be able to touch us. Just call me Marrie.
VOICE. My crazy White Girl.
GIRL. Call me Marrie, husband.
VOICE. Marrie. Marrie, will you kiss me now?
GIRL. Yes, husband.
   They kiss, caress, and begin to undress.
VOICE. Crazy Marrie.
GIRL. John Baptist.
VOICE. My little girl.

SCENE IV

The Projected Title: "Scene Four: Flight". A drum beats in darkness. WHITE GIRL *pretends to sleep by the second fire.* ALMIGHTY VOICE *enters at a run, drops to his knees. The drum fades.*

VOICE. White Girl, wake up.
GIRL. Go away. I'm sleeping here.

VOICE. Where's my Winchester?

GIRL. How should I know?

VOICE. Did my mother take it?

GIRL. Where have you been?

VOICE. I'll be right back.

GIRL. Have you been with the Rump's Daughter?

VOICE. I got to get my Winchester.

GIRL. Have you been with the Rump's Daughter?

VOICE. I'll go wake my mother.

GIRL. Answer me!

VOICE. What?

GIRL. I'm your wife now. Your only wife.

VOICE. White Girl, I was with your brother.

GIRL. You weren't with the Rump's Daughter?

VOICE. We were in jail.

GIRL. Jail?

VOICE. That Sergeant over at Duck Lake, he threw us in the guard house.

GIRL. But you went for treaty money.

VOICE. Well the Sergeant has it now. Somebody told them that cow I shot belonged to somebody.

GIRL. You're all wet. Here. Get warm.

VOICE. Hey girl, I been swimming.

GIRL. You got away.

VOICE. In the freezing Saskatchewan.

GIRL. What about Young Dust?

VOICE. He said it was warm there.

GIRL. You shouldn't have left him there. They threw you in jail for killing that cow.

VOICE. That cow belonged to the Great White Mother. This halfbreed told me the guard said no way would I rot in jail like my dirty chief of a father. The Guard said I'd hang for killing that cow!

GIRL. But that's crazy. They don't hang people over meat.

VOICE. I'm not going back to that guard house, White Girl.

GIRL. They can't take you there.

VOICE. They always come after you. My Dad's in jail at Prince Albert over the pieces of a plough. He hates their stupid farming, this stupid reserve. They even turn the prairie into a jail.

GIRL. They can't put the wind in prison.

VOICE. Sounding Sky used to mean warrior. Now it's hard labour.

GIRL. Here. Dry yourself. Get warm.

VOICE. But I got to go get my Winchester.

GIRL. You rest while I find you your Winchester. They can't cross the river so quick. And you need to take some of that beef with you.

VOICE. They'll catch me with it.

GIRL. You got to eat. And the Mounties aren't going to catch us.

VOICE. But you can't come.

GIRL. I'm coming with my husband.

VOICE. You'll slow me down.

GIRL. No I won't.

VOICE. But there's snow coming.

GIRL. Better for us. Two can be warmer than one. You know that. Lie down. Lie down, John Baptist. I'll get your Winchester.

VOICE. But White Girl, crazy one—

GIRL. Lie down, John Baptist, rest. I'll be ready soon. No, rest. Listen, John Baptist, I'm a better shot than your mother Spotted Calf. I got better eyes.

VOICE. This is crazy, girl.

GIRL. Both of us. Remember?

SCENE V

The projected title: "Scene Five: The Killing". ALMIGHTY VOICE *and* WHITE GIRL *sit by the third fire. A drifting beat comes and goes on the drum.*

GIRL. It's all gone. The beef's all gone.

VOICE. I don't really like beef.

GIRL. What's wrong? I didn't burn it.

VOICE. No. Cattle aren't like real meat. They're stupid.

GIRL. They're not buffalo.

VOICE. That's for sure. They don't taste right.

GIRL. I like it. It makes me feel full.

VOICE. I'll get something else soon. My wife's not going hungry.

GIRL. It's good to be hungry.

VOICE. It's better to be full.

GIRL. It reminds you you're alive. That's what my mother used to say.

VOICE. What's wrong?

GIRL. Young Dust said the snow was too deep. The treaty agent wouldn't send the supplies out. Last winter. My mother wouldn't eat. She wouldn't eat. While I was away at that school. She used to like the way I cook.

VOICE. I do too, White Girl.

GIRL. I would have cooked for her.

VOICE. Cook for me now, White Girl.

GIRL. I didn't really want to be there. We had to eat this mush made out of grass seeds.

VOICE. No meat?

GIRL. Mush.

VOICE. How about some tea then? It's hot enough. It'll make you feel full.

GIRL. That's all there is.

VOICE. Can we go see your father now? He likes his tea. He always has sugar.

GIRL. The ice was almost too thick this morning. I was afraid we'd have to melt snow.

VOICE. We better go soon.

GIRL. Snow takes too long.

VOICE. That Sergeant's not as stupid as he looks. He'll see we doubled back.

GIRL. Do you know what glass is? Like thin ice?

VOICE. What are you talking about, White Girl?

GIRL. Some of the walls at the school were made out of it.

VOICE. Made out of what?

GIRL. Glass. A wall you can see through. I didn't know it was there at first, the wall. I tried to crawl through. I saw the sky, the grass moving. Out there. I banged my face. The glass broke. Sharp pieces, too. That's what this is from.

VOICE. A place to kiss.

GIRL. You know what, John Baptist? I dreamed about you. I knew you would come.

VOICE. What's the matter?

GIRL. I was looking at you far away. Through a glass wall!

VOICE. The soldiers, they have these clear beads they look through. Far away comes real close. All the walking in between seems to disappear.

GIRL. It was like that. It was. But it was also like I was waiting in my father's tipi. I could see you coming, I saw the moonlight on the barrel of your Winchester.

VOICE. I was bringing meat, I bet, buffalo meat for my wife.

GIRL. No you weren't. No! Let go.

VOICE. What's the matter, White Girl?

GIRL. You shot and the tipi broke. All the sharp pieces fell down on you, worse than hail. I think it hurt you, I think you got hurt.

VOICE. Stop it, White Girl, stop it. Don't be afraid. I'm all right.

GIRL. That god. That god. I'm afraid.

VOICE. That stupid god can't hurt me. That god belongs in that place, in the school. You're here now, I'm here now. He's not.

GIRL. He's everywhere!

VOICE. I told you he's a lie.

GIRL. He's like the glass. He's hard. He cuts you down.

VOICE. I'm your husband now. I won't let him hurt you. He doesn't deserve you.

GIRL. I'm sorry. I'm sorry.

VOICE. Listen, crazy one. You married Almighty Voice, who's not afraid to say his name. Let your glass god hear it. Almighty Voice!—who has listened to our fathers and heard what they say. Almighty Voice who remembers our Creator and our people's ways. Almighty Voice knows how to fight for you. Do you hear what I'm saying? Do you?

GIRL. Yes. Yes, I do.

VOICE. Who is saying it?

GIRL. Almighty Voice.

VOICE. Remember who you are. Remember what your mother taught you.

GIRL. Almighty Voice, the husband of White Girl!

VOICE. I'll break your glass god for you.

GIRL. Keep your bad medicine!

VOICE. It's just a bad smell. A stink. Come on. I'll get the horse. Your father has the tea ready for us.

GIRL. Husband, look!

VOICE. Give me my Winchester. My wife'll have rabbit for breakfast.

He loads and exits. WHITE GIRL *watches him go, then builds up the fire. She hears a noise from another direction and looks and stops. A shot. She runs toward the place where* ALMIGHTY VOICE *exited. He enters, dead rabbit in hand.*

VOICE. (*laughing*) Look how fat! This'll make you full.

GIRL. Husband, be quiet.

ALMIGHTY VOICE *drops the rabbit.*

GIRL. It's the god. See his glass eye.

VOICE. It's the Sergeant, White Girl. Just the stupid Sergeant. What's he say?

GIRL. I can't understand him.

VOICE. That's that stupid halfbreed with him. Stay behind me, girl.

GIRL. He wants to make peace. There's the sign.

VOICE. Get down. He's got a gun.

GIRL. Where's the halfbreed going?

VOICE. Stay where you are!

GIRL. What about the horse?

VOICE. No time. Stay there! Where's the other one?

GIRL. I can't see. Over there.

VOICE. Circling around. Don't come any closer. (*he reloads his Winchester*)

GIRL. Leave us alone! Go away!

VOICE. I'm warning you!

GIRL. Husband—

VOICE. This gun's loaded!

GIRL. —the halfbreed's behind us.

VOICE. Keep close. I'm warning you! Stop there! Stay there! (*shooting*) You stupid!

GIRL. One shot. One shot, Almighty Voice!

VOICE. The other one?

GIRL. I told you glass breaks.

VOICE. Gone. Scared his horse, too. He'll bring more Mounties. There will be more from now on.

GIRL. Glass breaks so easily.

VOICE. Wife, look at me.

GIRL. I'm all right, husband.

VOICE. Come on.

GIRL. No. There will be more from now on. I'll slow you down.

VOICE. I can't leave you, girl.

GIRL. They won't hurt me. They'll be afraid to now.

VOICE. White Girl, look at me.

GIRL. They'll have to take me home. I'll tell everyone how it happened, how he wouldn't listen. They'll just take me home. I'll just slow them down. We can meet at my mother's—I mean your mother's house. My mother's gone. She died of hunger last winter. But I'm all right, Almighty Voice. And I know I have to go talk to your mother soon.

VOICE. What about?

GIRL. I want us to make her a grandchild. She has to tell me how to get ready. Women's stuff. I know I have to eat. (*she goes and picks up the rabbit*) You better go now.

ALMIGHTY VOICE *exits*. WHITE GIRL *takes the rabbit to the fire.*

SCENE VI

The projected title: "Scene Six: Mid-Winter Moon". A martial beat on the drum as the bloody moon rises. Then silence. WHITE GIRL *sits near the second fire while* ALMIGHTY VOICE *wanders between the fires.*

GIRL. Mister. Mister! Mister God! I see your glass eye. Eye-eye! Stinky breath. It's me. Marrie! Marrie, your wife. Wife wife wife! God, look at me like before. How they taught me at school. How how. Here's my hair. Look. Here's my skin. How how, husband god, see what a little girl I am. Great husband god, see what a little girl I am. Great White God of the ghost men, mother is here. Blood blood blood between my thighs. Yes, gimme, gimme, gimme something sweet. Oh yes, yes, you're rotten, rotten meat, but wifey wife will eat you up. Mister God, god, stupid god, this is what you want!

Come on! Come on, don't leave! I'm your little squaw. Eye-eye! See! Eye-eye, Mister God. Eye-eye!

VOICE. Don't talk, cousin. You're being stupid. No one would mistake you for a warrior. And your woman, she's so skinny, no one would call you a hunter either. Or a lover. Could your woman do what my woman has? Could she look those white men in the eyes? They took her back to Duck Lake and kept her in that guard house and she gave them lies for their lies. "Run, husband. We will meet later." She said that to me. Is it a surprise I think about her? I believe what she says. If she is crazy, we all should be. Not a word, Little Salteau! Who's the one who killed a Mountie?

GIRL. I am the wife of Almighty Voice. You don't know my name. You don't even wonder if I have one. I'm only a crazy squaw. You're watching me but you expect to see my husband. His is a name you know. Almighty Voice. John Baptist. You say these names of his over and over again, like the prayers you say to your glass-eyed god for the grace of your Great White Mother Victoria. But your prayers won't make him come. Mister God Mountie, you don't know what his name means.

VOICE. Your sister, Young Dust, she makes me remember how my father used to talk about the buffalo. Maybe because she likes meat so much. I'd like to feed her till she's fat. My father said everyone used to be like that. Everyone used to follow the buffalo. He hates farming. A man shouldn't be a bag of bones. My mother says he gets no meat. In Prince Albert. John Sounding Sky is in jail because his son mistook a Mountie for a cow!

GIRL. You're laughing with that halfbreed. "Let the crazy squaw go home. Easy to keep an eye on her there." So he unlocks the door, walks away to the fire where you play with your silver coin, your dollar. That's what you want to trade my husband's blood for. Why? What is its power? A coin is not the moon. Can't you see it's dead, Mister Mountie? Cold as the bullet my husband kills rabbits or enemies with.

VOICE. So my mother Spotted Calf is alone still, running things, hating it. She says there are too many women now. I think there aren't enough men. It's like a war but no one will say so, so there's never any peace. How many of our brothers are there still in Stoney Mountain? How many come home in the spring? My mother says it makes her children crazy, living on snow. Maybe she's right. Come on. Let's go make some blood flow tonight!

GIRL. You've got a bad look on your face, a blindness, a glassy gaze. What are you staring at? Your silver dollar? The fire? My husband's bullet. You'll stare 'til they all turn to glass. And what will you see through them then? That forever place you want to live, the one they promised me in school? I turn here in the wind toward the river and the moon is there, a woman with better things to do. She slips away from you, going home.

SCENE VII

The projected title: "Scene Seven: Honeymoon". The drum beats. The full moon sweeps down from the sky like a spotlight to show and surround the lovers, lying together on the ground.

GIRL. Almighty Voice, come on.

VOICE. Not again.

GIRL. I want to be sure.

VOICE. Let me sleep.

GIRL. This is the time to do it. Your mother said so.

VOICE. I don't want to know that. I don't want to do it for my mother.

GIRL. Do it for me. It's the best time now.

VOICE. I don't want to know that stuff.

GIRL. Young Dust dreamed we had a son.

VOICE. This is none of your brother's business.

GIRL. Come on, John Baptist.

VOICE. White Girl, we got to sleep.

GIRL. Almighty Voice, do you like my hand there?

VOICE. Don't. You keep this up, we'll fall asleep on the horse later.

GIRL. You fall off, you can fall on me.

VOICE. White Girl, we got to move on tonight. Little Salteau said those stupid Mounties are just south of here.

GIRL. They're hunting quail, not us. I like it here. I like how flat it is. Like your belly.

VOICE. White Girl, stop it.

GIRL. Come on, Almighty Voice.

VOICE. Do as your husband says. And don't laugh.

GIRL. The Mounties don't know we're here. Why worry?

VOICE. Go to sleep.

GIRL. They'll forget about you.

VOICE. I killed a Mountie. They don't give up.

GIRL. But he would have killed you.

VOICE. I know.

GIRL. Spring comes, the snow goes. Too many other things to do. Cows running away through the grass. Fresh meat, husband.

VOICE. Can't you be quiet, girl?

GIRL. Isn't this grass moving in the wind here on your flat prairie?

VOICE. I'm your husband, White Girl.

GIRL. Oh your wife likes to run in the grass, Almighty Voice.

VOICE. Stop it. Go to sleep.

GIRL. They can't see you as long as you're with me.

VOICE. We can't hide in that grass, little girl.

GIRL. We can hide. With me you're in the dark of the moon. It's what your mother talks about. When we're together, it's like we're inside a bead of glass made of wind. They can't get at us. It's my medicine, husband. In the dream—you were in the dream. That's all I can tell you.

VOICE. You fasted? When?

GIRL. The last blizzard. Your mother took me out. In that wind.

VOICE. The moon was dark then.

GIRL. She took me down to the river. I built a fire on the ice. She visited me every morning. And she sang to me.

VOICE. And she serves tea to the priest!

GIRL. And laughs at him. He expects her to give you away. That priest wants her to marry his god too.

VOICE. That's crazy.

GIRL. Instead she gets news of your father in Prince Albert.

VOICE. I didn't know. What does she say about my father? Is his cough any better? When One Arrow got back from the jail at Stoney Mountain, he was old. He told my father that the visions of warriors have no more power against the soldiers.

GIRL. He was old, husband. He was tired.

VOICE. Not even Riel's vision, and he was part white.

GIRL. It's the jail, husband. They watch you all the time. You can't move.

VOICE. I was there when he said it.

GIRL. And it's all stone.

VOICE. He gave away his rifle.

GIRL. You can't see anything but stones. You can't see anything, husband. You forget everything.

VOICE. How can you forget everything and be a man?

GIRL. You're not a man then. You're like a ghost. You're lost.

VOICE. I want to see my father. I'm going to Prince Albert.

GIRL. That's crazy.

VOICE. The Mounties won't know I'm there. Why worry?

GIRL. Your mother says someone's always watching him. You don't know that place.

VOICE. I'm going to talk to him.

GIRL. You have to hide. Your mother said so.

VOICE. Shut up about my mother! I don't want to hear it.

GIRL. She won't let you go.

VOICE. Am I a child again? Hiding behind women. How can you look at me?

GIRL. You're my husband.

VOICE. My father is a man. John Sounding Sky still means warrior. But Almighty Voice?

GIRL. He's a warrior.

VOICE. Does a warrior run away? Almighty Voice is a stupid old man, a ghost. He's here, there, nowhere.

GIRL. You can't go.

VOICE. I should be in Prince Albert. John Sounding Sky should be at home with Spotted Calf.

GIRL. They ache to hang Almighty Voice.

VOICE. What good am I here?

GIRL. I need you.

VOICE. What good am I to you, White Girl?

GIRL. I don't want to be alone.

VOICE. You can stay with my mother.

GIRL. Two women old with no men? Your mother will die like my mother did. You can't leave me too.

VOICE. Your father will take you.

GIRL. You're sending me home?

VOICE. He'll get you a better husband.

GIRL. He'll get me a worse one.

VOICE. Who? Who could that be?

GIRL. Any ghost man will do. You want me to die.

VOICE. You won't die!

GIRL. I will. For years. Kill me now. Be good to me, husband. Kill me now and then you can go, go and be hanged.

VOICE. You're pretty fierce, all right.

GIRL. Let go of me.

VOICE. For a little girl.

GIRL. I'll get you your Winchester.

VOICE. Stay here with me.

GIRL. You can kill me, husband. We'll both be dead.

VOICE. That's stupid. White Girl who has visions, stay here with me.

GIRL. What about your father?

VOICE. We'll find a way. My mother will help.

GIRL. You won't leave me?

VOICE. Hey, I'm here with you. In the dark of the moon. They can't get at us.

GIRL. Almighty Voice—

VOICE. Can't you be quiet, girl? Your husband doesn't want to sleep any more. He likes your hand here.

SCENE VIII

A projected title: "Scene Eight: The Hunting Moon". A gunshot. The social drum. Three more shots. ALMIGHTY VOICE *with his Winchester at the last fire, the dead one.* WHITE GIRL *with a baby-sized bundle in her arms, still illuminated by the moon.*

GIRL. You brought me home to your mother. It was time. Spotted Calf expected me. She took me into her new house. Other women were waiting. "Go away," she said. "Young Dust will bring you news." Someone, the Rump's

Daughter, might tell. It was dangerous. The Mounties—it was dangerous. You wanted to hide under the floor, under her bed like last winter. But she made you go. "You men shouldn't know women's stuff." You men. Little Salteau and Dubling came along. I heard you laughing. Off you rode to hunt somewhere, the grass new, blue green. I saw you through the glass in the window of that house. Going.

VOICE. Has he come? Tell him, wife, tell him how good a season it was everywhere along the Saskatchewan the winter before he was born. Tell him I always found game, never got cold. Till now. Say the ghost men shivered in their huts, too afraid of the wind to fire a shot. Tell him it can be like that again. Tell him, girl. Do you hear me? I wish you did.

Tell him how we visited and people would give his mother more to eat. Even people in the woods far up north. An old bull buffalo, chewy but sweet. You worried it might be their last one but ate anyway. Tell him Old Dust gave in, gave us lots of sugar for our tea, called me son, when he saw how fat you were. One day I remember. Cold, bright. Leather stiff as wood. Your belly had begun to curve. Your breath feathers, or smoke that fell, hugged the ground. I teased you, your belly like the iron stove at the store at Duck Lake. Tight as a drum. I felt him kick then. What a thump! I knew I had a son.

I wanted to dance.

ALMIGHTY VOICE *dances with the drum in celebration. Then, as* WHITE GIRL *speaks, his steps turn into a war dance and then into stillness. The moon around* WHITE GIRL *turns bloody.*

GIRL. They tell me you came across another cow. They say you wanted to feast me and the baby. So you shot the stupid thing. Some farmer heard your guns, didn't mind his own business. Him and his sons gave chase. I can hear you laughing, leading them into this bluff of poplars. And suddenly there's Mounties, soldiers, farmers everywhere. And someone shoots someone. I hope it was that farmer. They tell me you got no food, no water all day. They say someone else got shot. Maybe a Mountie. Young Dust said he heard you singing. War songs. He says you were dancing. There were ghost men all around that night. Farmers, soldiers, priests of the glass god. Over a hundred against Little Salteau, Dubling and Almighty Voice by the end. And two big iron guns. I saw them myself the second day. Spotted Calf and I stood watching. I wanted you to be anywhere else. Young Dust held the baby, reminded me to feed his nephew. I didn't notice I was full, aching. I have no milk now. (*She puts her bundle down.*) That night I saw my husband Almighty Voice again against that moon I had tried to forget. Then those two guns started firing and firing. Firing and firing. It was cold and the smoke would not go away. I seemed to see you sometime in the night, in the smoke, but even before morning broke, your mother was singing her death song.

SCENE IX

A projected title: "Scene Nine: His Vision". The drum beats in the night. The moon is low in the sky, pulsing. ALMIGHTY VOICE *lies by the dead fire, his leg badly wounded. The spectral tipi appears and the drum goes silent. Inside the tipi are* WHITE GIRL *and her baby, mother and child, a destination.*

ALMIGHTY VOICE *rises and uses his Winchester as a crutch to come to the tipi.* WHITE GIRL *comes out and shows him the baby and the baby cries. The moon turns white.* ALMIGHTY VOICE *dies.*

ACT II

A follow spot finds a title placard: "Act Two: Ghost Dance".

SCENE I

The spot shifts to a second title placard: "Scene One: Overture", then fades. Spectral light from the dead fire. ALMIGHTY VOICE, *now in white face as his own* GHOST, *continues his dance of celebration around the fire inside the last crescent of the moon. Scattered around the moon's half circle are ruined stools, three of which are still sturdy enough to be useful. On the one upright at the crescent's mid point a searching spot finds a seated figure and finding its head, finds white-gloved hands hiding its face. As the crescent moon fades, the hands open to reveal the white face that masks* WHITE GIRL *into the role of the* INTERLOCUTOR, *a Mountie and the Master of Ceremonies. In a glance their eyes meet. Sudden light shift to variety show lights, both the* GHOST *and the* INTERLOCUTOR *in follow spots. The* INTERLOCUTOR *adjusts her monocle.*

INTERLOCUTOR. Here, here? I said "Here, here." Hey dead man! Hey red man! Hey Indian!

GHOST. *Awas. Si-pwete.* [Go away. Go on.]

INTERLOCUTOR. "Here, here," I said. What's the meaning of this? Come on, use the Queen's tongue, or I'll sell you to a cigar store.

GHOST. *Awas kititin ni-nimihiton oma ota.* [Go away. I'm dancing here.]

INTERLOCUTOR. You dare call these furtive foot steps, these frenzied flailings of arms like wings, dancing! Stop it. It's nonsense.

GHOST. *Awena kiya? Kekwiy ka-ayimota-man?* [Who are you? What are you talking about?]

INTERLOCUTOR. Snap out of it, chief. (*slapping him with the gloves four times*)

GHOST. *Oweeya! Oweeya! Ya! Ya! Pakitinin awena kiya moya ki-kis-ke yimitin.* [Ow! Ow! Ow! Ow! Let go of me. Who are you? I don't know you.]

INTERLOCUTOR. You know very well who the hell I am. I don't have to remind you no show can begin without its master. Here, here. Stop I say. How dare you go faster.

GHOST. *Nahkee. Kawiya-(ekosi). Ponikawin poko ta kisisimoyan.* [Stop. Let me alone. I have to finish my dance.]

INTERLOCUTOR. I'll break the other leg for you, Kisse-Manitou-Wayou.

GHOST. *Tansi esi kiskeyitaman ni wiyowin?* [How do you know my name?]

INTERLOCUTOR. Names, names, they're all the same. Crees all wear feathers. Dead man, red man, Indian, *Kisse-Manitou-Wayou*, Almighty Voice, *Jean Baptiste*! Geronimo, Tonto, Calijah. Or most simply, Mister Ghost.

GHOST. Ghost?

INTERLOCUTOR. Boo! Almighty Ghost, Chief. Now we're speaking English.

GHOST. What? Who are you?

INTERLOCUTOR. How. You're supposed to say "How". You know. Hey Pontiac, how's the engine? Can't you stick to the script? You're too new at this ghost schtick to go speaking *ad liberatum*.

GHOST. Let me go. I don't know you. Let me dance.

INTERLOCUTOR. Here here. Stop, I say. How dare you! Do I have to remind you this colourful display, these exotic ceremonials belong later on in the program? Listen to me, Chief. One doesn't begin with a climax, an end. Unmitigated foolishness, I'll have you know. If you begin at the end, then where do you go? Do you know? No. Well? What have you got to say for yourself?

GHOST. How—

INTERLOCUTOR. That's more like it!

GHOST. How did I get here? What's going on?

INTERLOCUTOR. What's going on! The show. The Red and White Victoria Regina Spirit Revival show! These fine, kind folks want to know the truth, the amazing details and circumstance behind your savagely beautiful appearance. They also want to be entertained and enlightened and maybe a tiny bit thrilled, just a goose of frightened. They want to laugh and cry. They want to know the facts. And it's up to you and me to try and lie that convincingly. And since all the rest of our company is late for the curtain, this is your chance, your big break for certain.

GHOST. No, I won't dance for you.

INTERLOCUTOR. But you have to toe the line, Chief. We all do. Here. Let me smell your breath. Bah! Like death warmed over. I've warned you before. You choose to booze and you're back on the street where I found you.

GHOST. Leave me alone. Go away.

INTERLOCUTOR. Don't you realize you could be internationally known, the most acclaimed magic act of the century?

GHOST. What do you mean?

INTERLOCUTOR. The Vanishing Indian!

GHOST. Poof?

INTERLOCUTOR. Forget about faggots.

GHOST. I want to know how I got here.

INTERLOCUTOR. Gutter. Does that sound mean anything to you? Gutter?

GHOST. All I remember—

INTERLOCUTOR. Answer me, you sotted fancy dancer.

GHOST. My leg was gone.

INTERLOCUTOR. Come on, Chief, be a friend.

GHOST. It was! I used a branch from a sapling.

INTERLOCUTOR. Be a pal, Chiefy, dear.

GHOST. No, it was my gun for a crutch.

INTERLOCUTOR. This is a bit much for this early in the proceedings.

GHOST. Sometime in the night—

INTERLOCUTOR. Wait wait wait. I'd like to apologize to the ladies in the audience and suggest that this might be a prime opportunity to make use of our theatre's other facilities. The details of the following story may be not for the faint of heart, are in fact quite gory, and ordinarily it would be our custom to warn you and ask your permission before we proceed.

However—how-ever—as you can see, my peer here feels he must thrust the entire tale upon us. Once again, I apologize. Thank you for your attention. All right. Proceed.

GHOST. My legs were gone.

INTERLOCUTOR. His leg was gone!

GHOST. I must have screamed.

INTERLOCUTOR. Talk about Wounded Knee.

GHOST. But my throat was too dry.

INTERLOCUTOR. The bones were shattered, pulp. Not that that mattered.

GHOST. There was no sound in my mouth.

INTERLOCUTOR. Quite the come down for Almighty Vocal Cords.

GHOST. I couldn't sing my song.

INTERLOCUTOR. Oh lord, talented, too!

GHOST. My death song. I crawled out of the pit.

INTERLOCUTOR. And we're not talking orchestra pits out here in the sticks.

GHOST. We had dug it in the ground to protect us from the gunfire.

INTERLOCUTOR. Not much good compared to a couple of cannons, was it?

GHOST. There was smoke close to the ground.

INTERLOCUTOR. From the fires all around?

GHOST. I thought I might be able to make it across the open space.

INTERLOCUTOR. And was it really over a hundred men by then?

GHOST. Against Little Salteau, Dubling and me.

INTERLOCUTOR. Imagine. Red coats and wild Indians. What a spectacle! Where are my glasses?

GHOST. It was the middle of the night. I might get by if the watch was asleep.

INTERLOCUTOR. Not on duty? Now that's not very funny

GHOST. I had seen her watching, many times that day, beyond their lines. I got halfway across.

INTERLOCUTOR. And amazingly, no one saw him then. He might have made good his escape. Think about that. However—how-ever—he was bleeding a lot. Red blood oozing from red skin. Oh what a thrill! I'm not offending you, am I?

GHOST. She came to meet me.
INTERLOCUTOR. (*à la "Indian Love Call"*) When I'm calling you-oo-oo-oo-oo-oo-oo!
GHOST. No one could see her. My wife had denied their glass-eyed god. It was her medicine to be invisible.
INTERLOCUTOR. Wish my wife could do that. That's really interesting. Kissy Kisse-Manitou-Wayou? Did you give her some tongue!
GHOST. She told me about my son. She told me I would not be forgotten.
INTERLOCUTOR. How can I put this delicately? Your last meeting, your last touch. Your life dribbling out of you, hot and sticky. Big strong buck like you used to be. Was it savage love? Did you have a last quickie?
GHOST. I knew I could die then.
INTERLOCUTOR. She was some babe, eh?
GHOST. People would remember me.
INTERLOCUTOR. Give me some of the juicy details, Chief.
GHOST. My people would remember me.
INTERLOCUTOR. One must always strive for accuracy. Do you have documentation?
GHOST. I knew I could die then.
INTERLOCUTOR. Come on, Chief, speak up. Anybody got a cigar? Never mind.
GHOST. I could hear my mother, off on the hill, singing her song.
INTERLOCUTOR. Talent just runs in that family!
GHOST. Her death song.
INTERLOCUTOR. So does manic depression! Do we feel better now? We do remember you, Mister Almighty Ghost. The angry young man, the passionate lover, the wild and crazy Indian kid. A shocking but true tale of the frontier. Now don't you think this is just too touching, ladies and gentlemen? Too much for my refined sensibilities, that's a certainty. That wasn't too bad, Chief, considering. And now— (*she changes the title placard*)

SCENE II

The new placard reads: "Scene Two. Baritone Solo".

INTERLOCUTOR. Ladies and gentlemen, for your further edification and delight, a musical selection. Mister Almighty Ghost, the famous aboriginal voice, will now render for you the sweet ballad, "Lament of the Redskin Lover". Mister Ghost?
GHOST. (*in a spotlight*) What are you talking about?
INTERLOCUTOR. Go on, Mister Ghost. We wait upon you, sir. Sing. Sing.
GHOST. I don't know this.
INTERLOCUTOR. No memory at all? Here. It's number two on your lyric sheet, sir.
GHOST. Who are you?

INTERLOCUTOR. This is it, your last show. You're back on the street in the morning. The gutter? Here we go.

The INTERLOCUTOR stands behind the GHOST and guides him through the accompanying mime.

GHOST. (*to the tune of "Oh! Susanna"*)
I track the winter prairie for the little squaw I lost.
I'm missing all the kissing I had afore the frost.
I'm moping, oh I'm hoping oh, to hold her hand in mine.
My flower of Saskatchewan, oh we were doing fine.

GHOST & INTERLOCUTOR. In our tipi, oh we were so in love,
One Arrow was too narrow for my little squaw and me.

GHOST. I had a dream the other night, I saw her on a hill.

INTERLOCUTOR. My little squaw was shaking, the wind was standing still.

GHOST. The banic bread was in her mouth, and
blood was in her eye.
The moon so bright I lost my sight—

INTERLOCUTOR. —I pray she didn't die!

GHOST. On the prairie, oh how the white does blow!
Who makes it through the winter?
Not my little squaw or me.

INTERLOCUTOR. Nicely done. Thank you, thank you, Mister Ghost. You were almost your spooky self again.

GHOST. Thank you, Mister Interlocutor.

INTERLOCUTOR. Buck up, Mister Ghost. Isn't this all familiar? Might not, say, Buck and Squaw be the latest dance craze?

INTERLOCUTOR pulls GHOST into a short Hollywood Indian War Dance. GHOST resists. At the end GHOST grabs INTERLOCUTOR and looks into her eyes.

GHOST. This is what they've done to you.

INTERLOCUTOR. Thank you, thank you, Mister Ghost. A most original interpretation of the material. Gentle listeners, Mister Bones will now perform for you—

GHOST. Mister Bones? He the one with the dice?

INTERLOCUTOR. No, Mister Ghost. He's the one who's got rhythm.

GHOST. There's no one like that backstage, sir.

INTERLOCUTOR. No? Perhaps our friend Mister Tambo waits in the wings.

GHOST. That the Tamborine Man? Not even in the flies, sir. Nor, sir, is Mister Drum lurking below the trapdoor.

INTERLOCUTOR. No Mister Drum? Well, Mister Ghost—no! Wait!

The GHOST changes the placard.

SCENE III

The new placard reads "Scene Three: The Stump".

GHOST. Ladies and gentlemen, boys and girls, dogs and cats, we of the Pale-Faced Band of the Sweet Saskatchewaners are pleased to present for your information and concern our own Mister Interlocutor in the role of Mister Drum, a loyal citizen of our territory.

INTERLOCUTOR. Wait a moment, Mister Ghost. That is not my part.

GHOST. But you do know it by heart. This is your chance, sir, your big break for certain. Ladies and gentlemen, please welcome Mister Drum.

INTERLOCUTOR. Ahem. Ahem. I come before you this evening, my dear friends, full, full of concern. We have ourselves a problem. Dare I say an indigent Indian problem? Dear friends, the pampered redskins, they are the bad ones. Those tribes that have been cared for as if they were our equals, they, dear friends, are the first to turn and shed the blood of their benefactors. Noisemaker was petted, yes, even feted, my friends, and now raids our farms. Pricky Pinecone was paid to come up to our fine territory and what, dear friends, is his pursuit nowadays? Carnage! Large Prairie Dog who for years has sharpened his teeth by chewing on the bone of idleness, shows his gratitude by killing his priests for their holy wine. That is not communion, friends. Little Dump, a non-treaty Indian, has been, friends, provisioned
with all
necessaries and so gets to spend all his days gallivanting about the territory, shouting loudly and plotting mischief. And now, my dear friends, this Almighty Gas character joins in on the season's carnival of ruin. Oh friends, the petted Indians have proved the bad ones and this gives weight to the wise adage, friends, that the only good Indians are the dead ones.

GHOST. Bravo! Bravo, Mister Interlocutor, sir. Mister Drum could not have said it better.

INTERLOCUTOR. Thank you, Mister Ghost.

GHOST. No, thank *you*, Mister Interlocutor. I take your words to heart. My heart soars! We all thank you, sir. Don't we, ladies and gentles? Never a truer word was said. It is to our great benefit to know of this dread red threat to our well beings and livelihoods, this deadly hood, this Almighty Fart character. Dead Indians would be even better, sir, if they didn't stink that way.

INTERLOCUTOR. Thank you again, Mister Ghost, thank you again. I thank you too, ladies and gentle sirs. We will now return to the sequence of events as listed in your programs.

GHOST. But sir, there's still no sign of Messers Bone, Tambo, Drum, or any one. The entire company, sir, seems to be running on Indian Time!

INTERLOCUTOR. Would you now consider performing, Mister Ghost, for our attentive friends that charming curiosity you called a dance?

GHOST. No.

INTERLOCUTOR. Surely, Mister Ghost—

GHOST. Call me the late Almighty Voice. Call me an early redman. Call me, yes, even call me a ghost—but don't call me Shirley!

INTERLOCUTOR. You're the most spirited ghost I've ever met.

GHOST. You better believe it. There's a stir of dissatisfaction, sir, in the audience. Perhaps number seven?

INTERLOCUTOR. An excellent suggestion, Mister Ghost. An excellent selection, I assure you, my friends.

GHOST. But, sir, it calls for the entire company. And we, sir, are the skeleton crew!

SCENE IV

The INTERLOCUTOR *changes the title placard to "Scene Four: The Walkaround".*

INTERLOCUTOR. Ladies and gentlemen, for your delight and encouragement, Mister Ghost and Yours Truly will now present a martial interlude. In honour of all our heroic boys in uniform!

GHOST. I'll even honour those boys out of uniform.

INTERLOCUTOR. I appear first in the role of Mister Allan, leading the charge through the bluff. After the renegade!

GHOST. Hurrah! We're beating the bushes.

INTERLOCUTOR. Where are the cowards?

GHOST. Moo? Pow, pow!

INTERLOCUTOR. Ambush, vicious ambush!

GHOST. It appears Mister Allan's fallen off his horse!

INTERLOCUTOR. A bullet! A bullet shattered my arm.

GHOST. Bull! The bottle did him in.

INTERLOCUTOR. Then I take the part of the brave second in command, Mister Raven.

GHOST. Already shot on the wing.

INTERLOCUTOR. What?

GHOST. In his private parts!

INTERLOCUTOR. Not my leg?

GHOST. Groin, groin, gone!

INTERLOCUTOR. Oh where is the rest of my happy company?

GHOST. Retreat! Retreat! Buck up, my friend, there are but three of them.

INTERLOCUTOR. We've got them outnumbered. I, Mister Hockin, take charge. Surround the bluff!!

GHOST. But are you nine and the settlers enough?

INTERLOCUTOR. Postmaster Grundy here, volunteer, sir. We'll all of us beat them bushes again.

GHOST. March then. March south, men. They can't hide from you.

INTERLOCUTOR. Where have they gone? We had them surrounded.

GHOST. This could be embarrassing.

INTERLOCUTOR. East to west now. Shoulder to shoulder.

GHOST. Nothing. No one. Again?

INTERLOCUTOR. Here we go. These darn trees.

GHOST. Unpopular poplars?

INTERLOCUTOR. If they weren't so green. Fire would force them out.

GHOST. Say again.

INTERLOCUTOR. Fire!

GHOST. Bang bang! Bang bang, bang bang, bang bang! The mail comes late.

INTERLOCUTOR. Why?

GHOST. Postmaster Grundy got shot in the gut.

INTERLOCUTOR. What about Hockin?

GHOST. His heart got broken.

INTERLOCUTOR. And Kerr?

GHOST. Sorry, sir. Retreat! Retreat!

INTERLOCUTOR. I don't want to wait all day and all night.

GHOST. Too late.

INTERLOCUTOR. I could have got them.

GHOST. Reinforcements arrive!

INTERLOCUTOR. I could have got them alive!

GHOST. So can I play the one little, two little dozen Mounties?

INTERLOCUTOR. I'll take the roles of the two big guns!

GHOST. Bang bang? Boom boom. Doom doom!

INTERLOCUTOR. As well as the crowd of concerned civilians, including the disappointed—

GHOST. —I do so much for those ungrateful wretches—

INTERLOCUTOR. —farm instructor and his friend the ever hopeful—

GHOST. —Spare the rod and spoil the child!—

INTERLOCUTOR. —missionary priest. Well?

GHOST. It will be the least I can do then and an honour to represent the man's wife and mother as well as others from the One Arrow Reserve, Treaty Number Six.

INTERLOCUTOR. Perhaps, then, you will do the parts then of the young man and his ill-fated companions? Yes?

GHOST. No.

INTERLOCUTOR. Mister Ghost, sure—please listen to me and consider—

GHOST. Fuck you. I'm not going through that again for your entertainment.

INTERLOCUTOR. Mister Ghost—

GHOST. You do it.

INTERLOCUTOR. (*to the tune of "Derry Down"*)
Who is fighting the battle for everyone,—

GHOST. —is fighting the battle for everyone,—

INTERLOCUTOR. —fights blood thirsty redskins and wears a grin,—

GHOST. —not afeard of anything?—

GHOST & INTERLOCUTOR. Who rides high in the saddle and shoots a gun,
    rides high in the saddle and shoots a gun,
    shoots blood thirsty redskins and wears a grin,
    not afeard of anything?
    We have the guns, the guts, the wit.
    We know that you are stinking shit.
    We did it to the buffalo.
    Want to be next? Yes or no?
    We are the men with guns and bucks.
    We know that you are stupid fucks.
    We did it to the buffalo.
    Want to be next? Yes or no?

INTERLOCUTOR. Who is fighting the battle for everyone,
    is fighting the battle for everyone,
    shoots blood thirsty redskins and wears a grin,
    not afeard of anything?

GHOST. We have the guns, the guts, the wit.
    We know that you are stupid shit.
    We did it to the buffalo.
    Want to be next? Yes or no?

GHOST & INTERLOCUTOR. We are the men,
    well let's say it again,
    to get them heathen Indians.
    We are the ones,
    oh let's do it with guns,
    let's kill them stinking Indians.
    We are the ones,
    well let's do it with rum,
    let's get them redskin Indians.
    We are the men,
    oh let's say it again,
    to kill them damn dead Indians.

GHOST. Who rides high in the saddle and shoots a gun,
    rides high in the saddle and shoots a gun,
    shoots blood thirsty redskins and wears a grin,
    not afeard of anything?

INTERLOCUTOR. We have the guns, the guts, the wit.
    We know that you are stinking shit.
    We did it to the buffalo.
    Want to be next? Yes or No?

GHOST & INTERLOCUTOR. We have the bucks and you do not.
    Is it a wonder that you got shot?
    We have the bucks and you do not.
    Is it a wonder that you got shot?
    We have the bucks and you do not.

Is it a wonder that you got shot?
We have the bucks and you do not.
Is it a wonder that you got shot?

We have the blankets and the rum.
Oh did you say that you want some?

GHOST. Well, Mister Interlocutor, how do you feel now?

INTERLOCUTOR. No, Mister Ghost, how do you feel now?

GHOST. Well, Mister Interlocutor, I feel somewhat like a newspaper.

INTERLOCUTOR. You feel like a newspaper? How is that, Mister Ghost?

GHOST. I'm pale as a sheet of paper.

INTERLOCUTOR. A sheet of paper? With black eyes, Mister Ghost?

GHOST. Every one dotted, sir.

INTERLOCUTOR *hits* GHOST.

GHOST. And ultimately, sir, I am like a newspaper in that I am read all over—the countryside.

INTERLOCUTOR. Red all over, sir? A most colourful conceit. Bloody good, as our cousins would have it. Newspapers are our pass to an understanding of the reserve, the life of its denizens.

GHOST. And we don't have to go to the Indian agent to get them. The passes.

INTERLOCUTOR. Are you making one at me, sir? (*hitting him*) Did you read how we're teaching our primitive friends agriculture?

GHOST. That'll bring them down to earth.

INTERLOCUTOR. And we're giving them the benefit of our modern tongue.

GHOST. They'll need no other one, our kingdom come.

INTERLOCUTOR. Did you read how tranquil and subordinate they've become under our wise and humane government?

The GHOST *claps a "gunshot".*

INTERLOCUTOR. Was that a gun? A shot?

GHOST. Likely not. The Indian Agent won't give them any more ammunition until they put in a crop.

INTERLOCUTOR. What will they eat in the meantime?

GHOST. (*hitting himself*) Off to the hoose-gow with them! Lazy is as lazy does. So it says in the newspaper. Or the Bible. (*reprising "Derry Down"*)

Who is shooting in battle at every one
is shooting in battle at everyone,—

GHOST & INTERLOCUTOR. —fights blood thirsty redskins and wears a grin, not afeard of anything?—

GHOST. —We have the words, the pens, the laws.
We know that treaties are for fools.
We did it to the buffalo.
You want to be next?

SCENE V

The GHOST *reveals the next placard: "Scene Five: Tenor Solo".*

GHOST. And now, for the particular delectation of the ladies in the audience—

INTERLOCUTOR. What are you doing?

GHOST. —Mister Interlocutor will render in his most famous transvestatory manner—

INTERLOCUTOR. I won't do this.

GHOST. —as the Princess Porkly Haunches, he now sings "The Sioux Song".

INTERLOCUTOR. This is not a regular part of the program, ladies and gentlemen.

GHOST. And therefore we must show our gratitude to the Princess. Let us further encourage her, ladies and gentle sirs.

INTERLOCUTOR. (*to the tune of "Amazing Grace"*)
How beautiful
A man the moon.
I am what I am.
I'm not above
A buck for love.
What good is it? Sioux me.

A sparkling place
The city is.
My face is my face.
I must go far
Below zero.
What good is it? Sioux me.

My name is Sioux.
What did I do?
I never ever said
That red is what
I want to drink.
It goes right to my head.

How beautiful
A place the past.
We are where we are.
The redskin race
Finishes last.
What good is it? Sioux me.

GHOST. Thank you, thank you, Mister Interlocutor. An astonishingly touching masquerade. It seemed almost real. Is this a tear here, washing the war paint?

INTERLOCUTOR. Unhand me, sir. I'm not afraid of you.

GHOST. Boo is no go then. So how do you feel, Mister Interlocutor?

INTERLOCUTOR. I'm the Interlocutor here!

GHOST. How do you feel now?

INTERLOCUTOR. I know what to do. I know the order of the show.

GHOST. You do, do you?

INTERLOCUTOR. I want my happy company.

GHOST. They're even later than I am, sir. It's curtains for all of us!

INTERLOCUTOR. No, the show must go on.

GHOST. The audience is waiting. Mister Interlocutor?

INTERLOCUTOR. The playlet.

SCENE VI

The INTERLOCUTOR *reveals the placard: "Scene Six: The Playlet".*

GHOST. The playlet!

INTERLOCUTOR. Ladies and gentlemen, as a public service to the citizens at the forefront of our civilization, we now present a short drama of spiritual significance.

GHOST. Mister Interlocutor, in the continued absence of Mister Bones, will now render the role of Sweet Sioux.

INTERLOCUTOR. I dream. I dream, I do, of the bright lights of the city. Regina, she's the finest, the queen city of my dreams. But I promised Daddy, Daddy dear, I would keep up the homestead, I would be his little red pioneer. This on his deathbed. Sigh. Gangrene from an arrow. Oh horror!

GHOST. Shot by me, ha ha, in error. Oops!

INTERLOCUTOR. Mister Ghost now appears, in the infelicitous absence of Mister Tambo, in the role of the villainous Chief Magistrate.

GHOST. Ahem. Ahem. Give me some rum or I'll shoot you in the bum. I need fire water for a starter. Then off I go on a hunt or to court. Order, order, I say to the buffalo. Right between the eyes, I warn the prisoners. Tonight it's too late, too late for her.

INTERLOCUTOR. It is the eleventh hour. It is beyond my power to pay the mortgage on my Daddy's farm. Oh I am losing courage.

GHOST. Knocka knocka, Sweet Sioux.

INTERLOCUTOR. Who's there? At this hour.

GHOST. Knocka knocka.

INTERLOCUTOR. What would Daddy do?

GHOST. Answer the door.

INTERLOCUTOR. You think so?

GHOST. Knocka knocka, Sioux!

INTERLOCUTOR. Hello. Who's there?

GHOST. It is I, my dear. Your sweetheart, Chief Magistrate.

INTERLOCUTOR. You're no sweetheart to me.

GHOST. She's not all there up here. Sometimes she believes me.

INTERLOCUTOR. Stay away. What is it you want?

GHOST. The time is short. The deed on this land is about to come due. I was worried, my dear, about you.

INTERLOCUTOR. You were? Really?

GHOST. Do you have the necessary dollars?

INTERLOCUTOR. No—

GHOST. —Hooray!—

INTERLOCUTOR. —I'm sorry to say.

GHOST. I mean to say I'm here to help you.

INTERLOCUTOR. But at what price? A Chief doesn't become Magistrate without vice.

GHOST. Oh Sweet Sioux.

INTERLOCUTOR. What's a girl to do?

GHOST. Oh sweet Sweet Sioux.

INTERLOCUTOR. Oh, no, Chief Magistrate. I couldn't do that.

GHOST. Why not, my dear? She's done it before.

INTERLOCUTOR. I'm not that kind of girl. I only do it for love and/or marriage.

GHOST. Why buy the moo cow?

INTERLOCUTOR. I won't do it for meat anymore.

GHOST. I'll give the deed to you.

INTERLOCUTOR. Oh no. I couldn't do that. That would make me one of those women, nothing more than a squaw.

GHOST. A squaw? You mean like Buck and Squaw?

> *The* GHOST *pulls the* INTERLOCUTOR *into a reprise of the Hollywood Indian War Dance. The* INTERLOCUTOR *complies but keeps it short.*

INTERLOCUTOR. Midnight is about to strike!

GHOST. There goes the farm.

INTERLOCUTOR. But I keep my honour.

GHOST. Midnight strikes. The farm is mine. And what the hell, so are you!

INTERLOCUTOR. Oh no no! That would be—rape!

GHOST. Right you are! You're more intelligent than you appear.

INTERLOCUTOR. Rape, oh no!

GHOST. Oh yes, yes, Sweet Sioux! Talk about the Almighty Buck.

INTERLOCUTOR. Corporal? Corporal Coat? Mister Tambo? Mister Drum! Anybody!

GHOST. There's no one here to come to your aid.

INTERLOCUTOR. Stop! Stop, I know. It is I, I, Corporal Red Coat of the Mounted Police—

GHOST. —Aye, aye!—

INTERLOCUTOR. —cleverly disguised as Sweet Sioux in order to tempt the evil Chief Magistrate to show his true colours.

GHOST. Blast you, Corporal Red Coat. Talk about an Indian giver. Your feminine innocence, your eyes, had me completely convinced.

INTERLOCUTOR. It is now my duty to arrest you, Chief Magistrate.

GHOST. Corporal Coat, could I make you an offer?

INTERLOCUTOR. Oh more villainy. You're trying to bribe me.

GHOST. I offer you the deed to the farm for a taste of your feminine charms.

INTERLOCUTOR. How dare you, sir! Bang bang!

GHOST. Oh I am wounded, I am dying, mortifying, I am dead.

INTERLOCUTOR. Oh Corporal Coat.

GHOST. As my soul slips toward hell, I repent. Is it too late?

INTERLOCUTOR. Call me Red, miss.

GHOST. What a sorry end this is!

INTERLOCUTOR. I want to thank you.

GHOST. Jesus loves me!

INTERLOCUTOR. We can talk about that later on, Sioux.

GHOST. And suddenly my skin is white.

INTERLOCUTOR. Oh, Red, may I offer you some apple cider?

GHOST. Oh miracle! I'm heaven sent!

INTERLOCUTOR. I love you.

GHOST. Or are those wedding bells I hear?

INTERLOCUTOR. I love you, too, my dear. I'm beside myself with love.

GHOST. And as I say adieu to those two united souls, choirs of angels remind me how true it is said that the only good Indians are the ones who are sainted.

INTERLOCUTOR. Bravo, Mister Ghost. What a wonderful halo.

GHOST. It's old paint, Mister Interlocutor. Bravo to you, too, sir. I love your Sweet Sioux.

INTERLOCUTOR. As you were. Thank you, thank you, ladies and gentlemen. You're too kind.

GHOST. They're deaf, dumb and blinded by the light of the heavenly Ghost, sir.

INTERLOCUTOR. We hope our tale encouraged all and offended none.

GHOST. There ain't no nuns I can see out there, sir.

INTERLOCUTOR. We give you laughter and tears. We give hope to all who toil and are laden.

GHOST. For every girl, there is a guy.

INTERLOCUTOR. For every man, a maiden.

GHOST. For every nun, a holy Ghost.

SCENE VII

The GHOST, *on his way to the footlights, bumps into the placard stand and "Scene Seven: Duet" turns up.*

GHOST. Hi, my name's Almighty. Do you come here much?

INTERLOCUTOR. Mister Ghost, where are you going?

GHOST. I want to get in touch with the audience.

INTERLOCUTOR. Our final curtain has yet to descend, Mister Ghost.

GHOST. Speak for yourself. I want to make some new friends in the pit.

INTERLOCUTOR. You can't leave me too.

GHOST. Hiya. Will you help me down?

INTERLOCUTOR. Mister Ghost, I implore you.

GHOST. Mister Interlocutor, sir, or madam, I was forgetting about you.

INTERLOCUTOR. You can't go. I mean we do have some few ensuing numbers, Mister Ghost.

GHOST. The two of us? Go on without me.

INTERLOCUTOR. None of the rest of our happy company has come along.

GHOST. Look me in the eyes and ask.

INTERLOCUTOR. Please, Mister Ghost. Please.

GHOST. Mister Interlocutor, sir, how do you feel?

INTERLOCUTOR. How do I feel? With my hands! No, Mister Ghost, I feel this evening like the moon.

GHOST. You feel like the moon, Mister Interlocutor. How is that?

INTERLOCUTOR. Envious and pale of face and alone, Mister Ghost.

GHOST. I know how you feel, but you are mistaken.

INTERLOCUTOR. How am I mistaken, Mister Ghost?

GHOST. The Moon's an old woman. We call her Grandmother. (*to the tune of* "*God Save The Queen*")

> The Moon's an old woman
> A very wise woman.
> She's made of light!

GHOST & INTERLOCUTOR. She watches over us,
> Over the children
> Each of us is a child again
> In the coldest night.

INTERLOCUTOR. The Moon's a young woman
> A very new woman
> Made out of dark
> She's waiting for the light
> Just as a child might
> Wrapped warmly in a blanket and
> Not at all afraid.

GHOST. Well how do you feel now, Mister Interlocutor? Mister?

SCENE VIII

The INTERLOCUTOR, *fleeing the* GHOST, *bumps into the placard stand. "Scene Eight: Standup" turns up.*

GHOST. Sir!

INTERLOCUTOR. Did you know, Mister Ghost, that marriage is an institution?

GHOST. Yes, sir, I had heard that said.

INTERLOCUTOR. Well, sir, so is an insane asylum! Did you know, Mister Ghost, that love makes the world go round? Well, sir, so does a sock in the jaw! Which reminds me, sir. An Indian from Batoche came up to me the other day and said he hadn't had a bite in days. So I bit him! Do you know, sir, how many Indians it takes to screw in a light bulb?

GHOST. What's a light bulb?

INTERLOCUTOR. Good one, Mister Ghost, a very good one. Well then, sir, if it's night time here, it must be winter in Regina. Nothing could be finah than Regina in the wintah, sir. Am I making myself clear? Does this bear repeating? Does this buffalo repeating?

Almighty Gas, you say! Answer me, Mister Ghost. Answer! What! A fine time to demand a medium. It's very small of you, sir. I promise you I will large this in your face if you do not choose to co-operate. Tell me, is it true that the Indian brave will marry his wife's sister so he doesn't have to break in a new mother-in-law? Does it therefore follow, sir, that our good and great Queen Victoria keeps her Prince Albert in a can? That's where she keeps the Indians! Hear ye, hear ye! Don't knock off her bonnet and stick her in her royal rump with a sword, sir. The word, sir, is treason. Or are you drunk? Besotted! Be seated, sir. No! Standup! You sir, you, I recognize you now. You're that redskin! You're that wagon burner! That feather head, Chief Bullshit. No, Chief Shitting Bull! Oh, no, no. Blood-thirsty savage. Yes, you're primitive, uncivilized, a cantankerous cannibal! Unruly redman, you lack human intelligence! Stupidly stoic, sick, demented, foaming at the maws! Weirdly mad and dangerous, alcoholic, diseased, dirty, filthy, stinking, ill-fated degenerate race, vanishing, dying, lazy, mortifying, fierce, fierce and crazy, crazy, shit, shit, shit . . .

GHOST. What's a light bulb?

INTERLOCUTOR. Who are you? Who the hell are you?

GHOST. I'm a dead Indian. I eat crow instead of buffalo.

INTERLOCUTOR. That's good. That's very good.

SCENE IX

The lights shift from variety to spectral as the spotlight finds the placard: "Scene Nine: Finale".

INTERLOCUTOR. Who am I? Do you know?

GHOST. I recognized you by your eyes.

INTERLOCUTOR. Who am I?

GHOST. White Girl, my White Girl.

INTERLOCUTOR. Who? Who is that?

GHOST. My fierce, crazy little girl. My wife. *Ni-wikimakan.* [*My wife.*]

The INTERLOCUTOR *touches her face with her gloved hands as the* GHOST *embraces and releases her. The spotlight finds her face as her gloved hands begin to wipe the white face off, unmasking the woman inside. The* GHOST *removes one glove and throws it on the dead fire, she does the same with the other. The fire rekindles.*

GHOST. *Piko ta-ta-wi kisisomoyan ekwo.* [*I have to go finish dancing now.*]

INTERLOCUTOR. *Patima, Kisse-Manitou-Wayou.* [*Goodbye, Almighty Voice.*]

The GHOST *goes and dances in celebration to a drum. The woman removes the rest of the white face and costume, becoming* WHITE GIRL *again. She gathers the costume in her arms as the spotlight drifts away to become a full moon in the night.* WHITE GIRL *lifts a baby-sized bundle to the audience as the* GHOST *continues to dance in the fading lights.*

The end.

(1991)

Joan MacLeod   b. 1954

The Shape of a Girl

The Shape of a Girl is a one act, one character play. Braidie is a fifteen-year-old female. The running time is approximately eighty minutes; there is no intermission.

The original set was a gravel beach with a large and beautiful driftwood tree upstage.

> *Darkness, a bell sounds from the distance, spot up on* BRAIDIE, *she speaks to her absent brother Trevor.*

BRAIDIE
I woke up this morning to this sound. This sound that feels far away one second then from right inside my gut the next. Very pure with the potential to be extremely creepy. But before I've even opened my eyes this other thing worms its way in and wreaks its usual havoc: the voice of mum.

I tell you Trevor, she's gotten even worse since you left. She is yelling that THIS *is* IT. What IT is I still haven't figured out. At this point in my life being kicked out would be incredible. All I know is her voice chiseled, no burrowed into my brain before I was fully conscious. By the time I'm actually awake the voice of mum has reached this pitch that is making the panelling beside my bed vibrate. *Braidie—I have had* IT!

And then I remembered that day, that truly outstanding day Trevor when you told mum that in another life her voice is going to come back as an ear wig. I was thinking of that exact thing when that sound comes again and this time I know what it is. The blind are back, back at their summer camp across the bay—which is highly weird because it's hardly April. That sound is the gong that tells the blind folks to get up or come for porridge. It just seems like it's really close, sound carrying across water and all that.

And for some reason today, on this particular morning, at this particular point in time, after living on this stupid island my whole life, I am acutely aware for the first time that sound carries across water BOTH ways. Did that ever dawn on you? Did you ever have this really ugly image of mum's voice snaking around the blind camp? There they are: lying on their bunk beds, innocent as pie. *You're your own worst enemy!* That'll get them sitting up or worse yet shuffling off to the cook shack, mum's voice attacking them from above like some crow gone nuts. *Keep your shoulders back! You are walking like an ape!*

I am thinking of all these things Trevor and how I wish I could talk to you about it. I wish you were here, asleep in your room. You, big brother, with the unparalleled ability to sleep until three in the afternoon three months in a row; you who can drive all the way to your place in Whistler using only your peripheral vision. I am thinking of all this stuff then all of a sudden this seaplane lands, right outside the deck. I pretend, just like we always did, that the plane is here to kill us. BAM! BAM! BAM!—it'll dive-bomb the whole island. Bullets will explode the mattress around me, outline my arms, my legs.

That is how my day begins, that is how I greet the morning. And from across the water the gong from the camp sounds again. I think, briefly, very briefly, about actually going to school. I also contemplate apologizing to mum for the basic snarkiness of my disposition—all inherited of course— but she's already left for work. Then I'm pretending we're all Muslims or Buddhist monks or anything except who we are. And that the gong is calling us to prayer or at least ending this round.

That the sound means—STOP, don't move a muscle, help is on the way.

*

I watch the school bus come and go. I haven't been to school in a week now. Adrienne always waits until the last minute to climb aboard. She looks tall and grumpy. Mum says I need to make more friends. She reminds me that in grade five I almost had a heart attack because Adrienne and I had different teachers for the first time, the first time since preschool. In preschool Annie made a point of trying to let other kids sit beside Adrienne at circle and I'd just freak. And Annie and me, we'd have to go off together for a quiet time in her rocking chair. She smelled like play dough. I'd bury my head in her shirt and I'd blubber all over Annie. The world was ending. I love Adrienne so much I used to worry I was a lesbian and when dad would say stuff like *you two sure are joined at the hip!* I thought he was worried that I was a lesbian too.

If Adrienne jumped off the Lions Gate Bridge would you? All over the world, parents have been posing this question to their children forever. I used to think I'd want to be dead if mum or dad died. Now I actually imagine them dead so that I'll be able to stay out late and do what I want. If Adrienne jumped off the Lions Gate I wouldn't follow BUT—I would spend the rest of my life writing poems about her short one. And explaining the devastating effect that her death had on, well, her obviously. And me. I'm not the suicidal type. Even if I was a complete mess and my brain had turned to jello I wouldn't want anyone pulling the plug.

Mum would pull the plug on me in a second. Remember that Trevor. Make sure mum doesn't pull the plug.

So the bus is gone and mum is gone and even though it is my intention to at least try and write a poem I end up flipping on the TV. I watch one of those really bad shows about really bad things that happen to really depressingly normal people. We're still not allowed cable so the reception is just rancid—everybody's foreheads have gone alien and bodies all shivery—like when you'd try to zap down something racy from Pay. The show's called MOST DANGEROUS AND AWFUL MOMENTS EVER.

They're showing this speedboat, this speedboat in Florida somewhere and it's heading full speed, dead ahead, for this big bleacher full of spectators. God knows what the problem with the boat is but the guy driving it is yelling and waving his hands, warning the people in the stands to get the hell out of the way. The boat smashes right into the crowd—chaos. I tell you—blood and guts and totally nuts.

And I was thinking of this poet, this poet I have recently discovered called Stevie Smith. Not a guy Stevie, a girl Stevie. I was thinking of this thing she said that I loved, that reminded me of my friends and me. This thing about not waving but drowning. I was thinking of that when the rabbit ears sort of shake, almost like they're one of those divining things and all of a sudden the whole scene changes on the TV.

And there we are. A group of girls—just like me and Adrienne and Jackie and Amber. A group of girls with hair and jeans and jackets. *They are not waving, they are drowning.* And this group of girls on the TV starts waving, right on cue. Weird I'm thinking. This is highly weird.

And what feels even stranger is that the picture is actually clear for once, from the neck down at least. But their faces are blurry, smudged, almost as though someone has taken an eraser and tried to rub them out.

And then I realize who these girls are. They are supposed to look distorted because they are young offenders and we aren't allowed to see who they are. They are accused of assault, accused of murder, accused of killing another girl—a fourteen-year-old girl. One is wearing these big high heel runners like Amber's. They are all standing out front of the courthouse while the judge is taking a break. They are laughing like maniacs. Me and Adrienne often laugh like maniacs. Honestly, totally unprovoked.

Then the news guy starts talking about how one saw her dad murdered when she was six. And another girl's dad was also murdered. And I feel stupid to have ever thought we have anything in common. In fact it pisses me off that they are trying to pass themselves off as normal. And even though it's illegal to do so, I can imagine their faces: slutty eyes, chapped lips. Then one girl waves again and yells *hi* and you just know she's making goofy faces just like Adrienne and me did when we saw the Canucks, when we thought we were making our debut on national television.

I don't know why I have to find out more about those girls, I just do. They are all over the news. Always in a group, always from the back or with their jackets pulled over their heads. I don't want to look at the victim, it's too depressing. But she is everywhere too—as a baby with her dad, as a regular weird kid on holiday, then one of those blown up yearbook pictures that always mean someone is either a movie star or dead.

And then that gong across the bay starts ringing again. Except this time it sounds like a summons, like someone is calling me.

> *Lights up on set—*BRAIDIE *is on a beach, perhaps leaning against a log, looking out at the water, she is wearing jeans, a warm jacket, a tangle of blackberry vines and bush rise up steeply on the bank behind.*

Hello! I'm here . . . Attention: Braidie has landed.

> BRAIDIE *looks upstage.*

But up at the camp the shutters are all still up, the flag pole is bare, not a blind guy in sight. And you know that gong? It's just the same old bell. I was expecting something out of Tarzan. So it's me, solo. Braidie on the beach. Remember how much we used to love coming here to spy?

> BRAIDIE *holds her arms, straight out in front.*

Trevor, let's be blind.

Shutting her eyes.

Shut your eyes and you can hear the summer. The little kids arriving, so wired up. And the older ones with their dogs, those outstanding dogs. I love Buster but I've always felt he was an inferior species of animal. I mean I've never seen a seeing-eye dog eating goose shit or sniffing up another retriever.

A bell rings softly in the distance, BRAIDIE *opens her eyes and looks up the bank, watching a memory from years ago.*

Trevor? Did you hear that? Do you see? It's Sofie, twelve years old. The camp is deserted like now. It's winter. I am below her, also twelve. Adrienne is up the hill beside Sofie, always nearly one year older. Sofie wants to ring the bell because she thinks Adrienne might kill her and I think Adrienne might kill Sofie too. I watch Adrienne watching Sofie. Adrienne is so mad her mouth is shaking. Sofie is watching me. She has no idea my body has turned to concrete. I can't move and I can't shout. All I can do is see.

*

BRAIDIE *goes back in time, she is eight years old, she gallops around and around until she falls over, exhausted and happy.*

We are in love, we are all forever in love. We spend hours drawing them. We call ourselves by our new names in secret: Rainbow Rider, Lucky Lady, Thunder. We cram our pockets and lunchkits with them—piles and piles of ponies. Little brushes for their tiny pink manes, their purple tails.

Sofie is the new girl in grade two. Her horse name is Trotter and Toto and Lala and Gypsy. Because Sofie doesn't just fall in love with horses and have a horse name like the rest of us. Sofie becomes a horse or sometimes an entire herd of horses. She gallops out to the playground for recess; she trots down the halls. She talks by doing whinnies and stomping her feet. She even eats her lunch like it's a feed-bag, without using her hands.

We are amazed by Sofie, how she can spend hours, entire afternoons, down there on all fours. How she never cares about who sees. *Good little horsie.* That's what Adrienne says and then Adrienne is flying, having been bucked by Sofie the horse onto the couch. And then Rachel has a turn on Sofie's back and Sofie sends her flying too. We love Sofie the horse. We make tiny braids all over her head; we paint rainbows on her cheeks.

And then one day, one normal un-special day Adrienne comes to school and announces that it's penalty day. We don't know what penalty day is. Adrienne explains that on penalty day one girl is chosen and everyone is mean to that one girl for the whole day. *Why?* Adrienne doesn't know. It's just a part of school. Adrienne offers to go first. We get to be mean to her first. I want to go first too.

At first penalty day is hard to figure out. There are a lot of rules. The person we have to be mean to has fleas of course. Everyone has to write FP for flea proof on their hand.

BRAIDIE, *as a teenager again.*

You know something Trevor? By the end of grade four penalty day had become as complex as World War Two. But who the enemy was had become entirely simple. Now all the girls had FP written on their hands, all the girls but one. I don't know why it was Sofie. It just was.

*

It is the next day. BRAIDIE *is settling in on the beach.*

THE VOICE OF MUM came in weak today, this annoying little signal that was barely registering. I believe I told her I was sick—perhaps I surfaced long enough to tell her school was out of the question. I sense she senses that school and myself are on our last legs. Maybe I'll be like you, try home-schooling. Maybe I'll move up to Whistler too.

Mum and me did have a big blow out last night, a major blow out. She says to me, all weird and cheery—*the teen centre is having a dance this weekend. Why don't you go?* I point out I went last time and that it was BEYOND repulsive.

She points out that I never actually went inside, that I hung out with Adrienne in the parking lot. How does she know?

Because she drove by—MORE than once. She cruised the teen centre like an undercover cop or a pervert. Life with her is unbearable, a lesson in indignity.

In today's papers there are no pictures of those young offenders. I tell you—it's almost a relief. You remember when the girl was killed Trevor, you were still living here. How she was beat up by a group of girls and this guy and then finished off a few minutes later by that boy and this one girl who went back for more. The ones that watched the girl get beat up, they aren't accused of anything. To be accused you have to have gotten in there, down and dirty. I suppose that to be a teenager, even to be a little kid, is to often see very hideous behaviour from your peers.

If you reported everyone you would certainly have to watch your back at all times and look no one in the face, ever. You would have to go through your entire life using only your peripheral vision.

The girls who beat her up, the girls who are on trial for assault, they used to hang out at Walmart. They also hang out UNDER COVER. This sounds way cooler than it is. Because under cover really is just that—a covered area at the school just like we had for playing hopscotch when it rained. But these really are tough girls. They make like they are a gang and that they're all hooked up with the gangs in New York and L.A.

On Granville Mall once Adrienne and me were followed by some tough girls, these wipe out girls. They wanted us to give them some money and Adrienne said no way. They said they were going to get us. One gobbed on the back of Adrienne's jeans. But we weren't afraid of them. We just thought they were idiots.

These girls in Victoria, they're a mess. Some are in foster care, some have been doing the McFamily thing for a long long time. Some have already been up on charges, one for lighting fire to another girl's hair. The fight with the dead girl starts when someone butts out a cigarette on her forehead. This is terrible enough in itself but it also opens a door. *Look what*

I did? Now just watch, just wait and see . . . It's surreal. And that's not fair to say because it's exactly the opposite—it's totally real. I mean it happened. And what scares me, what freaks me right out Trevor is that I know the way in. I don't know how else to put it. I know the way in.

The human body is what? Eighty percent water? That kills me. We're like these melons with arms and legs. Well eighty percent of the female brain is pure crap. We're constantly checking each other out, deciding who goes where, who's at the bottom.

When I look at her picture, when I look at the picture of the dead girl in the paper, part of me gets it. And I hate it that I do; I hate to be even partly composed of that sort of information. But right now, if you put me in a room filled with girls, girls my age that I've never seen before in my life—I could divide them all up. I could decide who goes where and just where I fit in without anyone even opening their mouth. They could be from this island, they could be from Taiwan. It doesn't matter. Nobody would have to say a word. You know something Trevor? I could have divided up a room like that when I was in grade two. Grade fucking two.

*

When the lights come up BRAIDIE *is ten years old, being Adrienne, perhaps standing up the bank, up high.*

No one is to have contact of any kind with IT *from first period until lunch. If you have to address* IT *do so during homeroom. On the school bus* IT *has to sit on the fourth seat on the left. If* IT *talks to any boys it will be dealt with by me.* IT's *lunch today will be divided between Amber, Braidie and Jackie. Case closed.* IT *will make no comments and will not be allowed to look at me anymore as of now.*

BRAIDIE *leaps down.*

Adrienne then turns her back on Sofie, to show us she means business. Adrienne always means business. So the five of us sit there, waiting for the school bus.

Yesterday means nothing now; it means nothing that we spent all day Sunday together and had a good time. There is a brand new code every day. I spend most of my time trying to figure out what the code is.

—*What if she* . . .
—IT.
—*What if* IT *has to go to the bathroom.*

This is Amber interjecting when she shouldn't. Adrienne ignores her. Adrienne often ignores what isn't important. And it works.

Yesterday we let ourselves into one of the houses Adrienne's mum is trying to sell. *Let's take off our tops.* Adrienne is lifting up her tee-shirt. She is wearing a white bra covered in tiny pink flowers. Mine is identical. Sofie yanks up her blouse. She is wearing a rolled up undershirt.

—IT'S A SPORTS BRA, *says Sofie.*
—IT *thinks that's a bra.*
—DON'T CALL ME THAT.
—*Don't call me that.*

The house is freezing. The beds are all bare. The mattresses and the ocean silver. Something shitty's going to happen. Something shitty could happen here. *Tell* IT *to get us something from the fridge.* And Sofie does. She comes back with a box of baking soda and a jar of relish. The lousy food is Sofie's fault. Maybe she should've broken in early and stocked the fridge. I would've. I would've done that if I was in her position. But Sofie doesn't have a clue. She has no sense of how to avoid anything.

A sports bra, says Adrienne, *is a defense against guys. The really high end sports bras repel guys, totally impenetrable. A good sports bra will catapult guys across the room.* THAT *is* NOT *a sports bra. It's a little Miss Undie Undie shirt.*

Ha ha. Another one of Sofie's bad habits, ha-ha-ing all the time. She sticks her fingers into the jar of relish. *Ooohhhh Gross.* Adrienne practically has a heart attack. It is gross. Sofie slopping up a jar of hamburger relish. Except now Adrienne also finds it funny. And all of a sudden everyone is laughing and Sofie is allowed to be our friend again.

So we sit there all afternoon in our bras or our phony bras, fingers in the relish. Last year we took off all our clothes and sat together in a dry bathtub. I don't know why. We just did.

—*You have to swim across this lake to get there. Then you'll come to a little door in the side of a tree.*

This is Adrienne, doing what we always do. Designing a place, a home for the four of us. A dream house where we will all live together forever.

My dream house always looks the same—one big room that is divided by gauzy white curtains, sort of like a swishy hospital ward. There are no mothers and our dads will show up with supplies only when we want them to. Boys are banished. We do not want boys like the ones we see now, getting on the school bus. Adrienne, Sofie, Amber and me are first picked up and last home every day on the school bus.

BRAIDIE, *as a teenager again.*

You were there too Trevor. At the back with the boys: throwing pencil cases and shoes and sweaters out the window. You had a handmade sling shot that was the envy of everyone. And a pocketful of smooth black stones. You were always pummeling each other, always mouthing off to Gustaf the driver. So you probably didn't notice how we sat around Sofie. And how still she was, with her eyes straight ahead. Behind her Jackie was kicking her calves, something was smeared in her hair. The girls across from her were chanting but you'd have to listen hard to hear it. While you boys in the back were slugging it out we were in the front, almost still, always the good little girls.

*

A few days later.

The voice of mum and I went out for dinner last night. As usual Dad—also known as Planet Dad—is away on business, so it's going to be, and I quote—*just us girls.*

One would think that dinner would mean ordering food, eating food, paying for food. Not so. Mum insists, first, that we sit at the same table.

Two, that I don't read. Three, four, and five that I get my hair out of my face, sit up properly and stop looking as though I'm planning my escape. And six, she wants us to *reconnect*, have ourselves a little chat. I explain, patiently, that I'd rather be shot from a cannon than hang around and see what she really has up her stupid sleeve.

And so it comes out: the school has phoned her at work. They are seeking an explanation for my unexplained absences. I explain, patiently, that I am now homeschooling.

All apparently news to mum. And news to the school.

I am part way through stating just what I think homeschooling should be when the voice of mum jumps to her feet and starts doing the famous whisper-shriek. *This is the last straw, the end of the road, the end of the rope, the absolute limit.* Then she's goes. Leaves me sitting there alone with Terry the cook. Terry leers from the kitchen. He cleans his teeth with a business card and winks at me.

The Braidie Institute Of Higher Learning. Lesson One—Current Events

    BRAIDIE *holds up a newspaper.*

Girls Turning On Each Other
Bullied To Death
Girls Killing Girls

These are the headlines, these are what put us on the map. Like the Stanley Cup riots only worse, way worse.

The articles go on and on about how girls are getting meaner. The attacks more vicious. I look at those girls. I look at the pictures of those young offenders until the newspaper goes all squirrelly. If you look at them in bits they are regular girls: these lips, that hair, those kind of jeans.

If someone could invent a laser to zap the rotten parts they would be entirely normal. Young offenders. *Sorry—I didn't mean to offend you!* Adrienne and me would run into people on purpose on the ferry so that we could say that. *Oooops! No offense . . .* We thought that was hysterical.

A girl in the shape of a monster
A monster in the shape of a girl

That, Trevor, is poetry. It is also a riddle that gets played out in Victoria. Because that's how they treat her—like a monster. Only they're the monsters, get it? Because they phoned her up. *Guess what we're doing? Wanna come?* It's like wolves pretending to be some animal that's hurt, maybe a little calf or a goat. This wasn't a case of someone in the wrong place at the wrong time. This was planned, organized.

And the girl, she knows they're one scary bunch but she goes. Maybe she is pleased that someone phoned, someone wanted her to do something. *Let's meet here . . .* She even brings her pyjamas. Her pyjamas and diary and Charlie perfume are buckled into her black pack.

    BRAIDIE *goes back in time, she is twelve years old.*

Sofie walks like a cripple, little quarters of blood on her heel, soaking into her white socks. Sofie wears her runners too small because her feet are too big. She is accused of watching the girls get undressed in gym. But I watch too. I want to see who else has hair under their arms or who has thighs as big as mine. I talked to her after volley ball. I told her, I did the best I could.

—*Sofie don't go on the field trip.* See—I said it: in plain English.
—*Why?*
—*Just don't.*
—*But we have to write an essay.*

This is pure Sofie, putting homework ahead of life or death. I tell you—she's an extremely exasperating person. We are all going to see *Hamlet* for the field trip, at a theatre in town. It's not the real *Hamlet*; it's a phony version for kids.

FOR EMERGENCY ONLY—SORTIE DU SECOURS. I have studied that sign ever since I can remember. It is written over top of some windows in the bus. I sit three rows down from Sofie. Jackie and Adrienne are behind me.

Sofie is sitting with Lorna. Lorna's dad owns the store on our island; sometimes she works there. We don't know Lorna. We don't even think of Lorna as an actual person.

The ocean shrinks and glitters as we head over the Lions Gate. You can see where we live, lying out there in the strait, all wrapped up in mist. It looks uninhabited, prehistoric. Adrienne and Lorna have switched places. Adrienne is whispering something to Sofie. Sofie is looking dead ahead. Adrienne leans into Sofie so that Sofie is squished up against the side. Sofie's face turns grey.

FOR EMERGENCY ONLY. Sofie pushes the window on the bus. It fans out unnaturally from the bottom. Sofie hoists herself up, her head is out. Sofie is going to jump out the window. The ocean is hundreds of feet below.

I shut my eyes. And Sofie is falling, cannon-balling over the side of the bridge, her clothes parachute around her, a gigantic flower. I open my eyes. Sofie hasn't gone over the side of anything. Her bum is stuck in the window of the bus.

Amber and Adrienne and me and Jackie—we laugh so hard we nearly puke. Sofie is all weird and breathing heavy. Then she pushes out a sound that is hardly human. *Ha-ha.*

The bus driver is grabbing Sofie by the sweater. He pulls her in. *What the hell do you think you're doing?* Adrienne watches Sofie. *Nothing,* Sofie says. *Fooling around.*

Sofie isn't allowed to see the play. We watch Ophelia load herself up with flowers and sail off to meet her maker. We make burp noises except when Hamlet's around. Hamlet's cute.

When Hamlet gets going on one of his long speeches we go *oh oh oh oh* like we are Hamlet's own girlfriend. Then this lady usher comes and tells us we have to be quiet. She's a total bitch.

*

A few days later.

The first week is now history at the Braidie Institute. Two weeks now without Adrienne.

This is me without my friends. I am nothing, zero, zip. A black mark on the horizon.

If I had to I could live on this beach for a long time—live on berries and fish and kelp. Trevor, remember how we'd plant ourselves up there in the bank? The perfect camouflage—we would spy on the blind just doing their everyday stuff: the little kids going ballistic, the old guys sucking back the lemonade. Remember them swimming. Bobbing around in their life-jackets, unaware that the sun is descending in some spectacular fashion. They had that way of turning their faces up to the sky—all weird and happy.

It floored me Trevor. I mean I'm sure their lives are usually even more dull and shitty and hideous than the rest of us but I used to imagine myself blind—how careful I would be. For my eighteenth birthday I would be given a dog. I would call him Henry. *There goes Henry and Braidie.* I never think about all the stuff I wouldn't be able to do, what I wouldn't be able to see. For once I am focusing on only the positive. The voice of mum would be proud of me.

BRAIDIE *goes back in time, she is twelve years old.*

We are blind: Adrienne, Amber, Jackie and me. We have made a huge pile of sand and leaves. We cover our eyes with a pair of old panty hose and leap off the bank. We turn each other around and around to see if we can point in the right direction—at the beach, the mountains, each other. We feel each other's faces, stomachs, breasts. *Definitely Braidie.* If it wasn't winter I would swim away, swim blind into the middle of the sea.

This is boring. Adrienne takes off her blind fold. We take off ours. We climb up the bank and hide in the laurel leaves. We think about going to the store to steal something: gum, matches, bath oil bubbles that squish in our pockets and leak all over our shirts. Sometimes Adrienne steals change and cans of beer from the people she baby-sits for. I confine my crimes to the General Store and believe I am a slightly less bad person.

Adrienne goes to light a smoke then stops. *Look . . .* And we look out on the beach and there is Sofie. *What is* IT *doing?* We haven't seen Sofie in ages. *God, look at* IT*!* Adrienne makes it sound as if Sofie is out there killing something. I squint in on her but Sofie is just hunched over a little book. Maybe Sofie still draws pictures of horses. Maybe she also likes trying to write poems and stories. The possibility that Sofie and I might have even one thing in common makes a little shift in me.

I'm going to get It. Adrienne is climbing down the vines. Sofie looks up and in the wrong direction: pure Sofie. And Adrienne is right there, grabbing Sofie by the ponytail.

What do you think you're doing?

Nothing. Sofie slams her book shut, she examines her feet.

What's in the book?

Nothing.

And Sofie tries to run, to bolt down the beach. Adrienne still has a hold of her hair, she pushes Sofie down. Sofie's head makes a little smack sound on the rock. It sounds phony—like a slap in the movies. And then her head is bleeding and the blood looks phony too. And then we are all around Sofie. This is it. Adrienne is going to do something. And we are going to see. Then Adrienne is holding a covered elastic and a tangle of Sofie's hair.

Sofie is gone, running. And then everybody is running after her, someone is yelling *No No No . . . It isn't me.*

Sofie mashes open her jeans falling on the barnacles. She starts climbing back up the blackberries and Adrienne is right there, grabbing on to her ankle.

I understand too now what Sofie wants to do. Sofie is going to ring the bell at the blind camp. You can hear that bell all over the island. But then Adrienne screams and we all stop breathing.

We watch Adrienne slide down the bank while Sofie scrambles away. We peer down at Adrienne on the sand, all curled up and quiet. *She's dead.* Amber announces.

BRAIDIE, *as a teenager again.*

But I knew Adrienne had just been stalled, shot, hit by a smooth black stone. And that you were there, you were with us Trevor, up in the maple tree. How much did you know all along? How much did you see? Adrienne came back from the dead a moment later. *Your brother is such an asshole.* Adrienne knew it was you but somehow it becomes Sofie's fault too. *Sofie and Trevor probably do it together, do it twenty times a day.*

We all lay there on the sand, joined at the head, spokes in a wheel. In my pocket, a pink plastic diary and a key. Of course it belonged to Sofie. I didn't show it to anyone. But I felt entitled, I found it, it was mine to keep and mine to see.

What was Sofie doing as we lay there on the beach? Were the others thinking about her too? How she might be stumbling in the back door of her house, trying to keep the blood and the dirt from getting over everything. *I fell, I slipped, I whacked my head on an alder tree.* We all understand that Sofie telling the truth isn't even a remote possibility.

BRAIDIE *goes back in time, she is twelve years old.*

Jackie shifts down, rests her head on my stomach. I place my head on Adrienne's. We make a chain. First Amber laughs then Jackie, all around the circle. I can feel the laughter and the skin of Adrienne's body, warm against my ear. And then, I'm laughing too and when we stop there's just our breath, rising and falling. I match my breath to Adrienne's perfectly.

*

The next day.

Mum comes thundering down the stairs last night to announce she has given up. I point out, as calmly as possible—*If you're going to give up on someone you just give up. You don't tell them about it.* Mum goes berserk. All this screaming and crying and gnashing of teeth. Then she notices the pictures, some of the newspaper clippings tacked up around my room. *I'm studying.*

And then she's screaming—*Cut the lip! Cut all the nonsense about home schooling.* And she is inside my room, mine, for the first time in a year and a half. A complete violation of my rights. *What is this stuff?* She is looking at this cover from the Vancouver Province. At *least* SHE *has a nice haircut.*

She's a killer—I tell her.

And mum takes me by the shoulders—*Look*. She stares right into me, then her eyes fill up and she touches my cheek. *Braidie?* It's worse than anything, the voice of mum trying to be my buddy, trying to be half-way sweet.

Get out. Her hands drop to her side. *This is my room.* But she isn't moving. She gets me so pissed off I just start flailing.

—BRAIDIE *use your words.*

—*All right. Fuck you mother.*

And she gets it, she finally gets it. She slams the door behind her. She's giving up on me.

I look at the girl, the picture of the girl who did it. The one in Victoria who held her head underwater until all was quiet. The one who held a smoke in one hand and held the girl under with the other, her foot on her back. She bragged about it. Maybe she made the telling of it into a joke because she doesn't know how else to try it out. *Did you hear the one about . . .* Maybe she just snapped. I do that. I look at the picture again: she's a regular girl.

And she's hanging out on a Friday night in November, 1997—the moon is full, the air is clear. Usually the stars get lost in winter here. But on this night the stars are out, everyone is out, *under cover,* passing a joint, drinking vodka and sprite mixed in a can. Some are watching the sky and waiting because a Russian satellite is going to break through the earth's atmosphere tonight, right over Victoria. It will explode, light up all that black.

But this girl, this regular girl and one other girl are waiting for something else; they are waiting to teach someone a lesson. They've already phoned her up, they've called her out.

Because she is big, because she likes *that* boy. Because she is brown and she lost their book; because she doesn't fit and she lies. Because they can.

The girl they're going to get is miserable, that much is clear. Four different schools and two different foster homes in the past year. She keeps returning to family—her parents, her grandma and grandpa. And she keeps running away. And she doesn't know, doesn't get the plot, doesn't understand her part. So it starts.

The ones who watched, maybe they thought it wasn't real. Maybe as they yelled out or laughed they were actually frozen. Maybe they were so glad to not be that girl—whose hair is being held up to a lighter now—that they don't even know how to imagine shouting *stop.* Maybe they think that silence is the ticket, the only way to never end up like the girl.

Even the ones who didn't watch, who just heard about what happened, they carry the silence too—a dark present, passed hand to hand. When they get home maybe they will dream about being blind. Because they can't stand the replays anymore—how the girl looked up and begged for help.

Or maybe it's that boy in Burnaby last winter, how he wrote his goodbye note and climbed the rails on the Putallo Bridge.

Or maybe it's Sofie. Because just when you think it was all ancient history it starts again.

Trevor—remember how I went through the first five years of life hiding behind mum's bum whenever we were out in public? That's the trouble with staying silent. I can't move, even when I want to. And I start thinking Adrienne acts for me.

*

BRAIDIE *goes back in time, she is fourteen years old.*

It is dark now by 4:30. We miss the school bus on purpose so that we can hang out longer in town. *Mum—I'll be on the 6:30 ferry, pick me up . . .* I'm doing what I do every day after school, what I did practically every day in grade eight and in grade nine too. I am in the parking lot behind the school and I am waiting for Adrienne. High School is just like how movie stars describe making movies—there's a lot of waiting around.

It's raining hard; my hair is soaking wet—unbelievably ugly. There are about thirty of us hanging out. Some of the older guys have cars. These little pools of light—vibrating with music and bodies and smoke. And with Adrienne.

Right now she is in Justin Hannah's Dodge Caravan. She loves Justin and Justin, of course, treats her terribly. I think Justin is sort of an idiot. In fact I find a lot of Adrienne's guys are fairly gross.

Across from the parking lot everybody else lines up for the bus—shoving and smoking and fooling around. Except for one still shape, holding on to the bus sign like it's some sort of anchor. Sofie always has her hood up, rain or shine. From the back she looks like this giant version of ET. Sofie is something Adrienne seems to have forgotten. At lunch Sofie doesn't go to the cafeteria or behind the gym or the parking lot like the rest of us. She slinks along the edges of the halls; she walks away from the school. She walks around and around. She often eats lunch in a bus shelter, six blocks from our school. She doesn't hang out with other kids. She is certainly doing her very best to be invisible.

I have no idea why I feel I have to keep tabs on Sofie. I just do. Sometimes I follow her around. She has no idea; she has always been a fairly clued out individual. I go to the bus shelter after she's left to check it out. There are little rocks lined up along the sides and she's carved her initials—S.G.—into the seat. No doubt it all is charged with meaning in the weird world of Sofie. Maybe I'll give back her diary. I keep it at the back of my locker, just on the verge of handing it over. I never even finished reading the whole thing. It was too boring—just a regular girl. She doesn't let anyone in on anything.

I watch Sofie board the bus, always first on so that she can sit directly behind the driver. I watch the bus pull away just as Adrienne gets out of Justin's van.

Adrienne lights a cigarette and glares at me. Justin was supposed to give us a ride to the ferry but apparently now this is completely and totally out of the question. We walk—two and a half miles. I get home four hours late, the voice of mum waiting on the dock to tear a strip off of me.

*

A girl in the shape of a monster
A monster in the shape of a girl

It all starts again just three weeks ago, in the girls' bathroom. Right after home room. I walk in. I'm not doing anything, I'm minding my own business, I just have to pee. Sofie is there. Applying this goofy blue eye-liner in a goofy blue line. Then guess-who comes kicking her way out of the end cubicle. Adrienne's been crying; her eyes are rabbity pink. No doubt there has been some new atrocity between her and Justin. *Let's go*. That's me, trying to head her off but Adrienne has already seen Sofie.

—*What are you looking at?* Sofie goes blank. She turns and fixes her sights on the tampax machine. *I asked you a question*. But Sofie is still in statue mode, uninhabited. No doubt Sofie's entire school life is an out of body experience.

Adrienne drops her Atlas on Sofie's foot. Sofie doesn't blink.

—*Pick it up*.
—*Let's go*.
—*I said pick it up*.

Do something, say something, anything, fight. Do something, say something, anything, fight . . .

But Sofie just bends over. And I hate her. As soon as she does it I know she's lost. Adrienne kicks Sofie down on all fours. All the work she'd put into being invisible, down the drain. Sofie is entirely visible—her legs are pink, her underwear covered in little blue circles.

Lovely. Sofie the horse. Sofie tries to get up and Adrienne's boot comes down in the centre of Sofie's back. *Did I say you could get up?* Sofie tries to turn her head around but Adrienne grabs her by the shirt. *Maybe the horse needs a drink of water*. Adrienne pulls Sofie over to the toilet.

And yes, finally. Sofie's head is turning, twisting away from Adrienne and . . . turning toward me. *Braidie please*.

You do what you have to do.
You look down.
Like this.

And then you navigate your way to the door using only your peripheral vision.

When I walk down the hall, I feel all weird and pukey. I feel like everyone is staring at me. I don't go to English; I just walk around. And then I don't go to Math or P.E. At lunch I go looking for Sofie. I go to the bus shelter. S.G. still carved into the bench. Why wouldn't it be?

After school, when I get on the bus, Adrienne is waiting, waiting for me.

—*Adrienne. What happened?* But she doesn't know what I'm talking about, can't remember, just a regular day. *What happened to Sofie?*

—*Nothing happened.* I see the empty seat behind the driver on the bus, Sofie's seat. A tremor starts, way down low on the floor of the ocean. *With someone like Sofie you never have to actually* DO *anything.* My hands are shaking, the bus pulls out. *Shut up* says Adrienne. *Stop breathing like a pervert.*

But Adrienne seems miles away now, deflated, her face behind her hair all white and skinny.

And she's gone. The friend I loved is gone. All that's left is the shape of a girl.

FOR EMERGENCY ONLY. I push out the window and it fans out from the bottom unnaturally. I puke all down the side of the bus. The driver lets me off. I walk back to school. I go right into the girls' bathroom. I wash my face. When I turn off the tap I hear a sound, from the last cubicle.

Sofie is sitting on the lid of the toilet. Her lips all puffed up and purple. When she sees who it is, she covers her head. *Don't worry . . .* She's acting like I'm going to hit her, which is so crazy. *I never did anything.* I bet she wishes you were there Trevor, hiding out behind the tampax machine, waiting to get off a good shot at me.

Sofie rocks back and forth then all of a sudden she smashes her head into the side of the stall.

We did a good job. Even Sofie hates Sofie.

*

A bell sounds as in the beginning.

Sound carries across water. On that full moon night, in Victoria, the word goes out that a girl was killed, that girl. Maybe there are groups of kids in schoolyards, malls . . . *Really?* And by the time her body is found—hundreds of kids know and hundreds of kids don't tell. Who is the one who told the unthinkable to their mum or their teacher? Who marched into the police station and said *see here, enough is enough?* I'll bet you a million dollars everyone thinks it wasn't a girl.

*

I always thought it was the voice of mum that made you escape Trevor. But I'm wondering now if you moved to Whistler to get away from me. In fact you might be ecstatic to know I am well on my way to becoming the official island outcast. I just wanted you to know one thing. One tiny thing that'll probably be the end of me.

Mum is forcing me to abandon homeschooling. I agreed, on the condition, that the voice of mum no longer speak to me. So yesterday the now defunct Braidie Institute went on our first and last field trip—to the Island Community Preschool. Remember preschool? Remember what a big deal it was?

They have this snazzy new building now. I'm hanging out at the fence like some kind of psycho. Watching all these kids smash into each other on their trikes and kicking around in the mud puddles. All these nutty four-year-olds doing their usual things. And Annie comes out. Her hair is all gray now. But she is still the same because this boy is hanging off her arm by his teeth and she doesn't even notice. You can tell she still thinks all kids are just dandy.

Then Annie spots me. *Braidie!* You'd think I was God or something. You'd think I was the greatest thing she's ever seen. And Annie comes running over. She smells like play dough. She opens the gate for me.

A spot shines brightly in front of BRAIDIE; *she steps into the light.*

And I understand for the first time what I have to say and how long I've been practising.

I wish to report the behaviour of . . .
I fear for . . .
I'm scared. Scared for the safety of another girl.
That she might do something crazy. Her name is Sofie. She has been treated in a despicable way by many people . . . including me.

Annie doesn't say anything. For the longest time she just nods. And then when she finally does speak it's in this weird whisper because she probably hates me. She will go with me to my school, to the principal. I tell her—*okay*.

She holds me tightly. Maybe she thinks I'm going to escape. Her arms still fit around me.

*

A bell sounds again then BRAIDIE *looks up.*

Sound carries across water. The girl in Victoria is discovered after eight days, her body seen floating from the air above. The stories were endless, the stories about how it all happened. Most of them weren't true. The only real story is the one told by her body, silently. This bruising beneath her eyes, the black nose and cheeks. The broken arm and the star burnt into her forehead.

A bell sounds fourteen times.

Sometimes I dream she got away, swam straight out into the ocean, maybe floated off on a log boom. Where? Not south to the States, not here. I don't know how to imagine it; I don't know where her safe place might be. I only know how to go backwards.

BRAIDIE *goes back in time, she is eight years old.*

We are eight years old. We are all planting our toes in the edge of the water. We're at the blind beach, it's summer, the water is foamy and brown around our feet. We are all wearing life jackets. Adrienne, Amber, Sofie and me. The jackets make us feel like we can go anywhere, do anything—deep water, waves, you name it, all these possibilities.

We are brave, we are perfect—girls.

The End

(2001)

Appendix: Critical Approaches for Interpreting Literature

We are all critics. That is, we find ourselves in conversations about books, movies, and TV shows, conversations in which we express our likes and dislikes, approval and disapproval, often disagreeing with one another. You may devour romance novels in your spare time, while your best friend thinks those same novels are silly and a waste of time. Meanwhile, that friend seeks out the latest in experimental science fiction, which you find confusing and pointless. The two of you are coming from different tastes, for sure, but you are both taking different critical stances about what makes a book good. You value emotional involvement and absorption, as well as a satisfying beginning–middle–happy-ending structure, and that's what you get in romance novels. Your friend doesn't care at all about a predictable structure and an absorbing love story but values mental playfulness, challenge, and the element of surprise in her leisure reading. No one can say that one or the other is right. In using the word *criticism* in relation to the arts, we do not mean fault-finding as we do in everyday conversation; literary criticism has to do with interpretation of a work. Some literary criticism does evaluate or judge a work as good or bad, but appraisal is not the main point in most cases.

Just as friends can be separated into groups according to what they look for in leisure reading, literary critics can be loosely grouped according to what they look for in written works. They apply a systematic method to the interpretation of a piece and usually have a preferred method or combination of methods. For example, one critic may customarily think about a work in terms of how it reflects the historical period in which it was written, whereas another likes to focus on the images of femininity and masculinity depicted in the work. You can learn the various points of view that people use to interpret and judge literature. Probably some of them are the points of view you already use informally, and seeing them laid out in an orderly way will help you study and write about literature. You will want to be acquainted with all the standard approaches, because you need to match the critical point of view with the specific work you are studying. There is no one-size-fits-all option.

FORMALISM

A formalist critic looks at a piece of literature as complete within itself. The formalist approach appreciates the way in which all the features of a piece work together in a unified, meaningful whole. These features are, for the most part, what you study in this textbook: structure, imagery, character development, setting, language, and so on. The term *formalist*, instead of being directly related to the idea of formality, is related to the idea of *form*. In this book we encourage you to perceive the form and content of literature as deeply entwined. For example, as Chapter 13 suggests, rhythm and rhyme are considered for the way they enhance tone and meaning. A prominent technique of the formalist critic is *close reading*, which we have promoted in this textbook as essential in making a first attempt at interpreting literature.

A strictly formalist reading does not bring in outside sources. The main tools are imagination and skill in analyzing the various features of literature. Support for an interpretation comes from evidence within the poem, story, or play.

HISTORICAL APPROACHES

In contrast with formalism, several approaches emphasize that the writer was leading a life in a certain time in history, and that events in personal life and in the world affect the literature produced. Historical critics examine a work in the context of its time. They try to see the work as people in the original audience would have. For example, Kate Chopin's "The Story of an Hour," published in 1894, shocked its original nineteenth-century readers with its focus on a woman's attitude toward her stifling marriage to a benevolent patriarch. Women's expectation of independence is commonplace in our time, so it helps us understand the story to know that in its own day a sympathetic portrayal of Louise was considered outrageous.

Several types of historical approach are possible, focusing on specialized aspects of the past. These aspects may be biographical, cultural, or political.

BIOGRAPHICAL

Diaries, letters, journals, biographies, and autobiographies are tools of the critic who investigates how an author's life is reflected in his or her imaginative writing. Emily Dickinson's hermit-like seclusion in real life often serves to help illuminate her difficult poems because we can speculate on how her unusual solitude gave her an extraordinary point of view on things others take for granted or do not see at all. Similarly, we can appreciate Wilfred Owen's "Dulce et Decorum Est" more fully when we know that he served in World War I, was wounded in 1917 (shortly before the poem was written), and died in action in 1918. The powerful, detailed imagery of the poem is rooted in real-life experience.

CULTURAL

Cultural critics use materials beyond the standard biographical information and history books to examine literature. They are likely to look at cultural artifacts like the period's advertisements, architecture, journalism, campaign speeches, political tracts, fads, and popular literature such as comic books when they set a work in historical context. Jim Wong-Chu's poem "old chinese cemetery kamloops" lends itself to such an approach because the speaker tries to understand himself by identifying with his Chinese predecessors in Canada. Knowing how important ancestors are to the Chinese culture is an important element in understanding and interpreting the poem. The Chinese men buried in Kamloops were probably part of a crew of Chinese immigrants hired for scant wages to work on the railway. A cultural critic would be more likely than a formalist to examine a work of literature in terms of its time. For example, such a critic might argue that Jim Wong-Chu focuses on the cultural importance of the long-dead men not only to the persona but also to an entire cultural group's sense of themselves as Canadians.

MARXIST

Another historical point of view that may include judgment or evaluation of literature is the Marxist approach. Marxist critics take the stance that literature, driven by economic forces and class struggle, is an artifact of history. They see the fine arts as frequently a reflection of the values of the privileged class, endorsing the status quo rather than challenging it. A Marxist critic would probably point out that Russell Smith's "Serotonin" focuses on the concerns of a self-absorbed character and neglects people who have no leisure to spend so much time in an altered state of consciousness determining the nature of love. Many works of literature do lend themselves to a more fruitful Marxist analysis; for example, Pablo Neruda in his poem "The United Fruit Co." poignantly exposes the colonialism of American companies as they exploit the workers of South American nations.

PSYCHOLOGICAL APPROACHES

Timothy Findley's "Stones" could be approached from a psychological point of view. The father in the story shows signs of post-traumatic stress disorder (PTSD) following his experiences at Dieppe. People suffering from PTSD engage in thoughts and behaviours that interfere with their leading their everyday lives.

Because a grasp of human motivation is key to understanding so much literature, psychology comes into play continually, and many critics make a practice of looking at literature through the lenses of psychological theories. It is difficult to discuss a story like Willa Cather's "Paul's Case" without psychoanalyzing the main character, who seems narcissistic as well as manic-depressive. Freud's theories inform much psychological literary criticism, so explorations of characters' subconscious motivations, defences, inner conflicts, and symbolic acts are commonplace. The shock of being a witness to trauma is the experience of characters in Eugene McNamara's "Falling in Place," so an understanding of the psychological condition of post-traumatic stress disorder could help in a psychological approach to analyzing the story as well. Sometimes psychological critics use their tools not to examine the characters, but to analyze the author in their search for meaning in the literary work, and in such cases their pursuit combines the biographical and psychological approaches. It is never appropriate, however, to assume that in order to write about psychological disorders an author must have suffered from such a disorder. All judgments made about an author must be grounded in reliable and available information.

MYTHOLOGICAL AND ARCHETYPAL APPROACHES

Another approach is related to mass psychology rather than individual idiosyncrasies. Mythological or archetypal critics look at commonalities among dreams, myths, legends, religions, visual arts, and literature, and they see the same threads running through human imaginative work throughout the ages and across cultures. One such thread, for instance, is the quest or journey, during which the main character is challenged sorely (often three times), gaining wisdom and insight along the way to a heroic ending point (or not, having failed the challenge). Another thread is the hero who dies for the salvation of all humankind. Archetypal plots and characters are associated with the theories of the Swiss psychologist Carl Jung, who believed that every person is born equipped with a collective unconscious, a set of images including many universal fictional characters such as the wise old man, the fool, the trickster, the manly rescuer, the earth mother, and the mysterious stranger, as well as others. Our attraction to certain types of stories and characters comes from the way they appeal to our collective unconscious. Arnold Friend, the menacing yet magnetic visitor in Joyce Carol Oates's "Where Are You Going, Where Have You Been?" can be seen as a trickster archetype.

GENDER FOCUS

Drawing from psychological, sociological, and political thought as well as from literary studies, many critics in the twentieth and twenty-first centuries look at art through the lenses of gender. They ponder how sex roles, sexual identity, and relationships between the sexes affect the way that a work is written and read. A gender-based reading of Timothy Findley's "Stones" would emphasize that the relationship between the father and son is what it is because they are males in a society that expects certain behaviours from men. Within the fold of gender-focused critics are feminist critics, who would analyze the story in terms of women's strategies to cope with their powerlessness in the male-oriented world. Feminists explain the disparate experiences of the sexes by analyzing the effects of the differences in power, privilege, and expectations. Hisaye Yamamoto's "Seventeen Syllables" is ripe for a feminist approach, especially for understanding the mother's motivations. Feminist critics are interested in the images of women and men as presented in literature, often pointing out negative portrayals of women that might otherwise go unnoticed.

Another gender focus involves the lives and lifestyles of gay and lesbian authors, characters, and readers. As a minority culture, gays and lesbians have a distinctive experience that has often been ignored, despised, or treated as exotic. These attitudes frequently affect the way they write and are written about (or avoided). David Henry Hwang's *M. Butterfly* derives much of its impact from society's fear-driven attitudes toward homosexuality, gender roles, and ethnic stereotypes.

READER RESPONSE

The critical approaches discussed so far share the idea that a work of literature has a meaning, probably one that is stable and coherent. The last two we will take up do not share this idea, but focus on the variety of interpretation that is possible. The reader response approach accepts that each person brings his or her own experiences and points of view to bear while reading. No one reads a work in exactly the same way as anyone else, as you have probably noticed in discussions with classmates and friends. In fact, you may have read the same work differently within your own life as you got older. One of our colleagues claims that no one can possibly understand *Macbeth* before the age of thirty! Although reader response critics will not allow totally far-fetched interpretations of a work, they are interested in individuals' different reactions to ambiguous clues. For example, when J. Alfred Prufrock asks, "Do I dare to eat a peach?" one reader may think that Prufrock is worried about the embarrassing messiness of consuming a ripe peach, another may think that he fears looking greedy, and another may decide that the peach is a feminine symbol and Prufrock fears the sex act. All of these thoughts are defensible using other evidence within the poem, and all are probably projections of the reader's own fears.

DECONSTRUCTION

Deconstructionists take a step beyond reader response critics by viewing a work of literature as unstable and therefore vulnerable to being taken apart (de-constructed). Whereas formalists look for the way that all the elements of a piece fit together, deconstructionists look for the way these elements contradict each other and undermine coherence. Their point of view is rooted in a philosophy of language that suggests words are incapable of accurately expressing meaning, that every utterance contains a lie by omitting all other possible utterances at the moment. Other critical stances reject interpretations that cannot be supported by evidence within the work, but deconstructionists delight in bizarre and contradictory claims. For example, while most people view J. Alfred Prufrock as a timid, self-effacing, and fearful fellow, deconstructionists might ask why a timid person would present such a lengthy, detailed, self-absorbed introspection. They could argue that J. Alfred is a braggart and narcissist, enchanted with his own superhuman sensitivity.

WHERE DO YOU STAND?

As you read our brief summaries of critical approaches, you probably recognized the ones that you most regularly use when you think and write about literature. You may find it illuminating to try out some different approaches, especially when your usual tools are not working. You may also find it mind-expanding to look up work by other critics who share your favourite stance, learning from them how to use it more consciously and effectively. You can begin by reading an example of a formalist interpretation of Robert Hayden's "Those Winter Sundays" that we have reprinted in Chapter 13 or by examining the critical interpretation of Timothy Findley's writings about war and his concern with class distinction in Lorraine M. York's "Epilogue: *Stones*" reprinted in Chapter 5.

Glossary of Literary and Rhetorical Terms

Allegory A form of symbolism in which ideas or abstract qualities are represented as characters or events in a story, novel, or play. For example, in the medieval drama *Everyman*, Fellowship, Kindred, and Goods, the friends of the title character, will not accompany him on his end-of-life journey, and he must depend on Good Works, whom he has previously neglected.

Alliteration Repetition of the same consonant sounds, usually at the beginning of words:

> Blows out her furbelows,
> Her bustling boughs;
> —Dorothy Livesay

Allusion An indirect reference to some character or event in literature, history, or mythology that enriches the meaning of the passage. For example, the title of Alden Nowlan's poem "I, Icarus" is an ironic allusion to the figure in Greek mythology who fell into the sea after flying too close to the sun.

Ambiguity Something that may be validly interpreted in more than one way; double meaning.

Anapest *See* Meter.

Antagonist The character (or a force such as war or poverty) in a drama, poem, or work of fiction whose actions oppose those of the protagonist (hero or heroine).

Anticlimax A trivial event following immediately after significant events.

Apostrophe A poetic figure of speech in which a personification is addressed:

> Be strong, O paddle ! be brave, canoe !
> —Pauline Johnson

Archetype A recurring character type, plot, symbol, or theme of seemingly universal significance: the blind prophet figure, the journey to the underworld, the sea as source of life, the initiation theme.

Assonance The repetition of similar vowel sounds within syllables:

> To him who hears them grief beyond control
> —Archibald Lampman

Atmosphere *See* Mood.

Audience In composition, the readers for whom a piece of writing is intended.

Ballad A narrative poem in four-line stanzas, rhyming *x a x a*, often sung or recited as a folk tale. The *x* means that those two lines do not rhyme.

Blank Verse Unrhymed iambic pentameter, the line that most closely resembles speech in English:

> I have no use for measured, cadenced verse
> If you won't read. Icarus-like, I'll fall

> Against this page of snow, tumble blackly
> Across vision to drown in the white sea
> —George Elliott Clarke

Carpe Diem Literally, seize the day, a phrase applicable to many lyric poems advocating lustful living:

> Gather ye rosebuds while ye may,
> Old time is still a-flying:
> And this same flower that smiles today
> Tomorrow will be dying.
> —Robert Herrick

Catharsis In classical tragedy, the purging of pity and fear experienced by the audience at the end of the play; a "there but for the grace of the gods go I" sense of relief.

Chorus In Greek drama, a group (often led by an individual) that comments on or interprets the action of the play.

Climax The point toward which the action of a plot builds as the conflicts become increasingly intense or complex; the turning point.

Coherence In good writing, the orderly, logical relationship among the many parts—the smooth moving forward of ideas through clearly related sentences. *Also see* Unity.

Comedy A play, light in tone, designed to amuse and entertain, that usually ends happily, often with a marriage.

Comedy of Manners A risqué play satirizing the conventions of courtship and marriage.

Complication The rising action of a plot during which the conflicts build toward the climax.

Conceit A highly imaginative, often startling, figure of speech drawing an analogy between two unlike things in an ingenious way:

> In this sad state, God's tender bowels run
> Out streams of grace. . . .
> —Edward Taylor

Concrete That which can be touched, seen, or tasted; not abstract. Concrete illustrations make abstractions easier to understand.

Concrete Poetry Poetry whose meaning is conveyed not only through the words themselves but through unusual typography and patterns of letters, words, or symbols.

Conflict The antagonism between opposing characters or forces that causes tension or suspense in the plot.

Connotation The associations that attach themselves to many words, deeply affecting their literal meanings (e.g., *politician, statesman*).

Consonance Close repetition of the same consonant sounds preceded by different vowel sounds (*flesh/flash* or *breed/bread*). At the end of lines of poetry, this pattern produces half-rhyme.

Controlling Idea *See* Thesis.

Controlling Image In a short story, novel, play, or poem, an image that recurs and carries such symbolic significance that it embodies the theme of the work, as the boat does in Alistair MacLeod's story of the same name, and as the zero does in Lorna Crozier's "Poem about Nothing."

Convention An accepted improbability in a literary work, such as the dramatic aside, in which an actor turns from the stage and addresses the audience.

Couplet Two rhymed lines of poetry:

> For thy sweet love remembered such wealth brings
> That then I scorn to change my state with kings.
> —William Shakespeare

Crisis *See* Climax.

Dactyl *See* Meter.

Denotation The literal dictionary meaning of a word.

Denouement Literally, the "untying"; the resolution of the conflicts following the climax (or crisis) of a plot.

Diction Words chosen in writing or speaking.

Double Entendre A double meaning, one of which usually carries sexual suggestions, as in the country-western song about a truck driver who calls his wife long distance to say he is bringing his "big ol' engine" home to her.

Dramatic Irony *See* Irony.

Dramatic Monologue A poem consisting of a self-revealing speech delivered by one person to a silent listener; for instance, Robert Browning's "My Last Duchess."

Dramatic Point of View *See* Point of View.

Elegy A poem commemorating someone's death but usually encompassing a larger issue as well.

Empathy Literally, "feeling in"; the emotional identification that a reader or an audience feels with a character.

English Sonnet *See* Sonnet.

Epigram A short, witty saying that often conveys a bit of wisdom:

> Heaven for climate; hell for society.
> —Mark Twain

Epigraph A quotation at the beginning of a poem, novel, play, or essay that suggests the theme of the work.

Epilogue The concluding section of a literary work, usually a play, in which loose threads are tied together or a moral is drawn.

Epiphany A moment of insight in which something simple and commonplace is seen in a new way and, as James Joyce said, "its soul, its whatness leaps to us from the vestment of its appearance."

Episode In a narrative, a unified sequence of events; in Greek drama, the action between choruses.

Exposition That part of a plot devoted to supplying background information, explaining events that happened before the current action.

Fable A story, usually using symbolic characters and settings, designed to teach a lesson.

Falling Action In classical dramatic structure, the part of a play after the climax, in which the consequences of the conflict are revealed. *Also see* Denouement.

Figurative Language Words that carry suggestive or symbolic meaning beyond the literal level.

First-Person Point of View *See* Point of View.

Flashback Part of a narrative that interrupts the chronological flow by relating events from the past.

Flat Character In contrast to a well-developed round character, a flat one is stereotyped or shallow, not seeming as complex as real people; flat characters are often created deliberately to give them a symbolic role, like Faith in "Young Goodman Brown."

Foil A character, usually a minor one, who emphasizes the qualities of another one through implied contrast between the two.

Foot A unit of poetic rhythm. *See* Meter.

Foreshadowing Early clues about what will happen later in a narrative or play.

Formal Writing The highest level of usage, in which no slang, contractions, or fragments are used. Usually associated with the language of law and usually too lofty for undergraduate academic writing.

Free Verse Poetry that does not have regular rhythm, rhyme, or standard form.

Freewriting Writing without regard to coherence or correctness, intended to relax the writer and produce ideas for further writing.

Genre A classification of literature: drama, novel, short story, poem.

Hero/Heroine The character intended to engage most fully the audience's or reader's sympathies and admiration. *Also see* Protagonist.

Hubris Unmitigated pride, often the cause of the hero's downfall in Greek tragedy.

Hyperbole A purposeful exaggeration.

Iamb *See* Meter.

Image/Imagery Passages or words that stir feelings or memories through an appeal to the senses.

Informal Writing The familiar, everyday level of usage, which includes contractions and perhaps slang but precludes nonstandard grammar and punctuation.

Internal Rhyme The occurrence of similar sounds within the lines of a poem rather than just at the ends of lines:

> Too bright for our infirm delight
> —Emily Dickinson

Invention The process of generating subjects, topics, details, and plans for writing.

Irony Lack of agreement between expectation and reality.

Verbal irony involves a major discrepancy between the words spoken or written and the intended meaning. For example, Stephen Crane writes, "War is kind," but he means—and the poem shows—that war is hell.

Situational irony can stem quite literally from irony of situation. For example, in Thomas King's "Borders," the narrator and his mother remain in limbo between the Canadian and American checkpoints, neither border guard accepting the mother's insistence on "Blackfoot" as her citizenship. Situational irony can also involve the contrast between the hopes, aspirations, or fears of a character and the outcome of that person's actions or eventual fate. For example, in Timothy Findley's "Stones," the narrator's father goes off to war eagerly, only to return a broken man.

Dramatic irony involves the difference between what a character knows or believes and what the better-informed reader or audience knows to be true. For example, in Ethel Wilson's "The Window," while Mr. Willy is absorbed in philosophical thoughts about death he is unaware of being watched through his window by a violent thief.

Italian Sonnet *See* Sonnet.

Jargon The specialized words and expressions belonging to certain professions, sports, hobbies, or social groups. Sometimes any tangled and incomprehensible prose is called jargon.

Juxtaposition The simultaneous presentation of two conflicting images or ideas, designed to make a point of the contrast: for example, an elaborate and well-kept church surrounded by squalid slums.

Limited Point of View *See* Point of View.

Lyric A poem that primarily expresses emotion.

Metaphor A figure of speech that makes an imaginative comparison between two literally unlike things: Sylvia's face was a pale star.

Metaphysical Poetry A style of poetry (usually associated with seventeenth-century poet John Donne) that boasts intellectual, complex, and even strained images (called *conceits*), which frequently link the personal and familiar to the cosmic and mysterious. *Also see* Conceit.

Meter Recurring patterns of stressed and unstressed syllables in poetry. A metrical unit is called a *foot*. There are four basic patterns of stress: an *iamb*, or *iambic foot*, which consists of an unstressed syllable followed by a stressed one (*before, return*); a *trochee*, or *trochaic foot*, which consists of a stressed syllable followed by an unstressed one (*funny, double*); an *anapest*, or *anapestic foot*, which consists of two unstressed syllables followed by a stressed one (*contradict*); and a *dactyl*, or *dactylic foot*, which consists of a stressed syllable followed by two unstressed ones (*merrily, syllable*). One common variation is the *spondee*, or *spondaic foot*, which consists of two stressed syllables (*moonshine, football*).

Lines are classified according to the number of metrical feet they contain: *monometer* (one foot), *dimeter* (two feet), *trimeter* (three feet), *tetrameter* (four feet), *pentameter* (five feet), *hexameter* (six feet), and so on.

Metonymy A figure of speech in which the name of one thing is substituted for that of something else closely associated with it—for example, *Crown* for monarch or *the pen is mightier than the sword* (meaning written words are more powerful than military force).

Mood The emotional content of a scene or setting, usually described in terms of feeling: sombre, gloomy, joyful, expectant. *Also see* Tone.

Motif A pattern of identical or similar images recurring throughout a passage or entire work.

Myth A traditional story involving deities and heroes, usually expressing and inculcating the established values of a culture.

Narrative A story line in prose or verse.

Narrator The person who tells the story to the audience or reader. *Also see* Unreliable Narrator.

Objective Point of View *See* Point of View.
Ode A long, serious lyric focusing on a stated theme: "Ode on a Grecian Urn."
Omniscient Point of View *See* Point of View.
Onomatopoeia A word that sounds like what it names: *whoosh, clang, babble.*
Oxymoron A single phrase that juxtaposes opposite terms:

> the lonely crowd, a roaring silence.

Parable A story designed to demonstrate a principle or lesson using symbolic characters, details, and plot lines.
Paradox An apparently contradictory statement that, upon examination, makes sense:

> In my end is my beginning.
> —Motto of Mary, Queen of Scots

The motto is intelligible only in the context of Christian theology, which promises renewed life after death.
Paraphrase In prose, a restatement in different words, usually briefer than the original version; in poetry, a statement of the literal meaning of the poem in everyday language.
Parody An imitation of a piece of writing, copying some features such as diction, style, and form, but changing or exaggerating other features for humorous effect.
Pentameter A line of poetry that contains five metrical feet. *See* Meter.
Persona The person created by the writer to be the speaker of the poem or story. The persona is not usually identical to the writer—for example, a personally optimistic writer could create a cynical persona to narrate a story.
Personification Giving human qualities to nonhuman things:

> the passionate song of bullets and the banshee shrieks of shells
> —Stephen Crane

Phallic Symbol An image shaped like the male sex organ; suggests male potency or male dominance (*towers, snakes, spurs, jet planes, sleek cars*).
Plagiarism Carelessly or deliberately presenting the words or ideas of another writer as your own; literary theft.
Plot A series of causally related events or episodes that occur in a narrative or play. *Also see* Climax, Complication, Conflict, Denouement, Falling Action, Resolution, and Rising Action.
Point of View The angle or perspective from which a story is reported and interpreted. There are four common points of view that authors use:

First person—someone, often the main character, tells the story as he or she experienced it (and uses the pronoun *I*).

Omniscient—the narrator knows everything about the characters and events and can move about in time and place and into the minds of all the characters.

Limited—the story is limited to the observations, thoughts, and feelings of a single character (not identified as *I*).

Shifting—a limited view which can shift to the perspective of more than one character.

Objective or *dramatic*—the actions and conversations are presented in detail as they occur, more or less objectively, without any comment from the author or a narrator.

Unreliable—narrated from the point of view of a character unable or perhaps unwilling to give a fully accurate account.

Prewriting The process that writers use to gather ideas, consider audience, determine purpose, develop a thesis and tentative structure (plan), and generally prepare for the actual writing stage.

Primary Source The literary work under consideration by the reader.

Protagonist The main character in drama or fiction, sometimes called the hero or heroine.

Pun A verbal joke based on the similarity of sound between words that have different meanings:

> They went and *told* the sexton and the sexton *tolled* the bell.
> —Thomas Hood

Quatrain A four-line stanza of poetry, which can have any number of rhyme schemes.

Resolution The conclusion of the conflict in a fictional or dramatic plot. *Also see* Denouement *and* Falling Action.

Rhyme Similar or identical sounds between words, usually the end sounds in lines of verse (*brain/strain; liquor/quicker*).

Rhythm The recurrence of stressed and unstressed syllables in a regular pattern. *Also see* Meter.

Rising Action The complication and development of the conflict leading to the climax in a plot.

Round Character A literary character with sufficient complexity to be convincing, true to life.

Sarcasm A form of *verbal irony* that presents caustic and bitter disapproval in the guise of praise. *Also see* Irony.

Satire Literary expression that uses humour and wit to attack and expose human folly and weakness. *Also see* Parody.

Secondary Source Critical material from the library or the internet (*articles, reviews, books, sections of books*).

Sentimentality The attempt to produce an emotional response that exceeds the circumstances and to draw from the readers a stock response instead of a genuine emotional response.

Setting The time and place in which a story, play, or novel occurs. *Also see* Mood.

Shakespearean Sonnet *See* Sonnet.

Simile A verbal comparison in which a similarity is expressed directly, using *like* or *as*:

> houses leaning together like conspirators.
> —James Joyce

Also see Metaphor.

Situational Irony *See* Irony.

Soliloquy A speech in which a dramatic character reveals what is going through his or her mind by talking aloud to herself or himself. *Also see* Dramatic Monologue.

Sonnet A poem of fourteen ten-syllable lines, arranged in a pattern of rhyme schemes. The *English* or *Shakespearean sonnet* uses seven rhymes that divide the poem into three quatrains and a couplet: *a b a b, c d c d, e f e f, g g*. The *Italian sonnet* usually divides into an octave (eight lines) and a sestet (six lines) by using only five rhymes: *a b b a, a b b a, c d e c d e*. (The rhyme scheme of the sestet varies widely from sonnet to sonnet.)

Speaker The voice or person presenting a poem.

Spondee *See* Meter.

Standard English The language that is written and spoken by most educated persons of English-speaking countries.

Stereotype An oversimplified, commonly held image or opinion about a person, a race, or an issue.

Stilted Language Words and expressions that are too formal for the writing situation; unnatural, artificial language.

Structure The general plan, framework, or form of a piece of writing.

Style Individuality of expression, achieved in writing through the selection and arrangement of words and punctuation.

Subplot Secondary plot in a novel or play, usually reinforcing the main theme but sometimes just providing interest, excitement, or comic relief.

Symbol Something that suggests or stands for an idea, quality, or concept larger than itself: the lion is a symbol of courage; a voyage or journey can symbolize life; water suggests spirituality, dryness the lack thereof.

Synecdoche A figure of speech in which some prominent feature is used to name the whole, or vice versa—for example, *a sail in the harbour* (meaning a ship), or *call the law* (meaning call the law enforcement officers).

Synesthesia Figurative language in which two or more sense impressions are combined:

> blue uncertain stumbling buzz
> —Emily Dickinson

Syntax Sentence structure; the relationship between words and among word groups in sentences.

Theme The central or dominating idea advanced by a literary work, usually containing some insight into the human condition.

Thesis The main point or position that a writer develops and supports in a composition.

Tone The attitude a writer conveys toward his or her subject and audience. In poetry this attitude is sometimes called *voice*.

Tragedy A serious drama that relates the events in the life of a protagonist, or *tragic hero*, whose error in judgment, dictated by a *tragic flaw*, results in the hero's downfall and culminates in catastrophe. In less classical terms, any serious drama, novel, or short story that ends with the death or defeat of the main character may be called tragic.

Trochee *See* Meter.

Type Character A literary character who embodies a number of traits that are common to a particular group or class of people (a rebellious daughter, a stern father, a jealous lover).

Understatement A form of ironic expression that intentionally minimizes the importance of an idea or fact.

Unity The fitting together or harmony of all elements in a piece of writing. *Also see* Coherence.

Unreliable Narrator A viewpoint character who presents a biased or erroneous report that may mislead or distort a reader's judgments about other characters and actions; sometimes the unreliable narrator may be self-deceived.

Usage The accepted or customary way of using words in speaking and writing a language.

Verbal Irony *See* Irony.

Verisimilitude The appearance of truth or believability in a literary work.

Versification The mechanics of poetic composition, including such elements as rhyme, rhythm, meter, and stanza form.

Yonic Symbol An image shaped like the female breasts, uterus, or genitalia; suggests fecundity or female sexuality (*caves, pots, rooms, apples, full-blown roses*).

Biographical Notes

CHINUA ACHEBE (b. 1930) started out as a writer for the Nigerian Broadcasting Corporation, but his first novel, *Things Fall Apart* (1958), which depicts the conflicts of African and European culture in Nigeria, brought him international success. His fiction often deals with the legacy of colonialism in Africa, reflecting the civil war and violence that have racked Nigeria since it gained independence from British rule in 1963. Achebe has taught in Canada and at the University of Connecticut.

MATTHEW ARNOLD (1822–1888), born in Middlesex, England, studied classics at Oxford and later taught there. He was appointed inspector of schools for England and remained in that post for thirty-five years. As a poet, Arnold took his inspiration from Greek tragedies, Keats, and Wordsworth. An eminent social and literary critic in later years, he lectured in America in 1883 and 1886. His essay "The Function of Criticism" explains his shift from poet to critic.

MARGARET ATWOOD (b. 1939) was born in Ottawa and attended the University of Toronto and Radcliffe College, Harvard. Her vast list of publications includes criticism, poetry, short stories, and novels. Among her many awards are the 1985 Governor General's Award for her novel *The Handmaid's Tale*; the 1994 Trillium Award; the Commonwealth Writers' Prize and France's Chevalier dans l'Ordre des Arts et des Lettres for *The Robber Bride*; the 1996 Giller Prize for *Alias Grace*; and the 2000 Booker Prize for *The Blind Assassin*. "Death of a Young Son by Drowning" and "Dream 2: Brian the Still-Hunter" are from *The Journals of Susanna Moodie* (1970), Atwood's writings about this early Canadian figure.

W. H. AUDEN (1907–1973) was born in England but became a U.S. citizen in 1946. An extremely talented poet, he was a major literary voice of the 1930s, an "age of anxiety" that faced world war and global depression. Influenced by Freud, Auden often wrote about human guilt and fear, but he also celebrated the power of love to overcome anxiety. His volume of poetry *The Age of Anxiety* (1947) won the Pulitzer Prize. Auden also collaborated on verse plays and wrote librettos for operas.

MARGARET AVISON (b. 1918) was born in Galt, Ontario, and has worked as a librarian, editor, lecturer, and social worker. Her first poetry collection, *The Winter Sun* (1960), won the Governor General's Award, as did *No Time* (1989). Her collection *The Dumbfounding* (1966) and her poetry since mark a simplification of her poetic form and demonstrate a spiritual struggle that reflects her own dramatic embracing of Christianity in 1963. Avison's poem "The Swimmer's Moment" endorses the idea that everyone will come to a defining moment of decision and commitment.

SANDRA BIRDSELL (b. 1942) was born in Manitoba to a Russian-Mennonite mother and Métis father, the fifth of ten children. She now lives in Saskatchewan. Since 1982 she has published several books of short fiction and novels, all focusing on female characters in rural communities. In her story "The Wednesday Circle," ironic sentiments such as "Occasionally

"... in this room someone dares to speak the truth," spoken by a member of a Bible-reading sewing circle, illustrate Birdsell's satirical voice.

EARLE BIRNEY (1904–1995) was born in Alberta and was raised there and in rural BC. The influence of his early, very physically demanding work as a mountain guide and on survey teams and road crews can be seen throughout his fifteen volumes of poetry and two novels. After serving in the Canadian army in World War II, Birney taught in the English department at UBC until his retirement in 1965. His focus on medieval literature is evident in the Old English conventions of his poem "Anglosaxon Street."

WILLIAM BLAKE (1757–1827) was both artist and poet, though he achieved little success as either during his lifetime. Of the more than half a dozen books he wrote and illustrated, only one was published conventionally; his wife helped him print the rest. A mystic and visionary, Blake created his own mythology, complete with illustrations. His best-known volumes of poetry are *Songs of Innocence* (1789) and *Songs of Experience* (1794).

DIONNE BRAND (b. 1953) was born in Guayguayare, Trinidad, and moved to Toronto in 1970. Her publications include the prose poems of *No Language Is Neutral* (1990), the collection of essays *Bread out of Stone* (1994), and the novel *In Another Place, Not Here* (1996). Her 1997 poetry collection *Land to Light On* won the Governor General's Award. Her works cover race and gender as well as political and lesbian issues.

GWENDOLYN BROOKS (1917–2000) was an African-American poet whose work often focused on ghetto life. Although from a middle-class family, Brooks identified with poor blacks, and the simplicity of her poetic voice often mirrored the meagre circumstances of her subjects. Her second book of poetry, *Annie Allen* (1949), won the Pulitzer Prize in 1950, making Brooks the first African-American woman to receive this award. Brooks was named poet laureate of Illinois in 1969.

ROBERT BROWNING (1812–1889) was an English poet who experimented with diction and rhythm as well as with psychological portraits in verse. He secretly married Elizabeth Barrett, and they moved to Italy in 1846, partly to avoid her domineering father. Browning was a master of dramatic monologues, exemplified in "My Last Duchess." After the death of his wife, Browning returned to England, where he wrote what some consider his masterwork, *The Ring and the Book* (1868–1869).

GEORGE GORDON, LORD BYRON (1788–1824) was born in London of an aristocratic family and educated at Cambridge. He became a public figure, as much for his scandalous personal life as for his irreverent, satiric poetry. Rumours about an affair with his half-sister forced him to leave England in 1816. Byron died in Greece from a fever that he contracted while fighting for Greek independence. His masterpiece is the comic epic poem *Don Juan*, begun in 1819 and still unfinished when he died.

ANNE CARSON (b. 1950) lives in Montreal and instructs at McGill University, where she is director of graduate studies, classics. Her background in anthropology and the classics is evident in her work. *Glass and God* (1998), *Autobiography of Red* (1998), and *If Not, Winter: Fragments of Sappho* (2002) are among her many publications. The poem "God's Work" from her collection *The Truth about God* is suggestive of the Buddhist "no-mind" principle.

WILLA CATHER (1873–1947) moved from Virginia to Nebraska with her family when she was nine, and the hard-working immigrant people there became characters in some of her finest work, including *O Pioneers!* (1913) and *My Ántonia* (1918). After graduating from the University of Nebraska in 1895, she became a magazine editor in Pittsburgh. In 1906 she moved to New York to edit *McClure's Magazine*, and in 1911 she resigned that position to begin her writing career in earnest. Although she lived most of her life in New York with her long-time companion Edith Lewis, Cather never forgot the pioneer past that she discovered in Nebraska: its qualities of resourcefulness, industry, courage, and sympathy are celebrated in her works, especially in contrast to the crass materialism of modern society.

ANTON CHEKHOV (1860–1904), a multitalented man whose gifts were matched by his humanitarianism, was born in southern Russia, studied medicine in Moscow, and supported himself by writing humorous sketches. Later he ran a free clinic for peasants while gaining fame as a playwright. He established close ties with the famous Moscow Art Theater, where his great plays, including *Three Sisters* (1901) and *The Cherry Orchard* (1904), were produced. His emphasis on characterization and tragicomedy has influenced a generation of modern dramatists.

KATE CHOPIN (1851–1904) was born Kate O'Flaherty in St. Louis. After her father died when she was four, she was raised by her mother, grandmother, and great-grandmother, all widows. In 1870 she married Oscar Chopin and moved to New Orleans. Although she published numerous short stories in popular magazines, Chopin made her greatest impact with *The Awakening* (1899), a short novel that was widely banned in the United States. Her explorations of female sexuality and her championing of women's self-worth, both of which outraged readers at the turn of the century, are no longer shocking.

GEORGE ELLIOTT CLARKE (b. 1960) was born in Windsor, Nova Scotia. He won the 2001 Governor General's Award for his poetry collection *Execution Poems*. In this collection, as in much of his work, Clarke opens up Canada's history of racism, expressing its painful results in language that is at once modern and formal. He often does this, as his poem "Blank Sonnet" demonstrates, by writing in transformed traditional formats.

LEONARD COHEN (b. 1934) is a prolific poet, novelist, and songwriter. In his first major creative period his many works included the poetry collection *Let Us Compare Mythologies* (1954); two novels, *The Favourite Game* (1963) and *Beautiful Losers* (1966); a recording, *The Songs of Leonard Cohen* (1968); and the *Selected Poems* (1968), for which he won (and refused) a Governor General's Award. He released several new albums in the 1980s and received the Governor General's Award for Performing Arts in 1993.

STEPHEN CRANE (1871–1900) was born in Newark, the fourteenth child of a Methodist minister who died when Crane was nine. Leaving college early, he moved to New York City, where he observed firsthand the boozers and prostitutes who inhabited the slums. His first novel, *Maggie: A Girl of the Streets* (1893), drew on these observations. At age twenty-four, and with no military experience, he wrote *The Red Badge of Courage* (1895), a Civil War novel that made him famous and became an American classic.

LORNA CROZIER (b. 1948) was born in Swift Current, Saskatchewan, and received a B.A. from the University of Saskatchewan and an M.A. from the University of Alberta. Her poetry collection *Inventing the Hawk* (1992) won the Governor General's Award. Crozier currently teaches creative writing at the University of Victoria. She and poet Patrick Lane live together outside Victoria, BC.

E. E. CUMMINGS (1894–1962), born Edward Estlin Cummings in Cambridge, Massachusetts, is perhaps best known for his eccentric antipathy toward capital letters—a style copied by many poetry students. His volumes of poetry include *Tulips and Chimneys* (1923) and *95 Poems* (1958). During World War I, Cummings served as an ambulance driver in France and was mistakenly committed to a French prison camp for three months, an experience he recounted in the prose journal *The Enormous Room* (1922).

EMILY DICKINSON (1830–1886) is among the greatest of American poets. During most of her adult life, she was a recluse, confining herself to her father's Amherst, Massachusetts, home, wearing only white, and shunning company. She produced over 1700 lyrics, which are characterized by startling imagery, ellipses, and unexpected juxtapositions. Only seven of her poems were published in her lifetime—and those without her permission. Her influence is still felt in modern poetry.

JOHN DONNE (1572–1631) was the first and perhaps greatest of the metaphysical poets. In his youth, he wrote erotic lyrics and cynical love poems. A politically disastrous marriage ruined his civil career, but in 1615 he converted to Anglicanism and later became dean of St. Paul's Cathedral and the most influential preacher in England. In later years, he wrote religious sonnets, elegies, epigrams, and verse letters. Donne's use of complex conceits and compressed phrasing has influenced many twentieth-century poets, especially T. S. Eliot.

PAUL LAURENCE DUNBAR (1872–1906) was born in Dayton, Ohio, the son of former slaves. He graduated from high school but could not afford university and worked instead as an elevator operator. He published his first two books of poetry with his own money. He finally found a major publisher for *Lyrics of Lowly Life* (1896) and became the first African-American poet to win national recognition. Although the public seemed to prefer his dialect poems, Dunbar favoured those, like "We Wear the Mask," which are written in literary English.

T. S. ELIOT (1888–1965) was born in St. Louis, studied at Harvard, and emigrated to London, where he worked as a bank clerk and as an editor. In 1927 he became a British citizen and joined the Church of England. His landmark poem, *The Wasteland* (1922), influenced a generation of young poets. As a critic, he revived interest in John Donne and other metaphysical poets. In later years, he wrote verse plays, such as *Murder in the Cathedral* (1935) and *The Cocktail Party* (1950), and won the Nobel Prize for Literature in 1948.

LOUISE ERDRICH (b. 1954) was born in Minnesota and grew up in North Dakota as a member of the Turtle Mountain Chippewas. Her grandfather was the tribal chief and her parents taught in the Bureau of Indian Affairs School. After earning a degree in anthropology from Dartmouth College, she returned to North Dakota to teach, then studied creative writing at Johns Hopkins University. Her work explores Native American experience, particularly life on the reservation. Her novels *Love Medicine* (1984), *The*

Beet Queen (1986), *Tracks* (1988), and *Bingo Palace* (1994) have established Erdrich as one of America's most important writers. She has published collections of poetry, including *Jacklight* (1984) and *Baptism of Desire* (1989).

LAWRENCE FERLINGHETTI (b. 1919) was born in Yonkers, New York. As the owner of San Francisco's City Lights Bookstore and publisher of City Lights Books, he was an important figure in the San Francisco Renaissance even before his own poetry began to appear. He encouraged young writers by giving them a place in his bookshop where they could meet and read their poetry, and by publishing their work in his Pocket Book series of small paperbacks. His many volumes of poetry include *Pictures Gone World* (1955), *A Coney Island of the Mind* (1958), *Back Roads to Small Places* (1971), *Landscapes of Living & Dying* (1979), and *Endless Life: The Selected Poems* (1981).

TIMOTHY FINDLEY (1930–2002) was born in Toronto and lived in and out of the affluent Rosedale area he depicts in his short story "Stones." He wrote screenplays, scripts for radio and television (often with his life partner, William Whitehead), numerous novels, and two collections of short fiction. Some of Findley's writings focus on the horrors of war, and his characters struggle against a society that sanctions war among genders, classes, and nations.

PATRICK FRIESEN (b. 1946) was born into the Mennonite community of Steinbach, Manitoba, and lived in Winnipeg for many years. His publications include *Blasphemer's Wheel: Selected & New Poems* (which won the 1994 Manitoba Book of the Year Award), *A Broken Bowl* (a finalist for the 1997 Governor General's Award), and *The Breath You Take from the Lord* (2002). He lives in Vancouver and teaches creative writing at Kwantlen University College.

ROBERT FROST (1874–1963) is one of the most popular and respected of American poets. He was born in San Francisco, but when he was a young boy his family moved to New England. His poems are characterized by colloquial, restrained language that implies messages rather than openly stating them. His works include *A Boy's Will* (1913), *New Hampshire* (1923), *A Witness Tree* (1942), *Steeple Bush* (1947), and *In the Clearing* (1962). Frost was awarded four Pulitzer Prizes for his poetry.

ALLEN GINSBERG (1926–1997) grew up in Paterson, New Jersey, where his father taught high school English. After attending Columbia University, Ginsberg moved to San Francisco in the early 1950s and began his relationship with poet Peter Orlovsky. The appearance of the controversial *Howl and Other Poems* (1956) established Ginsberg as a major "beat" poet. In the 1960s, he gave public readings and became a prominent figure in civil rights rallies, the war resistance movement, and gay liberation. His other works include *Kaddish* (1961), *Reality Sandwiches* (1963), and *Collected Poems* (1980).

DONALD HALL (b. 1928) was born in Connecticut and attended both Harvard and Oxford universities. He was poetry editor of the *Paris Review* and professor of English at the University of Michigan before moving to rural New Hampshire. His first book of poems, *Exiles and Marriages* (1955), won several awards, including the Millay Award of the Poetry Society of America. Hall has also written children's books, several college textbooks, and a book about baseball.

THOMAS HARDY (1840–1928) was an architect in London when he first became interested in literature. At age thirty he began to write novels; he produced sixteen of them. When his novel *Jude the Obscure* (1895) was called immoral for criticizing marriage, Hardy became so angry that he wrote nothing but poetry for the rest of his life. Among his best-known novels are *The Return of the Native* (1878) and *Tess of the D'Urbervilles* (1891).

NATHANIEL HAWTHORNE (1804–1864) ranks with the great writers of fiction in English. His first publication, *Twice-Told Tales* (1837), a volume of richly symbolic tales about moral duty and human guilt, helped to establish the short story as a legitimate literary form. The appearance of his masterpiece of hidden guilt and redemption, *The Scarlet Letter* (1850), secured his position as one of America's foremost writers. His other major novels are *The House of the Seven Gables* (1851) and *The Blithedale Romance* (1852).

ROBERT HAYDEN (1913–1980), born Asa Bundy Sheffey in Detroit, was renamed by his foster parents. In the poetry of his first collection, *Heart-Shape in the Dust* (1940), he used facts about African-American history that he unearthed as a researcher for the Federal Writers' Project (1936–1940). Educated at Wayne State University and the University of Michigan, Hayden taught at Fisk University and returned to teach at Michigan. He considered his writing "a collective creation of prayer—a prayer for illumination, perfection."

MICHAEL HEALEY (b. 1963) is a Toronto-based playwright whose first play, *Kicked* (1998), won a Dora for Best New Play. *The Drawer Boy* (1999 Governor General's Award and Dora winner) evolved from *The Farm Show*, a collective creation begun in 1972 by Toronto actors.

SEAMUS HEANEY (b. 1939) has been cited as Ireland's best poet since Yeats. Heaney was born on a farm in Northern Ireland, and his early poetry communicates a strong sense of the physical environment of his youth. His later work, often dense and poignant, concerns the cultural implications of words and their historical contexts. Heaney now divides his time between Dublin and America, where he teaches at Harvard. His books of poetry include *Electric Light* (2001), *The Haw Lantern* (1997), *New Selected Poems 1966–1987* (1990), *Seeing Things* (1991), and *The Spirit Level* (1996). He received the Nobel Prize for Literature in 1995.

ERNEST HEMINGWAY (1899–1961) began his professional writing career as a reporter for newspapers in Kansas City and Toronto. In the 1920s he became a voice for the Lost Generation of expatriated Americans living in Paris. His direct, forceful style is exhibited in short stories and novels, which include *A Farewell to Arms* (1929), *For Whom the Bell Tolls* (1940), and *The Old Man and the Sea* (1954), which won the Pulitzer Prize. Hemingway was awarded the Nobel Prize for Literature in 1954.

GERARD MANLEY HOPKINS (1844–1889) was, like Emily Dickinson, a major poet who was not recognized during his lifetime. Born in Essex, England, he attended Oxford, converted to Catholicism, and became a Jesuit priest. He died of typhoid fever at age forty-four. Nearly thirty years later, his friend Robert Bridges published Hopkins's *Poems* (1918), having thought them too demanding for earlier readers. Hopkins developed his own theory of meter, called *sprung rhythm*, which focuses on the number of stressed syllables in a line and disregards the unstressed syllables.

A. E. HOUSMAN (1859–1936), after failing his finals at Oxford, became a clerk in the London Patent Office. An extremely capable scholar, he began publishing his studies of classical authors and was eventually appointed professor of Latin at London University and then at Cambridge. Housman's own poetry, admired for its exquisite simplicity and penetrating feeling, often deals with the tragedy of doomed youth. His poetic works include *A Shropshire Lad* (1896) and *Last Poems* (1922).

LANGSTON HUGHES (1902–1967), born in Joplin, Missouri, became a major contributor to the Harlem Renaissance by writing about black urban life. In his writing he achieved a cultivated artlessness by incorporating spirituals and blues into traditional verse forms. Hughes was the first black writer to make a living by composing radio plays, song lyrics, novels, plays, poetry, and children's books. His poetry collections include *The Weary Blues* (1926) and *One-Way Ticket* (1949).

DAVID HENRY HWANG (b. 1957), the son of immigrant Chinese-American parents, was born in Los Angeles and educated at Stanford University. His first play, *F.O.B.*, dramatizes the tensions between a "fresh-off-the-boat" Chinese immigrant and his assimilated friends. It won the 1981 Obie Award for best new off-Broadway play of the season. Hwang addressed similar issues in *The Dance and the Railroad* (1981) and *Rich Relations* (1986). *M. Butterfly* (1988), a brilliant critique of Western attitudes toward Asia, established Hwang as an important voice in American theatre. The play was a Broadway hit and claimed several major prizes, including the Tony Award for best play of the year. In 1993 it was made into a popular film starring Jeremy Irons.

RANDALL JARRELL (1914–1965) is recognized as one of the most powerful commentators on war in American literature. He flew as a pilot during World War II, and two of his collections of poetry—*Little Friend, Little Friend* (1945) and *Losses* (1948)—describe the war's profound effect on him. After the war he returned to his life as professor, poet, and critic. In later years he wrote four books for children, including *The Bat Poet* (1964). Jarrell was struck and killed by an automobile in 1965.

PAULINE JOHNSON (1861–1913) was born on the Six Nations Reserve near Brantford, Ontario. Her father, Chief George Henry Martin Johnson, was Mohawk and her mother, Emily Susanna Howells, English. Johnson was educated in English literary tradition by her mother and in Native stories by her grandfather, John Smoke Johnson. In 1886 she took the Mohawk name "Tekahionwake" and began touring North America and Europe, performing her poetry and dressing as a Mohawk princess when reading her Native poems. The tension brought about by her dual heritage is evident in much of her work.

BEN JONSON (1572–1637), the posthumous son of a Scottish minister, was raised and educated in London. After working as a bricklayer and serving as a soldier in Flanders, he married and became an actor and playwright. He became the self-appointed leader of a group of actors and writers who hung out at the Mermaid Tavern. One of his friends and associates was William Shakespeare. As a playwright, Jonson wrote brilliant satiric comedies, including *Volpone* (1606) and *The Alchemist* (1610). As a poet, he produced classical lyrics, odes, epigrams, and sonnets.

JAMES JOYCE (1882–1941) rejected his Irish Catholic heritage and left his homeland at age twenty. Though an expatriate most of his adult life, Joyce wrote almost exclusively about his native Dublin. His first book, *Dubliners* (1914), was a series of sharply drawn vignettes based on his experiences in Ireland, the homeland he later described as "a sow that eats its own farrow." His novel *Ulysses* (1933) was banned for a time in the United States because of its coarse language and frank treatment of sexuality.

JOHN KEATS (1795–1821) was a major figure in the romantic period of English poetry. His potential was cut short when he died of tuberculosis in Italy at the age of twenty-five. He began writing when he was eighteen, already having seen his mother die of consumption; his brother was to follow. Perhaps the haunting disease provided the spur to Keats's uncanny development. His poems, which are rich in imagery and dignified in expression, include "Ode on a Grecian Urn," "To Autumn," and "The Eve of St. Agnes."

THOMAS KING (b. 1943) was born in California and is of Cherokee and Greek descent. After travelling worldwide as a photojournalist, much like the protagonist in his 1989 novel *Medicine River*, he moved to Canada in 1980. His works include novels, short stories, children's books, and a series of lectures for CBC's *The Massey Lectures* (2003). He teaches creative writing and Native literature at the University of Guelph, Ontario. His short story "Borders" focuses on the arbitrary boundaries that Aboriginal people encounter in North America.

JOY KOGAWA (b. 1935) was born in Vancouver. She and her family were among the Japanese Canadians interned in the interior of BC (Slocan) and then Alberta (Coaldale) during World War II. As a result she became a political activist fighting for reparations for evacuated Japanese Canadians. Her short story "Obasan" was the basis for her novels *Obasan* (1981) and *Itsuka* (1992) and her children's book *Naomi's Road* (1986). She has published several other novels, and much of her poetry in her several collections reflects the effects of the internment.

MICHELE LALONDE (b. 1937) was born in Montreal. Focusing on the connection between language and culture, she quickly became a prominent writer in Quebec's political and intellectual circles. Until "the Quiet Revolution" in the 1960s, English was the language of business and industry in Quebec, and Lalonde speaks to this discrimination against francophones in her poem "Speak White."

ARCHIBALD LAMPMAN (1861–1899) was raised in the Rice Lake district of Ontario and was an acquaintance of Susanna Moodie and Catharine Parr Traill. After graduating from Trinity College in Toronto, he taught high school and then became a postal clerk, remaining in the civil service for the rest of his life. His marriage to Maud Playter in 1887 resulted in lifelong unhappiness, and he found solace in his associations with those who shared his intellectual interests and love of the wilderness, including poet Duncan Campbell Scott. His poetry reveals exquisite expression, and he is felt by many to have been the best poet of the Confederation period.

PATRICK LANE (b. 1939) was born in Nelson, BC. His collection *Poems, New and Selected* won the Governor General's Award in 1978, and he has published numerous other collections of poetry, a children's book, and a collection of stories titled *How Do You Spell Beautiful?* He has been a writer-in-residence and instructor at a number of institutions and currently lives outside Victoria, BC, with poet Lorna Crozier. His poem "The Bird" demonstrates his distinctively sparse, lyrical voice.

PHILIP LARKIN (1922–1985) came from a working-class background in the north of England. His past is reflected in his first volume of poems, *The North Ship* (1946), and his first two novels, *Jill* (1946) and *A Girl in Winter* (1947). Larkin, who once said, "Form holds little interest for me," became the leader of the British antiromantic movement. His poetry collection *The Less Deceived* (1955) treats conventional themes, like love and death, with searing wit and sophisticated roughness.

MARGARET LAURENCE (1926–1987), born Margaret Wemys in Neepawa, Manitoba, attended the University of Winnipeg. She later married engineer Jack Laurence, with whom she travelled to England (1949) and Africa (1950). Drawing upon her experiences in Africa, she published *A Tree for Poverty* (1954) and *The Tomorrow-Tamer* (1963). After separating from her husband, Laurence wrote her five-volume Manawaka series—*The Stone Angel*, *A Jest of God*, *The Fire-Dwellers*, the short story collection *A Bird in the House*, and *The Diviners*—set in fictional Manawaka, Manitoba. Her short stories are considered her most autobiographical works.

IRVING LAYTON (b. 1912), born in Romania, was raised in Montreal and educated at a variety of institutions, including Macdonald College, where he received a B.Sc. in agricultural science, a background evident in his poem "The Bull Calf." He is one of Canada's best-known authors and poets, the combined result of his voluminous publications and his controversial reputation as a spokesperson who challenges inert society and elitist academia on behalf of artists.

JOHN LENNON (1940–1980) was the acknowledged leader of the British rock group the Beatles. He described himself as the "hip" and "hallucinatory" side of the Lennon-McCartney composing team, with his hand most evident in such songs as "Strawberry Fields," "Revolution," and "Help!" After teaming with his second wife, Yoko Ono, he recorded political songs, such as "Imagine," "Give Peace a Chance," and "Come Together." Lennon was shot dead outside his New York City apartment.

DENISE LEVERTOV (1923–1997) was born in England and educated by her mother, who was Welsh, and her father, an Anglican priest converted from Judaism. She was a nurse in World War II, married an American novelist, and moved to the United States, where she discovered the work of William Carlos Williams and other free-form poets. Although her poetry focuses on politics, especially concern for women and the third world, much of it remains personal. Her collections include *The Jacob's Ladder* (1961), *The Freeing of the Dust* (1975), and *A Door in the Hive* (1989).

DOROTHY LIVESAY (1909–1996) was born in Winnipeg. Her work contends with social and political issues, the feminist movement, and, as evidenced in "Bartok and the Geranium," the individual woman and her domestic situation. The BC book prize in poetry is named in her honour, and she won the 1947 Governor General's Award for *Poems for the People*. Livesay was named an Officer of the Order of Canada in 1987. *Call My People Home* (1950), her documentary poem based on the internment of Japanese Canadians, was written for choral presentation. The images and metaphors of growth in her poetry speak of the enduring human spirit.

BILLIE LIVINGSTON (b. 1965) was born in Hamilton, Ontario, and grew up in Toronto and Vancouver, where she currently lives. Her poetry and short fiction, as well as a novel (*Going Down Swinging*, 2000), have been published in Canada, Australia, England, and the United States. The collection from which "Paperweight" is taken, *The Chick at the Back of the Church*, is gritty and tough yet unsentimental in the revelation of human relationships and family love; the poem itself features a persona who is both vulnerable and pugnacious.

RICHARD LOVELACE (1618–1657) was a wealthy, handsome, elegant Cavalier poet. Because of his loyal support of King Charles I, Lovelace was twice imprisoned by the Puritan Parliament during the English Civil War. He died in poverty in a London slum. Much of Lovelace's poetry is laboured and lifeless, but he did write several charming, graceful lyrics, such as "To Althea from Prison," "To Amarantha, That She Would Dishevel Her Hair," and "To Lucasta, on Going to the Wars."

GWENDOLYN MACEWEN (1941–1987) was born in Toronto, and at age seventeen published her first poem in *The Canadian Forum*. A year later she left school to concentrate on her writing and to teach herself languages, including Hebrew and Egyptian. She was the writer-in-residence at the University of Western Ontario (1984–85) and the University of Toronto (1986-87). MacEwen died in Toronto after a long struggle with alcoholism. In 1969 she won the Governor General's Award for *Shadow-Maker*; her most well-known collection is *The T. E. Lawrence Poems* (1982). In her poem "Icarus," MacEwen parallels the flight of Icarus with the creative process of the poet.

ALISTAIR MACLEOD (b. 1936) was born in North Battleford, Saskatchewan, but his family returned to their Cape Breton, Nova Scotia, farm when he was ten. In 1969 he became professor of English and creative writing at the University of Windsor, retiring in 2000. His collections of short stories, *The Lost Salt Gift of Blood* (1976) and *As Birds Bring Forth the Sun* (1986), have earned much acclaim, and his first novel, *No Great Mischief* (1999), won the International IMPAC Dublin Literary Award and the 2000 Trillium Award. All his writings attest to his Cape Breton heritage.

JOAN MACLEOD (b. 1954) was born in Vancouver and has been a playwright-in-residence and a creative writing instructor. Among her many plays are *Amigo's Blue Guitar*, winner of the 1997 Governor General's Award; *Hope Slide, Little Sister* (1999); *Jewel* (2002); and *The Shape of a Girl* (2001), which is grounded in the murder of Victoria student Reena Virk. MacLeod lives on Bowen Island, BC.

DAPHNE MARLATT (b. 1942) was born in Australia. She moved to Malaysia when she was three, and then to Vancouver in 1951. She has published non-fiction, including *Steveston Recollected: A Japanese-Canadian History* (1975) and *Opening Doors: Vancouver's East End* (1980). Her works of prose fiction include novels, such as *Ana Historic* (1988) and *Taken* (1996). She has published books of poetry, including *Touch to My Tongue* (1984), *Salvage* (1991), and collaborative works with Betsy Warland, *Double Negative* (1988) and *Two Women in a Birth* (1994). She currently lives in Victoria, BC.

ANDREW MARVELL (1621–1678), though not a Puritan himself, supported the Puritan cause in the English Civil War. He held a number of posts during the Commonwealth and was instrumental in saving John Milton from punishment after the Restoration. One of the metaphysical poets, Marvell is best known for his witty lyrics, which often present a tacit debate about opposing values. He has been called "the most major minor poet" in English.

PAUL MCCARTNEY (b. 1942) is the most successful survivor of the legendary rock group the Beatles. He and the late John Lennon established themselves as one of the twentieth century's best-loved songwriting teams, turning out an extraordinary number of pop standards within a very few years. Following the Beatles' breakup, McCartney continued as a solo artist and as the leader of the band Wings. The *Guinness Book of Records* lists him as the best-selling composer and recording artist of all time.

DON MCKAY (b. 1942) has published numerous collections of poetry, winning Governor General's Awards for *Birding, or Desire* (1983), *Night Field* (1991), and *Another Gravity* (2001). *Apparatus* (1997) was short-listed for the award. He has taught at the University of Western Ontario and the University of New Brunswick, and was the editor of *The Fiddlehead* magazine. McKay is currently the associate director of poetry, writing, and publishing at the Banff Centre for the Arts. He lives in Victoria, BC.

EUGENE MCNAMARA (b. 1930) was born in Chicago and is Professor Emeritus at the University of Windsor. He has published over a dozen volumes of poetry, several short story collections, and books of literary criticism. In the collection *Waterfalls,* from which "Falling in Place" is taken, he explores the connection between life and art and reveals the human vulnerabilities that make his characters compelling and his stories complex and poignant.

ANNE MICHAELS (b. 1958) was born in Toronto and for many years taught creative writing at the University of Toronto. Her collections of poetry include *The Weight of Oranges* (1986), *Miner's Pond* (1991), a finalist for the Governor General's Award, and *Skin Divers* (1999); her novel *Fugitive Pieces* (1997) won the Trillium Award and the Books in Canada First Novel Award, among others. Michaels uses a variety of styles and formats in her verse, which ranges from short love poems to longer lyrical narratives.

EDNA ST. VINCENT MILLAY (1892–1950) was born in Maine and educated at Vassar. In 1917 she moved to Greenwich Village and published her first book of poetry, *Renascence and Other Poems*. She won the Pulitzer Prize for *The Harp-Weaver* (1922), a collection that deals wittily and flippantly with love. Although Millay became politically involved and used her poetry to speak out for social causes, she is known best for her poems about the bittersweet emotions of love and the brevity of life.

SUSANNA MOODIE (1803–1885), born Susanna Strickland in London, England, immigrated with her husband and sister Catharine Parr Traill to Upper Canada in 1832. While in England, she published her first novel in 1822 and a collection of poetry in 1831. After unsuccessful attempts at bush farming and much misfortune, the Moodies moved to Belleville, Ontario. From 1829 to 1851 she published many poems and works of prose in literary magazines. The subject of her poem "XI. Brian, the Still-Hunter" is elaborated upon in her most famous work, *Roughing It in the Bush*. Margaret Atwood writes extensively on this early Canadian writer in her work *The Journals of Susanna Moodie* (1970).

DANIEL DAVID MOSES (b. 1952), a Delaware from the Six Nations Reserve in Grand River, Ontario, is a playwright, poet, and editor. His plays include *Coyote City*, a finalist for the 1991 Governor General's Award; *The Moon and Dead Indians* (1994); *The Indian Medicine Shows* (1995), which won the 1996 James Buller Memorial Award for Excellence in Aboriginal Theatre; and

Big Buck City (1998). *Almighty Voice and His Wife* (1991) is based on events that occurred in nineteenth-century Canada.

LISEL MUELLER (b. 1924), the daughter of two teachers, began writing poetry in Nazi Germany. Fearing that their anti-Fascist beliefs would result in persecution, her family fled the country when Mueller was fifteen, settling in Evansville, Indiana, where her father became a professor at the University of Evansville. Mueller received a degree from Evansville in 1944 and has since taught and lectured on creative writing at the University of Chicago, Elmhurst College, and Goddard College in Vermont. Her books include *The Need to Hold Still*, which won the 1981 National Book Award; *The Private Life*, which was the Lamont Poetry Selection in 1975; and *Alive Together*, which won the 1997 Pulitzer Prize for poetry.

BHARATI MUKHERJEE (b. 1940) views herself as an American writer, not an Asian-American one. She was born in Calcutta, India, but was educated there by Irish nuns and later went to school in England and Switzerland. She joined the famous Writers' Workshop at the University of Iowa in 1961, married and lived in Canada, and then returned to the United States, where she now lives and teaches. Mukherjee's topics do reflect a multicultural consciousness: three of her novels depict Indian women confronting the disparity between Indian and American cultures. Her short stories also focus on the immigrant experience.

ALICE MUNRO (b. 1931) grew up in rural Ontario. In her work she often focuses on small-town life, and particularly on the lives of women. Although her characters seem ordinary and self-conscious, they possess emotional lives of surprising depth. Munro specializes in short stories, claiming they allow her to present "intense, but not connected, moments of experience." Her collections include *Lives of Girls and Women* (1971), *The Progress of Love* (1986), *Friends of My Youth* (1990), *The Love of a Good Woman* (1998), and *Hateship, Friendship, Courtship, Loveship, Marriage* (2001) among others.

HOWARD NEMEROV (1920–1991) left his native New York to go to Harvard; he graduated in 1941 and went into military service as a pilot in World War II. After the war Nemerov worked as an editor and completed his first book of poems, *The Image and the Law* (1947). He spent the rest of his life as a college teacher, primarily at Washington University in St. Louis. In his verse Nemerov discovers witty, unexpected, often jarring connections between simple, unrelated objects. He wrote more than fifteen collections of poetry, several novels, a group of short stories, essays, and a memoir. *The Collected Poems of Howard Nemerov* won the Pulitzer Prize in 1978.

PABLO NERUDA (1904–1973) was born in Parral, Chile. Despite his reputation as one of the greatest Spanish-American poets in history, few of his works have been translated into English. Neruda was a radical poet who mixed meditations on political oppression with intensely personal lyrics about romantic love. He was awarded the Nobel Prize for Literature in 1971.

BP NICHOL (1944–1988) was born Barrie Phillip Nichol in Vancouver. He published numerous works that push the boundaries of writing, and although he worked in many forms, he is probably best known for his concrete poetry. He was a member of the Four Horsemen, a group that experimented with sound and poetry. In 1970 Nichol won the Governor General's Award for four different volumes of his poetry: *Still Water, The True Eventual Story of Billy the Kid, Beach Head,* and *The Cosmic Chef* (as editor). His poems "Blues" and "landscape: 1" demonstrate his concept of language as art.

ALDEN NOWLAN (1933–1983) was born in Windsor, Nova Scotia; he was self-educated and worked as a newspaperman. He published poetry, short stories, novels, and plays, and his poetry collection *Bread, Wine and Salt* (1967) won the Governor General's Award. Nowlan's work expresses his connection with his Nova Scotia origins and his love of the people. In 1969 he was writer-in-residence at the University of New Brunswick.

JOYCE CAROL OATES (b. 1938) was born in Lockport, New York, graduated from Syracuse University, and now teaches at Princeton. Fascinated by psychological and social disorder, Oates often explores the relationship between violence and love in American society. She has written over one hundred stories and nearly forty novels, as well as literary criticism and essays on boxing. Among her works are *A Garden of Earthly Delights* (1967), *them* (1969), *Bellefleur* (1980), and *Last Days* (1984).

FLANNERY O'CONNOR (1925–1964), afflicted with lupus erythematosus, spent most of her short life in Milledgeville, Georgia. After earning an M.F.A. from the University of Iowa, she returned to the family farm to raise peacocks and write about contemporary southern life in grotesquely comic terms. She produced two novels, *Wise Blood* (1952) and *The Violent Bear It Away* (1960), and two volumes of short stories, *A Good Man Is Hard to Find* (1955) and *Everything That Rises Must Converge* (1965).

MICHAEL ONDAATJE (b. 1943) was born in Sri Lanka, moved to England when he was ten, and relocated to Canada in 1962. Educated in Toronto and Kingston, he is perhaps best known as a novelist (*Coming through Slaughter, In the Skin of a Lion, The English Patient, Anil's Ghost*) but has written several books of poetry. *The Collected Works of Billy the Kid* shared the Governor General's Award for poetry in 1970; he won again for poetry in 1979. He and his wife, Linda Spalding, edit the literary journal *Brick*.

WILFRED OWEN (1893–1918) began writing poetry at the University of London. After teaching English in France for a few years, Owen returned to England and joined the army. He was wounded in 1917 and killed in action a few days before the armistice was declared in 1918. Owen's poems, published only after his death, are some of the most powerful and vivid accounts of the horrors of war to emerge from World War I.

P. K. PAGE (b. 1916) was born in England and raised in Calgary, Winnipeg, and Saint John, New Brunswick. Beginning in 1941 she published her poetry in a variety of literary magazines and journals. Following a move to Montreal, she married Arthur Irwin; the couple went on to live in Brazil, Australia, and Mexico, where, unable to write, Page began painting under the name P. K. Irwin. Her many works include the well-known *Cry Ararat: Poems New and Selected* (1967); *Brazilian Journal* (writings and paintings, 1987); *The Glass Air: Poems Selected and New* (1991); *Hologram: A Book of Glosas* (1994); and *The Hidden Room: Collected Poems* (1997).

DOROTHY PARKER (1893–1967), known best for her acerbic wit, was actually a serious editor and writer. Fired from *Vanity Fair* for writing harsh theatre reviews, she reviewed books for *The New Yorker*, which also published her stories, poems, and articles for over thirty years. Her lasting literary contributions include short stories such as "Big Blonde" and "The Waltz" and several collections of often sardonic verse.

MARJORIE PICKTHALL (1883–1922), born in Middlesex, England, immigrated to Canada with her parents in 1889. She was very successful as a lyric poet early in her career but published only two collections: *The Drift of Pinions* (1913) and *The Lamp of Poor Souls* (1916). Six other collections were published posthumously. The repetition, rhythm, and rhyme in "The Bird in the Room" demonstrate her movement toward a less traditional approach.

SYLVIA PLATH (1932–1963) was born in Boston, where her father taught at Boston University. Her early years were filled with honours and awards. She won a Fulbright Scholarship to Cambridge, where she met and married English poet Ted Hughes. But beneath the conventional success was a woman whose acute perceptions and intolerable pain led her to commit suicide at age thirty. Plath produced three volumes of powerful poetry and an autobiographical novel, *The Bell Jar* (1963).

KATHERINE ANNE PORTER (1890–1980) specialized in short fiction. She worked for several newspapers and did some acting until she was able to survive on her earnings as an author. Nurtured by academia, she received a number of honours and lectured at more than two hundred universities and colleges. Her finest collections are *Flowering Judas* (1930) and *Pale Horse, Pale Rider* (1939). Her only novel, *Ship of Fools* (1962), was made into an award-winning film. *The Collected Stories* (1965) won a Pulitzer Prize.

EZRA POUND (1885–1972), one of the most influential and controversial poets of our time, was born in Idaho, left America in 1908, and lived in Europe for much of his life. Pound's colossal ambition led him to found the imagist movement in poetry, to advise a galaxy of great writers (e.g., Eliot, Joyce, Yeats, and Frost), and to write numerous critical works. It also led to a charge of treason (for broadcasting propaganda for Mussolini) and to twelve years in a mental hospital. His poetry is collected in *Personae* (1949) and *The Cantos* (1976).

E. J. PRATT (1882–1964) is considered Canada's first modernist poet. His most famous work, *Towards the Last Spike*, is a long epic poem about the building of the Canadian Pacific Railway and its attendant physical and political struggles. "The Flight of the Geese" demonstrates Pratt's skill as an imagist poet.

AL PURDY (1918-2000) was born in Wooler, Ontario, and began publishing in the early 1960s. He was a poet, editor, travel writer, TV and radio playwright, and anthologist. Purdy won the Governor General's Award in 1965 for *The Cariboo Horses* and in 1986 for *Collected Poems, 1956–1986*. In 1982 he received the Order of Canada, and in 1987 he won the People's Poet Award for *Collected Poems*.

JAMES REANEY (b. 1926) was born in Easthope, Ontario, and is a poet, playwright, children's writer, and literary critic. He won Governor General's Awards for his poetry collections *The Red Heart* (1949), *A Suit of Nettles* (1958), and *Twelve Letters to a Small Town* (1962). Reaney's plays include *The Killdeer and Other Plays* (1962), and his dramatic Donnelly trilogy (1974–1975) has received much acclaim.

ADRIENNE RICH (b. 1929), who was born in Baltimore, graduated from Radcliffe College in 1951, the same year that her first book of poetry, *A Change of World*, appeared in the Yale Series of Younger Poets. The Vietnam War and her experience in teaching minority youth in New York City heightened Rich's political awareness, and she became increasingly involved in the women's movement. Her most recent books include *Dark*

Fields of the Republic: Poems 1991–1995 (1995), *Midnight Salvage: Poems 1995–1998* (1999), and *Fox: Poems 1998–2000* (2001).

DAVID ADAMS RICHARDS (b. 1950) was born in Newcastle, New Brunswick. Although he now lives in Toronto, it is New Brunswick's Mirimachi Valley that provides the setting for his novels and short stories. Richards writes about poor rural characters and their profound sense of duty, integrity, and spirituality, but his work often concerns the cost or the loss of these values. He has won many awards, including the Governor General's Award for *Nights below Station Street* (1988) and for the non-fiction *Lines beneath the Water* (1998). *For Those Who Hunt the Wounded Down* (1993) won the Thomas Raddall Award and was also made into a Gemini Award–winning film. *Mercy among the Children* (2001) won the Giller Prize.

SIR CHARLES G. D. ROBERTS (1860–1943) was one of the Confederation poets. His writing largely depicts the Canadian countryside, specifically New Brunswick, where he spent his childhood. He was well educated, yet he was in close contact with the backwoods, a duality shared by his contemporaries Archibald Lampman, Duncan Campbell Scott, and cousin Bliss Carman. Roberts's best-known works are *Orion* (1880), *Divers Tones* (1886), *Selected Poems* (1936), *Watchers of the Trails* (1904), *Hoof and Claw* (1913), and *History of Canada* (1897).

THEODORE ROETHKE (1908–1963) was born in Saginaw, Michigan, where he grew up surrounded by his father's twenty-five-acre greenhouse complex. While an undergraduate at the University of Michigan, he decided to pursue both poetry and teaching. A preoccupation with literal and symbolic growth pervades his poetry, as does a concern for nature and childhood. His collection *The Waking* (1953) won the Pulitzer Prize, and *Words for the Wind* (1958) received the National Book Award.

SINCLAIR ROSS (1908–1996) was born in Saskatchewan and travelled the small towns of that province as he worked for the Royal Bank of Canada. These towns, along with characters in typically strained relationships and nature with its devastating effects on the human spirit, fill his writing. His first novel, *As for Me and My House* (1941), as well as *The Lamp at Noon and Other Stories* (1968) and *The Race and Other Stories* (1982), offers visions of isolation and suffering in the prairies. The novel was not well received when it was first published, but it is now considered a Canadian classic.

CARL SANDBURG (1878–1967) was born in Galesburg, Illinois, and worked as a day labourer, soldier, political activist, and journalist. These experiences provided a rich palette of poetic colours to select from, and Sandburg painted boldly in vigorous free verse. His works include *Chicago Poems* (1916), *Cornhuskers* (1918), *The People, Yes* (1936), and *Harvest Poems* (1960). He also wrote a six-volume biography of Abraham Lincoln and four children's books, including the *Rootabaga Stories* (1922).

F. R. SCOTT (1899–1985) was born in Quebec City, the son of Confederation poet Frederick George Scott. Educated in Quebec and England, he returned to Canada to study law at McGill University. He became a social activist and is known for his satiric verse, including "All the Spikes but the Last" and "The Canadian Authors Meet." "The Laurentian Shield" reflects Scott's admiration for the Canadian landscape and its effects on the development of a Canadian voice.

WILLIAM SHAKESPEARE (1564–1616) is the most widely known author in all English literature. He was born in Stratford-on-Avon, probably attended grammar school there, and at eighteen married Anne Hathaway, who bore him three children. In 1585 or shortly thereafter, he went to London and began his apprenticeship as an actor. By 1594 he had won recognition as a poet, but it was in the theatre that he made his strongest reputation. Shakespeare produced perhaps thirty-five plays in twenty-five years, including historical dramas, comedies, romances, and great tragedies: *Hamlet* (1602), *Othello* (1604), *King Lear* (1605), and *Macbeth* (1606). His 154 sonnets are supreme examples of the form.

PERCY BYSSHE SHELLEY (1792–1822) married sixteen-year-old Harriet Westbrook in 1811, the same year he was expelled from Oxford for writing a pamphlet on atheism. In 1814 he went to France with Mary Wollstonecraft, later famous for writing *Frankenstein* (1818). He married Wollstonecraft in 1816, after Harriet committed suicide; they then settled in Italy, where Shelley wrote some of his best lyrics, including "Ozymandias." His other works include "Ode to the West Wind" and *Adonais*, an elegy to John Keats.

A. J. M. SMITH (1902–1980) was a modernist poet who changed the course of English-Canadian poetry. He denounced the reliance of the nation's poets on British and American models and advocated the creation of a uniquely Canadian form and voice. In his poem "The Wisdom of Old Jelly Roll," Smith demonstrates jazz rhythm through the spoken language of a jazz expert. Such poems also demonstrate that Canadian poets can and do write about more than Canadian landscape.

RUSSELL SMITH (b. 1963) was born in Johannesburg, South Africa, and was educated at the Université de Poitiers, the Université de Paris, and Queen's University. He has written novels, *How Insensitive* (1995), *Noise* (1998), and *Muriella Pent* (2004); a collection of short stories, *Young Men* (2000); and the illustrated fable *The Princess and the Whiskheads* (2004). He is a weekly columnist for *The Globe and Mail*.

STEVIE SMITH (1902–1971) was born Florence Margaret Smith in Hull, England. She worked as a secretary and occasionally as a writer and broadcaster for the BBC. She began publishing verse, which she often illustrated herself, in the 1930s but did not gain much recognition until 1962, when her *Selected Poems* appeared. Noted for her eccentricity and humour, Smith often aimed her satirical barbs at religion and made unexpected use of traditional hymns, songs, and nursery rhymes in her poems.

SOPHOCLES (ca. 496–ca. 405 BCE) wrote more than 120 plays, but only 7 have survived. Born in Colonus, near Athens, he studied under Aeschylus, the master of Greek tragedy. Sophocles did not question the justice of the gods; his plays assume a divine order that humans must follow. His strong-willed protagonists end tragically because of pride and lack of self-knowledge. His works include *Oedipus the King*, *Antigone*, *Electra*, and *Ajax*.

JOHN STEINBECK (1902–1968) was born in Salinas, California, where he worked as a fruit-picker and hod-carrier. Seeing firsthand the grief and misery caused by agricultural exploitation, he incorporated his sympathetic observations about oppressed workers into such novels as *The Grapes of Wrath*, which won the Pulitzer Prize in 1940. Other novels include *Of Mice and*

Men (1937), *Cannery Row* (1945), and *East of Eden* (1952). Steinbeck was awarded the Nobel Prize for Literature in 1962.

WALLACE STEVENS (1879–1955), born in Reading, Pennsylvania, was an insurance executive who wrote poetry almost as a hobby. He was forty-four when he published his first book of poems, *Harmonium* (1923). His elegant images often give substance to such abstract concepts as time, being, and meaning. A key figure in modernist literature, Stevens profoundly affected the writing of poetry in America. His *Collected Poems* (1954) won the Pulitzer Prize.

ALFRED, LORD TENNYSON (1809–1892), one of the most popular poets in Victorian England, showed his talents early, publishing his first volume at age eighteen. Encouraged to devote himself to poetry by friends at Cambridge, he was particularly close to Arthur Hallam, whose sudden death inspired the long elegy *In Memoriam* (1850). This work brought Tennyson lasting recognition: he was appointed poet laureate the year it appeared. His other works include *Locksley Hall* (1842) and *Idylls of the King* (1859–1885).

DYLAN THOMAS (1914–1953) was born in Wales. Shunning school to pursue a writing career, he published his first book of poetry at age twenty. Limited by his lack of a degree, he had trouble making a living as a writer, and his early life was marked by poverty and heavy drinking. Calling his poetry a "record of my struggle from darkness towards some measure of light," Thomas delighted in sound, sometimes at the expense of sense. His play *Under Milk Wood* (1954) is filled with his private, onomatopoeic language.

MIRIAM WADDINGTON (1917–2004) was born in Winnipeg and later lived in Montreal, where she wrote poetry and was a social worker. In 1960 she returned as a divorced single parent to Toronto, teaching English at York University and continuing in social work. In her early poetry she expresses broader social concerns, as in her poem "The Nineteen Thirties Are Over"; later, as seen in "Ten Years and More," she focuses on more personal issues.

BRONWEN WALLACE (1945–1989) was born and educated in Kingston, Ontario, and moved to Windsor, where as a political activist she worked with women's groups and unionists. After returning to Kingston in 1977, she continued her work with women's groups and began to teach. She published four books of poetry, and her collection of short stories *People You'd Trust Your Life To* (1990) was published posthumously. Her poetry often focuses on domestic life and the complications and miracles that lie just beneath the surface.

EDMUND WALLER (1606–1687) was an English poet and a wealthy member of Parliament. Despite a turbulent political career, he managed to write poetry that is smooth and effortlessly clear. His most famous poems include "Song" (1645), "On a Girdle" (1686), and "Of the Last Verses in the Book" (1686).

SHEILA WATSON (1909–1998) was born in New Westminster, BC, and although her publications are few, she is well known for her modernist novel, *The Double Hook*. This was the first Canadian work of fiction in which narrative event took second place to ideas and form. Between 1949 and 1951 Watson wrote four mythic short stories, including "Antigone," whose characters are related to Greek myths.

PHYLLIS WEBB (b. 1927) was born in Victoria, BC, and after moving to Toronto in 1965 she produced *Ideas*, the CBC Radio show. She has served as writer-in-residence at the University of Alberta and taught at UBC, the University of Victoria, and the Banff Centre. She currently lives on Saltspring Island, BC. Her most renowned poetry collection, *Naked Poems*, was published in 1965, and her selected poems entitled *The Vision Tree* (1982) won the Governor General's Award.

EUDORA WELTY (1909–2001), one of America's most distinguished writers of fiction, was born in Jackson, Mississippi, and attended the University of Wisconsin and Columbia University. Returning to Jackson in 1932, she worked for a radio station, several newspapers, and the Works Progress Administration (WPA) before launching her literary career. Welty's humour and astute observations give her portraits of small-town life a universal reality. Her awards include three O. Henry Prizes, a Pulitzer Prize (for *The Optimist's Daughter*, 1972), and the Howells Medal (for her *Collected Stories*, 1980).

WALT WHITMAN (1819–1892) was born on Long Island and worked as a printer, teacher, journalist, and carpenter. *Leaves of Grass* (1855) established his reputation after it was praised by Ralph Waldo Emerson. Whitman's celebration of human sexuality, expressed in experimental free verse, shocked his contemporaries. He revised *Leaves of Grass* throughout his lifetime, bringing out numerous editions. A great lover of his native land, Whitman honoured America in his poetry and in his essay *Democratic Vistas* (1871). His influence on modern poetry is inestimable.

RUDY WIEBE (b. 1934) has written nine novels and was made an Officer of the Order of Canada in 2000. He has won the Governor General's Award twice—in 1973 for *The Temptations of Big Bear* and in 1994 for *A Discovery of Strangers*. His 1998 work *Stolen Life: The Journey of a Cree Woman*, co-written with Yvonne Johnson, won the Viacom Canada Book Award. Wiebe writes about his Mennonite background, Aboriginals, and the Métis.

WILLIAM CARLOS WILLIAMS (1883–1963) spent almost his entire life as a physician in Rutherford, New Jersey. The "inarticulate poems" that he heard in the words of his patients inspired him to write, jotting down lines and phrases whenever he could find a moment. Williams wrote about common objects and experiences and imbued them with spiritual qualities. His works include *Pictures from Brueghel* (1962), which won a Pulitzer Prize, and his masterpiece, *Paterson* (1946–1958), a poem in five volumes.

ETHEL WILSON (1888–1980) lived in Vancouver and published her first short story in 1937. Her first novel, *Hetty Dorval* (1947), was published when she was fifty-nine. Three novels, two novellas, and a collection of short fiction, *Mrs. Golightly and Other Stories* (1961), followed. Wilson's prose is at once realistic and sarcastic. "The Window" expresses her view that, although the world can be a very unpredictable place, individuals often lead sterile lives.

JIM WONG-CHU (b. 1949) was born in Hong Kong and then brought to Vancouver in 1953 to be raised by relatives. He is a founding member of the Asian Canadian Writers' Workshop. His works include the poetry volume *Chinatown Ghosts* (1986). He is also the co-editor of the collection *Many Mouthed Birds: Contemporary Writing by Chinese Canadians* (1991). His collaboration with Lien Chao is *A New Chinese Canadian Anthology* (2003). In his poem "old chinese cemetery kamloops," Wong-Chu's persona steps back in history to better understand his life.

WILLIAM WORDSWORTH (1770–1850) was an English poet recognized for his use of common language and his love of nature. Educated at Cambridge

University, he lived for a time in France, where he fathered an illegitimate daughter and experienced the French Revolution firsthand. When he returned to England, he began writing in earnest. His works include *Lyrical Ballads* (1798), *Poems in Two Volumes* (1807), and *The Excursion* (1814). A leader of English romanticism, Wordsworth was named poet laureate in 1843.

RICHARD WRIGHT (1908–1960) was born near Natchez, Mississippi, attended school in Jackson, and moved to Memphis, where he worked odd jobs and began to write. In 1927 he moved to Chicago and joined the Federal Writers' Project in the 1930s. Like many writers of the time, Wright joined the Communist Party but quit after several years. In 1946 he moved to Paris. His works include story collections, *Uncle Tom's Children* (1938) and *Eight Men* (1961); a novel, *Native Son* (1940); and a two-part autobiography, *Black Boy* (1945) and *American Hunger* (1977).

HISAYE YAMAMOTO (b. 1921) was born in Redondo Beach, California. Before World War II she wrote for the Japan-California *Daily News*. When the United States entered the war, she and her family, like others of Japanese ancestry, were interned in a "relocation centre." After the war she wrote for the Los Angeles *Tribune*, a black weekly. She published her first short story in *The Partisan Review* in 1948. Yamamoto's stories usually concern rural Japanese Americans during the Depression of the 1930s.

WILLIAM BUTLER YEATS (1865–1939), one of the most important poets of the twentieth century, was born near Dublin and attended art school for a time but quit to devote himself to poetry. His early work is full of Irish myth, but he later turned to actual events and real people to speak for a "New Ireland" that "longs for psychological truth." He helped found the Irish National Theatre Society at the Abbey Theatre and served as a senator in the Irish Free State (1922–1928). Yeats was awarded the Nobel Prize for Literature in 1923.

JAN ZWICKY (b. 1955), was born in Calgary and received her Ph.D. in philosophy from the University of Toronto. She taught philosophy and creative writing at the University of New Brunswick and now teaches philosophy at the University of Victoria. Her many publications include *Songs for Relinquishing the Earth* (1996), which won the 1999 Governor General's Award, and *21 Small Songs* (2000). Zwicky's poetry reflects her background in philosophy and interest in music.

Credits

Chinua Achebe, "Dead Men's Path" from *Girls at War and Other Stories*. Copyright © 1972, 1973 by Chinua Achebe. Reprinted by permission of Harold Ober Associates Incorporated.

Margaret Atwood, "Dream 2: Brian the Still-Hunter" and "Death of a Young Son by Drowning" from *Selected Poems 1966–1984*, by Margaret Atwood. Copyright © 1990 Oxford University Press Canada. Reprinted by permission of the publisher.

Margaret Avison, "The Swimmer" from *A Swimmer's Moment* by Margaret Avison. Used by permission of Porcupine's Quill Press.

W.H. Auden, "Musée des Beaux Arts" and one stanza of "As I walked out one evening…" from *Collected Poems* by W.H. Auden. Copyright © 1940 and renewed 1968 by W.H. Auden. Reprinted with the permission of Random House, Inc.

Matsuo Basho, *A Haiku Journey: Basho's Narrow Road to a Far Province* translated by Dorothy Britton. Copyright © 1974, 1980, 2002 by Kodansha International Ltd.

Sandra Birdsell, "The Wednesday Circle" from *Agassiz Story* by Sandra Birdsell. Reprinted with the permission of McClelland & Stewart Ltd. *The Canadian Publishers*.

Earle Birney, "Anglosaxon Street" from *The Collected Poems of Earle Birney*. Reprinted with the permission of McClelland & Stewart Ltd. *The Canadian Publishers*.

Dionne Brand, "Land to Light On" from *Land to Light On* (Toronto, McClelland & Stewart Ltd. Reprinted with the permission of McClelland & Stewart Ltd. *The Canadian Publishers*.

Gwendolyn Brooks, "We Real Cool" from *Blacks* (Chicago, Illinois, Third World Press, 1991). Copyright © 1991 by Gwendolyn Brooks Blakely. Reprinted by consent of Brooks Permissions.

Taniguchi Buson, "Haiku" (trans. Harold G. Henderson) from *An Introduction to Haiku* by Harold G. Henderson. Copyright © 1958 by Harold G. Henderson. Reprinted with the permission of Doubleday, a division of Random House, Inc.

Anne Carson, "God's Work" from *Glass, Irony, and God* by Anne Carson. Copyright © by Anne Carson. Reprinted by permission of New Directions Publishing Corp.

Anton Chekhov, "The Proposal" from *The Plays of Anton Chekov* translated by Paul Schmidt. Copyright © 1997 by Paul Schmidt. Reprinted with the permission of HarperCollins Publishers, Inc.

George Elliott Clarke, "Blank Sonnet" from *Whylah Falls* by George Elliott Clarke. First pub. in 1990 by Polestar, an imprint of Raincoast Books.

Leonard Cohen, "A Kite Is a Victim" from *Stranger Music: Selected Poems and Songs* (McClelland & Stewart, 1993). Reprinted with the permission of McClelland & Stewart Ltd. *The Canadian Publishers*.

Lorna Crozier, "Poem About Nothing" from *The Garden Going On Without Us*. Reprinted with the permission of McClelland & Stewart Ltd. *The Canadian Publishers*.

e.e. cummings, "anyone lived in a pretty how town" from *Complete Poems: 1904–1962* by E.E. Cummings, edited by George J. Firmage. Copyright © 1940, 1968, 1991 by the Trustees for the E.E. Cummings Trust. Reprinted with the permission of Liveright Publishing Corporation.

Emily Dickinson, "Safe in Their Alabaster Chambers" and "Because I Could Not Stop for Death" and two stanzas from "Wild Nights" from *The Poems of Emily Dickinson*, Thomas H. Johnson, ed., Cambridge, Mass.: The Belknap Press of Harvard University Press. Copyright © 1951, 1955, 1979 by the President and Fellows of Harvard College. Reprinted by permission of the publishers and the Trustees of Amherst College.

T.S. Eliot, "The Hollow Men" and "The Love Song of J. Alfred Prufrock." Reprinted courtesy of Faber and Faber.

Louise Erdrich, "The Red Convertible" from *Love Medicine, New and Expanded Version* by Louise Erdrich. Copyright © 1984, 1993 by Louise Erdrich. Reprinted by permission of Henry Holt and Company, LLC.

Louise Erdrich, "Indian Boarding School: The Runaways." Copyright © 1984 by Louise Erdrich. Reprinted with the permission of The Wylie Agency, Inc.

Laurence Ferlinghetti, "Constantly Rising Absurdity" from *A Coney Island of the Mind*. Copyright © 1958 by Lawrence Ferlinghetti. Reprinted by permission of New Directions Publishing Corp.

Timothy Findley, "Stones" from *Stones*. Copyright © 1988 by Pebble Productions Inc. Reprinted by permission of Penguin Books Canada Limited.

Patrick Friesen, "pa poem 4: naked and nailed" from *Blasphemer's Wheel*. Copyright © 1994 Patrick Friesen. Reprinted by permission of Turnstone Press.

Robert Frost, "Design" from *The Poetry of Robert Frost*, edited by Edward Connery Lathem. Copyright © 1922, 1930, 1939, 1969 by Henry Holt and Company. Copyright © 1936, 1958 by Robert Frost, © 1967 by Leslie Frost Ballantine. Reprinted with the permission of Henry Holt and Company, LLC.

Allen Ginsberg, "A Supermarket in California" from *Collected Poems 1947–1980* by Allen Ginsberg. Copyright © 1955 by Allen Ginsberg. Reprinted with the permission of HarperCollins Publishers Inc.

Donald Hall, "My Son My Executioner" from *Old and New Poems* by Donald Hall. Copyright © 1990 by Donald Hall. Reprinted by permission of Houghton Mifflin Company. All rights reserved.

Robert Hayden, "Those Winter Sundays" from *Angle of Ascent: New and Selected Poems*. Copyright © 1966 by Robert Hayden. Used by permission of Liveright Publishing Corporation.

Michael Healey, "The Drawer Boy." Reprinted by permission of the playwright, Michael Healey, and the publisher, Playwrights Canada Press.

Seamus Heaney, "Digging" from *Selected Poems 1966–1987*. Copyright © 1980 by Seamus Heaney. Reprinted with the permission of Faber and Faber Ltd.

Ernest Hemingway, "Hills Like White Elephants" from *Men Without Women* by Ernest Hemingway. Copyright © 1927 by Charles Scribner's Sons, renewed © 1955 by Ernest Hemingway. Reprinted with permission of Scribner, an imprint of Simon & Schuster Adult Publishing Group.

David Huddle, "The 'Banked Fire' of Robert Hayden's 'Those Winter Sundays'" from *Touchstones: American Poets on a Favorite Poem*, Robert Pack and Jay Parini, eds. Reprinted with the permission of the author.

Langston Hughes, "Harlem (A Dream Deferred)" from *The Collected Poems of Langston Hughes* by Langston Hughes. Copyright © 1994 by The Estate of Langston Hughes. Reprinted with the permission of Alfred A. Knopf, a division of Random House, Inc.

David Henry Hwang, *M. Butterfly*. Copyright © 1986, 1987, 1988 by David Henry Hwang. Reprinted with the permission of Dutton Signet, a division of Penguin Group (USA) Inc.

Randall Jarrell, "The Death of the Ball Turret Gunner" from *The Complete Poems* by Randall Jarrell. Copyright © 1969, renewed 1997 by Mary von S. Jarrell. Reprinted by permission of Farrar, Straus and Giroux, LLC.

James Joyce, "Eveline" and "Araby" from *Dubliners*. Copyright © 1903, renewed by the Estate of James Joyce. Reproduced with the permission of the Estate of James Joyce.

Thomas King, "Borders" from *One Good Story, That One*. Copyright © 1991 Dead Dog Café Productions Inc. Reprinted with permission of the author.

Joy Kogawa, "Obasan," a short story by Joy Kogawa, is reprinted with the permission of the author. The subsequent novel, *Obasan*, was published first by Lester & Orpen Dennys, 1981, and is currently published by Penguin Canada.

Joy Kogawa, "Where There's a Wall" from *Women in the Woods* by Joy Kogawa (Mosaic Press).

Michele Lalonde, "Speak White." Reprinted by permission of the translator, D.G. Jones.

Patrick Lane, "The Bird." Copyright © Patrick Lane.

Philip Larkin, "Home Is So Sad" from *The Whitman Weddings*. Copyright © 1964 by Philip Larkin. Reprinted by permission of Faber and Faber Ltd.

Margaret Laurence, "To Set Our House in Order" from *A Bird in the House* by Margaret Laurence. Copyright © by Margaret Laurence. Reprinted by permission of McClelland & Stewart Ltd. *The Canadian Publishers*.

Irving Layton, "The Bull Calf" from *The Collected Poems of Irving Layton*. Reprinted with the permission of McClelland & Stewart Ltd. *The Canadian Publishers*.

"Eleanor Rigby," written by John Lennon and Paul McCartney. Northern Songs (PRS)/Sony/ATV Songs LLC. All rights on behalf of Northern Songs (PRS) administered by Sony/ATV Music Publishng Canada, 1121 Leslie St., Toronto, ON M3C 2J9. All rights reserved. Used by permission.

Denise Levertov, "O Taste and See" from *Poems 1960–1967*. Copyright © 1964 by Denise Levertov. Reprinted with the permission of New Directions Publishing Corporation.

Dorothy Livesay, "Bartok and the Geranium." Reproduced with the permission of Jay Stewart, Literary Executrix for the Estate of Dorothy Livesay.

Billie Livingston, "Paperweight" from *The Chick at the Back of the Church* (Roberts Creek, BC: Nightwood Editions, 2001).

CREDITS   855

Daphne Marlatt, "retrieving madrone" from *This Tremor Love Is* by Daphne Marlatt. Copyright © 2001. Reprinted with the permission of Talon Books Ltd.
Gwendolyn MacEwen, "Icarus." Copyright © 1961 by Gwendolyn MacEwan. Permission for use granted by the author's family.
Alistair MacLeod, "The Boat," from *The Lost Salt Gift of Blood* (Toronto, McClelland & Stewart, 1976). Reprinted by permission of McClelland & Stewart Ltd. *The Canadian Publishers*.
Joan MacLeod, *The Shape of a Girl*. Copyright © by Joan MacLeod. Reprinted with permission of Talon Books, Ltd.
Don McKay, "Icarus" from *Another Gravity* by Don McKay. Reprinted by permission of McClelland & Stewart Ltd. *The Canadian Publishers*.
Don McKay, "Glenn Gould Humming" from *Apparatus* by Don McKay. Reprinted by permission of McClelland & Stewart Ltd. *The Canadian Publishers*.
Eugene McNamara, "Falling in Place" from *Waterfalls* (Regina, Coteau Books, 2001). Reprinted with the permission of Coteau Books.
Anne Michaels, "There Is No City That Does Not Dream" from *Skin Divers* by Anne Michaels. Reprinted by permission of McClelland & Stewart Ltd. *The Canadian Publishers*.
Edna St. Vincent Millay, "First Fig" from *Fatal Interview* from *Collected Poems* (New York: Harper & Row, 1975). Copyright © 1923, 1931, 1951, 1958, by Edna St. Vincent Millay and Norma Millay Ellis. Reprinted with the permission of Elizabeth Barnett, literary executor.
Daniel David Moses, *Almighty Voice and His Wife*. Reprinted by permission of the playwright, Daniel David Moses, and the publisher, Playwrights Canada Press.
Lisel Mueller, "Things" from *Alive Together: New and Selected Poems*. Copyright © 1996 by Lisel Mueller. Reprinted by permission of Louisiana State University Press.
Bharati Mukherjee, "The Management of Grief" from *The Middleman and Other Stories* by Bharati Mukherjee. Copyright © Bharati Mukherjee, 1988. Reprinted by permission of Penguin Group (Canada), a Division of Pearson Penguin Canada Inc.
Alice Munro, "Boys and Girls," from *Dance of the Happy Shades*. Reproduced with permission of McGraw-Hill Ryerson Ltd.
Ogden Nash, "Common Sense," "The Cow," "Reflection on Ingenuity," "The Parent," and "Grandpa Is Ashamed." Copyright © 1931, 1931, 1940, 1933, 1962 by Ogden Nash, renewed. Copyright © by Linell Nash Smith and Isabel Nash Eberstadt. Reprinted by permission of Curtis Brown, Ltd.
Howard Nemerov, "The Goose Fish" from *The Collected Poems of Howard Nemerov*. Copyright © 1977 by Howard Nemerov. Reprinted with the permission of Margaret Nemerov.
Pablo Neruda, "The United Fruit Co." from *Neruda and Vallejo: Selected Poems*, translated by Robert Bly (Boston, MA: Beacon Press, 1971). Copyright © 1970 by Robert Bly. Reprinted with the permission of the translator.
bp Nichol, "landscape: 1" from *Zygal* (Coach House, 1985, 2001). Reprinted with the permission of the author's estate.
bp Nichol, "Blues" from *An H in the Heart* by bp Nichol. Reprinted by permission of McClelland & Stewart Ltd. *The Canadian Publishers*.
Alden Nowlan, "I, Icarus" and "A Middle-Aged Man in the Supermarket" from *Selected Poems* © 1967, 1974. Reprinted by permission of House of Anansi Press, Toronto.
Joyce Carol Oates, "Where Are You Going? Where Have You Been?" Copyright © 1970 by *Ontario Review*. Reprinted by permission of John Hawkins & Associates, Inc.
Flannery O'Connor, "A Good Man Is Hard to Find" from *A Good Man Is Hard to Find and Other Stories*. Copyright © 1953 by Flannery O'Connor and renewed 1981 by Regina O'Connor. Reprinted by permission of Harcourt, Inc.
Michael Ondaatje, "The Cinnamon Peeler" from *The Cinnamon Peeler* by Michael Ondaatje. Used by permission of the author.
P.K. Page, "Stories of Snow." Reprinted with the permission of The Porcupine's Quill, Inc.
Dorothy Parker, "One Perfect Rose" from *Complete Poems* by Dorothy Parker. Copyright © 1999 by The National Association for the Advancement of Colored People. Used by permission of Penguin, a division of Penguin Group (USA) Inc.
Sylvia Plath, "Daddy" from *Ariel*. Copyright © 1963 by Ted Hughes. Reprinted by permission of Faber and Faber Ltd.
Katherine Anne Porter, "The Jilting of Granny Weatherall" from *Flowering Judas and Other Stories*. Copyright © 1930 and renewed 1958 by Katherine Anne Porter. Reprinted by permission of Harcourt, Inc.
Ezra Pound, "In a Station of the Metro" from *Personae*. Copyright © 1926 by Ezra Pound. Reprinted with the permission of New Directions Publishing Corporation.

E.J. Pratt, "From Stone to Steel" from *E.J. Pratt, Complete Poems*, Sandra Djwa and R.G. Moyles, eds. (Toronto: University of Toronto Press, 1989).

Al Purdy, "The Dead Poet" from *Beyond Remembering: The Collected Poems of Al Purdy* (Harbour Publishing, 2000).

James Reaney, "School Globe" from *Selected Shorter Poems* copyright © 2003 by the author, is reprinted by permission of Beach Holme Publishing (formerly Press Porcépic) in Vancouver.

Adrienne Rich, "Aunt Jennifer's Tigers" from *The Fact of a Doorframe: Selected Poems 1950–2001* by Adrienne Rich. Copyright © 1951, 2002 by Adrienne Rich. Used by permission of W.W. Norton & Company, Inc.

David Adams Richards, "A Rural Place" from *Dancers at Night*. Reprinted by permission of Oberon Press.

Theodore Roethke, "My Papa's Waltz." (US ed. p. 473) from *The Collected Poems of Theodore Roethke*. Copyright © 1942 by Hearst Magazines, Inc. Used by permission of Doubleday, a division of Random House, Inc.

Mildred A. Rose, Spring Haiku "Affiliated with puddles …" and Spring Haiku "Rain in night London…" Copyright © by Mildred A. Rose. Originally published by The Music House Press, 1989. © Don Rose.

Sinclair Ross, "The Lamp at Noon" from *The Lamp at Noon* by Sinclair Ross. Reprinted by permission of McClelland & Stewart Ltd. *The Canadian Publishers*.

Carl Sandburg, "Fog" from *Chicago Poems* by Carl Sandburg. Copyright © 1916 by Holt, Rinehart and Winston and renewed 1944 by Carl Sandburg. Reprinted by permission of Harcourt, Inc.

Carl Sandburg, "Grass" from *Cornhuskers* by Carl Sandburg. Copyright © 1918 by Holt, Rinehart and Winston and renewed 1946 by Carl Sandburg. Reprinted by permission of Harcourt, Inc.

F.R. Scott, "Laurentian Shield" from *F.R. Scott: Selected Poems*. Reprinted with the permission of William Toye, literary executor for the Estate of F.R. Scott.

William Shakespeare, *Othello, The Moor of Venice*. Notes from "Othello" in *The Complete Works of Shakespeare*, 4th ed., by David Bevington. Copyright © 1992 by HarperCollins. Reprinted by permission of Pearson Education, Inc.

A.J.M. Smith, "The Wisdom of Old Jelly Roll," from *The Classic Shade* by A.J.M. Smith. Reprinted with permission of William Toye, literary executor for the Estate of A.J.M. Smith.

Russell Smith, "Serotonin." First published in *The Notebooks* (Doubleday, Canada).

Stevie Smith, "Not Waving but Drowning" from *Collected Poems of Stevie Smith*. Copyright © 1972 by Stevie Smith. Reprinted by permission of New Directions Publishing Corporation.

Sophocles, "Antigone" from *Three Theban Plays*, translated by Robert Fagles. Copyright © 1982 by Robert Fagles. Reprinted with the permission of Viking Penguin, a division of Penguin Group (USA) Inc.

John Steinbeck, "The Chrysanthemums" from *The Long Valley* by John Steinbeck. Copyright © 1937, renewed © 1965 by John Steinbeck. Used by permission of Viking Penguin, a division of Penguin Group (USA) Inc.

Wallace Stevens, "The Emperor of Ice Cream." from *The Collected Poems of Wallace Stevens*. Copyright © 1954 by Wallace Stevens and renewed 1982 by Holly Stevens. Reprinted with the permission of Alfred A. Knopf, a division of Random House, Inc.

Dylan Thomas, "Do Not Go Gentle into That Good Night" from *The Poems of Dylan Thomas*. Copyright © 1952 by the Trust for the Copyrights of Dylan Thomas. Reprinted by permission of David Higham Associates.

Miriam Waddington, "Ten Years and More" from *Miriam Waddington: Collected Poems*. Copyright © 1992 Oxford University Press Canada. Reprinted by permission of the publisher.

Bronwen Wallace, "The Woman in This Poem" from *Signs of the Former Tenant* (Oberon, 1983). Reprinted from by permission of Oberon Press.

Sheila Watson, "Antigone" from *The Tamarack Review*, Spring, 1959. With permission.

Phyllis Webb, "Sitting" and "Treblinka Gas Chamber." Copyright © Phyllis Webb. Reprinted with permission of Talon Books, Ltd.

Eudora Welty, "A Worn Path" from *A Curtain of Green and Other Stories*. Copyright © 1941 and renewed 1969 by Eudora Welty. Reprinted by permission of Harcourt, Inc.

Rudy Wiebe, "Where Is the Voice Coming From?" extracted from *River of Stone* by Rudy Wiebe. Copyright © 1995 Jackpine House Ltd. Reprinted by permission of Alfred A. Knopf Canada.

William Carlos Williams, "The Red Wheelbarrow" from *Collected Poems: 1909–1939, volume I*, copyright © 1938 by New Directions Publishing Corp. Reprinted by permission of New Directions Publishing Corporation.

Ethel Wilson, "The Window" from *Mrs. Golightly and Other Stories* by Ethel Wilson. Copyright © 1961 by Ethel Wilson. Reprinted by permission of The University of British Columbia.

Jim Wong-Chu, "old chinese cemetery kamloops" from *Chinatown Ghosts* (Arsenal Pulp Press, 1986). Reprinted with permission.

Richard Wright, "The Man Who Was Almost a Man" from *Eight Men* by Richard Wright. Copyright © 1940, © 1961 by Richard Wright; renewed © 1989 by Ellen Wright. Introduction by Paul Gilmore. Reprinted by permission of HarperCollins Publishers Inc.

Hisaye Yamamoto, "Seventeen Syllables" from *Seventeen Syllables and Other Stories*. Copyright © 1948 by Partisan Review, renewed © 1975 by Hisaye Yamamoto. Reprinted with the permission of Kitchen Table: Women of Color Press.

Lorraine York, "Epilogue: Stones" from *Front Lines: The Fiction of Timothy Findley* (ECW Press, 1991). Copyright © 1991. Reprinted by permission of ECW Press.

Jan Zwicky, "Musicians" from *Songs for Relinquishing the Earth* (Brick Books, 1998).

Index of Authors, Titles, and First Lines of Poems

Note: First lines of poems are set in quotation marks.

"About suffering they were never wrong," 436
Achebe, Chinua, 269
"Ah, look at all the lonely people!", 459
"Air smells of rhubarb, occasional," The (Clarke), 473
Almighty Voice and His Wife (Moses), 771
"alongthehorizongrewanunbrokenlineoftrees," 392
Anglosaxon Street (Birney), 433
Antigone (Sophocles), 484
Antigone (Watson), 237
"anyone lived in a pretty how town," 393
anyone lived in a pretty how town (cummings), 393
"Apparition of these faces in the crowd," The (Pound), 427
Araby (Joyce), 187
Arnold, Matthew, 415
"As I come loose, I realize," 474
Atwood, Margaret, 456
Auden, W.H., 436
"Aunt Jennifer's tigers prance across a screen," 448
Aunt Jennifer's Tigers (Rich), 448
Avison, Margaret, 441

"Banked Fire" of Robert Hayden's "Those Winter Sundays" (Huddle), 402–403
Bartok and the Geranium (Livesay), 375
"Because I could not stop for Death," 416
Because I Could Not Stop for Death (Dickinson), 416
"Bent double, like old beggars under sacks," 431
"Between my finger and my thumb," 457
Bird, The (Lane), 458
Bird in the Room, The (Pickthall), 426
"Bird you captured is dead," The (Lane), 458
Birdsell, Sandra, 300
Birney, Earle, 433
Blake, William, 409
Blank Sonnet (Clarke), 473
Blues (Nichol), 465
Bly, Robert, 435
Boat, The (MacLeod), 130
Borders (King), 307
Boys and Girls (Munro), 149
Brand, Dionne, 469
Brian, the Still-Hunter (XI) (Moodie), 413
Brooks, Gwendolyn, 392

Browning, Robert, 413
Bull Calf, The (Layton), 437
Byron, Lord George Gordon, 411

"Call the roller of big cigars," 425
Carson, Anne, 469
Cather, Willa, 174
Chekhov, Anton, 760
Chopin, Kate, 172
Chrysanthemums, The (Steinbeck), 214
Cinnamon Peeler, The (Ondaatje), 464
Clarke, George Elliott, 473
Cohen, Leonard, 452
"Constantly risking absurdity," 442
Constantly Risking Absurdity (Ferlinghetti), 442
Crane, Stephen, 422
Crozier, Lorna, 376
Cry from an Indian Wife (Johnson), 355
cummings, e.e., 393

Daddy (Plath), 448
"Dawn drizzle ended dampness steams from," 433
Dead Men's Path (Achebe), 269
Dead Poet, The (Purdy), 441
"Death, be not proud, though some have called thee," 406
Death, Be Not Proud (Donne), 406
Death of a Young Son by Drowning (Atwood), 456
Death of the Ball Turret Gunner (Jarrell), 438
"Degree of nothingness," The (Webb), 448
Design (Frost), 423
Dickinson, Emily, 416
Digging (Heaney), 457
"Do not go gentle into that good night," 438
Do Not Go Gentle into That Good Night (Thomas), 438
"Do not weep, maiden, for war is kind," 422
Donne, John, 406
Dover Beach (Arnold), 415
Drawer Boy, The (Healey), 535
Dream 2: Brain the Still-Hunter (Atwood), 456
Dulce et Decorum Est (Owen), 431
Dunbar, Paul Laurence, 423

Eagle, The (Tennyson), 413
Eleanor Rigby (Lennon and McCartney), 459
Eliot, T.S., 427
Emperor of Ice-Cream, The (Stevens), 425

859

Epilogue: *Stones* (York), 87
Erdrich, Louise, 330, 472
Eveline (Joyce), 191

Fagles, Robert, 484
Falling in Place (McNamara), 122
"fallingstars," 394
"Farewell, thou child of my right hand and joy," 407
"Feather and wax, the artful wings," 460
Ferlinghetti, Lawrence, 442
Findlay, Timothy, 69–70
First Fig (Millay), 430
Flea, The (Donne), 406
Flight of the Geese, The (Roberts), 419
Fog (Sandburg), 424
"Fog comes on little cat feet," The (Sandburg), 424
"For everyone the swimmer's moment at the whirlpool comes," 441
Friesen, Patrick, 467
"From my mother's sleep I fell into the State," 438
"From stone to bronze, from bronze to steel," 425
From Stone to Steel (Pratt), 425
Frost, Robert, 423

Ginsberg, Allen, 446
Glenn Gould, Humming (McKay), 462
"Glory be to God for dappled things," 417
"Go, lovely Rose," 356
Go, Lovely Rose (Waller), 356
God's Work (Carson), 469
Good Man Is Hard to Find, A (O'Connor), 258
Goose Fish, The (Nemerov), 443
Grass (Sandburg), 424

"Had we but world enough, and time," 407
Hall, Donald, 378
Hardy, Thomas, 354
Harlem (A Dream Deferred) (Hughes), 432
Hawthorne, Nathaniel, 163
Hayden, Robert, 437
"He, who navigated with success," 456
"He clasps the crag with crooked hands," 413
Healey, Michael, 534–535
Heaney, Seamus, 457
Hemingway, Ernest, 210
"Hidden in wonder and snow, or sudden with summer," 431
Hills Like White Elephants (Hemingway), 210
"Home is so sad. It stays as it was left," 444
Home Is So Sad (Larkin), 444
"Home's the place we head for in our sleep," 472
Hopkins, Gerard Manley, 417
Housman, A.E., 418
"How all men wrongly death to dignify," 433
Huddle, David, 403

Hughes, Lanston, 432
Hwang, David Henry, 579–580

I, Icarus (Nowlan), 451
"I found a dimpled spider, fat and white," 423
"I hear the low wind wash the softening snow," 419
"I met a traveller from an antique land," 411
"I pass a bunch of musicians in the street," 472
"I remember those carpenter's hands," 467
"I was altered in the placenta," 441
Icarus (MacEwen), 460
Icarus (McKay), 463
"I e," 465
"If I were a cinnamon peeler," 464
"I'm pretending to test the avocados for ripeness," 451
In a Station of the Metro (Pound), 427
Indian Boarding School: The Runaways (Erdrich), 472
"isn't sorry. We do not find him," 463

Jarrell, Randall, 438
Jilting of Granny Weatherall, The (Porter), 203
Johnson, Pauline, 355, 419
Jones, D.G., 453
Jonson, Ben, 407
Joyce, James, 187, 191

Keats, John, 411
King, Thomas, 307
Kite Is a Victim, A (Cohen), 452
Kogawa, Joy, 2–3, 453

Lalonde, Michele, 453
Lamb, The (Blake), 409
Lamp at Noon, The (Ross), 230
Lampman, Archibald, 374, 420
Land to Light On (Brand), 469
landscape: 1 (Nichol), 392
Lane, Patrick, 458
Larkin, Philip, 444
"Last autumn when they aired the house," 426
Laurence, Margaret, 91–92
Laurentian Shield (Scott), 431
Layton, Irving, 437
Lennon, John, 459
"Let me not to the marriage of true minds," 405
Let Me Not to the Marriage of True Minds (Shakespeare), 405
"Let us go then, you and I," 427
Levertov, Denise, 445
"like a child lost," 468
"Little Lamb, who made thee?", 409
Livesay, Dorothy, 375
Livingston, Billie, 474
Love Song of J. Alfred Prufrock, The (Eliot), 427
Lovelace, Richard, 407

INDEX OF AUTHORS, TITLES, AND FIRST LINES OF POEMS

M. Butterfly (Hwang), 580
MacEwen, Gwendolyn, 460
MacLeod, Alistair, 129–130
MacLeod, Joan, 803
"Man I saw in the forest," The (Atwood), 457
Man Who Was Almost a Man (Wright), 221
Management of Grief, The (Mukherjee), 289
"Margaret are you grieving," 417
"Mark but this flea, and mark in this," 406
Marlatt, Daphne, 462
Marvell, Andrew, 407
"Maybe this wide country just stretches your life to a thinness," 469
McCartney, Paul, 459
McKay, Don, 462
McNamara, Eugene, 121–122
Michaels, Anne, 473
Middle-Aged Man in the Supermarket (Nowlan), 451
Millay, Edna St. Vincent, 430
Moodie, Susanna, 413
"Moonlight in the kitchen is a sign of God," 469
Moses, Daniel David, 771
Mueller, Lisel, 445
Mukherjee, Bharati, 289
Munro, Alice, 149
Musée des Beaux Arts (Auden), 436
Musicians (Zwicky), 472
"My candle burns at both ends," 430
"My Forest Brave, my Red-skin love, farewell," 355
My Last Duchess (Browning), 413
"My mistress' eyes are nothing like the sun," 405
My Mistress' Eyes Are Nothing Like the Sun (Shakespeare), 405
My Papa's Waltz (Roethke), 354
"My son, my executioner," 378
My Son My Executioner (Hall), 378

Nemerov, Howard, 443
Neruda, Pablo, 435
Nichol, bp, 392, 465
"Nobody heard him, the dead man," 433
Noiseless Patient Spider, A (Whitman), 373
"not along with the music, which isn't listening," 462
Not Waving but Drowning (Smith), 433
Nowlan, Alden, 451
Nuns Fret Not (Woodsworth), 394
"Nuns fret not at their convent's narrow room," 394

"O 'Melia, my dear, this does everything crown!", 354
"O Rose, thou art sick!", 410
O Taste and See (Levertov), 445
Oates, Joyce Carol, 278
Obasan (Kogawa), 2–3
O'Connor, Flannery, 258
Ode on a Grecian Urn (Keats), 411

"O'er memory's glass I *see* his shadow flit," 413
old chinese cemetery kamloops (Wong-Chu), 468
On My First Son (Jonson), 407
"On the long shore, lit by the moon," 443
Ondaatje, Michael, 464
One Perfect Rose (Parker), 357
Othello, the Moor of Venice (Shakespeare), 669
Owen, Wilfred, 431
Ozymandias (Shelley), 411

pa poem 4: naked and nailed (Friesen), 467
Page, P.K., 439
Paperweight (Livingston), 474
Parker, Dorothy, 357
Paul's Case (Cather), 174
Pickthall, Marjorie, 426
Pied Beauty (Hopkins), 417
"Pile the bodies high at Austerlitz and Waterloo," 424
Plath, Sylvia, 448
Poem about Nothing (Crozier), 376
Porter, Katherine Anne, 203
Pound, Ezra, 427
Pratt, E.J., 425
Proposal, The (Chekhov), 760
Purdy, Al, 441

Reaney, James, 447
Red Convertible, The (Erdrich), 330
Red Wheelbarrow, The (Williams), 426
retrieving madrone (Marlatt), 462
Rich, Adrienne, 448
Richards, David Adams, 315
Roberts, Sir Charles G.D., 418
Roethke, Theodore, 354
Ross, Sinclair, 230
Ruined Maid, The (Hardy), 354
Rural Place, A (Richards), 315

"Safe in their Alabaster Chambers," 416
Safe in Their Alabaster Chambers (Dickinson), 416
Sailing to Byzantium (Yeats), 421
Sandburg, Carl, 424
School Globe, The (Reaney), 447
Scott, F.R., 431
"Sea is calm to-night," The (Arnold), 415
Second Coming, The (Yeats), 421
Serotonin (Smith), 337
Seventeen Syllables (Yamamoto), 249
Shakespeare, William, 374, 405, 669
"Shall I compare thee to a summer's day?", 374
Shall I Compare Thee to a Summer's Day? (Shakespeare), 374
Shape of a Girl, The (MacLeod), 803
"She lifts her green umbrellas," 375
"She walks in beauty, like the night," 411
She Walks in Beauty (Byron), 411

Shelley, Percy Bysshe, 411
Sick Rose, The (Blake), 410
"Single flow'r he sent me, since we met," A (Parker), 357
Sitting (Webb), 448
Smith, A.J.M., 433
Smith, Russell, 337
Smith, Stevie, 433
"so much depends upon a red wheel barrow," 426
"Sometimes when I hold our faded old globe," 447
Song My Paddle Sings, The (Johnson), 419
Sophocles, 484
"Speak white," 453
Speak White (Lalonde), 453
Spring and Fall (Hopkins), 417
Steinbeck, John, 214
Stevens, Wallace, 425
Stones (Findlay), 69
Stories of Snow (Page), 439
Story of an Hour, The (Chopin), 172
"Sundays too my father got up early," 437
Supermarket in California, A (Ginsberg), 446
Swimmer's Moment, The (Avison), 441

"take, take the arbutus, crazy-woman tree, she said, does," 462
"Tell me not, sweet, I am unkind," 407
Ten Years and More (Waddington), 440
Tennyson, Lord Alfred, 413
"That is no country for old men. The young," 421
"That's my last Duchess painted on the wall," 413
"There is no city that does not dream," 473
There Is No City That Does Not Dream (Michaels), 473
"There was a time when I could fly. I swear it," 451
"Thing could barely stand. Yet taken," The (Layton), 437
Things (Mueller), 445
Thomas, Dylan, 438
"Those in the vegetable rain retain," 439
Those Winter Sundays (Hayden), 437
"Thou still unravished bride of quietness," 411
"Time you won your town the race," The (Housman), 418
To an Athlete Dying Young (Housman), 418
To His Coy Mistress (Marvell), 407
To Lucasta, on Going to the Wars (Lovelace), 407
To Set Our House in Order (Laurence), 92
"Tonight the very horses springing by," 420
Treblinka Gas Chamber (Webb), 394
"Turning and turning in the widening gyre," 421
Tyger, The (Blake), 409
"Tyger, Tyger, burning bright," 409

United Fruit Co., The (Neruda), 435
Voices of Earth (Lampman), 374
Waddington, Miriam, 440
Wallace, Bronwen, 465
Waller, Edmund, 356
War Is Kind (Crane), 422
Watson, Sheila, 248
"We have not heard the music of the spheres," 374
"We real cool. We," 392
We Real Cool (Brooks), 392
We Wear the Mask (Dunbar), 423
"We wear the mask that grins and lies," 423
Webb, Phyllis, 394, 448
Wednesday Circle, The (Birdsell), 300
Welty, Eudora, 243
"West wind, blow from your prairie nest," 419
"What happened is, we grew lonely," 445
"What happens to a dream deferred?", 432
"What thoughts I have of you tonight, Walt Whitman, for I," 446
"When my husband lay dying a mountain," 440
"When the trumpet sounded, it was," 435
Where Are You Gonig, Where Have You Been? (Oates), 278
Where Is the Voice Coming From? (Wiebe), 272
"Where there's a wall," 453
Where There's a Wall (Kogawa), 453
"Whiskey on your breath,"The (Roethke), 354
Whitman, Walt, 373
Wiebe, Rudy, 272
Williams, William Carlos, 426
Wilson, Ethel, 194
Window, The (Wilson), 194
Winter Evening (Lampman), 420
Wisdom of Old Jelly Roll, The (Smith), 433
Woman in this Poem, The (Wallace), 465
Wong-Chu, Jim, 468
Wordsworth, William, 394, 410
"World is not with us enough," The (Levertov), 445
World Is Too Much with Us, The (Wordsworth), 410
"World is too much with us; late and soon," The (Wordsworth), 410
Worn Path, A (Welty), 243
Wright, Richard, 221

Yamamoto, Hisaye, 249
Yeats, William Butler, 421
York, Lorraine M., 87
"You do not do, you do not do," 448
Young Goodman Brown (Hawthorne), 163

"Zero is the one we didn't understand," 376
Zwicky, Jan, 472

Subject Index

abstract words, 525
active voice, 50
adjective form, 401–402
after-writing outline
   checking the outline, 40–41
   construction of, 40
   exercise, 42–43
   purpose of, 40
   sample, 41–42
agon (argument), 481
allegory, 825
alliteration, 390, 825
allusion, 825
ambiguity, 825
analysis, 11
analysis of poem, 362
anapest, 829
anapestic foot, 389, 829
antagonist, 481, 825
anticlimax, 825
apostrophe, 825
apron, 477
Arabic numbers, 663
archetypal approaches, 822
archetypal symbols, 90
archetype, 825
arena stage, 477
argument
   details, developing with, 22–23
   of interpretation, 21–22
articles, quotations from, 663
associations for meaning, 349–351
assonance, 390, 825
atmosphere
   see also mood
   critical writing ideas, 143–144
   described, 129
   examples of, 129
   organization of writing, 143
   prewriting stage, 142
   responsive writing ideas, 143
   writing about, 142–144
audience
   analysis of, 9
   defined, 825
   diversity of, 9
auditory images, 89
authors and their works, guides to, 636

balanced sentences, 144–145
ballad, 825
beginning of paper, 19
biographical approach, 820
blank verse, 825–826

CARL Uncover, 634
carpe diem, 826
catastrophe, 482
catharsis, 826
cause and effect, 45
central events, 20
central traits, 20
character
   central events, 20
   central traits, 20
   foil, 65
   general plan, 19–20
   in short fiction, 64–65
   writing paper on, 19–21
checklists
   accurate documentation, 643
   arguing an interpretation, 22
   peer evaluation checklist for revision, 39
   proofreading checklist, 54
   revision checklist, 46
chorus, 826
chronological order, 21
citation of sources, 27–28, 642
   see also MLA documentation style;
      Works Cited sample entries
clarity, 524–525
classical tragic hero. *See* tragic hero
cliché, 17
climax, 482, 826
closed form poetry, 390
clustering, 15, 15*f*–16*f*
coherence
   see also unity
   achieving coherence, 160
   checking for, 160–161
   defined, 826
   editing for, 161–162
   glosses, using, 160
   parallel structure, 44, 161–162
   repetition of key words, 44–45, 161
   revision for, 44–45, 160–161
   synonyms, 161
   techniques for, 45
combining sentences, 45–47
comedy, 482, 826
comedy of manners, 826
comparisons, 379
complication, 826
composing. *See* writing process
conceit, 826, 829
conciseness, combining sentences for, 46
conclusion
   description, 128
   echoing introduction, 128

SUBJECT INDEX

emphatic final sentence, 26
humour, 128
importance of, 26
irony, 128
postponing writing of, 26
psychological importance of, 128
quotation from story, 128
relate discussion to theme, 26
revision of, 128
thought-provoking ending, 128
writing ahead, 26
concrete, 826
concrete poetry, 826
conflict, 826
connotation, 51, 370, 826
consonance, 390, 826
context, and words, 402
contrast, 45, 379
controlling idea. *See* thesis
controlling image, 826–827
convention, 827
couplets, 390–391, 827
crisis. *See* climax
critical approaches
  archetypal approaches, 822
  biographical approach, 820
  cultural approach, 820–821
  deconstruction, 823–824
  formalism, 819–820
  gender focus, 822–823
  historical approaches, 820–821
  Marxist approach, 821
  mythological approach, 822
  psychological approaches, 821–822
  reader response approach, 823
critical comment, 23–24
critical focus, 23–24
critical questions
  reading plays, 480
  reading poetry, 350
  reading short fiction, 67
critical thinking, 11
critical writing ideas
  atmosphere, writing about, 143–144
  dramatic structure, 523–524
  generally, 36
  imagery and symbolism, 104
  modern hero, 575–576
  poetic form, 400
  poetic language, 380
  point of view, 127
  setting, writing about, 143–144
  structure of short fiction, 84
  symbolism, 104
  theme, 160
  tone, 363
cultural analysis, 578–579
cultural approach, 820–821

dactyl, 829
dactylic foot, 389, 829

databases, 634
deconstruction, 823–824
denotations, 51, 370, 827
denouement, 482, 827
details
  of argument, 22–23
  classification of, 159
  grouping, 83
  of plot, 23–24
  theme, relating to, 84, 159
dialogue, 476
diction, 827
dimeter, 829
direct quotation, 639
directed freewriting, 13, 13f
documentation checklist, 643
double entendre, 827
downstage, 477
drama
  see also plays
  agon (argument), 481
  criticism, guides to, 636
  fable, 481
  film, 479
  modern hero in. See modern hero
  plot, 481
  researched writing ideas, 641
  secondary sources. See research papers
  stage terminology, 477–478
dramatic irony, 829
dramatic monologue, 827
  see also soliloquy
dramatic point of view, 831
dramatic structure
  climax, 482
  components of, 481–482
  critical writing ideas, 523–524
  denouement, 482
  described, 481–482
  examples of, 482–520
  exposition, 482
  falling action, 482
  fundamental struggle, 481
  point of attack, 482
  prewriting, for analysis, 521
  quotations from play, 523
  responsive writing ideas, 523
  rewriting stage, 524–525
  rising action, 482
  student paper, sample, 525–531
  thesis, workable and argumentative, 522–523
  writing about, 521–524

echo transitions, 45
editing
  coherence, 161–162
  combining sentences, 45–47
  described, 45
  poetry, writing about, 363–364
  rearrangement for emphasis and variety, 47–48

research papers, 642–643
writing style, 49–52
electronic sources, 667
elegy, 827
ellipsis dots, 364
emotional meanings of words, 51
empathy, 827
emphasis
  and arrangement of points, 43–44
  editing for, 47–48
  repetition for, 48, 161
  transitional phrases for, 45
end of paper, 19
end punctuation, in poetry, 364
Engfish, 524
English sonnet, 832
epigram, 827
epigraph, 827
epilogue, 827
epiphany, 827
episode, 827
ERIC databases, 634, 667
essay, quotation from, 662
explication of poem, 362
exposition, 482, 827
expressive writing, and poetic form, 398–400
extended metaphor, 371

fable, 481, 827
falling action, 482, 827
  see also denouement
feedback, 38–39
feet. *See* foot
feminist critics, 822–823
figurative language, 828
figures of speech, 370–371
film, 479, 667
final draft, sample, 54–60
final sentence, 26
first draft
  after-writing outline, 40–43
  messy process, 27
  rescan, pausing to, 27
  sample student paper, 28
  sources, quoting from, 27–28
first-person plural, 52
first-person point of view, 120, 830
first-person singular, 52
flashback, 63, 828
flat character, 828
flats, 477
flow. *See* coherence
foil, 65, 828
foot
  see also meter
  anapestic foot, 389, 829
  dactylic foot, 389, 829
  defined, 828, 829
  iambic foot, 829
  kinds of feet, 389

number of, in poetic form, 389
number of feet, 389
spondaic foot, 829
trochaic foot, 389, 829
foreshadowing
  defined, 828
  in short fiction, 65
formal writing, 828
formalism, 819–820
free verse, 390, 391, 828
freewriting, 13, 13*f*, 828

gay and lesbian stereotypes, 823
gender focus, 822–823
generalizations, 22
genre, 828
glosses, 160
gustatory images, 89

Handbook for Writers of Research Papers (MLA), 364
hero
  see also protagonist
  defined, 828
  modern hero. See modern hero
  tragic hero, 533, 832
heroine, 481, 828
  see also protagonist
hexameter, 829
historical approaches
  biographical approach, 820
  cultural approach, 820–821
  Marxist approach, 821
homonyms, 401
hubris, 828
hyperbole, 828

iamb, 829
iambic foot, 829
idea development
  clustering, 15, 15*f*–16*f*
  critical thinking, 11
  directed freewriting, 13, 13*f*
  problem solving, 13–15
  self-questioning, 11–12
  suggestions, 35
ideas
  for critical writing, 36
  ordering of, 21
  parallel ideas, presentation of, 44
  for responsive writing, 36
imagery, 828
  in poetry, 372
  in short fiction, 89–90
images
  see also motif
  auditory images, 89
  categories of, 89
  defined, 828
  described, 89
  gustatory images, 89
  kinetic images, 89

866 SUBJECT INDEX

in short fiction, 65
tactile images, 89
thermal images, 89
visual images, 89
in medias res, 482
indexes, 634
informal writing, 828
informational notes, 642, 663
Infotrac SearchBank, 634
internal rhyme, 828
Internet research, 634–635, 667–668
interpretation, 21–22
introduction
   appealing opening, 25
   echoing in conclusion, 128
   importance of, 24
   postponing writing of, 24
   revision of, 104–105
   thesis, statement of, 25
invention, 11, 828
irony
   defined, 828
   dramatic irony, 829
   in short fiction, 65
   situational irony, 829
   verbal irony, 353, 828, 831
Italian sonnet, 832

jargon, 524–525, 829
Jung, Carl, 822
juxtaposition, 829

kinetic images, 89

library sources. *See* secondary sources
limited omniscient point of view, 120
limited point of view, 830
line numbers, 363–364
lines, classification of, 829
literal meaning, 348–349
literary criticism, 86
logic, and arrangement of points, 43–44
logical order, 21
lyric, 829

malapropisms, 402
Marxist approach, 821
metaphor
   see also simile
   defined, 829
   extended metaphor, 371
   in poetic language, 371
metaphorical ideas, 371
metaphysical poetry, 829
   see also conceit
meter
   see also foot
   defined, 829
   feet, number of, 389
   kinds of feet, 389
metonymy, 829
middle of paper, 19
misused words, 402

MLA documentation style
   abbreviations for pages, omission of, 663
   Arabic numbers, 663
   article, quotations from, 663
   book with single author, 662
   essay, quotations from, 662
   informational notes, 663
   lower case, use of, 663
   multiple volumes, 662
   multiple works by same author, 663
   novel, quotations from, 661
   period, spacing of, 663
   play, quotations from, 662
   poem, quotations from, 661
   publication, place of, 663
   samples of. See Works Cited sample entries
   short story, quotations from, 661
   Works Cited list, 661
MLA International Bibliography, 634, 635
modern hero
   critical writing ideas, 575–576
   example of, 534–573
   modern tragic hero, 534
   paragraph specifics, development of, 576
   prewriting stage, 574
   responsive writing ideas, 575
   rewriting stage, 576
   structure, choice of, 575
   thesis, choice of, 575
   writing about, 574–576
Modern Language Association (MLA), 27, 364
monometer, 829
mood, 829
   see also tone
motif
   defined, 829
   in short fiction, 65, 90
multisyllabic words, 524–525
myth, 829
mythological approach, 822

narrative, 829
narrator
   defined, 829
   shifting narrators, 120–121
   in short fiction, 119
   unreliable narrator, 120–121, 833
note-taking, 635
notecards, 637
novels
   quotations from, 661
   structure in, 68

objective point of view, 120, 831
ode, 830
omniscient point of view, 120, 830
online catalogue, 634
onomatopoeia, 830
open form poetry, 390, 391
organization
   atmosphere, writing about, 143
   basic approach, 19–21

SUBJECT INDEX 867

chronological order, 21
general plan, 19–20
logical order, 21
ordering of ideas, 21
research paper, 637
revision of, 144
setting, writing about, 143
traditional format, 19
outlines. *See* after-writing outline
oxymoron, 373, 830

parable, 830
paradox, 372–373, 830
parallel structure, 44
paraphrase, 348–349, 361, 639, 830
parody, 830
passive voice, 50–51
patterns, and structure, 83
peer review
guidelines, 38
peer review groups, 38–39
revision checklist, 39
pentameter, 829, 830
persona
critical writing ideas, 363
defined, 830
in poetry, 352, 353, 357–358
prewriting stage, 357–361
responsive writing ideas, 362
student paper, sample, 381–387
personification, 372, 830
phallic symbol, 90, 830
photocopies, 637
plagiarism, 48, 638–639, 830
plays
see also drama
dramatic structure. See dramatic structure
quotations from, 523, 662
reading plays. See reading plays
structure in, 68
plot
defined, 830
details of, vs. critical comments, 23–24
in drama, 481
in short stories, 62
and structure, 68
subplot, 63
poems. *See* poetry
poetic form
alliteration, 390
assonance, 390
closed forms, 390
consonance, 390
couplets, 390–391
critical writing ideas, 400
exact word, use of, 401–402
examples of, 392
exercise on poetic form, 390
experimenting with, 395–397
expressive writing ideas, 398–400
foot. See foot
free verse, 390, 391

meaning, relating to, 398
meter. See meter
open forms, 390, 391
poetic syntax, 391
prewriting stage, 395–397
published essay, sample, 402–404
quatrain, 390–391
rewriting stage, 400–402
rhyme, 388
rhythm, 388
sonnet, 391
stanzas, 390–391
style, revision of, 400–402
types of, 388
writing about, 397–400
poetic language
comparisons, 379
connotation, 370
contrasts, 379
critical writing ideas, 380
denotation, 370
descriptive terms, 380
diction, 381
examples of, 373
figures of speech, 370–373
imagery, 372
lively words, 380–381
metaphor, 371
oxymoron, 373
paradox, 372–373
personification, 372
prewriting stage, 378–379
responsive writing ideas, 379
simile, 371
style, 380–381
symbol, 372
vivid terms, 380
writing about, 379–380
poetic syntax, 391
poetry
analysis of poem, 362
associations for meaning, 349–351
criticism, guides to, 636
literal meaning, 348–349
personal experiences, and interpretation, 358
poetic form. See poetic form
poetic syntax, 391
quotations from, 363–364, 661
reading poetry, 348–350
structure in, 68
tone in, 353
writing about. See poetry, writing about
poetry, writing about
editing, 363–364
ellipsis dots, use of, 364
end punctuation, adjustment of, 364
explication of poem, 362
line numbers, 363–364
multiple lines, quotation of, 364
paraphrasing, 361
persona, 352, 353, 357–358
poetic form. See poetic form

SUBJECT INDEX

poetic language, 379–380
quotation of poem, 363–364
researched writing ideas, 641
slash marks, 363
speaker, identification of, 352
square brackets, use of, 364
student paper, sample, 365–369, 381–387
thesis, development of, 358–359, 360, 361
tone, 352–353, 357–361
understanding, need for, 361
verbal irony, 353
point of attack, 482
point of view
  critical writing ideas, 127
  defined, 830
  describing, 120
  dramatic point of view, 831
  examples of, 121
  first-person point of view, 120, 830
  identification of, 119
  limited omniscient point of view, 120
  limited point of view, 830
  objective point of view, 120, 831
  omniscient point of view, 120, 830
  prewriting to identify, 126
  responsive writing ideas, 127
  revisions, 128
  shifting narrators, 120–121
  shifting point of view, 830
  in short fiction, 63–64
  theme, relating to, 126
  unreliable narrator, 120–121
  unreliable point of view, 831
  writing about, 126–127
prewriting stage
  atmosphere, 141–142
  audience analysis, 9
  defined, 831
  dramatic structure, analysis of, 521
  ideas, development of, 11–15
  modern hero, 574
  patterns, determination of, 83
  persona, 357–361
  poetic form, experimenting with, 395–397
  poetic language, 378–379
  point of view, identification of, 126
  purpose of writing, 10–11
  reading for writing, 2
  setting, 141–142
  about structure, 83
  symbols, interpretation of, 102
  theme, 17–18, 157–158
  thesis ideas, 15–17
  thesis statement, 17–18
  tone, 357–361
primary sources
  citation of. See MLA documentation style
  defined, 831
  on Work Cited sheet, 28
  writing from. See dramatic structure; poetry, writing about; short fiction, writing about
problem solving, 13–15

proofreading
  checklist, 54
  described, 52
  friends' help, 53
  reading aloud, 53
  reading paper backwards, 52
  typical errors, 53
proscenium, 477
protagonist, 62, 481, 831
PsychINFO, 634
psychological approaches, 821–822
public access catalogue, 634
pun, 831

quatrain, 390–391, 831
quotations
  citation of, 27–28
  see also MLA documentation style
  in conclusion, 128
  direct quotation, 639
  integration of, 85
  introduction of, 639–640
  multiple lines of poetry, 364
  from play, 523
  of poem, in essay, 363–364
  from sources, 27–28

reader response approach, 823
reading aloud, 53, 476–477
reading plays
  critical questions for, 480
  drama on film, 479
  envisioning the action, 478–479
  listening to lines, 476–477
  visualization of scenes, 477–478
reading poetry
  associations for meaning, 349–351
  critical questions, 350
  literal meaning, 348–349
  paraphrase, 348–349
  positive attitude, 348
reading short fiction
  characters, study of, 64–65
  critical questions for, 67
  foils, 65
  point of view, 63–64
  recognizing images and symbols, 91
  setting, 64
  specialized literary techniques, 65
  structure, 62–63
  subplot, 63
  theme, discovery of, 66
  title, examination of, 66
rearrangement of points, 43–44
reference works
  in print, 635
  reading poetry, 351
  on symbols, 91
repetition
  for coherence, 44–45, 161
  for emphasis, 48, 161
research papers
  citation of sources, 642

SUBJECT INDEX 869

cultural analysis, 578–579
documentation checklist, 643
editing, 642–643
informational notes, 642
library sources, 631–632
MLA documentation style. See MLA documentation style
notecards, 637
organization, 637
photocopies, 637
plagiarism, avoiding, 638–639
prewriting stage, 632
quotations, introduction of, 639–640
researched writing ideas, 640–641
rewriting stage, 642
sample documented student papers, 642–653, 654–660
secondary sources. See secondary sources
thesis, development of, 632
thesis statement, 636–637
writing before researching, 637–638
research process, 631
researched writing ideas
drama, 641
poetry, 641
short fiction, 640
resolution, 831
see also denouement; falling action
responsive writing ideas
atmosphere, writing about, 143
dramatic structure, 523
generally, 36
imagery and symbolism, 103
modern hero, 575
poetic language, 379
point of view, 127
setting, writing about, 143
structure of short fiction, 84
symbolism, 103
theme, 159–160
tone, 362
restatement, 45
revision
abstract words, 525
after-writing outline, 40–43
balanced sentences, 144–145
checklist, 46
citation of sources, 642
clarity, 524–525
coherence, 160–161
conclusion, 127–128
described, 37–38
dramatic structure, 524–525
Engfish, 524
exact words in poetry, 401–402
feedback, 38–39
flow of writing, 44–45
glosses, 160
informational notes, 642
introduction, 104–105
jargon, 524–525
modern hero, writing about, 576

organization of ideas, 144
paragraph specifics, development of, 576
peer groups, 38–39
peer review, 38–39
poetic form, and style, 400–402
proofreading, 52–53
quotations, graceful integration of, 85
rearrangement of points, 43–44
repetition of key terms, 44–45
research papers, 642
sentence modelling, 145–146
strongest-point rule, 44
transitional phrases, 44, 45
rewriting process. *See* revision
rhyme
defined, 831
described, 389
effect of, 389
and poetic form, 388
rhythm
see also meter
defined, 831
and poetic form, 388
rising action, 482, 831
round character, 831

sample papers. *see* student papers
sarcasm
see also irony
defined, 831
in negative book reviews, 51
satire, 831
see also parody
secondary sources
see also research papers
authors and their works, guides to, 636
citation of. See MLA documentation style
databases, 634
defined, 831
described, 631–632
dramatic criticism, 636
fiction, criticism of, 636
guides to literary criticism, 636
indexes, 634
Internet research, 634–635
note-taking, 635
online catalogue, 634
poetry, criticism of, 636
public access catalogue, 634
reference works in print, 635
self-questioning, 11–12
sentence modelling, 145–146
sentences
balanced sentences, 144–145
combining, during editing stage, 45–47
short-short sentence, 48
sentimentality, 831
setting
see also mood
critical writing ideas, 143–144
defined, 831
described, 129

SUBJECT INDEX

examples of, 129
organization of writing, 143
prewriting stage, 142
responsive writing ideas, 143
in short fiction, 64
writing about, 142–144
Shakespearean sonnet, 832
shifting narrators, 120–121
shifting point of view, 830
short fiction
  characters, 64–65
  criticism, guide to, 636
  foreshadowing, 65
  images in, 65
  irony, 65
  motifs, 65
  plot, 62
  point of view, 63–64
  quotation from, 661
  reading short fiction. See reading short fiction
  setting, 64
  specialized literary techniques, 65
  structure, 62–63
  see also structure
  subplot, 63
  symbols, 65
  theme, 66
  title, 66
  writing about. See short fiction, writing about
short fiction, writing about
  atmosphere, 142–144
  critical interpretations, inclusion of, 86
  imagery, 89–104
  point of view, 126–127
  prewriting stage. See prewriting stage
  quotations, integration of, 85
  researched writing ideas, 640
  rewriting stage. See revision
  setting, 142–144
  structure, 83–85
  student paper, sample, 105–118
  symbolism, 90–102, 103–104
  theme, 147–161, 158–160
  thesis, 103
short-short sentence, 48
similarity, 45
simile, 371, 831
  see also metaphor
situational irony, 829
slash marks, 363
soliloquy, 831
  see also dramatic monologue
sonnet
  defined, 832
  described, 391
  English sonnet, 832
  Italian sonnet, 832
  Shakespearean sonnet, 832
sources
  citation of. See citation of sources
  electronic sources, 667

primary source, 831
see also primary sources
quoting from, 27–28
secondary source, 831
see also secondary sources
speaker
  defined, 832
  in poem, 352
  questions about, 357–358
spondaic foot, 829
spondee, 829
square brackets, 364
stage terminology, 477–478
standard English
  defined, 832
  use of, 52
stanzas
  closed form, 390
  couplets, 390–391
  free verse, 390, 391
  open forms, 391
  quatrain, 390–391
  sonnet, 391
stereotype, 832
stilted language, 832
strongest-point rule, 44
structure
  critical interpretations, inclusion of, 86
  critical writing ideas, 84
  defined, 832
  described, 68
  discovering structure, 68–69
  dramatic structure. See dramatic structure
  framework for writing, 83–84
  grouping details, 83
  modern hero, writing about, 575
  in novels, 68
  and pattern, 83
  in plays, 68
  and plot, 68
  in poems, 68
  prewriting for patterns, 83
  quotations, integration of, 85
  responsive writing ideas, 84
  rewriting stage, 85
  in short fiction, 62–63, 68
  theme, relating to, 84
  title, 69
  visible structural features, 69
  writing about, 83–85
student papers
  on drama (documented paper), 642–653
  on dramatic structure, 525–531
  final draft, sample, 54–60
  first draft, sample, 28
  on poetry, 365–369, 381–387
  on short fiction, 105–118
  on short fiction (documented paper), 654–660
style, 832
style of writing. *See writing style*
subject, *vs.* theme, 147

SUBJECT INDEX

subplot
  defined, 832
  in short fiction, 63
symbol
  archetypal symbols, 90
  defined, 832
  described, 90
  interpretation of, in prewriting, 102
  phallic symbol, 90
  in poetry, 372
  recognizing symbols, 91
  reference works on, 91
  in short fiction, 65
  yonic symbols, 90, 833
symbolism
  allegory, 825
  critical writing, 104
  details related to theme, 159
  responsive writing, 103
  in short fiction, 90–102
synecdoche, 832
synesthesia, 832
synonyms, 161, 401
syntax, 832

tactile images, 89
tetrameter, 829
theatre in the round, 477
theme
  cliché as, 17
  coherence, revising and editing for, 160–162
  in conclusion, 26
  critical writing ideas, 160
  defined, 147, 832
  details relating to, 84, 159
  determination of, 158
  examples of, 148
  finding the theme, 17–18
  prewriting stage, 158
  relating details to, 84
  responsive writing ideas, 159–160
  in short fiction, 66
  statement of, 147, 158
  vs. subject, 147
  writing about, 158–160
thermal images, 89
thesis
  argumentative, 522–523
  defined, 832
  in dramatic structure, 522–523
  idea development, 15–17
  in introduction, 25
  modern hero, writing about, 575
  poetry, writing about, 358–359, 360, 361
  relating part to whole, 16
  research papers, 632, 636–637
  statement, 17–18
  staying focused on, 18
  workable thesis, development of, 103
third-person approach, 52
title
  of short fiction, 66
  and structure, 69

tone
  critical writing ideas, 363
  in "A Cry from an Indian Wife"
    (Johnson), 360
  defined, 832
  describing tone, 353
  and emotion, 51
  in "Go, Lovely Rose" (Waller), 361
  in "One Perfect Rose" (Parker), 361
  in poetry, 352–353, 357–361
  prewriting stage, 357–361
  responsive writing ideas, 362
  student paper, sample, 381–387
  in "The Ruined Maid" (Hardy), 359
  verbal irony, 353
  and writing style, 51–52
traditional format, 19
tragedy, 832
tragic flaw, 832
tragic hero, 533, 832
transitional phrases, 44, 45
trimeter, 829
trochaic foot, 389, 829
trochee, 829
type character, 832
typical errors, 53

unclear language, 524–525
understatement, 833
unity, 833
  see also coherence
unreliable narrator, 120–121, 833
unreliable point of view, 831
upstage, 477
usage, 833

variety
  pattern, variations in, 47–48
  repetition for emphasis, 48
  short-short sentence, 48
verbal irony, 353
  defined, 828
  sarcasm as, 831
verbs
  active voice, 50
  during editing stage, 49
  passive voice, 50–51
verisimilitude, 833
versification, 833
villain, 481
visible structural features, 69
visual images, 89
voice
  active voice, 50
  defined, 832
  passive voice, 50–51

Wilson Indexes, 634
words
  abstract words, 525
  adjective form, 401–402
  choices in writing process, 49–50
  clarity, 524–525

SUBJECT INDEX

connotations, 51
and context, 402
denotations, 51
emotional meanings, 51
homonyms, 401
malapropisms, 402
misused words, 402
multisyllabic words, 524–525
synonyms, 161, 401
Works Cited list
  see also MLA documentation style
  hanging indentation, 28
  primary source, 28
Works Cited sample entries
  anonymous article, 665
  anonymous book, 664
  anonymous pamphlet, 666
  anthology, work in, 664
  article in periodical (Internet), 668
  article in periodical with continuous pagination, 665
  article in periodical with no volume number, 665
  article in periodical with separately paged issues, 665
  article in reference database, 667
  Bible, reference to, 666
  Dictionary of American Biography article, 665
  electronic sources, 667
  encyclopaedia article, signed, 665
  encyclopaedia article, unsigned, 665
  ERIC document, 667
  essays, 664
  films, 667
  Internet sources, 667–668
  lectures, 666
  multiple volumes, 664
  newspaper article, signed, 665
  newspaper article, unsigned, 665
  personal interview, 666
  personal letter, reference to, 666
  published letter, reference to, 666
  reprint of earlier edition, 663
  reviews, 666
  revised edition, 663
  single author, 663
  telephone interview, 666
  three or more authors, 664
  translations, 664
  two authors, 664
  unpublished letter, reference to, 666
writing
  critical writing, ideas for, 36
  for entertainment, 10
  as expression of feelings, 10
  to inform, 10
  as persuasion, 10
  purpose of, 10–11
  before researching, 637–638
  responsive writing, ideas for, 36
  about short fiction. See short fiction, writing about
writing process
  conclusion, 26–27
  critical focus, 23–24
  details, developing with, 22–23
  editing. See editing
  first draft, composition of, 27–28
  ideas for writing, 36
  interpretation, argument of, 21–22
  introduction, 24–25
  organization of ideas, 19–21
  prewriting. See prewriting stage
  rewriting. See revision
  suggestions for writing, 35
writing style
  active voice, 50
  balanced sentences, 144–145
  emotional meaning of words, 51
  first-person plural, 52
  first-person singular, 52
  passive voice, 50–51
  poetic language, 380–381
  revision of, and poetic form, 400–402
  standard English, 52
  third-person approach, 52
  tone, 51–52
  verbs, 49
  word choice, 49–50

yonic symbol, 90, 833